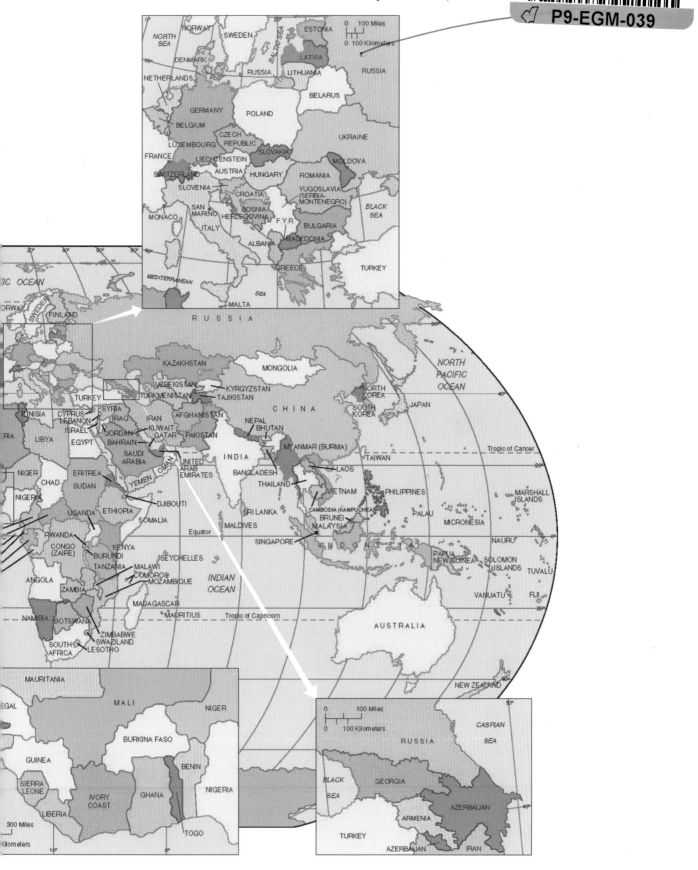

International Management

Culture, Strategy, and Behavior

Seventh Edition

Fred Luthans
University of Nebraska

Jonathan P. Doh
Villanova University

McGraw-Hill Irwin

Boston   Burr Ridge, IL   Dubuque, IA   New York   San Francisco   St. Louis
Bangkok   Bogotá   Caracas   Kuala Lumpur   Lisbon   London   Madrid   Mexico City
Milan   Montreal   New Delhi   Santiago   Seoul   Singapore   Sydney   Taipei   Toronto

INTERNATIONAL MANAGEMENT: CULTURE, STRATEGY, AND BEHAVIOR

Published by McGraw-Hill/Irwin, a business unit of The McGraw-Hill Companies, Inc., 1221 Avenue of the Americas, New York, NY, 10020. Copyright © 2009, 2006, 2003, 2000, 1997, 1994, 1991 by The McGraw-Hill Companies, Inc. All rights reserved. No part of this publication may be reproduced or distributed in any form or by any means, or stored in a database or retrieval system, without the prior written consent of The McGraw-Hill Companies, Inc., including, but not limited to, in any network or other electronic storage or transmission, or broadcast for distance learning.

Some ancillaries, including electronic and print components, may not be available to customers outside the United States.

This book is printed on acid-free paper.

1 2 3 4 5 6 7 8 9 0 QPD/QPD 0 9 8

ISBN 978-0-07-338119-0
MHID 0-07-338119-5

Publisher: *Paul Ducham*
Managing developmental editor: *Laura Hurst Spell*
Editorial assistant: *Sara Knox Hunter*
Director of marketing: *Rhonda Seelinger*
Lead project manager: *Christine A. Vaughan*
Senior production supervisor: *Debra Sylvester*
Lead designer: *Matthew Baldwin*
Senior media project manager: *Lynn M. Bluhm*
Cover images: © *Getty Images*
Typeface: *10/12 Times Roman*
Compositor: *Aptara, Inc.*
Printer: *Quebecor World Dubuque Inc.*

Library of Congress Cataloging-in-Publication Data

Luthans, Fred.
    International management : culture, strategy, and behavior. / Fred Luthans,
Jonathan P. Doh.—7th ed. / Fred Luthans, Jonathan P. Doh.
      p. cm.
    Rev. ed. of: International management / Richard M. Hodgetts, Fred Luthans
Jonathan Doh. 6th ed. 2006.
    Includes bibliographical references and index.
    ISBN-13: 978-0-07-338119-0 (alk. paper)
    ISBN-10: 0-07-338119-5 (alk. paper)
    1. International business enterprises—Management. 2. International business
enterprises—Management—Case studies. I. Doh, Jonathan P. II. Title.
HD62.4.H63 2009
658'.049—dc22
                                                                    2008001613

www.mhhe.com

Dedicated in Memory of

Richard M. Hodgetts
A Pioneer in International Management Education

Preface

hanges in the global business environment continue at an accelerated pace. The challenges for international management reflect this dynamism and the increasing unpredictability of global economic and political events. Continued reverberations from 9/11, the ongoing war in Iraq, tensions in Iran, North Korea, and Greater China, and concerns about conflicts in Africa and elsewhere represent some of the political and security concerns that characterize global affairs. On the economic front, trade tensions, failure to conclude important trade agreements, and continued criticism of offshoring and outsourcing pose additional challenges to global managers and multinational companies. While globalization and economic integration continue unabated, growing pressures regarding the distribution of the benefits of economic development have raised serious questions about the responsibilities of countries and corporations to the global "common good." In Latin America—and elsewhere—populist governments are questioning the efficacy of neoclassical solutions to economic problems and seeking to revisit some of the dramatic privatization and liberalization of earlier periods. Yet growth in global trade and investment and, especially, dramatic innovations in science and technology provide new and unexpected opportunities for global companies.

These often unpredictable developments underscore and reinforce the importance of understanding different cultures, national systems, and corporate management practices around the world. Students and managers now recognize that all business is global, and that the world is now interconnected not only geographically but also electronically and psychologically; it is hard to imagine any business or nonbusiness organization that is not directly affected by globalization. The challenge in today's uncertain geopolitical and economic environment is to learn and effectively practice international management. Past assumptions must always be tested and challenged, and best practices will continuously evolve in response to changing environmental and competitive conditions. Those with the knowledge and skills to apply international management concepts and insights will be taking a huge step toward gaining a competitive advantage over those who do not have such a perspective. They will be in a strong position to gain a broad understanding and to take specific steps for implementation of effective managing across cultures.

In the seventh edition of *International Management,* we have taken care to retain the effective foundation gained from research and practice over the past decades. At the same time, we have fully incorporated important new and emerging developments that have changed what international managers are currently facing and likely to face in the coming years. Of special importance is that students of international management understand what will be expected of them from the range of stakeholders with whom they interact.

Although we have extensive new material in this edition, as described below, we nevertheless have streamlined the text to make it even more user-friendly by taking out the final chapter, reducing the number of chapters from 15 to 14. We have also revised material to effectively provide a general overview of the broad global landscape before elaborating on country-specific elements. We have renamed the opening chapter *Globalization and International Linkages* to better represent the global perspective on critical issues for international managers. We continue to take a balanced approach in the seventh edition of *International Management: Culture, Strategy, and Behavior.* Whereas other texts stress culture, strategy, or behavior, we feel that our emphasis on all three and the resulting synergy has been a primary reason why the previous editions have been the market-leading international management text. Specifically, this edition has the following chapter distribution: environment (three chapters), culture (four chapters), strategy (four chapters), and organizational behavior/human resource management (three chapters). Because international management is such a dramatically changing field, all the chapters have been updated and improved. New, real-world examples and research results are integrated throughout the book, accentuating the experiential relevance of the straightforward content. As always, we emphasize a balance of research and application.

In particular for the seventh edition, we have incorporated important new content in the areas of offshoring and outsourcing, the globalization of human capital, strategy for emerging markets, international entrepreneurship, political and ethical differences around the world, negotiation, and other important developments in the international management field. Given the changing nature of global work, and the interconnected nature of the geographic, thematic, and functional challenges of global management, we have integrated many topical areas—such as offshoring and outsourcing—throughout the book to emphasize these trends as they pertain to today's and tomorrow's international managers. In this regard, we continue to increase emphasis on emerging markets, and the importance of global leaders such as Brazil, Russia, India, and China—the "BRIC" economies—as well as less developed areas in Africa, Asia, Central and Eastern Europe, Latin America, and the Middle East. We have also included the most current insights on the role of biotechnology in global business and the increasing importance of corporate social responsibility and sustainability in global management. We have incorporated the latest research on "green" management practices, the "emerging giant" multinationals from China and India, and the increasing prevalence and utility of "born global" strategies and strategies focused on "base of the pyramid" economies. On a more cross-cultural and behavioral level, we have incorporated the latest research on authentic leadership, positive organizational behavior, and findings of the comprehensive GLOBE study on cross-cultural leadership and included a discussion of how GLOBE's insights compare to Hofstede's classic cultural dimensions.

A continuing and highly relevant dimension of this edition is the addition of all new chapter-opening articles from *BusinessWeek*. These are very recent, relevant, short news stories to grab readers' interest and attention. A transition paragraph leads readers into the chapter topic. At the end of each chapter, there is a pedagogical feature titled "The World of *BusinessWeek*—Revisited." Here we pose several discussion questions based on the opening news article. Answering them requires readers to draw from the chapter material. Suggested answers to these discussion questions appear in the completely updated Instructor's Manual, where we also provide some multiple-choice and true-false questions that draw directly from the story for instructors who want to include this material in their tests.

Another end-of-chapter feature is the "Internet Exercise." The purpose of each exercise is to encourage students to use the Internet to find information from the Web sites of prominent MNCs to answer relevant questions about the chapter topic. An end-of-book feature is a series of skill-building and experiential exercises for aspiring international managers. These in-class exercises represent the various parts of the text (culture, strategy, and behavior) and provide hands-on experience.

The use of cases is featured and further enhanced in this edition. All cases have been updated and several have been added for this edition. The short within-chapter case illustrations—"In the International Spotlight" and "You Be the International Management Consultant"—can be read and discussed in class. The revised or newly added "Integrative Cases" positioned at the end of each part were created exclusively for this edition and provide opportunities for reading and analysis outside of class. Review questions provided for each case are intended to facilitate lively and productive written analysis or in-class discussion. Our "Brief Integrative Cases" typically explore a specific situation or challenge facing an individual or team. Our longer and more detailed "In-Depth Integrative Cases" provide a broader discussion of the challenges facing a company. These two formats allow maximum flexibility so that instructors can use the cases in a tailored and customized fashion. Accompanying each in-depth case is a short exercise that can be used in class to reinforce both the substantive topic and students' skills in negotiation, presentation, and analysis. The cases have been extensively updated and several are new to this edition. Cases concerning the global AIDS epidemic, HSBC, Nike, Wal-Mart, HP-Compaq, AirAsia, Chiquita, Coca-Cola, Microsoft, and others are unique to this book and specifically to this edition. (Of course, instructors also have access to McGraw-Hill's extensive Primis case database, which includes thousands of cases from major sources such as Harvard Business School, Ivey, Darden, and NACRA case databases.)

Along with the new or updated "International Management in Action" boxed application examples within each chapter and other pedagogical features at the end of each chapter (i.e., "Key Terms," "Review and Discussion Questions," "The World of *BusinessWeek*— Revisited," and "Internet Exercise"), the end-of-part brief and in-depth cases, and the end-of-book skill-building exercises and simulations provide the complete package for relating text material to the real world of international management. To help instructors teach international management, this text is accompanied by a revised and expanded Instructor's Resource Manual and Test Bank. This edition includes entirely new and high-caliber PowerPoint presentation slides for each chapter and a set of videos complementing many of the key concepts and examples from the text.

International Management is generally recognized to be the first "mainline" text of its kind. Strategy casebooks and specialized books in organizational behavior, human resources, and, of course, international business, finance, marketing, and economics preceded it, but there were no international management texts before this one, and it remains the market leader. We have had sustainability because of the effort and care put into the revisions. We hope you agree that the seventh edition continues the tradition and remains the best "world-class" text for the study of international management.

We would like to acknowledge those who have helped to make this book a reality. Special thanks go to our growing number of colleagues throughout the world who have given us many ideas and inspired us to think internationally. Closer to home, Luthans would like to give special recognition to two international management scholars. First is Henry H. Albers, former Chair of the Management Department at the University of Nebraska and former Dean at the University of Petroleum and Minerals, Saudi Arabia, to whom previous editions of this book were dedicated; and Sang M. Lee, currently Chair of the Management Department at Nebraska and President of the Pan Pacific Business Association. Doh would like to thank the Villanova School of Business and its leadership, especially Dean Jim Danko, and Herb Rammrath who generously endowed the Chair in International Business Jonathan now holds. Also, for this new edition we would like to thank Elizabeth Stewart for exemplary research assistance on the text and Courtney Asher for research support in preparation of the new and revised cases.

In addition, we would like to acknowledge the help that we received from the many reviewers from around the globe, whose feedback guided us in preparing the seventh edition of the text. These include Chi Anyansi-Archibong, North Carolina A&T State University; Lauryn Migenes, University of Central Florida; Jan Flynn, Georgia College and State University; Valerie S. Perotti, Rochester Institute of Technology; Joseph Richard Goldman, University of Minnesota; James P. Johnson, Rollins College; Juan F. Ramirez, Nova Southeastern University; Lawrence A. Beer, Arizona State University; Tope A. Bello, East Carolina University; and Irfan Ahmed, Sam Houston State University. Our thanks, too, to the reviewers of previous editions of the text: Alan N. Miller, University of Nevada, Las Vegas; Lawrence A. Beer, Arizona State University; Lauryn Migenes, University of Central Florida; Constance Campbell, Georgia Southern University; Timothy Wilkinson, University of Akron; Scott Kenneth Campbell, Georgia College & State University; Janet S. Adams, Kennesaw State University; William Newburry, Rutgers Business School; Dr. Dharma deSilva, Center for International Business Advancement (CIBA); Christine Lentz, Rider University; Yohannan T. Abraham, Southwest Missouri State University; Kibok Baik, James Madison University; R. B. Barton, Murray State University; Mauritz Blonder, Hofstra University; Gunther S. Boroschek, University of

Massachusetts–Boston; Charles M. Byles, Virginia Commonwealth University; Helen Deresky, SUNY Plattsburgh; Val Finnigan, Leeds Metropolitan University; David M. Flynn, Hofstra University; Robert T. Green, University of Texas at Austin; Jean M. Hanebury, Salisbury State University; Richard C. Hoffman, Salisbury State University; Johan Hough, University of South Africa; Mohd Nazari Ismail, University of Malaya; Robert Kuhne, Hofstra University; Robert C. Maddox, University of Tennessee; Douglas M. McCabe, Georgetown University; Jeanne M. McNett, Assumption College; Ray Montagno, Ball State University; Rebecca J. Morris, University of Nebraska–Omaha; Ernst W. Neuland, University of Pretoria; Yongsun Paik, Loyola Marymount University; Richard B. Peterson, University of Washington; Suzanne J. Peterson, University of Nebraska–Lincoln; Joseph A. Petrick, Wright State University; Richard David Ramsey, Southeastern Louisiana University; Mansour Sharif-Zadeh, California State Polytechnic University, Pomona; Jane H. Standford, Texas A&M–Kingsville University; Dale V. Steinmann, San Francisco State University; Randall Stross, San Jose State University; George Sutija, Florida International University; David Turnipseed, Georgia Southern College; Katheryn H. Ward, Chicago State University; Aimee Wheaton, Regis College; Marion M. White, James Madison University; Corinne Young, University of Tampa; and Anatoly Zhuplev, Loyola Marymount University.

Finally, thanks to the team at McGraw-Hill who worked on this book: Paul Ducham, Publisher; Laura Spell, Managing Developmental Editor; Sara Hunter, Editorial Assistant; Christine Vaughan, Project Manager; Gina Hangos, Production Supervisor; Lynn Bluhm, Media Project Manager; and Matthew Baldwin, Designer. Last but by no means least, we greatly appreciate the love and support provided by our families.

Fred Luthans and Jonathan P. Doh

LUTHANS DOH

The seventh edition of *International Management: Culture, Strategy, and Behavior* **is still setting the standard. Current authors Fred Luthans and Jonathan P. Doh have taken care to retain the effective foundation gained from research and practice over the past decades. At the same time, they have fully incorporated important new and emerging developments that have changed what international managers are currently facing and likely to face in the coming years.**

x

New and Enhanced Themes and Structure

- Thoroughly revised and updated chapters to reflect the most critical issues for international managers.
- Greater attention to and focus on a global perspective on international management.
- New, more streamlined format (14 chapters total).
- All new *BusinessWeek* opening cases on current international management challenges.
- Extensively revised and newly titled opening chapter on *globalization and international linkages*.
- New and updated discussions of offshoring and outsourcing and the globalization of human capital (Chapters 1, 2, 3, 14 and throughout cases and inserts).
- Greater emphasis on emerging markets, including the emerging market "giants" of China and India, as well as Brazil, Russia, and other developing countries in Africa, Asia, Central and Eastern Europe, Latin America, and the Middle East.

Thoroughly Revised and Updated Chapter Content

- Updated chapter on political/legal/technological environment with new material on political differences around the world and the global biotechnology revolution.
- Updated chapter on ethics and social responsibility with more extensive discussion of ethical differences among countries and sustainability as a major international management trend.
- More extensive coverage of Project GLOBE and its comparison to Hofstede's classic description of national cultural dimensions (Chapters 4, 13).
- More extensive discussion of differences in negotiation approaches across cultures (Chapter 7).
- Greater coverage of international entrepreneurship, "born global" strategies, and the challenges and opportunities for international strategy targeted to the developing "base of the pyramid" economies (Chapter 8).
- New coverage of the contribution of "authentic leadership" (Chapter 13) and "positive organizational behavior" (POB) (Chapter 14) to international management.

STILL SETTING THE STANDARD...

Thoroughly Updated New Cases, Inserts, Exercises, and Supplements

- New and/or updated country spotlights, "International Management in Action," features, and "You Be the International Management Consultant" sections.

- Thoroughly updated cases (not available elsewhere): *Pharmaceutical Companies, Intellectual Property, and the Global AIDS Epidemic; Advertising or Free Speech? The Case of Nike and Human Rights; Wal-Mart's Japan Strategy; Euro Disneyland* (with new supplement on Disney's other global ventures); *The HP–Compaq Merger and Its Global Implications; Can the Budget Airline Model Succeed in Asia? The Story of AirAsia;* and *Chiquita's Global Turnaround.*

- Brand new end-of-part cases developed exclusively for this edition (and not available elsewhere): *Coca-Cola in India; The Last Rajah: Ratan Tata and Tata's Global Expansion; Microsoft Opens the Gates: Patent Piracy, and Political Challanges in China;* and *HSBC in China.*

- Totally revised PowerPoint slides, Instructor's Manual, test bank, and videos.

About the Authors

FRED LUTHANS is the George Holmes Distinguished Professor of Management at the University of Nebraska–Lincoln. He is also a senior research scientist with Gallup Inc. He received his BA, MBA, and PhD from the University of Iowa, where he received the Distinguished Alumni Award in 2002. While serving as an officer in the U.S. Army from 1965–1967, he taught leadership at the U.S. Military Academy at West Point. He has been a visiting scholar at a number of colleges and universities and has lectured in most European and Pacific Rim countries. He has taught international management as a visiting faculty member at the universities of Bangkok, Hawaii, Henley in England, Norwegian Management School, Monash in Australia, Macau, Chemnitz in the former East Germany, and Tirana in Albania. A past president of the Academy of Management, in 1997 he received the Academy's Distinguished Educator Award. In 2000 he became an inaugural member of the Academy's Hall of Fame for being one of the "Top Five" all-time published authors in the prestigious Academy journals. Currently, he is co-editor-in-chief of the *Journal of World Business,* editor of *Organizational Dynamics,* co-editor of *Journal of Leadership and Organization Studies,* and the author of numerous books. His book *Organizational Behavior* (Irwin/McGraw-Hill) is now in its 10th edition. He is one of very few management scholars who is a Fellow of the Academy of Management, the Decision Sciences Institute, and the Pan Pacific Business Association, and he has been a member of the Executive Committee for the Pan Pacific Conference since its beginning 20 years ago. This committee helps to organize the annual meeting held in Pacific Rim countries. He has been involved with some of the first empirical studies on motivation and behavioral management techniques and the analysis of managerial activities in Russia; these articles have been published in the *Academy of Management Journal, Journal of International Business Studies, Journal of World Business,* and *European Management Journal.* Since the very beginning of the transition to a market economy after the fall of communism in Eastern Europe, he has been actively involved in management education programs sponsored by the U.S. Agency for International Development in Albania and Macedonia, and in U.S. Information Agency programs involving the Central Asian countries of Kazakhstan, Kyrgyzstan, and Tajikistan. Professor Luthans's most recent international research involves the relationship between psychological variables and attitudes and performance of managers and entrepreneurs across cultures. He is applying his positive approach to organization behavior (POB) and authentic leadership to effective global management.

JONATHAN P. DOH is the Herbert G. Rammrath Chair in International Business, founding Director of the Center for Global Leadership, and Associate Professor of Management at the Villanova School of Business. Jonathan teaches, does research, and serves as an executive instructor and consultant in the areas of international strategy and corporate responsibility. He is also Senior Associate at the Center for Strategic and International Studies and an occasional executive educator for Duke Corporate Education and the Aresty Institute of Executive Education at the Wharton Business School. Previously, he was on the faculty of American and Georgetown Universities and a senior trade official with the U.S. government, with responsibilities for the North American Free Trade Agreement. Jonathan is author or co-author of more than 40 refereed articles published in the top international business and management journals, 20 chapters in scholarly edited volumes, and more than 60 conference papers. Recent articles have appeared in journals such as *Academy of Management Review, California Management Review, Journal of*

International Business Studies, Organization Science, Sloan Management Review, and *Strategic Management Journal.* He is co-editor and contributing author of *Globalization and NGOs* (Praeger, 2003) and *Handbook on Responsible Leadership and Governance in Global Business* (Elgar, 2005) and co-author of the previous edition of *International Management: Culture, Strategy, and Behavior* (6th ed., McGraw-Hill/Irwin 2006), the best-selling international management text. His current research focus is on strategy for emerging markets, global corporate responsibility, and offshore outsourcing of services, and he is presently completing work on two books: *Multinationals and Development* (with Alan Rugman, Yale University Press), and *Corporations and NGOs: Conflict and Collaboration* (with Michael Yaziji, Cambridge University Press). Jonathan has also developed more than a dozen original cases and simulations published in books, journals, and case databases, and used at many leading universities, including, for example, at Dartmouth's Tuck School of Business. He has been a consultant or executive instructor for ABB, Anglo American plc, Bosch, Deutsche Bank, China Minsheng Bank, the Government of Thailand, HSBC, The Municipal Government of Shanghai, Medtronic, and Deloitte Touche, where he served as senior external adviser to the Global Energy Resource Group. He received his PhD from George Washington University in strategic and international management.

Brief Contents

Organizational Behavior and   **Part Four**
Human Resource Management

Skill-Building and Experiential Exercises

Contents

International Strategic Management   <u>**Part Three**</u>

Part Four   Organizational Behavior and Human Resource Management

Skill-Building and Experiential Exercises

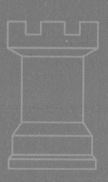

PART ONE

ENVIRONMENTAL
FOUNDATION

Chapter 1

GLOBALIZATION AND INTERNATIONAL LINKAGES

OBJECTIVES OF THE CHAPTER

The global economy has arrived. In nearly every country around the world, dramatically increasing numbers of large, medium, and even small corporations are going international, and a growing percentage of overall revenue is coming from overseas markets. This is true throughout North America, Europe, Asia, Latin America, Africa, and the Middle East. In addition, globalization is presenting challenges for governments, corporations, and communities around the world. As a result, international management— the process of applying management concepts and techniques in a multinational environment—is rapidly gaining importance.

Although globalization and international linkages have been part of history for centuries (see "International Management in Action: Tracing the Roots of Modern Globalization"), the principal focus of this opening chapter is to examine the process of globalization in the contemporary world. The rapid integration of countries and the acceleration of the Information Age have created a new, more integrated world and true global competition. These developments both create and influence the opportunities, challenges, and problems that managers in the international arena will face during the years ahead. Since the environment of international management is all-encompassing, this chapter is mostly concerned with the economic dimensions, while the following two chapters are focused on the political, legal, and technological dimensions and ethical and social dimensions, respectively. The specific objectives of this chapter are:

1. **ASSESS** the implications of globalization for countries, industries, firms, and communities.

2. **REVIEW** the major trends in global and regional integration.

3. **EXAMINE** the changing balance of global economic power and trade and investment flows among countries.

4. **ANALYZE** the major economic systems and recent developments among countries that reflect those systems.

The World of *BusinessWeek*

BusinessWeek

Emerging Giants

It's time to take a look at how globalization has come full circle. A new breed of ambitious multinationals is rising on the world scene from developing nations such as Brazil, China, India, Russia, and even Egypt and South Africa, presenting both challenges and opportunities for established global players.

Unlike Japanese and Korean conglomerates, which benefited from protection and big profits at home before they took on the world, these are mostly companies that have prevailed in brutally competitive domestic markets. As a result, these emerging champions must make profits at price levels unheard of in the U.S. or Europe. Indian generic drugmakers, for example, often charge customers in their home market as little as 1% to 2% of what people pay in the U.S.

Some already are marquee names. Lenovo Group, the Chinese computer maker, made waves last year by buying IBM's $11 billion PC business. Indian software outfits Infosys, Tata Consultancy Services, and Wipro have revolutionized the $650 billion technology services industry.

These companies are just the first wave. The biggest international cellular provider may soon be Mexico's América Móvil, which boasts more than 100 million Latin American subscribers. Hong Kong's Techtronic Industries Ltd. power tools fill the aisles of Home Depot Inc. with the brands it manufactures: Ryobi, Milwaukee, and RIDGID. Brazil's Embraer has surged past Canada's Bombardier as the world's No. 3 aircraft maker and is winning midsize-jet orders that otherwise would have gone to larger planes by Airbus and Boeing. Western telecom equipment leaders have long looked down on China's Huawei Technologies Co. as a mere copier of their designs. But last year, Huawei snared $8 billion in new orders, including contracts from British Telecommunications PLC for its $19 billion program to transform Britain's telecom network. The deal "sent a chill through the rest of the telecom manufacturers," says analyst Michael Howard of Infonetics Research Inc. in Campbell, California.

Many more companies are using their bases in the developing world as springboards to build global empires, such as Mexican cement giant Cemex, Indian drugmaker Ranbaxy, and Russia's Lukoil, which has hundreds of gas stations in New Jersey and Pennsylvania. "What is surprising is the amount of progress emerging-market companies have made in the last few years," says Harold L. Sirkin, senior vice president at Boston Consulting Group (BCG), which recently published a study based on data collected from 3,000 companies in 12 developing nations. BCG identified 100 emerging multinationals that appear positioned to "radically transform industries and markets around the world." The 100 had a combined $715 billion in revenue in 2005, $145 billion in operating profits, and a half-trillion dollars in assets. They have grown at a 24% annual clip in the past four years.

Their key advantages are access to some of the world's most dynamic growth markets and immense pools of low-cost resources, be they production workers, engineers, land, petroleum, or iron ore. The best of the pack are proving as innovative and expertly run as any in the business, astutely absorbing global consumer trends and technologies and getting new products to market faster than their rivals. Techtronic, for example, was the first to sell heavy-duty cordless tools powered by lightweight lithium ion batteries. Globalization and the Internet are ushering in this "seismic change" to the competitive landscape, says management guru Ram Charan. Because they can tap the same managerial talent, information, and capital as Western companies, "anyone from anywhere who sets his mind to it can really restructure an industry," Charan says.

U.S. corporations, of course, have weathered waves of new rivals before. The 1960s and '70s saw the rise of Western European industrial groups such as Unilever, Philips, Siemens, and Volkswagen. Then came Japanese giants such as Sony and Toyota, followed by South Korean powerhouses such as Hyundai and Samsung and Taiwanese electronics conglomerates in the '90s. Each time, chief executives found themselves caught off guard.

Yet this new group of game-changing companies is different on many levels. For starters, the new players are coming from many nations at once and deploying an array of strategies. They're also arriving from lands that, while growing fast, remain relatively poor. Germany and Japan were industrial powers before World War II and built on those strengths to reemerge as global heavyweights. By contrast, China and India have begun to emerge from extreme poverty only in recent decades. Per capita income in China is still just $1,300 a year. In India it's $620. That sounds like a huge handicap for companies from those nations: It implies low-income customers, meager capital, and hand-me-down technologies. It also means struggling with arcane regulations, corruption, and poor infrastructure.

Fit Survivors

Hardscrabble origins, though, can be a vital source of strength. These companies have learned to make money by developing reliable, easy-to-use goods and services at very low prices. And those skills have equipped them well for operating elsewhere in the Third World. Telcos such as Orascom and India's Bharti Telecom, for example, earn high margins while selling cellular service in some nations for 2 cents or 3 cents a minute, while América Móvil pioneered the use of pay-as-you-go cellular service that allows the masses to pay as little as $4.50 for a prepaid card. India has some of the lowest pharmaceutical prices in the world. The country has 101 brands of generic ciprofloxacin, used to treat bacterial infections such as pneumonia and anthrax, costing an average of 63 cents for 10 tablets of 500 mg each. That compares with $51 for generic ciprofloxacin in the U.S., according to Ranbaxy Laboratories. "By learning to compete in this environment, we have gained strength in development and marketing that helps us around the world," says Ranbaxy CEO Malvinder Mohan Singh.

The late 1990s proved to be a time of key opportunity for these companies. In the wake of financial crises in Asia, Latin America, and Russia, many Western companies and banks pulled back from all but a few developing nations. Well-run local players bought assets from retreating Westerners on the cheap and doggedly pursued opportunities from Nigeria to Pakistan to Colombia. From 1995 to 2003, the World Bank estimates, corporate investment from one developing nation to another more than tripled, to $47 billion annually. It probably has neared $60 billion since.

That leaves the new multinationals in a strong position. Over the next decade, the World Bank projects, developing nations' share of world gross domestic product is expected to grow from one-fifth to one-third. During the next two decades, predicts Goldman, Sachs & Co., China, India, Brazil, and Russia alone will add to their populations some 225 million consumers who earn at least $15,000 a year. That's more than the combined population of Germany and Japan. Of 1.2 billion new cellular-phone subscribers worldwide by 2010, estimates Pyramid Research in Cambridge, Massachusetts, 86% will be in developing nations. Chicago economic consultant Keystone India figures emerging markets will make up 69% of all new car sales by 2030, compared with 26% now.

Where they choose to fight, of course, the established multinationals still hold big advantages over the upstarts. Citibank, General Electric, Honda, HSBC, Motorola, Nokia, and Philips are masters at using low-cost manufacturing, engineering, and managerial talent from Bangalore to São Paulo. Few developing-nation companies have such management agility.

The best emerging multinationals have amassed piles of cash, have built global research and development networks, and boast world-class management. You get the idea how far some companies have come by touring Embraer's campus in São José dos Campos, the size of 55 soccer fields. On the floor of one hangar, dozens of workers in impeccable overalls put the finishing touches on three luxurious Legacy 600 corporate jets that seat up to 16 individuals. In a classroom perched above the assembly line, 30 engineers enrolled in the company's graduate aerospace program fine-tune a PowerPoint presentation on a hypothetical new jet they have designed after conducting exhaustive market research and cost-feasibility studies.

Local Heroes

Other emerging players are using their access to deep pools of low-cost local engineers and experience gained in developing nations to close the gap with Western incumbents. Just three years ago, Huawei was known in the U.S. mainly as the company that Cisco Systems Inc. caught copying its designs. But Huawei, which spent $558 million in R&D last year and employs 7,000 engineers at its sprawling Shenzhen campus, is winning respect globally. Last year 57% of its sales were outside China. It boasts a 15% market share in Asia and 9% in Latin America, cutting sharply into Cisco's lead in those regions. Huawei is the global leader in the rapidly

Major Emerging-Market Companies by Country		
Company	**Industry**	**Revenues (in billions)**
Brazil		
Petrobas	Oil and Gas	$56.3
CVRD	Mining	15.1
Embraer	Aerospace	3.8
Russia		
Gazprom	Oil and Gas	48.9
MMC Norilsk Nickel	Nonferrous Metals	7.2
Severstal	Steel	4.9
China		
China Mobile	Telecom Services	30.1
Shanghai Baosteel	Steel	15.8
Lenovo Group	Computers, IT Components	13.4
Haier	Home Appliances	12.8
Turkey		
Koc Holding	Diversified Industries	18.0
Mexico		
América Móvil	Telecom Services	17.0
Cemex	Building Materials	15.3
India		
Tata Motors	Autos	5.8
Tata Consultancy Services	IT Services	2.8
Ranbaxy Laboratories	Pharmaceuticals	1.2
Egypt		
Orascom Telecom	Telecom Services	3.3

growing equipment market for voice-over-Internet protocol service.

A raft of Indian companies also have gotten in position for a U.S. assault after building heft at the margins of the global economy. Ranbaxy may rank just No. 14 in the $28 billion U.S. market for prescription generic drugs. But it is a leader in nations like Nigeria and Brazil. It has earned goodwill by being one of the biggest suppliers of $1-a-day generic AIDS treatments to Africa at cost, and hopes to have its own new malaria drug on the market by 2008. It has also snapped up smaller generic drugmakers in Belgium, Italy, and Romania. When Ranbaxy first began to market its drugs in Europe, recalls CEO Singh, its sales staff was often kept waiting hours before skeptical purchasing managers would hear their pitch. Now, Ranbaxy is a top supplier in much of Europe, and 80% of its $1.2 billion in revenues comes from overseas. It has staff in 49 nations, plants in seven, and an R&D team of 1,100 at its 17-acre campus outside New Delhi. Ranbaxy's pipeline is the second biggest in the generic industry.

Western multinationals can respond by respecting the new competition. That is the attitude David C. Everitt, president of Deere's $10.5 billion agricultural division, is adopting toward Mahindra. Everitt concedes the Indian rival could someday pass Deere in global unit sales. Mahindra dominates the Indian market, which is bigger even than America's, and is especially strong in the small tractors that account for two-thirds of U.S. sales. But Deere also is picking up its game by, among other things, boosting R&D in higher-end tractors for mega-farms in the U.S., Europe, and Brazil, and expanding its own production in India and elsewhere. "We are not afraid of competition," Everitt says. "It gets the juices going and helps us find ways to be better."

Standing Pat

Another strategy is to refuse to cede ground either at home or abroad. Last year, Whirlpool Corp. agreed to pay a surprisingly high $2.8 billion to buy Maytag Corp. It wanted to keep Maytag out of the hands of China's Haier, which is ramping up in the U.S. and had made a rival bid. Cisco, meanwhile, is keeping up the pressure in China, Huawei's home market. Cisco continues to win large orders from Chinese corporations, has plowed $650 million into Chinese tech startups, and has forged a tie-up with local Huawei rival ZTE Corp.

Then there's always the strategy of joining the new challengers. Nortel Networks Ltd. and 3Com have formed telecom equipment and design ventures with Huawei. And Navistar International Corp. in Warrenville, Ill., has a joint venture with Mahindra to build trucks and buses for export. "These companies can be opportunities," says BCG's Sirkin, "if you can work with them."

No matter how the big U.S. companies respond, gone is the era when they could afford to wait for an emerging market to ripen, then count on their ability to roll over the unsophisticated local players. "If you don't participate in these markets, you not only miss opportunities but also are cut out of all the innovation that comes from competing there," says University of Michigan management strategist C. K. Prahalad. "Then you won't be able to withstand the pressure when these companies come and hit you here." Whether one chooses to confront or collaborate, the new multinationals are set to change the rules in industry after industry.

By Pete Engardio with Michael Arndt in Chicago and Geri Smith in São José dos Campos, Brazil

This story highlights how adept developing countries have become in their ability to compete in the global market. Companies from established markets invested in these regions for years in an attempt to profit from abundant cheap labor and resources and, more recently, to serve growing demand for consumer and capital goods. During economic crises, many firms withdrew their investments, enabling local contestants to snatch up inexpensive property and ultimately gain competitive advantage. Innovative strategies, which combine cultural perspective with tactics learned during the period of Western occupation, have facilitated the ability of developing countries to capitalize on their resources and spring into action. While established multinationals have the resources to respond to this challenge, companies from these emerging markets are dramatically changing the face of global competition, creating challenges for established multinationals in the years to come.

In this chapter, we examine the globalization phenomenon, the growing integration among countries and regions, the changing balance of global economic power, and examples of different economic systems. As you read this chapter, keep in mind that globalization is moving at a rapid pace and that all nations, including the United States, as well as individual companies and their managers, are going to have to keep a close watch on the current environment if they hope to be competitive in the years ahead.

■ Introduction

international management
Process of applying management concepts and techniques in a multinational environment and adapting management practices to different economic, political, and cultural environments.

MNC
A firm having operations in more than one country, international sales, and a nationality mix of managers and owners.

International management is the process of applying management concepts and techniques in a multinational environment and adapting management practices to different economic, political, and cultural environments. Managers experience some level of this in today's increasingly diverse organizations. International management is distinct from other forms of management in that the knowledge and insights about global issues and specific cultures are a requisite for success. Today more firms than ever are earning some of their revenue from international operations, even nascent organizations as illustrated in the opening article. Many of these companies are multinational corporations (MNCs).

An **MNC** is a firm that has operations in more than one country, international sales, and a nationality mix of managers and owners. One example is Dell Computer, which now has three manufacturing plants in Ireland, passing Intel as the country's largest foreign employer. Dell's importance to the Irish economy is evidenced by the company's contribution of at least 5.5 percent of Irish exports, 2 percent of GDP, and over 4 percent of all expenditure in the Irish economy.[1] A second is the Solectron Corporation of Milpitas, California, a leading provider of electronics manufacturing and integrated supply chain services. In 2006, Solectron announced it had opened a dedicated medical manufacturing facility in Singapore—the Singapore Medical Center of Excellence—to help manufacturers of medical equipment lower costs, improve quality, and increase flexibility and time to market.[2] A third is IBM, whose Global Services division, which acquired PriceWaterhouseCoopers' consulting arm, is now providing quality information technology (IT) and related services to clients in more countries than any industry rival. IBM's expansion in India has been dramatic, with its Indian workforce growing from 9,000 in 2004 to nearly 50,000 in 2007.[3] A fourth is General Electric (GE), which has operations in every major market worldwide, including Russia and China, where its businesses run the gamut from medical-imaging equipment to plastics and to insurance. GE recently spun off its business process outsourcing (BPO) business as Genpact, now India's largest BPO company with nearly 30,000 employees.[4] In 2003, GE opened its China Technology Center (CTC), a $64 million research and development (R&D) facility in Zhangjiang Hi-tech Park, Shanghai, where it conducts basic and applied research in a range of sectors, including plastics, medical instruments, and alternative energy. This move illustrates the growing trend of MNCs not only investing in manufacturing and distribution abroad but also locating basic R&D and high-value activities in foreign locations. Another example is not so well known. Gruma, based in Mexico, makes and distributes tortillas worldwide for companies such as Yum! Brands Inc. Just 31 percent of Gruma's sales are generated from its home country. The company has established local plants, including one in Shanghai, to better serve local tastes and secure the remaining 69 percent of sales. Its strategy has helped Gruma diversify its revenues, an approach that is especially beneficial as Mexico recently imposed price controls in Mexico on tortillas due to rising costs of corn.[5]

These companies are not alone. In recent years such well-known American MNCs as Avon Products, Chevron, Citicorp, Coca-Cola, Colgate Palmolive, Du Pont, Exxon-Mobil, Eastman Kodak, Gillette, Hewlett-Packard, McDonald's, Motorola, Ralston Purina, Texaco, the 3M Company, and Xerox have all earned more annual revenue in the international arena than they have stateside. GE, one of the world's largest companies, with 2006 revenue of more than $160 billion, saw its overseas revenue exceed domestic sales in 2007. Sales to developing markets alone are expected to reach $50 billion

Table 1–1

The World's Top Nonfinancial MNCs from Developed Countries, Ranked By Foreign Assets, 2004

(in millions of dollars)

Rank	Company Name	Home Economy	Foreign Assets	Total Assets	Foreign Sales	Total Sales
1	General Electric	United States	448,901	750,507	56,896	152,866
2	Vodaphone Group Plc	United Kingdom	247,850	258,626	53,307	62,494
3	Ford Motor	United States	179,856	305,341	71,444	171,652
4	General Motors	United States	173,690	479,603	59,137	193,517
5	British Petroleum Company Plc	United Kingdom	154,513	193,213	232,388	285,059
6	ExxonMobil	United States	134,923	195,256	202,870	291,252
7	Royal Dutch/ Shell Group	United Kingdom/ Netherlands	129,939	192,811	170,286	265,190
8	Toyota Motor Corp.	Japan	122,967	233,721	102,995	171,467
9	Total	France	98,719	144,636	123,265	152,353
10	France Telecom	France	85,669	131,204	24,252	58,554

Source: UNCTAD World Investment Report 2006, annex Table A.I.11.

by 2014. Table 1–1 lists the world's top nonfinancial companies ranked by foreign assets in 2004.

As mentioned in the opening article, companies from developing economies, such as India, Brazil, and China, are providing formidable competition to their North American, European, and Japanese counterparts. Names like Embraer, Lenovo, LG Electronics, Rambaxy, Telefonica, Santander, Reliance, Samsung, Grupo Televisa, Tata, and Infosys once unfamiliar are now becoming well-known global brands. Globalization and the rise of emerging markets' MNCs have brought prosperity to many previously underdeveloped parts of the world, notably the emerging markets of Asia. Tata Group has become India's biggest conglomerate, with a 2006 market capitalization of $56 billion. Tata's revenues in 2005 were $22 billion, 2.8 percent of the country's GDP. Tata employs 250,000 workers and has 28 publicly listed enterprises, including Tata Steel, Tata Consultancy Services, Tata Motors, and Tata Tea. Tata accounts for 5 percent of India's annual exports and is investing aggressively in Australia, Bangladesh, and South Africa to increase overseas income. Since 2000, Tata has acquired Daewoo CV (a truck manufacturer) in South Korea, Tetley Group of Britain, a steelmaker in Singapore, and a stake in a Spanish bus component company, Hispano Carrocera.[6]

As also discussed in the *BusinessWeek* article above and partly in response to the challenge of the growth of emerging markets' MNCs, many U.S., European, and Japanese companies are radically reshaping their business models. In a striking move, Cisco Systems, one of the world's largest producers of network equipment, such as routers, announced it would establish a "Globalization Center East" in Bangalore, India. This center will include all the corporate and operational functions of U.S. headquarters, which will be mirrored in India. Under this plan, which includes an investment of over $1.1 billion, one-fifth of Cisco's senior management will move to Bangalore.[7] Accenture, another leader in outsourcing, has nearly 100 expatriate managers in India, up from fewer than 12 in 2004, and will see overall Indian staffing levels surpass its U.S. head count by mid-2007.[8]

Table 1–2
The World's Top Nonfinancial MNCs from Developing Countries, Ranked by Foreign Assets, 2004
(in millions of dollars)

Rank	Company Name	Home Economy	Foreign Assets	Total Assets	Foreign Sales	Total Sales
1	Hutchison Whampoa Limited	Hong Kong, China	67,638	84,162	11,426	23,080
2	Petronas-Petroleum National Bhd	Malaysia	22,647	62,915	10,567	36,065
3	Singtel Ltd.	Singapore	18,641	21,626	5,396	7,722
4	Samsung Electronics Co., Ltd.	Republic of Korea	14,609	66,665	61,524	79,184
5	CITIC Group	China	14,452	84,744	1,746	6,413
6	Cemex S.A.	Mexico	13,323	17,188	5,412	8,059
7	LG Electronics, Inc.	Republic of Korea	10,420	28,903	36,082	41,782
8	China Ocean Shipping (Group) Co.	China	9,024	14,994	4,825	11,293
9	Petroleo Brasileiro S.A.-Petrobas	Venezuela	8,868	55,355	25,551	46,589
10	Jardine Matheson Holdings Ltd.	Hong Kong, China	7,141	10,555	10,555	8,988

Source: UNCTAD World Investment Report 2006, annex Table A.I.11.

These trends reflect the realities that firms are finding they must develop international management expertise. Managers from today's MNCs must learn to work effectively with those from many different countries. Moreover, as this decade unfolds, more and more small and medium-sized businesses will find that they are being affected by the trend toward internationalization. Many of these companies will be doing business abroad, and those that do not will find themselves doing business with MNCs operating locally. Table 1–2 lists the world's top nonfinancial companies from *developing* countries ranked by foreign assets in 2004.

■ Globalization and Internationalization

International business is not a new phenomenon; however, the volume of international trade has increased dramatically over the last decade. Today, every nation and an increasing number of companies buy and sell goods in the international marketplace. A number of developments around the world have helped fuel this activity.

Globalization, Antiglobalization, and Global Pressures

globalization
The process of social, political, economic, cultural, and technological integration among countries around the world.

Globalization can be defined as the process of social, political, economic, cultural, and technological integration among countries around the world. Globalization is distinctive from internationalization in that internationalization is the process of a business crossing national and cultural borders, while globalization is the vision of creating one world unit, a single market entity. Evidence of globalization can be seen in increased levels of trade, capital flows, and migration. Globalization has been facilitated by technological advances

Tracing the Roots of Modern Globalization

Globalization is often presented as a new phenomenon associated with the post–World War II period. In fact, globalization is not new. Rather, its roots extend back to ancient times. Globalization emerged from long-standing patterns of transcontinental trade that developed over many centuries. The act of barter is the forerunner of modern international trade. During different periods of time, nearly every civilization contributed to the expansion of trade.

Middle Eastern Intercontinental Trade

In ancient Egypt, the King's Highway or Royal Road stretched across the Sinai into Jordan and Syria and into the Euphrates Valley. These early merchants practiced their trade following one of the earliest codes of commercial integrity: *Do not move the scales, do not change the weights, and do not diminish parts of the bushel.* Land bridges later extended to the Phoenicians, the first middlemen of global trade. Over 2,000 years ago, traders in silk and other rare valued goods moved east out of the Nile basin to Baghdad and Kashmir and linked the ancient empires of China, India, Persia, and Rome. At its height, the Silk Road extended over 4,000 miles, providing a transcontinental conduit for the dissemination of art, religion, technology, ideas, and culture. Commercial caravans crossing land routes in Arabian areas were forced to pay tribute—a forerunner of custom duties—to those who controlled such territories. In his youth, the Prophet Muhammad traveled with traders, and prior to his religious enlightenment the founder of Islam himself was a trader. Accordingly, the Qur'an instructs followers to respect private property, business agreements, and trade.

Trans-Saharan Cross-Continental Trade

Early tribes inhabiting the triad cities of Mauritania, in ancient West Africa below the Sahara, embraced caravan trade with the Berbers of North Africa. Gold from the sub-Saharan area was exchanged for something even more prized—salt, a precious substance needed for retaining body moisture, preserving meat, and flavoring food. Single caravans, stretching 5 miles and including nearly 2,500 camels, earned their reputation as ships of the desert as they ferried gold powder, slaves, ivory, animal hides, and ostrich feathers to the northeast and returned with salt, wool, gunpowder, porcelain pottery, silk, dates, millet, wheat, and barley from the East.

China as an Ancient Global Trading Initiator

In 1421, a fleet of over 3,750 vessels set sail from China to cultivate trade around the world for the emperor. The voyage reflected the emperor's desire to collect tribute in exchange for trading privileges with China and Chi-

na's protection. The Chinese, like modern-day multinationals, sought to extend their economic reach while recognizing principles of economic equity and fair trade. In the course of their global trading, the Chinese introduced uniform container measurements to enable merchants to transact business using common weight and dimension measurement systems. Like the early Egyptians and later the Romans, they used coinage as an intermediary form of value exchange or specie, thus eliminating complicated barter transactions.

European Trade Imperative

The concept of the alphabet came to the Greeks via trade with the Phoenicians. During the time of Alexander the Great, transcontinental trade was extended into Afghanistan and India. With the rise of the Roman Empire, global trade routes stretched from the Middle East through central Europe, Gaul, and across the English Channel. In 1215 King John of England signed the Magna Carta, which stressed the importance of cross-border trade. By the time of Marco Polo's writing of *The Description of the World,* at the end of the 13th century, the Silk Road from China to the city-states of Italy was a well-traveled commercial highway. His tales, which chronicled journeys with his merchant uncles, gave Europeans a taste for the exotic, further stimulating the consumer appetite that propelled trade and globalization. Around 1340 Francisco Balducci Pegolotti, a Florentine mercantile agent, authored *Practica Della Mercatura (Practice of Marketing),* the first widely distributed reference on international business and a precursor to today's textbooks. The search for trading routes contributed to the Age of Discovery and encouraged Christopher Columbus to sail west in 1492.

Globalization in U.S. History

The Declaration of Independence, which set out grievances against the English crown upon which a new nation was founded, cites the desire to "establish Commerce" as a chief rationale for establishing an independent state. The king of England was admonished "For cutting off our trade with all parts of the world," providing one of the earliest antiprotectionist free-trade statements from the New World.

Globalization, begun as trade between and across territorial borders in ancient times, was historically and is even today the key driver of world economic development. The first paths in the creation of civilization were made in the footsteps of trade. In fact the word meaning "footsteps" in the old Anglo-Saxon language is *trada,* from which the modern English word *trade* is derived. Contemporary globalization is a new branch of a very old tree whose roots were planted in antiquity.

outsourcing
The subcontracting or contracting out of activities to endogenous organizations that had previously been performed by the firm.

in transnational communications, transport, and travel. Thomas Friedman, in his book *The World Is Flat,* identified 10 "flatteners" that have hastened the globalization trend, including the fall of the Berlin Wall, offshoring, and **outsourcing,** which have combined to dramatically intensify the effects of increasing global linkages.[9] Hence, in recent years, globalization has accelerated, creating both opportunities and challenges to global business and international management.

On the plus side, global trade and investment continue to grow, bringing wealth, jobs, and technology to many regions around the world. While some emerging countries have not benefited from globalization and integration, the emergence of MNCs from developing countries reflects the increasing inclusion of all regions of the world in the benefits of globalization. Yet, as the pace of global integration quickens, so have the cries against globalization and the emergence of new concerns over mounting global pressures.[10] These pressures can be seen in protests at the meetings of the World Trade Organization (WTO), International Monetary Fund (IMF), and other global bodies and in the growing calls by developing countries to make the global trading system more responsive to their economic and social needs. Nongovernmental organizations (NGOs) have become more active in expressing concerns about the potential shortcomings of economic globalization.[11]

Who benefits from globalization? Proponents believe that everyone benefits from globalization, as evidenced in lower prices, greater availability of goods, better jobs, and access to technology. Theoretically, individuals in established markets will strive for better education and training to be prepared for future positions, while citizens in emerging markets and underdeveloped countries will reap the benefits of large amounts of capital flowing into those countries which will stimulate growth and development. Critics disagree, noting that the high number of jobs moving abroad as a result of the **offshoring** of business services jobs to lower-wage countries does not inherently create greater opportunities at home and that the main winners of globalization are the company executives. Proponents claim that job losses are a natural consequence of economic and technological change and that offshoring actually improves the competitiveness of American companies and increases the size of the overall economic pie.[12] Critics point out that growing trade deficits and slow wage growth are damaging economies and that globalization may be moving too fast for some emerging markets, which could result in economic collapse. Moreover, critics argue that when production moves to countries to take advantage of lower labor costs or less regulated environments, it creates a "race to the bottom" in which companies and countries place downward pressure on wages and working conditions.[13]

offshoring
The process by which companies undertake some activities at offshore locations instead of in their countries of origin.

India is one country at the center of the globalization debate. As noted above, India has been the beneficiary of significant foreign investment, especially in services such as software and IT. Limited clean water, power, paved roadways, and modern bridges, however, are making it increasingly difficult for companies to expand. There have even been instances of substantial losses for companies using India as an offshore base, such as occurred when Nokia Corp. experienced the destruction of thousands of cellular phones due to a lack of storage space at an airport during a rainstorm. With India's public debt at 82 percent of GDP, the country now stands where China did a decade ago. It is possible that India will follow in China's footsteps and continue rapid growth in incomes and wealth; however, it is also possible that the challenges India faces are greater than the country's capacity to respond to them.[14]

This example illustrates just one of the ways in which globalization has raised particular concerns over environmental and social impacts. According to antiglobalization activists, if corporations are free to locate anywhere in the world, the world's poorest countries will relax or eliminate environmental standards and social services in order to attract first-world investment and the jobs and wealth that come with it. Proponents of globalization contend that even within the developing world, it is protectionist policies, not trade and investment liberalization, that result in environmental and social damage. They believe globalization will force higher-polluting countries such as China and

Outsourcing and Offshoring

The concepts of outsourcing and offshoring are not new, but practices are growing at an extreme rate. *Offshoring* refers to the process by which companies undertake some activities at offshore locations instead of in their countries of origin. *Outsourcing* is the subcontracting or contracting out of activities to endogenous organizations that had previously been performed within the firm and is a wholly different phenomenon. Often the two combine to create "offshore outsourcing." Offshoring began with manufacturing operations. Globalization jump-started the extension of offshore outsourcing of services, including call centers, R&D, information services, and even legal work. During 2006, Du Pont hired attorneys in Manila to oversee documentation in preparation for legal cases. The company hopes to save an estimated $6 million in legal spending by moving offshore and cutting documentation by 40 to 60 percent once everything is scanned and digitally saved. This is a risky venture as legal practices are not the same across countries, and

the documents may be too sensitive to rely on assembly-line lawyers. It also raises the question as to whether or not there are limitations to offshore outsourcing. Many companies, including Deutsche Bank, spread offshore outsourcing opportunities across multiple countries such as India and Russia for economic or political reasons. The advantages, concerns, and issues with offshoring span a variety of subjects. Throughout the text we will revisit the idea of offshore outsourcing as it is relevant. Here in Chapter 1 we see how skeptics of globalization wonder if there are benefits to offshore outsourcing, while in Chapter 2 we see how these are related to technology, and finally in Chapter 14 we see how offshore practices affect human resource management and the global distribution of work.

Source: Pete Engardio and Assif Shameen, "Let's Offshore the Lawyers," *BusinessWeek,* September 18, 2006, p. 42; and Tony Hallett and Andy McCue, "Why Deutsche Bank Spreads Its Outsourcing," *BusinessWeek,* March 15, 2007

Russia into an integrated global community that takes responsible measures to protect the environment. However, given the significant changes required in many developing nations to support globalization, such as better infrastructure, greater educational opportunities, and other improvements, most supporters concede that there may be some short-term disruptions. Over the long term, globalization supporters believe industrialization will create wealth that will enable new industries to employ more modern, environmentally friendly technology. We discuss the social and environmental aspects of globalization in more detail in Chapter 3.

These contending perspectives are unlikely to be resolved anytime soon. Instead, a vigorous debate among countries, MNCs, and civil society will likely continue and will affect the context in which firms do business internationally. Business firms operating around the world must be sensitive to different perspectives on the costs and benefits of globalization and adapt and adjust their strategies and approaches to these differences.

Global and Regional Integration

One important dimension of globalization is the increasing economic integration among countries brought about by the negotiation and implementation of trade and investment agreements. Here we provide a brief overview of some of the major developments in global and regional integration.

Over the past six decades, succeeding rounds of global trade negotiations have resulted in dramatically reduced tariff and nontariff barriers among countries. These efforts reached their crest in 1994 with the conclusion of the Uruguay Round of multilateral trade negotiations under the General Agreement on Tariffs and Trade (GATT) and the creation of the **World Trade Organization (WTO)** to oversee the conduct of trade around the world. The WTO is the global organization of countries that oversees rules and regulations for international trade and investment, including agriculture, intellectual property, services, competition, and subsidies. Recently, however, the momentum of global trade agreements has slowed. In December 1999, trade ministers from around

World Trade Organization (WTO) The global organization of countries that oversees rules and regulations for international trade and investment.

the world met in Seattle to launch a new round of global trade talks. In what later became known as the "Battle in Seattle," protesters disrupted the meeting, and developing countries who felt their views were being left out of the discussion succeeded in ending the discussions early and postponing a new round of trade talks. Two years later, in November 2001, the members of the WTO met again and successfully launched a new round of negotiations at Doha, Qatar, to be known as the "Development Round," reflecting the recognition by members that trade agreements needed to explicitly consider the needs of and impact on developing countries.[15] However, after a lack of consensus among WTO members regarding agricultural subsidies and the issues of competition and government procurement, progress slowed. At a meeting in Cancún in September 2003, a group of 20-plus developing nations led by Brazil and India united to press developed countries such as the United States, the European Union (EU), and Japan to reduce barriers to agricultural imports.[16] Failure to reach agreement resulted in another setback, and although there have been attempts to restart the negotiations, they have remained stalled.

Partly as a result of the slow progress in multilateral trade negotiations, the United States and many other countries have pursued bilateral and regional trade agreements. The United States, Canada, and Mexico make up the **North American Free Trade Agreement (NAFTA),** which in essence has removed all barriers to trade among these countries and created a huge North American market. A number of economic developments have occurred because of this agreement and are designed to promote commerce in the region. Some of the more important developments include (1) the elimination of tariffs as well as import and export quotas; (2) the opening of government procurement markets to companies in the other two nations; (3) an increase in the opportunity to make investments in each other's country; (4) an increase in the ease of travel between countries; and (5) the removal of restrictions on agricultural products, auto parts, and energy goods. Many of these provisions were implemented gradually. For example, in the case of Mexico, quotas on Mexican products in the textile and apparel sectors were phased out over time, and customs duties on all textile products were eliminated over 10 years. Negotiations between NAFTA members and many Latin American countries, such as Chile, have concluded, and others are ongoing. Moreover, other regional and bilateral trade agreements, including the U.S.–Singapore Free Trade Agreement, concluded in May 2003, and the U.S.–Central American Free Trade Agreement (CAFTA), later renamed CAFTA-DR to reflect the inclusion of the Dominican Republic in the agreement and concluded in May 2004, were negotiated in the same spirit as NAFTA. The U.S. Congress approved the CAFTA-DR in July 2005, and the president signed it into law on August 2, 2005. The CAFTA-DR has been approved by the legislatures in the Dominican Republic, El Salvador, Guatemala, Honduras, and Nicaragua. Costa Rica was the last of the Central American countries to approve the agreement by way of a closely fought referendum. The export zone created will be the United States' second largest free-trade zone in Latin America after Mexico. The United States is implementing the CAFTA-DR on a rolling basis as countries make sufficient progress to complete their commitments under the agreement. The agreement first entered into force between the United States and El Salvador on March 1, 2006, followed by Honduras and Nicaragua on April 1, 2006, Guatemala on July 1, 2006, and the Dominican Republic on March 1, 2007. The U.S. government continues to work with Costa Rica to ensure timely and full implementation of the agreement.

In addition, the 34 democratically elected governments of the Western Hemisphere had worked toward an agreement that was supposed to create the world's largest free-trade region by January 2005 as part of the **Free Trade Agreement of the Americas (FTAA).**[17] These negotiations, however, like those under the WTO, have stalled due to differences between developing countries, like Brazil, and developed nations, like the United States. Agreements like NAFTA and CAFTA not only reduce barriers to trade but also require additional domestic legal and business reforms in developing nations to protect property rights. Most of these agreements now include

North American Free Trade Agreement (NAFTA)
A free-trade agreement between the United States, Canada, and Mexico that has removed most barriers to trade and investment.

Free Trade Agreement of the Americas (FTAA)
A proposed free-trade agreement among the 34 democratically governed countries of the Western Hemisphere.

supplemental commitments on labor and the environment to encourage countries to upgrade their working conditions and environmental protections, although some critics believe the agreements do not go far enough in ensuring worker rights and environmental standards. Partly due to the stalled progress with the WTO and FTAA, the United States has pursued bilateral trade agreements with a range of countries, including, Australia, Bahrain, Chile, Colombia, Israel, Jordan, Malaysia, Morocco, Oman, Panama, Peru, and Singapore.[18]

The European Union (EU) has made significant progress over the past decade in becoming a unified market. In 2003 it consisted of 15 nations: Austria, Belgium, Denmark, Finland, France, Germany, Great Britain, Greece, the Netherlands, Ireland, Italy, Luxembourg, Portugal, Spain, and Sweden. In May 2004, 10 additional countries joined the EU: Cyprus, the Czech Republic, Estonia, Hungary, Latvia, Lithuania, Malta, Poland, Slovakia, and Slovenia.[19] On January 1, 2007, Romania and Bulgaria aceded to the EU, bringing current membership to 27 countries. Not only have most trade barriers between the members been removed, but a subset of European countries have adopted a unified currency called the *euro*. As a result, it is now possible for customers to compare prices between most countries and for business firms to lower their costs by conducting business in one, uniform currency. With access to the entire pan-European market, large MNCs can now achieve the operational scale and scope necessary to reduce costs and increase efficiencies. Even though long-standing cultural differences remain, the EU is more integrated as a single market than NAFTA, CAFTA, or the allied Asian countries. With many additional countries poised to join the EU, the resulting pan-European market will be one that no major MNC can afford to ignore.

> **European Union**
> A political and economic community consisting of 27 member states.

Although Japan has experienced economic problems since the early 1990s. it continues to be one of the primary economic forces in the Pacific Rim. Japanese MNCs want to take advantage of the huge, underdeveloped Asian markets. At the same time, China continues to be a major economic force, with some predictions that it will surpass the United States as the largest economy in the world by 2035.[20] Although all the economies in Asia are now feeling the impact of the economic uncertainty of the post-9/11 era and the Asian economic crisis of the late 1990s, Hong Kong, Taiwan, South Korea, and Singapore have been doing relatively well, and the Southeast Asia countries of Malaysia, Thailand, Indonesia, and even Vietnam are bouncing back to become major export-driven economies. The Association of Southeast Asian Nations (ASEAN), made up of Indonesia, Malaysia, the Philippines, Singapore, Brunei, Thailand, and in recent years Cambodia, Myanmar, and Vietnam is advancing trade and economic integration among these dynamic economies.

Central and Eastern Europe, Russia, and the other republics of the former Soviet Union currently are still trying to make stable transitions to market economies. Although the Czech Republic, Slovenia, Poland, and Hungary have accelerated this process through their accession to the EU, others (the Balkan countries, Russia, and the other republics of the former Soviet Union) still have a long way to go. However, all remain a target for MNCs looking for expansion opportunities. For example, after the fall of the Berlin Wall in 1989, Coca-Cola quickly began to sever its relations with most of the state-run bottling companies in the former communist-bloc countries. The soft drink giant began investing heavily to import its own manufacturing, distribution, and marketing techniques. To date, Coca-Cola has pumped billions into Central and Eastern Europe—and this investment is beginning to pay off. Its business in Central and Eastern Europe has been expanding at twice the rate of its other foreign operations.

Economic activity in Latin America continues to be volatile. Despite the continuing political and economic setbacks these countries periodically experience, economic and export growth continue in Brazil, Chile, and Mexico. In addition, while outside MNCs continually target this geographic area, there also is a great deal of cross-border investment between Latin American countries. Regional trade agreements are helping in this cross-border process, including NAFTA, which ties the Mexican economy more closely to the United States. The CAFTA agreement, signed August 5, 2006, between the United States and Central American countries presents new opportunities for bolstering trade, investment, services, and working conditions in the region. Within South America there are Mercosur, a common market created by Argentina, Brazil, Paraguay, and Uruguay, and the Andean Common Market, a subregional free-trade compact that is designed to promote economic and social integration and cooperation between Bolivia, Colombia, Ecuador, Peru, and Venezuela.

There also is recent economic progress among other less developed nations. A good example is India, which for years has had a love-hate relationship with multinational businesses. The Indian government has been known for its slow-moving bureaucracy, which has been a major stumbling block in attracting foreign capital. In recent years, however, there has been a dramatic turnaround in government policy, and a growing number of multinationals recently have been attracted to India. Much of this spurt has resulted from the Indian government's willingness to reduce the bureaucratic red tape that accompanies the necessary approvals to move forward with investments. In addition, business service jobs such as programmers and call-center operators are creating many new opportunities for Indians.

Those are specific, geographic examples of emerging internationalism. Equally important to this new climate of globalization, however, are broader trends that reflect the emergence of developing countries as major players in global economic power and influence.

The Shifting Balance of Economic Power in the Global Economy

Economic integration and the rapid growth of emerging markets are creating a shifting international economic landscape. Specifically, the developing and emerging countries of the world are now predicted to occupy increasingly dominant roles in the global economic system. In a widely cited report, Goldman Sachs argued that the economic potential of Brazil, Russia, India, and China (the "BRIC" economies) is such that they may become among the four most dominant economies by the year 2050, with China surpassing the United States in output by 2035. The Goldman Sachs global economics team released a follow-up report to its initial BRIC study in 2004, taking the analysis a step further by focusing on the impact that the growth of these four economies will have on global markets. In this report, they estimated that the BRIC economies' share of world growth could rise from 20 percent in 2003 to more than 40 percent in 2025. Also, their total weight in the world economy would rise from approximately 10 percent in 2004 to more than 20 percent in 2025. Furthermore, between 2005 and 2015 over 800 million people in these countries will have crossed the annual income threshold of $3,000. In 2025, it is calculated that approximately 200 million people in these economies will have annual incomes above $15,000. Therefore, the huge pickup in demand will not be restricted to basic goods but will impact higher-priced branded goods as well. According to the report, China, followed by India a decade later, will overtake the United States as the world's largest car market.[21]

The Economist Intelligence Unit has undertaken similar analyses, the result of which appear in summary form in Tables 1–3 and 1–4. Table 1–3 shows the world's largest economies in 2005 and 2020 (projected) using (current) market exchange rates. By this calculation, the United States would remain the largest global economic power by 2020, with China moving ahead of Japan as the second largest and India moving up to number seven. Viewing the data on a purchasing power parity (PPP) basis, a method which adjusts GDP to account for different prices in countries, a more dramatic picture is presented. Using this method, China would surpass the United States as the largest world economic power by 2020, and India would rank third. In both the Goldman Sachs and EIU scenarios, global growth over the next decade is heavily supported by Asia, as seen in Table 1–5. In addition, China and India will remain the most populous countries in the world in 2050, although India will surpass China as the most populous (Table 1–6).

Most African countries have not, to date, fully benefited from globalization. However, recent increases in the price of commodities, such as oil and gas, agricultural products, and mineral and mining products, have helped boost incomes and wealth in the African continent. Moreover, rapid population growth in many African countries, similar to growth in India and China in earlier periods, may suggest that African countries could constitute the next wave of dynamic emerging markets.

Table 1–3
The World's Largest Economies 2005 and 2020 (Projected) Measured by GDP at Market Exchange Rates
(in millions of dollars)

	2005		2020	
	GDP	Rank	GDP	Rank
United States	12,457	1	28,830	1
Japan	4,617	2	6,862	3
Germany	2,829	3	4,980	4
China	2,225	4	10,130	2
United Kingdom	2,213	5	4,203	5
France	2,132	6	3,536	6
Italy	1,720	7	2,543	10
Canada	1,122	8	2,206	11
Spain	1,119	9	2,146	12
South Korea	804	10	2,607	9
Brazil	787	11	1,600	13
India	759	12	3,228	7
Mexico	752	13	1,450	14
Russia	749	14	2,692	8

Source: From *Foresight 2020: Economic, Industry and Corporate Trends.* Copyright © 2006 The Economist Intelligence Unit. Reprinted with permission of The Economist Intelligence Unit via Copyright Clearance Center.

Global trade and investment continues to grow at a healthy rate, outpacing domestic growth in most countries. According to the World Trade Organization, merchandise exports rose by 13 percent to reach $10.2 trillion and commercial services exports rose by 10 percent to reach $2.4 trillion in 2005 over 2006.[22] **Foreign direct investment (FDI)**—the term used to indicate the amount invested in property, plant, and equipment

foreign direct investment (FDI)
Investment in property, plant, or equipment in another country.

Table 1–4
The World's Largest Economies 2005 and 2020 (Projected) Measured by GDP at Purchasing Power Parity
(in millions of dollars)

	2005		2020	
	GDP	Rank	GDP	Rank
United States	12,457	1	28,830	2
China	8,200	2	29,590	1
Japan	4,008	3	6,795	4
India	3,718	4	13,363	3
Germany	2,426	5	4,857	5
United Kingdom	1,962	6	4,189	6
France	1,905	7	3,831	7
Brazil	1,636	8	3,823	8
Italy	1,630	9	2,884	10
Russia	1,542	10	3,793	9
Spain	1,151	11	2,427	14
Canada	1,071	12	2,423	15
South Korea	1,067	13	2,837	11
Mexico	1,059	14	2,459	13

Source: From *Foresight 2020: Economic, Industry and Corporate Trends.* Copyright © 2006 The Economist Intelligence Unit. Reprinted with permission of The Economist Intelligence Unit via Copyright Clearance Center.

Table 1–5
Countries Expected to Contribute Most to Global Growth 2006–2020
(percent contribution)

China	26.7
United States	15.9
India	12.2
Brazil	2.4
Russia	2.3
Indonesia	2.3
South Korea	2.1
United Kingdom	1.9

Source: From *Foresight 2020: Economic, Industry and Corporate Trends.* Copyright © 2006 The Economist Intelligence Unit. Reprinted with permission of The Economist Intelligence Unit via Copyright Clearance Center.

in another country—also has been growing at a healthy rate. Global FDI inflows reached more than $11.5 trillion in 2005, with the United States receiving more than $1.7 trillion of this investment. Interestingly, in 2005 Hong Kong received more FDI than Germany, and China received nearly as much as Canada, showing the shifting balance of economic influence among developed and developing countries. Table 1–7 shows trade flows among major world regions in both absolute and percentage terms. Tables 1–8 and 1–9 show FDI inflows and outflows by leading developed and emerging economies.

As nations become more affluent, they begin looking for countries with economic growth potential where they can invest. Over the last two decades, for example, Japanese MNCs have invested not only in their Asian neighbors but also in the United States and the EU. European MNCs, meanwhile, have made large financial commitments in Japan and more recently in China and India, because they see Asia as having continued growth potential. American multinationals have followed a similar approach in regard to both Europe and Asia.

Table 1–6
Most Populous Countries in 1980, 2000, and 2050 (Projected) Ranked by Size

1980	2000	2050
China	China	India
Soviet Union	India	China
India	United States	United States
United States	Indonesia	Pakistan
Japan	Brazil	Indonesia
Indonesia	Russian Fed.	Nigeria
Germany	Pakistan	Bangladesh
Brazil	Bangladesh	Brazil
United Kingdom	Japan	Congo
Italy	Nigeria	Ethiopia
France	Mexico	Mexico
Bangladesh	Germany	Philippines

Source: UN.

Table 1-7
Trade Flows Among World Regions, 2005
(in billions of dollars or percent)

Origin	North America	South and Central America	Europe	Commonwealth of Independent States (CIS)	Africa	Middle East	Asia	World
Destination								
Value (in $billion)								
North America	824	87	238	7	18	34	270	1,478
South and Central America	118	86	68	6	10	6	48	355
Europe	398	58	3,201	109	112	122	332	4,372
Commonwealth of Independent States (CIS)	19	7	178	62	5	11	40	340
Africa	60	8	128	1	26	5	49	298
Middle East	66	3	87	3	15	54	281	538
Asia	608	51	498	37	54	89	1,424	2,779
World	2,093	301	4,398	224	240	321	2,443	10,159
Share of Regional Trade Flows in World Merchandise Exports								
North America	8.1	0.9	2.3	0.1	0.2	0.3	2.7	14.5
South and Central America	1.2	0.8	0.7	0.1	0.1	0.1	0.5	3.5
Europe	3.9	0.6	31.5	1.1	1.1	1.2	3.3	43.0
Commonwealth of Independent States (CIS)	0.2	0.1	1.8	0.6	0.0	0.1	0.4	3.3
Africa	0.6	0.1	1.3	0.0	0.3	0.1	0.5	2.9
Middle East	0.7	0.0	0.9	0.0	0.2	0.5	2.8	5.3
Asia	6.0	0.5	4.9	0.4	0.5	0.9	14.0	27.4
World	20.6	3.0	43.3	2.2	2.4	3.2	24.0	100.0

Source: WTO International Trade Statistics, 2006.

Table 1–8
World Foreign Direct Investment Inflows
(millions of dollars)

	2004	2005
Developed Economies		
(selected areas)		
United States	122,377	99,443
United Kingdom	56,214	164,530
Germany	15,113	32,663
France	31,371	63,576
Canada	1,533	33,822
Japan	7,816	2,775
Emerging Economies		
(selected areas)		
Hong Kong, China	34,032	35,897
China	60,630	72,406
Africa	17,199	30,672
Mexico	18,674	18,055
Brazil	18,146	15,066
Singapore	14,820	20,083
Russia	15,444	14,600
India	5,474	6,598
Malaysia	4,624	3,967
Vietnam	1,610	1,610
World	10,255,642	11,046,106

Source: UNCTAD World Investment Report 2006.

Table 1–9
World Foreign Direct Investment Outflows
(in millions of dollars)

	2004	2005
Developed Economies		
(selected areas)		
United States	222,437	−12,714
United Kingdom	94,862	101,099
Germany	1,883	45,634
France	57,006	115,668
Canada	43,254	34,083
Japan	30,951	45,781
Emerging Economies		
(selected areas)		
Hong Kong, China	45,716	32,560
China	1,805	11,306
Africa	1,885	1,054
Mexico	4,432	6,171
Brazil	9,807	2,517
Singapore	8,512	5,519
Russia	13,782	13,126
India	2,024	1,364
Malaysia	2,061	2,971
Vietnam	0	0
World	11,138,308	11,450,614

Source: UNCTAD World Investment Report 2006.

In addition to growth in international investment flows, international trade increased substantially over the last two decades. For example, in 1983 the United States exported slightly over $200 billion of goods and services and imported $269 billion of goods and services. By the end of 2006, U.S. exports were in the range of $1.4 trillion annually, and imports were close to $1.8 trillion.

EU trade also increased sharply. This is particularly true for exports and imports between EU members, both of which are now in excess of $2 trillion annually.[23] Japan, despite its ongoing economic problems, has also seen continual increases in its annual exports and imports.[24]

Emerging markets and established economies will continue to compete for higher GDP, as it represents purchasing power and will help level the playing field with trade and by attracting offshore outsourcing. The *percentage* of world trade that is accounted for by the four major trading blocs—the United States, the EU, China, and Japan—has remained fairly consistent. Over the last two decades this group's share of world exports and imports has remained in the range of 55–59 percent. Simply stated, this group accounts for most of the world's international trade, and the United States is the major economic power among these countries. In 2006, the United States imported $288 billion in goods from China but exported only about $55.2 billion, creating tensions in the U.S.-China trading relationship. These tensions have resulted in a call by some U.S. government officials for China to allow its currency to float in order to reduce the perceived price advantage of keeping the yuan at an artificially low value.

Finally, it is important to note that foreign investment and trade do not rely exclusively on MNCs exporting or setting up operations locally. In some cases, it is far easier to buy a domestic firm. Beer companies, for example, are finding that customers like local products, so rather than trying to sell them an imported beer, the MNC will invest in or buy a local brewery. Moreover, the name of the local company may remain the same, so that many local residents are unaware that the firm has changed hands. To illustrate this point, answer the following questions about well-known products sold in the United States; then check your answers at the end of the chapter:

1. Where is the parent company of Braun household appliances (electric shavers, coffee makers, etc.) located?
   a. Switzerland   *b.* Germany   *c.* the United States   *d.* Japan

2. The BIC pen company is
   a. Japanese   *b.* British   *c.* U.S.-based   *d.* French

3. The company that owns Häagen-Dazs ice cream is in
   a. Germany   *b.* the U.S.   *c.* Sweden   *d.* Japan

4. RCA television sets are produced by a company based in
   a. France   *b.* the United States   *c.* Malaysia   *d.* Taiwan

5. The firm that owns Green Giant vegetables is
   a. U.S.-based   *b.* Canadian   *c.* British   *d.* Italian

6. The owners of Godiva chocolate are
   a. U.S.-based   *b.* Swiss   *c.* Dutch   *d.* Swedish

7. The company that produces Vaseline is
   a. French   *b.* Anglo-Dutch   *c.* German   *d.* U.S.-based

8. Wrangler jeans are made by a company that is
   a. Japanese   *b.* Taiwanese   *c.* British   *d.* U.S.-based

9. The company that owns Holiday Inn is headquartered in
   a. Saudi Arabia   *b.* France   *c.* the United States   *d.* Britain

10. Tropicana orange juice is owned by a company that is headquartered in
    a. Mexico   *b.* Canada   *c.* the United States   *d.* Japan

This quiz helps illustrate how transnational today's MNCs have become. This trend is not restricted to firms in North America, Europe, or Asia. An emerging global community is becoming increasingly interdependent economically. Although there may be a true, totally integrated global market in the near future, at present *regionalization,* as represented by North America, Europe, Asia, and the less developed countries, is most descriptive of the world economy.

■ Economic Systems of the World and Regional Connections

Global Economies

The evolution of global economies has resulted in three main systems: market economies, command economies, and mixed economies. Recognizing opportunities in global expansion includes understanding the differences in these systems, as they affect issues such as consumer choice and managerial behavior.

Market Economy

A *market economy* exists when private enterprise reserves the right to own property and monitor the production and distribution of goods and services while the state simply supports competition and efficient practices. Management is particularly effective here since private ownership provides local evaluation and understanding, opposed to a nationally standardized archetype. This model contains the least restriction as the allocation of resources is roughly determined by the law of demand. Individuals within the community disclose wants, needs, and desires to which businesses may appropriately respond. A general balance between supply and demand sustains prices, while an imbalance creates a price fluctuation. In other words, if demand for a good or service exceeds supply, the price will inevitably rise, while an excess supply over consumer demand will result in a price decrease.[25]

Since the interaction of the community and firms guides the system, organizations must be as versatile as the individual consumer. Competition is fervently encouraged to promote innovation, economic growth, high quality, and efficiency. The government may prohibit such things as monopolies or restrictive business practices in order to maintain the integrity of the economy. Monopolies tend to stifle economic growth and consumer choice with the power to determine supply. A lack of competition allows monopolies to harbor all freedoms normally reserved for the public in this system. Factors such as efficiency of production and quality and pricing of goods can be chosen arbitrarily, leaving consumers without a choice and at the mercy of big business. The focus on how to best serve the customer is necessary for optimal growth as it ensures a greater penetration of niche markets.[26]

Command Economy

A *command economy* is comparable to a monopoly in the sense that the organization, in this case the government, has explicit control over the price and supply of a good or service. The particular goods and services offered are not necessarily in response to stated needs but are determined by the theoretical advancement of society. Businesses in this model are owned by the state to ensure that investments and practices are done in the best interest of the nation despite the often opposing outcomes. Management within this model ignores demographic information. Government subsidies provide firms with enough security so they cannot go out of business, which simply encourages a lack of efficiency or incentive to monitor costs. Devoid of private ownership, a command economy creates an environment where little motivation exists to improve customer service or introduce innovative ideas.[27]

History confirms the inefficiency and economic stagnation of this system with the dramatic decline of communism in the 1980s. Communist countries believe that the goals of the populous take precedence over individualism. While the communist regime once penetrated countries such as Ethiopia, Bulgaria, Hungary, Poland, and the former U.S.S.R., among others, it survives only in North Korea, Cuba, Laos, Vietnam, and China today. A desire to effectively compete in the global economy has resulted in the attempt to move away from communist markets, especially in China, which will be considered in greater depth later in the chapter.

Mixed Economy

A *mixed economy* is a combination of a market and command economy. While some aspects of this system include private ownership and the freedom and flexibility of the law of demand, other sectors are subject to government planning. The balance allows competition to strive while the government can extend assistance to individuals or companies. Regulations concerning minimum wage standards, social security, environmental protection, and the advancement of civil rights may raise the standard of living and ensure that those who are elderly, sick, or have limited skills are taken care of. Ownership of organizations seen as imperative to the nation may be transferred to the state to subsidize costs and allow the firm to flourish.[28]

Bolivia recently began nationalizing many of its natural resources from hydrocarbons, such as oil and natural gas, to minerals, such as tin smelter. The bold movement from the country with South America's second largest reserve of natural gas has and will continue to support future nationalization, whether it is simply that other resources are nationalized or that other countries follow suit. The latter is currently in effect, with Venezuela tightening control over its oil reserves, one of the largest long-term sources left in the world. While Venezuela and Bolivia may benefit from their decisions, there could be dire consequences for companies who rely on these exports. Bolivia's grandiose plans have rattled Brazil, Spain, Argentina, Britain, France, and the United States, which have had to reevaluate whether their changing relationship with Bolivia is worth the continued effort to extract natural resources.[29]

Below we discuss general developments in key world regions that reflect one or more of these economic systems and the impact of these developments on international management.

North America

As noted earlier, North America constitutes one of the four largest trading blocs in the world. The combined purchasing power of the United States, Canada, and Mexico is close to $12 trillion. Even though there will be more integration both globally and regionally, effective international management still requires knowledge of individual countries.

The free-market-based economy of this region allows for more freedom in decision-making processes of private firms. This allows for greater flexibility with decisions and low barriers for other countries to establish business but consequently results in facing higher barriers when attempting to move into other countries. Despite factors such as the Iraq War beginning in 2003, Hurricane Katrina in 2005, and high oil prices through 2005 and 2006, the U.S. economy continues to grow. U.S. MNCs have holdings throughout the world, and foreign firms are welcomed as investors in the U.S. market. U.S. firms maintain particularly dominant global positions in technology-intensive industries, including computing (hardware and services), telecommunications, media, and biotechnology. At the same time, foreign MNCs are finding the United States to be a lucrative market for expansion. Many foreign automobile producers, such as BMW, Honda, Nissan, and Toyota, have established a major manufacturing presence in the United States.

Canada is the United States' largest trading partner, a position it has held for many years. The United States also has considerable foreign direct investment in Canada, more than in any other country except the United Kingdom. This helps explain why most of the largest foreign-owned companies in Canada are totally or heavily U.S.-owned. The legal and business environment in Canada is similar to that in the United States, and the similarity helps promote trade between the two countries. Geography, language, and culture also help, as does NAFTA, which will assist Canadian firms in becoming more competitive worldwide. They will have to be able to go head to head with their U.S. and Mexican competitors as trade barriers are removed. It should result in greater efficiency and market prowess on the part of the Canadian firms, which must compete successfully or go out of business. In recent years, Canadian firms have begun investing heavily in the United States while gaining international investment from both the United States and elsewhere. Canadian firms also do business in many other countries, including Mexico, Great Britain, Germany, and Japan, where they find ready markets for Canada's vast natural resources, including lumber, natural gas, crude petroleum, and agriproducts.

By the early 1990s Mexico had recovered from its economic problems of the previous decade and had become the strongest economy in Latin America. In 1994, Mexico became part of NAFTA, and it appeared to be on the verge of becoming the major economic power in Latin America. Mexico now has 12 free-trade agreements with over 40 countries, including Guatemala, Honduras, El Salvador, the European Free Trade Area, and Japan.[30] In 2000 the 71-year hold of the Institutional Revolutionary Party on the presidency of the country came to an end, and many investors believe that the administration of Vicente Fox and his successor, Felipe Calderon, has been especially pro-business.

maquiladora
A factory, the majority of which are located in Mexican border towns, that imports materials and equipment on a duty- and tariff-free basis for assembly or manufacturing and re-export.

In the meantime, Mexico has built a very strong **maquiladora** industry. Long before NAFTA, this was an arrangement by the Mexican government that permitted foreign manufacturers to send materials to their Mexican-based plants, process or assemble the products, and then ship them back out of Mexico with only the value added being taxed. U.S. labor unions argue that this arrangement has cost many jobs in the United States, but the U.S. Department of Labor reports that maquiladora operations actually support jobs by helping U.S. firms maintain their international competitiveness.

Because of NAFTA, Mexican businesses are finding themselves able to take advantage of the U.S. market by replacing goods that were previously purchased from Asia. Mexican firms are now able to produce products at highly competitive prices thanks to lower-cost labor and proximity to the American market. Location has helped hold down transportation costs and allows for fast delivery. Mexican firms, taking advantage of a new arrangement that the government has negotiated with the EU, can now export goods into the European community without having to pay a tariff. The country's trade with both the EU and Asia is on the rise, which is important to Mexico as it wants to reduce its overreliance on the U.S. market.

South America

Over the years, countries in South America have had difficult economic problems. They have accumulated heavy foreign debt obligations and experienced severe inflation. Although most have tried to implement economic reforms reducing their debt, periodic economic instability and the emergence of populist leaders have had an impact on the attractiveness of countries in this region.

Brazil's economy has evolved into a flourishing system. Through 2006, GDP continued to rise, inflation decreased, and employment increased. This economy outweighs that of any other South American country and is quickly becoming a worldwide presence. Brazil continues to attract outside investors, partly drawn to opportunities created by Brazil's privatization of telecommunications and other infrastructure sectors. (See "International Management in Action: Telecommunications Privatization in Brazil.") General Electric has constructed $9 billion worth of electricity plants in the southern part of the country. At the same time, many other well-known companies have set up operations in Brazil, including Arby's, JCPenney, Kentucky Fried Chicken, McDonald's, and Wal-Mart.[31] All this international business activity should spell success. However, by the turn of the century, Brazil was experiencing difficulties in the volatile world economy, and its future remains uncertain.

Telecommunications Privatization in Brazil

www.v-brazil.com/business/
phone-privatization.html

Privatization has become the most widely used and most effective way to carry out reform in the telecommunications industry, liberating firms from the constraints imposed by the almost universal requirement that they operate as government-owned or highly regulated monopolies. The structure, organization, financial underpinnings, and operational environment of telecommunications firms have all been transformed. Many telecommunications companies have been allowed, for the first time in history, to become innovative, privately owned enterprises competing, sometimes fiercely, with one another both locally and, in some cases, globally. Brazil is an excellent example of a developing nation that has adopted mass privatization of the telecommunications industry.

Brazil's Telecommunications Act of 1997 marked the beginning of established regulatory conditions for competition in the industry. This privatization has resulted in sweeping changes to Brazil's telecom environment, including a rise in the telecommunications market and in the growth of the nation's infrastructure. The first privatization movement occurred on July 29, 1998, when the Brazilian government privatized the state-owned telecommunications sector, Telebras, for a total sale price of R$22.057 million or approximately US$19 billion. This included the sale of Brazil's single long-distance telecommunication provider, Embratel, which was purchased by a consortium led by MCI for $2.28 billion through its fully owned Brazilian subsidiary, Startel.

Today, competition exists in each of eight geographic regions and in the long-distance market, resulting in lower telecommunication prices for Brazilian consumers. Privatization has also created opportunities for U.S. and European telecommunication companies that have entered this burgeoning market, and should also help speed up Internet adoption rates. Since 2005, Brazil has expressed an interest in becoming a part of the digital movement and expects to bring the Internet to every citizen, which private telecommunication companies could capitalize on by bundling services (at a lower cost) in order to compete with global players. This has become increasingly important with cyber cafés now common in major cities such as Rio de Janerio and São Paulo.

One of the largest emerging countries with potential for a sustainable growth, Brazil has the biggest and most modern industrial park in Latin America. With continued assistance from Anatel, Brazil's regulatory agency similar to the FCC in the United States, Brazil's telecommunications market has been transformed from a monopoly to an open and competitive global market.

Chile's market-based economic growth has fluctuated between 3 and 6 percent over the last decade, creating uncertainty in its future. Despite this, Chile attracts a lot of foreign direct investment, mainly dealing with gas, water, electricity, and mining. It continues to participate in globalization by engaging in further trade agreements, including those with Mercosur, China, India, the EU, South Korea, and Mexico.[32]

Argentina has one of the strongest economies overall with abundant natural resources, a highly literate population, an export-oriented agricultural sector, and a diversified industrial base; however, it has suffered the recurring economic problems of inflation, external debt, capital flight, and budget deficits. While the economy continues to fluctuate, Argentina had a promising average GDP growth of 9 percent between 2003 and 2006, indicating solid growth potential.[33]

Despite the ups and downs, a major development in South America is the growth of intercountry trade, spurred on by the progress toward free-market policies. For example, beginning in 1995, 90 percent of trade among Mercosur members was duty-free. At the same time, South American countries are increasingly looking to do business with the United States. In fact, a survey of businesspeople from Argentina, Brazil, Chile, Colombia, and Venezuela found that the U.S. market, on average, was more important for them than any other. Some of these countries, however, also are looking outside the Americas for growth opportunities. Mercosur continues talks with the EU to create free trade between the two blocs, and Chile has joined the Asia-Pacific Economic Cooperation group.[34] These developments help illustrate the economic dynamism of South America and, especially in light of Asia's recent economic problems, explain why so many multinationals are interested in doing business within this part of the world.

Europe

Although often overshadowed in the past because of Asia's spectacular growth, major economic developments have occurred in Europe over the past decade. One interesting development has been the privatization of traditionally nationalized industries. Another has been the full emergence of the EU as an operational economic union, and yet another, the close economic linkages established between the EU and emerging Central and Eastern European countries. Including the former communist bloc, today Greater Europe is a trading area of about 550 million mostly middle-class consumers in at least 25 countries.

The EU   The ultimate objective of the EU is to eliminate all trade barriers among member countries (like between the states in the United States). This economic community eventually will have common custom duties as well as unified industrial and commercial policies regarding countries outside the union. Another goal that has finally largely become a reality is a single currency and a regional central bank. Since 2007, 27 countries comprise the EU, with 13 having adopted the euro. Another 11 countries, joining the EU in either 2004 or 2007, are legally bound to adopt the euro upon meeting the monetary convergence criteria.[35]

Such developments will allow companies based in EU nations that are able to manufacture high-quality, low-cost goods to ship them anywhere within the EU without paying duties or being subjected to quotas. This helps explain why many North American and Pacific Rim firms have established operations in Europe; however, all these outside firms are finding their success tempered by the necessity to address local cultural differences.

The challenge for the future of the EU is to absorb its eastern neighbors, the former communist-bloc countries. This could result in a giant, single European market. In fact, a unified Europe could become the largest economic market in terms of purchasing power in the world. In 2004 alone, Poland, the Czech Republic, and Hungary all joined the EU, improving economic growth, inflation, and employment rates throughout. Such a development is not lost on Asian and U.S. firms, which are working to gain a stronger foothold in Eastern European countries as well as the existing EU. In recent years, foreign governments have been very active in helping to stimulate and develop the market economies of Central and Eastern Europe to enhance their economic growth as well as world peace.

Central and Eastern Europe   In 1991, the Soviet Union ceased to exist. Each of the individual republics that made up the U.S.S.R. in turn declared their independence and now attempt to shift from a centrally planned to a market-based economy. The Russian Republic has the largest population, territory, and influence, but others, such as Ukraine, also are industrialized and potentially important in the global economy. Of most importance to the study of international management are the Russian economic reforms, the dismantling of Russian price controls (allowing supply and demand to determine prices), and privatization (converting the old communist-style public enterprises to private ownership).

Russia's economy continues to grow as poverty declines and the middle class expands. Direct investment in Russia, along with its membership in the International Monetary Fund (IMF), is helping to raise GDP and decrease inflation, offsetting the hyperinflation created from the initial attempt at transitioning to a market-based economy. In addition, the Group of Seven (the United States, Germany, France, England, Canada, Japan, and Italy) has pledged billions of dollars for humanitarian and other types of assistance. So while the Russian economy likely will have a number of years of painfully slow economic recovery and many recurrent problems, most economic experts predict that if the Russians can hold things together politically and maintain social order, the situation could improve in the long run.

Although these economic reforms are being implemented slowly, there are significant problems in Russia associated with growing crime of all kinds as well as political uncertainty. Many foreign investors feel that the risk is still too high. Russia is such a large market, however, and has so much potential for the future that many MNCs feel they must get involved, especially with a promising rise in GDP. There also has been a movement toward teaching Western-style business courses, as well as MBA programs in all the Central European countries, creating a greater preparation for trends in globalization.

In Hungary, state-owned hotels have been privatized, and Western firms, attracted by the low cost of highly skilled, professional labor, have been entering into joint ventures with local companies. MNCs also have been making direct investments, as in the case of General Electric's purchase of Tungsram, the giant Hungarian electric company. Another example is Britain's Telfos Holdings, which paid $19 million for 51 percent of Ganz, a Hungarian locomotive and rolling stock manufacturer. Still others include Suzuki's investment of $110 million in a partnership arrangement to produce cars with local manufacturer Autokonzern, Ford Motor's construction of a new $80 million car component plant, and Italy's Ilwa's $25 million purchase of the Salgotarjau Iron Works.

Poland had a head start on the other former communist-bloc countries. General political elections were held in June 1989, and the first noncommunist government was established well before the fall of the Berlin Wall. In 1990, the Communist Polish United Workers Party dissolved, and Lech Walesa was elected president. Earlier than its neighbors, Poland instituted radical economic reforms (characterized as "shock therapy"). Although the relatively swift transition to a market economy has been very difficult for the Polish people, with very high inflation initially, continuing unemployment, and the decline of public services, Poland's economy has done relatively well. However, political instability and risk, large external debts, a deteriorating infrastructure, and only modest education levels have led to continuing economic problems.

Although Russia, the Czech Republic, Hungary, and Poland receive the most media coverage and are among the largest of the former communist countries, others also are struggling to right their economic ships. A small but particularly interesting example is Albania. Ruled ruthlessly by the Stalinist-style dictator Enver Hoxha for over four decades following World War II, Albania was the last, but most devastated, Eastern European country to abandon communism and institute radical economic reforms. At the beginning of the 1990s, Albania started from zero. Industrial output initially fell over 60 percent, and inflation reached 40 percent monthly. Today, Albania still struggles but is slowly making progress.

The key for Albania and the other Eastern European countries is to maintain the social order, establish the rule of law, rebuild the collapsed infrastructure, and get factories and other value-added, job-producing firms up and running. Foreign investment must be forthcoming for these countries to join the global economy. A key challenge for Albania and the other "have-not" Eastern European countries will be to make themselves less risky and more attractive for international business.

Asia

Despite the severe economic downturn starting in 1997, Asia has mostly bounced back and promises to continue being one of the major players in the world economy. Because there are far too many nations to allow for comprehensive coverage here, the following provides insights into the economic status and international management challenges of selected Asian countries.

Japan   During the 1970s and 1980s, Japan's economic success had been without precedent. The country had a huge positive trade balance, the yen was strong, and the Japanese became recognized as the world leaders in manufacturing and consumer goods.

One objective of multicultural research is to learn more about the customs, cultures, and work habits of people in other countries. After all, a business can hardly expect to capture an overseas market without knowledge of the types of goods and services the people there want to buy. Equally important is the need to know the management styles that will be effective in running a foreign operation. Sometimes this information can change quite rapidly. For example, as Russia continues to move from a central to a market economy, management is constantly changing as the country attempts to adjust to increased exposure in the global environment. Russia entered into a strategic partnership with the United States in 2002. However, while U.S. perspectives of "partnerships" are flexible but are seen as inherently having some hierarchal structure, Russia sees "partnerships" as entailing equality, especially in the decision-making process. This may be a part of the reason Russia formed a strategic partnership with China in 2005, since both countries emerged from a communist regime and can understand similar struggles. Regardless, as Russia moves to privatize its organizations, the new partnership may pose a threat to the Americas and the West if efforts to understand each other and work together are abandoned.

It is evident that the United States and Russia differ on many horizons. Russian management is still based on authoritarian styles, where the managerial role is to pass orders down the chain of command, and there is little sense of responsibility, open communication, or voice in the decision-making process. Furthermore, while 64 percent of U.S. employees see retirement as an opportunity for a new chapter in life, only 15 percent of Russian employees feel that way, and another 23 percent see retirement as "the beginning of the end." Despite these differences, there are points of similarity that a U.S. firm can use as leverage when considering opening a business in Russia. About 46 percent of employees in both the United States and Russia would prefer a work schedule that fluctuates between work and leisure, mirroring a pattern of recurring sabbaticals. Also, Russia currently has a post–Cold War mentality, much like the United States experienced after the Great Depression of the 1930s. Looking back at history and incorporating the evolutionary knowledge can assist in understanding emerging economies.

These examples show the importance of studying international management and learning via systematic analysis and firsthand information how managers in other countries really do behave toward their employees and their work. Such analysis is critical in ensuring a strong foothold in effective international management.

Analysts ascribe Japan's phenomenal success to a number of factors. Some areas that have received a lot of attention are the Japanese cultural values supporting a strong work ethic and group/team effort, consensus decision making, the motivational effects of guaranteed lifetime employment, and the overall commitment that Japanese workers have to their organizations. However, at least some of these assumptions about the Japanese workforce have turned out to be more myth than reality, and some of the former strengths have become weaknesses in the new economy. For example, consensus decision making turns out to be too time-consuming in the new speed-based economy. Also, there has been a steady decline in Japan's overseas investments since the 1990s due to a slowing Japanese economy, poor management decisions, and other emerging economies, such as China.

Some of the early success of the Japanese economy can be attributed to the **Ministry of International Trade and Industry (MITI).** This is a governmental agency that identifies and ranks national commercial pursuits and guides the distribution of national resources to meet these goals. In recent years, MITI has given primary attention to the so-called ABCD industries: automation, biotechnology, computers, and data processing.

Another major reason for Japanese success may be the use of **keiretsus.** This Japanese term stands for the large, vertically integrated corporations whose holdings supply much of the assistance needed in providing goods and services to end users. Being able to draw from the resources of the other parts of the keiretsu, a Japanese MNC often can get things done more quickly and profitably than its international competitors.

Ministry of International Trade and Industry (MITI)
A Japanese government agency that identifies and ranks national commercial pursuits and guides the distribution of national resources to meet these goals.

keiretsu
An organizational arrangement in Japan in which a large group of vertically integrated companies bound together by cross-ownership, interlocking directorates, and social ties provide goods and services to end users.

Despite setbacks, Japan remains a formidable international competitor and is well poised in all three major economic regions: the Pacific Rim, North America, and Europe.

China China's GDP has remained strong, maintaining at least 8 percent growth and surpassing 10 percent in 2006. In the first quarter of 2007, GDP grew at a blistering 11.1 percent, causing some concerns that the Chinese government has been unable to tap the brakes on this rapid growth. China faces other formidable challenges, including a massive savings glut in the corporate sector, the globalization of manufacturing networks, vast developmental needs, and the requirement for 15–20 million new jobs annually to avoid joblessness and social unrest.[36]

China also remains a major risk for investors. The one country, two systems (communism and capitalism) balance is a delicate one to maintain, and foreign businesses are often caught in the middle. Most MNCs find it very difficult to do business in and with China, and many have yet to make a profit. Outside chemical producers have found themselves facing "registration fees" of $10,000 per product, and U.S. law firms operating in Shanghai were forced to close until the government granted them new licenses. German and Japanese banks have found that collecting loans from the government can be extremely difficult as well. In addition, some securities firms have learned that Chinese clients sometimes refuse to pay for trades that turn out to be losers, and there is no government protection for such actions.[37] Simply put, China remains a complicated and high-risk venture. Even so, MNCs know that China with its 1.3 billion people will be a major world market and that they must have a presence there.

Trade relations between China and developed countries and regions, such as the United States and the EU, remain tense. In 2007, Vice Premier Wu Yi rebuked the United States for its "misunderstanding about the reality in China." This followed a formal action at the WTO by U.S. Trade Representative Susan Schwab, who charged China with failing to live up to its trade obligations in the area of piracy and its refusal to grant fair market access to U.S. music, movies, DVDs, and books. In addition, legislation has been threatened in Congress (the Schumer-Graham bill) calling for a blanket tariff on all U.S. imports from China unless Beijing takes steps to revalue the yuan.[38]

Emerging Markets of Asia In addition to Japan and China, there are four other widely recognized economic powerhouses in Asia. Note that the traditional term "newly industrialized countries" (NICs) is not used because they are not really new anymore. South Korea, Hong Kong, Singapore, and Taiwan have arrived as major economic powers.

In South Korea, the major conglomerates, called **chaebols**, include such internationally known firms as Samsung, Daewoo, Hyundai, and the LG Group. Many key managers in these huge firms have attended universities in the West, where in addition to their academic programs they learned the culture, customs, and language. Now they are able to use this information to help formulate competitive international strategies for their firms. This will be very helpful for South Korea, which has shifted to privatizing a wide range of industries and withdrawing some of the restrictions on overall foreign ownership. The 2006 reports showed a solid economy with moderate growth, moderate inflation, low unemployment, an export surplus, and fairly equal distribution of income.

chaebols
Very large, family-held Korean conglomerates that have considerable political and economic power.

Bordering southeast China and now part of the People's Republic of China (PRC), Hong Kong has been the headquarters for some of the most successful multinational operations in Asia. Although it can rely heavily on southeast China for manufacturing, there is still uncertainty about the future and the role that the Chinese government intends to play in local governance.

Singapore is a major success story. Its solid foundation leaves only the question of how to continue expanding in the face of increasing international competition. To date, however, Singapore has emerged as an urban planner's ideal model and the leader and financial center of Southeast Asia. Taiwan has progressed from a labor-intensive economy to one that is dominated by more technologically sophisticated industries, including banking, electricity generation, petroleum refining, and computers. Although its economy has also been hit by the downturn in Asia, it continues to steadily grow.

Besides Singapore, other countries of Southeast Asia also should be recognized. Thailand, Malaysia, Indonesia, and now Vietnam (See "In the International Spotlight" in Chapter 2) have developed economically with a relatively large population base and inexpensive labor despite the lack of considerable natural resources. These countries were also known to have social stability, but in the aftermath of the economic crisis there has been considerable turmoil in this part of the world, especially in Indonesia, the fourth largest populated country in the world. Nevertheless, as other Asian countries have begun to level off and mature, these export-driven Southeast Asian countries remain attractive to outside investors. MNCs from around the globe all want to have a presence in these countries.

Other Developing and Emerging Countries and Regions

In contrast to the fully developed countries of North America, Europe, and Asia are the less developed countries (LDCs) around the world. An LDC typically is characterized by two or more of the following: low GDP, slow (or negative) GDP growth per capita, high unemployment, high international debt, a large population, and a workforce that is either unskilled or semiskilled. In some cases, such as in the Middle East, there also is considerable government intervention in economic affairs. Emerging markets are developing economies that exhibit sustained economic reform and growth.

India   With a population of about 1 billion and growing, India has traditionally had more than its share of political and economic problems. The recent trend of locating software and other higher-value-added services has helped to bolster a large middle- and upper-class market for goods and services and a GDP that is quickly reaching the level of China. India may soon be viewed as a fully developed country if it can withstand the intense growth period.

For a number of reasons, India is attractive to multinationals, and especially to U.S. and British firms. Many Indian people speak English and are very well educated and are known for advanced information technology expertise. Also, the Indian government is providing funds for economic development. For example, India is expanding its telecommunication systems and increasing the number of phone lines fivefold, a market that AT&T is vigorously pursuing. Many frustrations remain in doing business in India (see "In the International Spotlight" at the end of this chapter), but there is little question that the country will receive increased attention in the years ahead.

Middle East and Central Asia   Israel, the Arab countries, Iran, Turkey, and the Central Asian countries of the former Soviet Union are considered by the World Bank to be LDCs. Because of their oil, however, some of these countries are considered to be economically rich. Recently, this region has been in the world news because of the aftermath of the September 11, 2001, terrorist attack on the United States. However, these countries continue to try to balance the geopolitical, religious forces with economic viability and remain active in the international business arena. Students of international management should have a working knowledge of these countries' customs, culture, and management practices since most industrial nations rely, at least to some degree, on imported oil and since many people around the world work for international, and specifically Arab, employers.

The Arab and Central Asian countries rely almost exclusively on oil production. The price of oil greatly fluctuates, and the Organization of Petroleum Exporting Countries (OPEC) has trouble holding together its cartel. In recent years the price has been relatively high, and world demand is likely to keep it there. Arab countries have invested billions of dollars in U.S. property and businesses. Many people around the world, including those in the West, work for Arab employers. For example, the bankrupt United Press International was purchased by the Middle East Broadcasting Centre, a London-based MNC owned by the Saudis.

Africa   Even though they have considerable natural resources, on the whole African nations remain very poor and undeveloped, and international trade is not a major source of income. Although African countries do business with developed countries, it is on a limited scale. One major problem of doing business in the African continent is the overwhelming diversity of approximately 750 million people divided into 3,000 tribes that speak 1,000 languages and dialects. Also, political instability is pervasive, and this instability generates substantial risks for foreign investors.

In recent years, Africa, especially sub-Saharan Africa, has had a number of severe problems. In addition to tragic tribal wars, there has been the spread of terrible diseases such as AIDS and Ebola. In 2002–2003, the WTO agreed to relax intellectual property rights (IPR) rules to allow for greater and less costly access by African countries to antiviral AIDS medications (see the In-Depth Integrative Case at the end of Part I). While globalization has opened up new markets for developed countries, developing nations in Africa lack the institutions, infrastructure, and economic capacity to take full advantage of globalization. Other big problems include poverty, malnutrition, illiteracy, corruption, social breakdown, vanishing resources, overcrowded cities, drought, and homeless refugees. There is still hope in the future for Africa despite this bleak situation, because African countries remain virtually untapped. Not only are there considerable natural resources, but the diversity can also be used to its advantage. For example, many African people are familiar with the European cultures and languages of the former colonial powers (e.g., English, French, Dutch, and Portuguese), and this can serve them well in international business as they strive for continued growth. Uncertain times are ahead, but a growing number of MNCs are attempting to make headway in this vast land. Also, the spirit of these emerging countries has not been broken. There are continuing efforts to stimulate economic growth. Examples of what can be done include Togo, which has sold off many of its state-owned operations and leased a steel-rolling mill to a U.S. investor, and Guinea, which has sold off some of its state-owned enterprises and cut its civil service force by 30 percent. A special case is South Africa, where apartheid, the former white government's policies of racial segregation and oppression, has been dismantled and the healing process is progressing. Long-jailed former black president Nelson Mandela is recognized as a world leader. These significant developments have led to an increasing number of the world's MNCs returning to South Africa; however, there continue to be both social and economic problems that, despite Mandela's and his successors' best efforts, signal uncertain times for the years ahead. One major initiative is the country's Black Economic Empowerment (BEE) program, designed to reintegrate the disenfranchised majority into business and economic life.

Many African economies saw their growth accelerate in 2006–2007 due to higher commodity prices. According to the Economic Commission on Africa, African economies continued to sustain the growth momentum of previous years, recording an overall real GDP growth rate of 5.7 percent in 2006 compared to 5.3 percent in 2005 and 5.2 percent in 2004. This growth exceeded that of Latin America (4.8 percent) but was lower than that of developing Asia (8.7 percent).[39]

Table 1–10 ranks the top 10 countries globally by their "competitiveness" using a composite of several measures. Table 1–11 ranks emerging markets by several key indicators.

Table 1–10
World's Most Competitive Nations, 2006

Country	Rank
United States	1
Singapore	2
Hong Kong	3
Luxemburg	4
Denmark	5
Switzerland	6
Iceland	7
Netherlands	8
Sweden	9
Canada	10

Source: World Competitive Scoreboard, 2006.

Table 1–11
Market Potential Indicators Ranking for Emerging Markets, 2007

Countries	Market Size	Market Growth	Market Intensity	Market Consumption Capacity	Commercial Infrastructure	Economic Freedom	Market Receptivity	Country Risk
China	1	1	25	12	16	27	22	13
Hong Kong	24	20	1	13	2	6	2	2
Singapore	27	18	9	11	6	10	1	1
Taiwan	12	6	11	–	1	8	5	3
Israel	25	12	2	4	3	3	4	5
S. Korea	7	16	5	2	5	7	10	4
Czech Republic	23	9	13	3	4	2	9	6
Hungary	26	24	3	1	7	4	8	8
India	2	3	22	7	25	17	27	16
Poland	14	27	10	6	8	5	14	9
Turkey	9	7	12	10	12	16	18	20
Malaysia	20	2	26	19	10	20	3	11
Russia	3	15	23	16	9	25	19	17
Mexico	5	25	8	21	15	11	6	12
Thailand	17	11	18	14	20	15	7	15
Chile	21	19	17	23	13	1	12	10
Argentina	15	10	4	20	11	14	25	27
Saudi Arabia	13	4	27	–	14	22	11	7
Egypt	16	14	14	9	21	26	17	18
Pakistan	10	5	6	5	26	23	26	25
Indonesia	6	13	21	8	27	21	15	24
Phillipines	11	21	7	18	22	19	13	23
Brazil	4	26	20	24	17	13	24	19
S. Africa	8	17	15	25	24	9	20	14

Source: GlobalEdge.

The World of *BusinessWeek*—Revisited

Having read this chapter, you should now be more cognizant of the impacts of globalization and international linkages among countries, firms, and societies on international management. Although controversial, globalization appears unstoppable. The creation of free-trade agreements worldwide has helped to trigger economic gains in many developing nations. The consolidation and expansion of the EU will continue to open up borders and make it easier and more cost-effective for exporters from less developed countries to do business there. In Asia, formerly closed economies such as India and China have opened up, and other emerging Asian countries such as South Korea, Singapore, Malaysia, and Thailand have begun to bounce back from the economic crises of the late 1990s. In some instances, investment in developing countries has aided in their ability to gain a substantial foothold in the global market. Continued efforts to privatize, deregulate, and liberalize many industries will increase consumer choice and lower prices as competition increases. The rise of MNCs from emerging markets is one tangible example both of the increasing reach of globalization and heightened global competition for markets. Continued concerns over the negative spillovers from globalization will remain and may even grow in the coming years. In particular, concerns over offshoring of jobs from developed to developing countries has created insecurity in developed countries while generating economic opportunities in emerging economies.

In light of these developments, answer the following questions: (1) What are some of the pros and cons of globalization and free trade? (2) What challenges does the emergence of MNCs from developing countries pose for MNCs from developed countries? (3) Which regions of the world are most likely to benefit from globalization and integration in the years to come, and which may experience dislocations?

SUMMARY OF KEY POINTS

1. Globalization—the process of increased integration among countries—continues at an accelerated pace. More and more companies—including those from developing countries—are going global, creating opportunities and challenges for the global economy and international management. Globalization has become controversial in some quarters due to perceptions that the distribution of its benefits are uneven and due to the global distribution of economic activities as illustrated by offshoring. There have emerged sharp critics of globalization from academics, NGOs, and the developing world, yet the pace of globalization and integration continues unabated.

2. Economic integration is most pronounced in the triad of North America, Europe, and the Pacific Rim. The North American Free Trade Agreement (NAFTA) is turning the region into one giant market. In South America, there is an increasing amount of intercountry trade, sparked by Mercosur. Additionally, trade agreements such as the Central American

Free Trade Agreement (CAFTA) are linking countries of the Western Hemisphere together. In Europe, the expansion of the original countries of the European Union (EU) is creating a larger and more diverse union, with dramatic transformation of Central and Eastern European countries such as the Czech Republic, Poland, and Hungary. Asia is another major regional power, as reflected in the rapid growth shown not only by Japan but also the economies of China, India, and other emerging markets. Countries in Africa and the Middle East continue to face complex problems but still hold economic promise for the future. Emerging markets in all regions present both opportunities and challenges for international managers.

3. Different growth rates and shifting demographics are dramatically altering the distribution of economic power around the world. Notably, China's rapid growth will make it the largest economic power in the world by midcentury, if not before. India will be the most populous country in the

world, and other emerging markets will also become important players. International trade and investment have been increasing dramatically over the years. Major multinational corporations (MNCs) have holdings throughout the world, from North America to Europe to the Pacific Rim to Africa. Some of these holdings are a result of direct investment; others are partnership arrangements with local firms. Small firms also are finding that they must seek out international markets to survive in the future. MNCs from emerging markets are growing rapidly and expanding their global reach. The internationalization of nearly all business has arrived.

4. Different economic systems characterize different countries and regions. These systems, which include market, command, and mixed economies, are represented in different nations and have changed as economic conditions have evolved.

KEY TERMS

chaebols, *27*

European Union, *13*

foreign direct investment (FDI), *15*

Free Trade Agreement of the Americas (FTAA), *12*

globalization, *8*

international management, *6*

keiretsu, *26*

maquiladora, *22*

Ministry of International Trade and Industry (MITI), *26*

MNC, *6*

North American Free Trade Agreement (NAFTA), *12*

offshoring, *10*

outsourcing, *10*

World Trade Organization (WTO), *11*

REVIEW AND DISCUSSION QUESTIONS

1. How has globalization affected different world regions? What are some of the benefits and costs of globalization for different sectors of society (companies, workers, communities)?

2. How has NAFTA affected the economies of North America and the EU affected Europe? What importance do these economic pacts have for international managers in North America, Europe, and Asia?

3. Why are Russia and Eastern Europe of interest to international managers? Identify and describe some reasons for such interest.

4. Many MNCs have secured a foothold in Asia, and many more are looking to develop business relations there. Why does this region of the world hold such interest for international management? Identify and describe some reasons for such interest.

5. Why would MNCs be interested in South America, India, the Middle East and Central Asia, and Africa, the less developed and emerging countries of the world? Would MNCs be better off focusing their efforts on more industrialized regions? Explain.

6. MNCs from emerging markets (India, China, Brazil) are beginning to challenge the dominance of developed country MNCs. How might MNCs from North America, Europe, and Japan respond to these challenges?

ANSWERS TO THE IN-CHAPTER QUIZ

1. **c.** Procter & Gamble, a U.S.-based MNC that bought Gillette some years back owns the Braun company.

2. **d.** BIC SA is a French company.

3. **b.** The British MNC Grand Metropolitan PLC sold Häagen-Dazs to the Pillsbury Company of the United States.

4. **a.** Thomson SA of France produces RCA televisions.

5. **a.** Britain's Grand Metropolitan PLC also sold the Green Giant product line to the Pillsbury Company of the United States.

6. **a.** Godiva chocolate is owned by Campbell Soup, an American firm.

7. **b.** Vaseline is manufactured by the Anglo-Dutch MNC Unilever PLC.

8. **d.** Wrangler jeans are made by the VF Corporation based in the United States.

9. **d.** Holiday Inn is owned by Britain's Bass PLC, recently renamed Six Continents.

10. **c.** Tropicana orange juice was purchased by U.S.-based PepsiCo.

INTERNET EXERCISE: FRANCHISE OPPORTUNITIES AT McDONALD'S

One of the best-known franchise operations in the world is McDonald's; and in recent years the company has been working to expand its international presence. Why? Because the U.S. market is becoming saturated, and the major growth opportunities lie in the international arena. Visit the McDonald's Web site **www.mcdonalds.com** and find out what is going on in the company. Begin by perusing the latest annual report, and see how well the company is doing both domestically and internationally. Then turn to the franchise information that is provided, and find out how much it would cost to set up a franchise in the following countries: Belgium, Brazil, South Korea,

Mexico, Slovenia, and Turkey. Which seems the most attractive international investment? In addition to this group, in what other countries is the firm seeking franchisees? Would any of these seem particularly attractive to you as investor? Which ones? Why?

Then based on this assignment and the chapter material, answer these last three questions: (1) Will the fact that the euro has become the standard currency in the EU help or hinder a new McDonald's franchisee in Europe? (2) If there are exciting worldwide opportunities, why does McDonald's not exploit these itself instead of looking for franchises? (3) What is the logic in McDonald's expansion strategy?

India

India is located in southern Asia, with the Bay of Bengal on the east and the Arabian Sea on the west. One-sixth of the world's population (approximately 1 billion people) lives within the country's 1.27 million square miles. Though Hindi is the dominant language in terms of number of speakers (it is the mother tongue to over 40 percent of Indians), India is essentially a multilingual nation with more than 10 other languages spoken by 20 million people or more. These include Telugu, Tamil, Marathi, and Bengali. Most states are divided along linguistic lines, with different states accepting different "official" languages (one each). English serves as the national language among the educated Indians. Higher education in science and engineering is in English. The Indian economy derives only a quarter of its output from agriculture, with services contributing almost 55 percent. However, more than 70 percent of Indians are dire ctly or indirectly dependent on agriculture. Three-quarters of Indians live in over 600,000 villages. Many of these communities lack infrastructure such as roads, power, and telecommunications. Hence, India's rural population presents a huge untapped potential for many marketers. The country operates as a democratic republic since its independence in 1947. At that time, India was born of the partition of the former British Indian empire into the new countries of India and Pakistan. This division has been a source of many problems through the years. For example, much to the dismay of the world community, both countries had nuclear tests in a cold war atmosphere. Also, many millions of Indians still live at the lowest level of subsistence, and per capita income is very low. India's misaligned central and local public finances have contributed to an overall fiscal deficit of more than 10 percent of GDP.

In the past, doing business in India has been quite difficult. For example, it took PepsiCo three years just to set up a soft drink concentrate factory, and Gillette, the U.S. razor blade company, had to wait eight years for its application to enter the market to be accepted. Additionally, many MNCs have complained that there are too many barriers to effective operations. In the mid-1970s, the country changed its rules and required that foreign partners hold no more than 40 percent ownership in any business. As a result, some MNCs left India.

In recent years, the government has been relaxing its bureaucratic rules, particularly those relating to foreign investments. From 1981 to 1991, total foreign direct investment in India increased by $250 million, and between 1991 and 1993, it jumped by an additional $2.5 billion. In 2000, foreign direct investment exceeded $3 billion and by 2005

had reached $6.6 billion. Most of this investment has come from the United States and nonresident Indians. One reason for this change in the nation's policies toward business is that the government realizes many MNCs are making a critical choice: India or China? Any monies not invested in India may be lost to China forever. Additionally, it can be seen that foreign investments are having a very positive effect on the Indian economy. After the first big year of new investments (1991), India's annual GDP growth jumped to over 4 percent. In 2006, GDP increased by more than 8 percent.

With the disbandment of the "License Raj," a socialist-inspired system that made government permits mandatory for almost every aspect of business, the climate for foreign investment has improved markedly. Coca-Cola was able to get permission for a 100-percent-owned unit in India in eight weeks, and Motorola received clearance in two days to add a new product line—and did all of this via fax. Other companies that have reported rapid progress include DaimlerChrysler, Procter & Gamble, and Whirlpool. At the same time, however, not everything is roses. Many MNCs are still reporting problems.

The Indian government's new approach however is helping a great deal. In addition, there are other attractions. (1) a large number of highly educated people, especially in areas such as medicine, engineering, and computer science; (2) widespread use of English, long accepted as the international language of business; and (3) low wages and salaries, which often are 10 to 30 percent of those in the world's economic superpowers. While these factors will continue to have a positive impact, the growing debate over jobs outsourced from the United States could dampen some of the impressive growth prospect for India. In addition, the election upset of May 2004, in which the opposition National Congress Party defeated the ruling BJP Party, suggests Indians are concerned about attention to social needs, not just economic growth.

www.ib-net.com

Questions

1. What is the climate for doing business in India? Is it supportive of foreign investment?
2. How important is a highly educated human resource pool for MNCs wanting to invest in India? Is it more important for some businesses than for others?
3. Given the low per capita income of the country, why would you still argue for India to be an excellent place to do business in the coming years?

Here Comes the Competition

The Wadson Company is a management research firm headquartered in New Jersey. The company was recently hired by a large conglomerate with a wide range of products, ranging from toys to electronics and financial services. This conglomerate wants Wadson to help identify an acquisition target. The conglomerate is willing to spend up to $2.5 billion to buy a major company anywhere in the world.

One of the things the research firm did was to identify the amount of foreign direct investment in the United States by overseas companies. The research group also compiled a list of major acquisitions by non-U.S. companies. It gathered these data to show the conglomerate the types of industries and companies that are currently attractive to the international buyers. "If we know what outside firms are buying," the head of the research firm noted, "this can help us identify similar overseas businesses that may also have strong growth potential. In this way, we will not confine our list of recommendations to U.S. firms only." In terms of direct foreign investment by industry, the researchers found that the greatest investment was being made in manufacturing (almost $100 billion). Then, in descending order, came wholesale trade, petroleum, real estate, and insurance.

On the basis of this information, the conglomerate has decided to purchase a European firm. "The best acquisitions in the United States have already been picked," the president told the board of directors. "However, I'm convinced that there are highly profitable enterprises in Europe that are ripe for the taking. I'd particularly like to focus my attention on the UK and Germany." The board gave the president its full support, and the research firm will begin focusing on potential European targets within the next 30 days.

Questions

1. Is Europe likely to be a good area for direct investment during the years ahead?
2. Why is so much foreign money being invested in U.S. manufacturing? Based on your conclusions, what advice would be in order for the conglomerate?
3. If the conglomerate currently does not do business in Europe, what types of problems is it likely to face?

Chapter 2

THE POLITICAL, LEGAL, AND TECHNOLOGICAL ENVIRONMENT

The environment that international managers face is changing rapidly. The past is proving to be a poor indicator of what will happen in the future. Changes are not only more common now but also more significant than ever before, and these dramatic forces of change are creating new challenges. Although there are many dimensions in this new environment, most relevant to international management is the economic environment that was covered in the last chapter and the cultural environment covered in the chapters of Part 2. Also important are the political, legal and regulatory, and technological dimensions of the environment. The objective of this chapter is to examine how the political, legal and regulatory, and technological environments have changed in recent years. Some major trends in each that will help dictate the world in which international managers will compete also are presented. The specific objectives of this chapter are:

OBJECTIVES OF THE CHAPTER

1. INTRODUCE the basic political systems that characterize regions and countries around the world and offer brief examples of each.

2. PRESENT an overview of the legal and regulatory environment in which MNCs operate worldwide.

3. REVIEW key technological developments as well as their impact on MNCs now and in the future.

The World of *BusinessWeek*

BusinessWeek

How Yahoo China Missed Out on the Mainland

If any U.S. Internet company should have done well in China, it's Yahoo! Inc. The Net powerhouse was early on the mainland, establishing a unit there in 1999, well before most U.S.dot-com rivals. With Yahoo Japan, the company already had a big success in the region. And Yahoo co-founder Jerry Yang was born in Taiwan to a father from the mainland, making him something of a local hero.

Yet Yahoo China has suffered numerous management missteps and now trails competitors by a wide margin. The latest setback came on November 27, 2006 when President Xie Wen stepped down "for personal reasons" after just 42 days on the job.

Yahoo's travails in China hurt, and not just because Yang's reputation in the mainland might be tarnished. With more than 123 million people online, China is an important growth market for any Net company. Yahoo faces challenges at home in trying to catch Google Inc. in search ads and sheer buzz. So it's important that it succeed in China.

That goal looks more than elusive each day. The company got a black eye early this year when U.S. pundits and politicians pilloried it for cooperating with Chinese authorities in the arrest of a dissident who had a Yahoo China e-mail account. As a portal, Yahoo lags behind local rivals Sina.com and Sohu.com. So a year ago, Yahoo China decided to focus on search and redesigned its page with an uncluttered look similar to Google's. But after just five months, Yahoo switched back to the busier look of a portal. Today it's a distant third in search behind market leader Baidu.com. "Yahoo still hasn't made a major impact in China," says Duncan Clark, managing director of Beijing consulting firm BDA China Ltd.

To set things right, Yang last year transferred the China operation Alibaba.com, which runs online auction sites in the mainland. In exchange, Yahoo paid $1 billion for a 40% stake in Alibaba. The partnership has hardly been a stellar success. Yang and Alibaba CEO Jack Ma have known each other for years, but industry watchers say there have been disagreements between China managers and California headquarters, and Xie quit shortly after he and Ma returned from a trip to the U.S. to discuss strategy. Yahoo declined to comment, but a spokesman for Alibaba says there haven't been significant disputes.

Spyware Shenanigans

Yahoo China also faces accusations by a former executive that it spreads malware, software that installs itself without permission. The charges come from Zhou Hongyi, who became general manager in 2003 when Yahoo China bought Zhou's search engine. In August 2005, Zhou resigned and soon landed at Qihoo.com, a Net search outfit backed by U.S. venture funds such as Sequoia Capital. Qihoo distributes an anti-spyware program that identifies Yahoo China's toolbar as malware and zaps it from computers. Zhou says that while he worked at Yahoo, the strategy was to distribute the toolbar widely and get users to unwittingly visit sites via pop-up windows. Now he claims he wants to make amends with Qihoo's program. "I opened the Pandora's box, so I should do something to close it." Yahoo China has launched an unfair competition lawsuit against Zhou in Beijing. Zhou has filed a defamation suit of his own.

Despite turmoil, there's some good news. In November Yahoo China won a suit brought by the China Confederation of Anti-Rogue Software, a local anti-malware group. And Morgan Stanley analyst Richard Ji says Yahoo China registered a 16% increase in repeat visitors over the last

THE STAT	
China's search landscape*	
Baidu	62%
Google	25
Yahoo	5

*First choice of search engine
Data: China Internet Network Information Center

Source: From Bruce Einhorn, "How Yahoo Missed Out on the Mainland," *BusinessWeek*, December 18, 2006, p. 54. Reprinted with permission.

year, vs. 3% for Baidu and a drop of 2% for Google. "Although its market share is small," says Ji, Yahoo "is very sticky."

Source: **Reprinted with special permission from "How Yahoo Missed Out on the Mainland," by Bruce Einhom, *BusinessWeek*, December 18, 2006. Copyright © 2006 The McGraw-Hill Companies.**

The opening case provides an excellent example of some of the problems associated with globalization within the context of political, legal, and technological environments. Yahoo China has faced a myriad of obstacles from attaining market recognition and usage to facilitating the silencing of a nonconformist Chinese citizen. Simply networking and recognizing a market growth opportunity are not sufficient; effective strategies that acknowledge and respond to the political, legal, and technological environment are essential for successful integration. While disagreements will arise, partnerships must identify points of parity and evolve from there. Some instances, as illustrated here, prove that political and cultural barriers can provide an unfair advantage to home companies by pushing out international competition. Further, a negative reputation can result when companies acede to local pressures that are at variance with home market values. In an era of accelerating integration and technological advancement, political and legal developments in one region of the world can have profound impacts in many others. MNCs must therefore be sensitive to the changing political, legal, and technological landscape in which they operate.

■ Political Environment

The domestic and international political environments have a major impact on MNCs. As government policies change, MNCs must adjust their strategies and practices to accommodate the new perspectives and actual requirements. Moreover, in a growing number of regions and countries, governments appear to be less stable; therefore, these areas carry more risk than they have in the past. The assessment of political risk will be given specific attention in Chapter 10, but in this chapter we focus on general political systems with selected areas used as illustrations relevant to today's international managers.

The political system or system of government in a country greatly influences how it manages and conducts business. We discussed in Chapter 1 how the government regulates business practices via economic systems. Here we review the general systems currently in place throughout the world. Political systems vary greatly between nation-states across the world. The issue with understanding how to conduct international management practices extends beyond general knowledge of the governmental practices, as this is a surface evaluation. Underlying the actions of a government are the ideologies, or the ideas reflecting the beliefs and values which influence the behavior and culture of nations and political systems.[1] Effective management occurs when the philosophies are recognized.

An evaluation of a political system can be approached from two dimensions. The first dimension focuses on the rights of citizens based on a system of government ranging from fully democratic to totalitarian. The other dimension centers on whether the focus of the political system is on individuals or a broader collective. The first dimension is known as the *ideology* of the system, while the second focuses on the degree to which the system stresses individualism or collectivism. Since no pure form of government exists in any category, we can assume that there are many points of intersection between these two extremes. The observed correlation suggests that democratic societies emphasize individualism, while totalitarian societies lean toward collectivism.[2]

Ideologies

individualism
The political philosophy that people should be free to pursue economic and political endeavors without constraint.

Individualism   Adopters of **individualism** adhere to the philosophy that people should be free to pursue economic and political endeavors without constraint. This means that government interest should not solely influence individual behavior. In a business context, this is synonymous with capitalism and is connected to a free-market society, as discussed in Chapter 1, which states that encouraging diversity or competition, compounded with private ownership, will stimulate productivity over homogeneity and communal ownership. It has been argued that private property is more successful, progressive, and productive than communal property due to increased incentives for maintenance and focus on care for individually owned property. The idea is that working in a group requires less energy per person to achieve the same goal, but an individual will work as hard as he or she has to in order to survive in a competitive environment. Simply following the status quo will stunt progress, while competing will increase creativity and progress. Modern managers may witness this when dealing with those who adopt an individualist philosophy and then must work in a team situation. Research has shown that team performance is negatively influenced by those who consider themselves individualistic; however competition stimulates motivation and encourages increased efforts to achieve goals.[3]

The groundwork for this ideology was founded long ago. Philosophers such as David Hume (1711–1776), Adam Smith (1723–1790), and even Aristotle (384–322 BC) contributed to these principles. While philosophers created the foundation for this belief system, it can be witnessed through modern practice. Eastern Europe, the former Soviet Union, areas of Latin America, Great Britain, and Sweden all have moved toward the idea that the betterment of society is related to the level of freedom individuals have in pursuing economic goals, along with some indication of general individual freedoms and self-expression without governmental constraint. The most well-known movement in Britain toward privatization was led by Prime Minister Margaret Thatcher. During her 11 years in office (1979–1990), she successfully transferred ownership of many companies from the state to individuals, and reduced the government-owned portion of gross national product from 10 to 3.9 percent.[4] She was truly a pioneer in the movement toward a capitalistic society, which has since spread across Europe. International managers must remain alert as to how political changes may impact their business, as a continuous struggle for a foothold in government power often shifts leaders in office. For example, Britain's economy improved under the leadership of Tony Blair; however, his support of the Iraq War severely weakened his position.

Europe has added complexity to the political environment with the unification of the EU, which celebrated its 50th "birthday" in 2007. MNCs cannot avoid political risks even when doing business with individual countries because of what the EU may dictate. It is important to realize that there are vast cultural differences, which will be discussed in Chapter 5, but also that the fate of the EU members is interdependent. Now, whatever happens to one can often influence the others. A good example is provided by France and Germany. Today, Franco-German relations are the cornerstone of a united Europe. The two are tied closely together in a number of ways. For instance, each is among the other's largest trading partners, so each has a vested interest in the other doing well. MNCs doing business in either country find that they must focus on developments in both nations, as well as in the EU at large. Simply put, Europe is no longer a group of fragmented countries; it is a giant and expanding interwoven region in which international management must be aware of what is happening politically, not only in the immediate area of operations but also throughout the continent.[5] The EU consists of not only countries that adhere to individualistic orientations but also those that show collectivist ideals.

Collectivism

Collectivism views the needs or goals of society at large as more important than individual desires.[6] The reason there is no one rigid form of collectivism is because societal goals and the decision of how to keep people focused on them differ greatly among national cultures. The Greek philosopher Plato (427–347 BC) believed that individual rights should be sacrificed and property should be commonly owned. While on the surface one may assume that this leads to a classless society, Plato believed that classes should still exist and that the best suited should rule over the people. Many forms of collectivism do not adhere to that rule.

> **collectivism**
> The political philosophy that views the needs or goals of society as a whole as more important than individual desires.

Collectivism emerged in Germany and Italy as "national socialism," or fascism. *Fascism* is an authoritarian political ideology (generally tied to a mass movement) that considers individual and other societal interests inferior to the needs of the state and seeks to forge a type of national unity, usually based on ethnic, religious, cultural, or racial attributes. Various scholars attribute different characteristics to fascism, but the following elements are usually seen as its integral parts: nationalism, authoritarianism, militarism, corporatism, collectivism, totalitarianism, anticommunism, and opposition to economic and political liberalism.

We will explore individualism and collectivism again in Chapter 4 in the context of national cultural characteristics.

Socialism

Socialism directly refers to a society in which there is government ownership of institutions but profit is not the ultimate goal. It can be viewed as a moderate example of collectivism in practice. In addition to historically communist states such as China, North Korea, and Cuba, socialism has been practiced to varying degrees in recent years in a more moderate form—"democratic socialism"—by Great Britain's Labour Party, Germany's Social Democrats, as well as in France, Spain, and Greece.[7]

> **socialism**
> A moderate form of collectivism in which there is government ownership of institutions, and profit is not the ultimate goal.

Modern socialism draws on the philosophies of Karl Marx (1818–1883), Friedrich Engels (1820–1895), and Vladimir Ilyich Lenin (1870–1924). Marx believed that governments should own businesses because in a capitalistic society only a few would benefit, and it would probably be at the expense of others in the form of not paying due wages to laborers. He contested for a classless society where everything was essentially communal. However, socialism is lax in its convictions, and therefore forms of it are seen as unstable, which is why it branched off into two extremes: communism and social democracy.

Communism is an extreme form of socialist thought which was realized through violent revolution and was committed to the idea of a worldwide communist state. During the 1970s, most of the world's population lived in communist states. The Communist Party encompassed the former Soviet Union, China, and nations in Eastern Europe, Southeast Asia, Africa, and Latin America. Also included were countries such as Cuba, Nicaragua, Cambodia, Laos, and Vietnam. Today much of the communist collective has disintegrated. The extent to which China still exhibits communism is in the form of limiting individual political freedom. China has begun to move away from this belief in the economic and business realm because it has discovered the failure of communism as an economic system due to the tendency of common goals to stunt progression and individual creativity.

Some transitioning countries, such as Russia, are postcommunist but still show signs of an authoritarian government. Russia presents one of the most extreme examples of how the political environment impacts international management. Poorly managed approaches to challenging aspects of the economic and political transition resulted in neglect, corruption, and confusing changes in economic policy.[8] Devoid of funds and experiencing regular gas pipeline leaks, toxic drinking water, pitted roads, and electricity shutoffs, Russia did not present attractive investment opportunities. Yet more companies are taking the risk because of increasing ease of entry, the new attempt at dividing and privatizing the Unified Energy System, and the movement by the Kremlin to begin government funding for the good of society including education, housing, and health care.[9] The challenge for the Russian government is to keep the economy on an even keel while attracting more foreign investment.

One of the biggest problems in Russia and in other transition economies is corruption, which we will discuss in greater depth in Chapter 3. The European Bank for Reconstruction and Development reports that almost one-third of firms doing business in Russia indicate they are required to give bribes in order to do business and that these monies add more than 4 percent to the overall cost of doing business there.[10] As more MNCs invest in Russia, these unethical practices will face increasing scrutiny if political forces can be contained. To date, many multinationals feel that the risk is too great, especially with corruption continuing to spread throughout the country. Despite the Kremlin's support of citizens, Russia is in danger of becoming a unified corrupt system.[11] Still most view Russia as they do China: Both are markets that are too large and potentially too lucrative to ignore. This is especially true since the May 2004 agreement between Russia and the EU for Russia's entry into the WTO. See Table 2-1 for a list of key elements in this agreement. Russia still has a long way to go, since a 2006 index of political democracy published by the Economist Intelligence Unit ranked Russia at 102 out of 167 countries.[12]

Social democracy refers to a socialist movement that achieved its goals through nonviolent revolution. This system was pervasive in such Western nations as Australia, France, Germany, Great Britain, Norway, Spain, and Sweden, as well as in India and Brazil. While social democracy was a great influence on these nations at one time or another, in practice it was not as viable as anticipated. Businesses that were nationalized were quite inefficient due to the guarantee of funding and the monopolistic structure. Citizens noticed a hike in both taxes and prices, which was contrary to the public interest and the good of the people. The 1970s and 1980s brought about a response to this unfair structure with the success of Britain's Conservative Party and Germany's Christian Democratic Party which adopted free-market ideals. Margaret Thatcher, as mentioned above, was a great leader in this movement toward privatization. Although many businesses have been privatized, Britain still has a central government that adheres to the ideal of social democracy. Whether Britain will remain a central government is up for debate. Britain already extends government influence whenever its efficiency and integrity are under question, much to the chagrin of Home Secretary John Reid, who has witnessed the disappointment of constant restructuring. While the movement for Britain to become less centralized may not be immediate, the continued disappointment of having to restructure and still not living up to expectations may make that a reality soon.[13]

Table 2–1
Key Elements of Russia's WTO Accession Deal with the EU

Tariffs

Russia will not exceed an average tariff level of 7.6% for industrial goods, 11% for fishery products, and 13% for agricultural goods.
Tariff rate quotas for fresh and frozen meat and poultry will be around €600 million ($720 million) per year.

Energy

Russian gas prices to domestic industrial users will gradually be increased.
Russia's state gas corporation, Gazprom, will retain its export monopoly. Export duties on gas will be capped at 30%.

Airlines

Russia will revamp the charges currently applied to EU airlines flying over Siberia to make them cost-based and nondiscriminatory.

Banking

Russia will maintain a ban on foreign banks opening branches.
Under existing rules, foreign banks are allowed to open only wholly or partly owned subsidiaries.

Services

Russia has committed to cross-border provision and commercial establishment of certain services.
Sectors include telecoms, transport, financial services, postal, construction, distribution, environmental, news agency, and tourism.

Source: Reuters.

It is important to note here the difference between the nationalization of businesses and nationalism. The nationalization of businesses is the transference of ownership of a business from individuals or groups of individuals to the government. This may be done for several reasons: The ideologies of the country encourage the government to extract more money from the firm, the government believes the firm is hiding money, the government has a large investment in the company, or the government wants to secure wages and employment status because jobs would otherwise be lost. Nationalism, on the other hand, is an ideal in and of itself whereby an individual is completely loyal to his or her nation. People who are a part of this mindset gather under a common flag for such reasons as language or culture. The confusing aspect is that it can be associated with both individualism and collectivism. Nationalism exists in the United States, where there is a national anthem and all citizens gather under a common flag, even though individualism is practiced in the midst of a myriad of cultures and extensive diversity. Nationalism also exists in China, due mostly to the movement against Japan in the mid-1930s and the communist victory in 1949 when communist leader Mao Tse-tung gathered communists and peasants to fight under a common goal. This ultimately led to the People's Republic of China and showed how nationalism is also a part of collectivism.[14]

Political Systems

Democracy **Democracy,** with its European roots and strong presence in Northern and Western Europe, refers to the system in which the government is controlled by the citizens either directly or through elections. Essentially, every citizen should be involved in decision-making processes. The representative government ensures individual freedom since anyone who is eligible may have a voice in the choices made.

A democratic society cannot exist without at least a two-party system. Once elected, the representative is held accountable to the electorate for his or her actions, and this

democracy
A political system in which the government is controlled by the citizens either directly or through elections.

ultimately limits governmental power. Individual freedoms, such as freedom of expression and assembly, are secured. Further protections of citizens include impartial public service, such as a police force and court systems which also serve the government and, in turn, the electorate, though they are not directly affiliated with any political party. Finally, while representatives may be re-elected, the number of terms are often limited, and the elected representative may be voted out during the next election if he or she does not sufficiently adhere to the goals of the majority ruling.[15] As mentioned above, a social democracy combines a socialist ideology with a democratic political system, a situation that has characterized many modern European states as well as some in Latin America and other regions.

Totalitarianism **Totalitarianism** refers to a political system in which there is only one representative party which exhibits control over every facet of political and human life. Power is often maintained by suppression of opposition, which can be violent. George Orwell illustrated an extreme example of this with his fictional writings in *1984*. The government warned that Big Brother was watching at all times, and any hint of opposition would result in harsh "rehabilitation."

totalitarianism
A political system in which there is only one representative party which exhibits control over every facet of political and human life.

While Orwell's fictional writings were quite ominous, they do mirror some of the practices throughout history in totalitarian societies. Media censorship, political repression, and denial of rights and civil liberties are dominant ideals. If there is opposition to government, the response is imprisonment or even worse tactics, often torture. This may be used as a form of rehabilitation or simply a warning to others who may question the government.

Since only one party within each entity exists, there are many forms of totalitarian government. The most common is communist totalitarianism, whose basis we discussed in the collectivism section of ideologies. Most dictatorships under the Communist Party disintegrated by 1989, but as noted above, aspects of this form of government are still found in Cuba, North Korea, Laos, Vietnam, and China. The evolution of modern global business has substantially altered the political systems in Vietnam, Laos, and China, each of which has moved toward a more market-based and pluralistic environment, but each still exhibits some oppression of citizens through denial of civil liberties. The political environment in China is very complex because of the government's desire to balance national, immediate needs with the challenge of a free-market economy and globalization. Since joining the WTO in 2001, China has made trade liberalization a top priority. However, MNCs still face a host of major obstacles when doing business with and in China. For example, government regulations severely hamper multinational activity and favor domestic companies, which results in questionable treatment such as longer document processing times for foreign firms.[16] This makes it increasingly difficult for MNCs to gain the proper legal footing. The biggest problem may well be that the government does not know what it wants from multinational investors, and this is what accounts for the mixed signals and changes in direction that it continually sends. This increases the importance of knowledgeable international managers.

China may therefore be moving further away from its communist affiliation as it begins supporting a more open, democratic society. China will continue to monitor antigovernment actions and practices, but there is a discernible shift toward greater tolerance of individual freedoms.[17] For now, China continues to challenge the capabilities of current international business theory as it transitions through a unique system favoring high governmental control yet striving to unleash a more dynamic market economy.[18]

Though the most common, the totalitarian form of government exhibited in China is not the only one. Other forms of totalitarianism exhibit some form of oppression as well. Parties or individuals that govern an entity based on religious principles will ultimately oppress religious and political expression of its citizens. An example of this can be seen mainly in the Middle Eastern nations of Iran or Saudi Arabia, where the laws and government are based on Islamic principles. Conducting business in the Middle East is, in many ways, similar to operating a business in the Western world.

The Arab countries have been a generally positive place to do business, as many of these nations are seeking modern technology and most have the financial ability to pay for quality services. Worldwide fallout from the war on terrorism, the Afghanistan and Iraq wars, and the ongoing Israel-Arab conflicts, however, have raised tensions in the Middle East considerably, making the business environment there risky and potentially dangerous.

One final form of totalitarianism, sometimes refered to as "right-wing," allows for some economic (but not political) freedoms. While it directly opposes socialist and communist ideas, this form may gain power and support from the military, often in the form of a military leader imposing a government "for the good of the people." This results in military officers filling most government positions. Such military regimes ruled in Germany and Italy from the 1930s to 1940s and persisted in Latin America and Asia until the 1980s when the latter moved toward a democratic form of ruling. Recent examples include Myanmar, where the Military has ruled since the suspension of democracy in 1962.

■ Legal and Regulatory Environment

One reason why today's international environment is so confusing and challenging for MNCs is that they face many different laws and regulations in their global business operations. These factors affect the way businesses are developed and managed within host nations, so special consideration must be paid to the subtle differences in the legal codes from one country to another. Adhering to disparate legal frameworks sometimes prevents large MNCs from capitalizing on manufacturing economies of scale and scope within these regions. In addition, the sheer complexity and magnitude require special attention. This, in turn, results in slower time to market and greater costs. MNCs must take time to carefully evaluate the legal framework in each market in which they do business before launching products or services in those markets.

There are four foundations on which laws are based around the world. Briefly summarized, these are:

1. **Islamic law**. This is law derived from interpretation of the Qur'an and the teachings of the Prophet Muhammad. It is found in most Islamic countries in the Middle East and Central Asia.

2. **Socialist law.** This law comes from the Marxist socialist system and continues to influence regulations in former communist countries, especially those from the former Soviet Union, as well as present-day China, Vietnam, North Korea, and Cuba. Since socialist law requires most property to be owned by the state or state-owned enterprises, MNCs have traditionally shied away from these countries.

3. **Common law.** This comes from English law, and it is the foundation of the legal system in the United States, Canada, England, Australia, New Zealand, and other nations.

4. **Civil or code law.** This law is derived from Roman law and is found in the non-Islamic and nonsocialist countries such as France, some countries in Latin America, and even Louisiana in the United States.

With these broad statements serving as points of departure, the following sections discuss basic principles and examples of the international legal environment facing MNCs today.

Basic Principles of International Law

When compared with domestic law, international law is less coherent because its sources embody not only the laws of individual countries concerned with any dispute but also treaties (universal, multilateral, or bilateral) and conventions (such as the

Islamic law
Law that is derived from interpretation of the Qur'an and the teachings of the Prophet Muhammad and is found in most Islamic countries.

socialist law
Law that comes from the Marxist socialist system and continues to influence regulations in countries formerly associated with the Soviet Union as well as China.

common law
Law that derives from English law and is the foundation of legislation in the United States, Canada, and England, among other nations.

civil or code law
Law that is derived from Roman law and is found in the non-Islamic and nonsocialist countries.

principle of sovereignty
An international principle of law which holds that governments have the right to rule themselves as they see fit.

nationality principle
A jurisdictional principle of international law which holds that every country has jurisdiction over its citizens no matter where they are located.

territoriality principle
A jurisdictional principle of international law which holds that every nation has the right of jurisdiction within its legal territory.

protective principle
A jurisdictional principle of international law which holds that every country has jurisdiction over behavior that adversely affects its national security, even if the conduct occurred outside that country.

doctrine of comity
A jurisdictional principle of international law which holds that there must be mutual respect for the laws, institutions, and governments of other countries in the matter of jurisdiction over their own citizens.

act of state doctrine
A jurisdictional principle of international law which holds that all acts of other governments are considered to be valid by U.S. courts, even if such acts are illegal or inappropriate under U.S. law.

Geneva Convention on Human Rights or the Vienna Convention of Diplomatic Security). In addition, international law contains unwritten understandings that arise from repeated interactions among nations. Conforming to all the different rules and regulations can create a major problem for MNCs. Fortunately, much of what they need to know can be subsumed under several broad and related principles that govern the conduct of international law.

Sovereignty and Sovereign Immunity   The **principle of sovereignty** holds that governments have the right to rule themselves as they see fit. In turn, this implies that one country's court system cannot be used to rectify injustices or impose penalties on another unless that country agrees. So while U.S. laws require equality in the workplace for all employees, U.S. citizens who take a job in Japan cannot sue their Japanese employer under the provisions of U.S. law for failure to provide equal opportunity for them.

International Jurisdiction   International law provides for three types of jurisdictional principles. The first is the **nationality principle,** which holds that every country has jurisdiction (authority or power) over its citizens no matter where they are located. Therefore, a U.S. manager who violates the American Foreign Corrupt Practices Act while traveling abroad can be found guilty in the United States. The second is the **territoriality principle,** which holds that every nation has the right of jurisdiction within its legal territory. Therefore, a German firm that sells a defective product in England can be sued under English law even though the company is headquartered outside England. The third is the **protective principle,** which holds that every country has jurisdiction over behavior that adversely affects its national security, even if that conduct occurred outside the country. Therefore, a French firm that sells secret U.S. government blueprints for a satellite system can be subjected to U.S. laws.

Doctrine of Comity   The **doctrine of comity** holds that there must be mutual respect for the laws, institutions, and governments of other countries in the matter of jurisdiction over their own citizens. Although this doctrine is not part of international law, it is part of international custom and tradition.

Act of State Doctrine   Under the **act of state doctrine,** all acts of other governments are considered to be valid by U.S. courts, even if such acts are inappropriate in the United States. As a result, for example, foreign governments have the right to set limits on the repatriation of MNC profits and to forbid companies from sending more than this amount out of the host country back to the United States.

Treatment and Rights of Aliens   Countries have the legal right to refuse admission of foreign citizens and to impose special restrictions on their conduct, their right of travel, where they can stay, and what business they may conduct. Nations also can deport aliens. For example, the United States has the right to limit the travel of foreign scientists coming into the United States to attend a scientific convention and can insist they remain within 5 miles of the hotel. After the horrific events of 9/11, the U.S. government began greater enforcement of laws related to illegal aliens. As a consequence, closer scrutiny of visitors and temporary workers, including expatriate workers from India and elsewhere who have migrated to the United States for high-tech positions, may result in worker shortages.[19]

Forum for Hearing and Settling Disputes   This is a principle of U.S. justice as it applies to international law. At their discretion, U.S. courts can dismiss cases brought before them by foreigners; however, they are bound to examine issues including where the plaintiffs are located, where the evidence must be gathered, and where the property to be used in restitution is located. One of the best examples of this principle is the Union Carbide pesticide plant disaster in Bhopal, India. Over 2,000 people were killed and thousands left permanently injured when a toxic gas enveloped 40 square kilometers around the plant. The New York Court of Appeals sent the case back to India for resolution.

Examples of Legal and Regulatory Issues

The principles described above help form the international legal and regulatory framework within which MNCs must operate. The following examines some examples of specific laws and situations that can have a direct impact on international business.

Foreign Corrupt Practices Act   During the special prosecutor's investigation of the Watergate scandal in the early 1970s, a number of questionable payments made by U.S. corporations to public officials abroad were uncovered. These bribes became the focal point of investigations by the U.S. Internal Revenue Service, Securities and Exchange Commission (SEC), and Justice Department. This concern over bribes in the international arena eventually culminated in the 1977 passage of the **Foreign Corrupt Practices Act (FCPA),** which makes it illegal to influence foreign officials through personal payment or political contributions. The objectives of the FCPA were to stop U.S. MNCs from initiating or perpetuating corruption in foreign governments and to upgrade the image of both the United States and its businesses abroad.

> **Foreign Corrupt Practices Act (FCPA)**
> An act that makes it illegal to influence foreign officials through personal payment or political contributions; made into U.S. law in 1977 because of concerns over bribes in the international business arena.

Critics of the FCPA feared the loss of sales to foreign competitors, especially in those countries where bribery is an accepted way of doing business. Nevertheless, the U.S. government pushed ahead and attempted to enforce the act. Some of the countries that were named in early bribery cases under the law included Algeria, Kuwait, Saudi Arabia, and Turkey. The U.S. State Department tried to convince the SEC and Justice Department not to reveal countries or foreign officials who were involved in its investigations for fear of creating internal political problems for U.S. allies. Although this political sensitivity was justified for the most part, several interesting developments occurred: (1) MNCs found that they could live within the guidelines set down by the FCPA and (2) many foreign governments actually applauded these investigations under the FCPA, because it helped them crack down on corruption in their own country.

One analysis reported that since passage of the FCPA, U.S. exports to "bribe prone" countries actually increased.[20] Investigations reveal that once bribes were removed as a key competitive tool, more MNCs were willing to do business in that country. This proved to be true even in the Middle East, where many U.S. MNCs always assumed that bribes were required to ensure contracts. Evidence shows that this is no longer true in most cases; and in cases where it is true, those companies that engage in bribery face a strengthened FCPA that now allows the courts to both fine and imprison guilty parties.[21]

Bureaucratization   Very restrictive foreign bureaucracies are one of the biggest problems facing MNCs. This is particularly true when bureaucratic government controls are inefficient and left uncorrected. A good example is Japan, whose political parties feel more beholden to their local interests than to those in the rest of the country. As a result, it is extremely difficult to reorganize the Japanese bureaucracy and streamline the ways things are done, because so many politicians are more interested in the well-being of their own districts than in the long-term well-being of the nation as a whole. In turn, parochial actions create problems for MNCs trying to do business there. The administration of Prime Minister Junichiro Koizumi of Japan tried to reduce some of this bureaucracy.[22] Certainly the long-running recessionary economy of the country is inspiring reforms in the nation's antiquated banking system, opening up the Japanese market to more competition.[23]

Japanese businesses are also becoming more aware of the fact that they are dependent on the world market for many goods and services and that when bureaucratic red tape drives up the costs of these purchases, local consumers pay the price. These businesses are also beginning to realize that government bureaucracy can create a false sense of security and leave them unprepared to face the harsh competitive realities of the international marketplace.

A good example was provided during the mid-1990s when the value of the yen rose sharply and resulted in a decline in international sales by local businesses. Foreign purchasers were unwilling to buy Japanese products that cost 30–40 percent more than they did a few years earlier. At the same time, foreign firms exporting goods into the Japanese market found that they could easily compete because their prices were lower than those of Japanese producers whose costs were pegged to the high-value yen. As a result, Chrysler cut the price of its Jeep Cherokee by 10 percent and sales rose; and American computer manufacturers such as Compaq and IBM, largely on the basis of price, were able to double their share of the Japanese market. Since that time the yen has declined in market value, and local businesses have been able to recapture some lost market share. However, local firms still face greater international competition than ever before.

Additionally, Japan now faces new problems. One of these is that the cost of doing business in Japan is often higher than in other Asian countries. As a result, there has been a recent trend by MNCs toward buying from these less expensive sources. In an effort to deal with this new challenge, the Japanese will have to continue to cut bureaucratic red tape and open their markets to foreign competition. The pressure that has been put on Japan to open its markets in the long run will drive down its own costs of doing business and enable it to remain competitive against world-class organizations.

Privatization   Another example of the changing international regulatory environment is the current move toward privatization by an increasing number of countries. The German government, for example, has sped up privatization and deregulation of its telecommunications market. This has opened a host of opportunities for MNCs looking to create joint ventures with local German firms. Additionally, the French government is putting some of its businesses on the sale block. Meanwhile, in China the government has ordered the military to close or sell off between 10,000 and 20,000 companies that earn an estimated $9.5 billion annually. Known collectively as PLA Inc., the Chinese Army's business interests stretch from Hong Kong to the United States and include five-star hotels, paging services, golf courses, and Baskin-Robbins ice cream franchises. When the government cut the military budget during the early 1990s, it allowed the army to make up the shortfall by earning commercial revenue. However, now the government has decided that the army must exit this end of the business and let the free market take over.[24] As described in Chapter 1's "International Management in Action: Telecommunications Privatization in Brazil," many developing countries are privatizing their telecommunications monopolies to provide greater competition and access to service.

Regulation of Trade and Investment

The regulation of international trade and investment is another area in which individual countries use their legal and regulatory policies to affect the international management environment. The rapid increase in trade and investment has raised concerns among countries that others are not engaging in fair trade, based on the fundamental principles of international trade as specified in the WTO and other trade and investment agreements. Specifically, international trade rules require countries to provide "national treatment," which means that they will not discriminate against others in their trade relations. Unfortunately, many countries engage in government support (subsidies) and other types of practices that distort trade. For example, many developing countries require that foreign MNCs take on local partners in order to do business. Others mandate that MNCs employ a certain percentage of local workers or produce a specific amount in their country. These

The United States Goes to the Mat

The trade relationship between the United States and China is unbalanced to say the least. In 2006, the United States accumulated a $233 billion deficit with China and claims that an extremely undervalued yuan and government subsidies and regulations that favor Chinese MNCs are the main sources of the problem. This is not the first time the United States has voiced complaints. For a number of years, the United States has negotiated with China in an attempt to open its markets and be accorded the same access as the Chinese MNCs. The United States should hold some leverage in these exchanges, since about 60 percent of China's exports are produced from companies that are in whole or part owned by foreign investors; however, the emerging economy still does not operate on market-based values.

U.S. administrations have pushed hard to level the playing field for trading with China. The main strategy has been threats to impose tariffs on Chinese imports. Two petitions put forth in 1991 were quickly rejected, but now that the United States has so much stock in China's growth, it is placing more pressure on the World Trade Organization (WTO). In 2006 the United States and the European Union joined forces to file a complaint that tariff policies in China unfairly block foreign-made auto parts and U.S. imports. Independently, the United States decided to focus responses on specific industries.

NewPage Corporation of Dayton, Ohio, initiated a "countervailing duty" case in 2006 against both Shandong Chenming Paper Holdings and Gold East Paper of China over glossy paper exports. NewPage claimed that government subsidies not only boosted exports, but made those exported goods unfairly inexpensive. WTO rules strictly prohibit governments from using subsidies as a way to support exports; however, China's "non-market" economy status had previously provided some protection from these actions.

China can respond to these claims in a number of ways. One response has been that China will rewrite the nation's tax code and eventually eliminate tax breaks to Chinese businesses. Another has been to draft a plan to buy $12.5 billion of U.S. goods, from mechanical to agricultural. Countervailing had been set at 10.9 percent for Shandong Chenming Paper Holdings, 20.35 percent for Gold East Paper, and 18.16 percent for all other paper companies, and they can be paid by posting bonds or directly depositing cash with U.S. Customs. Understandably, China is not ecstatic about this ruling and may resort to legal action under the WTO. Furthermore, there is a chance that there will be a reduction of glossy paper exports to the United States, and instead those exports will be diverted to other countries or regions. The worst scenario could result in China abandoning the U.S.

market. However, even though glossy paper imports did rise from $29 million in 2004 to $224 million in 2006, they still only account for less than 1 percent of all Chinese imports.

In September 2006, the United States and China announced they had created a "strategic economic dialogue" to provide an overarching framework for bilateral economic dialogue and future economic relations. Bilateral issues such as pressing China for floating exchange rates, greater intellectual property rights, and increasing market access were at the top of the U.S. agenda for this forum, which was added to a range of existing mechanisms for addressing trade and economic issues between the United States and China, including the Joint Commission on Commerce and Trade (JCCT) between the U.S. Department of Commerce, the U.S. Trade Representative, and the Chinese vice premier responsible for trade and the Joint Economic Committee between the U.S. Department of the Treasury and the Chinese Ministry of Finance. In May 2007, Treasury Secretary Henry Paulsen announced that under the dialogue, the United States and China reached agreements to cooperate more closely in the areas of financial services, aviation, energy, and the environment. Just prior to this announcement, China said it would allow the yuan to appreciate further against other currencies, although Congress expressed disappointment that further progress was not made in intellectual property protection.*

The future of these claims and disagreements are uncertain. The United States believes that continued undervaluation of the yuan and subsidies or regulations that favor domestic Chinese companies and protect them from foreign competition maintain a very unlevel playing field. There is evidence of monopolies in aviation, steel, and telecommunication, but the United States has begun chipping away at other, more manageable fields. The United States also recognizes that China is an economic powerhouse and that an excess of tariffs could result in a trade war. It is evident that the EU and the United States would like to break down trade walls and be a part of the lucrative Chinese market, but they may need the added support of the WTO for effective negotiations.

The steps being taken by the U.S. government and the EU are important in opening up the Chinese market. Much needs to be done, however, and the U.S. government believes that success in this area will require it to "go to the mat" with China. The outcome promises to be interesting and vital to the success of world trade.

*Michael, M. Phillips, "Congress Fumes as China Talks Show Few Gains," *Wall Street Journal,* May 24, 2007, p. A1.

practices are not limited to developing countries. Japan, the United States, and many European countries use product standards, "buy local" regulations, and other policies to protect domestic industries and restrict trade.

In addition, most trade agreements require that countries extend most-favored-nation status such that trade benefits accorded one country (such as tariff reductions under the WTO) are accorded all other countries that are parties to that agreement. The emergence of regional trade arrangements has called into question this commitment because, by definition, agreements among a few countries (NAFTA, EU) preference those members over those who are not part of these trading "blocs." In addition, as discussed in Chapter 1, many countries engage in antidumping actions intended to offset the practice of trading partners "dumping" products at below cost or home market price, as well as countervailing duty actions intended to offset foreign government subsidization. In each case, there is evidence that many countries abuse these laws to protect domestic industries, something the WTO has been more vigilant in monitoring in recent years.

■ Technological Environment and Global Shifts in Production

Technological advancements not only connect the world at lightning speed but also aid in the increased quality of products, information gathering, and R&D. Manufacturing, information processing, and transportation are just a few examples of where technology improves organizational and personal business. The need for instant communication increases exponentially as global markets expand. MNCs need to keep their businesses connected; this is becoming increasingly easier as technology contributes to "flattening the world." Thomas Friedman, in his book *The World Is Flat,* writes that such events as the introduction of the Internet or the World Wide Web, along with mobile technologies, open sourcing, and work flow software distribution, not only enable businesses and individuals to access vast amounts of information at their fingertips in real time but are also resulting in the world flattening into a more level playing field.[25]

Trends in Technology, Communication, and Innovation

Innovation of the microprocessor could be considered the foundation of much of the technological and computing advancements seen today.[26] The creation of a digital framework allowed high-power computer performance at low cost. This then gave birth to such breakthroughs as the development of enhanced telecommunication systems, which will be explored in greater depth later in the chapter. Now, computers, telephones, televisions, and wireless forms of communication have merged to create multimedia products and allow users anywhere in the world to communicate with one another. The Internet allows one to obtain information from literally billions of sources. The number of people who use cellular phones is greater than ever, and in countries such as Finland, Norway, and Sweden over half the population are cellular subscribers.[27]

Global connections do not necessarily level the playing field, however. The challenge of integrating telecom standards has become an issue for MNCs in China. Qualcomm Corporation had wanted to sell China narrowband CDMA (code division multiple access) technology; however, Qualcomm was unsuccessful in convincing the government that it could build enough products locally. This doomed its plans for CDMA production in China, a technology that is in use in the United States and a few other countries. Instead, China's current network, the world's largest mobile network, will use primarily GSM technology that is popular in Europe.[28] Furthermore, concepts like the open-source model allow for free and legal sharing of software and code, which may be utilized by underdeveloped countries in an attempt to gain competitive advantage while minimizing costs. India exemplifies this practice as it continues to increase its adoption of the Linux operating system (OS) in place of the global standard Microsoft Windows. The state of Kerala is shifting the software of its 2,600 high schools to the Linux system, which will enable a user to configure it to his or her needs. This may create a generation of adept programmers, but it could soon be an obsolete system. Microsoft is attempting to develop India-specific software to allow for more versatility and pricing flexibility, which may be necessary to avoid the potential of India's emerging technological hub falling short of its potential.[29]

There also exists a great potential for disappointment as the world relies more and more on digital communication and imaging. The world is connected by a vast network of cables which we do not see because they are either buried underground or under water. One disruption occurred off the shores of Asia on December 26, 2006, when undersea cables were destroyed by rock slides, cutting phone and Internet connections in Taiwan, China, South Korea, Japan, and India. The fact that so many were reliant on a mere 4-inch-thick cable shows the potential risks associated with greater global connectivity. Restoration of some services to most of the affected areas was accomplished within 12 hours of the earthquake by rerouting digital traffic through Europe to the United States with other network cables.[30]

The possibilities of digital and wireless technologies are vast. Researchers at the Massachusetts Institute of Technology have recently discovered a way to wirelessly recharge batteries, a phenomenon they call "WiTricity."[31] Microsoft also introduced "Surface" at a 2007 conference, a touch-screen computer that looks like a tabletop and does not have a keyboard. Wireless compatible phones, cameras, music players, and so on will be able to exchange data between the unit and the computer with just a few simple hand motions.[32]

We have reviewed general influences of technology here, but what are some of the make specific dimensions of technology? What are other ways in which technology will affect international management? Here, we explore some of the dimensions of the technological environment currently facing international management with a closer look at biotechnology, e-business, telecommunications, and the connection between technology, outsourcing, and offshoring.

In addition to the trends discussed above, other specific ways in which technology will affect international management in the next decade include:

1. Rapid advances in biotechnology that are built on the precise manipulation of organisms, which will revolutionize the fields of agriculture, medicine, and industry.

2. The emergence of nanotechnology, in which nanomachines will possess the ability to remake the whole physical universe.

3. Satellites that will play a role in learning. For example, communication firms will place tiny satellites into low orbit, making it possible for millions of people, even in remote or sparsely populated regions such as Siberia, the Chinese desert, and the African interior, to send and receive voice, data, and digitized images through handheld telephones.

4. Automatic translation telephones, which will allow people to communicate naturally in their own language with anyone in the world who has access to a telephone.

5. Artificial intelligence and embedded learning technology, which will allow thinking that formerly was felt to be only the domain of humans to occur in machines.

6. Silicon chips containing up to 100 million transistors, allowing computing power that now rests only in the hands of supercomputer users to be available on every desktop.

7. Supercomputers that are capable of 1 trillion calculations per second, which will allow advances such as simulations of the human body for testing new drugs and computers that respond easily to spoken commands.[33]

The development and subsequent use of these technologies have greatly benefited the mostly developed countries in which they were first deployed. However, the most positive effects should be seen in developing countries where inefficiencies in labor and production impede growth. Although all these technological innovations will affect international management, specific technologies will have especially pronounced effects in transforming economies and business practices. The following discussion highlights some specific dimensions of the technological environment currently facing international management.

Biotechnology

The digital age has given rise to such innovations as computers, cellular phones, and wireless technology. Advancements within this realm allow for more efficient communication and productivity to the point where the digital world has extended its effect from information systems to biology. **Biotechnology** is the integration of science and technology, but more specifically it is the creation of agricultural or medical products through industrial use and manipulation of living organisms. At first glance, it appears that the fusion of these two disciplines could breed a modern bionic man immune to disease, especially with movements toward technologically advanced prosthetics, cell regeneration through stem cell research, or laboratory-engineered drugs to help prevent or cure diseases such as HIV or cancer.

For example, China has already begun to use stem cells at the clinical level, since there are fewer cultural and political barriers to prevent this medical procedure there. Attracting worldwide patients, this treatment has alleviated suffering from spinal injuries, cerebral palsy, multiple sclerosis, and other ailments.[34] Stem cell research is not universally accepted. Those who object pinpoint ethical issues, a topic considered in detail in Chapter 3, including what factors determine the stage in which life begins. Scientists are beginning to side-step this roadblock by finding new, innovative ways to regenerate cells. Recently, three research teams from the United States and Japan have discovered a way to take mature cells, such as skin cells, and essentially turn back the clock. The cells reverse their growth process until they mirror embryonic cell structures, becoming a clean slate. Cells can then be reprogrammed to grow into anything from a nerve to a heart. While this has not yet been attempted in humans, it is a new market discovery bringing us one step closer to an era of fighting health issues.[35]

Pharmaceutical competition is also prevalent on the global scale with China's raw material reserve and the emergence of biotech companies such as Genentech and the new Merck, after its acquisition of Swiss biotech company Serono. India is emerging as a major player, with its largest, mostly generic, pharmaceutical company Ranbaxy's ability to produce effective and affordable drugs.[36] While pharmaceutical companies mainly manufacture drugs through a process similar to that of organic chemistry, biotech companies attempt to discover genetic abnormalities or medicinal solutions through exploring organisms at the molecular level or formulating compounds from inorganic materials that mirror organic substances. DNA manipulation in the laboratory extends beyond human research. As mentioned above, another aspect of biotech research is geared toward agriculture. Demand for ethanol in the United States is on the rise due to uncertain future oil supplies, making corn-derived ethanol a viable alternative. Yet, using corn as a fuel alternative will not only increase the cost of fuel but also create an imbalance between consumable corn and stock used for biofuel.[37] For this and many other reasons, global companies like Monsanto are collaborating with others such as BASF AG to work toward creating genetically modified seeds such as drought-tolerant corn and herbicide-tolerant soybeans.[38] Advancements in this industry include nutritionally advanced crops that may help alleviate world hunger.[39]

Aside from crops, the meat industry can also benefit from this process. The outbreak of mad cow disease in Great Britain sparked concern when evidence of the disease spread throughout Western Europe; however, the collaborative work of researchers in the United States and Japan may have engineered a solution to the problem by eliminating the gene which is the predecessor to making the animal susceptible to this ailment.[40] Furthermore, animal cloning, which simply makes a copy of pre-existing DNA, could boost food production by producing more meat or dairy-producing animals. The first evidence of a successful animal clone was Dolly, born in Scotland in 1996. Complications

---

biotechnológy

The integration of science and technology to create agricultural or medical products through industrial use and manipulation of living organisms.

arose, and Dolly aged at an accelerated rate, indicating that while she provided hope, there still existed many flaws in the process. While the United States is the only country that allows cloned animal products to be incorporated in the food supply, other countries actively cloning animals include Australia, Italy, China, South Korea, Japan, and New Zealand.[41] The world is certainly changing, and the trend toward technological integration is far from over. Whether one desires laser surgery to correct eyesight, a vaccine for emerging viruses, or more nutritious food, there is a biotechnology firm competing to be the first to achieve these goals. Hunger and poor health care is a worldwide issue, and advancement in global biotechnology is working to raise the standards.

E-Business

As the Internet becomes increasingly widespread, it is having a dramatic effect on international commerce. For example, millions of Americans have purchased books from Amazon.com, and the company has now expanded its operations around the world. So have a host of other electronic retailers (e-tailers) which are discovering that their home-grown retailing expertise can be easily transferred and adapted for the international market.[42] Dell Computer has been offering B2C (electronic business–to-consumer) goods and services in Europe for a number of years, and the automakers are now beginning to move in this direction. Most automotive firms sell custom cars online.[43] Other firms are looking to use e-business to improve their current operations. For example, Deutsche Bank has overhauled its entire retail network with the goal of winning affluent customers across the continent.[44] Yet the most popular form of e-business is for business-to-business (B2B) dealings, such as placing orders and interacting with suppliers worldwide. Business-to-consumer (B2C) transactions will not be as large, but this is an area where many MNCs are trying to improve their operations.

The area of e-business that will most affect global customers is e-retailing and financial services. For example, customers can now use their keyboard to pay by credit card, although security remains a problem. However, the day is fast approaching when electronic cash (e-cash) will become common. This scenario already occurs in a number of forms. A good example is prepaid smart cards, which are being used mostly for telephone calls and public transportation. An individual can purchase one of these cards and use it in lieu of cash. This idea is blending with the Internet, allowing individuals to buy and sell merchandise and transfer funds electronically. The result will be global digital cash, which will take advantage of existing worldwide markets that allow buying and selling on a 24-hour basis.

This technological development also will have a major impact on financial institutions. After all, who will need the local corner ATM when they can tap into their funds through the Internet? Similarly, companies will not have to wait for their money from buyers, thus eliminating (or at least substantially reducing) bad debts while increasing their working capital. Therefore, if General Electric shipped $12 million of merchandise to Wal-Mart in Hong Kong with payment due on delivery, the typical 7- to 10-day waiting period between payment and collection of international transactions would, for all intents and purposes, be eliminated.[45]

Of course, e-cash creates many problems, and it will take some time for these to be resolved. For example, if a Mexican firm pays for its merchandise in pesos, there must be some system for converting these pesos into U.S. dollars. At present, such transactions are handled through regulated foreign exchange markets. In the near future, these transactions likely will be denominated in a single, conventional currency and exchanged at conventional market rates. It is equally likely, however, that the entire system of transactions eventually will become seamless and require no processing through foreign exchange markets. One expert explained it this way:

> Ideally, the ultimate e-cash will be a currency without a country (or a currency of all countries), infinitely exchangeable without the expense and inconvenience of conversion between local denominations. It may constitute itself as a wholly new currency with its own denomination— the "cyber dollar," perhaps. Or, it may continue to fix itself by reference to a traditional currency,

in which case the American dollar would seem to be the likeliest possibility. Either way, it is hard to imagine that the existence of an international, easy-to-use, cheap-to-process, hard-to-tax electronic money will not then force freer convertibility on traditional currencies.[46]

Telecommunications

One of the most important dimensions of the technological environment facing international management today is telecommunications. To begin with, it no longer is necessary to hardwire a city to provide residents with telephone service. This can be done wirelessly, thus allowing people to use cellular phones, pagers, and other telecommunications services. As a result, a form of technologic leapfrogging is occurring, in which regions of the world are moving from a situation where phones were unavailable to one where cellular is available everywhere, including rural areas, due to the quick and relatively inexpensive installation of cellular infrastructure. In addition, technology is merging the telephone and the computer. As a result, in Europe and Asia growing numbers of people are now accessing the Web through their cell phones. While this development has not attracted a large market in the United States, over 125 million Asians and 50 million Europeans now use this service.[47] Over the next decade, the merging of the Internet and wireless technology will radically change the ways people communicate.[48] Wireless technology is also proving to be a boon for less developed countries, such as in South America and Eastern Europe where customers once waited years to get a telephone installed.

One reason for this rapid increase in telecommunications services is many countries believe that without an efficient communications system their economic growth may stall. Additionally, governments are accepting the belief that the only way to attract foreign investment and know-how in telecommunications is to cede control to private industry. As a result, while most telecommunications operations in the Asia-Pacific region were state-run a decade ago, a growing number are now in private hands. Singapore Telecommunications, Pakistan Telecom, Thailand's Telecom Asia, Korea Telecom, and Globe Telecom in the Philippines all have been privatized, and MNCs have helped in this process by providing investment funds. Today, NYNEX holds a stake in Telecom Asia; Bell Atlantic and Ameritech each own 25 percent of Telecom New Zealand; and Bell South has an ownership position in Australia's Optus. At the same time, Australia's Telestra is moving into Vietnam, Japan's NTT is investing in Thailand, and Korea Telecom is in the Philippines and Indonesia.

Many governments are reluctant to allow so much private and foreign ownership of such a vital industry; however, they also are aware that foreign investors will go elsewhere if the deal is not satisfactory. The Hong Kong office of Salomon Brothers, a U.S. investment bank, estimates that to meet the expanding demand for telecommunication service in Asia, companies will need to considerably increase the investment, most of which will have to come from overseas. MNCs are unwilling to put up this much money unless they are assured of operating control and a sufficiently high return on their investment.

Developing countries are eager to attract telecommunication firms and offer liberal terms. Cable & Wireless of Great Britain has opened an office in Hanoi. In Hong Kong, while the local telephone monopoly will not lose its grip on international services until 2006, its monopoly on local services has ended, and private groups are competing to provide service.

Technology, Outsourcing, and Offshoring

As MNCs use advanced technology to help them communicate, produce, and deliver their goods and services internationally, they face a new challenge: how technology will affect the nature and number of their employees. Some informed observers note that technology already has eliminated much and in the future will eliminate even more of the work being done by middle management and white-collar staff. Mounting cost pressures resulting from increased globalization of competition and profit expectations exerted by investors have placed pressure on MNCs to outsource or offshore production to take advantage of lower labor and other costs.[49] In the past century, machines replaced millions of manual laborers, but those who worked with their minds were able to thrive and survive. During the past three decades in particular, employees in blue-collar, smokestack industries such as steel and autos have been downsized by technology, and the result has been a permanent restructuring of the number of employees needed to run factories efficiently. In the 1990s, a similar trend unfolded in the white-collar service industries (insurance, banks, and even government). Most recently, this trend has affected high-tech companies, after the dot-com bubble burst, hundreds of thousands of jobs were lost.

Some experts predict that in the future technology has the potential to displace employees in all industries, from those doing low-skilled jobs to those holding positions traditionally associated with knowledge work. For example, voice recognition is helping to replace telephone operators; the demand for postal workers has been reduced substantially by address-reading devices; and cash-dispensing machines can do 10 times more transactions in a day than bank tellers, so tellers can be reduced in number or even eliminated entirely in the future. Also, expert (sometimes called "smart") systems can eliminate human thinking completely. For example, American Express has an expert system that performs the credit analysis formerly done by college-graduate financial analysts. In the medical field, expert systems can diagnose some illnesses as well as doctors can, and robots capable of performing certain operations are starting to be used.

Emerging information technology also makes work more portable. As a result, MNCs have been able to move certain production activities overseas to capitalize on cheap labor resources. This is especially true for work that can be easily contracted with overseas locations. For example, low-paid workers in India and Asian countries now are being given subcontracted work such as labor-intensive software development and code-writing jobs. A restructuring of the nature of work and of employment is a result of such information technology; Figure 2–1 identifies some winners and losers in the workforce in recent years.

The new technological environment has both positives and negatives for MNCs and societies as a whole. On the positive side, the cost of doing business worldwide should decline thanks to the opportunities that technology offers in substituting lower-cost machines for higher-priced labor. Over time, productivity should go up, and prices should go down. On the negative side, many employees will find either their jobs eliminated or their wages and salaries reduced because they have been replaced by machines and their skills are no longer in high demand. This job loss from technology can be especially devastating in developing countries. However, it doesn't have to be this way. A case in point is South Africa's showcase for automotive productivity, the Delta Motor Corporation's Opel Corsa plant in Port Elizabeth. To provide as many jobs as possible, this world-class operation automated only 23 percent, compared to more than 85 percent auto assembly in European and North America.[50] Also, some industries can add jobs. For example, the positive has outweighed the negative in the computer and information technology industry, despite its ups and downs. Specifically, employment in the U.S. computer software industry has increased over the last decade. In less developed countries such as India, a high-tech boom in recent years has created jobs and opportunities for a growing number of people.[51] Additionally, even though developed countries such as Japan and the United States are most affected by technological displacement of workers, both nations still lead the world in creating new jobs and shifting their traditional industrial structure toward a high-tech, knowledge-based economy.

The precise impact that the advanced technological environment will have on international management over the next decade is difficult to forecast. One thing is certain, however; there is no turning back the technological clock. MNCs and nations alike must evaluate the impact of these changes carefully and realize that their economic performance is closely tied to keeping up with, or ahead of, rapidly advancing technology.

The World of *BusinessWeek*—Revisited

As the *BusinessWeek* article at the beginning of this chapter illustrates, political, legal, and technological environments can alter the landscape of global companies. Yahoo's responses to these environments affected its ability to gain

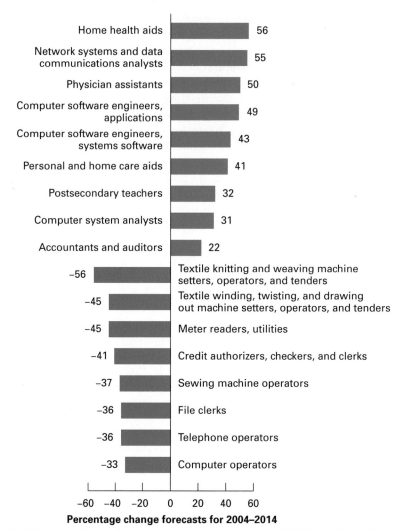

Figure 2–1

Winners and Losers in Selected Occupations: Percentage Change Forecasts for 2004–2014

Home health aids — 56
Network systems and data communications analysts — 55
Physician assistants — 50
Computer software engineers, applications — 49
Computer software engineers, systems software — 43
Personal and home care aids — 41
Postsecondary teachers — 32
Computer system analysts — 31
Accountants and auditors — 22

−56 Textile knitting and weaving machine setters, operators, and tenders
−45 Textile winding, twisting, and drawing out machine setters, operators, and tenders
−45 Meter readers, utilities
−41 Credit authorizers, checkers, and clerks
−37 Sewing machine operators
−36 File clerks
−36 Telephone operators
−33 Computer operators

Percentage change forecasts for 2004–2014

Source: U.S. Bureau of Labor Statistics, www.bls.gov/opub/mlr/2005/11/art5full.pdf.

market share in China and adversely influenced global perceptions and investment. Now more than ever, international managers need to be aware of how differing political, legal, and technological environments are affecting their business and how globalization, security concerns, and other developments influence these environments. Changes in political, legal, and environmental conditions also open up new business opportunities but close some old ones.

In light of the information you have learned from reading this chapter, you should have a good understanding of these environments and some of the ways in which they will affect companies doing business abroad. Drawing on this knowledge, answer the following questions: (1) How will changes in the political and legal environment in China affect U.S. MNCs conducting business there? (2) How might rules governing data privacy and free speech affect future investment by Internet companies such as Yahoo? (3) How does technology result in greater integration and dependencies among economies, political systems, and financial markets?

SUMMARY OF KEY POINTS

1. The global political environment can be understood via an appreciation of ideologies and political

systems. Ideologies, including individualism and collectivism, reflect underlying tendencies in society. Political systems, including democracy and totalitarianism, incorporate ideologies into political structures. There are fewer and fewer purely collectivist or socialist societies, although totalitarianism still exists in several countries and regions. Many countries are experiencing transitions from more socialist to democratic systems, reflecting related trends discussed in Chapter 1 toward more market-oriented economic systems.

2. The current legal and regulatory environment is both complex and confusing. There are many different laws and regulations to which MNCs doing business internationally must conform, and each nation is unique. Also, MNCs must abide by the laws of their own country. For example, U.S. MNCs must obey the rules set down by the Foreign Corrupt Practices Act. Privatization and regulation of

trade also affect the legal and regulatory environment in specific countries.

3. The technological environment is changing quickly and is having a major impact on international business. This will continue in the future. For example, digitization, higher-speed telecommunication, and advancements in biotechnology offer developing countries new opportunities to leapfrog into the 21st century. New markets are being created for high-tech MNCs that are eager to provide telecommunications service. Technological developments also impact both the nature and the structure of employment, shifting the industrial structure toward a more high-tech, knowledge-based economy. MNCs that understand and take advantage of this high-tech environment should prosper, but they also must keep up, or ahead, to survive.

KEY TERMS

act of state doctrine, *44*

biotechnology, *50*

civil or code law, *43*

collectivism, *39*

common law, *43*

democracy, *41*

doctrine of comity, *44*

Foreign Corrupt Practices Act (FCPA), *45*

individualism, *38*

Islamic law, *43*

nationality principle, *44*

principle of sovereignty, *44*

protective principle, *44*

socialism *39*

socialist law, *43*

territoriality principle, *44*

totalitarianism, *42*

REVIEW AND DISCUSSION QUESTIONS

1. In what ways do different ideologies and political systems influence the environment in which MNCs operate? Would these challenges be less for those operating in the EU than for those in Russia or China? Why or why not?

2. How do the following legal principles impact MNC operations: the principle of sovereignty, the nationality principle, the territoriality principle, the protective principle, and principle of comity?

3. How will advances in technology and telecommunications affect developing countries? Give some specific examples.

4. Why are developing countries interested in privatizing their telecommunications industries? What opportunities does privatization have for telecommunication MNCs?

INTERNET EXERCISE: HITACHI GOES WORLDWIDE

Hitachi products are well known in the United States, as well as in Europe and Asia. However, in an effort to continue maintaining its international momentum, the Japanese MNC is continuing to push forward into new markets while also developing new products. Visit the MNC at its Web site **www.hitachi.com,** and examine some of the latest developments that are taking place. Begin by reviewing the firm's current activities in Asia, specifically Hong Kong and Singapore. Then look at how it is doing business in North America. Finally, read about its Euro-

pean operations. All of these are available at this Web site. Then answer these three questions: (1) What kinds of products does the firm offer? What are its primary areas of emphasis? (2) In what types of environments does it operate? Is Hitachi primarily interested in developed markets, or is it also pushing into newly emerging markets? (3) Based on what it has been doing over the last two to three years, what do you think Hitachi's future strategy will be in competing in the environment of international business during the first decade of the new millennium?

Vietnam

Located in Southeast Asia, the Socialist Republic of Vietnam is bordered to the north by the People's Republic of China, to the west by Laos and Cambodia, and to the east and south by the South China Sea. The country is a mere 127,000 square miles but has a population of almost 84.5 million. The language is Vietnamese, and the principal religion Buddhism, although there are a number of small minorities, including Confucian, Christian (mainly Catholic), Caodist, Daoist, and Hoa Hao. In recent years, the country's economy has been up and down, but average annual per capita income still is in the hundreds of dollars as the peasants remain very poor.

One of the reasons that Vietnam has lagged behind its fast-developing neighbors in Southeast Asia, such as Thailand and Malaysia, is its isolation from the industrial West, and the United States in particular, because of the Vietnam War. From the mid-1970s, the country had close relations with the U.S.S.R., but the collapse of communism there forced the still-communist Vietnamese government to work on establishing stronger economic ties with other countries. The nation recently has worked out many of its problems with China, and today, the Chinese have become a useful economic ally. Vietnam would most like to establish a vigorous trade relationship with the United States, however. Efforts toward this end began over a decade ago, but because of lack of information concerning the many U.S. soldiers still unaccounted for after the war, it was not until 1993 that the United States permitted U.S. companies to take part in ventures in Vietnam that were financed by international aid agencies. Then, in 1994, the U.S. trade embargo was lifted, and a growing number of American firms began doing business in Vietnam.

Caterpillar began supplying equipment for a $2 billion highway project. Mobil teamed with three Japanese partners to begin drilling offshore. Exxon, Amoco, Conoco, Unocal, and Arco negotiated production-sharing contracts with Petro Vietnam. General Electric opened a trade office and developed plans to use electric products throughout the country. AT&T began working to provide long-distance service both in and out of the country. Coca-Cola began bottling operations. Within the first 12 months, 70 U.S. companies obtained licenses to do business in Vietnam. Besides the United States, the largest investors have been Singapore, Taiwan, Japan, South Korea, and Hong Kong, which collectively have put over $22 billion into the country. Most recently, Intel signed a $1 billion deal to build a 500,000 square foot semiconductor assembly plant in Vietnam. Plans state that construction should be completed by 2009, and an estimated 4,000 jobs could be created throughout the process, adding solid footing to Vietnam's attempt at competing in the global market.

Over the past couple of years, Vietnamese authorities have acted swiftly to implement the structural reforms needed to modernize the national economy and to produce more competitive exports for sale in the global economy. In July 2000 the United States and Vietnam signed a bilateral trade agreement that opens up trade and foreign investment in Vietnam and gives Vietnamese exporters access to the vast U.S. market. The treaty, which entered into force near the end of 2001, is also expected to increase foreign direct investment from the United States over the next decade. This, in turn, should help stimulate direct investment from other pro-trade societies around the world. As in China, many U.S. firms have found doing business in Vietnam frustrating because of the numerous and ever-changing bureaucratic rules enacted by the communist government officials; but these concerns are beginning to subside with the induction of Vietnam into the World Trade Organization on January 11, 2007. After 11 years of preparation, with 8 years of negotiation, Vietnam finally became the 150th member of the WTO. As a result, Vietnam should experience continued economic stimulus through its liberalizing reforms. Overall, this opportunity may open the market to foreign investors who were unsure of the risks involved in entering Vietnam. Vietnam's accession to the WTO provides a context of greater certainty and predictability in the business and broader economic environment.

Questions

1. In what way does the political environment in Vietnam pose both an opportunity and a threat for American MNCs seeking to do business there?

2. Why are U.S. multinationals so interested in going into Vietnam? How much potential does the country offer? Conversely, how much benefit can Vietnam derive from a business relationship with U.S. MNCs?

3. Will there be any opportunities in Vietnam for high-tech American firms? Why or why not?

A Chinese Venture

The Darby Company is a medium-sized communications technology company headquartered on the west coast of the United States. Among other things, Darby holds a patent on a mobile telephone that can operate effectively within a 5-mile radius. The phone does not contain state-of-the-art technology, but it can be produced extremely cheaply. As a result, the Chinese government has expressed interest in manufacturing and selling this phone throughout its country.

Preliminary discussions with the Chinese government reveal some major terms of the agreement that it would like to include: (1) Darby will enter into a joint venture with a local Chinese firm to manufacture the phones to Darby's specifications; (2) these phones will be sold throughout China at a 100 percent markup, and Darby will receive 10 percent of the profits; (3) Darby will invest $35 million in building the manufacturing facility, and these costs will be recovered over a five-year period; and (4) the government in Beijing will guarantee that at least 100,000 phones are sold every year, or it will purchase the difference.

The Darby management is not sure whether this is a good deal. In particular, Darby executives have heard all sorts of horror stories regarding agreements that the Chinese government has made and then broken. The company also is concerned that once its technology is understood, the Chinese will walk away from the agreement and start making these phones on their own. Because the technology is not state-of-the-art, the real benefit is in the low production costs, and the technological knowledge is more difficult to protect.

For its part, the Chinese government has promised to sign a written contract with Darby, and it has agreed that any disputes regarding enforcement of this contract can be brought, by either side, to the World Court at the Hague for resolution. Should this course of action be taken, each side would be responsible for its own legal fees, but the Chinese have promised to accept the decision of the court as binding.

Darby has 30 days to decide whether to sign the contract with the Chinese. After this time, the Chinese intend to pursue negotiations with a large telecommunications firm in Europe and try cutting a deal with it. Darby is more attractive to the Chinese, however, because of the low cost of producing its telephone. In any event, the Chinese are determined to begin mass-producing cellular phones in their country. "Our future is tied to high-tech communication," the Chinese minister of finance recently told Darby's president. "That is why we are so anxious to do business with your company; you have quality phones at low cost." Darby management is flattered by these kind words but still unsure if this is the type of business deal in which it wants to get involved.

Questions

1. How important is the political environment in China for the Darby Company? Explain.

2. If a disagreement arises between the two joint-venture partners and the government of China reneges on its promises, how well protected is Darby's position? Explain.

3. Are the economic and technological environments in China favorable for Darby? Why or why not?

Chapter 3

ETHICS AND SOCIAL RESPONSIBILITY

OBJECTIVES OF THE CHAPTER

Recent concerns about ethics and social responsibility transcend national borders. In this era of globalization MNCs must be concerned with how they carry out their business and their social role in foreign countries. This chapter examines business ethics and social responsibility in the international arena, and it looks at some of the critical social issues that will be confronting MNCs in the years ahead. The discussion includes ethical decision making in various countries, regulation of foreign investment, the growing trends toward environmental sustainability, and current responses to social responsibility by today's multinationals. The specific objectives of this chapter are:

1. **EXAMINE** ethics in international management and some of the major ethical issues and problems confronting MNCs in selected countries.

2. **DISCUSS** some of the pressures on and actions being taken by selected industrialized countries and companies to be more socially and environmentally responsive to world problems.

3. **EXPLAIN** some of the initiatives to bring greater accountability to corporate conduct and limit the impact of corruption around the world.

The World of *BusinessWeek*

BusinessWeek

Beyond the Green Corporation

For years, the term "sustainability" has carried a lot of baggage. Put simply, it's about meeting humanity's needs without harming future generations. It was a favorite cause among economic development experts, human rights activists, and conservationists. But to many U.S. business leaders, sustainability just meant higher costs and smacked of earnest U.N. corporate-responsibility conferences and the utopian idealism of Western Europe. Now, sustainability is "right at the top of the agendas" of more U.S. CEOs, especially young ones, says McKinsey Global Institute Chairman Lenny Mendonca.

More than PR

You can tell something is up just wading through the voluminous sustainability reports most big corporations post on their Web sites. These lay out efforts to cut toxic emissions, create eco-friendly products, help the poor, and cooperate with nonprofit groups. As recently as five years ago, such reports—if they appeared at all—were usually transparent efforts to polish the corporate image. Now there's a more sophisticated understanding that environmental and social practices can yield strategic advantages in an interconnected world of shifting customer loyalties and regulatory regimes.

Embracing sustainability can help avert costly setbacks from environmental disasters, political protests, and human rights or workplace abuses—the kinds of debacles suffered by Royal Dutch Shell PLC in Nigeria and Unocal in Burma. "Nobody has an idea when such events can hit a balance sheet, so companies must stay ahead of the curve," says Matthew J. Kiernan, CEO of Innovest Strategic Value Advisors. Innovest is an international research and advisory firm whose clients include large institutional investors.

The roster of advocates includes Jeffrey Immelt, CEO of General Electric Co., who is betting billions to position GE as a leading innovator in everything from wind power to hybrid engines. Wal-Mart Stores Inc., long assailed for its labor and global sourcing practices, has made a series of high-profile promises to slash energy use overall, from its stores to its vast trucking fleets, and purchase more electricity derived from renewable sources. GlaxoSmithKline discovered that, by investing to develop drugs for poor nations, it can work more effectively with those governments to make sure its patents are protected. Dow Chemical Co. is increasing R&D in products such as roof tiles that deliver solar power to buildings and water treatment technologies for regions short of clean water. "There is 100% overlap between our business drivers and social and environmental interests," says Dow CEO Andrew N. Liveris.

Striking that balance is not easy. Many noble efforts fail because they are poorly executed or never made sense to begin with. Sustainability can be a hard proposition for investors, too. Decades of experience show that it's risky to pick stocks based mainly on a company's long-term environmental or social-responsibility targets. Nevertheless, new sets of metrics, which Innovest and others designed to measure sustainability efforts, have helped convince CEOs and boards that they pay off. Few Wall Street analysts, for example, have tried to assess how much damage Wal-Mart's reputation for poor labor and environmental practices did to the stock price. But New York's Communications Consulting Worldwide (CCW), which studies issues such as reputation, puts it in stark dollars and cents. CCW calculates that if Wal-Mart had a reputation like that of rival Target Corp., its stock would be worth 8.4% more, adding $16 billion in market capitalization.

Serious money is lining up behind the sustainability agenda. Assets of mutual funds that are designed to invest in companies meeting social responsibility criteria have swelled from $12 billion in 1995 to $178 billion in 2005, estimates trade association Social Investment Forum.

Why the sudden urgency? The growing clout of watchdog groups making savvy use of the Internet is one factor. New environmental regulations also play a powerful role. Electronics manufacturers slow to wean their factories and products off toxic materials, for example, could be at a serious disadvantage as Europe adopts additional, stringent restrictions. American energy and utility companies that don't cut fossil fuel reliance could lose if Washington joins the rest of the industrialized world in ordering curbs on greenhouse gas emissions. Such developments help explain why Exxon Mobil Corp., long opposed to linking government policies with global warming theories, is now taking part in meetings to figure out what the U.S. should do to cut emissions.Rising investor demand for information on sustainability has spurred a flood of new research. Goldman Sachs, Deutsche Bank Securities, UBS, Citigroup, Morgan Stanley, and other brokerages have formed dedicated teams assessing how companies are affected by everything from climate change and social pressures in emerging markets to governance records. "The difference in interest between three years ago and now is extraordinary," says former Goldman Sachs Asset Management CEO David Blood.

Perhaps the most ambitious effort is by Innovest, founded in 1995 by Kiernan, a former KPMG senior partner. Besides conventional financial performance metrics, Innovest studies 120 different factors, such as energy use, health and safety records, litigation, employee practices, regulatory history, and management systems for dealing with supplier problems. It uses these measures to assign grades ranging from AAA to CCC, much like a bond rating, to 2,200 listed companies.

Some of Innovest's conclusions are counterintuitive. Hewlett-Packard and Dell both rate AAA, for example; market darling Apple gets a middling BBB on the grounds of weaker oversight of offshore factories and lack of a "clear environmental business strategy." An Apple spokesman contests that it is a laggard, citing the company's leadership in energy-efficient products and in cutting toxic substances.

Weighing the Efforts

BP seems to disprove the sustainability thesis altogether. CEO John Browne has preached environmentalism for a decade, and BP consistently ranked atop most sustainability indexes. Yet in the past two years it has been hit with a refinery explosion that killed 15 in Texas, a fine for safety violations at a refinery in Ohio, a major oil pipeline leak in Alaska, and a U.S. Justice Dept. probe into suspected manipulation of oil prices. Browne has recently announced his retirement. BP's shares have slid 10% since late April. Exxon's are up around 12%.

Innovest still rates BP a solid AA, while labeling Exxon a riskier BB. And PetroChina? Innovest gives it a CCC. Here's why: BP wins points for plowing $8 billion into alternative energies to diversify away from oil and engages community and environmental groups. Exxon has done less to curb greenhouse gas emissions and promote renewables and has big projects in trouble spots like Chad. "I would still say Exxon is a bigger long-term risk," says Innovest's Kiernan. PetroChina is easier to justify. Begin with its safety record: A gas well explosion killed 243 people in 2003; another fatal explosion in 2005 spewed toxic benzene into a river, leaving millions temporarily without water. PetroChina has been slow to invest in alternative energy, Innovest says, and its parent company has big bets in the Sudan.

Do Innovest's metrics make a reliable guide for picking stocks? Dozens of studies have looked for direct relationships between a company's social and environmental practices and its financial performance. So far the results are mixed, and Kiernan admits Innovest can't prove a causal link. That's little help to portfolio managers who must post good numbers by year-end. "The crux of the problem is that we are looking at things from the long term, but we're still under short-term review from our clients," says William H. Page, who oversees socially responsible investing for State Street Global Advisors.

Talking a Good Fight

Yet Kiernan and many other experts maintain sustainability factors are good proxies of management quality. "They show that companies tend to be more strategic, nimble, and better equipped to compete in the complex, high-velocity global environment," Kiernan explains.

Still, BP's woeful performance highlights a serious caveat to the corporate responsibility crusade. Companies that talk the most about sustainability aren't always the best at executing. Ford Motor Co. is another case in point. Former CEO William C. Ford Jr. has championed green causes for years. He famously spent $2 billion overhauling the sprawling River Rouge (Mich.) complex, putting on a 10-acre grass roof to capture rainwater. Ford also donated $25 million to Conservation International for an environmental center.

But Ford was flat-footed in the area most important to its business: It kept churning out gas-guzzling SUVs and pickups. "Having a green factory was not Ford's core issue. It was fuel economy," says Andrew S. Winston, director of a Yale University corporate environmental strategy project and co-author of the book *Green to Gold.* The corporate responsibility field is littered with lofty intentions that don't pay off. As a result, many CEOs are unsure what to do exactly. "This is uncomfortable territory because most CEOs have not been trained to sense or react to the broader landscape," says McKinsey's Mendonca. "For the first time, they are expected to be statesmen as much as they are functional business leaders." Adding to the complexity, says Harvard's Porter, each company must custom-design initiatives that fit its own objectives.

Dow Chemical is looking at the big picture. CEO Liveris cites global water scarcity as a field in which Dow can "marry planetary issues with market opportunity." The U.N. figures 1.2 billion people lack access to clean water. Dow says financial solutions could help 300 million of them. That could translate into up to $3 billion in sales for Dow, which has a portfolio of cutting-edge systems for filtering minute contaminants from water. Philips Electronics also is building strategies around global megatrends. By 2050, the U.N. predicts, 85% of people will live in developing nations. But shortages of health care are acute. Among Philips' many projects are medical vans that reach remote villages, allowing urban doctors to diagnose and treat patients via satellite. Philips has also developed low-cost water-purification technology and a smokeless wood-burning stove that could reduce the 1.6 million deaths annually worldwide from pulmonary diseases linked to cooking smoke. "For us, sustainability is a business imperative," says Philips Chief Procurement Officer Barbara Kux, who chairs a sustainability board that includes managers from all business units.

Such laudable efforts, even if successful, may not help managers make their numbers next quarter. But amid turbulent global challenges, they could help investors sort long-term survivors from the dinosaurs.

Source: **Reprinted with special permission from "Beyond the Green Corporation," by Pete Engardio, *BusinessWeek,* January 29, 2007. Copyright © 2007 The McGraw-Hill Companies.**

This article demonstrates how many corporations are shifting their focus from traditional market-responsive supply and demand models to a broader consideration of social and environmental responsibilities and obligations. As economic growth continues unabated, natural resources are being used at a much more rapid rate than they once were. Greater emphasis on resource conservation, a higher standard of living, and growing public opinion that social and environmental considerations are an important element of businesses' role in society are prompting MNCs to respond. MNCs are realizing that consumer needs extend beyond simple goods and services, and social factors such as environmental sustainability and concerns over public health are front and center in many consumers' minds. There is also increasing evidence that social and environmental practices can yield positive financial returns, especially over the longer term.

Who's Doing Well by Doing Good

SOME LEADERS What does it mean to say a company, its products, or its processes are "sustainable"? Here is a list of top-rated companies by industry:

AUTOMOBILES		COMMUNICATIONS EQUIPMENT	
TOYOTA	The maker of the top-selling Prius hybrid leads in developing efficient gas-electric vehicles.	NOKIA	Makes phones for handicapped and low-income consumers. A leader in phasing out toxic materials.
RENAULT	Integrates sustainability throughout organization. Has fuel-efficient cars and factories.	ERICSSON	Eco-friendly initiatives include wind- and fuel-cell-powered telecom systems in Nigerian villages.
VOLKSWAGEN	A market leader in small cars and clean diesel technologies.	MOTOROLA	Good disclosure of environmental data. Takes back used equipment in Mexico, U.S., and Europe.
COMPUTERS & PERIPHERALS		**FINANCIAL SERVICES**	
HEWLETT-PACKARD	Despite board turmoil, the company rates high on ecological standards and digital tech for the poor.	ABN AMRO	Involved in carbon-emissions trading. Finances everything from micro enterprises to biomass fuels.
TOSHIBA	At forefront of developing eco-efficient products, such as fuel cells for notebook PC batteries.	HSBC	Lending guidelines for forestry, freshwater, and chemical sectors factor in social, ecological risks.
DELL	Among the first U.S. PC makers to take hardware back from consumers and recycle it for free.	ING	Weighs sustainability in project finance. Helps developing nations improve financial institutions.
HEALTH CARE		**HOUSEHOLD DURABLES**	
FRESENIUS MEDICAL CARE	Discloses costs of its patient treatment in terms of energy and water use and waste generated.	PHILIPS ELECTRONICS	Top innovator of energy-saving appliances, lighting, and medical gear and goods for developing world.
IMS HEALTH	Places unusual emphasis on environmental issues in its global health consulting work.	SONY	Is ahead on green issues and ensuring quality, safety, and labor standards of global suppliers.
QUEST DIAGNOSTICS	Has diversity program promoting businesses owned by minorities, women, and veterans.	MATSUSHITA ELECTRIC	State-of-the-art green products. Eliminated 96% of the most toxic substances in its global operations.
OIL & GAS		**PHARMACEUTICALS**	
ROYAL DUTCH SHELL	Since Nigerian human rights woes in '90s, leads in community relations. Invests in wind and solar.	ROCHE	Committed to improving access to medicine in poor nations. Invests in drug research for Third World.
NORSK HYDRO	Cut greenhouse gas emissions 32% since 1990. Strong in assessing social, environmental impact.	NOVO NORDISK	Sells diabetes drugs in poor nations at deep discounts. Helps upgrade clinics, public education.
SUNCOR ENERGY	Ties with aboriginals help it deal with social and ecological issues in Canada's far north.	GLAXO-SMITHKLINE	One of few pharmas to devote R&D to malaria and T.B. First to offer AIDS drugs at cost.
RETAIL		**UTILITIES**	
MARKS & SPENCER	Buys local product to cut transit costs and fuel use. Good wages and benefits help retain staff.	FPL	Largest U.S. solar generator. Has 40% of wind-power capacity. Strong shareholder relations.
HOME RETAIL GROUP	High overall corporate responsibility standards have led to strong consumer and staff loyalty.	IBERDROLA	Since Scottish Power takeover, renewable energy accounts for 17% of capacity. Wants that to grow.
AEON	Environmental accounting has saved $5.6 million. Good employee policies in China and SE Asia.	SCOTTISH & SOUTHERN	Aggressively discloses environmental risk, including air pollution and climate change.

SOME LAGGARDS Concentrating on the bottom line makes companies postpone important changes. It can also lead to poor public relations. Here are a few companies that received lower marks:

ALLEGHENY ENERGY Reliance on coal poses risk if U.S. passes greenhouse gas rules.

BANK OF CHINA Hit by recent corruption cases, but bank says it has since improved governance.

GENERAL MOTORS Trails Toyota and Honda in fuel-efficient cars. High reliance on SUVs.

NINTENDO Slow to grapple with how emerging environmental, safety, and labor standards will affect offshore suppliers.

PETROCHINA Lacks transparent environmental programs. Safety record includes fatal gas leak and benzene plant explosion.

SURGUTNEFTEGAZ Plagued by shareholder suits. Lacks public environmental policy.

WAL-MART The mass retailer has made great strides with ambitious green initiatives, but the company's image remains tarnished by criticisms of labor and offshore sourcing practices.

Data: Innovest Strategic Value Advisors

Source: Adapted from Pete Engardio, "Beyond the Green Corporation," *BusinessWeek,* January 29, 2007, pp. 50–64. Reprinted with permission.

More broadly, recent scandals have called attention to the perceived lack of ethical values and corporate governance standards in business. In addition, assisting impoverished countries by helping them gain a new level of independence is both responsible and potentially profitable. Indeed, corporate social responsibility is becoming more than just good moral behavior. It can assist in avoiding future economic and environmental setbacks and may be the key to keeping companies afloat.

■ Ethics and Social Responsibility

The ethical behavior of business and the broader social responsibilities of corporations have become major issues in the United States and all countries around the world. Ethical scandals and questionable business practices have received considerable media attention and aroused the public's concern about ethics in international business and attention to the social impact of business operations.

Ethics and Social Responsibility in International Management

ethics
The study of morality and standards of conduct.

Unbiased ethical decision-making processes are imperative to modern international business practices. It is difficult to determine a universal ethical standard when the views and norms in one country can vary substantially from others. **Ethics,** the study of morality and standards of conduct, is often the victim of subjectivity as it yields to the will of cultural relativism, or the belief that the ethical standard of a country is based on the culture that created it and that moral concepts lack universal application.[1]

The adage, "When in Rome, do as the Romans do," is derived from the idea of cultural relativism and suggests that businesses and the managers should behave in accordance with the ethical standards of the country they are active in, regardless of MNC headquarter location. It is necessary, to some extent, to rely on local teams to execute under local rule; however, this can be taken to extremes. While a business whose only objective is to make a profit may opt to take advantage of these differences in norms and standards in order to legally gain leverage over the competition, it may find that negative consumer opinion about ethical business practices, not to mention potential legal action, could affect the bottom line. Dilemmas that arise from conflicts between ethical standards of a country and business ethics, or the moral code guiding business behavior, are most evident in employment and business practices, recognition of human rights, including women in the workplace, and corruption. The newer area of corporate social responsibility (CSR) is closely related to ethics. However, we discuss CSR issues separately. Ethics is the study of or the learning process involved in understanding morality, while CSR involves taking action. Furthermore, the area of ethics has a lawful component and infers right and wrong in a legal sense, while CSR is based more on voluntary actions. Business ethics and CSR may be therefore viewed as two complementary dimensions of a company's overall social profile and position.

Employment and Business Practices

Political, economic, and cultural differences emphasize how difficult it is to instill a universal foundation of employment practices. It does not make much sense to standardize compensation packages within an MNC that spans both developed and underdeveloped nations. Elements such as working conditions, expected consecutive work hours, and labor regulations also create challenges in deciding which employment practice is the most appropriate. For example, the low cost of labor entices businesses to look to China; however, workers in China are not well paid, and to meet the demand for output, they often are forced to work 12-hour days, 7 days a week. In some cases, children are used for this work. Child labor initially invokes negative associations and is considered an unethical employment practice. This is not true for every country, as 26 percent of children in Africa and an approximate 122 million children in Asia between the ages of

Ethical Business Practices at Johnson & Johnson

The corporate credo of Johnson & Johnson follows:

We believe our first responsibility is to the doctors, nurses and patients, to mothers and fathers and all others who use our products and services. In meeting their needs everything we do must be of high quality. We must constantly strive to reduce our costs in order to maintain reasonable prices. Customers' orders must be serviced promptly and accurately. Our suppliers and distributors must have an opportunity to make a fair profit.

We are responsible to our employees, the men and women who work with us throughout the world. Every-one must be considered as an individual. We must respect their dignity and recognize their merit. They must have a sense of security in their jobs. Compensation must be fair and adequate, and working conditions clean, orderly and safe. We must be mindful of ways to help our employees fulfill their family responsibilities. Employees must feel free to make suggestions and complaints. There must be equal opportunity for employment, development and advancement for those qualified. We must provide competent management, and their actions must be just and ethical.

We are responsible to the communities in which we will live and work and to the world community as well. We must be good citizens—support good works and charities and bear our fair share of taxes. We must encourage civic improvements and better health and education. We must maintain in good order the property we are privileged to use, protecting the environment and natural resources.

Johnson & Johnson (J&J) has experienced its fair share of ethical dilemmas over the past 25 years. The first occurred in 1982 in Chicago, Illinois, when bottles of extra-strength Tylenol capsules were found to be laced with cyanide. J&J looked to its credo of 'the customer always comes first,' and quickly responded to the tragedy only three days after the second tainted bottle was discovered. A recall of an estimated 31 million bottles swept the nation, along with J&J's wallet as it experienced losses of about $100 million and an almost 30 percent drop, bringing it to single digits, in market share for pain relievers. By 1986 an almost full recovery showed J&J with a 33 percent market share for pain relievers when another unfortunate poisoning occurred. At this point, J&J recalled all Tylenol capsules and still maintained 96 percent of sales despite the setback. J&J is often cited for its impressive response to this crisis. More recently, J&J disclosed that "improper payments in connection with the sale of medical devices" were made in some units. Adding insult to injury, Janssen, a J&J subsidiary, inappropriately marketed a psychiatric product targeted for use in children, resulting in a combined $117 million in costs to the Texas Medicaid program. How has Johnson & Johnson continued to be a profitable company?

One may argue that its impeccable response time and dedication to accept responsibility for its actions maintains the respect and loyalty of customers. What could be some other factors?

Source: Reprinted with permission of Johnson & Johnson.

5 and 17 work to help support their families.[2] In certain countries it is necessary for children to work due to low wages. UNICEF and the World Bank recognize that in some instances family survival depends on all members working and that intervention is necessary only when the child's developmental welfare is compromised.[3]

Business practices in China continue to be questionable as there is evidence of piracy, counterfeiting, and industrial spying. One reason for the existence of counterfeiting is that China does not have clear definitions for or laws against it.[4] Some of this may also be due to cultural relativism, because what the United States sees as piracy in a wealthy country based on individualism (see Chapter 2), China may see as an affordable alternative within collectivist practices, outside the question of ethics. For example, in China up to 90 percent of the Microsoft Windows operating systems in use are pirated copies. As China's economy begins to flourish, it is expected that more people who can afford the system will be willing to purchase it at full cost, resulting in the dissipation of such perceived unethical behavior.[5] During 2002, there were also laws implemented in an attempt to curb music, film, and software piracy. Another issue is that Chinese-backed industrial spying on outside MNCs has increased over the years. Finally, joint ventures have been in danger when Chinese partners break such agreements and walk off with patents or capital, or simply start an operation that is in direct competition with the venture.

Japan has also experienced its fair share of ethical issues in business. Japanese cabinet members have accepted questionable payments and favors. The Japanese banking system has failed to take corrective action when disbursing loans and has continued to operate despite being technically bankrupt. Finally, some Japanese firms have systematically concealed customer complaints for over 20 years even though many knew of the cover-up or have worked toward encouraging employees to mislead government inspectors.

All this conjures the question, How much responsibility do MNCs have in changing these practices? Should they adopt the regulations in the country of origin or yield to those in the country of operation? One remedy could be to instill a business code of ethics that extends to all countries, or to create contracts for situations that may arise. However, this is not as simple as it appears. Levi Strauss experienced this issue in the early 1990s with its suppliers from Bangladesh. Children under the age of 14 were working at two locations, which did not violate the law in Bangladesh, but did go against the policy of Levi Strauss. Ultimately, Levi Strauss decided to continue paying the wages of the children and secured a position for them once they reached the age of 14, after their return from schooling.[6] While the level of involvement is hard to standardize, having a basic set of business ethics and appropriately applying it to the culture in which one is managing is a step in the right direction. Managers need to be cautious not to blur the lines of culture in these situations. The Prince of Wales was once quoted as saying, "Business can only succeed in a sustainable environment. Illiterate, poorly trained, poorly housed, resentful communities, deprived of a sense of belonging or of roots, provide a poor workforce and an uncertain market."[7] Businesses face much difficulty in attempting to balance organizational and cultural roots with the advancement of globalization.

One recent phenomenon in response to globalization has been to offshore not just low-cost labor-intensive practices, as described in Chapter 1, but to transfer a large percentage of current employees of all types to foreign locations. The inexpensive labor available through offshore outsourcing in India has aided many institutions, but has also put a strain on some industries, particularly home-based technology services. Accenture, a company specializing in management consulting, technology services, and outsourcing, moved almost 22 percent of its employees to India by August 2007 in hopes of avoiding dwindling revenues and stock prices due to the continuous investment in India. With labor costs in India at less than half of those in the United States, Accenture is already gaining the competitive advantage by offering similar low-cost services, but with consulting expertise that is not yet matched by Indian cohorts. Accenture recognized the rising competition early, and careful strategies have enabled it to maintain, if not gain, a foothold in India.[8]

The transfer of the labor force overseas creates an interesting dynamic in the scope of ethics and corporate responsibility. While most international managers concern themselves with understanding the social culture in which the corporation is enveloped and how that can mesh with the corporate culture, this recent wave involves the extension of an established corporate culture into a new social environment. The difference here is that the individuals being moved offshore are part of a corporate citizenship, meaning that they will identify with the corporation and not necessarily the outside environment; the opposite occurs when the firm moves to another country and seeks to employ local citizens. Accenture proves that it is possible to succeed with such an effort, but as more and more companies follow suit, other questions and concerns may arise. How will the two cultures work together? Will employees adhere to the work schedule of the home or the host country? Will the host country be open or reluctant to an influx of new citizens? The latter may not be a current concern due to the infrequency of offshoring, but MNCs may face a time when they have to consider more than just survival of the company, but also bear in mind the effects these choices will have on both cultures.

Human Rights

Human rights issues present challenges for MNCs as there is currently no universally adopted standard of what constitutes acceptable behavior. It is difficult to list all rights inherent to humanity since there is considerable subjectivity involved and cultural differences exist among societies. Some basic rights include life, freedom from slavery or torture, freedom of opinion and expression, and a general ambiance of nondiscriminatory practices.[9] One violation of human rights that resonated with MNCs and made them question whether to move operations into China was the violent June 1989 crackdown on student protesters in Beijing's Tiananmen Square. Despite this horrific event, MNCs observed too many growth opportunities in China, although friction still exists between countries with high and low human rights standards. Even South Africa is beginning to experience the healing process of transitioning to higher human rights standards after the 1994 dismantling of the apartheid, the former white government's policies of racial segregation. Unfortunately, human rights violations are still rampant worldwide. For several decades, for example, Russia has experienced widespread human trafficking, but this practice has accelerated in recent years.[10] Here, we take a closer look at women in the workplace.

Women's rights can be considered a subset of human rights. While the number of women in the workforce has increased substantially worldwide, most are still experiencing the effects of a "glass ceiling," meaning that it is difficult, if not impossible, to reach the upper management positions. Japan is a good example, since both harassment and a glass ceiling exist in the workplace. Sexual harassment remains a major social issue in Japan partly because Japanese managers do not understand why it is a moral issue or how the work environment would be improved if it did not exist. There are no laws against sexual harassment in Japan, and many male managers regard female employees as mere assistants, creating a more difficult obstacle course in the attempt to move up the corporate ladder. Many women college graduates in Japan are still offered only secretarial or dead-end jobs. Japanese management still believes that women will quit and get married within a few years of employment, leading to a two-track recruiting process: one for men and one for women.[11]

Equal employment opportunities may be more troubled in Japan than other countries, but the glass ceiling is pervasive throughout the world. Today, women earn less than men for the same job in the United States, although progress has been made in this regard. France, Germany, and Great Britain have seen an increase in the number of women not only in the workforce but also in management positions. Unfortunately, women in management tend to represent only the lower level and do not seem to have the resources to move up in the company. This is partially due to social factors and perceived levels of opportunity or lack thereof. The United States, France, Germany, and Great Britain all have equal opportunity initiatives, whether they are guaranteed by law or are represented by growing social groups. Despite the existence of equal opportunity in French and German law, the National Organization for Women in the United States, and British legislation, there is no guarantee that initiatives will be implemented. It is a difficult journey as women attempt to make their mark in the workplace, but soon it may be possible for them to break through the glass ceiling.

Corruption

As noted in Chapter 2, government corruption is a pervasive element in the international business environment. Recently publicized scandals in Russia, China, Pakistan, Lesotho, South Africa, Costa Rica, Egypt, and elsewhere underscore the extent of corruption glob-ally, especially in the developing world. However, a number of initiatives have been taken by governments and companies to begin to stem the tide of corruption.[12]

The Foreign Corrupt Practices Act (FCPA) makes it illegal for U.S. companies and their managers to attempt to influence foreign officials through personal payments or political contributions. Prior to passage of the FCPA, some American multinationals had engaged in this practice, but realizing that their stockholders were unlikely to approve of these tactics, the firms typically disguised the payments as entertainment expenses, consulting fees, and so on. Not only does the FCPA prohibit these activities, but the U.S. Internal Revenue Service also continually audits the books of MNCs. Those firms that take deductions for such illegal activities are subject to high financial penalties, and individuals who are involved can even end up going to prison.

Strict enforcement of the FCPA has been applauded by many people, but some critics wonder if such a strong social responsibility stance has hurt the competitive ability of American MNCs. On the positive side, many U.S. multinationals have now increased the amount of business in countries where they used to pay bribes. Additionally, many institutional investors in the United States have made it clear that they will not buy stock in companies that engage in unethical practices and will sell their holdings in such firms. Given that these institutions have hundreds of billions of dollars invested, senior-level management must be responsive to their needs.

Looking at the effect of the FCPA on U.S. multinationals, it appears that the law has had far more of a positive effect than a negative one. Given the growth of American MNCs in recent years, it seems fair to conclude that bribes are not a basic part of business in many countries, for when multinationals stopped this activity, they were still able to sell in that particular market. On the other hand, this does not mean that bribery and corruption is a thing of the past. Figure 3–1 gives the latest corruption index of countries around the world. Notice that the United States ranks 20th in this independent analysis.

Figure 3–1

Corruption Index: Ranking of Least Corrupt to Most

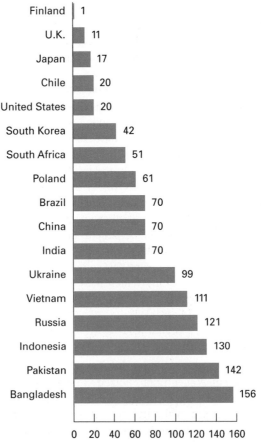

Source: Adapted from Transparency International, CPI Table, www.transparency.org/news_room/in_focus/2006/cpi_2006__1/cpi_table.

Yet bribery continues to be a problem for U.S. MNCs. In complying with the provisions of the FCPA, U.S. firms must be aware of changes in the law that make FCPA violators subject to Federal Sentencing Guidelines. When two Lockheed Corporation executives were found guilty of paying a $1 million bribe to a member of the Egyptian parliament in order to secure the sale of aircraft to the Egyptian military, one of the executives was sentenced to probation and fined $20,000 and the other, who initially fled prosecution, was fined $125,000 and sentenced to 18 months in prison.[13]

Another development that promises to give teeth to "antibribing" legislation is the recent formal agreement by a host of industrialized nations to outlaw the practice of bribing foreign government officials. The treaty, which initially included 29 nations that belong to the Organization for Economic Cooperation and Development (OECD), marked a victory for the United States, which outlawed foreign bribery two decades previously but had not been able to persuade other countries to follow its lead. As a result, American firms had long complained that they lost billions of dollars in contracts each year to rivals that bribed their way to success.[14]

This treaty does not outlaw most payments to political party leaders. In fact, the treaty provisions are much narrower than U.S. negotiators wanted, and there undoubtedly will be ongoing pressure from the American government to expand the scope and coverage of the agreement. For the moment, however, it is a step in the direction of a more ethical and level playing field in global business. Additionally, in summing up the impact and value of the treaty, one observer noted that:

> For their part, business executives say the treaty…reflects growing support for anti-bribery initiatives among corporations in Europe and Japan that have openly opposed the idea. Some of Europe's leading industrial corporations, including a few that have been embroiled in recent allegations of bribery, have spoken out in favor of tougher measures and on the increasingly corrosive effect of corruption.[15]

In addition to the 29 members of the OECD, a number of developing countries, including Argentina, Brazil, Bulgaria, Chile, and the Slovak Republic, have signed on to the OECD agreement. Latin American countries have established the Organization of American States (OAS) Inter-American Convention Against Corruption, which entered into force in March 1997, and more than 25 Western Hemisphere countries are signatories to the convention, including Argentina, Brazil, Chile, Mexico, and the United States. As a way to prevent the shifting of corrupt practices to suppliers and intermediaries, the Transparent Agents Against Contracting Entities (TRACE) standard was developed after a review of the practices of 34 companies. It applies to business intermediaries, including sales agents, consultants, suppliers, distributors, resellers, subcontractors, franchisees, and joint-venture partners, so that final producers, distributors, and customers can be confident that no party within a supply chain has participated in corruption.

Both governments and companies have made important steps in their efforts to stem the spread of corruption, but much more needs to be done in order to reduce and eventually eliminate the impact of corruption on companies and the broader societies in which they operate.[16]

■ Corporate Social Responsibility and Sustainability

In addition to expectations that they adhere to specific ethical codes and principles, corporations are under increasing pressure to contribute to the societies and communities in which they operate and to adopt more socially responsible business practices throughout their entire range of operations. **Corporate social responsibility (CSR)** can be defined as the actions of a firm to benefit society beyond the requirements of the law and the direct interests of the firm.[17] It is difficult to provide a list of obligations since the social, economic, and environmental expectations of each company will be based on the desires of the stakeholders. Pressure for greater attention to CSR has emanated from a range of stakeholders, including civil society (the broad societal

corporate social responsibility (CSR) The actions of a firm to benefit society beyond the requirements of the law and the direct interests of the firm.

A growing number of multinationals are taking action against counterfeiting and piracy in China due to the continued pervasiveness of the issue. Within hours of the time goods are on the street, many find that counterfeiters are already developing their own version of a product—and in many cases, these clones look just like the original. Today, there are fake cans of Coca-Cola, fake McDonald's hamburger restaurants, fake versions of the Jeeps that Chrysler manufactures with a joint-venture partner in Beijing, and fake Gillette razor blades.

Personal care product companies such as Henkl of Germany and Procter & Gamble of the United States estimate that about a quarter of the goods bearing their names in China are fake. Nike says that its potential annual losses in China resulting from counterfeit operations are about the size of its legitimate business in the United States. And pharmaceutical firms find that their drugs are often copied and distributed under their own name. Pfizer began selling Viagra in China in July 2000. By the end of the year, three local producers had introduced ripped-off versions of the pill, and within the next 90 days another 30 companies had done so as well. Overall, an estimated three-quarters of a trillion dollars are lost in profits, future business opportunities, and taxes from global effects of counterfeiting.

Chinese law dictates that one must be found both producing and distributing counterfeited goods to be charged with a crime, and in the case of goods such as CDs, one must be caught with at least 500 units. However, even when counterfeiters are caught, the Chinese government often does very little about it. The Gillette Razor Blade Company provides a good example of this. The Huaxing Razor Blade Factory was producing Gillette look-alike blades and packaging them in the same blue package used by Gillette. After Chinese authorities raided the factory, they fined the company $3,500 and told management that it was illegal to produce counterfeit blades and that they were to stop. Five months later, when it became evident that the company was still manufacturing the blades, there was a second raid, followed by a fine of $3,300. At that time, the manager was asked why he not only kept producing the blades but also used the same packaging as before. He remarked that he did not want to throw away packaging that had already been printed. "We didn't want to waste it," he said.

Will such a "slap on the wrist" type of enforcement stop the counterfeiting? It is unlikely, because the fines are small compared with the revenues being generated. However, the Chinese government is beginning to make amends. For example, pharmaceutical companies have collaborated with China's Ministry of Public Security, or the police, to tip it off about pirating factories so the police can subsequently raid the facilities. Some cases have shown that when MNCs have complained that counterfeiters have gone back to their old ways, inspectors have refused to take any additional action, arguing that "we already addressed that issue and we are now moving on to other matters." Such an attitude worries MNCs, because they feel there is no protection for their intellectual properties and they fear uncertain relationships with Chinese cohorts. This became evident during plans for a 2007 Global Forum on Intellectual Property Protection and Innovation. The United States originally filed claims with the World Trade Organization over antipiracy issues in China as well as restrictions on distribution of foreign movies, music, and printed materials within the market. Companies such as Siemens USA, Intel, Nokia, and Time Warner backed these claims and joined forces to take action in this process. Other companies that were a part of the Business Software Alliance and the Pharmaceutical Research and Manufacturers of America did not support this since they had made their own advances independently. Microsoft is one good example of these companies.

Microsoft experienced massive unrealized profit losses in China when computers were being shipped out and distributed without operating systems installed. Most consumers installed either Linux, a free operating system, or pirated copies of Microsoft Windows XP. Bill Gates saw an opportunity not only to counter the piracy efforts but also to collaborate with China and form a partnership. In 2002, Bill Gates originally stated that over three years, Microsoft would invest $750 million in Chinese software companies. This was modified in 2006 when new plans stated that $900 million would be invested over five years. The goal is to reduce piracy rates and establish Windows as the primary operating system. While investments will not directly curb piracy, the Microsoft-China relations have negotiated an indirect cessation. During 2006, China required all new PCs to be shipped with preinstalled and legal operating systems, and while most may opt for the free Linux system, some specified that it must be Windows XP. Currently, about 70 percent of Lenovo-brand PCs have Microsoft Windows XP preinstalled, showing that more headway may be made through working together. A detailed analysis of this case is included in Part 3 of the book.

Unless foreign investors can convince the government of China to take more stringent steps toward pirating and counterfeiting, companies will continue to experience losses in China. In the final analysis, it appears that China will have to get tough on pirates and counterfeiters...or else.

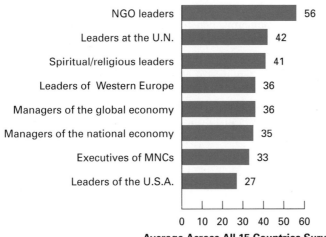

NGO leaders — 56
Leaders at the U.N. — 42
Spiritual/religious leaders — 41
Leaders of Western Europe — 36
Managers of the global economy — 36
Managers of the national economy — 35
Executives of MNCs — 33
Leaders of the U.S.A. — 27

0 10 20 30 40 50 60

Average Across All 15 Countries Surveyed

Figure 3–2

Trust in Leaders: Percentage Saying "A Lot" and "Some Trust"

Source: From *Voice of the People Survey, 2003.* Reprinted with permission of Gallup International.

interests in a given region or country) and from **nongovernmental organizations (NGOs).** These groups have urged MNCs to be more responsive to the range of social needs in developing countries, including concerns about working conditions in factories or service centers and the environmental impacts of their activities.[18] As a result of recent ethics scandals and concerns about the lack of corporate responsibility, according to World Economic Forum's Gallup International Poll released in November 2002, leaders of NGOs are the most trusted of the eight leadership categories tested, while leaders of MNCs and leaders of the United States were the least trusted (see Figure 3–2).[19]

Shell, Johnson & Johnson, and many other MNCs take their CSR commitment seriously. These firms have integrated their response to CSR pressures into their core business strategies and operating principles around the world (see the section "Response to Social Obligations" and the Internet exercise later in this chapter).

nongovernmental organizations (NGOs) Private, not-for-profit organizations that seek to serve society's interests by focusing on social, political, and economic issues such as poverty, social justice, education, health, and the environment.

Sustainability

In the boardroom, the term **sustainability** may first be associated with financial investments or the hope of steadily increasing profits, but for a growing number of companies, this term means the same to them as it does to an environmental conservationist. As we saw from the *BusinessWeek* article at the beginning of the chapter, business practices bringing the least harm to the environment and the most benefit to society have evolved into an organizational priority.[20] Partially this is due to corporations recognizing that dwindling resources will eventually halt productivity, but the World Economic Forum in Davos, Switzerland, has also played a part in bringing awareness to this timely subject. While the January 24, 2007, gathering obviously put profit at the top of the agenda, it was closely followed by the concern of global warming and environmentally damaging practices, marking a new era with sustainability as a high priority concern.[21]

While the United States has the Environmental Protection Agency to provide information about and enforce environmental laws,[22] the United Nations also has a division dedicated to the education, promotion, facilitation, and advocacy of sustainable practices and environmentally sound concerns called the United Nations Environment Programme (UNEP).[23] The degree to which global awareness and concern is rising extends beyond laws and regulations, as corporations are now taking strides to be leaders in this "green" movement.

sustainability Development that meets humanity's needs without harming future generations.

Wal-Mart, one of the most well known, penetrating, and pervasive global retailers, has begun to recognize the numerous benefits of the adage, "Think globally, act locally." Working with environmentalists, it discovered that many changes in production and supply chain practices could reduce waste and pollution and therefore reduce costs. By cutting back on packaging, Wal-Mart could save an estimated $2.4 million a year, 3,800 trees, and 1 million barrels of oil. Over 60,000 suppliers compete to put their products on Wal-Mart shelves, which means that this company has a strong influence on how manufacturers do business. Executives in Japanese supermarkets are learning from this precedent, and Wal-Mart is attempting to change global standards as it offers higher prices to coffee growers in Brazil and increases pressures on the factory owners in China to reduce energy and fuel costs.[24] Management styles again are changing as agendas are refocused on not only seeing the present but also looking to the future of human needs and the environment.

NGOs, MNCs, and Ethical Balance

The emergence of organized civil society and NGOs has dramatically altered the business environment globally and the role of MNCs within it. Although social movements have been part of the political and economic landscape for centuries, the emergence of NGO activism in the United States during the modern era can be traced to mid-1984, when a range of NGOs, including church and community groups, human rights organizations, and other antiapartheid activists, built strong networks and pressed U.S. cities and states to divest their public pension funds of companies doing business in South Africa. This effort, combined with domestic unrest, international governmental pressures, and capital flight, posed a direct, sustained, and ultimately successful challenge to the white minority rule, resulting in the collapse of apartheid.

Since then, NGOs generally have grown in number, power, and influence. Large global NGOs such as Save the Children, Oxfam, CARE, World Wildlife Fund, and Conservation International are active in all parts of the world. Their force has been felt in a range of major public policy debates, and NGO activism has been responsible for major changes in corporate behavior and governance. Some observers now regard NGOs as a counterweight to business and global capitalism. NGO criticisms have been especially sharp in relation to the activities of MNCs, such as Nike, Levi's, Chiquita, and others whose sourcing practices in developing countries have been alleged to exploit low-wage workers, take advantage of lax environmental and workplace standards, and otherwise contribute to social and economic problems. Two recent examples illustrate the complex and increasingly important impact of NGOs on MNCs.

In January 2004, Citigroup announced it would no longer finance certain projects in emerging markets identified by the Rainforest Action Network (RAN) as damaging to the environment. This announcement came after several years of aggressive pressure and lobbying by RAN, including full-page advertising in daily newspapers showing barren landscapes and blackened trees, lobbying by film and television personalities urging consumers to cut up their credit cards, blockades of Citigroup branches, and campaigns involving schoolchildren who sent cards to Citigroup's chairman, Sanford Weil, asking him to stop contributing to the extinction of endangered species.[25] After heavy lobbying from NGOs, in August 2003, the U.S. pharmaceutical industry dropped its opposition to relaxation of intellectual property provisions under the WTO to make generic, low-cost antiviral drugs available to developing countries facing epidemics or other health emergencies[26] (see the In-Depth Integrated Case at the end of Part 1).

Many NGOs recognize that MNCs can have positive impacts on the countries in which they do business, often adhering to higher standards of social and environmental responsibility than local firms. In fact, MNCs may be in a position to transfer "best practices" in social or environmental actions from their home to host countries' markets.

In some instances, MNCs and NGOs collaborate on social and environmental projects and in so doing contribute both to the well-being of communities and to the reputation of the MNC. The emergence of NGOs that seek to promote ethical and socially responsible business practices is beginning to generate substantial changes in corporate management, strategy, and governance.

Response to Social Obligations

MNCs are increasingly engaged in a range of responses to growing pressures to contribute positively to the social and environmental progress of the communities in which they do business. One response is the agreements and codes of conduct in which MNCs commit to maintain certain standards in their domestic and global operations. These agreements, which include the U.N. Global Compact (see Table 3–1), the Global Reporting Initiative, the social accountability "SA8000" standards, and the ISO 14000 environmental quality standards, provide some assurances that when MNCs do business around the world, they will maintain a minimum level of social and environmental standards in the workplaces and communities in which they operate.[27] These codes help offset the real or perceived concern that companies move jobs to avoid higher labor or environmental standards in their home markets. They may also contribute to the raising of standards in the developing world by "exporting" higher standards to local firms in those countries.

Individual companies have also taken steps to develop strong ethical principles and integrate social responsibility into their business operations, often with the help of

---

Table 3–1
Principles of the Global Compact

Human Rights

Principle 1: Support and respect the protection of international human rights within their sphere of influence.

Principle 2: Make sure their own corporations are not complicit in human rights abuses.

Labor

Principle 3: Freedom of association and the effective recognition of the right to collective bargaining.

Principle 4: The elimination of all forms of forced and compulsory labor.

Principle 5: The effective abolition of child labor.

Principle 6: The elimination of discrimination with respect to employment and occupation.

Environment

Principle 7: Support a precautionary approach to environmental challenges.

Principle 8: Undertake initiatives to promote greater environmental responsibility.

Principle 9: Encourage the development and diffusion of environmentally friendly technologies.

Anticorruption

Principle 10: Business should work against all forms of corruption, including extortion and bribery.

Source: Reprinted by permission of the United Nations Global Compact.

NGOs.[28] For example, a number of pharmaceutical companies, in the attempt to increase access to AIDS medications, have initiated or expanded alliances with the very NGOs that opposed them over the issue of relaxing intellectual property rights (IPR) regulations. Once an agreement was reached, these NGOs, such as Doctors Without Borders and Oxfam, helped the companies deliver drugs to the target populations and to restore the companies' legitimacy, which had been damaged as a result of their initial opposition to modification of the IPR rules.

Hewlett-Packard has initiated a series of "i-communities" in economically deprived areas such as the town of Kuppam in the state of Andhra Pradesh, India. These communities use public-private-NGO partnerships to enhance economic development through technology. NGOs promote the projects and enlist community support. HP is able to use the projects to build markets, test products, and expand global marketing knowledge.[29] The experience provides HP with valuable knowledge about how to identify and negotiate with rural customers and positions it to improve its ability to do business in rural markets of India and other countries in the future. In addition, HP has received positive reputation effects in development circles. Mattel's board of directors independently contracts with the International Center for Corporate Accountability, an NGO, to provide unscheduled on-site audits of its factories and its first- and second-tier suppliers to determine compliance with the company's Global Manufacturing Principles. Motorola is engaged in efforts to certify literally thousands of suppliers to meet its global corporate responsibility standards. In some instances, it has accepted suppliers' standards as meeting or exceeding those of Motorola itself.

Hence, companies are very actively trying both to respond to pressure to be more socially responsible and to develop proactive strategies to demonstrate their commitment to social and environmental progress around the world, especially in developing countries.[30]

Corporate Governance

The global ethical and governance scandals have placed corporations under intense scrutiny regarding their oversight and accountability. Corporate governance is increasingly high on the agenda for directors, investors, and governments alike in the wake of financial collapses and corporate scandals in recent years. The collapses and scandals have not been limited to a single country, or even a single continent, but have been a global phenomenon. **Corporate governance** can be defined as the system by which business corporations are directed and controlled.[31] The corporate governance structure specifies the distribution of rights and responsibilities among different participants in the corporation—such as the board, managers, shareholders, and other stakeholders—and spells out the rules and procedures for making decisions on corporate affairs. By doing this, it also provides the structure through which the company objectives are set and the means of attaining those objectives and monitoring performance.

corporate governance
The system by which business corporations are directed and controlled.

Governance rules and regulations differ among countries and regions around the world. For example, the U.K. and U.S. systems have been termed "outsider" systems because of dispersed ownership of corporate equity among a large number of outside investors. Historically, although institutional investor ownership was predominant, institutions generally did not hold large shares in any given company; hence they had limited direct control.[32] In contrast, in an insider system, such as that in many continental European countries, ownership tends to be much more concentrated, with shares often being owned by holding companies, families, or banks. In addition, differences in legal systems, as described in Chapter 2, also affect shareholders' and other stakeholders' rights and, in turn, the responsiveness and accountability of corporate managers to these constituencies. Notwithstanding recent scandals, in general, North American and European systems are considered comparatively responsive to shareholders and other stakeholders. In regions with less well developed legal and institutional protections and poor property rights, such as some countries in Asia, Latin America, and Africa, forms of "crony capitalism" may emerge in which weak corporate governance and government interference can lead to poor performance, risky financing patterns, and macroeconomic crises.

Corporate governance will undoubtedly remain high on the agenda of governments, investors, NGOs, and corporations in the coming years, as pressure for accountability and responsiveness continues to increase.

International Assistance

In addition to government- and corporate-sponsored ethics and social responsibility practices, governments and corporations are increasingly collaborating to provide assistance to communities around the world through global partnerships. This assistance is particularly important for those parts of the world that have not fully benefited from globalization and economic integration. Using a cost-benefit analysis of where investments would have the greatest impact, a recent study identified the top priorities around the world for development assistance. The results of this analysis are presented in Table 3–2. Controlling and preventing AIDS, fighting malnutrition, reducing subsidies and trade restrictions, and controlling malaria are shown to be the best investments. Governments, international institutions, and corporations are involved in several ongoing efforts to address some of these problems.[33]

At the United Nations Millennium Summit in September 2000, world leaders placed development at the heart of the global agenda by adopting the Millennium Development Goals (see Table 3–3). The eight Millennium Development Goals constitute an ambitious agenda to significantly improve the human condition by 2015. The goals set clear targets for reducing poverty, hunger, disease, illiteracy, environmental degradation, and discrimination against women.[34] For each goal, a set of targets and indicators have been defined and are used to track the progress in meeting the goals.

Table 3–2
Copenhagen Consensus Development Priorities

Project Rating		Challenge	Opportunity
Very good	1	Diseases	Control of HIV/AIDS
	2	Malnutrition	Providing micro nutrients
	3	Subsidies and trade	Trade liberalization
	4	Diseases	Control of malaria
Good	5	Malnutrition	Development of new agricultural technologies
	6	Sanitation and water	Small-scale water technology for livelihoods
	7	Sanitation and water	Community-managed water supply and sanitation
	8	Sanitation and water	Research on water productivity in food production
	9	Government	Lowering the cost of starting a new business
Fair	10	Migration	Lowering barriers to migration for skilled workers
	11	Malnutrition	Improving infant and child nutrition
	12	Malnutrition	Reducing the prevalence of low birth weight
	13	Diseases	Scaled-up basic health services
Bad	14	Migration	Guest-worker programs for the unskilled
	15	Climate	"Optimal" carbon tax
	16	Climate	The Kyoto protocol
	17	Climate	Value-at-risk carbon tax

Source: Copenhagen Consensus.

Note: Some of the proposals were not ranked.

> ### Table 3–3
> ### The U.N. Millennium Development Goals
>
> Goal 1: Eradicate extreme poverty and hunger.
> Goal 2: Achieve universal primary education.
> Goal 3: Promote gender equality and empower women.
> Goal 4: Reduce child mortality.
> Goal 5: Improve maternal health.
> Goal 6: Combat HIV/AIDS, malaria, and other diseases.
> Goal 7: Ensure environmental sustainability.
> Goal 8: Develop a Global Partnership for Development.
>
> *Source:* www.unmillenniumproject.org.

A more specific initiative is the Global Fund to Fight AIDS, Tuberculosis and Malaria, which was established in 2001. By July 2003, more than $2 billion had been contributed by developed countries to the Global Fund. In addition to leading country donors that included the United States, the EU, individual European countries, and Japan, the Gates Foundation contributed $100 million, and other corporations are being solicited for contributions. In April 2002, the Global Fund made its first awards to programs in over 40 countries, totaling $616 million.[35]

Through these and other efforts, MNCs, governments, and international organizations are providing a range of resources to communities around the world to assist them as they respond to the challenges of globalization and development. International managers will increasingly be called upon to support and contribute to these initiatives.

The World of *BusinessWeek*—Revisited

The *BusinessWeek* article that opens this chapter outlines corporate efforts toward building a more sustainable business and natural environment. It emphasizes the importance of adopting initiatives which aid impoverished countries and reduce ecological impact. In this chapter we focused on ethics and social responsibility in global business activities, including the role of governments, MNCs, and NGOs in advancing greater ethical and socially responsible behavior. MNCs' new focus on environmental sustainability and "doing well by doing good" is an important dimension of this broad trend.

Global ethical and governance scandals have rocked the financial markets and implicated dozens of individual companies. New corporate ethics guidelines passed in the United States have forced many MNCs to take a look at their own internal ethical practices and make changes accordingly. Lawmakers in Europe and Asia have also made adjustments in rules over corporate financial disclosure. The continuing trend toward globalization and free trade appears to be encouraging development of a set of global ethical, social responsibility, and anticorruption standards. This may actually help firms cut compliance costs as they realize that economies have common global frameworks. The old message, "This is how we've always done business," will have to give way to a new standard of ethical conduct.

Having read the chapter, answer the following questions: (1) Do governments and companies in developed countries have an ethical responsibility to contribute to economic growth and social development in developing countries? (2) Are governments, companies, or NGOs best equipped to provide this assistance? (3) Do corporations have a responsibility to use their "best" ethics and social responsibility practices when they do business in other countries, even if those countries' practices are different?

SUMMARY OF KEY POINTS

1. Ethics is the study of morality and standards of conduct. It is important in the study of international management because ethical behavior often varies from one country to another. Ethics manifests itself in the ways societies and companies address issues such as employment conditions, human rights, and corruption. A danger in international management is the ethical relativism trap—"When in Rome, do as the Romans do."

2. During the years ahead, multinationals likely will become more concerned about being socially responsible. NGOs are forcing the issue. Countries are passing laws to regulate ethical practices and

governance rules for MNCs. MNCs are being more proactive (often because they realize it makes good business sense) in making social contributions in the regions in which they operate and in developing codes of conduct to govern ethics and social responsibility. One area in which companies have been especially active is in pursuing strategies that blend environmental sustainability and business objectives.

3. MNCs—in conjunction with governments and NGOs—are also contributing to international development assistance and working to ensure that corporate governance practices are sound and effective.

KEY TERMS

corporate governance, *72*

corporate social responsibility (CSR), *67*

ethics, *62*

nongovernmental organizations (NGOs), *69*

sustainability, *69*

REVIEW AND DISCUSSION QUESTIONS

1. What lessons can U.S. multinationals learn from the political and bribery scandals in Japan that can be of value to them in doing business in this country? Discuss two.

2. In recent years, some prominent spokespeople have argued that those who work for the U.S. government in trade negotiations should be prohibited for a period of five years from accepting jobs as lobbyists for foreign firms. Is this a good idea? Why or why not?

3. How do ethical practices differ in the United States and in European countries such as France and

Germany? What implications does your answer have for U.S. multinationals operating in Europe?

4. Why are many MNCs reluctant to produce or sell their goods in China? What role can the Chinese government play in helping to resolve this problem?

5. Why are MNCs getting involved in corporate social responsibility? Are they displaying a sense of social responsibility, or is this merely a matter of good business? Defend your answer.

INTERNET EXERCISE: SOCIAL RESPONSIBILITY AT JOHNSON & JOHNSON AND HP

In this chapter, the social responsibility actions of companies such as Johnson & Johnson and Hewlett-Packard (HP) were discussed.

At Johnson & Johnson, social responsibility flows from the company's credo. Consult the box "A Closer Look," above, and go to the J&J Web site, **www.jnj.com,** to the sections "Our Credo" and "Social Responsibility." Then answer these questions: (1) Which stakeholders are most important to J&J and why? (2) How does J&J ensure that all its many operating companies adhere to the credo? (3) What are the main areas of social responsibility activities for J&J, and how do they relate to the credo?

At Hewlett-Packard, "global citizenship" means engaging in public-private partnerships and demonstrating model behavior and activities in governance, environmental policy and practices, community engagement models, and "e-inclusion initiatives." Go to the HP Web site, **www.hp.com,** to the sections on global citizenship and e-inclusion. Then answer these questions: (1) What does it mean to be a global citizen at HP? (2) How does HP measure and evaluate its success in global citizenship? (3) What is e-inclusion, and what are some specific examples of projects that advance HP's e-inclusion goals?

Saudi Arabia

Saudi Arabia is a large Middle Eastern country covering 865,000 square miles. Part of its east coast rests on the Persian Gulf, and much of the west coast rests along the Red Sea. One of the countries on its border is Iraq. After Iraq's military takeover of Kuwait in August 1990, Iraq threatened to invade Saudi Arabia. This, of course, did not happen, and Saudi Arabia was not an Iraqi target during the U.S.-led war in Iraq during 2003–2004. However, accusations stemming from rumors of terrorists financing activities have made Saudi Arabia a focus in the global war on terrorism, and Saudi Arabia itself was the target of terrorist attacks in 2003–2004.

There are approximately 22 million people in Saudi Arabia, and the annual per capita income is around $11,500. This apparent prosperity is misleading because most Saudis are poor farmers and herders who tend their camels, goats, and sheep. In recent years, however, more and more have moved to the cities and have jobs connected to the oil industry. Nearly all are Arab Muslims. The country has the two holiest cities of Islam: Mecca and Medina. The country depends almost exclusively on the sale of oil (it is the largest exporter of oil in the world) and has no public debt. The government is a monarchy, and the king makes all important decisions but is advised by ministers and other government officials. Royal and ministerial decrees account for most of the promulgated legislation. There are no political parties.

Recently, Robert Auger, the executive vice president of Skyblue, a commercial aircraft manufacturing firm based in Kansas City, had a visit with a Saudi minister. The Saudi official explained to Auger that the government planned to purchase 10 aircraft over the next two years. A number of competitive firms were bidding for the job. The minister went on to explain that despite the competitiveness of the situation, several members of the royal family were impressed with Auger's company. The firm's reputation for high-quality performance aircraft and state-of-the-art technology gave it the inside track. A number of people are involved in the decision, however, and in the minister's words, "Anything can happen when a committee decision is being made."

The Saudi official went on to explain that some people who would be involved in the decision had recently suffered large losses in some stock market speculations on the London Stock Exchange. "One relative of the King, who will be a key person in the decision regarding the purchase of the aircraft, I have heard, lost over $200,000 last week alone. Some of the competitive firms have decided to put together a pool of money to help ease his burden. Three of them have given me $100,000 each. If you were to do the same, I know that it would put you on a par with them, and I believe it would be in your best interests when the decision is made." Auger was stunned by the suggestion and told the minister that he would check with his people and get back to the minister as soon as possible.

As soon as he returned to his temporary office, Auger sent a coded message to headquarters asking management what he should do. He expects to have an answer within the next 48 hours. In the interim, he has had a call from the minister's office, but Auger's secretary told the caller that Auger had been called away from the office and would not be returning for at least two days. The individual said he would place the call again at the beginning of this coming week. Meanwhile, Auger has talked to a Saudi friend whom he had known back in the United States and who is currently an insider in the Saudi government. Over dinner, Auger hinted at what he had been told by the minister. The friend seemed somewhat puzzled about what Auger was saying and indicated that he had heard nothing about any stock market losses by the royal family or pool of money being put together for certain members of the decision-making committee. He asked Auger, "Are you sure you got the story straight, or as you Americans say, is someone pulling your leg?"

Questions

1. What are some current issues facing Saudi Arabia? What is the climate for doing business in Saudi Arabia today?
2. Is it legal for Auger's firm to make a payment of $100,000 to help ensure this contract?
3. Do you think other firms are making these payments, or is Auger's firm being singled out? What conclusion can you draw from your answer?
4. What would you recommend that Skyblue do?

It Sounds a Little Fishy

For the past two years, the Chicago-based Brattle Company has been thinking about going international. Two months ago, Brattle entered into negotiations with a large company based in Paris to buy one of its branches in Lyon, France. This would give Brattle a foreign subsidiary. Final arrangements on the deal should be completed within a month, although a few developments have occurred that concern the CEO of Brattle, Angela Scherer.

The most serious concern resulted from a conversation that Scherer had with one of the Lyon firm's largest customers. This customer had been introduced to Scherer during a dinner that the Paris headquarters gave in her honor last month. After the dinner, Scherer struck up a conversation with the customer to assure him that when Brattle took over the Lyon operation, it would provide the same high-quality service as its predecessor. The customer seemed interested in Scherer's comments and then said, "Will I also continue to receive $10,000 monthly for directing my business to you?" Scherer was floored; she did not know what to say. Finally she stammered, "That's something I think you and I will have to talk about further." With that, the two shook hands and the customer left. Scherer has not been back in touch with the customer since the dinner and is unsure of what to do next.

The other matter that has Scherer somewhat upset is a phone call from the head of the Lyon operation last week. This manager explained that his firm was very active in local affairs and donated approximately $5,000 a month to charitable organizations and philanthropic activities. Scherer is impressed with the firm's social involvement but wonders whether Brattle will be expected to assume these obligations. She then told her chief financial officer, "We're buying this subsidiary as an investment, and we are willing to continue employing all the local people and paying their benefits. However, I wonder if we're going to have any profits from this operation after we get done with all the side payments for nonoperating matters. We have to cut back a lot of extraneous expenses. For example, I think we have to cut back much of the contribution to the local community, at least for the first couple of years. Also, I can't find any evidence of payment of this said $10,000 a month to that large customer. I wonder if we're being sold a bill of goods, or has it been paying him under the table? In any event, I think we need to look into this situation more closely before we make a final decision on whether to buy this operation."

Questions

1. If Scherer finds out that the French company has been paying its largest customer $10,000 a month, should Brattle back out of the deal? If Brattle goes ahead with the deal, should it continue to make these payments?

2. If Scherer finds out that the customer has been making up the story and no such payments were actually made, what should she do? What if this best customer says he will take his business elsewhere?

3. If Brattle buys the French subsidiary, should Scherer continue to give $5,000 monthly to the local community? Defend your answer.

Colgate's Distasteful Toothpaste

Colgate is a well-known consumer products company based in New York. Its present products are in the areas of household and personal care, which include laundry detergents such as Ajax and Fab, health care products manufactured for home health care, and specialty products such as Hill pet food. The household products segment represents approximately 75 percent of company revenues, while the specialty segment accounts for less than 7 percent. Colgate's value has been set in excess of $5.6 billion. Through both recessionary and recovery periods in the United States, Colgate has always been advocated by investment analysts as a good long-term stock.

Colgate's domestic market share has been lagging for several years. In the 1970s, when diversification seemed to be the tool to hedge against risk and sustain profits, Colgate bought companies in various industries, including kosher hot dogs, tennis and golf equipment, and jewelry. However, such extreme diversification diverted the company's attention away from its key moneymaking products: soap, laundry detergents, toothpaste, and other household products. The product diversification strategy ended in 1984 when Reuben Mark became CEO. At the young age of 45, he ordered the sale of parts of the organization that deviated too far from Colgate's core competency of personal and household products. He followed consultant Tom Peters's prescription for excellence: "Stick to the knitting."

Colgate's International Presence

Colgate traditionally has had a strong presence overseas. The company has operations in Australia, Latin America, Canada, France, and Germany. International sales presently represent one-half of Colgate's total revenue. In the past, Colgate always made a detailed analysis of each international market for demand. For instance, its entry into South America required an analysis of the type of product that would be most successful based on the dental hygiene needs of South American consumers. Because of this commitment to local cultural differences, the company has the number-one brand of toothpaste worldwide, Total.

To gain a strong share of the Asian market without having to build its own production plant, Colgate bought a 50 percent partnership in the Hawley and Hazel group in August 1985 for $50 million. One stipulation of this agreement was that Colgate had no management prerogatives: Hawley and Hazel maintained the right to make the major decisions in the organization. This partnership turned out to be very lucrative for Colgate, with double-digit millions in annual sales.

Enter the Distasteful Toothpaste

Hawley and Hazel is a chemical products company based in Hong Kong. The company was formed in the early part of the twentieth century, and its only product of note, believe it or not, was called "Darkie" toothpaste. Over the years, this had been one of the popular brands in Asia and had a dominant presence in markets such as Taiwan, Hong Kong, Singapore, Malaysia, and Thailand.

"Darkie" toothpaste goes back to the 1920s. The founder of this product, on a visit to the United States, loved Al Jolson, then a very popular black-faced entertainer (i.e., a white person with black makeup on his face). The founder decided to re-create the spirit of this character in the form of a trademark logo for his toothpaste because of the character's big smile and white teeth. When the founder returned to Asia, he trademarked the name "Darkie" to go along with the logo. Since the 1920s, there has been strong brand loyalty among Asians for this product. One housewife in Taipei whose family used the product for years remarked, "The toothpaste featuring a Black man with a toothy smile is an excellent advertisement."

The Backlash Against Colgate

"Darkie" toothpaste had been sold in Asia for about 65 years. After Colgate became partners with Hawley and Hazel and its distasteful product, however, there was a wave of dissatisfaction with the logo and name from U.S. minorities and civil rights groups. There really has been no definite source on how this issue was passed to U.S. action groups and the media; however, a book entitled *Soap Opera: The Inside Story of Procter and Gamble* places responsibility in the hands of Procter & Gamble in an effort to tarnish Colgate's image and lower its market share.

The Americans' irate response to "Darkie" was a surprise to the Hawley and Hazel group. The product had always been successful in their Asian markets, and there had been no complaints. In fact, the success of "Darkie" had led the firm to market a new product in Japan called "Mouth Jazz," which had a similar logo. A spokesperson for Hawley and Hazel remarked, "There had been no problem before, you can tell by the market share that it is quite well received in Asia."

ICCR, the Interfaith Center on Corporate Responsibility, started the fight against Colgate about 10 years ago when it received a package of "Darkie" toothpaste from a consumer in Thailand. ICCR is composed of institutional investors that influence corporations through stock ownership. At the time the movement against Colgate's racially offensive product started, three members of ICCR already owned a small amount of stock in the company, and they filed a shareholder petition against Colgate requesting a change in the logo and name.

In a letter to Colgate, the ICCR executive director summarized the position against the distasteful toothpaste as follows:

> "Darkie" toothpaste is a 60-year-old product sold widely in Hong Kong, Malaysia, Taiwan and other places in the Far East. Its packaging includes a top-hatted and gleaming-toothed smiling likeness of Al Jolson under the words "Darkie" toothpaste. As you know, the term "Darkie" is deeply offensive. We would hope that in this new association with the Hawley and Hazel Chemical Company, that immediate action will be taken to stop this product's name so that a U.S. company will not be associated with promoting racial stereotypes in the Third World.

In response to this letter, R. G. S. Anderson, Colgate's director of corporate development, replied, "No plans exist or are being contemplated that would extend marketing and sales efforts for the product in Colgate subsidiaries elsewhere or beyond this Far East area." Anderson then went on to explain that Darkie's founder was imitating Al Jolson and that in the Chinese view, imitation was the "highest form of flattery." The ICCR then informed Colgate that if the logo was not changed, the organization would create a media frenzy and help various civil rights action groups in a possible boycott.

Because Colgate still refused to remove the logo, ICCR did form a coalition with civil rights groups such as the NAACP and the National Urban League to start protest campaigns. The protest took many forms, including lobbying at the state and local levels. At one point, after heavy lobbying by the ICCR, the House of Representatives in Pennsylvania passed a resolution urging Colgate to change the name and logo. Similar resolutions had been proposed in the U.S. Congress.

The pressures at home placed Colgate in a difficult position, especially as it had no management rights in its agreement with Hawley and Hazel. In the Asian market, neither Colgate nor Hawley and Hazel had any knowledge of consumer dissatisfaction because of racial offensiveness, despite the fact that the local Chinese name for

"Darkie" (pronounced *hak ye nga goh*) can be translated as "Black Man Toothpaste." The logo seemed to enhance brand loyalty. One Asian customer stated, "I buy it because of the Black man's white teeth."

The demographics of the Asian market may help to explain the product's apparent acceptance. There are a relatively small number of Africans, Indians, Pakistanis, and Bangladeshis in the region; therefore, the number of people who might be offended by the logo is low. Also, some people of color did not seem disturbed by the name. For example, when asked about the implications of "Darkie" toothpaste, the secretary of the Indian Chamber of Commerce noted, "It doesn't offend me, and I'm sort of dark-skinned."

Initially, Colgate had no intentions of forcing Hawley and Hazel to change the product. R. G. S. Anderson issued another formal statement to the ICCR as follows: "Our position . . . would be different if the product were sold in the United States or in any Western English-speaking country; which, as I have stated several times, will not happen." Hawley and Hazel concurred with the stance. The alliance was very fearful of a loss of market share and did not believe that the complaints were issues relevant to Pacific Rim countries. A spokesperson for the alliance referred to the protest campaign as "a U.S. issue." The trade-off for revamping a successful product was deemed to be too risky and costly.

Colgate's Change of Heart

The issue did not go away. As U.S. leaders in Congress began to learn about this very offensive logo and name, the pressure on Colgate mounted. Interestingly, however, the value of Colgate's stock increased throughout this period of controversy. Wall Street seemed oblivious to the charges against Colgate, and this was another reason why Colgate took no action. Colgate management believed that an issue about overseas products should not have a negative effect on the company's domestic image. However, pressures continued from groups such as the Congressional Black Caucus, a strong political force. Colgate finally began to waver, but because of its agreement with Hawley and Hazel, it felt helpless. As one Colgate executive remarked, "One hates to let exogenous things drive your business, but you sometimes have to be aware of them."

Colgate CEO Reuben Mark eventually became very distressed over the situation. He was adamantly against racism of any kind and had taken actions to exhibit his beliefs. For instance, he and his wife had received recognition for their involvement in a special program for disadvantaged teenagers. He commented publicly about the situation as follows: "It's just offensive. The morally right thing dictates that we must change. What we have to do is find a way to change that is least damaging to the economic interests of our partners." He also publicly stated that Colgate had been trying to change the package since 1985, when it bought into the partnership.

Colgate's Plan of Action to Repair the Damage

The protest campaign initiated by ICCR and carried further by others definitely caused Colgate's image to be tarnished badly in the eyes not only of African Americans but of all Americans. To get action, some members of the Congressional Black Caucus (including Rep. John Conyers, D-Mich.) even bypassed Colgate and tried to negotiate directly with Hawley and Hazel. To try to repair the damage, two years after ICCR's initial inquiry, Colgate, in cooperation with Hawley and Hazel, finally developed a plan to change the product. In a letter to ICCR, CEO Mark stated, "I and Colgate share your concern that the caricature of a minstrel in black-face on the package and the name 'Darkie' itself could be considered racially offensive." Colgate and Hawley and Hazel then proposed some specific changes for the name and logo. Names considered included Darlie, Darbie, Hawley, and Dakkie. The logo options included a dark, nondescript silhouette and a well-dressed black man. The alliances decided to test-market the options among their Asian consumers; however, they refused to change the Chinese name ("Black Man Toothpaste"), which is more used by their customers.

They decided that changes would be implemented over the course of a year to maintain brand loyalty and avoid advertising confusion with their customers. There was the risk that loyal customers would not know if the modified name/logo was still the same toothpaste that had proven itself through the years. Altogether, the process would take approximately three years, test marketing included. Colgate also decided to pay for the entire change process, abandoning its initial suggestion that the change be paid for by Hawley and Hazel.

Colgate and Hawley and Hazel then made a worldwide apology to all insulted groups. Although Hawley and Hazel was slow to agree with the plan, a spokesperson emphasized that racial stereotyping was against its policy. It also helped that Hawley and Hazel would pay no money to make the needed changes. It felt that the product was too strong to change quickly; thus, three years was not too long to implement the new logo and name fully into all Asian markets. Further, it insisted that as part of the marketing campaign, the product advertising use the fol-lowing statement in Chinese, "Only the English name is being changed. Black Man Toothpaste is still Black Man Toothpaste."

Response Worldwide

Colgate and Hawley and Hazel still suffer from the effects of their racially offensive product. In 1992, while dealing with its own civil rights issues, the Chinese government placed a ban on Darlie toothpaste because of the product's violation of China's trademark laws. Although the English name change was implemented across all markets, the retained Chinese name and logo still were deemed derogatory by the Chinese, and the government banned the product. Also, Eric Molobi, an African National Congress representative, was outraged at the toothpaste's logo on a recent visit to the Pacific Rim. When asked if Darlie toothpaste would be marketed in his country, the South African representative replied, "If this company found itself in South Africa it would not be used. There would be a permanent boycott."

Today, the name of Colgate cannot be found anywhere on the packaging of what is now called Darlie toothpaste. In a strategic move, Colgate has distanced itself completely away from the controversial product. In the Thailand and Indonesia health-products markets, Colgate even competes against Darlie toothpaste with its own brand.

Questions for Review

1. Identify the major strategic and ethical issues faced by Colgate in its partnership with Hawley and Hazel.

2. What do you think Colgate should have done to handle the situation?

3. Is it possible for Colgate and Hawley and Hazel to change the toothpaste's advertising without sacrificing consumer brand loyalty? Is that a possible reason for Colgate's not responding quickly to domestic complaints?

4. In the end, was a "no management rights" clause good for Colgate? What could have happened during the negotiations process to get around this problem?

Source: Reprinted with permission of Alisa L. Mosley.

Brief Integrative Case 2

Advertising or Free Speech?
The Case of Nike and Human Rights

Nike Inc., the global leader in the production and marketing of sports and athletic merchandise including shoes, clothing, and equipment, has enjoyed unparalleled worldwide growth for many years. Consumers around the world recognize Nike's brand name and logo. As a supplier to and sponsor of professional sports figures and organizations, and as a large advertiser to the general public, Nike is widely known. It was a pioneer in offshore manufacturing, establishing company-owned assembly plants and engaging third-party contractors in developing countries.

In 1996, *Life* magazine published a landmark article about the labor conditions of Nike's overseas subcontractors, entitled, "On the playgrounds of America, Every Kid's Goal is to Score: In Pakistan, Where children stitch soccer balls for Six Cents an hour, their goal is to Survive." Accompanying the article was a photo of a 12-year-old Pakistani boy stitching a Nike embossed soccer ball. The photo caption noted that the job took a whole day, and the child was paid US$.60 for his effort. Up until this time, the general public was neither aware of the wide use of foreign labor nor familiar with the working arrangements and treatment of laborers in developing countries. Since then, Nike has become a poster child for the questionable unethical use of offshore workers in poorer regions of the world. This label has continued to plague the corporation as many global human interest and labor rights organizations have monitored and often condemned Nike for its labor practices around the world.

Nike executives have been frequent targets at public events, especially at universities where students have pressed administrators and athletic directors to ban products that have been made under "sweatshop" conditions. Indeed, at the University of Oregon, a major gift from Phil Knight, Nike's CEO, was held up in part because of student criticism and activism against Nike on campus.[1]

In 2003 the company employed 86 compliance officers (up from just 3 in 1996) to monitor its plant operations and working conditions and ensure compliance with its published corporate code of conduct. Even so, the stigma of past practices—whether perceived or real—remains emblazoned on its image and brand name. Nike found itself constantly defending its activities, striving to shake this reputation and perception.

In 2002 Marc Kasky sued Nike, alleging that the company knowingly made false and misleading statements in its denial of direct participation in abusive labor conditions abroad. Through corporate news releases, full-page ads in major newspapers, and letters to editors, Nike defended its conduct and sought to show that allegations of misconduct were unwarranted. The action by the plaintiff, a local citizen, was predicated on a California state law prohibiting unlawful business practices. He alleged that Nike's public statements were motivated by marketing and public relations and were simply false. According to the allegation, Nike's statements misled the public and thus violated the California statute. Nike countered by claiming its statements fell under and within the protection of the First Amendment, which protects free speech. The state court concluded that a firm's public statements about its operations have the effect of persuading consumers to buy its products and therefore are, in effect, advertising. Therefore, the suit could be adjudicated on the basis of whether Nike's pronouncements were false and misleading. The court stated that promoting a company's reputation was equivalent to sales solicitation, a practice clearly within the purview of state law. The majority of justices summarized their decision by declaring, "because messages in question were directed by a commercial speaker to a commercial audience, and because they made representations of fact about the speaker's own business operations for the purpose of promoting sales of its products, we conclude that these messages are commercial speech for purposes of applying state laws barring false and misleading commercial messages" (*Kasky v. Nike Inc.*, 2002). The conclusion reached by the court was that statements by a business enterprise to promote its reputation must, like advertising, be factual representations and that companies have a clear duty to speak truthfully about such issues.[2]

In January 2003 the U.S. Supreme Court agreed to hear Nike's appeal of the *Kasky v. Nike Inc.* from the California Supreme Court. In particular, the U.S. Supreme court agreed to rule on whether Nike's previous statements about the working conditions at its subcontracted, overseas plants were in fact "commercial speech" and, separately, whether a private individual (such as Kasky) has the right to sue on those grounds. Numerous amici briefs were filed on both sides. Supporters of Kasky included California, as well as 17 other states, Ralph Nader's Public Citizen Organization, California's AFL/CIO, and

California's attorney general. Nike's friends of the court included the American Civil Liberties Union, the Business Roundtable, the U.S. Chamber of Commerce, other MNCs including Exxon/Mobil and Microsoft, and the Bush administration (particularly on the grounds that it does not support private individuals acting as public censors).[3]

Despite the novelty of this First Amendment debate and the potentially wide-reaching effects for big business (particularly MNCs), the U.S. Supreme Court dismissed the case (6 to 3) in June 2003 as "improvidently granted" due to procedural issues surrounding the case. In their dissenting opinion, Justices Stephen G. Breyer and Sandra Day O'Connor suggested that Nike would likely win the appeal at the U.S. Supreme Court level. In both the concurring and dissenting opinions, Nike's statements were described as a mix of "commercial" and "noncommercial" speech.[4] This suggested to Nike, as well as other MNCs, that if the Court were to have ruled on the substantive issue, Nike would gave prevailed.

Although this case has set no nationwide precedent for corporate advertising about business practices or corporate social responsibility (CSR) in general, given the sensitivity of the issue, Nike has allowed its actions to speak louder than words in recent years. As part of its international CSR profile, Nike has assisted relief efforts (donating $1 million to tsunami relief in 2004) and advocated fair wages and employment practices in its outsourced operations. Nike claims that it has not abandoned production in certain countries in favor of lower-wage labor in others and that its factory wages abroad are actually in accordance with local regulations, once one accounts for purchasing power and cost-of-living differences.[5] The Nike Foundation, a nonprofit organization supported by Nike, is also an active supporter of the Millennium Development Goals, particularly those directed at improving the lives of adolescent girls in developing countries (specifically Bangladesh, Brazil, China, Ethiopia, and Zambia) through better health, education, and economic opportunities.[6]

As part of its domestic CSR profile, Nike is primarily concerned with keeping youth active, presumably for health, safety, educational, and psychological/esteem reasons. Nike has worked with Head Start (2005) and Special Olympics Oregon (2007), as well as created its own community program, NikeGO, to advocate physical activity among youth. Furthermore, Nike is committed to domestic efforts such as Hurricane Katrina relief and education, the latter through grants made by the Nike School Innovation Fund in support of the Primary Years Literacy Initiative.[7]

Despite Nike's impressive CSR profile, if the California State Supreme Court decision is sustained and sets a global precedent, Nike's promotion or "advertisement" of its global CSR initiatives could still be subjected to legal challenge. This could create a minefield for multinational firms. It would effectively elevate statements on human rights treatment by companies to the level of corporate marketing and advertising. Under these conditions, it might be difficult for MNCs to defend themselves against allegations of human rights abuses. In fact, action such as the issuance and dissemination of a written company code of conduct could fall into the category of advertising declarations. Although *Kasky v. Nike* was never fully resolved in court, the issues that it raised remain to be addressed by global companies.

Also to be seen is what effect a court decision would have on Nike's financial success. Despite the publicity of the case, at both the state and Supreme Court levels, and the lingering criticism about its labor practices overseas, Nike has maintained strong and growing sales and profits. The company has expanded its operations into different types of clothing and sports equipment and has continued to choose successful athletes to advertise its gear. Nike has shown no signs of slowing down, suggesting that its name and logo have not been substantially tarnished in the global market.

Questions for Review

1. What ethical issues faced by MNCs in their treatment of foreign workers could bring allegations of misconduct in their operations?

2. Would the use of third-party independent contractors insulate MNCs from being attacked? Would that practice offer MNCs a good defensive shield against charges of abuse of "their employees"?

3. Do you think that statements by companies that describe good social and moral conduct in the treatment of their workers are part of the image those companies create and therefore are part of their advertising message? Do consumers judge companies and base their buying decision on their perceptions of corporate behavior and values? Is the historic "made in" question (e.g., "Made in the USA") now being replaced by a "made by" inquiry (e.g., "Made *by* Company X" or "Made *for* Company X by Company Y")?

4. Given the principles noted in the case, how can companies comment on their positive actions to promote human rights so that consumers will think well of them? Would you propose that a company (a) do nothing, (b) construct a corporate code of ethics, or (c) align itself with some of the universal covenants or compacts prepared by international agencies?

5. What does Nike's continued financial success, in spite of the lawsuit, suggest about consumers' reactions to negative publicity? Have American

media and NGOs exaggerated the impact of a firm's labor practices and corporate social responsibility on its sales? How should managers of a MNC respond to such negative publicity?

Source: This case was prepared by Lawrence Beer, W. P. Carey School of Business, Arizona State University as the basis for class discussion.

Pharmaceutical Companies, Intellectual Property, and the Global AIDS Epidemic

In August 2003, after heavy lobbying from nongovernmental organizations (NGOs) such as Doctors Without Borders, the U.S. pharmaceutical industry finally dropped its opposition to relaxation of the intellectual property rights (IPR) provisions under World Trade Organization (WTO) regulations to make generic, low-cost antiviral drugs available to developing countries like South Africa facing epidemics or other health emergencies.[1] Although this announcement appeared to end a three-year dispute between multinational pharmaceutical companies, governments, and NGOs over the most appropriate and effective response to viral pandemics in the developing world, the specific procedures for determining what constitutes a health emergency had yet to be worked out. Nonetheless, the day after the agreement was announced, the government of Brazil said it would publish a decree authorizing imports of generic versions of patented AIDS drugs that the country said it could no longer afford to buy from multinational pharmaceutical companies. Although the tentative WTO agreement would appear to allow such production under limited circumstances, former U.S. trade official Jon Huenemann remarked, "They're playing with fire. . . . The sensitivities of this are obvious and we're right on the edge here."[2]

Despite the role of developed and developing country governments, NGOs, large pharmaceutical companies, and their generic competitors in crafting this agreement, it was unclear how it would be implemented and whether action would be swift enough to stem the HIV/AIDS epidemic ravaging South Africa and many other countries.

The AIDS Epidemic and Potential Treatment

In 2003, HIV/AIDS was the number-one cause of death among young adults aged 15–19 around the world. According to the World Health Organization (WHO), in 2003 there were approximately 40 million people living with AIDS, with 5 million newly infected, and 3 millions deaths (see Table 1). Since 1980, AIDS has killed more than 25 million people. HIV is especially deadly because it often remains dormant in an infected person for years without showing symptoms and is transmitted to others often without the knowledge of either person. HIV leads to AIDS when the virus attacks the immune system and cripples it, making the person vulnerable to diseases.[3]

The health of a nation's population is closely correlated with its economic wealth. Poor countries lack resources for health care generally, and for vaccination in particular.

Table 1 Regional HIV/AIDS Statistics, 2003

	Adults and Children Living with HIV/AIDS	Adults and Children Newly Infected with HIV	Adult Prevalence Rate [%]*	Adult and Child Deaths Due to AIDS
Sub-Saharan Africa	25.0–28.2 million	3.0–3.4 million	7.5–8.5	2.2–2.4 million
North Africa and Middle East	470,000–730,000	43,000–67,000	0.2–0.4	35,000–50,000
South and South-East Asia	4.6–8.2 million	610,000–1.1 million	0.4–0.8	330,000–590,000
East Asia and Pacific	700,000–1.3 million	150,000–270,000	0.1–0.1	32,000–58,000
Latin America	1.3–1.9 million	120,000–180,000	0.5–0.7	49,000–70,000
Caribbean	350,000–590,000	45,000–80,000	1.9–3.1	30,000–50,000
Eastern Europe and Central Asia	1.2–1.8 million	180,000–280,000	0.5–0.9	23,000–37,000
Western Europe	520,000–680,000	30,000–40,000	0.3–0.3	2,600–3,400
North America	790,000–1.2 million	36,000–54,000	0.5–0.7	12,000–18,000
Australia and New Zealand	12,000–18,000	700–1,000	0.1–0.1	<100
TOTAL	40 million	5 million	1.1%	3 million
	[34–46 million]	[4.2–5.8 million]	[0.9–1.3]	[2.5–3.5 million]

*The proportion of adults [15 to 49 years of age] living with HIV/AIDS in 2003, using 2003 population numbers. The ranges around the estimates in this table define the boundaries within which the actual numbers lie, based on the best available information. These ranges are more precise than those of previous years, and work is under way to increase even further the precision of the estimates.

Source: World Health Organization.

Table 2   **Prices (in $) of Daily Dosage of ARV, April 2000**

Drug	U.S.A.	Côte d'Ivoire	Uganda	Brazil	Thailand
Zidovudine	10.12	2.43	4.34	1.08	1.74
Didanosine	7.25	3.48	5.26	2.04	2.73
Stavudine	9.07	4.10	6.19	0.56	0.84
Indinavir	14.93	9.07	12.79	10.32	NA
Saquinavir	6.5	4.82	7.37	6.24	NA
Efavirenz	13.13	6.41	NA	6.96	NA

Source: UNAIDS, *2000 Report on the Global HIV/AIDS Epidemic.*

They are unable to provide sanitation and to buy drugs for those who cannot afford them. They also have lower levels of education, and therefore people are less aware of measures needed to prevent the spread of disease.[4] There is no cure or vaccine for AIDS. Therefore, public health experts place a high priority on prevention. However, only a small percentage of the funds targeted to prevent AIDS was deployed in developing countries.

Drugs help combat AIDS by prolonging the lives of those infected and by slowing the spread of the disease. These drugs significantly reduce deaths in developed countries. Treatment, however, is very expensive. As with most medicines, manufacturers hold patents for drugs, thereby limiting competition from generic products and allowing firms to price well above manufacturing costs in order to recoup R&D investment and make a fair profit.

In 2000–2001, a year's supply of a "cocktail" of antiretroviral (ARV) drugs used to fight AIDS cost between $10,000 and $12,000 in developed countries, putting it beyond the reach of those in most developing countries, where per capita income is a fraction of this cost (see Tables 2 and 3).[5] This discrepancy provokes strong reactions. Dr. James Orbinski, president of Doctors Without Borders (Médecins Sans Frontières), an international humanitarian nongovernmental organization (NGO) that won the 1999 Nobel Peace Prize, lamented, "The poor

Table 3   **Estimated Number of People in 2002 Who Needed "Triple Therapy" AIDS Treatment, Compared with the Number Who Received Treatment (in thousands)**

	In Need of Treatment	Received Treatment
Latin America and the Caribbean	370	196
North Africa and Middle East	7	3
Eastern Europe and Central Asia	80	7
Asia Pacific	1,000	43
Sub-Saharan Africa	**4,100**	**50**

Source: UNAIDS, *2002 Report on the Global HIV/AIDS Epidemic.*

have no consumer power, so the market has failed them. I'm tired of the logic that says: 'He who can't pay dies.'"[6]

AIDS in Southern Africa

In sub-Saharan Africa, approximately 26 million people are living with AIDS. Of the 3 million AIDS deaths globally in 2003, approximately two-thirds or 2.2 million were in sub-Saharan Africa (see Table 1).[7] The disease took a heavy toll on women and children. By the end of 2003, more than 2 million children were infected in the region and a disproportionate percentage of infected adults were women.

Most HIV transmission among southern Africans occurred through sexual activity rather than blood transfusion or use of infected needles. As a result of historic and economic factors, there are large numbers of single migrant male communities in southern Africa. These communities, many of whom served the mining industry, are at great risk of AIDS transmission, especially with easy access to alcohol and commercial sex workers (prostitutes).[8]

There is great stigma attached to AIDS in southern Africa. On International AIDS Day in 1998, Gugu Dlamini, a South African AIDS activist, declared on television that she was HIV-positive and was subsequently stoned to death for having shamed her community. Dr. Peter Piot, head of UNAIDS (the AIDS program of the United Nations), pointed out the tragic irony in the situation: Some of those who murdered Dlamini probably had AIDS but didn't know it—25 percent of her community was infected.[9]

In the nation of South Africa, one out of every nine residents has HIV/AIDS. The disease had slashed South African life expectancy from 66 years to below 50, a level not seen since the late 1950s. Large pharmaceutical companies and the U.S. government resisted calls to relax intellectual property laws that were thought to limit the provision of low-cost AIDS treatments. South African president Thabo Mbeki himself had been accused of engaging in "denial" as he had disputed established wisdom regarding the source of and treatment for AIDS. Meanwhile, South Africans continued to die from the

Table 4   2003 Global Pharmaceutical Sales by Region

World Audited Market	2003 Sales ($bn)	% Global Sales ($)	% Growth (constant $)
North America	229.5	49%	+11%
European Union	115.4	25	8
Rest of Europe	14.3	3	14
Japan	52.4	11	3
Asia, Africa, and Australasia	37.3	8	12
Latin America	17.4	4	6
Total	$466.3bn	100%	+9%

Source: IMS World Review (2004).

disease, and the South African economy also suffered direct and indirect costs from the disease's ravaging effects.[10]

The Global Pharmaceutical Industry, R&D, and Drug Pricing

Most of the global $466 billion of pharmaceutical sales in 2003 were in the developed countries of North America, Japan, and Western Europe (see Table 4). Leading pharmaceutical companies were large and profitable (see Table 5), although all of them have come under pressure from a range of factors—most notably, calls for lower health care costs in most major industrialized countries. Drug discovery was a long, expensive, and uncertain process. In recent years, the development of a new drug, starting with laboratory research and culminating in FDA approval, was estimated to take 10 to 15 years and cost around $800 million on average. Only 30 percent of drugs marketed were reported to earn revenues that matched average R&D costs.[11]

Like most for-profit firms, pharmaceutical companies pursue opportunities with high profit potential. A spokesman for Aventis, a French-German pharmaceutical company, said, "We can't deny that we try to focus on top markets—cardiovascular, metabolism, anti-infection, etc. But we're an industry in a competitive environment—we have a commitment to deliver performance for shareholders."[12] The industry tended to focus on diseases prevalent in its major markets. Drug patents enable companies to charge prices several times the variable manufacturing costs and generate hefty margins to help recover R&D costs and deliver profits. Drugs tend to be relatively price insensitive during the period of patent protection.

Prices vary considerably across markets, as illustrated by the price of fluconazole, an antifungal agent as well as a cure for cryptococcal meningitis, which attacked 9 percent of people with AIDS and killed them within a month. According to a study by Doctors Without Borders, in 2000, wholesale prices for fluconazole averaged $10 per pill and ranged from $3.60 in Thailand to $27 in Guatemala. Pfizer, who reportedly earned $1 billion annually on fluconazole, claimed the range was narrower ($6). Prices were considerably lower in countries that did not uphold foreign patents for pharmaceuticals. In India, Bangladesh, and Thailand it was sold by generic manufacturers for prices ranging from 30 to 70 cents.[13] (Some of the countries that didn't recognize patents for pharmaceuticals did have laws for patent protection of other products.)

The pharmaceutical industry was criticized for spending large sums on sales, marketing, and lobbying. Pfizer's spokesman, Brian McGlynn, countered, "yes, we spend a lot of money on advertising and marketing. But we don't sell soda pop. It's an enormous transfer of knowledge from our lab scientists to doctors, through those sales reps."[14] Companies also spent heavily on lobbying governments on issues such as government–managed prescription drug plans for the elderly, which could create pressure to cap drug prices, and on strengthening and enforcing intellectual property protections.

WTO and Intellectual Property Rights[15]

Intellectual property rights (IPR) grant investors rights for original creations. The goal of IPR protection is to stimulate creativity and innovation, and to provide incentives and funding for R&D. In general, copyrights are protected for literary and artistic works extending 70 years after the author's death. Trademarks can be protected indefinitely if they continue to be distinctive. Inventions, industrial designs, and trade secrets are protected through patents for a finite period, usually 20 years. Intellectual property rights, such as patents, prevent people from using inventors' creations without permission.

Table 5   2001 Financials for Selected Pharmaceutical Companies ($bn)

	Merck	Pfizer	GlaxoSmithKline
Country	U.S.	U.S.	U.K.
Revenue	47.7	32.3	29.7
COGS	29.0	5.0	6.9
SG&A	6.2	11.3	12.2
R&D	2.5	4.8	3.8
Net income	7.3	7.8	4.4

Source: Sushil Vachani, "South Africa and the AIDS Epidemic," *Vilkapala* 29, no. 1 (January–March 2004), p. 104; and company annual reports.

The WTO's Agreement on Trade-Related Aspects of Intellectual Property Rights (TRIPS), which was agreed to under the Uruguay Round of the GATT (1986–1994), attempted to bring conformity among different nations' protection of IPR. TRIPS covered five basic areas (see Exhibit 1). Patent protection extended a minimum of 20 years. Governments could deny patent protection on certain grounds (e.g., public order or morality) or for certain classes of inventions (e.g., surgical methods, plants, and so on). If the patent holder abused the rights granted by the patent (e.g., by refusing to supply the product to the market), the government could, under prescribed conditions, issue compulsory licenses that allowed competitors to produce the product.[16]

Also under TRIPS, a country that is in a state of medical emergency could resort to two actions: compulsory licensing, under which it could have generic products manufactured while paying a royalty to the patent holder, and parallel importing, which meant importing legally produced copies of a product that were cheaper in a foreign country than in the importing country. However, the WTO guidelines did not define a medical emergency. Developing countries' view of what constituted a medical emergency was substantially different from that held by drug companies and the U.S. government.

Despite being a country with 85,000 AIDS patients,[17] Brazil responded to international pressures and passed a law recognizing patents in 1996. This law specified that products commercialized anywhere before May 15, 1997, would forever remain unpatented in Brazil. The Brazilian government encouraged local companies to produce unlicensed copies of several AIDS drugs, which it bought from them to distribute to its patients free of charge in a policy of universal access. AIDS deaths were halved between 1996 and 1999. Between 1996 and 2000, local production, together with bulk imports, reduced annual treatment costs by 80 percent for double therapy (a cocktail of two AIDS drugs, both nucleosides) and by about 35 percent for triple therapies (two nucleosides and a protease inhibitor or non-nucleoside).[18]

For drugs that had valid patents in Brazil, the government attempted to negotiate lower prices. When negotiations between Merck and the Brazilian government over prices of the drug Stocrin initially stalled, the government threatened to license the drug compulsorily under the provisions of Brazilian law. When Merck learned a copy was being developed in a government lab, it threatened to file a lawsuit. The U.S. government filed a complaint with the WTO, but Brazil refused to budge.[19] President Fernando Cardoso defended the patent-breaking practice, suggesting that this approach was not one of commercial interest, but rather a moral issue that could not be solved by the market alone. The pharmaceutical industry association's position on intellectual property rights was summarized as follows:

Exhibit 1   Broad Areas Covered by the WTO Agreement on Trade-Related Aspects of Intellectual Property Rights (TRIPS)

1. Basic principles
   a. National treatment. Equal treatment of foreign and domestic nationals.
   b. Most-favored-nation treatment. Equal treatment of nationals of all WTO members.
   c. Technological progress. Intellectual property rights had to strike a balance between technological innovation and technology transfer. The objective was to enhance economic and social welfare by making both producers and users benefit.
2. How to provide adequate protection.
3. Enforcement.
4. Dispute settlement.
5. Special transitional arrangements. WTO agreements took effect January 1, 1995. Developed countries were given one year to bring their laws and practices in line with TRIPS. Developing countries were given 5 years and least developed countries 11 years.

Source: WTO, www.wto.org/english/tratop_e/trips_e/trips_e.htm.

Strong intellectual property protection is the key to scientific, technological and economic progress. Such protection is the *sine qua non* of a vibrant and innovative pharmaceutical industry—and thus to patients—in the United States and around the world. Without such protection, far fewer drugs would be developed, fewer generic copies would be manufactured, and the flow of medicines to the public would be greatly slowed—to the detriment of patients, public health, and economic development throughout the world.[20]

Pharmaceutical companies were worried about more than losing contributions from sales of a drug faced with a knockoff in a specific country. They feared a domino effect—compulsory licensing spreading across developing countries and sharply hurting profits in multiple markets. Even more alarming was the prospect that prices in developed countries might sink either because of a gray market in generics or because of pressure to cap prices as information on the significant price differential between countries became widely available and developed-country consumers clamored for lower prices.

Drug Pricing in Developing Countries: Government, Industry, and NGO Perspectives[21]

Dr. Christopher Ouma, who cared for AIDS patients in a Kenyan public hospital, pointed out that half his patients couldn't pay the $2.60 daily bed charge. He usually didn't tell patients' families about the existence of drugs to treat AIDS. "This is where the doctor's role goes from caregiver to undertaker," he added. "You talk to them about the cheapest method of burial. Telling them about the drugs is always kind of a cruel joke."[22]

Drug companies had been reluctant to provide AIDS drugs to developing countries at prices much lower than those charged in developed countries. They expressed concern that distributing drugs in unregulated and unreliable environments could risk creating new strains of drug-resistant HIV. In 1997, South Africa passed a law to permit compulsory licensing of essential drugs. Pharmaceutical companies including Bristol-Myers Squibb and Merck sued the South African government in an attempt to delay implementation of the law.

The Clinton administration lobbied the South African government to reverse its decision. U.S. Trade Representative Charlene Barshefsky placed South Africa on the "301 watch list," which puts a nation on notice that U.S. trade sanctions will be imposed if it doesn't change its policies.[23]

The *Washington Post* reported, "Critics have accused U.S. trade policy of placing the profits of drug companies above public health, moving to block poor countries from manufacturing the drugs themselves, despite international laws that permit countries to do so when facing a public health emergency."[24] The British newspaper *Guardian* referred to the U.S. government's actions as "trade terrorism" and called for efforts to "defend developing countries against U.S. aggression."[25] The World Bank official who oversaw the Bank's African health investments and its annual $800 million drug procurement said the drug-price structure "shows an increasing disconnect with the needs of the majority of the people in the world."[26]

As the U.S. government began to exert pressure on developing countries through the WTO and unilaterally, AIDS activists and NGOs, such as Doctors Without Borders, Act-Up, Health Action International, and the Consumer Project on Technology, swung into action. They targeted the public appearances of Vice President Al Gore during his presidential campaign. In September 1999, the administration backed off from the threats of placing trade sanctions against South Africa. The administration informed the South African government it would not object to issuance of compulsory licenses for essential drugs provided this was done within WTO guidelines.

In December 1999, President Bill Clinton told members of the WTO that the U.S. government would show "flexibility" and allow countries to obtain cheaper drugs during health emergencies on a case-by-case basis.[27] NGOs immediately called on the U.S. government to end trade pressure on poor countries in health care industry disputes.[28] Over the following year, the U.S. government declared it would not block compulsory licenses in the rest of sub-Saharan Africa and Thailand, and elsewhere on a selected basis.

In the summer of 2000, at the 13th International AIDS Conference in Durban, South Africa, Boehringer Ingelheim, a German pharmaceutical company, offered to make its AIDS drug, Viramune, available for free. Bristol-Myers Squibb, Merck, and Glaxo Wellcome made similar offers. NGOs and developing governments, however, criticized the companies for making the announcements without consulting and working with the concerned governments, and for placing restrictions on distribution.[29] Doctors Without Borders suggested the industry focus on "concrete action" rather than publicity. Jack Watters, Pfizer's medical director for Africa, defended the conditions of the company's pilot free-drug program in South Africa: "We want to evaluate how much impact the program has on survival." The company was also concerned about corruption and diversion of supplies. He added, "There's no guarantee that the drug will find its way to the people who need it most."[30]

NGO activists continued to press the U.S. government, the WTO, and the pharmaceutical industry to make it easier for developing countries to produce or import generics. Robert Weissman, co-director of Essential Action, a Washington NGO, said, "There's a global health crisis of historic proportions, and there's an existing set of treatments that allow people to live indefinitely with the disease. But instead of trying to deliver medicine to the sick, we are worrying about the intellectual rights of the pharmaceutical companies." He added, "The overriding point is that, no matter what kind of charity companies dole out, countries should have the right to make generic drugs."[31] Some felt that if the pharmaceutical industry really wanted to make its products available it should drop its lawsuit against the South African government.

In spring 2001, three U.S. pharmaceutical companies—Merck, Bristol-Myers Squibb, and Abbott—announced they would sell HIV drugs to developing countries at cost. GlaxoSmithKline offered 90 percent discounts.[32] Merck planned to use the United Nations Human Development Index and offer the lowest prices to countries that received "low" rankings or had an AIDS infection rate of 1 percent or higher. It offered Brazil, which didn't fall in that category, prices about 75 percent higher. Still, this was a steep discount compared to U.S. prices. Merck would sell efavirenz in Brazil for $920 per year per patient (compared to $4,700 in the United States) and Crixivan for $1,029 ($6,000 in the United States).[33] In October 2002, Merck announced further cuts in the price for Stocrin from the (already reduced) price of $1.37 per patient per day to $0.95 per patient per day in the poorest, hardest-hit countries. The price for middle-development countries with less than 1 percent HIV prevalence would be $2.10 per patient per day, down from $2.52.

On September 5, 2002, GlaxoSmithKline announced an additional price cut for antiretroviral drugs and malaria drugs for poor countries. The British company said it would cut the prices of its HIV/AIDS drugs by as much as 33 percent and the prices of its antimalarial drugs by as much as 38 percent in developing countries to help health workers fight two of the deadliest diseases that afflict the developing world. Under the new pricing plan, GlaxoSmithKline said it would supply its AIDS and anti-malarial drugs at not-for-profit prices to the public sector, nongovernmental organizations, aid agencies, the United Nations, and the Global Fund to Fight AIDS, Tuberculosis and Malaria. To prevent cut-price drugs from being reimported into the West, Glaxo said it would seek regulatory approval to provide special packaging for the cut-price drugs.

Indian generic manufacturers, such as Cipla, offered among the lowest prices in the world. Over the years Cipla had developed a range of pharmaceuticals. It began exporting in 1946 when it sold a hypertension drug to an American company. In 1985 the U.S. FDA approved Cipla's bulk drug manufacturing facilities. Cipla's net income in 2001–2002 was $48 million on sales of $292 million. Its major export markets were the Americas (41%), Europe (24%), and the Middle East and Africa (12% each). In late 2001 Cipla agreed to supply a three-drug antiretroviral combination to Nigeria for $350 per person per year.[34] The Nigerian government initiated a $4 million pilot program covering 10,000 adults and 5,000 children in which it planned to charge patients $120 per year and cover the remaining cost from government funds.[35]

In March 2002 the WHO released its first list of companies that are regarded as manufacturers of safe AIDS drugs. The head of UNAIDS, Dr. Peter Piot, hoped the list would pave the way for patients to "gain greater access to affordable HIV medicines of good quality." Of the 41 drugs listed, 26 were sold by multinationals and 10 by Cipla.

In October 2002, the Global Fund announced that it would encourage developing countries to buy cheap generic drugs instead of expensive branded ones. Anxious to maximize the impact on its limited resources, the Fund announced it would impose three conditions on recipient nations: that they purchase the cheapest drugs, that they only buy drugs of guaranteed quality, and that they comply with international laws and their own laws. It was unclear, however, how this last provision squared with the WTO TRIPS agreement.

The Global Fund

In April 2001, while addressing an African summit in Nigeria, U.N. Secretary General Kofi Annan proposed creation of a global fund to combat AIDS. He stressed the need to ratchet up spending on fighting AIDS in developing countries from the current $1 billion level to $7–10 billion. He noted that pharmaceutical companies were beginning to accept that "generic medication can be produced where it can save lives." The previous week pharmaceutical companies had dropped their lawsuit against the South African government over patent laws.[36]

The proposal attracted significant support from world leaders. In May 2001, President George W. Bush announced $200 million in seed money for the fund. The following month, addressing delegates from 180 nations at a U.N. conference, U.S. Secretary of State Colin Powell declared, "No war on the face of the world is more destructive than the AIDS pandemic. I was a soldier. I know of no enemy in war more insidious or vicious than AIDS, an enemy that poses a clear and present danger to the world." He added, "We hope this seed money will generate billions more from donors all over the world, and more will come from the United States as we learn where our support can be most effective."

The Global Fund, set up as an independent corporation, was broadened to address not just AIDS but tuberculosis and malaria as well. By July 2003, more than $2 billion had been paid in by developed countries (see Table 6). In addition to leading country donors that included the United States, the EU, individual European countries, and Japan, the Gates Foundation contributed $100 million. In April 2002, the Global Fund made its first awards, totaling $616 million, to programs in 40 countries. Slightly more than half was designated for Africa. Experts predicted that the Fund's success hinged on how effective it proved to be as a "hard-nosed judge of its grantees' performance."

In October 2003, the Fund announced it would slow the pace of its awards to one round per year because it had fallen short of its fund-raising goals and was concerned about running out of money. The Fund announced it had received pledges through 2008 of about $5.2 billion, well short of its $8–$10 billion goal.[37] The decision came as the Fund announced $623 million in grants to 71 disease prevention and treatment programs in about 50 countries. This round of grants, the third, was substantially smaller than the $884 million awarded in January 2003. In June 2003, it was announced that Jack Valenti, longtime lobbyist for the motion picture industry, would assume the presidency of a group set up to raise money for the fund.

Table 6 **Leading Donors (Paid to Date) to the Global Fund, July 2004**

Country	$m
U.S.A.	623
EU	401
France	304
Japan	230
Italy	215
U.K.	173
Gates Foundation	100

Source: theglobalfundatm.org.

Pressure Mounts

In June 2002, two weeks before the 14th International AIDS Conference in Barcelona, the WTO council responsible for intellectual property extended until 2016 the transition period during which least-developed countries (LDCs) did not have to provide patent protection for pharmaceuticals.[38] Previously they'd been expected to comply by 2006. (See Exhibit 2 for a list of least-developed countries.)

The delegates from the 194 countries left the July 2002 International AIDS Conference in Barcelona with cautious optimism. Joep Lange, president of the International AIDS Society, said, "If we can get Coca-Cola and cold beer to every remote corner of Africa, it should not be impossible to do the same with drugs." However the conference wasn't without protests. Activists tore down the European Union exhibition stand, demanding larger contributions to the Global Fund. They heckled U.S. Health Secretary Tommy Thompson, demanding the United States do more to improve health systems in developing countries.

The World Health Organization estimated that given the public health infrastructure in developing countries, the maximum that could be spent productively each year by 2005 was about $9 billion. This assumed $4.8 billion for prevention and $4.2 billion for treatment. It also estimated that with a commitment of $4.8 billion per year to prevention, 29 million infections could probably be avoided by 2010.

Several challenges remained. Drug prices had fallen significantly, but not low enough for everyone. While the large pharmaceutical companies were selling antiretroviral combinations for about $1,200 per person per year in some developing countries, the lowest generic prices out of India were $209. Health economists estimated that prices needed to fall as low as $30–$40 per person per year for drugs to reach the poorest recipients. Such low prices were unlikely to materialize anytime soon. NGOs, such as Doctors Without Borders, were expected to push for optimizing use of scarce funds by deploying Global Fund allocations for purchase of generics only. Tough decisions needed to be made about the allocation of resources between AIDS and other diseases, and between prevention and treatment of AIDS.

In early August 2003, the South African government reversed its policy on AIDS, signed the Global Fund, and announced production of its first generic AIDS drug. Aspen Pharmacare, a South African firm, announced it would be the initial provider of generic treatments. Backed by many activist groups, including the influential Treatment Action Campaign, revisions to the $41 million deal detailed an operational plan to make the drugs available by the end of September 2003. South African president Thabo Mbeki finally agreed to the long-standing proposal after a recent World Bank report predicted "a complete economic collapse" within four generations if the government didn't act swiftly.

The 2003 WTO Agreement and Its Aftermath

In August 2003, the United States and other WTO members announced that they had finalized a solution to streamline the supply of disease-fighting medications to poor countries. As part of the compromise deal, the United States agreed to language that would allow compulsory licensing only for "genuine health reasons" and not for commercial advantage. This appeared to prompt action.

On December 10, 2003, Britain's GlaxoSmithKline and Germany's Boehringer Ingelheim agreed to expand the licensing of their patented AIDS drugs to three generic manufacturers in South Africa and other African countries as part of an out-of-court settlement with South Africa's Treatment Action Campaign. In return, the South African Competition Commission, a government body that monitors free-market practices, agreed to drop a yearlong probe into whether the companies had overcharged for their AIDS drugs. Glaxo and Boehringer Ingelheim already had existing agreements with a fourth generic manufacturer, South Africa's Aspen Pharmacare. Under the settlement pact in South Africa, Glaxo also agreed to cap royalty fees at no more than 5 percent of net sales and to extend the generic licenses to the private and public sectors. It said it would allow the generic licensees to export AIDS drugs manufactured in South Africa to 47 sub-Saharan African countries. The Competition Commission said it had not asked for a fine or administrative penalty against Glaxo, which is the world's largest maker of AIDS medicines.[39]

Shareholder activists have also begun to put pressure on companies to provide more comprehensive reporting

Exhibit 2   Countries Classified as Least-Developed by WTO

Angola	Djibouti	Maldives	Sierra Leone
Bangladesh	Gambia	Mali	Solomon Islands
Benin	Guinea	Mauritania	Tanzania
Burkina Faso	Guinea Bissau	Mozambique	Togo
Burundi	Haiti	Myanmar	Uganda
Central African Republic	Lesotho	Niger	Zambia
Chad	Madagascar	Rwanda	
Congo	Malawi	Senegal	

about their potential to support efforts to fight AIDS. In March 2004, a consortium of religious investors forwarded shareholder resolutions at four top drug makers, asking the companies to assess how much charity work they are doing for HIV and AIDS in developing countries and to estimate how much the epidemic could affect their businesses. The Interfaith Center on Corporate Responsibility (ICCR) and roughly 30 religious groups requested that pharmaceutical companies offer shareholders a report of their conclusions six months after the annual meetings. Although the boards of directors at Pfizer, Merck, and Abbott said they opposed the measure, Coca-Cola's board said it supported a similar shareholder proposal to assess the business risks associated with the HIV/AIDS epidemic.[40]

2005: Making the WTO Agreement Official and Its Aftermath

At the end of 2005, members of the WTO approved changes to the intellectual property agreement making permanent the August 2003 "waiver" which facilitated access for developing countries to cheaper, generic versions of patented medications.[41] Director-General Pascal Lamy said, "This is of particular personal satisfaction to me, since I have been involved for years in working to ensure that the TRIPS Agreement is part of the solution to the question of ensuring the poor have access to medicines."[42]

According to the NGO group Doctors Without Borders, prices of first-line treatments have dropped from more than $10,000 to as little as $150 a year since 2000 largely due to competition from generics.[43] Brazil and Thailand have been able to launch successful national AIDS programs because key pharmaceuticals were not patent protected and could be locally produced for very low costs. Still, the method of implementation at the national or regional trade level of TRIPS can still cause problems.

In early 2006, Bristol-Myers Squibb (BMY) announced an agreement for technology transfer and voluntary license with generic manufacturers Aspen Pharmacare and Emcure Pharmaceuticals for atazanavir, first approved for combination therapy in the United States in June 2003. Peter R. Dolan, Bristol-Myers Squibb's CEO, highlighted his company's commitment to the global fight against AIDS: "In Sub-Saharan Africa, where the HIV/AIDS pandemic has been especially devastating, we've taken a broad-based approach to addressing the AIDS crisis, including providing our AIDS medicines at no profit prices and committing to ensure our patents do not prevent inexpensive treatment in the region."[44] Under the deal, the generic company will set prices in Africa and India.

Generic drug manufacturers have lowered the costs of some much-needed drugs to developing countries, but often new drugs are still priced much higher than old treatments, and are hence unavailable in many of the countries with the most need. Doctors Without Borders

spoke out in March 2006 against what it calls the standard practice of drug companies marketing less adapted drugs to African, Asian, and Latin American countries, while reserving new and improved drugs for more wealthy countries.[45] The NGO specifically criticized Abbot Laboratories' lopinavir/ritonavir, which does not need refrigeration but is only available in the United States at a cost of US $9,687 per patient per year. Doctors Without Borders worker Dr. Helen Bygrave commented, "It's a cruel irony that although this drug—with no need for refrigeration—seems to have been designed for places like Nigeria, it is not available here."[46]

In December 2005, the WHO released a statement urging countries to adopt a policy of free access at the point of service delivery to HIV care and treatment, including antiretroviral therapy.[47] This recommendation came in the wake of a 2005 endorsement by G8 leaders and U.N. member states to provide universal access to HIV treatment and care by 2010. During a similar effort, the "3 by 5" program, which aimed to provide treatment for 3 million patients in 50 developing countries by the conclusion of 2005, it had become apparent that charging users at the point of service undermines efforts to provide universal care.

The number of people receiving antiretroviral aid has increased under the 3 by 5 program, but not to desired levels. More than 1 million people in developing countries received antiretroviral treatment in 2005, and expanded treatment helped to prevent 250,000–350,000 deaths.[48] Still, the global number of people with AIDS continued to rise. At the end of 2005, 40.3 million people were estimated to be living with AIDS.[49]

Pressure Mounts Again

The increasing severity of the AIDS epidemic, compounded by the constant lack of access to drugs, has recently prompted more drastic action among some developing countries. In January 2007 Thailand, a nation with nearly half a million residents infected with HIV, announced its intentions to break the patent on an important AIDS drug (Kaletra) produced by Abbott Laboratories,[50] setting a precedent for other nations such as Brazil, Indonesia, and the Philippines. Abbott retaliated by revoking the introduction of seven new drugs in Thailand. Doctors Without Borders called Abbott's reaction "callous," and Abbott has since backed down.

The U.N. and World Bank have openly supported Thailand's landmark patent-breaking decision as part of its serious treatment of AIDS within its new health program.[51] The global impact of Thailand's decision is likely to be magnified by subsequent policy changes by other countries; for instance, Brazil renounced the patent on a Merck AIDS drug in May 2007 (after years of threatening to do so).[52] Although the U.S.-Brazil Business Council warns that this IPR violation might deter future business investment from Brazil, the government still went through with the decision, likely prompted by Thailand's precedent as well as Merck's inability to offer what Brazil viewed as a satisfactory discount on patented drug purchases.[53]

The increased global effort to fight HIV/AIDS has been supported by other organizations. Among others, the Clinton Foundation has recently stepped up its work with drug companies to lower prices of AIDS medications. In October 2003, former president Bill Clinton first announced a landmark program to attack two of the toughest obstacles to treating AIDS in the developing world: high drug prices and low-quality health infrastructures. The Clinton Foundation HIV/AIDS Initiative reached a deal with four generic-drug companies, including one in South Africa, to slash the price of antiretroviral AIDS medicine. In April 2004, Clinton's foundation announced that these special drug prices were being extended from the initial 16 countries in the Caribbean and Africa to any country supported by UNICEF, the World Bank, and the U.N.-administered Global Fund to Fight AIDS, Tuberculosis, and Malaria. "With these agreements, we are one step closer to making sure future generations can live without the scourge of AIDS," Clinton said in a statement released by his U.S.-based foundation.

In May 2007 the Foundation struck a deal with Cipla and Matrix Laboratories to lower prices on "second-line" AIDS drugs.[54] The Clinton Foundation, which is financed by Unitaid (an organization of 20 nations that donate a portion of airline tax revenues for HIV/AIDS programs in developing countries), provides access to lower-priced AIDS drugs for approximately 65,000 people in 65 countries worldwide.[55]

Under the Clinton Foundation agreement, five generic-drug manufacturers—Pharmacare Holdings of South Africa and the Indian companies Cipla, Hetero Drugs, Ranbaxy Laboratories, and Matrix Laboratories—provide basic HIV treatment for as little as $140 per person per year, one-third to one-half of the lowest price available elsewhere. Diagnostic tests are supplied by five different companies and include machines, training, chemicals, and maintenance at a price that is up to 80 percent cheaper than the normal market price. "This new partnership works to break down some of the barriers—such as price, supply and demand—that are impeding access to lifesaving AIDS medicines and diagnostics in developing countries," said UNICEF Executive Director Carol Bellamy.[56]

Questions for Review

1. Do pharmaceutical companies have a responsibility to distribute drugs for free or at low cost in developing countries? What are the main arguments for and against such an approach?

2. What are the principal arguments of pharmaceutical companies that oppose making exceptions to IPR laws for developing countries? What are the arguments by NGOs and others for relaxing IPR laws?

3. What impact would you expect South Africa's decision to levy duties on drug imports from Western nations to have on the international distribution of drugs to South Africa?

4. In June 2002, the WTO extended the transition period during which least-developed countries (LDCs) had to provide patent protection for pharmaceuticals. In your opinion, was this an appropriate change in policy or a dangerous precedent? What could be some of the negative ramifications of this resolution? What about the effects for other industries?

5. Given the initiatives announced by global development and aid organizations and among pharmaceutical companies themselves, was it necessary to relax IPR rules in order to ensure that adequate supplies of AIDS medications would be available for distribution in the developing world?

6. What role do MNCs have in providing funding or other assistance to international organizations such as the Global Fund?

Exercise

Although the WTO has now agreed to relax intellectual property rules in order to facilitate the production and distribution of inexpensive generic antivirals, the conditions under which this provision allows for production or importation of generics ("genuine health reasons") are not entirely clear. The WTO is to hold a hearing for interested parties to provide input about how these rules should be implemented. Your group represents the interests of one of the key stakeholders (see table) and will be responsible for arguing that stakeholder's position.

Team	Stakeholder
1	The WTO
2	Doctors Without Borders (NGO)
3	CIPLA (Indian generic manufacturer)
4	GlaxoSmithKline (representing pharma companies)
5	Government of Brazil (representing developing countries)
6	The Clinton Foundation HIV/AIDS Initiatives

Discuss with your group the major points to make to advance your perspectives. Come prepared to make a five-minute presentation summarizing how you would like the WTO to implement the new rules. The WTO group should ask questions during the hearing. It should then take 10 minutes to deliberate and come up with a proposed plan incorporating the interests of all of the stakeholders.

Source: © McGraw-Hill Irwin. This case was prepared by Jonathan Doh and Erik Holt of Villanova University with research assistance by Courtney Asher as the basis for class discussion. It is not intended to illustrate either effective or ineffective managerial capability or administrative responsibility. The authors thank Sushil Vachani for comments, suggestions, and input.

PART TWO

THE ROLE
OF CULTURE

Chapter 4

THE MEANINGS AND DIMENSIONS OF CULTURE

A major challenge of doing business internationally is to adapt effectively to different cultures. Such adaptation requires an understanding of cultural diversity, perceptions, stereotypes, and values. In recent years, a great deal of research has been conducted on cultural dimensions and attitudes, and the findings have proved useful in providing integrative profiles of international cultures. However, a word of caution must be given when discussing these country profiles. It must be remembered that stereotypes and overgeneralizations should be avoided; there are always individual differences and even subcultures within every country.

This chapter examines the meaning of culture as it applies to international management, reviews some of the value differences and similarities of various national groups, studies important dimensions of culture and their impact on behavior, and examines country clusters. The specific objectives of this chapter are:

1. DEFINE the term *culture*, and discuss some of the comparative ways of differentiating cultures.

2. DESCRIBE the concept of cultural values, and relate some of the international differences, similarities, and changes occurring in terms of both work and managerial values.

3. IDENTIFY the major dimensions of culture relevant to work settings, and discuss their effects on behavior in an international environment.

4. DISCUSS the value of country cluster analysis and relational orientations in developing effective international management practices.

The World of *BusinessWeek*

BusinessWeek

New Tech, Old Habits

Despite World-Class IT Networks, Japanese and Korean Workers Are Still Chained to Their Desks

Masanori Goto was in for a culture shock when he returned to Japan after a seven-year stint in New York. The 42-year-old public relations officer at cellular giant NTT DoCoMo logged many a late night at his Manhattan apartment, using his company laptop to communicate with colleagues 14 time zones away. Now back in Tokyo, Goto has a cell phone he can use to send quick e-mails after hours, but he must hole up at the office late into the night if he needs to do any serious work. The reason: His bosses haven't outfitted him with a portable computer. "I didn't realize that our people in Japan weren't using laptops," he says. "That was a surprise."

A few hundred miles to the west, in Seoul, Lee Seung Hwa also knows what it's like to spend long hours chained to her desk. The 33-year-old recently quit her job as an executive assistant at a carmaker because, among other complaints, her company didn't let lower-level employees log on from outside the office. "I could have done all the work from home, but managers thought I was working hard only if I stayed late," says Lee.

These days, information technology could easily free the likes of Goto and Lee. Korea and Japan are world leaders in broadband access, with connection speeds that put the U.S. to shame. And their wireless networks are state of the art, allowing supercharged Web surfing from mobile phones and other handhelds, whether at a café, in the subway, or on the highway. But when it comes to taking advantage of connectivity for business, Americans are way ahead.

For a study in contrasts, consider the daily commute. American trains are packed with businesspeople furiously tapping their BlackBerrys or Treos, squeezing a few extra minutes into their workdays. In Tokyo or Seoul, commuters stare intently at their cell phone screens, but they're usually playing games, watching video clips, or sending Hello Kitty icons to friends. And while advertising for U.S. cellular companies emphasizes how data services can make users more productive at work, Asian carriers tend to stress the fun factor.

Why? Corporate culture in the Far East remains deeply conservative, and most businesses have been slow to mine the opportunities offered by newfangled communications technologies. One big reason is the premium placed on face time at the office. Junior employees are reluctant to leave work before the boss does for fear of looking like slackers. Also, Confucianism places greater stock on group effort and consensus-building than on individual initiative. So members of a team all feel they must stick around if there is a task to complete. "To reap full benefits from IT investment, companies must change the way they do business," says Lee Inn Chan, vice-president at SK Research Institute, a Seoul management think tank funded by cellular carrier SK Telecom. "What's most needed in Korea and Japan is an overhaul in business processes and practices."

Time, Not Task

In these countries, if you're not in the office, your boss simply assumes you're not working. It doesn't help that a lack of clear job definitions and performance metrics makes it difficult for managers to assess the productivity of employees working off site. "Performance reviews and judgments are still largely time-oriented here, rather than task-oriented as in the West," says Cho Bum Coo, a Seoul-based executive partner at business consulting firm Accenture Ltd.

Even tech companies in the region often refuse to untether workers from the office. Camera-maker Canon Inc. for instance, dispensed with flextime four years ago after employees said it interfered with communications, while Samsung stresses that person-to-person contact is far more effective than e-mail. In Japan, many companies say they are reluctant to send workers home with their laptops for fear that proprietary information might go astray. Canon publishes a 33-page code of conduct that includes a cautionary tale of a worker who loses a notebook computer loaded with sensitive customer data on his commute. At Korean companies SK

Telecom, Samsung Electronics, and lg Electronics, employees must obtain permission before they can carry their laptops out of the office. Even then, they often are barred from full access to files from work. And while just about everyone has a cell phone that can display Web pages or send e-mails, getting into corporate networks is complicated and unwieldy.

The result: Korean and Japanese white-collar workers clock long days at the office, often toiling till midnight and coming in on weekends. "In my dictionary there's no such thing as work/life balance as far as weekdays are concerned," says a Samsung Electronics senior manager who declined to be named. Tom Coyner, a consultant and author of *Mastering Business in Korea: A Practical Guide,* says: "Even your wife would think you were not regarded as an important player in the office if you came home at five or six."

These factors may be preventing Japan and Korea from wringing more productivity out of their massive IT investments. Both countries place high on lists of global innovators. For instance, Japan and Korea rank No. 2 and No. 6, respectively, out of 30 nations in terms of spending on research and development, according to the Organization for Economic Cooperation and Development. And the Geneva-based World Intellectual Property Organization says Japan was second and Korea fourth in international patent filings. But when it comes to the productivity of IT users, both countries badly lag the U.S., says Kazuyuki Motohashi, a University of Tokyo professor who is an expert on technological innovation. "Companies in Japan and Korea haven't made the structural changes to get the most out of new technologies," he says.

Still, a new generation of managers rising through the ranks may speed the transformation. These workers are tech-savvy and often more individualistic, having come from smaller families. Already, some companies are tinkering with changes to meet their needs. SK Telecom abolished titles for all midlevel managers in the hopes that this would spur workers to take greater initiative. Japan's NEC Corp. is experimenting with telecommuting for 2,000 of its 148,000 employees. And in Korea, CJ 39 Shopping, a cable-TV shopping channel, is letting 10% of its call-center employees work from home.

Foreign companies are doing their bit to shake things up. In Korea, IBM has outfitted all of its 2,600 employees with laptops and actively encourages them to work off site.

The system, which was first introduced in 1995, has allowed the company to cut back on office space and reap savings of $2.3 million a year. One beneficiary is Kim Yoon Hee. The procurement specialist reports to the office only on Tuesdays and Thursdays. On other days, calls to her office phone are automatically routed to her laptop, so she can work from home. "It would have been difficult for me to remain employed had it not been for the telecommuting system," says Kim, 35, who quit a job at a big Korean company seven years ago because late nights at the office kept her away from her infant daughter. "This certainly makes me more loyal to my company."

Source: **Reprinted with special permission from "New Tech, Old Habits," by Moon Ihlwan and Kenji Hall,** *BusinessWeek,* **March 26, 2007. Copyright © 2007 The McGraw-Hill Companies.**

The opening article shows how culture can have a great impact on business practices. We discussed in Chapter 2 how technological advances are connecting the world and providing opportunities to conduct business from any location. While some cultures have embraced this as a way to support greater work-life balance, we see here that other cultures have not yet fully incorporated all that technology has to offer, due to enduring differences in national culture. Knowledge is expanding at a more rapid pace, allowing some individuals to work outside the office, yet some cultures do not value or support that trend. International managers need to keep in mind that practices around the world differ greatly, and requesting a worker to perform a task in one culture may involve challenges not faced in another. MNCs that are aware of the cultures in which they do business will be better equipped to balance the needs of the consumers, workers, and business to hopefully create an environment of productivity, loyalty, and understanding.

■ The Nature of Culture

The word *culture* comes from the Latin *cultura*, which is related to cult or worship. In its broadest sense, the term refers to the result of human interaction.[1] For the purposes of the study of international management, **culture** is acquired knowledge that people use to interpret experience and generate social behavior.[2] This knowledge forms values, creates attitudes, and influences behavior. Most scholars of culture would agree on the following characteristics of culture:

culture
Acquired knowledge that people use to interpret experience and generate social behavior. This knowledge forms values, creates attitudes, and influences behavior.

1. *Learned.* Culture is not inherited or biologically based; it is acquired by learning and experience.
2. *Shared.* People as members of a group, organization, or society share culture; it is not specific to single individuals.
3. *Transgenerational.* Culture is cumulative, passed down from one generation to the next.
4. *Symbolic.* Culture is based on the human capacity to symbolize or use one thing to represent another.
5. *Patterned.* Culture has structure and is integrated; a change in one part will bring changes in another.
6. *Adaptive.* Culture is based on the human capacity to change or adapt, as opposed to the more genetically driven adaptive process of animals.[3]

Because different cultures exist in the world, an understanding of the impact of culture on behavior is critical to the study of international management.[4] If international managers do not know something about the cultures of the countries they deal with, the results can be quite disastrous. For example, a partner in one of New York's leading private banking firms tells the following story:

> I traveled nine thousand miles to meet a client and arrived with my foot in my mouth. Determined to do things right, I'd memorized the names of the key men I was to see in Singapore. No easy job, inasmuch as the names all came in threes. So, of course, I couldn't resist showing off that I'd done my homework. I began by addressing top man Lo Win Hao with plenty of

well-placed Mr. Hao's—sprinkled the rest of my remarks with a Mr. Chee this and a Mr. Woon that. Great show. Until a note was passed to me from one man I'd met before, in New York. Bad news. "Too friendly too soon, Mr. Long," it said. Where diffidence is next to godliness, there I was, calling a room of VIPs, in effect, Mr. Ed and Mr. Charlie. I'd remembered everybody's name—but forgot that in Chinese the surname comes *first* and the given name *last*.[5]

Cultural Diversity

There are many ways of examining cultural differences and their impact on international management. Culture can affect technology transfer, managerial attitudes, managerial ideology, and even business-government relations. Perhaps most important, culture affects how people think and behave. Table 4–1, for example, compares the most important cultural values of the United States, Japan, and Arab countries. A close look at this table shows a great deal of difference among these three cultures. Culture affects a host of business-related activities, even including the common handshake. Here are some contrasting examples:

Culture	Type of Handshake
United States	Firm
Asian	Gentle (shaking hands is unfamiliar and uncomfortable for some; the exception is the Korean, who usually has a firm handshake)
British	Soft
French	Light and quick (not offered to superiors); repeated on arrival and departure
German	Brusk and firm; repeated on arrival and departure
Latin American	Moderate grasp; repeated frequently
Middle Eastern	Gentle; repeated frequently[6]
South Africa	Light/soft; long and involved

In overall terms, the cultural impact on international management is reflected by basic beliefs and behaviors. Here are some specific examples where the culture of a society can directly affect management approaches:

- *Centralized vs. decentralized decision making.* In some societies, top managers make all important organizational decisions. In others, these decisions are diffused throughout the enterprise, and middle- and lower-level managers actively participate in, and make, key decisions.

Table 4–1
Priorities of Cultural Values: United States, Japan, and Arab Countries

United States	Japan	Arab Countries
1. Freedom	1. Belonging	1. Family security
2. Independence	2. Group harmony	2. Family harmony
3. Self-reliance	3. Collectiveness	3. Parental guidance
4. Equality	4. Age/seniority	4. Age
5. Individualism	5. Group consensus	5. Authority
6. Competition	6. Cooperation	6. Compromise
7. Efficiency	7. Quality	7. Devotion
8. Time	8. Patience	8. Patience
9. Directness	9. Indirectness	9. Indirectness
10. Openness	10. Go-between	10. Hospitality

Note: "1" represents the most important cultural value, "10" the least.
Source: Adapted from information found in F. Elashmawi and Philip R. Harris, *Multicultural Management* (Houston: Gulf Publishing, 1993), p. 63.

- *Safety vs. risk.* In some societies, organizational decision makers are risk-averse and have great difficulty with conditions of uncertainty. In others, risk taking is encouraged, and decision making under uncertainty is common.

- *Individual vs. group rewards.* In some countries, personnel who do outstanding work are given individual rewards in the form of bonuses and commissions. In others, cultural norms require group rewards, and individual rewards are frowned on.

- *Informal vs. formal procedures.* In some societies, much is accomplished through informal means. In others, formal procedures are set forth and followed rigidly.

- *High vs. low organizational loyalty.* In some societies, people identify very strongly with their organization or employer. In others, people identify with their occupational group, such as engineer or mechanic.

- *Cooperation vs. competition.* Some societies encourage cooperation between their people. Others encourage competition between their people.

- *Short-term vs. long-term horizons.* Some cultures focus most heavily on short-term horizons, such as short-range goals of profit and efficiency. Others are more interested in long-range goals, such as market share and technologic development.

- *Stability vs. innovation.* The culture of some countries encourages stability and resistance to change. The culture of others puts high value on innovation and change.

These cultural differences influence the way that international management should be conducted. "International Management in Action: Business Customs in South Africa" provides some examples from a country where many international managers are unfamiliar with day-to-day business protocol.

Another way of depicting cultural diversity is through visually separating its components. Figure 4–1 provides an example by using concentric circles. The outer ring consists of the explicit artifacts and products of the culture. This level is observable and consists of such things as language, food, buildings, and art. The middle ring contains the norms and values of the society. These can be both formal and informal, and they are designed to help people understand how they should behave. The inner circle contains the basic, implicit assumptions that govern behavior. By understanding these assumptions, members of a culture are able to organize themselves in a way that helps them

Figure 4–1

A Model of Culture

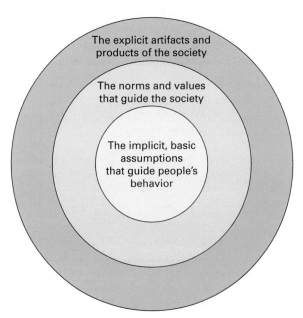

The explicit artifacts and products of the society

The norms and values that guide the society

The implicit, basic assumptions that guide people's behavior

Business Customs in South Africa

The proper methods for conducting business in Africa can vary greatly depending on the region. As mentioned in Chapter 2, Africa consists of many traditions often within the same area. Adding further complication is the propensity for northern regions of Africa to mirror Islamic fundamentals. For simplicity, we will focus on some suggestions with regard to business customs in South Africa:

1. Arrange a meeting before discussing business over the phone. Most South Africans prefer face-to-face interactions. Be prepared for informal small talk before and during the meeting to be better acquainted. In most cases, first meetings are less about business and more about establishing a relationship. Sincere inquiries about family or discussion of topics such as sports (e.g., rugby, cricket, or soccer) are encouraged; avoid talking about racial politics as it is viewed as taboo.

2. Appointments should be made as far in advance as possible. There is a chance that senior-level managers may be unavailable on short notice, but last-minute arrangements occur often. South Africans are early risers, so breakfast and lunch meetings are quite common. If you have a few meetings scheduled, be sure to allow ample time between them as the view of time is more lax in this area and meetings are prone to being postponed.

3. When introduced, maintain eye contact, shake hands, and provide business cards to everyone. Do not sit until invited to do so. Men and women do not shake hands as often in South Africa, so wait for women to initiate handshakes. Women visiting the country who extend their hand may not have it taken by a South African male; do not take this as a rude response.

4. Since women are not yet in senior level positions in South Africa, female representatives may encounter condescending behavior or "tests" that would not be extended to male counterparts. Men are expected to leave a room before the women as a "protective" measure, and when a woman or elder enters the room, men are expected to stand.

5. After establishing a trustworthy relationship, make business plans clear, including deadlines, since these are seen as more fluid than contractual. Be sure to keep a tone of negotiation while keeping figures manageable. Negotiation is not their strong point, and an aggressive approach will not prove to be successful. Maintain a win-win strategy.

6. Patience is very important when dealing with business. Never interrupt a South African. Be prepared for a long lag-time between business proposition and acceptance or rejection. Decision-making procedures include a lot of discussion between top managers and subordinates, resulting in slow processes.

7. Keep presentations short, and do away with flashy visuals. Follow up and be clear that you intend to continue relations with the business or individual; a long-term business relationship is valued with South Africans.

Source: www.kwintessential.co.uk/resources/global-etiquette/south-africa-country-profile.html; Going Global Inc., "Cultural Advice," *South Africa Career Guide, 2006.* Accessed at content.epnet.com.ps2.villanova.edu/pdf18_21/pdf/2006/ONI/01Jan06/22291722.pdf.

increase the effectiveness of their problem-solving processes and interact well with each other. In explaining the nature of the inner circle, Trompenaars and Hampden-Turner have noted that:

> The best way to test if something is a basic assumption is when the [situation] provokes confusion or irritation. You might, for example, observe that some Japanese bow deeper than others… If you ask why they do it the answer might be that they don't know but that the other person does it too (norm) or that they want to show respect for authority (value). A typical Dutch question that might follow is: "Why do you respect authority?" The most likely Japanese reaction would be either puzzlement or a smile (which might be hiding their irritation). When you question basic assumptions you are asking questions that have never been asked before. It might lead others to deeper insights, but it also might provoke annoyance. Try in the USA or the Netherlands to raise the question of why people are equal and you will see what we mean.[7]

Figure 4–2

Comparing Cultures as Overlapping Normal Distributions

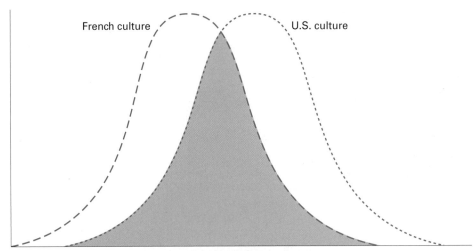

French culture   U.S. culture

Source: Adapted from Fons Trompenaars and Charles Hampden-Turner, *Riding the Waves of Culture: Understanding Diversity in Global Business,* 2nd ed. (New York: McGraw-Hill, 1998), p. 25.

A supplemental way of understanding cultural differences is to compare culture as a normal distribution, as in Figure 4–2, and then to examine it in terms of stereotyping, as in Figure 4–3. French culture and American culture, for example, have quite different norms and values. So the normal distribution curves for the two cultures have only limited overlap. However, when one looks at the tail ends of the two curves, it is possible to identify stereotypical views held by members of one culture about the other. The stereotypes are often exaggerated and used by members of one culture in describing the other, thus helping reinforce the differences between the two while reducing the likelihood of achieving cooperation and communication. This is one reason why an understanding of national culture is so important in the study of international management.

Figure 4–3

Stereotyping from the Cultural Extremes

How the Americans see the French:

- arrogant
- flamboyant
- hierarchical
- emotional

How the French see the Americans:

- naive
- aggressive
- unprincipled
- workaholic

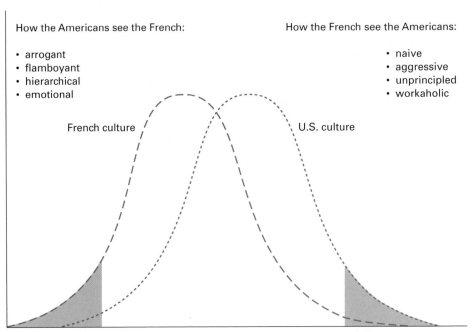

French culture   U.S. culture

Source: Adapted from Fons Trompenaars and Charles Hampden-Turner, *Riding the Waves of Culture: Understanding Diversity in Global Business,* 2nd ed. (New York: McGraw-Hill, 1998), p. 23.

Values in Culture

A major dimension in the study of culture is values. **Values** are basic convictions that people have regarding what is right and wrong, good and bad, important and unimportant. These values are learned from the culture in which the individual is reared, and they help direct the person's behavior. Differences in cultural values often result in varying management practices. Table 4–2 provides an example. Note that U.S. values can result in one set of business responses and that alternative values can bring about different responses.

values
Basic convictions that people have regarding what is right and wrong, good and bad, important and unimportant.

Value Differences and Similarities Across Cultures   Personal values have been the focus of numerous intercultural studies. In general, the findings show both differences and similarities between the work values and managerial values of different cultural groups. For example, one study found differences in work values between Western-oriented and tribal-oriented black employees in South Africa.[8] The Western-oriented group accepted most of the tenets of the Protestant work ethic, but the tribal-oriented group did not. The results were explained in terms of the differences of the cultural backgrounds of the two groups.

Differences in work values also have been found to reflect culture and industrialization. Researchers gave a personal-values questionnaire (PVQ) to over 2,000 managers in five countries: Australia ($n = 281$), India ($n = 485$), Japan ($n = 301$), South Korea ($n = 161$), and the United States ($n = 833$).[9] The PVQ consisted of 66 concepts related to business goals, personal goals, ideas associated with people and groups of people, and ideas about general topics. Ideologic and philosophic concepts were included to represent major value systems of all groups. The results showed some significant differences between the managers in each group. U.S. managers placed high value on the tactful acquisition of influence and on regard for others. Japanese managers placed high value on deference to superiors, company commitment, and the cautious use of aggressiveness and control. Korean managers placed high value on personal forcefulness and aggressiveness and low

Table 4–2
U.S. Values and Possible Alternatives

U.S. Cultural Values	Alternative Values	Examples of Management Function Affected
Individuals can influence the future (where there is a will there is a way).	Life follows a preordained course, and human action is determined by the will of God.	Planning and scheduling.
Individuals should be realistic in their aspirations.	Ideals are to be pursued regardless of what is "reasonable."	Goal setting and career development.
We must work hard to accomplish our objectives (Puritan ethic).	Hard work is not the only prerequisite for success. Wisdom, luck, and time are also required.	Motivation and reward system.
A primary obligation of an employee is to the organization.	Individual employees have a primary obligation to their family and friends.	Loyalty, commitment, and motivation.
Employees can be removed if they do not perform well.	The removal of an employee from a position involves a great loss of prestige and will rarely be done.	Promotion.
Company information should be available to anyone who needs it within the organization.	Withholding information to gain or maintain power is acceptable.	Organization, communication, and managerial style.
Competition stimulates high performance.	Competition leads to imbalances and disharmony.	Career development and marketing.
What works is important.	Symbols and the process are more important than the end point.	Communication, planning, and quality control.

Source: Adapted from information found in Philip R. Harris and Robert T. Moran, *Managing Cultural Differences* (Houston: Gulf Publishing, 1991), pp. 79–80.

value on recognition of others. Indian managers put high value on the nonaggressive pursuit of objectives. Australian managers placed major importance on values reflecting a low-key approach to management and a high concern for others.[10] In short, value systems across national boundaries often are different.

At the same time, value similarities exist between cultures. In fact, research shows that managers from different countries often have similar personal values that relate to success. England and Lee examined the managerial values of a diverse sample of U.S. ($n = 878$), Japanese ($n = 312$), Australian ($n = 301$), and Indian ($n = 500$) managers. They found that:

1. There is a reasonably strong relationship between the level of success achieved by managers and their personal values.

2. It is evident that value patterns predict managerial success and could be used in selection and placement decisions.

3. Although there are country differences in the relationships between values and success, findings across the four countries are quite similar.

4. The general pattern indicates that more successful managers appear to favor pragmatic, dynamic, achievement-oriented values, while less successful managers prefer more static and passive values. More successful managers favor an achievement orientation and prefer an active role in interaction with other individuals who are instrumental to achieving the managers' organizational goals. Less successful managers have values associated with a static and protected environment in which they take relatively passive roles.[11]

"International Management in Action: Common Personal Values" discusses these findings in more depth.

Values in Transition   Do values change over time? George England found that personal value systems are relatively stable and do not change rapidly.[12] However, changes are taking place in managerial values as a result of both culture and technology. A good example is the Japanese. Reichel and Flynn examined the effects of the U.S. environment on the cultural values of Japanese managers working for Japanese firms in the United States. In particular, they focused attention on such key organizational values as lifetime employment, formal authority, group orientation, seniority, and paternalism. Here is what they found:

1. Lifetime employment is widely accepted in Japanese culture, but the stateside Japanese managers did not believe that unconditional tenure in one organization was of major importance. They did believe, however, that job security was important.

2. Formal authority, obedience, and conformance to hierarchic position are very important in Japan, but the stateside managers did not perceive obedience and conformity to be very important and rejected the idea that one should not question a superior. However, they did support the concept of formal authority.

3. Group orientation, cooperation, conformity, and compromise are important organizational values in Japan. The stateside managers supported these values but also believed it was important to be an individual, thus maintaining a balance between a group and a personal orientation.

4. In Japan, organizational personnel often are rewarded based on seniority, not merit. Support for this value was directly influenced by the length of time the Japanese managers had been in the United States. The longer they had been there, the lower their support for this value.

5. Paternalism, often measured by a manager's involvement in both personal and off-the-job problems of subordinates, is very important in Japan. Stateside Japanese managers disagreed, and this resistance was positively associated with the number of years they had been in the United States.[13]

Common Personal Values

One of the most interesting findings about successful managers around the world is that while they come from different cultures, many have similar personal values. Of course, there are large differences in values within each national group. For example, some managers are very pragmatic and judge ideas in terms of whether they will work; others are highly ethical-moral and view ideas in terms of right or wrong; still others have a "feeling" orientation and judge ideas in terms of whether they are pleasant. Some managers have a very small set of values; others have a large set. Some have values that are related heavily to organization life; others include a wide range of personal values; others have highly group-oriented values. There are many different value patterns; however, overall value profiles have been found within successful managers in each group. Here are some of the most significant:

U.S. managers

- Highly pragmatic
- High achievement and competence orientation
- Emphasis on profit maximization, organizational efficiency, and high productivity

Japanese managers

- Highly pragmatic
- Strong emphasis on size and growth
- High value on competence and achievement

Korean managers

- Highly pragmatic
- Highly individualistic
- Strong achievement and competence orientation

Australian managers

- High moral orientation
- High humanistic orientation
- Low value on achievement, success, competition, and risk

Indian managers

- High moral orientation
- Highly individualistic
- Strong focus on organization compliance and competence

The findings listed here show important similarities and differences. Most of the profiles are similar in nature; however, note that successful Indian and Australian managers have values that are distinctly different. In short, although values of successful managers within countries often are similar, there are intercountry differences. This is why the successful managerial value systems of one country often are not ideal in another country.

There is increasing evidence that individualism in Japan is on the rise, indicating that Japanese values are changing—and not just among managers outside the country. The country's long economic slump has convinced many Japanese that they cannot rely on the large corporations or the government to ensure their future. They have to do it for themselves. As a result, today a growing number of Japanese are starting to embrace what is being called the "era of personal responsibility." Instead of denouncing individualism as a threat to society, they are proposing it as a necessary solution to many of the country's economic ills. A vice-chairman of the nation's largest business lobby summed up this thinking at the opening of a recent conference on economic change when he said, "By establishing personal responsibility, we must return dynamism to the economy and revitalize society."[14] This thinking is supported by Lee and Peterson's research which reveals that a culture with a strong entrepreneurial orientation is important to global competitiveness, especially in the small business sector of an economy. So this current trend may well be helpful to the Japanese economy in helping it meet foreign competition at home.[15]

The focus here has been on Japan due to the concrete experiential and experimental evidence. While Japanese cultures and values continue to evolve, other countries such as China are just beginning to undergo a new era. We discussed in Chapter 2 how China is moving away from a collectivist culture, and it appears as though even China is not sure what cultural values it will adhere to. Confucianism was worshipped for over 2,000 years, but the powerful messages through Confucius's teachings were overshadowed in a world where profit became a priority. Now, Confucianism is slowly gaining popularity once again, emphasizing respect for authority, concern for others, balance, harmony, and overall order. While this may provide sanctuary for some, it poses problems within the government, since it will have to prove its worthiness to remain in power. As long as China continues to prosper, hope for a unified culture may be on the horizon. Many are still concerned with the lack of an alternative if China's growth is stunted, creating even more confusion in the journey to maintain cultural values.[16]

■ Hofstede's Cultural Dimensions

Some researchers have attempted to provide a composite picture of culture by examining its subparts, or dimensions. In particular, Dutch researcher Geert Hofstede identified four dimensions, and later a fifth dimension, of culture that help explain how and why people from various cultures behave as they do.[17] His initial data were gathered from two questionnaire surveys with over 116,000 respondents from over 70 different countries around the world—making it the largest organizationally based study ever conducted. The individuals in these studies all worked in the local subsidiaries of IBM. As a result, Hofstede's research has been criticized because of its focus on just one company; however, he has countered this criticism. Hofstede is well aware of

> the amazement of some people about how employees of a very specific corporation like IBM can serve as a sample for discovering something about the culture of their countries at large. "We know IBMers," they say, "they are very special people, always in a white shirt and tie, and not at all representative of our country." The people who say this are quite right. IBMers do not form representative samples from national populations.... However, samples for cross-national comparison need not be representative, as long as they are functionally equivalent. IBM employees are a narrow sample, but very well matched. Employees of multinational companies in general and of IBM in particular form attractive sources of information for comparing national traits, because they are so similar in respects other than nationality: their employers..., their kind of work, and—for matched occupations—their level of education. The only thing that can account for systematic and consistent differences between national groups *within* such a homogenous multinational population is nationality itself; the national environment in which people were brought up *before* they joined this employer. Comparing IBM subsidiaries therefore shows national culture differences with unusual clarity.[18]

Hofstede's massive study continues to be a focal point for additional research. The four now-well-known dimensions that Hofstede examined were (1) power distance, (2) uncertainty avoidance, (3) individualism, and (4) masculinity. The more recent fifth dimension of time orientation is not as well known, but it was added to help describe the long- versus short-term orientations of cultures.[19] The East Asian countries were found to have longer-term orientations while the U.S. and U.K. were found to have relatively short-term orientations. While such time orientations are important to our understanding of cultures, the original four dimensions have received the most attention and are therefore the primary focus here.

Power Distance

power distance
The extent to which less powerful members of institutions and organizations accept that power is distributed unequally.

Power distance is "the extent to which less powerful members of institutions and organizations accept that power is distributed unequally."[20] Countries in which people blindly obey the orders of their superiors have high power distance. In many societies, lower-level employees tend to follow orders as a matter of procedure. In societies with high power distance, however, strict obedience is found even at the upper levels; examples include Mexico, South Korea, and India. For example, a senior Indian executive with a PhD from a prestigious U.S. university related the following story:

> What is most important for me and my department is not what I do or achieve for the company, but whether the [owner's] favor is bestowed on me.... This I have achieved by saying "yes" to everything [the owner] says or does.... To contradict him is to look for another job.... I left my freedom of thought in Boston.[21]

The effect of this dimension can be measured in a number of ways. For example, organizations in low-power-distance countries generally will be decentralized and have flatter organization structures. These organizations also will have a smaller proportion of supervisory personnel, and the lower strata of the workforce often will consist of highly qualified people. By contrast, organizations in high-power-distance countries will tend to be centralized and have tall organization structures. Organizations in high-power-distance countries will have a large proportion of supervisory personnel, and the people at the lower levels of the structure often will have low job qualifications. This latter structure encourages and promotes inequality between people at different levels.[22]

Uncertainty Avoidance

Uncertainty avoidance is "the extent to which people feel threatened by ambiguous situations and have created beliefs and institutions that try to avoid these.[23] Countries populated with people who do not like uncertainty tend to have a high need for security and a strong belief in experts and their knowledge; examples include Germany, Japan, and Spain. Cultures with low uncertainty avoidance have people who are more willing to accept that risks are associated with the unknown, that life must go on in spite of this. Examples here include Denmark and Great Britain.

The effect of this dimension can be measured in a number of ways. Countries with high-uncertainty-avoidance cultures have a great deal of structuring of organizational activities, more written rules, less risk taking by managers, lower labor turnover, and less ambitious employees.

Low-uncertainty-avoidance societies have organization settings with less structuring of activities, fewer written rules, more risk taking by managers, higher labor turnover, and more ambitious employees. The organization encourages personnel to use their own initiative and assume responsibility for their actions.

uncertainty avoidance
The extent to which people feel threatened by ambiguous situations and have created beliefs and institutions that try to avoid these.

Individualism

We discussed individualism and collectivism in Chapter 2 in reference to political systems. **Individualism** is the tendency of people to look after themselves and their immediate family only.[24] Hofstede measured this cultural difference on a bipolar continuum with individualism at one end and collectivism at the other. **Collectivism** is the tendency of people to belong to groups or collectives and to look after each other in exchange for loyalty.[25]

Like the effects of the other cultural dimensions, the effects of individualism and collectivism can be measured in a number of different ways.[26] Hofstede found that wealthy countries have higher individualism scores and poorer countries higher collectivism scores (see Table 4–3 for the 74 countries used in Figure 4–4 and subsequent figures). Note that in Figure 4–4, the United States, Canada, Australia, Denmark, and Sweden, among others, have high individualism and high GNP. Conversely, Indonesia, Pakistan, and a number of South American countries have low individualism (high collectivism) and low GNP. Countries with high individualism also tend to have greater support for the Protestant work ethic, greater individual initiative, and promotions based on market value. Countries with low individualism tend to have less support for the Protestant work ethic, less individual initiative, and promotions based on seniority.

individualism
The tendency of people to look after themselves and their immediate family only.

collectivism
The tendency of people to belong to groups or collectives and to look after each other in exchange for loyalty.

Masculinity

Masculinity is defined by Hofstede as "a situation in which the dominant values in society are success, money, and things."[27] Hofstede measured this dimension on a continuum ranging from masculinity to femininity. Contrary to some stereotypes and connotations, **femininity** is the term used by Hofstede to describe "a situation in which the dominant values in society are caring for others and the quality of life."[28]

Countries with a high masculinity index, such as the Germanic countries, place great importance on earnings, recognition, advancement, and challenge. Individuals are encouraged to be independent decision makers, and achievement is defined in terms of recognition and wealth. The workplace is often characterized by high job stress, and many managers believe that their employees dislike work and must be kept under some degree of control. The school system is geared toward encouraging high

masculinity
A cultural characteristic in which the dominant values in society are success, money, and things.

femininity
A cultural characteristic in which the dominant values in society are caring for others and the quality of life.

Table 4–3
Countries and Regions Used in Hofstede's Research

Arabic-speaking countries (Egypt, Iraq, Kuwait, Lebanon, Libya, Saudi Arabia, United Arab Emirates)	Ecuador	Panama
	Estonia	Peru
	Finland	Philippines
	France	Poland
	Germany	Portugal
	Great Britain	Romania
	Greece	Russia
Argentina	Guatemala	Salvador
Australia	Hong Kong (China)	Serbia
Austria		Singapore
Bangladesh	Hungary	Slovakia
Belgium Flemish (Dutch speaking)	India	Slovenia
	Indonesia	South Africa
Belgium Walloon (French speaking)	Iran	Spain
	Ireland	Suriname
Brazil	Israel	Sweden
Bulgaria	Italy	Switzerland French
Canada Quebec	Jamaica	Switzerland German
Canada total	Japan	Taiwan
Chile	Korea (South)	Thailand
China	Luxembourg	Trinidad
Colombia	Malaysia	Turkey
Costa Rica	Malta	United States
Croatia	Mexico	Uruguay
Czech Republic	Morocco	Venezuela
Denmark	Netherlands	Vietnam
East Africa (Ethiopia, Kenya, Tanzania, Zambia)	New Zealand	West Africa (Ghana, Nigeria, Sierra Leone)
	Norway	
	Pakistan	

Source: From Hofstede and Hofstede, *Cultures and Organizations: Software of the Mind.* Copyright © 2005 The McGraw-Hill Companies, Inc. Reprinted with permission.

performance. Young men expect to have careers, and those who do not often view themselves as failures. Historically, fewer women hold higher-level jobs, although this is changing. The school system is geared toward encouraging high performance.

Countries with a low masculinity index (Hofstede's femininity dimension), such as Norway, tend to place great importance on cooperation, a friendly atmosphere, and employment security. Individuals are encouraged to be group decision makers, and achievement is defined in terms of layman contacts and the living environment. The workplace tends to be characterized by low stress, and managers give their employees more credit for being responsible and allow them more freedom. Culturally, this group prefers small-scale enterprises, and they place greater importance on conservation of the environment. The school system is designed to teach social adaptation. Some young men and women want careers; others do not. Many women hold higher-level jobs, and they do not find it necessary to be assertive.

Integrating the Dimensions

A description of the four dimensions of culture is useful in helping to explain the differences between various countries, and Hofstede's research has extended beyond this focus and

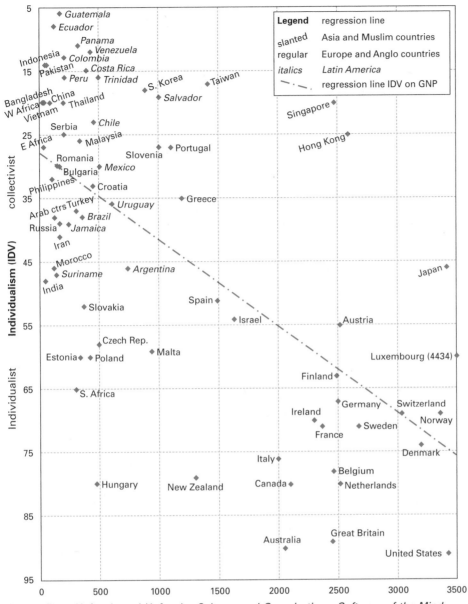

Source: From Hofstede and Hofstede, *Cultures and Organizations: Software of the Mind.*
Copyright © 2005 The McGraw-Hill Companies, Inc. Reprinted with permission.

shown how countries can be described in terms of pairs of dimensions. In Hofstede's and later research, pairings and clusters can provide useful summaries for international managers. It is always best to have an in-depth understanding of the multicultural environment, but the general groupings outline common ground that one can use as a starting point. Figure 4–5, which incorporates power distance and individualism, provides an example.

Upon first examination of the cluster distribution, the data may appear confusing. However, they are very useful in depicting what countries appear similar in values, and to what extent they differ with other country clusters. The same countries are not always clustered together in subsequent dimension comparisons. This indicates that while some beliefs overlap between cultures, it is where they diverge that makes groups unique to manage.

In Figure 4–5, the United States, Australia, Canada, Britain, Denmark, and New Zealand are located in the lower-left-hand quadrant. Americans, for example, have very high individualism and relatively low power distance. They prefer to do things for

Figure 4–5

Power Distance Versus Individualism

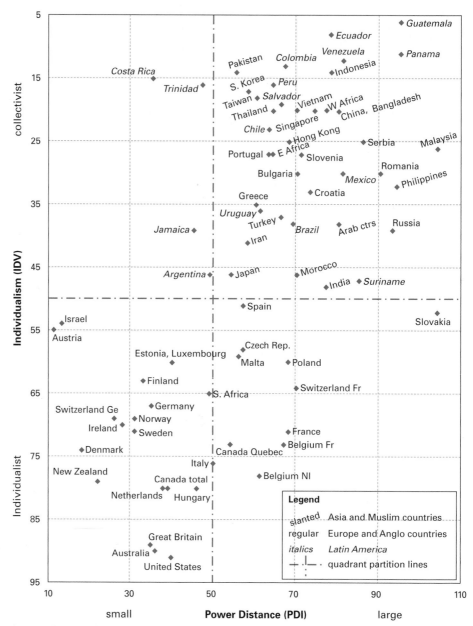

themselves and are not upset when others have more power than they do. The other countries, while they may not be a part of the same cluster, share similar values. Conversely, many of the underdeveloped or newly industrialized countries, such as Colombia, Hong Kong, Portugal, and Singapore, are characterized by large power distance and low individualism. These nations tend to be collectivist in their approach.

Figure 4–6 plots the uncertainty-avoidance index for the 74 countries against the power-distance index. Once again, there are clusters of countries. Many of the Anglo nations tend to be in the upper-left-hand quadrant, which is characterized by small power distance and weak uncertainty avoidance (they do not try to avoid uncertainty). In contrast, many Latin countries (in both Europe and the Western Hemisphere), Mediterranean countries, and Asian nations (e.g., Japan and Korea) are characterized by high power distance and strong uncertainty avoidance. Most other Asian countries are characterized by large power distance and weak uncertainty avoidance.

Figure 4–7 plots the position of 74 countries in terms of uncertainty avoidance and masculinity femininity. The most masculine country is Japan, followed by the Germanic

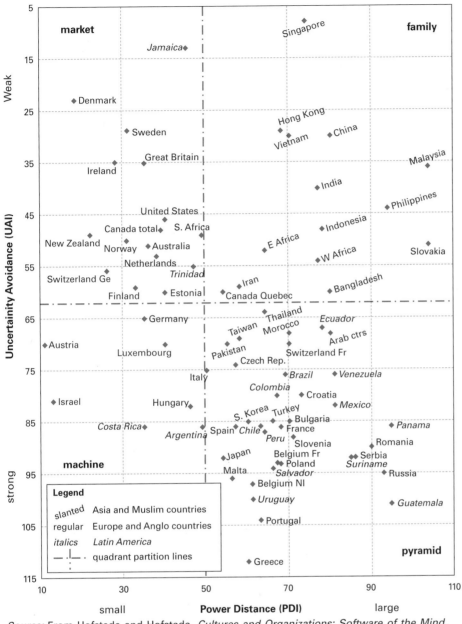

Figure 4–6

Power Distance Versus Uncertainty Avoidance

Source: From Hofstede and Hofstede, *Cultures and Organizations: Software of the Mind.*
Copyright © 2005 The McGraw-Hill Companies, Inc. Reprinted with permission.

countries (Austria, Switzerland, Germany) and Latin countries (Venezuela, Mexico, Italy). Many countries in the Anglo cluster, including Ireland, Australia, Great Britain, and the United States, have moderate degrees of masculinity. So do some of the former colonies of Anglo nations, including India, South Africa, and the Philippines. The Northern European cluster (Denmark, Sweden, Norway, the Netherlands) has low masculinity, indicating that these countries place high value on factors such as quality of life, preservation of the environment, and the importance of relationships with people over money.

The integration of these cultural factors into two-dimensional plots helps illustrate the complexity of understanding culture's effect on behavior. A number of dimensions are at work, and sometimes they do not all move in the anticipated direction. For example, at first glance, a nation with high power distance would appear to be low in individualism, and vice versa, and Hofstede found exactly that (see Figure 4–5). However, low uncertainty avoidance does not always go hand in hand with high masculinity, even though those who are willing to live with uncertainty will want rewards such as money and power and accord low value to the quality of work life and caring for others (see Figure 4–7). Simply

Figure 4–7

Masculinity Versus Uncertainty Avoidance

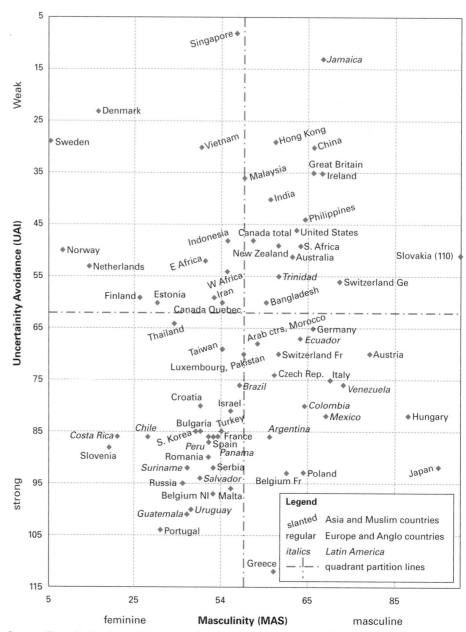

Source: From Hofstede and Hofstede, *Cultures and Organizations: Software of the Mind.* Copyright © 2005 The McGraw-Hill Companies, Inc. Reprinted with permission.

put, empirical evidence on the impact of cultural dimensions may differ from commonly held beliefs or stereotypes. Research-based data are needed to determine the full impact of differing cultures.

■ Trompenaars's Cultural Dimensions

The Hofstede cultural dimensions and country clusters are widely recognized and accepted in the study of international management. A more recent description of how cultures differ, by another Dutch researcher, Fons Trompenaars, is receiving increasing attention as well. Trompenaars's research was conducted over a 10-year period and published in 1994.[29] He administered research questionnaires to over 15,000 managers from 28 countries and received usable responses from at least 500 in each nation; the 23 countries in his research are presented in Table 4–4. Building heavily on value orientations and the relational orientations of

Table 4–4
Trompenaars's Country Abbreviations

Abbreviation	Country
ARG	Argentina
AUS	Austria
BEL	Belgium
BRZ	Brazil
CHI	China
CIS	Former Soviet Union
CZH	Former Czechoslovakia
FRA	France
GER	Germany (excluding former East Germany)
HK	Hong Kong
IDO	Indonesia
ITA	Italy
JPN	Japan
MEX	Mexico
NL	Netherlands
SIN	Singapore
SPA	Spain
SWE	Sweden
SWI	Switzerland
THA	Thailand
UK	United Kingdom
USA	United States
VEN	Venezuela

well-known sociologist Talcott Parsons,[30] Trompenaars derived five relationship orientations that address the ways in which people deal with each other; these can be considered to be cultural dimensions that are analogous to Hofstede's dimensions. Trompenaars also looked at attitudes toward both time and the environment, and the result of his research is a wealth of information helping explain how cultures differ and offering practical ways in which MNCs can do business in various countries. The following discussion examines each of the five relationship orientations as well as attitudes toward time and the environment.[31]

Universalism vs. Particularism

Universalism is the belief that ideas and practices can be applied everywhere without modification. **Particularism** is the belief that circumstances dictate how ideas and practices should be applied. In cultures with high universalism, the focus is more on formal rules than on relationships, business contracts are adhered to very closely, and people believe that "a deal is a deal." In cultures with high particularism, the focus is more on relationships and trust than on formal rules. In a particularist culture, legal contracts often are modified, and as people get to know each other better, they often change the way in which deals are executed. In his early research, Trompenaars found that in countries such as the United States, Australia, Germany, Sweden, and the United Kingdom, there was high universalism, while countries such as Venezuela, the former Soviet Union, Indonesia, and China were high on particularism. Figure 4–8 shows the continuum.

In follow-up research, Trompenaars and Hampden-Turner uncovered additional insights regarding national orientations on this universalism-particularism continuum. They did this by presenting the respondents with a dilemma and asking them to make a decision. Here is one of these dilemmas along with the national scores of the respondents:[32]

> You are riding in a car driven by a close friend. He hits a pedestrian. You know he was going at least 35 miles per hour in an area of the city where the maximum allowed speed is 20 miles per hour. There are no witnesses. His lawyer says that if you testify under oath that he was driving 20 miles per hour it may save him from serious consequences. What right has your friend to expect you to protect him?

universalism
The belief that ideas and practices can be applied everywhere in the world without modification.

particularism
The belief that circumstances dictate how ideas and practices should be applied and that something cannot be done the same everywhere.

Figure 4–8

Trompenaars's Relationship Orientations on Cultural Dimensions

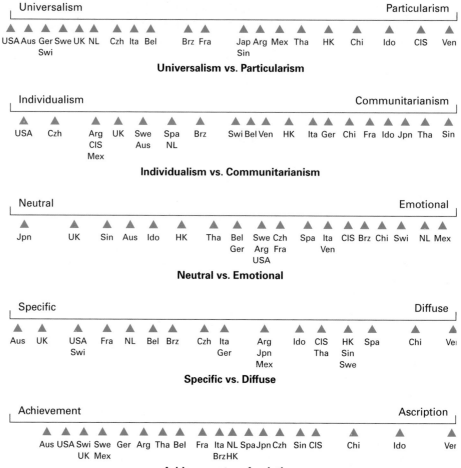

Source: Adapted from information found in Fons Trompenaars, *Riding the Waves of Culture* (New York: Irwin, 1994); Charles M. Hampden-Turner and Fons Trompenaars, "A World Turned Upside Down: Doing Business in Asia," in *Managing Across Cultures: Issues and Perspectives,* ed. Pat Joynt and Malcolm Warner (London: International Thomson Business Press, 1996), pp. 275–305.

(*a*) My friend has a definite right as a friend to expect me to testify to the lower figure.
(*b*) He has some right as a friend to expect me to testify to the lower figure.
(*c*) He has no right as a friend to expect me to testify to the lower figure.

With a high score indicating strong universalism (choice *c*) and a low score indicating strong particularism (choice *a*), here is how the different nations scored:

Universalism (no right)	
Canada	96
United States	95
Germany	90
United Kingdom	90
Netherlands	88
France	68
Japan	67
Singapore	67
Thailand	63
Hong Kong	56
Particularism (some or definite right)	
China	48
South Korea	26

As noted earlier, respondents from universalism cultures (e.g., North America and Western Europe) felt that the rules applied regardless of the situation, while respondents from particularism cultures were much more willing to bend the rules and help their friend.

Based on these types of findings, Trompenaars recommends that when individuals from particularist cultures do business in a universalistic culture, they should be prepared for rational, professional arguments and a "let's get down to business" attitude. Conversely, when individuals from universalist cultures do business in a particularist environment, they should be prepared for personal meandering or irrelevancies that seem to go nowhere and should not regard personal, get-to-know-you attitudes as mere small talk.

Individualism vs. Communitarianism

Individualism and communitarianism are key dimensions in Hofstede's earlier research. Although Trompenaars derived these two relationships differently than Hofstede does, they still have the same basic meaning, although in his more recent work Trompenaars has used the word *communitarianism* rather than *collectivism*. For him, individualism refers to people regarding themselves as individuals, while **communitarianism** refers to people regarding themselves as part of a group, similar to the political groupings discussed in Chapter 2. As shown in Figure 4–8, the United States, former Czechoslovakia, Argentina, the former Soviet Union (CIS), and Mexico have high individualism. These findings of Trompenaars are particularly interesting, because they differ somewhat from those of Hofstede, as reported in Figure 4–5. Although the definitions are not exactly the same, the fact that there are differences (e.g., Mexico and Argentina are moderately collectivistic in Hofstede's findings but individualistic in Trompenaars's research) points out that cultural values may be changing (i.e., even though Hofstede has added some countries and updated his findings, they still may be dated). For example, with Mexico now part of NAFTA and the global economy, this country may have moved from dominant collectivistic or communitarianistic cultural values to more individualist values. Trompenaars also found that the former communist countries of Czechoslovakia and the Soviet Union now appear to be quite individualistic, which of course is contrary to assumptions and conventional wisdom about the former communist bloc. In other words, Trompenaars points out the complex, dynamic nature of culture and the danger of overgeneralization.

In his most recent research, and again using the technique of presenting respondents with a dilemma and asking them to make a decision, Trompenaars posed the following situation. If you were to be promoted, which of the two following issues would you emphasize most: (a) the new group of people with whom you will be working or (b) the greater responsibility of the work you are undertaking and the higher income you will be earning? The following reports the latest scores associated with the individualism of option *b*—greater responsibility and more money.[33]

communitarianism
Refers to people regarding themselves as part of a group.

Individualism (emphasis on larger responsibilities and more income)

Canada	77
Thailand	71
United Kingdom	69
United States	67
Netherlands	64
France	61
Japan	61
China	54
Singapore	50
Hong Kong	47

Communitarianism (emphasis on the new group of people)

Malaysia	38
Korea	32

These findings are somewhat different from those presented in Figure 4–8 and show that cultural changes may be occurring more rapidly than many people realize. For example, the latest findings show Thailand very high on individualism (possibly indicating an increasing entrepreneurial spirit/cultural value), whereas the Thais were found to be low on individualism a few years before, as shown in Figure 4–8. At the same time, it is important to remember that there are major differences between people in high-individualism societies and those in high-communitarianism societies. The former stress personal and individual matters; the latter value group-related issues. Negotiations in cultures with high individualism typically are made on the spot by a representative, people ideally achieve things alone, and they assume a great deal of personal responsibility. In cultures with high communitarianism, decisions typically are referred to committees, people ideally achieve things in groups, and they jointly assume responsibility.

Trompenaars recommends that when people from cultures with high individualism deal with those from communitarianism cultures, they should have patience for the time taken to consent and to consult, and they should aim to build lasting relationships. When people from cultures with high communitarianism deal with those from individualist cultures, they should be prepared to make quick decisions and commit their organization to these decisions. Also, communitarianists dealing with individualists should realize that the reason they are dealing with only one negotiator (as opposed to a group) is that this person is respected by his or her organization and has its authority and esteem.

Neutral vs. Emotional

neutral culture
A culture in which emotions are held in check.

emotional culture
A culture in which emotions are expressed openly and naturally.

A **neutral culture** is one in which emotions are held in check. As seen in Figure 4–8, both Japan and the United Kingdom are high-neutral cultures. People in these countries try not to show their feelings; they act stoically and maintain their composure. An **emotional culture** is one in which emotions are openly and naturally expressed. People in emotional cultures often smile a great deal, talk loudly when they are excited, and greet each other with a great deal of enthusiasm. Mexico, the Netherlands, and Switzerland are examples of high emotional cultures.

Trompenaars recommends that when individuals from emotional cultures do business in neutral cultures, they should put as much as they can on paper and submit it to the other side. They should realize that lack of emotion does not mean disinterest or boredom, but rather that people from neutral cultures do not like to show their hand. Conversely, when those from neutral cultures do business in emotional cultures, they should not be put off stride when the other side creates scenes or grows animated and boisterous, and they should try to respond warmly to the emotional affections of the other group.

Specific vs. Diffuse

specific culture
A culture in which individuals have a large public space they readily share with others and a small private space they guard closely and share with only close friends and associates.

diffuse culture
A culture in which public space and private space are similar in size and individuals guard their public space carefully, because entry into public space affords entry into private space as well.

A **specific culture** is one in which individuals have a large public space they readily let others enter and share and a small private space they guard closely and share with only close friends and associates. A **diffuse culture** is one in which public space and private space are similar in size and individuals guard their public space carefully, because entry into public space affords entry into private space as well. As shown in Figure 4–8, Austria, the United Kingdom, the United States, and Switzerland all are specific cultures, while Venezuela, China, and Spain are diffuse cultures. In specific cultures, people often are invited into a person's open, public space; individuals in these cultures often are open and extroverted; and there is a strong separation of work and private life. In diffuse cultures, people are not quickly invited into a person's open, public space, because once they are in, there is easy entry into the private space as well. Individuals in these cultures often appear to be indirect and introverted, and work and private life often are closely linked.

An example of these specific and diffuse cultural dimensions is provided by the United States and Germany. A U.S. professor, such as Robert Smith, PhD, generally would be called "Doctor Smith" by students when at his U.S. university. When shopping, however, he might be referred to by the store clerk as "Bob," and he might even ask the clerk's advice regarding some of his intended purchases. When golfing, Bob might just be one of the guys, even to a golf partner who happens to be a graduate student in his department. The reason for these changes in status is that, with the specific U.S. cultural values, people have large public spaces and often conduct themselves differently depending on their public role. At the same time, however, Bob has private space that is off-limits to the students who must call him "Doctor Smith" in class. In high-diffuse cultures, on the other hand, a person's public life and private life often are similar. Therefore, in Germany, Herr Professor Doktor Schmidt would be referred to that way at the university, local market, and bowling alley—and even his wife might address him formally in public. A great deal of formality is maintained, often giving the impression that Germans are stuffy or aloof.

Trompenaars recommends that when those from specific cultures do business in diffuse cultures, they should respect a person's title, age, and background connections, and they should not get impatient when people are being indirect or circuitous. Conversely, when individuals from diffuse cultures do business in specific cultures, they should try to get to the point and be efficient, learn to structure meetings with the judicious use of agendas, and not use their titles or acknowledge achievements or skills that are irrelevant to the issues being discussed.

Achievement vs. Ascription

An **achievement culture** is one in which people are accorded status based on how well they perform their functions. An **ascription culture** is one in which status is attributed based on who or what a person is. Achievement cultures give high status to high achievers, such as the company's number-one salesperson or the medical researcher who has found a cure for a rare form of bone cancer. Ascription cultures accord status based on age, gender, or social connections. For example, in an ascription culture, a person who has been with the company for 40 years may be listened to carefully because of the respect that others have for the individual's age and longevity with the firm, and an individual who has friends in high places may be afforded status because of whom she knows. As shown in Figure 4–8, Austria, the United States, Switzerland, and the United Kingdom are achievement cultures, while Venezuela, Indonesia, and China are ascription cultures.

Trompenaars recommends that when individuals from achievement cultures do business in ascription cultures, they should make sure that their group has older, senior, and formal position holders who can impress the other side, and they should respect the status and influence of their counterparts in the other group. Conversely, he recommends that when individuals from ascription cultures do business in achievement cultures, they should make sure that their group has sufficient data, technical advisers, and knowledgeable people to convince the other group that they are proficient, and they should respect the knowledge and information of their counterparts on the other team.

achievement culture
A culture in which people are accorded status based on how well they perform their functions.

ascription culture
A culture in which status is attributed based on who or what a person is.

Time

Aside from the five relationship orientations, another major cultural difference is the way in which people deal with the concept of time. Trompenaars has identified two different approaches: sequential and synchronous. In cultures where *sequential* approaches are prevalent, people tend to do only one activity at a time, keep appointments strictly, and show a strong preference for following plans as they are laid out and not deviating from them. In cultures where *synchronous* approaches are common, people tend to do more than one activity at a time, appointments are approximate and may be changed at a moment's notice, and schedules generally are subordinate to relationships. People in synchronous-time cultures often will stop what they are doing to meet and greet individuals coming into their office.

A good contrast is provided by the United States, Mexico, and France. In the United States, people tend to be guided by sequential-time orientation and thus set a schedule and stick to it. Mexicans operate under more of a synchronous-time orientation and thus tend to be much more flexible, often building slack into their schedules to allow for interruptions. The French are similar to the Mexicans and, when making plans, often determine the objectives they want to accomplish but leave open the timing and other factors that are beyond their control; this way, they can adjust and modify their approach as they go along. As Trompenaars noted, "For the French and Mexicans, what was important was that they get to the end, not the particular path or sequence by which that end was reached."[34]

Another interesting time-related contrast is the degree to which cultures are past- or present-oriented as opposed to future-oriented. In countries such as the United States, Italy, and Germany, the future is more important than the past or the present. In countries such as Venezuela, Indonesia, and Spain, the present is most important. In France and Belgium, all three time periods are of approximately equal importance. Because different emphases are given to different time periods, adjusting to these cultural differences can create challenges.

Trompenaars recommends that when doing business with future-oriented cultures, effective international managers should emphasize the opportunities and limitless scope that any agreement can have, agree to specific deadlines for getting things done, and be aware of the core competence or continuity that the other party intends to carry with it into the future. When doing business with past- or present-oriented cultures, he recommends that managers emphasize the history and tradition of the culture, find out whether internal relationships will sanction the types of changes that need to be made, and agree to future meetings in principle but fix no deadlines for completions.

The Environment

Trompenaars also examined the ways in which people deal with their environment. Specific attention should be given to whether they believe in controlling outcomes (inner-directed) or letting things take their own course (outer-directed). One of the things he asked managers to do was choose between the following statements:

1. What happens to me is my own doing.
2. Sometimes I feel that I do not have enough control over the directions my life is taking.

Managers who believe in controlling their own environment would opt for the first choice; those who believe that they are controlled by their environment and cannot do much about it would opt for the second.

Here is an example by country of the sample respondents who believe that what happens to them is their own doing:[35]

United States	89%
Switzerland	84%
Australia	81%
Belgium	76%
Indonesia	73%
Hong Kong	69%
Greece	63%
Singapore	58%
Japan	56%
China	35%

In the United States, managers feel strongly that they are masters of their own fate. This helps account for their dominant attitude (sometimes bordering on aggressiveness) toward the environment and discomfort when things seem to get out of control. Many Asian cultures do not share these views. They believe that things move in waves or natural shifts and one must "go with the flow," so a flexible attitude, characterized by a willingness to compromise and maintain harmony with nature, is important.

Trompenaars recommends that when dealing with those from cultures that believe in dominating the environment, it is important to play hardball, test the resilience of the opponent, win some objectives, and always lose from time to time. For example, representatives of the U.S. government have repeatedly urged Japanese automobile companies to purchase more component parts from U.S. suppliers to partially offset the large volume of U.S. imports of finished autos from Japan. Instead of enacting trade barriers, the United States was asking for a quid pro quo. When dealing with those from cultures that believe in letting things take their natural course, it is important to be persistent and polite, maintain good relationships with the other party, and try to win together and lose apart.

Cultural Patterns or Clusters

Like Hofstede's work, Trompenaars's research lends itself to cultural patterns or clusters. Table 4–5 relates his findings to the five relational orientations. It is useful to compare Hofstede and Trompenaars, because of the overlapping information. For example, Hofstede's

Table 4–5
Cultural Groups Based on Trompenaars's Research

Relationship	Anglo Cluster	
	United States	United Kingdom
Individualism (I) Communitarianism (C)	I	I
Specific relationship (S) Diffuse relationship (D)	S	S
Universalism (U) Particularism (P)	U	U
Neutral relationship (N) Emotional relationship (E)	E	N
Achievement (Ach) Ascription (As)	Ach	Ach

Relationship	Asian Cluster				
	Japan	China	Indonesia	Hong Kong	Singapore
Individualism (I) Communitarianism (C)	C	C	C	C	C
Specific relationship (S) Diffuse relationship (D)	D	D	D	D	D
Universalism (U) Particularism (P)	P	P	P	P	P
Neutral relationship (N) Emotional relationship (E)	N	E	N	N	N
Achievement (Ach) Ascription (As)	As	As	As	As	As

Relationship	Latin American Cluster			
	Argentina	Mexico	Venezuela	Brazil
Individualism (I) Communitarianism (C)	I	I	C	I
Specific relationship (S) Diffuse relationship (D)	D	D	D	S
Universalism (U) Particularism (P)	P	P	P	U
Neutral relationship (N) Emotional relationship (E)	N	N	N	E
Achievement (Ach) Ascription (As)	Ach	Ach	As	As

(continued)

Table 4–5 *(continued)*
Cultural Groups Based on Trompenaars's Research

Relationship	Latin European Cluster			
	France	Belgium	Spain	Italy
Individualism (I) Communitarianism (C)	C	C	I	C
Specific relationship (S) Diffuse relationship (D)	S	S	D	S
Universalism (U) Particularism (P)	U	U	P	U
Neutral relationship (N) Emotional relationship (E)	E	E	N	E
Achievement (Ach) Ascription (As)	As	As	Ach	As

Relationship	Germanic Cluster			
	Austria	Germany	Switzerland	Czechoslovakia
Individualism (I) Communitarianism (C)	I	C	C	C
Specific relationship (S) Diffuse relationship (D)	S	D	S	S
Universalism (U) Particularism (P)	U	U	U	U
Neutral relationship (N) Emotional relationship (E)	N	E	E	N
Achievement (Ach) Ascription (As)	Ach	Ach	As	Ach

Source: Adapted from information in Fons Trompenaars, *Riding the Waves of Culture* (New York: Irwin, 1994).

country assessments included India but not China. Trompenaars, conversely, shows results for China but not India. Conventional times require international managers to become familiar with beliefs and traditions in both areas, since they play a significant role in the new world economy (see Chapter 1). Further examination of Table 4–5 shows that while general clusters can be formed, there still exists inherent, significant differences within. For example, Brazil is considered to be a part of the Latin American cluster, though some of the unique findings suggest that Brazil is more independent than strictly "Latin American." The Latin European grouping mirrors similar results, with Italy showing some preferences that are different from both France and Belgium and with Spain displaying distinguishing characteristics as compared to the other three in the cluster.

The work of Hofstede and Trompenaars provides a springboard, not a definitive characterization, of how to view groups of countries, partially because some of their information intersects and partially because they seem to fill in the blanks left by the other research. Future investigations may be in order, since culture is extremely hard to effectively categorize with so few dimensions due to the complicated nature of the underlying motivations of societies. Furthermore, as the world becomes more integrated due to globalization, it can be postulated that cultures are beginning to change in order to effectively play the game. The results shown in this chapter are still very relevant to current beliefs, since it takes quite some time for an entire country's culture to be significantly altered. It is just as important to recognize that influences on countries that were not present during these studies could alter some perspectives and to keep in mind that not all people within a country adhere to cultural beliefs. In other words, when seeking out business opportunities abroad, one should become familiar with the individuals involved and not simply use stereotypes or generalizations to communicate effectively.

Overall, Table 4–5 shows that a case can be made for cultural similarities between clusters of countries. With only small differences, Trompenaars's research helps support and, more important, extend the work of Hofstede. Such research provides a useful point of departure for recognizing cultural differences, and it provides guidelines for doing business effectively around the world.

■ Integrating Culture and Management: The GLOBE Project

The **GLOBE** (Global Leadership and Organizational Behavior Effectiveness) research program reflects an additional approach to measuring cultural differences. The GLOBE project extends and integrates previous analyses of cultural attributes and variables. At the heart of the project is the study and evaluation of nine different cultural attributes using middle managers from 951 organizations in 62 countries.[36] A team of 170 scholars worked together to survey over 17,000 managers in three industries: financial services, food processing, and telecommunications. When developing the measures and conducting the analysis, they also used archival measures of country economic prosperity and of the physical and psychological well-being of the cultures studied. Countries were selected so that every major geographic location in the world was represented. Additional countries, including those with unique types of political and economic systems, were selected to create a complete and comprehensive database upon which to build the analyses.[37] This research has been considered among the most sophisticated in the field to date, and a collaboration of Hofstede and GLOBE researchers could provide an influential outlook on the major factors characterizing global cultures.[38]

The GLOBE study is interesting because its nine constructs were defined, conceptualized, and operationalized by a multicultural team of researchers. In addition, the data in each country were collected by investigators who were either natives of the cultures studied or had extensive knowledge and experience in those cultures.

GLOBE (Global Leadership and Organizational Behavior Effectiveness) A multicountry study and evaluation of cultural attributes and leadership behaviors among more than 17,000 managers from 951 organizations in 62 countries.

Culture and Management

GLOBE researchers adhere to the belief that certain attributes that distinguish one culture from others can be used to predict the most suitable, effective, and acceptable organizational and leader practices within that culture. In addition, they contend that societal culture has a direct impact on organizational culture and that leader acceptance stems from tying leader attributes and behaviors to subordinate norms.[39]

The GLOBE project set out to answer many fundamental questions about cultural variables shaping leadership and organizational processes. The meta-goal of GLOBE was to develop an empirically based theory to describe, understand, and predict the impact of specific cultural variables on leadership and organizational processes and the effectiveness of these processes. Overall, GLOBE hopes to provide a globally standard guideline that allows managers to focus on local specialization. Specific objectives include answering these fundamental questions:[40]

- Are there leader behaviors, attributes, and organizational practices that are universally accepted and effective across cultures?
- Are there leader behaviors, attributes, and organizational practices that are accepted and effective in only some cultures?
- How do attributes of societal and organizational cultures affect the kinds of leader behaviors and organizational practices that are accepted and effective?
- What is the effect of violating cultural norms that are relevant to leadership and organizational practices?
- What is the relative standing of each of the cultures studied on each of the nine core dimensions of culture?
- Can the universal and culture-specific aspects of leader behaviors, attributes, and organizational practices be explained in terms of an underlying theory that accounts for systematic differences across cultures?

GLOBE's Cultural Dimensions

The GLOBE project identified nine cultural dimensions:[41]

1. *Uncertainty avoidance* is defined as the extent to which members of an organization or society strive to avoid uncertainty by reliance on social norms, rituals, and bureaucratic practices to alleviate the unpredictability of future events.

2. *Power distance* is defined as the degree to which members of an organization or society expect and agree that power should be unequally shared.

3. *Collectivism I: Societal collectivism* refers to the degree to which organizational and societal institutional practices encourage and reward collective distribution of resources and collective action.

4. *Collectivism II: In-group collectivism* refers to the degree to which individuals express pride, loyalty, and cohesiveness in their organizations or families.

5. *Gender egalitarianism* is defined as the extent to which an organization or a society minimizes gender role differences and gender discrimination.

6. *Assertiveness* is defined as the degree to which individuals in organizations or societies are assertive, confrontational, and aggressive in social relationships.

7. *Future orientation* is defined as the degree to which individuals in organizations or societies engage in future-oriented behaviors such as planning, investing in the future, and delaying gratification.

8. *Performance orientation* refers to the extent to which an organization or society encourages and rewards group members for performance improvement and excellence.

9. *Humane orientation* is defined as the degree to which individuals in organizations or societies encourage and reward individuals for being fair, altruistic, friendly, generous, caring, and kind to others.

The first six dimensions have their origins in Hofstede's cultural dimensions. The collectivism I dimension measures societal emphasis on collectivism; low scores reflect individualistic emphasis, and high scores reflect collectivistic emphasis by means of laws, social programs, or institutional practices. The collectivism II scale measures in-group (family or organization) collectivism such as pride in and loyalty to family or organization and family or organizational cohesiveness. In lieu of Hofstede's masculinity dimension, the GLOBE researchers developed the two dimensions they labeled *gender egalitarianism* and *assertiveness.* Likewise, the future orientation, performance orientation, and humane orientation measures have their origin in past research.[42] These measures are therefore integrative and combine a number of insights from previous studies. Recently, further analysis has been conducted with regard to corporate social responsibility (CSR), a topic discussed in detail in Chapter 3.[43]

GLOBE Country Analysis

The initial results of the GLOBE analysis are presented in Table 4–6. The GLOBE analyses correspond generally with those of Hofstede and Trompenaars, although with some variations resulting from the variable definitions and methodology. Hofstede critiqued the GLOBE analysis, pointing out key differences between the research methods; Hofstede was the sole researcher and writer of his findings, while GLOBE consisted of a team of perspectives; Hofstede focused on one institution and surveyed employees, while GLOBE interviewed managers across many corporations, and so on. The disparity of the terminology between these two, coupled with the complex research, makes it challenging to compare and fully reconcile these two approaches.[44] Other assessments have pointed out that Hofstede may have provided an introduction into the psychology of culture, but further research is necessary in this changing world. While the GLOBE analysis is sometimes seen as complicated, but so are cultures and perceptions. An in-depth understanding of all facets of culture is difficult, if not impossible, to attain, but GLOBE provides a current comprehensive overview of general stereotypes that can be further analyzed for greater insight.[45]

Table 4–6
GLOBE Cultural Variable Results

Variable	Highest Ranking	Medium Ranking	Lowest Ranking
Assertiveness	Spain, U.S.	Egypt, Ireland	Sweden, New Zealand
Future orientation	Denmark, Canada	Slovenia, Egypt	Russia, Argentina
Gender differentiation	South Korea, Egypt	Italy, Brazil	Sweden, Denmark
Uncertainty avoidance	Austria, Denmark	Israel, U.S.	Russia, Hungary
Power distance	Russia, Spain	England, France	Denmark, Netherlands
Collectivism/societal	Denmark, Singapore	Hong Kong, U.S.	Greece, Hungary
In-group collectivism	Egypt, China	England, France	Denmark, Netherlands
Performance orientation	U.S., Taiwan	Sweden, Israel	Russia, Argentina
Humane orientation	Indonesia, Egypt	Hong Kong, Sweden	Germany, Spain

Examination of the GLOBE project has resulted in an extensive breakdown of how managers behave and how different cultures can yield managers with similar perspectives in some realms, with quite divergent opinions in other sectors. One example, as illustrated in Figure 4–9, shows how managers in Brazil compare to managers in the United States in a web structure, based on factors such as individualism, consciousness of social and professional status, and risky behaviors. Brazilian managers are typically class and status-conscious, rarely conversing with subordinates on a personal level within or outside of work. They are known for avoiding conflict within groups and risky endeavors and tend to exhibit group dynamics with regard to decision-making processes. Managers in the United States, on the other hand, do not focus intensely on different class or status levels. They are more likely to take risks, and while it appears as though they are more individualistic, the graph implies a

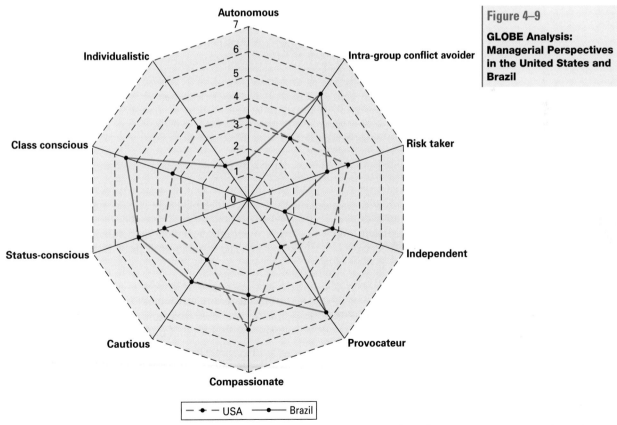

Figure 4–9

GLOBE Analysis: Managerial Perspectives in the United States and Brazil

Source: From Mansour Javidan, Peter W. Dorfman, et. al., "In the Eye of the Beholder: Cross Cultural Lessons in Leadership from Project GLOBE," *Perspectives—Academy of Management* 20, No. 1 (2006), p. 76. Reproduced with permission of Academy of Management via Copyright Clearance Center.

more tolerant attitude than direct single-person decision-making structure. Here, both Brazil and the United States show how it is important to have group communication on some level. While Americans value mutual respect and open dialogue, Brazilians may see this behavior as unacceptable, even aggressive, if discussion discloses a large amount of information and includes members from different groups, or subordinate and managerial positions.[46]

It has been suggested that if Americans are preparing to do business in Brazil, the representatives should spend an ample amount of time getting to know the Brazilian executives. Be sure to show respect for top managers, and inform subordinates of any plans or changes, encouraging feedback. Managers still make the final decisions, and it is very unlikely that workers will provide any suggestions, but they also do not appreciate simply being told what to do. In other words, family structures, including in-group structures, are very important to Brazilians, but the head of the household still has the last word. Finally, stress short-term, risk-aversive goals to maintain vision and interest in business proposals.[47]

We will explore additional implications of the GLOBE findings as they relate to managerial leadership in Chapter 13.

The World of *BusinessWeek*—Revisited

The article that opens this chapter illustrates the importance of MNCs gaining an understanding of the cultures of the countries in which they do business. With proper understanding, companies can more appropriately invest in equipment and the people within the culture to provide better management and an overall better way of life. Having read this chapter, you should understand the impact culture has on the actions of MNCs, including general management practices and relations with employees and customers, and on maintaining overall reputation.

Based on your reading of the article and on Hofstede's and Trompenaars's cultural dimensions, answer the following questions: (1) What dimensions contribute to the differences between how Americans and Japanese or Korean workers use current technology? (2) What are some ways Israel may respond to using such technology? (3) How could managers alter decisions to allow Japanese or Korean workers to experience more of a work-life balance?

SUMMARY OF KEY POINTS

1. Culture is acquired knowledge that people use to interpret experience and generate social behavior. Culture also has the characteristics of being learned, shared, transgenerational, symbolic, patterned, and adaptive. There are many dimensions of cultural diversity, including centralized vs. decentralized decision making, safety vs. risk, individual vs. group rewards, informal vs. formal procedures, high vs. low organizational loyalty, cooperation vs. competition, short-term vs. long-term horizons, and stability vs. innovation.

2. Values are basic convictions that people have regarding what is right and wrong, good and bad, important and unimportant. Research shows that there are both differences and similarities between the work values and managerial values of different cultural groups. Work values often reflect culture and industrialization, and managerial values are highly related to success. Research shows that values tend to change over time and often reflect age and experience.

3. Hofstede has identified and researched four major dimensions of culture: power distance, uncertainty avoidance, individualism, and masculinity. Recently, he has added a fifth dimension, time orientation. Each will affect a country's political and social system. The integration of these factors into two-dimensional figures can illustrate the complexity of culture's effect on behavior.

4. In recent years, researchers have attempted to cluster countries into similar cultural groupings to study similarities and differences. Through analyzing the relationship between two dimensions, as Hofstede illustrated, two-dimensional maps can be created to show how countries differ and where they overlap.

5. Research by Trompenaars has examined five relationship orientations: universalism vs. particularism, individualism vs. communitarianism, affective vs. neutral, specific vs. diffuse, and achievement vs. ascription. Trompenaars also looked at attitudes

toward time and toward the environment. The result is a wealth of information helping to explain how cultures differ as well as practical ways in which MNCs can do business effectively in these environments. In particular, his findings update those of Hofstede while helping support the previous work by Hofstede on clustering countries.

6. Recent research undertaken by the GLOBE project has attempted to extend and integrate cultural attributes and variables as they relate to managerial leadership and practice. These analyses confirm much of the Hofstede and Trompenaars research, with greater emphasis on differences in managerial leadership styles.

KEY TERMS

achievement culture, *115*

ascription culture, *115*

collectivism, *105*

communitarianism, *113*

culture, *96*

diffuse culture, *114*

emotional culture, *114*

femininity, *105*

GLOBE, *119*

individualism, *105*

masculinity, *105*

neutral culture, *114*

particularism, *111*

power distance, *104*

specific culture, *114*

uncertainty avoidance, *105*

universalism, *111*

values, *101*

REVIEW AND DISCUSSION QUESTIONS

1. What is meant by the term *culture*? In what way can measuring attitudes about the following help differentiate between cultures: centralized or decentralized decision making, safety or risk, individual or group rewards, high or low organizational loyalty, cooperation or competition? Use these attitudes to compare the United States, Germany, and Japan. Based on your comparisons, what conclusions can you draw regarding the impact of culture on behavior?

2. What is meant by the term *value*? Are cultural values the same worldwide, or are there marked differences? Are these values changing over time, or are they fairly constant? How does your answer relate to the role of values in a culture?

3. What are the four major dimensions of culture studied by Geert Hofstede? Identify and describe each. What is the cultural profile of the United States? Of Asian countries? Of Latin American countries? Of Latin European countries? Based on your comparisons of these four profiles, what conclusions can you draw regarding cultural challenges

facing individuals in one group when they interact with individuals in one of the other groups? Why do think Hofstede added the fifth dimension of time orientation?

4. As people engage in more international travel and become more familiar with other countries, will cultural differences decline as a roadblock to international understanding, or will they continue to be a major barrier? Defend your answer.

5. What are the characteristics of each of the following pairs of cultural characteristics derived from Trompenaars's research: universalism vs. particularism, neutral vs. emotional, specific vs. diffuse, achievement vs. ascription? Compare and contrast each pair.

6. How did project GLOBE build on and extend Hofstede's analysis? What unique contributions are associated with project GLOBE?

7. In what way is time a cultural factor? In what way is the need to control the environment a cultural factor? Give an example for each.

INTERNET EXERCISE: DAIMLER-CHRYSLER, HELPING THE WORLD MOVE

Daimler-Chrysler was born through the merger of the German company Daimler-Benz AG and the American company Chrysler Corporation in 1998. In order to maintain an increase in market segment sales, Daimler-Chrysler has had to effectively manage across cultures from the United States to South Africa. Visit the Daimler-Chrysler Web site at **www.daimlerchrysler.com** to see where factories reside for each car group. Compare

and contrast the similarities and differences in these markets. Then answer these three questions: (1) How do you think cultural differences affect the way the firm operates in South Africa and in the United States? (2) In what way is culture a factor in auto sales? (3) Is it possible for a car company to transcend national culture and produce a global automobile that is accepted by people in every culture? Why or why not?

Taiwan

Taiwan is an island located 100 miles off the southeast coast of the China mainland. Taiwan is only 13,900 square miles, and with a population of approximately 23 million, it has one of the highest population densities in the world. In 1949, the communists under Mao Zedong defeated the Nationalists under Chiang Kai-shek, and the latter government moved to Taiwan, where it established dominance. The People's Republic of China still considers Taiwan to be a breakaway province, and tensions between the two flare up frequently.

The government of Taiwan was totally controlled by the Nationalists until 1996 when the first democratic election was held. In 2000 the Democratic Progressive Party candidate, Chen Shui-bian, was elected president for a four-year term, although the Nationalist Party continued to hold over 50 percent of the seats in the country's parliament, the Legislative Yuan. He was reelected by a narrow margin in March 2004, though it has been suggested that an assassination attempt may have been staged in order to win sympathy votes, which has created some tension over the validity of his position as president. The country's gross domestic product is approximately $680.5 billion, and per capita GDP is around $29,500. In the late 1990s many Asian economies slowed sharply, caught in a vicious economic crisis. Japan, South Korea, Indonesia, Thailand, and Malaysia all saw their GDP growth decline, and some of them, especially Japan, still run budget deficits as high as 10 percent of GDP. Taiwan, on the other hand, had steady GDP growth in the range of 6 percent throughout this period. In particular, the country's economy has been managed carefully through a combination of tight exchange controls, low foreign debt, conservative fiscal policies, and relatively austere and transparent banking.

Taiwan is one of the 15 largest trading powers in the world, which its 2002 induction into the World Trade Organization has helped maintain, and one of the strongest sectors of its economy is information technology. The value of computer-related products produced in Taiwan is over $35 billion annually. Taiwanese manufacturers build two-thirds of the motherboards and keyboards sold worldwide, in addition to 60 percent of the monitors and almost 40 percent of the notebook PCs. A number of major high-tech firms have set up operations on the island, including Sun Microsystems, Microsoft, and Intel. All three realized that costs here are lower than in most other places, and the quality of the workforce would allow them to produce state-of-the-art products. Other firms, including locally based manufacturers, also followed this strategy. As a result, by the mid-1990s Taiwan had leapfrogged South Korea in the production of PCs. Some of this success was a result of Taiwanese firms entering into a series of private-label contracts with U.S. importers.

By the late 1990s Taiwan-based chipmakers were investing billions of dollars annually in semiconductor fabrication plants. By 2002 annual investment in research, development, and new capacity was in excess of $17 billion. The world is so dependent on Taiwan for computer-related equipment that when a devastating earthquake hit the island in September 1999, the global information technology (IT) market shuddered and the price of PC chips rose sharply. Although the IT companies emerged relatively unscathed, the incident served to underscore the importance of Taiwan's semiconductor, electronic components, and PC industry. During the first decade of the millennium the importance of Taiwan in these areas is likely to grow.

The success of the IT companies is likely a reflection of personal cultural values, such as high motivation, hard work, and patience. The people of Taiwan are very humble and family-oriented to the point where an individual who brings shame upon himself or herself will unintentionally shame the entire family. It is obvious that *guan-xi* (pronounced "qwon-she"), or personal relationships, are very important to the citizens of Taiwan, a factor that managers need to take into consideration when conducting business in this land based on friendliness and respect for others.

www.gio.gov.tw,
www.careerjournaleurope.com

Questions

1. What are some current issues facing Taiwan? What is the climate for doing business in Taiwan today?
2. In terms of cultural dimensions, is Taiwan much different from the United States? (Use Figure 4–7 in your answer.) Why or why not?
3. In what way might culture be a stumbling block for firms seeking to set up businesses in Taiwan?
4. How are the three high-tech firms mentioned in this discussion managing to sidestep or overcome cultural barriers?

A Jumping-Off Place

A successful, medium-sized U.S. manufacturing firm in Ohio has decided to open a plant near Madrid, Spain. The company was attracted to this location for three reasons. First, the firm's current licensing agreement with a German firm is scheduled to come to an end within six months, and the U.S. manufacturer feels that it can do a better job of building and selling heavy machinery in the EU than the German firm. Second, the U.S. manufacturer invested almost $300 million in R&D over the last three years. The result is a host of new patents and other technological breakthroughs that now make this company a worldwide leader in the production of specialized heavy equipment. Third, labor costs in Spain are lower than in most other EU countries, and the company feels that this will prove extremely helpful in its efforts to capture market share in Greater Europe.

Because this is the manufacturer's first direct venture into the EU, it has decided to take on a Spanish partner. The latter will provide much of the on-site support, such as local contracts, personnel hiring, legal assistance, and governmental negotiations. In turn, the U.S. manufacturer will provide the capital for renovating the manufacturing plant, the R&D technology, and the technical training.

If the venture works out as planned, the partners will expand operations into Italy and use this location as a jumping-off point for tapping the Central and Eastern European markets. Additionally, because the cultures of Spain and Italy are similar, the U.S. manufacturer feels that staying within the Latin European cultural cluster can be synergistic. Plans for later in the decade call for establishing operations in northern France, which will serve as a jumping-off point for both Northern Europe and other major EU countries, such as Germany, the Netherlands, and Belgium. However, the company first wants to establish a foothold in Spain and get this operation working successfully; then it will look into expansion plans.

Questions

1. In what way will the culture of Spain be different from that of the United States? In answering this question, refer to Figures 4–5, 4–6, and 4–7.

2. If the company expands operations into Italy, will its experience in Spain be valuable, or will the culture be so different that the manufacturer will have to begin anew in determining how to address cultural challenges and opportunities? Explain.

3. If the firm expands into France, will its previous experiences in Spain and Italy be valuable in helping the company address cultural challenges? Be complete in your answer.

Chapter 5

MANAGING ACROSS CULTURES

OBJECTIVES OF THE CHAPTER

Traditionally, both scholars and practitioners assumed the universality of management. There was a tendency to take the management concepts and techniques that worked at home into other countries and cultures. It is now clear, from both practice and cross-cultural research, that this universality assumption, at least across cultures, does not hold up. Although there is a tendency in a borderless economy to promote a universalist approach, there is enough evidence from many cross-cultural researchers to conclude that the universalist assumption that may have held for U.S. organizations and employees is not generally true in other cultures.[1]

The overriding purpose of this chapter is to examine how MNCs can and should manage across cultures. This chapter puts into practice Chapter 4 on the meaning and dimensions of culture and serves as a foundation and point of departure for Chapters 8 and 9 on strategic management. The first part of this chapter addresses the traditional tendency to attempt to replicate successful home-country operations overseas without taking into account cultural differences. Next, attention is given to cross-cultural challenges, focusing on how differences can impact multinational management strategies. Finally, the cultures in specific countries and geographic regions are examined. The specific objectives of this chapter are:

1. **EXAMINE** the strategic dispositions that characterize responses to different cultures.

2. **DISCUSS** cross-cultural differences and similarities.

3. **REVIEW** cultural differences in select countries and regions, and note some of the important strategic guidelines for doing business in each.

The World of *BusinessWeek*

BusinessWeek

The Arab World Wants Its MTV

And U.S. Media Giant Viacom Aims to Deliver It, as well as Nickelodeon, Comedy Central and More

Matthew Noujaim lives and breathes hip-hop. But the 19-year-old Beirut university student, who raps about "anything and everything, including the Arab cause" in English and Arabic, has struggled to get his music noticed. Although rap is hugely popular among Middle Eastern youth, it's still underground and largely ignored by the region's record labels, radio stations, and music television channels. "There's lots of good hip-hop made here that never gets played," Noujaim says. "No one's willing to promote local talent."

That's about to change. MTV Arabia, a new 24-hour free satellite channel, will begin broadcasting in Arabic across the Middle East on Nov. 16. The Viacom-owned network's flagship show, *Hip HopNa* ("my hip-hop"), will be co-hosted by Saudi rapper Qusai Khidr and Palestinian-American producer Farid Nassar, aka Fredwreck, who has worked with Snoop Dogg, 50 Cent, and other marquee names. The show will visit 10 cities across the Middle East in search of talent, giving would-be Arab rap stars an international platform. Noujaim won the show's first competition, and Fredwreck has produced one of his tracks. "This is a music genre that is bubbling underneath the surface here, and we want to claim it as our own," says Bhavneet Singh, head of emerging markets for MTV Networks International.

Globalization a Go-Go

How will the likes of Justin Timberlake and Rihanna go down in a region that's not exactly brimming with goodwill toward Americans? Better than you might think. Middle

Eastern youth may not agree with U.S. politics, but they can't get enough of Western music and fashion. "The myth about the Arab world is that people go to bed at night hating the U.S. and wake up hating Israel," says James Zogby, president of the Arab American Institute, a think tank in Washington. "But go to any mall in Saudi Arabia, and you'll see kids in jeans and baseball caps hanging out at Starbucks and McDonald's. Globalization is real."

For Viacom, MTV Arabia is just the beginning. The region is attractive because it's awash in petrodollars and two-thirds of the population is under 25. Viacom has signed a 10-year licensing deal between MTV Networks and Tecom Investments, controlled by Dubai's ruler. On Oct. 12, Viacom planned to announce another decade-long licensing deal with Tecom for children's channel Nickelodeon Arabia. That's set for the second half of 2008, and the company reckons an Arabic version of Comedy Central won't be far behind. Also under discussion: Paramount Pictures productions in the region and licensing of Nick's characters for clothing, toys, and games. "The Middle East may be the world's most underappreciated growth story," says Viacom Chairman Sumner M. Redstone. No wonder U.S. media giants are pouring in. NBC Universal in May struck a licensing deal for a $2.2 billion amusement park in Dubai. Days later, Viacom announced plans to create a Nickelodeon section in Dubailand, a $2.5 billion development in the emirate that aims to be the world's largest theme park when it opens in 2011. And in September, Warner Bros. Entertainment announced a multibillion-dollar deal in Abu Dhabi that includes film production, a Warner Bros. theme park and hotel, and a chain of cinemas.

The Westerners will face plenty of homegrown competition. More than 50 music TV channels broadcast in the region. The dominant player, Rotana, owned by Saudi Prince Al Waleed bin Talal, is also the Middle East's largest record label and has exclusive contracts with most top-selling pop and folk artists. But MTV is betting it will win viewers by offering an alternative. "No one in this market is going out and asking the viewers what they want," says Abdullatif Al Sayegh, CEO of Arab Media Group, the Tecom unit that runs the channel. "We're spending our time in malls and cafés talking to young people; we're not getting our ideas from watching TV."

MTV Arabia is the biggest test to date of the network's two-decade-old localization strategy. MTV's flagship music channel has seen its American TV ratings slip and has struggled online. Management believes the biggest growth will come overseas, and the network now pumps out a blend of international and local tunes from Russia to Indonesia to Pakistan. That has helped MTV and sister operations, such as VH1 and Nickelodeon, reach 508 million households in 161 countries. "This isn't going to be MTV U.S.," Bill Roedy, vice-chairman of MTV Networks, says of the latest offering. "It is Arabic MTV made by Arabs for Arabs."

That means it'll be pretty tame by American standards. At noon every Friday, Islam's holiest day, the channel will air an animated call to prayer. During peak family viewing hours from 8 to 11 p.m., shows will introduce audiences to acts from the West and from other emerging markets such as India and Pakistan. And there will be Arabic versions of popular MTV shows such as *Made,* which gives young people coaching in fields like cooking and film.

"Edgy and Fun"

Later in the evening things will loosen up a bit. *Al Hara* ("the neighborhood") is an Arabic version of *Barrio 19,* a program that shows what young people do for fun. In the Middle East, that apparently includes dune-bashing (driving all-terrain vehicles over, and into, steep sand dunes) and water soccer, played in what looks like a vast inflatable kiddie pool. Says Rasha Al Emam, the 30-year-old Saudi woman who heads MTV Arabia's programming production: "The idea is to encourage kids to go out and do something edgy and fun instead of sitting around smoking a *shisha,*" or waterpipe.

While plenty of U.S. and European videos will never make it into the line-up, others will be sanitized for the Arab audience. At MTV Arabia's offices, a vast warehouse in Dubai, editors from across the region pore over clips frame by frame to remove offensive content. Bad language? Bleep it out. Shots of kissing, revealing outfits à la Britney Spears, or people on a bed? Blur them, or insert some less racy bit of the video.

That'll be fine with Maram Alhabib. The 23-year-old Saudi studying special education at Jeddah's Dar Al Hekma University loves metal group Seether and American

SUMNER OF ARABIA
Viacom chief Redstone has big plans for the Middle East

TELEVISION Launching MTV Arabia in November, with Nickelodeon to follow in 2008. Arabic Comedy Central under discussion.

LICENSING Selling rights to use SpongeBob SquarePants, Dora the Explorer, and other Nick characters for toys and clothing.

FILM Exploring Dubai-based production of Paramount titles and co-production deals for Arabic-language films.

DIGITAL Planning to put MTV on the Net and on phones. Similar deals for Nickelodeon and other brands being considered.

HOTELS Considering Nickelodeon-branded hotel in Dubai as part of a global relationship with Marriott.

THEME PARKS Planning Nickelodeon-branded section in Dubailand, the world's largest amusement park, set to open in 2011.

alternative band Three Doors Down, but she finds many music videos to be too provocative. "The Arab channels are boring, they all play the same music and a lot of the videos . . . are all about seduction," she says. "If MTV focuses on music and issues Arabs care about, people will watch."

Source: Reprinted with special permission from "The Arab World Wants Its MTV," by Kerry Capell, *BusinessWeek*, October 11, 2007, online edition. Copyright © 2007 The McGraw-Hill Companies.

This news story highlights the current effects of globalization, and the complexity of understanding and managing cultural differences within and across borders. Knowledge of cultural differences, introduced in Chapter 2, is imperative for international managers as they discover ways to manage and oversee operations outside of their home country. We discussed in Chapter 2 how the political landscape can affect MNC movement into other countries. While Middle Eastern people may not have the same political beliefs as Americans, there is a palpable interest in the social and cultural norms in the United States, creating an interesting dynamic. International managers should be aware that while some practices may appeal to other cultures, the message cannot be literally translated from one language and cultural context to another. Media coverage in the Arab countries is considered tame by U.S. standards, and Viacom is carefully taking that into consideration as it begins to offer channels such as MTV, Nickelodeon, and possibly Comedy Central to current Arab networks. It may prove to be challenging for the company to more aggressively incorporate pop culture into the Arab communities, even as the demand for that content appears to be growing. How can two countries that have such different views share the same interests? This chapter provides insight into uncovering similarities and differences across cultures and using those insights to develop international management approaches that are effective and responsive to local cultures.

■ The Strategy for Managing Across Cultures

As MNCs become more transnational, their strategies must address the cultural similarities and differences in their varied markets.[2] A good example is provided by Renault, the French auto giant. For years Renault manufactured a narrow product line that it sold primarily in France. Because of this limited geographic market and the fact that its cars continued to have quality-related problems, the company's performance was at best mediocre. Several years ago, however, Renault made a number of strategic decisions that dramatically changed the way it did business. Among other things, it bought controlling stakes in Nissan Motor of Japan, Samsung of South Korea, and Dacia, the Romanian automaker. The company also built a $1 billion factory in Brazil to produce its successful

Megane sedan and acquired an idle factory near Moscow to manufacture Renaults for the eastern European market.

Today, Renault is a multinational automaker with operations on four continents. The challenge the company now faces is to make all these operations profitable. This will not be easy. Nissan's profits are unpredictable, and while it has had a good run since 1999, profits plummeted by 54 percent in early 2007, leading board members to forgo bonuse.[3] Meanwhile Dacia is operating in one of Europe's most dismal economies. Even so, Dacia has manufactured what some call a genuine world car, known as the Logan. This simple, compact vehicle is sold at an affordable price in European markets and has recently been introduced in India. Renault maintains innovative strategies by offering the Logan under either the Dacia, Renault, or Nissan name, depending on the market.[4] Now it needs to further straighten out its international operations and get everything working in harmony.[5] One of the recent steps it has taken to do this is the decision to meld its own sales organizations with those of Nissan in Europe, thus creating one well-integrated, efficient sales force on the continent. Another step has been to start producing Nissan models in its Brazilian plant, so that it can expand its South American offerings by more efficiently using current facilities. One of the company's long-term goals is by 2010 to have 10 common platforms, or underbodies, that will allow it to build Renaults and Nissans everywhere, while maintaining the look, feel, and identity of its separate brands.[6] At the same time the firm is working to improve its effectiveness in dealing with governments, unions, and employees, as well as to understand the cultural differences in customer preferences in Europe, Asia, and the Americas. Renault will certainly face challenges, as the recent market has not been working in its favor. New car registrations in Europe have fallen, and even with new car sales increasing due to the Logan, the European market has greatly hurt profits.[7] Adding insult to injury, Ford Motors, which has experienced global losses for years, is becoming the industry leader in the Russian market, outpacing the seasoned Renault options already offered.[8] Renault's recent experiences underscore the need to carefully consider different national cultures and practices when developing international strategies.

Strategic Predispositions

Most MNCs have a cultural strategic predisposition toward doing things in a particular way. Four distinct predispositions have been identified: ethnocentric, polycentric, regiocentric, and geocentric.

A company with an **ethnocentric predisposition** allows the values and interests of the parent company to guide strategic decisions. Firms with a **polycentric predisposition** make strategic decisions tailored to suit the cultures of the countries where the MNC operates. A **regiocentric predisposition** leads a firm to try to blend its own interests with those of its subsidiaries on a regional basis. A company with a **geocentric predisposition** tries to integrate a global systems approach to decision making. Table 5–1 provides details of each of these orientations.

If an MNC relies on one of these profiles over an extended time, the approach may become institutionalized and greatly influence strategic planning. By the same token, a predisposition toward any of these profiles can provide problems for a firm if it is out of step with the economic or political environment. For example, a firm with an ethnocentric predisposition may find it difficult to implement a geocentric strategy, because it is unaccustomed to using global integration. Commonly, successful MNCs use a mix of these predispositions based on the demands of the current environment described in the chapters in Part 1.

Meeting the Challenge

Despite the need for and tendency of MNCs to address regional differentiation issues, many MNCs are committed to a **globalization imperative**, which is a belief that one worldwide approach to doing business is the key to both efficiency and effectiveness.

ethnocentric predisposition
A nationalistic philosophy of management whereby the values and interests of the parent company guide strategic decisions.

polycentric predisposition
A philosophy of management whereby strategic decisions are tailored to suit the cultures of the countries where the MNC operates.

geocentric predisposition
A philosophy of management whereby the company tries to integrate a global systems approach to decision making.

regiocentric predisposition
A philosophy of management whereby the firm tries to blend its own interests with those of its subsidiaries on a regional basis.

globalization imperative
A belief that one worldwide approach to doing business is the key to both efficiency and effectiveness.

Table 5–1
Orientation of an MNC Under Different Profiles

	Orientation of the Firm			
	Ethnocentric	**Polycentric**	**Regiocentric**	**Geocentric**
Mission	Profitability (viability)	Public acceptance (legitimacy)	Both profitability and public acceptance (viability and legitimacy)	Same as regiocentric
Governance	Top-down	Bottom-up (each subsidiary decides on local objectives)	Mutually negotiated between region and its subsidiaries	Mutually negotiated at all levels of the corporation
Strategy	Global integration	National responsiveness	Regional integration and national responsiveness	Global integration and national responsiveness
Structure	Hierarchical product divisions	Hierarchical area divisions, with autonomous national units	Product and regional organization tied through a matrix	A network of organizations (including some stakeholders and competitor organizations)
Culture	Home country	Host country	Regional	Global
Technology	Mass production	Batch production	Flexible manufacturing	Flexible manufacturing
Marketing	Product development determined primarily by the needs of home country customers	Local product development based on local needs	Standardize within region, but not across regions	Global product, with local variations
Finance	Repatriation of profits to home country	Retention of profits in host country	Redistribution within region	Redistribution globally
Personnel practices	People of home country developed for key positions everywhere in the world	People of local nationality developed for key positions in their own country	Regional people developed for key positions anywhere in the region	Best people everywhere in the world developed for key positions everywhere in the world

Source: From Balaji S. Chakravarthy and Howard V. Perlmutter, "Strategic Planning for a Global Business," *Columbia Journal of World Business,* Summer 1985, pp. 5–6. Copyright © 1985 Elsevier. Reprinted with permission.

One study, involving extensive examination of 115 medium and large MNCs and 103 affiliated subsidiaries in the United States, Canada, France, Germany, Japan, and the United Kingdom, found an overwhelming majority used the same strategies abroad as at home.[9]

Despite these tendencies to use home strategies, effective MNCs are continuing their efforts to address local needs. A number of factors are helping facilitate this need to develop unique strategies for different cultures, including:

1. The diversity of worldwide industry standards such as those in broadcasting, where television sets must be manufactured on a country-by-country basis.

2. A continual demand by local customers for differentiated products, as in the case of consumer goods that must meet local tastes.

3. The importance of being an insider, as in the case of customers who prefer to "buy local."

4. The difficulty of managing global organizations, as in the case of some local subsidiaries that want more decentralization and others that want less.

5. The need to allow subsidiaries to use their own abilities and talents and not be restrained by headquarters, as in the case of local units that know how to customize products for their market and generate high returns on investment with limited production output.

By responding to the cultural needs of local operations and customers, MNCs find that regional strategies can be used effectively in capturing and maintaining worldwide market niches. One example is Sony, which you may become more familiar with after completing the Internet exercise at the end of the chapter. One of the best examples is Warner-Lambert, which has manufacturing facilities in Belgium, France, Germany, Italy, Ireland, Spain, and the United Kingdom. Each plant is specialized and produces a small number of products for the entire European market; in this way, each can focus on tailoring products for the unique demands of the various markets.

The globalization vs. national responsiveness challenge is even more acute when marketing cosmetics and other products that vary greatly in consumer use. For example, marketers sell toothpaste as a cosmetic product in Spain and Greece but as a cavity-fighter in the Netherlands and United States. Soap manufacturers market their product as a cosmetic item in Spain but as a functional commodity in Germany. Moreover, the way in which the marketing message is delivered also is important. For example:

- Germans want advertising that is factual and rational; they fear being manipulated by "the hidden persuader." The typical German spot features the standard family of two parents, two children, and grandmother.
- The French avoid reasoning or logic. Their advertising is predominantly emotional, dramatic, and symbolic. Spots are viewed as cultural events—art for the sake of money—and are reviewed as if they were literature or films.
- The British value laughter above all else. The typical broad, self-deprecating British commercial amuses by mocking both the advertiser and consumer.[10]

In some cases, however, both the product and the marketing message are similar worldwide. This is particularly true for high-end products, where the lifestyles and expectations of the market niche are similar regardless of the country. Heineken beer, Hennessey brandy, Porsche cars, and the *Financial Times* all appeal to consumer niches that are fairly homogeneous regardless of geographic locale. The same is true at the lower end of the market for goods that are impulse purchases, novel products, or fast foods, such as Coca-Cola's soft drinks, Levi's jeans, pop music, and ice-cream bars. In most cases, however, it is necessary to modify products as well as the market approach for the regional or local market. One analysis noted that the more marketers understand about the way in which a particular culture tends to view emotion, enjoyment, friendship, humor, rules, status, and other culturally based behaviors, the more control they have over creating marketing messages that will be interpreted in the desired way.

Figure 5–1 provides an example of the role that culture should play in advertising by recapping the five relationship orientations identified through Trompenaars's research (see Chapter 4). Figure 5–1 shows how value can be added to the marketing approach by carefully tailoring the advertising message to the particular culture. For example, advertising in the United States should target individual achievement, be expressive and direct, and appeal to U.S. values of success through personal hard work. On the other hand, the focus in China and other Asian countries should be much more indirect and subtle, emphasizing group references, shared responsibility, and interpersonal trust.

The need to adjust global strategies for regional markets presents three major challenges for most MNCs. First, the MNC must stay abreast of local market conditions and sidestep the temptation to assume that all markets are basically the same. Second, the MNC must know the strengths and weaknesses of its subsidiaries so that it can provide these units with the assistance needed in addressing local demands. Third, the multinational must give the subsidiary more autonomy so that it can respond to changes in local demands. "International Management in Action: Ten Key Factors for MNC Success" provides additional insights into the ways that successful MNCs address these challenges.

Figure 5–1

Trompenaars's Cultural Dimensions and Advertising: Adjusting the Message for Local Meaning

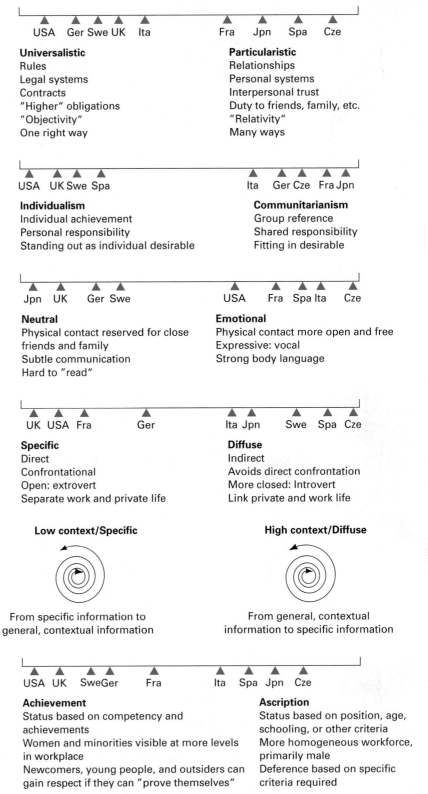

Universalistic
Rules
Legal systems
Contracts
"Higher" obligations
"Objectivity"
One right way

Particularistic
Relationships
Personal systems
Interpersonal trust
Duty to friends, family, etc.
"Relativity"
Many ways

Individualism
Individual achievement
Personal responsibility
Standing out as individual desirable

Communitarianism
Group reference
Shared responsibility
Fitting in desirable

Neutral
Physical contact reserved for close friends and family
Subtle communication
Hard to "read"

Emotional
Physical contact more open and free
Expressive: vocal
Strong body language

Specific
Direct
Confrontational
Open: extrovert
Separate work and private life

Diffuse
Indirect
Avoids direct confrontation
More closed: Introvert
Link private and work life

Low context/Specific

From specific information to general, contextual information

High context/Diffuse

From general, contextual information to specific information

Achievement
Status based on competency and achievements
Women and minorities visible at more levels in workplace
Newcomers, young people, and outsiders can gain respect if they can "prove themselves"

Ascription
Status based on position, age, schooling, or other criteria
More homogeneous workforce, primarily male
Deference based on specific criteria required

Source: Lisa Hoecklin, *Managing Cultural Differences: Strategies for Competitive Advantage* (Workingham, England: Addison-Wesley, 1995), p. 107, which is drawn from information found in Fons Trompenaars, *Riding the Waves of Culture: Understanding Diversity in Global Business* (New York: Irwin, 1994).

Ten Key Factors for MNC Success

Why are some international firms successful while others are not? Some of the main reasons are that successful multinational firms take a worldwide view of operations, support their overseas activities, pay close attention to political winds, and use local nationals whenever possible. These are the overall findings of a report that looked into the development of customized executive education programs. Specifically, there are 10 factors or guidelines that successful global firms seem to employ. Successful global competitors:

1. See themselves as multinational enterprises and are led by a management team that is comfortable in the world arena.

2. Develop integrated and innovative strategies that make it difficult and costly for other firms to compete.

3. Aggressively and effectively implement their worldwide strategy and back it with large investments.

4. Understand that innovation no longer is confined to the United States and develop systems for tapping innovation abroad.

5. Operate as if the world were one large market rather than a series of individual, small markets.

6. Have organization structures that are designed to handle their unique problems and challenges and thus provide them the greatest efficiency.

7. Develop a system that keeps them informed about political changes around the world and the implications of these changes on the firm.

8. Have management teams that are international in composition and thus better able to respond to the various demands of their respective markets.

9. Allow their outside directors to play an active role in the operation of the enterprise.

10. Are well managed and tend to follow such important guidelines as sticking close to the customer, having lean organization structures, and encouraging autonomy and entrepreneurial activity among the personnel.

■ Cross-Cultural Differences and Similarities

As shown in Chapter 4, cultures can be similar or quite different across countries. The challenge for MNCs is to recognize and effectively manage the similarities and differences. For instance, the way in which MNCs manage their home businesses often should be different from the way they manage their overseas operations.[11] After recognizing the danger for MNCs of drifting toward parochialism and simplification because of cultural differences, the discussion in this section shifts to some examples of cultural similarities and differences and how to effectively manage across cultures by a contingency approach.

Parochialism and Simplification

Parochialism is the tendency to view the world through one's own eyes and perspectives. This can be a difficult problem for many international managers, who often come from advanced economies and believe that their state-of-the-art knowledge is more than adequate to handle the challenges of doing business in less developed countries. In addition, many of these managers have a parochial point of view fostered by their background.[12] A good example is provided by Randall and Coakley, who studied the impact of culture on successful partnerships in the former Soviet Union. Initially after the breakup of the Soviet Union, the republics called themselves the Commonwealth of Independent States (CIS). Randall and Coakley found that while outside MNC managers typically entered into partnerships with CIS enterprises with a view toward making them efficient and profitable, the CIS managers often brought a different set of priorities to the table.

> Commenting on their research, Randall and Coakley noted that the way CIS managers do business is sharply different from that of their American counterparts. CIS managers are still emerging from socially focused cultural norms embedded in their history, past training and

parochialism
The tendency to view the world through one's own eyes and perspectives.

work experiences which emphasize strategic values unlike those that exist in an internationally market-driven environment. For example, while an excess of unproductive workers may lead American managers to lay off some individuals for the good of the company, CIS managers would focus on the good of the working community and allow the company to accept significant profit losses as a consequence. This led the researchers to conclude:

> As behavioral change continues to lag behind structural change, it becomes imperative to understand that this inconsistency between what economic demands and cultural norms require manifests problems and complexities far beyond mere structural change. In short, the implications of the different perspectives on technology, labor, and production . . . for potential partnerships between U.S. and CIS companies need to be fully grasped by all parties entering into any form of relationship.[13]

simplification

The process of exhibiting the same orientation toward different cultural groups.

Simplification is the process of exhibiting the same orientation toward different cultural groups. For example, the way in which a U.S. manager interacts with a British manager is the same way in which he or she behaves when doing business with an Asian executive. Moreover, this orientation reflects one's basic culture. Table 5–2 provides an example, showing several widely agreed-on, basic cultural orientations and the range of variations for each. Asterisks indicate the dominant U.S. orientation. Quite obviously, U.S. cultural values are not the same as those of managers from other cultures; as a result, a U.S. manager's attempt to simplify things can result in erroneous behavior. Here is an example of a member of the purchasing department of a large European oil company who was negotiating an order with a Korean supplier:

> At the first meeting, the Korean partner offered a silver pen to the European manager. The latter, however, politely refused the present for fear of being bribed (even though he knew about the Korean custom of giving presents). Much to our manager's surprise, the second meeting began with the offer of a stereo system. Again the manager refused, his fear of being bribed probably heightened. When he gazed at a piece of Korean china on the third meeting, he finally realized what was going on. His refusal had not been taken to mean: "let's get on with business right away," but rather: "If you want to get into business with me, you had better come up with something bigger."[14]

Table 5–2
Six Basic Cultural Variations

Orientations	Range of Variations
What is the nature of people?	Good (changeable/unchangeable) A mixture of good and evil* Evil (changeable/unchangeable)
What is the person's relationship to nature?	Dominant* In harmony with nature Subjugation
What is the person's relationship to other people?	Lineal (hierarchic) Collateral (collectivist) Individualist*
What is the modality of human activity?	Doing* Being and becoming Being
What is the temporal focus of human activity?	Future* Present Past
What is the conception of space?	Private* Mixed Public

Note: *Indicates the dominant U.S. orientation.
Source: Adapted from the work of Florence Rockwood Kluckhohn and Fred L. Stodtbeck.

Understanding the culture in which they do business can make international managers more effective.[15] Unfortunately, when placed in a culture with which they are unfamiliar, most international managers are not culturally knowledgeable, so they often misinterpret what is happening. This is particularly true when the environment is markedly different from the one in which they live. Consider, for example, the difference between the cultures in Malaysia and the United States. Malaysia has what could be called a high-context culture, which possesses characteristics such as:

1. Relationships between people are relatively long lasting, and individuals feel deep personal involvement with each other.
2. Communication often is implicit, and individuals are taught from an early age to interpret these messages accurately.
3. People in authority are personally responsible for the actions of their subordinates, and this places a premium on loyalty to both superiors and subordinates.
4. Agreements tend to be spoken rather than written.
5. Insiders and outsiders are easily distinguishable, and outsiders typically do not gain entrance to the inner group.

These Malaysian cultural characteristics are markedly different from those of low-context cultures such as the United States, which possess the following characteristics:

1. Relationships between individuals are relatively short in duration, and in general, deep personal involvement with others is not valued greatly.
2. Messages are explicit, and individuals are taught from a very early age to say exactly what they mean.
3. Authority is diffused throughout the bureaucratic system, and personal responsibility is hard to pin down.
4. Agreements tend to be in writing rather than spoken.
5. Insiders and outsiders are not readily distinguished, and the latter are encouraged to join the inner circle.[16]

These differences are exacerbated by the fact that Malaysian culture is based on an amalgamation of diverse religions, including Hinduism, Buddhism, and Islam. Since it is predominantly Muslim, the consumption of alcohol is forbidden. That, coupled with the belief that success and failure are the will of God, may create issues with American managers attempting to make deals, as Malaysians will focus less on facts and more on intuitive feelings.[17] At the same time, it is important to realize that while there are cultural differences, there also are similarities. Therefore, in managing across cultures, not everything is totally different. Some approaches that work at home also work well in other cultural settings.

Similarities Across Cultures

When internationalization began to take off in the 1970s, many companies quickly admitted that it would not be possible to do business in the same way in every corner of the globe. There was a secret hope, however, that many of the procedures and strategies that worked so well at home could be adopted overseas without modification. This has proved to be a false hope. At the same time, some similarities across cultures have been uncovered by researchers. For example, a co-author of this text (Luthans) and his associates studied through direct observation a sample of managers ($n = 66$) in the largest textile factory in Russia to determine their activities.[18] Like U.S. managers studied earlier, Russian managers carried out traditional management, communication, human resources, and networking activities. The study also found that, as in the United States, the relative attention given to the networking activity increased the Russian managers' opportunities for promotion, and that communication activity was a significant predictor of effective performance in both Russia and the United States.[19]

Besides the similarities of managerial activities, another study at the same Russian factory tested whether organizational behavior modification (O.B.Mod.) interventions that led to performance improvements in U.S. organizations would do so in Russia.[20] As with the applications of O.B.Mod. in the United States, Russian supervisors were trained to administer social rewards (attention and recognition) and positive feedback when they observed workers engaging in behaviors that contributed to the production of quality fabric. In addition, Russian supervisors were taught to give corrective feedback for behaviors that reduced product quality. The researchers found that this O.B.Mod. approach, which had worked so well in the United States, produced positive results in the Russian factory. They concluded that "the class of interventions associated with organizational behavior modification are likely to be useful in meeting the challenges faced by Russian workers and managers are given initial support by the results of this study."[21]

In another cross-cultural study, this time using a large Korean sample (1,192 employees in 27 large Korean firms), Luthans and colleagues analyzed whether demographic and situational factors identified in the U.S.-based literature had the same antecedent influence on the commitment of Korean employees.[22] As in the U.S. studies, Korean employees' position in the hierarchy, tenure in their current position, and age all related to organizational commitment. Other similarities with U.S. firms included (1) as organizational size increased, commitment declined; (2) as structure became more employee-focused, commitment increased; and (3) the more positive the perceptions of organizational climate, the greater the employee commitment. The following conclusion was drawn:

> This study provides beginning evidence that popular constructs in the U.S. management and organizational behavior literature should not be automatically dismissed as culture bound. Whereas some organizational behavior concepts and techniques do indeed seem to be culture specific . . . a growing body of literature is demonstrating the ability to cross-culturally validate other concepts and techniques, such as behavior management. . . . This study contributed to this cross-cultural evidence for the antecedents to organizational commitment. The antecedents for Korean employees' organizational commitment were found to be similar to their American counterparts.[23]

Many Differences Across Cultures

We have stressed throughout the text how different cultures can be from one another and how important it is for MNCs to understand the points of disparity. Here, we look at some differences from a human resources perspective, a topic which will be covered in depth in Chapter 14. We introduce human resource management (HRM) here as a way to illustrate that the cultural foundations utilized in the selection of employees can further form the culture that international managers will oversee. In other words, understanding the HRM strategies before becoming a manager in the industry can aid in effective performance. The focus here is more from a socially cultural perspective; the organizational perspective will be discussed further in Chapter 14.

Despite similarities between cultures in some studies, far more differences than similarities have been found. In particular, MNCs are discovering that they must carefully investigate and understand the culture where they intend to do business and modify their approaches appropriately.

Sometimes these cultures are quite different from the United States—as well as from each other! One human resource management example has been offered by Trompenaars, who examined the ways in which personnel in international subsidiaries were appraised by their managers. The head office had established the criteria to be used in these evaluations but left the prioritization of the criteria to the national operating company. As a result, the outcome of the evaluations could be quite different from country to country because what was regarded as the most important criterion in one subsidiary might be ranked much lower on the evaluation list of another subsidiary. In the case of Shell Oil, for example, Trompenaars found that the firm was using a HAIRL system of appraisal. The five criteria in this acronym stood for (a) helicopter—the capacity to take a broad view from above; (b) analysis—the ability to evaluate situations logically and completely; (c) imagination—the ability to be creative and think outside the box; (d) reality—the ability to use information realistically; and (e) leadership—the ability to effectively galvanize and inspire personnel. When Shell's operating companies in four countries were asked to prioritize from top to bottom these five criteria, the results were as follows:

Netherlands	France	Germany	Britain
Reality	Imagination	Leadership	Helicopter
Analysis	Analysis	Analysis	Imagination
Helicopter	Leadership	Reality	Reality
Leadership	Helicopter	Imagination	Analysis
Imagination	Reality	Helicopter	Leadership

Quite obviously, personnel in different operating companies were being evaluated differently. In fact, no two of the operating companies in the four countries had the same criterion at the top of their lists. Moreover, the criterion at the top of the list for operating companies in the Netherlands—reality—was at the bottom of the list for those in France; and the one at the top of the list in French operating companies—imagination—was at the bottom of the list of the Dutch firms. Similarly, the German operating companies put leadership at the top of the list and helicopter at the bottom, while the British companies did the opposite! In fact, the whole list for the Germans is in the exact reverse order of the British list.[24]

Other HRM differences can be found in areas such as wages, compensation, pay equity, and maternity leave. Here are some representative examples.

1. The concept of an hourly wage plays a minor role in Mexico. Labor law requires that employees receive full pay 365 days a year.

2. In Austria and Brazil, employees with one year of service are automatically given 30 days of paid vacation.

3. Some jurisdictions in Canada have legislated pay equity—known in the United States as comparable worth—between male- and female-intensive jobs.

4. In Japan, compensation levels are determined by using the objective factors of age, length of service, and educational background rather than skill, ability, and performance. Performance does not count until after an employee reaches age 45.

5. In the United Kingdom, employees are allowed up to 40 weeks of maternity leave, and employers must provide a government-mandated amount of pay for 18 of those weeks.

6. In 87 percent of large Swedish companies, the head of human resources is on the board of directors.[25]

These HRM practices certainly are quite different from those in the United States, and U.S. MNCs need to modify their approaches when they go into these countries if they hope to be successful. Compensation plans in particular provide an interesting area of contrast across different cultures.

Drawing on the work of Hofstede (see Chapter 4), it is possible to link cultural clusters and compensation strategies. Table 5–3 shows a host of different cultural groupings, including some in Asia, the EU, and Anglo countries. Each cluster requires a different approach to formulating an effective compensation strategy, and after analyzing each such cluster, we suggest that:

1. In Pacific Rim countries, incentive plans should be group-based. In high-masculinity cultures (Japan, Hong Kong, Malaysia, the Philippines, Singapore), high salaries should be paid to senior-level managers.

Table 5–3
Cultural Clusters in the Pacific Rim, EU, and United States

	Power Distance	Individualism	Masculinity	Uncertainty Avoidance
Pacific Rim				
Hong Kong, Malaysia, Philippines, Singapore	+	–	+	–
Japan	+	–	+	+
South Korea, Taiwan	+	–	–	+
EU and United States				
France, Spain	+	+	–	+
Italy, Belgium	+	+	+	+
Portugal	+	–	–	+
Greece	+	–	+	+
Denmark, Netherlands	–	+	+	–
Germany	–	+	+	+
Great Britain, Ireland, United States	–	–	+	+

Note: + indicates high or strong; – indicates low or weak.

Source: Based on research by Hofstede and presented in Richard M. Hodgetts and Fred Luthans, "U.S. Multinationals' Compensation Strategies for Local Management: Cross-Cultural Implications," *Compensation and Benefits Review,* March–April 1993, p. 47. Reproduced with permission of Sage Publications, Inc. via Copyright Clearance Center.

2. In EU nations such as France, Spain, Italy, and Belgium, compensation strategies should be similar. In the latter two nations, however, significantly higher salaries should be paid to local senior-level managers because of the high masculinity index. In Portugal and Greece, both of which have a low individualism index, profit-sharing plans would be more effective than individual incentive plans, while in Denmark, the Netherlands, and Germany, personal-incentive plans would be highly useful because of the high individualism in these cultures.

3. In Great Britain, Ireland, and the United States, managers value their individualism and are motivated by the opportunity for earnings, recognition, advancement, and challenge. Compensation plans should reflect these needs.[26]

Figure 5–2 shows how specific HRM areas can be analyzed contingently on a country-by-country basis. Take, for example, the information on Japan. When it is contrasted with U.S. approaches, a significant number of differences are found. Recruitment and selection in Japanese firms often are designed to help identify those individuals who will do the best job over the long run. In the United States, people often are hired based on what they can do for the firm in the short run, because many of them eventually will quit or be downsized. Similarly, the Japanese use a great deal of cross-training, while the Americans tend to favor specialized training. The Japanese use group performance appraisal and reward people as a group; at least traditionally, Americans use manager-subordinate performance appraisal and reward people as individuals. In Japan, unions are regarded as partners; in the United States, management and unions view each other in a much more adversarial way. Only in the area of job design, where the Japanese use a great deal of participative management and autonomous work teams, are the Americans beginning to employ a similar approach. The same types of differences can be seen in the matrix of Figure 5–2 among Japan, Germany, Mexico, and China.

Figure 5–2	A Partially Completed Contingency Matrix for International Human Resource Management

	Japan	Germany	Mexico	China
Recruitment and selection	• Prepare for long process • Ensure that your firm is "here to stay" • Develop trusting relationship with recruit	• Obtain skilled labor from government subsidized apprenticeship program	• Use expatriates sparingly • Recruit Mexican nationals at U.S. colleges	• Recent public policy shifts encourage use of sophisticated selection procedures
Training	• Make substantial investment in training • Use general training and cross-training • Training is everyone's responsibility	• Reorganize and utilize apprenticeship programs • Be aware of government regulations on training	• Use bilingual trainers	• Careful observations of existing training programs • Utilize team training
Compensation	• Use recognition and praise as motivator • Avoid pay for performance	• Note high labor costs for manufacturing	• Consider all aspects of labor cost	• Use technical training as reward • Recognize egalitarian values • Use "more work more pay" with caution
Labor relations	• Treat unions as partners • Allow time for negotiations	• Be prepared for high wages and short work week • Expect high productivity from unionized workers	• Understand changing Mexican labor law • Prepare for increasing unionization of labor	• Tap large pool of labor cities • Lax labor laws may become more stringent
Job design	• Include participation • Incorporate group goal setting • Use autonomous work teams • Use uniform, formal approaches • Encourage co-worker input • Empower teams to make decision	• Utilize works councils to enhance worker participation	• Approach participation cautiously	• Determine employee's motives before implementing participation

Source: From Fred Luthans, Paul A. Marsnik, and Kyle W. Luthans, "A Contingency Matrix Approach to IHRM," *Human Resource Management Journal* 36, no. 2, 1997. Reprinted with permission of John Wiley & Sons, Inc.

These differences should not be interpreted to mean that one set of HRM practices is superior to another. In fact, recent research from Japan and Europe shows these firms often have a higher incidence of personnel-related problems than U.S. companies. For example, one study found that Japanese MNCs ($n = 34$) and European MNCs ($n = 23$) had more problems than U.S. MNCs ($n = 24$) in such areas as (1) home-country personnel who possessed sufficient international management skills; (2) home-country personnel who wanted to work abroad; (3) difficulty in attracting high-caliber local nationals; and (4) high turnover of local employees. Additionally, when compared with Japanese MNCs, U.S. multinationals had less friction and better communication between their home-country expatriates and local employees, and there were fewer complaints by local employees regarding their ability to advance in the company.[27]

Figure 5–2 clearly indicates the importance of MNCs using a contingency approach to HRM across cultures. Not only are there different HRM practices in different cultures, but there also are different practices within the same cultures. For instance, one study involving 249 U.S. affiliates of foreign-based MNCs found that in general, affiliate HRM practices closely follow local practices when dealing with the rank and file but even more closely approximate parent-company practices when dealing with upper-level management.[28] In other words, this study found that a hybrid approach to HRM was being used by these MNCs.

Aside from the different approaches used in different countries, it is becoming clear that common assumptions and conventional wisdom about HRM practices in certain countries no longer are valid. For example, for many years, it has been assumed that Japanese employees do not leave their jobs for work with other firms, that they are loyal to their first employer, and that it would be virtually impossible for MNCs operating in Japan to recruit talent from Japanese firms. Recent evidence, however, reveals that job-hopping among Japanese employees is increasingly common. One report concluded:

> While American workers, both the laid-off and the survivors, grapple with cutbacks, one in three Japanese workers willingly walks away from his job within the first 10 years of his career, according to the Japanese Institute of Labor, a private research organization. And many more are thinking about it. More than half of salaried Japanese workers say they would switch jobs or start their own business if a favorable opportunity arose, according to a survey by the Recruit Research Corporation.[29]

These findings clearly illustrate one important point: Managing across cultures requires careful understanding of the local environment, because common assumptions and stereotypes may not be valid. Cultural differences must be addressed, and this is why cross-cultural research will continue to be critical in helping firms learn how to manage across cultures.[30]

■ Cultural Differences in Selected Countries and Regions

Chapter 4 introduced the concept of country clusters, which is the idea that certain regions of the world have similar cultures. For example, the way that Americans do business in the United States is very similar to the way that British do business in England. Even in this Anglo culture, however, there are pronounced differences, and in other clusters, such as in Asia, these differences become even more pronounced. "International Management in Action: Managing in Hong Kong" depicts such differences. Chapter 1 examined some important worldwide developments, and the next sections focus on cultural highlights and differences in selected countries and regions that provide the necessary understanding and perspective for effective management across cultures.

Doing Business in China

The People's Republic of China (PRC or China, for short) has had a long tradition of isolation. In 1979, Deng Xiaoping opened this country to the world. Although his bloody 1989 put-down of protesters in Tiananmen Square was a definite setback for progress, China is rapidly trying to close the gap between itself and economically advanced nations and to establish itself as a power in the world economy. As noted in Chapter 1, China is actively trading in world markets, is a member of the WTO, and is a major trading partner of the United States. Despite this global presence, many U.S. and European multinationals still find that doing business in the PRC can be a long, grueling process.[31] Very few outside firms have yet to make a profit in China. One primary reason is that Western-based MNCs do not appreciate the important role and impact of Chinese culture.

Managing across cultures has long been recognized as a potential problem for multinationals. To help expatriates who are posted overseas deal with a new culture, many MNCs offer special training and coaching. Often, however, little is done to change expatriates' basic cultural values or specific managerial behaviors. Simply put, this traditional approach could be called the *practical school of management thought,* which holds that effective managerial behavior is universal and a good manager in the United States also will be effective in Hong Kong or any other location around the world. In recent years, it generally has been recognized that such an approach no longer is sufficient, and there is growing support for what is called the *cross-cultural school of management thought,* which holds that effective managerial behavior is a function of the specific culture. As Black and Porter pointed out, successful managerial action in Los Angeles may not be effective in Hong Kong.

Black and Porter investigated the validity of these two schools of thought by surveying U.S. managers working in Hong Kong, U.S. managers working in the United States, and Hong Kong managers working in Hong Kong. Their findings revealed some interesting differences. The U.S. managers in Hong Kong exhibited managerial behaviors similar to those of their counterparts back in the United States; however, Hong Kong managers had managerial behaviors different from either group of U.S. managers. Commenting on these results, the researchers noted:

This study . . . points to some important practical implications. It suggests that American firms and the practical school of thought may be mistaken in the assumption that a good manager in Los Angeles will necessarily do fine in Hong Kong or some other foreign country. It may be that because firms do not include in their selection criteria individual characteristics such as cognitive flexibility, cultural flexibility, degree of ethnocentricity, etc., they end up sending a number of individuals on international assignments who have a tendency to keep the same set of managerial behaviors they used in the U.S. and not adjust or adapt to the local norms and practices. Including the measurement of these characteristics in the selection process, as well as providing cross-cultural training before departure, may be a means of obtaining more effective adaptation of managerial behaviors and more effective performance in overseas assignments.

Certainly the study shows that simplistic assumptions about culture are erroneous and that what works in one country will not necessarily produce the desired results in another. If MNCs are going to manage effectively throughout the world, they are going to have to give more attention to training their people about intercultural differences.

Experienced executives report that the primary criterion for doing business in China is technical competence. For example, in the case of MNCs selling machinery, the Chinese want to know exactly how the machine works, what its capabilities are, and how repairs and maintenance must be handled. Sellers must be prepared to answer these questions in precise detail. This is why successful multinationals send only seasoned engineers and technical people to the PRC. They know that the questions to be answered will require both knowledge and experience, and young, fresh-out-of-school engineers will not be able to answer them.

A major cultural difference between the PRC and many Western countries is the issue of time. The Chinese tend to be punctual, so it is important that those who do business with them arrive on time, as discussed in Chapter 4. During meetings, such as those held when negotiating a contract, the Chinese may ask many questions and nod their assent at the answers. This nodding usually means that they understand or are being polite; it seldom means that they like what they are hearing and want to enter into a contract. For this reason, when dealing with the Chinese, one must keep in mind that patience is critically important. The Chinese will make a decision in their own good time, and it is common for outside businesspeople to make several trips to China before a deal is finally concluded. Moreover, not only are there numerous meetings, but sometimes these are unilaterally canceled at the last minute and rescheduled. This often tries the patience of outsiders and is inconvenient in terms of rearranging travel plans and other problems.

Another important dimension of Chinese culture is **guanxi,** which means "good connections."[32] In turn, these connections can result in such things as lower costs for

guanxi
In Chinese, it means "good connections."

doing business.[33] Yet guanxi goes beyond just lower costs. Yi and Ellis surveyed Hong Kong and PRC Chinese managers and found that both groups agreed that guanxi networking offered a number of potential benefits, including increased business, higher sales revenue, more sources of information, greater prospecting opportunities, and the facilitation of future transactions.[34] In practice, guanxi resembles nepotism, where individuals in authority make decisions on the basis of family ties or social connections rather than objective indices. Tung has reported that:

> In a survey of 2,000 Chinese from Shanghai and its surrounding rural community, 92% of the respondents confirmed that *guanxi* played a significant role in their daily lives. Furthermore, the younger generation tended to place greater emphasis on *guanxi*. In fact, *guanxi* has become more widespread in the recent past. . . . Most business practitioners who have experience in doing business with East Asians will readily agree that in order to succeed in these countries "who you know is more important than what you know." In other words, having connections with the appropriate individuals and authorities is often more crucial than having the right product and/or price.[35]

Additionally, outsiders doing business in China must be aware that Chinese people will typically argue that they have the guanxi to get a job done, when in reality they may or may not have the necessary connections.

In China, it is important to be a good listener. This may mean having to listen to the same stories about the great progress that has been made by the PRC over the past decade. The Chinese are very proud of their economic accomplishments and want to share these feelings with outsiders.

When dealing with the Chinese, one must realize they are a collective society in which people pride themselves on being members of a group. This is in sharp contrast to the situation in the United States and other Western countries, where individualism is highly prized. For this reason, one must never single out a Chinese and praise him or her for a particular quality, such as intelligence or kindness, because doing so may embarrass the individual in the presence of his or her peers. It is equally important to avoid using self-centered conversation, such as excessive use of the word "I," because it appears that the speaker is trying to single him- or herself out for special consideration.

The Chinese also are much less animated than Westerners. They avoid open displays of affection, do not slap each other on the back, and are more reticent, retiring, and reserved than North or South Americans. They do not appreciate loud, boisterous behavior, and when speaking to each other, they maintain a greater physical distance than is typical in the West.

Cultural highlights that affect doing business in China can be summarized and put into some specific guidelines as follows:

1. The Chinese place values and principles above money and expediency.[36]

2. Business meetings typically start with pleasantries such as tea and general conversation about the guest's trip to the country, local accommodations, and family. In most cases, the host already has been briefed on the background of the visitor.

3. When a meeting is ready to begin, the Chinese host will give the appropriate indication. Similarly, when the meeting is over, the host will indicate that it is time for the guest to leave.

4. Once the Chinese decide who and what are best, they tend to stick with these decisions. Therefore, they may be slow in formulating a plan of action, but once they get started, they make fairly good progress.

5. In negotiations, reciprocity is important. If the Chinese give concessions, they expect some in return. Additionally, it is common to find them slowing down negotiations to take advantage of Westerners desiring to conclude arrangements as quickly as possible. The objective of this tactic is to extract further concessions. Another common ploy used by the Chinese is to pressure the other party during final arrangements by suggesting that this counterpart

has broken the spirit of friendship in which the business relationship originally was established. Again, through this ploy, the Chinese are trying to
gain additional concessions.

6. Because negotiating can involve a loss of face, it is common to find Chinese
carrying out the whole process through intermediaries. This allows them to
convey their ideas without fear of embarrassment.[37]

7. During negotiations, it is important not to show excessive emotion of any kind.
Anger or frustration, for example, is viewed as antisocial and unseemly.

8. Negotiations should be viewed with a long-term perspective. Those who will do
best are the ones who realize they are investing in a long-term relationship.[38]

While these are the traditional behaviors of Chinese businesspeople, the transitioning
economy (see Chapter 1) has also caused a shift in business culture, which is beginning
to affect working professionals' private lives. Performance, which was once based on
effort, is now being evaluated from the angle of results as the country continues to maintain its flourishing profits. While traditional Chinese culture focused on family first,
financial and material well-being has become a top priority. This performance orientation
has increased stress and contributed to growing incidences of burnout, depression, substance abuse, and other ailments. Some U.S. companies have attempted to curb these
psychological ailments by offering counseling; however, this service is not as readily
accepted by the Chinese. Instead of bringing attention to the "counseling" aspect, firms
instead promote "workplace harmony" and "personal well-being services."[39] This suggests that while some aspects of Chinese culture are changing, international managers
must recognize the foundational culture of the country and try to deal with such issues
according to local beliefs.

Doing Business in Russia

As pointed out in Chapter 1, the Russian economy has experienced severe problems,[40]
and the risks of doing business there cannot be overstated.[41] At the same time, however,
by following certain guidelines, MNCs can begin to tap the potential opportunities. Here
are some suggestions for being successful in Russia:

1. Build personal relationships with partners. Business laws and contracts do
not mean as much in Russia as they do in the West. When there are contract
disputes, there is little protection for the aggrieved party because of the time
and effort needed to legally enforce the agreement. Detailed contracts can be
hammered out later on; in the beginning, all that counts is friendship.

2. Use local consultants. Because the rules of business have changed so much
in recent years, it pays to have a local Russian consultant working with the
company. Russian expatriates often are not up to date on what is going on
and, quite often, are not trusted by local businesspeople who have stayed in
the country. So the consultant should be someone who has been in Russia
all the time and understands the local business climate.

3. Consider business ethics. Ethical behavior in the United States is not always
the same as in Russia. For example, it is traditional in Russia to give gifts to
those with whom one wants to transact business, an approach that may be
regarded as bribery in the United States.

4. Be patient. In order to get something done in Russia, it often takes months
of waiting. Those who are in a hurry to make a quick deal are often sorely
disappointed.

5. Stress exclusivity. Russians like exclusive arrangements and often negotiate
with just one firm at a time. This is in contrast to Western businesspeople
who often "shop" their deals and may negotiate with a half-dozen firms at
the same time before settling on one.

6. Remember that personal relations are important. Russians like to do business face to face. So when they receive letters or faxes, they often put them on their desk but do not respond to them. They are waiting for the businessperson to contact them and set up a personal meeting.

7. Keep financial information personal. When Westerners enter into business dealings with partners, it is common for them to share financial information with these individuals and to expect the same from the latter. However, Russians wait until they know their partner well enough to feel comfortable before sharing financial data. Once trust is established, then this information is provided.

8. Research the company. In dealing effectively with Russian partners, it is helpful to get information about this company, its management hierarchy, and how it typically does business. This information helps ensure the chances for good relations because it gives the Western partner a basis for establishing a meaningful relationship.

9. Stress mutual gain. The Western idea of "win-win" in negotiations also works well in Russia. Potential partners want to know what they stand to gain from entering into the venture.

10. Clarify terminology. For-profit business deals are new in Russia, so the language of business is just getting transplanted there. As a result, it is important to double-check and make sure that the other party clearly understands the proposal, knows what is expected and when, and is agreeable to the deal.[42]

11. Be careful about compromising or settling things too quickly, because this is often seen as a sign of weakness. During the Soviet Union days, everything was complex, and so Russians are suspicious of anything that is conceded easily. If agreements are not reached after a while, a preferred tactic on their part is to display patience and then wait it out. However, they will abandon this approach if the other side shows great patience because they will realize that their negotiating tactic is useless.

12. Written contracts are not as binding to Russians as they are to Westerners. Like Asians, Russians view contracts as binding only if they continue to be mutually beneficial. One of the best ways of dealing with this is to be able to continually show them the benefits associated with sticking to the deal.[43]

These 12 steps can be critical to the success of a business venture in Russia. They require careful consideration of cultural factors, and it often takes a lot longer than initially anticipated. However, the benefits may be worth the wait. And when everything is completed, there is a final cultural tradition that should be observed: Fix and reinforce the final agreements with a nice dinner together and an invitation to the Russians to visit your country and see your facilities.[44]

Doing Business in India

In recent years, India has begun to attract the attention of large MNCs. Unsaturated consumer markets, coupled with cheap labor and production locations, have helped make India a desirable market for global firms.[45] The government continues to play an important role in this process, although recently many of the bureaucratic restrictions have been lifted as India works to attract foreign investment and raise its economic growth rate.[46] In addition, although most Indian businesspeople speak English, many of their values and beliefs are markedly different from those in the West. Thus, understanding Indian culture is critical to successfully doing business in India.

Shaking hands with male business associates is almost always an acceptable practice. U.S. businesspeople in India are considered equals, however, and the universal method of greeting an equal is to press one's palms together in front of the chest and say *namaste,* which means "greetings to you." Therefore, if a handshake appears to be improper, it always is safe to use *namaste.*

Western food typically is available in all good hotels. Most Indians do not drink alcoholic beverages, or if they do, they tend to prefer liquor and avoid the popular Western choice of beer, and many are vegetarians or eat chicken but not beef. Therefore, when foreign businesspeople entertain in India, the menu often is quite different from that back home. Moreover, when a local businessperson invites an expatriate for dinner at home, it is not necessary to bring a gift, although it is acceptable to do so. The host's wife and children usually will provide help from the kitchen to ensure that the guest is well treated, but they will not be at the table. If they are, it is common to wait until everyone has been seated and the host begins to eat or asks everyone to begin. During the meal, the host will ask the guest to have more food. This is done to ensure that the person does not go away hungry; however, once one has eaten enough, it is acceptable to politely refuse more food.

For Western businesspeople in India, shirt, trousers, tie, and suit are proper attire. In the southern part of India, where the climate is very hot, a light suit is preferable. In the north during the winter, a light sweater and jacket are a good choice. Indian businesspeople, on the other hand, often will wear local dress. In many cases, this includes a *dhoti,* which is a single piece of white cloth (about five yards long and three feet wide) that is passed around the waist up to half its length and then the other half is drawn between the legs and tucked at the waist. Long shirts are worn on the upper part of the body. In some locales, such as Punjab, Sikhs will wear turbans, and well-to-do Hindus sometimes will wear long coats like the Rajahs. This coat, known as a *sherwani,* is the dress recognized by the government for official and ceremonial wear. Foreign businesspeople are not expected to dress like locals, and in fact, many Indian businesspeople will dress like Europeans. Therefore, it is unnecessary to adopt local dress codes.

When doing business in India, one will find a number of other customs useful to know, such as:

1. It is important to be on time for meetings.
2. Personal questions should not be asked unless the other individual is a friend or close associate.
3. Titles are important, so people who are doctors or professors should be addressed accordingly.
4. Public displays of affection are considered to be inappropriate, so one should refrain from backslapping or touching others.
5. Beckoning is done with the palm turned down; pointing often is done with the chin.
6. When eating or accepting things, use the right hand because the left is considered to be unclean.
7. The *namaste* gesture can be used to greet people; it also is used to convey other messages, including a signal that one has had enough food.
8. Bargaining for goods and services is common; this contrasts with Western traditions, where bargaining might be considered rude or abrasive.[47]

Finally, it is important to remember that Indians are very tolerant of outsiders and understand that many are unfamiliar with local customs and procedures. Therefore, there is no need to make a phony attempt to conform to Indian cultural traditions. Making an effort to be polite and courteous is sufficient.[48]

Doing Business in France

Many in the United States believe that it is more difficult to get along with the French than with other Europeans. This feeling probably reflects the French culture, which is markedly different from that in the United States. In France, one's social class is very important, and these classes include the aristocracy, the upper bourgeoisie, the upper-middle bourgeoisie, the middle, the lower middle, and the lower. Social interactions are affected by class stereotypes, and during their lifetime, most French people do not encounter much change in social status. Unlike an American, who through hard work and success can move from the lowest economic strata to the highest, a successful French person might, at best, climb one or two rungs of the social ladder. Additionally, the French are very status conscious, and they like to provide signs of their status, such as knowledge of literature and the arts; a well-designed, tastefully decorated house; and a high level of education.

The French also tend to be friendly, humorous, and sardonic (sarcastic), in contrast to Americans, for example, who seldom are sardonic. The French may admire or be fascinated with people who disagree with them; in contrast, Americans are more attracted to those who agree with them. As a result, the French are accustomed to conflict and during negotiations accept that some positions are irreconcilable and must be accepted as such. Americans, on the other hand, believe that conflicts can be resolved and that if both parties make an extra effort and have a spirit of compromise, there will be no irreconcilable differences. Moreover, the French often determine a person's trustworthiness based on his or her firsthand evaluation of the individual's character. This is in marked contrast to Americans, who tend to evaluate a person's trustworthiness based on past achievements and other people's evaluations of this person.

In the workplace, many French people are not motivated by competition or the desire to emulate fellow workers. They often are accused of not having as intense a work ethic as, for example, Americans or Asians. Many French workers frown on overtime, and statistics show that on average, they have the longest vacations in the world (four to five weeks annually). On the other hand, few would disagree that they work extremely hard in their regularly scheduled time and have a reputation for high productivity. Part of this reputation results from the French tradition of craftsmanship. Part of it also is accounted for by a large percentage of the workforce being employed in small, independent businesses, where there is widespread respect for a job well done.

Most French organizations tend to be highly centralized and have rigid structures. As a result, it usually takes longer to carry out decisions. Because this arrangement is quite different from the more decentralized, flattened organizations in the United States, both middle- and lower-level U.S. expatriate managers who work in French subsidiaries often find bureaucratic red tape a source of considerable frustration. There also are marked differences at the upper levels of management. In French companies, top managers have far more authority than their U.S. counterparts, and they are less accountable for their actions. While top-level U.S. executives must continually defend their decisions to the CEO or board of directors, French executives are challenged only if the company has poor performance. As a result, those who have studied French management find that they take a more autocratic approach.[49]

In countries such as the United States, a great deal of motivation is derived from professional accomplishment. Americans realize there is limited job and social security in their country, so it is up to them to work hard and ensure their future. The French do not have the same view. While they admire Americans' industriousness and devotion to work, they believe that quality of life is what really matters. As a result, they attach a great deal of importance to leisure time, and many are unwilling to sacrifice the enjoyment of life for dedication to work.

The values and beliefs discussed here help to explain why French culture is so different from that in other countries. Some of the sharp contrasts with the United States, for example, provide insights regarding the difficulties of doing business in France. Additional cultural characteristics, such as the following, also help explain the difficulties that outsiders may encounter in France:

1. When shaking hands with a French person, use a quick shake with some pressure in the grip. A firm, pumping handshake, which is so common in the United States, is considered to be uncultured.

2. It is extremely important to be on time for meetings and social occasions. Being "fashionably late" is frowned on.

3. During a meal, it is acceptable to engage in pleasant conversation, but personal questions and the subject of money are never brought up.

4. Great importance is placed on neatness and taste. Therefore, visiting businesspeople should try very hard to be cultured and sophisticated.[50]

5. The French tend to be suspicious of early friendliness in the discussion and dislike first names, taking off jackets, or disclosure of personal or family details.

6. In negotiations the French try to find out what all of the other side's aims and demands are at the beginning, but they reveal their own hand only late in the negotiations.

7. The French do not like being rushed into making a decision, and they rarely make important decisions inside the meeting. In fact, the person who is ultimately responsible for making the decision is often not present.

8. The French tend to be very precise and logical in their approach to things, and will often not make concessions in negotiations unless their logic has been defeated. If a deadlock results, unlike Americans, who will try to break the impasse by suggesting a series of compromises by both sides, the French tend to remain firm and simply restate their position.[51]

Doing Business in Brazil

Brazil is considered a Latin American country, but it is important to highlight this nation since some characteristics make it markedly different to manage as compared to other Latin American countries.[52] Brazil was originally colonized by Portugal, and remained affiliated with its parent country until 1865. Even though today Brazil is extremely multicultural, the country still demonstrates many attributes derived from its Portuguese heritage, including its official language. For example, the Brazilian economy was once completely centrally controlled like many other Latin American countries, yet was motivated by such Portuguese influences as flexibility, tolerance, and commercialism.[53] This may be a significant reason behind its successful economic emergence.

Brazilians have a relaxed work ethic, often respecting those who inherit wealth and have strong familial roots over those seeking entrepreneurial opportunities. They view time in a very relaxed manner, so punctuality is not a strong suit in this country. Overall, the people are very good-natured and tend to avoid confrontation but seek out risky endeavors. Appearances in some realms are held in high regard, which can sometimes confuse managers attempting to form business relationships.

Here are some factors to consider when pursuing business in Brazil:

1. Physical contact is acceptable as a form of communication. Brazilians tend to stand very close to others when having a conversation, and will touch the person's back, arm, or elbow as a greeting or sign of respect.

2. Face-to-face interaction is preferred as a way to communicate, so avoid simply e-mailing or calling. Do not be surprised if meetings begin anywhere from 10 to 30 minutes after the scheduled time, since Brazilians are not governed by the clock. Greet with a pleasant demeanor, and accept any offering of *cafezinho,* or small cups of Brazilian coffee, as it is one indication of a relaxed, social setting.

3. Brazilians tend not to trust others, so be sure to form a strong relationship before bringing up business issues. Be yourself, and be honest, since rigid exteriors or putting on a show is not revered. Close relationships are extremely important, since they will do anything for friends, hence the

expression, "For friends, everything. For enemies, the law." Showing interest in their personal and professional life is greatly appreciated, especially if international representatives speak some Portuguese.

4. Appearance is very important, as it will reflect both you and your company. Be sure to have polished shoes. Men should wear conservative dark suits, shirts, and ties. Women should dress nicely, but avoid too conservative or formal attire. Think fashion. Brazilian managers often wonder, for example, if Americans make so much money, why do they dress like they are poor?

5. Patience is key. Many processes are long and drawn out, including negotiations. Expressing frustration or impatience and attempting to speed up procedures may lose the deal. It is worth waiting out, as Brazilians will be very committed and loyal once an agreement is reached.

6. The slow processes and relaxed atmosphere do not imply that it is acceptable to be ill-prepared. Presentations should be informative and expressive, as Brazilians respond to such emotional cues. Consistency is important. Be prepared to state your case multiple times. It is common for Brazilians to bring a lot of people to attend negotiations, mostly to observe and learn. Subsequent meetings may include members of higher management, requiring a rehashing of information.[54]

Doing Business in Arab Countries

The intense media attention given to the Iraq War, terrorist actions, and continuing conflicts in the Middle East have pointed out that Arab cultures are distinctly different from Anglo cultures.[55] Americans often find it extremely hard to do business in Arab countries, and a number of Arab cultural characteristics can be cited for this difficulty.

One is the Arab view of time. In the United States, it is common to use the cliché, "Time is money." In Arab countries, a favorite expression is *Bukra insha Allah,* which means "Tomorrow if God wills," an expression that explains the Arabs' fatalistic approach to time. Arabs believe that Allah controls time, in contrast to Westerners, who believe that they control their own time. As a result, if Arabs commit themselves to a date in the future and fail to show up, they feel no guilt or concern because they believe they have no control over time in the first place.

A word of caution on overgeneralizing is needed here and in all the examples used throughout this chapter's discussion of cultural characteristics. There are many Arabs who are very particular about promises and appointments. There are also many Arabs who are very proactive and not fatalistic. The point is that there are always exceptions, and stereotyping in cross-cultural dealings is unwarranted.

Another Arab cultural belief that generally holds is that destiny depends more on the will of a supreme being than on the behavior of individuals. A higher power dictates the outcome of important events, so individual action is of little consequence. This thinking affects not only Arabs' aspirations but also their motivation. Also of importance is that the status of Arabs largely is determined by family position and social contact and connections, not necessarily by their own accomplishments. This view helps to explain why some Middle Easterners take great satisfaction in appearing to be helpless. In fact, helplessness can be used as a source of power, for in this area of the world, the strong are resented and the weak compensated. Here is an example:

> In one Arab country, several public administrators of equal rank would take turns meeting in each other's offices for their weekly conferences, and the host would serve as chairman. After several months, one of these men had a mild heart attack. Upon his recovery, it was decided to hold the meetings only in his office, in order not to inconvenience him. From then on, the man who had the heart attack became the permanent chairman of the conference. This individual appeared more helpless than the others, and his helplessness enabled him to increase his power.[56]

This approach is quite different from that in the United States, where the strong tend to be compensated and rewarded. If a person was ill, such as in this example, the individual would be relieved of this responsibility until he or she had regained full health. In the interim, the rest of the group would go on without the sick person, and he or she may lose power.

Another important cultural contrast between Arabs and Americans is that of emotion and logic. Arabs often act based on emotion; in contrast, those in an Anglo culture are taught to act on logic. Many Arabs live in unstable environments where things change constantly, so they do not develop trusting relationships with others. Americans, on the other hand, live in a much more predictable environment and develop trusting relationships with others.

Arabs also make wide use of elaborate and ritualized forms of greetings and leave-takings. A businessperson may wait past the assigned meeting time before being admitted to an Arab's office. Once there, the individual may find a host of others present; this situation is unlike the typical one-on-one meetings that are so common in the United States. Moreover, during the meeting, there may be continuous interruptions, visitors may arrive and begin talking to the host, and messengers may come in and go out on a regular basis. The businessperson is expected to take all this activity as perfectly normal and remain composed and ready to continue discussions as soon as the host is prepared to do so.

Business meetings typically conclude with an offer of coffee or tea. This is a sign that the meeting is over and that future meetings, if there are to be any, should now be arranged.

Unlike the case in many other countries, titles are not in general use on the Arabian Peninsula, except in the case of royal families, ministers, and high-level military officers. Additionally, initial meetings typically are used to get to know the other party. Business-related discussions may not occur until the third or fourth meeting. Also, in contrast to the common perception among many Western businesspeople who have never been to an Arab country, it is not necessary to bring the other party a gift. If this is done, however, it should be a modest gift. A good example is a novelty or souvenir item from the visitor's home country.

Arabs attach a great deal of importance to status and rank. When meeting with them, one should pay deference to the senior person first. It also is important never to criticize or berate anyone publicly. This causes the individual to lose face, and the same is true for the person who makes these comments. Mutual respect is required at all times.

Other useful guidelines for doing business in Arab cultures include:

1. It is important never to display feelings of superiority, because this makes the other party feel inferior. No matter how well someone does something, the individual should let the action speak for itself and not brag or put on a show of self-importance.

2. One should not take credit for joint efforts. A great deal of what is accomplished is a result of group work, and to indicate that one accomplished something alone is a mistake.

3. Much of what gets done is a result of going through administrative channels in the country. It often is difficult to sidestep a lot of this red tape, and efforts to do so can be regarded as disrespect for legal and governmental institutions.

4. Connections are extremely important in conducting business. Well-connected businesspeople can get things done much faster than their counterparts who do not know the ins and outs of the system.

5. Patience is critical to the success of business transactions. This time consideration should be built into all negotiations, thus preventing one from giving away too much in an effort to reach a quick settlement.

6. Important decisions usually are made in person, not by correspondence or telephone. This is why an MNC's personal presence often is a prerequisite for success in the Arab world. Additionally, while there may be many people

who provide input on the final decision, the ultimate power rests with the person at the top, and this individual will rely heavily on personal impressions, trust, and rapport.[57]

The World of *BusinessWeek*—Revisited

As the *BusinessWeek* article at the beginning of the chapter demonstrates, doing business in different cultures presents MNCs with a variety of challenges. Television is not managed in the same manner in Arab countries as it is in the United States, and media content has historically been quite different. There are related political differences which also reflect cultural distinctions. Viacom is attempting to be responsive to local demands without offending national cultural traditions and mores. As we saw in Chapter 4, the Arabic and U.S. cultures differ on many dimensions, which may constrain Viacom's growth. Viacom must carefully consider these differences and incorporate those considerations into when and how it introduces MTV and other programming in the Arab world.

Now that you have read this chapter, you should have a good understanding of the importance and difficulties of managing across cultures. Using this knowledge as a platform, answer the following questions: (1) In what ways could Viacom's research with regard to television programming (i.e., asking consumers directly) help its market entry and management strategy? Do you think it will be successful with current management strategies in the Arab television industry? (2) How do the cultural differences and similarities play a role in introducing MTV to the Arab culture? (3) How would you characterize Viacom's approach to moving into this market in terms of the four basic predispositions?

SUMMARY OF KEY POINTS

1. One major problem facing MNCs is that they sometimes attempt to manage across cultures in ways similar to those of their home country. MNC dispositions toward managing across cultures can be characterized as (1) ethnocentric, (2) polycentric, (3) regiocentric, and (4) geocentric. These different approaches shape how companies adapt and adjust to cultural pressures around the world.

2. One major challenge when dealing with cross-cultural problems is that of overcoming parochialism and simplification. Parochialism is the tendency to view the world through one's own eyes and perspectives. Simplification is the process of exhibiting the same orientation toward different cultural groups. Another problem is that of doing things the same way in foreign markets as they are done in domestic markets. Research shows that in some cases, this approach can be effective; however, effective cross-cultural manage-

ment more commonly requires approaches different than those used at home. One area where this is particularly evident is human resource management. Recruitment, selection, training, and compensation often are carried out in different ways in different countries, and what works in the United States may have limited value in other countries and geographic regions.

3. Doing business in various parts of the world requires the recognition and understanding of cultural differences. Some of these differences revolve around the importance the society assigns to time, status, control of decision making, personal accomplishment, and work itself. These types of cultural differences help to explain why effective managers in China or Russia often are quite different from those in France, and why a successful style in the United States will not be ideal in Arab countries.

KEY TERMS

ethnocentric predisposition, *129*

geocentric predisposition, *129*

globalization imperative, *129*

guanxi, *141*

parochialism, *133*

polycentric predisposition, *129*

regiocentric predisposition, *129*

simplification, *134*

REVIEW AND DISCUSSION QUESTIONS

1. Define the four basic predispositions MNCs have toward their international operations.

2. If a locally based manufacturing firm with sales of $350 million decided to enter the EU market by setting up operations in France, which orientation would be the most effective: ethnocentric, polycentric, regiocentric, or geocentric? Why? Explain your choice.

3. In what way are parochialism and simplification barriers to effective cross-cultural management? In each case, give an example.

4. Many MNCs would like to do business overseas in the same way that they do business domestically. Do research findings show that any approaches that work well in the United States also work well in other cultures? If so, identify and describe two.

5. In most cases, local managerial approaches must be modified for doing business overseas. What are three specific examples that support this statement? Be complete in your answer.

6. What are some categories of cultural differences that help make one country or region of the world different from another? In each case, describe the value or norm and explain how it would result in different behavior in two or more countries. If you like, use the countries discussed in this chapter as your point of reference.

INTERNET EXERCISE: SONY'S APPROACH

Sony is a multinational corporation that sells a wide variety of goods in the international marketplace. These range from electronics to online games to music—and the Japanese MNC is even in the entertainment business (Sony Pictures Entertainment), producing offerings for both the big screen as well as for television. Visit the MNC's Web site at **www.sony.com**, and read about some of the latest developments in which the company is engaged. Pay close attention to its new offerings in the areas of electronics, television shows, movies, music, and online games. Then answer these three questions: (1) What type of cultural challenges does Sony face when it attempts to market its products worldwide? Is demand universal for all these offerings, or is there a "national responsiveness/globalization" challenge, as discussed in the chapter, that must be addressed? (2) Investigate the Sony credit card that the company is now offering online. Is this a product that will have worldwide appeal, or is it more likely to be restricted to more economically advanced countries? (3) In managing its far-flung enterprise, what are two cultural challenges that the company is likely to face and what will it need to do to respond to these?

Mexico

Located directly south of the United States, Mexico covers an area of 756,000 square miles. It is the third-largest country in Latin America and the thirteenth-largest in the world. The most recent estimates place the population at around 107 million, and this number is increasing at a rate of about 1.4 percent annually. As a result, today Mexico is one of the "youngest" countries in the world. Approximately 55 percent of the population is under the age of 20, while a mere 4 percent is 65 years of age or older.

Today, even though the economy is uncertain as in the rest of the world, Mexico has made itself attractive for foreign investment. Trade agreements with the United States and Canada (NAFTA), the EU, Japan, and dozens of Latin American countries have begun to fully integrate the Mexican economy into the global trading system. Multinationals in a wide variety of industries, from computers to electronics and from pharmaceuticals to manufacturing, have invested billions of dollars in the country. Telefonica, the giant Spanish telecommunications firm, is putting together a wireless network across Latin America, and Mexico is one of the countries that it has targeted for investment. Meanwhile, manufacturers not only from the United States but also from Asia to Europe have helped sustain Mexico's booming maquiladora assembly industry. By the turn of the century over 1.2 million people were employed in this industry, including 600,000 in the two border states of Baja California and Chihuahua.

Thomson SA, the French consumer electronics firm, has three plants in the border states that make export TVs and digital decoder boxes. And like a growing number of MNCs located in Mexico, the firm is now moving away from importing parts and materials from outside and producing everything within the country. One reason for this move is that under the terms of the North American Free Trade Agreement only parts and materials originating in one of the three NAFTA trading partners are now allowed to enter the processing zones duty-free. Anything originating outside these three countries is subject to tariffs of as much as 25 percent. So the French MNC Thomson is building a picture-tube factory in Baja California so that it will no longer have to import dutiable tubes from Italy. In many cases, imported items from the European Union, however, are allowed to enter duty-free because in 1999 Mexico signed a free-trade agreement with the EU. As a result, a host of firms, including Philips Electronics and Siemens, poured large amounts of investment into the country. At the same time Mexico also has begun negotiating another free-trade pact with the four Nordic countries, raising the likelihood that firms such as Nokia, Ericsson, and Saab-Scania will also invest heavily in the country.

While many European MNCs are now investing in Mexico, the United States still remains the largest investor. Over 60 percent of all outside investment is by U.S. firms. Asian companies, in particular Japanese MNCs, also have large holdings in the country, although these firms have been scaling back in recent years because of the import duties and the fact that Mexican labor costs are beginning to rise, thus making it more cost-effective to produce some types of goods in Asia and export them to North America. The largest investments in Mexico are in the industrial sector (around 60 percent of the total) and services (around 30 percent).

One of the major benefits of locating in Mexico is the highly skilled labor force that can be hired at fairly low wages when compared with those paid elsewhere, especially in the United States. Additionally, manufacturing firms that have located there report high productivity growth rates and quality performance. A study by the Massachusetts Institute of Technology on auto assembly plants in Canada, the United States, and Mexico reported that Mexican plants performed well. Another by J. D. Power and Associates noted that Ford Motor's Hermisillo plant was the best in all of North America. Computer and electronic firms are also finding Mexico to be an excellent choice for new expansion plants. Intel, for example, invested approximately $1.5 billion to upgrade plants in 2007. The technology industry must be very innovative to stay competitive. Intel operates out of many countries, but an investment of this size shows that Mexico is extremely valuable, and operations here will continue for years to come.
www.mexicool.com

Questions

1. Why would multinationals be interested in setting up operations in Mexico? Give two reasons.

2. Would cultural differences be a major stumbling block for U.S. MNCs doing business in Mexico? For European firms? For Japanese firms? Explain your answer.

3. Why might MNCs be interested in studying the organizational culture in Mexican firms before deciding whether to locate there? Explain your logic.

Beijing, Here We Come!

A large toy company located in Canada is considering a business arrangement with the government of China (PRC). Although company representatives have not yet visited the PRC, the president of the firm recently met with their representatives in Ottawa and discussed the business proposition. The Canadian CEO learned that the PRC government would be quite happy to study the proposal, and the company's plan would be given a final decision within 90 days of receipt. The toy company now is putting together a detailed proposal and scheduling an on-site visit.

The Canadian firm would like to have the mainland Chinese manufacture a wide variety of toys for sale in Asia as well as in Europe and North America. Production of these toys requires a large amount of labor time, and because the PRC is reputed to have one of the largest and least expensive workforces in the world, the company believes that it can maximize profit by having the work done there. For the past five years, the company has had its toys produced in Taiwan. Costs there have been escalating recently, however, and because 45 percent of the production expense goes for labor, the company is convinced that it will soon be priced out of the market if it does not find another source.

The company president and three officers plan on going to Beijing next month to talk with government officials. They would like to sign a five-year agreement with a price that will not increase by more than 2 percent annually. Production operations then will be turned over to the mainland Chinese, who will have a free hand in manufacturing the goods.

The contract with the Taiwanese firm runs out in 90 days. The company already has contacted this firm, and the latter understands that its Canadian partner plans to terminate the arrangement. One major problem is that if it cannot find another supplier soon, it will have to go back to the Taiwanese firm for at least two more years. The contract stipulates that the agreement can be extended for another 24 months if the Canadian firm makes such a request; however, this must be done within 30 days of expiration of the contract. This is not an alternative that appeals to the Canadians, but they feel they will have to take it if they cannot reach an agreement with the mainland Chinese.

Questions

1. What is the likelihood that the Canadians will be able to reach an agreement with the mainland Chinese and not have to go back to their Taiwanese supplier? Explain.

2. Are the Canadians making a strategically wise decision in letting the Chinese from the PRC handle all the manufacturing, or should they insist on getting more actively involved in the production process? Defend your answer.

3. What specific cultural suggestions would you make to the Canadians regarding how to do business with the mainland Chinese?

Chapter 6

ORGANIZATIONAL CULTURES AND DIVERSITY

OBJECTIVES OF THE CHAPTER

The previous two chapters focused on national cultures. The overriding objective of this chapter is to examine the interaction of national culture (diversity) and organizational cultures and to discuss ways in which MNCs can manage the often inherent conflicts between national and organizational cultures. Many times, the cultural values and resulting behaviors that are common in a particular country are not the same as those in another. To be successful, MNCs must balance and integrate the national cultures of the countries in which they do business with their own organizational culture. Employee relations, which includes how organizational culture responds to national culture or diversity, deals with internal structures and defines how the company manages. Customer relations, associated with how national culture reacts to organizational cultures, reflects how the local community views the company from a customer service and employee satisfaction perspective.

Although the field of international management has long recognized the impact of national cultures, only recently has attention been given to the importance of managing organizational cultures and diversity. This chapter first examines common organizational cultures that exist in MNCs, and then presents and analyzes ways in which multiculturalism and diversity are being addressed by the best, world-class multinationals. The specific objectives of this chapter are:

1. **DEFINE** exactly what is meant by *organizational culture,* and discuss the interaction of national and MNC cultures.

2. **IDENTIFY** the four most common categories of organizational culture that have been found through research, and discuss the characteristics of each.

3. **PROVIDE** an overview of the nature and degree of multiculturalism and diversity in today's MNCs.

4. **DISCUSS** common guidelines and principles that are used in building multicultural effectiveness at the team and the organizational levels.

The World of *BusinessWeek*

BusinessWeek

BMW's Dream Factory

Sharing the Wealth, Listening to Even the Lowest-Ranking Workers, and Rewarding Risk Have Paid Off Big Time

The car looks like the victim of some mad scientist's experiment gone awry. Inside a research lab in Munich, a BMW 5 Series sedan is splayed open, with electronic gadgets and wires spewing in all directions. The project: an onboard computer that will recognize you, then seek out information you want and entertainment you love. While you sleep, your BMW will scour the Net—via Wi-Fi and other connections—collecting, say, 15 minutes of new jazz followed by a 10-minute podcast on the energy industry. It may sound far-fetched, but for BMW's research wizards it's yet another way to woo customers by personalizing cars. This intelligent machine will grow to know you better every day, constantly learning what you like by monitoring your choices. The brains of the system might even tag along with you on a business trip in the form of a "smart card," instructing the Bimmer you rent in Beijing to load up your daily fix of news and music. When Hans-Joerg Vögel, the 38-year-old project chief, hops in the car's front seat and fires it up, his excitement is palpable. Launching into a riff on the wonders of melding the virtual world with the nuts and bolts of an automobile, Vögel says the next generation of BMW 5 Series and 7 Series sedans will be the most Net-savvy cars on the road. And if he's right, it'll be because Vögel had the vision to see the importance of the technology and the gumption to build it so everyone at the automaker could recognize its potential. "We are encouraged to make decisions on our own and defend them," says Vögel. "Risk-taking is part of the job."

Vögel's project is only a tiny part of BMW's vast innovation machine. Just about everyone working for the Bavarian automaker—from the factory floor to the design studios to the marketing department—is encouraged to speak out. Ideas bubble up freely, and there is never a penalty for proposing a new way of doing things, no matter how outlandish. BMW, says Ulrich Steger, a professor of management at the International Institute for Management Development in Lausanne, Switzerland, is "a fine-tuned learning system."

True Believers

That's no small accomplishment, and it has fueled BMW's growth over the past decade from a boutique European automaker to a global leader in premium cars. Although BMW, with $59.2 billion in sales last year, is much smaller than its American rivals, the U.S. auto giants could still learn a thing or two from the Bavarians. Detroit's rigid and bloated bureaucracies are slow to respond to competitive threats and market trends, while BMW's management structure is flat, flexible, entrepreneurial—and fast. That explains why, at the very moment GM and Ford appear to be in free fall, BMW is more robust than ever. The company has become the industry benchmark for high-performance premium cars, customized production, and savvy brand management, making it the envy of Mercedes-Benz, Audi, and Lexus and the subject of Harvard Business School case studies. Even mighty Toyota Motor Corp. regularly dispatches engineers to BMW's factories to see how the company cranks out 1.3 million customized cars a year.

Few companies have been as consistent at producing an ever-changing product line, with near-flawless quality, that consumers crave. BMW has redefined luxury design with its 7 Series, created a mania for its Mini, and maintained some of the widest margins in the industry. A sporty four-wheel-drive coupe and a svelte minivan called the Luxury Sport Cruiser are slated to roll off the production line in 2008. Those models promise to continue BMW's run of cool cars under its new chief executive, Norbert Reithofer, who took over in September. (His predecessor, Helmut Panke, stepped down upon reaching the mandatory retirement age of 60.) Says Reithofer: "We push change through the organization to ensure its strength. There are always better solutions."

Virtually everyone at BMW is expected to help find those solutions. When demand for the 1 Series compact soared, plant manager Peter Claussen volunteered to temporarily use his brand new factory—which had been designed for the 3 Series—to crank out 5,000 of the compacts, and he quickly figured out how to do it while maintaining all-important quality. Last year line workers in Munich suggested adding a smaller diesel engine in the 5 Series, arguing that it would have enough oomph to handle like a Bimmer and be a big seller among those on a tighter budget. They were right. And Panke once insisted that all six members of the management board take an advanced driving course so they would have a better feel for BMW cars.

Much of BMW's success stems from an entrepreneurial culture that's rare in corporate Germany, where management is usually top-down and the gulf between workers and managers is vast. BMW's 106,000 employees have become a nimble network of true believers with few hierarchical barriers to hinder innovation. From the moment they set foot inside the company, workers are inculcated with a sense of place, history, and mission. Individuals from all strata of the corporation work elbow to elbow, creating informal networks where they can hatch even the most unorthodox ideas for making better Bimmers or boosting profits. The average BMW buyer may not know it, but when he slides behind the wheel, he is driving a machine born of thousands of impromptu brainstorming sessions. BMW, in fact, might just be the chattiest auto company ever. "The difference at BMW is that [managers] don't think we have all the right answers," says Claussen, manager of the company's new Leipzig factory, a 21st century cathedral of light and air designed by avant garde architect Zaha M. Hadid. "Our job is to ask the right questions."

It may sound trite, but it sure seems to work. Last year the company sprinted past its stumbling archrival, Mercedes-Benz, in global sales of its BMWs, Minis, and Rolls-Royces. (The German company bought the Rolls name in 1999.) More impressive, BMW's 8.1% operating margins make the automaker one of the most profitable in the industry. In the first half of 2006, BMW's sales rose 10.2%, to $32 billion, while pretax earnings jumped 44.5%, to $3.2 billion, despite a strong euro and punishing increases in raw material costs.

That's not to say this freewheeling idea factory hasn't made its share of blunders over the years. In 2001, BMW alienated customers with its iDrive control system. The device was designed to help drivers quickly move through hundreds of information and entertainment functions with a single knob, but it proved incomprehensible to many buyers. That misstep could seem minor, though, if BMW were to fail to artfully navigate the challenges ahead. Rival Audi is narrowing the gap with BMW in Europe by churning out a new generation of stylish, high-performance cars that have topped consumer polls. Toyota's Lexus also has BMW in its sights as it makes a move to gain in Europe with sportier, better-handling cars. "We will be challenged—no question," says Reithofer. "We have to take Lexus seriously."

A profit squeeze could just as easily trip up the company in the eyes of investors. To prove he has the right stuff, Reithofer is going to have to boost margins even as the cost of materials soars. Down the line the high price of oil and concerns about global warming could make "the ultimate driving machine" a lot less appealing when compared with gas-sipping, eco-friendly cars. The premium market "means extravagance by definition," something consumers may start to reject, says Garel Rhys, a professor of automotive economics at Cardiff University in Wales. Yet BMW's greatest danger could be its own growth and success. Says Ralf Kalmbach, a partner at Munich management consultant Roland Berger: "Losing its culture to sheer size is a major risk."

In BMW's favor is an enduring sense that things can go badly wrong. New hires quickly learn that the BMW world as they know it began in 1959. That's when the company nearly went bankrupt and was just a step away from being acquired by Mercedes. That long-ago trauma remains the pivotal moment in BMW folklore. "We never forget 1959," says Reithofer. "It's in our genes, and it drives our performance." If it weren't for a bailout by Germany's wealthy Quandt family—still the controlling shareholder, with a 46.6% stake—and a pact with labor to keep the company afloat, BMW wouldn't exist today. "Near-death experiences are very healthy for companies," says David Cole, a partner at the Center for Automotive Research in Ann Arbor, Michigan "BMW has been running scared for years."

The story of 1959 is told and retold at each orientation of new plant workers. Works Council Chief Manfred Schloch, a 26-year veteran, holds up old, grainy black-and-white photos of two models from the 1950s. The big one was too pricey for a struggling postwar Germany. The other, a tiny two-seater, looked like a toy and was too small to be practical, even by the standards of that era. The company badly misjudged the market, he says. As if handling an ancient, sacred parchment, Schloch pulls out a yellowed, typewritten 1959 plan for turning the company around with a new class of sporty sedans. Schloch then hands out photos of Herbert Quandt and the labor leader of the period, Kurt Golda. "I explain how we rebuilt the company with Quandt's money and the power of the workforce," says Schloch. "And I tell them that's the way it works today, too."

BMW's Keys to Getting the Most out of Its Workforce

DEEP-SIX THE EGOS Rigorously screen new hires for their ability to thrive as part of a team. Promote young talent but hold back perks until they've shown their stuff.

BUILD A SHARED MYTHOLOGY New hires learn about 1959, when BMW nearly went bankrupt. Its recovery remains the centerpiece of company lore, inspiring a deep commitment to innovation.

WORSHIP THE NETWORK Teams from across the company work elbow to elbow in open, airy spaces, helping them to create informal networks where they hatch ideas quickly and resolve disagreements.

WORK OUTSIDE THE SYSTEM The sleek Z4 coupe exists because a young designer's doodle inspired a team to push his concept even though management had already killed the program.

KEEP THE DOOR OPEN From the factory floor to the executive suite, everyone is encouraged to speak out. Ideas bubble up freely, and even the craziest proposals will get a hearing.

Happy Workers, Better Cars

BMW derives much of its strength from an almost unparalleled labor harmony rooted in that long-ago pact. In 1972, years before the rest of Europe Inc. began to think about pay for performance, the company cut workers in on its profits. It set up a plan that distributes as much as one and a half months' extra pay at the end of the year, provided BMW meets financial targets. In return, the workforce is hyperflexible. When a plant is introducing new technology or needs a volume boost, it's not uncommon for workers from other BMW factories to move into temporary housing far from home for months and put in long hours on the line. Union bosses have made it easy for BMW to quickly adjust output to meet demand. Without paying overtime, the company can crank up production to as much as 140 hours a week or scale it back to as little as 60 hours. The system lets the company provide unprecedented job security, and no one at BMW can remember any layoffs—ever. Since 2000, BMW has hired 12,000 new workers even as General Motors Corp. and Ford Motor Co. have slashed tens of thousands of jobs.

That helps explain why landing a job at BMW is to many Germans what getting into Harvard is for American high school students. The company's human resources department receives more than 200,000 applications annually. Those who make it to an interview undergo elaborate daylong drills in teams that screen out big egos. For the lucky few who are hired, a Darwinian test of survival ensues. BMW promotes talented managers rapidly and provides little training along the way, forcing them to reach out to others to learn the ropes. With no one to coach them in a new job, managers are forced to stay humble and work closely with subordinates and their peers, minimizing traditional corporate turf battles. Anyone who wants to push an innovative new idea learns the key to success fast. "You can go into fighting mode or you can ask permission and get everyone to support you," says Stefan Krause, BMW's 44-year-old chief financial officer. "If you do it without building ties, you will be blocked."

That BMW's spectacular Leipzig factory was ever built is a testament to the power of such ties. When plant manager Claussen first proposed a competition to lure top architects, headquarters was aghast. "People said to me, 'What's wrong with these guys in Leipzig?'" recalls Krause. "'We don't need beautiful buildings, we need productive buildings.'" But Claussen convinced Krause and others that the unconventional approach wouldn't just produce a pretty factory but one whose open, airy spaces would improve communications between line workers and managers and create an environment that helps the company build cars better.

Even before Claussen began pushing his architectural vision, others were busy designing the inner workings of the plant. Newly minted engineer Jan Knau was only 27 in 2000 when he was asked to come up with a flexible assembly line for the factory. Knau, then just a junior associate, rang up BMW's top 15 assembly engineers, inviting them to a two-day workshop at a BMW retreat near the Austrian Alps. The calls paid off. After a series of marathon sessions that included discussions of every facet of the ideal assembly line, Knau sketched a design with four "fingers," or branches, off the main spine. The branches could extend to add equipment needed to build new models, making it possible to keep giant robots along the main line in place rather than moving them for each production change, an expensive and time-consuming process.

Leipzig opened in May 2005, joining Claussen's vision of teamwork enhanced through design to Knau's smart engineering concepts. With pillars of sunlight streaming through soaring glass walls, architect Hadid's design looks more like an art museum than a car factory. Open workspaces cascade over two floors like a waterfall. Unfinished car bodies move along a track, bathed in ethereal blue light, that runs above offices and a smart-looking, open cafeteria. If the parade of half-finished cars slows, engineers feel the pulse of the plant change and can quickly investigate the problem. And weekly quality audits—in a plaza workers pass on their way to lunch—ensure that everyone is quickly aware of any production snafus. The combination of togetherness and openness sparks impromptu encounters among line workers, logistics engineers, and quality experts. "They meet simply because their paths cross naturally," says Knau. "And they say, 'Ah, glad I ran into you, I have an idea.'"

The flexibility of BMW's factories allows for a dizzying choice of variations on basic models. At Leipzig, for instance, parts ranging from dashboards and seats to axles and front ends snake onto overhead conveyer belts to be lowered into the assembly line in precise sequence according to customers' orders. BMW buyers can select everything from engine type to the color of the gear-shift box to a seemingly limitless number of interior trims—and then change their mind and order a completely different configuration as little as five days before production begins. Customers love it. They request some 170,000 changes a month in their orders, mostly higher-priced options such as a bigger engine or a more luxurious interior. There are so many choices that line workers assemble exactly the same car only about once every nine months.

That kind of individualization would swamp most automakers with budget-busting complexity. But BMW has emerged as a sort of anti-Toyota. One excels in simplifying automaking. The other excels in mastering complexity and tailoring cars to customers' tastes. That's what differentiates BMW from Lexus and the rest of the premium pack. "BMW drivers never change to other brands," says Yoichi Tomihara, president of Toyota Deutschland, who concedes that Toyota lags behind BMW in the sort of customization that creates emotional appeal.

Bottom-up ideas help keep BMW's new models fresh and edgy year after year. Young designers in various company studios from Munich headquarters to DesignWorks in Los Angeles are constantly pitted against one another in heated competitions. Unlike many car companies, where a design chief dictates a car's outlines to his staff, BMW designers are given only a rough goal but are otherwise free to come up with their best concepts.

To get the most out of its people, BMW likes to throw together designers, engineers, and marketing experts to work intensively on a single project. The redesign of the Rolls-Royce Phantom, for instance, was dubbed "The Bank" since the 10 team members worked out of an old bank building at London's Marble Arch, where dozens of Rollses roll by daily. "We took designers from California and Munich and put them in a new environment" to immerse them in the Rolls Royce culture, says Ian Cameron, Rolls's chief designer. The result was the 2003 Phantom, a 19-foot edifice on wheels that remains true to Rolls's DNA but with 21st century lines and BMW's technological muscle under the hood. With sales of the $350,000 car running at about 700 a year, the Phantom is the best-seller in the superluxury segment, outstripping both the Bentley Arnage and the Mercedes Maybach.

Much of BMW's innovation, though, doesn't come via formal programs such as The Bank. In 2001 management decided to pull the plug on the disappointing Z3 sports coupe. But that didn't stop a 33-year-old designer named Sebastian Trübsbach from doodling a sketch of what a Z3 successor might look like. Ulrich Bruhnke, head of BMW's high-performance division, loved it. In Trübsbach's drawing, Bruhnke saw a car that could rival Porsche's Cayman S in performance but at a lower price. He persuaded a few designers and engineers to carve out some time for the renegade project. Next, Bruhnke gathered a team to map out the business case. The small group toiled for 10 months to build a prototype.

The moment of truth came in November 2004, at a top-secret test track near Munich. Cars were lined up so the board could examine their styling and proportions in natural light. Only one was covered by a tarp. Panke approached the mystery model. "What is this interesting silhouette?" he asked Bruhnke, who invited his boss to take a look. Panke

yanked back the cloth, exposing a glittering, bronze metallic prototype for what would become the Z4 coupe. Bruhnke breathed a sigh of relief when he saw Panke's eyes light up as they swept over the car's curved surfaces. Panke and the board quickly gave the go ahead, and the Z4 coupe sped to production in just 17 months, hitting showrooms this summer. Bingo. BMW's idea factory wins again.

By Gail Edmondson

Source: **Reprinted with special permission from "BMW's Dream Factory,"** *BusinessWeek,* **October 16, 2006. Copyright © 2006 The McGraw-Hill Companies.**

The opening article illustrates how a single organizational culture can thrive across many countries. BMW is an especially interesting case since the organizational culture is so different from the culture in the country where it first began. We have seen from Chapters 4 and 5 that German workers tend to experience a top-down form of management, but the open communication style at BMW seems to translate into any language. Referencing the near bankruptcy of the company has motivated employees immensely. Furthermore, the managerial behavior of "asking the right questions" instead of simply making decisions and allocating responsibilities encourages active participation, and has resulted in impressive creativity among those who would otherwise be silent employees in other companies. BMW not only manages money well but also shows that it cares about the employees. This is evident through the relative absence of lay-offs, which many other automotive companies experience on a regular basis. Even the work space has been designed in such a way to promote community. It seems clear why people want to join the BMW group: They are not simply taking home a paycheck for a hard day of work; they become an integral part of a second family. This has created a sense of ambition to keep the company alive and has been the key to how BMW has continued to be so innovative.

In this chapter we will explore the nature and characteristics of organizational culture as it relates to doing business in today's global context. In addition, strategies and guidelines for establishing a strong organizational culture in the presence of diversity are presented.

■ The Nature of Organizational Culture

The chapters in Part 1 provided the background on the external environment, and the chapters so far in this part have been concerned with the external culture. Regardless of whether this environment or cultural context affects the MNC, when individuals join an MNC, not only do they bring their national culture, which greatly affects their learned beliefs, attitudes, values, and behaviors, with them, but they also enter into an organizational culture. Employees of MNCs are expected to "fit in." For example, at PepsiCo, personnel are expected to be cheerful, positive, enthusiastic, and have committed optimism; at Ford, they are expected to show self-confidence, assertiveness, and machismo.[1] Regardless of the external environment or their national culture, managers and employees must understand and follow their organization's culture to be successful. In this section, after first defining organizational culture, we analyze the interaction of national and organizational cultures. An understanding of this interaction has become recognized as vital to effective international management.

organizational culture
Shared values and beliefs that enable members to understand their roles and the norms of the organization.

Definition and Characteristics

Organizational culture has been defined in several different ways. In its most basic form, organizational culture can be defined as the shared values and beliefs that enable members to understand their roles and the norms of the organization. A more detailed definition is offered by organizational cultural theorist Edgar Schein, who defines it as a pattern of shared basic assumptions that the group learned as it solved its problems of external adaptation and internal integration, and that has worked well enough to be considered valid and, therefore, to be taught to new members as the correct way to perceive, think, and feel in relation to those problems.[2]

Regardless of how the term is defined, a number of important characteristics are associated with an organization's culture. These have been summarized as:

1. Observed behavioral regularities, as typified by common language, terminology, and rituals.

2. Norms, as reflected by things such as the amount of work to be done and the degree of cooperation between management and employees.

3. Dominant values that the organization advocates and expects participants to share, such as high product and service quality, low absenteeism, and high efficiency.

4. A philosophy that is set forth in the MNC's beliefs regarding how employees and customers should be treated.

5. Rules that dictate the dos and don'ts of employee behavior relating to areas such as productivity, customer relations, and intergroup cooperation.

6. Organizational climate, or the overall atmosphere of the enterprise, as reflected by the way that participants interact with each other, conduct themselves with customers, and feel about the way they are treated by higher-level management.[3]

This list is not intended to be all inclusive, but it does help illustrate the nature of organizational culture.[4] The major problem is that sometimes an MNC's organizational culture in one country's facility differs sharply from organizational cultures in other countries. For example, managers who do well in England may be ineffective in Germany, despite the fact that they work for the same MNC. In addition, the cultures of the English and German subsidiaries may differ sharply from those of the home U.S. location. Effectively dealing with multiculturalism within the various locations of an MNC is a major challenge for international management.

A good example is provided by the German MNC Hoechst AG, the very large chemical company that employs more people on the other side of the Atlantic than in Germany. As its chairman has noted, "We are not merely a German company with foreign interests. One could almost say we are a nonnational company." And because of the high labor costs in Germany, the firm has been expanding its operations to lower-cost regions. It has also been selling some of its German operations while purchasing businesses in other countries. In the process, Hoechst has also made its top management less German. For example, a Brazilian and an American are members of the firm's nine-member board. The company is also trying to change its culture through new performance-based pay programs. However, getting people to buy into the new culture has proved a challenge.

In some cases companies have deliberately maintained two different business cultures because they do not want one culture influencing the other. A good example is JCPenney, the giant department store chain. When this well-known retailer bought control of Renner, a Brazilian retail chain with 20 stores, it used a strategy that is not very common when one company controls another. Rather than impose its own culture on the chain, Penney's management took a back seat. Recognizing Renner's reputation for value and service among its middle-class customers, Penney let the Brazilian managers continue to run the stores while it provided assistance in the form of backroom operations, merchandise presentation, logistics, branding, and expansion funds. In a country where fashion is constantly evolving, Renner is able to keep up with the market by changing fashion lines seven to eight times a year. The company also provides rapid checkout service, credit cards to individuals who earn as little as $150 a month, and interest-free installment plans that allow people to pay as little as $5 a month toward their purchases. Thanks to Penney's infusion of capital, in the first two years Renner opened 30 more stores and sales jumped from $150 million to over $300 million. The company proved to be profitable for a while; however, the run did not last forever, and JCPenney sold its controlling interest in the company in 2005.

Interaction Between National and Organizational Cultures

There is a widely held belief that organizational culture tends to moderate or erase the impact of national culture. The logic of such conventional wisdom is that if a U.S. MNC set up operations in, say, France, it would not be long before the French employees began to "think like Americans." In fact, evidence is accumulating that just the opposite may be true. Hofstede's research found that the national cultural values of employees have a significant impact on their organizational performance, and that the cultural values employees bring to the workplace with them are not easily changed by the organization. So, for example, while some French employees would have a higher power distance than Swedes and some a lower power distance, chances are "that if a company hired locals in Paris, they would, on the whole, be less likely to challenge hierarchical power than would the same number of locals hired in Stockholm."[5]

Andre Laurent's research supports Hofstede's conclusions.[6] He found that cultural differences actually are more pronounced among foreign employees working within the same multinational organization than among personnel working for firms in their native lands. Nancy Adler summarized these research findings as follows:

> When they work for a multinational corporation, it appears that Germans become more German, Americans become more American, Swedes become more Swedish, and so on. Surprised by these results, Laurent replicated the research in two other multinational corporations, each with subsidiaries in the same nine Western European countries and the United States. Similar to the first company, corporate culture did not reduce or eliminate national differences in the second and third corporations. Far from reducing national differences, organization culture maintains and enhances them.[7]

There often are substantial differences between the organizational cultures of different subsidiaries, and of course, this can cause coordination problems. For example, when the Upjohn Company of Kalamazoo, Michigan, merged with Pharmacia AB of Sweden, which also has operations in Italy, the Americans failed to realize some of the cultural differences between themselves and their new European partners. As was reported in *The Wall Street Journal,* "Swedes take off the entire month of July for vacation, virtually en masse, and Italians take off August. Everyone in *Europe* knows, that is, but apparently hardly anyone in Kalamazoo, Michigan, does."[8] As a result, a linkup that was supposed to give a quick boost to the two companies, solving problems such as aging product lines and pressure from giant competitors, never got off the ground. Things had to be rescheduled, and both partners ended up having to meet and talk about their cultural differences, so that each side better understood the "dos and don'ts" of doing business with the other.

When the two firms first got together, they never expected these types of problems. Upjohn, with household names such as Rogaine and Motrin, had no likely breakthroughs in its product pipeline, so it was happy to merge with Pharmacia. The latter had developed a solid roster of allergy medicines, human-growth hormone, and other drugs, but its distribution in the United States was weak and its product line was aging. So a merger seemed ideal for both firms. The big question was how to bring the two companies together. Given that Pharmacia had recently acquired an Italian firm, there was a proposal by the European group that there be three major centers—Kalamazoo, Stockholm, and Milan—as well as a new headquarters in London. However, this arrangement had a number of built-in problems. For one, the executives in Italy and Sweden were accustomed to reporting to local bosses. Second, the people in London did not know a great deal about how to coordinate operations in Sweden and Italy. American cultural values added even more problems in that at Upjohn workers were tested for drug and alcohol abuse, but in Italy waiters pour wine freely every afternoon in the company dining room, and Pharmacia's boardrooms were stocked with humidors for executives who liked to light a cigar during long meetings. Quite obviously, there were cultural differences that had to be resolved by the companies. In the end, Pharmacia and Upjohn said they would meld the different cultures and attitudes and get on with their growth plans. However, one thing is certain: The different cultures of the merged firms created a major challenge.

Organizational culture clashes often occur when a purchasing company does not fully understand the true operations of the business acquired. Take DaimlerChrysler, for example. The company evaluated the performance of both Nissan and Mitsubishi and found Nissan to be a riskier investment due to a high debt load and a weak keiretsu, or network. Mitsubishi, on the other hand, had a very strong keiretsu, which piqued more interest. What German owner DaimlerChrysler did not anticipate was that the organizational Japanese culture of Mitsubishi hindered management from relaying bad news. DaimlerChrysler therefore did not act very aggressively to change the culture, as it assumed that operations would prove to be affluent. Poor managerial decisions and a reluctance to comply with investor requests, such as closing plants in Japan and Australia and shift some production to China for greater efficiency, resulted in an expected $660 million loss for Mitsubishi in 2004. Nissan, however, still showed signs of profitability. The keiretsu that Nissan was associated with could not afford to bail the company out of any impending turmoil, so Nissan had to fight to stay afloat. DaimlerChrysler had no idea what hit it, since management did not inform the company of hard times, and the idea of a strong keiretsu proved to be more of a false sense of security than a guarantee of prosperity.[9]

In examining and addressing the differences between organizational cultures, Hofstede provided the early database of a set of proprietary cultural-analysis techniques and programs known as DOCSA (Diagnosing Organizational Culture for Strategic Application). This approach identifies the dimensions of organizational culture summarized in Table 6–1. It was found that when cultural comparisons were made

Table 6–1
Dimensions of Corporate Culture

Motivation	
Activities	**Outputs**
To be consistent and precise. To strive for accuracy and attention to detail. To refine and perfect. Get it right.	To be pioneers. To pursue clear aims and objectives. To innovate and progress. Go for it.

Relationship	
Job	**Person**
To put the demands of the job before the needs of the individual.	To put the needs of the individual before the needs of the job.

Identity	
Corporate	**Professional**
To identify with and uphold the expectations of the employing organizations.	To pursue the aims and ideals of each professional practice.

Communication	
Open	**Closed**
To stimulate and encourage a full and free exchange of information and opinion.	To monitor and control the exchange and accessibility of information and opinion.

Control	
Tight	**Loose**
To comply with clear and definite systems and procedures.	To work flexibly and adaptively according to the needs of the situation.

Conduct	
Conventional	**Pragmatic**
To put the expertise and standards of the employing organization first. To do what we know is right.	To put the demands and expectations of customers first. To do what they ask.

Source: Adapted from a study by the Diagnosing Organizational Culture for Strategic Application (DOCSA) group and reported in Lisa Hoecklin, *Managing Cultural Differences: Strategies for Competitive Advantage,* (Workingham, England: Addison-Wesley), 1995, p. 146.

Figure 6–1

Europeans' Perception of the Cultural Dimensions of U.S. Operations (A) and European Operations (B) of the Same MNC

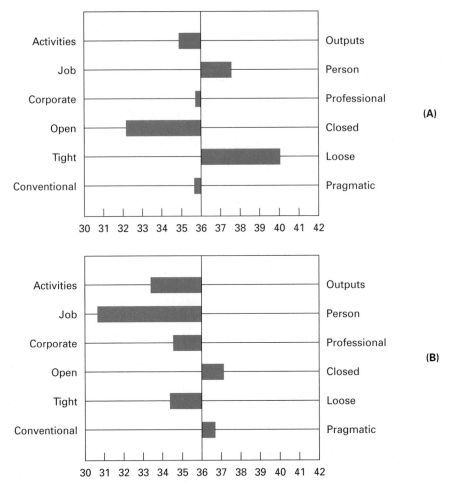

Source: Adapted from a study by the Diagnosing Organizational Culture for Strategic Application (DOCSA) group and reported in Lisa Hoecklin, *Managing Cultural Differences: Strategies for Competitive Advantage,* (Workingham, England: Addison-Wesley), 1995, p. 147–148.

between different subsidiaries of an MNC, different cultures often existed in each one. Such cultural differences within an MNC could reduce the ability of units to work well together. An example is provided in Figure 6–1, which shows the cultural dimensions of a California-based MNC and its European subsidiary as perceived by the Europeans. A close comparison of these perceptions reveals some startling differences.

The Europeans viewed the culture in the U.S. facilities as only slightly activities oriented (see Table 6–1 for a description of these dimensions), but they saw their own European operations much more heavily activities oriented. The U.S. operation was viewed as moderately people oriented, but their own relationships were viewed as very job oriented. The Americans were seen as having a slight identification with their own organization, while the Europeans had a much stronger identification. The Americans were perceived as being very open in their communications; the Europeans saw themselves as moderately closed. The Americans were viewed as preferring very loose control, while the Europeans felt they preferred somewhat tight control. The Americans were seen as somewhat conventional in their conduct, while the Europeans saw themselves as somewhat pragmatic. If these perceptions are accurate, then it obviously would be necessary for both groups to discuss their cultural differences and carefully coordinate their activities to work well together.

This analysis is relevant to multinational alliances. It shows that even though an alliance may exist, the partners will bring different organizational cultures with them. Lessem and Neubauer, who have portrayed Europe as offering four distinct ways of

Table 6–2
European Management Characteristics

Dimension	Characteristic			
	Western (United Kingdom)	**Northern (France)**	**Eastern (Germany)**	**Southern (Italy)**
Corporate	Commercial	Administrative	Industrial	Familial
Management attributes				
Behavior	Experiential	Professional	Developmental	Convivial
Attitude	Sensation	Thought	Intuition	Feeling
Institutional models				
Function	Salesmanship	Control	Production	Personnel
Structure	Transaction	Hierarchy	System	Network
Societal ideas				
Economics	Free market	Dirigiste	Social market	Communal
Philosophy	Pragmatic	Rational	Holistic	Humanistic
Cultural images				
Art	Theatre	Architecture	Music	Dance
Culture	(Anglo-Saxon)	(Gallic)	(Germanic)	(Latin)

Source: Adapted from Ronald Lessen and Fred Neubauer, *European Management Systems,* McGraw-Hill, London, 1994 and reported in Lisa Hoecklin, *Managing Cultural Differences: Strategies for Competitive Advantage,* (Workingham, England: Addison-Wesley), 1995, pp. 149.

dealing with multiculturalism (based on the United Kingdom, French, German, and Italian characteristics), provide an example, and Table 6–2 briefly describes each of these sets of cultural characteristics. A close examination of the differences highlights how difficult it can be to do business with two or more of these groups, because each group perceives things differently from the others. Another example is the way in which negotiations occur between groups; here are some contrasts between French and Spanish negotiators:[10]

French	Spanish
Look for a meeting of minds.	Look for a meeting of people.
Intellectual competence is very important.	Social competence is very important.
Persuasion through carefully prepared and skilled rhetoric is employed.	Persuasion through emotional appeal is employed.
Strong emphasis is given to a logical presentation of one's position coupled with well-reasoned, detailed solutions.	Socialization always precedes negotiations, which are characterized by an exchange of grand ideas and general principles.
A contract is viewed as a well-reasoned transaction.	A contract is viewed as a long-lasting relationship.
Trust emerges slowly and is based on the evaluation of perceived status and intellect.	Trust is developed on the basis of frequent and warm interpersonal contact and transaction.

Such comparisons also help explain why it can be difficult for an MNC with a strong organizational culture to break into foreign markets where it is not completely familiar with divergent national cultures. "International Management in Action: Doing Things the Wal-Mart Way" provides an illustration. When dealing with these challenges, MNCs must work hard to understand the nature of the country and institutional practices to both moderate and adapt their operations in a way that accommodates the company and customer base. The Brief Integrative Case on the merger in Europe at the end of Part 2 considers the scenario of an MNC establishing itself in a foreign market where there is only local competition. Furthermore, it demonstrates the sensitivities

Doing Things the Wal-Mart Way, Germans Say, "Nein vielen Dank"

www.walmart.com,
www.businessweek.com

Across the globe, Wal-Mart employees engage in the "Wal-Mart cheer" to start their day. It is a way to show inclusivity and express their pride in the company, and can be heard in many different languages. Wal-Mart not only operates in 14 countries but is also a leader in diversity in the workplace. In June 2007, Wal-Mart was named one of the top 50 companies for diversity by *DiversityInc Magazine*. Despite Wal-Mart's multinational presence and representation, its internal culture proved to be less than satisfactory to the German market.

Wal-Mart has experienced a fair share of negative PR over the years, so it is no surprise that some may have adverse reactions to news of Wal-Mart moving into the neighborhood. Before the unflattering buzz, Wal-Mart discovered that even the best intentions can fall flat. Wal-Mart entered the German market in 1997 and stressed the idea of friendly service with a smile, where the customers always come first. Even before the employees walked onto the sales room floor, employee dissatisfaction became clear.

The pamphlet which outlined the workplace code of ethics was simply translated from English to German, but the message was not expressed the way Wal-Mart had intended. It warned employees of potential supervisor-employee relationships, implying sexual harassment, and encouraged reports of "improper behavior," which spoke more to legal matters. The Germans interpreted this to mean that there was a ban on any romantic relationships in the workplace and saw the reporting methods as more of a way to rat out co-workers than benefit the company. As we saw in Chapter 3, ethical values in one country may not be the same as in another, and Wal-Mart experienced this firsthand. Another employee relations issue that arose dealt with local practices. Wal-

Mart has never been open to unionized employees, so when the German operations began dealing with workers' councils and adhering to co-determination rules, a common practice there, Wal-Mart was less than willing to listen to suggestions as to how to improve employee working conditions. As if this was not enough, Wal-Mart soon experienced problems with customer relations as well.

Doing things the Wal-Mart way included smiling at customers and assisting them by bagging their groceries at the Supercenter locations. This policy presented problems in the German environment. Male employees who were ordered to smile at customers were often seen as flirtatious to male customers, and Germans do not like strangers handling their groceries. These are just a few reasons that customers did not enjoy their shopping experience. This does not mean that everything Wal-Mart attempted was wrong. Products which are popular in Germany were available on the shelves in place of products that would be common in other countries. Enhanced distribution processes guaranteed availability of most requested items, and efficiency was pervasive.

Despite good intentions and numerous attempts to improve the German stores, the Wal-Mart culture proved to be a poor fit for the German market, and Wal-Mart vacated Germany in 2006. Unfortunately, Wal-Mart learned the hard way that in the retail or service industry, local customs are often more important than a strong, unyielding organizational culture. The challenge to incorporate everyone into the Wal-Mart family certainly fell short of expectations. If the Wal-Mart culture does not become more flexible, or locally relevant, it may be chastised from numerous global markets, and the company could hear, "no, thank you" in even more languages as it continues to expand.

and challenges when simultaneously integrating different national and organizational cultures. A large part of this process calls for carefully understanding the nature of the various organizational cultures, and the next section examines the different types in detail.

■ Organizational Cultures in MNCs

Organizational cultures of MNCs are shaped by a number of factors, including the cultural preferences of the leaders and employees. In the international arena, some MNCs have subsidiaries that, except for the company logo and reporting procedures, would not be easily recognizable as belonging to the same multinational.[11]

Given that many recent international expansions are a result of mergers or acquisition, the integration of these organizational cultures is a critical concern in international management. Numeroff and Abrahams have suggested that there are four steps that are critical in this process: (1) The two groups have to establish the purpose, goal, and focus of their merger. (2) Then they have to develop mechanisms to identify the most important organizational structures and management roles. (3) They have to determine who has authority over the resources needed for getting things done. (4) They have to identify the expectations of all involved parties and facilitate communication between both departments and individuals in the structure.

> Companies all over the world are finding out firsthand that there is more to an international merger or acquisition than just sharing resources and capturing greater market share. Differences in workplace cultures sometimes temporarily overshadow the overall goal of long-term success of the newly formed entity. With the proper management framework and execution, successful integration of cultures is not only possible, but the most preferable paradigm in which to operate. It is the role of the sponsors and managers to keep sight of the necessity to create, maintain, and support the notion of a united front. It is only when this assimilation has occurred that an international merger or acquisition can truly be labeled a success.[12]

In addition, there are three aspects of organizational functioning that seem to be especially important in determining MNC organizational culture: (1) the general relationship between the employees and their organization; (2) the hierarchical system of authority that defines the roles of managers and subordinates; and (3) the general views that employees hold about the MNC's purpose, destiny, goals, and their places in them.[13] When examining these dimensions of organizational culture, Trompenaars suggested the use of two continua. One distinguishes between equity and hierarchy; the other examines orientation to the person and the task. Along these continua, which are shown in Figure 6–2, he identifies and describes four different types of organizational cultures: family, Eiffel Tower, guided missile, and incubator.[14]

In practice, of course, organizational cultures do not fit neatly into any of these four, but the groupings can be useful in helping examine the bases of how individuals relate to each other, think, learn, change, are motivated, and resolve conflict. The following discussion examines each of these cultural types.

Family Culture

Family culture is characterized by a strong emphasis on hierarchy and orientation to the person. The result is a family-type environment that is power-oriented and headed by a

family culture
A culture that is characterized by a strong emphasis on hierarchy and orientation to the person.

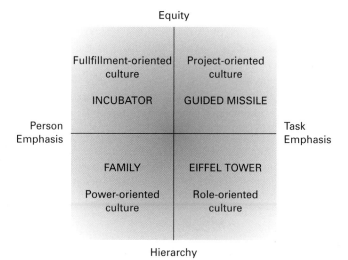

Figure 6–2

Organizational Cultures

Source: Adapted from Fons Trompenaars, *Riding the Waves of Culture: Understanding Diversity in Global Business* (Burr Ridge, IL: Irwin, 1994), p. 154.

leader who is regarded as a caring parent and one who knows what is best for the personnel. Trompenaars found that this organizational culture is common in countries such as Turkey, Pakistan, Venezuela, China, Hong Kong, and Singapore.[15]

In this culture, personnel not only respect the individuals who are in charge but look to them for both guidance and approval as well. In turn, management assumes a paternal relationship with personnel, looks after employees, and tries to ensure that they are treated well and have continued employment. Family culture also is characterized by traditions, customs, and associations that bind together the personnel and make it difficult for outsiders to become members. When it works well, family culture can catalyze and multiply the energies of the personnel and appeal to their deepest feelings and aspirations. When it works poorly, members of the organization end up supporting a leader who is ineffective and drains their energies and loyalties.

This type of culture is foreign to most managers in the United States, who believe in valuing people based on their abilities and achievements, not on their age or position in the hierarchy. As a result, many managers in U.S.-based MNCs fail to understand why senior-level managers in overseas subsidiaries might appoint a relative to a high-level, sensitive position even though that individual might not appear to be the best qualified for the job. They fail to realize that family ties are so strong that the appointed relative would never do anything to embarrass or let down the family member who made the appointment. Here is an example:

> A Dutch delegation was shocked and surprised when the Brazilian owner of a large manufacturing company introduced his relatively junior accountant as the key coordinator of a $15 million joint venture. The Dutch were puzzled as to why a recently qualified accountant had been given such weighty responsibilities, including the receipt of their own money. The Brazilians pointed out that the young man was the best possible choice among 1,200 employees since he was the nephew of the owner. Who could be more trustworthy than that? Instead of complaining, the Dutch should consider themselves lucky that he was available.[16]

Eiffel Tower Culture

Eiffel Tower culture
A culture that is characterized by strong emphasis on hierarchy and orientation to the task.

Eiffel Tower culture is characterized by strong emphasis on hierarchy and orientation to the task. Under this organizational culture, jobs are well defined, employees know what they are supposed to do, and everything is coordinated from the top. As a result, this culture—like the Eiffel Tower itself—is steep, narrow at the top, and broad at the base.

Unlike family culture, where the leader is revered and considered to be the source of all power, the person holding the top position in the Eiffel Tower culture could be replaced at any time, and this would have no effect on the work that organization members are doing or on the organization's reasons for existence. In this culture, relationships are specific, and status remains with the job. Therefore, if the boss of an Eiffel Tower subsidiary were playing golf with a subordinate, the subordinate would not feel any pressure to let the boss win. In addition, these managers seldom create off-the-job relationships with their people, because they believe this could affect their rational judgment. In fact, this culture operates very much like a formal hierarchy—impersonal and efficient.

> Each role at each level of the hierarchy is described, rated for its difficulty, complexity, and responsibility, and has a salary attached to it. There then follows a search for a person to fill it. In considering applicants for the role, the personnel department will treat everyone equally and neutrally, match the person's skills and aptitudes with the job requirements, and award the job to the best fit between role and person. The same procedure is followed in evaluations and promotions.[17]

Eiffel Tower culture most commonly is found in northwestern European countries. Examples include Denmark, Germany, and the Netherlands. The way that people in this culture learn and change differs sharply from that in the family culture. Learning involves the accumulation of skills necessary to fit a role, and organizations will use qualifications in deciding how to schedule, deploy, and reshuffle personnel to meet their needs. The organization also will employ such rational procedures as assessment centers, appraisal systems, training and development programs, and job rotation in managing its human resources. All these procedures help ensure that a formal hierarchic or bureaucracy-like approach works well. When changes need to be made, however, the Eiffel Tower culture often is ill-equipped to handle things. Manuals must be rewritten, procedures changed, job descriptions altered, promotions reconsidered, and qualifications reassessed.

Because the Eiffel Tower culture does not rely on values that are similar to those in most U.S. MNCs, U.S. expatriate managers often have difficulty initiating change in this culture. As Trompenaars notes:

> An American manager responsible for initiating change in a German company described to me the difficulties he had in making progress, although the German managers had discussed the new strategy in depth and made significant contributions to its formulation. Through informal channels, he had eventually discovered that his mistake was not having formalized the changes to structure or job descriptions. In the absence of a new organization chart, this Eiffel Tower company was unable to change.[18]

Guided Missile Culture

Guided missile culture is characterized by strong emphasis on equality in the workplace and orientation to the task. This organizational culture is oriented to work, which typically is undertaken by teams or project groups. Unlike the Eiffel Tower culture, where job assignments are fixed and limited, personnel in the guided missile culture do whatever it takes to get the job done. This culture gets its name from high-tech organizations such as the National Aeronautics and Space Administration (NASA), which pioneered the use of project groups working on space probes that resembled guided missiles. In these large project teams, more than a hundred different types of engineers often were responsible for building, say, a lunar landing module. The team member whose contribution would be crucial at any given time in the project typically could not be known in advance. Therefore, all types of engineers had to work in close harmony and cooperate with everyone on the team.

To be successful, the best form of synthesis must be used in the course of working on the project. For example, in a guided missile project, formal hierarchical considerations are given low priority, and individual expertise is of greatest importance. Additionally, all team members are equal (or at least potentially equal), because their relative contributions to the project are not yet known. All teams treat each other with respect, because they may need the other for assistance. This egalitarian and task-driven organizational culture fits well with the national cultures of the United States and United Kingdom, which helps explain why high-tech MNCs commonly locate their operations in these countries.

Unlike family and Eiffel Tower cultures, change in guided missile culture comes quickly. Goals are accomplished, and teams are reconfigured and assigned new objectives. People move from group to group, and loyalties to one's profession and project often are greater than loyalties to the organization itself.

Trompenaars found that the motivation of those in guided missile cultures tends to be more intrinsic than just concern for money and benefits. Team members become enthusiastic about, and identify with, the struggle toward attaining their goal. For example, a project team that is designing and building a new computer for the Asian market may be highly motivated to create a machine that is at the leading edge of technology, user-friendly, and likely to sweep the market. Everything else is secondary

guided missile culture
A culture that is characterized by strong emphasis on equality in the workplace and orientation to the task.

to this overriding objective. Thus, both intragroup and intergroup conflicts are minimized and petty problems between team members set aside; everyone is so committed to the project's main goal that no one has time for petty disagreements. As Trompenaars notes:

> This culture tends to be individualistic since it allows for a wide variety of differently specialized persons to work with each other on a temporary basis. The scenery of faces keeps changing. Only the pursuit of chosen lines of personal development is constant. The team is a vehicle for the shared enthusiasm of its members, but is itself disposable and will be discarded when the project ends. Members are garrulous, idiosyncratic, and intelligent, but their mutuality is a means, not an end. It is a way of enjoying the journey. They do not need to know each other intimately, and may avoid doing so. Management by objectives is the language spoken, and people are paid for performance.[19]

Incubator Culture

incubator culture
A culture that is characterized by strong emphasis on equality and orientation to the person.

Incubator culture is the fourth major type of organizational culture that Trompenaars identified, and it is characterized by strong emphasis on equality and personal orientation. This culture is based heavily on the existential idea that organizations per se are secondary to the fulfillment of the individuals within them. This culture is based on the premise that the role of organizations is to serve as incubators for the self-expression and self-fulfillment of their members; as a result, this culture often has little formal structure. Participants in an incubator culture are there primarily to perform roles such as confirming, criticizing, developing, finding resources for, or helping complete the development of an innovative product or service. These cultures often are found among start-up firms in Silicon Valley, California, or Silicon Glen, Scotland. These incubator-type organizations typically are entrepreneurial and often founded and made up by a creative team who left larger, Eiffel Tower–type employers. They want to be part of an organization where their creative talents will not be stifled.

Incubator cultures often create environments where participants thrive on an intense, emotional commitment to the nature of the work. For example, the group may be in the process of gene splitting that could lead to radical medical breakthroughs and extend life. Often, personnel in such cultures are overworked, and the enterprise typically is underfunded. As breakthroughs occur and the company gains stability, however, it starts moving down the road toward commercialization and profit. In turn, this engenders the need to hire more people and develop formalized procedures for ensuring the smooth flow of operations. In this process of growth and maturity, the unique characteristics of the incubator culture begin to wane and disappear, and the culture is replaced by one of the other types (family, Eiffel Tower, or guided missile).

As noted, change in the incubator culture often is fast and spontaneous. All participants are working toward the same objective. Because there may not yet be a customer who is using the final output, however, the problem itself often is open to redefinition, and the solution typically is generic, aimed at a universe of applications. Meanwhile, motivation of the personnel remains highly intrinsic and intense, and it is common to find employees working 70 hours a week—and loving it. The participants are more concerned with the unfolding creative process than they are in gathering power or ensuring personal monetary gain. In sharp contrast to the family culture, leadership in this incubator culture is achieved, not gained by position.

The four organizational cultures described by Trompenaars are "pure" types and seldom exist in practice. Rather the types are mixed and, as shown in Table 6–3, overlaid with one of the four major types of culture dominating the corporate scene. Recently, Trompenaars and his associates have created a questionnaire designed to identify national patterns of corporate culture as shown in Figure 6–3.

Table 6–3
Summary Characteristics of the Four Corporate Cultures

Characteristic	Corporate Culture			
	Family	**Eiffel Tower**	**Guided Missile**	**Incubator**
Relationships between employees	Diffuse relationships to organic whole to which one is bonded.	Specific role in mechanical system of required interaction.	Specific tasks in cybernetic system targeted on shared objectives.	Diffuse, spontaneous relationships growing out of shared creative process.
Attitude toward authority	Status is ascribed to parent figures who are close and powerful.	Status is ascribed to superior roles that are distant yet powerful.	Status is achieved by project group members who contribute to targeted goal.	Status is achieved by individuals exemplifying creativity and growth.
Ways of thinking and learning	Intuitive, holistic, lateral, and error correcting.	Logical, analytical, vertical, and rationally efficient.	Problem centered, professional, practical, cross-disciplinary.	Process oriented, creative, ad hoc, inspirational.
Attitudes toward people	Family members.	Human resources.	Specialists and experts.	Co-creators.
Ways of changing	"Father" changes course.	Change rules and procedures.	Shift aim as target moves.	Improvise and attune.
Ways of motivating and rewarding	Intrinsic satisfaction in being loved and respected.	Promotion to greater position, larger role.	Pay or credit for performance and problems solved.	Participation in the process of creating new realities.
	Management by subjectives.	Management by job description.	Management by objectives.	Management by enthusiasm.
Criticism and conflict resolution	Turn other cheek, save other's face, do not lose power game.	Criticism is accusation of irrationalism unless there are procedures to arbitrate conflicts.	Constructive task-related only, then admit error and correct fast.	Improve creative idea, not negate it.

Source: Adapted from Fons Trompenaars and Charles Hampden-Turner, *Riding the Waves of Culture: Understanding Diversity in Global Business,* 2nd ed. (New York: McGraw-Hill, 1998), p. 183.

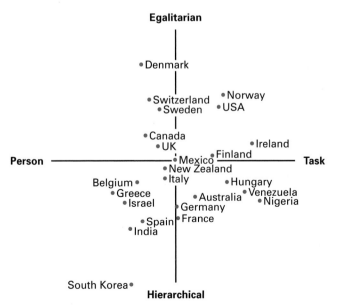

Figure 6–3

National Patterns of Corporate Culture

Source: Adapted from Fons Trompenaars and Charles Hampden-Turner, *Riding the Waves of Culture: Understanding Diversity in Global Business,* 2nd ed. (New York: McGraw-Hill, 1998), p. 184.

In recent years, growing numbers of multinationals have begun to expand their operations, realizing that if they do not increase their worldwide presence now, they likely will be left behind in the near future. In turn, this has created a number of different challenges for these MNCs, including making a fit between their home organizational culture and the organizational cultures at local levels in the different countries where the MNC operates. Matsushita provides an excellent example of how to handle this challenge with its macro-micro approach. This huge, Japanese MNC has developed a number of guidelines that it uses in setting up and operating its more than 150 industrial units. At the same time, the company complements these macro guidelines with on-site micro techniques that help create the most appropriate organizational culture in the subsidiary.

At the macro level, Matsushita employs six overall guidelines that are followed in all locales: (1) Be a good corporate citizen in every country, among other things, by respecting cultures, customs, and languages. (2) Give overseas operations the best manufacturing technology the company has available. (3) Keep the expatriate head count down, and groom local management to take over. (4) Let operating plants set their own rules, fine-tuning manufacturing processes to match the skills of the workers. (5) Create local research and development to tailor products to markets. (6) Encourage competition between overseas outposts and with plants back home.

Working within these macro guidelines, Matsushita then allows each local unit to create its own culture. The Malaysian operations are a good example. Matsushita has erected 23 subsidiaries in Malaysia which collectively consist of about 30,000 employees. Less than 1 percent of the employee population, however, is Japanese. From these Malaysian operations, Matsushita has been producing more than 1.3 million televisions and 1.8 million air conditioners annually, and 75 percent of these units are shipped overseas. To produce this output, local plants reflect Malaysia's cultural mosaic of Muslim Malays, ethnic Chinese, and Indians. To accommodate this diversity, Matsushita cafeterias offer Malaysian, Chinese, and Indian food, and to accommodate Muslim religious customs, Matsushita provides special prayer rooms at each plant and allows two prayer sessions per shift.

How well does this Malaysian workforce perform for the Japanese MNC? In the past, the Malaysian plants' slogan was "Let's catch up with Japan." Today, however, these plants frequently outperform their Japanese counterparts in both quality and efficiency. The comparison with Japan no longer is used. Additionally, Matsushita has found that the Malaysian culture is very flexible, and the locals are able to work well with almost any employer. Commenting on Malaysia's multiculturalism, Matsushita's managing director notes, "They are used to accommodating other cultures, and so they think of us Japanese as just another culture. That makes it much easier for us to manage them than some other nationalities."

Today, Matsushita faces a number of important challenges, including remaining profitable in a slow-growth, high-cost Japanese economy. Fortunately, this MNC is doing extremely well overseas, which is buying it time to get its house in order back home. A great amount of this success results from the MNC's ability to nurture and manage overseas organizational cultures (such as in Malaysia) that are both diverse and highly productive.

■ Managing Multiculturalism and Diversity

As the "International Management in Action" box on Matsushita indicates, success in the international arena often is greatly determined by an MNC's ability to manage both multiculturalism and diversity.[20] Both domestically and internationally, organizations find themselves leading workforces that have a variety of cultures (and subcultures) and consist of a largely diverse population of women, men, young and old people, blacks, whites, Latins, Asians, Arabs, Indians, and many others.

Phases of Multicultural Development

The effect of multiculturalism and diversity will vary depending on the stage of the firm in its international evolution. Table 6–4 depicts the characteristics of the major phases in this evolution. For example, Adler has noted that international cultural diversity has minimal impact on domestic organizations, although domestic multiculturalism has a highly significant impact. As firms begin exporting to foreign clients, however, and

Table 6–4
The Evolution of International Corporations

Characteristics/ Activities	Phase I (Domestic Corporations)	Phase II (International Corporations)	Phase III (Multinational Corporations)	Phase IV (Global Corporations)
Primary orientation	Product/service	Market	Price	Strategy
Competitive strategy	Domestic	Multidomestic	Multinational	Global
Importance of world business	Marginal	Important	Extremely important	Dominant
Product/service	New, unique	More standardized	Completely standardized (commodity)	Mass-customized
	Product engineering emphasized	Process engineering emphasized	Engineering not emphasized	Product and process engineering
Technology	Proprietary	Shared	Widely shared	Instantly and extensively shared
R&D/sales	High	Decreasing	Very low	Very high
Profit margin	High	Decreasing	Very low	High, yet immediately decreasing
Competitors	None	Few	Many	Significant (few or many)
Market	Small, domestic	Large, multidomestic	Larger, multinational	Largest, global
Production location	Domestic	Domestic and primary markets	Multinational, least cost	Imports and exports
Exports	None	Growing, high potential	Large, saturated	Imports and exports
Structure	Functional divisions	Functional with international division	Multinational lines of business	Global alliances, hierarchy
	Centralized	Decentralized	Centralized	Coordinated, decentralized
Primary orientation	Product/service	Market	Price	Strategy
Strategy	Domestic	Multidomestic	Multinational	Global
Perspective	Ethnocentric	Polycentric/ regiocentric	Multinational	Global/multicentric
Cultural sensitivity	Marginally important	Very important	Somewhat important	Critically important
With whom	No one	Clients	Employees	Employees and clients
Level	No one	Workers and clients	Managers	Executives
Strategic assumption	"One way"/ one best way	"Many good ways," equifinality	"One least-cost way" simultaneously	"Many good ways"

Source: From *International Dimensions of Organizational Behavior*, 2nd Edition by Nancy J. Adler, 1991, pp. 7–8. Reprinted with permission of South-Western, a division of Thomson Learning: www.thomsonrights.com.

become what she calls "international corporations" (Phase II in Table 6–4), they must adapt their approach and products to those of the local market. For these international firms, the impact of multiculturalism is highly significant. As companies become what she calls "multinational corporations" (Phase III), they often find that price tends to dominate all other considerations, and the direct impact of culture may lessen slightly. For those who continue this international evolution and become full-blown "global corporations" (Phase IV), the impact of culture again becomes extremely important. Notes Adler:

> Global firms need an understanding of cultural dynamics to plan their strategy, to locate production facilities and suppliers worldwide, to design and market culturally appropriate

Figure 6–4

Locations of International Cross-Cultural Interaction

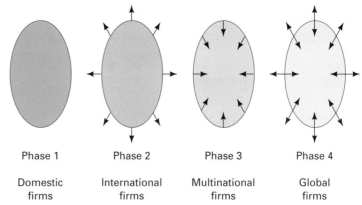

Phase 1   Phase 2   Phase 3   Phase 4

Domestic   International   Multinational   Global
firms   firms   firms   firms

Source: From *International Dimensions of Organizational Behavior*, 2nd Edition by Nancy J. Adler, 1991, pp. 7–8. Reprinted with permission of South-Western, a division of Thomson Learning: www.thomsonrights.com.

products and services, as well as to manage cross-cultural interaction throughout the organization—from senior executive committees to the shop floor. As more firms today move from domestic, international, and multinational organizations to operating as truly global organizations and alliances, the importance of cultural diversity increases markedly. What once was "nice to understand" becomes imperative for survival, let alone success.[21]

As shown in Figure 6–4, international cultural diversity traditionally affects neither the domestic firm's organizational culture nor its relationship with its customers or clients. These firms work domestically, and only domestic multiculturalism has a direct impact on their dynamics as well as on their relationship to the external environment.

Conversely, among international firms, which focus on exporting and producing abroad, cultural diversity has a strong impact on their external relationships with potential buyers and foreign employees. In particular, these firms rely heavily on expatriate managers to help manage operations; as a result, the diversity focus is from the inside out. This is the reverse of what happens in multinational firms, where there is less emphasis on managing cultural differences outside the firm and more on managing cultural diversity within the company. This is because multinational firms hire personnel from all over the world. Adler notes that these multinational firms need to develop cross-cultural management skills up the levels of the hierarchy. As shown in Figure 6–4, this results in a diversity focus that is primarily internal.

Global firms need both an internal and an external diversity focus (again see Figure 6–4). To be effective, everyone in the global organization needs to develop cross-cultural skills that allow them to work effectively with internal personnel as well as external customers, clients, and suppliers.

Types of Multiculturalism

For the international management arena, there are several ways of examining multiculturalism and diversity. One is to focus on the domestic multicultural and diverse workforce that operates in the MNC's home country. In addition to domestic multiculturalism, there is the diverse workforce in other geographic locales, and increasingly common are the mix of domestic and overseas personnel found in today's MNCs. The following discussion examines both domestic and group multiculturalism and the potential problems and strengths.

Domestic Multiculturalism   It is not necessary for today's organizations to do business in another country to encounter people with diverse cultural backgrounds. Culturally distinct populations can be found within organizations almost everywhere in the world. In Singapore, for example, there are four distinct cultural and linguistic groups: Chinese, Eurasian, Indian, and Malay. In Switzerland, there are four distinct ethnic communities: French, German, Italian, and Romansch. In Belgium, there are two linguistic groups: French and Flemish. In the United States, millions of first-generation immigrants have brought both their languages and their cultures. In Los Angeles, for example, there are more Samoans than on the island of Samoa, more Israelis than in any other city outside Israel, and more first- and second-generation Mexicans than in any other city except Mexico City. In Miami, over one-half the population is Latin, and most residents speak Spanish fluently. More Puerto Ricans live in New York City than in Puerto Rico.

It is even possible to examine domestic multiculturalism within the same ethnic groups. For example, Lee, after conducting research in Singapore among small Chinese family businesses, found that the viewpoints of the older generation differ sharply from those of the younger generation. Older generations tend to stress hierarchies, ethics, group dynamics and the status quo, while the younger generations focus on worker responsibility, strategy, individual performance, and striving for new horizons. For example, members of the older generation claim that they have more experience, that the boss should take care of workers, that workers should be involved in all processes and accept majority rule, and that structures should maintain stability. Members of the younger generation, on the other hand, feel that they have more education, accentuate the importance of employee performance and problem-solving abilities, believe that work should be appropriately allocated to maximize potential, and pursue opportunities that lead to growth and achievement.[22] These differences can slow organizational processes as one generation considers the other to be ineffective in its methods. Managers, therefore, need to consider employees on an individual basis and try to compile techniques that convey a common message, ultimately maximizing productivity while satisfying everyone across the ages.

In short, there is considerable multicultural diversity domestically in organizations throughout the world, and this trend will continue. For example, the U.S. civilian labor force of the next decade will change dramatically in ethnic composition. In particular, there will be a significantly lower percentage of white males in the workforce and a growing percentage of women, African Americans, Hispanics, and Asians.

Group Multiculturalism There are a number of ways that diverse groups can be categorized. Four of the most common include:

1. **Homogeneous groups,** in which members have similar backgrounds and generally perceive, interpret, and evaluate events in similar ways. An example would be a group of male German bankers who are forecasting the economic outlook for a foreign investment.

2. **Token groups,** in which all members but one have the same background. An example would be a group of Japanese retailers and a British attorney who are looking into the benefits and shortcomings of setting up operations in Bermuda.

3. **Bicultural groups,** in which two or more members represent each of two distinct cultures. An example would be a group of four Mexicans and four Canadians who have formed a team to investigate the possibility of investing in Russia.

4. **Multicultural groups**, in which there are individuals from three or more different ethnic backgrounds. An example is a group of three American, three German, three Uruguayan, and three Chinese managers who are looking into mining operations in Chile.

homogeneous group
A group in which members have similar backgrounds and generally perceive, interpret, and evaluate events in similar ways.

token group
A group in which all members but one have the same background, such as a group of Japanese retailers and a British attorney.

bicultural group
A group in which two or more members represent each of two distinct cultures, such as four Mexicans and four Taiwanese who have formed a team to investigate the possibility of investing in a venture.

multicultural group
A group in which there are individuals from three or more different ethnic backgrounds, such as three U.S., three German, three Uruguayan, and three Chinese managers who are looking into mining operations in South Africa.

As the diversity of a group increases, the likelihood of all members perceiving things in the same way decreases sharply. Attitudes, perceptions, and communication in general may be a problem. On the other hand, there also are significant advantages associated with the effective use of multicultural, diverse groups. Sometimes, local laws require a certain level of diversity in the workplace. More and more, people are moving to other countries to find the jobs that match their skills. International managers need to be cognizant of the likelihood that they will oversee a group that represents many cultures, not just the pervasive culture associated with that country. The following sections examine the potential problems and the advantages of workplace diversity.

Potential Problems Associated with Diversity

Overall, diversity may cause a lack of cohesion that results in the unit's inability to take concerted action, be productive, and create a work environment that is conducive to both efficiency and effectiveness. These potential problems are rooted in people's attitudes.

An example of an attitudinal problem in a diverse group may be the mistrust of others. For example, many U.S. managers who work for Japanese operations in the United States complain that Japanese managers often huddle together and discuss matters in their native language. The U.S. managers wonder aloud why the Japanese do not speak English. What are they talking about that they do not want anyone else to hear? In fact, the Japanese often find it easier to communicate among themselves in their native language, and because no Americans are present, the Japanese managers ask why they should speak English. If there is no reason for anyone else to be privy to our conversation, why should we not opt for our own language? Nevertheless, such practices do tend to promote an attitude of mistrust.

Another potential problem may be perceptual. Unfortunately, when culturally diverse groups come together, they often bring preconceived stereotypes with them. In initial meetings, for example, engineers from economically advanced countries often are perceived as more knowledgeable than those from less advanced countries. In turn, this perception can result in status-related problems, because some of the group initially are regarded as more competent than others and likely are accorded status on this basis. As the diverse group works together, erroneous perceptions often are corrected, but this takes time. In one diverse group consisting of engineers from a major Japanese firm and a world-class U.S. firm, a Japanese engineer was assigned a technical task because of his stereotyped technical educational background. The group soon realized that this particular Japanese engineer was not capable of doing this job, because for the last four years, he had been responsible for coordinating routine quality and no longer was on the technologic cutting edge. His engineering degree from the University of Tokyo had resulted in the other members perceiving him as technically competent and able to carry out the task; this perception proved to be incorrect.

A related problem is inaccurate biases. For example, it is well known that Japanese companies depend on groups to make decisions. Entrepreneurial behavior, individualism, and originality are typically downplayed.[23] However, in a growing number of Japanese firms this stereotype is proving to be incorrect.[24] Here is an example.

> Mr. Uchida, a 28-year-old executive in a small software company, dyes his hair brown, keeps a sleeping bag by his desk for late nights in the office and occasionally takes the day off to go windsurfing. "Sometimes I listen to soft music to soothe my feelings, and sometimes I listen to hard music to build my energy," said Mr. Uchida, who manages the technology-development division of the Rimnet Corporation, an Internet access provider. "It's important that we always keep in touch with our sensibilities when we want to generate ideas." The creative whiz kid, a business personality often prized by corporate America, has come to Japan Inc. Unlikely as it might seem in a country renowned for its deference to authority and its devotion to group solidarity, freethinkers like Mr. Uchida are popping up all over the workplace. Nonconformity is suddenly in.[25]

Still another potential problem with diverse groups is inaccurate communication, which could occur for a number of reasons. One is misunderstandings caused by words used by a speaker that are not clear to other members. For example, in a diverse group in which one of the authors was working, a British manager told her U.S. colleagues, "I will fax you this report in a fortnight." When the author asked the Americans when they would be getting the report, most of them believed it would be arriving in four days. They did not know that the common British word *fortnight* (14 nights) means two weeks.

Another contribution to miscommunication may be the way in which situations are interpreted. Many Japanese nod their heads when others talk, but this does not mean that they agree with what is being said. They merely are being polite and attentive. In many societies, it is impolite to say no, and if the listener believes that the other person wants a positive answer, the listener will say yes even though this is incorrect. As a result, many U.S. managers find out that promises made by individuals from other cultures cannot be taken at face value—and in many instances, the other individual assumes that the American realizes this!

Diversity also may lead to communication problems because of different perceptions of time. For example, many Japanese will not agree to a course of action on the spot. They will not act until they have discussed the matter with their own people, because they do not feel empowered to act alone. Many Latin managers refuse to be held to a strict timetable, because they do not have the same time urgency that U.S. managers do. Here is another example, as described by a European manager:

> In attempting to plan a new project, a three-person team composed of managers from Britain, France, and Switzerland failed to reach agreement. To the others, the British representative appeared unable to accept any systematic approach; he wanted to discuss all potential problems before making a decision. The French and Swiss representatives agreed to examine everything before making a decision, but then disagreed on the sequence and scheduling of operations. The Swiss, being more pessimistic in their planning, allocated more time for each suboperation than did the French. As a result, although everybody agreed on its validity, we never started the project. If the project had been discussed by three Frenchmen, three Swiss, or three Britons, a decision, good or bad, would have been made. The project would not have been stalled for lack of agreement.[26]

Advantages of Diversity

While there are some potential problems to overcome when using culturally diverse groups in today's MNCs, there also are a host of benefits to be gained.[27] In particular, there is growing evidence that culturally diverse groups can enhance creativity, lead to better decisions, and result in more effective and productive performance.[28]

One main benefit of diversity is the generation of more and better ideas. Because group members come from a host of different cultures, they often are able to create a greater number of unique (and thus creative) solutions and recommendations. For example, a U.S. MNC recently was preparing to launch a new software package aimed at the mass consumer market. The company hoped to capitalize on the upcoming Christmas season with a strong advertising campaign in each of its international markets. A meeting of the sales managers from these markets in Spain, the Middle East, and Japan helped the company revise and better target its marketing effort. The Spanish manager suggested that the company focus its campaign around the coming of the Magi (January 6) and not Christmas (December 25), because in Latin cultures, gifts typically are exchanged on the date that the Magi brought their gifts. The Middle East manager pointed out that most of his customers were not Christians, so a Christmas campaign would not have much meaning in his area. Instead, he suggested the company focus its sales campaign around the value of the software and how it could be useful to customers and not worry about getting the product shipped by early

December. The Japanese manager concurred with his Middle East colleague but suggested that some of the colors being proposed for the sales brochure be changed to better fit with Japanese culture. Thanks to these ideas, the sales campaign proved to be one of the most effective in the company's history.

groupthink
Social conformity and pressures on individual members of a group to conform and reach consensus.

A second major benefit is that culturally diverse groups can prevent **groupthink,** which is social conformity and pressures on individual members of a group to conform and reach consensus. When this occurs, group participants believe that their ideas and actions are correct and that those who disagree with them are either uninformed or deliberately trying to sabotage their efforts. Multicultural diverse groups often are able to avoid this problem, because the members do not think similarly or feel pressure to conform. As a result, they typically question each other, offer opinions and suggestions that are contrary to those held by others, and must be persuaded to change their minds. Therefore, unanimity is achieved only through a careful process of deliberation. Unlike homogeneous groups, where everyone can be "of one mind," diverse groups may be slower to reach a general consensus, but the decision may be more effective.

Diversity in the workplace enhances more than the internal operations. A common belief is that anyone will have insight to and connect better with others of the same nationality or cultural background. This tends to result in quickly building trust and understanding one another's preferences. Therefore, if the customer base is comprised of many cultures, it may benefit the company to have representatives from corresponding nationalities. The U.S. multinational cosmetic firm Avon adopted this philosophy over a decade ago. When Avon observed an increase in the number of Korean shoppers at one of its U.S. locations, it quickly employed Korean sales staff.[29] This shows that the external environment, even in the MNC home country, can encompass many cultures that managers should bear in mind. Expanding diversity in the workplace to better serve the customer means that even local managers have an international exposure, further emphasizing the importance of learning about the cultural surroundings.

Building Multicultural Team Effectiveness

Multiculturally diverse teams have a great deal of potential, depending on how they are managed. As shown in Figure 6–5, Dr. Carol Kovach,who conducted research on the importance of leadership in managing cross-cultural groups, reports that if cross-cultural groups are led properly, they can indeed be highly effective; unfortunately, she also found that if they are not managed properly, they can be highly ineffective. In other words, diverse groups are more powerful than single-culture groups. They can hurt the organization, but if managed effectively, they can be the best.[30] The following sections provide the conditions and guidelines for managing diverse groups in today's organizations effectively.

Figure 6–5

Group Effectiveness and Culture

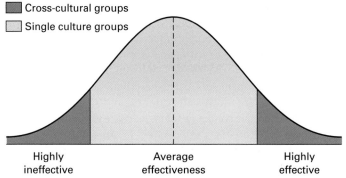

Source: From *International Dimensions of Organizational Behavior*, 2nd Edition by Nancy J. Adler, 1991, pp. 7–8. Reprinted with permission of South-Western, a division of Thomson Learning: www.thomsonrights.com.

Understanding the Conditions for Effectiveness   Multicultural teams are most effective when they face tasks requiring innovativeness. They are far less effective when they are assigned to routine tasks. As Adler explains:

> Cultural diversity provides the biggest asset for teams with difficult, discretionary tasks requiring innovation. Diversity becomes less helpful when employees are working on simple tasks involving repetitive or routine procedures. Therefore, diversity generally becomes more valuable during the planning and development of projects (the "work" stage) and less helpful during their implementation (the "action" stage). The more senior the team members, the more likely they are to be working on projects that can benefit from diversity. Diversity is therefore extremely valuable to senior executive teams, both within and across countries.[31]

To achieve the greatest amount of effectiveness from diverse teams, activities must be determined by the stage of team development, as mentioned earlier in the chapter (e.g., entry, working, and action). For example, in the entry stage, the focus should be on building trust and developing team cohesion. This can be a difficult task for diverse teams, whose members are accustomed to working in different ways. For example, Americans, Germans, and Swiss typically spend little time getting to know each other; they find out the nature of the task and set about pursuing it on their own without first building trust and cohesion. This contrasts sharply with individuals from Latin America, Southern Europe, and the Middle East, where team members spend a great deal of initial time getting to know each other. This contrast between task-oriented and relationship-oriented members of a diverse team may slow progress due to communication and strategic barriers. To counteract this problem, it is common in the entry stage of development to find experienced multicultural managers focusing attention on the team members' equivalent professional qualifications and status. Once this professional similarity and respect are established, the group can begin forming a collective unit.

In the work stage of development, attention may be directed more toward describing and analyzing the problem or task that has been assigned. This stage often is fairly easy for managers of multicultural teams, because they can draw on the diversity of the members in generating ideas. As noted earlier, diverse groups tend to be most effective when dealing with situations that require innovative approaches.

In the action stage, the focus shifts to decision making and implementation. This can be a difficult phase, because it often requires consensus building among the members. In achieving this objective, experienced managers work to help the diverse group recognize and facilitate the creation of ideas with which everyone can agree. In doing so, it is common to find strong emphasis on problem-solving techniques such as the nominal group technique (NGT), where the group members individually make contributions before group interaction and consensus are reached.

Using the Proper Guidelines   A summary, along with some specific guidelines, can be helpful as a quick reference when deciding how to manage a culturally diverse team. Here are some of the most useful:

1. Team members must be selected for their task-related abilities and not solely based on ethnicity. If the task is routine, homogeneous membership often is preferable; if the task is innovative, multicultural membership typically is best.

2. Team members must recognize and be prepared to deal with their differences. The goal is to facilitate a better understanding of cross-cultural differences and generate a higher level of performance and rapport. In doing so, members need to become aware of their own stereotypes, as well as those of the others, and use this information to better understand the real differences that exist between them. This can then serve as a basis for determining how each individual member can contribute to the overall effectiveness of the team.

3. Because members of diverse teams tend to have more difficulty agreeing on their purpose and task than members of homogeneous groups, the team leader must help the group to identify and define its overall goal. This goal is most useful when it requires members to cooperate and develop mutual respect in carrying out their tasks.

4. Members must have equal power so that everyone can participate in the process; cultural dominance always is counterproductive. As a result, managers of culturally diverse teams distribute power according to each person's ability to contribute to the task, not according to ethnicity.

5. It is important that all members have mutual respect for each other. This often is accomplished by managers choosing members of equal ability, making prior accomplishments and task-related skills known to the group, and minimizing early judgments based on ethnic stereotypes.

6. Because teams often have difficulty determining what is a good or a bad idea or decision, managers must give teams positive feedback on their process and output. This feedback helps the members see themselves as a team, and it teaches them to value and celebrate their diversity, recognize contributions made by the individual members, and trust the collective judgment of the group.

World-class organizations use such an approach, and one good example is NUMMI (New United Motor Manufacturing), a joint venture between General Motors and Toyota that transformed an out-of-date GM plant in Fremont, California, into a world-class organization. This joint-venture partnership, formed over 20 years ago, continues to be a success story of how a culturally diverse workforce can produce state-of-the-art automobiles. The successful approach to culturally diverse work teams at NUMMI was built around four principles:

1. Both management and labor recognized that their futures were interdependent, thus committing them to a mutual vision.

2. Employees felt secure and trusted assurances that they would be treated fairly, thus enabling them to become contributors.

3. The production system formed interdependent relationships throughout the plant, thus helping to create a healthy work environment.

4. The production system was managed to transform the stress and conflict of everyday life into trust and mutual respect.[32]

In achieving success at NUMMI, Toyota sent trainers from Japan to work with its U.S. counterparts and teach the production system that would be used throughout the plant. During this period, both groups searched for points of agreement, establishing valuable relationships in the process. In addition, the Japanese taught the Americans some useful techniques for increasing productivity, including how to focus on streamlining operations, reduce waste, and blame mistakes on the situation or themselves (not on team members).

In overcoming multicultural differences at NUMMI, several changes were introduced—for example, (1) reserved dining rooms were eliminated, and all managers now eat in a communal cafeteria; (2) all reserved parking spaces were eliminated; and (3) GM's 80 job classifications were collapsed into only 3 to equalize work and rewards and ensure fairness. Commenting on the overall success of the joint venture, it was noted that

> Toyota managers resisted temptations to forge ahead with a pure version of the system. Both the Japanese and Americans learned as they went. By adopting a "go slow" attitude, the Japanese and Americans remained open to points of resistance as they arose and navigated around them. By tolerating ambiguity and by searching for consensus, Toyota managers established the beginnings of mutual respect and trust with the American workers and managers.[33]

NUMMI is only one example of the many successful multicultural workforces producing world-class goods and services. In each case, however, effective multinationals rely on the types of guidelines that have been highlighted in this discussion.

The World of *BusinessWeek*—Revisited

The *BusinessWeek* article that introduces the chapter shows how a company can form an inviting culture that embodies the advantages of diversity. Having read the chapter, you should have a clearer understanding of how organizational cultures behave to maximize employee potential in a multicultural environment. BMW employees are motivated to perform duties outside of their normal job descriptions because of the strong internal culture that focuses on humble management and individual voices. BMW is also able to customize its operations to local markets by understanding the needs of those societies. In other words, its internal culture works well with the external cultures it encounters. The inquisitive management, creative tendencies, and inclusive atmosphere are just a few of the reasons why BMW receives over 200,000 employment applications annually and why the hiring procedures are so competitive. Recruiters work hard to find local talent that is the best fit for the company, and employees work hard to stay there.

It is common for a rigid business structure to face difficulties when opening operations in other countries. The same is true in instances when an uninformed company from one culture merges with or acquires a company with very different beliefs and practices. There are many ways a company can fail, but is BMW's method the only way to succeed? Using what you have learned from this chapter, answer the following: (1) What has BMW done differently from other companies with strong internal cultures that has allowed it to succeed across countries where others have failed? (2) According to Adler's research, based on BMW's behavior, what stage(s) could it be in? (3) What could that say about the age and innovation of the company? (4) Which countries exhibit a similar national culture as compared to BMW's internal structure?

SUMMARY OF KEY POINTS

1. Organizational culture is a pattern of basic assumptions that are developed by a group as it learns to cope with its problems of external adaptation and internal integration and that are taught to new members as the correct way to perceive, think, and feel in relation to these problems. Some important characteristics of organizational culture include observed behavioral regularities, norms, dominant values, philosophy, rules, and organizational climate.

2. Organizational cultures are shaped by a number of factors. These include the general relationship between employees and their organization, the hierarchic system of authority that defines the roles of managers and subordinates, and the general views that employees hold about the organization's purpose, destiny, goals, and their place in the organization. When examining these differences, Trompenaars suggested the use of two continua: equity-hierarchy and person-task orientation, resulting in four basic types of organizational cultures: family, Eiffel Tower, guided missile, and incubator.

3. Family culture is characterized by strong emphasis on hierarchic authority and orientation to the person. Eiffel Tower culture is characterized by strong emphasis on hierarchy and orientation to the task. Guided missile culture is characterized by strong emphasis on equality in the workplace and orientation to the task. Incubator culture is characterized by strong emphasis on equality and orientation to the person.

4. Success in the international arena often is heavily determined by a company's ability to manage multiculturalism and diversity. Firms progress through four phases in their international evolution: (1) domestic corporation, (2) international corporation, (3) multinational corporation, and (4) global corporation.

5. There are a number of ways to examine multiculturalism and diversity. One is by looking at the domestic multicultural and diverse workforce that operates in the MNC's home country. Another is by examining the variety of diverse groups that exist in MNCs, including homogeneous groups, token groups, bicultural groups, and multicultural groups. Several potential problems as well as advantages are associated with multicultural, diverse teams.

6. A number of guidelines have proved to be particularly effective in managing culturally diverse groups. These include careful selection of the members, identification of the group's goals, establishment of equal power and mutual respect among the participants, and delivering positive feedback on performance. A good example of how these guidelines have been used is the NUMMI joint venture created by General Motors and Toyota.

KEY TERMS

bicultural group, *173*

Eiffel Tower culture, *166*

family culture, *165*

groupthink, *176*

guided missile culture, *167*

homogeneous group, *173*

incubator culture, *168*

multicultural group, *173*

organizational culture, *158*

token group, *173*

REVIEW AND DISCUSSION QUESTIONS

1. Some researchers have found that when Germans work for a U.S. MNC, they become even more German, and when Americans work for a German MNC, they become even more American. Why would this knowledge be important to these MNCs?

2. When comparing the negotiating styles and strategies of French versus Spanish negotiators, a number of sharp contrasts are evident. What are three of these, and what could MNCs do to improve their position when negotiating with either group?

3. In which of the four types of organizational cultures—family, Eiffel Tower, guided missile, incubator—would most people in the United States feel comfortable? In which would most Japanese feel comfortable? Based on your answers, what conclusions could you draw regarding the importance of understanding organizational culture for international management?

4. Most MNCs need not enter foreign markets to face the challenge of dealing with multiculturalism. Do you agree or disagree with this statement? Explain your answer.

5. What are some potential problems that must be overcome when using multicultural, diverse teams in today's organizations? What are some recognized advantages? Identify and discuss two of each.

6. A number of guidelines can be valuable in helping MNCs to make diverse teams more effective. What are five of these? Additionally, what underlying principles guided NUMMI in its effective use of multicultural teams? Were the principles used by NUMMI similar to the general guidelines identified in this chapter, or were they significantly different? Explain your answer.

INTERNET EXERCISE: HEWLETT-PACKARD'S INTERNATIONAL FOCUS

Mention the name Hewlett-Packard, or HP for short, and people are likely to think of printers—an area where the MNC has managed to excel worldwide in recent years. However, HP has many other offerings besides printers and has rapidly expanded its product line into the international arena over the last decade.

Visit its Web site at **www.hp.com**, and review some of the latest developments. In particular, pay close attention to its product line and international expansion. Then choose three different countries where the firm is doing business: one from the Americas, one from Europe, and one from Southeast Asia or India. (The sites are all presented in the local language, so you might want to make India your choice because this site is in English.) Compare and contrast the product offerings and ways in which HP goes about marketing itself over the Web in these locations. What do you see as some of the major differences? Second, using Figure 6–2 and Table 6–3 as your guide, in what way are differences in organizational cultures internationally likely to present significant challenges to HP's efforts to create a smooth-running international enterprise? What would you see as two of the critical issues with which management will have to deal? Third, what are two steps that you think HP will have to take in order to build multicultural team effectiveness? What are two guidelines that can help it do this?

Japan

Japan is located in eastern Asia, and it comprises a curved chain of more than 3,000 islands. Four of these—Hokkaido, Honshu, Shikoku, and Kyushi—account for 89 percent of the country's land area. The population of Japan is approximately 128 million, with over 12 million people living in the nation's capital, Tokyo. According to the *CIA World Factbook*, the country's gross domestic product in 2006 was approximately $33,100 per capita. The country has been in the throes of an economic recession that has been going on for over 10 years, with an annual growth rate of 2.2 percent. While economic conditions have been slowly improving, Japan's huge government debt, which is approaching 175 percent of GDP, and the aging of the population are two long-term problems that must be addressed. There is hope for Japan, which made some good investment choices that brought significant returns in early 2007.

Surprisingly, Japan has become a fashion mecca. Spanish clothing company Zara, Swedish brand H&M, French designer Louis Vuitton, and American jeweler Tiffany & Co. are very popular and prosperous throughout Japan. The new generation of fashion aficionados also makes Japan a country to watch. Japan is usually associated with a minimalist nature, not owning more than is necessary. In Tokyo, however, younger people are beginning to express themselves by quickly purchasing any item that appears to be part of a new trend, only to abandon it for the next craze in the blink of an eye. Investment in Japan has been supported by this phenomenon, since many fashion companies use Japan as their new testing ground before launching expensive lines in other markets. While New York City in the United States was once considered the primary region to try out new styles, experience has shown that what catches on in Japan often works across the globe as well and that the Japanese are much faster to respond to new products. This does not imply that everything that is tested in Japan will work worldwide. For example, bags with bubbly, cartoon printing containing the likes of Hello Kitty or indistinguishable characteristics that thrive in the *kawaii*, or "cute," market segment may not make a profit elsewhere. Essentially, there are times when Japan is distinctly ahead of the crowd, and it may take quite some time for the rest of the world to catch up.

Considering workplace ethics and customs in the home, most would not immediately think of Japan as such a vogue region. For instance, in business, employees often dress conservatively, are well groomed, and do not leave the work space until after the boss has left, which can be many hours after the office has officially closed. In fact, it is usually embarrassing for a worker to leave the moment the office closes, since that is seen as leaving "early," and it singles out the employee. Homes can be small, with little extra room for extravagant purchases, though with gift giving so prevalent in the country, it is unpredictable what someone else may procure for your household. These reasons and many more would imply that the Japanese would not want to call more attention to themselves. However, as Japan continues to move toward individualistic tendencies, citizens may be scrambling to find a way to express their own unique voice.

www.japanlink.com, www.businessweek.com

Questions

1. Based on their home country, how might the organizational cultures of the four companies mentioned be distinct from one another, and in what ways could they be the same?

2. If the first two companies and the last two companies want to form joint ventures (Zara with H&M, and Louis Vuitton with Tiffany & Co.), what could be some potential ways the organizational cultures interact?

3. What types of problems might a culturally diverse top management team at headquarters create for the two joint ventures? Give some specific examples. How could these problems be overcome?

4. How could work structures and schedules of these companies at their respective headquarters affect operations in Japan? In what ways are they different or similar?

A Good-Faith Effort Is Needed

Excelsior Manufacturing is a medium-sized firm located in the northeastern part of the United States. Excelsior has long been known as a high-quality, world-class producer of precision tools. Recently, however, this MNC has been slowly losing market share in Europe because many EU companies are turning to other European firms to save on taxes and transportation costs. Realizing that it needed a European partner if it hoped to recapture this lost ground, Excelsior began looking to buy a firm that could provide it with a strong foothold in this market. After a brief search, the MNC made contact with Quality Instrumentation, a Madrid-based firm that was founded five years ago and has been growing at 25 percent annually. Excelsior currently is discussing a buyout with Quality Instrumentation, and the Spanish firm appears to be interested in the arrangement as it will provide it with increased technology, a quality reputation, and more funding for European expansion.

Next week, owners of the two companies are scheduled to meet in Madrid to discuss purchase price and potential plans for integrating their overall operations. The biggest sticking point appears to be a concern for meshing the organizational cultures and the work values and habits of the two enterprises. Each is afraid that the other's way of doing business might impede overall progress and lead to wasted productivity and lost profit. To deal with this issue, the president of Excelsior has asked his management team to draft a plan that could serve as a guide in determining how both groups could coordinate their efforts.

On a personal level, the head of Excelsior believes that it will be important for the Spanish management team to understand that if the Spaniards sell the business, they must be prepared to let U.S. managers have final decision-making power on major issues, such as research and development efforts, expansion plans, and customer segmentation. At the same time, the Americans are concerned that their potential European partners will feel they are being told what to do and resist these efforts. "We're going to have to make them understand that we must work as a unified team," the president explained to his planning committee, "and create a culture that will support this idea. We may not know a lot about working with Spaniards, and they may not understand a great deal about how Americans do things, but I believe that we can resolve these differences if we put forth a good-faith effort."

Questions

1. What do you think some of the main organizational culture differences between the two companies would be?

2. Why might the cultural diversity in the Spanish firm not be as great as that in the U.S. firm, and what potential problems could this create?

3. What would you recommend be done to effectively merge the two organizational cultures and ensure they cooperate harmoniously? Offer some specific recommendations.

Chapter 7

CROSS-CULTURAL COMMUNICATION AND NEGOTIATION

Communication takes on special importance in international management because of the difficulties in conveying meanings between parties from different cultures. The problems of misinterpretation and error are compounded in the international context. Chapter 7 examines how the communication process in general works, and it looks at the downward and upward communication flows that commonly are used in international communication. Then the chapter examines the major barriers to effective international communication and reviews ways of dealing with these communication problems. Finally, one important dimension of international communication, international negotiation, is examined, with particular attention to how negotiation approaches and strategies must be adapted to different cultural environments. The specific objectives of this chapter are:

OBJECTIVES OF THE CHAPTER

1. **DEFINE** the term *communication,* examine some examples of verbal communication styles, and explain the importance of message interpretation.

2. **ANALYZE** the common downward and upward communication flows used in international communication.

3. **EXAMINE** the language, perception, and culture of communication and nonverbal barriers to effective international communications.

4. **PRESENT** the steps that can be taken to overcome international communication problems.

5. **DEVELOP** approaches to international negotiations that respond to differences in culture.

6. **REVIEW** different negotiating and bargaining behaviors that may improve negotiations and outcomes.

The World of *BusinessWeek*

BusinessWeek

Skype Goes Mobile

Skype's New Cell Phone Will Deliver Mobile Access to Its Service: The Beleaguered Carrier Hopes to Jump-Start Revenues Overseas

B it by bit, big names in the computing world are barging into the cell-phone business. First came Apple's game-changing iPhone. Next came word that Google is creating its own software platform for a new breed of cell phones. Now Skype, which popularized free and cheap phone calls over the Internet, is set to launch a customized cell phone developed jointly with 3 Mobile, a wireless carrier in Europe, Asia, and Australia.

Code-named the "white phone," the Skype handset will be introduced by late October in Britain, Italy, Hong Kong, and Australia, and will reach 3's other five markets later, *BusinessWeek* has learned. There are no immediate plans to bring the device to North America, though the companies may try to license it to other carriers or sell versions straight to consumers for them to use on other networks.

The iSkoot Button

What may be most striking about the device is that it's being pushed by a mobile carrier at a time when most of the wireless industry is anxiously fighting to preserve its business model against a siege of new technologies and players. The major wireless carriers are fearful of upstart technologies that are slashing once-robust revenue streams from traditional home and office telephones, so they've made it impossible to use Internet phone services on most of their phones. Indeed, Vonage and other providers of VoIP technology will have signed up more than 15 million U.S. homes and businesses by year-end, generating nearly $5 billion of revenue for 2007, says research firm

TeleGeography. But on cell phones, VoIP is hard to find. "There are a lot of reasons why mobile VoIP has not yet taken off—and they differ by region," says Stephan Beckert, a TeleGeography analyst. "In the U.S., a key reason is that mobile operators are deliberately trying to keep their customers from being able to use it."

The Skype cell phone, developed with a software outfit named iSkoot, is equipped with multimedia capabilities and high-speed data for mobile Web browsing. But its most prominent feature is a big button right above the regular keypad to activate Skype's popular service for long-distance and international calls. A press on that button triggers an iSkoot-developed application that brings up a list of a user's Skype "buddies" and regular phone contacts. A click on any entry in that list dials the call.

Skype's Challenge: Turning Appeal Into Profits

Skype is betting that easy mobile access to its service could spur more overseas call traffic, a revenue-producing business where growth has slumped sharply. Though Skype boasts 246 million accounts, only about one-quarter to one-third of those customers are thought to be regular users, and the vast majority of their calls are free. Skype has struggled to turn its popularity into profits since it was acquired two years ago by eBay, which recently acknowledged it overpaid by $1.4 billion for the business.

Calls on the Skype cell phone will cost the same as on a computer or Skype cordless phone: free when speaking to other Skype users, pennies per minute when users dial regular phone numbers in most countries. 3 Mobile, owned by Hong Kong's Hutchison Whampoa, won't charge extra to use the Skype feature. But customers will need to spend a certain amount per month for other services, such as regular mobile calls, ringtones, or text messaging.

A cheap international connection could prove to be a potent draw for wireless users. Currently, few mobile phone subscribers are willing to pay the quarters and dollars per minute charged by cellular companies for international calls. That means 3 Mobile is putting little international revenue at risk by moving to the Skype model. Another intriguing twist: Since eBay owns the online payment service PayPal, success with the Skype phone could provide a springboard for using a cell phone or other handheld device to pay for items, as if it's a charge or debit card. That's been an elusive goal for the wireless industry except in a handful of countries such as Japan and Korea.

A Tough Sell with Carriers

But even if it widens the path being carved by Apple and Google, the Skype phone is really more of a back-to-basics concept. The iPhone adds sleek Web browsing and the simplicity of an iPod music player to a phone. The gPhone seeks to bring Google's expertise, finding information and showing related ads, to a mobile handset. By contrast, the Skype phone is first and foremost about plain old phone calls.

Whatever the nature of these new services and phones, Apple, Skype, and even handset makers like Nokia have found that it's difficult to get them into consumers' hands without the aid of mobile carriers—and their cooperation is rare. In the case of Internet calling, the industry's uneasiness has been especially palpable.

Mobile carriers such as AT&T specifically prohibit VoIP on their phones in their terms of service. Verizon and Sprint Nextel have battered Vonage with patent infringement suits that may have as much to do with nudging the Internet phone company toward bankruptcy as protecting their intellectual property. And

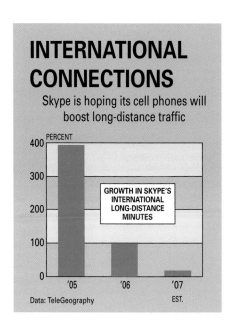

INTERNATIONAL CONNECTIONS

Skype is hoping its cell phones will boost long-distance traffic

GROWTH IN SKYPE'S INTERNATIONAL LONG-DISTANCE MINUTES

Data: TeleGeography

earlier this year, one of the top U.S. cellular companies put a last-minute kibosh on a plan by iSkoot to announce that its Skype application worked on some of that carrier's handsets. The carrier told iSkoot it was still determining its policy toward not only Skype, but VoIP in general.

The arrival of the Skype phone is but the latest sign of evolution in wireless, and counter measures by the cel-

lular carriers a ready reminder that there won't be a revolution any time soon.

By Bruce Meyerson

The opening article illustrates how new technology and media can create new ways of communicating. These new technologies, however, also challenge existing approaches, setting up the potential for conflict that must be resolved through negotiation or other means. Inexpensive global communication via the Internet is evolving to include handheld cellular devices, threatening some existing companies such as Verizon and Sprint Nextel. While companies such as Vonage and Skype are trying to spread the word and let customers know that their technology could work on current networks, the corresponding cellular providers are working against such efforts and claiming that these innovations are an infringement on their own property. North American telecom providers do not plan to sell Skype phones, a decision that may emanate from the absence of successful negotiation among the various countries and companies to determine how they might benefit from this new innovation. Skype is developing partners and collaborators in some areas, while also creating conflict and disagreement with other telecom providers. Skype has been a major vehicle in accelerating global communications. Although the company encourages communication across cultures, it is still subject to differences in negotiation and communication approaches in these different regions, as well as the legacies of different legal and regulatory approaches to communication. If Skype plans to expand its international operations, it may have to negotiate with some of the existing cellular providers that are currently blocking its expansion. How could Skype effectively bring its cellular phone technology to other countries in ways that are compatible with the communication styles, policies, and practices of those nations?

In this chapter, we explore communication and negotiation styles across cultures, emphasizing the importance of understanding different approaches to the development of effective international communication and negotiation strategies.

■ The Overall Communication Process

communication

The process of transferring meanings from sender to receiver.

Communication is the process of transferring meanings from sender to receiver. On the surface, this appears to be a fairly straightforward process. On analysis, however, there are a great many problems in the international arena that can result in the failure to transfer meanings correctly.

Verbal Communication Styles

One way of examining the ways in which individuals convey information is by looking at their communication styles. In particular, as has been noted by Hall, context plays a key role in explaining many communication differences.[1] **Context** is information that surrounds a communication and helps convey the message. In high-context societies, such as Japan and many Arab countries, messages are often highly coded and implicit. As a result, the receiver's job is to interpret what the message means by correctly filtering through what is being said and the way in which the message is being conveyed. This approach is in sharp contrast to low-context societies such as the United States and Canada, where the message is explicit and the speaker says precisely what he or she means. These contextual factors must be considered when marketing messages are being developed in disparate societies. For example, promotions in Japan should be subtle and convey a sense of community (high context). Similar segments in the United States, a low-context environment, should be responsive to expectations for more explicit messages.

context

Information that surrounds a communication and helps to convey the message.

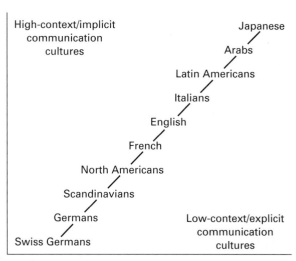

Source: Adapted from Martin Rosch, "Communications: Focal Point of Culture," *Management International Review* 27, no. 4 (1987), p. 60. Used with permission.

Figure 7–1

Explicit-Implicit Communication: An International Comparison

Figure 7–1 provides an international comparison of high-context/implicit and low-context/explicit societies. In addition, Table 7–1 presents some of the major characteristics of communication styles.

Indirect and Direct Styles   In high-context cultures, messages are implicit and indirect. One reason is that those who are communicating—family, friends, co-workers, clients—tend to have both close personal relationships and large information networks. As a result, each knows a lot about others in the communication network; they do not have to rely on language alone to communicate. Voice intonation, timing, and facial expressions can all play roles in conveying information.

Table 7–1
Major Characteristics of Verbal Styles

Verbal Style	Major Variation	Interaction Focus and Content	Cultures in Which Characteristic Is Found
Indirect vs. direct	Indirect	Implicit messages	Collective, high context
	Direct	Explicit messages	Individualistic, low context
Succinct vs. elaborate	Elaborate	High quantity of talk	Moderate uncertainty avoidance, high context
	Exacting	Moderate amount of talk	Low uncertainty avoidance, low context
	Succinct	Low amount of talk	High uncertainty avoidance, high context
Contextual vs. personal	Contextual	Focus on the speaker and role relationships	High power distance, collective, high context
	Personal	Focus on the speaker and personal relationships	Low power distance, individualistic, low context
Affective vs. instrumental	Affective	Process-oriented and receiver-focused language	Collective, high context
	Instrumental	Goal-oriented and sender-focused language	Individualistic, low context

In low-context cultures, people often meet only to accomplish objectives. Since they do not know each other very well, they tend to be direct and focused in their communications.

One way of comparing these two kinds of culture—high context and low context—is by finding out what types of questions are typically asked when someone is contacted and told to attend a meeting. In a high-context culture it is common for the person to ask, "Who will be at this meeting?" so he or she knows how to prepare for appropriate personal interactions. In contrast, in a low-context culture the individual is likely to ask, "What is the meeting going to be about?" so he or she knows how to properly organize for the engagement. In the high-context society, the person focuses on the environment in which the meeting will take place. In the low-context society, the individual is most interested in the objectives that are to be accomplished at the meeting.

Elaborate to Succinct Styles   There are three degrees of communication quantity—elaborate, exacting, and succinct. In high-context societies, the elaborate style is often very common. There is a great deal of talking, description includes much detail, and people often repeat themselves. This elaborate style is widely used in Arabic countries.

The exacting style is more common in nations such as England, Germany, and Sweden, to name three. This style focuses on precision and the use of the right amount of words to convey the message. If a person uses too many words, this is considered exaggeration; if the individual relies on too few, the result is an ambiguous message.

The succinct style is most common in Asia, where people tend to say few words and allow understatements, pauses, and silence to convey meaning. In particular, in unfamiliar situations, communicators are succinct in order to avoid risking a loss of face.

Researchers have found that the elaborating style is more popular in high-context cultures that have a moderate degree of uncertainty avoidance. The exacting style is more common in low-context, low-uncertainty-avoidance cultures. The succinct style is more common in high-context cultures with considerable uncertainty avoidance.

Contextual and Personal Styles   A contextual style is one that focuses on the speaker and relationship of the parties. For example, in Asian cultures people use words that reflect the role and hierarchical relationship of those in the conversation. As a result, in an organizational setting, speakers will choose words that indicate their status relative to the status of the others. Commenting on this idea, Yoshimura and Anderson have noted that white-collar, middle-management employees in Japan, commonly known as salarymen, quickly learn how to communicate with others in the organization by understanding the context and reference group of the other party:

> A salaryman can hardly say a word to another person without implicitly defining the reference groups to which he thinks both of them belong. . . . [This is because] failing to use proper language is socially embarrassing, and the correct form of Japanese to use with someone else depends not only on the relationship between the two people, but also on the relationship between their reference groups. Juniors defer to seniors in Japan, but even this relationship is complicated when the junior person works for a much more prestigious organization (for example, a government bureau) than the senior. [As a result, it is] likely that both will use the polite form to avoid social embarrassment.[2]

A personal style focuses on the speaker and the reduction of barriers between the parties. In the United States, for example, it is common to use first names and to address others informally and directly on an equal basis.

Researchers have found that the contextual style is often associated with high-power-distance, collective, high-context cultures. Examples include Japan, India, and Ghana. In contrast, the personal style is more popular in low-power-distance, individualistic, low-context cultures. Examples include the United States, Australia, and Canada.

Affective and Instrumental Styles   The affective style is characterized by language that requires the listener to carefully note what is being said and to observe how the sender is

Table 7–2
Verbal Styles Used in 10 Select Countries

Country	Indirect vs. Direct	Elaborate vs. Succinct	Contextual vs. Personal	Affective vs. Instrumental
Australia	Direct	Exacting	Personal	Instrumental
Canada	Direct	Exacting	Personal	Instrumental
Denmark	Direct	Exacting	Personal	Instrumental
Egypt	Indirect	Elaborate	Contextual	Affective
England	Direct	Exacting	Personal	Instrumental
Japan	Indirect	Succinct	Contextual	Affective
Korea	Indirect	Succinct	Contextual	Affective
Saudi Arabia	Indirect	Elaborate	Contextual	Affective
Sweden	Direct	Exacting	Personal	Instrumental
United States	Direct	Exacting	Personal	Instrumental

Source: Anne Marie Francesco and Barry Allen Gold, *International Organizational Behavior: Text, Readings, Cases, and Skills,* 1st Edition © 1998. Electronically reproduced by permission of Pearson Education, Inc., Upper Saddle River, New Jersey.

presenting the message. Quite often the meaning that is being conveyed is nonverbal and requires the receiver to use his or her intuitive skills in deciphering what is being said. The part of the message that is being left out may be just as important as the part that is being included. In contrast, the instrumental style is goal-oriented and focuses on the sender. The individual clearly lets the other party know what he or she wants the other party to know.

The affective style is common in collective, high-context cultures such as the Middle East, Latin America, and Asia. The instrumental style is more commonly found in individualistic, low-context cultures such as Switzerland, Denmark, and the United States.

Table 7–2 provides a brief description of the four verbal styles that are used in select countries. A close look at the table helps explain why managers in Japan can have great difficulty communicating with their counterparts in the United States and vice versa: The verbal styles do not match in any context.

Interpretation of Communications

The effectiveness of communication in the international context often is determined by how closely the sender and receiver have the same meaning for the same message.[3] If this meaning is different, effective communication will not occur. A good example is the U.S. firm that wanted to increase worker output among its Japanese personnel. This firm put an individual incentive plan into effect, whereby workers would be given extra pay based on their work output. The plan, which had worked well in the United States, was a total flop. The Japanese were accustomed to working in groups and to being rewarded as a group. In another case, a U.S. firm offered a bonus to anyone who would provide suggestions that resulted in increased productivity. The Japanese workers rejected this idea, because they felt that no one working alone is responsible for increased productivity. It is always a group effort. When the company changed the system and began rewarding group productivity, it was successful in gaining support for the program.

A related case occurs when both parties agree on the content of the message but one party believes it is necessary to persuade the other to accept the message. Here is an example:

> Motorola University recently prepared carefully for a presentation in China. After considerable thought, the presenters entitled it "Relationships do not retire." The gist of the presentation was that Motorola had come to China in order to stay and help the economy to create wealth. Relationships with Chinese suppliers, subcontractors and employees would

constitute a permanent commitment to building Chinese economic infrastructure and earning hard currency through exports. The Chinese audience listened politely to this presentation but was quiet when invited to ask questions. Finally one manager put up his hand and said: "Can you tell us about pay for performance?"[4]

Quite obviously, the Motorola presenter believed that it was necessary to convince the audience that the company was in China for the long run. Those in attendance, however, had already accepted this idea and wanted to move on to other issues.

Still another example has been provided by Adler, who has pointed out that people doing business in a foreign culture often misinterpret the meaning of messages. As a result, they arrive at erroneous conclusions as in the following story of a Canadian doing business in the Middle East. The Canadian was surprised when his meeting with a high-ranking official was not held in a closed office and was constantly interrupted:

> Using the Canadian-based cultural assumptions that (a) important people have large private offices with secretaries to monitor the flow of people into the office, and (b) important business takes precedence over less important business and is therefore not interrupted, the Canadian interprets the . . . open office and constant interruptions to mean that the official is neither as high ranking nor as interested in conducting the business at hand as he had previously thought.[5]

■ Communication Flows

Communication flows in international organizations move both down and up. However, as Figure 7–2 humorously, but in many ways accurately, portrays, there are some unique differences in organizations around the world.

Downward Communication

downward communication
The transmission of information from superior to subordinate.

Downward communication is the transmission of information from manager to subordinate. The primary purpose of the manager-initiated communication flow is to convey orders and information. Managers use this channel to let their people know what is to be done and how well they are doing. The channel facilitates the flow of information to those who need it for operational purposes.

In Asian countries, as noted earlier, downward communication is less direct than in the United States. Orders tend to be implicit in nature. Conversely, in some European countries, downward communication is not only direct but extends beyond business matters. For example, one early study surveyed 299 U.S. and French managers regarding the nature of downward communication and the managerial authority they perceived themselves as having. This study found that U.S. managers basically used downward communication for work-related matters. A follow-up study investigated matters that U.S. and French managers felt were within the purview of their authority.[6] The major differences involved work-related and nonwork-related activities: U.S. managers felt that it was within their authority to communicate or attempt to influence their people's social behavior only if it occurred on the job or it directly affected their work. For example, U.S. managers felt that it was proper to look into matters such as how much an individual drinks at lunch, whether the person uses profanity in the workplace, and how active the individual is in recruiting others to join the company. The French managers were not as supportive of these activities. The researcher concluded that "the Americans find it as difficult [as] or more difficult than the French to accept the legitimacy of managerial authority in areas unrelated to work."[7]

Harris and Moran have noted that when communicating downward with nonnative speakers, it is extremely important to use language that is easy to understand and allows the other person to ask questions. Here are 10 suggestions that apply not only for downward but for all types of communication:

1. Use the most common words with their most common meanings.
2. Select words that have few alternative meanings.

There are a number of different "organization charts" that have been constructed to depict international organizations. An epigram is a poem or line of verse that is witty or satirical in nature. The following organization designs are epigrams that show how communication occurs in different countries. In examining them, remember that each contains considerable exaggeration and humor, but also some degree of truth.

In America, everyone thinks he or she has a communication pipeline directly to the top.

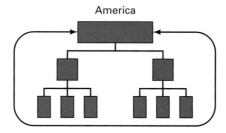

There are so many people in China that organizations are monolithic structures characterized by copious levels of bureaucracy. All information flows through channels.

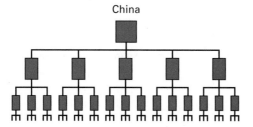

At the United Nations everyone is arranged in a circle so that no one is more powerful than anyone else. Those directly in front or behind are philosophically aligned, and those nearby form part of an international bloc.

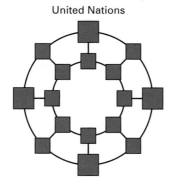

In France some people in the hierarchy are not linked to anyone, indicating how haphazard the structure can be.

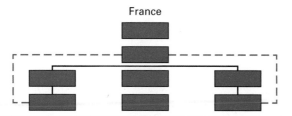

Figure 7–2

Communication Epigrams

Source: Adapted from Simcha Ronen, *Comparative and Multinational Management* (New York: Wiley, 1986), pp. 318–319. The epigrams in turn were derived from a variety of sources, including Robert M. Worchester of the U.K.-based Market and Opinion Research International (MORI), Ole Jacob Raad of Norway's PM Systems, and anonymous managers.

3. Strictly follow the basic rules of grammar—more so than would be the case with native speakers.

4. Speak with clear breaks between the words so that it is easier for the person to follow.

5. Avoid using words that are esoteric or culturally biased such as "he struck out" or "the whole idea is Mickey Mouse" because these clichés often have no meaning for the listener.

6. Avoid the use of slang.

7. Do not use words or expressions that require the other person to create a mental image such as "we were knee deep in the Big Muddy."

8. Mimic the cultural flavor of the nonnative speaker's language, for example, by using more flowery communication with Spanish-speaking listeners than with Germans.

9. Continually paraphrase and repeat the basic ideas.

10. At the end, test how well the other person understands by asking the individual to paraphrase what has been said.[8]

Upward Communication

upward communication
The transfer of meaning from subordinate to superior.

Upward communication is the transfer of information from subordinate to superior. The primary purpose of this subordinate-initiated upward communication is to provide feedback, ask questions, or obtain assistance from higher-level management. In recent years, there has been a call for and a concerted effort to promote more upward communication in the United States. In other countries, such as in Japan, Hong Kong, and Singapore, upward communication has long been a fact of life. Managers in these countries have extensively used suggestion systems and quality circles to get employee input and always are available to listen to their people's concerns.

Here are some observations from the approach the Japanese firm Matsushita uses in dealing with employee suggestions:

> Matsushita views employee recommendations as instrumental to making improvements on the shop floor and in the marketplace. [It believes] that a great many little people, paying attention each day to how to improve their jobs, can accomplish more than a whole headquarters full of production engineers and planners. Praise and positive reinforcement are an important part of the Matsushita philosophy. . . . Approximately 90 percent of . . . suggestions receive rewards; most only a few dollars per month, but the message is reinforced constantly: "Think about your job; develop yourself and help us improve the company." The best suggestions receive company-wide recognition and can earn substantial monetary rewards. Each year, many special awards are also given, including presidential prizes and various divisional honors.[9]

Matsushita has used the same approach wherever it has established plants worldwide, and the strategy has proved very successful. The company has all its employees begin the day by reciting its basic principles, beliefs, and values, which are summarized in Table 7–3, to reinforce in all employees the reason for the company's existence and to provide a form of spiritual fabric to energize and sustain them. All employees see themselves as important members of a successful team, and they are willing to do whatever is necessary to ensure the success of the group.

Outside these Asian countries, upward communication is not as popular. For example, in South America, many managers believe that employees should follow orders and not ask a lot of questions. German managers also make much less use of this form of communication. In most cases, however, evidence shows that employees prefer to have downward communication at least supplemented by upward channels. Unfortunately, such upward communication does not always occur because of a number of communication barriers.

> **Table 7–3**
> **Matsushita's Philosophy**
>
> **Basic Business Principles**
> To recognize our responsibilities as industrialists, to foster progress, to promote the general welfare of society, and to devote ourselves to the further development of world culture.
>
> **Employees Creed**
> Progress and development can be realized only through the combined efforts and cooperation of each member of the company. Each of us, therefore, shall keep this idea constantly in mind as we devote ourselves to the continuous improvement of our company.
>
> **The Seven Spiritual Values**
> 1. National service through industry
> 2. Fairness
> 3. Harmony and cooperation
> 4. Struggle for betterment
> 5. Courtesy and humility
> 6. Adjustment and assimilation
> 7. Gratitude

■ Communication Barriers

A number of common communication barriers are relevant to international management. The more important include language, culture, perception, and nonverbal communication.

Language Barriers

Knowledge of the home country's language (the language used at the headquarters of the MNC) is important for personnel placed in a foreign assignment. If managers do not understand the language that is used at headquarters, they likely will make a wide assortment of errors. Additionally, many MNCs now prescribe English as the common language for internal communication, so that managers can more easily convey information to their counterparts in other geographically dispersed locales.[10] Despite such progress, however, language training continues to lag in many areas, although in an increasing number of European countries, more and more young people are becoming multilingual.[11] Table 7–4 shows the percentage of European students who are studying English, French, or German.

Language education is a good beginning, but it is also important to realize that the ability to speak the language used at MNC headquarters is often not enough to ensure that the personnel are capable of doing the work. Stout recently noted that many MNCs worldwide place a great deal of attention on the applicant's ability to speak English without considering if the person has other necessary skills, such as the ability to interact well with others and the technical knowledge demanded by the job.[12] Additionally, in interviewing people for jobs, he has noted that many interviewers fail to take into account the applicant's culture. As a result, interviewers misinterpret behaviors such as quietness or shyness and use them to conclude that the applicant is not sufficiently confident or self-assured. Still another problem is that nonnative speakers may know the language but not be fully fluent, so they end up asking questions or making statements that convey the wrong message. After studying Japanese for only one year, Stout began interviewing candidates in their local language and made a number of mistakes. In one case, he reports, "a young woman admitted to having an adulterous affair—even though this was not even close to the topic I was inquiring about—because of my unskilled use of the language."[13]

Written communication has been getting increased attention, because poor writing is proving to be a greater barrier than poor talking. For example, Hildebrandt has found that among U.S. subsidiaries studied in Germany, language was a major problem when subsidiaries were sending written communications to the home office. The process often

Table 7–4			
Multilingualism in the EU Classroom			
	Percentage of Pupils in General Second-ary Education Learning English, French, or German as a Foreign Language, 2004		
	English	**French**	**German**
Finland	99	13	26
Germany	94	23	–
Denmark	99	15	85
Spain	97	37	2
France	97	–	18
Belgium	70	52	15
Greece	97	39	20
Italy	88	31	5
Romania	92	86	11
Britain	–	34	14
Ireland	–	68	21
Poland	80	6	46

Source: Eurostat (2007).

involved elaborate procedures associated with translating and reworking the report. Typical steps included (1) holding a staff conference to determine what was to be included in the written message; (2) writing the initial draft in German; (3) rewriting the draft in German; (4) translating the material into English; (5) consulting with bilingual staff members regarding the translation; and (6) rewriting the English draft a series of additional times until the paper was judged to be acceptable for transmission. The German managers admitted that they felt uncomfortable with writing, because their command of written English was poor. As Hildebrandt noted:

> All German managers commanding oral English stated that their grammatical competence was not sufficiently honed to produce a written English report of top quality. Even when professional translators from outside the company rewrote the German into English, German middle managers were unable to verify whether the report captured the substantive intent or included editorial alterations.[14]

Problems associated with the translation of information from one language to another have been made even clearer by Schermerhorn, who conducted research among 153 Hong Kong Chinese bilinguals who were enrolled in an undergraduate management course at a major Hong Kong university. The students were given two scenarios written in either English or Chinese. One scenario involved a manager who was providing some form of personal support or praise for a subordinate. The research used the following procedures:

> [A] careful translation and back-translation method was followed to create the Chinese language versions of the research instruments. Two bilingual Hong Kong Chinese, both highly fluent in English and having expertise in the field of management, shared roles in the process. Each first translated one scenario and the evaluation questions into Chinese. Next they translated each other's Chinese versions back into English, and discussed and resolved translation differences in group consultation with the author. Finally, a Hong Kong professor read and interpreted the translations correctly as a final check of equivalency.[15]

The participants were asked to answer eight evaluation questions about these scenarios. A significant difference between the two sets of responses was found. Those who were queried in Chinese gave different answers from those who were queried in English. This led Schermerhorn to conclude that language plays a key role in conveying information between cultures and that in cross-cultural management research, bilingual individuals should not be queried in their second language.

Cultural Barriers

Closely related to the language barriers are cultural barriers. For example, research by Sims and Guice compared 214 letters of inquiry written by native and nonnative speakers of English to test the assumption that cultural factors affect business communication. Among other things, the researchers found that nonnative speakers used exaggerated politeness, provided unnecessary professional and personal information, and made inappropriate requests of the other party. Commenting on the results and implications of their study, the researchers noted that their investigation

> indicated that the deviations from standard U.S. business communication practices were not specific to one or more nationalities. The deviations did not occur among specific nationalities but were spread throughout the sample of nonnative letters used for the study. Therefore, we can speculate that U.S. native speakers of English might have similar difficulties in international settings. In other words, a significant number of native speakers in the U.S. might deviate from the standard business communication practices of other cultures. Therefore, these native speakers need specific training in the business communication practices of the major cultures of the world so they can communicate successfully and acceptably with readers in those cultures.[16]

Research by Scott and Green has extended these findings, showing that even in English-speaking countries, there are different approaches to writing letters. In the United States, for example, it is common practice when constructing a bad-news letter to start out "with a pleasant, relevant, neutral, and transitional buffer statement; give the reasons for the unfavorable news before presenting the bad news; present the refusal in a positive manner; imply the bad news whenever possible; explain how the refusal is in the reader's best interest; and suggest positive alternatives that build goodwill."[17] In Great Britain, however, it is common to start out by referring to the situation, discussing the reasons for the bad news, conveying the bad news (often quite bluntly), and concluding with an apology or statement of regret (something that is frowned on by business-letter experts in the United States) designed to keep the reader's goodwill. Here is an example:

> Lord Hanson has asked me to reply to your letter and questionnaire of February 12 which we received today.
>
> As you may imagine, we receive numerous requests to complete questionnaires or to participate in a survey, and this poses problems for us. You will appreciate that the time it would take to complete these requests would represent a full-time job, so we decided some while ago to decline such requests unless there was some obvious benefit to Hanson PLC and our stockholders. As I am sure you will understand, our prime responsibility is to look after our stockholders' interests.
>
> I apologize that this will not have been the response that you were hoping for, but I wish you success with your research study.[18]

U.S. MNC managers would seldom, if ever, send that type of letter; it would be viewed as blunt and tactless. However, the indirect approach that Americans use would be viewed by their British counterparts as overly indirect and obviously insincere.

On the other hand, when compared to Asians, many American writers are far more blunt and direct. For example, Park, Dillon, and Mitchell reported that there are pronounced differences between the ways in which Americans and Asians write business letters of complaint. They compared the approach used by American managers for whom English is a first language, who wrote international business letters of complaint, with the approach of Korean managers for whom English is a second language, who wrote the same types of letters. They found that American writers used a direct organizational pattern and tended to state the main idea or problem first before sharing explanatory details that clearly related to the stated problem. In contrast, the standard Korean pattern was indirect and tended to delay the reader's discovery of the main point. This led the researchers to conclude that the U.S.-generated letter might be regarded as rude by Asian readers, while American readers might regard the letter from the Korean writer as vague, emotional, and accusatory.[19]

Perceptual Barriers

perception
A person's view of reality.

Perception is a person's view of reality. How people see reality can vary and will influence their judgment and decision making.[20] One example involves Japanese stockbrokers who perceived that the chances of improving their career would be better with U.S. firms, so they changed jobs. Another involves Hong Kong hoteliers who began buying U.S. properties because they had the perception that if they could offer the same top-quality hotel service as back home, they could dominate their U.S. markets. These are examples of how perceptions can play an important role in international management. Unfortunately, misperceptions also can become a barrier to effective communication. For example, when the Clinton administration decided to allow Taiwan President Lee Tenghui to visit the United States, the Chinese (PRC) government perceived this as a threatening gesture and took actions of its own. Besides conducting dangerous war games very near Taiwan's border as a warning to Taiwan not to become too bold in its quest for recognition as a sovereign nation, the PRC also snubbed U.S. car manufacturers and gave a much-coveted $1 billion contract to Mercedes-Benz of Germany.[21] The following sections provide examples of perception barriers in the international arena.

Advertising Messages   One way that perception can prove to be a problem in international management communication is evident when one person uses words that are misinterpreted by the other. Many firms have found to their dismay that a failure to understand home-country perceptions can result in disastrous advertising programs. Here are two examples:

> Ford . . . introduced a low cost truck, the "Fiera," into some Spanish-speaking countries. Unfortunately, the name meant "ugly old woman" in Spanish. Needless to say, this name did not encourage sales. Ford also experienced slow sales when it introduced a top-of-the-line automobile, the "Comet," in Mexico under the name "Caliente." The puzzling low sales were finally understood when Ford discovered that "caliente" is slang for a street walker.[22]
>
> One laundry detergent company certainly wishes now that it had contacted a few locals before it initiated its promotional campaign in the Middle East. All of the company's advertisements pictured soiled clothes on the left, its box of soap in the middle, and clean clothes on the right. But, because in that area of the world people tend to read from the right to the left, many potential customers interpreted the message to indicate the soap actually soiled the clothes.[23]

There have been countless other advertising blunders. Some speak to the political crowd, such as when Mercedes-Benz introduced its Grand Sports Tourer, or Mercedes GST, in Canada. Canadians were not very impressed, since they used the letters GST to refer to Canadian socialism. Other times, the advertising is simply offensive. Bacardi, for example, advertised the fruity drink "Pavian" in Germany, believing that it was *tres chic*. "Pavian" to the German population, however, meant "baboon." Needless to say, sales did not exceed expectations. The food and beverage industry may have experienced the worst string. The Coors slogan "Turn It Loose" dismayed the Spanish who thought it would cause intestinal problems. In Taiwan, Pepsi's "Come alive with Pepsi" frightened consumers, since it literally meant "Pepsi will bring your ancestors back from the grave." Finally, even though Kentucky Fried Chicken is performing better in the Chinese market than in America, its catchphrase "Finger-licking good" was originally translated as "Eat your fingers off."[24]

Managers must be very careful when they translate messages. As mentioned earlier in the chapter, some common phrases in one country will not mean the same in others. It is evident from the examples provided that errors in translation occur frequently, but many MNCs can still come out on top.

View of Others   Perception influences communication when it deals with how individuals "see" others. A good example is provided by the perception of foreigners who reside in the United States. Most Americans see themselves as extremely friendly, outgoing, and kind, and they believe that others also see them in this way. At the same time, many are not aware of the negative impressions they give to others, especially in the light of September 11,

Doing It Right the First Time

Like other countries of the world, Japan has its own business customs and culture. And when someone fails to adhere to these traditions, the individual runs the risk of being perceived as ineffective or uncaring. The following addresses three areas that are important in being correctly perceived by one's Japanese counterparts.

Business Cards

The exchange of business cards is an integral part of Japanese business etiquette, and Japanese businesspeople exchange these cards when meeting someone for the first time. Additionally, those who are most likely to interface with non-Japanese are supplied with business cards printed in Japanese on one side and a foreign language, usually English, on the reverse side. This is aimed at enhancing recognition and pronunciation of Japanese names, which are often unfamiliar to foreign businesspeople. Conversely, it is advisable for foreign businesspeople to carry and exchange with their Japanese counterparts a similar type of card printed in Japanese and in their native language. These cards can often be obtained through business centers in major hotels.

When receiving a card, it is considered common courtesy to offer one in return. In fact, not returning a card might convey the impression that the manager is not committed to a meaningful business relationship in the future.

Business cards should be presented and received with both hands. When presenting one's card, the presenter's name should be facing the person who is receiving the card so the receiver can easily read it. When receiving a business card, it should be handled with care, and if the receiver is sitting at a conference or other type of table, the card should be placed in front of the individual for the duration of the meeting.

It is considered rude to put a prospective business partner's card in one's pocket before sitting down to discuss business matters.

Bowing

Although the handshake is increasingly common in Japan, bowing remains the most prevalent formal method of greeting, saying goodbye, expressing gratitude, or apologizing to another person. When meeting foreign businesspeople, however, Japanese will often use the handshake or a combination of both a handshake and a bow, even though there are different forms and styles of bowing, depending on the relationship of the parties involved. Foreign businesspeople are not expected to be familiar with these intricacies, and therefore a deep nod of the head or a slight bow will suffice in most cases. Many foreign businesspeople are unsure whether to use a handshake or to bow. In these situations, it is best to wait and see if one's Japanese counterpart offers a hand or prefers to bow and then to follow suit.

Attire

Most Japanese businessmen dress in conservative dark or navy blue suits, although slight variations in style and color have come to be accepted in recent years. As a general rule, what is acceptable business attire in virtually any industrialized country is usually regarded as good business attire in Japan as well. Although there is no need to conform precisely to the style of dress of the Japanese, good judgment should be exercised when selecting attire for a business meeting. If unsure about what constitutes appropriate attire for a particular situation, it is best to err on the conservative side.

2001, and the Iraq War, which has at times shaken the world view of the United States. Another example is the way in which people act, or should act, when initially meeting others. "International Management in Action: Doing It Right the First Time" provides some insights regarding how to conduct oneself when doing business in Japan.

Another example of how the perceptions of others affect communication occurs in the way that some international managers perceive their subordinates. For example, a study examined the perceptions that German and U.S. managers had of the qualifications of their peers (those on the same level and status), managers, and subordinates in Europe and Latin America.[25] The findings showed that both the German and the U.S. respondents perceived their subordinates to be less qualified than their peers. However, although the Germans perceived their managers to have more managerial ability than their peers, the Americans felt that their South American peers in many instances had qualifications equal to or better than the qualifications of their own managers. Quite obviously, this perception will affect how U.S. expatriates communicate with their South American peers, as well as how the expatriates communicate with their bosses.

Another study found that Western managers have more favorable attitudes toward women as managers than Asian or Saudi managers do.[26] This perception obviously affects the way these managers interact and communicate with their female counterparts. The same is true in the case of many Japanese managers, who, according to one survey, still regard women as superfluous to the effective running of their organizations and generally continue to not treat women as equals.[27]

The Impact of Culture

Besides language and perception, another major barrier to communication is culture, a topic that was given detailed attention in Chapter 4. Culture can affect communication in a number of ways, and one way is through the impact of cultural values.

Cultural Values   One expert on Middle Eastern countries notes that people there do not relate to and communicate with each other in a loose, general way as do those in the United States. Relationships are more intense and binding in the Middle East, and a wide variety of work-related values influence what people in the Middle East will and will not do.

> In North American society, the generally professed prevalent pattern is one of nonclass-consciousness, as far as work is concerned. Students, for example, make extra pocket money by taking all sorts of part-time jobs—manual and otherwise—regardless of the socioeconomic stratum to which the individual belongs. The attitude is uninhibited. In the Middle East, the overruling obsession is how the money is made and via what kind of job.[28]

These types of values indirectly, and in many cases directly, affect communication between people from different cultures. For example, one would communicate differently with a "rich college student" from the United States than with one from Saudi Arabia. Similarly, when negotiating with managers from other cultures, knowing the way to handle the deal requires an understanding of cultural values.[29]

Another cultural value example is the way that people use time. In the United States, people believe that time is an asset and is not to be wasted. This is an idea that has limited meaning in some other cultures. Various values are reinforced and reflected in proverbs that Americans are taught from an early age. These proverbs help to guide people's behavior. Table 7–5 lists some examples.

Misinterpretation   Cultural differences can cause misinterpretations both in how others see expatriate managers and in how the latter see themselves. For example, U.S. managers doing business in Austria often misinterpret the fact that local businesspeople always

---

Table 7–5
U.S. Proverbs Representing Cultural Values

Proverb	Cultural Value
A penny saved is a penny earned.	Thriftiness
Time is money.	Time thriftiness
Don't cry over spilt milk.	Practicality
Waste not, want not.	Frugality
Early to bed, early to rise, makes one healthy, wealthy, and wise.	Diligence; work ethic
A stitch in time saves nine.	Timeliness of action
If at first you don't succeed, try, try again.	Persistence; work ethic
Take care of today, and tomorrow will take care of itself.	Preparation for future

Source: Drawn from Nancy J. Adler, *International Dimensions of Organizational Behavior,* 2nd ed. (Boston: PWS-Kent Publishing, 1991), pp. 79–80.

address them in formal terms. They may view this as meaning that they are not friends or are not liked, but in fact, this formalism is the way that Austrians always conduct business. The informal, first-name approach used in the United States is not the style of the Austrians.

Culture even affects day-to-day activities of corporate communications.[30] For example, when sending messages to international clients, American managers have to keep in mind that there are many things that are uniquely American and overseas managers may not be aware of them. As an example, daylight savings time is known to all Americans, but many Asian managers have no idea what the term means. Similarly, it is common for American managers to address memos to their "international office" without realizing that the managers who work in this office regard the American location as the "international" one! Other suggestions that can be of value to American managers who are engaged in international communications include:

- Be careful not to use generalized statements about benefits, compensation, pay cycles, holidays, or policies in your worldwide communications. Work hours, vacation accrual, general business practices, and human resource issues vary widely from country to country.

- Since most of the world uses the metric system, be sure to include converted weights and measures in all internal and external communications.

- Keep in mind that even in English-speaking countries, words may have different meanings. Not everyone knows what is meant by "counterclockwise," or "quite good."

- Remember that letterhead and paper sizes differ worldwide. The $8\frac{1}{2} \times 11$ inch page is a U.S. standard, but most countries use an A4 ($8\frac{1}{4} \times 11\frac{1}{2}$ inch) size for their letterhead, with envelopes to match.

- Dollars are not unique to the United States. There are Australian, Bermudian, Canadian, Hong Kong, Taiwanese, and New Zealand dollars, among others. So when referring to American dollars, it is important to use "US$."

Many Americans also have difficulty interpreting the effect of national values on work behavior. For example, why do French and German workers drink alcoholic beverages at lunchtime? Why are many European workers unwilling to work the night shift? Why do overseas affiliates contribute to the support of the employees' work council or donate money to the support of kindergarten teachers in local schools? These types of actions are viewed by some people as wasteful, but those who know the culture of these countries realize that such actions promote the long-run good of the company. It is the outsider who is misinterpreting why these culturally specific actions are happening, and such misperceptions can become a barrier to effective communication.

Nonverbal Communication

Another major reason for perception problems is accounted for by **nonverbal communication,** which is the transfer of meaning through means such as body language and use of physical space. Table 7–6 summarizes a number of dimensions of nonverbal communication. The general categories that are especially important to communication in international management are kinesics, proxemics, chronemics, and chromatics.

Kinesics   **Kinesics** is the study of communication through body movement and facial expression. Primary areas of concern include eye contact, posture, and gestures. For example, when one communicates verbally with someone in the United States, it is good manners to look the other person in the eye. This area of communicating through the use of eye contact and gaze is known as **oculesics.** In some areas of the world oculesics is an important consideration because of what people should not do, such as stare at others or maintain continuous eye contact, because it is considered impolite to do these things.

nonverbal communication
The transfer of meaning through means such as body language and the use of physical space.

kinesics
The study of communication through body movement and facial expression.

oculesics
The area of communication that deals with conveying messages through the use of eye contact and gaze.

Table 7–6
Common Forms of Nonverbal Communication
1. Hand gestures, both intended and self-directed (autistic), such as the nervous rubbing of hands.
2. Facial expressions, such as smiles, frowns, and yawns.
3. Posture and stance.
4. Clothing and hair styles (hair being more like clothes than like skin, both subject to the fashion of the day).
5. Interpersonal distance (proxemics).
6. Eye contact and direction of gaze, particularly in "listening behavior".
7. "Artifacts" and nonverbal symbols, such as lapel pins, walking sticks, and jewelry.
8. Paralanguage (though often in language, just as often treated as part of nonverbal behavior—speech rate, pitch, inflections, volume).
9. Taste, including symbolism of food and the communication function of chatting over coffee or tea, and oral gratification such as smoking or gum chewing.
10. Cosmetics: temporary—powder; permanent—tattoos.
11. Time symbolism: what is too late or too early to telephone or visit a friend, or too long or too short to make a speech or stay for dinner.
12. Timing and pauses within verbal behavior.

Source: From John C. Condon and Fathi S. Yousef, *An Introduction To Intercultural Communication,* 1st Edition. Published by Allyn and Bacon, Boston, MA. Copyright © 1975 by Pearson Education. Reprinted by permission of the publisher.

Another area of kinesics is posture, which can also cause problems. For example, when Americans are engaged in prolonged negotiations or meetings, it is not uncommon for them to relax and put their feet up on a chair or desk, but this is insulting behavior in the Middle East. Here is an example from a classroom situation:

> In the midst of a discussion of a poem in the sophomore class of the English Department, the professor, who was British, took up the argument, started to explain the subtleties of the poem, and was carried away by the situation. He leaned back in his chair, put his feet up on the desk, and went on with the explanation. The class was furious. Before the end of the day, a demonstration by the University's full student body had taken place. Petitions were submitted to the deans of the various facilities. The next day, the situation even made the newspaper headlines. The consequences of the act, that was innocently done, might seem ridiculous, funny, baffling, incomprehensible, or even incredible to a stranger. Yet, to the native, the students' behavior was logical and in context. The students and their supporters were outraged because of the implications of the breach of the native behavioral pattern. In the Middle East, it is extremely insulting to have to sit facing two soles of the shoes of somebody.[31]

Gestures are also widely used and take many different forms. For example, Canadians shake hands, Japanese bow, Middle Easterners of the same sex kiss on the cheek. Communicating through the use of bodily contact is known as **haptics,** and it is a widely used form of nonverbal communication.

haptics
Communicating through the use of bodily contact.

Sometimes gestures present problems for expatriate managers because these behaviors have different meanings depending on the country. For example, in the United States, putting the thumb and index finger together to form an "O" is the sign for "okay." In Japan, this is the sign for money; in southern France, the gesture means "zero" or "worthless"; and in Brazil, it is regarded as a vulgar or obscene sign. In France and Belgium, snapping the fingers of both hands is considered vulgar; in Brazil, this gesture is used to indicate that something has been done for a long time. In Britain, the "V for victory" sign is given with the palm facing out; if the palm is facing in, this roughly means "shove it"; in non-British countries, the gesture means two of something and often is used when placing an order at a restaurant.[32] Gibson, Hodgetts, and Blackwell found that many foreign students attending school in the United States have trouble communicating because they are unable to interpret some of the most common nonverbal gestures.[33] A survey group of 44 Jamaican, Venezuelan, Colombian, Peruvian, Thai, Indian, and Japanese students at two major universities were given pictures of 20 universal cultural gestures, and each was asked to describe the nonverbal gestures illustrated. In 56 percent of the choices the respondents either gave an interpretation that was markedly different from that of Americans or reported that the nonverbal gesture had no meaning in their culture. These findings help to reinforce the need to teach expatriates about local nonverbal communication.

Proxemics   **Proxemics** is the study of the way that people use physical space to convey messages. For example, in the United States, there are four "distances" people use in communicating on a face-to-face basis (see Figure 7–3.) **Intimate distance** is used for very confidential communications. **Personal distance** is used for talking with family and close friends. **Social distance** is used to handle most business transactions. **Public distance** is used when calling across the room or giving a talk to a group.

One major problem for Americans communicating with people from the Middle East or South America is that the intimate or personal distance zones are violated. Americans often tend to be moving away in interpersonal communication with their Middle Eastern or Latin counterparts, while the latter are trying to physically close the gap. The American cannot understand why the other is standing so close; the latter cannot understand why the American is being so reserved and standing so far away. The result is a breakdown in communication.

Office layout is another good example of proxemics. In the United States, the more important the manager, the larger the office, and often a secretary screens visitors and keeps away those whom the manager does not wish to see. In Japan, most managers do not have large offices, and even if they do, they spend a great deal of time out of the office and with the employees. Thus, the Japanese have no trouble communicating directly with their superiors. A Japanese manager's staying in his office would be viewed as a sign of distrust or anger toward the group.

Another way that office proxemics can affect communication is that in many European companies, no wall separates the space allocated to the senior-level manager from that of the subordinates. Everyone works in the same large room. These working conditions often are disconcerting to Americans, who tend to prefer more privacy.

Chronemics   **Chronemics** refers to the way in which time is used in a culture. When examined in terms of extremes, there are two types of time schedules: monochronic and polychronic. A **monochronic time schedule** is one in which things are done in a linear fashion. A manager will address Issue A first and then move on to Issue B. In these societies, time schedules are very important, and time is viewed as something that can be controlled and should be used wisely. In individualistic cultures such as the United States,

---

proxemics
The study of the way people use physical space to convey messages.

intimate distance
Distance between people that is used for very confidential communications.

personal distance
In communicating, the physical distance used for talking with family and close friends.

social distance
In communicating, the distance used to handle most business transactions.

public distance
In communicating, the distance used when calling across the room or giving a talk to a group.

chronemics
The way in which time is used in a culture.

monochronic time schedule
A time schedule in which things are done in a linear fashion.

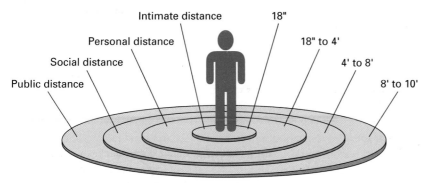

Figure 7–3

Personal Space Categories for Those in the United States

Intimate distance — 18"
Personal distance — 18" to 4'
Social distance — 4' to 8'
Public distance — 8' to 10'

Source: Adapted from Richard M. Hodgetts and Donald F. Kuratko, *Management,* 2nd ed. (San Diego, CA: Harcourt Brace Jovanovich, 1991), p. 384.

Great Britain, Canada, and Australia, as well as many of the cultures in Northern Europe, managers adhere to monochronic time schedules.

polychronic time schedule
A time schedule in which people tend to do several things at the same time and place higher value on personal involvement than on getting things done on time.

This is in sharp contrast to **polychronic time schedules,** which are characterized by people tending to do several things at the same time and placing higher value on personal involvement than on getting things done on time. In these cultures, schedules are subordinated to personal relationships. Regions of the world where polychronic time schedules are common include Latin America and the Middle East.

When doing business in countries that adhere to monochronic time schedules, it is important to be on time for meetings. Additionally, these meetings typically end at the appointed time so that participants can be on time for their next meeting. When doing business in countries that adhere to polychronic time schedules, it is common to find business meetings starting late and finishing late.

chromatics
The use of color to communicate messages.

Chromatics   Chromatics is the use of color to communicate messages. Every society uses chromatics, but colors that mean one thing in the United States may mean something entirely different in Asia. For example, in the United States it is common to wear black when one is in mourning, while in some locations in India people wear white when they are in mourning. In Hong Kong red is used to signify happiness or luck and traditional bridal dresses are red; in the United States it is common for the bride to wear white. In many Asian countries shampoos are dark in color because users want the soap to be the same color as their hair and believe that if it were a light color, it would remove color from their hair. In the United States shampoos tend to be light in color because people see this as a sign of cleanliness and hygiene. In Chile a gift of yellow roses conveys the message "I don't like you," but in the United States it says quite the opposite.

Knowing the importance of chromatics can be very helpful because, among other things, it can avoid embarrassing situations. A good example is the American manager in Peru who upon finishing a one-week visit to the Lima subsidiary decided to thank the assistant who was assigned to him. He sent her a dozen red roses. The lady understood the faux pas, but the American manager was somewhat embarrassed when his Peruvian counterpart smilingly told him, "It was really nice of you to buy her a present. However, red roses indicate a romantic interest!"

■ Achieving Communication Effectiveness

A number of steps can be taken to improve communication effectiveness in the international arena. These include improving feedback systems, providing language and cultural training, and increasing flexibility and cooperation.

Improve Feedback Systems

One of the most important ways of improving communication effectiveness in the international context is to open up feedback systems. Feedback is particularly important between parent companies and their affiliates. There are two basic types of feedback systems: personal (e.g., face-to-face meetings, telephone conversations, and personalized e-mail) and impersonal (e.g., reports, budgets, and plans). Both systems help affiliates keep their home office aware of progress and, in turn, help the home office monitor and control affiliate performance as well as set goals and standards.

At present, there seem to be varying degrees of feedback between the home offices of MNCs and their affiliates. For example, one study evaluated the communication feedback between subsidiaries and home offices of 63 MNCs headquartered in Europe, Japan, and North America.[34] A marked difference was found between the way that U.S. companies communicated with their subsidiaries and the way that European and Japanese firms did. Over one-half of the U.S. subsidiaries responded that they received monthly feedback from their reports, in contrast to less than 10 percent of the European and

Japanese subsidiaries. In addition, the Americans were much more inclined to hold regular management meetings on a regional or worldwide basis. Seventy-five percent of the U.S. companies had annual meetings for their affiliate top managers, compared with less than 50 percent for the Europeans and Japanese. These findings may help explain why many international subsidiaries and affiliates are not operating as efficiently as they should. The units may not have sufficient contact with the home office. They do not seem to be getting continuous assistance and feedback that are critical to effective communication.

Provide Language Training

Besides improving feedback systems, another way to make communication more effective in the international arena is through language training. Many host-country managers cannot communicate well with their counterparts at headquarters. Because English has become the international language of business, those who are not native speakers of English should learn the language well enough so that face-to-face and telephone conversations and e-mail are possible. If the language of the home office is not English, this other language also should be learned. As a U.S. manager working for a Japanese MNC recently told one of the authors, "The official international language of this company is English. However, whenever the home-office people show up, they tend to cluster together with their countrymen and speak Japanese. That's why I'm trying to learn Japanese. Let's face it. They say all you need to know is English, but if you want to really know what's going on, you have to talk *their* language."

Written communication also is extremely important in achieving effectiveness. As noted earlier, when reports, letters, and e-mail messages are translated from one language to another, preventing a loss of meaning is virtually impossible. Moreover, if the communications are not written properly, they may not be given the attention they deserve. The reader will allow poor grammar and syntax to influence his or her interpretation and subsequent actions. Moreover, if readers cannot communicate in the language of those who will be receiving their comments or questions about the report, their messages also must be translated and likely will lose further meaning. Therefore, the process can continue on and on, each party failing to achieve full communication with the other. Hildebrandt has described the problems in this two-way process when an employee in a foreign subsidiary writes a report and then sends it to his or her boss for forwarding to the home office:

> The general manager or vice president cannot be asked to be an editor. Yet they often send statements along, knowingly, which are poorly written, grammatically imperfect, or generally unclear. The time pressures do not permit otherwise. Predictably, questions are issued from the States to the subsidiary and the complicated bilingual process now goes in reverse, ultimately reaching the original . . . staff member, who receives the English questions retranslated.[35]

Language training would help to alleviate such complicated communication problems.

Provide Cultural Training

It is very difficult to communicate effectively with someone from another culture unless at least one party has some understanding of the other's culture.[36] Otherwise, communication likely will break down. This is particularly important for multinational companies that have operations throughout the world.[37] Although there always are important differences between countries, and even between subcultures of the same country, firms that operate in South America find that the cultures of these countries have certain commonalities. These common factors also apply to Spain and Portugal. Therefore, a basic understanding of Latin cultures can prove to be useful throughout a large region of the world. The same is true of Anglo cultures, where norms and values tend to be somewhat similar from one country to another. When a multinational has operations in South America, Europe, and Asia, however, multicultural training becomes necessary. "International Management in Action: Communicating in Europe" provides some specific examples of cultural differences.

As Chapter 4 pointed out, it is erroneous to generalize about an "international" culture, because the various nations and regions of the globe are so different. Training must be conducted on a regional or country-specific basis. Failure to do so can result in continuous communication breakdown.[38] Chapter 14 will give considerable attention to cultural training as part of selection for overseas assignments and human resource development.

Increase Flexibility and Cooperation

Effective international communications require increased flexibility and cooperation by all parties.[39] To improve understanding and cooperation, each party must be prepared to give a little.[40] Take the case of International Computers Ltd., a mainframe computer firm that does a great deal of business in Japan. This firm urges its people to strive for successful collaboration in their international partnerships and ventures. At the heart of this process is effective communication. As put by Kenichi Ohmae:

> We must recognize and accept the inescapable subtleties and difficulties of intercompany relationships. This is the essential starting point. Then we must focus not on contractual or equity-related issues but on the quality of the people at the interface between organizations. Finally, we must understand that success requires frequent, rapport-building meetings by at least three organizational levels: top management, staff, and line management at the working level.[41]

■ Managing Cross-Cultural Negotiations

negotiation
Bargaining with one or more parties for the purpose of arriving at a solution acceptable to all.

Closely related to communications but deserving special attention is managing negotiations.[42] **Negotiation** is the process of bargaining with one or more parties to arrive at a solution that is acceptable to all. It has been estimated that managers can spend 50 percent or more of their time on negotiation processes.[43] Therefore, it is a learnable skill that is imperative not only for the international manager but for the domestic manager as well, since more and more domestic businesses are operating in multicultural environments (see Chapter 6). Negotiation often follows assessing political environments and is a natural approach to conflict management. Often, the MNC must negotiate with the host country to secure the best possible arrangements. The MNC and the host country will discuss the investment the MNC is prepared to make in return for certain guarantees or concessions. The initial range of topics typically includes critical areas such as hiring practices, direct financial investment, taxes, and ownership control. Negotiation also is used in creating joint ventures with local firms and in getting the operation off the ground. After the firm is operating, additional areas of negotiation include expansion of facilities, use of more local managers, additional imports or exports of materials and finished goods, and recapture of profits.

On a more macro level of international trade are the negotiations conducted between countries. The current balance-of-trade problem between the United States and China is one example. The massive debt problems of less developed countries and the opening of trade with Eastern European and newly emerging economies are other current examples.

Types of Negotiation

distributive negotiations
Bargaining that occurs when two parties with opposing goals compete over a set value.

People enter into negotiations for a multitude of reasons, but the nature of the goal determines what kind of negotiation will take place. There are two types of negotiations that we will discuss here: distributive and integrative negotiation. **Distributive negotiations** occur when two parties with opposing goals compete over a set value.[44] Consider a person who passes a street vendor and sees an item he likes but considers the price, or set value, a bit steep. The goal of the buyer is to procure the item at the lowest price,

Communicating in Europe

In Europe, many countries are within easy commuting distance of their neighbors, so an expatriate who does business in France on Monday may be in Germany on Tuesday, Great Britain on Wednesday, Italy on Thursday, and Spain on Friday. Each country has its own etiquette regarding how to greet others and conduct oneself during social and business meetings. The following sections examine some of the things that expatriate managers need to know to communicate effectively.

France

When one is meeting with businesspeople in France, promptness is expected, although tardiness of 5 to 10 minutes is not considered a major gaffe. The French prefer to shake hands when introduced, and it is correct to address them by title plus last name. When the meeting is over, a handshake again is proper manners.

French executives try to keep their personal and professional lives separate. As a result, most business entertaining is done at restaurants or clubs. When gifts are given to business associates, they should appeal to intellectual or aesthetic pursuits as opposed to being something that one's company produces for sale on the world market. In conversational discussions, topics such as politics and money should be avoided. Also, humor should be used carefully during business meetings.

Germany

German executives like to be greeted by their title, and one should never refer to someone on a first-name basis unless invited to do so. When introducing yourself, do not use a title, just state your last name. Business appointments should be made well in advance, and punctuality is important. Like the French, the Germans usually do not entertain clients at home, so an invitation to a German manager's home is a special privilege and always should be followed with a thank-you note. Additionally, as is the case in France, one should avoid using humor during business meetings. They are very serious when it comes to business, so be as prepared as possible and keep lighthearted banter to the German hosts' discretion.

Great Britain

In Britain, it is common to shake hands on the first meeting, and to be polite one should use last names and appropriate titles when addressing the host, until invited to use their first name. Punctuality again is important to the British, so be prepared to be on time and get down to business fairly quickly. The British are quite warm, though, and an invitation to a British home is more likely than in most areas of Europe. You should always bring a gift if invited to the host's house; flowers, chocolates, or books are acceptable.

During business meetings, suits and ties are common dress; however, striped ties should be avoided if they appear to be a copy of those worn by alumni of British universities and schools or by members of military or social clubs. Additionally, during social gatherings it is a good idea not to discuss politics, religion, or gossip about the monarchy unless the British person brings the topic up first.

Italy

In traditional companies, executives are referred to by title plus last name. It is common to shake hands when being introduced, and if the individual is a university graduate, the professional title *dottore* should be used.

Business appointments should be made well in advance, and if you expect to be late, call the host and explain the situation. In most cases, business is done at the office, and when someone is invited to a restaurant, this invitation is usually done to socialize and not to continue business discussions. If an expatriate is invited to an Italian home, it is common to bring a gift for the host, such as a bottle of wine or a box of chocolates. Flowers are also acceptable, but be sure to send an uneven number and avoid chrysanthemums, a symbol of death, and red roses, a sign of deep passion. Be sure to offer high-quality gifts with the wrapping done well, as the Italians are very generous when it comes to gifts. It is not a common practice to exchange them during business, but it is recommended that you are prepared. During the dinner conversation, there is a wide variety of acceptable topics, including business, family matters, and soccer.

Spain

It is common to use first names when introducing or talking to people in Spain, and close friends typically greet each other with an embrace. Appointments should be made in advance, but punctuality is not essential.

If one is invited to the home of a Spanish executive, flowers or chocolates for the host are acceptable gifts. If the invitation includes dinner, any business discussions should be delayed until after coffee is served. During the social gathering, some topics that should be avoided include religion, family, and work. Additionally, humor rarely is used during formal occasions.

Characteristic	Distributive Negotiations	Integrative Negotiations
Objective	Claim maximum value	Create and claim value
Motivation	Individual-selfish benefit	Group-cooperative benefit
Interests	Divergent	Overlapping
Relationship	Short term	Long term
Outcome	Win-lose	Win-win

Table 7–7
Negotiation Types and Characteristics

Source: Adapted from *Harvard Business Essentials: Negotiation* (Boston: Harvard Business School Press, 2003), pp. 2–6.

getting more value for his money, while the goal of the seller is to collect as much as possible to maximize profits. Both are trying to get the best deal, but what translates into a gain by one side is usually experienced as a loss by the other, otherwise known as a *win-lose* situation. The relationship is focused on the individual and based on a short-term interaction. More often than not, the people involved are not friends, or at least their personal relationship is put aside in the matter. Information also plays an important role, since you do not want to expose too much and be vulnerable to counterattack.

Research has shown that first offers in a negotiation can be good predictors of outcomes, which is why it is important to have a strong initial offer.[45] This does not imply that overly greedy or aggressive behavior is acceptable; this could be off-putting to the other negotiator, causing her to walk away. In addition to limiting the amount of information you disclose, it can be advantageous to know a little about the other side.

Integrative negotiation involves cooperation between the two groups to integrate interests, create value, and invest in the agreement. Both groups work toward maximizing benefits for both sides and distributing those benefits. This method is sometimes called the *win-win* scenario, which does not mean that everyone receives exactly what they wish for, but instead that the compromise allowed both sides to keep what was most important and still gain on the deal. The relationship in this instance tends to be more long term, since both sides take time to really get to know the other side and what motivates them. The focus is on the group, reaching for a best-case outcome where everyone benefits. Table 7–7 provides a summary of the two types of negotiation. This is the most useful tactic when dealing with business negotiation, so from this point on, we assume the integrative approach.

integrative negotiation
Bargaining that involves cooperation between two groups to integrate interests, create value, and invest in the agreement.

The Negotiation Process

Several basic steps can be used to manage the negotiation process. Regardless of the issues or personalities of the parties involved, this process typically begins with planning.

Planning   Planning starts with the negotiators' identifying the objectives they would like to attain. Then they explore the possible options for reaching these objectives. Research shows that the greater the number of options, the greater the chances for successful negotiations. While this appears to be an obvious statement, research also reveals that many negotiators do not alter their strategy when negotiating across cultures.[46] Next, consideration is given to areas of common ground between the parties. Other major areas include (1) the setting of limits on single-point objectives, such as deciding to pay no more than $10 million for the factory and $3 million for the land; (2) dividing issues into short- and long-term considerations and deciding how to handle each; and (3) determining the sequence in which to discuss the various issues.

Interpersonal Relationship Building   The second phase of the negotiation process involves getting to know the people on the other side. This "feeling out" period is characterized by the desire to identify those who are reasonable and those who are not. In contrast to negotiators in many other countries, those in the United States often give little attention to this phase; they want to get down to business immediately, which often is an ineffective approach. Adler notes:

> Effective negotiators must view luncheon, dinner, reception, ceremony, and tour invitations as times for interpersonal relationship building, and therefore as key to the negotiating process. When American negotiators, often frustrated by the seemingly endless formalities, ceremonies, and "small talk," ask how long they must wait before beginning to "do business," the answer is simple: wait until your opponents bring up business (and they will). Realize that the work of conducting a successful negotiation has already begun, even if business has yet to be mentioned.[47]

Exchanging Task-Related Information   In this part of the negotiation process, each group sets forth its position on the critical issues. These positions often will change later in the negotiations. At this point, the participants are trying to find out what the other party wants to attain and what it is willing to give up.

Persuasion   This step of negotiations is considered by many to be the most important. No side wants to give away more than it has to, but each knows that without giving some concessions, it is unlikely to reach a final agreement. The success of the persuasion step often depends on (1) how well the parties understand each other's position; (2) the ability of each to identify areas of similarity and difference; (3) the ability to create new options; and (4) the willingness to work toward a solution that allows all parties to walk away feeling they have achieved their objectives.

Agreement   The final phase of negotiations is the granting of concessions and hammering out a final agreement. Sometimes, this phase is carried out piecemeal, and concessions and agreements are made on issues one at a time. This is the way negotiators from the United States like to operate. As each issue is resolved, it is removed from the bargaining table, and interest is focused on the next. Asians and Russians, on the other hand, tend to negotiate a final agreement on everything, and few concessions are given until the end. Simply put, to negotiate effectively in the international arena, it is necessary to understand how cultural differences between the parties affect the process.

Cultural Differences Affecting Negotiations

In negotiating effectively, it is important to have a sound understanding of the other side's culture. One reason is because individuals have a tendency toward in-group favoring. Whether the association resides with the home company or culture, one should be familiar with the other side to better empathize.[48] The cultural aspects managers should consider include communication patterns, time orientation, and social behaviors.[49] A number of useful steps can help in this process. One negotiation expert recommends the following:

1. Do not identify the counterpart's home culture too quickly. Common cues (e.g., name, physical appearance, language, accent, location) may be unreliable. The counterpart probably belongs to more than one culture.
2. Beware of the Western bias toward "doing." In Arab, Asian, and Latin groups, ways of being (e.g., comportment, smell), feeling, thinking, and talking can shape relationships more powerfully than doing.
3. Try to counteract the tendency to formulate simple, consistent, stable images.

4. Do not assume that all aspects of the culture are equally significant. In Japan, consulting all relevant parties to a decision is more important than presenting a gift.

5. Recognize that norms for interactions involving outsiders may differ from those for interactions between compatriots.

6. Do not overestimate your familiarity with your counterpart's culture. An American studying Japanese wrote New Year's wishes to Japanese contacts in basic Japanese characters but omitted one character. As a result, the message became "Dead man, congratulations."[50]

Other useful examples have been offered by Trompenaars and Hampden-Turner, who note that a society's culture often plays a major role in determining the effectiveness of a negotiating approach. This is particularly true when the negotiating groups come from decidedly different cultures such as an ascription society and an achievement society. As noted in Chapter 4, in an ascription society status is attributed based on birth, kinship, gender, age, and personal connections. In an achievement society, status is determined by accomplishments. As a result, each side's cultural perceptions can affect the outcome of the negotiation. Here is an example:

> Sending whiz-kids to deal with people 10–20 years their senior often insults the ascriptive culture. The reaction may be: "Do these people think that they have reached our own level of experience in half the time? That a 30-year-old American is good enough to negotiate with a 50-year-old Greek or Italian?" Achievement cultures must understand that some ascriptive cultures, the Japanese especially, spend much on training and in-house education to ensure that older people actually are wiser for the years they have spent in the corporation and for the sheer number of subordinates briefing them. It insults an ascriptive culture to do anything which prevents the self-fulfilling nature of its beliefs. Older people are held to be important *so that* they will be nourished and sustained by others' respect. A stranger is expected to facilitate this scheme, not challenge it.[51]

U.S. negotiators have a style that often differs from that of negotiators in many other countries. Americans believe it is important to be factual and objective. In addition, they often make early concessions to show the other party that they are flexible and reasonable. Moreover, U.S. negotiators typically have authority to bind their party to an agreement, so if the right deal is struck, the matter can be resolved quickly. This is why deadlines are so important to Americans. They have come to do business, and they want to get things resolved immediately.

A comparative example would be the Arabs, who in contrast to Americans, with their logical approach, tend to use an emotional appeal in their negotiation style. They analyze things subjectively and treat deadlines as only general guidelines for wrapping up negotiations. They tend to open negotiations with an extreme initial position. However, the Arabs believe strongly in making concessions, do so throughout the bargaining process, and almost always reciprocate an opponent's concessions. They also seek to build a long-term relationship with their bargaining partners. For these reasons, Americans typically find it easier to negotiate with Arabs than with representatives from many other regions of the world.

Another interesting comparative example is provided by the Chinese. In initial negotiation meetings, it is common for Chinese negotiators to seek agreement on the general focus of the meetings. The hammering out of specific details is postponed for later get-togethers. By achieving agreement on the general framework within which the negotiations will be conducted, the Chinese seek to limit and focus the discussions. Many Westerners misunderstand what is happening during these initial meetings and believe the dialogue consists mostly of rhetoric and general conversation. They are wrong and quite often are surprised later on when the Chinese negotiators use the agreement on the framework and principles as a basis for getting agreement on goals—and then insist that all discussions on concrete arrangements be in accord with these agreed-upon goals. Simply put, what is viewed as general conversation by many Western negotiators is regarded by

Table 7–8

Negotiation Styles from a Cross-Cultural Perspective

Element	United States	Japanese	Arabians	Mexicans
Group composition	Marketing oriented	Function oriented	Committee of specialists	Friendship oriented
Number involved	2–3	4–7	4–6	2–3
Space orientation	Confrontational; competitive	Display harmonious relationship	Status	Close, friendly
Establishing rapport	Short period; direct to task	Longer period; until harmony	Long period; until trusted	Longer period; discuss family
Exchange of information	Documented; step by step; multimedia	Extensive; concentrate on receiving side	Less emphasis on technology, more on relationship	Less emphasis on technology, more on relationship
Persuasion tools	Time pressure; loss of saving/making money	Maintain relationship references; intergroup connections	Go-between; hospitality	Emphasis on family and on social concerns; goodwill measured in generations
Use of language	Open, direct, sense of urgency	Indirect, appreciative, cooperative	Flattery, emotional, religious	Respectful, gracious
First offer	Fair ±5 to 10%	±10 to 20%	±20 to 50%	Fair
Second offer	Add to package; sweeten the deal	−5%	−10%	Add an incentive
Final offer package	Total package	Makes no further concessions	−25%	Total
Decision-making process	Top management team	Collective	Team makes recommendation	Senior manager and secretary
Decision maker	Top management team	Middle line with team consensus	Senior manager	Senior manager
Risk taking	Calculated personal responsibility	Low group responsibility	Religion based	Personally responsible

Source: Lillian H. Chaney and Jeanette S. Martin, *International Business Communication*, 3rd Edition © 2004. Electronically reproduced by permission of Pearson Education, Inc., Upper Saddle River, New Jersey.

the Chinese as a formulation of the rules of the game that must be adhered to throughout the negotiations. So in negotiating with the Chinese, it is important to come prepared to ensure that one's own agenda, framework, and principles are accepted by both parties.

Before beginning any negotiations, negotiators should review the negotiating style of the other parties. (Table 7–8 provides some insights regarding negotiation styles of the Americans, Japanese, Arabs, and Mexicans.) This review should help to answer certain questions: What can we expect the other side to say and do? How are they likely to respond to certain offers? When should the most important matters be introduced? How quickly should concessions be made, and what type of reciprocity should be expected? These types of questions help effectively prepare the negotiators. In addition, the team will work on formulating negotiation tactics. "International Management in Action: Negotiating with the Japanese" demonstrates such tactics, and the following discussion gets into some of the specifics.

Sometimes, simply being familiar with the culture is still falling short of being aptly informed. We discussed in Chapter 2 how the political and legal environment of a country can have an influence over an MNC's decision to open operations, and those external factors are good to bear in mind when coming to an agreement. Both parties may believe that the goals have been made clear, and on the surface a settlement may deliver positive results. However, the subsequent actions taken by either company could prove to exhibit even more barriers. Take Pirelli, an Italian tire maker that acquired

Continental Gummiwerke, its German competitor. Pirelli purchased the majority holdings of Continental's stock, a transaction which would translate into Pirelli having control of the company if it occurred in the United States. When Pirelli attempted to make key managerial decisions for its Continental unit, it discovered that in Germany, the corporate governance in place allows German companies to block such actions, regardless of the shareholder position. Furthermore, the labor force has quite a bit of leverage with its ability to elect members of the supervisory board, which in turn chooses the management board.[52] Pirelli essentially lost on an investment; that is, unless Continental can be profitable under its current management. If Pirelli had known that this was going to happen, it probably would have reconsidered. One solution could be for Pirelli's management to begin some positive rapport with the labor force to try and sway viewpoints internally. The better option, though, would be for international managers to be as informed as possible and avoid trouble before it occurs.

Negotiation Tactics

A number of specific tactics are used in international negotiation. The following discussion examines some of the most common.

Location   Where should negotiations take place? If the matter is very important, most businesses will choose a neutral site. For example, U.S. firms negotiating with companies from the Far East will meet in Hawaii, and South American companies negotiating with European firms will meet halfway, in New York City. A number of benefits derive from using a neutral site. One is that each party has limited access to its home office for receiving a great deal of negotiating information and advice and thus gaining an advantage on the other. A second is that the cost of staying at the site often is quite high, so both sides have an incentive to conclude their negotiations as quickly as possible. (Of course, if one side enjoys the facilities and would like to stay as long as possible, the negotiations could drag on.) A third is that most negotiators do not like to return home with nothing to show for their efforts, so they are motivated to reach some type of agreement.

Time Limits   Time limits are an important negotiation tactic when one party is under a time constraint. This is particularly true when this party has agreed to meet at the home site of the other party. For example, U.S. negotiators who go to London to discuss a joint venture with a British firm often will have a scheduled return flight. Once their hosts find out how long these individuals intend to stay, the British can plan their strategy accordingly. The "real" negotiations are unlikely to begin until close to the time that the Americans must leave. The British know that their guests will be anxious to strike some type of deal before returning home, so the Americans are at a disadvantage.

Time limits can be used tactically even if the negotiators meet at a neutral site. For example, most Americans like to be home with their families for Thanksgiving, Christmas, and the New Year holiday. Negotiations held right before these dates put Americans at a disadvantage, because the other party knows when the Americans would like to leave.

Buyer-Seller Relations   How should buyers and sellers act? As noted earlier, Americans believe in being objective and trading favors. When the negotiations are over, Americans walk away with what they have received from the other party, and they expect the other party to do the same. This is not the way negotiators in many other countries think, however.

The Japanese, for example, believe that the buyers should get most of what they want. On the other hand, they also believe that the seller should be taken care of through reciprocal favors. The buyer must ensure that the seller has not been "picked clean." For example, when many Japanese firms first started doing business with large U.S. firms, they were unaware of U.S. negotiating tactics. As a result, the Japanese thought the

Some people believe that the most effective way of getting the Japanese to open up their markets to the United States is to use a form of strong-arm tactics, such as putting the country on a list of those to be targeted for retaliatory action. Others believe that this approach will not be effective, because the interests of the United States and Japan are intertwined and we would be hurting ourselves as much as them. Regardless of which group is right, one thing is certain: U.S. MNCs must learn how to negotiate more effectively with the Japanese. What can they do? Researchers have found that besides patience and a little table pounding, a number of important steps warrant consideration.

First, business firms need to prepare for their negotiations by learning more about Japanese culture and the "right" ways to conduct discussions. Those companies with experience in these matters report that the two best ways of doing this are to read books on Japanese business practices and social customs and to hire experts to train the negotiators. Other steps that are helpful include putting the team through simulated negotiations and hiring Japanese to assist in the negotiations.

Second, U.S. MNCs must learn patience and sincerity. Negotiations are a two-way street that require the mutual cooperation and efforts of both parties. The U.S. negotiators must understand that many times, Japanese negotiators do not have full authority to make on-the-spot decisions. Authority must be given by someone at the home office, and this failure to act quickly should not be interpreted as a lack of sincerity on the part of the Japanese negotiators.

Third, the MNC must have a unique good or service. So many things are offered for sale in Japan that unless the company has something that is truly different, persuading the other party to buy it is difficult.

Fourth, technical expertise often is viewed as a very important contribution, and this often helps to win concessions with the Japanese. The Japanese know that the Americans, for example, still dominate the world when it comes to certain types of technology and that Japan is unable to compete effectively in these areas. When such technical expertise is evident, it is very influential in persuading the Japanese to do business with the company.

These four criteria are critical to effective negotiations with the Japanese. MNCs that use them report more successful experiences than those who do not.

Americans were taking advantage of them, whereas the Americans believed they were driving a good, hard bargain.

The Brazilians are quite different from both the Americans and Japanese. Researchers have found that Brazilians do better when they are more deceptive and self-interested and their opponents more open and honest than they are.[53] Brazilians also tend to make fewer promises and commitments than their opponents, and they are much more prone to say no. However, Brazilians are more likely to make initial concessions. Overall, Brazilians are more like Americans than Japanese in that they try to maximize their advantage, but they are unlike Americans in that they do not feel obligated to be open and forthright in their approach. Whether they are buyer or seller, they want to come out on top.

Negotiating for Mutual Benefit

When managers enter a negotiation with the intent to win and are not open to flexible compromises, it can result in a stalemate. Ongoing discussion with little progress can increase tensions between the two groups and create an impasse where groups become more frustrated and aggressive, and no agreement can be reached.[54] Ultimately, too much focus on the plan with little concern for the viewpoint of the other group can lead to missed opportunities. It is important to keep objectives in mind and on the forefront, but it should not be a substitute for constructive discussions. Fisher and Ury, authors of the book *Getting to Yes,* present five general principles to help avoid such disasters: (1) separate the people from the problem, (2) focus on interests rather than positions, (3) generate a variety of options before settling on an agreement (as mentioned earlier in this section), (4) insist that the agreement be based on objective criteria, and (5) stand your ground.[55]

Separating the People from the Problem   Often, when managers spend so much time getting to know the issue, many become personally involved. Therefore, responses to a particular position can be interpreted as a personal affront. In order to preserve the personal relationship and gain a clear perspective of the issue, it is important to distinguish the problem from the individual.

When dealing with people, one barrier to complete understanding is the negotiating parties' perspectives. Negotiators should try to put themselves in the other's shoes. Avoid incidences of blame, and keep the atmosphere positive by attempting to alter proposals to better translate the objectives. The more inclusive the process, the more willing everyone will be to find a solution that is mutually beneficial.

Emotional factors arise as well. Negotiators often experience some level of an emotional reaction during the process, but it is not seen by the other side. Recognize your own emotions, and be open to hearing and accepting emotional concerns of the other party. Do not respond in a defensive manner or give in to intense impulses. Ignoring the intangible tension is not recommended; try to alleviate the situation through sympathetic gestures such as apologies.

As mentioned earlier, communication is imperative to reaching an agreement. Talk to each other, instead of just rehashing grandiose aspects of the proposal. Listen to responses, and avoid passively sitting there while formulating a response. When appropriate, summarize the key points by vocalizing your interpretation to the other side to ensure correct evaluation of intentions.

Overall, don't wait for issues to arise and react to them. Instead, go into discussion with these guidelines already in play.

Focusing on Interests over Positions   The position one side takes can be expressed through a simple outline, but still does not provide the most useful information. Focusing on interests gives one insight into the motivation behind why a particular position was chosen. Digging deeper into the situation by both recognizing your own interests and becoming more familiar with others' interests will put all active partners in a better position to defend their proposal. Simply stating, "This model works, and it is the best option," may not have much leverage. Discussing your motivation, such as, "I believe our collaboration will enhance customer satisfaction, which is why I took on this project," will help others see the *why*, not just the *what*.

Hearing the incentive behind the project will make both sides more sympathetic, and may keep things consistent. Be sure to consider the other side, but maintain focus on your own concerns.

Generating Options   Managers may feel pressured to come to an agreement quickly for many reasons, especially if they hail from a country that puts a value on time. If negotiations are with a group that does not consider time constraints, there may be temptation to only have a few choices to narrow the focus and expedite decisions. It turns out, it is better for everyone to have a large number of options in case some proposals prove to be unsatisfactory.

How do groups go about forming these proposals? First, they can meet to brainstorm and formulate creative solutions through a sort of invention process. This includes shifting thought focus among stating the problem, analyzing the issue, pondering general approaches, and strategizing the actions. After creating the proposals, the groups can begin evaluating the options and discuss improvements where necessary. Try to avoid the win-lose approach by accentuating the points of parity. When groups do not see eye to eye, find options that can work with both viewpoints by "look[ing] for items that are of low cost to you and high benefit to them, and vice versa."[56] By offering proposals that the other side will agree to, you can pinpoint the decision makers and tailor future suggestions toward them. Be sure to support the validity of your proposal, but not to the point of being overbearing.

Using Objective Criteria   In cases where there are no common interests, avoid tension by looking for objective options. Legitimate, practical criteria could be formed by using reliable third-party data, such as legal precedent. If both parties would accept being bound to certain terms, then chances are the suggestions were derived from objective criteria. The key is to emphasize the communal nature of the process. Inquire about why the other group chose its particular ideas. It will help you both see the other side and give you a spring-board from which you can argue your views, which can be very persuasive. Overall, effective negotiations will result from international managers who are flexible but do not fold to external pressures.

These are just general guidelines to abide by to try and reach a mutual agreement. The approaches will be more effective if the group adhering to the outline was the one with more power. Fisher and Ury also looked at what managers should do if the other party has the power.

Standing Ground   Every discussion will have some imbalance of power, but there is something negotiators can do to defend themselves. It may be tempting to create a "bottom line," or lowest possible set of options that one will accept, but it does not necessarily accomplish the objective. When negotiators make a definitive decision before engaging in discussion, they may soon find out that the terms never even surface. That is not to say that their bottom line is below even the lowest offer, but instead that without working with the other negotiators, they cannot accurately predict the proposals that will be devised. So what should the "weaker" opponent do?

The reason two parties are involved in a negotiation is because they both want a situation that will leave them better off than before. Therefore, no matter how long negotiations drag on, neither side should agree to terms that will leave it worse off than its best alternative to a negotiated agreement, or BANTA. Clearly defining and understanding the BANTA will make it easier to know when it is time to leave a negotiation and empower that side. An even better scenario would be if the negotiator learns of the other side's BANTA. As Fisher and Ury say: "Developing your BANTA thus not only enables you to determine what is a minimally acceptable agreement, it will probably raise that minimum."[57]

Even the most prepared manager can walk into a battle zone. At times, negotiators will encounter rigid, irritable, caustic, and selfish opponents. A positional approach to bargaining can cause tension, but the other side can opt for a principled angle. This entails a calm demeanor and a focus on the issues. Instead of counterattacking, redirect the conversation to the problem, and do not take any outbursts as personal attacks. Inquire about their reasoning and try to take any negative statements as constructive. If no common ground is reached, a neutral third party can come in to assess the desires of each side and compose an initial proposal. Each group has the right to suggest alternative approaches, but the third-party person has the last word in what the true "final draft" is. If the parties decide it is still unacceptable, then it is time to walk away from negotiations.

Fisher and Ury compiled a comprehensive guide as to how to approach negotiations. While no guideline has a 100 percent effective rate, their method helps gain a position where both sides win.

Bargaining Behaviors

Closely related to the discussion of negotiation tactics are the different types of bargaining behaviors, including both verbal and nonverbal behaviors. Verbal behaviors are an important part of the negotiating process, because they can improve the final outcome. Research shows that the profits of the negotiators increase when they make high initial offers, ask a lot of questions, and do not make many verbal commitments until the end of the negotiating process. In short, verbal behaviors are critical to the success of negotiations.

Use of Extreme Behaviors   Some negotiators begin by making extreme offers or requests. The Chinese and Arabs are examples. Some negotiators, however, begin with an initial position that is close to the one they are seeking. The Americans and Swedes are examples here.

Is one approach any more effective than the other? Research shows that extreme positions tend to produce better results. Some of the reasons relate to the fact that an extreme bargaining position (1) shows the other party that the bargainer will not be exploited; (2) extends the negotiation and gives the bargainer a better opportunity to gain information on the opponent; (3) allows more room for concessions; (4) modifies the opponent's beliefs

Table 7–9
Cross-Cultural Differences in Verbal Behavior of Japanese, U.S., and Brazilian Negotiators

Behavior and Definition	Number of Times Tactic Was Used in a Half-Hour Bargaining Session		
	Japanese	United States	Brazilian
Promise. A statement in which the source indicated an intention to provide the target with a reinforcing consequence which source anticipates target will evaluate as pleasant, positive, or rewarding.	7	8	3
Threat. Same as promise, except that the reinforcing consequences are thought to be noxious, unpleasant, or punishing.	4	4	2
Recommendation. A statement in which the source predicts that a pleasant environmental consequence will occur to the target. Its occurrence is not under the source's control.	7	4	5
Warning. Same as recommendation except that the consequences are thought to be unpleasant.	2	1	1
Reward. A statement by the source that is thought to create pleasant consequences for the target.	1	2	2
Punishment. Same as reward, except that the consequences are thought to be unpleasant.	1	3	3
Positive normative appeal. A statement in which the source indicates that the target's past, present, or future behavior was or will be in conformity with social norms.	1	1	0
Negative normative appeal. Same as positive normative appeal, except that the target's behavior is in violation of social norms.	3	1	1
Commitment. A statement by the source to the effect that its future bids will not go below or above a certain level.	15	13	8
Self-disclosure. A statement in which the source reveals information about itself.	34	36	39
Question. A statement in which the source asks the target to reveal information about itself.	20	20	22
Command. A statement in which the source suggests that the target perform a certain behavior.	8	6	14
First offer. The profit level associated with each participant's first offer.	61.5	57.3	75.2
Initial concession. The differences in profit between the first and second offer.	6.5	7.1	9.4
Number of no's. Number of times the word "no" was used by bargainers per half-hour.	5.7	9.0	83.4

Source: Adapted from John L. Graham, "The Influence of Culture on the Process of Business Negotiations in an Exploratory Study," *Journal of International Business Studies,* Spring 1983, p. 88. Reproduced with permission of Palgrave Macmillan.

about the bargainer's preferences; (5) shows the opponent that the bargainer is willing to play the game according to the usual norms; and (6) lets the bargainer gain more than would probably be possible if a less extreme initial position had been taken.

Although the use of extreme position bargaining is considered to be "un-American," many U.S. firms have used it successfully against foreign competitors. When Peter Ueberroth managed the Olympic Games in the United States in 1984, he turned a profit of well over $100 million—and that was without the participation of Soviet-bloc countries, which would have further increased the market potential of the games. In past Olympiads, sponsoring countries had lost hundreds of millions of dollars. How did Ueberroth do it? One way was by using extreme position bargaining. For example, the Olympic Committee felt that the Japanese should pay $10 million for the right to televise the games in the country, so when the Japanese offered $6 million for the rights, the Olympic Committee countered with $90 million. Eventually, the two sides agreed on $18.5 million. Through the effective use of extreme position bargaining, Ueberroth got the Japanese to pay over three times their original offer, an amount well in excess of the committee's budget.

Promises, Threats, and Other Behaviors Another approach to bargaining is the use of promises, threats, rewards, self-disclosures, and other behaviors that are designed to influence the other party. These behaviors often are greatly influenced by the culture. Graham conducted research using Japanese, U.S., and Brazilian businesspeople and found that they employed a variety of different behaviors during a buyer-seller negotiation simulation.[58] Table 7–9 presents the results.

The table shows that Americans and Japanese make greater use of promises than Brazilians. The Japanese also rely heavily on recommendations and commitment. The Brazilians use a discussion of rewards, commands, and self-disclosure more than Americans and Japanese. The Brazilians also say no a great deal more and make first offers that have higher-level profits than those of the others. Americans tend to operate between these two groups, although they do make less use of commands than either of their opponents and make first offers that have lower profit levels than their opponents'.

Nonverbal Behaviors Nonverbal behaviors also are very common during negotiations. These behaviors refer to what people do rather than what they say. Nonverbal behaviors sometimes are called the "silent language." Typical examples include silent periods, facial gazing, touching, and conversational overlaps. As seen in Table 7–10, the

---

Table 7–10
Cross-Cultural Differences in Nonverbal Behavior of Japanese, U.S., and Brazilian Negotiators

Behavior and Definition	Number of Times Tactic Was Used in a Half-Hour Bargaining Session		
	Japanese	**United States**	**Brazilian**
Silent period. The number of conversational gaps of 10 seconds or more per 30 minutes.	5.5	3.5	0
Facial gazing. The number of minutes negotiators spend looking at their opponent's face per randomly selected 10-minute period.	1.3 minutes	3.3 minutes	5.2 minutes
Touching. Incidents of bargainers' touching one another per half-hour (not including handshakes).	0	0	4.7
Conversational overlaps. The number of times (per 10 minutes) that both parties to the negotiation would talk at the same time.	12.6	10.3	28.6

Source: Adapted from John L. Graham, "The Influence of Culture on the Process of Business Negotiations in an Exploratory Study," *Journal of International Business Studies,* Spring 1983, p. 88. Reproduced with permission of Palgrave Macmillan.

Japanese tend to use silent periods much more often than either Americans or Brazilians during negotiations. In fact, in this study, the Brazilians did not use them at all. The Brazilians did, however, make frequent use of other nonverbal behaviors. They employed facial gazing almost four times more often than the Japanese and almost twice as often as the Americans. In addition, although the Americans and Japanese did not touch their opponents, the Brazilians made wide use of this nonverbal tactic. They also relied heavily on conversational overlaps, employing them more than twice as often as the Japanese and almost three times as often as Americans. Quite obviously, the Brazilians rely very heavily on nonverbal behaviors in their negotiating.

The important thing to remember is that in international negotiations, people use a wide variety of tactics, and the other side must be prepared to counter or find a way of dealing with them. The response will depend on the situation. Managers from different cultures will give different answers. Table 7–11 provides some examples of the types of characteristics needed in effective negotiators. To the extent that international managers have these characteristics, their success as negotiators should increase.

Table 7–11
Culture-Specific Characteristics Needed by International Managers for Effective Negotiations

U.S. managers	Preparation and planning skill
	Ability to think under pressure
	Judgment and intelligence
	Verbal expressiveness
	Product knowledge
	Ability to perceive and exploit power
	Integrity
Japanese managers	Dedication to job
	Ability to perceive and exploit power
	Ability to win respect and confidence
	Integrity
	Listening skill
	Broad perspective
	Verbal expressiveness
Chinese managers (Taiwan)	Persistence and determination
	Ability to win respect and confidence
	Preparation and planning skill
	Product knowledge
	Interesting
	Judgment and intelligence
Brazilian managers	Preparation and planning skill
	Ability to think under pressure
	Judgment and intelligence
	Verbal expressiveness
	Product knowledge
	Ability to perceive and exploit power
	Competitiveness

Source: Adapted from Nancy J. Adler, *International Dimensions of Organizational Behavior,* 2nd ed. (Boston: PWS-Kent Publishing, 1991), p. 187, and from material provided by Professor John Graham, School of Business Administration, University of Southern California, 1983.

The World of *BusinessWeek*—Revisited

The opening *BusinessWeek* article introduced a situation that demonstrates the challenges of international communication and negotiation. The simple but revolutionary approach to communication offered by Skype has the potential to undermine the basic business model of other providers by providing free services which would cut profitability. In other words, customers will begin to question why they pay such a premium for services that are available for free. Some countries and cultures are open to the new technology offered through Skype, such as in Europe, Asia, and Australia, indicating that either the customer needs are different or the political and market environment is more accepting of the competition. If Skype is to become successful in expanding its operations to other countries, it will have to understand the social and business culture involved and effectively communicate its objectives and even negotiate with some carriers that it currently views as competitors.

A key to success in today's global economy is being able to communicate effectively within and across national boundaries and to engage in effective negotiations across cultures. Considering Skype's situation, along with what you have read in this chapter, answer the following questions: (1) How is cultural communication in Luxembourg (where Skype is headquartered) similar to that in other parts of Europe and Asia? How is it different? (2) What kind of managerial relationships could you assume exist between Skype and 3 Mobile? Between Skype and Verizon (assuming Skype is similar to Vonage)? Justify your answer. (3) What kind of negotiations could Skype engage in to enter the North American market? How does culture play a role?

SUMMARY OF KEY POINTS

1. Communication is the transfer of meaning from sender to receiver. The key to the effectiveness of communication is how accurately the receiver interprets the intended meaning.

2. Communicating in the international business context involves both downward and upward flows. Downward flows convey information from superior to subordinate; these flows vary considerably from country to country. For example, the downward system of organizational communication is much more prevalent in France than in Japan. Upward communication conveys information from subordinate to superior. In the United States and Japan, the upward system is more common than in South America or some European countries.

3. The international arena contains a number of communication barriers. Some of the most important are language, perception, culture, and nonverbal communication. Language, particularly in written communications, often loses considerable meaning during interpretation. Perception and culture can result in people's seeing and interpreting things differently, and as a result, communication can break down.

Nonverbal communication such as body language, facial expressions, and use of physical space, time, and even color often varies from country to country and, if improper, often results in communication problems.

4. A number of steps can be taken to improve communication effectiveness. Some of the most important include improving feedback, providing language and cultural training, and encouraging flexibility and cooperation. These steps can be particularly helpful in overcoming communication barriers in the international context and can lead to more effective international management.

5. Negotiation is the process of bargaining with one or more parties to arrive at a solution that is acceptable to all. There are two basic types of negotiation: distributive negotiation involves bargaining over opposing goals while integrative negotiation involves cooperation aimed at integrating interests. The negotiation process involves five basic steps: planning, interpersonal relationship building, exchanging task-related information, persuasion, and agreement. The way in which the

process is carried out often will vary because of cultural differences.

6. There are a wide variety of tactics used in international negotiating. These include location, time limits, buyer-seller relations, verbal behaviors, and nonverbal behaviors.

7. Negotiating for mutual benefit includes separating the people from the problem, focusing on interests rather than positions, generating a variety of options, insisting that the agreement be based on objective criteria, and standing ground.

KEY TERMS

chromatics, *202*

chronemics, *201*

communication, *186*

context, *186*

distributive negotiations, *204*

downward communication, *190*

haptics, *200*

integrative negotiation, *206*

intimate distance, *201*

kinesics, *199*

monochronic time schedule, *201*

negotiation, *204*

nonverbal communication, *199*

oculesics, *199*

perception, *196*

personal distance, *201*

polychronic time schedule, *202*

proxemics, *201*

public distance, *201*

social distance, *201*

upward communication, *192*

REVIEW AND DISCUSSION QUESTIONS

1. How does explicit communication differ from implicit communication? What is one culture that makes wide use of explicit communication? Implicit communication? Describe how one would go about conveying the following message in each of the two cultures you identified: "You are trying very hard, but you are still making too many mistakes."

2. One of the major reasons that foreign expatriates have difficulty doing business in the United States is that they do not understand American slang. A business executive recently gave the authors the following three examples of statements that had no direct meaning for her because she was unfamiliar with slang: "He was laughing like hell." "Don't worry; it's a piece of cake." "Let's throw these ideas up against the wall and see if any of them stick." Why did the foreign expat have trouble understanding these statements, and what could be said instead?

3. Yamamoto Iron & Steel is considering setting up a minimill outside Atlanta, Georgia. At present, the company is planning to send a group of executives to the area to talk with local and state officials regarding this plant. In what way might misperception be a barrier to effective communication between the representatives for both sides? Identify and discuss two examples.

4. Diaz Brothers is a winery in Barcelona. The company would like to expand operations to the United States and begin distributing its products in the Chicago area. If things work out well, the company then will expand to both coasts. In its business dealings in the Midwest, how might culture prove to be a communication barrier for the

company's representatives from Barcelona? Identify and discuss two examples.

5. Why is nonverbal communication a barrier to effective communication? Would this barrier be greater for Yamamoto Iron & Steel (question 3) or Diaz Brothers (question 4)? Defend your answer.

6. For U.S. companies going abroad for the first time, which form of nonverbal communication barrier would be the greatest, kinesics or proxemics? Why? Defend your answer.

7. If a company new to the international arena was negotiating an agreement with a potential partner in an overseas country, what basic steps should it be prepared to implement? Identify and describe them.

8. What elements of the negotiation process should be done with only your group? What events should take place with all sides present? Why?

9. An American manager is trying to close a deal with a Brazilian manager, but has not heard back from him for quite some time. The American is getting very nervous that if he waits too long, he is going to miss out on any backup options due to waiting for the Brazilian. What should the American do? How can the American tell it is time to drop the deal? Give some signs that suggest negotiations will go no further.

10. Wilsten Inc. has been approached by a Japanese firm that wants exclusive production and selling rights for one of Wilsten's new high-tech products. What does Wilsten need to know about Japanese bargaining behaviors to strike the best possible deal with this company? Identify and describe five.

INTERNET EXERCISE: WORKING EFFECTIVELY AT TOYOTA

In 2006 Toyota's Camry was the best-selling car in the United States, and the firm's share of the American automobile market was solid. However, the company is not resting on its laurels. Toyota has expanded worldwide and is now doing business in scores of countries. Visit the firm's Web site and find out what it has been up to lately. The address is **www.toyota.com.** Then take a tour of the company's products and services including cars, air services, and sports vehicles. Next, go to the jobs section site, and see what types of career opportunities there are at Toyota. Finally, find out what Toyota is doing in your particular locale. Then, drawing upon this information and the material you read in the chapter, answer these three questions: (1) What type of communication and negotiation challenges do you think you would face if you worked for Toyota and were in constant communication with home-office personnel in Japan? (2) What type of communication training do you think the firm would need to provide to you to ensure that you were effective in dealing with senior-level Japanese managers in the hierarchy? (3) Using Table 7–1 as your guide, what conclusions can you draw regarding communicating with the Japanese managers, and what guidelines would you offer to a non-Japanese employee who just entered the firm and is looking for advice and guidance regarding how to communicate and negotiate more effectively?

China

China, with more than 1.3 billion people, is the world's most populous country and has a rapidly growing economy. Economic development has proceeded unevenly. Urban coastal areas, particularly in the southeast, are experiencing more rapid economic development than other areas of the country. China has a mixed economy, with a combination of state-owned and private firms. A number of state-owned enterprises (SOEs) have undergone partial or full privatization in recent years. The Chinese government has encouraged foreign investment—in some sectors of the economy and subject to constraints—since the 1980s, defining several "special economic zones" in which foreign investors receive preferable tax, tariff, and investment treatment.

In March 2003, a long-expected transition in China's political leadership took place. Hu Jintao assumed the country's presidency as well as chairmanship of the ruling Communist Party. Wen Jinbao became the new premier. Former president Jiang Zemin retained the chairmanship of the Central Military Commission.

With China's entry into the World Trade Organization in November 2001, the Chinese government made a number of specific commitments to trade and investment liberalization that, when fully implemented, will substantially open the Chinese economy to foreign firms. In telecommunications, this means the lifting or sharp reduction of tariffs and foreign ownership limitations, although China will retain the right to limit foreign majority ownership of telecom firms. There are still lingering concerns about China's enforcement of intellectual property protection and its willingness to fully open access to its telecommunications market.

China's real GDP grew by 9.1 percent in 2003, an impressive performance given the SARS epidemic and the generally sluggish conditions in the global economy. This growth brought China's GDP to $1.41 trillion and, for the first time, boosted per capita GDP above $1,000. Indeed, there are concerns that China's economy may be growing too fast: Economic growth continues and even hit an astounding 10.7 percent in 2006. China began its attempt to cut carbon emissions under the Kyoto protocol in 2003. The country has a maximum level of carbon emissions it is allowed to expel before it starts purchasing "carbon credits" or "allowances" to emit more gases. It is not known exactly how much China spends for these extra allowances, but China does account for about 75 percent of carbon credit sales under Kyoto. This may have a significant impact on China's growth rate. Layoffs have been part of the restructuring of the SOEs, for many were severely overstaffed. The layoffs have created unemployment, recorded as 4.5 percent of the urban population in 2005, which is a burden on the government budget as the government begins to provide social benefits that were previously the responsibility of the SOEs. The geographic concentration of privately owned industry in the urban centers along the coast also has created social strains. Today, China's investment laws seek to channel foreign investment into infrastructure building, industries involving advanced technologies, and high-value-added export-oriented products.

In June 2003, Bruce Claflin, CEO of struggling networking company 3Com Corp., caused quite a stir by announcing a joint alliance with China's Huawei Technologies—just weeks after Huawei had been sued on a range of intellectual property rights (IPR) violations by 3Com's Silicon Valley neighbor Cisco Systems. The suit claims that Huawei's products include some of Cisco's carefully guarded source code and that Huawei infringes on copyrights related to Cisco's computer commands.

According to Claflin, 3Com's negotiations with Huawei began in mid-2002, long before Cisco filed suit. Although he admits that the deal took some by surprise, Claflin insists that it was a "no brainer." "Let's face it, people have the perception of China as a low-tech, low-cost kind of place. But my first impression was that this was truly a great technology company. It blows your mind when everyone thinks China is all about exploiting low-cost labor."

Claflin believes that Cisco's argument of IPR infringement is more complicated than it sounds: "There are two courts they care about: the court of law and the court of public opinion. I bet there's not one company out there that doesn't somehow infringe on Cisco in some way." Cisco says it respects 3Com as a rival and is hopeful that 3Com's promise that products sold by the Huawei-3Com joint venture won't infringe on Cisco's patents will come to pass. Still, it's quite possible that Cisco will file suit against the joint venture, raising questions about IPR protections in China and the United States. **english.peopledaily.com.cn**

Questions

1. Do you think China will continue to achieve record growth? What factors could hurt its prospects?

2. Today, because of an abundance of cheap labor, China is a hot destination for global corporate outsourcing. Do you think this will still be the case a decade from now? Why or why not?

3. What communication and negotiation challenges may have arisen in the three-way exchanges among Cisco, 3Com, and Huawei?

4. Can 3Com take any proactive measures to help limit the possibility of Cisco moving forward with litigation?

Foreign or Domestic?

Connie Hatley is a very successful businesswoman who has holdings in a wide variety of industries. Hatley recently was approached by one of the Big Three automakers and offered a multidealership arrangement. In return for investing $50 million in facilities, the auto manufacturer would be willing to give her five dealerships spread throughout the United States. These locations, for the most part, are in rural areas, but over the next decade, these locales likely will become much more populated. In addition, the company pointed out that a large percentage of new cars are purchased by individuals who prefer to buy in rural locations, because prices at these dealerships tend to be lower. Hatley has been seriously considering the offer, although she now has a competitive alternative.

A South Korean auto manufacturer has approached Hatley and offered her the same basic deal. Hatley indicated that she was wary of doing business with a foreign firm so far away, but the Korean manufacturer presented her with some interesting auto sales data: (1) Between 1981 and 2001, the South Korean share of the U.S. auto market went from 0 to over 3 percent. (2) South Korean automakers are capturing market share in the United States at a faster rate than any other competitor. (3) New technology is being incorporated into these Korean-built cars at an unprecedented rate, and the quality is among the highest in the industry. (4) Although the Big Three (GM, Ford, and DaimlerChrysler) hold a large share of the U.S. auto market, their market share among those 45 years of age or younger is declining and being captured by foreign competitors. (5) The South Korean firm intends to increase its share of the U.S. market by 20 percent annually.

Hatley is very impressed with these data and forecasts. Recently, however, the Korean auto company's sales and market share have been declining; she is uneasy about having to deal with someone located halfway around the world. "If I don't receive scheduled deliveries, whom do I call?" she asked one of her vice presidents. "Also, we don't speak their language. If there is a major problem, how are we going to really communicate with each other? I like the proposal, and I'd take it if I were sure that we wouldn't have communication problems. However, $50 million is a lot of money to invest. If a mistake is made, I'm going to lose a fortune. They did experience some problems last year, and their sales were off that year. Of course, if the South Koreans are right in their long-range forecasts and I have no major problems dealing with them, my return on investment is going to be almost 50 percent higher than it will be with the U.S. manufacturer."

Questions

1. What specific types of communication problems might Hatley encounter in dealing with the South Koreans?

2. Can these communication problems be resolved, or are they insurmountable and will simply have to be tolerated?

3. Based on communication problems alone, should Hatley back away from the deal or proceed? Give your recommendation; then defend it.

4. What negotiation approaches might Hatley use if she wants to continue with the deal in order to increase her confidence that it will be successful?

Cross-Cultural Conflicts in the Corning-Vitro Joint Venture

Vitro is a Mexican glass manufacturer located in Monterrey, Mexico. Vitro's product line concentrates on drinkware but includes dozens of products, from automobile windshields to washing machines. Vitro has a long history of successful joint ventures and is globally oriented.

Corning Inc. is most famous for its oven-ready glassware; however, Corning has diversified into fiber optics, environmental products, and laboratory services. Like Vitro, Corning has a long history of successful joint ventures and globalization. Vitro and Corning share similar corporate cultures and customer-oriented philosophies.

After realizing such similarities and looking to capitalize on NAFTA by accessing the Mexican market, Corning Inc. entered into a joint venture with Vitro in the fall of 1992. The similarities in history, philosophy, culture, goals, and objectives of both companies would lead to the logical conclusion that this alliance should be an instant success. However, as Francisco Chevez, an analyst with Smith Barney Shearson in New York, said, "The cultures did not match . . . it was a marriage made in hell." As history reveals, Corning and Vitro dissolved the joint venture 25 months after the agreement. Both companies still have an interest in maintaining the relationship and continue to distribute each other's products.

A further look at the strategic history of Corning and the joint venture between Corning and Vitro will lead to a better understanding of the difficulties that are involved in creating and maintaining foreign alliances. A more in-depth investigation also will reveal the impact of culture on business transactions.

The Strategic History of Corning

Corning Inc. has been an innovative leader in foreign alliances for over 73 years. One of the company's first successes was an alliance with St. Gobain, a French glassmaker, to produce Pyrex cookware in Europe during the 1920s. Corning has formed approximately 50 ventures over the years. Only 9 have failed, which is a phenomenal number considering one recent study found that over one-half of foreign and national alliances do not succeed. Over the last five years, Corning's sales from joint ventures were over $3 billion, which contributed more than $500 million to its net income.

Corning enters into joint ventures for two primary reasons, which are best explained through examples of its past ventures. The first is to gain access to markets that it cannot penetrate quickly enough to obtain a competitive advantage. Corning currently has multiple ventures that exemplify market penetration. Samsung-Corning is an alliance in which Corning provided its distinctive competency of television tube production while Samsung provided expansion into the television market. Corning was able to achieve a strong market share in the Asian market, with sales in excess of $500 million.

The second reason is to bring its technology to market. For example, the strategic alliance of Corning with Mitsubishi led to the creation of Cometec Inc. Corning produces the ceramic substrates in automotive catalytic converters. The venture employs coating technology developed by Mitsubishi that extends Corning's business into stationary pollution control. Corning reports that the venture is quite successful.

Corning's CEO, James R. Houghton, summarizes the major criteria for deciding whether an equity venture is likely to succeed as follows:

1. You need a solid business opportunity.
2. The two partners should make comparable contributions to the new enterprise.
3. The new enterprise should have a well-defined scope and no major conflicts with either parent company.
4. The management of each parent firm should have the vision and confidence to support the venture through its inevitable rough spots.
5. An autonomous operating team should be formed.
6. Responsibility cannot be delegated.

Houghton also emphasizes that the most important dimension of a successful joint venture is trust between the partners.

Corning's track record indicates that it has been able to establish and run a large number of joint ventures successfully. What went wrong with the recent Vitro venture? Vitro and Corning seemed to have similar operating procedures, and Vitro's product line complemented Corning's consumer business. Therefore, how could a seemingly perfect alliance fail so miserably? Probing deeper into the Corning-Vitro joint venture reveals the important role that culture may play in international alliances.

Background on the Corning-Vitro Joint Venture

The Corning-Vitro venture seemed to be ideal. However, a strong Mexican peso, increased overseas competition, and strong cultural differences spelled trouble for the alliance. The economic problems are understandable, but the cultural differences should have been given more attention before the alliance was entered into.

Although both companies appeared so similar on the surface, they really were quite different. Cultural clashes erupted from the very beginning of the venture because of differing approaches to work. One example was in the marketing area. Vitro's sales approach was less aggressive than the Americans at Corning thought necessary; the slower, deliberate approach to sales in Mexico was a result of the previously highly controlled Mexican economy. Corning's more quick-action-oriented and aggressive sales approach had developed from decades of competition.

Once in the venture, the Mexicans thought the Americans were too forward, and the Americans believed that their Mexican partners wasted time being too polite. The Americans perceived the Mexican characteristics to include an unwillingness to acknowledge problems and faults. With respect to speed, the Mexicans thought Corning moved too quickly, while the Americans thought Vitro moved too slowly.

Another obvious cultural difference was the conflicting styles and time allotment for decision making. Vitro is bureaucratic and hierarchical, and loyalty is to family members and patrons in the ranks of the company. Decisions often are left either to a member of the controlling family or to top executives, while middle-level managers seldom are asked to contribute their opinions, let alone to make important decisions. Mr. Loose (Corning's chief executive of the joint venture) observed, "If we were looking at a distribution decision, or a customer decision, we would have a group of people in a room, they would do an assessment, figure alternatives and make a decision, and I as chief executive would never know about it. My experience on the Mexican side is that someone in the organization would have a solution in mind, but then the decision had to be kicked up a few levels."

These examples indicate that culture was an especially sensitive issue between Corning and Vitro, and the alliance was not able to overcome these problems. Corning felt that the cross-cultural differences were depriving both companies of the flexibility to take the fast management action that is necessary in the dynamic business climate of both countries. Vitro basically agreed. Corning gave Vitro back its $130 million investment, and the joint venture was called off. The companies still recognize the opportunity to continue business with each other, however. They have changed their relationship into a mutual distribution of each other's products.

The Aftermath of the Breakup

Vitro and Corning each responded publicly to the dissolution of their alliance, and each indicated the strong differences in culture. Corning wanted to discuss the problems and learn from them, while Vitro was hesitant to criticize anyone, especially a visible U.S. partner like Corning. The Mexicans preferred to concentrate on continuation of the marketing arrangement between the companies. Houghton, the Corning CEO, openly spoke of the alliance as one that stopped making sense. He stated that cross-cultural differences inhibited the potential of the alliance. Corning's chief executive of the venture, Mr. Loose, openly acknowledged the different decision-making styles between the two cultures. Vitro executives were defensive and disappointed that Mr. Loose had expressed his views so frankly in public. "It is unfortunate that he made those comments," said an anonymous Vitro executive. The president of Vitro, Eduardo Martens, flatly denied that the cultural differences were any greater than in other alliances. In an interview with the *Harvard Business Review,* however, he admitted, "Business in Mexico is done on a consensus basis, very genteel and sometimes slow by U.S. standards."

Corning feels it learned a lesson in the failed Vitro alliance; both foreign and domestic alliances require additional skills and more management time. CEO Houghton says that alliances carry a lot of risk and misunderstandings, but they can be significantly beneficial to the operations of a company if they are done carefully and selectively. Corning continues to analyze why the cultural differences with Vitro were too strong to overcome.

Questions for Review

1. Identify and discuss Corning's strategic predisposition toward a joint venture with Vitro.

2. Cultural clashes among partners in joint ventures are not a new issue. Discuss why an MNC, and specifically Corning, would be interested in fully understanding the culture of a potential partner before deciding on an alliance.

3. If Corning and Vitro had decided to remain in the alliance, how could they have overcome their differences to make the partnership a success?

4. Discuss why both companies would continue to distribute each other's products after the joint venture failed. What impact might the public statements about the failure have on this relationship?

Source: This case was prepared by Professor Cara Okleshen of the University of Georgia as the basis for class discussion. It is not intended to illustrate either effective or ineffective managerial capability or administrative responsibility.

Coca-Cola in India

Coca-Cola is a brand name known throughout the entire world. It covers 60 percent of the $1.6 billion soft drink market. In 2006–2007, Coca-Cola faced some difficult challenges in the region of Kerala, India. The company was accused of using water that contained pesticides in its bottling plants in Kerala. An environmental group, the Center for Science and Environment (CSE), found 57 bottles of Coke and Pepsi products from 12 Indian states that contained unsafe levels of pesticides.[1]

The Kerala minister of health, Karnataka R. Ashok, imposed a ban on the manufacture and sale of Coca-Cola products in the region. Coca-Cola then arranged to have its drinks tested in a British lab, and the report found that the amount of pesticides found in Pepsi and Coca-Cola drinks was harmless to the body.[2] Coca-Cola then ran numerous ads to regain consumers' confidence in its products and brand. However these efforts did not satisfy the environmental groups or the minister of health.

India's Changing Marketplace

During the 1960s and 1970s, India's economy was facing many challenges, growing only an average of 3–3.5 percent per year. There were numerous obstacles hindering foreign companies from investing in India, and many restrictions on economic activity which caused huge difficulties for Indian firms and disinterest among foreign investors. For many years the government had problems with implementing reform, and in overcoming bureaucratic and political divisions. Business activity was traditionally undervalued in India; leisure is typically given more value than work. Stemming from India's colonial legacy, Indians are highly suspicious of foreign investors. Indeed, there have been a few well-publicized disputes between the Indian government and foreign investors.[3]

More recently, however, many Western companies are finding an easier time doing business in India.[4] In 1991, many restrictions were eased, and economic reforms came into force. With more than 1 billion consumers, India has become an increasingly attractive market.[5] From 2003–2006, foreign investment doubled to $6 billion, and some say it will double again by 2009. Imported goods have become a status symbol for the middle class.[6] Over the past three years, India's economy has grown at 8-plus percent, but the country needs more investment in manufacturing if it hopes to improve the lives of the 350 million living in poverty.[7]

Coca-Cola and Other Soft Drink Investment in India

Coca-Cola has faced previous confrontations with the Indian government. In 1977, Coke pulled out of India when the government demanded its secret formula.[8]

Circumstances have dramatically improved over the years for soft drink providers of India. Coke and Pepsi have invested nearly $2 billion in India over the years. They employ about 12,500 people directly and support 200,000 indirectly through their purchases of sugar, packaging material, and shipping services. Coke is India's number one consumer of mango pulp for its local soft drink offerings.[9] From 1994 to 2003, Coca-Cola sales in India more than doubled.

Royal Crown Cola (RC Cola) is the world's third largest brand of soft drinks. The brand was purchased in 2000 by Cadbury Schweppes and entered the Indian market in 2003. For production in India, the company hired three licensing and franchising bottlers. In order to ensure that it was not implicated in the pesticide accusations associated with Pepsi and Coke, RC Cola immediately had its groundwater tested by the testing institute, SGS India Pvt Ltd.[10]

The Charges Against Coke

The pesticide issue began in 2002, in Plachimada, India. Villagers thought that water levels had sunk and the drinking water was contaminated by Coke's plant. They launched a vigil at the plant, and two years later, Coke's license was canceled. Coca-Cola's recent pesticide issue began at a bottling plant in Mehdiganj. The plant was accused of exploiting the groundwater and polluting it with toxic metals.[11] Karnataka R. Ashok, the health minister of Kerala, India, banned the sale of all Coca-Cola and PepsiCo products, claiming that the drinks contained unsafe levels of pesticides.

The alleged contamination of the water launched a debate on everything from pesticide-polluted water to India's middle-class addiction to unhealthy, processed foods. "It's wonderful," said Sunita Narin, director of CSE; "Pepsi and Coke are doing our work for us. Now the whole nation knows that there is a pesticide problem."[12]

Coca-Cola fought back against the accusations. "No Indian soft drink makers have been tested for similar violations even though pesticides could be in their products such as milk and bottled teas. If pesticides are in the groundwater, why isn't anyone else being tested? We are continuously being challenged because of who we are," said Atul Singh, CEO of Coca-Cola India.[13]

Some believe that Coca-Cola was targeted to bring the subject of pesticides in consumer products to light. "If you target multinational corporations, you get more publicity," adds Arvind Kumar, a researcher at the watchdog group Toxic Links. "Pesticides are in everything in India."[14]

India's Response to the Allegations

After CSE's discovery of the unsafe levels of pesticides,[15] some suggested the high levels of pesticides came from sugar, which is 10 percent of the soft drink content. However laboratories found the sugar samples to be pesticide free.[16]

Kerala is run by a communist government and a chief minister who still claims to have a revolutionary objection to the evils of capitalism.[17] Defenders of Coca-Cola claim that this is a large reason for the pesticide findings in Coca-Cola products. After the ban was placed on all Coca-Cola and PepsiCo products in the region of Kerala, Coca-Cola took its case to the state court to defend its products and name. The court said that the state government had no jurisdiction to impose a ban on the manufacture and sale of products.[18] Kerala then lifted the statewide ban on Coke products.[19]

Pepsi's Experience in India

PepsiCo has had an equally noticeable presence in India; and it is not surprising that the company has weathered the same accusations as its rival, Coca-Cola. In addition to claims of excessive water use, a CSE pesticide study, performed in August 2006, accused Pepsi of having 30 times the "unofficial" pesticide limit in its beverages (Coke was claimed to be 27 times the limit in this study).[20] These findings, coupled with the original 2003 CSE study that first tarnished the cola companies' image, have prompted numerous consumers to stop their cola consumption. Some have even taken to the streets, burning pictures of Pepsi bottles in protest.

Indra Nooyi, CEO of PepsiCo Inc. and a native of India, is far too familiar with the difficulties of water contamination and shortages. Yet, in light of the recent claims made against Pepsi, she has expressed frustration with the exaggerated CSE findings (local tea and coffee have thousands of times the alleged pesticide level found in Pepsi products) and the disproportionate reaction to Pepsi's water-use practices (pointing out that soft drinks and bottled water account for less than 0.04 percent of industrial water usage in India).[21]

In order to reaffirm the safety and popularity of its products, Pepsi has taken on a celebrity-studded ad campaign across India, as well as continued its legacy of corporate social responsibility (CSR). Some of Pepsi's CSR efforts have involved digging village wells, "harvesting" rainwater, and teaching better techniques for growing rice and tomatoes.[22] Pepsi has also initiated efforts to reduce water waste at its Indian facilities.

Although Pepsi sales are back on the rise, Nooyi realizes that she should have acted sooner to counteract CSE's claims about Pepsi products. From here on out, the company must be more attentive to its water-use practices; but Nooyi also notes, "We have to invest, too, in educating communities in how to farm better, collect water, and then work with industry to retrofit plants and recycle."[23]

Coke's Social Responsibility Commitments

Coca-Cola has recently employed The Energy and Resources Institute (TERI) to assess its operations in India. These investigations have been conducted based

Table 1 A Timeline of Coca-Cola in Kerala, India

1977:	Coca-Cola pulls out of India when the government demands its secret formula.
1991:	Restrictions are eased in India for easier international business development.
1999:	A report is published by the All-Indian Coordinated Research Program stating that 20% of all Indian food commodities exceed the maximum pesticide residue level and 43% of milk exceeds the maximum residue levels of DDT.
2002:	Villagers in Plachimada, India, make the accusation that Coke's bottling plant is contaminating their drinking water.
2003:	The Center for Science and Environment produces a study that finds unsafe levels of pesticides in Coca-Cola products in India.
January 2004:	Parliament in India forms a Joint Parliamentary Committee to investigate the charges by the CSE.
March 2004:	A Coca-Cola bottling facility is shut down in Plachimada, India.
2004:	Indian government announces new regulations for carbonated soft drinks based on European Union standards.
2005:	Coca-Cola co-founds the Global Water Challenge, develops the Global Community-Watershed Partnership, and establishes the Ethics and Compliance Committee.
August 2006:	The CSE produces another report finding 57 Coke and Pepsi products from 12 Indian states that contain unsafe pesticide levels.
September 2006:	India's high court overturns the ban on the sale of Coke products in Kerala.

on claims that Coca-Cola has engaged in unethical production practices in India. These alleged practices include causing severe water shortages, locating water-extracting plants in "drought prone" areas, further limiting water access by contaminating the surrounding land and groundwater, and irresponsibly disposing of toxic waste. Colleges and universities throughout the United States, U.K., and Canada have joined in holding the company accountable for its overseas business practices by banning Coca-Cola products on their campuses until more positive results are reported. However, critics argue that TERI's assessment will undoubtedly be biased since the organization has been largely funded by the Coca-Cola Company.[24]

Coca-Cola stands behind the safety of its products. "Multinational corporations provide an easy target," says Amulya Ganguli, a political analyst in New Delhi. "These corporations are believed to be greedy, devoted solely to profit, and uncaring about the health of the consumers." There is also a deeply rooted distrust of big business and particularly foreign big business in India.[25] This is a reminder that there will continue to be obstacles, as there were in the past, to foreign investments in India.

In order to reaffirm their presence in India, Coke and Pepsi have run separate ads insisting that their drinks are safe. Coke's ad said, "Is there anything safer for you to drink?" and invited Indians to visit its plants to see how the beverage is made.[26] Nevertheless, in July 2006, Coke reported a 12 percent decline in sales.[27]

Coca-Cola has taken various initiatives to improve the drinking water conditions for those around the world. It has formally pledged support for the United Nations Global Compact and co-founded the Global Water Challenge, which improves water access and sanitation in countries in critical need. It is improving energy and efficiency through the use of hydrofluorocarbon-free insulation for 98 percent of new refrigerate sales and marketing equipment.

Specifically in India, Coke has stated that "More than 1/3 of the total water that is used in operations is renewed and returned to groundwater systems."[28] Coca-Cola is installing 270 devices to catch rainwater, and plans to install 50 more water-catching devices this year. The company will also be distributing a kit that works to improve the water-use efficiency to its bottlers.[29] Inspecting its own water-use habits, Coca-Cola has vowed to reduce the amount of water it uses in its bottling operations. As of June 2007, Coca-Cola had reduced the amount of water needed to make one liter of Coke to 2.54 liters (compared with 3.14 liters five years earlier).[30]

At the June 2007 annual meeting of the World Wildlife Fund (WWF) in Beijing, Coca-Cola announced its multiyear partnership with the organization "to conserve and protect freshwater resources." E. Neville Isdell, chairman and CEO of the Coca-Cola Company, said, "Our goal is to replace every drop of water we use in our beverages and their production. For us that means reducing the amount of water used to produce our beverages, recycling water used for manufacturing processes so it can be returned safely to the environment, and replenishing water in communities and nature through locally relevant projects." Coca-Cola hopes to spread these practices to other members of its supply chain, particularly the sugar cane industry. The Coca-Cola-WWF partnership is also focused on climate protection and protection of seven of the world's "most critical freshwater basins," including the Yangtze in China. Although Coca-Cola's corporate social responsibility has included other projects with the WWF in the past, it hopes that this official partnership will help achieve larger-scale results.[31] Figures 1 and 2 show Coca-Cola's declining water use on a per-plant and systemwide basis.

Figure 1

Coca-Cola's Water Use: Average Plant Ratios

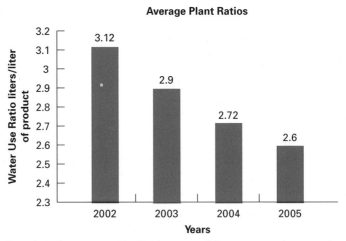

Source: The Coca-Cola Company, *2005 Environmental Report,* www.thecocacolacompany.com/citizenship/environmental_report2005.pdf.

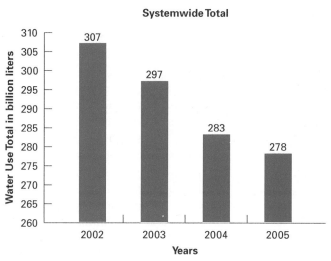

Systemwide Total

Source: The Coca-Cola Company, *2005 Environmental Report,* www.thecocacolacompany. com/citizenship/environmental_report2005.pdf.

Figure 2

Coca-Cola's Water Use: Systemwide Total

Coca-Cola has also established EthicsLine, which is a global Web and telephone information and reporting service that allows anyone to report confidential information to a third party. Service is toll free—24 hours a day—and translators are available. Coca-Cola is currently working on promoting nutrition and physical education by launching programs throughout the world. It is also focusing on improving standards through the global water challenge and enhancing global packaging to make it more environmentally friendly.

During the past decade, the Coca-Cola Company has invested more than US$1 billion in India, making it one of India's top international investors. Almost all the goods and services required to produce and market Coca-Cola are made in India. The Coca-Cola Company directly employs approximately 6,000 local people in India; and indirectly, its business in India creates employment for more than 125,000 people.[32]

Lessons Learned

Yet Coca-Cola was caught off guard by its experience in India. Coke did not fully appreciate how quickly local politicians would attack Coke in light of the test results, nor did it respond quickly enough to the anxieties of its consumers. The company failed to realize how fast news travels in modern India. India represents only about 1 percent of Coca-Cola's global volume, but it is central to the company's long-term growth strategy. The company needed to take action fast.[33]

In what Coke thought to be a respectful and immediate time frame, it formed committees in India and the United States. The committees worked on rebuttals and had their own labs commission the tests, and then they commented in detail. Coke also directed reporters to Internet blogs full of entries that were pro-Coke. Critics say that Coke focused too much on the charges instead of winning back the support of its customers. "Here people interpret silence as guilt," said Mr. Seth, Coke's Indian public relations expert.

Ms. Bjorhus, the Coke communications director, said she could now see how the environmental group had picked Coca-Cola as a way of attracting attention to the broader problem of pesticide contamination in Indian food products. Coca-Cola stands behind its products as being pesticide free. It is now up to the Indian consumer to decide the success of Coca-Cola in the future years.

The Global Water Challenge

In 2007, one out of every five people globally lacked access to clean drinking water.[34] In August 2006, an international conference was held in Stockholm, Sweden, to discuss global water issues. A UN study reported that many large water corporations have decreased their investments in developing countries because of high political and financial risks. Even nations that have been abundant in water supplies are experiencing significant reductions. These reductions are believed to be caused by two factors: the decline in rainfall and increased evaporation of water due to global warming and the loss of the wetlands. Water is something that affects every person each and every day. The executive director of the Stockholm Water Institute, Anders Berntell, noted that water affects the areas of agriculture, energy, transportation, forestry, trade, financing, and social and political security. The Food and Agriculture Organization points out, "Agriculture is the world's largest water consumer. Any water crisis will therefore also create a food crisis."

There have been attempts to improve the water conditions around the world. The United Nations recently released the *World Water Development Report*. This report was compiled by 24 UN agencies and claimed that, in actuality, only 12 percent of the funds targeted for water and sanitation improvement reached those most in need. The United Nations stated that more than 1.1 billion people still lack access to improved water resources, where nearly two-thirds of the 1.1 billion live in Asia.[35] In China, nearly a quarter of the population is unable to access clean drinking water. Over half of China's major waterways are also polluted. The Institute of Public and Environmental Affairs reported that 34 foreign-owned or joint-venture companies, including Pepsi, have caused water pollution problems in China. Ma Jun, the institute's founder, said, "We're not talking about very high standards. These companies are known for their commitment to the environment."[36]

With businesses expanding globally every day, water is an imperative resource that will increasingly affect all industries in the following years. With water conditions improving at a slower rate than business development, businesses will have not only to take on the responsibility of finding an adequate supply of the diminishing resource but also take on the added burden of making sure the water is safe for all to consume. This responsibility is going to be an additional cost to companies, but a necessary one that will prevent loss of sales in the future. Coca-Cola's specific situation in India is a reminder for all global corporations.

Questions for Review

1. What aspects of U.S. and Indian culture may have been a cause of Coke's difficulties in India?

2. How might Coca-Cola have responded differently when this situation first occurred, especially in terms of reacting to negative perceptions among Indians of Coke and other MNCs?

3. If Coca-Cola wants to obtain more of India's soft drink market, what changes does it need to make?

4. How might companies like Coca-Cola and PepsiCo demonstrate their commitment to working with different cultures and respecting the cultural and natural environment of those societies?

Source: This case was prepared by Jaclyn Johns of Villanova University under the supervision of Professor Jonathan Doh as the basis for class discussion. It is not intended to illustrate either effective or ineffective managerial capability or administrative responsibility. Research assistance was provided by Courtney Asher.

Euro Disneyland

On January 18, 1993, Euro Disneyland chairperson Robert Fitzpatrick announced he would leave that post on April 12 to begin his own consulting company. Quitting his position exactly one year after the grand opening of Euro Disneyland, Fitzpatrick's resignation removed U.S. management from the helm of the French theme park and resort.

Fitzpatrick's position was taken by a Frenchman, Philippe Bourguignon, who had been Euro Disneyland's senior vice president for real estate. Bourguignon, 45 years old, faced a net loss of FFr 188 million for Euro Disneyland's fiscal year, which ended September 1992. Also, between April and September 1992, only 29 percent of the park's total visitors were French. Expectations were that closer to half of all visitors would be French.

It was hoped that the promotion of Philippe Bourguignon would have a public relations benefit for Euro Disneyland—a project that has been a publicist's nightmare from the beginning. One of the low points was at a news conference prior to the park's opening when protesters pelted Michael Eisner, CEO of the Walt Disney Company, with rotten eggs. Within the first year of operation, Disney had to compromise its "squeaky clean" image and lift the alcohol ban at the park. Wine is now served at all major restaurants.

Euro Disneyland, 49 percent owned by Walt Disney Company, Burbank, California, originally forecasted 11 million visitors in the first year of operation. In January 1993 it appeared attendance would be closer to 10 million. In response, management temporarily slashed prices at the park for local residents to FFr 150 ($27.27) from FFr 225 ($40.91) for adults and to FFr 100 from FFr 150 for children in order to lure more French during the slow, wet winter months. The company also reduced prices at its restaurants and hotels, which registered occupancy rates of just 37 percent.

Bourguignon also faced other problems, such as the second phase of development at Euro Disneyland, which was expected to start in September 1993. It was unclear how the company planned to finance its FFr 8–10 billion cost. The company had steadily drained its cash reserves (FFr 1.9 billion in May 1993) while piling up debt (FFr 21 billion in May 1993). Euro Disneyland admitted that it and the Walt Disney Company were "exploring potential sources of financing for Euro Disneyland." The company was also talking to banks about restructuring its debts.

Despite the frustrations, Eisner was tirelessly upbeat about the project. "Instant hits are things that go away quickly, and things that grow slowly and are part of the culture are what we look for," he said. "What we created in France is the biggest private investment in a foreign country by an American company ever. And it's gonna pay off."

In the Beginning

Disney's story is the classic American rags-to-riches story, which started in a small Kansas City advertising office where Mickey was a real mouse prowling the unknown Walt Disney floor. Originally, Mickey was named Mortimer, until a dissenting Mrs. Disney stepped in. How close Mickey was to Walt Disney is evidenced by the fact that when filming, Disney himself dubbed the mouse's voice. Only in later films did Mickey get a different voice. Disney made many sacrifices to promote his hero-mascot, including selling his first car, a beloved Moon Cabriolet, and humiliating himself in front of Louis B. Mayer. "Get that mouse off the screen!" was the movie mogul's reported response to the cartoon character. Then, in 1955, Disney had the brainstorm of sending his movie characters out into the "real" world to mix with their fans, and he battled skeptics to build the very first Disneyland in Anaheim, California.

When Disney died in 1966, the company went into virtual suspended animation. Its last big hit of that era was 1969's *The Love Bug*, about a Volkswagen named Herbie. Today, Disney executives trace the problem to a tyrannical CEO named E. Cardon Walker, who ruled the company from 1976 to 1983, and to his successor, Ronald W. Miller. Walker was quick to ridicule underlings in public and impervious to any point of view but his own. He made decisions according to what he thought Walt would have done. Executives clinched arguments by quoting Walt like the Scriptures or Marx, and the company eventually supplied a little book of the founder's sayings. Making the wholesome family movies Walt would have wanted formed a key article of Walker's creed. For example, a poster advertising the unremarkable *Condorman* featured actress Barbara Carrera in a slit skirt. Walker had the slit painted over. With this as the context, studio producers ground out a thin stream of tired, formulaic movies that fewer and fewer customers would pay to see. In mid-1983, a similar low-horsepower approach to television production led to CBS's cancellation of the hour-long program *Walt Disney,* leaving the company without a regular network show for the first time in 29 years. Like a reclusive hermit, the company lost touch with the contemporary world.

Ron Miller's brief reign was by contrast a model of decentralization and delegation. Many attributed Miller's ascent to his marrying the boss's daughter rather than to any special gift. To shore Miller up, the board installed Raymond L. Watson, former head of the Irvine Co., as part-time chairperson. He quickly became full time.

Miller sensed the studio needed rejuvenation, and he managed to produce the hit film *Splash,* featuring an apparently (but not actually) bare-breasted mermaid, under the newly devised Touchstone label. However, the reluctance of freelance Hollywood talent to accommodate Disney's narrow range and stingy compensation often kept his sound instincts from bearing fruit. "Card [Cardon Walker] would listen but not hear," said a former executive. "Ron [Ron Miller] would listen but not act."

Too many box office bombs contributed to a steady erosion of profit. Profits of $135 million on revenues of $915 million in 1980 dwindled to $93 million on revenues of $1.3 billion in 1983. More alarmingly, revenues from the company's theme parks, about three-quarters of the company's total revenues, were showing signs of leveling off. Disney's stock slid from $84.375 a share to $48.75 between April 1983 and February 1984.

Through these years, Roy Disney Jr. simmered while he watched the downfall of the national institution that his uncle, Walt, and his father, Roy Disney Sr., had built. He had long argued that the company's constituent parts all work together to enhance each other. If movie and television production weren't revitalized, not only would that source of revenue disappear but the company and its activities would also grow dim in the public eye. At the same time the stream of new ideas and characters that kept people pouring into the parks and buying toys, books, and records would dry up. Now his dire predictions were coming true. His own personal shareholding had already dropped from $96 million to $54 million. Walker's treatment of Ron Miller as the shining heir apparent and Roy Disney as the idiot nephew helped drive Roy to quit as Disney vice president in 1977, and to set up Shamrock Holdings, a broadcasting and investment company.

In 1984, Roy teamed up with Stanley Gold, a tough-talking lawyer and a brilliant strategist. Gold saw that the falling stock price was bound to flush out a raider and afford Roy Disney a chance to restore the company's fortunes. They asked Frank Wells, vice chairperson of Warner Bros., if he would take a top job in the company in the event they offered it. Wells, a lawyer and a Rhodes scholar, said yes. With that, Roy knew that what he would hear in Disney's boardroom would limit his freedom to trade in its stock, so he quit the board on March 9, 1984. "I knew that would hang a 'For Sale' sign over the company," said Gold.

By resigning, Roy pushed over the first of a train of dominoes that ultimately led to the result he most desired. The company was raided, almost dismantled, greenmailed, raided again, and sued left and right. But it miraculously emerged with a skilled new top management with big plans for a bright future. Roy Disney proposed Michael Eisner as the CEO, but the board came close to rejecting Eisner in favor of an older, more buttoned-down candidate. Gold stepped in and made an impassioned speech to the directors. "You see guys like Eisner as a little crazy . . . but every studio in this country has been run by crazies. What do you think Walt Disney was? The guy was off the goddamned wall. This is a creative institution. It needs to be run by crazies again."[1]

Meanwhile Eisner and Wells staged an all-out lobbying campaign, calling on every board member except two, who were abroad, to explain their views about the company's future. "What was most important," said Eisner, "was that they saw I did not come in a tutu, and that I was a serious person, and I understood a P&L, and I knew the investment analysts, and I read *Fortune.*"

In September 1984, Michael Eisner was appointed CEO and Frank Wells became president. Jeffrey Katzenberg, the 33-year-old, maniacal production chief, followed Fisher from Paramount Pictures. He took over Disney's movie and television studios. "The key," said Eisner, "is to start off with a great idea."

Disneyland in Anaheim, California

For a long time, Walt Disney had been concerned about the lack of family-type entertainment available for his two daughters. The amusement parks he saw around him were mostly filthy traveling carnivals. They were often unsafe and allowed unruly conduct on the premises. Disney envisioned a place where people from all over the world would be able to go for clean and safe fun. His dream came true on July 17, 1955, when the gates first opened at Disneyland in Anaheim, California.

Disneyland strives to generate the perfect fantasy. But magic does not simply happen. The place is a marvel of modern technology. Literally dozens of computers, huge banks of tape machines, film projectors, and electronic controls lie behind the walls, beneath the floors, and above the ceilings of dozens of rides and attractions. The philosophy is that "Disneyland is the world's biggest stage, and the audience is right here on the stage," said Dick Hollinger, chief industrial engineer at Disneyland. "It takes a tremendous amount of work to keep the stage clean and working properly."

Cleanliness is a primary concern. Before the park opens at 8 a.m., the cleaning crew will have mopped, hosed, and dried every sidewalk, street, floor, and counter. More than 350 of the park's 7,400 employees come on duty at 1 a.m., to begin the daily cleanup routine. The thousands of feet that walk through the park each day and

*Stephen Koepp, "Do You Believe in Magic?" *Time,* April 25, 1988, pp.66–73.

chewing gum do not mix; gum has always presented major cleanup problems. The park's janitors found long ago that fire hoses with 90 pounds of water pressure would not do the job. Now they use steam machines, razor scrapers, and mops towed by Cushman scooters to literally scour the streets and sidewalks daily.

It takes one person working a full eight-hour shift to polish the brass on the Fantasyland merry-go-round. The scrupulously manicured plantings throughout the park are treated with growth retarding hormones to keep the trees and bushes from spreading beyond their assigned spaces and destroying the carefully maintained five-eighths scale modeling that is utilized in the park. The maintenance supervisor of the Matterhorn bobsled ride personally walks every foot of track and inspects every link of tow chain every night, thus trusting his or her own eyes more than the $2 million in safety equipment that is built into the ride.

Eisner himself pays obsessive attention to detail. Walking through Disneyland one Sunday afternoon, he peered at the plastic leaves on the Swiss Family Robinson tree house noting that they periodically wear out and need to be replaced leaf by leaf at a cost of $500,000. As his family strolled through the park, he and his eldest son Breck stooped to pick up the rare piece of litter that the cleanup crew had somehow missed. This old-fashioned dedication has paid off. Since opening day in 1955, Disneyland has been a consistent moneymaker.

Disney World in Orlando, Florida

By the time Eisner arrived, Disney World in Orlando was already on its way to becoming what it is today—the most popular vacation destination in the United States. But the company had neglected a rich niche in its business: hotels. Disney's three existing hotels, probably the most profitable in the United States, registered unheard-of occupancy rates of 92 percent to 96 percent versus 66 percent for the industry. Eisner promptly embarked on an ambitious $1 billion hotel expansion plan. Two major hotels, Disney's Grand Floridian Beach Resort and Disney's Caribbean Beach Resort, were opened during 1987–89. Disney's Yacht Club and Beach Resort along with the Dolphin and Swan Hotels, owned and operated by Tishman Realty & Construction, Metropolitan Life Insurance, and Aoki Corporation opened during 1989–90. Adding 3,400 hotel rooms and 250,000 square feet of convention space made it the largest convention center east of the Mississippi.

In October 1982, Disney made a new addition to the theme park—the Experimental Prototype Community of Tomorrow, or EPCOT Center. E. Cardon Walker, then president of the company, announced that EPCOT would be a "permanent showcase, industrial park, and experimental housing center." This new park consists of two large complexes: Future World, a series of pavilions designed to show the technological advances of the next 25 years, and World Showcase, a collection of foreign "villages."

Tokyo Disneyland

It was Tokyo's nastiest winter day in four years. Arctic winds and 8 inches of snow lashed the city. Roads were clogged and trains slowed down. But the bad weather didn't keep 13,200 hardy souls from Tokyo Disneyland. Mikki Mausu, better known outside Japan as Mickey Mouse, had taken the country by storm.

Located on a fringe of reclaimed shoreline in Urayasu City on the outskirts of Tokyo, the park opened to the public on April 15, 1983. In less than one year, over 10 million people had passed through its gates, an attendance figure that has been bettered every single year. On August 13, 1983, 93,000 people helped set a one-day attendance record that easily eclipsed the old records established at the two parent U.S. parks. Four years later, records again toppled as the turnstiles clicked. The total this time: 111,500. By 1988, approximately 50 million people, or nearly half of Japan's population, had visited Tokyo Disneyland since its opening. The steady cash flow pushed revenues for fiscal year 1989 to $768 million, up 17 percent from 1988.

The 204-acre Tokyo Disneyland is owned and operated by Oriental Land under license from the Walt Disney Co. The 45-year contract gives Disney 10 percent of admissions and 5 percent of food and merchandise sales, plus licensing fees. Disney opted to take no equity in the project and put no money down for construction.

Exhibit 2   Investor's Snapshot: The Walt Disney Company (December 1989)

Sales (latest four quarters)	$4.6 billion
Change from year earlier	Up 33.6%
Net profit	$703.3 million
Change	Up 34.7%
Return on common stockholders' equity	23.4%
Five year average	20.3%
Stock price average (last 12 months)	$60.50–$136.25
Recent share price	$122.75
Price/Earnings Multiple	27
Total return to investors (12 months to 11/3/89)	90.6%

Source: Fortune, December 4, 1989.

"I never had the slightest doubt about the success of Disneyland in Japan," said Masatomo Takahashi, president of Oriental Land Company. Oriental Land was so confident of the success of Disney in Japan that it financed the park entirely with debt, borrowing ¥180 billion ($1.5 billion at February 1988 exchange rates). Takahashi added, "The debt means nothing to me," and with good reason. According to Fusahao Awata, who co-authored a book on Tokyo Disneyland: "The Japanese yearn for [American culture]."

Soon after Tokyo Disneyland opened in April 1983, five Shinto priests held a solemn dedication ceremony near Cinderella's castle. It is the only overtly Japanese ritual seen so far in this sprawling theme park. What visitors see is pure Americana. All signs are in English, with only small *katakana* (a phonetic Japanese alphabet) translations. Most of the food is American style, and the attractions are cloned from Disney's U.S. parks. Disney also held firm on two fundamentals that strike the Japanese as strange—no alcohol is allowed and no food may be brought in from outside the park.

However, in Disney's enthusiasm to make Tokyo a brick-by-brick copy of Anaheim's Magic Kingdom, there were a few glitches. On opening day, the Tokyo park discovered that almost 100 public telephones were placed too high for Japanese guests to reach them comfortably. And many hungry customers found countertops above their reach at the park's snack stands.

"Everything we imported that worked in the United States works here," said Ronald D. Pogue, managing director of Walt Disney Attractions Japan Ltd. "American things like McDonald's hamburgers and Kentucky Fried Chicken are popular here with young people. We also wanted visitors from Japan and Southeast Asia to feel they were getting the real thing," said Toshiharu Akiba, a staff member of the Oriental Land publicity department.

Still, local sensibilities dictated a few changes. A Japanese restaurant was added to please older patrons. The Nautilus submarine is missing. More areas are covered to protect against rain and snow. Lines for attractions had to be redesigned so that people walking through the park did not cross in front of patrons waiting to ride an attraction. "It's very discourteous in Japan to have people cross in front of somebody else," explained James B. Cora, managing director of operations for the Tokyo project. The biggest differences between Japan and America have come in slogans and ad copy. Although English is often used, it's "Japanized" English—the sort that would have native speakers shaking their heads while the Japanese nod happily in recognition. "Let's Spring" was the motto for one of their highly successful ad campaigns.

Pogue, visiting frequently from his base in California, supervised seven resident American Disney managers who work side by side with Japanese counterparts from Oriental Land Co. to keep the park in tune with the Disney doctrine. American it may be, but Tokyo Disneyland appeals to such deep-seated Japanese passions as cleanliness, order, outstanding service, and technological wizardry. Japanese executives are impressed by Disney's detailed training manuals, which teach employees how to make visitors feel like VIPs. Most worth emulating, say the Japanese, is Disney's ability to make even the lowliest job seem glamorous. "They have changed the image of dirty work," said Hakuhodo Institute's Sekizawa.

Disney Company did encounter a few unique cultural problems when developing Tokyo Disneyland:

> *The problem:* how to dispose of some 250 tons of trash that would be generated weekly by Tokyo Disneyland visitors?
> *The standard Disney solution:* trash compactors.
> *The Japanese proposal:* pigs to eat the trash and be slaughtered and sold at a profit.
> James B. Cora and his team of some 150 operations experts did a little calculating and pointed out that it would take 100,000 pigs to do the job. And then there would be the smell . . .
> The Japanese relented.

The Japanese were also uneasy about a rustic-looking Westernland, Tokyo's version of Frontierland. "The Japanese like everything fresh and new when they put it in," said Cora. "They kept painting the wood and we kept saying, 'No, it's got to look old.'" Finally the Disney crew took the Japanese to Anaheim to give them a firsthand look at the Old West.

Tokyo Disneyland opened just as the yen escalated in value against the dollar, and the income level of the Japanese registered a phenomenal improvement. During this era of affluence, Tokyo Disneyland triggered an interest in leisure. Its great success spurred the construction of "leisure-lands" throughout the country. This created an increase in the Japanese people's orientation toward leisure. But demographics are the real key to Tokyo Disneyland's success. Thirty million Japanese live within 30 miles of the park. There are three times more than the number of people in the same proximity to Anaheim's Disneyland. With the park proven such an unqualified hit, and nearing capacity, Oriental Land and Disney mapped out plans for a version of the Disney-MGM studio tour next door. This time, Disney talked about taking a 50 percent stake in the project.

Building Euro Disneyland

On March 24, 1987, Michael Eisner and Jacques Chirac, the French prime minister, signed a contract for the building of a Disney theme park at Marne-la-Vallee. Talks between Disney and the French government had dragged on for more than a year. At the signing, Robert Fitzpatrick, fluent in French, married to the former Sylvie Blondet, and the recipient of two awards from the French government, was introduced as the president of Euro Disneyland. He was expected to be a key player in wooing support from the French establishment for the theme park. As one analyst put it, Disney selected him to set up the park because he is "more French than the French."

Disney had been courted extensively by Spain and France. The prime ministers of both countries ordered their governments to lend Disney a hand in its quest for a site. France set up a five-person team headed by Special Advisor to Foreign Trade and Tourism Minister Edith Cresson, and Spain's negotiators included Ignacio Vasallo, Director-General for the Promotion of Tourism. Disney pummeled both governments with requests for detailed information. "The only thing they haven't asked us for is the color of the tourists' eyes," moaned Vasallo.

The governments tried other enticements too. Spain offered tax and labor incentives and possibly as much as 20,000 acres of land. The French package, although less generous, included spending of $53 million to improve highway access to the proposed site and perhaps speeding up a $75 million subway project. For a long time, all that smiling Disney officials would say was that Spain had better weather while France had a better population base.

Officials explained that they picked France over Spain because Marne-la-Vallee is advantageously close to one of the world's tourism capitals, while also being situated within a day's drive or train ride of some 30 million people in France, Belgium, England, and Germany. Another advantage mentioned was the availability of good transportation. A train line that serves as part of the Paris Metro subway system ran to Torcy, in the center of Marne-la-Vallee, and the French government promised to extend the line to the actual site of the park. The park would also be served by A-4, a modern highway that runs from Paris to the German border, as well as a freeway that runs to Charles de Gaulle airport.

Once a letter of intent had been signed, sensing that the French government was keen to not let the plan fail, Disney held out for one concession after another. For example, Disney negotiated for VAT (value-added tax) on ticket sales to be cut from a normal 18.6 percent to 7 percent. A quarter of the investment in building the park would come from subsidized loans. Additionally, any disputes arising from the contract would be settled not in French courts but by a special international panel of arbitrators. But Disney did have to agree to a clause in the contract which would require it to respect and utilize French culture in its themes.

The park was built on 4,460 acres of farmland in Marne-la-Vallee, a rural corner of France 20 miles east of Paris known mostly for sugar beets and Brie cheese. Opening was planned for early 1992, and planners hoped to attract some 10 million visitors a year. Approximately $2.5 billion was needed to build the park, making it the largest single foreign investment ever in France. A French "pivot" company was formed to build the park with starting capital of FFr 3 billion, split 60 percent French and 40 percent foreign, with Disney taking 16.67 percent. Euro Disneyland was expected to bring $600 million in foreign investment into France each year.

As soon as the contract had been signed, individuals and businesses began scurrying to somehow plug into the Mickey Mouse money machine—all were hoping to benefit from the American dream without leaving France. In fact, one Paris daily, *Liberation,* actually sprouted mouse ears over its front-page flag.

The $1.5 to $2 billion first phase investment would involve an amusement complex including hotels and restaurants, golf courses, and an aquatic park in addition to a European version of the Magic Kingdom. The second phase, scheduled to start after the gates opened in 1992, called for the construction of a community around the park, including a sports complex, technology park, conference center, theater, shopping mall, university campus, villas, and condominiums. No price tag had been put on the second phase, although it was expected to rival, if not surpass, the first phase investment. In November 1989, Fitzpatrick announced that the Disney–MGM Studios, Europe would also open at Euro Disneyland in 1996, resembling the enormously successful Disney–MGM Studios theme park at Disney World in Orlando. The new studios would greatly enhance the Walt Disney Company's strategy of increasing its production of live action and animated filmed entertainment in Europe for both the European and world markets.

"The phone's been ringing here ever since the announcement," said Marc Berthod of EpaMarne, the government body that oversees the Marne-la-Vallee region. "We've gotten calls from big companies as well as small—everything from hotel chains to language interpreters all asking for details on Euro Disneyland. And the individual mayors of the villages around here have been swamped with calls from people looking for jobs," he added.

Euro Disneyland was expected to generate up to 28,000 jobs, providing a measure of relief for an area that had suffered a 10 percent–plus unemployment rate for the previous year. It was also expected to light a fire under France's construction industry, which had been particularly hard hit by France's economic problems over the previous year. Moreover, Euro Disneyland was expected to attract many other investors to the depressed outskirts of Paris. International Business Machines (IBM) and Banque National de Paris were among those already building in the area. In addition one of the new buildings going up was a factory that would employ 400 outside workers to wash the 50 tons of laundry expected to be generated per day by Euro Disneyland's 14,000 employees.

The impact of Euro Disneyland was also felt in the real estate market. "Everyone who owns land around here is holding on to it for the time being, at least until they know what's going to happen," said Danny Theveno, a spokesman for the town of Villiers on the western edge of Marne-la-Vallee. Disney expected 11 million visitors in the first year. The break-even point was estimated to be between 7 and 8 million. One worry was that Euro Disneyland would cannibalize the flow of European visitors to Walt Disney World in Florida, but European travel agents said that their customers were still eagerly signing up for Florida, lured by the cheap dollar and the promise of sunshine.

Exhibit 3   Chronology of the Euro Disneyland Deal

1984–85	Disney negotiates with Spain and France to create a European theme park. Chooses France as the site.
1987	Disney signs letter of intent with the French government.
1988	Selects lead commercial bank lenders for the senior portion of the project. Forms the Société en Nom Collectif (SNC). Begins planning for the equity offering of 51% of Euro Disneyland as required in the letter of intent.
1989	European press and stock analysts visit Walt Disney World in Orlando. Begin extensive news and television campaign. Stock starts trading at 20–25 percent premium from the issue price.

Source: Geraldine E. Willigan, "The Value-Adding CFO: An Interview with Disney's Gary Wilson," *Harvard Business Review,* January–February 1990, pp. 85–93.

Protests of Cultural Imperialism

Disney faced French communists and intellectuals who protested the building of Euro Disneyland. Ariane Mnouchkine, a theater director, described it as a "cultural Chernobyl." "I wish with all my heart that the rebels would set fire to Disneyland," thundered a French intellectual in the newspaper *La Figaro.* "Mickey Mouse," sniffed another, "is stifling individualism and transforming children into consumers." The theme park was damned as an example of American "neoprovincialism."

Farmers in the Marne-la-Vallee region posted protest signs along the roadside featuring a mean looking Mickey Mouse and touting sentiments such as "Disney go home," "Stop the massacre," and "Don't gnaw away our national wealth." Farmers were upset partly because under the terms of the contract, the French government would expropriate the necessary land and sell it without profit to the Euro Disneyland development company.

While local officials were sympathetic to the farmers' position, they were unwilling to let their predicament interfere with what some called "the deal of the century." "For many years these farmers have had the fortune to cultivate what is considered some of the richest land in France," said Berthod. "Now they'll have to find another occupation."

Also less than enchanted about the prospect of a magic kingdom rising among its midst was the communist-dominated labor federation, the Confédération Générale du Travail (CGT). Despite the job-creating potential of Euro Disney, the CGT doubted its members would benefit. The union had been fighting hard to stop the passage of a bill which would give managers the right to establish flexible hours for their workers. Flexible hours were believed to be a prerequisite to the profitable operation of Euro Disneyland, especially considering seasonal variations.

However, Disney proved to be relatively immune to the anti-U.S. virus. In early 1985, one of the three state-owned television networks signed a contract to broadcast two hours of dubbed Disney programming every Saturday evening. Soon after, *Disney Channel* became one of the top-rated programs in France.

In 1987, the company launched an aggressive community relations program to calm the fears of politicians, farmers, villagers, and even bankers that the project would bring traffic congestion, noise, pollution, and other problems to their countryside. Such a public relations program was a rarity in France, where businesses make little effort to establish good relations with local residents. Disney invited 400 local children to a birthday party for Mickey Mouse, sent Mickey to area hospitals, and hosted free trips to Disney World in Florida for dozens of local officials and children.

"They're experts at seduction, and they don't hide the fact that they're trying to seduce you," said Vincent Guardiola, an official with Banque Indosuez, one of the 17 banks wined and dined at Orlando and subsequently one of the venture's financial participants. "The French aren't used to this kind of public relations—it was unbelievable." Observers said that the goodwill efforts helped dissipate initial objections to the project.

Financial Structuring at Euro Disneyland

Eisner was so keen on Euro Disneyland that Disney kept a 49 percent stake in the project, while the remaining 51 percent of stock was distributed through the London, Paris, and Brussels stock exchanges. Half the stock under the offer was going to the French, 25 percent to the English, and the remainder distributed in the rest of the European community. The initial offer price of FFr 72 was considerably higher than the pathfinder prospectus estimate because the capacity of the park had been slightly extended. Scarcity of stock was likely to push up the price, which was expected to reach FFr 166 by opening day in 1992. This would give a compound return of 21 percent.

Walt Disney Company maintained management control of the company. The U.S. company put up $160 million of its own capital to fund the project, an investment which soared in value to $2.4 billion after the popular stock offering in Europe. French national and local authorities, by comparison, were providing about $800 million in low-interest loans and poured at least that much again into infrastructure.

Other sources of funding were the park's 12 corporate sponsors, and Disney would pay them back in kind. The "autopolis" ride, where kids ride cars, features coupes emblazoned with the "Hot Wheels" logo. Mattel Inc., sponsor of the ride, was grateful for the boost to one of its biggest toy lines.

The real payoff would begin once the park opened. The Walt Disney Company would receive 10 percent of admission fees and 5 percent of food and merchandise revenue, the same arrangement as in Japan. But in France, it would also receive management fees, incentive fees, and 49 percent of the profits.

A Saloman Brothers analyst estimated that the park would pull in 3 to 4 million more visitors than the 11 million the company expected in the first year. Other Wall Street analysts cautioned that stock prices of both Walt Disney Company and Euro Disney already contained all the Euro optimism they could absorb. "Europeans visit Disney World in Florida as part of an 'American experience,'" said Patrick P. Roper, marketing director of Alton Towers, a successful British theme park near Manchester. He doubted they would seek the suburbs of Paris as eagerly as America and predicted attendance would trail Disney projections.

The Layout of Euro Disneyland

Euro Disneyland is determinedly American in its theme. There was an alcohol ban in the park despite the attitude among the French that wine with a meal is a God-given right. Designers presented a plan for a Main Street USA based on scenes of America in the 1920s, because research indicated that Europeans loved the Prohibition era. Eisner decreed that images of gangsters and speakeasies were too negative. Though made more ornate and Victorian than Walt Disney's idealized Midwestern small town, Main Street remained Main Street. Steamships leave from Main Street through the Grand Canyon Diorama en route to Frontierland.

The familiar Disney Tomorrowland, with its dated images of the space age, was jettisoned entirely. It was replaced by a gleaming brass and wood complex called Discoverland, which was based on themes of Jules Verne and Leonardo da Vinci. Eisner ordered $8 or $10 million in extras to the "Visionarium" exhibit, a 360-degree movie about French culture which was required by the French in their original contract. French and English are the official languages at the park, and multilingual guides are available to help Dutch, German, Spanish, and Italian visitors.

With the American Wild West being so frequently captured on film, Europeans have their own idea of what life was like back then. Frontierland reinforces those images. A runaway mine train takes guests through the canyons and mines of Gold Rush country. There is a paddle wheel steamboat reminiscent of Mark Twain, Indian explorer canoes, and a phantom manor from the Gold Rush days.

In Fantasyland, designers strived to avoid competing with the nearby European reality of actual medieval towns, cathedrals, and chateaux. While Disneyland's castle is based on Germany's Neuschwanstein and Disney World's is based on a Loire Valley chateau, Euro Disney's

Le Château de la Belle au Bois Dormant, as the French insisted Sleeping Beauty be called, is more cartoonlike with stained glass windows built by English craftspeople and depicting Disney characters. Fanciful trees grow inside as well as a beanstalk.

The park is criss-crossed with covered walkways. Eisner personally ordered the installation of 35 fireplaces in hotels and restaurants. "People walk around Disney World in Florida with humidity and temperatures in the 90s and they walk into an air-conditioned ride and say, 'This is the greatest,'" said Eisner. "When it's raining and miserable, I hope they will walk into one of these lobbies with the fireplace going and say the same thing."

Children all over Europe were primed to consume. Even one of the intellectuals who contributed to *Le Figaro's* Disney-bashing broadsheet was forced to admit with resignation that his 10-year-old son "swears by Michael Jackson." At Euro Disneyland, under the name "Captain EO," Disney just so happened to have a Michael Jackson attraction awaiting him.

Food Service and Accommodations at Euro Disneyland

Disney expected to serve 15,000 to 17,000 meals per hour, excluding snacks. Menus and service systems were developed so that they varied both in style and price. There is a 400-seat buffeteria, 6 table service restaurants, 12 counter service units, 10 snack bars, 1 Discovery food court seating 850, 9 popcorn wagons, 15 ice-cream carts, 14 specialty food carts, and 2 employee cafeterias. Restaurants were, in fact, to be a showcase for American foods. The only exception to this is Fantasyland which re-creates European fables. Here, food service will reflect the fable's country of origin: Pinocchio's facility having German food; Cinderella's, French; Bella Notte's, Italian; and so on.

Exhibit 4 **The Euro Disneyland Resort**

5,000 acres in size

30 attractions

12,000 employees

6 hotels (with 5,184 rooms)

10 theme restaurants

414 cabins

181 camping sites

Source: Roger Cohen, "Threat of Strikes in Euro Disney Debut," *New York Times,* April 10, 1992, p. 20.

Of course recipes were adapted for European tastes. Since many Europeans don't care much for very spicy food, Tex-Mex recipes were toned down. A special coffee blend had to be developed which would have universal appeal. Hot dog carts would reflect the regionalism of American tastes. There would be a ball park hot dog (mild, steamed, a mixture of beef and pork), a New York hot dog (all beef, and spicy), and a Chicago hot dog (Vienna-style, similar to bratwurst).

Euro Disneyland has six theme hotels which would offer nearly 5,200 rooms on opening day, a campground (444 rental trailers and 181 camping sites), and single family homes on the periphery of the 27-hole golf course.

Disney's Strict Appearance Code

Antoine Guervil stood at his post in front of the 1,000-room Cheyenne Hotel at Euro Disneyland, practicing his "Howdy!" When Guervil, a political refugee from Haiti, said the word, it sounded more like "Audi." Native French speakers have trouble with the aspirated "h" sound in words like "hay" and "Hank" and "howdy." Guervil had been given the job of wearing a cowboy costume and booming a happy, welcoming howdy to guests as they entered the Cheyenne, styled after a Western movie set.

"Audi," said Guervil, the strain of linguistic effort showing on his face. This was clearly a struggle. Unless things got better, it was not hard to imagine objections from Renault, the French car company that was one of the corporate sponsors of the park. Picture the rage of a French auto executive arriving with his or her family at the Renault-sponsored Euro Disneyland, only to hear the doorman of a Disney hotel advertising a German car.

Such were the problems Disney faced while hiring some 12,000 people to maintain and populate its Euro Disneyland theme park. A handbook of detailed rules on acceptable clothing, hairstyles, and jewelry, among other things, embroiled the company in a legal and cultural dispute. Critics asked how the brash Americans could be so insensitive to French culture, individualism, and privacy. Disney officials insisted that a ruling that barred them from imposing a squeaky-clean employment standard could threaten the image and long-term success of the park.

"For us, the appearance code has a real effect from a product identification standpoint," said Thor Degelmann, vice president for human resources for Euro Disneyland. "Without it we wouldn't be presenting the Disney product that people would be expecting."

The rules, spelled out in a video presentation and detailed in a guide handbook, went beyond height and weight standards. They required men's hair to be cut above the collar and ears with no beards or mustaches. Any tattoos must be covered. Women must keep their hair in one "natural color" with no frosting or streaking, and they may make only limited use of makeup like mascara. False eyelashes, eyeliners, and eye pencil were completely off limits. Fingernails can't pass the end of the fingers. As for jewelry, women can wear only one earring in each ear, with the earring's diameter no more than three-quarters of an inch. Neither men nor women can wear more than one ring on each hand. Further, women were required to wear appropriate undergarments and only transparent panty hose, not black or anything with fancy designs. Though a daily bath was not specified in the rules, the applicant's video depicted a shower scene and informed applicants that they were expected to show up for work "fresh and clean each day." Similar rules are in force at Disney's three other theme parks in the United States and Japan.

In the United States, some labor unions representing Disney employees have occasionally protested the company's strict appearance code, but with little success. French labor unions began protesting when Disneyland opened its "casting center" and invited applicants to "play the role of [their lives]" and to take a "unique opportunity to marry work and magic." The CGT handed out leaflets in front of the center to warn applicants of the appearance code, which they believed represented "an attack on individual liberty." A more mainstream union, the Confédération Française Démocratique du Travail (CFDT) appealed to the Labor Ministry to halt Disney's violation of "human dignity." French law prohibits employers from restricting individual and collective liberties unless the restrictions can be justified by the nature of the task to be accomplished and are proportional to that end.

Degelmann, however, said that the company was "well aware of the cultural differences" between the United States and France and as a result had "toned down" the wording in the original American version of the guidebook. He pointed out that many companies, particularly airlines, maintained appearance codes just as strict. "We happened to put ours in writing," he added. In any case, he said that he knew of no one who had refused to take

Exhibit 5 **What Price Mickey?**

	Euro Disneyland	Disney World, Orlando
Peak Season Hotel Rates		
4-person room	$97 to $345	$104–$455
Campground Space		
	$48	$30–$49
One-Day Pass		
Children	$26	$26
Adults	$40	$33

Source: BusinessWeek, March 30, 1992.

the job because of the rules and that no more than 5 percent of the people showing up for interviews had decided not to proceed after watching the video, which also detailed transportation and salary.

Fitzpatrick also defended the dress code, although he conceded that Disney might have been a little naive in presenting things so directly. He added, "Only in France is there still a communist party. There is not even one in Russia any more. The ironic thing is that I could fill the park with CGT requests for tickets."

Another big challenge lay in getting the mostly French "cast members," as Disney calls its employees, to break their ancient cultural aversions to smiling and being consistently polite to park guests. The individualistic French had to be molded into the squeaky-clean Disney image. Rival theme parks in the area, loosely modeled on the Disney system, had already encountered trouble keeping smiles on the faces of the staff, who sometimes took on the demeanor of subway ticket clerks.

The delicate matter of hiring French citizens as opposed to other nationals was examined in the more than two-year-long preagreement negotiations between the French government and Disney. The final agreement called for Disney to make a maximum effort to tap into the local labor market. At the same time, it was understood that for Euro Disneyland to work, its staff must mirror the multi-country makeup of its guests. "Casting centers" were set up in Paris, London, Amsterdam, and Frankfurt. "We are concentrating on the local labor market, but we are also looking for workers who are German, English, Italian, Spanish, or other nationalities and who have good communication skills, are outgoing, speak two European languages—French plus one other—and like being around people," said Degelmann.

Stephane Baudet, a 28-year-old trumpet player from Paris, refused to audition for a job in a Disney brass band when he learned he would have to cut his ponytail. "Some people will turn themselves into a pumpkin to work at Euro Disneyland," he said. "But not me."

Opening Day at Euro Disneyland

A few days before the grand opening of Euro Disneyland, hundreds of French visitors were invited to a preopening party. They gazed perplexed at what was placed before them. It was a heaping plate of spare ribs. The visitors were at the Buffalo Bill Wild West Show, a cavernous theater featuring a panoply of "Le Far West," including 20 imported buffaloes. And Disney deliberately didn't provide silverware. "There was a moment of consternation," recalls Fitzpatrick. "Then they just kind of said, 'The hell with it,' and dug in." There was one problem. The guests couldn't master the art of gnawing ribs and applauding at the same time. So Disney planned to provide more napkins and teach visitors to stamp with their feet.

On April 12, 1992, the opening day of Euro Disneyland, *France-Soir* enthusiastically predicted Disney dementia. "Mickey! It's madness," read its front-page headline, warning of chaos on the roads and suggesting that people may have to be turned away. A French government survey indicated that half a million might turn up with 90,000 cars trying to get in. French radio warned traffic to avoid the area.

By lunchtime on opening day, the Euro Disneyland car park was less than half full, suggesting an attendance of below 25,000, less than half the park's capacity and way below expectations. Many people may have heeded the advice to stay home or, more likely, were deterred by a one-day strike that cut the direct rail link to Euro Disneyland from the center of Paris. Queues for the main rides, such as Pirates of the Caribbean and Big Thunder Mountain rail-road, were averaging around 15 minutes less than on an ordinary day at Disney World, Florida.

Disney executives put on a brave face, claiming that attendance was better than at first days for other Disney theme parks in Florida, California, and Japan. However, there was no disguising the fact that after spending thousands of dollars on the preopening celebrations, Euro Disney would have appreciated some impressively long traffic jams on the auto route.

Other Operating Problems

When the French government changed hands in 1986, work ground to a halt, as the negotiator appointed by the Conservative government threw out much of the ground work prepared by his Socialist predecessor. The legalistic approach taken by the Americans also bogged down talks, as it meant planning ahead for every conceivable contingency. At the same time, right-wing groups who saw the park as an invasion of "chewing-gum jobs" and U.S. pop culture also fought hard for a greater "local cultural context."

On opening day, English visitors found the French reluctant to play the game of queuing. "The French seem to think that if God had meant them to queue, He wouldn't have given them elbows," they commented. Different cultures have different definitions of personal space, and Disney guests faced problems of people getting too close or pressing around those who left too much space between themselves and the person in front.

Disney placed its first ads for work bids in English, leaving small- and medium-sized French firms feeling like foreigners in their own land. Eventually, Disney set up a data bank with information on over 20,000 French and European firms looking for work and the local Chamber of Commerce developed a video text information bank with Disney that small- and medium-sized companies through France and Europe would be able to tap into. "The work will come, but many local companies have got to learn that they don't simply have the right to a chunk of work without competing," said a chamber official.

Efforts were made to ensure that sooner, rather than later, European nationals take over the day-to-day running of the park. Although there were only 23 U.S. expatriates among the employees, they controlled the show and held most of the top jobs. Each senior manager had the task of choosing his or her European successor.

Disney was also forced to bail out 40 subcontractors who were working for the Gabot-Eremco construction contracting group, which had been unable to honor all of its commitments. Some of the subcontractors said they faced bankruptcy if they were not paid for their work on Euro Disneyland. A Disney spokesperson said that the payments would be less than $20.3 million and the company had already paid Gabot-Eremco for work on the park. Gabot-Eremco and 15 other main contractors demanded $157 million in additional fees from Disney for work that they said was added to the project after the initial contracts were signed. Disney rejected the claim and sought government intervention. Disney said that under no circumstances would it pay Gabot-Eremco and accused its officers of incompetence.

As Bourguignon thought about these and other problems, the previous year's losses and the prospect of losses again in the current year, with their negative impact on the company's stock price, weighed heavily on his mind.

Questions for Review

1. Using Hofstede's four cultural dimensions as a point of reference, what are some of the main cultural differences between the United States and France?

2. In what way has Trompenaars's research helped explain cultural differences between the United States and France?

3. In managing its Euro Disneyland operations, what are three mistakes that the company made? Explain.

4. Based on its experience, what are three lessons the company should have learned about how to deal with diversity? Describe each.

Source: This case was prepared by Research Assistant Sonali Krishna under the direction of Professors J. Stewart Black and Hal B. Gregersen as the basis for class discussion. It is not intended to illustrate either effective or ineffective managerial capability or administrative responsibility. Reprinted by permission of the authors.

Beyond Tokyo: Disney's Expansion in Asia

After its success with Tokyo Disneyland in the 1980s, Disney began to realize the vast potential of the Asian market. The theme park industry throughout Asia has been very successful in recent years, with a range of regional and international companies all trying to enter the market. Disney has been one of the major participants, opening Hong Kong Disneyland in 2005 and discussing future operations in at least three other Asian cities.

Disney in China

After Disney's success in Tokyo, China, in particular, became a serious option for its next theme park venture in light of the country's impressive population and economic growth throughout the 1990s. Successful sales associated with the Disney movie, *The Lion King,* in 1996 also convinced Disney officials that China was a promising location. However, consumer enthusiasm for theme parks in China was at a low in the late 1990s. "Between 1993 and 1998, more than 2,000 theme parks had been opened in China," and "many projects were swamped by excessive competition, poor market projections, high costs, and relentless interference from local officials," forcing several hundred to be closed.[2] Nevertheless, Disney continued to pursue plans in both Shanghai and Hong Kong.

Shanghai, known as the "Paris of the Orient," was an attractive site for Disney officials because of its growing commercialization and industrialization and its already extant transportation access. The projected $1 billion project was scheduled to be built across the Huangpu River from Shanghai's world-famous waterfront promenade, the Bund, on a 200-square-mile expanse called The Pudong New Area. The first phase of construction included a Magic Kingdom park, while an EPCOT-style theme park was to be added after at least five years of operations.[3]

A Disney theme park in Shanghai would be mutually beneficial for the company and the nation of China. From Disney's perspective, it would gain access to one of the world's largest potential markets (and also compete with Universal Studios' new theme park). From the perspective of Chinese government officials, Disney's park would be a long-awaited mark of international success for a communist nation.[4]

Initially planners hoped to have a Disneyland operating in Shanghai prior to the World Expo in 2010. However the project stalled, and as of late 2006, "the chances of Beijing approving the project have shrunk since Shanghai's Communist Party boss was implicated in a big corruption investigation in September [2005]". This led Disney to consider other options for the construction of a new park.[5]

Hong Kong Disneyland

Plans in Hong Kong, which culminated in the opening of Hong Kong Disneyland in September 2005, began after the 1997–1998 Asian financial crisis. Despite the poor economic condition of Hong Kong in the late 1990s, Disney was still optimistic about prospects for a theme park in the "city of life." Hong Kong, already an international tourist destination, would draw Disneyland patrons primarily from China, Taiwan, and Southeast Asia.

The official park plans were announced in November 1999 as a joint venture between the Walt Disney Company and the Hong Kong SAR Government. Unlike its experience in Tokyo, where Disney handed the reins over completely to a foreign company (the Oriental Land Company), Disney decided to take more direct control over this new park. The park was built on Lantau Island at Penny's Bay, within the 6-mile stretch separating the international airport and downtown. Hong Kong Disneyland was estimated to create 18,000 jobs upon opening and ultimately 36,000 jobs. The first phase of the park was to include a 10 million annual visitor Disneyland-based theme park, 2,100 hotel rooms, and a 300,000-square-foot retail, dining and entertainment complex.[6]

In order to make the park "culturally sensitive," Jay Rasulo, president of Walt Disney Parks & Resorts, announced that Hong Kong Disneyland would be trilingual with English, Cantonese, and Mandarin. The park would also include a fantasy garden for taking pictures with the Disney characters (popular among Asian tourists), as well as more covered and rainproof spaces to accommodate the "drizzly" climate.[7]

Unfortunately, Disney soon realized that its attempts at cultural sensitivity had not gone far enough. For instance, the decision to serve shark fin soup, a local favorite, greatly angered environmentalists. The park ultimately had to remove the dish from its menus. Park executives also failed to plan for the large influx of visitors around the Chinese New Year in early 2006, forcing them to turn away numerous patrons who had valid tickets. Unsurprisingly, this led to customer outrage and negative media coverage of the relatively new theme park.

Other criticisms of the park have included its small scale and slow pace of expansion. Hong Kong Disneyland only has 16 attractions and "one classic Disney thrill ride, Space Mountain, compared to 52 at Disneyland Resort Paris [formerly Euro Disneyland]."[8] However the government has made plans to increase the size of the park by acquiring land adjacent to the existing facilities. Likely due to its small size and fewer attractions, Hong Kong Disneyland only pulled in 5.2 million guests during its first 12 months, less than the estimated 5.6 million.[9] Failure to meet its projected levels of attendance and guest spending could cause the park to look toward other sources of funding for these expansions.

Other Asian Ventures

The Walt Disney Company has also looked into building other theme parks and resorts in Asia. Based on its successful operation of two theme parks in the United States (at Anaheim and Orlando), Disney believes that it can have more than one park per region. Another strategically located park in Asia, officials agreed, would not compete with Tokyo Disneyland or Hong Kong Disneyland, but rather bring in a new set of customers.

One such strategic location is the state of Johor in Malaysia. Malaysian officials wanted to develop Johor in order to rival its neighbor, Singapore, as a tourist attraction. (Singapore built two large casino resorts in 2006.) However, Disney claimed to have no existing plans or discussions for building a park in Malaysia. Alannah Goss, a spokeswoman for Disney's Asian operations based in Hong Kong, said, "We are constantly evaluating strategic markets in the world to grow our park and resort business and the Disney brand. We continue to evaluate markets but at this time, we have no plans to announce regarding a park in Malaysia."[10]

Singapore, in its effort to expand its tourism industry, had also expressed interest in being host to the next Disneyland theme park. Although rumors of a Singapore Disneyland were quickly dismissed, some reports suggested there were exploratory discussions of locations at either Marina East or Seletar. Residents of Singapore expressed concern that the park would not be competitive, even against the smaller-scale Hong Kong Disneyland. Their primary fears included limited attractions (based on size and local regulations), hot weather, and high ticket prices.

Disney's Future in Asia

Although Disney is wise to enter the Asian market with its new theme parks, it still faces many obstacles. One is finding the right location. Lee Hoon, professor of tourism management at Yanyang University in Seoul noted, "Often, more important than content is whether a venue is located in a metropolis, whether it's easily accessible by public transportation." Often tied to issues of location is the additional threat of competition, both from local attractions and those of other international corporations. It seems that Asian travelers are loyal to their local attractions, evidenced by the success of South Korea's Everland theme park and Hong Kong's own Ocean Park (which brought in more visitors than Hong Kong Disneyland in 2006).[11] The stiff competition of the theme park industry in Asia will center on not only which park can create a surge of interest in its first year but also which can build a loyal base of repeat customers.

Despite its already large size, the Asian theme park industry is still developing. Disney officials will need to be innovative and strategic in order to maintain sales. After Universal Studios in Japan witnessed a 20 percent drop in attendance between 2001 and 2006 and Hong Kong Disneyland failed to meet its estimated attendance level in 2006, Disney officials might want to think twice about building additional parks in Asia.[12]

Questions for Review

1. What cultural challenges are posed by Disney's expansion into Asia? How are these different from those in Europe?

2. How do cultural variables influence the location choice of theme parks around the world?

3. What location would you recommend for Disney's next theme park in Asia? Why?

Source: This case was prepared by Courtney Asher under the supervision of Professor Jonathan Doh of Villanova University as the basis for class discussion. It is not intended to illustrate either effective or ineffective managerial capability or administrative responsibility.

Wal-Mart's Japan Strategy

In March 2002, Wal-Mart first entered the Japanese market by acquiring a $46 million stake in Seiyu, the nation's fifth-largest supermarket retailer.[1] Another main player in the deal was Sumitomo Corp., a leading trading company in Japan. Sumitomo's solid business base and knowledge of the retail sector was viewed as helping Wal-Mart effectively enter and expand in this unique market. As part of the deal, Sumitomo increased its stake in Seiyu to 15.6 percent.

Although Seiyu's existing distribution channels gave Wal-Mart an established local partner, two years after the initial entry, its success was unclear. In September 2003, Seiyu forecast a loss of $83 million for the March–December period, blaming a poor economic environment and an unfavorable produce climate.[2] While Wal-Mart is confident of its decision, the two companies have a different approach to management strategy, operations, and marketing. Wal-Mart specializes in large-scale general merchandise stores, mainly in suburban areas. Seiyu had traditionally focused on profitable grocery stores in city-center locations. Over time, Wal-Mart is expected to move away from these locations and focus on opening new open-spaced outlets.

In addition to meeting its quantitative goals, Wal-Mart's ability to effectively relate to Seiyu's employees will be an integral piece of the mix. Japanese and Americans have many distinct sociocultural differences, and these variations must be understood and properly managed by those who will be overseeing Seiyu's operations. In the final analysis, Wal-Mart's lasting success will hinge on its ability to understand cultural nuances and properly convey its message to both Japanese consumers and employees alike.

Wal-Mart's International Expansion

Wal-Mart has traditionally been one of the largest and most admired global companies (see Tables 1, 2, and 3), although in recent years it has come under recent criticism for its hard-ball expansion strategy, wage and working conditions, and alleged discrimination in employment practices. Relying on long-term opportunities outside of its domestic market to expand sales, Wal-Mart is slowly and steadily making its way in many international regions, including China, Mexico, and especially Japan (see Tables 4 and 5). As of late 2003, if ranked separately, Wal-Mart's international division would have been

number 33 on the Fortune 500 list. According to John Menzer, Wal-Mart's international division president and CEO, "our challenge is to rake up one-third of the company's sales, and take our global scale to the local level."[3] While Wal-Mart has been successful in making some inroads overseas, its success has been far from universal. For example, in Mexico, China, and the U.K., the company's efforts to offer the lowest price to customers backfired because of resistance from established retailers. In Mexico, three of the largest domestic retailers constructed a joint buying and operational alliance solely to compete with Wal-Mart.[4]

So far, labor advocates and environmentalists have created headaches for the U.S. behemoth, making continued expansion both cumbersome and expensive. For instance, in 2006, Wal-Mart faced a strong public relations campaign from the All-China Federation of Trade Unions (ACFTU) over Wal-Mart's refusal to let its workers in China unionize. Wal-Mart was eventually forced to concede, perhaps because the Chinese government also lent its weight to the ACFTU's campaign in its effort to establish unions in all foreign-funded enterprises throughout the country. As of October 2006, almost 6,000 of Wal-Mart China's 30,000 employees were union members.[5] Despite its public battle with the ACFTU, *Fortune China* and Watson Wyatt still voted Wal-Mart China as one of the "Top 10 Best Companies to Work for" in 2005.[6] As Wal-Mart continues to expand its global operations, analysts are curious to see how the company is received and whether consumers' opinions in fragmented market settings are able to move past their desire for lower prices.

In its quest for global expansion outside of Japan, Wal-Mart has entered other locations including Mexico, China, South Korea, Germany, Hong Kong, and Indonesia. Wal-Mart has experienced varied levels of success. Its operations in Hong Kong lasted only two years during the 1990s, and it ended operations in Indonesia in the mid-90s after rioting incidents in Jakarta. Wal-Mart also owned approximately 16 stores in South Korea and 85 in Germany; however, it sold off these operations in 2006 in order to focus greater attention on its Japanese market.[7] Reasons for exiting the Korean and German markets included merchandise that failed to match consumer tastes, distribution and re-badging problems, and strong customer loyalties to other brands.

Wal-Mart has had a more successful experience in Mexico. In 1991 Wal-Mart entered into a joint venture with retail conglomerate Cifra and opened a Sam's Club in Mexico City. In 1997 it gained a majority position in the company and in 2001 changed the store name to Wal-Mart de Mexico, or more commonly, "Wal-Mex." In addition to its 195 Wal-Mart Supercenters and Sam's Club warehouses, Wal-Mex also operates Bodega food and general merchandise discount stores, Superama supermarkets, Suburbia apparel stores, and Vips and El Portón restaurants. The majority of its stores are located in and around Mexico City; however, it does business in over 145 cities throughout Mexico.

Wal-Mex has shown no signs of slowing down. In 2005 Wal-Mart opened 93 new stores and saw a 13.7 percent increase in net sales overall. As of February 2007, it operated 889 stores in Mexico and had plans to open another 125 that year.[8] In late 2006 the company was also approved by Mexico's Finance Ministry to open its own bank. In a country where 80 percent of citizens have never had a bank account due to high fees, "Banco Wal-Mart de Mexico Adelante" will add much-needed competition to the financial services industry and hopefully lowering the traditionally high fees.[9] Wal-Mex's plans for future growth involve more heavily targeting the 16–24-year-old age group, which constitutes 55 percent of Mexico's population.

Though not as easy as its experience in Mexico, Wal-Mart has also found decent success in China. Wal-Mart entered the Chinese market in 1996 when it opened a Supercenter and Sam's Club in Shenzen. As of late 2006 the company had expanded to 73 stores in 36 cities. In order to cater to its Chinese shoppers, Wal-Mart has introduced "retail-tainment" and attempted to create a more hands-on shopping experience.[10] China's Tourism Bureau even named one underground Wal-Mart store a tourist destination.[11]

In addition to its own stores, Wal-Mart has had a stake in the Taiwanese Bounteous Company Ltd., which owned the popular chain of Trust-Mart stores.[12] In late 2006, *The Wall Street Journal* publicized a $1 billion deal between Wal-Mart and Bounteous, in which Wal-Mart would acquire Trust-Mart's 100 stores over the course of three years. In light of Wal-Mart's slowing U.S. sales and the termination of its operations in Germany and South Korea, the company's expansion in China is quite timely. Like its operations in Mexico, Wal-Mart has also entered the Chinese financial service industry, by introducing a credit card with Bank of Communications Ltd. in late 2006.[13]

Wal-Mart's expansions have not gone unnoticed. Domestic Chinese rivals have also built up their businesses in order to compete. In 2005 Shanghai Bailan Group purchased four rival supermarkets and department stores and now operates over 5,000 stores. China Resources Enterprise has hired away managers from foreign chains and cut staff in order to increase its profitability.[14] While these efforts signal greater competition for Wal-Mart in particular, they are necessary for domestic companies to survive in China's $841 billion retail market,[15] which has been increasingly competitive ever since the country joined the WTO and dropped restrictions on foreign retailers.

Wal-Mart Enters Japan

Japan, home of the world's second-largest consumer market, has been aggressively targeted by Wal-Mart as a key piece in its international strategy. Historically, reaching Japan's fickle customer base has been quite a challenge. In Japan, consumers often equate bad quality with low prices. Not so in the United States. But Wal-Mart isn't naive. It realizes that changing consumer perceptions won't be easy or cheap, especially in the wake of recent competitive moves intended to counter its entrance into the nation of the rising sun. Succeeding where many large corporations have failed before it means that Wal-Mart has to be able to capture a distinct place in the hearts and minds of the Japanese customer as, specifically, a retail destination that offers an abundance of quality goods at rock-bottom prices.

The timing seemed right for Wal-Mart's expansion to Japan. The Japanese economy had been in the midst of a prolonged recession but was showing some signs of recovery. The country seemed ready for a discount retailer which could provide lower-priced goods for cash-strapped consumers. In 2002, the nation's economy grew just 1.6 percent while household income dropped. During the quarter ending September 30, 2003, household income dropped 1.4 percent, and consumer spending flattened. With the country experiencing deflationary forces in the prices of consumer goods, Wal-Mart hoped it would begin to attract more and more bargain-hungry consumers.

Although real estate prices dropped substantially over the past couple of years, they are still relatively high. Rather than build massive supercenter-size stores, Japanese retailers often stick with smaller shops that are easier to open in densely populated urban areas. Through the Seiyu ownership, Wal-Mart has been able to avoid upfront building costs, giving itself a swift advantage over hobbled Japanese retailers. Nevertheless, Wal-Mart's ultimate challenge will lie in its ability to convince Japanese consumers that its everyday low prices don't translate into poor product quality.

Retail Environment in Japan

Japan is the second-largest and one of the wealthiest economies in the world, with a GDP at purchasing power parity of $4.22 trillion and per-capita GDP of about

Table 1   **Wal-Mart Balance Sheet as of December 31, 2006**

Wal-Mart Corporation Consolidated Balance Sheet (in millions)

	2006	2005	2004	2003
Assets				
Cash and equivalents	6,414	5,488	5,199	2,758
Accounts receivable	2,662	1,715	1,254	2,108
Inventories	32,191	29,447	26,612	24,891
Total current assets	43,824	38,491	34,421	30,483
PP&E (net)	75,875	65,408	56,410	48,700
Total assets	138,187	120,223	105,405	94,685
Liabilities and Shareholders' Equity				
Accounts payable	25,373	21,671	19,425	17,140
Notes payable	4,595	3,759	2,904	4,538
Accrued liabilities	13,465	12,155	10,671	8,945
Total current liabilities	48,826	42,888	37,840	32,617
Long-term debt	26,429	20,087	17,102	16,607
Total liabilities	85,016	70,827	61,782	55,348
Shareholders' equity	53,171	49,396	43,623	39,337
Total liabilities and shareholders' equity	138,187	120,223	105,405	94,685

Source: Wal-Mart 2003, 2005, and 2006 Annual Reports.

Table 2   **Wal-Mart Income Statement, December 31, 2006**

Wal-Mart Income Statement (in millions, except per share amounts)

	2006	2005	2004	2003
Net revenue	312,427	285,222	256,329	244,524
Cost of sales	240,391	219,793	198,747	191,838
SG&A	56,733	51,248	44,909	41,043
Interest expense	1,172	986	832	925
Interest provisions	5,803	5,589	5,118	4,487
Net income	11,231	10,267	9,054	8,039
Basic EPS	$2.68	$2.41	$2.08	$1.81
Diluted EPS	$2.68	$2.41	$2.07	$1.81
Dividends per share	$0.60	$0.52	$0.36	$0.30

Source: Wal-Mart 2003 and 2006 Annual Reports.

Table 3   **The 10 Most Admired Global Companies**

2004			2007		
Rank Company		**Country**	**Rank Company**		**Country**
1 **Wal-Mart Stores**		**U.S.**	1 General Electric		U.S.
2 General Electric		U.S.	2 Toyota Motor		Japan
3 Microsoft		U.S.	3 Procter & Gamble		U.S.
4 Johnson & Johnson		U.S.	4 Johnson & Johnson		U.S.
5 Berkshire Hathaway		U.S.	5 Apple		U.S.
6 Dell		U.S.	6 Berkshire Hathaway		U.S.
7 IBM		U.S.	7 FedEx		U.S.
8 Toyota Motor		Japan	8 Microsoft		U.S.
9 Procter & Gamble		U.S.	9 BMW		Germany
10 FedEx		U.S.	10 PepsiCo		U.S.
			. . .		
			13 **Wal-Mart Stores**		**U.S.**

Source: www.fortune.com.

Table 4   Wal-Mart's History

1962: First Wal-Mart opens in Rogers, Arkansas.

1968: Wal-Mart moves outside Arkansas with stores in Sikeston, Missouri, and Claremore, Oklahoma.

1969: Company incorporated as Wal-Mart Stores Inc.

1977: Wal-Mart makes first acquisition, 16 Mohr-Value stores in Michigan and Illinois.

1981: Wal-Mart makes second acquisition, 92 Kuhn's Big K stores.

1983: First Sam's Club opens in Midwest City, Oklahoma; U.S. Woolco stores acquired.

1985: Grand Central Stores acquired.

1988: David Glass named CEO of Wal-Mart Stores Inc.; first supercenter opens in Washington, Missouri; Supersaver units acquired.

1990: Wal-Mart becomes nation's number-one retailer; McLane Co. of Temple, Texas, acquired.

1991: Western Merchandisers Inc. of Amarillo, Texas, acquired; "Sam's American Choice" brand products introduced; Wal-Mart enters first international market with the opening of a unit in Mexico City.

1992: Sam Walton dies; S. Robson Walton named chairman of the board; Wal-Mart enters Puerto Rico.

1993: Wal-Mart International division formed with Bobby Martin as president; 91 Pace Warehouse clubs acquired.

1994: 122 Woolco stores in Canada acquired; three value clubs open in Hong Kong.

1995: Wal-Mart enters its 50th state—Vermont; enters Argentina and Brazil.

1996: Wal-Mart enters China through a joint-venture agreement.

1997: Wal-Mart has first $100 billion year, with sales totaling $105 billion.

1998: Wal-Mart introduces Neighborhood Market concept in Arkansas; acquires 21 Wertkauf units in Germany; enters Korea.

1999: Wal-Mart acquires 74 Interspar units in Germany and ASDA Group PLC in the United Kingdom.

2000: H. Lee Scott named president and CEO; Progressive Grocer names Wal-Mart its Retailer of the Year.

2002: Wal-Mart purchases a 34 percent interest in Japanese retailer Seiyu Ltd., with options to purchase up to 66.7 percent of the company.

2003: Wal-Mart sells McLane Co. subsidiary to Berkshire Hathaway Inc.; *Fortune* magazine names Wal-Mart most-admired company.

2004: Wal-Mart again named most-admired company, and also presented with the Corporate Patriotism Award for exceptional dedication to raising awareness and support of U.S. service members and their families.

2005: Wal-Mart expands to more than 6,200 facilities worldwide, including 3,800 international units. Along with launching the Acres for America program to conserve wildlife habitats, Wal-Mart opens experimental stores in the U.S. that conserve energy and natural resources and reduce pollution.

2007: Wal-Mart drops to no. 13 on *Fortune*'s magazine's most-admired company list.

Source: Walmart.com and author's research.

Table 5   International Distribution Coverage as of December 31, 2006
Wal-Mart Stores Inc. Global Distribution Coverage

Country	Number of Stores				
	2002	2003	2004	2005	2006
Argentina	12	11	11	11	11
Brazil	25	22	25	149	295
South Korea	15	15	15	16	16
Canada	220	213	235	262	278
Mexico	625	552	623	679	774
Puerto Rico	21	52	53	54	54
China	31	26	34	43	56
Germany	92	94	92	91	88
United Kingdom	296	258	267	282	315

Source: Wal-Mart 2003, 2004, 2005, and 2006 Annual Reports.

$33,100 (Exhibit 1). Japan's retail market has its own culture-specific quirks that are often difficult for outsiders to fully grasp. The sector has produced a few causalities in recent years, including the painful structuring of retailing bellwethers such as Mycal and Daiei.[16] With many of its global competitors struggling, Wal-Mart sensed an opportunity to strike in Japan. Concerned over past market-entry failures, Wal-Mart deliberated for over four years before purchasing a minority stake in Seiyu.[17] This sluggish pace has given many new and existing retailers adequate time to react to Wal-Mart's entrance. Archrival Carrefour, the world's second-largest retail chain, entered Japan about a month before Wal-Mart with its first store in Makuhari. Ostensibly, Carrefour's move was designed to steal market share from fledgling retail players before the U.S. retail giant had a chance to streamline with Seiyu. Big, traditional Japanese retail outlets have suffered from rising competition from newly emerging stores such as Uniglo leveraging low prices of imported goods. In addition, a decline in personal spending, in juxtaposition with a poor economic climate, has given discount retailers some traction with consumers who now need their money to work longer and harder.

Wal-Mart was initially concerned by Carrefour's preemptive entrance, but it was confident it had learned from past mistakes and knew that getting to market faster didn't necessarily equate to being better. For example, in Germany, where retail regulations and swift price competition are both fierce, Wal-Mart reacted before its inventory systems were in place, and the result was substantial operating losses.[18] While such a deliberate strategy might cost the firm some advantages, international head John Menzer believed the bit-by-bit approach was the way to go in Japan. "We've been criticized for going too slowly (in Japan). But we have to do it step-by-step. In the end, it seemed that Wal-Mart's approach was superior to that of Carrefour, who left Japan in 2005 after suffering a $264 million loss in four years.[19]

Exhibit 1 Japan at a Glance, 2002

Land Area: 374,744 square miles

Location: East Asia

Population: 127.4 million (13.8% younger than 15; 65.2% between ages 15–65; 21% 65 and older)

Capital and largest city: Tokyo (population 12.57 million)

GDP: $4.22 trillion

GDP composition by sector: Agriculture 1.6%, Industry 25.3%, Services 73.1%

Per capita GDP: $33,100

GDP real growth rate: 2.2%

Labor force: 66.4 million

Unemployment: 4.1%

Inflation: 0.3%

Source: The CIA World Factbook.

Japan's multilayered distribution networks have notoriously made selling merchandise more expensive for retailers. This is unfamiliar territory for Wal-Mart, which demands supplier accreditation before even considering the product line in the United States. Its ultimate goal is to eventually supersede the current network of suppliers and wholesalers. With a weak economy, suppliers may be convinced to sell direct in an attempt to produce incremental cash flows. For a while, Seiyu did not own a fleet of trucks or distribution warehouses, so Wal-Mart was content with working with wholesalers during the short term. Typically, wholesalers' margins are between 7 and 20 percent, according to Jerry Black, managing director of global practices for Kurt Salmon and Associates, an Atlanta retail-consulting company. In 2006, Seiyu opened its own distribution center in Tokyo, using new Wal-Mart technology. If Wal-Mart is eventually able to supersede the wholesaler segment in Japan entirely, it will be in a much better position to distribute goods at a cheaper cost, which will enable it to pass along some of the price savings to customers. Changing the nature of the supply chain process in Japan will not be easy and is sure to be met with stiff resistance. According to Black, suppliers must decide whether they want to rock the boat by going to Wal-Mart directly.

A majority of the competition reacted swiftly as news of Wal-Mart's entrance began to surface. Aeon, a midsize retail player, began making adjustments as early as 2001. Along with remodeling existing stores and creating labor efficiencies, Aeon began a campaign to eliminate all middlemen from its supply chain.[20] Convincing suppliers to go direct has been quite a challenge, but Aeon has managed to get more than 20 existing partners to come on board and approximately 20 more are waiting in the wings. A survey by Goldman Sachs in 2003 found prices on Aeon's nongrocery items were approximately 9.4 percent below the local average, identical to discounts Wal-Mart has been offering through Seiyu stores.[21]

Ito-Yokado, Japan's leading supermarket retailer, did not react to Wal-Mart's entry in the same fashion. Ito was convinced that quality is what sells in Japan, and the firm launched an aggressive marketing campaign entitled "Made in Japan" to convey its message. By labeling quality products with a traditional Japanese symbol, the rising sun, Ito-Yokado hoped to bring a sense of Japanese national pride to the surface. "Ito-Yokado isn't offering everyday low prices. It's offering higher quality," explained Yoshinobu Naito, an Ito-Yokado board member.[22] Ito has also balked at the idea of developing supercenters because it believes that land rates are still cost-prohibitive. Moreover, Ito has not reduced its staff as a means of cutting costs. It steadfastly believes that Japanese customers demand a quick entry and exit from its stores and eliminating staff would delay this process.

Entry Strategy: Too Slow or Just Right?

Wal-Mart has been very forthcoming about its entrance in Japan: slow and steady. Greg Penner, senior VP and CFO, Wal-Mart Japan, claimed that Wal-Mart's stake in Seiyu would grow from its current 37 percent to 50 percent by December 2005 and to 67 percent by December 2007.[23] On target with its ownership plans, Wal-Mart captured a 53 percent majority stake in Seiyu in 2005. Drawing from its past international experiences in Germany and Mexico, and given the psychological dynamic of the Japanese consumer, Penner believes that the current strategy is the best way to avoid growing pains and mistakes made in Germany and Mexico.

In a land where department stores rule, Wal-Mart sees great potential. However, there is concern that such a deliberate pace will give the competition time to create barriers. Driving the strategy is the installation of Wal-Mart's Retail Link operation, a JIT inventory replenishment system shared between retailer and supplier, effectively eliminating the wholesaler and speeding up payables and receivables collections.[24] However, since getting burned in Germany and Mexico by cutting corners, Wal-Mart has been more than calculating in developing its infrastructure capabilities in Japan. According to Carl Steidtmann, chief economist at Deloitte Research, retail software will have to be translated into Japanese and Japanese suppliers and retailers will have to go through a transformation to adapt to Wal-Mart's technology-focused management systems.[25] Many analysts believe that a tight inventory management system is imperative if Wal-Mart is to become successful in Japan. Another obstacle to overcome is Japan's multilayered distribution system. While Wal-Mart is quick to bypass such networks within the United States, personal interaction when doing business is much more prevalent in Japan, making these distribution layers more difficult to supersede.

After a careful round of evaluations, Wal-Mart believed Seiyu was the partner best suited for its entry strategy. The logic was simple. By working through a local partner, Wal-Mart believed it could better wade through Japan's long and costly network of suppliers, which has long frustrated many other foreign investors. "Wal-Mart has to change the system from the inside out," said Seth Sulkin, president of Pacifica Malls K.K., which develops shopping centers in Japan. Since only the biggest Japanese retailers have leverage with manufacturers, partnering with an existing market leader should prove invaluable when attempting to negotiate direct deals. Moreover, Wal-Mart avoids having to build stores and can take advantage of Seiyu's well-recognized brand.

Starting in early 2000, Seiyu began divesting itself from failing formats and businesses and was able to develop some financial stability. With 414 stores and more than $9 billion in sales, a strong customer base, and heavy

saturation in the Tokyo area, where real estate prices are exorbitant, Seiyu made a very attractive target. Furthermore, Seiyu's strength in food retailing gave Wal-Mart a natural extension for its supercenters, where food products are the most prominent. However, Seiyu is loaded with debt, with a debt-to-capital ratio more than twice the industry average. In the half year that ended in August 2003, Seiyu lost $77 million as sales slipped roughly 4 percent from the same period a year earlier. In 2005 Wal-Mart saw a 17.7 billion yen loss, followed by a 55.8 billion yen loss in 2006.[26] Wal-Mart claimed that its net losses were due to a one-time write-off of assets and that it has, in fact, experienced some success. In the first half of 2006, comparative store sales (which delete effects for store openings and closings) rose 1.4 percent, the first year-on-year gain in 14 years.[27] Regardless of its performance, Wal-Mart has pledged to stay in Japan and continue with its improvements. For instance, Wal-Mart pushed Seiyu to reduce the number of planned store closings from five to three because it believed it could make productivity gains in some of these existing outlets.

Penner strongly believes that over time Japanese customers will begin to see the value in Wal-Mart's unique selling proposition, one where low prices rule.[28] Wal-Mart hopes its "Every Day Low Prices" moniker will have a substantial impact given the troubled Japanese economy. So far that hasn't happened. Seiyu currently operates as a high-low retailer; it offers special promotions to its customers depending on the day. For example, Seiyu stores run 100-yen specials on certain items on Tuesdays. It also offers one-day sales by way of newspaper inserts, or coupons, called "chirashi."[29] This on-again, off-again promotional strategy is in sharp contrast with Wal-Mart's everyday deals. Executives believe it will take both time and effort to convince loyal Seiyu customers that rock-bottom prices are available every day. Eventually, Wal-Mart hopes customers will realize that the company doesn't offer lower-quality products at low prices but quality products close to the manufacturing cost of other retailers. In the meantime, in an effort to erase the stereotype that low prices mean low quality, Seiyu has remodeled many of its stores to look "less frumpy" and even added more expensive items to its shelves for its less price-conscious customers.[30]

Labor and Human Resources Challenges

Labor costs have also been a problem. In response, Wal-Mart developed a five-year plan to reduce full-time employee hours by about 40 percent, partly through early retirement and an increase in part-time staff. By the end of 2005, 80 percent of Seiyu's labor force was part time, and in the process, it had cut wage costs by 7.6 percent in 2004.[31] Furthermore, Seiyu announced that it planned on cutting jobs by up to 40 percent, some 2,500 jobs, over a three-year period beginning in mid-2003.[32] The remaining employees would have to begin to learn to sell the Wal-Mart way.

To reinforce the importance of selling correctly, Wal-Mart has put store managers through weeklong training sessions and has flown hundreds of Seiyu workers to company headquarters in Arkansas. "Japanese might think what we're doing is very tough, but they have to realize that this is the world standard," said Seiyu's CEO Masao Kiuchi. Workers receive quite a bit of "cultural training" to teach them to be more outspoken, upbeat, and goal-oriented.

However, trainees have had a more difficult time with Wal-Mart's practice of continually praising co-workers. In a society where being humble is paramount, many workers have had difficulty accepting this type of praise. While achieving employee buy-in has been difficult at times, Jeff McAllister, Wal-Mart COO in Japan, is confident that their plan is working. "Once they understand what you want them to do, you get follow-through."[33] By computerizing all Seiyu's operations, remodeling dilapidated stores, and retraining staff, Wal-Mart will be in a better position to capitalize on the future.

The Wal-Mart Effect

In recent years, Japan's economy has been one of the poorest performers among developed nations, making the playing field well suited for Wal-Mart's deal-oriented businesses. Department store leaders Seibu, Mitsukoshi, and Takashimaya have all experienced flat growth in recent years. Each has been able to generate over $1 billion in sales, but rates of return and margins remain low as supply-chain expenses creep upward. As a result, most retailers are burdened by high debt, resulting in higher department store prices. If Wal-Mart were able to construct supplier agreements in Japan similar to those in the United States, then it would have a huge advantage over its competitors in its ability to price low. Moreover, the Japanese market appears to be ready for value chains. A growing numbers of 100-yen stores, which are equivalent to dollar stores in the United States, are already popping up in major markets all over Japan.[34] Some retailers have seen this coming and are in the midst of a consolidation boom in an attempt to add both breadth and depth to fight Wal-Mart's size and strength. In June 2003, Seibu Department stores and Sogo Co. merged to form Millennium Retailing Inc., becoming one of Japan's largest department store groups.[35]

While these huge department stores are concerned about Wal-Mart's entrance, it doesn't appear to be keeping all of them up at night. Koji Nose, president of Mitsukoshi U.S.A., said, "Wal-Mart will have an effect, but not a big impact."[36] Wal-Mart's ability to find appropriate locations for its stores will have a material impact. Since the Japanese travel mostly by railroad instead of in cars, the firm is hoping to secure locations on edges of big cities where commuters shop. Most downtown cities in Japan are heavily saturated with retail shops, so finding alternative locations will be integral to getting top-of-mind awareness among consumers.

What's Next for Wal-Mart?

If Wal-Mart is able to duplicate what it has done in the United States, it may change the way consumer goods are sold and distributed in Japan. Cutting costs and streamlining its supply chain are two main priorities already in the works. Its partnerships with Seiyu and Sumitomo have already given Wal-Mart a large foothold in Japan's multidimensional distribution system.[37] If Wal-Mart is able to effectively skip the middleman, then it should be able to pass lower costs along to the customer. According to Bill Wertz, Wal-Mart's director of international corporate affairs, "We're reorganizing Seiyu in a style more consistent with Wal-Mart in the U.S."[38] Wal-Mart executives have been actively involved in the corporate transformation of Seiyu, but Seiyu's executives will continue to run the business. This corporate transformation and restructuring have hurt Seiyu in its competition with local rivals. Retail rival Aeon, free from such costs, has been able to pour more money into product innovation for its stores. Aeon will continue to pose a threat to Seiyu since purchasing a significant stake in the retail group, Daiei, in early 2007. The new Aeon-Daiei alliance will exceed 6 trillion yen in sales to become the country's largest retail group.[39]

In support of its international operations, Wal-Mart announced the opening of a Global Procurement (GP) USA Export Office in February 2003 at world headquarters in Arkansas. The GP USA Export Office now sources products from over 70 countries and in so doing provides a service to those domestic suppliers who have been unable to navigate through restrictive import regulations in foreign countries. "We see the GP USA Export Office as a window to new markets," said Ken Easton, Wal-Mart's senior VP of global procurement. "We want to sell American products globally, but we will also need to work with the U.S. government to break down barriers that we encounter." Wal-Mart has opened global procurement offices in 23 countries, though it notably has yet to open one in Japan.[40]

Although Wal-Mart has divested itself of its operations in other countries, namely South Korea and Germany, it says it is committed to staying in Japan. The retail sector in Japan remains in flux, as sales in hypermarkets, discount stores, and convenience stores are on the rise while supermarket sales are in decline. However the "Japan Food & Drug Report" for the fourth quarter of 2006 forecasted a 6.8 percent growth in grocery sales in Japan by 2010, which should give Seiyu greater confidence in the Japanese retail market as a whole.[41]

Wal-Mart is confident it can make significant inroads in Japan under its low-price model. As Japanese customers become more value conscious, there arises a huge opportunity for discount retailers to capitalize on changing cultural conditions.

Mounting attacks on Wal-Mart, both at home and abroad, have forced the company to make changes to its overall business profile, in addition to its specific corporate global strategies in countries like Mexico, China, and Japan. These criticisms have caused Wal-Mart to decline in public favor, as evidenced by its falling rating on *Fortune's* "Most Admired Companies" list. (See Table 3.)

Most famously, Wal-Mart has dealt with a sex-discrimination lawsuit, filed by six female employees in 2001. The plaintiffs submitted data claiming that women earned 5 to 15 percent less than their male counterparts in Wal-Mart jobs, leading a San Francisco federal district court judge to rule that the case would become a class action suit in 2004. The suit, now comprised of 1.6 million female workers, is open to any woman who has been a Wal-Mart employee since 1998.[42] Wal-Mart has fought to reverse the class action decision as recently as early 2007, but its attempts have been unsuccessful. On its Web site, the company claims, "Wal-Mart is a wonderful place for women and minorities to work, and isolated complaints, such as those noted in the Wal-Mart discrimination case, that arise from its three-thousand-plus locations do not change this fact."[43] Its Web site also states that 60 percent of its associates and 40 percent of its managers are women. Perhaps to counter the negative publicity of the discrimination lawsuit, Wal-Mart also opened a diversity office in November 2003.[44]

Wal-Mart has also had a tough battle with unions, and not just in China. U.S. labor unions have claimed that Wal-Mart lowers workers' standard of living and "pulverizes" unionized grocery stores with its low food prices. They claim that Wal-Mart associates that support a family live below the poverty line and that the company's health care benefits are incomplete; fewer than half of Wal-Mart employees are insured (bringing the burden onto taxpayers). In October 2002, a coalition of 30 U.S. unions and left-wing groups began their anti-Wal-Mart campaign, which urged shoppers to boycott the store and lobbied towns not to let Wal-Mart in.[45] Despite the negative impact these campaigns have had on Wal-Mart's image, it has had little trouble attracting shoppers with its low prices or attracting workers with the promise of a career in a fast-growing company. As CEO H. Lee Scott described it, "at Wal-Mart you can—without a high-school degree—start as a cart pusher in the parking lot and end up being a store manager, district manager, a regional vice-president. You have wonderful opportunities at Wal-Mart."[46]

As the world's largest retailer, Wal-Mart has also come under attack from environmentalists. The company has had to pay millions of dollars to state and federal regulators for violation of air and water pollution laws.[47] Lobbyists from the World Wildlife Federation, the Natural Resources Defense Council, and Greenpeace, and even Al Gore, have all visited the company's Bentonville headquarters. Although some environmentalists are still skeptical about the credibility of Wal-Mart's initiatives (calling it "green-washing"), there is no denying the company's commitment. It planned to invest $500 million in sustainability projects which include increasing the efficiency of its vehicle fleet and reducing electricity use and solid waste at its stores.[48] Wal-Mart has also taken to buying and selling more organic products and engaging in sustainable agribusiness. In February 2007, Scott unveiled Wal-Mart's latest plan, "Sustainability 360," which includes goals to reduce packaging by 5 percent by 2013 and encourage sustainability practices in markets around the globe.[49] Wal-Mart's other environmentally friendly initiatives include clean air (the Clean Air Initiative), protection of wildlife habitats (Acres for America), renewable energy, and experimental "green" stores.

Although Wal-Mart continues to see growth abroad, it is too early to tell how reactions to its labor and environmental criticisms—and its newfound commitment to environmental protection and sustainability—will affect its global image, including its success in specific markets such as Japan.

Questions for Review

1. How would you characterize Wal-Mart's approach to global management?

2. Do you agree with Wal-Mart's entry strategy in Japan? What are some of the inherent risks? Do you think that a faster market entry would be more effective?

3. In your opinion, what is the single most important thing Wal-Mart can do to ensure success in Japan? Explain.

4. Do you think Wal-Mart is doing enough cross-cultural training with its Seiyu employees? What are the greatest challenges Wal-Mart faces in relating to its Japanese employees?

5. How can Wal-Mart respond to some of the negative impressions of its employment practices in the United States so that these perspectives do not follow it as it expands internationally?

Exercise

Pair up with a classmate. One of you will play the role of head of a retail distribution firm in Japan, while the other plays the role of a marketing strategist for Wal-Mart Stores Inc. Debate and discuss the pros and cons of entering and participating in the Japanese distribution system and the difficulties that must be overcome.

Source: This case was prepared by Professor Jonathan Doh and Erik Holt of Villanova University with research assistance by Courtney Asher as the basis for class discussion. It is not intended to illustrate either effective or ineffective managerial capability or administrative responsibility.

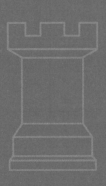

PART THREE

INTERNATIONAL
STRATEGIC
MANAGEMENT

Chapter 8

STRATEGY FORMULATION AND IMPLEMENTATION

OBJECTIVES OF THE CHAPTER

All major MNCs formulate and implement strategies that result from a careful analysis of both external and internal environments. In this process, an MNC will identify the market environment for its goods and services and then evaluate its ability and competitive advantage to capture the market. The success of this strategic planning effort will largely depend on accurate forecasting of the external environment and a realistic appraisal of internal company strengths and weaknesses. In recent years, MNCs have relied on their strategic plans to help refocus their efforts by abandoning old domestic markets and entering new global markets. This strategic global planning process has been critical in their drive to gain market share, increase profitability, and, in some cases, survive. Strategies can be formulated from any level of management, but middle management plays a key role in ensuring that decisions are put into subsequent action.

Chapter 5 addressed overall management across cultures. This chapter focuses on strategic management in the international context, and the basic steps by which a strategic plan is formulated and implemented are examined. The specific objectives of this chapter are:

1. **DISCUSS** the meaning, needs, benefits, and approaches of the strategic planning process for today's MNCs.

2. **UNDERSTAND** the tension between pressures for global integration and national responsiveness and the four basic options for international strategies.

3. **IDENTIFY** the basic steps in strategic planning, including environmental scanning, internal resource analysis of the MNC's strengths and weaknesses, and goal formulation.

4. **DESCRIBE** how an MNC implements the strategic plan, such as how it chooses a site for overseas operations.

5. **REVIEW** the three major functions of marketing, production, and finance that are used in implementing a strategic plan.

6. **EXPLAIN** specialized strategies appropriate for emerging markets and international new ventures.

The World of *BusinessWeek*

BusinessWeek

Why Nokia Is Leaving Moto in the Dust

Phones for High- and Low-End Consumers, a Great Supply Chain, and Cash—the Finnish Company Has It All (except the iPhone)

Pop singer Alicia Keys and Ramkishen Pyarelal, proprieter of a Mumbai tea stall, may not have a lot in common. But they both carry Nokia mobile phones. If you want to know why Motorola is in such trouble these days, the celebrity and the Indian street merchant provide a big part of the answer.

From stylish $750 handsets with built-in global-positioning receivers to $45 basic models with black-and-white displays, Nokia saturates the booming mobile-phone market in a way neither Moto nor any other competitor has been able to duplicate. Nokia's formidable lineup of some 100 models is just one of many reasons why more than one out of every three handsets in the world traces its origins to the Helsinki suburb of Espoo.

The former producer of rubber boots and timber, which famously made a risky decision in 1992 to focus on mobile technology, seems to be doing everything right these days. Nokia's supply-chain management may be the best of any company in the world. It has a big head start in fast-growing markets such as China and India. And it has $9.5 billion in cash and practically no debt, so it can invest far more than rivals on developing new products or conquering new markets—and thus build even more intimidating economies of scale. "We are about to report our billionth customer, so we must be doing something right," says Anssi Vanjoki, a Nokia executive committee member responsible for multimedia devices.

Shock-Resistant

Thanks to those advantages, Nokia's global market share has climbed to 37%, and some in the industry think it could hit 40% this year. "If there's a time when that goal looks realistic, it's now," says Gartner analyst Carolina Milanesi.

Motorola managers can take some comfort in recalling that Nokia, too, has endured some devastating crises. Back in 1995, its manufacturing system nearly collapsed under the weight of rapid growth. And in 2003, Nokia was slow to introduce clamshell-style phones and color displays. From the fourth quarter of 2003 to the first quarter of 2004, its market share plunged from 34.6% to 28.4%, according to market watcher Strategy Analytics.

Similar woes have driven other mobile-phone producers from the market. Onetime contenders such as Panasonic, Philips, and Siemens (which later sold its phone division to Taiwan's BenQ) today have market shares below 1% each. But under former Chief Executive Officer Jorma Ollila and his successor, Olli-Pekka Kallasvuo, the stoic Finns emerged even stronger. By diversifying its products and its geographical reach, Nokia now seems far less vulnerable to shocks than it was three years ago. "Nokia has definitely learned from that experience," says Neil Mawston, an analyst with Strategy Analytics. "They have spread their risk a lot more."

All Things to All Consumers

One lesson Nokia learned was that it doesn't pay to rely too heavily on a few top-selling models. Motorola, by contrast, became overly dependent on the Razr. Nokia has nailed both the high and low ends of the market and pretty much everything in between. For affluent buyers who want the latest technology, the $750 top-of-the-line N95 includes an Internet browser, music player, GPS satellite receiver, and the ability to connect to Wi-Fi networks as well as standard cellular services.

Even Nokia's entry-level phones offer extras that appeal to Mumbai tea sellers and vast numbers of other low-income people enjoying their first taste of telecommunications.

Its $45 model 1200, for example, can go more than two weeks without a recharge and has a built-in flashlight, handy for people who live in homes without electricity.

The company has invested hundreds of millions of dollars building distribution systems and networks of retailers in developing countries, including vans that bump along the rural roads of India between stops for instruction on how to use mobile phones. As a result, it's the No. 1 handset supplier in China and India and is growing fast in Africa, the industry's next frontier. Meanwhile, Motorola's low-cost phone for India has been a flop despite a $35 price tag, in part because its limited features didn't convey a sense of status to potential buyers.

Supply-Chain Smarts

Perhaps most impressive is that Nokia has managed the shift to low-cost phones while maintaining healthy profit margins. The company earned an operating profit of 16.8% on mass-market mobile phones in the first quarter of 2007, a modest decline from 18.5% a year earlier. But that doesn't even include Nokia's high-end multimedia devices, which had a profit margin of 18.8%. In the most recent quarter, net profits were $1.3 billion on sales of $13.4 billion. When Nokia reports second-quarter results on Aug. 2—figures analyst Richard Windsor of Nomura Securities in London—profits should climb 11% on a 7% increase in revenues.

Nokia makes money at the low end because of its superefficient manufacturing systems. It also keeps costs and complexity under control by sharing components among devices and designing phones that have fewer parts than competing models. Such practices pushed Nokia to the No. 1 spot this year in Boston consultancy AMR Research's annual survey of top supply-chain operators, ahead of logistics champions such as Toyota and Wal-Mart. (Motorola was a respectable No. 12 in the ranking, which was based in part on a poll of supply-chain executives.) Analysts say even low-cost Chinese producers such as Huawei Technologies can't match the efficiency of Nokia, which operates its own factories in Vietnam, India, and other low-wage countries.

Not the iPhone, but So What?

To be sure, Nokia still has weaknesses. Its Eseries devices for the corporate e-mail crowd lag rivals such as Research In Motion's BlackBerry and are unprofitable. Swedish rival Ericsson is far ahead of Nokia's joint venture with Siemens in the market for base stations and other mobile infrastructure. And in design, Nokia faces a serious challenge from Apple and its hot iPhone. Nokia has only a few touch-screen products and none as advanced as the iPhone, with its glass surface and finger-operated interface.

It's not the first time a competitor has challenged Nokia for classiness: see LG Electronics' Chocolate Phone or Samsung's elegant superthin handsets. But time and again, the Finns' consistently excellent distribution, manufacturing, and marketing have prevailed. It will take more than one cool phone to threaten Nokia's dominance.

"Maybe the iPhone will be very successful," says Martin Garner, director of wireless intelligence for London market researcher Ovum. "Does that knock Nokia off its perch? I don't think so."

By Jack Ewing with Nandini Lakshman in Mumbai

Source: **Reprinted with special permission from "Why Nokia is Leaving Moto in the Dust,"** *BusinessWeek,* **July 19, 2007. Copyright © 2007 The McGraw-Hill Companies.**

Strategic management—the formulation and implementation of a strategy—is a critical function in today's global business environment. As seen in the opening *BusinessWeek* story, Nokia consistently improved its supply chain operations by using its knowledge of the industry and pushing efficiency. Nokia has consistently innovated in its product offerings, and has been open to tailoring products to particular geographic and demographic segments. Its foothold in emerging markets has allowed it to capture increasing shares of the world's most dynamic markets. Offering an array of phones, from less expensive yet high functioning units to more expensive phones with the latest technology, Nokia has been able to satisfy local markets without sacrificing profits. While other companies may surpass Nokia with technological offerings, its ability to develop efficient global platforms while simultaneously responding to local markets may be the key to long-term success.

This chapter will examine how multinational corporations use strategic management in their global operations. When formulated and implemented wisely, strategic management sets the course for a company's future. It should answer two simple questions, "Where are we going?" and "How are we going to get there?" Some strategies are consistent across markets, while others must be adapted to regional situations, but in either case, a firm's global strategy should support decision making in all major operations. In Nokia's case, those questions seem to have been asked and answered; Nokia just needs to be sure to reevaluate strategies periodically and make necessary adjustments to keep the vision clear.

As you read this chapter, think of yourself as a manager in a large mobile-phone firm. How might you go about developing a strategic plan to capture greater market share and expand the types of products you are selling? There are some basic steps involved in creating a strategy, but first, let us take a look at what strategic management is and why it is so important.

■ Strategic Management

strategic management
The process of determining an organization's basic mission and long-term objectives, then implementing a plan of action for attaining these goals.

Strategic management is the process of determining an organization's basic mission and long-term objectives and then implementing a plan of action for pursuing this mission and attaining these objectives. For most companies, regardless of how decentralized, the top management team is responsible for setting the strategy. Middle management has sometimes been viewed as primarily responsible for the strategic implementation process, but now companies are realizing how imperative all levels of management are to the entire process. For example, Volvo discovered that while managers do inform team members of new strategic plans, the most informed, enthusiastic and effective managers were those who were involved in the entire process.[1] Another good example was provided in the opening article in Chapter 6, where BMW is integrating all levels of management into strategic and operational decision making.

As companies go international, strategic processes take on added dimensions. A good example is provided by Citibank (a unit of Citicorp), which opened offices in China in 1902 and continued to do business there until 1949, when communists took power. However, in 1984 Citibank quietly returned, and over the last two decades the firm has been slowly increasing its presence in China.[2] Some ways Citibank has done this include opening new branches, expanding the employee base, and increasing stakes in local companies such as Shanghai Pudon Development Bank Co.[3] The Chinese banking environment is closely regulated by the government, and Citibank's activities are currently restricted to making local currency loans to foreign multinationals and their joint-venture partners. As a result, the bank does only about 20 percent as much business here as it does in South Korea. However, China's admission into the World Trade Organization (WTO) is changing all of this. Under WTO provisions, elite local corporations such as the personal computer maker Legend, electronic goods manufacturer Konda, consumer appliance maker Haier, and telecom service provider China Telecom will all be able to turn to foreign banks for local currency loans. This will give Citibank a major opportunity to expand operations. Additionally, under WTO rules the bank is allowed to offer consumer financial services such as credit cards and home mortgages. Citibank believes that there is a large pent-up demand for credit cards, especially among businesspeople and yuppies who now carry around thick wads of currency to pay their bills and make purchases. Another opportunity Citibank sees is in the area of business-to-business (B2B) commerce. As more Chinese firms conduct commerce over the Internet, there will be an increase in Net-related financial services. Citibank has now hooked up with U.S.-based B2B site Commerce One to run its Net-based payment systems, and the bank believes that it can provide this same service for Chinese exporters.

Despite the huge potential market in China, however, Citibank is aware of the risks. In 1995 the firm was chosen as one of the first foreign banks to be issued a local-currency license. The bank felt certain that this was the opportunity it needed to break into the retail market, but this did not happen. In order to protect its domestic banks from competition, the government imposed a limit on the number of branches that foreign banks could open as well as to whom they could lend money and in what amounts. Quite simply, Citibank's opportunities were very limited. Will China being a member of the WTO change all of this? It might, but there are still a great many risks associated with doing business there. In particular, executives know that if foreign banks are given unrestricted access to China's retail customers, havoc could develop. It is estimated that Chinese customers have over $500 billion in savings. If these customers were to begin taking their money out of local banks and putting it into foreign ones, China's banks would be forced to stop lending to the country's state-owned enterprises (SOEs), most of which are losing money. In turn, these SOEs would go bankrupt and unemployment would skyrocket. The four major state-owned commercial banks currently control 70 percent of all financial assets in China, and approximately 30 percent of all their loans are uncollectible. So the Chinese government is unlikely to move quickly to open up the banking market. Nevertheless, Citibank sees China as a major market and is developing strategies to increase its presence there and ride out any financial storms. In order to do this, the bank will need a well-formulated strategic plan.

While this chapter focuses on the larger picture of strategic planning, it is important to remember that all stages of organizational change incorporate levels of strategy from planning to implementation. This includes innovative ways to improve a product to expanding to international operations.

The Growing Need for Strategic Management

One of the primary reasons that MNCs such as Citibank need strategic management is to keep track of their increasingly diversified operations in a continuously changing international environment. This need is particularly obvious when one considers the amount of foreign direct investment (FDI) that has occurred in recent years. Statistics reveal that FDI has grown three times faster than trade and four times faster than world gross domestic product (GDP).[4] These developments are resulting in a need to coordinate and integrate diverse operations with a unified and agreed-on focus. There are many examples of firms that are doing just this.

One is Ford Motor, which has reentered the market in Thailand and is beginning to build a strong sales force and to garner market share. The firm's strategic plan here is based on offering the right combination of price and financing to a carefully identified market segment. In particular, Ford is working to keep down the monthly payments so that customers can afford a new vehicle. Ford has also been very active in Vietnam, where only a small percentage of population currently has personal income to afford a car.

Another example of the growing need for strategic management is provided by Bertelsmann AG, the giant German book publisher that has entered the Chinese market.[5] Bertelsmann has created a giant book club that could dramatically change the way Chinese buy books. Since the late 1990s, this club has signed up over 1.5 million members, opened dozens of retail stores, and sold almost 10 million volumes. Moreover, Bertelsmann is now adding 2,000 new members every day, a growth rate that is easily sustainable given that approximately 180 million Chinese read books on a regular basis. The company's strategic plan calls for continual expansion, driven by a wide assortment of books, low costs, and home delivery. In fact, things are going so well for Bertelsmann in China that the company has now sent salespeople to South Korea to lay the groundwork for a book club there and has plans for expanding to Japan, India, and Thailand.[6] Furthermore, Bertelsmann has employed other global strategies, one of which resulted in the acquisition of Time Inc.'s stakes in online book-of-the-month clubs, making it the dominating operator of book, music and DVD clubs in the U.S. market.[7]

A third example of the growing need for strategic management is offered by the highly profitable GE Capital, which has been expanding rapidly in Europe. Since the mid-1980s the company has amassed assets in excess of $50 billion, much of this in the last several years. The firm began years ago by helping customers purchase General Electric products, but it has now expanded widely and provides diverse services ranging from equipment financing for middle-market firms to consumer finance, to reinsurance. Relying on a well-coordinated strategic plan, the company sets targets for each of its stand-alone businesses. Overall, GE Capital looks for at least a 20 percent annual return on capital and strong growth. The approach flouts some time-honored traditions, as seen by the fact that each business handles its customers independently. So one customer can have multiple relationships with GE Capital.[8] And while this type of strategic planning approach may seem questionable to some, the company has been very successful using it. Revenues have been growing sharply, and annual earnings in recent years have been in excess of $5 billion.[9]

Benefits of Strategic Planning

Now that the needs for strategic planning have been explored, what are some of the benefits? Many MNCs are convinced that strategic planning is critical to their success, and these efforts are being conducted both at the home office and in the subsidiaries. For example, one study found that 70 percent of the 56 U.S. MNC subsidiaries in Asia and Latin America had comprehensive 5- to 10-year plans.[10] Others found that U.S., European, and Japanese subsidiaries in Brazil were heavily planning-driven[11] and that Australian manufacturing companies use planning systems that are very similar to those of U.S. manufacturing firms.[12]

Do these strategic planning efforts really pay off? To date, the evidence is mixed. Certainly, that the strategic plan helps an MNC to coordinate and monitor its far-flung operations must be viewed as a benefit. Similarly, that the plan helps an MNC to deal with political risk problems (see Chapter 10), competition, and currency instability cannot be downplayed.

Despite some obvious benefits, there is no definitive evidence that strategic planning in the international arena always results in higher profitability, especially when

MNCs try to use home strategies across different cultures (see Chapter 6). Most studies that report favorable results were conducted at least a decade ago. Moreover, many of these findings are tempered with contingency-based recommendations. For example, one study found that when decisions were made mainly at the home office and close coordination between the subsidiary and home office was required, return on investment was negatively affected.[13] Simply put, the home office ends up interfering with the subsidiary, and profitability suffers.

Another study found that planning intensity (the degree to which a firm carries out strategic planning) is an important variable in determining performance.[14] Drawing on results from 22 German MNCs representing 71 percent of Germany's multinational enterprises, the study found that companies with only a few foreign affiliates performed best with medium planning intensity. Those firms with high planning intensity tended to exaggerate the emphasis, and profitability suffered. Companies that earned a high percentage of their total sales in overseas markets, however, did best with a high-intensity planning process and poorly with a low-intensity process. Therefore, although strategic planning usually seems to pay off, as with most other aspects of international management, the specifics of the situation will dictate the success of the process.

Approaches to Formulating and Implementing Strategy

Four common approaches to formulating and implementing strategy are (1) focusing on the economic imperative; (2) addressing the political imperative; (3) emphasizing the quality imperative; and (4) implementing an administrative coordination strategy.

Economic Imperative   MNCs that focus on the **economic imperative** employ a worldwide strategy based on cost leadership, differentiation, and segmentation. Middle managers are the key to stimulating profit growth within a company, so expanding those efforts on an international level is a necessary tool to learn for today's new managers.[15] Many of these companies typically sell products for which a large portion of value is added in the upstream activities of the industry's value chain. By the time the product is ready to be sold, much of its value has already been created through research and development, manufacturing, and distribution. Some of the industries in this group include automobiles, chemicals, heavy electrical systems, motorcycles, and steel. Because the product is basically homogeneous and requires no alteration to fit the needs of the specific country, management uses a worldwide strategy that is consistent on a country-to-country basis.

The strategy also is used when the product is regarded as a generic good and therefore does not have to be sold based on name brand or support service. A good example is the European PC market. Initially, this market was dominated by such well-known companies as IBM, Apple, and Compaq. However, more recently, clone manufacturers have begun to gain market share. This is because the most influential reasons for buying a PC have changed. A few years ago, the main reasons were brand name, service, and support. Today, price has emerged as a major input into the purchasing decision. Customers now are much more computer literate, and they realize that many PCs offer identical quality performance. Therefore, it does not pay to purchase a high-priced name brand when a lower-priced clone will do the same things. As a result, the economic imperative dominates the strategic plans of computer manufacturers.

Another economic imperative concept that has gained prominence in recent years is global sourcing, which is proving very useful in formulating and implementing strategy.[16] A good example is provided by the way in which manufacturers are reaching into the supply chain and shortening the buying circle. Li & Fung, Hong Kong's largest export trading company, is one of the world's leading innovators in the development of supply chain management, and the company has managed to use its expertise to whittle costs to the bone. Instead of buying fabric and yarn from one company and letting that firm work on keeping its costs as low as possible, Li & Fung gets actively involved in managing

economic imperative
A worldwide strategy based on cost leadership, differentiation, and segmentation.

the entire process. How does it keep costs down for orders it receives from The Limited? The chairman of the company explained the firm's economic imperative strategy this way:

> We come in and look at the whole supply chain. We know The Limited is going to order 100,000 garments, but we don't know the style or the colors yet. The buyer will tell us that five weeks before delivery. The trust between us and our supply network means that we can reserve undyed yarn from the yarn supplier. I can lock up capacity at the mills for the weaving and dying with the promise that they'll get an order of a specified size; five weeks before delivery, we will let them know what colors we want. Then I say the same thing to the factories, "I don't know the product specs yet, but I have organized the colors and the fabric and the trim for you, and they'll be delivered to you on this date and you'll have three weeks to produce so many garments."
>
> I've certainly made life harder for myself now. It would be easier to let the factories worry about securing their own fabric and trim. But then the order would take three months, not five weeks. So to shrink the delivery cycle, I go upstream to organize production. And the shorter production time lets the retailer hold off before having to commit to a fashion trend. It's all about flexibility, response time, small production runs, small minimum-order quantities, and the ability to shift direction as the trends move.[17]

political imperative
Strategic formulation and implementation utilizing strategies that are country-responsive and designed to protect local market niches.

Political Imperative   MNCs using the **political imperative** approach to strategic planning are country-responsive; their approach is designed to protect local market niches. "International Management in Action: Point/Counterpoint" demonstrates this political imperative. The products sold by MNCs often have a large portion of their value added in the downstream activities of the value chain. Industries such as insurance and consumer packaged goods are examples—the success of the product or service generally depends heavily on marketing, sales, and service. Typically, these industries use a country-centered or multi-domestic strategy.

A good example of a country-centered strategy is provided by Thums Up, a local drink that Coca-Cola bought from an Indian bottler in 1993. This drink was created back in the 1970s, shortly after Coca-Cola pulled up stakes and left India. In the ensuing two decades the drink, which is similar in taste to Coke, made major inroads in the Indian market. But when Coca-Cola returned and bought the company, it decided to put Thums Up on the back burner and began pushing its own soft drink. However, local buyers were not interested. They continued to buy Thums Up, and Coca-Cola finally relented. Today Thums Up is the firm's biggest seller and fastest-growing brand in India, and the company spends more money on this soft drink than it does on any of its other product offerings, including Coke.[18] As one observer noted, "In India the 'Real Thing' for Coca-Cola is its Thums Up brand." Recently, Coke has encountered challenges in India, as described in the Part 2 case.

quality imperative
Strategic formulation and implementation utilizing strategies of total quality management to meet or exceed customers' expectations and continuously improve products or services.

Quality Imperative   A **quality imperative** takes two interdependent paths: (1) a change in attitudes and a raising of expectation for service quality and (2) the implementation of management practices that are designed to make quality improvement an ongoing process.[19] Commonly called *total quality management,* or simply TQM, the approach takes a wide number of forms, including cross-training personnel to do the jobs of all members in their work group, process re-engineering designed to help identify and eliminate redundant tasks and wasteful effort, and reward systems designed to reinforce quality performance.

TQM covers the full gamut, from strategy formulation to implementation. TQM can be summarized as follows:

1. Quality is operationalized by meeting or exceeding customer expectations. Customers include not only the buyer or external user of the product or service but also the support personnel both inside and outside the organization who are associated with the good or service.
2. The quality strategy is formulated at the top management level and is diffused throughout the organization. From top executives to hourly employees,

A good example of the political imperative in action is the Kodak-Fuji dispute. Kodak has accused Fuji of blocking its growth in the Japanese market. Fuji has responded by arguing that Kodak has long held a monopoly-type position in the United States. This debate began when Kodak complained to the U.S. government and asked for help in further opening the door to the Japanese market. Kodak's argument included the following points:

1. Unlike film manufacturers in the United States, film manufacturers in Japan sell directly not to retailers or photofinishers but to distributors, and Fuji has close ties with the four dominant distributors. Fuji holds an equity position in two of them and gives all four both rebates and cash payments.

2. Fuji controls 430 Japanese wholesale photofinishing labs through ownership, loans, rebates, and other forms of operational support. Additionally, the Japanese government has helped establish the system to impede Kodak.

3. Kodak has invested $750 million in Japan and garnered less than 10 percent of the market.

4. Fuji uses profits from the Japanese market to subsidize the dumping of its products in other countries, thus effectively reducing Kodak's worldwide market share.

5. The Japanese government has not vigorously enforced antimonopoly legislation, and this has helped Fuji establish distribution dominance.

These charges are answered by Fuji, which contends that Kodak uses many tactics that prevent Fuji from gaining U.S. market share. These include:

1. Kodak gives U.S. retailers rebates and upfront payments that effectively exclude competitors. For example, Kodak offered Genovese Drug Stores of Glen Cove, New York, $40,000 plus rebates if the company would carry no branded film but Kodak, use only Kodak paper and processing chemicals, and give Kodak 80 percent of the chain's shelf-space allotment for film.

2. Kodak holds 70 percent of the U.S. wholesale photofinishing market through ownership and by giving discounts, advertising dollars, and other investments to land exclusive accounts.

3. Fuji has invested $2 billion in the United States and holds less than 11 percent of the market.

4. Kodak's worldwide operating profit margin over the last two decades is 13 percent, close to Fuji's 15.5 percent.

5. The U.S. government has not vigorously enforced consent decrees that were created to limit Kodak's U.S. marketing practices and ensure that Kodak did not gain an unfair advantage over competitors.

Will the U.S. government prevail in its efforts to help Kodak? Will Fuji be able to make further gains in the U.S. market? What role will political intervention play? These questions are yet to be answered. In the meantime, the two firms continue to compete—and cooperate. Together, they currently are developing a "smart film"—a new system that offers small cameras and film that can record information to improve the quality of processing. Whatever the outcome of their market-share argument, this strategic cooperative effort likely will continue.

everyone operates under a TQM strategy of delivering quality products or services to internal and external customers. Middle managers will better understand and implement these strategies if they are a part of the process.

3. TQM techniques range from traditional inspection and statistical quality control to cutting-edge human resource management techniques, such as self-managing teams and empowerment.[20]

Many MNCs make quality a major part of their overall strategy, because they have learned that this is the way to increase market share and profitability. Take the game console industry, for example. Nintendo lived in the shadow of Sony's PlayStation success as it fought for market share with the GameCube. Years later, Nintendo proved to have superior game console quality when it introduced the Wii. Now, the tables have turned, and it is Sony which is scrambling after its less than successful launch of the

PlayStation 3. In fact, Nintendo is now challenging Sony's market leadership and shares in Nintendo were up more than 50% through the first half of 2007, thanks to the combined sales of the Wii and the handheld DS systems.[21]

The auto industry is also a good point of reference. While the U.S. automakers have dramatically increased their overall quality in recent years to close the gap with Japanese auto quality, Japanese firms continue to have fewer safety recalls. Toyota and Honda continue to be ranked very high by American consumers, and Nissan's recent market performance shows that the firm is also a major competitor in this market.[22]

Another example of firms using quality as an integral part of their strategy is provided by Nortel, the Canadian telecom equipment manufacturer. A few years ago Nortel concluded that there would be a growing demand for optical networking technology to send and retrieve data. Investing heavily in research and development and acquiring companies with the technologies needed to complement these efforts, the company was able to create a reliable and affordable system just in time to meet a huge demand.

> Fiber-optic networks per se are nothing new. Major phone companies like AT&T, WorldCom, and Sprint have been installing fiber for years, mostly across long distances—spanning continents and crossing the ocean floors. . . . But in the past few years the rise of the Internet has created an explosion in data traffic and hence in the demand for bandwidth, or carrying capacity, by the world's telecom companies. Instead of just transporting phone conversations from Tupelo to Topeka, telecom networks are also being used to transmit e-mail, Web pages, and video to multiple locations all over the world. This vast quantity of information eats up enormous amounts of network capacity. So telecoms need to start lighting up all their fiber to handle the burgeoning load.[23]

Today, Nortel's high-quality system helps account for the fact that in 2001 the firm controlled over 40 percent of the global market for optical equipment. Its nearest competitor, Lucent, had a mere 15 percent share.

Simultaneously, a growing number of MNCs are finding that they must continually revise their strategies and make renewed commitment to the quality imperative because they are being bested by emerging market forces. Motorola, for example, found that its failure to anticipate the industry's switch to digital cell technology was a costly one.[24] In 1998 the company dominated the U.S. handset market, and its StarTAC was popular worldwide. Five years later the firm's share of the $160 billion global market for handsets had shrunk from 22 percent to 10 percent and was continuing to fall, while Nokia, Ericsson, and Samsung in particular, with smaller, lighter, and more versatile offerings, were now the dominant players.[25] The lesson is clear: The quality imperative is neverending, and MNCs such as Motorola must meet this strategic challenge or pay the price.

administrative coordination
Strategic formulation and implementation in which the MNC makes strategic decisions based on the merits of the individual situation rather than using a predetermined economically or politically driven strategy.

Administrative Coordination   An **administrative coordination** approach to formulation and implementation is one in which the MNC makes strategic decisions based on the merits of the individual situation rather than using a predetermined economic or political strategy. A good example is provided by Wal-Mart, which has expanded rapidly into Latin America in recent years. While many of the ideas that worked well in the North American market served as the basis for operations in the Southern Hemisphere, the company soon realized that it was doing business in a market where local tastes were different and competition was strong.

Wal-Mart is counting on its international operations to grow 25–30 percent annually, and Latin American operations are critical to this objective. Despite this objective, the company has faced losses in several of its Latin American businesses as it strives to adapt to the local markets. The firm is learning, for example, that the timely delivery of merchandise in places such as São Paulo, where there are continual traffic snarls and the company uses contract truckers for delivery, is often far from ideal. Another challenge is finding suppliers who can produce products to Wal-Mart's specification for easy-to-handle packaging and quality control. A third challenge is learning to adapt to the culture.

For example, in Brazil, Wal-Mart brought in stock-handling equipment that did not work with standardized local pallets. It also installed a computerized bookkeeping system that failed to take into account Brazil's wildly complicated tax system.

Many large MNCs work to combine the economic, political, quality, and administrative approaches to strategic planning. For example, IBM relies on the economic imperative when it has strong market power (especially in less developed countries), the political and quality imperatives when the market requires a calculated response (European countries), and an administrative coordination strategy when rapid, flexible decision making is needed to close the sale. Of the four, however, the first three approaches are much more common because of the firm's desire to coordinate its strategy both regionally and globally.

Global vs. Regional Strategies

A fundamental tension in international strategic management is the question of when to pursue global or regional (or local) strategies. This is commonly referred to as the *globalization vs. national responsiveness conflict.* As used here, **global integration** is the production and distribution of products and services of a homogeneous type and quality on a worldwide basis.[26] To a growing extent, the customers of MNCs have homogenized tastes, and this has helped to spread international consumerism. For example, throughout North America, the EU, and Japan, there has been a growing acceptance of standardized yet increasingly personally customized goods such as automobiles and computers. This goal of efficient economic performance through a globalization and mass customization strategy, however, has left MNCs open to the charge that they are overlooking the need to address national responsiveness through Internet and intranet technology.

National responsiveness is the need to understand the different consumer tastes in segmented regional markets and respond to different national standards and regulations imposed by autonomous governments and agencies.[27] For example, in designing and building cars, international manufacturers now carefully tailor their offerings in the American market. Toyota's "full-size" T100 pickup proved much too small to attract U.S. buyers. So the firm went back to the drawing board and created a full-size Tundra pickup that is powered by a V-8 engine and has a cabin designed to "accommodate a passenger wearing a 10-gallon cowboy hat." Honda has developed its new Model X SUV with more Americanized features, including enough interior room so that travelers can eat and sleep in the vehicle. Mitsubishi has abandoned its idea of making a global vehicle and has brought out its new Montero Sport SUV in the U.S. market with the features it learned that Americans want: more horsepower, more interior room, more comfort. Meanwhile, Nissan is doing what many foreign carmakers would have thought to be unthinkable just a few years ago. Today, U.S. engineers and product designers are now completely responsible for the development of most Nissan vehicles sold in North America. Among other things, they are asking children between the ages of 8 and 15, in focus-group sessions, for ideas on storage, cup holders, and other refinements that would make a full-size minivan more attractive to them.[28]

National responsiveness also relates to the need to adapt tools and techniques for managing the local workforce. Sometimes what works well in one country does not work in another, as seen by the following example:

> An American computer company introduced pay-for-performance in both the USA and the Middle East. It worked well in the USA and increased sales briefly in the Middle East before a serious slump occurred. Inquiries showed that indeed the winners among salesmen in the Middle East had done better, but the vast majority had done worse. The wish for their fellows to succeed had been seriously eroded by the contest. Overall morale and sales were down. Ill-will was contagious. When the bosses discovered that certain salespeople were earning more than they did, high individual performances also ceased. But the principal reason for eventually abandoning the system was the discovery that customers were being loaded up with products they could not sell. As A tried to beat B to the bonus, the care of customers began to slip, with serious, if delayed, results.[29]

global integration
The production and distribution of products and services of a homogeneous type and quality on a worldwide basis.

national responsiveness
The need to understand the different consumer tastes in segmented regional markets and respond to different national standards and regulations imposed by autonomous governments and agencies.

Figure 8–1

Global Integration vs. National Responsiveness

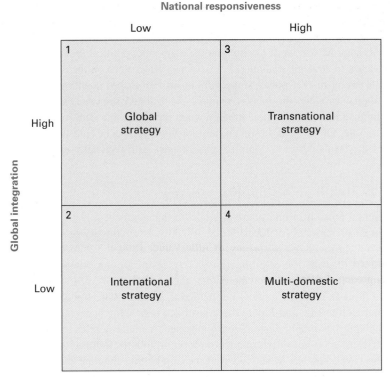

National responsiveness

	Low	High

Source: Adapted from information in Christopher A. Bartlett and Sumantra Ghoshal, *Managing Across Borders: The Transnational Solution,* 2nd ed. (Boston: Harvard Business School Press, 1998).

Global Integration vs. National Responsiveness Matrix   The issue of global integration vs. national responsiveness can be further analyzed conceptually via a two-dimensional matrix. Figure 8–1 provides an example.

The vertical axis in the figure measures the need for global integration. Movement up the axis results in a greater degree of economic integration. Global integration generates economies of scale (takes advantage of large size) and also capitalizes on further lowering unit costs (through experience curve benefits) as a firm moves into worldwide markets selling its products or services. These economies are captured through centralizing specific activities in the value-added chain. They also occur by reaping the benefits of increased coordination and control of geographically dispersed activities.

The horizontal axis measures the need for multinationals to respond to national responsiveness or differentiation. This suggests that MNCs must address local tastes and government regulations. The result may be a geographic dispersion of activities or a decentralization of coordination and control for individual MNCs.

Figure 8–1 depicts four basic situations in relation to the degrees of global integration vs. national responsiveness. Quadrants 1 and 4 are the simplest cases. In quadrant 1, the need for integration is high and awareness of differentiation is low. In terms of economies of scale, this situation leads to **global strategies** based on price competition. A good example of this is Matsushita, which has standardized many aspects of its operations and marketing over the years, including its name. To gain global recognition, Matsushita changed the name of all its products to then have the Panasonic brand. Even before that, Matsushita, along with the Toshiba Corporation, the Victor Company of Japan and others, worked to standardize the digital videocassette recording (VCR) industry. Matsushita's strong global distribution network, companywide mission statements, financial control, and ability to get to the market quickly allowed the company to offer the VCR at an economy of scale and, in turn, gained a sizable portion of the market.[30] In this quadrant-1 type of environment, mergers and acquisitions often occur.

global strategy
Integrated strategy based primarily on price competition.

**Table 8–1
Areas for Formulation of MNC Goals**

Profitability
Level of profits
Return on assets, investment, equity, sales
Yearly profit growth
Yearly earnings per share growth

Marketing
Total sales volume
Market share—worldwide, region, country
Growth in sales volume
Growth in market share
Integration of country markets for marketing efficiency and effectiveness

Operations
Ratio of foreign to domestic production volume
Economies of scale via international production integration
Quality and cost control
Introduction of cost-efficient production methods

Finance
Financing of foreign affiliates—retained earnings or local borrowing
Taxation—minimizing tax burden globally
Optimum capital structure
Foreign exchange management—minimizing losses from foreign fluctuations

Human Resources
Recruitment and selection
Development of managers with global orientation
Management development of host-country nationals
Compensation and benefits

Profitability and marketing goals almost always dominate the strategic plans of today's MNCs. Profitability, as shown in Table 8–1, is so important because MNCs generally need higher profitability from their overseas operations than they do from their domestic operations. The reason is quite simple: Setting up overseas operations involves greater risk and effort. In addition, a firm that has done well domestically with a product or service usually has done so because the competition is minimal or ineffective. Firms with this advantage often find additional lucrative opportunities outside their borders. Moreover, the more successful a firm is domestically, the more difficult it is to increase market share without strong competitive response. International markets, however, offer an ideal alternative to the desire for increased growth and profitability.

Another reason that profitability and marketing top the list is that these tend to be more externally environmentally responsive, whereas production, finance, and personnel functions tend to be more internally controlled. Thus, for strategic planning, profitability and marketing goals are given higher importance and warrant closer attention. Ford's European operations offer an example. In recent years the automaker has been losing market share in the EU. In an effort to turn things around, the MNC scaled back production capacity and announced that it intends to push market share above 10 percent, reversing a trend that has seen its slice of the European auto pie drop from almost 12 percent in the 1980s to just over 6 percent recently.[40] In order to reach this objective,

Ford closed plants, cut its European workforce, and transferred vehicle production to more efficient factories. After cutting costs, the company launched a proactive strategy to increase market share.[41]

Ford in Europe has been working to create a fresh image by offering new models, designing a totally revised advertising campaign, and developing a revised dealership network. However, these adjustments have been costly and contributed to poor financial performance. Ford announced losses in its European market through 2003, which included a $1.1 billion loss for that year. While Ford broke even in 2004 and showed promise with slight profits in 2005, 2006 again proved shaky, and it is clear that continuous strategy implementation will be necessary to keep generating positive numbers.[42]

Once the strategic goals are set, the MNC will develop specific operational goals and controls, usually through a two-way process at the subsidiary or affiliate level. Home-office management will set certain parameters, and the overseas group will operate within these guidelines. For example, the MNC headquarters may require periodic financial reports, restrict on-site decisions to matters involving less than $100,000, and require that all client contracts be cleared through the home office. These guidelines are designed to ensure that the overseas group's activities support the goals in the strategic plan and that all units operate in a coordinated effort.

■ Strategy Implementation

strategy implementation
The process of providing goods and services in accord with a plan of action.

Once formulated, the strategic plan next must be implemented. **Strategy implementation** provides goods and services in accord with a plan of action. Quite often, this plan will have an overall philosophy or series of guidelines that direct the process. In the case of Japanese electronic-manufacturing firms entering the U.S. market, Chang has found a common approach:

> To reduce the risk of failure, these firms are entering their core businesses and those in which they have stronger competitive advantages over local firms first. The learning from early entry enables firms to launch further entry into areas in which they have the next strongest competitive advantages. As learning accumulates, firms may overcome the disadvantages intrinsic to foreignness. Although primary learning takes place within firms through learning by doing, they may also learn from other firms through the transfer or diffusion of experience. This process is not automatic, however, and it may be enhanced by membership in a corporate network: in firms associated with either horizontal or vertical business, groups were more likely to initiate entries than independent firms. By learning from their own sequential entry experience as well as from other firms in corporate networks, firms build capabilities in foreign entry.[43]

International management must consider three general areas in strategy implementation. First, the MNC must decide where to locate operations. Second, the MNC must carry out entry and ownership strategies (discussed in Chapter 9). Finally, management must implement functional strategies in areas such as marketing, production, and finance.

Location Considerations for Implementation

In choosing a location, today's MNC has two primary considerations: the country and the specific locale within the chosen country. Quite often, the first choice is easier than the second, because there are many more alternatives from which to choose a specific locale.

The Country   Traditionally, MNCs have invested in highly industrialized countries, and research reveals that annual investments have been increasing substantially. In 1993, over $325 billion was spent on mergers and acquisitions worldwide. By 1997, the annual total had jumped to $1.6 trillion, although in the last few years it has dropped significantly and showed signs of growth again, ending at $1.2 trillion in 2006.[44] Much of this investment, especially by American MNCs, has been in Europe, Canada, and Mexico.

In the case of Japan, multinational banks and investors from around the world have been looking for properties that are being jettisoned by Japanese banks that are trying to unload some of their distressed loans. The Japanese commercial property market collapsed starting in the mid-1990s, creating many opportunities for investors. One was U.S.-based MNC Bankers Trust, which bought a large plot of properties of a failed affiliate of Nippon Credit Bank Ltd. Bankers Trust paid $220 million for properties that had a face value of $2.2 billion.[45] Nonbanking MNCs are also actively engaged in mergers and acquisitions in Japan. Intuit Inc. of Menlo Park, California, purchased a financial software specialist in Japan for $52 million in stock and spent $30 million for the Nihon Mikon Company, which sells small business accounting software. These purchases point to a new trend in Japan—the acquisition of small firms. However, many larger purchases have also been made, as seen in Table 8–2.

Foreign investors are also pouring into Mexico, although this investment activity has generated some political controversy in the United States.[46] One reason is that it is a gateway to the American and Canadian markets. A second reason is that Mexico is a very cost-effective place in which to manufacture goods. A third is that the declining value of the peso in the late 1990s hit many Mexican businesses hard and left them vulnerable to mergers and acquisitions—an opportunity not lost on many large multinationals.

> Britain's B.A.T. Industries PLC took control of Cigarrera La Moderna, Mexico's tobacco giant, in a $1.5 billion deal. A few days earlier, Philip Morris Cos. increased its stake in the second-largest tobacco company, Cigarros La Tabacalera Mexicana SA, to 50% from about 29% for $400 million. In June, Wal-Mart Stores Inc. announced plans to acquire control of Mexico's largest retailer, Cifra SA, in a deal valued at more than $1 billion. In July, Procter & Gamble Co. acquired a consumer-products concern, Loreto y Pena Pobre, for $170 million. Bell Atlantic Co. has acquired full control of its cellular-phone partner, Grupo Iusacell SA, with total investments of more than $1 billion. The list goes on and on and is expected to keep growing.[47]

MNCs often invest in advanced industrialized countries because they offer the largest markets for goods and services. In addition, the established country or geographic locale may have legal restrictions related to imports, encouraging a local presence. Japanese firms, for example, in complying with their voluntary export quotas of cars to the United States as well as responding to dissatisfaction in Washington regarding the continuing trade imbalance with the United States, have established U.S.-based assembly plants. In Europe, because of EU regulations for outsiders, most U.S. and Japanese MNCs have operations in at least one European country, thus ensuring access to the European community at large. In fact, the huge U.S. MNC ITT now operates in each of the original 12 EU countries.

Table 8–2
Representative MNC Acquisitions in Japan

Glaxo Wellcome	Purchased the remaining 50 percent of its Nippon Glaxo affiliate for $537 million.
Ford Motor	Picked up an additional 9 percent of Mazda, bringing its stake to 33.4 percent, for $430 million.
BASF	The German drugmaker purchased 51 percent of Hokuriku Seiyaku for $294 million.
Grande Group	The Singapore firm acquired 70 percent of Nakamichi for $286 million.
GE Capital	Bought 80 percent of Narubeni Car System, an auto-loan business, for $80 million.
Semi-Tech Group	The Hong Kong high-tech company put out $167 million for an additional 11 percent of Akai Electric.
Boehringer Ingelheim	The German firm acquired 9 percent of SS Pharmaceutical for $71 million.
Amersham International	The British drugmaker acquired 30 percent of Nihon Mediphysics for $76 million.

Another consideration in choosing a country is the amount of government control. Traditionally, MNCs from around the world refused to do business in Eastern European countries with central planning economies. The recent relaxing of the trade rules and move toward free-market economies in the republics of the former Soviet Union and the other Eastern European nations, however, have encouraged MNCs to rethink their positions; more and more are making moves into this largely untapped part of the global market. The same is true in India, although the political climate can be volatile and MNCs must carefully weigh the risks of investing here.

Still another consideration in selecting a country is restrictions on foreign investment. Traditionally, countries such as China and India have required that control of the operation be in the hands of local partners. MNCs that are reluctant to accept such conditions will not establish operations there.

In addition to these considerations, MNCs will examine the specific benefits offered by host countries, including low tax rates, rent-free land and buildings, low-interest or no-interest loans, subsidized energy and transportation rates, and a well-developed infrastructure that provides many of the services found back home (good roads, communication systems, schools, health care, entertainment, and housing). These benefits will be weighed against any disincentives or performance requirements that must be met by the MNC, such as job-creation quotas, export minimums for generating foreign currency, limits on local market growth, labor regulations, wage and price controls, restrictions on profit repatriation, and controls on the transfer of technology. Commenting on the overall effect of these potential gains and losses, Garland and Farmer noted:

> These incentives and disincentives often make operations abroad less amenable to integration on a global basis; essentially they may alter a company's strategy for the region. They affect, for example, a firm's make-or-buy decision, intracorporate transfer policies (e.g., between subsidiaries or between headquarters and the subsidiaries), both horizontal and vertical sourcing arrangements, and so on. In effect, they weaken the MNC's mandate for global efficiency by encouraging the firm to suboptimize.[48]

Local Issues   Once the MNC has selected the country in which to locate, the firm must choose the specific locale. A number of factors influence this choice. Common considerations include access to markets, proximity to competitors, availability of transportation and electric power, and desirability of the location for employees coming in from the outside.

One study found that in selecting U.S. sites, both German and Japanese firms place more importance on accessibility and desirability and less importance on financial considerations.[49] However, financial matters remain important: Many countries attempt to lure MNCs to specific locales by offering special financial packages.

Another common consideration is the nature of the workforce. MNCs prefer to locate near sources of available labor that can be readily trained to do the work. A complementary consideration that often is unspoken is the presence and strength of organized labor. Japanese firms in particular tend to avoid heavily unionized areas.

Still another consideration is the cost of doing business. Manufacturers often set up operations in rural areas, commonly called "greenfield locations," which are much less expensive and do not have the problems of urban areas. Conversely, banks often choose metropolitan areas, because they feel they must have a presence in the business district.

Some MNCs opt for locales where the cost of running a small enterprise is significantly lower than that of running a large one. In this way, they spread their risk, setting up many small locations throughout the world rather than one or two large ones. Manufacturing firms are a good example. Some production firms feel that the economies of scale associated with a large-scale plant are more than offset by potential problems that can result should economic or political difficulties develop in the country. These firms' strategy is to spread the risk by opting for a series of small plants throughout a wide geographic region.[50] This location strategy can also be beneficial for stockholders.

Research has found that MNCs with a presence in developing countries have significantly higher market values than MNCs that operate only in countries that have advanced economies.[51]

The Role of the Functional Areas in Implementation

To implement strategies, MNCs must tap the primary functional areas of marketing, production, and finance. The following sections examine the roles of these functions in international strategy implementation.

Marketing   The implementation of strategy from a marketing perspective must be determined on a country-by-country basis. What works from the standpoint of marketing in one locale may not necessarily succeed in another. In addition, the specific steps of a marketing approach often are dictated by the overall strategic plan, which in turn is based heavily on market analysis.

German auto firms in Japan are a good example of using marketing analysis to meet customer needs. Over the past 15 years, the Germans have spent millions of dollars to build dealer, supplier, and service-support networks in Japan, in addition to adapting their cars to Japanese customers' tastes. Volkswagen Audi Nippon has built a $320 million import facility on a deepwater port. This operation, which includes an inspection center and parts warehouse, can process 100,000 cars a year. Mercedes and BMW both have introduced lower-priced cars to attract a larger market segment, and BMW now offers a flat-fee, three-year service contract on any new car, including parts. At the same time, German manufacturers work hard to offer first-class service in their dealerships. As a result, German automakers in recent years sell almost three times as many cars in Japan as their U.S. competitors do.

The Japanese also provide an excellent example of how the marketing process works. In many cases, Japanese firms have followed a strategy of first building up their market share at home and driving out imported goods. Then, the firms move into newly developed countries, honing their marketing skills as they go along. Finally, the firms move into fully developed countries, ready to compete with the best available. This pattern of implementing strategy has been used in marketing autos, cameras, consumer electronics, home appliances, petrochemicals, steel, and watches. For some products, however, such as computers, the Japanese have moved from their home market directly into fully developed countries and then on to the newly developing nations. Finally, the Japanese have gone directly to developed countries to market products in some cases, because the market in Japan was too small. Such products include color TVs, videotape recorders, and sewing machines. In general, once a firm agrees on the goods it wants to sell in the international marketplace, then the specific marketing strategy is implemented.

The implementation of marketing strategy in the international arena is built around the well-known "four Ps" of marketing: product, price, promotion, and place. As noted in the example of the Japanese, firms often develop and sell a product in local or peripheral markets before expanding to major overseas targets. If the product is designed specifically to meet an overseas demand, however, the process is more direct. Price largely is a function of market demand.[52] For example, the Japanese have found that the U.S. microcomputer market is price-sensitive; by introducing lower-priced clones, the Japanese have been able to make headway, especially in the portable laptop market. The last two Ps, promotion and place, are dictated by local conditions and often left in the hands of those running the subsidiary or affiliate. Local management may implement customer sales incentives, for example, or make arrangements with dealers and salespeople who are helping to move the product locally.

Production   Although marketing usually dominates strategy implementation, the production function also plays a role. If a company is going to export goods to a foreign market, the production process traditionally has been handled through domestic operations. In recent years, however, MNCs have found that whether they are exporting or producing the goods locally in the host country, consideration of worldwide production is important. For example, goods may be produced in foreign countries for export to other nations. Sometimes, a plant will specialize in a particular product and export it to all the MNC's markets; other times, a plant will produce goods only for a specific locale, such as Western Europe or South America. Still other facilities will produce one or more components that are shipped to a larger network of assembly plants. That last option has been widely adopted by pharmaceutical firms and automakers such as Volkswagen and Honda.

As mentioned in the first part of the chapter, if the firm operates production plants in different countries but makes no attempt to integrate its overall operations, the company is known as a multi-domestic. A recent trend has been away from this scattered approach and toward global coordination of operations.

Finally, if the product is labor-intensive, as in the case of microcomputers, then the trend is to farm the product out to low-cost sites such as Mexico or Brazil, where the cost of labor is relatively low and the infrastructure (electric power, communications systems, transportation systems) is sufficient to support production. Sometimes, multiple sources of individual components are used; in other cases, one or two sources are sufficient. In any event, careful coordination of the production function is needed when implementing the strategy, and the result is a product that is truly global in nature.

Finance   Use of the finance function to implement strategy normally is developed at the home office and carried out by the overseas affiliate or branch. When a firm went international in the past, the overseas operation commonly relied on the local area for funds, but the rise of global financing has ended this practice. MNCs have learned that transferring funds from one place in the world to another, or borrowing funds in the international money markets, often is less expensive than relying on local sources. Unfortunately, there are problems in these transfers.

Such a problem is representative of those faced by MNCs using the finance function to implement their strategies. One of an MNC's biggest recent headaches when implementing strategies in the financial dimension has been the revaluation of currencies. For example, in the late 1990s the U.S. dollar increased in value against the Japanese yen. American overseas subsidiaries that held yen found their profits (in terms of dollars) declining. The same was true for those subsidiaries that held Mexican pesos when that government devalued the currency several years ago. When this happens, a subsidiary's profit will decline. After its initial introduction in 1999, the euro declined against the U.S. dollar, but when the dollar subsequently came under pressure, the euro regained strength. One of the more recent examples of financial issues is the expansive U.S. trade deficit with China, where the potentially undervalued yuan has played a role. Whether there has been poor economic planning by the United States or miscalculated currency by China is still being worked out.[53]

When dealing with the inherent risk of volatile monetary exchange rates, some MNCs have bought currency options that (for a price) guarantee convertibility at a specified rate. Others have developed countertrade strategies, whereby they receive products in exchange for currency. For example, PepsiCo received payment in vodka for its products sold in Russia. Countertrade continues to be a popular form of international business, especially in less developed countries and those with nonconvertible currencies.

■ Specialized Strategies

In addition to the basic steps in strategy formulation, the analysis of which strategies may be appropriate based on the globalization vs. national responsiveness framework, and the specific processes in strategy implementation, there are some circumstances that may require specialized strategies. Two that have received considerable attention in recent years are strategies for developing and emerging markets and strategies for international entrepreneurship and new ventures.

Strategies for Emerging Markets

Emerging economies have assumed an increasingly important role in the global economy and are predicted to compose more than half of global economic output by mid-century. Partly in response to this growth, MNCs are directing increasing attention to those markets. Foreign direct investment (FDI) flows into developing countries—one measure of increased integration and business activity between developed and emerging economies—grew from $23.7 billion in 1990 to $204.8 billion in 2001, a ninefold increase, helping to contribute to growth in the stock of FDI in developing countries from 5 percent to 20.5 percent of GDP over this same period.[54] FDI inflows into developing countries reached $334 billion in 2005.[55] In particular, the "big emerging markets"—Mexico, Brazil, Argentina, South Africa, Poland, Turkey, India, Indonesia, China, and South Korea—have captured the bulk of investment and business interest from MNCs and their managers.[56]

At the same time, emerging economies pose exceptional risks due to their political and economic volatility and their relatively underdeveloped institutional systems. These risks show up in corruption, failure to enforce contracts, red tape and bureaucratic costs, and general uncertainty in the legal and political environment.[57] MNCs must adjust their strategy to respond to these risks. For example, in these risky markets, it may be wise to engage in arm's-length or limited equity investments or to maintain greater control of operations by avoiding joint ventures or other shared ownership structures. In other circumstances, it may be wiser to collaborate with a local partner who can help buffer risks through its political connections.[58] Some of the factors relating to these conditions will be discussed in Chapters 9 and 10. However, two unique types of strategies for emerging markets deserve particular attention here.

First-Mover Strategies   Recent research has suggested that entry order into developing countries may be particularly important given the transitional nature of these markets. In general, in particular industries and economic environments, significant economies are associated with first-mover or early-entry positioning—being the first or one of the first to enter a market. These include capturing learning effects important for increasing market share, achieving scale economies that accrue from opportunities for capturing that greater share, and development of alliances with the most attractive (or in some cases the only) local partner. In emerging economies that are undergoing rapid changes such as privatization and market liberalization, there may be a narrow window of time within which these opportunities can be best exploited. In these conditions, first-mover strategies allow entrants to preempt competition, establish beachhead positions, and influence the evolving competitive environment in a manner conducive to their long-term interests and market position.

One study analyzed these benefits in the case of China, concluding that early entrants have reaped substantial rewards for their efforts, especially when collaborations with governments provided credible commitments that the deals struck in those early years of liberalization would not later be undone. First-mover advantages in some other transitional markets, such as Russia and Eastern Europe, are not so clear. Moreover, there may be substantial risks to premature entry—that is, entry before the basic legal, institutional, and political frameworks for doing business have been established.[59]

Privatization presents a particularly powerful case supporting the competitive effects of first-mover positioning. First movers who succeed in taking over newly privatized state-owned enterprises, such as telecom and energy firms, possess a significant advantage over later entrants, especially when market liberalization is delayed and the host government provides protection to the newly privatized incumbent firms. This was the case in 1998 when the Mexican government accepted a $1.757 billion bid for a minority (20.4 percent) but controlling interest in Telefonos de Mexico (Telmex) from an international consortium composed of Grupo Carso, Southwestern Bell, and France

Cable et Radio, an affiliate of France Telecom. Although the Mexican market subsequently opened to competition, Telmex and its foreign partners (the first movers) maintained monopoly control over local networks and were able to bundle local and long-distance service, cross-market, and cross-subsidize, giving Telmex a strong advantage. Moreover, the Mexican government was responsive to providing the Telmex consortium protection and financial support for infrastructure investment, and it did so partly by charging new carriers to help Telmex pay for improvements needed for the long-distance network. In addition, Telmex was able to charge relatively high fees to connect to its network, and the long delay between the initial privatization and market opening allowed these advantages to persist.[60]

base of the pyramid strategy
Strategy targeting low-income customers in developing countries.

Strategies for the "Base of the Pyramid"   Another area of increasing focus for MNCs is the 4 to 5 billion potential customers around the world who have heretofore been mostly ignored by international business, even within emerging economies, where most MNCs target only the wealthiest consumers. Although FDI in emerging economies has grown rapidly, most has been directed at the big emerging markets previously mentioned—China, India, and Brazil—and even there, most MNC emerging-market strategies have focused exclusively on the elite and emerging middle-class markets, ignoring the vast majority of people considered too poor to be viable customers.[61] Because of this focus, MNC strategies aimed at tailoring existing practices and products to better fit the needs of emerging-market customers have not succeeded in making products and services available to the mass markets in the developing world—the 4–5 billion people at the bottom of the economic pyramid who represent fully two-thirds of the world's population. Figure 8–4 shows the distribution of population and income around the world.

A group of researchers and companies have begun exploring the potentially untapped markets at the base of the pyramid (BOP). They have found that incremental adaptation of existing technologies and products is not effective at the BOP and that the BOP forces MNCs to fundamentally rethink their strategies.[62] Companies must consider smaller-scale strategies and build relationships with local governments, small entrepreneurs, and nonprofits rather than depend on established partners such as central governments and large local companies. Building relationships directly and at the local level contributes to the reputation and fosters the trust necessary to overcome the lack of formal institutions such as intellectual property rights and the rule of law. The BOP may also be an ideal environment for incubating new, leapfrog technologies, including

Figure 8–4

The World Population and Income Pyramid

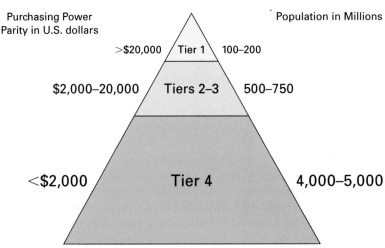

Source: Adapted from C. K. Prahalad and Stuart L. Hart, "The Fortune at the Bottom of the Pyramid," *Strategy + Business* 26 (2002), pp. 54–67.

How Telecom Is Revolutionizing Economies at the Base of the Pyramid

Developed countries have been exposed to advanced cellular technology for years. System upgrades, new phones, and alternative network frequencies have made many phones and plans virtually obsolete. Some phone companies, however, are taking a back-to-basics approach and using Africa as a springboard to launch strategies.

Many impoverished regions in Africa are known for dirt roads that flood during rainy season, a lack of electricity and indoor plumbing, and a general disconnect in communications with the rest of the world. Telecom is about to change all of that. In an area where people make $2 or less a day, mobile phones are being offered on a pay-as-you-go basis. Phones can be purchased for $20 or less, incoming calls are free as long as the phone is activated, and text messages are usually free. Many villagers will have the minimum balance on their account and simply text message, buy a SIM card (computer chip) and borrow other phones, wait for incoming calls, or "flash" another person by calling and letting it ring, but hanging up before the other person answers. With all these efforts from the villagers to keep cost at a minimum after the telecom companies have already cut their costs so much, it would seem as though this is a losing battle for company profitability. However, expanding the coverage to other base-of-pyramid areas could stimulate the economy and make up for low per-customer fees by massively increasing scale.

People who are trying to run a business in Africa, whether they are selling agricultural goods or handmade crafts, often run into the issue of delivering products to places where clients are not available or disposing of excess inventory because potential customers cannot

be reached. As mobile technology becomes available, business owners can contact their clients and set up specific times and areas to meet and exchange goods, saving time and money. As word of mouth spreads, other customers can call the business to quickly and easily find out more information. Fishermen, for example, may come on shore to sell what they have caught. If they do not have a way of informing others in the area that fresh fish is coming to the dock, they may have to dispose of the fish they could not sell. On the other hand, if the fishermen know they will be able to sell all that they have caught, they can become more profitable or lower prices for consumers so that everyone benefits. Either way, it stimulates the local economies and frees more time and money to be spent on community and communication.

Telecom has not only stimulated the economy but also enriched the lives of consumers. Now, people can spend more time on what is important to them. They are able to transfer money via cellular phones, which saves trips to the bank and ensures that family and friends are financially cared for. There is an extremely high growth potential in this market, as many impoverished people are avid phone users. These populations will also be contributing to economies of scale, as the world moves from its current 3 billion mobile users to an estimated 5 billion by 2015. Telecom and Africa have shown that even the poorest of areas can pave the road to an enriching future.

Source: Reprinted with special permission from "How Telecom is Revolutionizing Economies at the Base of Pyramid," *BusinessWeek,* Copyright © 2007 The McGraw-Hill Companies.

"disruptive" technologies that reduce environmental impacts and increase social benefit such as renewable energy and wireless telecom. Finally, business models forged successfully at the base of the pyramid have the potential to travel profitably to higher-income markets because adding cost and features to a low-cost model may be easier than removing cost and features from high-cost models.[63] This last finding has significant implications for the globalization–national responsiveness framework introduced at the beginning of the chapter and for the potential for MNCs to achieve a truly transnational strategy.

The BOP strategy is challenging to implement. Companies have to offer affordable goods that are highly available in a community that is willing to accept the product. Most importantly, however, is that the company must bring awareness of the product to the general populous. Balancing these is not a simple task, since advertising and efficient distribution networks, for example, cost a significant amount, yet the companies cannot add a high price tag. Furthermore, illiteracy issues, poor infrastructure, corruption, and nonexistent distribution channels often associated with poverty-stricken societies deter companies from wanting to invest. Despite the many barriers, companies can be successful. Smart Communications Inc. saw that there was a great opportunity to expand in the Philippines, where about half the population lived in poverty. In 2002, the market forecasted that approximately 30 percent of the population would be using mobile phones by 2008. Smart offered pay-as-you-go phones that could be recharged using a microchip that was already in the cellular phones, making it possible to recharge "over the air." The company then began to offer pricing plans that consisted of extremely small increments, so even the low-income consumer could take advantage of the opportunity. It worked in Smart's favor, as more and more people began using the service daily, and the cellular industry reached a 30 percent margin in 2004, changing forecasts to a shocking 70 percent mobile phone usage rate by 2008. Smart's parent company experienced a more than tenfold increase in profits in 2004 as compared to 2003, due in large part to focusing on the very lucrative market at the base of the pyramid.[64] To learn more about how mobile technology is reaching impoverished countries, see "International Management in Action: How Telecom Is Revolutionizing Economies at the Base of the Pyramid."

Entrepreneurial Strategy and New Ventures

In addition to strategies that must be tailored for the particular needs and circumstances in emerging economies, another condition that calls for specialized strategies is the international management activities of entrepreneurial and new-venture firms. Most international management activities take place within the context of medium-large MNCs, but, increasingly, small and medium companies, often in the form of new ventures, are getting involved in international management. This has been made possible by advances in telecommunication and Internet technologies and by greater efficiencies and lower costs in shipping, allowing firms that were previously limited to local or national markets to access international customers. These new access channels, however, suggest particular strategies that must be customized and tailored to the unique situations and resource limitations of small, entrepreneurial firms.[65]

international entrepreneurship
A combination of innovative, proactive, and risk-seeking behavior that crosses national boundaries and is intended to create value for organizations.

International Entrepreneurship   **International entrepreneurship** has been defined as "a combination of innovative, proactive, and risk-seeking behavior that crosses national borders and is intended to create value in organizations."[66] The internationalization of the marketplace and the increasing number of entrepreneurial firms in the global economy have created new opportunities for small and new-venture firms to accelerate internationalization. This international entrepreneurial activity is being observed in even the smallest and newest organizations. Indeed, one study among 57 privately held Finnish electronics firms during the mid-1990s showed that firms that internationalize after they are established domestically must overcome a number of barriers to that international expansion, such as their domestic orientation, internal domestic political ties, and domestic decision-making inertia. In contrast, firms that internationalize earlier face fewer barriers to learning about the international environment.[67] Thus, the earlier in its existence that an innovative firm internationalizes, the faster it is likely to grow both overall and in foreign markets.

However, despite this new access, there remain limitations to international entrepreneurial activities. In another study, researchers show that deploying a technological learning advantage internationally is no simple process. They studied more than 300 private independent and corporate new ventures based in the United States. Building on past research about the advantages of large, established multinational enterprises, their results from 12 high-technology industries show that greater diversity of national environments is associated with increased technological learning opportunities even for new ventures, whose internationalization is usually thought to be limited.[68] In addition, the breadth, depth, and speed of technological learning from varied international environments is significantly enhanced by formal organizational efforts to integrate knowledge throughout a firm such as cross-functional teams and formal analysis of both successful and failed projects. Further, the research shows that venture performance (growth and return on equity) is improved by technological learning gained from international environments.

International New Ventures and "Born-Global" Firms Another dimension of the growth of international entrepreneurial activities is the increasing incidence of international new ventures, or "born globals"—firms that engage in significant international activity a short time after being established. Building on an empirical study of small firms in Norway and France, researchers found that more than half of the exporting firms established there since 1990 could be classified as "born globals."[69] Examining the differences between newly established firms with high or low export involvement levels revealed that a decision maker's global orientation and market conditions are important factors.

Another study highlighted the critical role of innovative culture, as well as knowledge and capabilities, in this unique breed of international, entrepreneurial firm. An analysis of case studies and surveys revealed key strategies that engender international success among these innovative firms.[70] Successful born-global firms leverage a distinctive mix of orientations and strategies that allow them to succeed in diverse international markets. Firms whose possession of the foundational capabilities of international entrepreneurial orientation and international marketing orientation engender the development of a specific collection of organizational strategies. The most important business strategies employed by born-global firms are global technological competence, unique-products development, quality focus, and leveraging of foreign distributor competences.[71]

There is a difference between born-global firms and born-international firms, as one study showed. Born-international firms tend to export products close to markets, and revenues from these outside markets contribute 25 percent or less of total revenues. Truly born-global firms, however, tend to distribute goods to distant markets in multiple regions, and revenues from international activities tend to surpass 25 percent. It has been found that truly born-global firms tend to survive longer than other seemingly global companies.[72] However, being born global can simply be seen as accelerated internationalization. Another study compared born-global firms to those which sought out joint ventures or acquisitions (see Chapter 9) as a method to expand internationally. Results showed that while the market responds more positively to joint ventures or "partnerships," the extent to which a born global is successful greatly depends on how developed the area is that the company is moving into. In other words, while the market appreciates already established firms because they are familiar, if a startup does not have the capital to partner with well-known organizations and the international markets are open, then born-global companies may show slightly lower returns in the beginning, but this is not an indicator of survival or ultimate success.[73]

One clear example of a born-global firm is California-based Amazon.com. Like most U.S. Internet firms, Amazon.com has been able to distribute its products and services on an international scale from the outset. Although differing levels of cultural similarities and technological sophistication impact Amazon's potential for success internationally, the Internet as a medium has removed certain entry barriers that have historically restricted quick market entry.[74] Another example is New York–based online trading and investing services E*Trade. The company was able to bring in revenues from 33 countries in only three years, clearly making it a global brand. Allowing customers to actively participate in their investments while offering multilingual technical and professional customer support allowed E*Trade to integrate its services in many countries. The simplified Web site does not bombard consumers with extraneous information, and allows each person to trade as much or as little as desired, making it inherently customized. It has not been a success story for its entire existence, however. The company was in danger of being left behind when it could not get out of the red, but in 2005, the company was able to become profitable due to the low cost of Internet business and its extremely diverse customer base. The Internet is clearly one of the easiest and most efficient methods of becoming global quickly, but it is important that awareness is brought to the business, or it too can be lost in the digital maze of the World Wide Web.[75] Now more than ever, born global as a corporate strategy is becoming more attractive and less risky.

The World of *BusinessWeek*—Revisited

Looking back to the *BusinessWeek* article that opens this chapter, it is easy to see why Nokia's global strategic management has worked for the company. While it faltered for a period because it fell behind in developing the newest cell phone designs and technology, the company did not allow the temporary setback to throw it off track. While it is difficult to reach the pinnacle of an effective strategy, it is very easy to fall short, which is why periodic reevaluations are necessary. Nokia should be very sensitive to competitive threats, because while Nokia's shortcomings are not an impediment in the current market, it could fall behind again if competitors respond better to changing markets.

Drawing on the need and benefits of strategic management, answer these questions: (1) Which imperative is likely to be relatively most important to MNCs in the coming decade: economic, political, or quality? (2) When MNCs scan the environment, what are two key areas for consideration that they must address? (3) How would you characterize Nokia's strategy within the globalization–national responsiveness framework? (4) To what extent has Nokia used a base-of-pyramid approach? How would it affect the company if low-income markets turned out to be a bust?

SUMMARY OF KEY POINTS

1. There is a growing need for strategic management among MNCs. Some of the primary reasons include: foreign direct investment is increasing; planning is needed to coordinate and integrate increasingly diverse operations via an overall focus; and emerging international challenges require strategic planning.

2. A strategic plan can take on an economic focus, a political focus, a quality focus, an administrative coordination focus, or some variation of the four. The global integration–national responsiveness framework defines the four basic strategies employed by MNCs: international, global, multi-domestic, and transnational. Although transnational is often the preferred strategy, it is also the most difficult to implement.

3. Strategy formulation consists of several steps. First, the MNC carries out external environmental scanning to identify opportunities and threats. Next, the firm conducts an internal resource analysis of company strengths and weaknesses. Strategic goals then are formulated in light of the results of these external and internal analyses.

4. Strategy implementation is the process of providing goods and services in accord with the predetermined plan of action. This implementation typically involves such considerations as deciding where to locate operations, carrying out an entry and ownership strategy, and using functional strategies to implement the plan. Functional strategies focus on marketing, production, and finance.

5. Strategies for emerging markets and international entrepreneurship/new ventures may require specialized approaches targeted to these unique circumstances.

KEY TERMS

administrative coordination, *258*

base of the pyramid strategy, *272*

born-global firms, *275*

economic imperative, *255*

environmental scanning, *262*

global integration, *259*

global strategy, *260*

international entrepreneurship, *274*

international strategy, *261*

key success factor (KSF), *264*

multi-domestic strategy, *261*

national responsiveness, *259*

political imperative, *256*

quality imperative, *256*

strategic management, *252*

strategy implementation, *266*

transnational strategy, *261*

REVIEW AND DISCUSSION QUESTIONS

1. Of the four imperatives discussed in this chapter—economic, political, quality, and administration—which would be most important to IBM in its efforts to make inroads in the Pacific Rim market? Would this emphasis be the same as that in the United States, or would IBM be giving primary attention to one of the other imperatives? Explain.

2. Define *global integration* as used in the context of strategic international management. In what way might globalization be a problem for a successful national organization that is intent on going international? In your answer, provide an example of the problem.

3. Some international management experts contend that globalization and national responsiveness are diametrically opposed forces, and that to accommodate one, a multinational must relax its efforts in the other. In what way is this an accurate statement? In what way is it incomplete or inaccurate?

4. Consider that both a retail chain and a manufacturing company want to expand overseas. What environmental factors would have the most impact on these companies? What ratio of environmental scanning to internal analysis should each employ? What key factors of success differentiate the two?

5. Anheuser-Busch is attempting to expand in India, where beer is hardly ever consumed and liquor dominates the market. What areas should be targeted for strategic goals? What could be some marketing implications in the Indian market?

6. What particular conditions that MNCs face in emerging markets may require specialized strategies? What strategies might be most appropriate in response? How might a company identify opportunities at the "base of the pyramid" (i.e., low-income markets)?

7. What conditions have allowed some firms to be born global? What are some examples of born-global companies?

8. Mercedes changed its U.S. strategy by announcing that it is developing cars for the $30,000 to $45,000 price range (as well as its typical upper-end cars). What might have accounted for this change in strategy? In your answer, include a discussion of the implications from the standpoints of marketing, production, and finance.

INTERNET EXERCISE: FINDING OUT WHAT MAKES FUJITSU TICK

Fujitsu is the world's third-largest IT service provider. It offers consulting services, goods to doctors and health care systems and grocery store chains, and business or personal office solutions. Go to Fujitsu's Web site at **www.fujitsu.com** to see background of the firm and the products it offers. Then answer these questions: How do you think international strategic management is reflected in what you see on the Web site? What major strategic planning steps would Fujitsu need to carry out in order to remain a world leader with such diverse offerings? What potential threat, if it occurred, would prove most disastrous for Fujitsu, and what could the company do to deal with the possibility of this negative development?

Poland

Poland is the sixth-largest country in Europe. It is bordered by Germany, the Czech Republic, and Slovakia in the west and south and by the former Soviet Union republics of Ukraine in the south, Belarus in the east, and Lithuania in the northeast. The northwest section of the country is located on the Baltic Sea. Named after the Polane, a Slavic tribe that lived more than a thousand years ago, Poland has beautiful countryside and rapidly growing cities. Rolling hills and rugged mountains rise in southern Poland.

There are approximately 39 million Poles, and GDP is around $337 billion. While the agriculture industry contributes to 4.1 percent of GDP and 16.1 percent of labor force, a shift to industry and services has made Poland attractive to MNCs. There are many facets that make Poland attractive, one of which is that the central location to other European countries provides MNCs with easy access to competitive markets nearby.

Throughout the 1990s the United States and other Western countries supported the growth of a free-enterprise economy by reducing Poland's foreign debt burden, providing economic aid, and lowering trade barriers. Poland graduated from USAID assistance in 2000. As a result of Poland's growth and investment-friendly climate, the country has received over $65 billion in direct foreign investment since 1990. However, the government continues to play a strong role in the economy, as seen in excessive red tape and the high level of politicization in many business decisions. Investors complain that state regulation is not transparent or predictable. The economy suffers from a lack of competition in many sectors, notably telecommunications. In early 2002, the government announced a new set of economic reforms designed in many ways to complete the process launched in 1990. The package acknowledges the need to improve Poland's investment climate, particularly the conditions for small and medium-sized enterprises, and better prepare the economy to compete as an EU member.

Despite continuing problems, the Poles have made some progress in establishing a viable economy. To take advantage of this economic situation, a medium-sized Canadian manufacturing firm has begun thinking about renovating a plant near Warsaw and building small power tools for the expanding Central and Eastern European market. The company's logic is fairly straightforward. There appears to be no competition in this niche, because there has been little demand for power tools in this area. As the postcommunist countries continue to struggle in their transition to a market economy, they will have to increase their productivity if they hope to compete with Western European nations. Small power tools are one of the products they will need to accomplish this goal.

Other than the lack of competition, why would Poland seem so attractive to companies such as the Canadian power tool firm? The people of Poland have a great deal to offer. The highly educated populous includes a great deal of individuals who are multilingual and are extremely hard working, second only to Korea in hours worked per year. Furthermore, low labor costs in a country where almost 15 percent of the people are still unemployed is a huge incentive. Poland also has a vast modern transportation system including seaports, major airports, railroad systems, and roadways. The government also attempts to bring in new companies by offering grants or tax exemptions. And while the firm considers moving the manufacturing to Poland, it can also consider the vast successful R&D projects that are already in progress in the country, including institutions such as Siemens, Avio, IBM, Intel, Motorola, GlaxoSmithKline, and more.

Finally, there likely will be little competition for the next couple of years, because small power tools do not carry a very large markup and no other manufacturer is attempting to tap what the Canadian firm views as "an emerging market for the 21st century." However, a final decision on this matter is going to have to wait until the company has made a thorough evaluation of the market and the competitive nature of the industry.
www.poland.pl

Questions

1. What are some current issues facing Poland? What is the climate for doing business in Poland today?

2. Is the Canadian manufacturing firm using an economic, political, or quality imperative approach to strategy?

3. How should the firm carry out the environmental scanning process? Would the process be of any practical value?

4. What are two key factors for success that will be important if this project is to succeed?

Go East, Young People, Go East

Amanda Brendhart, Jose Gutierrez, and Rhoda Schreiber founded and are partners in a small electronics firm, Electronic Visions, that has developed and patented some state-of-the-art computer components. Visions has had moderate success selling these components to large U.S.-based computer manufacturers. The biggest problem is that in recent months, the computer market has begun to turn soft, and many of the manufacturers are offering substantial discounts to generate sales. Therefore, although Visions has found an increasing demand for its product, it now is grossing less money than it was several months ago.

To increase both sales and profit, the partners have decided to expand into Asia. Although this region is known for its low-cost computer production, the group believes that countries such as China, Malaysia, and Thailand soon will become more lucrative markets, because the U.S. government will make these countries open their doors to imports more fully. If trade barriers are removed, the partners are convinced that they can export the goods at very competitive prices. In addition, the partners intend to find a partner in each market so that they have someone to help with the marketing and financing of the product. Of course, if the components can be produced more cheaply with local labor, the partnership is willing to forgo exporting and have everything produced locally.

At present, the group is trying to answer three questions. First, what is the best entry strategy to use in reaching the Asian markets? Second, what type of marketing strategy will be most effective? Third, if production must be coordinated between the United States and an overseas country, what is the best way to handle this? The partners believe that over the next two months, they will have a very good idea of what is going to happen regarding the opening of Asian markets. In the interim, they intend to work up a preliminary strategic plan that they can use to guide them.

Questions

1. What type of entry and ownership approach would you recommend? Defend your choice.

2. How could the partners use the four Ps of marketing to help implement strategy?

3. If production must be globally coordinated, will Visions have a major problem? Why or why not?

Chapter 9

ENTRY STRATEGIES AND ORGANIZATIONAL STRUCTURES

The success of an international firm can be greatly affected by how it enters and operates in new markets and by the overall structure and design of its operations. There are a wide variety of entry strategies and organizational structures and designs from which to choose. Selecting the most appropriate strategy and structure depends on a number of factors, such as the desire of the home office for control over its foreign operations and the demands placed on the overseas unit by both the local market and the personnel who work there.

This chapter first discusses some entry strategies and systems of ownership which MNCs may have to choose from when deciding to expand abroad. With regard to the organization itself, the chapter presents and analyzes traditional organizational structures for effective international operations. Then it explores some of the new, nontraditional organizational arrangements stemming from mergers, joint ventures, and the Japanese concept of keiretsu. The specific objectives of this chapter are:

1. **DESCRIBE** how an MNC develops and implements entry strategies and ownership structures.

2. **EXAMINE** the major types of entry strategies and organizational structures used in handling international operations.

3. **ANALYZE** the advantages and disadvantages of each type of organizational structure, including the conditions that make one preferable to others.

4. **DESCRIBE** the recent, nontraditional organizational arrangements coming out of mergers, joint ventures, keiretsus, and other new designs including electronic networks and product development structures.

5. **EXPLAIN** how organizational characteristics such as formalization, specialization, and centralization influence how the organization is structured and functions.

The World of *BusinessWeek*

BusinessWeek

Gazprom Loosens Its Grip

Nine Months After Stating It Would Develop the Shtokman Field Alone, the Russian Giant Has Made a Deal with France's Total, and Hints at Others

A change of heart. That's the first phrase that springs to mind after news that Russia's Gazprom is once again selecting foreign partners to help it develop Shtokman, a giant gas field beneath the Barents Sea.

On July 13, Gazprom signed a deal with French oil giant Total that will leave full ownership of Shtokman in Gazprom's hands but give Total a 25% stake in an operating company that will finance the exploration and build the infrastructure for extracting and transporting gas. It's significant that the unusual structure will allow Total to show a quarter of Shtokman's reserves on its books. Such booked reserves are an important element in investors' valuations of oil and gas companies.

Gazprom has also said that it may offer an additional 24% of the project to other foreign investors. The announcement comes just nine months after Gazprom declared that it would develop Shtokman alone, breaking off years of negotiations with potential foreign participants in the project.

Breakthrough Technologies Needed

Gazprom's about-face over Shtokman is just the latest reminder of Russia's unpredictable ways—though it's less surprising than the earlier plan to go it alone. Analysts have said all along that Gazprom would need foreign expertise to develop the field, which will require some $20 billion in investment to extract an estimated 3.7 trillion cubic meters of gas.

"It's impossible for Gazprom to commission such a large field, in a very harsh environment, and located offshore, where Russia has very little experience. They need breakthrough technologies," says Valery Nesterov, oil and gas analyst at Troika Dialog, an investment bank in Moscow.

The decision to admit Total into the project is also consistent with the overall pattern now emerging in Russia's energy sector. In recent years the country has re-nationalized much of the industry, squeezing foreign investors out of majority ownership of big projects. But it has also signaled a willingness to admit foreigners as junior partners to the two big state energy players, Gazprom and Rosneft.

Shell on the Scene

There's plenty of evidence that major foreign investors are happy to play by the new rules. The Shtokman deal is the third major partnership between a Western energy company and a Russian state corporation announced in as many weeks. On June 22, Gazprom reached a deal with British Petroleum to settle a long-running dispute over the Kovykta oil and gas field in Siberia, under which Gazprom and BP formed a global partnership to explore joint energy projects.

Then, on July 9, Shell and Rosneft, Russia's state oil company, announced that they were forming a strategic partnership to develop oil projects in Russia. Shell is already partners with Gazprom in the Sakhalin 2 oil and gas project in the Pacific, after Shell was pressured to sell a controlling interest in the project to Gazprom last December. Shell retained a 25% stake in the project, with a further 24% held by two Japanese companies, Mitsui and Mitsubishi.

Not Angry Anymore

The news that Gazprom is now softening its position over Shtokman is therefore consistent with Russia's strategy elsewhere. "All the recent deals show that Russia is getting tougher on foreign investors, but on the other hand the rules of the game are becoming more transparent and predictable," says Nesterov. It's a model Russia is expected to follow in the future, too, particularly as it moves to develop far-flung offshore fields in the Arctic Ocean and the Pacific, from which much of its future energy growth will come.

For foreign energy companies eager to replace their dwindling reserves, a minority stake in a huge Russian project is a big consolation prize for playing a junior role. Hence the shock last October when Gazprom announced that it would keep Shtokman all to itself. That decision appears to have been prompted in part by pique over the refusal of European governments to support Russia's ambitions to increase its stake in EADS, the pan-European aerospace concern.

It's a reminder, also, of the extent to which big investments in Russian energy are tied into international politics—one reason the rules of the game are never likely to be 100% clear for foreign investors, even though the broad outlines of Russia's energy policy are becoming more apparent. Some commentators have attributed the decision to invite Total into the Shtokman project to personal talks between Putin and new French President Nikolas Sarkozy.

What About the U.S.?

Putin may have figured that the election of a new French leader was a good chance to mend fences with a major European country at a time when Russia's foreign relations have become strained with the West. "Company managements don't often know themselves what's going to happen, because the end decision might have more of a political element to it than a commercial one," says Chris Weafer, chief strategist at Russia's Alfa Bank.

In particular, it's still not clear whether Russia's change of heart also extends to U.S. companies Chevron and ConocoPhilips that also had been negotiating for inclusion in the Shtokman project. Originally they seemed destined for major roles, with Russia eager to ship Shtokman's gas, in liquid form, to the East Coast of the U.S.

Yet last year, amid disagreements with the U.S. over Russia's bid to join the World Trade Organization, Russia abruptly changed its plans and announced that it would ship all of Shtokman's gas to Europe. Gazprom's latest announcement hints that a liquefied natural gas project may once again be back on the agenda, but the details are still sketchy.

The recent deals suggest that European companies may have a head start when it comes to developing relationships with Russia's expanding state energy companies. Strained political relations between Russia and the U.S. mean that U.S. investors may not receive as warm a welcome.

By Jason Bush

The opening story is a good example of the entry and organizational challenges a company may face when looking to expand overseas. Gazprom stated that it intended to build the Shtokman project alone after growing weary of endless negotiations, but it soon found that limited capital and technology, along with little knowledge of developing such an expansive project in an offshore environment, would require the company to seek outside assistance. Gazprom has used this strategy before as it partnered with both Shell and BP for various gas and oil projects, although in each case Gazprom has backed away from its commitments. Russia's strong position as a leading source of increasingly valuable energy assets puts it in a strong negotiating position in influencing the terms of foreign companies' entry strategies and operational structures in Russia (see Chapter 7 for more on negotiation). As a result, Gazpron often retains full control and ownership of organizations created through these joint ventures with the help of strong political influence by the Russian government (a topic reviewed in Chapter 10). While some contracts are not completely traditional, since Gazprom may fully own the subsidiary and only offer a 25 percent interest to the partnering company, the agreements benefit both organizations to some extent. Total may not own any of the gas extracted from Shtokman, but it will recognize returns if it decides to invest in the project. Allowing Gazprom to have control over managerial decisions in Shtokman may put Total at risk, but simply turning down the agreement could leave Total with nothing, especially if other companies are interested in the contract. There are advantages and disadvantages to all parties involved, regardless of the specific strategy chosen. The next section introduces some of these strategies and structures, and their positive and negative implications.

■ Entry Strategies and Ownership Structures

There are a number of common entry strategies and ownership structures in international operations. The most common entry approaches are wholly owned subsidiaries, mergers and acquisitions, alliances and joint ventures, licensing agreements, franchising, and basic export and import operations. Depending on the situation, any one of these can be a very effective way to implement an MNC's strategy. We first look at exporting and importing, since it is not only one of the oldest approaches, but one that requires the least investment by the MNC.

Export/Import

As noted in the discussion in Chapter 8 on international entrepreneurship and new ventures, exporting and importing often are the only available choices for small and new firms wanting to go international.[1] These choices also provide an avenue for larger firms that want to begin their international expansion with a minimum of investment. The paperwork associated with documentation and foreign-currency exchange can be turned over to an export management company to handle, or the firm can handle things itself by creating its own export department. The firm can turn to major banks or other specialists that, for a fee, will provide a variety of services, including letters of credit, currency conversion, and related financial assistance.

A number of potential problems face firms that plan to export. For example, if a foreign distributor does not work out well, some countries have strict rules about dropping that distributor. So an MNC with a contractual agreement with a distributor could be stuck with that distributor. If the firm decides to get more actively involved, it may make direct investments in marketing facilities, such as warehouses, sales offices, and transportation equipment, without making a direct investment in manufacturing facilities overseas.

When importing goods, many MNCs make deals with overseas suppliers that can provide a wide assortment. It is common to find U.S. firms purchasing supplies and components from Korea, Taiwan, and Hong Kong. In Europe, there is so much trade between EU countries that the entire process seldom is regarded as "international" in focus by the MNCs that are involved.

Exporting and importing can provide easy access to overseas markets; however, the strategy usually is transitional in nature. If the firm continues to do international business, it will get more actively involved in terms of investment.

Wholly Owned Subsidiary

A **wholly owned subsidiary** is an overseas operation that is totally owned and controlled by an MNC. This option is often pursued by smaller companies, especially if international or transaction costs, such as the cost of negotiating and transferring information, are high.[2]

The primary reason for the use of fully owned subsidiaries is a desire by the MNC for total control and the belief that managerial efficiency will be better without outside partners. Due to the sole ownership, it has been found that profits can be higher with this venture and that there are clearer communications and shared visions. However, there are some drawbacks. Typically, wholly owned subsidiaries face a high risk with such a large investment in one area and are not very efficient with entering multiple countries or markets. This can also lead to low international integration or multinational involvement.[3] Furthermore, host countries often feel that the MNC is trying to gain economic control by setting up local operations but refusing to take in local partners. Some countries are concerned that the MNC will drive out local enterprises. In dealing with these concerns, many newly developing countries prohibit fully owned subsidiaries. Another drawback is that home-country unions sometimes oppose the creation of foreign subsidiaries, which they see as an attempt to "export jobs," particularly when the MNC exports goods to another country and then decides to set up manufacturing operations there. As a result, today many multinationals opt for a merger, alliance, or joint venture rather than a fully owned subsidiary.[4]

wholly owned subsidiary
An overseas operation that is totally owned and controlled by an MNC.

Mergers/Acquisitions

In recent years, a growing number of multinationals have acquired (fully or in part) their subsidiaries through **mergers/acquisitions.** MNCs may choose this route in order to quickly expand resources or construct high-profit products in a new market.[5] Purchasing a majority interest in another company is an expedient way to expand. For example, when Procter & Gamble (P&G) purchased Gillette for $57 billion, P&G gained a large portion of the market share as the company grew by 20 percent.[6] While this example illustrates two companies that reside in the same country, international agreements can yield similar results, as seen in the opening case at the beginning of the chapter.

A cross-border example is British Petroleum's (BP) acquisition of Amoco for $48.2 billion.[7] A string of international acquisitions and mergers once made BP one of the largest and most profitable companies in the world.[8] Despite turmoil in the North American market, including a 2005 refinery blast in Texas and oil spills in Alaska, the company still remains promising as it works toward improving operations.[9] Although cross-border mergers and acquisitions remain a popular strategy for entering international markets, the challenges of premerger agreements and postmerger integration are substantial. Cultural differences (see Chapter 6) and time constraints are the two most pervasive barriers.[10] Even before agreements are reached, time is of great concern. While managers do not want to force negotiations or rush a potential subsidiary's decision, waiting too long could result in missed opportunities due to bids from competitors or a rapid change in the market. Once a merger or acquisition occurs, managers may find it difficult to clearly communicate new operational goals to the foreign subsidiary, which not only highlights cultural differences but also adds time to a company's activities.

merger/acquisition
The cross-border purchase or exchange of equity involving two or more companies.

Transition costs also pose a problem in the postmerger environment. In 2006, France telecommunication company Alcatel merged with U.S. telecommunication company Lucent in an $11.6 billion deal. Alcatel-Lucent, which provides hardware, software, and services in the telecommunication industry, exhibited a disappointing $460 million loss in early 2007. This counteracted the original purpose of the merger, namely to deflect worldwide competition, since other companies such as Ericsson had been experiencing a gain in profits and were then better equipped to weaken the already stumbling newborn. Alcatel-Lucent attributes the loss to postmerger complications due to heavy investments which were necessary to migrate customer networks. The future of this company is bleak for the moment, as the quarter resulted in a 9.3 percent drop in share price, so managers need to be wary of such common complications and attempt to move forward by increasing communication and operational efficiency.[11]

Alliances and Joint Ventures

alliance
Any type of cooperative relationship among different firms.

joint venture (JV)
An agreement under which two or more partners own or control a business.

An **alliance** is any type of cooperative relationship among different firms. An international alliance is comprised of two or more firms from different countries. Some alliances are temporary; others are more permanent. A **joint venture (JV)** can be considered a specific type of alliance agreement under which two or more partners own or control a business. An international joint venture (IJV) is a JV comprised of two or more firms from different countries. Alliances and joint ventures can take a number of different forms, including cross-marketing arrangements, technology-sharing agreements, production-contracting deals, and equity agreements. In some instances, two parties may create a third, independent entity expressly for the purpose of developing a collaborative relationship outside their core companies. Alliances and joint ventures, like mergers and acquisitions, can pose substantial managerial challenges. We discuss some of these at the end of the chapter and again in Chapter 10.

There are two types of alliances and joint ventures. The first type is the *nonequity venture,* which is characterized by one group's merely providing a service for another. The group providing the service typically is more active than the other. Examples include a consulting firm that is hired to provide analysis and evaluation and then make its recommendations to the other party, an engineering or construction firm that contracts to design or build a dam or series of apartment complexes in an undeveloped area of a partner's country, or a mining firm that has an agreement to extract a natural resource in the other party's country.

The second type is the *equity joint venture,* which involves a financial investment by the MNC in a business enterprise with a local partner. Many variations of this arrangement adjust the degree of control that each of the parties will have and the amount of money, technological expertise, and managerial expertise each will contribute.[12]

Most foreign firms are more interested in the amount of control they will have over the venture than in their share of the profits. Many local partners feel the same way, and this can result in problems. Nevertheless, alliances and joint ventures have become very popular in recent years because of the benefits they offer to both parties. Some of the most commonly cited advantages include:

1. *Improvement of efficiency.* The creation of an alliance or joint venture can help the partners achieve economies of scale and scope that would be difficult for one firm operating alone to accomplish. Additionally, the partners can spread the risks among themselves and profit from the synergies that arise from the complementarity of their resources.[13]

2. *Access to knowledge.* In alliances and joint ventures each partner has access to the knowledge and skills of the others. So one partner may bring financial and technological resources to the venture while another brings knowledge of the customer and market channels.

3. *Political factors.* A local partner can be very helpful in dealing with political risk factors such as a hostile government or restrictive legislation.

4. *Collusion or restriction in competition.* Alliances and joint ventures can help partners overcome the effects of local collusion or limits that are being put on foreign competition. By becoming part of an "insider" group, foreign partners manage to transcend these barriers.[14]

As noted above, alliance and joint-venture partners often complement each other and can thus reduce the risks associated with their undertaking. A good example is European truck manufacturing and auto component industries. Firms in both groups have found that the high cost of developing and building their products can be offset through joint ventures. In particular, some partners to these ventures have contributed financial assistance, while others provide the distribution networks needed to move the product through channels. In March 2004, the joint venture between Alcatel and Fujitsu was awarded a $500 million contract to build a submarine cable network connecting Southeast Asia, the Middle East, and Western Europe.[15] Sharing risks, resources, and capabilities can often position two companies to gain more success together than alone.

Although much negotiation may be necessary before an alliance or joint-venture agreement is hammered out, the final result must be one that both sides can accept.[16] Many successful examples of such agreements have emerged in recent years. One of the most complex was the General Motors–Toyota agreement, which involved scores of groups and thousands of individuals. Other examples include General Motors's venture with the Polish government to build Opels in Poland, L.L.Bean's decision to sell clothing and equipment under a joint-venture agreement with two Japanese companies in Tokyo, Occidental Petroleum's joint venture in a northern China coal mining project, and Sony and America Online's joint venture for linking Sony's PlayStation 2 video game machine to the Internet.[17]

Alliances and joint ventures are proving to be particularly popular as a means for doing business in emerging-market economies. For example, in the early 1990s, foreigners signed more than 3,000 joint-venture agreements in Eastern Europe and the former republics of the Soviet Union, and interest remains high today. Careful analysis must be undertaken to ensure that the market for the desired goods and services is sufficiently large, that all parties understand their responsibilities, and that all are in agreement regarding the overall operation of the venture. If these problems can be resolved, the venture stands a good chance of success. "International Management in Action: Joint Venturing in Russia" illustrates some of the problems that need to be overcome for a joint venture to be successful. Some of the other suggestions that have been offered by researchers regarding participation in strategic alliances include:

1. Know your partners well before an alliance is formed.

2. Expect differences in alliance objectives among potential partners headquartered in different countries.

3. Realize that having the desired resource profiles does not guarantee that they are complementary to your firm's resources.

4. Be sensitive to your alliance partner's needs.

5. After identifying the best partner, work on developing a relationship that is built on trust, an especially important variable in some cultures.[18]

Licensing

Another way to gain market entry, which may also be considered a form of alliance, is to acquire the right to a particular product by getting an exclusive license to make or sell the good in a particular geographic locale. A **license** is an agreement that

license
An agreement that allows one party to use an industrial property right in exchange for payment to the other party.

Joint Venturing in Russia

Joint venturing is becoming an increasingly popular strategy for setting up international operations. Russia is particularly interested in these arrangements because of the benefits they offer for attracting foreign capital and helping the country tap its natural resource wealth. However, investors are finding that joint venturing in Russia and the other republics of the former Soviet Union can be fraught with problems. For example, Royal Dutch Shell was recently pressured to give up its majority stake in Sakhalin Island to Gazprom. In addition, BP has been forced to renegotiate its contracts with its Russian joint-venture partner, TNK. New laws will require foreign investors interested in Russian energy projects to pair with Kremlin-approved organizations, further empowering the Russian company and government. Kremlin power is not the only problem facing joint-venture investors in Russia. Others include the following:

1. Many Russian partners view a joint venture as an opportunity to travel abroad and gain access to foreign currency; the business itself often is given secondary consideration.

2. Finding a suitable partner, negotiating the deal, and registering the joint venture often take up to a year, mainly because the Russians are unaccustomed to some of the basic steps in putting together business deals.

3. Russian partners typically try to expand joint ventures into unrelated activities.

4. Russians do not like to declare profits, because a two-year tax holiday on profits starts from the moment the first profits are declared.

5. The government sometimes allows profits to be repatriated in the form of counter-trade. However, much of what can be taken out of the country has limited value, because the government keeps control of those resources that are most salable in the world market.

These representative problems indicate why there is reluctance on the part of some MNCs to enter into joint ventures in Russia. As one of them recently put it, "The country may well turn into an economic sink hole." As a result, many MNCs are wary of potential contracts and are proceeding with caution.

allows one party to use an industrial property right in exchange for payment to the other party. In a typical arrangement, the party giving the license (the licensor) will allow the other (the licensee) to use a patent, a trademark, or proprietary information in exchange for a fee. The fee usually is based on sales, such as 1 percent of all revenues earned from an industrial motor sold in Asia. The licensor typically restricts licensee sales to a particular geographic locale and limits the time period covered by the arrangement. The firm in this example may have an exclusive right to sell this patented motor in Asia for the next five years. This allows the licensor to seek licensees for other major geographic locales, such as Europe, South America, and Australia.

Licensing is used under a number of common conditions. For example, the product typically is in the mature stage of the product life cycle, competition is strong, and profit margins are declining. Under these conditions, the licensor is unlikely to want to spend money to enter foreign markets. However, if the company can find an MNC that is already there and willing to add the product to its own current offerings, both sides can benefit from the arrangement. A second common instance of licensing is evident when foreign governments require newly entering firms to make a substantial direct investment in the country. By licensing to a firm already there, the licensee avoids entry costs. A third common condition is that the licensor usually is a small firm that lacks financial and managerial resources. Finally, companies that spend a relatively large share of their revenues on research and development (R&D) are likely to be licensors, and those that spend very little on R&D are more likely to be licensees. In fact, some small R&D firms make a handsome profit every year by developing and licensing new products to large firms with diversified product lines.

Some licensors use their industrial property rights to develop and sell goods in certain areas of the world and license others to handle other geographic locales. This provides the licensor with a source of additional revenues, but the license usually is not good for much more than a decade. This is a major disadvantage of licensing. In particular, if the product is very good, the competition will develop improvement patents that allow it to sell similar goods or even new patents that make the current product obsolete. Nevertheless, for the period during which the agreement is in effect, a license can be a very low-cost way of gaining and exploiting foreign markets. Table 9–1 provides some comparisons between licensing and joint ventures and summarizes the major advantages and disadvantages of each.

Franchising

Closely related to licensing is franchising. A **franchise** is a business arrangement under which one party (the franchisor) allows another (the franchisee) to operate an enterprise using its trademark, logo, product line, and methods of operation in return for a fee. Franchising is widely used in the fast-food and hotel-motel industries. The concept is very adaptable to the international arena, and with some minor adjustments for the local market, it can result in a highly profitable business. In fast foods, McDonald's, Burger King, and Kentucky Fried Chicken have used franchise arrangements to expand their markets from Paris to Tokyo and from Cairo to Caracas. In the hotel business, Holiday Inn, among others, has been very successful in gaining worldwide presence through the effective use of franchisees.

Franchise agreements typically require payment of a fee up front and then a percentage of the revenues. In return, the franchisor provides assistance and, in some instances, may require the purchase of goods or supplies to ensure the same quality of goods or services worldwide. Franchising can be beneficial to both groups: It provides the franchisor with a new stream of income and the franchisee with a time-proven concept and products or services that can be quickly brought to market.

franchise
A business arrangement under which one party (the franchisor) allows another (the franchisee) to operate an enterprise using its trademark, logo, product line, and methods of operation in return for a fee.

■ The Organization Challenge

A natural outgrowth of general international strategy formulation and implementation and specific decisions about how best to enter international markets is the question of how best to structure the organization for international operations. A number of MNCs have recently been rethinking their organizational approaches to international operations.

Dell computers was seen as number one in the PC industry for years, until it faced a series of challenges that resulted in management changes and a new CEO in 2004. Dell continued to focus on direct sales, technical offerings, and simple displays, ignoring the growing market of enhanced microprocessors and the use of portable laptops for entertainment value. Hewlett-Packard (HP), which sold its units in over 110,000 retail stores worldwide, became the world's largest computer maker in 2006, knocking Dell out of the number-one spot. Dell continued to lose market share until it made efforts to change the organization. Michael Dell, the company's founder, returned as CEO in 2007, and now Dell is attempting a face-lift. Customer service may be available in person, as opposed to the endless maze of technical service representatives, and computers are being offered in an array of colors, as opposed to the standard gray. Dell has also made agreements with numerous retail outlets to offer PCs in stores, including Wal-Mart for the U.S. market, Carphone Warehouse Group PLC in the U.K., and Bic Camera Inc. in Japan.[19] While it would seem that in the technological age it may be better for certain companies to solely offer products online, some consumers want to experience a PC before purchasing it, especially with the emphasis on entertainment. Hopefully Dell has not waited too long to change its organization

Table 9–1
Partial Comparison of Global Strategic Alliances

Strategy	Organization Design	Advantages	Disadvantages	Critical Success Factors	Strategic Human Resources Management
Licensing—manufacturing industries	Technologies	Early standardization of design; Ability to capitalize on innovations; Access to new technologies; Ability to control pace of industry evolution	New competitors created; Possible eventual exit from industry; Possible dependence on licensee	Selection of licensee unlikely to become a competitor; Enforcement of patents and licensing agreements	Technical knowledge; Training of local managers on-site
Licensing—servicing and franchises	Geography	Fast market entry; Low capital cost	Quality control; Trademark protection	Partners compatible in philosophies/values; Tight performance standards	Socialization of franchisees and licensees with core values
Joint ventures—specialization across partners	Function	Learning a partner's skills; Economies of scale; Quasivertical integration; Faster learning	Excessive dependence on partner for skills; Deterrent to internal investment	Tight and specific performance criteria; Entering a venture as "student" rather than "teacher" to learn skills from partner; Recognizing that collaboration is another form of competition to learn new skills	Management development and training; Negotiation skills; Managerial rotation
Joint venture—shared value-adding	Product or line of business	Strengths of both partners pooled; Faster learning along value chain; Fast upgrading of technologic skills	High switching costs; Inability to limit partner's access to information	Decentralization and autonomy from corporate parents; Long "courtship" period; Harmonization of management styles	Team-building; Acculturation; Flexible skills for implicit communication

Source: From David Lei and John W. Slocum Jr., "Global Strategic Alliances: Payoffs and Pitfalls," *Organizational Dynamics,* Winter 1991, p. 48. Copyright © 1991 Elsevier. Reprinted with permission.

and marketing strategies to more traditional methods, and can continue to be a major competitor without losing too much specialization.

Another example of worldwide reorganizing is provided by Coca-Cola, which now delegates a great deal of authority for operations to the local level. This move is designed to increase the ability of the worldwide divisions to respond to their local markets. As a result, decisions related to advertising, products, and packaging are handled by international division managers for their own geographic regions. As an example, in Turkey the regional division has introduced a new pear-flavored drink, while Coke's German operation launched a berry-flavored Fanta. This "local" approach was designed to help Coke improve its international reputation, although Coke's new management is rethinking some aspects of this approach in the face of increasing cost pressures.[20] Even so, Coke continues to diversify its offerings, despite an initial increase in cost. In Brazil, for example, Coke was losing market share as local soda companies were offering low-priced carbonated beverages. Coke offered only three bottle sizes, and simply cutting the price of those did not seem to gain anything for the company. Now, Coke offers 18 different sizes in Brazil, which include many reusable glass bottles that can be returned for credit. While this has not increased market share, it has boosted profits.[21]

A third example of how firms are meeting international challenges through reorganization is provided by Li & Fung, Hong Kong's largest export trading company and an innovator in the development of supply chain management. The company has global suppliers worldwide that are responsible for providing the firm with a wide range of consumer goods ranging from toys to fashion accessories to luggage. In recent years Li & Fung reorganized and now manages its day-to-day operations through a group of product managers who are responsible for their individual areas. This new organizational arrangement emerged in a series of steps. In the late 1970s, the company was a regional sourcing agent. Big international buyers would come to Li & Fung for assistance in getting materials and products because the MNC was familiar with the producers throughout Asia and it knew the complex government regulations and how to successfully work through them. The MNC then moved into a more sophisticated stage in which it began developing the entire process for the buyer from concept to prototype to delivery of the goods. By the late 1980s, however, Hong Kong had become a very expensive place to manufacture products, and Li & Fung changed its approach and began organizing around a new concept called "dispersed manufacturing," which draws heavily on dissection of the value chain and coordinating the operations of many suppliers in different geographic locations. For example, when the MNC receives an order from a European retailer to produce a large number of dresses, it has to decide where to buy the yarn in the world market, which companies should get the orders to weave and dye the cloth, where supplemental purchases such as buttons and zippers should be made, and how final shipment must be made to the customer. Commenting on this overall process, the company president noted:

> This is a new type of value added, a truly global product that has never been seen before. The label may say "Made in Thailand," but it's not a Thai product. We dissect the manufacturing process and look for the best solution at each step. We're not asking which country can do the best job overall. Instead, we're pulling apart the value chain and optimizing each step—and we're doing it globally. Not only do the benefits outweigh the costs of logistics and transportation, but the higher value added also lets us charge more for our services. We deliver a sophisticated product and we deliver it fast. If you talk to the big global consumer products companies, they are all moving in this direction—toward being best on a global scale.[22]

■ Basic Organizational Structures

The preceding examples of Dell, Coca-Cola, and Li & Fung show how MNCs are dramatically reorganizing their operations to compete more effectively in the international arena. As with other MNCs following this strategic route, a number of basic organization structures need to be considered. In many cases, the designs are similar to those used domestically; however, significant differences may arise depending on the nature and

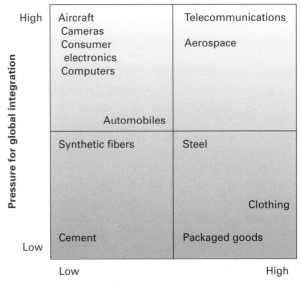

Source: Adapted from Paul W. Beamish, J. Peter Killing, Donald J. LeCraw, and Harold Crookell, *International Management: Text and Cases* (Homewood, IL: Irwin, 1991), p. 99.

scope of the overseas businesses and the home office's approach to controlling the operation. Ideally, an overseas affiliate or subsidiary will be designed to respond to specific concerns, such as production technology or the need for specialized personnel. The overall goal, however, is to meet the needs of both the local market and the home-office strategy of globalization.

Figure 9–1 illustrates how the pressures for global integration and local responsiveness play out in a host of industries. As an MNC tries to balance these factors, an if-then contingency approach can be used. *If* the strategy needed to respond quickly to the local market changes, *then* there will be accompanying change in the organizational structure. Despite the need for such a flexible, fast-changing, contingency-based approach, most MNCs still slowly evolve through certain basic structural arrangements in international operations. The following sections examine these structures, beginning with initial, pre-international patterns.[23]

Initial Division Structure

Many firms make their initial entry into international markets by setting up a subsidiary or by exporting locally produced goods or services. A subsidiary is a common organizational arrangement for handling finance-related businesses or other operations that require an on-site presence from the start. In recent years, many service organizations have begun exporting their expertise. Examples include architectural services, legal services, advertising, public relations, accounting, and management consulting. Research and development firms also fall into this category, exporting products that have been successfully developed and marketed locally.

An export arrangement is a common first choice among manufacturing firms, especially those with technologically advanced products. Because there is little, if any, competition, the firm can charge a premium price and handle sales through an export manager. If the company has a narrow product line, the export manager usually reports directly to the head of marketing, and international operations are coordinated by this department. If the firm has a broad product line and intends to export a number of different products into the international market, the export manager will head a separate department and often report directly to the president. These two arrangements work well as long as the company has little competition and is using international sales only to supplement domestic efforts.

If overseas sales continue to increase, local governments often exert pressure in these growing markets for setting up on-site manufacturing operations. A good example is the General Motors joint venture in China, where a large percentage of all parts are made locally. Additionally, many firms find themselves facing increased competition. Establishing foreign manufacturing subsidiaries can help the MNC deal with both local government pressures and the competition. The overseas plants show the government that the firm wants to be a good local citizen. At the same time, these plants help the MNC greatly reduce transportation costs, thus making the product more competitive. This new structural arrangement often takes a form similar to that shown in Figure 9–2. Each foreign subsidiary is responsible for operations within its own geographic area, and the head of the subsidiary reports either to a senior executive who is coordinating international operations or directly to the home-office CEO.

International Division Structure

If international operations continue to grow, subsidiaries commonly are grouped into an **international division structure,** which handles all international operations out of a division that is created for this purpose. In other words, a unit is added on simply to deal with international issues, while the original organizational structure is left intact. This structural arrangement is useful as it takes a great deal of the burden off the chief executive officer for monitoring the operations of a series of overseas subsidiaries as well as domestic operations. The head of the international division coordinates and monitors overseas activities and reports directly to the chief executive on these matters. Figure 9–3 provides an example. PepsiCo reorganized its international soft drink division into six such geographic business units covering 150 countries in which Pepsi does business. Each geographic unit has self-sufficient operations and broad local authority.

Companies still in the developmental stages of international business involvement are most likely to adopt the international division structure. Others that use this structural arrangement include those with small international sales, limited geographic diversity, or few executives with international expertise.

A number of advantages are associated with use of an international division structure. The grouping of international activities under one senior executive ensures that the international focus receives top management attention. The structural arrangement allows the company to develop an overall, unified approach to international operations, and the arrangement helps the firm develop a cadre of internationally experienced managers.

Use of this structure does have a number of drawbacks, however. The structure separates the domestic and international managers, which can result in two different camps with divergent objectives. Also, as the international operation grows larger,

international division structure
A structural arrangement that handles all international operations out of a division created for this purpose.

Figure 9–3

An International Division Structure

(Partial Organization Chart)

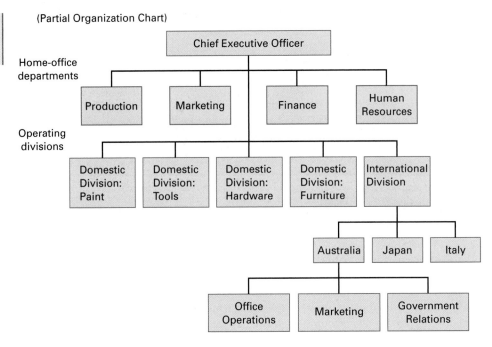

the home office may find it difficult to think and act strategically and to allocate resources on a global basis; thus, the international division is penalized. Finally, most research and development efforts are domestically oriented, so ideas for new products or processes in the international market often are given low priority.

Global Structural Arrangements

MNCs typically turn to global structural arrangements when they begin acquiring and allocating their resources based on international opportunities and threats. The global structural arrangement differs from the international division structure because while both have an international scope, the former focuses on greater expansion and integration. This international perspective signifies a major change in management strategy, and it is supported by the requisite changes in organization structure. It is important to remember that a structural framework is chosen only after the basic strategy is formulated, not vice versa. Global structures come in three common types: product, area, and functional.

global product division
A structural arrangement in which domestic divisions are given worldwide responsibility for product groups.

Global Product Division   A **global product division** is a structural arrangement in which domestic divisions are given worldwide responsibility for product groups. Figure 9–4 provides an illustration. As shown, the manager who is in charge of product division C has authority for this product line on a global basis. This manager also has internal functional support related to the product line. For example, all marketing, production, and finance activities associated with product division C are under the control of this manager.

The global product divisions operate as profit centers. The products generally are in the growth stage of the product life cycle, so they need to be promoted and marketed carefully. In doing so, global product division managers generally run the operation with considerable autonomy; they have the authority to make many important decisions. However, corporate headquarters usually will maintain control in terms of budgetary constraints, home-office approval for certain decisions, and mainly "bottom-line" (i.e., profit) results.

A global product structure provides the most benefits when the need for product specification or differentiation is high. This often occurs when companies offer a variety of products, the customer base is extremely diverse, or goods must be modified to match

(Partial Organization Chart)

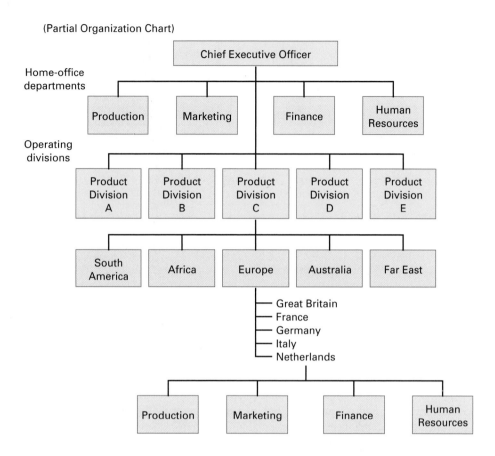

Figure 9–4

A Global Product Division Structure

local tastes (e.g. food or toys). Creating divisions which specialize in each product set results in efficient alterations, especially since marketing, production and finance can be coordinated on a product-by-product basis. Furthermore, if a product is in a different life cycle (mature vs. growth stage) across regions, in the global product divisions can ensure that each location responds appropriately. Other advantages of a global product division structure can be summarized as follows:

> It preserves product emphasis and promotes product planning on a global basis; it provides a direct line of communication from the customer to those in the organization who have product knowledge and expertise, thus enabling research and development to work on development of products that serve the needs of the world customer; and it permits line and staff managers within the division to gain an expertise in the technical and marketing aspects of products assigned to them.[24]

Unfortunately, the approach also has some drawbacks. One is the necessity of duplicating facilities and staff personnel within each division. A second is that division managers may pursue currently attractive geographic prospects for their products and neglect other areas with better long-term potential. A third is that many division managers spend too much time trying to tap the local rather than the international market, because it is more convenient and they are more experienced in domestic operations.

Global Area Division   Instead of a global product division, some MNCs prefer to use a **global area division.** In this structure, illustrated in Figure 9–5, global operations are organized based on a geographic rather than a product orientation. This approach often signals a major change in company strategy, because now international operations are put on the same level as domestic operations. In other words, European or Asian operations are just as important to the company as North American operations.

global area division
A structure under which global operations are organized on a geographic rather than a product basis.

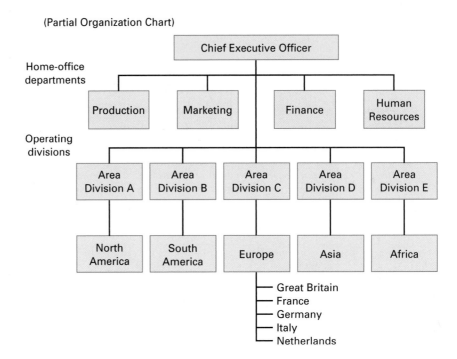

(Partial Organization Chart)

For example, when British Petroleum purchased Standard Oil of Ohio, the firm revised its overall structure and adopted a global area division structure. Under this arrangement, global division managers are responsible for all business operations in their designated geographic area. The chief executive officer and other members of top management are charged with formulating strategy that ensures that the global divisions all work in harmony.

A global area division structure most often is used by companies that are in mature businesses and have narrow product lines. These product lines often are differentiated based on geographic area. For example, the product has a strong demand in Europe but not in South America, or the type of product that is offered in France differs from that sold in England. This is different from the global product divisions because each division focuses on regional tastes and offers specialized products for and within that area, as opposed to focusing on a product set and discovering where it can survive and subsequently distributing it to that region. In addition, the MNC usually seeks high economies of scale for production, marketing, and resource-purchase integration in that area. Thus, by manufacturing in this region rather than bringing the product in from somewhere else, the firm is able to reduce cost per unit and get the good to market at a very competitive price. The geographic structure allows the division manager to cater to the tastes of the local market and make rapid decisions to accommodate environmental changes. A good example is food products. In the United States, soft drinks have less sugar than in South America, so the manufacturing process must be slightly different in these two locales. Similarly, in England, people prefer bland soups, but in France, the preference is for mildly spicy. In Turkey, Italy, Spain, and Portugal, people like dark, bitter coffee; in the United States, people prefer a milder, sweeter blend. In Europe, Canada, and the United States, people prefer less spicy food; in the Middle East and Asia, they like more heavily spiced food. A global area structure allows the geographic unit in a foods company to accommodate such local preferences.

The primary disadvantage of the global area division structure is the difficulty encountered in reconciling a product emphasis with a geographic orientation. For example, if a product is sold worldwide, a number of different divisions are responsible for sales. This lack of centralized management and control can result in increased

(Partial Organization Chart)

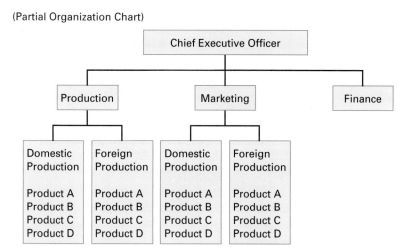

Figure 9–6

A Global Functional Structure

costs and duplication of effort on a region-by-region basis. A second drawback is that new research and development efforts often are ignored by division groups because they are selling goods that have reached the maturity stage. Their focus is not on the latest technologically superior goods that will win in the market in the long run but on those that are proven winners and now are being marketed conveniently worldwide.

Global Functional Division

A **global functional division** organizes worldwide operations based primarily on function and secondarily on product. This approach is not widely used other than by extractive companies, such as oil and mining firms. Figure 9–6 provides an example.

A number of important advantages are associated with the global functional division structure. These include (1) an emphasis on functional expertise, (2) tight centralized control, and (3) a relatively lean managerial staff. There also are some important disadvantages: (1) Coordination of manufacturing and marketing often is difficult; (2) managing multiple product lines can be very challenging because of the separation of production and marketing into different departments; and (3) only the chief executive officer can be held accountable for the profits. As a result, the global functional process structure typically is favored only by firms that need tight, centralized coordination and control of integrated production processes and firms that are involved in transporting products and raw materials from one geographic area to another.

global functional division
A structure that organizes worldwide operations primarily based on function and secondarily on product.

Mixed Organization Structures

Some companies find that neither a global product, an area, or a functional arrangement is satisfactory. They opt for a **mixed organization structure,** which combines all three into an MNC that supplements its primary structure with a secondary one and, perhaps, a tertiary one. For example, if a company uses a global area approach, committees of functional managers may provide assistance and support to the various geographic divisions. Conversely, if the firm uses a global functional approach, product committees may be responsible for coordinating transactions that cut across functional lines. In other cases, the organization will opt for a matrix structure that results in managers' having two or more bosses. Figure 9–7 illustrates this structure. In this arrangement, the MNC coordinates geographic and product lines through use of a matrix design.

In recent years, mixed organization structures have become increasingly popular. Sony's electronic businesses, including personal computers and cable-television set-top boxes, have been unified in one group. The company has also created a new division that will focus exclusively on the mobile phone business. In addition, the firm has

mixed organization structure
A structure that is a combination of a global product, area, or functional arrangement.

(Partial Organization Chart)

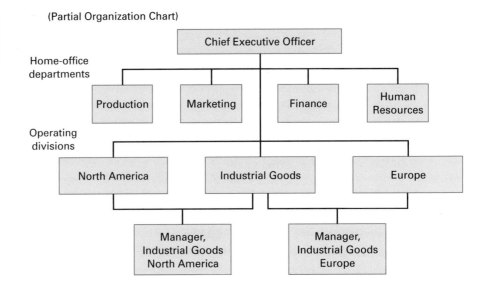

created a management group called the "Global Hub" that will coordinate strategy across a host of Sony units including financial services, games, Internet services, and entertainment. Quite clearly, the company feels that it needs a mixed structure in order to juggle all its worldwide holdings. Many other companies use a mixed structure, and one survey has found that more than one-third of the responding firms employ this organizational arrangement while nearly one-fifth utilize global product divisions and only about one-tenth exhibit initial division structures. Many advantages can be gleaned from a mixed organization structure. In particular, it allows the organization to create the specific type of design that best meets its needs. However, there are shortcomings associated with matrix structures. The most important is that as the matrix design's complexity increases, coordinating the personnel and getting everyone to work toward common goals often become difficult; too many groups go their own way. Thus, many MNCs have not opted for a matrix structure; they have found that simple, lean structures are the best design for them.

Transnational Network Structures

transnational network
structure
A multinational structural
arrangement that combines
elements of function,
product, and geographic
designs, while relying on a
network arrangement to
link worldwide
subsidiaries.

Besides matrix structures, another alternative international organizational design to recently emerge is the **transnational network structure.** This is designed to help MNCs take advantage of global economies of scale while also being responsive to local customer demands. The design combines elements of classic functional, product, and geographic structures while relying on a network arrangement to link the various worldwide subsidiaries. This configuration may appear very similar to the matrix, but it is much more complex. While the matrix may use more than one strategy to supplement inefficient operations, it is still fairly centralized in the sense that decisions are balanced between the main headquarters and international subsidiaries. Transnational networks, however, are convoluted integrations of business functions and communications where decisions are made at the local level, but each grouping informs headquarters and sometimes each other. At the center of the transnational network structure are nodes, which are units charged with coordinating product, functional, and geographic information. Different product line units and geographical area units have different structures depending on what is best for their particular operations. A good example of how the transnational network structure works is provided by N.V. Philips, which has operations in more than 60 countries and produces a diverse product line ranging from light bulbs to defense systems. In all, the company has eight product divisions with a varying number of subsidiaries in each—

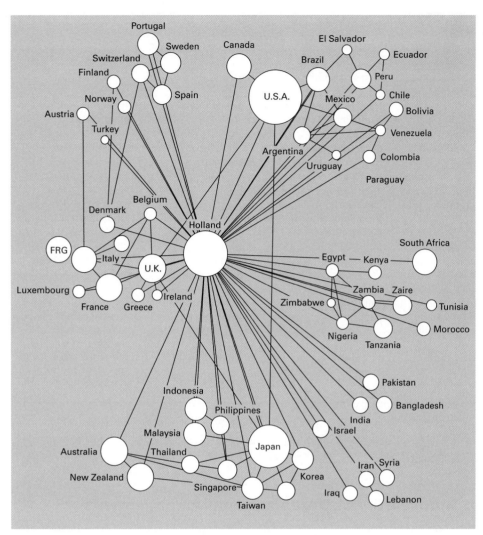

Source: See S. Ghoshal and C. A. Bartlett, "The Multinational Corporation as an Interorganizational Network," *Academy of Management Review,* October 1990, pp. 603–625.

and the focus of these subsidiaries varies considerably. Some specialize in manufacturing, others in sales; some are closely controlled by headquarters, and others are highly autonomous.

The basic structural framework of the transnational network consists of three components: dispersed subunits, specialized operations, and interdependent relationships. *Dispersed subunits* are subsidiaries that are located anywhere in the world where they can benefit the organization. Some are designed to take advantage of low factor costs, while others are responsible for providing information on new technologies or consumer trends. *Specialized operations* are activities carried out by subunits that focus on particular product lines, research areas, and marketing areas, and are designed to tap specialized expertise or other resources in the company's worldwide subsidiaries. *Interdependent relationships* are used to share information and resources throughout the dispersed and specialized subunits.

The transnational network structure is difficult to draw in the form of an organization chart because it is complex and continually changing. However, Figure 9–8 provides a view of N.V. Philips's network structure. These complex networks can be compared to some of the others that have been examined earlier in this chapter by looking

Table 9–2
Control Mechanisms Used in Select Multinational Organization Structures

Type of Multinational Structure	Output Control	Bureaucratic Control	Decision-Making Control	Cultural Control
International division structure	Profit control.	Have to follow company policies.	Typically there is some centralization.	Treated like all other divisions.
Global area division	Use of profit centers.	Some policies and procedures are necessary.	Local units are given autonomy.	Local subsidiary culture is often the most important.
Global product division	Unit output for supply; sales volume for sales.	Tight process controls are used to maintain product quality and consistency.	Centralized at the product-division headquarters level.	Possible for some companies, but not always necessary.
Matrix structure	Profit responsibility is shared with product and geographic units.	Not very important.	Balanced between the global area and product units.	Culture must support the shared decision making.
Transnational network structure	Used for supplier units and for some independent profit centers.	Not very important.	Few decisions are centralized at headquarters; most are centralized in the key network nodes.	Organization culture transcends national cultures, supports sharing and learning, and is the most important control mechanism.

at the ways in which the enterprise attempts to exercise control. Table 9–2 provides such a comparison.

■ Nontraditional Organizational Arrangements

In recent years, MNCs have increasingly expanded their operations in ways that differ from those used in the past. These include acquisitions, joint ventures, keiretsus, and strategic alliances. These organizational arrangements do not use traditional hierarchical structures and therefore cannot be shown graphically. The following sections describe how they work.

Organizational Arrangements from Mergers and Acquisitions

A recent development affecting the way that MNCs are organized is the increased use of mergers and acquisitions (M&As). In recent years, the annual value of worldwide M&As has reached as high as $6 trillion! One reason for this large figure is that a growing number of major MNCs are merging with, or being acquired by, other giant multinationals. In the past decade, for example, British Petroleum acquired Amoco for $48.2 billion, while on a smaller scale Renault took over Samsung Motors for $350 million and the assumption of $200 million of Samsung debt.[25] In other cases, MNCs have taken an equity position but have not purchased the entire company. For example, Ford Motor owns 75 percent of Aston Martin Lagonda of Britain, 49 percent of Autolatina of Brazil, and 34 percent of Mazda of Japan.[26]

In each of these examples, the purchasing MNCs fashioned a structural arrangement that attempts to promote synergy while encouraging local initiative by the acquired firm. The result is an organization design that draws on the more traditional structures that have been examined here but still has a unique structure specifically addressing the needs of the two firms.

Organizational Arrangements from Joint Ventures and Strategic Alliances

Other examples of recent organizational arrangements include joint-venture and strategic alliance agreements in which each party contributes to the undertaking and coordinates its efforts for the overall benefit of the venture.[27] These arrangements can take a variety of forms,[28] although the steps that are followed in creating and operating them often have a fair amount of similarity.[29] One good example of a joint venture is CALICA, which has two partners: Vulcan Materials, the leading firm in the U.S. aggregate materials market, and Grupo ICA of Mexico.[30] Working together, the two companies coordinate their activities in mining, shipping, distributing, and marketing gravel for use in highway and building construction. Another example is provided by Coca-Cola and Procter & Gamble (P&G). Coke has run behind Pepsi in snacks and noncarbonated drinks and recently considered buying Quaker Oats in order to strengthen itself in these areas. However, the $16 billion sales price was too high, so Coke entered into a joint venture with P&G.

These joint ventures require carefully formulated structures that allow each partner to contribute what it does best and to coordinate their efforts efficiently. In the case of Coke and P&G, this calls for clearly spelling out the responsibilities of all parties and identifying the authority that each will have for meeting specific targets.[31]

One of the main objectives in developing the structure for joint ventures is to help the partners address and effectively meld their different values, management styles, action orientation, and organization preferences. Figure 9–9 illustrates how Western and Asian firms differ in these four areas; the figure also is useful for illustrating the types of considerations that need to be addressed by MNCs from the same area of the world. Consider, for example, Matsushita Electric Industrial and Hitachi Ltd. The two agreed to join forces to develop new technology in three areas: smart cards, home network systems, and recyclable and energy-efficient consumer electronics.[32] The two firms will need to structure their organizational interface carefully to ensure effective interaction, coordination, and cooperation.

Organizational Arrangements from Keiretsus

Still another type of newly emerging organizational arrangement is the **keiretsu,** which is a large, often vertically integrated group of companies that cooperate and work closely with each other. A good example is the Mitsubishi Group, a keiretsu that consists of companies that are bound together not by authority relationships but rather by cross-ownership, long-term business dealings, interlocking directorates, and social ties (many of the senior executives were college classmates). There are three flagship firms in the group: Mitsubishi Corporation, which is a trading company; Mitsubishi Bank, which finances the keiretsu's operations; and Mitsubishi Heavy Industries, which is a leading worldwide manufacturer. In addition, hundreds of other Mitsubishi-related companies contribute to the power of the keiretsu.

The Japanese are not the only ones using this organizational arrangement. Large U.S. MNCs are creating their own type of keiretsus. Ford Motor, for example, now focuses its attention only on automotive and financial services and has divested itself of most other businesses. In the process of reorganizing, Ford has created a giant, keiretsu-like arrangement that includes research and development (R&D), parts production, vehicle assembly, financial services, and marketing. For example, in R&D, Ford belongs to eight consortia that conduct research in areas such as improved engineering techniques, materials, and electric-car batteries. In parts production, Ford has equity stakes in Cummins (engines), Excel Industries (windows), and Decoma International (body parts, wheels), and it relies on these firms as major suppliers. In vehicle assembly, Ford has ownership interests in Europe, South America, and Asia and uses these arrangements to both manufacture and sell autos in these parts of the world. In financial services, Ford has seven wholly owned units that cover a wide gamut, from consumer credit to commercial lending.

keiretsu
In Japan, an organizational arrangement in which a large, often vertically integrated group of companies cooperate and work closely with each other to provide goods and services to end users; members may be bound together by cross-ownership, long-term business dealings, interlocking directorates, and social ties.

Figure 9–9

A Comparison of Asian and Western Management Features

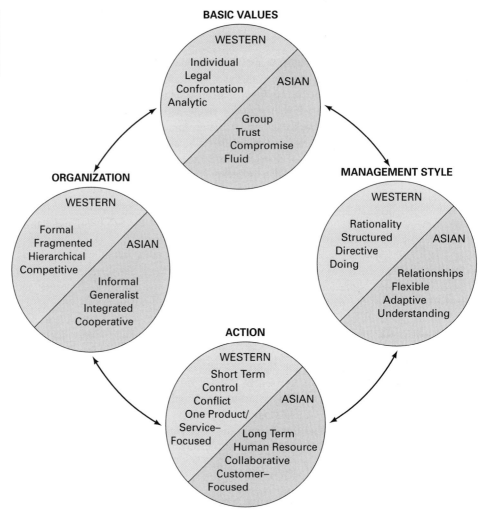

Source: From Frederic Swierczek and Georges Hirsch, "Joint Ventures in Asia and Multicultural Management," *European Management Journal,* June 1994, p. 203. Reprinted with permission of *European Management Journal.*

Ford is not alone. Today, more and more U.S. firms are cooperating to improve their competitiveness and offset the impact of foreign keiretsus that have been rapidly moving across the continuum of business activity, from upstream R&D to downstream marketing. For example, in the area of research, there now are more than 250 R&D consortia in the United States that are sharing both costs and information.[33] In design and production, manufacturers and suppliers are becoming partners; for example, at John Deere, workers now team up with their counterparts at suppliers such as the McLaughlin Body Company to improve quality and cut costs. In the financing area, large companies such as Digital Equipment, IBM, and Novellus Systems are taking equity positions or lending money to their strategic suppliers to ensure high-quality parts and on-time delivery. In the marketing area, manufacturers and suppliers are selling and servicing each other's products. For example, Mazda buys vehicles from Ford for sale in the United States, and vice versa. Furthermore, local keiretsu chapters are growing across the United States, including Seattle, Washington, and Boulder, Colorado. A total of 11 chapters exist today, where members pay a fee and attend Keiretsu Forums where the fees are pooled and investments are decided upon as a group. Having an extensive network so close to home has helped many, while the others are waiting for a time when they will need assistance as well.[34]

In fact, strategic partners and outsourcers are so important to the success of many MNCs that it is common to find them giving their partners direct access to their own computer systems. In this way, for example, an outsourcer can quickly determine the MNC's supply needs and adjust its own production schedule to meet these demands. This same type of close working B2B arrangement is used when providing services. For example, IBM works closely with the giant French MNC Thomson Multimedia SA, managing the firm's data centers, desktops, help desk, disaster recovery, and support services.[35]

Many companies are finding that M&As do not work out or they involve a considerable financial risk because of the high sales price. Joint ventures and strategic alliances are a good alternative. They provide MNCs with the opportunity to access a wide variety of competencies, thus reducing their own costs while ensuring that they have a reliable provider. In addition, joint ventures and strategic alliances help promote cooperation between the participating organizations; and as the positive effects of these keiretsu-like arrangements continue to spread, more and more MNCs will be drawn to them.[36]

The Emergence of the Electronic Network Form of Organization

Over the last few years there has been a major increase in the number of "electronic freelancers"—individuals who work on a project for a company, usually via the Internet, and move on to other employment when the assignment is done. In a way, these individuals represent a new type of electronic network organization, "temporary companies" that serve a particular, short-term purpose and then go on to other assignments. There are numerous examples.

> Consider the way many manufacturers are today pursuing radical outsourcing strategies, letting external agents perform more of their traditional activities. The U.S. computer-display division of the Finnish company Nokia, for example, chose to enter the U.S. display market with only five employees. Technical support, logistics, sales, and marketing were all subcontracted to specialists around the country. The fashion accessories company Topsy Tail, which has revenues of $80 million but only three employees, never even touches its products through the entire supply chain. It contracts with various injection-molding companies to manufacture its goods; uses design agencies to create its packaging; and distributes and sells its products through a network of independent fulfillment houses, distributors, and sales reps. Nokia's and Topsy Tail's highly decentralized operations bear more resemblance to the network model of organization than to the traditional industrial model.[37]

Many multinationals are beginning to rely increasingly on electronic freelancers (e-lancers, for short) to perform key tasks for them. In the case of General Motors, for example, outsourcers via computers work very closely with the company in providing both design and engineering assistance. The rise of the multinational university is yet another example. Growing numbers of academic institutions from Europe to North America are now offering both undergraduate and graduate courses, and in some cases full-fledged degree programs, via the Internet. In staffing these courses, the universities rely heavily on e-lancers with PhD degrees who are responsible for delivering the course online. In most cases, the university has little face-to-face contact with these e-lancers. Everything is done via computers.

These electronic network organizations are now becoming increasingly prominent. MNCs are realizing that the outsourcing function can be delivered online. Examples include design specifications, analytical computations, and consulting reports. So, in a way, this new structure is a version of the matrix design discussed earlier in the chapter. The major difference is that many of the people in the structure not only are temporary, contingent employees but never see each other and communicate exclusively in an electronic environment.

Organizing for Product Integration

Another recent organizing development is the emergence of designs that are tailored toward helping multinationals integrate product development into their worldwide operations. In the recent past, the use of cross-functional coordination was helpful in achieving this goal. However, MNCs have found that this arrangement results in people spending less time within their functions and thus becoming less knowledgeable regarding developments that are occurring in their specialized areas. A second shortcoming of the cross-functional approach is that it often leads to product teams becoming autonomous and thus failing to integrate their overall efforts with the organization at large.

Toyota created a structure that combines a highly formalized system with new structural innovations that ensure that projects are flexibly managed and, at the same time, able to benefit from the learning and experiences of other projects. In accomplishing this, Toyota employs six organizational mechanisms.

One of these is called mutual adjustment. In most companies this is achieved by assigning people to a specific project and having them meet face to face and work out a plan of action for designing the new product. At Toyota, however, design engineers are not assigned to specific projects; rather they remain in their functional area and typically communicate through written messages. This approach ensures that all members remain dedicated to their primary functional area and that they communicate succinctly and directly with each—thus saving time.

A second mechanism employed by Toyota is the use of direct, technically skilled supervisors. In a typical arrangement, design engineers are led by individuals who are no longer doing engineering work; they are primarily responsible for seeing that others do this work. However, at Toyota supervisors remain highly skilled in the technical side of the work and are responsible for mentoring, training, and developing their engineers. So if anyone has a design-related problem, the supervisor is technically skilled and can provide this assistance.

A third mechanism is the use of integrative leadership. In typical product design structures, the manager in charge has full authority and relies on the engineering personnel to get the work done within time, cost, and quality parameters. At Toyota, however, these managers are responsible for coordinating the work of the functional specialists and serving less as a manager than as a lead designer on the entire project. In this way, they serve as the glue that binds together the whole process.

In typical design operations, engineers are hired from universities or from other companies where they have gained experience, and they remain in their engineering position indefinitely. At Toyota most of the technical training is provided in-house, and people are rotated within only one function such as body engineers who work on auto-body subsystems for most, if not all, of their careers. As a result, they are able to get more work done faster because they do not have to communicate and coordinate continually with their counterparts regarding what needs to be done. They are so familiar with their jobs that they know what needs to be done.

Another organizational difference is that in typical design work each new product calls for a new development process, and there are complex forms and bureaucratic procedures for ensuring that everything is done correctly. At Toyota, standard milestones are created by the project leader, and simple forms and procedures are employed so that the work can be done simply and efficiently.

A final difference is that in many organizations design standards are obsolete and rigid. At Toyota, these standards are maintained by the people who are doing the work and are continually changed to meet new design demands.

The organizational approach used at Toyota is being carefully studied by other world-class auto manufacturers, who are coming to realize that the old way of organizing for product design is not sufficiently effective for dealing with the competitive challenges of the new millennium. In particular, a new organizational emphasis has to be placed on better blending the personnel and the work. Commenting on all of this, a group of experts who studied Toyota's approach wrote:

> The success of Toyota's system rides squarely on the shoulders of its people. Successful product development requires highly competent, highly skilled people with a lot of hands-on experience, deep technical knowledge, and an eye for the overall system. When we look at all the things that Toyota does well, we find two foundations for its product-development system: chief engineers using their expertise to gain leadership, and functional engineers using their expertise to reduce the amount of communication, supervision, trial and error, and confusion in the process. All the other coordinating mechanisms and practices serve to help highly skilled engineers do their job effectively. By contrast, many other companies seem to aspire to develop systems "designed by geniuses to be run by idiots." Toyota prefers to develop and rely on the skill of its personnel, and it shapes its product-development process around this central idea: people, not systems, design cars.[38]

The Changing Role of Information Technology in Organizing

Another major change that is taking place in the way multinationals organize themselves is related to the role of information technology (IT). After a slow start, Japanese firms are leading the way in redefining how IT will be used in the future. One of the major differences between IT in American multinationals and in their Japanese counterparts is that in Japan, IT is not seen as something special or different, but rather is viewed as being part of a fully integrated picture. In the process, Japanese firms carefully target how they are going to use information technology and try hard to neither overrate nor underrate its role and importance. A good contrast is provided by Seven-Eleven Japan and NSK, one of the world's leading bearings and auto component manufacturers.

In the case of Seven-Eleven Japan, the company has aggressively invested in IT and uses this system to monitor and meet customer needs. Japanese consumers place a high premium on product freshness. Many years ago the company began using its IT system to create a just-in-time arrangement that relies on multiple daily deliveries of products. Today, each store's fresh food changes over entirely three times a day, which allows managers to change their unit's physical layout throughout the day as the flow of customers shifts from housewives to students to working people. Moreover, the company's just-in-time system allows the stores to be extraordinarily responsive to consumers' shifting tastes. For example, if a particular kind of take-out lunch sells out by noon, extra stock can be in the store within an hour. Conversely, if it is raining, the IT system will remind cash register operators to put umbrellas on sale next to each register. This level of responsiveness is made possible by a sophisticated point-of-sale data-collection system and an electronic ordering system that links individual stores to a central distribution center.

In the case of NSK, the company uses a combination of highly integrated technology systems and low-tech systems. For example, for simulation and analysis in component design, engineers rely on the firm's flexible-engineering information control system and an array of databases and expert systems. Quality engineers use handheld terminals to monitor quality data, which are automatically recorded from in-line sensors and inspection machines. Salespeople can search sophisticated databases and narrow the range of products that they will suggest to a customer. At the same time, NSK has a number of low-technology islands where the personnel use machinery and equipment that are over a decade old and rely on their own judgment in making decisions and processing information. By choosing the best mix of information technology, the company is able to maintain its competitiveness.[39]

Other contrasts between the ways in which IT issues are addressed by Western firms and Japanese companies are provided in Table 9–3. A close analysis of these contrasts shows that the integration of IT into the overall organizing process can have a dramatic effect on the performance of an organization.

Table 9–3
Contrasting Approaches to Using Information Technology: Western and Japanese Views

Key Issue	How Western Firms Address the Matter	How Japanese Firms Address the Matter
How to decide upon the information systems needed by the business.	Develop an IT strategy that aligns with the company's business strategy.	Determine the basic way the firm competes, driven particularly by its operations goals, and use this to determine the IT investment.
How to determine if the investments in IT are worthwhile.	Adapt the capital budgeting process to manage and evaluate the IT investment.	Judge investments based on operational performance improvements.
When trying to improve a business process, how technology fits into management's thinking.	Assume that technology offers the smartest, cheapest way to improve performance.	Identify a performance goal and then select a technology that will help the firm achieve this goal in a way that supports the people doing the work.
How IT users and IT specialists should connect in the organization.	Teach specialists about business goals and develop technically adept, business-savvy chief information officers.	Encourage integration by rotating managers through the IT function and giving IT oversight to executives who oversee other functions.
How systems to improve organization performance can be designed.	Design the most technically elegant system possible and ask employees to adapt to it.	Design a system that makes use of the tacit and explicit knowledge that employees already possess.

Source: Adapted from M. Bensaou and Michael Earl, "The Right Mind-Set for Managing Information Technology," *Harvard Business Review,* September–October 1998, p. 121.

■ Organizational Characteristics of MNCs

Although MNCs have similar organizational structures, they do not all operate in the same way. A variety of factors that help explain the differences have been identified.[40] These include overall strategy, employee attitudes, and local conditions. Of particular significance to this discussion are the organizational characteristics of formalization, specialization, and centralization.

Formalization

formalization
The use of defined structures and systems in decision making, communicating, and controlling.

Formalization is the use of defined structures and systems in decision making, communicating, and controlling. Some countries make greater use of formalization than others; in turn, this affects the day-to-day organizational functioning. One large research study of Korean firms found that, unlike employees in the United States, Korean workers perceive more positive work environments when expectations for their jobs are set forth more strictly and formally. In short, Koreans respond very favorably to formalization.[41] Korean firms tend to be quite formal, but this may not hold throughout Asia. For example, a study that investigated whether Japanese organizations are more formalized than U.S. organizations found that although Japanese firms tend to use more labor-intensive approaches to areas such as book-keeping and office-related work than their U.S. counterparts, no statistical data support the contention that Japanese firms are more formalized.[42]

Another study of U.S. and Japanese firms in Taiwan divided formalization into two categories: objective and subjective.[43] Objective formalization was measured by things such as the number of different documents given to employees, organizational charts, information booklets, operating instructions, written job descriptions, procedure manuals, written policies, and work-flow schedules and programs. Subjective formalization was measured by the extent to which goals were vague and unspecified, use of informal controls, and use of culturally induced values in getting things done.

Commenting on differences in the use of formalization, the researchers concluded that American and Japanese firms appear to have almost the same level of written goals or objectives for subordinates, written standards of performance appraisals, written schedules, programs, and work specifications, written duties, authority and accountability. However, managers in Japanese firms perceive less formalization than do managers in American firms. Less reliance on formal rules and structure in Japanese firms is also revealed by the emphasis on face-to-face or behavioral mode of control indicated by the ratio of foreign expatriates to total employees in subsidiaries.[44]

The study also found that U.S. MNCs tend to rely heavily on budgets, financial data, and other formalized tools in controlling their subsidiary operations. This contrasts with Japanese MNCs, in which wider use is made of face-to-face, informal controls. These findings reveal that although the outward structural design of overseas subsidiaries may appear to be similar, the internal functioning in characteristics such as formalization may be quite different.

In recent years, this formal-informal characteristic of organizations has become the focal point of increased attention.[45] One reason is that MNCs now realize there are two dimensions of formality-informality that must be considered: internal and external. Moreover, to a large degree, these formal-informal relationships require effective networking of a different type. As Yoshino and Rangan noted, there are

two approaches that firms that must compete globally—and that includes most major firms— employ to achieve the layering of competitive advantages: (1) development of extensive *internal networks* of international subsidiaries in major national or regional markets and (2) forging *external networks* of strategic alliances with firms around the world. These approaches are not mutually exclusive, and increasingly firms are striving to build both types of networks.[46]

What is particularly interesting about these networking relationships is that each places a different set of demands on the MNC. In particular, external networking with joint-venture partners often involves ambiguous organizational mandates, less emphasis on systems and more on people, and ambiguous lines of authority. This is a marked difference from internal networking characteristics, where formality is much stronger than informality and the enterprise can rely on a shared vision, clear organizational mandates, and well-developed systems and lines of authority.[47] Table 9–4 summarizes the characteristics of these internal and external networks.

Specialization

As an organizational characteristic, **specialization** is the assigning of individuals to specific, well-defined tasks. Specialization in an international context can be classified into horizontal and vertical specialization.

Horizontal specialization assigns jobs so that individuals are given a particular function to perform, and people tend to stay within the confines of this area. Examples include jobs in areas such as customer service, sales, recruiting, training, purchasing, and

specialization
An organizational characteristic that assigns individuals to specific, well-defined tasks.

horizontal specialization
The assignment of jobs so that individuals are given a particular function to perform and tend to stay within the confines of this area.

Table 9–4
Internal vs. External Networks

Managerial Dimensions	Internal Network	External Network
Shared vision	Yes	No
Animating mindset	Cooperation	Cooperation and competition
Organizational mandates	Clear	Ambiguous
Organizational objective	Global optimization	Develop win-win approaches
Emphasis on systems	More	Less
Emphasis on people	Less	More
Lines of authority	Clear	Ambiguous at best

Source: Information drawn from Michael Yoshino and N. S. Rangan, *Strategic Alliances* (Boston: Harvard Business School Press, 1995), p. 203.

marketing research. When there is a great deal of horizontal specialization, personnel will develop functional expertise in one particular area.

vertical specialization
The assignment of work to groups or departments where individuals are collectively responsible for performance.

Vertical specialization assigns work to groups or departments where individuals are collectively responsible for performance. Vertical specialization also is characterized by distinct differences between levels in the hierarchy such that those higher up are accorded much more status than those farther down, and the overall structure usually is quite tall.

In the earlier, comparative study of 55 U.S. and 51 Japanese manufacturing plants, Japanese organizations had lower functional specialization of employees. Specifically, three-quarters of the functions listed were assigned to specialists in the U.S. plants, but less than one-third were assigned in the Japanese plants.[48] Later studies with regard to formalization have echoed this finding on specialization.

By contrast, studies find that the Japanese rely more heavily on vertical specialization. They have taller organization structures in contrast to the flatter designs of their U.S. counterparts. Japanese departments and units also are more differentiated than departments and units in U.S. organizations. Vertical specialization can be measured by the amount of group activity as well, such as in quality circles. Japanese firms make much greater use of quality circles than the U.S. firms. Vertical specialization also can result in greater job routinization. Because one is collectively responsible for the work, strong emphasis is placed on everyone's doing the job in a predetermined way, refraining from improvising, and structuring the work so that everyone can do the job after a short training period. Again, Japanese organizations make much wider use of job routinization than do U.S. organizations.

Centralization

centralization
A management system in which important decisions are made at the top.

decentralization
Pushing decision making down the line and getting the lower-level personnel involved.

Centralization is a management system in which important decisions are made at the top. In an international context, the value of centralization will vary according to the local environment and the goals of the organization. Many U.S. firms tend toward **decentralization,** pushing decision making down the line and getting the lower-level personnel involved. German MNCs centralize strategic headquarter-specific decisions independent of the host country and decentralize operative decisions in accordance with the local situation in the host country. "International Management in Action: Organizing in Germany" describes how relatively small German MNCs have been very successful with such a decentralization strategy. In some cases, large firms have also been very successful using a decentralized approach. Nokia, for example, has been described as "one of the least hierarchical big companies on earth, a place where it is often profoundly unclear who's in charge."[49] This hands-off approach promotes creativity, entrepreneurial effort, and personal responsibility. At the same time, however, in order to prevent operations from spinning out of control, the company exercises very tight financial discipline.

In contrast, researchers have found that Japanese organizations delegate less formal authority than their U.S. counterparts but permit greater involvement in decisions by employees lower in the hierarchy. At the same time, the Japanese manage to maintain strong control over their lower-level personnel by limiting the amount of authority given to the latter and carefully controlling and orchestrating worker involvement and participation in quality circles.[50] Other studies show similar findings.[51] When evaluating the presence of centralization by examining the amount of autonomy that Japanese give to their subordinates, one study concluded:

> In terms of job autonomy, employees in American firms have greater freedom to make their decisions and their own rules than in Japanese firms.... Results show that managers in American firms perceive a higher degree of delegation than do managers in Japanese firms. Also, managers in American firms feel a much higher level of participation in the coordinating with other units, ... in influencing the company's policy related to their work, and in influencing the company's policy in areas not related to their work.[52]

The finding related to influence is explained in more detail in Table 9–5. U.S. managers in Taiwanese subsidiaries felt that they had greater influence than did their Japanese counterparts. Moreover, when statistically analyzed, these data proved to be significant.

Organizing in Germany

www.stihlusa.com/chainsaws

Like every other place in the world, Europe in general and Germany in particular have gone through economic ups and downs. German labor unions, the most powerful in Europe, were having to give ground, and major corporations were scaling back operations and reporting losses. At the same time, a number of medium- and small-sized German companies continued to be some of the most successful in the world. Part of this success resulted from their carefully designed decentralized organization structures, a result of company efforts to remain close to the customer. The goal of these German MNCs is to establish operations in overseas locales where they can provide on-site assistance to buyers. Moreover, these subsidiaries in most cases are wholly owned by the company and have centralized controls on profits.

A common practice among German MNCs is to overserve the market by providing more than is needed. For example, when the auto firm BMW entered Japan, its initial investment was several times higher than that required to run a small operation; however, its high visibility and commitment to the market helped to create customer awareness and build local prestige.

Another strategy is to leave expatriate managers in their positions for extended periods of time. In this way, they become familiar with the local culture and thus the market, and they are better able to respond to customer needs as well as problems. As a result, customers get to know the firm's personnel and are more willing to do repeat business with them.

Still another strategy the German MNCs use is to closely mesh the talents of the people with the needs of the customers. For example, there is considerable evidence that most customers value product quality, closeness to the customer, service, economy, helpful employees, technologic leadership, and innovativeness. The German firms will overperform in the area that is most important and thus further bond themselves to the customer.

A final strategy is to develop strong self-reliance so that when problems arise, they can be handled with in-house personnel. This practice is a result of German companies' believing strongly in specialization and concentration of effort. They tend to do their own research and to master production and service problems so that if there is a problem, they can resolve it without having to rely on outsiders.

How well do these German organizing efforts pay off? Many of these relatively small companies hold world market shares in the 70 to 90 percent range. These are companies that no one has ever heard of, such as Booder (fish-processing machines), Gehring (honing machines), Korber/Hauni (cigarette machines), Marklin & Cle (model railways), Stihl (chain saws), and Webasto (sunroofs for cars). Even so, every one of these companies is the market leader not only in Europe but also throughout the world, and in some cases its relative market strength is up to 10 times greater than that of the nearest competitor.

Table 9–5
Managers' Influence in U.S. and Japanese Firms in Taiwan

Managers' Work-Related Activity	U.S. Firm Average	Japanese Firm Average
Assigning work to subordinates	4.72	3.96
Disciplining subordinates	4.07	3.82
Controlling subordinates' work (quality and pace)	3.99	3.82
Controlling salary and promotion of subordinates	3.81	3.18
Hiring and placing subordinates	3.94	3.24
Setting the budget for own unit	3.45	3.16
Coordinating with other units	3.68	3.52
Influencing policy related to own work	3.22	2.85
Influencing policy not related to own work	2.29	1.94
Influencing superiors	3.02	3.00

Note: The highest score of means is 5 (very great influence); the lowest score is 1 (very little influence). The *T*-value for all scores is significant at the .01 level.

Source: Adapted from Rhy-song Yeh and Tagi Sagafi-nejad, "Organizational Characteristics of American and Japanese Firms in Taiwan," *National Academy of Management Proceedings* (New Orleans, 1987), p. 114.

Putting Organizational Characteristics in Perspective

MNCs tend to organize their international operations in a manner similar to that used at home. If the MNC tends to have high formalization, specialization, and centralization at its home-based headquarters, these organizational characteristics probably will occur in the firm's international subsidiaries.[53] Japanese and U.S. firms are good examples. As the researchers of the comparative study in Taiwan concluded: "Almost 80 percent of Japanese firms and more than 80 percent of American firms in the sample have been operating in Taiwan for about ten years, but they maintain the traits of their distinct cultural origins even though they have been operating in the same (Taiwanese) environment for such a long time."[54]

These findings also reveal that many enterprises view their international operations as extensions of their domestic operations, thus disproving the widely held belief that convergence occurs between overseas operations and local customs. In other words, there is far less of an "international management melting pot" than many people realize. European countries are finding that as they attempt to unify and do business with each other, differing cultures (languages, religions, and values) are very difficult to overcome. A major challenge for the years ahead will be bringing subsidiary organizational characteristics more into line with local customs and cultures.

The World of *BusinessWeek*—Revisited

In this chapter, a number of different entry strategies and organizational arrangements are discussed. Some of these are fairly standard approaches used by MNCs; others represent hybrid or flexible arrangements. Increasingly, entry modes and organizational structures involve collaborative relationships in which control and oversight are shared. After reviewing Gazprom's strategies, consider the following questions: (1) What type of organizational structure does Gazprom have? (2) Will many companies benefit from a joint venture with Gazprom? Why or why not? (3) How is the political environment in Russia influencing the entry strategies and organizational structures that are emerging?

SUMMARY OF KEY POINTS

1. MNCs pursue a range of entry strategies in their international operations. These include wholly owned subsidiaries, mergers and acquisitions, alliances and joint ventures, licensing and franchising, and exporting. In general, the more cooperative forms of entry (alliances, joint ventures, mergers, licensing) are on the rise.

2. A number of different organizational structures are used in international operations. Many MNCs begin by using an export manager or subsidiary to handle overseas business. As the operation grows or the company expands into more markets, the firm often will opt for an international division structure. Further growth may result in adoption of a global structural arrangement, such as a global production division, global area division structure, global functional division, or a mixture of these structures.

3. Although MNCs still use the various structural designs that can be drawn in a hierarchical manner, they recently have begun merging or acquiring other firms or parts of other firms, and the resulting organizational arrangements are quite different from those of the past. The same is true of the many joint ventures now taking place across the world. One change stems from the Japanese concept of keiretsu, which involves the vertical integration and cooperation of a group of companies. Other examples of new MNC organizational arrangements include the emergence of electronic networks, new approaches to organizing for production development, and the more effective use of IT.

4. A variety of factors help to explain differences in the way that international firms operate. Three organizational characteristics that are of particular importance are formalization, specialization, and centralization. These characteristics often vary from country to country, so that Japanese firms will conduct operations differently from U.S. firms. When MNCs set up international subsidiaries, they often use the same organizational techniques they do at home without necessarily adjusting their approach to better match the local conditions.

KEY TERMS

alliance, *284*

centralization, *306*

decentralization, *306*

formalization, *304*

franchise, *287*

global area division, *293*

global functional division, *295*

global product division, *292*

horizontal specialization, *305*

international division structure, *291*

joint venture (JV), *284*

keiretsu, *299*

license, *285*

merger/acquisition, *283*

mixed organization structure, *295*

specialization, *305*

transnational network structure, *296*

vertical specialization, *306*

wholly owned subsidiary, *283*

REVIEW AND DISCUSSION QUESTIONS

1. One of the most common entry strategies for MNCs is the joint venture. Why are so many companies opting for this strategy? Would a fully owned subsidiary be a better choice?

2. A small manufacturing firm believes there is a market for handheld tools that are carefully crafted for local markets. After spending two months in Europe, the president of this firm believes that his company can create a popular line of these tools. What type of organization structure would be of most value to this firm in its initial efforts to go international?

3. If the company in question 2 finds a major market for its products in Europe and decides to expand into Asia, would you recommend any change in its organization structure? If yes, what would you suggest? If no, why not?

4. If this same company finds after three years of international effort that it is selling 50 percent of its output overseas, what type of organizational structure would you suggest for the future?

5. Why are keiretsus popular? What benefits do they offer? How can small international firms profit from these structures? Give an example.

6. In what way do formalization, specialization, and centralization have an impact on MNC organization structures? In your answer, use a well-known firm such as IBM or Ford to illustrate the effects of these three characteristics.

INTERNET EXERCISE: ORGANIZING FOR EFFECTIVENESS

Every MNC tries to drive down costs by getting its goods and services to the market in the most efficient way. Good examples include auto firms such as Ford Motor and Volkswagen, which have worldwide operations. In recent years Ford has begun expanding into Europe and VW has begun setting up operations in Latin America. By building cars closer to the market, these companies hope to reduce their costs and be more responsive to local needs. At the same time this strategy requires a great deal of organization and coordination. Visit the Web sites of both firms and examine the scope of their operations. The address for Ford Motor is **www.ford.com,** and for Volkswagen it is **www.vw.com**. Then, based on your findings, answer these questions: What type of organizational arrangement(s) do you see the two firms using in coordinating their worldwide operations? Which of the two companies has the more modern arrangement? Do you think this increases that firm's efficiency, or does it hamper the company's efforts to contain costs and be more competitive? Why?

Australia

Australia is the smallest continent but the sixth-largest country in the world. It lies between the Indian and Pacific oceans in the Southern Hemisphere and has a landmass of almost 3 million square miles (around 85 percent the size of the United States). Referred to as being "down under" because it lies entirely within the Southern Hemisphere, it is a dry, thinly populated land. The outback is famous for its bright sunshine, enormous numbers of sheep and cattle, and unusual wildlife, such as kangaroos, koalas, platypuses, and wombats. Over 20 million people live in this former British colony. Although many British customs are retained, Australians have developed their own unique way of life. One of the world's most developed countries, Australia operates under a democratic form of government somewhat similar to that of Great Britain. Gross domestic product is over $644 billion, with the largest economic sectors being services (70 percent), trade, and manufacturing.

A large financial services MNC in the United States has been examining the demographic and economic data of Australia. This MNC has concluded that there will be increased demand for financial services in Australia during the next few years. As a result, the company is setting up an operation in the capital, Canberra, which is slightly inland from Sydney and Melbourne, the two largest cities.

This financial services firm began in Chicago and now has offices in seven countries. Many of these foreign operations are closely controlled by the Chicago office. The overseas personnel are charged with carefully following instructions from headquarters and implementing centralized decisions. However, the Australian operation will be run differently. Because the country is so large and the population spread along the coast and to Perth in the west, and because of the "free spirit" cultural values of the Aussies, the home office feels compelled to give the manager of Australian operations full control over decision making. This manager will have a small number of senior-level managers brought from the United States, but the rest of the personnel will be hired locally. The office will be given sales and profit goals, but specific implementation of strategy will be left to the manager and his or her key subordinates on site.

The home office believes that in addition to providing direct banking and credit card services, the Australian operation should seek to gain a strong foothold in insurance and investment services. As the country continues to grow economically, this sector of the industry should increase relatively fast. Moreover, few multinational firms are trying to tap this market in Australia, and those that are doing so are from British Commonwealth countries. The CEO believes that the experience of the people being sent to Australia (the U.S. expatriates) will be particularly helpful in developing this market. He recently noted, "We know that the needs of the Australian market are not as sophisticated or complex as those in the United States, but we also know that they are moving in the same direction as we are. So we intend to tap our experience and knowledge and use it to garner a commanding share of this expanding market."

www.csu.edu.au/australia

Questions

1. What are some current issues facing Australia? What is the climate for doing business in Australia today?

2. What type of organizational structure arrangement is the MNC going to use in setting up its Australian operation?

3. Can this MNC benefit from any of the new organizational arrangements, such as a joint venture, the Japanese concept of keiretsu, or electronic networks?

4. Will this operation be basically centralized or decentralized?

Getting In on the Ground Floor

The EU currently is developing a strategy that will help member countries beat back the threat of U.S. and Asian competition and develop a strong technological base for new product development. European multinational firms currently are strong in a number of different areas. For example, Germany's Hoechst and BASF and Switzerland's Sandoz and Hoffman-LaRoche are major companies in chemicals and pharmaceutics. Philips of the Netherlands invented compact discs and is dominant in the television market. Many strong European-based MNCs could provide a solid base for the EU to defend itself from outside economic invasion.

Ruehter Laboratories, a high-tech R&D firm located in New Jersey, holds a number of important pharmaceutic patents and would like to expand its operation worldwide. The company is considering buying a small but highly profitable Dutch insulin maker. "This acquisition will help us enter the European market by getting in on the ground floor," noted the president.

Although the Dutch firm is quite small, it has strong R&D prowess and likely will play a major role in bio-technology research during the years ahead. Ruehter has talked to the Dutch firm, and the two have arrived at a mutually acceptable selling price. While waiting for the lawyers to work out the final arrangements, Ruehter intends to reorganize its overall operations so that the home-office management can work more closely with its new Dutch subsidiary. There are two areas that Ruehter intends to address in its reorganization efforts: (1) how the subsidiary will be structurally integrated into the current organization and (2) whether there can be any joint R&D efforts between the two groups.

Questions

1. What type of organization design would you recommend that Ruehter use?

2. If there were joint R&D efforts, would this be a problem?

Chapter 10

MANAGING POLITICAL RISK, GOVERNMENT RELATIONS, AND ALLIANCES

OBJECTIVES OF THE CHAPTER

Firms go international to become more competitive and profitable. Unfortunately, many risks accompany internationalization. One of the biggest emerges from the political situation of the countries in which the MNC does business. Terrorism is also a worldwide concern which can create a large barrier to MNC entry or survival in a country. MNCs must be able to assess political risk and conduct skillful negotiations. An overview of the political environment in selected areas of the world has already been provided in Chapter 2. This chapter specifically examines the impact of political risk on MNCs and their subsequent decisions in managing it. One major way is through effective evaluation and risk reduction. This process extends from risk identification and quantification to the formulation of appropriate responses, such as integration and protective and defensive techniques.

This chapter also describes the process for developing productive relationships with governments and for managing alliances with foreign partners, many of which are influenced by home- and host-government relations. The specific objectives of this chapter are:

1. EXAMINE how MNCs evaluate political risk.

2. PRESENT some common methods used for managing and reducing political risk.

3. DISCUSS strategies to mitigate political risk and develop productive relations with governments.

4. DESCRIBE challenges to and strategies for effectively managing alliances.

The World of *BusinessWeek*

BusinessWeek

So Much Gold, So Much Risk

Unrest Makes Freeport's Dependence on One Indonesian Mine Especially Precarious

James R. "Jim Bob" Moffett and Richard C. Adkerson are in the enviable business of sitting on a literal gold mine. They run Freeport-McMoRan Copper & Gold Inc., which owns the rights to excavate Grasberg, a remote, beautiful, controversial site high in the mountains of Papua, Indonesia, that is the world's second-largest copper source and biggest gold deposit. As those metals have soared in value, Grasberg has become a veritable mint. Since 2001, Freeport's profits have quadrupled, to $935 million on $4.2 billion in revenues, helping it land the No. 35 spot on the BusinessWeek 50 list of top corporate performers. In the same period, investors have enjoyed a fivefold rise in Freeport shares, along with a flood of special dividends and stock buybacks.

It is a straightforward business, but also an enormously risky one: Grasberg provides some 90% of New Orleans–based Freeport's revenues and virtually all of its profits. Freeport has no immediate plans to diversify its considerable political or financial risk. Despite ample cash and opportunity, the company has so far passed on taking any meaningful stake in other locations or products. Instead, Adkerson, who is president and CEO, appears willing to milk Grasberg for what he reckons will be 40 more years of strong production. Meanwhile, it falls to Moffett, Freeport's chairman and head of its Indonesian operating arm, to keep the relationship with whoever's in power amicable. He has managed to pull that off since the discovery of Grasberg in 1988, despite an association with the dictator Suharto, a revolution, simmering disquiet among Papuan locals, and scads of human-rights and environmental abuse allegations.

But in recent weeks, having all those golden eggs in one basket has looked particularly precarious. After a relatively serene couple of years, relations with the Papuans heated up in March. Locals were blocked from panning for gold in a river carrying Grasberg's residue, and protesters barricaded a key access road, halting operations for three days. Four security people were killed in related protests in Papua's capital city, Jayapura. Indonesian officials are concerned enough about resurgent Papuan separatists, who have been agitating against Jakarta for some 40 years, that more security and military personnel have been deployed to the province.

Earlier this month came a scathing report from the Indonesian Forum for the Environment, an influential watchdog coalition. Among many allegations: that the local operating company, PT Freeport Indonesia, has improperly disposed of more than 1 billion tons of residue in local river systems and dumped 1.3 billion tons of waste rock containing toxic materials, creating dangerous acid runoff and landslides.

In an interview with *BusinessWeek,* Adkerson says that Freeport's practices in Indonesia are highly responsible and comply with local environmental law. And he's almost blasé about the political risk. "We worked through the change of government in 1998 [when Suharto was ousted], the Asian financial crisis, the telecom bust, and through times of very low metals prices," says Adkerson, 59. He and Moffett, 67, have big personal stakes in the outcome: Not counting options, Adkerson owns 500,000 shares outright (worth about $30 million), and Moffett owns 1.2 million ($73 million).

Bigger Question Mark

Despite Adkerson's optimism, *BusinessWeek* has learned that Freeport officials have been so consumed with the recent unrest that they put on hold the next phase of a company-sponsored human-rights audit that was to start in April. Prakash Sethi, president of the International Center for Corporate Accountability Inc., says the audit and a second one meant to target the many companies that support and service Freeport's operations at Grasberg will be delayed for at least several months. "We won't send our people in until we're sure that stability is restored," he says.

WILD RIDE

Freeport-McMoRan relies on its huge mine in Papua, Indonesia, for some 90% of its revenues and, as a result, is exposed to the country's shifting political winds. Freeport's market cap has yo-yoed dramatically in the past 10 years:

Data: Bloomberg Financial Markets

Source: www.businessweek.com/magazine/content/06_22/b3986087.htm.

But it's the Indonesian government that's potentially more unsettling to investors than Papuan rebels. Several politicians and grassroots organizations are pushing President Susilo Bambang Yudhoyono to emulate Venezuela's Hugo Chavez and seize a bigger chunk of the bounty from his country's natural resources. At this point, though, most local businesspeople think Freeport's long-term contract will be respected. They say that Yudhoyono is pro-growth, and to win over new investors, he needs to continue setting a good example with current ones. Adkerson is confident the government will stick by its contract with Freeport, which supports 18,000 jobs and pays more than $1 billion in taxes.

The Grasberg-or-bust strategy has come with real marketplace consequences. Freeport's junk-level bond rating of BB- from Standard & Poor's would surely be higher given the company's enormous cash flow, but it "reflects the political and legal risks of operating in Indonesia and the company's limited operating diversity," S&P says. And Freeport's stock, despite its huge run, sells at a steep discount (about 12 times earnings) to some industry peers whose bets are hedged with multiple mines in different locales. Casting its entire lot with Grasberg ensures Freeport won't be short of metal reserves, or controversy, for the foreseeable future.

By Mark Morrison, with Assif Shameen in Singapore

Indonesia is one of the riskiest countries to do business in, yet Freeport has operated there for many years. While political risk is perceived to be high by investors and the general market, Freeport's largest concern is with the people, not the government. Grasberg has proved to be a virtual temple of riches, and locals now desire a share of the profits. From citizens blockading entry to Grasberg and halting mining, to pressuring the government to tighten control and demand a larger share of operations, many believe that Freeport will be forced to provide a greater share of its take to the locals. The company must be doing something right, as it has survived many phases of political unrest. The key now is to maintain government relations so the company can continue to mine without major disruption. The company is showing caution with its employees and further operations, but it is clear that both the Indonesian government and Freeport need each other to survive. If Indonesia can uphold contracts and not yield to unreasonable pressures from multiple parties for a share of the revenue, it may attract future investment from MNCs, ensuring long-term returns. With everyone mutually benefitting, a cooperative relationship can continue, and there will be no need for power plays. Not all MNCs are so confident about international investment in countries with political unrest. MNCs must be able to evaluate and manage political risks on a global scale and contemplate the potential of alliances and other long-term cooperative relationships, such as in the opening article, to help mitigate risks. In this chapter, we explore strategies for evaluating political risks, managing government relations, and developing and managing alliances with private and public partners.

■ The Nature and Analysis of Political Risk

Both domestic and international political developments have a major impact on MNCs' strategic plans. MNCs face hazards that originate directly from variation and unpredictability in political and governance systems. The state and its various institutions and agencies continue to pose a direct threat to multinational corporations through policy shifts in taxation or regulation, through outright or de facto expropriation, or by allowing the exploitation of assets by local firms. As government policies change, MNCs must adjust their strategies and practices to accommodate the new perspectives and actual requirements. Moreover, in a growing number of geographic regions and countries, governments appear to be less stable; therefore, these areas carry more risk than they did in the past. Applied to international management, **political risk** is the unanticipated likelihood that a multinational corporation's foreign investment will be constrained by a host government's policies. Since the terrorist attacks of 9/11, political risk assessment has become especially vital to MNCs. Today, almost all countries are interested in sustaining investment from MNCs.[1] Yet political risks persist, especially in the emerging economies of the world, which continue to struggle with political and institutional instability. The presence of policy and control mechanisms, coupled with historic treatment of MNCs within these nations, allows firms to evaluate the inherent risk of doing business there. Examples of risk factors include freezing the movement of assets out of the host country, placing limits on the remittance of profits or capital, devaluing the currency, appropriating assets, and refusing to abide by the contractual terms of agreements previously signed with the MNC. As rapid globalization continues, MNCs must be aware of the political risk factors present in doing business abroad and develop strategies to respond to them.

In the case of China, for example, the government was for several years very anxious to see the country admitted to the World Trade Organization (WTO). Yet even after its entry into the WTO, China began making decisions that were in its own best short-run interests but created new political risks for MNCs doing business there. One analysis noted:

> A series of recent moves by Chinese authorities—price controls, currency restrictions, limits on sale of state-owned companies—seem to reflect a slowdown in the nation's effort to

political risk
The unanticipated likelihood that a business's foreign investment will be constrained by a host government's policy.

shift from a planned to a market economy. Whether such steps are justifiably cautious or simply timid, economists and business executives agree that they are likely to further deter trade and investment in the near future. Today, China's central bank announced new restrictions on foreign exchange transactions, an attempt to control the flow of convertible currency out of the country. Officially described as a crackdown on illegal transactions, the moves will effectively make it more difficult for both domestic and international companies to move money in and out of China.[2]

Some of the policies have since been relaxed; however, political risk still continues to be a major consideration for multinationals doing business there. As was brought out in Chapter 3, industrial piracy continues to be a big problem, and the Chinese government has yet to take effective action against it. For example, Procter & Gamble estimates that it loses $150 million in sales annually because of counterfeit brands. One reason for the reluctance of the Chinese government to take action may well be that state-owned factories are some of the biggest counterfeiters. Yamaha estimates that five of every six JYM 150-A motorcycles and ZY125 scooters bearing its name in China are fake; some state-owned factories turn out copies four months after Yamaha introduces a new model.[3] Sometimes, counterfeiters are so efficient that the fake goods reach the market even before the actual product. Nike, for example, experienced this with its Air Max 360 when someone at the China office stole blueprints and began manufacturing. This is not the first instance of fake Nikes being sold in China and abroad. The company often receives shipments of shoes or returns from customers which bear the very recognizable swoosh logo, but are in fact cheap knockoffs of the original. China is not making a concerted effort to cease this behavior, even though nearly 20 percent of shoes with the swoosh logo are fakes. The country is capable of stopping such operations, which is exhibited by its ability to stave off counterfeit Olympic gear as it prepares to host the 2008 Olympics. This, however, only serves to aggravate those companies whose products continue to be pirated.[4]

Another common complaint is the way rules and regulations are interpreted. A Mitsubishi factory manager, commenting on the fact that customs officials continually offer contradictory rulings, said, "One day one official will say I do not need to pay duty, the next day, a different official will say I have to."[5] Another growing concern is government censorship. All advertisements must be approved by censors who carefully screen ads to ensure that they are culturally and politically correct.[6] Even the Internet and cellular multimedia usage is monitored and censored to some extent. In a world where technology allows networks to share information freely, China continues to set regulations that will restrict what it considers "harmful information." Internet search providers that operate in China, such as Google and Yahoo, already block content that Chinese authorities find questionable, even troublesome, and certain Web sites are restricted across the country.[7] Multinationals are also concerned about the pressure that the Chinese government puts on businesses to do things a particular way. MNCs in Hong Kong, now governed by the PRC, have reported meddling by Beijing.[8]

These types of actions by the Chinese increase the political risk of doing business in China. On the other side of the coin, Chinese MNCs must also assess the political risk inherent in doing business in the United States. The U.S. government has begun to review its trade policy with China. In particular, American trade officials claim that China has taken for granted its relationship with the United States and warn that if markets there are not opened for American goods, there will be reciprocal action against Chinese firms that are selling in the United States.[9] Given the enormous trade deficit that the United States has with China, this situation could end up creating major political risks for Chinese MNCs doing business in the politically stable but very risky United States. In fact, tensions continue to rise as U.S. politicians have become frustrated by China's unwillingness to revalue the Yuan and concerns have grown over the safety of goods imported from China. Specifically, tainted pet food imported from China and a massive toy recall by Matell have caused many in the United States to question the safety and reliability of Chinese products.[10]

Macro and Micro Analysis of Political Risk

macro political risk analysis
Analysis that reviews major political decisions likely to affect all enterprises in the country.

micro political risk analysis
Analysis directed toward government policies and actions that influence selected sectors of the economy or specific foreign businesses in the country.

Firms evaluate political risk in a number of ways. One is through **macro political risk analysis,** which reviews major political decisions that are likely to affect all business conducted in the country. For example, China's decision regarding restrictions on foreign-exchange transactions is a macro political risk because it affects all MNCs. **Micro political risk analysis** is directed toward government policies and actions that influence selected sectors of the economy or specific foreign businesses. China's government policies regarding investment in the telecommunications industry fall into the micro political risk category. The following two sections examine both of these areas—macro and micro political risk—in more depth.

Macro Risk Issues and Examples In recent years, macro risk analysis has become of increasing concern to MNCs because of the growing number of countries that are finding their economies in trouble, as in Southeast Asia, or, even worse, that are unable to make the transition to a market-driven economy. A good example of the latter is Russia, which has been tightening controls on the flow of foreign currencies. This decision represents a change in direction from the free-market principles that Russia had been following in order to ensure that it continued to receive assistance from the International Monetary Fund.

Other examples of developments that fall within the realm of macro political risk are provided by India, a country whose legal system is stymied by a labyrinth of laws and bureaucratic red tape. In recent years, the Indian high courts have had a backlog of over 3 million cases. Moreover, approximately one-third of these cases have been winding their way through the legal system for more than five years. So while the government touts the fact that Indian law offers strong protection to foreign firms against counterfeiters, an MNC finding that it must rely on the Indian judicial system to enforce its proprietary rights is likely to be sadly disappointed. As a result, many MNCs accept this risk as a price of doing business in India and formulate strategies for managing the problem. A good example is provided by the Timken Company of Canton, Ohio, which makes bearings and alloy steel. When Timken found that the Indian market was rampant with fake Timken products, the MNC's initial reaction was to sue the counterfeiters. However, after realizing how long this would take, the MNC opted for a different strategy. Management switched the packaging of its products from cardboard boxes to heat-sealed plastic with eight-color printing and a hologram that could not be forged. Result: Within months the counterfeit market began drying up.

Timken is not alone; there are many counterfeit operations in India because the slow-moving judicial system encourages noncompliance. In fact, some counterfeiters have found that by filing countersuits, they can tie up a case in court for years. For example, Ziff Davis Publishing, an American unit of Japan's Softbank Corporation, brought suit against a former Indian licensee for continuing to publish one of its computer magazines even though the license had expired. The defendant frivolously countersued, arguing that the magazine was generic and not proprietary. A similar brazen example hit Time Warner, owner of cable-television movie channel Home Box Office (HBO). This MNC won a temporary injunction preventing an Indian company from calling its movie channel Cable Box Office (CBO), so that firm changed its name to Cable Video Opera (CVO).

Many other newly emerging economies besides the big countries of China, Russia, and India also present macro political risks for MNCs. In Vietnam, for example, the communist government earned a bad name among foreign investors because of all the pitfalls they have to face. Until recently the Vietnamese government required all foreign investors to establish joint ventures with local partners. But even with this arrangement, getting things done proved to be extremely slow and difficult because of the numerous levels of bureaucracy to be dealt with. One international manager described his MNC's experience this way: "The negotiations would follow a serpentine path, with breakthroughs in one session often being erased in the next."[11] To date, macro political risks in Vietnam remain high, although there is little risk of political instability. Investors continue to proceed with caution, which may be a wise approach in an economy that could prove to be challenging for an increasingly integrated global marketplace.[12]

Another example of a macro consideration of political risk is an analysis of what would happen to a company's investment if opposition government leaders were to take control. In the 1970s U.S. companies in Iran failed to forecast the fall of the shah and rise of Khomeini. As a result, they lost their investment. Because of this Iranian experience, the situation in Iraq under militant dictator Saddam Hussein and the subsequent instability after his removal, and the terrorist attack on New York by ethnic Middle Easterners, many multinationals now are very reluctant to invest very heavily in most Middle Eastern countries. Recently, the government of Iran appeared to be interested in attracting foreign investment, but there is still a great deal of concern that this region is too politically explosive. Central, if not Eastern, Europe appears to be a better bet, as seen by the millions of dollars that MNCs have poured into transitionary postcommunist countries such as Hungary and Poland. This geographic region also is regarded as politically risky, however, as shown in the continuing conflict in the Balkans, the breakup of Czechoslovakia into the independent Czech Republic and Slovak Republic, the continuing problems in the former Soviet republics, and the political instability in the entire region. As a result, many multinationals have been tempering their expansion plans in these transitionary, still emerging economies. Recent populist governments somewhat hostile to capitalism and foreign investment have emerged in a number of Latin American countries, including Bolivia, Ecuador, and Venezuela. In some cases, these governments have effectively forced divestment by foreign multinationals, as was the case in Venezuela in the petrochemical sector.

Still another area of consideration in macro political risk is government corruption, which we discussed in Chapters 2 and 3. Common examples include bribery and the use of government rules and regulations that require the inclusion of certain locals in lucrative business deals. In fact, one of the most commonly cited reasons for the severe economic problems in Indonesia in recent years is the corrupt practices of the government. Because the family of former president Suharto was involved in virtually every big business deal that took place under his regime, many loans and major projects were approved by banks and government agencies simply because these family members were part of the process. However, when these loans or projects ran into trouble, more money was poured in to shore up things—and no one dared to challenge these unsound decisions.

What are the most and the least corrupt nations in the world? Table 10–1 provides the results of a survey of 85 nations that ranked countries based on a wide variety of criteria. About half the nations in the world were omitted from the survey because of the absence of reliable data. The United States ended up in 20th position, illustrating that even the U.S. has work to do in improving its business environment.

Micro Risk Issues and Examples   Micro risk issues often take such forms as industry regulation, taxes on specific types of business activity, and restrictive local laws. The essence of these micro risk issues is that some MNCs are treated differently from others. A good example is the situation faced by MNCs importing steel into the U.S. market. In 1992 American steelmakers filed more than 80 complaints against 20 nations on a single day. They charged that foreign steelmakers were dumping their products in the U.S. market at artificially low prices. In 1998, the industry again demanded action against foreign producers who, in the first six months of that year, had doubled their imports into the American market. Domestic producers charged that steelmakers in Brazil, Japan, and Russia were dumping steel in the United States at unfairly low prices. What was even more troubling was that the American producers were in the process of negotiating with big auto and appliance makers for the steel that is sold under long-term contracts. Since steel prices had dropped sharply because of the alleged "dumping," the American firms were concerned that they would end up getting locked into contracts that offered very little, if any, profit.

Table 10–1
The 2006 Transparency International Corruption Perceptions Index

Country Rank	Country	Country Rank	Country
1	Finland	40	Jordan
	Iceland	41	Hungary
3	New Zealand	42	Mauritius
4	Denmark		South Korea
5	Singapore	44	Malaysia
6	Sweden	45	Italy
7	Switzerland	46	Czech Republic
8	Norway		Kuwait
9	Australia		Lithuania
	Netherlands	49	Latvia
11	Austria		Slovakia
	Luxembourg	51	South Africa
	United Kingdom		Tunisia
14	Canada	53	Dominica
15	Hong Kong	54	Greece
16	Germany	55	Costa Rica
17	Japan		Namibia
18	France	57	Bulgaria
	Ireland		El Salvador
20	Belgium	59	Colombia
	Chile	60	Turkey
	United States	61	Jamaica
23	Spain		Poland
24	Barbados	63	Lebanon
	Estonia		Seychelles
26	Macao		Thailand
	Portugal	66	Belize
28	Malta		Cuba
	Slovenia		Grenada
	Uruguay	69	Croatia
31	United Arab Emirates	70	Brazil
			China
32	Bhutan		Egypt
	Qatar		Ghana
34	Israel		India
	Taiwan		Mexico
36	Bahrain		Peru
37	Botswana		Saudi Arabia
	Cyprus		Senegal
39	Oman		

Source: Transparency International, http://www.transparency.org/news_room/in_
focus/2006/cpi_2006__1/cpi_table.

The American steelmakers were insisting that their government force foreign producers to raise their prices.[13] The George W. Bush administration did ultimately impose tariffs on steel, but these were, in part, subsequently rescinded. This experience underscores the uncertainty and volatility associated with micro political risks.

A related development is the impact of WTO and EU regulations on American MNCs. For example, the WTO recently ruled that the United States' 1916 Anti-Dumping

Act violates global trade regulations and cannot be used by American firms to fend off imports.[14] Meanwhile on the European continent, the European Commission is investigating complaints by PepsiCo and other competitors that Coca-Cola has improperly attempted to shut down sales of its rivals.[15] The EU also examines all major mergers and acquisitions and has the authority to block such actions. For example, the EU refused to allow the General Electric (GE) and Honeywell merger, one of the best examples of globalization (the EU was able to stop the actions of perhaps the most powerful U.S. firm) as well as political risk (GE needed to better assess and manage the risk posed by the politicians and government bureaucrats in Brussels). Other examples include the EU's denying Volvo and Scania approval to merge and preventing Alcan Aluminum of Canada, Pechiney of France, and the Alusuisse Lonza Group of Switzerland, the world's three largest aluminum companies, from merging.[16] There has only been one other occurrence of the EU denying a merger since 2001, namely the hostile bid by Ryanair to purchase Ireland's Aer Lingus. The motivation behind refuting the deal was to avoid a monopoly, as the merger would result in Ryanair controlling more than 80 percent of European flights.[17] These regulatory actions are good examples of the types of micro risk issues that MNCs face from industry regulation.

Still another example of micro political risk is provided by countries in South America that face continued indebtedness and have introduced a variety of policies to promote exports and discourage imports. MNCs that feel they cannot abide by these policies will stay out; however, some that are looking for a location from which to produce and export goods will view these same government policies as very attractive. Table 10–2 lists criteria that MNCs could use to evaluate the degree of political risk.

Table 10–2
A Guide to Evaluation of Political Risk

External factors affecting subject country:
  Prospects for foreign conflict
  Relations with border countries
  Regional instabilities
  Alliances with major and regional powers
  Sources of key raw materials
  Major foreign markets
  Policy toward United States
  U.S. policy toward country
  Internal groupings (points of power)

Government in power:
  Key agencies and officials
  Legislative entrenched bureaucracies
  Policies—economic, financial, social, labor, etc.
  Pending legislation
  Attitude toward private sector
  Power networks

Political parties (in and out of power):
  Policies
  Leading and emerging personalities
  Internal power struggles
  Sector and area strengths
  Future prospects for retaining or gaining power

Other important groups:
  Unions and labor movements
  Military, special groups within military
  Families
  Business and financial communities
  Intelligentsia
  Students
  Religious groups
  Media
  Regional and local governments
  Social and environmental activists
  Cultural, linguistic, and ethnic groups
  Separatist movements
  Foreign communities
  Potential competitors and customers

Internal factors:
  Power struggles among elites
  Ethnic confrontations
  Regional struggles
  Economic factors affecting stability (consumer inflation, price and wage controls, unemployment, supply shortages, taxation, etc.)
  Anti-establishment movements
  Factors affecting a specific project (custom-designed for each project)

Note: Information in the table is an abridged version of Probe's Political Agenda Worksheet, which may serve as a guide for corporate executives initiating their own political evaluations. Probe International is located in Stamford, CT.

Source: From Benjamin Weinger, "What Executives Should Know About Political Risk," *Management Review,* January 1992, p. 20. Reproduced with permission of American Management Association via Copyright Clearance Center.

Terrorism and Its Overseas Expansion

terrorism
The use of force or violence against others to promote political or social views.

Terrorism has existed for centuries, but has become more of a concern over the last few years, especially in the United States in light of the September 11, 2001, attacks. **Terrorism** is the use of force or violence against others to promote political or social views. The ultimate goal is for government and citizens to change policies and ultimately yield to the beliefs of the terrorist group.[18] Three types of terrorism exist: classic, amateur, and religiously motivated.[19] *Classic terrorism* entails a specific, well-defined objective carried out by well-trained, professional, underground members. *Amateur terrorism* tends to occur once and often has poorly defined objectives, and therefore members are not as committed. *Religiously motivated terrorism* binds individuals through very strong core beliefs, regardless of how well defined the objectives are. The latter tends to be more chaotic and scattered, since the individuals involved are extremely passionate about the cause, despite the lack of clear intents.

Due to the political motivation of terrorist attacks, MNCs need to be wary of the combative environment that may exist when they seek to engage in overseas expansion. For example, the Al Qaeda group has attacked areas in Yemen, Pakistan, Kuwait, Tunisia, and Kenya, to name a few. Palestinian suicide bombers have blown up buses in Israel. Australian tourists were killed in a massive attack in Bali, and a restaurant in the Philippines was the target of similar assaults. Furthermore, the United States has invaded Afghanistan and Iraq, which has also harmed political relations with countries that did not agree with those actions.[20] There have also been violent uprisings in Africa and bombings in the U.K., and in 2004, a terrorist group took over a school in Russia, resulting in the deaths of about 325 people when the Russian military recaptured the school.[21]

It is clear that terrorism within a country can have a significant impact on the MNC. If a country has a high occurrence of terrorist attacks in commercial businesses, companies will be extremely wary about setting up operations. Typically, terrorists target areas or businesses that are of high status or those that have great influence on initiating change. While terrorists now use an extensive array of attack methods, they tend to avoid institutions with high security, since most attacks on private businesses are either driven by the amateur terrorist or those that are religiously motivated.[22] Therefore, while there is no way to guarantee that companies can fully avoid harm, it is best for MNCs to completely evaluate the political environment, install modern security systems, compile a crisis handbook, and prepare employees for situations that may arise.

Analyzing the Expropriation Risk

expropriation
The seizure of businesses by a host country with little, if any, compensation to the owners.

indigenization laws
Laws that require nationals to hold a majority interest in an operation.

Expropriation is the seizure of businesses with little, if any, compensation to the owners. Such seizures of foreign enterprises by developing countries were quite common in the old days. In addition, some takeovers were caused by **indigenization laws,** which required that nationals hold a majority interest in the operation. In the main, expropriation is more likely to occur in non-Western countries that are poor, relatively unstable, and suspicious of foreign multinationals.

Some firms are more vulnerable to expropriation than others. Often, those at greatest risk are in extractive, agricultural, or infrastructural industries such as utilities and transportation, because of their importance to the country. In addition, large firms often are more likely targets than small firms, because more is to be gained by expropriating from large firms.

MNCs can take a wide variety of strategies to minimize their chances of expropriation. They can bring in local partners. They can limit the use of high technology so that if the firm is expropriated, the country cannot duplicate the technology. They also can acquire an affiliate that depends on the parent company for key areas of the operation, such as financing, research, and technology transfer, so that no practical value exists in seizing the affiliate.

The Role of Operational Profitability in Risk Analysis

Although expropriation is a major consideration, most MNCs are more directly concerned with operational profitability. Will they be able to make the desired return on investment? A number of government regulations can have a negative impact on profitability. Requiring MNCs to use domestic suppliers instead of bringing in components or raw materials from other company-owned facilities or purchasing them more cheaply in the world market is one such regulation. Another is a restriction on the amount of profit that can be taken out of the country. A third is the wages and salaries that must be paid to the employees. Despite these difficulties, MNCs have become very interested in designing models and frameworks to understand and manage their political risk.

■ Managing Political Risk and Government Relations

For well over two decades, businesses have been looking for ways to manage their political risk. Quite often, the process begins with a detailed analysis of the various risks with which the MNC will be confronted, including development of a comprehensive framework that identifies the various risks and then assigns a quantitative risk or rating factor to them.

Developing a Comprehensive Framework or Quantitative Analysis

A comprehensive framework for managing political risk should consider all political risks and identify those that are most important. Schmidt has offered a three-dimensional framework that combines political risks, general investments, and special investments.[23] Figure 10–1 illustrates this framework, and the following sections examine each dimension in detail.

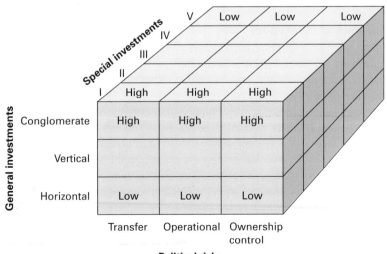

Figure 10–1

A Three-Dimensional Framework for Assessing Political Risk

Source: David A. Schmidt, "Analyzing Political Risk," *Business Horizons,* August 1986, p. 50. Copyright 1986 Elsevier. Reprinted with premission.

transfer risks
Government policies that
limit the transfer of capital,
payments, production,
people, and technology in
and out of the country.

operational risks
Government policies and
procedures that directly
constrain management and
performance of local
operations.

ownership-control risks
Government policies or
actions that inhibit
ownership or control of
local operations.

Political Risks   Political risks can be broken down into three basic categories: transfer risks, operational risks, and ownership-control risks. **Transfer risks** stem from government policies that limit the transfer of capital, payments, production, people, and technology in or out of the country. Examples include tariffs on exports and imports as well as restrictions on exports, dividend remittance, and capital repatriation. **Operational** risks result from government policies and procedures that directly constrain the management and performance of local operations. Examples include price controls, financing restrictions, export commitments, taxes, and local sourcing requirements. **Ownership-control risks** are brought about by government policies or actions that inhibit ownership or control of local operations. Examples include foreign-ownership limitations, pressure for local participation, confiscation, expropriation, and abrogation of proprietary rights. For example, the Russian government canceled an agreement with the Exxon Corporation that would have allowed the firm to tap huge oil deposits in the country's far north. The Russian minister for natural resources cited "legal irregularities" as the reason for the decision. As a result, the $1.5 billion project came to a grinding halt. Commenting on the government's action, one Western investment banker in Russia said that "it raises the question of whether a deal is a deal in Russia, because Exxon is meticulous to a fault in following the letter of the law."[24] In any event, the decision provides a good example of ownership-control risks. Still another is provided in "International Management in Action: Sometimes It's All Politics."

General Nature of Investment   The general nature of investment examines whether the company is making a conglomerate, vertical, or horizontal investment (see Figure 10–1). In a **conglomerate investment,** the goods or services produced are not similar to those produced at home. These types of investments usually are rated as high risk, because foreign governments see them as providing fewer benefits to the country and greater benefits to the MNC than other investments. **Vertical investments** include the production of raw materials or intermediate goods that are to be processed into final products. These investments run the risk of being taken over by the government because they are export-oriented, and governments like a business that helps them generate foreign capital. **Horizontal investments** involve the production of goods or services that are the same as those produced at home. These investments typically are made with an eye toward satisfying the host country's market demands. As a result, they are not very likely to be takeover targets.

conglomerate investment
A type of high-risk
investment in which goods
or services produced are
not similar to those
produced at home.

vertical investment
The production of raw
materials or intermediate
goods that are to be
processed into final
products.

horizontal investment
An MNC investment in
foreign operations to
produce the same goods or
services as those produced
at home.

Special Nature of Investment   The special nature of foreign direct investment relates to the sector of economic activity, technological sophistication, and pattern of ownership. There are three sectors of economic activity: (1) the primary sector, which consists of agriculture, forestry, and mineral exploration and extraction; (2) the industrial sector, consisting of manufacturing operations; and (3) the service sector, which includes transportation, finance, insurance, and related industries. Technological sophistication consists of science-based industry and non-science-based industry. The difference between them is that science-based industry requires the continuous introduction of new products or processes. Patterns of ownership relate to whether the business is wholly or partially owned.

The special nature of foreign direct investments can be categorized as one of five types (see Figure 10–1). Type I is the highest-risk venture; type V is the lowest-risk venture. This risk factor is assigned based on sector, technology, and ownership. Primary sector industries usually have the highest risk factor, service sector industries have the next highest, and industrial sector industries have the lowest. Firms with technology that is not available to the government should the firm be taken over have lower risk than those with technology that is easily acquired. Wholly owned subsidiaries have higher risk than partially owned subsidiaries.

Sometimes It's All Politics

One of the biggest problems in doing business internationally is that yesterday's agreement with a government may be canceled or delayed by today's politicians who disagree with that earlier decision. Enron, the now bankrupt Houston-based U.S. energy consortium, discovered this when its power project in Dabhol, India, became the focal point of political interest. India's economic nationalists began accelerating a campaign to scrap a high-profile, U.S.-backed power project despite warnings of potential damage to the confidence of foreign investors in the country. These politicians wanted to abandon the $2.8 billion deal as well as all other power projects in the country that had been approved under the government's "fast track" provisions. The contract for the two-stage, 2,000+ megawatt plant was signed before the current politicians came to power in Maharashtra, the state where Dabhol is located.

What effect would this political move have on foreign investment in India? A number of foreign investors indicated that if the Enron project were canceled, they would review their investment plans for the country. A survey of international energy companies by the East-West Center in Hawaii found that of 13 Asian economies, India's investment climate ranked fifth from the bottom for power-sector investment. This seemed to have little effect on the politicians, who proceeded to cancel the project. Members of the political opposition, who supported the project, called it a mere political ploy designed to appeal to voters in the upcoming elections, and they urged foreign investors to sit tight and ride out the political storm. Many of these investors appeared to be apprehensive about taking such advice, and Enron announced plans for taking the case to international arbitration to reclaim the $300 million it had invested in the project—as well as $300 million in damages.

Eventually things were straightened out, but only for a while. More recently the Maharashtra State Electric Board defaulted on $64 million in unpaid power bills. The board said that the company was charging too much for power, and Enron served notice that it would terminate the power supply contract and pull out. As of fall 2002,

following Enron's own collapse, the power purchase agreement was to be reworked, and the foreign investors—Enron's creditors, GE, and Bechtel—were looking to divest their stakes in the venture, scrambling to recover whatever they could from the project.

The political climate in India is not unique. Russia also offers its share of jitters to investors. In particular, many joint ventures that were created during the Gorbachev era now are having problems. A good example is Moscow's Radisson-Slavjanskaya Hotel venture, in which American Business Centers of Irvine, California, owns a 40 percent stake. American Business Centers manages several floors of offices in the hotel, and now that the venture is making money, it appears that the Irvine firm's Russian partners and the Radisson hotel people are trying to oust them. The president of American Business Centers claims that his partners feel they do not need him any longer.

The dilemma faced by American Business Centers is becoming increasingly common in Russia. For example, the Seattle-based firm Radio Page entered into a joint venture with Moscow Public Telephone Network and another Russian company to offer paging services. Together, they built a system of telephone pagers in the Moscow region. Radio Page held a 51 percent stake. When annual revenues hit $5 million and the venture was on the verge of making $1 million, the agreement began to unravel. The Russian partners demanded control of the operation and even threatened to pull the critical radio frequencies if they did not get their way.

There is little that foreign joint-venture firms doing business in high-risk countries can do except try to negotiate with their partners. For instance, the political situation in Russia is so unstable that support from one government ministry may be offset by opposition from another, or, worse yet, the individuals supporting the foreign firm may be ousted from their jobs tomorrow. Economic considerations tend to be the main reason why firms seek international partners, but sometimes it seems that everything boils down to politics and the risks associated with dealing in this political environment.

Using a framework similar to that provided in Figure 10–1 helps MNCs to manage their political risks. A way to complement this framework approach is to give specific risk ratings to various criteria.

Quantifying the Variables in Managing Political Risk   Some MNCs attempt to manage political risk through a quantification process in which a range of variables are simultaneously analyzed to derive an overall rating of the degree of political risk in a given jurisdiction. This would allow an MNC, for example, to compare how risky a particular venture would be in Russia and in Argentina.

Factors that are typically quantified reflect the political and economic environment, domestic economic conditions, and external economic conditions. Each factor

Table 10–3
Criteria for Quantifying Political Risk

| Major Area | Criteria | Scores | |
		Minimum	Maximum
Political and economic environment	1. Stability of the political system	3	14
	2. Imminent internal conflicts	0	14
	3. Threats to stability emanating from the outside world	0	12
	4. Degree of control of the economic system	5	9
	5. Reliability of the country as a trading partner	4	12
	6. Constitutional guarantees	2	12
	7. Effectiveness of public administration	3	12
	8. Labor relations and social peace	3	15
Domestic economic conditions	9. Size of population	4	8
	10. Per capita income	2	10
	11. Economic growth during previous 5 years	2	7
	12. Prospective growth during next 3 years	3	10
	13. Inflation during previous 2 years	2	10
	14. Accessibility of domestic capital market to foreigners	3	7
	15. Availability of high-quality local labor	2	8
	16. Possibility of giving employment to foreign nationals	2	8
	17. Availability of energy resources	2	14
	18. Legal requirements concerning environmental protection	4	8
	19. Traffic system and communication	2	14
External economic relations	20. Restrictions imposed on imports	2	10
	21. Restrictions imposed on exports	2	10
	22. Restrictions imposed on foreign investments in the country	3	9
	23. Freedom to set up or engage in partnerships	3	9
	24. Legal protection for brands and products	3	9
	25. Restrictions imposed on monetary transfers	2	8
	26. Reevaluations against the home market currency during previous 5 years	2	7
	27. Development of the balance of payments	2	9
	28. Drain on foreign funds through oil and other energy imports	3	14
	29. International financial standing	3	8
	30. Restrictions imposed on the exchange of local money into foreign currencies	2	8

Source: From E. Diehtl and H. G. Koglmayr, "Country Risk Ratings," *Management International Review,* Vol. 26, No. 4, 1986, p. 6. Reprinted with permission.

is given a minimum or maximum score, and the scores are tallied to provide an overall evaluation of the risk. Table 10–3 provides an example of a quantitative list of political risk criteria.

Techniques for Responding to Political Risk

Once political risk has been analyzed by a framework, quantitative analysis, or both, the MNC then will attempt to manage the risk further through a carefully developed response. The MNC can also proactively improve its relationship with governments by means of preemptive political strategies to mitigate risk before it appears. Three related strategies should be considered: (1) relative bargaining power analysis; (2) integrative, protective, and defensive techniques; and (3) proactive political strategies.

Relative Bargaining Power Analysis The theory behind relative bargaining power is quite simple. The MNC works to maintain a bargaining power position stronger than that of the host country. A good example arises when the MNC has proprietary technology that will be unavailable to the host country if the operation is expropriated or the firm is forced to abide by government decisions that are unacceptable to it. Over time, of course, this technology may become common, and the firm will lose its bargaining power. To prevent this from happening, the firm will work to develop new technology that again establishes the balance of power in its favor. As long as the host country stands to lose more than it will gain by taking action against the company, the firm has successfully minimized its political risk by establishing an effective bargaining position. Figure 10–2 provides an example. As long as the MNC's bargaining power remains at or above the diagonal line, the government will not intervene. At point E in the figure, this power declines, and the host country will begin to intervene.[25]

Gaining bargaining power depends on many factors, such as the host country's perception of the MNC's size, experience, and legitimacy. Furthermore, the ability to bargain and achieve security does not necessarily mean that the MNC must be aggressive or engage in a "power play." As seen in the opening case, it is possible for both sides involved to maintain a balance of bargaining power, creating a cooperative relationship that can survive beyond technological advancements. Enticing the host country with products or services which could benefit it in the short run could result in retaliatory actions if the MNC is not able to innovate or the host country grows weary of a lack of power.

Integrative, Protective, and Defensive Techniques   Another way that MNCs attempt to protect themselves from expropriation or minimize government interference in their operations is to use integration and the implementation of protective and defensive techniques. **Integrative techniques** are designed to help the overseas operation become part of the host country's infrastructure. The objective is to be perceived as "less foreign" and thus unlikely to be the target of government action. Some of the most integrative techniques include (1) developing good relations with the host government and other local political groups; (2) producing as much of the product locally as possible with the use of in-country suppliers and subcontractors, thus making it a "domestic" product; (3) creating joint ventures and hiring local people to manage and run the operation; (4) doing as much local research and development as possible; and (5) developing effective labor-management relations.

> **integrative techniques**
> Techniques that help the overseas operation become a part of the host country's infrastructure.

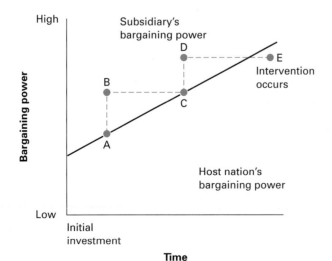

Figure 10–2

Relative Bargaining Power over Time

Source: Adapted from Thomas A. Pointer, "Political Risk: Managing Government Intervention," in *International Management: Text and Cases,* ed. Paul W. Beamish, J. Peter Killing, Donald J. LeCraw, and Harold Crookell (Homewood, IL: Irwin, 1991), p. 125.

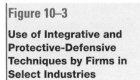

Figure 10–3

Use of Integrative and Protective-Defensive Techniques by Firms in Select Industries

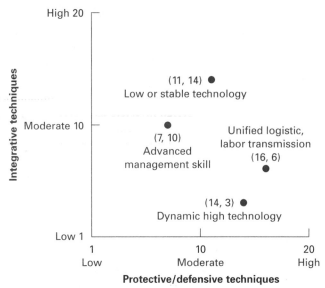

Source: Adapted from Ann Gregory, "Firm Characteristic and Political Risk Reduction in Overseas Ventures," *National Academy of Management Proceedings* (New York, 1982), p. 77.

MNCs should be cognizant of how integrated they become in foreign markets. It is recommended that managers seek to maintain close ties between the subsidiary and the parent company, and not fully integrate into the host country. There is no guarantee that host countries will completely treat the MNC as a domestic company, making true competition difficult. Therefore, other, more distant techniques may be beneficial.

protective and defensive techniques
Techniques that discourage the host government from interfering in operations.

Protective and defensive techniques are designed to discourage the host government from interfering in operations, mainly by avoiding complex ties to the host country's economy. In contrast to the integrative techniques, these actually encourage nonintegration of the enterprise in the local environment. Examples include (1) doing as little local manufacturing as possible and conducting all research and development outside the country; (2) limiting the responsibility of local personnel and hiring only those who are vital to the operation; (3) raising capital from local banks and the host government as well as outside sources; and (4) diversifying production of the product among a number of countries.

Companies are more likely to use a protective-defensive strategy or a balance over completely integrating into another country, as illustrated in Figure 10–3. Organizations with an emphasis on innovative technology, such as Microsoft, prefer a protective technique as a way to safeguard against actions such as counterfeiting. MNCs that have products which are labor-intensive and have a high value to weight ratio also prefer protective methods, though there exists some integration. Here, strong global marketing systems are needed to sell the product, which is why integration occurs on some level despite the more cost-efficient method of either manufacturing in the home country or simply outsourcing construction to lower-wage regions.

Developing countries do not hold advanced management skills in as high regard as developed countries. For this reason, when selling products such as food, which requires advanced marketing and management skills, it is best to employ a mixed strategy (see Figure 10–3). That is, integration is necessary in order to effectively manufacture the product to local tastes and advertise, and there is little need for the company to distance operations from the host country. Finally, industries that utilize little technology, such as steel manufacturers, exhibit the strongest integrative technique while still employing a defensive strategy. These companies require integration to ensure long-term production for projects, but may not desire to become completely enveloped in the host country's economy due to possibilities such as the host government suddenly requiring a greater share of profits generated by the MNC.

Proactive Political Strategies   As mentioned at the beginning of the chapter, despite the general trend of developing countries seeking MNC investment, many developing-country governments continue to engage in practices that effectively overturn or renege on past deals.[26] In the last half of the 1990s, leaders of a number of countries in which autocratic or dictatorial governments controlled negotiations with foreign investors were toppled. The ousting of leaders in Peru, Indonesia, Malaysia, the Philippines, and Venezuela led to a backlash against incumbent foreign investors and forced many project leaders to withdraw or renegotiate the terms of their investments.[27]

In Indonesia, President Suharto's 30 years of dictatorial and nepotistic government were totally discredited, and investors whose reputations were closely associated with his legacy face a challenging environment for preserving the economic viability of their presence. For example, the government of Indonesia reneged on its commitment to buy power from two projects sponsored by MidAmerica Energy Holdings, arguing that the projects, both of which were awarded on a sole-source contract basis under the Suharto regime, were overpriced and the government simply could not afford to pay.[28] Recently, Indonesia's minister of mines and energy, Purnamo Yusgiantora, said his government would fight in U.S. courts to release $130 million being held in a Bank of America escrow account after Karaha Bodas, a power developer, won an arbitration award in its dispute with the Indonesian government over cancellation of a geothermal plant that Karaha had agreed to build in collaboration with Indonesia's state electricity company.[29] The Bolivian government rescinded a 40-year contract with Aguas del Tunari—a consortium that included London-based International Water Ltd., Bechtel Enterprise Holdings, Italy's Montedison Energy Services, Spain's Abengoa Servicios Urbanos, and four of Bolivia's largest construction companies—to supply water to Cochabamba, Bolivia's third-largest city.

Often the challenges and complexity associated with governments' tendency to seek to renegotiate investment rules and contracts are worsened by the participation of both national and subcentral governments in the project. In India, Brazil, and, increasingly, China, states and provinces wield significant power, and this has been a particular problem in the development and financing of power, water, and transport projects. The Linha Amarela project in Rio de Janeiro, an urban expressway that begins in the residential area of Rio and provides a direct link to the downtown area, was initially bid with an official traffic estimate of around 55,000 cars per day in 1993–1994. However, when construction was complete and the road opened for business in 1998, traffic exceeded that amount, reaching 80,000 vehicles per day in early 2001. When the new mayor of Rio, Cesar Maia, took office on January 1, 2001, he issued a number of decrees overturning policies of his predecessor. One of these decrees unilaterally dropped the toll by 20 percent, squeezing the foreign owner of the concession.

In addition to the approaches mentioned above, how else can MNCs respond to such unpredictable government decisions? Because government policies can have a significant impact on business activities and many governments face competing pressures from a range of stakeholders, corporations must adopt various **proactive political strategies** both to affect government policy and to respond to competitors' efforts to influence that policy. Comprehensive strategies are especially important in unstable and transitional policy environments.[30] These strategies are designed, in part, to develop and maintain ongoing favorable relationships with government policy makers as a tool to mitigate risk before it becomes unmanageable. Broadly, strategies may include leveraging bilateral, regional, and international trade and investment agreements, drawing on bilateral and multilateral financial support, and using project finance structures to separate project exposure from overall firm risk. They also can include entering markets early in the privatization-liberalization cycle (the first-mover strategy discussed in Chapter 8), establishing a local presence and partnering with local firms, and pursuing preemptive stakeholder management strategies to secure relationships with all relevant actors.[31]

More specific proactive political strategies include formal lobbying, campaign financing, seeking advocacy through the embassy and consulates of the home country,

proactive political strategies
Lobbying, campaign financing, advocacy, and other political interventions designed to shape and influence the political decisions prior to their impact on the firm.

and more formal public relations and public affairs activities such as grassroots campaigning and advertising.[32] Strategies must vary based on the particular political system (parliamentary vs. nonparliamentary), distribution of power (highly centralized vs. decentralized), and other variations in political systems.[33] However, MNCs have the option of purchasing political risk insurance, which could be used across cultures and systems and protect the company from inherent uncertainty. This option has been available for decades, but many have not utilized it because risk assessment is so subjective and unpredictable, that most companies choose to forgo coverage.[34] MNCs that are concerned with currency convertibility issues, political unrest, or exporting matters may want to take a closer look. Insurance terms range anywhere from 3 to 15 years or more and can cover up to $80 million per risk.[35] As an MNC increases exporting or overseas operations, the benefits of coverage may outweigh the cost of the insurance.

Developing and maintaining ongoing relationships with political actors, including officials in power and in opposition parties, and with the range of stakeholders, including NGOs and others, can help buffer host-government actions that may constrain or undermine MNC strategies and plans.[36] In the previous examples, had investors made low-level contacts with opposition groups, they may have aggravated existing relationships with government but secured some protections for the future. Knowing when—and how—to exercise such relationships is a difficult but necessary strategy.

How does an MNC know which strategy to pursue? There is no straightforward answer to this question, since strategic responses rely on a multitude of factors. The nature of the industry, the firm's technological capabilities, local conditions in a host country, management skills and philosophies, logistics, and labor transmission are just a few ways decisions are impacted. No one strategy is guaranteed to work, but building a relationship with all parties involved could assist in the betterment of any method an MNC employs.

■ Managing Alliances

Another dimension of management strategy related to political risk and government relations is managing relationships with alliance partners. Some partners may be current or former state-owned enterprises; others may be controlled or influenced by government agencies. For example, in China, most foreign investors have some sort of alliance or joint-venture relationships with Chinese state-owned enterprises. Motorola, one of the most active investors in China, has many alliances with state-owned enterprises, such as its joint venture with Nanjing Panda Electronics to produce a personal computer. The heart of the computer will be Motorola's Power PC chip, the major rival to Intel's Pentium.[37] In 2004, Siemens AG chief executive Heinrich von Pierer announced a sweeping expansion of the company's business in China using its more than 45 joint ventures as the primary vehicle for expansion.[38] As mentioned in Chapter 9, alliances and joint ventures can significantly improve the success of MNC entry and operation in many international markets, especially emerging economies. Managing the relationships inherent in alliances, especially when governments are involved, can be especially challenging.

The Alliance Challenge

A rich and increasingly diverse recent literature has examined the motivations for collective action through international strategic alliances (ISAs). Researchers have begun to focus on specific explanations of ISA formation, the conditions that appear to lead to better or worse ISA performance and endurance, and the primary factors motivating firms to enter into such relationships.[39] Motivating factors include faster entry and payback, economies of scale and rationalization, complementary technologies and patents, and co-opting or blocking competition.[40]

In the strategic alliance literature, several researchers have argued that learning can be a powerful force in the initial motivations for, and ultimate success of, ISAs.[41] Some kinds of local knowledge cannot be internalized simply as a result of an MNC operating in a foreign market; acquisition of some kinds of local knowledge requires indigenous-firm experience through partnerships or alliances. Collaboration facilitates rapid market entry by allowing firms to share costs and risks, combine product and market complementarities, and reduce time-to-market.[42]

How an alliance relationship is developed is largely a function of interfirm negotiation. Alliances are an arena where both value-claiming activities (competitive, distributive negotiation) and value-creating activities (collaborative, integrative negotiation) take place. In order to lay claim to a larger share of the alliance pie, firms tend to seek an advantage over their partners. Firms do this by possessing superior resources or alternatives beyond the scope of the alliance. However, in order to create a "larger pie" through the combination of partner-firm resources and activities, firms must balance authority, allowing each firm to dictate certain activities within the alliance, and to commit to sharing and reciprocity where each partner firm plays some decision-making role. In these instances, alliance partners can create value through specialization gains or when the rationalization of redundant activities results in enhanced performance for the partners.[43]

A fundamental challenge of alliances is managing operations with partners from different national cultures. Cultural differences may create uncertainties and misunderstandings in the relationship, which may lead to conflict and even dissolution of the venture. Indeed, an alliance may be viewed as a temporal structure designed to address a particular problem during a period in time; all alliances eventually outlast their purpose.

Differences in the cultural backgrounds of partners cause problems in alliances and international joint ventures (IJVs). One study tried to determine whether some differences are more disruptive than others. The researchers found that differences in uncertainty avoidance and in long-term orientation, in particular, cause problems (see Chapter 4 for cultural dimensions). These differences have a negative impact on survival and decrease the likelihood that firms will enter a foreign country through an alliance rather than a wholly owned subsidiary.[44] Apparently, these differences, which translate into differences in how partners perceive and adapt to opportunities and threats in their environment, are more difficult to resolve than differences along other cultural dimensions. Perhaps cultural differences in power distance, individualism, and masculinity are more easily resolved because they are mainly reflected in different attitudes toward the management of personnel—something firms can make explicit. In a study of Mexican firms with experience in alliances with U.S. counterparts, Mexican managers were found to view a balance of authority as a positive contributor to alliance performance, while authority advantage—even when to the benefit of the Mexican partner at the expense of the U.S. partner—was viewed as having a negative impact on performance.[45]

Successful management of alliances depends on situational conditions, management instruments, and performance criteria. Success factors may include partner selection, cooperation agreement, management structure, acculturation process, and knowledge management.[46] In particular, partner selection and task selection criteria have been identified as critical variables that influence alliance success or failure. Choosing the right partners and defining the scope and limit to the alliance appear to be the most important elements in determining if an alliance will succeed or fail.

One difficult but important aspect of successful alliance management is preparation for the likely eventual termination of the alliance.[47] Many firms are caught off guard when their partners are better prepared to deal with issues related to termination of the alliance than they are. After studying two dozen successful alliance "divorces," a group of researchers identified a number of legal and business issues that were critical to successful divorces. Legal issues include the conditions of termination, the disposition of assets and liabilities, dispute resolution, distributorship arrangements, protection of proprietary information and property, and rights over sales territories and obligations to customers. Business issues include the basic decision to exit, people-related issues, and relations with the host government. Alliances, like individual businesses, experience a life cycle, as illustrated in Figure 10–4. Recognizing the point at which your alliance exists in the life cycle can help determine a proactive strategy to sustain the relationship and work towards a common goal.

Figure 10–4 | Alliance Life Cycle

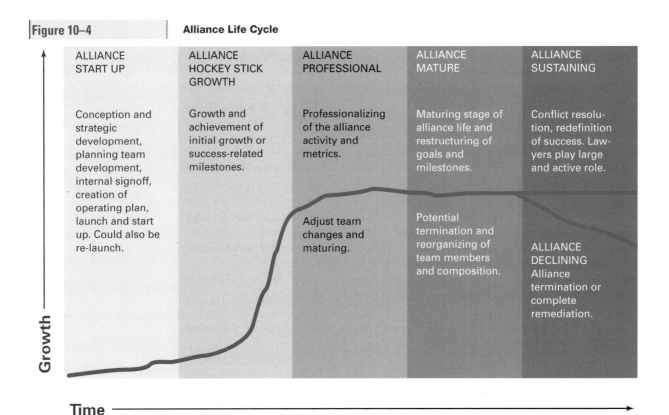

Source: From Larraine Segil, "Metrics to Successfully Manage Alliances," *Strategy & Leadership,* Vol. 22, No. 5, 2005, p. 47. Reprinted with permission of the author.

The Role of Host Governments in Alliances

As previously mentioned, host governments are active in mandating that investors take on partners, and these mandates can pose managerial and operational challenges for MNCs. Many host governments require investors to share ownership of their subsidiaries with local partners—in some cases, state-owned or state-controlled partners. These mandates can include specific requirements that investors select local state-owned firms (China) or that investors form joint ventures to meet local regulatory requirements where restrictions or local-content rules apply (Central and Eastern Europe).[48]

Even when host governments do not require alliances or joint venture as a condition for entry, many MNCs find that having alliance or joint-venture partners is advantageous to their entry and expansion. This is especially so in highly regulated industries such as banking, telecommunications, and health care. In a study conducted of alliances among global telecommunications firms, firms were found to establish alliances with local partners primarily to gain market access and to contend with local regulations.[49] In another study, also of telecommunications projects in emerging markets, firms were found to take on local partners as a way to cope with emerging-market environments characterized by arbitrary and unpredictable corruption.[50]

Even when alliances are dissolved, host governments can have a role. In particular, the host government of a partner may be unwilling to permit the alliance to terminate. It could object to the termination in an overt way, such as not permitting a foreign partner to sell its interest in the alliance.[51] There are also subtle ways to discourage a partner from leaving an alliance, such as blocking the repatriation of the foreign partner's investments in the alliance. It is also important to consider carefully the long-term effects of terminating an alliance on the ability of the company to do business in the same host country in the future.

In sum, host governments have a substantial role in the terms under which alliances are initially formed, the way in which they are managed, and even the terms of their dissolution. MNCs must be aware of these influences and use carefully crafted strategies to manage host-government involvement in their alliances.

Examples of Challenges and Opportunities in Alliance Management

Alliances and joint ventures are increasingly common modes of entry and operation in international business. A number of recent examples illustrate the challenges and opportunities associated with managing alliances.

A good example is provided by Ford Motor and Mazda. For a number of years the two have had a strategic alliance. Today, with guidance from its American partner, Mazda is trimming costs and introducing a host of popular new models in Asia. At the same time, the company is beginning to gain ground in both North America and Europe. Part of this success is accounted for by Ford executives who reined in Mazda's freewheeling engineers and forced them to share auto platforms and to source more components overseas. Mazda also began following Ford's advice to use customer clinics, thus helping the company to develop low-priced, compact sport vehicles that are proving very popular in the Japanese market. Over the next few years, Mazda intends to continue growing its market shares in North America and Europe. The two firms are also working closely together in Asia.

Starbucks Coffee International of Seattle, Washington, recently developed a joint venture with the Beijing Mei Da Coffee Company to open coffee houses in China. Getting local consumers to switch from tea to coffee is likely to be a major challenge. However, for the moment, the joint venture is focusing on the training of local managers who will run the coffee shops. Recruits are sent to Tacoma, Washington, to learn how to make the various types of Starbucks coffee and to get a firsthand look at the company's culture. As one of the general managers for the Mei Da Company put it, "People don't go to Starbucks for the coffee but for the experience. Focusing on the development of employees so that they can deliver that experience is our priority for now."[52] Part of Starbucks's strategy is also to show the new recruits that there are career and personal development opportunities in this new venture. This is an important area of emphasis for the firm because there is a major shortage of management personnel in China. As a result, many companies raid the management ranks of others, offering lucrative financial arrangements to those who are willing to change companies. One way that Starbucks is trying to deal with this is by encouraging the trainees to take responsibility, question the system, take risks, and make changes that will keep the customers coming back. Many foreign MNCs in China want the employees to do as they are told. Starbucks believes that its IJV emphasis on developing talent will give it an edge—and discourage people from leaving for higher financially attractive offers.

As these examples show, multinationals are and will be making a host of decisions related to IJVs. In Russia, the current trend is to renegotiate many of the old agreements and seek smaller deals that entail less bureaucratic red tape and are easier to bring to fruition. At the same time, the U.S. administration is trying to create a plan for providing assistance to the former Soviet republics, and this likely will generate increased interest in the use of IJVs.

Besides the former Soviet Union, other areas of the world previously closed to foreign investment are beginning to open up. One of these is Vietnam, which had a very auspicious beginning in the early 1990s when investors began flocking there. During this time period, Japan's Idemitsu Oil Development Company signed a deal with the Vietnamese government that gave the company the right to explore an offshore oil and gas field in the Gulf of Tonkin. A number of U.S. companies also targeted Vietnam for investment, and Citibank and Bank of America both were approved for branch status by the government. The bulk of their business was to be in wholesale banking and, in the case of Bank of America, advising the government on financing the rebuilding of the nation's weak power sector. Other firms that began giving serious consideration to Vietnam included AT&T, Coca-Cola, General Electric, ExxonMobil, and Ralston Purina, to name but five. As a result, by 1996 the country was attracting over $8 billion annually in foreign direct investment (FDI). In the late 1990s and early 2000s, however, FDI dropped sharply.

In 2000, the Vietnam General Department of Statistics reported that annual FDI was in the range of a mere $300 million. Despite its promises, the bureaucratic communist government had not created an attractive environment. Ford Motor, for example, had spent over $100 million to build a factory near Hanoi, but because of pressure from its local rival, the Vietnam Motor Corporation, it had taken 16 months for Ford to get approval to sell its Laser sedan. By the end of 2000, the company had sold fewer than 1,000 vehicles, a far cry from the 14,000 that had been initially projected.[53] Many other firms reported similar experiences. Consequently, the Vietnamese government tried to turn things around by undertaking domestic economic reform, pursuing international trade agreements, and encouraging foreign investment, especially joint ventures.[54] Among other things, the country's coffee production was skyrocketing, and Vietnam exported over 20 percent of its coffee to the United States; so it is in the best interests of the country to open its markets. At the same time, a growing number of multinationals were reexamining Vietnam's potential and looking to create strategic alliances that will help them establish a foothold in one of the more promising emerging economies in Asia.[55] After several years, this approach seemed to be paying off. Vietnam had passed a domestic enterprise law and investment law easing and clarifying foreign investment and business rules, including those pertaining to joint ventures, signed a trade agreement with the United States, and, in 2005, joined the WTO. As a result, foreign investment was once again on the rise, reaching nearly $10 billion in 2006. In 2002, Ford sold 3,685 vehicles worth about $95 million; by 2004, the company was selling more than 5,000 vehicles annually, surpassing Toyota as the best-selling brand.[56]

The World of *BusinessWeek*—Revisited

A wide range of risks emanate from the political environment in which MNCs operate, and firms can employ an equally diverse set of strategies to mitigate those risks and improve their relations with governments. Freeport's situation in Indonesia underscores these risks and the range of responses to them. Whether the progress Freeport has experienced is due to a shift in politics or simply an effective choice in strategy is something only time can tell. The fact is that relying so heavily on a country riddled with unstable political situations is extremely risky, and companies need to protect themselves against such uncertainty. The article conveys the importance of mitigating risk by securing solid government and broaden societal relationships. While Indonesia is interested in seeking outside investment, countries that are not in good standing with the Indonesian government may find that expansion is difficult, if not impossible. Good political risk assessment and strong government relations are crucial to success in today's global environment.

After reading this chapter and considering the challenges associated with business in Indonesia, answer the following questions: (1) What are two main concerns that MNCs should evaluate when doing business in Indonesia? (2) How can MNCs protect themselves from government action? (3) What proactive political strategies might help protect MNCs from future changes in the political environment? (4) How might alliances and joint ventures reduce risk and help relationships with government actors and other stakeholders?

SUMMARY OF KEY POINTS

1. Political risk is the likelihood that the foreign investment of a business will be constrained by a host government's policies. In dealing with this risk, companies conduct both macro and micro political risk analyses. Specific consideration is given to changing host-government policies, expropriation, and operational profitability risk.

2. MNCs attempt to manage their political risk in two basic ways. One is by developing a comprehensive framework for identifying and describing these risks.

This includes consideration of political, operational, and ownership-control risks. A second is by quantifying the variables that help constitute the risk.

3. Common risk management strategies are the use of relative bargaining power, integrative, protective, and defensive techniques, and proactive political strategies.

4. Effective alliance management includes careful selection of partners, defining the tasks and scope of the alliance, addressing cross-cultural differ ences, and responding to host-government requirements.

KEY TERMS

conglomerate investment, *322*

expropriation, *320*

horizontal investment, *322*

indigenization laws, *320*

integrative techniques, *325*

macro political risk analysis, *316*

micro political risk analysis, *316*

operational risks, *322*

ownership-control risks, *322*

political risk *314*

proactive political strategies, *327*

protective and defensive
   techniques, *326*

terrorism, *320*

transfer risks, *322*

vertical investment, *322*

REVIEW AND DISCUSSION QUESTIONS

1. What types of political risk would a company entering Russia face? Identify and describe three. What types of political risk would a company entering France face? Identify and describe three. How are these risks similar? How are they different?

2. Most firms attempt to quantify their political risk, although they do not assign specific weights to the respective criteria. Why is this approach so popular? Would the companies be better off assigning weights to each of the risks being assumed? Defend your answer.

3. How has terrorism impacted foreign interest in Iran and Saudi Arabia, considering the vast oil reserves

that are there? How have terrorist attacks affected political relationships between countries such as the United States and Russia?

4. If a high-tech firm wanted to set up operations in Iran, what steps might it take to ensure that the subsidiary would not be expropriated? Identify and describe three strategies that would be particularly helpful. How might proactive political strategies help protect firms from future changes in the political environment?

5. What are some of the challenges associated with managing alliances? How do host governments affect these?

INTERNET EXERCISE: MOTOROLA IN CHINA

Asia still offers great opportunities for multinational firms. However, given the slowdown that has occurred in this region in recent years, there are also great risks associated with doing business there. The large American-based MNC Motorola has determined that the opportunities are worth the risk and has staked a large claim in China and is determined to be a major player in the emerging Asian market. Visit Motorola's Web site at **www.motorola.com** and focus your attention on what

this well-known MNC is now doing in Asia. Drawing from specific information obtained from the Web site, this chapter, and your reading of the current news, answer these questions: What political risks does Motorola face in Asia, particularly China? How can Motorola manage these risks? How can effective international negotiating skills be of value to the firm in reducing its political risk and increasing its competitive advantage in this area of the world?

Brazil

After three centuries under the rule of Portugal, Brazil became an independent nation in 1822. By far the largest and most populous country in South America, Brazil has overcome more than a half century of military intervention in the governance of the country to pursue industrial and agricultural growth and the development of the interior.

After crafting a fiscal adjustment program and pledging progress on structural reform, Brazil received a $41.5 billion IMF-led international support program in November 1998. In January 1999, the Brazilian Central Bank announced that the *real* would no longer be pegged to the U.S. dollar. The consequent devaluation helped moderate the downturn in economic growth in 1999, and the country posted moderate GDP growth in 2000. Economic growth slowed considerably in 2001–2003—to less than 2 percent—because of a slowdown in major markets and the hiking of interest rates by the Central Bank to combat inflationary pressures. President Luiz Inácio Lula da Silva, who took office on January 1, 2003, has given priority to reforming the complex tax code, trimming the overblown civil service pension system, and continuing the fight against inflation. By exploiting vast natural resources and a large labor pool, Brazil is today South America's leading economic power and a regional bellwether as it continues toward a free-market society.

After winning a landslide victory in 2002 on a campaign to revamp the economy and battle for the poor, President Lula da Silva reassured worried investors when he continued his predecessor's plan of strict financial austerity. Instead of catching the jitters as predicted, the country's bond and stock markets enjoyed stellar returns in 2003 and are still going strong. But within a year, pressure was mounting on Lula da Silva to keep true to his populist roots. After riding a wave of popular support through his first year, Lula da Silva faced sharp criticism from within his own Workers' Party and governing coalition as well as from ordinary voters. Lula has also gained a reputation for being thin-skinned when it comes to criticism; he expelled a foreign journalist critical of his policies. Some feel betrayed by Lula da Silva's rejection of the socialist policies that the Workers' Party has always fought for. In a March 2004 opinion poll, only 28 percent of Brazilians voiced support for the government, down

from 41 percent in December. Despite this downturn, Lula da Silva was reelected in 2006, and received more votes than any other Brazilian elected president. Both the right and the left are frustrated with economic performance, although Brazil's economy has recently benefited from strong commodity prices and is expected to grow 4–5% in 2008 and 2009. In addition, Brazil has emerged as a leader of developing countries concerned about the imbalance in global trade rules, and Brazil led the "Group of 20" countries responsible for slowing progress in the Doha development round of global trade talks. Because of the same concerns, Brazil also dimmed prospects for a hemisphere-wide free-trade agreement—to the frustration of the United States and other countries, which went ahead with bilateral and regional FTAs to fill the gap.

Brazil's policies toward energy and telecommunications firms that entered the country as part of the privatization wave have also raised concerns. BellSouth, with operations in 10 Latin American countries—Argentina, Uruguay, Colombia, Venezuela, Chile, Peru, Ecuador, Panama, Nicaragua, and Guatemala—announced recently it would sell its operation in southern Brazil. It has more than 11 million subscribers in the region, making it the largest U.S. wireless player there and the second-largest player after Mexico's América Móvil. AES Corporation also pulled out some of its electricity investments because of general instability in the region, difficult labor relations, and lawsuits over service disruptions brought on by illegal line cutting by consumers wanting free electricity. Yet, Brazil's current government has taken a generally moderate stance and continues to push through economic reform.

Questions

1. In your opinion, why is there still political uncertainty in Brazil?

2. What strategy would be the most useful to companies interested in Brazilian investment?

3. Considering the economic and political environment, what types of companies would benefit the most by expanding operations to Brazil?

4. How should BellSouth, AES, and other companies address concerns about government policies in Brazil?

Rushing into Russia

As Russia continues to succeed with a decentralized economy and foreign investors flood in, a Chicago, Illinois–based computer chip manufacturer decides that it may be time to expand operations overseas. The company has a series of patents that provide legal protection and allow it to dominate a small but growing segment of the computer market. Its sales estimates reached $147 million within three years, but it believes that this could rise to $200 million if it was to expand internationally. Adam Smith, CEO of the company, had previously considered China and India for their cheap labor, but decided that their rapid growth and intense international interest would just lead to a higher bidding price. Furthermore, there are far fewer direct competitors expanding in Russia, whereas technological parts and services industries are already pervasive in other emerging countries. Adam recalls a time when Russia experienced high human trafficking, corruption, and general political instability, but he believes that with so much international interest in Russia, these issues must be curbed by this point in time.

Adam is confident that a deal will be accepted by Russia as it continues to welcome foreign investment to maintain economic growth. A state-of-the-art plant could help to reduce unemployment further and provide an inflow of needed capital. However, the banker is concerned that because of the political risks and uncertainty in Eastern Europe in general and Russia in particular, the company may either lose its investment through government expropriation or find itself unable to get profits out of the country. Given that the company will have to invest approximately $20 million, the venture could seriously endanger the company's financial status.

Adam understands these risks but believes that with the help of an international management consultant, he can identify and minimize the problems. "I'm determined to push ahead," he told the banker, "and if there is a good chance of making this project a success, I'm going to Russia."

Questions

1. What are some of the political risks that Adam's firm will face if he decides to go ahead with this venture? Identify and describe two or three.

2. Using Figure 10–3, what strategy would you recommend that the firm use? Why?

3. In his negotiations with the Russian government, what suggestions or guidelines would you offer to Adam? Identify and describe two or three.

Chapter 11

MANAGEMENT DECISION AND CONTROL

OBJECTIVES OF THE CHAPTER

Although they are not directly related to internationalization, decision making and controlling are two management functions that play critical roles in international operations. In *decision making,* a manager chooses a course of action among alternatives. In *controlling,* the manager evaluates results in relation to plans or objectives and decides what action, if any, to take. How these functions are carried out is influenced by the international context. An organization can employ a centralized or decentralized management system depending on such factors as company philosophy or competition. The company also has an array of measures and tools it can use to evaluate firm performance and restructuring options. As with most international operations, culture plays a significant role in what is important in both decision-making processes and control features, and can affect MNC decisions when forming relationships with subsidiaries.

This chapter examines the different decision-making and controlling management functions used by MNCs, notes some of the major factors that account for differences between these functions, and identifies the major challenges of the years ahead. The specific objectives of this chapter are:

1. **PROVIDE** comparative examples of decision making in different countries.

2. **PRESENT** some of the major factors affecting the degree of decision-making authority given to overseas units.

3. **COMPARE** and **CONTRAST** direct controls with indirect controls.

4. **DESCRIBE** some of the major differences in the ways that MNCs control operations.

5. **DISCUSS** some of the specific performance measures that are used to control international operations.

The World of *BusinessWeek*

BusinessWeek

The Race to Build Really Cheap Cars

The Newest Thing on Four Wheels Is Sturdy, Inexpensive, and Probably Not Made in the U.S.

How cheap is cheap? Renault-Nissan Chief Executive Carlos Ghosn is betting that for autos, the magic number is under $3,000. At a plant-opening ceremony in India Apr. 4, he was already talking up the industry's next challenge: a future model that would sport a sticker price as low as $2,500—about 40% less than the least expensive subcompact currently on the market. Renault-Nissan is the first global automaker to take up the gauntlet thrown down in 2003 by India's Tata Motors, which plans to launch a $2,500 car next year. Both are leading a race to the bottom that could affect the business every bit as much as Henry Ford's Model T did a century ago.

After years of making their mass-market cars more expensive, the world's automakers have abruptly shifted into reverse. With stagnant growth in the U.S., Europe, and Japan, they are now eyeing emerging markets for new opportunities. That means redesigning the car for buyers who might otherwise be able to afford only a motorcycle. And outdated, stripped-down models won't do. Demand is surging for basic cars that combine modern comfort with safety at a fraction of today's cost. The rush to build a modern, no-frills car could do for autos what airlines like Southwest Airlines Co. and JetBlue Airways Corp. have done for travel, and H&M and Zara have done for fashion. Low-cost cars are "the single most important trend in the automotive industry today," says Vikas Tibrewala, the Paris-based executive director of the Monitor Group consultancy.

Whatever the lowest sticker price turns out to be, the discounting trend will hit cars across the board, from minis to SUVs. Renault already has a runaway hit with its bare-bones Logan sedan. The automaker began offering the roomy Logan in Europe for just $7,200 in 2004—some 40% less than rival sedans—and has since sold 450,000 of the cars in 51 countries. Workers at its sprawling Dacia plant near the Romanian city of Pitesti and a newer plant in Russia toil in round-the-clock shifts but still can't meet demand. "With the Logan we have the product and we have the lead," says Ghosn.

A $3,000 car for Asian markets, built in low-cost India with a local partner, is the next logical step. "The main weakness of today's global automakers is that they are incapable of delivering a car that fulfills basic needs at a very low price," says Ghosn. "The people who have these skills are in India and China."

Cutting Costs to the Bone

That realization is now dawning on the industry's giants. When Tata made its vow to build a $2,500 car, many Western auto executives ridiculed the project, dubbing it a four-wheel bicycle. They aren't laughing anymore. Tata's model is a real car with four doors, a 33-horsepower engine, and a top speed of around 80 mph. The automaker claims it will even pass a crash test. And while the car probably won't win any beauty contests, it's no ugly duckling either, according to the handful of industry insiders who have been given a glimpse. The rest is top secret, but Tata engineers are already testing a prototype as the clock ticks toward a late 2008 launch. The key is India's low-cost engineers and their prodigious ability to trim needless spending to the bone, a skill developed by years of selling to the bottom of the pyramid. "You have to cut costs on everything—seats, materials, components—the whole package," says Tata Group Chairman Ratan N. Tata.

There's no lack of potential customers: Hundreds of millions of Chinese, Indians, Brazilians, Russians, and others will likely join the middle class in the coming decade, and cars are sure to be at the top of their shopping lists. As a result, the global car market is polarizing: The luxury segment continues to grow, cheap cars boom, and everything else gets squeezed. By 2012, the market for vehicles priced under $10,000 is likely to reach 18 million cars, or a fifth of world auto sales, according to Roland Berger Strategy Consultants. That's up from 12 million today.

So far this year, every major carmaker has announced its own 21st century Model T project. Toyota, Volkswagen, Fiat, and Peugeot have all vowed to build cut-rate Logan-killers. General Motors Corp. intends to use its Korean subsidiary, GM Daewoo, to design a model that will sell for about $7,000. Chrysler is developing low-cost cars with Chinese manufacturer Chery. Korea's Hyundai Motor Co. is making India its global hub for small-car production and expects to double its output to 600,000 cars annually by year-end, many of them destined for Europe. "Automakers will have to live with a trend of lower-cost vehicles. It is difficult but that's where the demand is," says David Nicholas (Nick) Reilly, president of GM Asia Pacific. The average retail price for many compacts will probably sink to $9,000, while minis will go for around $7,000, Reilly predicts. That's about 15% below current model prices.

Car manufacturers, of course, have always sought to cut costs and pack more value into each new-model generation to stay competitive. But now, emerging markets like India offer cheap engineering, inexpensive parts-sourcing, and low-cost manufacturing. For its new car, for example, Tata should be able to slash the cost of the engine to about $700, or 50% lower than a Western-developed equivalent, says one consultant close to the company. Combine Indian brainpower with Western innovation in design, materials, and processes, and the potential exists for a quantum leap in cost-reduction without major sacrifices in quality. Tata and Renault's Indian partner Mahindra & Mahindra Ltd. are already doing engineering work for global automakers at cut-rate prices. Tata, for example, is working on a coupe for a major Western customer.

Lessons for Big Cars

Another new factor in the low-cost car segment is the possibility of huge volumes that can drive profits. Ultra-cheap cars historically have not sold in large numbers. In 2005, low-cost cars represented less than 1% of new-vehicle sales in the U.S., according to Roland Berger. By contrast, emerging markets, which held little appeal for the major car brands even 10 years ago, now offer a volume bonanza that can make even cheap cars profit spinners. In India alone, some 1.6 million motorcycle and scooter riders are likely to buy a car over the next five years, the Berger study estimates. India's auto market is set to double to 3.3 million cars by 2014, while China's will grow 140% over the same period, to 16.5 million cars, according to J.D. Power Automotive Forecasting. That kind of demand makes dirt-cheap cars viable. "The real trick and idea behind the low-cost segment is to increase volume as much as possible to bring costs down," says Alfredo Altavilla, CEO for Fiat Powertrain Technologies. (Fiat signed a technical partnership with Tata Motors in February.)

What automakers learn from experimenting with discount cars may well shape how more expensive models are made. To make a success of the Logan, Renault manufactured in low-cost Romania. It developed a design that reduced the total number of parts and made assembly a cinch. It stripped out sophisticated electronics, dispensed with high-tech curved windshields, and even saved $3 per vehicle by using identical rear-view mirrors on each side. The biggest breakthrough: Renault was able to eliminate expensive prototypes and the pricey tooling involved in building them. As a result, it could move directly from digital mockup to production, an innovation that saved the French car company $40 million. Now Renault has figured out how to eliminate physical prototypes for all of its models.

Toyota is working on a bottom-of-the-line car with an expected sticker price of under $7,000 that could hit emerging markets such as India and Brazil by 2009. Toyota's management is banking on breakthroughs in new materials, manufacturing, and low-cost factories. If the Japanese company's engineers do their job, the cost-saving strategies will be deployed in everything from Corollas to Lexus SUVs. "When I asked for the low-cost development project two years ago, I wanted to see technology that would be applied to other vehicles as well," says Toyota President Katsuaki Watanabe. A prototype is expected this spring. A successful Toyota venture in this segment could "scramble all the eggs in emerging markets," says Fiat's Altavilla.

What's at Stake

To automakers' astonishment, cheap cars are also proving to be just as popular in established markets as they are in the developing world. Renault originally expected to sell the Logan only in Eastern Europe and other emerging markets. But in 2005, the automaker started offering it across Western Europe. Buyers have flooded showrooms to get behind the wheel of the no-frills model. Yesterday's cheap cars (remember the laughably bad Yugo?) failed to take off in the West because of poor quality. The new generation of cheap cars will be sturdy and reliable and will appeal to Western consumers who want to spend money on things other than transport. "It's all about price for performance," says Frankfurt music

teacher Elmar Kolle, who in November replaced his Ford Mondeo with a marine-blue Logan sedan. "I'd have to pay 5,000 euros [$6,500] more for a comparable car" from another manufacturer.

The shift to cut-rate wheels is jarring for an industry that has fixated for at least a decade on premium cars and their fat margins. BMW earns an estimated $3,300 per car on average, vs. Logan's $400 per car, according to Ferdinand Dudenhöffer, director of the German Center for Automotive Research. And when you get down to a sub-$3,000 sticker price, some experts say it'll be tough to cover the cost of the parts involved. "Any way you look at it, it will be difficult to be profitable," says David Cole, chairman of the Center for Automotive Research in Ann Arbor, Mich.

So why bother? Western automakers who don't join the fray risk being shut out of the growth in emerging markets. Even worse, they could give ambitious challengers a dangerous foothold in the West—not unlike the one they gave the Japanese by ignoring their low-cost, fuel-efficient models in the 1970s. China's Geely makes a model for $3,900 and it's aiming to export a car to the U.S. by 2010. Suzuki Motor Corp., which sells cars starting at $4,400 in India, will launch a new compact in 2008 and export it to Europe. Tata's $8,500 Indica compact sedan already sells in southern and eastern Europe. "The Chinese and Indians are coming," says Patrick Pelata, chief of strategy and product planning at Renault. "If we don't do our job, we will give them a huge slice of market share. We have to keep moving."

The majority of low-cost cars will range from $5,000 to $10,000, depending on size and features. Analysts say adding equipment required for safety and emissions control in Western markets would automatically bring the price of a cheap Chinese or Indian car up to $6,000 to $7,000. Many cars in India, for example, are sold without airbags or antilock brakes, standard features in the West. "There is a huge cost element to safety," says Hormazd Sorabjee, editor of *Autocar India*, noting that crash-test facilities alone are a gigantic investment.

Still, India remains the chief test bed and battleground for really cheap cars. Hyundai uses its plant outside Chennai as a global hub for its small-car production. By tapping local suppliers and manufacturing, the Korean upstart is able to offer a popular entry-level subcompact, the Santro, at a starting price of $6,300 in India, while still making features such as air conditioning and power steering standard. Moving along the pristine, high-tech production lines of its Chennai plant are also cars for export to Europe, Russia, and Latin America. Outside the plant, a vast sea of new cars, some 65% of them earmarked for export markets, fills Hyundai's orderly lots. "My only problem," says Lheem Heung-Soo, managing director of Hyundai India, "is limited capacity." He's ramping up production fast: So are all his rivals.

How Low Can You Go?

HYUNDAI Chose India as its global hub for small-auto production; expects to double plant capacity to 600,000

TATA MOTORS Plans to unveil the world's cheapest car, costing roughly $2,500, by year-end 2008

TOYOTA Working on a sub-$7,000 car for emerging markets, likely to be built in India or Brazil

SUZUKI Its sub-$10,000 offerings make it India's leader, with 44% of the market; already exports to Europe

CHRYSLER Inked alliance with China's Chery to develop cheap cars for Chrysler and Dodge

VOLKSWAGEN Developing a car based on its Polo subcompact to compete with the Logan from Renault

GM Building low-cost cars in Korea; may use Chevrolet brand for a cut-rate car to launch in emerging markets in 2010

RENAULT Pioneered segment with the $6,000 Logan built in Romania; now rolling out global production

By Gail Edmondson, with Ian Rowley in Tokyo, Nandini Lakshman in Mumbai, David Welch in Detroit, and Dexter Roberts in Beijing.

Source: **Reprinted with special permission from "The Race to Build Really Cheap Cars," by Gail Edmondson, et al.,** *BusinessWeek.* **Copyright © 2007 The McGraw-Hill Companies.**

The opening article illustrates how important managerial decisions are to company performance. The move by Renault-Nissan to enter the extremely inexpensive car market is a timely decision in response to Tata Motors (India) and Chery (China), two companies that have been leaders in this field. The decisions to aggressively cut costs and reduce prices are revolutionizing the automotive industry; however, it is not clear if these low-cost, no-frill cars will be accepted by the marketplace. Managerial decisions to cut costs at every level in the supply chain may raise questions about whether there are control systems in place to ensure quality, safety, and reliability. In addition, these low-cost cars result in dramatically lower per-unit profits, changing the balance of scale and profit such that automotive producers must sell hundreds of thousands of vehicles in order to ensure overall profitability. The growing market of price-sensitive consumers does appear to provide a great opportunity to be the leader in market share for inexpensive car sales. So which is better for a company to have, high profit margins or greater market share? The answer depends on numerous factors, many of which we discuss in this chapter and are the foundation that drives managerial decisions. One such factor is the level of control international managers have over operations. Any car company that becomes a part of this race will have to decide on how much control it has on such aspects as price, operational costs, and quality. How much can the company cut profits and still maintain quality? How safe can the vehicle be with the current budget? It is important for international managers to be involved on some level, as illustrated by a recent incident regarding China's Chery Amulet and a safety test performed by a lab owned by Russia's car maker OAO Avtovaz, a direct competitor of the Chery. Tests showed that the car was not safe for people to drive. Chery conducted its own test and found that the car was safer than previously reported, but initial word had already spread.[1] Companies need to evaluate the decisions and control systems that support informed business decision making and global profitability but that maintain sufficient control over production and execution in each target market.

■ Decision-Making Process and Challenges

decision making
The process of choosing a course of action among alternatives.

Managerial **decision-making** processes, the method of choosing a course of action among alternatives, is a common business practice becoming more and more relevant for the international manager as globalization becomes more pervasive. The process is often linear, though looping back is common, and consists of general phases outlined in Figure 11–1. The degree to which managers are involved in this procedure depends on the structure of the subsidiaries and the locus of decision making. If decision making is centralized, most important decisions are made at the top; if decision making is decentralized, decisions are delegated to operating personnel. Decision making is used to solve a myriad issues, including helping the subsidiary respond to economic and political demands of the host country. Decisions which are heavily economic in orientation concentrate on such aspects as return on investment (ROI) for overseas operations. In other instances, cultural differences can both inspire and motivate the process and outcome.

Figure 11–1

Decision-Making Process

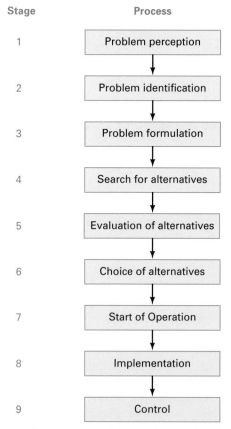

Stage	Process
1	Problem perception
2	Problem identification
3	Problem formulation
4	Search for alternatives
5	Evaluation of alternatives
6	Choice of alternatives
7	Start of Operation
8	Implementation
9	Control

Source: From Jette Schramm-Nielsen, "Cultural Dimensions of Decision Making: Denmark and France Compared," *Journal of Managerial Psychology* 16, No. 6, 2001, p. 408. Reprinted with premission of Emerald Insight.

For example, Ford Motor designed and built an inexpensive vehicle, the Ikon, for the Indian market. Engineers took apart the Ford Fiesta and totally rebuilt the car to address buyer needs. Some of the changes that were made included raising the amount of rear headroom to accommodate men in turbans, adjusting doors so that they opened wider in order to avoid catching the flowing saris of women, fitting intake valves to avoid auto flooding during the monsoon season, toughening shock absorbers to handle the pockmarked city streets, and adjusting the air-conditioning system to deal with the intense summer heat.[2] As a result of these decisions, the car is selling very well in India.

The way in which decision making is carried out will be influenced by a number of factors. We will first look at some of the factors, then provide some comparative examples in order to illustrate some of these differences.

Factors Affecting Decision-Making Authority

A number of factors will influence international managers' conclusions about retaining or delegating decision making to a subsidiary. Table 11–1 lists some of the most important situational factors, and the following discussion evaluates the influential aspects.

One of the major concerns for organizations is how efficient the processes are which are put in place. The size of a company can have great importance in this realm. Larger organizations may choose to centralize authority for critical decisions in order to ensure efficiency through greater coordination and integration of operations. An example of this occurred after PetroChina's initial public offering (IPO) in 2001. The company consisted of 53 subsidiaries which then had sub-subsidiaries. Overall, there were more than 100 bank accounts which ultimately belonged to PetroChina, and the company was losing money by thinly spread resources. Through consolidation, the company realized over $241 million in savings and achieved greater efficiency.[3] The same holds true for companies that have a high degree of interdependence, since there is a greater need for coordination. This is especially relevant when organizations provide a large investment since they prefer to keep track of progress. It is quite common for the investing company to send home-office personnel to the subsidiary and report on the situation, and for

Table 11–1
Factors That Influence Centralization or Decentralization of Decision Making in Subsidiary Operations

Encourage Centralization	Encourage Decentralization
Large size	Small size
Large capital investment	Small capital investment
Relatively high importance to MNC	Relatively low importance to MNC
Highly competitive environment	Stable environment
Strong volume-to-unit-cost relationship	Weak volume-to-unit-cost relationship
High degree of technology	Moderate to low degree of technology
Strong importance attached to brand name, patent rights, etc.	Little importance attached to brand name, patent rights, etc.
Low level of product diversification	High level of product diversification
Homogeneous product lines	Heterogeneous product lines
Small geographic distance between home office and subsidiary	Large geographic distance between home office and subsidiary
High interdependence between the units	Low interdependence between the units
Fewer highly competent managers in host country	More highly competent managers in host country
Much experience in international business	Little experience in international business

subsidiary managers to submit periodic reports. Both of the above scenarios imply that the subsidiary is of great importance to the MNC, and it is customary in these situations for subsidiary managers to clear any decisions with the home office before implementation. In fact, MNCs often will hire someone who they know will respond to their directives and will regard this individual as an extension of the central management staff.

Another efficiency checkpoint arises when competition is high. In domestic situations, when competition increases, management will decentralize authority and give the local manager greater decision-making authority. This reduces the time that is needed for responding to competitive threats. In the international arena, however, sometimes the opposite approach is used. As competition increases and profit margins are driven down, home-office management often seeks to standardize product and marketing decisions to reduce cost and maintain profitability. Many upper-level operating decisions are made by central management and merely implemented by the subsidiary, although in some instances, companies still opt to decentralize operations if product diversification is necessary. An example of a newly centralized company is Cadbury. Cadbury recently decided to shed 15 percent of its workforce by closing 12 of its 81 factories, dropping the beverage sector of its subsidiaries, and centralizing the management of its larger brands such as Trident, Dentyne, and Halls in order to better compete against candy rivals Hershey and Wrigley's.[4] Cadbury products also have a strong volume-to-unit cost relationship, as the low-cost edibles are purchased often. Firms that are able to produce large quantities will have lower cost per unit than those that produce at smaller amounts, and home-office management will often take the initiative to oversee sourcing, marketing, and overall strategy to keep subsidiary costs down.

Efficient processes become increasingly important as diversification or differences between the parent and subsidiary increase. This refers not only to specific products and services that may need to be tailored to geographic areas but also to the socioeconomic, political, legal, and cultural environments in which the subsidiary exists. In this case, the subsidiary would have superior staff and resources which would only become increasingly skilled in manufacturing and marketing products at the local level over time. Decentralization is emphasized here, and there exists a direct relationship between the physical distance and different environments between the parent and subsidiary and the level of decentralization. In other words, the farther apart the two units in either geographical area or cultural beliefs, the higher the level of decentralization.

Experience proves to be a simple indicator of efficiency. For example, if the subsidiary has highly competent local managers, the chances for decentralization are increased, because the home office has more confidence in delegating to the local level and less to gain by making all the important decisions. Conversely, if the local managers are inexperienced or not highly effective, the MNC likely will centralize decision making and make many of the major decisions at headquarters. Furthermore, if the firm itself has a great deal of international experience, its operations will likely be more centralized as it has already exhibited a high efficiency level and increasing management decision making at the local level may slow processes.

Protection of goods and services is also important to an MNC. It would not be a very lucrative experience to spend valuable time and money on R&D processes only to have competitors successfully mimic products and essentially take away market share. For this reason and many others, it is common for MNCs to centralize operations when dealing with sophisticated levels of technology. This is particularly true for high-tech, research-intensive firms such as computer and pharmaceutical companies, which do not want their technology controlled at the local level. Furthermore, a company is likely to centralize decision-making processes when there are important brand names or patent rights involved as it wants to create as much protection as possible.

In some areas of operation, MNCs tend to retain decision making at the top (centralization); other areas fall within the domain of subsidiary management (decentralization). It is most common to find finance, research and development, and strategic planning decisions being made at MNC headquarters and the subsidiaries working within the parameters established by the home office. In addition, when the subsidiary is selling new products in growing markets, centralized decision making is more likely. As the product line matures and the subsidiary managers gain experience, however, the company will start to rely more on decentralized decision making. These decisions involve planning and budgeting systems, performance evaluations, assignment of managers to the subsidiary, and use of coordinating committees to mesh the operations of the subsidiary with the worldwide operations of the MNC. The right degree of centralized or decentralized decision making can be critical to the success of the MNC.

Cultural Differences and Comparative Examples of Decision Making

Culture, whether outside or within the organization (see Chapters 2 and 6, respectively), has an effect on how individuals and businesses perceive situations and subsequently react. This knowledge raises the question: Do decision-making philosophies and practices differ from country to country? Research shows that to some extent they do, although there also is evidence that many international operations, regardless of foreign or domestic ownership, use similar decision-making norms.

One study showed that French and Danish managers do not approach the decision-making process in the same manner.[5] The French managers tend to spend ample time on searching for and evaluating alternatives (see Figure 11–1), exhibiting rationality and intelligence in each option. While the French approach each opportunity with a sense of creativity and logic, they tend to become quite emotionally charged rather quickly if challenged. Middle managers report to higher-level managers who ultimately make the final decision. Therefore, the individualistic nature of the French creates an environment in which middle managers vie for the recognition and praise of the upper management. Furthermore, middle-management implementation of ideas tends to be lacking since that stage is often seen as boring, practical work which lacks the prestige managers strive to achieve. Control, discussed later in the chapter, is quite high in the French firms at every level, so where implementation fails, control will compensate.

Danish managers tend to emphasize different stages in the decision-making process (see Figure 11–1). They do not spend as much time searching or analyzing alternatives to optimize production but instead choose the option that can be started and implemented quickly and still bring about the relative desired results. They are less emotionally responsive and tend to take a straightforward approach. Danes do not emphasize control in operations, since it tends to be a sign that management lacks confidence in the areas that "require" high control. The cooperative as opposed to individualistic emphasis in Danish corporations coupled with a results-oriented environment breeds a situation in which decisions are made quickly and middle managers are given autonomy.

Overall, the pragmatic nature of the Danes and the French need for intellectual prowess mark why each is more adept at different stages of the decision-making process. The French tend to be better at stages 4, 5, and 9, while the Danes are more adept at stages 6, 7, and 8 (see Figure 11–1). As one Danish manager in France says:

> They [Danes and Frenchmen] do not analyze and synthesize the same way. The French tend to think that the Danes are not thorough enough, and the Danes tend to think that the French are too complicated. At his desk, the Frenchman tends to keep on working on the case. He seems not to agree neither with his surroundings nor with himself. This means that when he has analyzed a case and has come to a conclusion, then he would like to go over it once more. I think that Frenchmen think in a more synthetic way...and he has a tendency to say: "well, yes, but what if it can still be done in another maybe smarter way." This means that in fact he is wasting time instead of making improvements.[6]

In Germany, managers focus more on productivity and quality of goods and services than on managing subordinates, which often translates into companies pursuing long-term approaches. In addition, management education is highly technical, and a legal system called **codetermination** requires workers and their managers to discuss major decisions. As a result, German MNCs tend to be fairly centralized, autocratic, and hierarchical. Scandinavian countries also have codetermination, but the Swedes focus much more on quality of work life and the importance of the individual in the organization. As a result, decision making in Sweden is decentralized and participative.

codetermination
A legal system that requires workers and their managers to discuss major decisions.

ringisei
A Japanese term that means "decision making by consensus."

The Japanese are somewhat different from the Europeans, though they still employ a long-term focus. They make heavy use of a decision-making process called **ringisei,** or decision making by consensus.

> Under this system any changes in procedures and routines, tactics, and even strategies of a firm are organized by those directly concerned with those changes. The final decision is made at the top level after an elaborate examination of the proposal through successively higher levels in the management hierarchy, and results in acceptance or rejection of a decision only through consensus at every echelon of the management structure.[7]

Sometimes Japanese consensus decision making can be very time-consuming. However, in practice most Japanese managers know how to respond to "suggestions" from the top and to act accordingly—thus saving a great deal of time. Many outsiders misunderstand how Japanese managers make such decisions. In Japan, what should be done is called **tatemae;** what one really feels, which may be quite different, is **honne.** Because it is vital to do what others expect in a given context, situations arise that often strike Westerners as a game of charades. Nevertheless, it is very important in Japan to play out the situation according to what each person believes others expect to happen.

tatemae
A Japanese term that means "doing the right thing" according to the norm.

honne
A Japanese term that means "what one really wants to do."

To clarify this complicated but important Japanese decision-making process, here is a specific example offered by a Japanese scholar of a Mr. Seward, a Western employee of a Japanese firm:

> [Mr. Seward] joined a meeting as one of eight employees tasked with deciding where to go for a company trip. When the result of the vote was taken, it appeared that the group favored going to a place named Izu. At this point, one of the president's secretaries spoke up, saying, "The president wants to visit Suwa." In a tense atmosphere a second vote was taken, considering the president's opinion, and it turned out that the entire group, except Seward, voted for Suwa. Mr. Seward protested the procedure, insisting that, if members were forced to follow the president's opinion, there was no point in meeting and voting, but his objections were overridden and the company trip was set for Suwa.[8]

Many Westerners would ask why the president did not simply send out a memo announcing the destination of the meeting. The answer is that, for the president, having the meeting and taking a vote was *tatemae*—the right thing to do according to the normal procedure for reaching this kind of decision. At the same time, going to Suwa was *honne*—what the president wanted to do. Similarly, for the Japanese members of the committee, voting for Suwa was *tatemae* once the president's desires were made clear, while going to Izu was *honne,* what the employees really wanted to do. Obviously such culturally based subtleties make understanding whether decision making is centralized or decentralized across cultures very difficult.

Another cultural difference is how managers view time in the decision-making process. As we saw from the French-Danish example earlier, the French do not value time as much as their counterparts. The French want to ensure that the best alternative was put into action, whereas the Danes want to act first and take advantage of opportunities. This is key in many international decision-making processes, as globalization has opened the door to extreme competition, and all players need to be able to both identify and make the most of profitable prospects. Renesas Technology, a Japanese chip manufacturer for semiconductors created through the merger of Hitachi and Mitsubishi, provides a good example of how companies, and cultures, are beginning to focus more on timely decisions. Satoru Ito, president of Renesas, had previously worked in U.S. operations prior to this position, and witnessed how the U.S. "take-charge" approach cut decision time and made firms more profitable. The Japanese desired a more aggressive approach to the market; however, the corporate and countrywide culture is such that decisions go through a multilevel process that can last for a long period. In the chip and semiconductor field, reactions and changes must occur quickly, or products could be rendered virtually obsolete as competition soars ahead. Renesas has subsequently cut decision-making time in half compared to other Japanese companies by merging two cultures: the consensus-oriented, long-term focused Japanese methods with Western-style proactive, short-term focused measures, such as training programs at every level in the company that seek to reinvent the company every year. This creation of a new culture has proved to be very difficult, but quite worth the effort as Renesas has become the number-three semiconductor company in the world behind Intel and Samsung.[9]

Total Quality Management Decisions

To achieve world-class competitiveness, MNCs are finding that a commitment to total quality management is critical. **Total quality management (TQM)** is an organizational strategy and accompanying techniques that result in delivery of high-quality products or services to customers.[10] The concept and techniques of TQM, which were introduced in Chapter 8 in relation to strategic planning, also are relevant to decision making and controlling.

> **total quality management (TQM)**
> An organizational strategy and the accompanying techniques that result in the delivery of high-quality products or services to customers.

One of the primary areas where TQM is having a big impact is in manufacturing. For example, in recent years, U.S. automakers have greatly improved the quality of their cars, but the Japanese have continuously improved quality and thus still have the lead. A number of TQM techniques have been successfully applied to improve the quality of manufactured goods. One is the use of concurrent engineering/interfunctional teams in which designers, engineers, production specialists, and customers work together to develop new products. This approach involves all the necessary parties and overcomes what used to be an all-too-common procedure: The design people would tell the manufacturing group what to produce, and the latter would send the finished product to retail stores for sale to the customer. Today, MNCs taking a TQM approach are customer-driven. They use TQM techniques to tailor their output to customer needs, and they require the same approach from their own suppliers.[11] IBM followed a similar approach in developing its AS/400 computer systems. Customer advisory councils were created to provide input, test the product, and suggest refinements. The result was one of the most successful product launches in the company's history.

A particularly critical issue is how much decision making to delegate to subordinates. TQM uses employee **empowerment.** Individuals and teams are encouraged to generate and implement ideas for improving quality and are given the decision-making authority and necessary resources and information to implement them. Many MNCs have had outstanding success with empowerment. For example, General Electric credits employee empowerment for cutting in half the time needed to change product-mix production of its dishwashers in response to market demand.

> **empowerment**
> The process of giving individuals and teams the resources, information, and authority they need to develop ideas and effectively implement them.

Another TQM technique that MNCs are successfully employing to develop and maintain world-class competitiveness is rewards and recognition. These range from increases in pay and benefits to the use of merit pay, discretionary bonuses, pay-for-skills and knowledge plans, plaques, and public recognition. The important thing to realize is that the rewards and recognition approaches that work well in one country may be ineffective in another. For example, individual recognition in the United States may be appropriate and valued by workers, but in Japan, group rewards are more appropriate as Japanese do not like to be singled out for personal praise. Similarly, although putting a picture or plaque on the wall to honor an individual is common practice in the United States, these rewards are frowned on in Finland, for they remind the workers that their neighbors, the Russians, used this system to encourage people to increase output (but not necessarily quality), and while the Russian economy is beginning to make headway, it was once in shambles in part due to the poor decision-making process and control and resulting poor quality.

Still another technique associated with TQM is the use of ongoing training to achieve continual improvement. This training takes a wide variety of forms, ranging from statistical quality control techniques to team meetings designed to generate ideas for streamlining operations and eliminating waste. In all cases, the objective is to apply what the Japanese call **kaizen,** or continuous improvement. By adopting a TQM

> **kaizen**
> A Japanese term that means "continuous improvement."

Table 11–2
The Emergence of New Beliefs Regarding Quality

Old Myth	New Truth
Quality is the responsibility of the people in the Quality Control Department.	Quality is everyone's job.
Training is costly.	Training does not cost; it saves.
New quality programs have high initial costs.	The best quality programs do not have up-front costs.
Better quality will cost the company a lot of money.	As quality goes up, costs come down.
The measurement of data should be kept to a minimum.	An organization cannot have too much relevant data on hand.
It is human to make mistakes.	Perfection—total customer satisfaction—is a standard that should be vigorously pursued.
Some defects are major and should be addressed, but many are minor and can be ignored.	No defects are acceptable, regardless of whether they are major or minor.
Quality improvements are made in small, continuous steps.	In improving quality, both small and large improvements are necessary.
Quality improvement takes time.	Quality does not take time; it saves time.
Haste makes waste.	Thoughtful speed improves quality.
Quality programs are best oriented toward areas such as products and manufacturing.	Quality is important in all areas, including administration and service.
After a number of quality improvements, customers are no longer able to see additional improvements.	Customers are able to see all improvements, including those in price, delivery, and performance.
Good ideas can be found throughout the organization.	Good ideas can be found everywhere, including in the operations of competitors and organizations providing similar goods and services.
Suppliers need to be price competitive.	Suppliers need to be quality competitive.

Source: Reported in Richard M. Hodgetts, *Measures of Quality and High Performance* (New York: American Management Association, 1998), p. 14.

perspective and applying the techniques discussed earlier, MNCs find that they can both develop and maintain a worldwide competitive edge. A good example is Zytec, the world-class, Minnesota-based manufacturer of power supplies. The customer base for Zytec ranges from the United States to Japan to Europe. One way in which the firm ensures that it maintains a total quality perspective is to continually identify client demands and then work to exceed these expectations. Another is to totally revise the company's philosophy and beliefs regarding what quality is all about and how it needs to be implemented. Table 11–2 provides some examples of the new thinking that is now emerging regarding quality.

Indirectly related to TQM is ISO 9000: International Standards Organization (ISO) certification to ensure quality products and services. Areas that are examined by the ISO certification team include design (product or service specifications), process control (instruction for manufacturing or service functions), purchasing, service (e.g., instructions for conducting after-sales service), inspection and testing, and training. ISO 9000 certification is becoming a necessary prerequisite to doing business in the EU, but it also is increasingly used as a screening criterion for bidding on contracts or getting business in the United States and other parts of the world. For example, after a year of hard work, Foxboro Corporation, based in Massachusetts, obtained certification, and its business greatly increased.

Decisions for Attacking the Competition

Another series of key decisions relates to MNC actions that are designed to attack the competition and gain a foothold in world markets. "International Management in Action:

Kodak's Corner" gives an example. Another is General Motors's decision to establish production operations on a worldwide basis and to be a major player throughout Asia, Australia, Europe, and South America, as well as in select areas of Africa. As a result of this decision, the company is now closing U.S. factories and building new assembly plants abroad. Between 1995 and 1999 GM opened a host of new facilities including a plant in Brazil that has an annual capacity of 120,000 units, as well as factories in Poland, India, Mexico, Thailand, and Shanghai, each of which has annual capacity of 100,000 units. By locating closer to the final customer and offering a well-designed and efficiently built car, the company has been able to increase its worldwide market share, thus more than offsetting the downturn it has encountered in the U.S. market, where overall share has dropped below 30 percent.

GM's expansion decisions, in many cases, have been designed to help it capture the lower end of the market with small, inexpensive cars. However, the company is also intent on appealing to the upper-level buyer as well, as seen by its decision to sell Cadillacs in Europe. This market is quite different from that in the United States. European buyers of luxury cars often settle for far less comfort and expect far more handling and performance. GM hopes to appeal to these buyers with many of the changes it introduced into the Cadillac Sevilles that it is selling in Europe. Differences between this car and the version marketed in the United States include (1) right-hand drive for the United Kingdom; (2) less interior clutter (e.g., unobtrusive cup holders); (3) simpler, more elegant interiors; (4) shorter overall length; (5) tighter suspension, wider wheel tracks, and better tires for high-speed driving; and (6) floor-mounted gearshift levers for automatic transmission.[12]

Will this decision result in greater sales for Cadillac in Europe? Unfortunately, Europeans have not fully embraced the Cadillac, and projected sales have fallen. The luxury-car market in Europe is highly competitive, and Europeans take pride in placing performance over comfort. Buyers like tight steering, rear-wheel drive, and smaller cars that provide greater gas mileage. Cadillac is not known for any of these. Nor does the car have a reputation for high-speed performance, something that people on the continent like, given that on European freeways it is common to find the traffic moving at 80–100 miles per hour. GM's extremely popular Opel may be able to make up for the losses with Cadillac. Now, GM is attempting to offer Opel compact models in North America, a move that seems timely, given high gasoline prices.[13]

Another example of decision making for attacking the competition is provided by BMW. While GM is trying to tap the upper market, BMW has made the decision to move down the line and gain small-car market share. The company is building small cars with a sales price in the range of $20,000. By sharing engines, gearboxes, and electrical systems from its other offerings, the firm intends to reduce its development and production costs and offer a reliable and competitively priced auto.[14] Other firms, including Mercedes and Audi, have done this and have not been particularly profitable, but BMW believes that it can succeed where they have not. BMW's introduction of the MINI Cooper is an interesting example of the integration of efficiency, sportiness, and nostalgia.

NEC offers a third example of how decision making is being used for attacking the competition. In 2001 the company held 8 percent of the world market for mobile transmitting infrastructure and was vying with major competitors such as Ericsson, Lucent, Nokia, and Nortel. Most of NEC's revenues come from its contracts with NTT, Japan's phone monopoly. However, the company is moving aggressively into the worldwide arena. Its prowess in fiber optics resulted in its winning a big AT&T network installation contract, and as the demand for fiber optics increases, NEC intends to exploit this strength.[15] The firm recently announced that it had developed a fiber-optic cable that is four times more powerful than that currently on the market. The company is also a world leader in manufacturing mobile handsets and the semiconductors used in mobiles and other devices. Its folding phones, for example, account for 40 percent of the Internet-capable handset market in Japan, and NEC is looking to expand its international sales of these products.

Kodak's Corner

Kodak has used various strategies to gain market share for quite some time. One short-term attempt to expand growth in Japan occurred when Kodak filed a complaint with the U.S. government, accusing its main competitor, Fuji, of blocking Kodak from the Japanese market. Since that time, Kodak has focused on long-term efforts that, in this technological age, will require fine tuning at every turn.

Kodak attempted to corner the camera market by creating inexpensive cameras that utilized digital imagery. Creating cameras that produced high-quality photos without the need to purchase film or go through the process of getting the pictures developed would seemingly allow Kodak to surpass its competitors and create a niche. Changes were necessary in order to implement these ideas. First, Kodak had to accept that its film sales would diminish greatly unless the products were offered in another market, and management needed to reorganize the business. A digital imaging unit was created, pooling the firm's digital talent into one division. Disposable camera offerings were expanded to include under-water, panoramic, and tel-ephoto options. The company acquired Ofoto Inc., an online photography service, to expand operations. Kodak hoped these investments would prove to be lucrative, but the future was uncertain.

Unfortunately, the company did not excel in digital camera sales, and other poor choices simply made expansion more difficult for the firm. The difficulty in generating research and development breakthroughs proved to be challenging, as illustrated by Kodak's unsuccessful effort to market a photo CD. This product required that users purchase a unit that could plug into a TV for $500, and the unit itself cost $20 per CD. The sole function was to be able to view photos from the CD on your television, which consumers did not find beneficial, though some companies did purchase the package.

Despite failed attempts in certain digital technologies and a series of losses that led to numerous job cuts, Kodak refused to yield. The company sold its health care business in order to increase revenue, and its film group has benefited from movie-film growth. Currently, Kodak is taking advantage of the growing market of digital photo printing and installing kiosks in Wal-Mart, the world's largest photo processor. The plan only focuses on the U.S. market for now, where Kodak is already the leader in digital-photo kiosks, with 80,000 units already in place. Kodak has also manufactured a new home ink-jet printer that uses less expensive ink than competitors. If this project is successful, then Kodak will certainly have the market on home-office printing technology.

Kodak's online EasyShare Gallery (formerly Ofoto) has been rated number one in print quality by such reviewers as *PC World*. The service offers superior storing and sharing of photos and allows consumers to order customized prints with ease, ranging in specs from delivery options to photo size. The company also created a new digital camera that can wirelessly communicate with printers and the Internet, which means that pictures can be sent to friends, family, online photo galleries, or a home printer at the touch of a button. While Kodak may have issues transitioning from film to digital cameras, management hopes that the superior photo quality and online technological advances will secure its own corner in the market.

Intel is another good example. The company has made a number of interesting decisions designed to stymie the competition. One is to bring out a new version of its Pentium chip at a much lower-than-expected price and cut the prices of its other chips, thus creating a strong demand for its products and forcing competitors to cut their prices. In a market where overall demand has been slowing, this strategy wreaks havoc on the competition. At the same time, lower prices mean that Intel must sell more products in order to increase revenues. One of the ways in which the firm is trying to do this is with an extension of its Xeon microprocessor family, which is aimed at more powerful desktop workstations and server systems than the firm has targeted in the past. Intel's server offerings generally were used in relatively lightweight machines such as those that serve up Web pages. This new push is designed to provide chips that are used in midsize servers, such as those that run databases, as well as in some larger systems used in mission-critical tasks. These machines typically cost millions of dollars and run on dozens of microprocessors operating in parallel.[16] The company also teamed up with Hewlett-Packard to develop the Itanium chip, which offers greater speed because it can process 64 bits of data at a time rather than 32 bits. Working with HP, Intel is building servers for telecommunications and making three-in-one chips that have the ability to radically reduce the size of cell phones and handheld computers.

■ Decision and Control Linkages

Decision making and **controlling** are two vital and often interlinked functions of international management. For example, Siemens has long been praised for its engineering abilities, but its slow market response has left the company struggling to reach internal earnings targets, which it has fallen short of for years. Klaus Kleinfeld took over as CEO in 2005 in an attempt to change management and profits. Almost immediately, Kleinfeld was able to encourage faster decision-making processes and stressed a customer spotlight as passionate as Siemens's technology focus. This proved successful, as 2006 sales increased by 16 percent and profits by 35 percent. There are also constant discussions about expansion, including building cement plants in Yemen or improving plants in Russia. Most would believe that the German company would be pleased by the turn of events, but the U.S. management style that Kleinfeld has employed does not sit well with the parent company, especially as questions arose over specific growth strategies. The culture clash has led to Kleinfeld stepping down, but not before a foundation of change was implemented. Whether the company returns to slow responses and lack of control is something only time can tell, but Siemens's taste of success may be enough to accept its new aggressive posture.[17]

Another example is provided by Boeing and General Motors, two well-known MNCs that signed major deals with the Chinese government. Boeing agreed to sell the Chinese Civil Aviation Administration five 777-200 jetliners for approximately $685 million; and General Motors finalized a $1.3 billion joint venture with a Shanghai automotive company to build Buick Century and Regal cars in China. The Boeing deal came after the giant aerospace MNC had been shut out of a number of contract bids in China and offers strong promise of even more business from the Chinese government. The GM deal is a 50-50 venture between the automotive MNC and the Shanghai Automotive Industry Corporation, a state-owned company. Both these developments are viewed by the management decision makers of the respective American-based MNCs as opportunities to further open the China market and with proper controls increase their sales growth and profitability.[18]

Still another example is offered by Universal Studios Japan. In an effort to attract visitors to its Osaka location, this new theme park was specially built based on feedback from Japanese tourists at Universal parks in Orlando and Los Angeles. The company wanted to learn what these visitors liked and disliked and then use this information in its Osaka park. One theme clearly emerged: The Japanese wanted an authentic American experience but also expected the park to cater to their own cultural preferences. In the process, thousands of decisions were made regarding what to include and what to leave out. For example, seafood pizza and gumbo-style soup were put on the menu, but a fried-shrimp concoction with colored rice crackers was rejected. In a musical number based on the movie *Beetlejuice,* it was decided that the main character should talk in Japanese and his sidekicks would speak and sing in English. The decision to put in a restaurant called Shakin's, based on the 1906 San Francisco earthquake, was not a good idea because Osaka has had terrible earthquakes that killed thousands of people.

Other decisions were made to give the park a uniquely Japanese flavor. The nation's penchant for buying edible souvenirs inspired a 6,000-square-foot confection shop packed with Japanese sweets such as dinosaur-shaped bean cakes. Restrooms include Japanese-style squat toilets. Even the park layout caters to the tendency of Japanese crowds to flow clockwise in an orderly manner, contrary to more-chaotic U.S. crowds that steer right. And on the Jurassic Park water slide, millions of dollars were spent to widen the landing pond, redesign boat hulls, and install underwater wave-damping panels to reduce spray. Why? Many fastidious Japanese don't like to get wet, even on what's billed as one of the world's biggest water slides.[19]

Over the next few years, as Universal Studios Japan evaluates park revenues and feedback from visitors, it will be able to judge how well it is doing in giving customers

controlling
The process of evaluating results in relation to plans or objectives and deciding what action, if any, to take.

an American experience in an environment that also addresses cultural considerations. After a period of reduced attendance, the company has discovered that creating an emotional connection between the consumer and the park, instead of focusing on the power of Hollywood, encourages people to frequent the park. The quick and adept response to profit losses shows that it has a concrete idea on how to deal with other cultures. In fact, plans are already in place to open Universal Studios in Dubai, Singapore, and South Korea.[20]

■ The Controlling Process

As indicated earlier in this chapter, controlling involves evaluating results in relation to plans or objectives and deciding what action to take. An excellent illustration is Mitsubishi's purchase of 80 percent of Rockefeller Center in the late 1980s. The Japanese firm paid $1.4 billion for this choice piece of Manhattan real estate, and it looked like a very wise decision. Over the next six years, however, depressed rental prices and rising maintenance costs resulted in Mitsubishi sinking an additional $500 million into the project. Finally, in late 1995, the company decided it had had enough and announced that it was walking away from the investment. Mitsubishi passed ownership to Rockefeller Center Properties Inc., the publicly traded real-estate investment trust that held the mortgage on the center. The cost of keeping the properties was too great for the Japanese firm, which decided to cut its losses and focus efforts on more lucrative opportunities elsewhere.

Another example is provided by Dana Corporation, the giant auto parts supply company, which in the last few years sold off some of its units, bought others, and refocused its business. Among the units that Dana sold were its clutch and transmission operation and heavy frame operations. In each case the company's control process indicated that the unit had low return on sales or investment, slow growth, operating losses, or eroding market share. At the same time, Dana purchased a piston rings and cylinder liners unit, a transmission unit, and a couple of axle units. The company provides complete integrated systems engineering to auto manufacturers worldwide, and it is the largest independent supplier of fluid transfer, fluid power, and materials transfer components and systems in the vehicular and industrial markets.[21] The company had sales of $8.6 billion in 2005, but has since filed for Chapter 11 bankruptcy. As the company strives to restructure the organization, it continues to be a leader among drivetrain, chassis, structural, and engine technologies suppliers.[22]

Another example of how the control process is being used by MNCs is in the personal computer (PC) business. Until the mid-1990s, PCs were built using the traditional model shown in Figure 11–2. Today the direct-sales model and the hybrid model are the most common (see Figure 11–2). PC firms are finding that they must keep on the cutting edge more than any other industry because of the relentless pace of technological change. This is where the control function becomes especially critical for success. For example, stringent controls keep the inventory in the system as small as possible. PCs are manufactured using a just-in-time approach (as in the case of a customer who orders the unit and has it made to specifications) or an almost just-in-time approach (as in the case of a retailer who orders 30 units and sells them all within a few weeks). Because technology in the PC industry changes so quickly, any units that are not sold in retail outlets within 60 days may be outdated and must be severely discounted and sold for whatever the market will bear. In turn, these costs are often assumed by the manufacturer. As a result, PC manufacturers are very much inclined to build to order or to ship in quantities that can be sold quickly. In this way the firm's control system helps ensure that inventory moves through the system and profitability does not suffer.[23]

In many ways, the control function is conceptually and practically similar to decision making. Like decision making, the approaches used by multinationals in controlling their operations have long been an area of interest. Of particular concern has been how companies attempt to control their overseas operations to become integrated, coordinated units.

Figure 11–2 | **Models of PC Manufacturing**

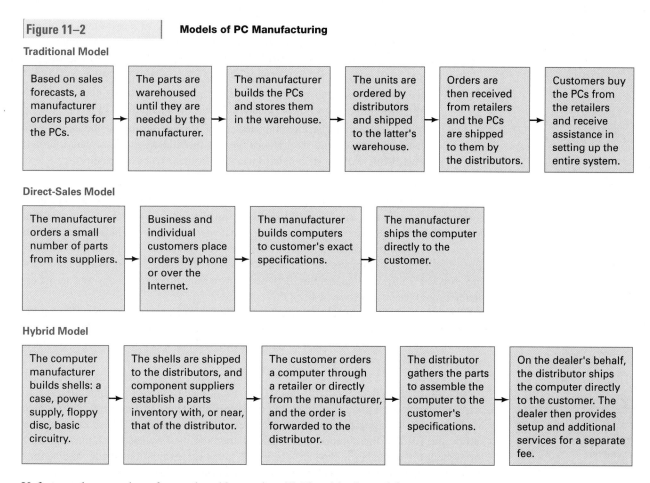

Traditional Model

| Based on sales forecasts, a manufacturer orders parts for the PCs. | → | The parts are warehoused until they are needed by the manufacturer. | → | The manufacturer builds the PCs and stores them in the warehouse. | → | The units are ordered by distributors and shipped to the latter's warehouse. | → | Orders are then received from retailers and the PCs are shipped to them by the distributors. | → | Customers buy the PCs from the retailers and receive assistance in setting up the entire system. |

Direct-Sales Model

| The manufacturer orders a small number of parts from its suppliers. | → | Business and individual customers place orders by phone or over the Internet. | → | The manufacturer builds computers to customer's exact specifications. | → | The manufacturer ships the computer directly to the customer. |

Hybrid Model

| The computer manufacturer builds shells: a case, power supply, floppy disc, basic circuitry. | → | The shells are shipped to the distributors, and component suppliers establish a parts inventory with, or near, that of the distributor. | → | The customer orders a computer through a retailer or directly from the manufacturer, and the order is forwarded to the distributor. | → | The distributor gathers the parts to assemble the computer to the customer's specifications. | → | On the dealer's behalf, the distributor ships the computer directly to the customer. The dealer then provides setup and additional services for a separate fee. |

Unfortunately, a number of control problems arise: (1) The objectives of the overseas operation and the corporation conflict. (2) The objectives of joint-venture partners and corporate management are not in accord. (3) Degrees of experience and competence in planning vary widely among managers running the various overseas units. (4) There are basic philosophic disagreements about the objectives and policies of international operations, largely because of cultural differences between home- and host-country managers. The following discussion examines the various types of control that are used in international operations and the approaches that are often employed in dealing with these types of problems.

Types of Control

There are two common, complementary ways of looking at how MNCs control operations. One way is by determining whether the enterprise chooses to use internal or external control in devising its overall strategy. The other is by looking at the ways in which the organization uses direct and indirect controls.

Internal and External Control   From an internal control standpoint, an MNC will focus on the things that it does best. At the same time, of course, management wants to ensure that there is a market for the goods and services that it is offering. So the company first needs to find out what the customers want and be prepared to respond appropriately. This requires an external control focus. Naturally, every MNC will give consideration to both internal and external perspectives of control. However, one is often given more attention than the other. In explaining this idea, Trompenaars and Hampden-Turner set forth four management views regarding how a control strategy should be devised and implemented:

1. No one dealing with customers is without a strategy of sorts. Our task is to find out which of these strategies work, which don't, and why. Devising our own strategy in the abstract and imposing it downwards only spreads confusion.

2. No one dealing with customers is without a strategy of sorts. Our task is to find out which of these strategies work and then create a master strategy from proven successful initiatives by encouraging and combining the best.

3. To be a leader is to be the chief deviser of strategy. Using all the experience, information, and intelligence we can mobilize, we need to devise an innovative strategy and then cascade it down the hierarchy.

4. To be a leader is to be the chief deviser of strategy. Using all the experience, information, and intelligence we can mobilize, we must create a broad thrust, while leaving it to subordinates to fit these to customer needs.

Trompenaars and Hampden-Turner ask managers to rank each of these four statements by placing a "1" next to the one they feel would most likely be used in their company, a "2" next to the second most likely, on down to a "4" next to the one that would be the last choice. This ranking helps managers better see whether they use an external or an internal control approach. Answer 1 focuses most strongly on an external-directed approach and rejects the internal control option. Answer 3 represents the opposite. Answer 2 affirms a connection between an external-directed strategy and an inner-directed one, whereas answer 4 does the opposite.[24]

Cultures differ in the control approach they use. For example, among U.S. multinationals it is common to find managers using an internal control approach. Among Asian firms an external control approach is more typical. Table 11–3 provides some contrasts between the two.

direct controls
The use of face-to-face or personal meetings for the purpose of monitoring operations.

Direct Controls   **Direct controls** involve the use of face-to-face or personal meetings to monitor operations. A good example is International Telephone and Telegraph (ITT), which holds monthly management meetings at its New York headquarters. These meetings are run by the CEO of the company, and reports are submitted by each ITT unit manager throughout the world. Problems are discussed, goals set, evaluations made, and actions taken that will help the unit to improve its effectiveness.

Table 11–3
The Impact of Internal- and External-Oriented Cultures on the Control Process

Key Differences Between . . .

Internal Control	External Control
Often dominating attitude bordering on aggressiveness toward the environment.	Often flexible attitude, willing to compromise and keep the peace.
Conflict and resistance mean that a person has convictions.	Harmony, responsiveness, and sensibility are encouraged.
The focus is on self, function, one's own group, and one's own organization.	The focus is on others such as customers, partners, and colleagues.
There is discomfort when the environment seems "out of control" or changeable.	There is comfort with waves, shifts, and cycles, which are regarded as "natural."

Tips for Doing Business with . . .

Internally Controlled (for externals)	Externally Controlled (for internals)
Playing "hardball" is legitimate to test the resilience of an opponent.	Softness, persistence, politeness, and long, long patience will get rewards.
It is most important to "win your objective."	It is most important to maintain one's relationships with others.
Win some, lose some.	Win together, lose apart.

Source: Adapted from Fons Trompenaars and Charles Hampden-Turner, *Riding the Waves of Culture: Understanding Diversity in Global Business,* 2nd ed. (New York: McGraw-Hill, 1998), pp. 160–161.

Another common form of direct control is visits by top executives to overseas affiliates or subsidiaries. During these visits, top managers can learn firsthand the problems and challenges facing the unit and offer assistance.

A third form is the staffing practices of MNCs. By determining whom to send overseas to run the unit, the corporation can directly control how the operation will be run. The company will want the manager to make operating decisions and handle day-to-day matters, but the individual also will know which decisions should be cleared with the home office. In fact, this approach to direct control sometimes results in a manager who is more responsive to central management than to the needs of the local unit.

A fourth form is the organizational structure itself. By designing a structure that makes the unit highly responsive to home-office requests and communications, the MNC ensures that all overseas operations are run in accord with central management's desires. This structure can be established through formal reporting relationships and chain of command (who reports to whom).

Indirect Controls **Indirect controls** involve the use of reports and other written forms of communication to control operations. One of the most common examples is the use of monthly operating reports that are sent to the home office. Other examples, which typically are used to supplement the operating report, include financial statements, such as balance sheets, income statements, cash budgets, and financial ratios that provide insights into the unit's financial health. The home office will use these operating and financial data to evaluate how well things are going and make decisions regarding necessary changes. Three sets of financial statements usually are required from subsidiaries: (1) statements prepared to meet the national accounting standards and procedures prescribed by law and other professional organizations in the host country; (2) statements prepared to comply with the accounting principles and standards required by the home country; and (3) statements prepared to meet the financial consolidation requirements of the home country.

> **indirect controls**
> The use of reports and other written forms of communication to control operations.

Indirect controls are particularly important in international management because of the great expense associated with direct methods. Typically, MNCs will use indirect controls to monitor performance on a monthly basis, whereas direct controls are used semiannually or annually. This dual approach often provides the company with effective control of its operations at a price that also is cost-effective.

Approaches to Control

International managers can employ many different approaches to control. These approaches typically are dictated by the MNC's philosophy of control, the economic environment in which the overseas unit is operating, and the needs and desires of the managerial personnel who staff the unit. Working within control parameters, MNCs will structure their processes so that they are as efficient and effective as possible. Typically, the tools that are used will give the unit manager the autonomy needed to adapt to changes in the market as well as to attract competent local personnel. These tools will also provide for coordination of operations with the home office, so that the overseas unit is in harmony with the MNC's strategic plan.

Some control tools are universal. For example, all MNCs use financial tools in monitoring overseas units. This was true as long as three decades ago, when the following was reported:

> The cross-cultural homogeneity in financial control is in marked contrast to the heterogeneity exercised over the areas of international operations. American subsidiaries of Italian and Scandinavian firms are virtually independent operationally from their parents in functions pertaining to marketing, production, and research and development; whereas, the subsidiaries of German and British firms have limited freedom in these areas. Almost no autonomy on financial matters is given by any nationality to the subsidiaries.[25]

Some Major Differences MNCs control operations in many different ways, and these often vary considerably from country to country. For example, how British firms monitor their overseas operations often is different from how German or French firms do. Similarly, U.S. MNCs tend to have their own approach to controlling, and it differs from both European and Japanese approaches. When Horovitz examined the key characteristics of top management control in Great Britain, Germany, and France, he found that British controls had four common characteristics: (1) Financial records were sophisticated and heavily emphasized. (2) Top management tended to focus its attention on major problem areas and did not get involved in specific, detailed matters of control. (3) Control was used more for general guidance than for surveillance. (4) Operating units had a large amount of marketing autonomy.[26]

This model was in marked contrast to that of German managers, who employed very detailed control and focused attention on all variances large and small. These managers also placed heavy control on the production area and stressed operational efficiency. In achieving this centralized control, managers used a large central staff for measuring performance, analyzing variances, and compiling quantitative reports for senior executives. Overall, the control process in the German firms was used as a policing and surveillance instrument. French managers employed a control system that was closer to that of the Germans than to the British. Control was used more for surveillance than for guiding operations, and the process was centrally administered. Even so, the French system was less systematic and sophisticated.[27]

How do U.S. MNCs differ from their European counterparts? One comparative study found that a major difference is that U.S. firms tend to rely much more heavily on reports and other performance-related data. Americans make greater use of output control, and Europeans rely more heavily on behavioral control. Commenting on the differences between these two groups, the researcher noted: "This pattern appears to be quite robust and continues to exist even when a number of common factors that seem to influence control are taken into account."[28] Some specific findings from this study include:

1. Control in U.S. MNCs focuses more on the quantifiable, objective aspects of a foreign subsidiary, whereas control in European MNCs tends to be used to measure more qualitative aspects. The U.S. approach allows comparative analyses between other foreign operations as well as domestic units; the European measures are more flexible and allow control to be exercised on a unit-by-unit basis.

2. Control in U.S. MNCs requires more precise plans and budgets in generating suitable standards for comparison. Control in European MNCs requires a high level of companywide understanding and agreement regarding what constitutes appropriate behavior and how such behavior supports the goals of both the subsidiary and the parent firm.

3. Control in U.S. MNCs requires large central staffs and centralized information-processing capability. Control in European MNCs requires a larger cadre of capable expatriate managers who are willing to spend long periods of time abroad. This control characteristic is reflected in the career approaches used in the various MNCs. Although U.S. multinationals do not encourage lengthy stays in foreign management positions, European MNCs often regard these positions as stepping-stones to higher offices.

4. Control in European MNCs requires more decentralization of operating decision making than does control in U.S. MNCs.

5. Control in European MNCs favors short vertical spans or reporting channels from the foreign subsidiary to responsible positions in the parent.[29]

As noted in the discussion of decision making, these differences help explain why many researchers have found European subsidiaries to be more decentralized than U.S. subsidiaries. Europeans rely on the managerial personnel they assign from headquarters to run the unit properly. Americans tend to hire a greater percentage of local management people and control operations through reports and other objective, performance-related data. The difference results in Europeans' relying more on socioemotional control systems and Americans' opting for task-oriented, objective control systems.

Evaluating Approaches to Control   Is one control approach any better than the other? The answer is that each seems to work best for its respective group. Some studies predict that as MNCs increase in size, they likely will move toward the objective orientation of the U.S. MNCs. Commenting on the data gathered from large German and U.S. MNCs, the researchers concluded:

> Control mechanisms have to be harmonized with the main characteristics of management corporate structure to become an integrated part of the global organization concept and to meet situational needs. Trying to explain the differences in concepts of control, we have to consider that the companies of the U.S. sample were much larger and more diversified.... Accordingly, they use different corporate structures, combining operational units into larger units and integrating these through primarily centralized, indirect, and task-oriented control.... The German companies have not (yet) reached this size and complexity, so a behavioral model of control seems to be fitting.[30]

Approaches to control also differ between U.S. and Japanese firms. For example, one study surveyed the attitudes of a large sample of Japanese and U.S. controllers and line managers. Respondents were drawn from the 500 largest industrial firms in both countries. Some of the results are presented in Table 11–4.

One overall finding of the research was that Japanese controllers and managers prefer less participation in the control process than their U.S. counterparts. In addition, the Japanese have longer-term planning horizons, view budgets as more of a communication device than a controlling tool, and prefer more slack in their budgets than the Americans. These results are extremely important in terms of adapting U.S. approaches to Japanese-owned subsidiaries. The study results suggest the following:

> U.S. managers who wish to design control systems for foreign divisions in Japan (or vice-versa) may wish to consider modifications to the typical domestic system, or they should at least be aware of the potential differences in responses to the system in the areas of budget development, evaluation against budgets, long-run/short-run orientation of budgets, the use of budget slack, and the use of analytic tools in developing inputs to the budget process to name a few.[31]

It is also important to understand why Japanese managers act as they do. Yoshimura and Anderson conducted a detailed analysis of white-collar middle managers in Japan in order to determine what foreign managers need to know about these "salarymen." One thing that the researchers found was that Japanese managers place human relationships ahead of economic efficiency. As a result, when Western managers try to penetrate Japanese markets by offering superior technology or lower price as their levers, they often find that these strategies do not work. If a Japanese company has had a satisfactory relationship with a supplier, the company may continue doing business with this firm even if it means accepting higher costs. Second, when dealing with a Japanese company, nothing is more important than a supplier's ability to meet this customer's expectations. When salarymen complain about non-Japanese companies and the products or service they provide, they usually contend that consistency is missing:

> They want their suppliers to understand customer expectations without being told explicitly, and they want assurance that even "unreasonable" expectations, such as midnight service, will be met. They don't want their relationship manager changed frequently because of turnover; a new contact may not understand their expectations immediately. Japanese overseas subsidiaries do business with their traditional suppliers because they want to maintain continuity in relationships, even if lower-cost local firms are available. The Japanese believe that, in the long run, if both parties contribute to the relationship in good faith, results will take care of themselves.[32]

Table 11–4
Selected Beliefs Related to Planning and Control

| | Statement of Results—Average Responses | | | |
| | Japan | | United States | |
	Managers	Controllers	Managers	Controllers
To be useful in performance evaluation of managers, a budget must be revised continuously throughout the year.	3.07	3.14	2.70	2.48
It is important that budgets be very detailed.	3.38	3.31	2.93	2.97
It is appropriate to charge other activities when budgeted funds are used up.	3.01	2.91	1.96	1.52
Budgets should be developed from the bottom up rather than from the top down.	3.13	3.01	3.68	3.96
Budgets are useful in communicating the goal and planned activities of the company.	4.54	4.68	4.11	4.23
Budgets are useful in coordinating activities of various departments.	4.24	4.46	3.78	4.02
A manager who fails to attain the budgets should be replaced.	2.56	2.67	2.00	1.92
Top management should judge a manager's performance mainly on the basis of attaining budget profit.	3.25	3.38	2.27	2.07
It is important that executive compensation depend on a comparison of actual and budgeted performance.	3.18	3.18	3.55	3.56
It is important that managers who perform exceptionally well receive more money than other managers in similar positions.	3.84	3.92	4.28	4.14
It is important for a manager to have quantitative or analytic skills as opposed to people skills.	3.12	3.15	2.04	1.96
The best way to determine the value of capital projects is through the use of quantitative analysis.	3.61	3.80	3.23	3.37

Note: The response scale was as follows:

Strongly disagree	1
Disagree	2
Neutral	3
Agree	4
Strongly agree	5

Source: Adapted from Lane Daley, James Jiambalvo, Gary L. Sundem, and Yasumasa Kondo, "Attitudes Toward Financial Control Systems in the United States and Japan," *Journal of International Business Studies,* Fall 1985, pp. 100–102.

Another thing that the researchers discovered is that sometimes performance results are not as high as they could be because of the fear of embarrassing others in the organization. For example, even though some decisions might result in higher returns on investment for the company, if these decisions put others in a bad light, they will not be made. This means that if a bank has two groups that are charged with buying and selling foreign currency and one of the groups concludes that the U.S. dollar is going to decline against the Japanese yen, it would be wise for this group to sell those dollars and buy yen. On the other hand, if there is another group in the bank that has a large position in dollars and will be unable to unload this currency very quickly, the first group might refuse to sell its dollars because this would end up making the group that held dollars look foolish, and this is something that Japanese salarymen try very hard to avoid.

In fact, the avoidance of embarrassment—saving "face"—is one reason that many Japanese firms focus on long-term objectives rather than short-term ones. While their pronouncements seem to emphasize the long-term orientation of their company, in truth this approach is a way of deflecting embarrassment. After all, no one knows what will happen in the long run, so by pretending to be highly interested in 50-year goals, the management sidesteps any likelihood that its current performance will be criticized. It can always argue that in the long run it will achieve high-level performance despite the fact that it is not doing very well at present. So in deciding which form of control to use, MNCs must determine whether they want a more bureaucratic or a more cultural control approach; and from the cultural perspective, it must be remembered that this control will vary across subsidiaries.

■ Performance Evaluation as a Mechanism of Control

A number of performance measures are used for control purposes. Three of the most common evaluate financial performance, quality performance, and personnel performance.

Financial Performance

Financial performance evaluation of a foreign subsidiary or affiliate usually is based on profit and return on investment. **Profit** is the amount remaining after all expenses are deducted from total revenues. **Return on investment (ROI)** is measured by dividing profit by assets; some firms use profit divided by owners' equity (returns on owners' investment, or ROOI) in referring to the return-on-investment performance measure. In any case, the most important part of the ROI calculation is profits, which often can be manipulated by management. Thus, the amount of profit directly relates to how well or how poorly a unit is judged to perform. For example, if an MNC has an operation in both country A and country B and taxes are lower in country A, the MNC may be able to benefit if the two units have occasion to do business with each other. This benefit can be accomplished by having the unit in country A charge higher prices than usual to the unit in country B, thus providing greater net profits to the MNC. Simply put, sometimes differences in tax rates can be used to maximize overall MNC profits. This same basic form of manipulation can be used in transferring money from one country to another, which can be explained as follows:

> Transfer prices are manipulated upward or downward depending on whether the parent company wishes to inject or remove cash into or from a subsidiary. Prices on imports by a subsidiary from a related subsidiary are raised if the multinational company wishes to move funds from the receiver to the seller, but they are lowered if the objective is to keep the funds in the importing subsidiary.... Multinational companies have been known to use transfer pricing for moving excess cash from subsidiaries located in countries with weak currencies to countries with strong currencies in order to protect the value of their current assets.[33]

The so-called bottom-line (i.e., profit) performance of subsidiaries also can be affected by a devaluation or revaluation of local currency. For example, if a country devalues its currency, then subsidiary export sales will increase, because the price of these goods will be lower for foreign buyers, whose currencies now have greater purchasing power. If the country revalues its currency, then export sales will decline because the price of goods for foreign buyers will rise, since their currencies now have less purchasing power in the subsidiary's country. Likewise, a devaluation of the currency will increase the cost of imported materials and supplies for the subsidiary, and a revaluation will decrease these costs because of the relative changes in the purchasing power of local currency. Because devaluation and revaluation of local currency are outside the control of the overseas unit, bottom-line performance sometimes will be a result of external conditions that do not accurately reflect how well the operation actually is being run.

profit
The amount remaining after all expenses are deducted from total revenues.

return on investment (ROI)
Return measured by dividing profit by assets.

Of course, not all bottom-line financial performance is a result of manipulation or external economic conditions. Sometimes other forces account for the problem. For example, one of Volkswagen's goals for a recent year was to earn a pretax 6.5 percent on revenues. The firm fell far short of this goal, earning only 3.5 percent before taxes. One reason for this poor performance was that labor costs in Lower Saxony, where approximately half its workforce is located, are very high. Workers here produce only 40 vehicles per employee annually in contrast to the VW plant in Navarra, Spain, which turns out 79 vehicles per employee per year. Why doesn't VW move work to lower-cost production sites? The major reason is that the state of Lower Saxony owns 19 percent of the company's voting stock, so the workers' jobs are protected.[34] Simply put, relying solely on financial results to evaluate performance can result in misleading conclusions.

Quality Performance

Just as quality has become a major focus in decision making, it also is a major dimension of the modern control process of MNCs. The term *quality control (QC)* has been around for a long time, and it is a major function of production and operations management. Besides the TQM techniques of concurrent engineering/interfunctional teams, employee empowerment, reward/recognition systems, and training, discussed earlier in this chapter in the context of decision making, another technique more directly associated with the control function is the use of quality circles, which have been popularized by the Japanese. A **quality control circle (QCC)** is a group of workers who meet on a regular basis to discuss ways of improving the quality of work. This approach has helped many MNCs improve the quality of their goods and services dramatically.

> **quality control circle (QCC)**
> A group of workers who meet on a regular basis to discuss ways of improving the quality of work.

Why are Japanese-made goods of higher quality than the goods of many other countries? The answer cannot rest solely on technology, because many MNCs have the same or superior technology or the financial ability to purchase it. There must be other causal factors. "International Management in Action: How the Japanese Do Things Differently" gives some details about these factors. One study attempted to answer the question by examining the differences between Japanese and U.S. manufacturers of air conditioners.[35] In this analysis, many of the commonly cited reasons for superior Japanese quality were discovered to be inaccurate. One theory was that the Japanese focus their production processes on a relatively limited set of tasks and narrow product lines, but this was not so. Nor was support found for the commonly held belief that single sourcing provided Japanese firms with cost advantages over those using multiple sourcing; the firms studied regularly relied on a number of different suppliers. So what were the reasons for the quality differences?

One reason was the focus on keeping the workplace clean and ensuring that all machinery and equipment were properly maintained. The Japanese firms were more careful in handling incoming parts and materials, work-in-process, and finished products than their U.S. counterparts. Japanese companies also employed equipment fixtures to a greater extent than did U.S. manufacturers in ensuring proper alignment of parts during final assembly.

The Japanese minimized worker error by assigning new employees to existing work teams or pairing them with supervisors. In this way, the new workers gained important experience under the watchful eye of someone who could correct their mistakes.

Another interesting finding was that the Japanese made effective use of QCCs. Quality targets were set, and responsibility for their attainment then fell on the circle while management provided support assistance. This was stated by the researcher as follows:

> In supporting the activities of their QCCs, the Japanese firms in this industry routinely collected extensive quality data. Information on defects was compiled daily, and analyzed for trends. Perhaps most important, the data were made easily accessible to line workers, often in the form of publicly posted charts. More detailed data were available to QCCs on request.[36]

How the Japanese Do Things Differently

Japanese firms do a number of things extremely well. One is to train their people carefully, a strategy that many successful U.S. firms also employ. Another is to try to remain on the technological cutting edge. A third, increasingly important because of its uniqueness to the Japanese, is to keep a keen focus on developing and bringing to market goods that are competitively priced.

In contrast to Western firms, many Japanese companies use a "target cost" approach. Like other multinational firms, Japanese companies begin the new product development process by conducting marketing research and examining the characteristics of the product to be produced. At this point, however, the Japanese take a different approach. The traditional approach used by MNCs around the world is next to go into designing, engineering, and supplier pricing and then to determine if the cost is sufficiently competitive to move ahead with manufacturing. Japanese manufacturers, in contrast, first determine the price that the consumer most likely will accept, and then they work with design, engineering, and supply people to ensure that the product can be produced at this price. The other major difference is that after most firms manufacture a product, they will engage in periodic cost reductions. The Japanese, however, use a kaizen approach, which fosters continuous cost-reduction efforts.

The critical difference between the two systems is that the Japanese get costs out of the product during the planning and design stage. Additionally, they look at profit in terms of product lines rather than just individual goods, so a consumer product that would be rejected for production by a U.S. or European firm because its projected profitability is too low may be accepted by a Japanese firm because the product will attract additional customers to other offerings in the line. A good example is Sony, which decided to build a smaller version of its compact personal stereo system and market it to older consumers. Sony knew that the profitability of the unit would not be as high as usual, but it went ahead because the product would provide another market niche for the firm and strengthen its reputation. Also, a side benefit is that once a product is out there, it may appeal to an unanticipated market. This was the case with Sony's compact personal stereo system. The unit caught on with young people, and Sony's sales were 50 percent greater than anticipated. Had Sony based its manufacturing decision solely on "stand-alone" profitability, the unit never would have been produced.

These approaches are not unique to Japanese firms. Foreign companies operating in Japan are catching on and using them as well. A good example is Coca-Cola Japan. Coke is the leading company in the Japanese soft drink market, which sees the introduction of more than 1,000 new products each year. Most offerings do not last very long, and a cost accountant might well argue that it is not worth the effort to produce them. However, Coca-Cola introduces one new product a month. Most of these sodas, soft drinks, and cold coffees survive less than 90 days, but Coke does not let the short-term bottom line dictate the decision. The firm goes beyond quick profitability and looks at the overall picture. Result: Coca-Cola continues to be the leading soft drink firm in Japan despite competition that often is more vigorous than that in the United States.

This finding pointed out an important difference between Americans and Japanese. The Japanese pushed data on quality down to the operating employees in the quality circles, whereas Americans tended to aggregate the quality data into summary reports aimed at middle and upper management.

Another important difference is that the Japanese tend to build in early warning systems so that they know when something is going wrong. Incoming field data, for example, are reviewed immediately by the quality department, and problems are assigned to one of two categories: routine or emergency. Special efforts then are made to resolve the emergency problems as quickly as possible. High failure rates attributable to a single persistent problem are identified and handled much faster than they would be in U.S. firms.

Still another reason is that the Japanese work closely with their suppliers so that the latter's quality increases. In fact, research shows that among suppliers that have contracts with both American and Japanese auto plants in the United States, the Japanese plants get higher performance from their suppliers than do the Americans.[37] The Japanese are able to accomplish this because they work closely with their suppliers and help them develop lean manufacturing capabilities. Some of the steps that Japanese manufacturers take in doing this include (1) leveling their own production schedules in order to avoid

Table 11–5
Performance of Suppliers When Serving U.S. and Japanese-Owned Auto Plants

Performance Indicators	Chrysler Suppliers ($n = 26$)	Ford Suppliers ($n = 42$)	GM Suppliers ($n = 23$)	Honda Suppliers ($n = 22$)	Nissan Suppliers ($n = 16$)	Toyota Suppliers ($n = 37$)
Inventory turnover	28.3	24.4	25.5	38.4	49.2	52.4
Work-in-process	3.0	3.9	7.2	4.0	3.8	3.0
Finished-goods storage time	4.8	5.4	6.6	5.3	4.9	3.2
Inventory on the truck	2.1	4.5	2.6	2.8	2.08	1.61
Inventory maintained at the customer's site	3.5	4.8	3.1	4.0	2.8	2.3
Percentage change in manufacturing costs compared to the previous year	0.69%	0.58%	0.74%	−0.9%	−0.7%	−1.3%
Percentage of late deliveries	4.4%	7.70%	3.04%	2.11%	1.08%	0.44%
Emergency shipping cost (per million sales dollars) in previous year	$1,235	$446	$616	$423	$379	$204

Source: Adapted from Jeffrey K. Liker and Yen-Chun Wu, "Japanese Automakers, U.S. Suppliers and Supply-Chain Superiority," *Sloan Management Review,* Fall 2000, p. 84.

big spikes in demand, thus allowing their suppliers to hold less inventory; (2) encouraging their suppliers to ship only what is needed by the assembly plant at a particular time, even if this means sending partially filled trucks; and (3) creating a disciplined system of delivery time windows during which all parts have to be received at the delivery plant. A close look at Table 11–5 shows that the 91 suppliers who were working for both Japanese and American auto firms performed more efficiently for their Japanese customers than for their American customers.

Management attitudes toward quality also were quite different. The Japanese philosophy is: "Anything worth doing in the area of quality is worth overdoing." Workers are trained for all jobs on the line, even though they eventually are assigned to a single workstation. This method of "training overkill" ensures that everyone can perform every job perfectly and results in two important outcomes: (1) If someone is moved to another job, he or she can handle the work without any additional assistance. (2) The workers realize that management puts an extremely high value on the need for quality. When questioned regarding whether their approach to quality resulted in spending more money than was necessary, the Japanese managers disagreed. They believed that quality improvement was technically possible and economically feasible. They did not accept the common U.S. strategy of building a product with quality that was "good enough."

These managers were speaking only for their own firms, however. Some evidence shows that, at least in the short run, an overfocus on quality may become economically unwise. Even so, firms must remember that quality goods and services lead in the long run to repeat business, which translates into profits and growth. From a control standpoint, the major issue is how to identify quality problems and resolve them as efficiently as possible. One approach that has gained acceptance in the United States is outlined by Genichi Taguchi, one of the foremost authorities on quality control. Taguchi's method is to dispense with highly sophisticated statistical methods unless more fundamental ways do not work. Figure 11–3 compares the use of the Taguchi method and the traditional method to identify the cause of defects in the paint on a minivan hood. The Taguchi

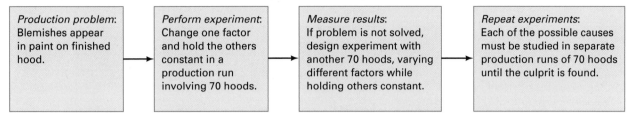

Figure 11–3 | **Solving a Quality Problem: Taguchi Method vs. Traditional Method**

Traditional Method Possible causes are studied one by one while holding the other factors constant.

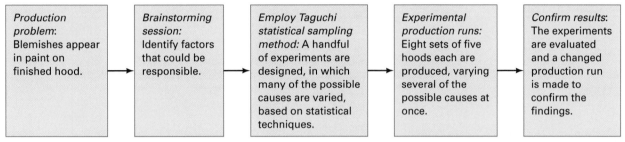

Taguchi Method Brainstorming and a few bold experiments seek to quickly find the problem.

Source: From information reported in John Holusha, "Improving Quality, the Japanese Way," *New York Times,* July 20, 1988, p. 35.

approach to solving quality control problems is proving to be so effective that many MNCs are adopting it. They also are realizing that the belief that Japanese firms will correct quality control problems regardless of the cost is not true. As Taguchi puts it, "the more efficient approach is to identify the things that can be controlled at a reasonable cost in an organized manner, and simply ignore those too expensive to control."[38] To the extent that U.S. MNCs can do this, they will be able to compete on the basis of quality.

Personnel Performance

Besides financial techniques and the emphasis on quality, another key area of control is personnel performance evaluation. This type of evaluation can take a number of different forms, although there is a great deal of agreement from firm to firm about the general criteria to be measured. Table 11–6 provides a list of the 50 most-admired global companies. What makes these MNCs so successful? Consultants at the Hay Group made an analysis of the best global firms and identified seven common themes:

1. Top managers at the most-admired companies take their mission statements seriously and expect everyone else to do the same.
2. Success attracts the best people—and the best people sustain success.
3. The top companies know precisely what they are looking for.
4. These firms see career development as an investment, not a chore.
5. Whenever possible, these companies promote from within.
6. Performance is rewarded.
7. The firms are genuinely interested in what their employees think, and they measure work satisfaction often and thoroughly.[39]

One of the most common approaches to personnel performance evaluation is the periodic appraisal of work performance. Although the objective is similar from country to country, how performance appraisals are done differs. For example, effective employee performance in one country is not always judged to be effective in another. Awareness of international differences is particularly important when expatriate managers evaluate local managers on the basis of home-country standards. A good example comes out of a survey

Table 11–6
The 50 Most-Admired Global Companies, 2007

Rank	Company	Country
1	General Electric	U.S.
2	Toyota Motor	Japan
3	Procter & Gamble	U.S.
4	Johnson & Johnson	U.S.
5	Apple	U.S.
6	Berkshire Hathaway	U.S.
7	FedEx	U.S.
8	Microsoft	U.S.
9	BMW	Germany
10	PepsiCo	U.S.
11	IBM	U.S.
12	Target	U.S.
13	Wal-Mart Stores	U.S.
14	United Parcel Service	U.S.
15	Costco Wholesale	U.S.
16	Walt Disney	U.S.
17	Singapore Airlines	Singapore
18	Exxon Mobil	U.S.
19	Boeing	U.S.
20	Nokia	Finland
21	Citigroup	U.S.
22	Bank of America	U.S.
23	Honda Motor	Japan
24	Coca-Cola	U.S.
25	Caterpillar	U.S.
26	Nestlé	Switzerland
27	Dell	U.S.
28	Toyota Industries	Japan
29	Intel	U.S.
30	Tesco	Britain
31	Dupont	U.S.
32	Cisco Systems	U.S.
33	Walgreens	U.S.
34	Samsung Electronics	South Korea
35	Anheuser-Busch	U.S.
36	BP	Britain
37	Best Buy	U.S.
38	Siemens	Germany
39	Home Depot	U.S.
40	L'Oréal	France
41	Sony	Japan
42	Motorola	U.S.
43	Hewlett-Packard	U.S.
44	Northwestern Mutual	U.S.
45	Lowe's	U.S.
46	Canon	Japan
47	Deere	U.S.
48	HSBC Holdings	Britain
49	Xerox	U.S.
50	Dow Chemical	U.S.

Source: "The 50 Most Admired Companies in the World," (2007 All-Stars), *Fortune International,* March 19, 2007. Copyright © 2007 Time Inc. All rights reserved.

that found Japanese managers in U.S.-based manufacturing firms gave higher evaluations to Japanese personnel than to Americans. The results led the researcher to conclude: "It seems that cultural differences and diversified approaches to management in MNCs of different nationalities will always create a situation where some bias in performance appraisal may exist."[40] Dealing with these biases is a big challenge facing MNCs.

Another important difference is how personnel performance control actually is conducted. A study that compared personnel control approaches used by Japanese managers in Japan with those employed by U.S. managers in the United States found marked differences.[41] For example, when Japanese work groups were successful because of the actions of a particular individual, the Japanese manager tended to give credit to the whole group. When the group was unsuccessful because of the actions of a particular individual, however, the Japanese manager tended to perceive this one employee as responsible. In addition, the more unexpected the poor performance, the greater was the likelihood that the individual would be responsible. In contrast, individuals in the United States typically were given the credit when things went well and the blame when performance was poor.

Other differences relate to how rewards and monitoring of personnel performance are handled. Both U.S. and Japanese managers offered greater rewards and more freedom from close monitoring to individuals when they were associated with successful performance, no matter what the influence of the group on the performance. The Americans carried this tendency further than the Japanese in the case of rewards, including giving high rewards to a person who was a "lone wolf."[42]

A comparison of these two approaches to personnel evaluation shows that the Japanese tend to use a more social or group orientation, while the Americans are more individualistic (for more, see Chapter 4). The researchers found that overall, however, the approaches were quite similar and that the control of personnel performance by Japanese and U.S. managers is far more similar than different.

Such similarity also can be found in assessment centers used to evaluate employees. An **assessment center** is an evaluation tool that is used to identify individuals with the potential to be selected or promoted to higher-level positions. Used by large U.S. MNCs for many years, these centers also are employed around the world. A typical assessment center would involve simulation exercises such as these: (1) in-basket exercises that require managerial attention; (2) a committee exercise in which the candidates must work as a team in making decisions; (3) business decision exercises in which participants compete in the same market; (4) preparation of a business plan; and (5) a letter-writing exercise. These forms of evaluation are beginning to gain support, because they are more comprehensive than simple checklists or the use of a test or an interview and thus better able to identify those managers who are most likely to succeed when hired or promoted.

> **assessment center**
> An evaluation tool used to identify individuals with the potential to be selected or promoted to higher-level positions.

The World of *BusinessWeek*—Revisited

This chapter focuses on two areas that are essential to any company joining the race to make extremely inexpensive vehicles: management decision and control systems. Competitors following Tata Motors's lead will vary in performance depending on how their decision-making processes are carried out. Any company attempting to be first to market will have to have efficient processes in place, and the internal structure may not support those efforts. Other aspects will also need to be considered, including whether cars will be manufactured at the local level or mass-produced in one location and distributed to target markets. These decisions have major implications for the budget, which has an influence over how much overall control the company retains in its global operations. Even if the company cannot afford to have control over all aspects of manufacturing and testing, outsourcing to other companies at critical periods, such as safety tests, could pose challenges to reputation and market acceptance.

Having reviewed the opening case and the principal considerations in international management decision making and control, answer the following questions: (1) How might differences in national and corporate culture impede timely decisions and control processes among existing and potential competitors in the low-cost car market? (2) To what extent should total quality management and quality control be considered when manufacturing inexpensive cars? Consider the business and institutional environment of the countries these cars will be offered in when answering. (3) Would it be better to enter the inexpensive car market early and defend your position or to enter later and attack competition? Cite specific decision and control processes to justify your answer.

SUMMARY OF KEY POINTS

1. Decision making involves choosing from among alternatives. Some countries tend to use more centralized decision making than others, so that more decisions are made at the top of the MNC than are delegated to the subsidiaries and operating levels.

2. A number of factors help influence whether decision making will be centralized or decentralized, including company size, amount of capital investment, relative importance of the overseas unit to the MNC, volume-to-unit-cost relationship, level of product diversification, distance between the home office and the subsidiary, and the competence of managers in the host country.

3. There are a number of decision-making challenges with which MNCs currently are being confronted. These include total quality management (TQM)

decisions and strategies for attacking the competition, among others.

4. Controlling involves evaluating results in relation to plans or objectives and then taking action to correct deviations. MNCs control their overseas operations in a number of ways. Most combine direct and indirect controls. Some prefer heavily quantifiable methods, and others opt for more qualitative approaches. Some prefer decentralized approaches; others opt for greater centralization.

5. Three of the most common performance measures used to control subsidiaries are in the financial, quality, and personnel areas. Financial performance typically is measured by profit and return on investment. Quality performance often is controlled through quality circles. Personnel performance typically is judged through performance evaluation techniques.

KEY TERMS

assessment center, *363*

codetermination, *343*

controlling, *349*

decision making, *340*

direct controls, *352*

empowerment, *345*

honne, *344*

indirect controls, *353*

kaizen, *345*

profit, *357*

quality control circle (QCC), *358*

return on investment (ROI), *357*

ringisei, *344*

tatemae, *344*

total quality management (TQM), *345*

REVIEW AND DISCUSSION QUESTIONS

1. A British computer firm is acquiring a smaller competitor located in Frankfurt. What are two likely differences in the way these two firms carry out the decision-making process? How could these differences create a problem for the acquiring firm? Give an example in each case.

2. Which cultures would be more likely to focus on external controls? Which cultures would consider direct controls to be more important than indirect controls?

3. How would you explain a company's decision to employ centralized decision-making processes and

decentralized control processes, considering the two are so interconnected? Provide an industry example of where this may occur.

4. How are U.S. multinationals trying to introduce total quality management into their operations? Give two examples. Would a U.S. MNC doing business in Germany find it easier to introduce TQM concepts into German operations, or would there be more receptivity to them back in the United States? Why? What if the U.S. multinational were introducing these ideas into a Japanese subsidiary?

5. In what ways could an accelerated decision-making process harm a company? Using Figure 11–1, which stage(s) do you think would be most in danger of being overlooked?

6. A company practices personnel performance evaluation through reviewing financial decisions management has made, specifically focusing on ROI. How is this approach beneficial to the company? Which aspects could the company be neglecting? Which cultures are most likely to employ this method? Which cultures would avoid this tactic?

INTERNET EXERCISE: LOOKING AT THE BEST

In Table 11–6, the 50 most-admired global companies are listed. Each company uses decision making and controlling to help ensure its success in the world market. Visit two of these company sites: Sony and Nokia. The addresses are **www.sony.com** and **www.nokia.com.** Carefully examine what these firms are doing. For example, what markets are they targeting? What products and services are they offering? What new markets are they entering? Then after you are as familiar with their operations as possible, answer these two questions: (1) What types of factors may influence future management decision making in these two companies? (2) What types of control criteria would you expect these companies to use in evaluating their operations and determining how well they are doing?

Spain

Spain, which covers 195,000 square miles, is located on the Iberian Peninsula at the southwest corner of Europe; its southernmost tip is directly across from Morocco. The country has a population of approximately 40.5 million and a gross domestic product of about $1.1 trillion ($27,400 per capita). Until the mid-1990s, Spain, known for its sunny climate, colorful bullfights, and storybook castles, was one of the most underdeveloped countries in Western Europe. Now it is an industrialized country whose economy relies heavily on trade, manufacturing, and services. Many of the old Spanish customs, such as taking a siesta (nap or rest) after lunch, are less common. Since 1978 the government has been a constitutional monarchy. The king is head of state and commander in chief of the armed forces, but legislative power rests in a bicameral parliament consisting of a congress of deputies and a senate.

The Spanish culture is one that places a great deal of emphasis on pride. When people work together, they try to avoid situations that will taint the relationship through criticism or cause either party embarrassment. Typically, in business, this means that control is very important as it signifies a certain level of prosperity. However, there are some instances where Spanish businesspeople will claim that everything is in order when it is not, as a way of saving face. Furthermore, the Spanish are not known to be risk takers, and approach ventures with caution. These factors are quite significant to companies hoping to expand operations in Spain.

Investors Limited, a partnership based in Hong Kong and headed by Stanley Wong, owns 17 medium and large hotels throughout Asia and a total of 9 others throughout the United Kingdom, France, and Germany. The group now plans on buying a large hotel in Madrid. This hotel was built at the turn of the 20th century but was completely refurbished in 1990 at a cost of $20 million. The current owners have decided that the return on investment, which has been averaging 5.2 percent annually, is too small to justify continuing the operation. They have offered the hotel to Investors Limited for $60 million. One-half is payable immediately, and the rest would be paid in equal annual installments over five years.

Stanley Wong believes that this would be a good investment and has suggested to his partners that they accept the offer. "Europe is going to boom during the new millennium," he told them, "and Spain is going to be an excellent investment. This hotel is one of the finest in Madrid, and we are going to more than triple our investment by the end of the decade."

In the past, the partnership has handled all hotel investments in the same way. A handful of company-appointed managers are sent in to oversee general operations and monitor financial performance, and all other matters continue to be handled by those personnel who were with the hotel before acquisition. The investment group intends to handle the Madrid operation in the same way. "The most important thing," Stanley noted recently, "is that we keep control of key areas of performance such as costs and return on investment. If we do that and continue to offer the best possible service, we'll come out just fine."

www.sispain.org, www.red2000.com/spain

Questions

1. What are some current issues facing Spain? What is the climate for doing business in Spain today?

2. Do you think Investors Limited, in running the hotel, should use centralized or decentralized decision making?

3. In what ways will Spanish business culture affect the decision-making time in negotiations with Investors Limited? How will it affect control decisions?

4. What are some likely differences between the control measures that Investors Limited would use and those that typically are used in countries such as Spain?

Expansion Plans

Kranden & Associates is a very successful porcelain-manufacturing firm based in San Diego. The company has six world-renowned artists who design fine-crafted porcelain statues and plates that are widely regarded as collectibles. Each year, the company offers a limited edition of new statues and plates. Last year, the company made 30 new offerings. On average, 2,500 items of each line are produced, and they usually are sold within six months. The company does not produce more than this number to avoid reducing the value of the line to collectors; however, the firm does believe that additional statues and plates could be sold in some areas of the world without affecting the price in North America. In particular, the firm is thinking about setting up production facilities in Rio de Janeiro, Brazil, and Paris, France.

The production process requires skilled personnel, but there are people in both Rio de Janeiro and Paris who can do this work. The basic methods can be taught to these people by trainers from the U.S. plant, because the production process will be identical.

The company intends to send three managers to each of its overseas units to handle setup operations and get the production process off the ground. This should take 12 to 18 months. Once this is done, one person will be left in charge, and the other two will return home.

The company believes that it will be able to sell just as much of the product line in Europe as it does in the United States. The South American market is estimated to be one-half that of the United States. Over the last five years, Kranden has had a return on investment of 55 percent. The company charges premium prices for its porcelain but still has strong demand for its products because of the high regard collectors and investors have for the Kranden line. The quality of its statues and plates is highly regarded, and the firm has won three national and two international awards for creativity and quality in design and production over the past 18 months. Over the last 10 years, the firm has won 17 such awards.

Questions

1. In managing its international operations, should the firm use centralized or decentralized decision making?

2. Would direct or indirect controls be preferable in managing these operations?

3. What kinds of performance measures should the company use in controlling these international operations?

Microsoft Opens the Gates: Patent, Piracy, and Political Challenges in China

In the mid-1980s, Microsoft made its first foray into the Greater China region, a region consisting of Hong Kong, the People's Republic of China, and Taiwan. It was not until 1992, however, that Microsoft entered the mainland by opening a sales office in Beijing. Lured by China's phenomenal economic growth and Chinese engineering talent, Microsoft has progressively deepened its involvement in China. By 2007, it had a global support center in Shanghai, a major research lab in Beijing, and employed more than 2,000 individuals throughout the country.

Along the way, Microsoft has faced significant challenges, such as the widespread piracy of its products, Chinese government pressures to transfer its technology, host government promotion of competitor products, discriminatory procurement practices by subnational authorities in China, and strong encouragement to enter into joint ventures (JVs) with local firms. To manage these challenges, Microsoft's top executives have built relationships with top Chinese leaders and the firm has invested heavily in China and built alliances with a number of Chinese technology companies. From time to time, Microsoft has lobbied the U.S. government to pressure China to enhance its protection of the intellectual property rights (IPR) of foreign companies.

The operating environment in China has been, at times, quite trying for Microsoft. Indeed, Microsoft senior counsel Fred Tipson said in November 2006, "We have to decide if the persecuting of bloggers reaches a point that it's unacceptable to do business there."[1] Even so, Microsoft is likely to plow ahead in its quest to profit from China. China's double-digit GDP growth rates and status as the world's second-largest PC market, and Microsoft's expectations that software sales will surge by 20 percent in 2007 suggest any other course of action is highly unlikely. Over the longer term, Microsoft's ability to tap China's riches will depend upon factors such as the country's continued economic growth, the development of the country's indigenous technology sector, and the extent to which foreign governments exert pressure on China.

Risks Facing Software Firms Operating in China

In 2001 China joined the World Trade Organization (WTO). Pursuant to its WTO agreements, China committed itself to honor the IPR—e.g., patents, copyrights, and trademarks—of foreign companies, including software firms. China quickly moved to make the requisite legal changes, but software piracy rates still ran an astounding 92 percent in 2004. The next year they fell to 86 percent, dropping to an improved but still troubling level of 82 percent by 2006.[2] Aside from piracy, software enterprises generally face great risks in defending their IPR in China. Specific challenges include an unclear specification of IPR enforcement responsibilities among government agencies, weak criminal sanctions, corruption, localism, and poor education about the requirements of IPR.

Beyond China's weak protection of IPR, foreign software firms operating in China must deal with a government deeply concerned about the development of China's technology sector.[3] In February 2006, for example, China's State Council (Cabinet) identified software as one of eleven sectors for prioritization. Nine months later, nine Chinese ministries, including the Ministry of Commerce, issued a document designed to boost China's software exports to $10 billion by 2010. Given this, it is not surprising that the government has moved to build up China's software sector. Its initiatives include subsidies, the provision of training, support for alternatives such as open source application software, efforts to create Chinese software standards, and preferential government procurement policies.

Foreign software firms also must contend with a strong undercurrent of Chinese nationalism. This nationalism can make government units, firms, and individuals reluctant to buy foreign products or do business with foreign firms. Even if it does not have this effect, nationalism can lead to extreme sensitivity about the behaviors of foreign businesses. At the extreme, it can even engender worries about the impact of foreign software firms on national security and national independence.[4]

Exploring Microsoft

Founded in 1975, Microsoft is the world's largest standalone software maker. Microsoft operating systems, such as Vista and XP, run on 90 percent of all PCs worldwide. Aside from operating system software for PCs, Microsoft offers systems software for servers and devices like personal digital assistants (PDAs) and mobile phones. Microsoft also develops security and collaboration software for the business market, diverse application software, including the

Microsoft Office productivity suite, computer games and operates Web sites such as MSN.com. While Microsoft is primarily a software company, it derives significant revenues from hardware items such as the Xbox gaming system and computer peripherals such as keyboards.

Although no longer the high-growth stock it once was, Microsoft registered very healthy results in 2006. Its revenues were $44.28 billion, almost $4.5 billion more than the previous year. Furthermore, the software giant's net income ran an impressive $12.59 billion. These results gave the company a return on equity of 28.5 percent, far better than many of its peers. While the financial picture has remained bright, Microsoft has long recognized the need to develop new sources of growth in order to deal with the maturation of the American market, regulatory challenges like the EU's antitrust action against Microsoft, and the rise of new competitors such as Google.

Microsoft took its first steps overseas in 1978 by establishing a sales office in Japan. Within 12 months Microsoft moved into Europe by signing a sales arrangement with Belgian firm Vector International. In 1982 Microsoft established a subsidiary in England, following the next year with the opening of subsidiaries in France and Germany and the purchase of a distributor in Australia. Two years later, Microsoft initiated its first production facility outside the United States in Dublin, Ireland. In 1986 the firm turned its attention to Latin America by establishing a subsidiary in Mexico. Three years later, Microsoft opened its European headquarters in France. In 1990 the firm deepened its involvement in the Asia Pacific by striking distribution arrangements in Indonesia, Malaysia, and Singapore and by opening a research and development center in Japan. In 1997 Microsoft opted to set up a research laboratory in England. One year later, Microsoft opened a development center in India, its largest outside of the United States. Expanding its presence in India, Microsoft opened a support center in Bangalore in 2003. Thereafter, Microsoft worked to build up its presence in China and other areas.

Microsoft's Quest to Excel in China[5]

Microsoft did not station its first employee in China until around 1991. A U.S.-China accord in 1992 on IPR spurred Microsoft to intensify its pursuit of opportunities in China. Subsequently, Microsoft opened a representative office and signed an agreement with various Chinese PC producers to preload its software on their computers. In 1994, then Microsoft Chairman and CEO, Bill Gates, visited China to launch Chinese Windows. Following a frosty reception by Chinese elites who felt Microsoft was not giving China due deference, Gates did an about face and pursued a more cooperative relationship with Beijing. Still, Microsoft did not shy away from aggressive measures to defend its interests. For example, it cheered efforts by the Office of the U.S. Trade Representative to obtain new IPR enforcement commitments from the Chinese government.

In November 1998, Microsoft and China opened Microsoft Research China, the company's second

Table 1 **Microsoft Timeline**

1975:	Microsoft is founded.
1981:	MS-DOS debuts on IBM's first PC.
1983:	Microsoft introduces MS Word, MS Windows, and the Microsoft mouse.
1985:	Microsoft sells the first retail version of Windows. Revenues reach almost $140 million.
1986:	Microsoft holds its IPO.
1989:	Microsoft launches Microsoft Office, a suite of business software including Excel.
1990:	Microsoft becomes the first software company to exceed $1 billion in revenues. U.S. Federal Trade Commission begins investigation into possible anticompetitive sales practices by Microsoft.
1993:	Microsoft launches Windows NT, a platform for network servers.
1995:	Microsoft introduces its Windows 95 operating system and its online MSN service. Revenues reach almost $6 billion.
1997:	U.S. Justice Department sues Microsoft for violating a 1994 consent decree relating to the licensing of Windows. A U.S. district court orders Microsoft to unbundle Windows 95 from its Internet browser.
2000:	Judge Thomas Jackson rules Microsoft a monopoly and orders breakup of the company and changes in its sales practices.
2001:	Microsoft launches Windows XP and the Xbox gaming system. U.S. Appeals Court overturns Jackson's breakup ruling.
2004:	European Union (EU) determines Microsoft is guilty of anticompetitive practices, fines it $613 million, orders it to share code, end certain practices, and untie certain music players from Windows.
2005:	Microsoft hits nearly $40 billion in revenues.
2006:	EU fines Microsoft $358 million for noncompliance with its 2004 ruling.
2007:	Microsoft releases Vista, its latest operating system and makes its largest ever acquisition, a $6 billion purchase of online marketing firm aQuantive.

Source: Author's compilation.

international research lab and first research facility in Asia. Around the same time, Microsoft established a major support center in Shanghai. Michael Rawding, Microsoft's Greater China regional director gushed, "China is the most populous country in the world, and it's becoming an ever more important location for information technology.... It's very important for Microsoft to understand and really be in the forefront of what's happening there."[6] The next year, though, Microsoft returned to a more confrontational path when it sued a Chinese company, Yadu Science and Technology, for piracy. The episode became a debacle for Microsoft, which not only lost the case but also suffered a public relations defeat.

While pressing for more progress on software piracy, Microsoft embraced a policy of cooperation. In this vein, it lobbied vigorously in 2000 for China's WTO accession and, in the same year, launched a simplified character version of Chinese Windows 2000. Relations with China were still antagonistic, though, because the Chinese government actively began to champion Linux (an open source operating system software) as an alternative to Microsoft's products. Chen Chong, a deputy minister in the Ministry of Information Industries, stated that China's support for Linux would "break the monopoly of the Windows operating system in the Chinese market."

There was reluctance, too, at the municipal level to embrace Microsoft. For example, in December 2001, the Beijing Municipal government shunned Microsoft by awarding operating system software contracts for 2,000 PCs to Red Flag Linux, a local Linux developer. On the bright side, Microsoft signed agreements with four leading Chinese computer makers—Legend, TCL, Tsinghua Tongfang, and Great Wall—to preinstall Windows XP on their machines. As well, it signed an accord with the Shanghai Municipal government, whereby it agreed to help develop Shanghai's software sector, expand its Shanghai regional support center into a global support center, and train thousands of software architects. Furthermore, it became the first foreign firm to become a member of the Chinese Software Industry Association.

In 2002 Microsoft entered into its first Chinese JV, Zhongguancun Software, with two Chinese firms—Centergate and Stone group. The deal was small but represented a change for Microsoft, which typically shunned such ventures. The same year, Microsoft signed a three-year, $750 million deal with China's State Development & Planning Commission, which committed Microsoft to invest in education and training, academic and research cooperation, and local software companies. Over the next two years, Microsoft agreed to let the Chinese government see the source code for the Windows operating system and all Office 2003 products (lest there be hidden security holes), signed a large investment and cooperation deal with the Beijing Commission on Science & Technology, and struck strategic partnership deals with various Chinese firms such as Petro China.[7] Despite Microsoft's efforts, the Chinese government continued to discriminate against the company by requiring all ministries to purchase Linux-based software.[8]

In 2005 Microsoft MSN announced a partnership with Shanghai Alliance Investment Ltd. (SAIL) to launch the MSN China online portal for delivering MSN products and services to customers in China. Concurrently, Microsoft developed a partnership with a Chinese mobile software and services firm (TSSX) to enable the delivery of MSN Mobile products and services. According to Tim Chen, CEO of Microsoft China, "creating a joint venture for MSN China and SAIL and our transaction with TSSX signifies the importance Microsoft attaches to the China market."[9] Eager to tap new sources of growth outside the maturing U.S. market, Microsoft worked in 2005 and into 2006 to conclude new agreements with Chinese PC manufacturers, develop new partnerships, and better its relations with the Chinese government.

As for commercial contracts, Microsoft signed deals worth almost $2 billion with Chinese PC makers Founder Technology Group, Lenovo, Tsinghua Tongfang, and TCL Group to preinstall Windows. With respect to partnerships, Microsoft began to license technology to Chinese firms. As a sign of bettering relations, Microsoft signed a five-year multibillion dollar agreement in April 2006 to outsource hardware production to Chinese firms as well as invest in others. Along similar lines, Microsoft signed a training, technology provision, and local investment agreement with the Guangzhou government in July. Microsoft's chief technology officer, Craig Mundie, noted that Microsoft was willing to continue to invest in China "even though the climate for our business has been suboptimal" because China was a priority for the firm both as a market and as a source of technology.[10]

Analysts partly attributed these favorable deals with Chinese PC firms and the Chinese government's 2006 decision to require all PC manufacturers to have legitimate operating systems to Microsoft's concerted overtures toward China. Tellingly, during his April 2006 visit to the United States, Chinese President Hu Jintao opted to meet with Bill Gates before meeting with President George Bush Jr. Moreover, during his tour of Microsoft's headquarters in Redmond, Washington, Hu complimented Gates as a friend of China.

At the beginning of 2007, Microsoft announced that it would set up an R&D facility in Shanghai to bolster its MSN offerings in China. Microsoft's relatively small $20 million investment was symbolically important, given that it was the company's first overseas MSN R&D venture. In April 2007, Bill Gates announced that Microsoft planned to double its R&D staffing in Beijing and Shanghai.[11] Microsoft China CEO Chen told the *China Daily*, "our core strategy is to implement a unified strategy, get rooted in China and grow with the local economy."[12] In May, it was reported that Lenovo had inked a new $1.3 billion software deal with Microsoft, following its $1 billion-plus deal in 2006.

The Vista for Microsoft in China

Going forward, China represents an immensely attractive market for Microsoft, a critical battleground, and a source of rich talent. China's 110 million Internet users, 350 million mobile phone subscribers, and 20 million PC sales in 2006 underscore its attractiveness as a software market. Bill Gates has repeatedly commented on China's immense scientific talent, most recently when receiving an honorary degree from Qinghua University in April 2007. There is little chance that the company will leave China despite Microsoft CFO John Connor's 2004 comment that "we can still be successful without large-scale China growth."[13]

In the future, software piracy will present a continuing challenge to Microsoft's growth in China. One reason is that the still high cost of Microsoft's software will encourage piracy. Another challenge for Microsoft is the fact that China's respect for IPR is still relatively underdeveloped. Yet another potential challenge is China's antimonopoly law, whose potential impact on the software giant remains unclear.

Over the longer term, analysts expect that Beijing's 2006 decision to require Chinese PC manufacturers to preinstall legal operating systems on all new PCs as well as various government agencies' decisions to require the purchase of only PCs preloaded with software will aide Microsoft's prospects. Also in Microsoft's favor are rising incomes that enable consumers to pay more, the improving legal environment for IPR, and the rise of an indigenous Chinese high-tech sector which can profit from IPR. Finally, Microsoft's extensive efforts to nurture partnerships, deepen its relations with China, and build a Microsoft-oriented software sector in China through training, certification, and the like should bolster the company's prospects.

Microsoft has come a long way since 1998 when Bill Gates reportedly said, "although about three million computers get sold every year in China, people don't pay for the software.... Someday they will...as long as they're going to steal it, we want them to steal ours. They'll get sort of addicted, and then we'll somehow figure out how to collect."[14] As one article put it, "Microsoft's investment [in China] can be best described with an old Chinese proverb 'give in order to take.' By doing so, Microsoft finally sees the twilight of making profit in China."[15]

Table 2 China's Closed Gates

$295	Price for a basic, legal copy of Microsoft Vista in China
$1.30 to $4.00	Price of a pirated copy of Microsoft Vista on the street in China
86%	Percentage of software on Chinese computers that is pirated
70%	Percentage of software on Chinese government computers that is pirated
$3.8 billion	Estimated software losses to piracy in China in 2005

Source: San Francisco Chronicle.

Questions for Review

1. What are the risks that Microsoft has faced in operating in China and dealing with the Chinese government? Do you see these risks as increasing, diminishing, or changing in the future? Are these risks unique to China or present in other developing countries?

2. What approaches did Microsoft take to manage its political risks in China? Why might it have favored some of these techniques versus others? Which do you feel worked best? What should Microsoft do going forward?

3. In its dealings with China, Microsoft frequently had to deal with lower levels of government. What special types of challenges and opportunities did this present?

4. Do other firms have the same risk management options as Microsoft? If so, why? If not, why not?

5. Is Microsoft creating serious risks by supporting, financing, and transferring technology to local Chinese software firms? How might Microsoft manage these risks?

Source: This case was prepared by Professor Jean-Marc Blanchard of San Francisco State University as the basis for class discussion.

The Last Rajah: Ratan Tata and Tata's Global Expansion

Among Asia's business titans, Ratan N. Tata stands out for his modesty. The chairman of the Tata Group—India's biggest conglomerate, with businesses ranging from software, cars, and steel to phone service, tea bags, and wristwatches—usually drives himself to the office in his $12,500 Tata Indigo Marina wagon. He prefers to spend weekends in solitude with his two dogs at a beachfront home he designed himself. And disdainful of pretense, he travels alone even on long business trips, eschewing the retinues of aides who typically coddle corporate chieftains. But the 69-year-old Tata also has a daredevil streak. An avid aviator, he often flies his own Falcon 2000 business jet around India. And in February he caused a sensation at the Aero India 2007 air show by co-piloting Lockheed F-16 and Boeing F-18 fighter jets.

Tata's business dealings reflect the bolder side of his personality. In the past four years he has embarked on an investment binge that is building his group from a once-stodgy regional player into a global heavyweight. Since 2003, Tata has bought the truck unit of South Korea's Daewoo Motors, a stake in one of Indonesia's biggest coal mines, and steel mills in Singapore, Thailand, and Vietnam. It has taken over a slew of tony hotels, including New York's Pierre, the Ritz-Carlton in Boston, and San Francisco's Camden Place. The 2004 purchase of Tyco International's undersea telecom cables for $130 million, a price that in hindsight looks like a steal, turned Tata into the world's biggest carrier of international phone calls. With its $91 million buyout of British engineering firm Incat International, Tata Technologies now is a major supplier of outsourced industrial design for American auto and aerospace companies, with 3,300 engineers in India, the United States, and Europe.

The crowning deal to date has been Tata Steel's $13 billion takeover in April of Dutch-British steel giant Corus Group, a target that would have been unthinkable just a few years ago. In one swoop, the move greatly expands Tata Steel's range of finished products, secures access to automakers across the United States and Europe, and boosts its capacity fivefold, with mills added in Pennsylvania and Ohio.

Now, a new gambit may catapult Tata into the big leagues of global auto manufacturing: The company is said to be weighing a bid for Jaguar Cars and Land Rover, which Ford Motor Co. wants to sell. On top of all this,

the group plans $28 billion in capital investments at home over the next five years in steel, autos, telecom, power, chemicals, and more. "We rescaled our thinking in terms of growth," Tata says over tea at Bombay House, the group's headquarters since 1926, a tranquil oasis with well-worn marble floors, a vast collection of modern Indian art, and staffers who circulate with bowls of vanilla ice cream every day at 3 p.m. "We just forced and cajoled our businesses to make this happen."

Spiritual Cement

The forcing and cajoling have worked brilliantly. The market value of the 18 listed Tata companies has swelled to $62 billion, from $12 billion, since 2003. Group sales and profits have doubled, to $29 billion and $2.8 billion, respectively. The three big companies that account for 75 percent of sales—Tata Steel, Tata Motors, and Tata Consultancy Services—are enjoying some of their best years ever. And in May, Tata Tea netted $523 million in profit when Coca-Cola Co. (KO) paid $1.2 billion for its 30 percent stake in Energy Brands Inc., the maker of Glacéau Vitamin Water. Not bad for a purchase made just nine months earlier. "This is a transformed Tata," says Rajeev Gupta, managing director of private equity shop Carlyle Advisory Partners.

The global push began four years ago. After a rocky first decade as chairman, Tata commissioned a sweeping review to plot strategy, including a study comparing India with China. He was struck by the sheer audacity of Chinese projects. "Whether they built a port or a highway, they did it big, the kind of scale that caused skeptics to say, 'My God, this is over the top,'" he says. "But China always grew into it." India, he concluded, should also think big—and so should Tata Group. By leveraging India's vast potential, he thought, the company could shift into turbocharged expansion to become a global heavyweight.

Tata is arguably the most important among a new pack of multinationals charging out of big developing nations such as China, Brazil, and Russia. These emerging giants can tap into abundant low-cost labor, tech talent, and mineral resources, while cutting their teeth in the world's biggest growth markets. Brimming with cash and confidence, they also are starting to export innovative business models honed in some of the planet's most challenging places to operate.

Building an organization with a coherent vision and capable of succeeding in so many industries and so many markets, though, is a daunting task. Asia has witnessed the rise of many soup-to-nuts behemoths that thrived when economic tides were high, such as Korea's Daewoo, Thailand's Charoen Pokphand, and Indonesia's Salim Group. Most eventually fell apart. The real test for Tata, too, is likely to come when India's boom abates and battles for talent and market share involving both aggressive Indian rivals and deep-pocketed multinationals intensify. But unlike most other Asian groups, "Tata already has proved it can survive turmoil and constantly reinvent itself," says Harvard Business School professor Tarun Khanna, who has closely studied the group for a decade.

At the center of the empire is Tata himself. An architecture graduate from Cornell University in 1962, he serves as the group's chief dealmaker, visionary, and spiritual cement. He joined the company after college, then steadily rose through the ranks. He took over 16 years ago—after the death of his gregarious uncle, J. R. D. Tata—just as India began dismantling decades of socialist-style business controls. Tata has overseen sharp downsizing, risky plunges into auto manufacturing and telecom, and a transformation of the conglomerate's insular and lethargic management culture. Now he wants to prove Tata companies can compete in the rich West as well as in the unpredictable but hugely promising markets of the developing world. What's more, Tata wants to set the group solidly on a path to achieving all this before he retires.

The barrel-chested tycoon hasn't named a successor or said when he plans to step down. He'll turn 70 in December, but he still has a vicelike handshake, and associates are amazed at his command of numbers and technical details of the various Tata companies. That makes his failure to designate a successor all the more disconcerting. Some even question whether his departure might spur the group's breakup. "Who will be the glue?" worries one veteran insider. "Will there even be a central leader?"

Ratan could even be the last Tata to oversee the group. The Tata family tree, on display at a company museum, stretches back 800 years through generations of Parsi priests, an Indian minority descended from Persians. It ends with Ratan—single and childless—and his siblings. Younger brother Jimmy and three half-sisters aren't involved in Tata businesses. His reclusive half-brother, Noel, runs a Tata-owned retail chain, but it's unclear whether he's tycoon timber. Succession "is a problem," Ratan acknowledges. "I am involved in more issues than I think I should be." When he does step down, Ratan Tata will leave a big void. Even though he and other family members own just 3 percent of shares in Tata Sons, the private holding company with controlling stakes in its businesses, Tata himself chairs key units including Tata Motors and Tata Steel. He is intimately involved in all

major deals and pushed for acquisitions such as Corus. The ventures into passenger cars and telecom are his babies. And Tata is instrumental in hatching new businesses, bouncing ideas gleaned from his travels to managers for follow-up.

Ratan Tata serves another vital function: While at ease with lawyers and investment bankers, he remains firmly planted in the developing world. He is a passionate promoter of corporate social responsibility, a mission that dates to the group's founding in the 1870s by Tata's great-grandfather, Jamsetji Tata. The founder was a pioneering industrialist, philanthropist, and fervent nationalist who traveled to the United States with a swami, meeting the tycoons of the day. He opened India's first textile mill, in large part to wean Indians from their industrial dependence on Britain, which until then had milled much of the subcontinent's cotton and then shipped the high-cost cloth back to the colonies. Tata offered worker benefits such as child care and pensions long before most companies in the West, and later one of Jamsetji's sons helped bankroll a young Mahatma Gandhi while he agitated in South Africa for the rights of immigrant Indians.

To this day, the Tata Group remains devoted to good works: Charitable trusts own 66 percent of the shares in parent Tata Sons, and many of its companies fund grassroots antipoverty projects that seem far removed from their core businesses. Ask the chairman to name the group's biggest challenges and he quickly cites two: "Talent, and retaining our value system as we get bigger and more diverse. We have to increase the management bandwidth, and with the same ethical standards."

He also concedes that the group is much less focused than he envisioned back in 1991, when he pledged to pare it from scores of companies to just a dozen or so. Tata did dump marginal businesses—cosmetics, paints, and cement—but entered retail, telecom, biotech, and others. Today, Tata Group comprises nearly 100 companies with 300 subsidiaries in 40 businesses. Slimming the group down "is one area where I have not succeeded in what I set out to do," he admits.

"I'm Not Moving"

His hope is that Tata's unorthodox structure will give individual companies the agility to respond to new opportunities and threats. "The organization is a lot lighter than a Western conglomerate," says Alan Rosling, a Briton who spearheads international expansion for Tata. "There is no central strategy. We don't even have consolidated financial statements." The group is bound together by the small staffs of Tata Sons and another holding company, Tata Industries. These two, chaired by Ratan, provide strategic vision, control the Tata brand, and lend a hand on big deals. And Tata Sons can raise cash to launch new businesses or help fund purchases such as Corus. In 2004 it pulled in $1.3 billion by floating a 10 percent share in Tata Consultancy Services.

Bombay House also exerts influence through the Group Corporate Office, another Ratan invention. The nine senior executives in this unit sit on the boards of Tata companies and act as "stewards," mentoring managers and promoting corporate responsibility values. For example, former Tata Tea and Indian Hotels chief R. K. Krishna Kumar helped incubate Ginger Hotels, a new chain of budget inns offering free Internet and cable TV for about $25 in India's most expensive business hubs—one-tenth of what most business hotels charge. R. Gopalakrishnan, who retired from Unilever's Indian affiliate in 1998, is chairman of a new Tata drug-research company and has advised fertilizer maker Tata Chemicals on an ambitious new strategy to market everything from seeds to low-cost insurance by setting up a network of stores and working with poor farmers to improve crop yields. Bombay House "offers guidance and sets perspective," says Satish Pradhan, who heads the Tata Group's sprawling management training center in Pune. "We hand-hold the businesses in a nonintrusive manner."

The chief steward, though, clearly is Ratan Tata. He negotiates major deals and steeps himself in the details of automaking, telecom, or steel. "He has a tremendous technological brain," says Tata Steel Managing Director B. Muthuraman. He's also not afraid of a fight. During a strike at Tata Motors' Pune plant, militant unionists assaulted Tata managers and occupied a section of the city. "If you put a gun to my head," Tata declared, "you had better take the gun away or pull the trigger, because I'm not moving." Tata signed a deal with a rival union and broke the strike after a confrontation between police and the militants. "While he doesn't look it," says Muthuraman, "he's one of the toughest people I've ever known."

The transformation of Tata Steel illustrates his impact. In the early 1990s, when India started opening to global competition, the 100-year-old company was saddled with antiquated plants, a bloated payroll, and "no market orientation . . . we were a good study in demise," recalls Muthuraman. Over the years, Tata cut the workforce from 78,000 to 38,000 and spent $2.5 billion on modernization. A decade later, Tata Steel had become one of the world's most efficient and profitable producers and began to acquire rivals. "Ratan was the chief architect" of the Corus deal, says Muthuraman. "I was worried about the magnitude and the amount of money. But he instilled confidence." The strategy: Because Tata is one of the few big steelmakers with its own abundant coal and iron ore reserves, it can produce raw steel at low cost in India and then ship it to Corus' first-rate mills in the West to make finished products.

But Tata Steel highlights the challenges of balancing Old World ways with New Economy realities. Jamshedpur, the company's home base in northern India, resembles a time capsule of a more paternalistic industrial age, a leafy city of genteel colonial-era structures and wide boulevards hacked from the jungle in 1908. Tata spends some $40 million a year supplying all civic services and schools, even though it employs just 20,000 of Jamshedpur's 700,000 residents. And in its downsizing program, workers who agreed to early retirement got full pay until age 60 and lifelong health care.

Tata Steel also spends millions annually on education, health, and agricultural development projects in 800 nearby villages. In Sidhma Kudhar, for instance, a dusty outpost of whitewashed stone houses with thatched roofs, the 32 families until two years ago subsisted on a single crop of low-grade rice and the $1 a day they could earn by stripping branches from nearby hills. Thanks to funds from Tata, they now have irrigation systems that allow them to grow rice crops and a variety of vegetables. The hillsides are now covered with thousands of mahogany and teak seedlings for future income, as well as jatropha bushes, whose seeds can be used for biofuel. Most children now attend classes in the refurbished school, and the village has three televisions, powered by Tata solar units that also supply enough juice for electric lights and clocks.

Such generosity will be put to the test now that Tata owns struggling Corus. The deal loads the Indian steelmaker with $7.4 billion in debt, and absorbing Corus' higher-cost operations will weaken margins. One key question is what to do with Corus mills such as the one at Port Talbot in Wales, which employs 3,000 workers. Tata says it will proceed with Corus' plans for the mill. But the union representing most Corus workers wants Tata Steel to invest an additional $600 million in Port Talbot to ensure it will remain competitive so it won't have to cut jobs. A delegation of 20 Corus labor reps visited Jamshedpur in April to meet the mill's new owners, but Tata executives declined to give guarantees. "We were extremely impressed by their workforce and commitment to social responsibility," says labor leader Michael Leahy. "But how will they be able to translate those principles into the British and European context? They couldn't answer that."

A bid for Jaguar and Land Rover might present an even more daunting challenge. The Ford assets would give Tata a luxury brand and a big boost in SUVs, but it would be an uphill climb to restore Jaguar's luxury cachet, which was damaged by sharing basic designs with Ford. Tata executives, who won't confirm their interest in Jaguar and Land Rover, have downplayed auto ambitions in the United States, citing the high cost of entry and their commitments in emerging markets. And an attempt to sell small cars under the Rover name in Britain lasted just two years amid complaints about quality. Tata Motors, which once made only trucks, surprised skeptics with the success of the Indica, an affordable passenger car developed from scratch and rolled out in the 1990s. The Indica is now India's number-two car and is selling well in South Africa, Spain, and Italy. Tata also will soon start exporting cars and trucks through a venture with Fiat (FIA) and is eyeing a similar project in South America. The company had another big hit in 2006 with the Ace, a bare-bones truck for less than $6,000. Tata already is boosting its output from 75,000 minitrucks to 250,000.

Inevitable Stumbles

Ratan's big passion, though, is the "one lakh" car. (One lakh is 100,000 rupees. And that many rupees equals about $2,500.) Since the mid-1990s, he has wanted to develop reliable but supercheap vehicles, a project he believes could ultimately revolutionize the auto industry and make India a major economic power. Tata personally supervised the project and traveled frequently to Tata Motors' development center in Pune to check on progress. Originally he envisioned a fundamentally new kind of vehicle—one made of plastics, for example, that didn't even resemble what we think of today as a car. He concedes that the spartan, oval-shaped model to be launched in early 2008 doesn't meet his lofty aims. It's made of steel. And it looks like, well, a car. To get the price to $2,500, engineers shrunk the size and stripped out frills such as reclining seats and a radio. "There is not a lot of innovation," he says. "We didn't reinvent the business."

Tata has similar ambitions to reinvent solar energy. Tata BP Solar Ltd., a $260 million venture with British energy giant British Petroleum (BP), supplies buildings in Germany with rooftop solar-electric systems. But in developing nations, the company sees a vast market in bringing affordable power to villages that are off the power grid. The company has introduced low-cost, solar-powered water pumps, refrigerators, and $30 lanterns that burn for two hours on a day's charge. And it has fitted 50,000 homes with $300 systems that can power two lights, a hot plate, a fan, and a 14-inch TV. "But this is a drop in the ocean," says Tata BP Solar CEO K. Subramanya. "We ought to be touching millions."

There is little question that the opportunities for Tata in India and abroad are staggering. But can the group succeed on all these fronts simultaneously? The interesting dilemmas will come when the Indian economy slows and some Tata affiliates inevitably stumble. Future managers could look at expensive burdens such as Jamshedpur and rural-development projects as tempting targets for cuts when times get tight. Tata companies could lose interest in low-cost goods for the masses without a passionate promoter as group chairman. And the group could take a tougher look at businesses to spin off.

For the foreseeable future, though, these are nonissues. Though Tata vows that he "won't carry this on endlessly," he says he will stay on at least two years beyond when he chooses a successor. So he seems likely to fulfill the last big item on his agenda: building a network of companies capable of thriving in 21st-century global competition while still adhering to traditional values long after the departure of Ratan Tata.

Go-Go Tata

Since beginning a global push four years ago, India's once-plodding Tata Group has expanded aggressively at home and abroad in a wide range of industries. Some of its major holdings:

	2007 REVENUES	2007 PROFITS
TATA MOTORS		
Building a new car plant and sharply boosting output of its small truck, the Ace. A new venture with Fiat will co-produce 150,000 cars and 250,000 trucks annually. The biggest gamble: a $2,500 people's car to be launched in 2008.	$7.2 BILLION (+36%)	$490 MILLION (+26%)
TATA STEEL		
Bought mills in Singapore, Thailand, and Vietnam, and is now expanding in India. With its $13 billion purchase of Corus, Europe's No. 2 steelmaker, capacity should reach 50 million tons by 2010, behind only Arcelor Mittal.	$6.6 BILLION (+99%)	$923 MILLION (+33%)
TATA CONSULTANCY SERVICES		
Riding the software and tech services outsourcing boom, TCS has grown explosively in the past five years. Now it's developing its own software for transportation, retail, finance, and other industries.	$4.2 BILLION (+41%)	$930 MILLION (+43%)

All figures for fiscal year ended Mar. 31, 2007

FORD/BLOOMBERG NEWS

Questions for Review

1. How do the Tata Group's strategies in its home market differ from its international ventures? Do you think joint ventures are essential for Tata's future success?

2. What have been Ratan Tata's most important strategic initiatives for the company? Should his successor follow in his footsteps or pursue new paths for growth?

3. What risks might Tata face in its global expansion? How might it manage their risks?

Source: Reprinted with special permission from Pete Engardio, "The Last Rajah: India's Ratan Tata Aims to Transform His Once-Stodgy Conglomerate Into a Global Powerhouse. But Can It Thrive After He Steps Down?" with Nandini Lakshman in Mumbai. *BusinessWeek,* August 2, 2007. Copyright © 2007 by the McGraw-Hill Companies, Inc.

The HP-Compaq Merger and Its Global Implications

Introduction

Two years after its multibillion-dollar merger with Compaq Computer, Hewlett-Packard's performance failed to appease Wall Street. Despite reporting profit for the third quarter of 2003, HP's numbers did not meet analysts' expectations. As a result, company shares slid more than 10 percent. HP was quick to blame weak sales, a sluggish overseas economy, and low prices of personal computers for its financial shortfall. An ominous quote from CEO Carly Fiorina summarized this position and future prospects: "We don't see a rapid upturn in information technology spending."[1] The analyst community was quick to criticize. Needham & Co. analyst Charlie Wolf remarked, "It looks like the party is over. HP went through its restructuring and now they have to behave like an adult. It seems like they are so far incapable of doing so."[2] Soundview Technology Group's John B. Jones explained, "Carly Fiorina has lost credibility with Wall Street because she did not always acknowledge the company's weaknesses, preferring to put the brightest spin on results that have sometimes been uneven."[3]

In May 2003, shortly before the one-year anniversary of Hewlett's huge $19 billion merger with Compaq, two separate research firms reported that the combined HP-Compaq had lost the top spot in the worldwide personal computer marketplace to Dell. Although HP tried to play down the news, its impact was clear to industry observers: "Dell has clearly been the biggest beneficiary of this merger," said Forrester analyst Rob Enderle.[4] Also of great concern is the health of the global technology sector. "When the merger happened, people thought the global market for technology couldn't get any worse, but in some ways it has," comments Yankee Group analyst Andrew Efstathiou.[5]

By late 2004, confidence in Fiorina had reached rock bottom, and in February 2005 she was forced to resign. This was not the end of turmoil for HP. In late 2006, a scandal involving board members leaking inside information to journalists and an order by the board chair to spy on and engage in illegal "pretexting" were exposed. By 2007, however, CEO Mark Heard was able to report very positive results, and HP seemed to be back on track. One dimension of the merger that did not receive substantial attention was the challenge of integrating HP's and Compaq's disparate global operations. More than any other of HP's many challenges, this one must be confronted if the new HP is to succeed.

HP History

Hewlett-Packard was founded in 1939 in a garage by Bill Hewlett and David Packard, with $538 of working capital.[6] After a string of failures, their company's first successful product, an audio oscillator better than anything on the market, earned a U.S. patent and an order from Disney Studios for eight units to help produce the animated film *Fantasia.* On November 6, 1957, HP had its first public stock offering. Net revenues were $30 million with 1,778 employees and 373 products. In the 1960s, HP was listed on the New York and Pacific exchanges as "HWP" and had its first appearance on *Fortune* magazine's list of the 500 largest U.S. companies.

In 1967, HP started operations in Boeblingen, Germany, introducing a noninvasive fetal heart monitor that helped babies by detecting fetal distress during labor. In the 1970s, revenues increased to $365 million with over 16,000 employees. In the 1980s, revenues again increased to $6.5 billion with over 85,000 employees. In the late 1980s, the firm introduced the HP-85 and HP LaserJet printers. The latter is the company's most successful single product, now considered a standard for laser printing. In the 1990s, HP opened research facilities in Tokyo, Japan. Net revenues reached $13.2 billion with over 91,000 employees. Today HP is a multinational company with 156,000 employees worldwide. HP is a technology solutions provider to consumers, businesses, and institutions globally. The company's offerings span IT infrastructure, personal computing and access devices, global services, and imaging and printing for consumers, enterprises, and small and medium businesses.[7] HP remains a world leader in servers, printers, printer supplies, and PCs. However, swift competition from Dell, especially in servers and PCs, has upped the scales in the technology marketplace. Exhibit 1 presents a time line of HP's history and development. Tables 1 and 2 present combined HP financials for 2001, 2003, and 2006.

Compaq History

Compaq Computer Corporation was founded in February 1982 by Rod Canion, Jim Harris, and Bill Murto. All three were senior managers at Texas Instruments who left and invested $1,000 each to form their own company. Sketched on a paper place mat in a Houston pie shop, the first product was a portable personal computer able to run all the software being developed then for the IBM PC.[8]

Prior to the merger with HP, Compaq had begun to move away from Internet-related markets to concentrate on software and services in hopes of surviving a sagging PC business.[9] As part of the shift, Compaq unveiled a plan to quit making its own computer chips and instead rely solely on microprocessors made by chipmaker Intel Corp. In mid-2001, Compaq set up a solutions unit to focus on telecommunications, financial services, retail, and government and education with a goal of reaching health care, life sciences, media and entertainment, and manufacturing markets within six to nine months.

In July 2001, Compaq announced that it would cut 1,500 jobs because of sluggish sales. "It is now clear that the economic slowdown is spreading overseas, and we will therefore move more swiftly and go even deeper in our structural cost reduction programs," said Compaq chairman and CEO Michael Capellas in mid-2001.[10] The total job reduction in 2001 amounted to 8,500 positions,

Exhibit 1 **HP Time Line**

1939: Hewlett-Packard Co. is founded.

1957: Goes public and issues shares.

1966: HP Laboratories is established as the company's central research facility. HP manufactures its first computer, used for in-house testing.

1972: Branches into business computing with HP 300 minicomputer, which introduces the era of distributed data processing. Also, HP launches the first handheld scientific calculator, the HP 35.

1982: Introduces the HP 9000, the first desktop mainframe.

1984: Enters the printer business with its own line of ink-jet and LaserJet printers.

1994: Collaborates with Intel to develop a common 64-bit microprocessor architecture.

1999: Hires Carly Fiorina, a former Lucent executive, as CEO.

2001: Announces plan to merge with Compaq.

Table 1 **HP Balance Sheet Before and After Merger**

Hewlett-Packard Company and Subsidiaries Consolidated B/S (in millions)

	2006	2003*	2001
Assets			
Cash and equivalents	16,400	14,118	4,197
Other current assets	10,779	8,454	5,094
Total current assets	48,264	40,996	21,305
PP&E (net)	6,863	6,482	4,397
Long-term investments and other assets	6,649	7,980	6,882
Total assets	81,981	74,708	32,584
Liabilities and Shareholders Equity			
Accounts payable	12,102	9,285	3,791
Notes payable	2,705	1,080	1,722

Table 2 **HP Income Statements, Before and After Merger**

Hewlett-Packard Company and Subsidiaries I/S (in millions, except per share amounts)

	2006	2003*	2001
Net revenue	91,658	73,061	45,226
Cost of revenues	85,098	70,165	43,787
Operating income	6,560	2,896	1,439
Total interest expense/other income	631	–8	–737
(Benefit from) provision for taxes	993	349	78
Net income	6,198	2,593	408
Basic EPS	2.23	0.83	0.21
Diluted EPS	2.18	0.83	0.21

*Begin Combined HP-Compaq data.

Source: HP 2003 and 2006 Annual Reports.

Exhibit 2 Compaq Time Line

1982: Compaq Computer Corp. is founded.

1983: Initial public offering raises $66 million.

1986: Pioneers 386-based desktop systems.

1989: Introduces its first notebook PC, the Compaq LTE, and its first server, the Compaq Systempro.

1991: Co-founder and chairman Rod Canion is ousted by the company board and replaced by Eckhard Pfeiffer.

1995: Acquires two networking product providers, Thomas-Conrad Corp. and NetWorth.

1997: Acquires Tandem Computer Inc., which focuses on high-end nonstop computing; also acquires remote access provider Microcom.

1998: Acquires Digital Equipment Corp.

1999: Pfeiffer quits; Compaq appoints former Oracle executive Michael Capellas as president and CEO.

2001: Compaq announces decision to shift its entire 64-bit series of AlphaServers to Intel's new Itanium processor by 2004.

2001: Announces plans to merge with HP.

or 12 percent of the company's global workforce. According to Capellas, Compaq's revenue shortfall in 2001 was largely due to aggressive pricing and currency issues in Europe. Clearly, Compaq was affected more by conditions overseas than were many of its rivals, because of the breadth of its international operations. Moving forward, the outlook did not look promising. Businesses had little need to upgrade their existing machines for basic word processing, spreadsheets, and Internet access, and consumers were more interested in broadband access than in faster PCs. Exhibit 2 presents a time line of Compaq's history and development.

HP's International Operations

HP's computer products include eight manufacturing divisions in North America, Europe, and Asia, with sales and support in more than 110 countries.[11]

HP's global market strategy allows the company to expand in different countries in two distinct ways. First, HP allows practically anyone with Internet access to log on under the URL and order online. Sixty-five percent of all Internet sites are published exclusively in English. A visitor to HP's Web site, however, can select the country where he or she lives and read the pages in a language other than English. Also available are software updates, technical support through e-mail, and 24/7 customer support for each country that HP serves.

The New HP

The consolidated HP is organized into four business groups:[12]

- *Enterprise Systems Group:* Servers, storage, networking technology, and management software required to build infrastructure solutions.

- *HP Services:* Consulting and services to IT infrastructures.

- *Imaging and Printing Group:* Internet-savvy printers, digital imaging solutions, and digital publishing systems.

- *Personal Systems Group:* Personal computers, notebooks, handheld devices, personal storage, emerging Internet-access devices, and mobility technology.

Since the merger, highly complementary products between HP and Compaq have been phased out. HP believed that the new entity would be capable of delivering a superior product portfolio, one that would have been impossible without the merger. However, the merger was not free from challenges.

Merger critics pointed out that Dell leapfrogged HP in the PC race during 2003. In addition, for the first couple of quarters after consummating the deal, HP saw its earnings suffer. In addition, 17,000 global employees were laid off as a result of the merger. Nevertheless, the news in 2003 looked a little brighter. HP managed to post a 50 percent increase in profits in the fourth quarter of 2002, though sales did not meet expectations. Even more important, the company landed some high-profile contracts for its international consulting and outsourcing services. In March 2003, it snagged a $243 million, five-year deal to provide helpdesk and related services to Telecom Italia. In early April, it announced a tentative agreement to provide some $3 billion worth of global outsourcing services to consumer-goods maker Procter & Gamble over the next decade.

In the international government sector, HP won contracts with the state treasury of Slovakia, the employment agency ANPE in France, the Belgian Federal Portal, the Swedish government, the ministry of the interior in Bulgaria, and the European Parliament.[13] It captured more than 50 percent of the market in Spain for state-of-the-art hospital information systems. In sum, HP says it scored some 200 outsourcing deals within a year of the merger. "Services is one place where the merger has paid off already," according to Forrester analyst Rob Enderle in 2003. "Some of those bigger contracts, they would not have been able to get without having the Compaq consultants on board."[14]

However, in some areas, the positive merger results were less evident. The company's revenue slipped 9 percent from 2002, compared with the company's forecast that revenues would decline only 4.5 percent over the period. Although HP has cut operating expenses, it was still behind in growing its business. Jeff Clarke, HP's executive vice president of global operations, blamed the revenue decline on the overall state of the technology industry, stating that the average for the tech sector was an 18 percent slump in revenue.[15] Because 25 percent of HP's revenues comes from consumer products such as PCs and printers, the firm is quite vulnerable to soft consumer spending worldwide.

According to the analyst community, a lack of worldwide integration hampered attempts to create a unified HP. In some places, the company remained divided evenly between Compaq and HP, even down to being able to find distinct groups of employees where integration was supposed to have occurred. In addition, the lasting presence of the Compaq brand on a line of upgraded Presario computers, though it is not part of the corporate name, indicated that many integration issues still needed to be solved.

Despite initial uncertainty, there were many positives following the merger. In less than a year, HP was able to cut more than $3.1 billion worth of expenses. This figure was well beyond the $2.5 billion that Carly Fiorina predicted before the merger. Predictably, almost half of the savings came from cutting approximately 17,000 jobs between the two companies. Additional savings came from the elimination of duplicate operations. HP vice president of e-business Marius Haas, a former Compaq executive, told *E-Commerce Times* that integration in the online space was ahead of schedule only one year after the merger.[16] Haas, who began working on the integration plan a full year before the deal went through, said his business unit was responsible for two of the four main objectives of the merger's first phase: the launching of the HP.com e-commerce site and the creation of an intranet for unified corporate communications. Behind the scenes, other integration efforts had greatly reduced the number of different Web applications in use. Haas believes top-down management directives emphasizing that the integration plan was "sacred" helped accelerate the pace of change.[17] Exhibit 3 presents a time line of key developments since the HP-Compaq merger.

Exhibit 3   HP-Compaq Time Line

2002:	HP and Compaq merge on May 3. The new HP serves over 1 billion customers in 162 countries.
2004:	HP ranks 11th on the Fortune 500 list.
2005:	HP chairman and CEO, Carly Fiorina, is forced out. Mark Hurd is named CEO and president. HP introduces the Halo Collaboration Studio and establishes a research lab in China.
2006:	Information leak is revealed, and Mark Hurd replaces Patricia Dunn as chairman of the board. HP acquires Mercury Interactive Corp., its largest software acquisition to date.
2007:	In the first quarter, HP surpasses Dell in PC sales.

Source: HP Web site.

HP and Developing Country Communities

In mid-2001, Carly Fiorina's proclamation that HP would be a company committed to global citizenship prompted the creation of an e-inclusion vision for HP. This vision was based on the premise that technology, in conjunction with communities, could help people learn, work, and thrive. The Internet has enabled firms to cross cultural boundaries by offering products and support on a global level. However, in some regions, technology infrastructure is not yet suitable enough to capitalize on the cost benefits of the Internet. Sponsored by HP, "i-communities" use public and private partnerships to boost economic development through technology while building markets, testing products, and honing the global savvy of HP leaders.[18]

Essentially, an "i-community" is a collaborative arrangement between the government and nonprofit or community-based organizations in a specific region to figure how information and communications technology can be used to accelerate sustainable economic development. Although there is a philanthropic component, HP has taken the time to closely link these projects with the company's overall global strategy. Keenly aware that its best growth opportunities depend on the infrastructure development of poorer nations, HP's international growth strategy focuses on the adoption of HP products in these regions. HP believes that it will reap both short- and long-term gains by helping these individual communities become self-sufficient in the digital age. Over the next couple of years, HP plans to aggressively target schools and train more teachers.[19] HP's ultimate goal is to have a sustainable project with limited corporate involvement. By doing so, HP believes that it will forge strong relationships with the communities that become actively involved, and the outcome will be a trusted and more powerful brand image.

In spring 2004, HP's first commercial e-inclusion was ready for deployment.[20] The company had developed 12 products based on the needs of the communities in which it operates. This new project, based on experimentation in the Kuppam i-community in south India and Dikhotole Digital Village in Johannesburg, South Africa, will focus on delivering educational tools to the underprivileged. According to Maureen Conway, vice president of e-inclusion and emerging-market solutions at HP, "The focus of the work in India and in South Africa is to add to our business. So we are not going into this with philanthropic dollars, but with strategic business development dollars."[21]

Through these alliances, HP encourages local governments to begin expanding their technology infrastructure, hoping that the expansion will open new market opportunities for HP. Eventually, HP would like to have culturally relevant, sustainable solutions in each of the regions it serves. "Philanthropy, to be effective, has to be sustainable," explained former CEO Carly Fiorina. "In the end, the most sustainable motivation there is, is enlightened self-interest."[22]

Problems and Challenges of Global Management

Of great concern to HP was how the merger would affect the totality of its international operations. With overall revenues down initially, HP executives were quick to point out that lower sales in the United States were offset by strong growth in HP's Asia-Pacific and European businesses. In the Asia-Pacific region, concerns over the breadth of Compaq's current operations in comparison with those of HP raised doubts about the new entity's ability to seamlessly integrate the two companies' corporate cultures.

Before the merger, HP operated as a single Asia-Pacific entity, and Compaq's operations were split into three separate geographic locations—Australia/New Zealand, ASEAN/India, and China/Japan. Luckily, the corporate headquarters of both companies were located in Singapore, and that has helped expedite some of the consolidation issues. Because both firms owned a solid presence in the Asia-Pacific region, the merger reduced the competitive nature of the market, especially in the PC arena. Lillian Tay, an Asian hardware platform analyst, believed the merger didn't have much "inherent business value." Even if she is right, it has been imperative for the merged companies to effectively communicate their combined offering to the public, in order to capitalize on the solid growth present in the region.[23]

In February 2002, the Gartner Group surveyed 700 IT resellers across 11 countries in the Asia-Pacific region in order to gauge their opinion of the proposed merger (see Table 3). At the time of the survey, almost 60 percent believed the merger would be beneficial or make no difference, but it was clear that not all countries were thrilled

by the idea of a unified HP-Compaq. HP must continue to develop and communicate a clearly defined channel strategy for each country. This, in turn, will help deliver an appropriate product mix in each region HP serves.

In the Philippines, HP has begun an initiative aimed at beefing up its presence all over the country. The company believes that through its "HP Stores" it can offer better direct service support to its customers. These stores are fully owned by HP, unlike most traditional computer hubs. Besides functioning as service centers, the stores serve as a product depot, making promotion and distribution easier in the region. Ultimately, these locations will be run by HP's reseller and distribution partners. By 2004, successful implementation had already occurred in other countries, including Thailand (13 stores), Malaysia (10 stores), and Indonesia (11 stores). Eventually, HP would like to have eight HP stores in the Philippines.[24]

In Europe, the merger resulted in a combined market share of 22 to 23 percent for personal computers but close to 47 percent for power servers and disk storage units in 2002.[25] HP believed the merger would have a substantial impact on the European enterprise computing and consulting markets; it hoped to become a one-stop shop destination for corporate customers. The European Commission approved the merger in early 2002 after competition experts found that it would not pose a detriment to Europe's IT sector. The commission agreed that HP would not be in a suitable position to raise prices, because of the lack of significant barriers to entry in this space.

For HP to continue making inroads in Europe, it must be ready for more swift competition from IBM, Dell, and Fujitsu-Siemens. Although rocky at first, the HP-Compaq merger has brought positive changes to HP's global strategy. Integrating two large organizations is challenging, and in an environment of fast-changing technology, fierce competition, and declining entry barriers, the challenge can be formidable.

Table 3 Assessment of HP-Compaq Merger, Asia-Pacific Reseller Survey, 2002 (in percent)

	Good	Bad	No Difference	No Comment
Asia-Pacific	38.4	21.4	18.3	21.9
Australia	23.6	20.0	34.5	21.9
China	67.3	32.7	0.0	0.0
Hong Kong	37.0	8.7	30.4	23.9
India	43.3	9.0	14.9	32.8
South Korea	36.4	36.4	20.5	6.7
Malaysia	46.8	12.8	10.6	29.8
New Zealand	29.8	31.9	17.0	21.3
Philippines	41.7	27.8	22.2	8.3
Singapore	29.3	17.1	12.2	41.4
Taiwan	28.6	11.4	14.3	45.7
Thailand	40.0	13.3	20.0	26.7

Source: Gartner (March 2002) as cited in "Asian Resellers Welcome HP/Compaq Merger," www.internetnews.com/ent-news/article.php/992921, March 18, 2002.

The New HP's Leadership

After its 2002 merger with Compaq, sales and stocks did not seem to improve much, if at all. Investor disappointment grew, and the blame landed on CEO Carly Fiorina, for engineering an unnecessary and unsuccessful business venture. Fiorina had been with HP since 1999 and was *Fortune's* "Most Powerful Woman in Business" since 1998. However her reputation as CEO of the newly merged HP was under serious revision. In late 2004, Fiorina told analysts that HP had, on three occasions, seriously considered breaking up the company. HP stock was also performing poorly compared to rivals Dell and IBM. Right before HP announced Fiorina's departure, HP stock was trading at 13 times 2005 earnings estimates while IBM and Dell shares were trading at 17 and 26 times forecasts, respectively.[26] When HP stock rose after Fiorina was let go, one analyst commented, "The Street had lost all faith in her and the market's hope is that anyone will be better."[27]

In March 2005, HP announced Mark Hurd as its new CEO and president. From the outset, Hurd was a very different leader for HP. Unlike Fiorina, who was ousted on account of HP's underperformance, Hurd has been known for "underpromising and overdelivering."[28] Hurd has preferred a more behind-the-scenes approach to leading HP and also a less centralized business practice, relying more heavily on individual business managers rather than company consultants. As for breaking up the company, Hurd commented, "I'm not working on spinning out the PC business or on spinning out the printer business. It's not happening. And you can quote me."[29]

HP's other recent leadership issue—information leaks from its board of directors—was soon to follow. Even before Fiorina's departure, it was evident that someone on the board had been leaking information. When HP's long-term strategy was revealed on CNET (an online technology site) in January 2006, Patricia Dunn, HP's chairman of the board, was determined to find the guilty party. She launched a private investigation, using controversial methods to track phone patterns of the board members. Dunn revealed George (Jay) Keyworth at a board meeting in May 2006. Though the board voted to have Keyworth resign, he initially refused, citing invasion of privacy and illegal investigation methods.[30] Finally, in two separate press releases, HP announced that Keyworth would resign after 21 years with the company and that Mark Hurd would replace Dunn as chairman of the board in January 2007. One press release said, "The board does not believe that Dr. Keyworth's contact with CNET in January 2006 was vetted through appropriate channels, but also recognizes that [it] was undertaken in an attempt to further HP's interests.... Dunn expressed regret for the intrusion into his privacy."[31]

HP's New Global Strategy

Despite its initially unimpressive merger with Compaq and its high-profile leadership changes, HP has made some serious revisions to its global business strategy. In June 2005, HP announced Todd Bradley as the new executive vice president of its Personal Systems Group (PSG), which includes the company's notebook and desktop PCs, handhelds, monitors, workstations, and related support services.[32] HP knew that it had to do more than slash prices and lay off workers in order to compete with Dell in the PC market, both at home and abroad. Bradley had previously worked at palmOne, Gateway, and FedEx. At Gateway he ran operations in Europe, Africa, and the Middle East. "Todd Bradley is an outstanding executive with a long track record of growing businesses, executing against plans and exceeding targets," said CEO and President Mark Hurd.[33]

Bradley's first remedy for the newly merged and stagnating company was to focus on PC sales at retail stores rather than online. He argued that HP was directing too many resources to online sales, where it faced the steepest competition from Dell. By focusing on retail, where Dell had no presence, HP was better positioned. In order to convince consumers that retail shopping was the optimal way to purchase a PC, Bradley approved a new ad campaign: "The Computer Is Personal Again." Ads featured celebrities such as hip-hop icon Jay-Z and fashion designer Vera Wang. Bradley's justification of the campaign was that PCs "aren't just a commodity that you run out and buy on the Internet. People are going to want to touch it and feel it and understand how it connects."[34] Although some HP executives argued that the campaign was too loud for the company's conservative image, Bradley reiterated his primary goal: to increase HP's profits.

HP has done a number of things to boost its retail sales. The company increased the percentage of its marketing funds that go toward in-store promotions from 40 percent in 2005 to 55 percent in 2006.[35] The company's online ads now urge customers to visit their local retailers to buy HP products. One retailer with which HP has worked closely is Best Buy. In 2006, Best Buy offered HP the opportunity to design a new notebook PC exclusively for its stores. Aimed at female consumers, it was one of the top-selling notebooks priced over $1,000 during the 2006 holiday season. Bradley also pursued an increase in retail sales abroad by negotiating with retailers and resellers in China and India to increase shelf-space for HP products overseas.[36]

Dell, along with HP's domestic rivals (including Sony, Gateway, and Acer), could no longer ignore the surge in HP's retail sales. In May 2007, Dell decided to enter the retail market by signing a deal to sell its PCs in Wal-Mart stores across the country. Dell even opened its own retail store in Dallas in July 2006, although the company has not announced intentions of opening any others.

Another one of Bradley's strategies for the new HP was to focus on the sales of "attention-getting" products. Some critics argued that, by doing so, the company was ignoring its corporate business. Nevertheless, in November 2005, Bradley brought in Phil McKinney, chief technology officer of HP's wireless business, to identify promising projects in HP labs and get them into retail stores quickly.[37] HP's new TouchSmart PC, introduced in January 2007, was a big success. Its price was three times higher than that of a basic PC and its sales in the first five months on the market exceeded internal estimates. In order to compete with Dell's custom-PC market, HP also took measures to target its new touch-screen technology to specific retailers such as fashion designers.

In addition to new products and marketing strategies, Bradley also focused company resources on cleaning up the merged HP-Compaq supply chain. He closed seven PC manufacturing plants to consolidate operations, as well as instituted weekly progress reports to locate delivery bottlenecks. Bradley established communication networks between employees who order parts and PCs, and updated the software that helps the company forecast its global supply and demand so that it could speed up or slow down manufacturing of certain models. Results of the cleanup included happier customers and a 30 percent rise in on-time deliveries during the 2006 fiscal year.[38]

Bradley's initiatives at HP since 2005 have brought the company success, especially in its ever-present competition with Dell. While Dell's stock dropped by 32 percent between 2005 and 2007, HP's stock doubled. More importantly, in the first quarter of 2007, HP surpassed Dell as the leader of the PC industry. HP's market share rose from 14.9 to 17.6 percent, while Dell's fell from 16.4 to 13.9 percent.[39] As a result, in June 2007, Dell announced its first layoffs since 2001.

Although HP has finally begun to see the success from its merger with Compaq, it must keep in mind the dynamic nature of the PC industry. With frequent changes in distribution tactics and consumer preferences, HP will look to innovate, integrate, and respond to dynamic market changes.

Questions for Review

1. Do you believe the new HP has communicated its combined offering effectively in its international markets? What else needs to be done?

2. What are some of the entry and organizational challenges that the new HP faces?

3. How has HP's move to a direct-selling model helped it battle Dell overseas? What else has Bradley done to help HP surpass Dell? Do you think HP's success will continue?

4. What has HP done to respond to soft consumer spending worldwide? How have the HP Stores and its other retail initiatives been effective in generating new business?

5. How much of an impact do you feel HP's i-communities have had on the company's sales? Do you think this form of international corporate social responsibility will contribute to the bottom line? Explain.

6. In your opinion, what were the three most significant accomplishments Carly Fiorina and her management team were able to achieve by merging HP and Compaq? What else should she and her team have done to make the merger more successful? What has Mark Hurd and his team done differently?

7. How has HP been affected by its leadership changes and challenges? What do these portend for HP's global success?

Exercise

Divide into groups of two. One person will represent HP, and the other person will represent Compaq. Debate and discuss the major issues surrounding the merging of two large corporate entities. Specifically, what are some of the integration challenges in Europe, given the political and economic environment?

Source: This case was prepared by Professor Jonathan Doh and Erik Holt of Villanova University as the basis for class discussion. Courtney Asher provided research assistance. It is not intended to illustrate either effective or ineffective managerial capability or administrative responsibility.

Can the Budget Airline Model Succeed in Asia?
The Story of AirAsia

Synopsis

In September 2001, Anthony Fernandes left his job as vice president and head of Warner Music's Southeast Asian operations, one of the most visible and prominent positions in Asia's music industry. He reportedly cashed in his stock options, took out a mortgage on his house, and lined up investors to take control of a struggling Malaysian airline with two jets and US$37 million in debt. Three days later, terrorists destroyed the World Trade Center.[1]

Within two years, AirAsia demonstrated that the low-fare model epitomized by Southwest and JetBlue in the United States, and by Ryanair and easyJet in Europe, has great potential in the Asian marketplace. In fact, AirAsia's success spawned numerous imitators and competitors. Yet questions remain as to whether the low-fare model can succeed and expand in Asia. Even if healthy market demand continues, it is unclear whether the influx of many new entrants will result in a shakeout such as has occurred in North America and Europe, compromising AirAsia's future in this increasingly competitive market.[2]

The Rise of Low-Fare Airlines in Asia

Following late on the global trend, low-fare airlines (LFAs) are rapidly emerging across Asia. In 2000, Skymark emerged in Japan, followed quickly by Air Do. Carriers modeled on leading American and European budget airlines also emerged in Thailand (PBAir and Air Andaman) and in Cambodia (Siem Reap Air). In late 2001, AirAsia was relaunched in Malaysia as a no-frills operation. In the Philippines, Cebu Pacific Airways, also expressly modeled on Southwest, focused on cost containment by selling online and operating out of secondary airports. India's first budget airline, Air Deccan, was launched in late August 2003.

LFAs have begun to make inroads into a number of Asian markets, but the long-term survival of these carriers depends on their ability to compete with Asia's traditional, full-service airlines. The prevailing sentiment among some of the Asian majors, expressed by the Asia Pacific Airlines Association in early 2003, is that "no-frill fliers are not a threat to Asian airlines."

Market Liberalization in the Asia-Pacific Region

Just a few years ago, most observers questioned whether Asia would ever emerge as a viable market for no-frills budget carriers similar to the United States' Southwest and Europe's Ryanair and easyJet. Recently, however, the environment changed dramatically. According to Peter Harbison of the Centre for Asia Pacific Aviation, a Sydney, Australia, consultancy, "The key ingredient is liberalization."[3]

Air transport liberalization in the Asia-Pacific region began in the 1990s when Australia deregulated its domestic market. Virgin Blue was one of the few carriers that survived this initial battle with incumbents, and it has succeeded in establishing its position in the market. New Zealand was one of the first countries to privatize its national flag carrier and embrace airline liberalization. More recently, India and Japan have pursued deregulation of air transport in order to stimulate competition. Elsewhere in Asia, several countries have publicly embraced liberalization in the form of reciprocal access agreements: Singapore, Malaysia, Taiwan, South Korea, Brunei, and Pakistan all have open-skies air service agreements with the United States. In Taiwan and South Korea, liberalization measures in the late 1980s and early 1990s spawned the birth of carriers that are now major players in their countries' air service sectors, both domestic and international. In Thailand, the domestic market has undergone deregulation, and new private players are looking to expand. Indonesia has witnessed the emergence of a large number of new entrants, following government moves to allow more competition.

In India, Pakistan, Bangladesh, Nepal, the Philippines, and Malaysia, domestic markets underwent varying forms of deregulation in the early-to-mid-1990s, and today, despite some glitches, passengers generally experience much greater choice in domestic travel. The People's Republic of China has also been opening up its air transport market and system. Foreign investors are now permitted to enter joint ventures with, or buy stock of, domestic Chinese airlines. The first outside investment in China was George Soros's US$25 million acquisition of a 25 percent stake in Hainan Airlines in 1995. China Eastern and China Southern Airlines have also issued shares on international capital markets.[4] In Hong Kong, restrictions barring more than one locally based airline from operating on a particular route have been eased. These moves were long overdue in a region that has been resistant to change in the airline sector.

ASEAN leaders have announced plans to fully liberalize air travel by 2008. However, there are doubts as to whether that deadline will be met since countries are allowed to opt out and delay liberalization until 2015. Still, according to the Centre for Asia Pacific Aviation, many, ASEAN states are prepared to open the skies between their capital cities in 2008.[5]

Low-Fare Airlines in Japan

Japan was the first Asian country to experience a real boom in both domestic and international travel in the 1960s. Since then, Japan has retained the status of the largest air travel market among all Asia-Pacific countries as a result of the combination of its population size and a steadily growing disposable income. Japanese air travel growth rates increased rapidly until the late 1980s, when the market became more mature and reached a plateau. The total Japanese travel market (both international and domestic) grew by only 6 percent from 1990 to 2000, which indicates that it was saturated with the product offered by the traditional full-service carriers.[6] Japan undertook comprehensive deregulation and liberalization in a range of sectors throughout the 1990s, partly as a strategy to jump-start its stagnant economy. One sector that was partly liberalized was air transport. Future growth in air transport could come from the introduction of the new business model represented by low-cost, low-fare carriers. Although the total supply of seats provided by the LFAs in the Japanese domestic market is still very small when compared to Japan Airlines (JAL) and All Nippon Airways (ANA), the two large traditional carriers, the potential for growth is significant as long as new entrants can successfully compete both with the full-service majors and with intermodal competition from high-speed rail.

Skymark Airlines, Japan's first real LFA, pursued a business model similar to JetBlue and easyJet's differentiated LFA approach rather than the traditional Southwest or Ryanair no-frills, price leadership model. Skymark was established in 1996 and commenced operations in 1998. By 2007, it was flying between five domestic points in Japan—Haneda (Tokyo), Sapporo, Kobe, Fukuoka and Naha on Okinawa—and operating an international charter service to Seoul. It had a fleet of nine aircraft, six Boeing 767s and three Boeing 737s. The service is basic although all aircraft are equipped with a satellite TV entertainment system. Skymark's onboard product is further differentiated through offering a small number of first-class seats on some routes, e.g., 12 seats out of 309 on its Fukuoka route. Such additional features put Skymark closer to a hybrid LFA model. An advanced entertainment system draws parallels with the JetBlue onboard TV model, while the availability of business-class seats places Skymark in the same category as AirTran and Spirit in the United States.[7]

Another distinction from the classic LFA model is Skymark's weekend charter operations from Tokyo to Seoul. The charter business is only secondary to Skymark, so it uses aircraft downtime to operate Korea charters at night or early in the morning, thereby maximizing total aircraft utilization. The distribution network includes all channels, such as direct reservation lines, Internet, and travel agents. The tickets for Korea charters can be purchased only through travel agents.

Low-Fare Airlines in Malaysia

The emergence of the LFA model in Malaysia has been a result of deregulation and of the Malaysian government's desire to release Malaysia Airlines (MAS) from having to serve its perpetually money-losing domestic routes. Malaysia's geographic position provides natural conditions that encourage air travel, but only 6 percent of the adult population traveled by air in 2001.[8] This low figure indicated an underdeveloped aviation market that could be grown significantly through the introduction of low fares on domestic routes.

The policy of highly regulated domestic fares has been long maintained by the Malaysian government.[9] Such a policy created many headaches for the management of MAS, which "has reportedly been losing up to US$79 million annually" on its domestic routes.[10] The initial success of AirAsia may partly validate the Malaysian government's role in encouraging a LFA into its domestic market. However, the government-controlled MAS is starting to show concern about that same success. In fall 2002, MAS introduced discounted fares on limited seats on domestic routes. After its initial failure, AirAsia was transformed from a money-losing full-service airline into a low-cost, low-fare airline when a new group of investors, Tune Air Sdn Bhd, bought the shares and half the share of liabilities in the original airline in September 2001.[11]

How did Malaysians react to the introduction of this new business model? The anecdotal evidence points out that they were as eager to embrace it as residents of the United States, U.K., and Ireland were when they were first given an opportunity to travel for a fraction of historical fares.[12] Conor McCarthy, AirAsia's operations director and a former director of operations for Ryanair, has specifically noted that the management of AirAsia has been encouraged by the similarities between the consumer market in Malaysia and in Ireland, Britain, and Germany when Ryanair first entered those markets.[13] One traveler offered the following comment on an online discussion site after traveling on AirAsia in March 2003 from Kuala Lumpur to Penang: "It is good to see the no-frills model finally making headway

Table 1 **Fleet Comparisons Among Asia, North America, and Europe in 2006**

Aircraft/ Region	Asia	North America	Europe
Wide-body fleet	70%	22%	23%
Narrow-body fleet	29%	77%	77%

Source: AAPA, ATA, and AEA.

in the Asia-Pacific region. No food, total scrum for the plane at the boarding announcement, crammed seats . . . but for the equivalent of around US$15, you can't complain. . . . Let's hope that the governments around the region put consumer interests ahead of protecting state-owned airlines."[14]

Table 1 provides a comparison of the types of aircraft in use in major world regions, underscoring the relative underdevelopment of the Asian market where narrow-body fleets, typically used for shorter haul intraregional service, are not widely used.

The Rise of AirAsia

The emergence of Malaysian-based AirAsia resembles the story of Ryanair, the Irish low-cost carrier that has dramatically altered the passenger air transport landscape in Europe since the mid-1990s. Both carriers underwent a remarkable transformation from money-losing regional operators into profitable low-cost, low-fare airlines. AirAsia was initially launched in 1996 as a full-service regional airline offering slightly cheaper fares than its main competitor, Malaysia Airlines.[15] This business model failed because AirAsia could neither sufficiently stimulate the market nor attract enough passengers away from Malaysia Airlines to establish its own market niche.

Fernandes's Entrepreneurial Venture

Anthony Fernandes had a history of going his own way. Shipped off to boarding school in Britain to become a doctor like his father, Fernandes rebelled, earning an accounting degree and landing a job with the Virgin Group instead. Eventually he left Virgin for Warner Music, which sent him back to Malaysia in 1992. In 1997, he became vice president for the company's Southeast Asian operations. By 2001, however, he had tired of the politics at what had become AOL Time Warner and decided to start his own airline. This came as no surprise to those who knew him. Unlike many kids who aspired to becoming airline pilots, from an early age Fernandes had wanted to own his own airline.[16]

On a trip to Europe, he met Conor McCarthy, Ryanair's former director of group operations.[17] Fernandes had envisioned a low-cost airline competing on long-haul routes. McCarthy encouraged him to focus closer to home. In late 2001, AirAsia was up for sale. Founded in 1996 as Malaysia's second airline, AirAsia had been beset by problems from the beginning and failed to turn a profit. Fernandes enlisted leading low-cost-airline experts to restructure AirAsia's business model, and he persuaded McCarthy to join the executive team and become one of the investors.[18]

The investors announced an agreement on September 8, 2001, to buy AirAsia for a symbolic one ringgit (26 cents) and to assume 50 percent of net liabilities, or around 40 million ringgit.[19] Paradoxically, the September 11 attacks resulted in lower costs for purchasing and leasing used airplanes. The new AirAsia was relaunched in January 2002 with three B737 aircraft as a low-fare, low-cost domestic airline. Its value proposition was described as "a Ryanair operational strategy, a Southwest people strategy, and an easyJet branding strategy."[20]

Fulfilling his boyhood dream, Tony Fernandes was running an airline company in which he had a personal stake of around 35 percent.

AirAsia's Strategy and Operations

AirAsia focuses on ensuring a very low cost structure as a cornerstone of its business strategy. It has been able to achieve a cost per average-seat-kilometer (ASK) of 2.5 cents, half that of Malaysia Airlines and Ryanair and a third that of easyJet.[21]

One important distinction of AirAsia's revenue model from the traditional LFAs comes from its active involvement in selling holiday packages marketed through its Web site and various tour operator partners. While enabling the carrier to reach more market segments with its product portfolio, this strategy must also add other costs usually associated with selling blocks of seats to the charter operators.[22]

Fernandes acknowledged that the timing of the AirAsia start-up in the aftermath of the tragic events of September 11, 2001, helped ensure the lowest possible cost structure, with both leasing and operating aircraft costs sharply declining year over year. By 2007, AirAsia was handling 51,000 passengers a day with a fleet of 54 planes, offering fares as low as 50 Malaysia ringgit (less than US$15).[23] The revenue formula of AirAsia mostly follows the traditional low-fare approach; only three different fare types are offered.[24] AirAsia's focus on Internet bookings and ticketless travel allows it to emphasize simplicity for the customer while securing low distribution costs. With the average fare 40 to 60 percent lower than the fares of its full-service competitor, AirAsia has been able to achieve strong market stimulation in the domestic Malaysian air market.[25]

For example, when AirAsia started out, the lowest fare it offered for the trip from Kuala Lumpur to Penang started at 39 ringgit. The same trip by bus cost 40 ringgit and increased to about 80 ringgit if traveling by car. The introduction of such supercompetitive fares began to produce the same market growth effect that was achieved by the entry of Ryanair (in its low-fare form) into the U.K.–Ireland air travel market—travelers' switching from sea to air transportation. In the case of Malaysia, consumers are increasingly switching from bus to air travel. Starting with two planes bought from a Malaysian conglomerate in late 2001, the airline had expanded to 54 aircraft by 2007. This was impressive growth, but it also raised concern because other LFAs have faced their most serious challenges when they attempted to expand too fast.[26]

AirAsia has expanded quickly. The airline handled 3.2 million passengers in 2004, up from 2.1 million in 2003 and 1.1 million in 2002. During the 2006 fiscal year, AirAsia carried almost three times that number: 9.3 million passengers. The company quickly repaid its inherited debt and was profitable from the outset. Its profit margins (before interest, depreciation, amortization, and aircraft leasing costs) have been as high as 35 percent, among the highest in the world, according to Michael McGhee, CSFB's airline analyst.

Reaction to AirAsia's Success

The Malaysian government was initially supportive of AirAsia so long as it was taking over previously money-losing domestic routes and serving as a benchmark for the restructuring of Malaysia Airlines. AirAsia's plans to enter the traditionally profitable intraregional markets to Thailand and other neighboring countries met with less enthusiasm from the Malaysian government. The Malaysian regulatory authorities faced the knotty problem of accommodating the growth plans of a new LFA at the cost of reducing the market value of government-owned Malaysia Airlines. In 2006, Malaysia Airlines made a deal to pay AirAsia $236 million as compensation for giving up domestic routes, as well as a $5 million subsidy to service some rural routes.[27]

Nevertheless, given the uncertainty about its ability to fly outside of Malaysia, AirAsia sought creative ways to expand its market coverage by targeting cross-border markets. AirAsia has entered into a number of joint ventures, which now include Thai AirAsia, Indonesia AirAsia, flyasianxprss (FAX), and AirAsia X.[28] In its cross-border joint ventures with Indonesia and Thailand, AirAsia has urged harmonization of national regulations in the areas of pilot hours and maintenance oversight. AirAsia has also won greater favor with the Malaysian government, which endorsed AirAsia X (AirAsia's low-cost, long-haul airline) and built the region's first low-cost terminal at Kuala Lampur International Airport in March 2006.[29]

The Malaysian towns serviced by AirAsia might attract residents of neighboring countries to try AirAsia when they travel to Kuala Lumpur if they can save half the airfare by taking a simple car trip across the border. This possibility elicited a response from some of AirAsia's competitors, most notably Singapore Airlines (SIA), Asia's largest carrier by market capitalization. Singapore announced a low-fare subsidiary, and a former SIA deputy chairman, Lim Chin Beng, registered "Valuair" in June 2003, intending to operate as Singapore's third airline. Thai Airways International also announced its LFA as a joint venture with another company.[30] In 2007 Sri Lanka is expected to launch its first two low-cost airlines, Air South Asia (formerly Holiday Air) and Mihin Lanka. In sum, AirAsia is causing competitive ripples that are likely to grow in scale and scope. (See Table 2.)

Recent Activity and Future Progress

Going International and Incumbent Competition

In January 2004, AirAsia started its first international service, from Kuala Lumpur to the Thai holiday island of Phuket. In February, it began flying from Johor Bahru across the border from Singapore. In 2005, it started flying to Indonesia, a country with 235 million potential passengers. Expansion to India and China is reportedly also under discussion, two markets with a combined population of 2.5 billion.

At the same time, incumbents are striking back. Of the 50 low-cost airlines currently serving East, South, and Southeast Asia, many come from spin-offs of traditional airlines. For example, Thai Airways announced an international carrier, Nok, and Singapore Airlines established its own budget airline, Tiger Airways, with the founders of Ryanair. In 2004, Australia's Qantas said that it was starting a new Singapore-based low-fare airline, subsequently called Jetstar. Qantas invested about 50 million Singapore dollars (US$30 million) for a 49 percent stake in the new airline; Temasek Holdings, the powerful investment arm of the Singapore government, owns 19 percent; and two local businessmen hold the remainder. Although Temasek owns roughly 57 percent of Singapore Airlines, Temasek officials denied that its ownership in the two carriers represented a conflict of interest. "We think this new player will increase the pie," said Rachel Lin, a spokeswoman for Temasek. "Our interest is strictly for financial returns; we see both of them as potentially attractive investments." Moreover, as the government moved to defend its role as a hub for air travel by building an airport terminal designed to accommodate budget airlines, Singapore's founding prime minister and elder statesman, Lee Kuan Yew, warned Singapore Airlines that the government intended to protect Changi Airport's competitiveness, even at the flag carrier's expense.[31]

Some believe the incumbents in Asia—like those in the United States—face inherent disadvantages in their ability to compete on cost and price because they do not have the cost discipline or the culture of budget start-ups. Thai Airways hired an advertising executive to run Nok, apparently

Table 2 **AirAsia Fact Sheet 2007**

Holding company	Tune Air Sdn Bhd
Operating company	AirAsia Sdn Bhd
Business description	Asia's first low-fare, no-frills airline to introduce "ticket-less" traveling, AirAsia will be unveiling more incentives in the future to encourage more air travel among Malaysians.
Head office	AirAsia Berhad Mezzanine Floor, LCC Terminal Jalan KLIA S3, Southern Support Zone Kuala Lumpur International Airport 64000 Sepang Selangor Darul Ehsan Malaysia
Established	December 12, 2001, Tune Air Sdn Bhd officially acquired 99.25 percent equity (51.68 million shares) of AirAsia from DRB-Hicom, making it the official holding company.
Chairman/director	YBhg Dato' Pahamin A. Rajab
Chief executive officer/director	Tony Fernandes
Directors	Encik Aziz Bakar, Conor McCarthy, John Francis Tierney, Tan Sri Dato' (Dr.) Navaratnam, Dato' Paul Leong, Encik Fam Lee, Datuk Alias Bin Ali, and Paul Da Vall.
Employees	2,680
Customer base	16,000,000
Cities served	Alor Star, Kedah Bali, Indonesia Bandung, Indonesia Bangkok, Thailand Bintulu, Sarawak Brunei, Brunei Chiang Mai, Thailand Hanoi, Vietnam Jakarta, Indonesia Johor Bahru, Johor Kota Kinabalu, Sabah Kota Bharu, Kelantan Kuala Terengganu, Terengganu Kuching, Sarawak Labuan, Sabah Langkawi, Kedah Macau (Guangzhou) Manila (Clark), Philippines Medan, Indonesia Miri, Sarawak Padang, Indonesia Palembang, Indonesia Penang Phuket, Thailand Phnom Penh, Cambodia Sandakan, Sabah Sibu, Sarawak Siem Reap, Cambodia Surabaya, Indonesia Solo, Indonesia Tawau, Sabah Wilayah Persekutuan Kuala Lumpur Wilayah Persekutuan Labuan
Fleet	34 Boeing 737-300 aircraft, and 20 Airbus 320s
Available seats	148 seats on Boeings, 180 seats on Airbuses (Daily flights are available to all destinations.)

Source: Company Web site.

with the intention of mimicking Tony Fernandes, but its choice appears to lack Fernandes's marketing and operational ability. Eric Kohn, who was number two at Deutsche BA, initially organized as a German-based low-price offshoot of British Airways, argues that established carriers are not set up to succeed in the low-cost space: "People at big airlines don't have accountability or a focus on costs. It is a lot easier to start an airline from scratch than to take a legacy airline and make a profit."[32]

"We feel pretty vindicated," Fernandes said in a telephone interview from his office at Kuala Lumpur International Airport. "A lot of people laughed at us at first."[33] Fernandes disputes analysts' warning that AirAsia is likely to run into more difficulties as it goes more international. "I don't see why it makes any difference," he said. As for Asia's relative lack of bilateral agreements to allow new carriers to ferry passengers from country to country, Fernandes says competition for tourist revenue is pushing more countries to open up.

AirAsia's Recent Progress

As more and more countries open their skies, AirAsia has been quick to start up cross-border joint ventures. AirAsia prompted increased passenger travel with its 2007–2008 "To Malaysia with Love" campaign. The campaign celebrates 50 years of nationhood for Malaysia, and offers travelers affordable fares "starting from MYR0.50, available for all destinations to/from its Malaysian hubs."[34] Cheaper airfare has also been made possible by the low-cost carrier terminal at Kuala Lampur Airport, which is expected to serve 10 million passengers annually.

In addition to growing its passenger travel, AirAsia has also expanded into cargo transportation. In May 2007 the airline made an agreement with the cargo management company Leisure Cargo. One of AirAsia's regional directors commented on the new partnership, saying, "cargo plays an integral part of our ancillary income and we foresee cargo to be one of the key drivers with significant contribution towards the company's bottom line."[35] This new agreement will serve 18 destinations, made possible by the airline's Airbus 320s carrying both passengers and cargo.

Another landmark development for AirAsia was becoming a publicly traded company. After deferring its decision on a public listing during 2004 to focus on domestic and regional expansion, AirAsia finally went public on November 22 of that year. When it did, its IPO was worth US$226 million.[36] It was one of the largest public offerings in Malaysia, and brought the company RM717.4 (US$188.8 million) for its future expansion.[37]

The Low-Fare Future in Asia

Views on whether low-cost airlines will continue to flourish in Asia vary. Three factors—regulation, population, and demographics—drive this calculus. Although the target consumer base for AirAsia is enormous—500 million

people live within three hours of AirAsia's hubs in Kuala Lumpur and Bangkok, more than Western Europe's entire population—the failure of Asia's regulatory environment to keep pace and the uncertain demand for low-cost services create uncertainty.

Those who sell airplanes, airports, or advice tend to be of the opinion that low-cost carriers will redraw Asia's socioeconomic map, offering affordable international travel to millions and thereby fostering the integration of a region divided by water, politics, and poor infrastructure. Analysts who see a large and growing market predict that low-cost carriers will tap pent-up demand among less affluent Asians who typically travel by bus and hardly expect attentive service. Since the global economy peaked in the second half of 2006, Asian carriers have seen increased success. "We're seeing that people in Asia travel as soon as they have some extra money in their pocket, and the last two to three years has dramatically increased the amount of average disposable income among the populace," said Don Birth, president and CEO of Abacus, a distribution services provider.[38] Although incomes are lower in Asia than in Europe, Timothy Ross, an analyst for UBS, says that the region's lower average incomes should boost rather than constrain demand for cheap fares.

Other analysts argue that there have traditionally been too few bilateral agreements that allow new, low-cost carriers to fly between countries and too few of the satellite airports that the airlines need to keep costs low. In that vein, low-cost airlines such as AirAsia are hoping for increased cross-border travel as they anxiously await the 2008 deadline for the multilateral liberalization agreement between 10 ASEAN countries. "2007 will be an important year for liberalisation of aviation access in Asia. Liberalisation tends to be infectious, and the germs of change are in the air," concluded Mr. Harbison, the executive chairman of the Centre for Asia Pacific Aviation.[39]

The pattern in other regions suggests that once rules start to relax, growth follows. In the United States, budget carriers saw passenger numbers rise nearly 50 percent in the five years following deregulation, compared with 4 percent for traditional airlines. Low-cost carriers now have over a third of the market. In Australia, Virgin Blue took only three years to win a 30 percent market share.[40]

The growth of low-fare carriers has great potential to spill over into the broader tourist and business travel economy: More air passengers generate higher demand for more hotel rooms. This connection has been seen in Australia, where Virgin Blue took nearly one-third of the domestic market from Qantas Airways (which responded in part by setting up Jetstar). This has resulted in a sharp upturn in demand for economy hotels such as Accor. "In many cases, it's entirely new business that wouldn't have happened if it weren't for cheap air tickets," says Peter Hook, general manager for communications at Accor Asia Pacific.[41] In addition, low-fare carriers may offer options for Asian travelers to mix business with pleasure, as many North American and European business travelers do, by extending trips or bringing family members to accompany them. Ultimately, Fernandes pointed out, low-cost airlines in Asia have an advantage in that Asia has almost no interregional highways and no high-speed international rail. "There's a lot of sea in between," he said. "Air travel is the only way to develop interconnectivity in Asia."

But competition is growing. In addition to the many upstart carriers and joint ventures with majors, some significant players from outside the region are also making rumbles. After his success with Virgin Blue, Richard Branson expressed interest in investing in a low-fare operation specifically in Asia. David Bonderman, an airline financier who helped found Ireland's Ryanair, took a stake in Tiger Airways, Singapore Airlines' budget venture. So far, Hong Kong–based Cathay Pacific Airways is one of the few regional heavyweights to say it isn't likely to enter the fray.[42]

With all of the new competitors for low-cost air travel in the region, AirAsia will need to stay ahead. In order to do so, it will be important to focus on profits, not just cost cutting, in order to win investors, thereby increasing capital. According to the Centre for Asia Pacific Aviation, "with financial experts predicting that funding aircraft acquisitions with equity and affordable debt will be much more difficult in the near future, only those airlines that have exhibited an ability to wisely increase capacity will be able to grow their operations."[43]

Questions for Review

1. What opportunities exist in the Asia-Pacific region for the entrance of new low-fare airlines? How might demand for low-fare service differ in the Asia-Pacific region and in North America and Europe?

2. Do governments pose a significant obstacle to the expansion of low-fare airlines in Asia?

3. Compare AirAsia's strategy with the strategies of Southwest and Ryanair. How is it similar to and different from the strategies of those carriers?

4. Did Tony Fernandes weigh the range of political, economic, and operational risks when he took over AirAsia? What risks might he have overlooked?

5. How would you describe Tony Fernandes's entrepreneurial strategy?

6. How should AirAsia respond to the challenges posed by (a) new low-fare carriers entering the Asian marketplace and (b) low-fare strategies pursued by incumbent carriers?

7. How do you think the Asian passenger air transport marketplace will shake out? What lessons can be drawn from the North American and European experience?

Exercise

Anthony Fernandes and his team are preparing to enter a new Asian market through strategic alliance with an indigenous partner company and are presenting the case to investors and workers. Break into three groups representing the key stakeholders: AirAsia management, shareholders, and employees. The AirAsia management group should make the case for the alliance to support expansion, describe the impact of this expansion on future earnings growth, and support this pitch with specific information about opportunities in the new Asian market. The groups representing workers and investors should ask questions and seek clarification about the validity of the expansion plans, the financial and operational implications, and the likely overall market and customer receptivity to the alliance.

Source: Reprinted with permission of Thomas Lawton.

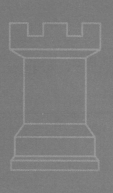

PART FOUR

ORGANIZATIONAL BEHAVIOR AND HUMAN RESOURCE MANAGEMENT

Chapter 12

MOTIVATION ACROSS CULTURES

OBJECTIVES OF THE CHAPTER

Motivation is closely related to the performance of human resources in modern organizations. Although the motivation process may be similar across cultures, there are clear differences in motivation that are culturally based. What motivates employees in the United States may be only moderately effective in Japan, France, or Nigeria. Therefore, although motivation in the workplace is derived from the need to stimulate and encourage employee performance, an international context requires country-by-country, or at least regional, examination of differences in motivation.

This chapter examines motivation as a psychological process and explores how motivation can be used to understand and improve employee performance. It also identifies and describes internationally researched work-motivation theories and discusses their relevance for international human resource management. The specific objectives of this chapter are:

1. **DEFINE** *motivation,* and explain it as a psychological process.

2. **EXAMINE** the hierarchy-of-needs, two-factor, and achievement motivation theories, and assess their value to international human resource management.

3. **DISCUSS** how an understanding of employee satisfaction can be useful in human resource management throughout the world.

4. **EXAMINE** the value of process theories in motivating employees worldwide.

5. **RELATE** the importance of job design, work centrality, and rewards to understanding how to motivate employees in an international context.

The World of *BusinessWeek*

BusinessWeek

India's Talent Gets Loads of TLC

Its Labor Supply Is No Longer Endless. The Smartest Companies Look for Creative Ways to Satisfy Ambitions

A visit to Infosys Technologies' Mysore campus highlights the extraordinary measures Indian companies are resorting to these days to attract and retain top talent. The 334-acre site boasts a multiplex theater shaped like a giant white dome, four huge food courts, 96 hotel-like guest houses, and a stylish activity center with a gym, pool hall, and eight-lane bowling alley. Last year the outsourcing company trained 20,000 recruits in everything from software writing to teamwork. Expansions under way will enable Infosys to train twice as many. "When I heard IBM's presentation at a job fair, they talked a lot about their brand and innovation but not much about training," says Sanjay Joshi, 22, a graduate of MS Ramaiah Institute of Technology in Bangalore. "That's why being at Infosys is the Indian middle-class dream."

Building showpiece campuses the size of many U.S. colleges is just one way big Indian employers are battling to hold on to budding engineers, designers, and finance specialists. Not long ago, India's skilled labor supply seemed limitless. Today, companies face high turnover, escalating salaries, and shortages of qualified workers and managers. Less than a quarter of companies surveyed in 2006 in India by McKinsey & Co. said they were meeting recruiting needs. By 2010, McKinsey predicts, India will face a shortfall of 500,000 staff capable of doing work for multinationals.

The scale of the human-resources challenge is dizzying. Six years ago, for example, Accenture Ltd. had 250 workers in India. By this fall, it expects to reach 35,000. To keep staffers happy, Accenture assigns each a career counselor and offers some 10,000 online courses, from languages to Harvard Business School classes. "People here are driven," says Rahul Varma, Accenture's senior human resources director in India.

Satisfying high career expectations can be tough. Just a few years ago, IBM, Microsoft, Hewlett-Packard, and Coca-Cola could lure all the top Indian grads they needed on the strength of their names. "Now multinationals are losing talent because they made false promises about careers," says Soumen Basu, who heads Manpower's India office. Some companies have grown so fast that it's common to find 25-year-olds managing 23-year-olds who are managing 21-year-olds. But as India's tech services industry matures, such rapid advancement can't be guaranteed.

So companies look for creative ways to satisfy ambitions. Hyderabad-based Satyam Computer Services Ltd. has grown from 9,000 to 42,000 workers in four years while annual sales have more than tripled, to $1.46 billion. Satyam has created 1,773 business units, many with modest sales. Each is headed by its own chief executive, who bears responsibility for boosting productivity, reducing costs, and fostering innovation.

That means a lot to engineers such as Karthikeyan Natarajan, 32, who joined Satyam in 2003. Now he heads a 20-person group designing kitchen appliances and aerospace components. His office is adorned with certificates showing he has completed international programs in skills such as quality control and global leadership. He says he is often approached by big U.S. info tech companies, but thinks he's better off at Satyam. "I could double or triple my salary in no time," Natarajan says. "But I could make that jump and stop learning. I don't want to be in a comfort zone."

Perhaps the cheapest way for companies to cultivate loyalty is to build ties with employees' families. Satyam and others encourage parents to visit the workplace. When a worker gets recognized, Satyam calls or sends letters of thanks to the parents. "If U.S. parents received a phone call saying their kid is doing well, they would be shocked," says Ed Cohen, a Booz Allen Hamilton vet who now runs Satyam's leadership school. "Here, it goes a long way to locking people into a firm." In the escalating war for Indian brainpower, any edge can be important.

By Pete Engardio

Source: **Reprinted with special permission from "India's Talent Gets Loads of TLC,"** *BusinessWeek,* **August 9, 2007. Copyright © 2007 by McGraw-Hill Companies.**

This opening news story illustrates the importance for MNCs to provide motivational incentives to their employees. As turnover rates increase in India, companies must focus on development of managers and other employees and create a climate in which job satisfaction is high to ensure worker retention. In some instances, relationships are maintained even after workers leave, as the company hopes that the positive rapport will lure talent back to previous positions. While financial factors influence Indian workers, continued education is even more highly valued. As MNCs shift from simply finding inexpensive employment bases to discovering new ways to enhance employee satisfaction, important questions begin to surface. Why does a relationship with an employee's family make a difference? What motivates workers in different cultures? What do they consider important with regard to employee satisfaction? In this chapter we discuss the background, research, and implications of motivating international managers and others across cultures. Employees typically seek more than just fair compensation. They want to believe that they are making a difference. Effectively motivating across cultures can create competitive advantages that are difficult for competitors to match.

■ The Nature of Motivation

motivation
A psychological process through which unsatisfied wants or needs lead to drives that are aimed at goals or incentives.

intrinsic
A determinant of motivation by which an individual experiences fulfillment through carrying out an activity and helping others.

extrinsic
A determinant of motivation by which the external environment and result of the activity are of greater importance due to competition and compensation or incentive plans.

Motivation is a psychological process through which unsatisfied wants or needs lead to drives that are aimed at goals or incentives. Figure 12–1 shows this motivation process. The three basic elements in the process are needs, drives, and goal attainment. The determinants of motivation could be **intrinsic,** by which an individual experiences fulfillment through carrying out an activity and helping others, or **extrinsic,** by which the external environment and result of the activity are of greater importance due to competition and compensation or incentive plans.[1] A person with an unsatisfied need will undertake goal-directed behavior to satisfy the need. Motivation is an important topic in international human resource management, because many MNC managers assume they can motivate their overseas personnel with the same approaches that are used in the home country. Is this true, or do major differences require tailor-made, country-by-country motivation programs? As described in earlier chapters (especially Chapter 4), there obviously are some motivational differences caused by culture. The major question is, Are these differences highly significant, or can an overall theory of work motivation apply throughout the world? Considerable research on motivating human resources has looked at motivation in a large number of countries; however, before reviewing these findings, two generally agreed-on starting assumptions about work motivation in the international arena should be discussed.

The Universalist Assumption

The first assumption is that the motivation process is universal, that all people are motivated to pursue goals they value—what the work-motivation theorists call goals with "high valence" or "preference." The process is universal; however, culture influences the specific content and goals that are pursued. For example, one analysis suggests that the key incentive for many U.S. workers is money; for Japanese employees, it is respect and power; and for Latin American workers, it is an array of factors including family considerations, respect, job status, and a good personal life. Similarly, the primary interest of the U.S. worker is him- or herself; for the Japanese, it is group interest; and for the Latin American employee, it is the interest of the employer.[2] Simply put, motivation differs across cultures. Adler sums up the case against universality:

> Unfortunately, American as well as non-American managers have tended to treat American theories as the best or only way to understand motivation. They are neither. American motivation theories, although assumed to be universal, have failed to provide consistently useful explanations outside the United States. Managers must therefore guard against imposing domestic American theories on their multinational business practices.[3]

In the United States, personal and professional achievement is an important desire, and individual success through promotions and increased earnings may be an important goal. In China, group affiliation is an important need, and harmony is an important goal. Therefore, the ways to motivate U.S. employees are quite different from those used with Chinese workers. The motivational process is the same, but the needs and goals are not because of differences between the two cultures. This conclusion was supported in a study by Welsh, Luthans, and Sommer that examined the value of extrinsic rewards, behavioral management, and participative techniques among Russian factory workers. The first two motivational approaches worked well to increase worker performance, but the third did not. The researchers noted that

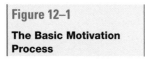

Figure 12–1

The Basic Motivation Process

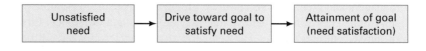

this study provides at least beginning evidence that U.S.-based behavioral theories and techniques may be helpful in meeting the performance challenges facing human resources management in rapidly changing and different cultural environments. We found that two behavioral techniques—administering desirable extrinsic rewards to employees contingent upon improved performance, and providing social reinforcement and feedback for functional behaviors and corrective feedback for dysfunctional behaviors—significantly improved Russian factory workers' performance. By the same token, the study also points out the danger of making universalist assumptions about U.S.-based theories and techniques. In particular, the failure of the participative intervention does not indicate so much that this approach just won't work across cultures, as that historical and cultural values and norms need to be recognized and overcome for such a relatively sophisticated theory and technique to work effectively.[4]

At the same time, it is important to remember that as a growing number of countries begin moving toward free-market economies and as new opportunities for economic rewards emerge, the ways in which individuals in these nations are motivated will change. Commenting on the management of Chinese personnel, for example, Sergeant and Frenkel pointed out that new labor laws now allow both state enterprises and foreign-invested Chinese enterprises to set their own wage and salary levels. However, companies have to be careful about believing that they can simply go into the marketplace, pay high wages, and recruit highly motivated personnel. In particular, the researchers note that:

> Devising reward packages for Chinese employees has been difficult because of the range and complexity of nonwage benefits expected by workers as a legacy of the "iron rice bowl" tradition. However, health and accident insurance, pensions, unemployment and other benefits are increasingly being taken over by the state. There are two cultural impediments to introducing greater differentials in pay among workers of similar status: importance accorded to interpersonal harmony which would be disrupted by variations in earnings; and distrust of performance appraisals because in state enterprises evaluations are based on ideological principles and *guanxi* [connections].[5]

So some of what foreign MNCs would suspect about how to motivate Chinese employees is accurate, but not all. The same is true, for example, about Japanese employees. Many people believe that all Japanese firms guarantee lifetime employment and that this practice is motivational and results in a strong bond between employer and employee. In truth, much of this is a myth. Actually, less than 28 percent (and decreasing) of the workforce has any such guarantee, and in recent years a growing number of Japanese employees have been finding that their firms may do the best they can to ensure jobs for them but will not guarantee jobs if the company begins to face critical times. As in the West, when a Japanese firm has a crisis, people are often let go. This was clearly seen in recent years when the Japanese economy was stalled and the country's joblessness rate hit new highs.[6]

The Assumption of Content and Process

The second starting assumption is that work-motivation theories can be broken down into two general categories: content and process. **Content theories** explain work motivation in terms of *what* arouses, energizes, or initiates employee behavior. **Process theories** of work motivation explain *how* employee behavior is initiated, redirected, and halted.[7] Most research in international human resource management has been content-oriented, because these theories examine motivation in more general terms and are more useful in creating a composite picture of employee motivation in a particular country or region. Process theories are more sophisticated and tend to focus on individual behavior in specific settings. Thus, they have less value to the study of employee motivation in international settings, although there has been some research in this area as well. By far the majority of research studies in the international arena have been content-driven, but this chapter examines research findings from both the content and the process theories.

content theories of motivation
Theories that explain work motivation in terms of what arouses, energizes, or initiates employee behavior.

process theories of motivation
Theories that explain work motivation by how employee behavior is initiated, redirected, and halted.

The next section examines work motivation in an international setting by focusing on the three content theories that have received the greatest amount of attention: the hierarchy-of-needs theory, the two-factor motivation theory, and the achievement motivation theory. Then attention is focused on three process theories: equity theory, goal-setting theory, and expectancy theory. Each offers important insights regarding the motivation process of personnel in international settings.

■ The Hierarchy-of-Needs Theory

The hierarchy-of-needs theory is based primarily on work by Abraham Maslow, a well-known humanistic psychologist now deceased.[8] Maslow's hierarchy of needs has received a great deal of attention in the U.S. management and organizational behavior field and from international management researchers, who have attempted to show its value in understanding employee motivation throughout the world.[9]

The Maslow Theory

Maslow postulated that everyone has five basic needs, which constitute a need hierarchy. In ascending order, beginning with the most basic need, they are physiological, safety, social, esteem, and self-actualization needs. Figure 12–2 illustrates this hierarchy.

Physiological needs are basic physical needs for water, food, clothing, and shelter. Maslow contended that an individual's drive to satisfy these physiological needs is greater than the drive to satisfy any other type of need. In the context of work motivation, these physiological needs often are satisfied through the wages and salaries paid by the organization.

Safety needs are desires for security, stability, and absence of pain. Organizations typically help personnel to satisfy these needs through safety programs and equipment and by providing security through medical insurance, unemployment and retirement plans, and similar benefits.

Social needs are needs to interact and affiliate with others and the need to feel wanted by others. This desire for "belongingness" often is satisfied on the job through social interaction within work groups in which people give and receive friendship. Social needs can be satisfied not only in formally assigned work groups but also in informal groups.

Esteem needs are needs for power and status. Individuals need to feel important and receive recognition from others. Promotions, awards, and feedback from the boss lead to feelings of self-confidence, prestige, and self-importance.

Self-actualization needs are desires to reach one's full potential, to become everything that one is capable of becoming as a human being. In an organization, an individual may achieve self-actualization not through promotion but instead by mastering his or her environment and setting and achieving goals.[10]

physiological needs
Basic physical needs for water, food, clothing, and shelter.

safety needs
Desires for security, stability, and the absence of pain.

social needs
Desires to interact and affiliate with others and to feel wanted by others.

esteem needs
Needs for power and status.

self-actualization needs
Desires to reach one's full potential, to become everything one is capable of becoming as a human being.

Figure 12–2

Maslow's Need Hierarchy

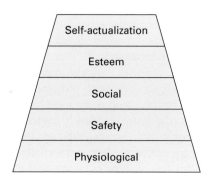

Maslow's theory rests on a number of basic assumptions. One is that lower-level needs must be satisfied before higher-level needs become motivators. A second is that a need that is satisfied no longer serves as a motivator. A third is that there are more ways to satisfy higher-level needs than there are ways to satisfy lower-level needs. Some of these assumptions came from Maslow's original work, some came from others' work, and some were modifications by Maslow himself. These assumptions have driven much of the international research on the theory.

International Findings on Maslow's Theory

Do people throughout the world have needs that are similar to those described in Maslow's need hierarchy? Research generally shows that they do. For example, in a classic study undertaken by Haire, Ghiselli, and Porter, a sample of 3,641 managers from 14 countries was surveyed. This study is quite dated but remains the most comprehensive and relevant one for showing different cultural impacts on employee motivation. Countries in this survey included the United States, Argentina, Belgium, Chile, Denmark, England, France, Germany, India, Italy, Japan, Norway, Spain, and Sweden.[11] With some minor modification, the researchers examined the need satisfaction and need importance of the four highest-level needs in the Maslow hierarchy. Esteem needs were divided into two groups: esteem and autonomy. The former included needs for self-esteem and prestige; the latter, desires for authority and for opportunities for independent thought and action.

The results of the Haire group's study showed that all these needs were important to the respondents across cultures. It should be remembered, however, that the subjects in this huge international study were managers, not rank-and-file employees. Upper-level needs were of particular importance to these managers. The findings for select country clusters (Latin Europe, United States/United Kingdom, and Nordic Europe) show that autonomy and self-actualization were the *most important* needs for the respondents. Interestingly, these same managers reported that those were the needs with which they were *least satisfied,* which led Haire and his associates to conclude:

> It appears obvious, from an organizational point of view, that business firms, no matter what country, will have to be concerned with the satisfaction of these needs for their managers and executives. Both types of needs were regarded as relatively quite important by managers, but, at the present time at least, the degree to which they were fulfilled did not live up to their expectations.[12]

Each country or geographic region appears to have its own need-satisfaction profile. When using this information to motivate managers, MNCs would be wise to consider the individual country's or region's profile and adjust their approach accordingly.

Some researchers have suggested that Maslow's hierarchy is too Western, and a more collectivist, Eastern perspective is necessary. Nevis believes that the Maslow hierarchy reflects a culture that is Western-oriented and focused on the inner needs of individuals.[13] Obviously, not all cultures function in this way: Asian cultures emphasize the needs of society. Nevis suggested that a Chinese hierarchy of needs would have four levels, which from lowest to highest would be (1) belonging (social), (2) physiological, (3) safety, and (4) self-actualization in the service of society, as seen in Figure 12–3. If this is true, MNCs attempting to do business in China must consider this revised hierarchy and determine how they can modify their compensation and job-design programs to accommodate the requisite motivational needs. In any event, Nevis's idea is worth considering, because it forces the multinational firm to address work motivation based on those cultural factors that are unique to it.

Figure 12–3

Collectivist Need Hierarchy

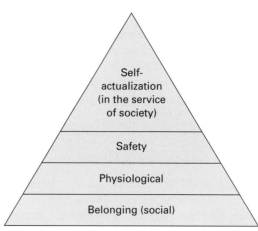

Source: Patrick A. Gambrel and Rebecca Cianci, "Maslow's Hierarchy of Needs: Does It Apply in a Collectivist Culture," *Journal of Applied Management and Entrepreneurship* 8, no. 2 (April 2003), p. 157. Reprinted with permission.

The discussion so far indicates that even though the need-hierarchy concept is culturally specific, it offers a useful way to study and apply work motivation internationally. However, the well-known Dutch researcher Geert Hofstede and others have suggested that need-satisfaction profiles are *not* a very useful way of addressing motivation, because there often are so many different subcultures within any given country that it may be difficult or impossible to determine which culture variables are at work in any particular work setting. The Haire and follow-up studies dealt only with managers. Hofstede found that job categories are a more effective way of examining motivation. He reported a linkage between job types and levels and the need hierarchy. Based on survey results from over 60,000 people in more than 50 countries who were asked to rank a series of 19 work goals (see Tables 12–1 and 12–2), he found that:

- The top four goals ranked by professionals corresponded to "high" Maslow needs.
- The top four goals ranked by clerks corresponded to "middle" Maslow needs.
- The top four goals ranked by unskilled workers corresponded to "low" Maslow needs.
- Managers and technicians showed a mixed picture—having at least one goal in the "high" Maslow category.[14]

The tables from Hofstede's research show that self-actualization and esteem needs rank highest for professionals and managers, and that security, earnings, benefits, and physical working conditions are most important to low-level, unskilled workers. These findings illustrate that job categories and levels may have a dramatic effect on motivation and may well offset cultural considerations. As Hofstede noted, "There are greater differences between job categories than there are between countries when it comes to employee motivation."[15]

In deciding how to motivate human resources in different countries or help them to attain need satisfaction, researchers such as Hofstede recommend that MNCs focus most heavily on giving physical rewards to lower-level personnel and on creating for middle- and upper-level personnel a climate in which there is challenge, autonomy, the ability to use one's skills, and cooperation. Some companies are finding innovative ways to create motivation throughout the organization, from lower-level employees to middle management, by altering HR strategies. "International Management in Action: McDonald's New Latin Flavor" provides an example of how

Rank	Goal	Questionnaire Wording

Table 12–1
Top-Ranking Goals for Professional Technical Personnel from a Large Variety of Countries

Rank	Goal	Questionnaire Wording
1	Training	Have training opportunities (to improve your present skills or learn new skills)
2	Challenge	Have challenging work to do—work from which you can get a personal sense of accomplishment
3	Autonomy	Have considerable freedom to adopt your own approach to the job
4	Up-to-dateness	Keep up-to-date with the technical developments relating to your job
5	Use of skills	Fully use your skills and abilities on the job
6	Advancement	Have an opportunity for advancement to higher-level job
7	Recognition	Get the recognition you deserve when you do a good job
8	Earnings	Have an opportunity for high earnings
9	Cooperation	Work with people who cooperate well with one another
10	Manager	Have a good working relationship with your manager
11	Personal time	Have a job which leaves you sufficient time for your personal or family life
12	Friendly department	Work in a congenial and friendly atmosphere
13	Company contribution	Have a job which allows you to make a real contribution to the success of your company
14	Efficient department	Work in a department which is run efficiently
15	Security	Have the security that you will be able to work for your company as long as you want to
16	Desirable area	Live in an area desirable to you and your family
17	Benefits	Have good fringe benefits
18	Physical conditions	Have good physical working conditions (good ventilation and lighting, adequate work space, etc.)
19	Successful company	Work in a company which is regarded in your country as successful

Source: From Geert H. Hofstede, "The Colors of Collars," *Columbia Journal of World Business,* September 1972, p. 74. Copyright © 1972 Elsevier. Reprinted with permission.

focusing on employees can both increase sales for the company and keep personnel on board.

Overall, there seems to be little doubt that need-hierarchy theory is useful in helping to identify motivational factors for international human resource management. This theory alone is not sufficient, however. Other content theories, such as the two-factor theory, add further understanding and effective practical application for motivating personnel.

Table 12–2
The Four Most Important Goals Ranked by Occupational Group and Related to the Need Hierarchy

Goals Ranked in "Need Hierarchy"	Professionals (Research Laboratories)	Professionals (Branch Offices)	Managers	Technicians (Branch Offices)	Technicians (Manufacturing Plants)	Clerical Workers (Branch Offices)	Unskilled Workers (Manufacturing Plants)
High—Self-Actualization and Esteem Needs							
Challenge	1	2	1	3	3		
Training		1		1			
Autonomy	3	3	2				
Up-to-dateness	2	4		4			
Use of skills	4						
Middle—Social Needs							
Cooperation			3/4			1	
Manager			3/4		4	2	
Friendly department						3	
Efficient department						4	
Low—Security and Physiological Needs							
Security				2	1		2
Earnings					2		3
Benefits							4
Physical conditions							1

Source: From Geert H. Hofstede, "The Colors of Collars," *Columbia Journal of World Business,* September 1972, p. 78. Copyright © 1972 Elseveir. Reprinted with permission.

■ The Two-Factor Theory of Motivation

The two-factor theory was formulated by well-known work-motivation theorist Frederick Herzberg and his colleagues. Like Maslow's theory, Herzberg's has been a focus of attention in international human resource management research over the years. This two-factor theory is closely linked to the need hierarchy.

The Herzberg Theory

The **two-factor theory of motivation** holds that two sets of factors influence job satisfaction: hygiene factors and motivators. The data from which the theory was developed were collected through a critical incident methodology that asked the respondents to answer two basic types of questions: (1) When did you feel particularly good about your job? (2) When did you feel exceptionally bad about your job? Responses to the first question generally related to job content and included factors such as achievement, recognition, responsibility, advancement, and the work itself. Herzberg called these job-content factors **motivators.** Responses to the second question related to job context and included factors such as salary, interpersonal relations, technical supervision, working conditions, and company policies and administration. Herzberg called these job-context variables **hygiene factors.** Table 12–3 lists both groups of factors. A close look at the two lists shows that the motivators are heavily psychological and relate to Maslow's upper-level needs and the hygiene factors are environmental in nature and relate more to Maslow's lower-level needs. Table 12–4 illustrates this linkage.

two-factor theory of motivation
A theory that identifies two sets of factors that influence job satisfaction: hygiene factors and motivators.

motivators
In the two-factor motivation theory, job-content factors such as achievement, recognition, responsibility, advancement, and the work itself.

hygiene factors
In the two-factor motivation theory, job-context variables such as salary, interpersonal relations, technical supervision, working conditions, and company policies and administration.

Table 12–3
Herzberg's Two-Factor Theory

Hygiene Factors	Motivators
Salary	Achievement
Technical supervision	Recognition
Company policies and administration	Responsibility
Interpersonal relations	Advancement
Working conditions	The work itself

Table 12–4
The Relationship Between Maslow's Need Hierarchy and Herzberg's Two-Factor Theory

Maslow's Need Hierarchy	Herzberg's Two-Factor Theory
Self-actualization	Motivators
	Achievement
	Recognition
	Responsibility
Esteem	Advancement
	The work itself
Social	Hygiene factors
	Salary
	Technical supervision
Safety	Company policies and administration
	Interpersonal relations
Physiological	Working conditions

International Management in Action

McDonald's New Latin Flavor

www.hewittassociates.com/intl/na/en-us/
KnowledgeCenter/Magazine/vol9_iss1/
departments-upclose.html

McDonald's was once the leader of "fast and friendly" service, according to customer opinions of Latin American restaurants. Over time, the company saw its margins quickly shrinking, and in some areas of Latin America, competitors were edging ahead. With managerial turnover at 40 percent, and an astounding 90 to 100 percent turnover rate among employees between 16 and 18 years old, it was clear that motivation and morale were too low for a sustainable work environment. Clearly, something had to change.

In the past, organizational operations were carried out on a country-by-country basis, where initiatives were created to mirror the specific region in a way McDonald's calls "freedom within a framework." The stagnant sales and dissatisfied employees indicated that while the company could survive, altering initiatives could lead to further success. The human resources department recognized its crucial role in changing the atmosphere, and soon plans emerged. First, it modified the HR board to include one member from each country. This provided efficient communication, collaboration, and coordination among the Latin American countries. A three-year plan was then set in place, accentuating a continuous-improvement mentality which would keep processes and employee satisfaction in check. However, no plan is effective unless it is put into action.

McDonald's began a point reward system in which each store was allotted a base number of points, depending on sales for that store. A competitive structure was then furthered by allowing lower-level employees to increase points by filling out operational surveys, a tactic used to promote product knowledge and enhance employee skills. These points could then be cashed in for prizes such as backpacks and even an iPod. Furthermore, global recognition programs were instilled that rewarded top-performing employees. For example, McDonald's sent the top 300 performers from around the world to the Turin Winter Olympics, where crew members attended various McDonald's sponsored events and, of course, Olympic games. Managers were also given the opportunity to profit from their actions, and the company stressed creativity throughout the

process. Periodic meetings among regional managers allowed each to share "best practices" that have helped each store, and company strategies were often brought to the table to better inform those in charge. A Latin American Ray Krok Award program was created to bring the top 1 percent of managers in the region to McDonald's headquarters, where participants had a chance to meet with top executives and engage in forums. The company further encouraged success through offering managers the opportunity to take business classes at surrounding universities and work toward a degree. Furthermore, managers engaged in training courses which shifted focus from administrative work to customers and employees under the assumption that given a more hands-on approach, personnel can better understand and achieve organizational and personal satisfaction goals.

McDonald's seems to have made all the right moves. Employees at every level are more motivated, and it shows in the numbers. After implementing the new HR strategy, sales in Latin America initially increased by 13 percent and continued to grow by 11.6 percent the next year. More crew members and managers remained at the stores as well, with turnover reducing to 70 percent and 25 percent, respectively. Furthermore, employee surveys indicated that there was an increase of overall commitment to the company by 9 percent, far surpassing the goal of 3–4 percent projected by the company.

Latin America sent a strong message to McDonald's without having to say a word. Personnel originally did not feel challenged and therefore sought other lucrative endeavors. McDonald's global strategy clearly was not universal, and in order to successfully integrate, local responses were imperative (see Chapter 8). The company's ability to balance its global HR standardization with regional cultures proved to be beneficial to all. Motivating personnel to achieve goals through rewards programs keeps morale high, and could save McDonald's a great deal of money as retention rates rise and the need for new worker training declines. Employees have had a taste of the revised HR programs, and it shows they like the new Latin flavor.

The two-factor theory holds that motivators and hygiene factors relate to employee satisfaction. This relationship is more complex than the traditional view that employees are either satisfied or dissatisfied. According to the two-factor theory, if hygiene factors are not taken care of or are deficient, there will be dissatisfaction (see Figure 12–4). Importantly, however, if hygiene factors are taken care of, there may be no dissatisfaction, but there also may be no satisfaction. Only when motivators are present will there be satisfaction. In short, hygiene factors help prevent dissatisfaction (thus the term *hygiene,* as it is used in the health field), but only motivators lead to satisfaction. Therefore, according to this theory, efforts to motivate human resources

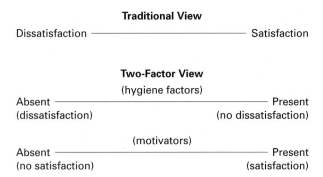

Figure 12–4

Views of Satisfaction/ Dissatisfaction

must provide recognition, a chance to achieve and grow, advancement, and interesting work.

Before examining the two-factor theory in the international arena, it is important to note that Herzberg's theory has been criticized by some organizational-behavior academics. One criticism surrounds the classification of money as a hygiene factor and not as a motivator. There is no universal agreement on this point. Some researchers report that salary is a motivator for some groups, such as blue-collar workers, or those for whom money is important for psychological reasons, such as a score-keeping method for their power and achievement needs.

A second line of criticism is whether Herzberg developed a total theory of motivation. Some argue that his findings actually support a theory of job satisfaction. In other words, if a company gives its people motivators, they will be satisfied; if it denies them motivators, they will not be satisfied; and if the hygiene factors are deficient, they may well be dissatisfied. Much of the international research on the two-factor theory discussed next is directed toward the satisfaction-dissatisfaction concerns rather than complex motivational needs, drives, and goals.

International Findings on Herzberg's Theory

International findings related to the two-factor theory fall into two categories. One consists of replications of Herzberg's research in a particular country. This research asks whether managers in country X give answers similar to those in Herzberg's original studies. In the other category are cross-cultural studies that focus on job satisfaction. This research asks what factors cause job satisfaction and how do these responses differ from country to country. The latter studies are not a direct extension of the two-factor theory, but they do offer insights regarding the importance of job satisfaction in international human resource management.

Two-Factor Replications A number of research efforts have been undertaken to replicate the two-factor theory, and in the main, they support Herzberg's findings. George Hines, for example, surveyed 218 middle managers and 196 salaried employees in New Zealand using ratings of 12 job factors and overall job satisfaction. Based on these findings, he concluded that "the Herzberg model appears to have validity across occupational levels."[16]

Another similar study was conducted among 178 managers in Greece who were Greek nationals. Overall, this study found that Herzberg's two-factor theory of job satisfaction generally held true for these managers. The researchers summarized their findings as follows:

> As far as job dissatisfaction was concerned, no motivator was found to be a source of dissatisfaction. Only categories traditionally designated as hygiene factors were reported to be sources of dissatisfaction for participating Greek managers. . . . Moreover . . . motivators . . . were more important contributors to job satisfaction than to dissatisfaction . . . (66.8% of

the traditional motivator items . . . were related to satisfaction and 31.1% were related to dissatisfaction). Traditional hygiene factors, as a group, were more important contributors to job dissatisfaction than to job satisfaction (64% of the responses were related to dissatisfaction and 36% were related to satisfaction).[17]

Another study tested the Herzberg theory in an Israeli kibbutz (communal work group). Motivators there tended to be sources of satisfaction and hygiene factors sources of dissatisfaction, although interpersonal relations (a hygiene factor) were regarded more as a source of satisfaction than of dissatisfaction. The researcher was careful to explain this finding as a result of the unique nature of a kibbutz: Interpersonal relations of a work and nonwork nature are not clearly defined, thus making difficult the separation of this factor on a motivator-hygiene basis. Commenting on the results, the researcher noted that "the findings of this study support Herzberg's two-factor hypothesis: Satisfactions arise from the nature of the work itself, while dissatisfactions have to do with the conditions surrounding the work."[18]

Similar results on the Herzberg theory have been obtained by research studies in developing countries. For example, one study examined work motivation in Zambia, employing a variety of motivational variables, and found that work motivation was a result of six factors: work nature, growth and advancement, material and physical provisions, relations with others, fairness/unfairness in organizational practices, and personal problems. These variables are presented in Figure 12–5. They illustrate that, in general, the two-factor theory of motivation was supported in this African country.[19] Furthermore, a study performed in Romania indicated that hygiene factors (salary, working conditions, and supervision), though important, were not the driving forces in deciding to accept a senior manager position. The most important aspects of a job to Romanians were how much recognition and appreciation they would receive. This was followed by a desire for salary incentives, though the need for increased knowledge and skills, along with being involved in teams and improving competence and self development, was also significant.[20]

Cross-Cultural Job-Satisfaction Studies   A number of cross-cultural studies related to job satisfaction also have been conducted in recent years. These comparisons show that Herzberg-type motivators tend to be of more importance to job satisfaction than

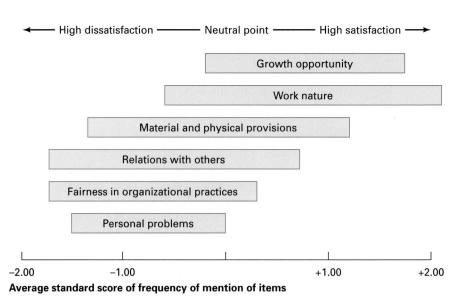

Figure 12–5

Motivation Factors in Zambia

Source: Adapted from Peter D. Machungwa and Neal Schmitt, "Work Motivation in a Developing Country," *Journal of Applied Psychology,* February 1983, p. 41. Reprinted with permission of the American Psychological Association and the author.

Figure 12–6 | **Selected Countries Hygiene and Motivation**

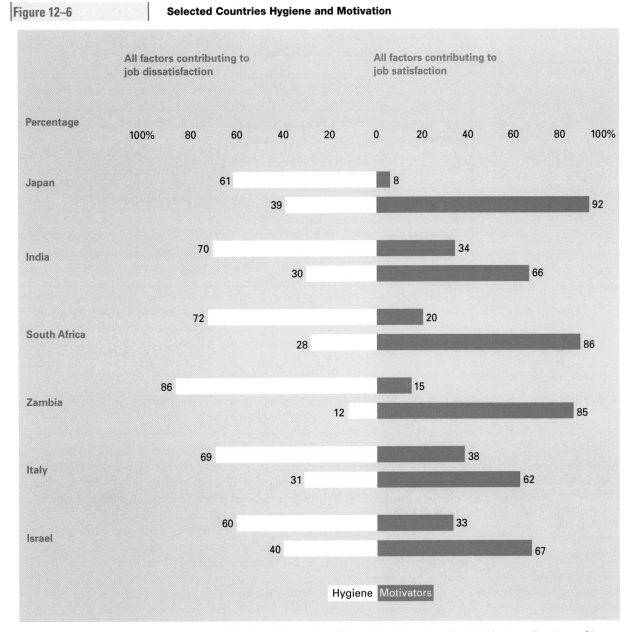

are hygiene factors. A comparison from selected Herzberg's studies is provided in Figure 12–6. This shows that hygiene is strongly associated with factors that relate to job dissatisfaction (or avoidance of), and motivation correlates with factors that drive job satisfaction. This is also evident in research, as seen in one study that administered the Job Orientation Inventory (JOI) to MBA candidates from four countries.[21] As seen in Table 12–5, the relative ranking placed hygiene factors at the bottom of the list and motivators at the top. What also is significant is that although Singapore students do not fit into the same cultural cluster as the other three groups in the study, their responses were similar. These findings provide evidence that job-satisfaction-related factors may not always be culturally bounded.[22]

Another, more comprehensive study of managerial job attitudes investigated the types of job outcomes that are desired by managers in different cultures. Data were

Table 12–5
The Results of Administering the JOI to Four Cross-Cultural Groups

	Relative Rankings			
	United States (*n* = 49)	Australia (*n* = 58)	Canada (*n* = 25)	Singapore (*n* = 33)
Achievement	2	2	2	2
Responsibility	3	3	3	3
Growth	1	1	1	1
Recognition	10	10	8	9
Job status	7	7	7	7
Relationships	5	5	10	6
Pay	8	8	6	8
Security	9	9	9	10
Family	6	6	5	5
Hobby	4	4	4	4

Source: From G. E. Popp, H. J. Davis, and T. T. Herbert, "An International Study of Intrinsic Motivation Composition," *Management International Review,* Vol. 26, No. 3 1986, p. 31. Reprinted with permission.

job-context factors
In work motivation, those factors controlled by the organization, such as conditions, hours, earnings, security, benefits, and promotions.

job-content factors
In work motivation, those factors internally controlled, such as responsibility, achievement, and the work itself.

gathered from lower- and middle-management personnel who were attending management development courses in Canada, the United Kingdom, France, and Japan.[23] The researchers sought to identify the importance of 15 job-related outcomes and how satisfied the respondents were with each other. The results indicated that job content is more important than job context. Organizationally controlled factors (**job-context factors,** such as conditions, hours, earnings, security, benefits, and promotions) for the most part did not receive as high a ranking as internally mediated factors (**job-content factors,** such as responsibility, achievement, and the work itself).

The data also show that managers from the four countries differ significantly regarding both the perceived importance of job outcomes and the level of satisfaction experienced on the job with respect to these outcomes. These differences are useful in shedding light on what motivates managers in these countries and, in the case of MNCs, in developing country-specific human resource management approaches. The most striking contrasts were between the French and the British. Commenting on the applicability of this research to the formulation of motivational strategies for effective human resource management, the researchers noted the following:

> The results suggest . . . that efforts to improve managerial performance in the UK should focus on job content rather than on job context. Changes in the nature of the work itself are likely to be more valued than changes in organizational or interpersonal factors. Job enrichment programs which help individuals design their own goals and tasks, and which downplay formal rules and structure, are more likely to improve performance in an intrinsically oriented society such as Britain, where satisfaction tends to be derived from the job itself, than in France, where job context factors such as security and fringe benefits are more highly valued. The results suggest that French managers may be more effectively motivated by changing job situation factors, as long as such changes are explicitly linked to performance.[24]

In summary, Herzberg's two-factor theory appears to reinforce Maslow's need hierarchy through its research support in the international arena. As with the application of Maslow's theory, however, MNCs would be wise to apply motivation-hygiene theory on a country-by-country or a regional basis. Although there are exceptions, such as France, there seems to be little doubt that job-content factors are more important than job-context factors in motivating not only managers but also lower-level employees around the world, as Hofstede pointed out.

■ Achievement Motivation Theory

In addition to the need-hierarchy and two-factor theories of work motivation, achievement motivation theory has been given a relatively great amount of attention in the international arena. Achievement motivation theory has been more applied to the actual practice of management than the others, and it has been the focus of some interesting international research.

The Background of Achievement Motivation Theory

Achievement motivation theory holds that individuals can have a need to get ahead, to attain success, and to reach objectives. Note that like the upper-level needs in Maslow's hierarchy or like Herzberg's motivators, the need for achievement is learned. Therefore, in the United States, where entrepreneurial effort is encouraged and individual success promoted, the probability is higher that there would be a greater percentage of people with high needs for achievement than, for example, in China, Russia, or Eastern European countries,[25] where cultural values have not traditionally supported individual, entrepreneurial efforts.

> **achievement motivation theory**
> A theory which holds that individuals can have a need to get ahead, to attain success, and to reach objectives.

Researchers such as the late Harvard psychologist David McClelland have identified a characteristic profile of high achievers.[26] First, these people like situations in which they take personal responsibility for finding solutions to problems. They want to win because of their own efforts, not because of luck or chance. Second, they tend to be moderate risk takers rather than high or low risk takers. If a decision-making situation appears to be too risky, they will learn as much as they can about the environment and try to reduce the probability of failure. In this way, they turn a high-risk situation into a moderate-risk situation. If the situation is too low risk, however, there usually is an accompanying low reward, and they tend to avoid situations with insufficient incentive.

Third, high achievers want concrete feedback on their performance. They like to know how well they are doing, and they use this information to modify their actions. High achievers tend to gravitate into vocations such as sales, which provide them with immediate, objective feedback about how they are doing. Finally, and this has considerable implications for human resource management, high achievers often tend to be loners, and not team players. They do not form warm, close relationships, and they have little empathy for others' problems. This last characteristic may distract from their effectiveness as managers of people.

Researchers have discovered a number of ways to develop high-achievement needs in people. These involve teaching the individual to do the following: (1) obtain feedback on performance and use this information to channel efforts into areas where success likely will be attained; (2) emulate people who have been successful achievers; (3) develop an internal desire for success and challenges; and (4) daydream in positive terms by picturing oneself as successful in the pursuit of important objectives.[27] Simply put, the need for achievement can be taught and learned.

Before examining international research on achievement motivation theory, it is important to realize that the theory has been cited as having a number of shortcomings. One is that it relies almost solely on the projective personality Thematic Apperception Test (TAT) to measure individual achievement, and a number of recent studies have questioned the validity and reliability of this approach.[28] Another concern is that achievement motivation is grounded in individual effort, but in many countries group harmony and cooperation are critically important to success. Simply put, the original theory does not satisfactorily explain the need for achievement in cultures in which individual accomplishment is neither valued nor rewarded.[29]

International Findings on Achievement Motivation Theory

A number of international researchers have investigated the role and importance of high-achievement needs in human resource management.[30]

Early research among Polish industrialists found that many of them were high achievers.[31] The average high-achievement score was 6.58, quite close to U.S. managers' average score of 6.74. This led some to conclude there is evidence that managers in countries as diverse as the United States and those of the former Soviet bloc in Central Europe have high needs for achievement.[32] In later studies, however, researchers did *not* find a high need for achievement in Central European countries. One study, for example, surveyed Czech industrial managers and found that the average high-achievement score was 3.32, considerably lower than that of U.S. managers.[33] Because the need for achievement is learned, differences in these samples can be attributed to cultural differences. By the same token, given the dramatic, revolutionary changes that occurred in Central and Eastern Europe with the end of communism and of centrally planned economies, one could argue that the achievement needs of postcommunist Europeans, now able to be freely expressed, may well be high today. The important point is that because achievement is a learned need and thus largely determined by the prevailing culture, it is not universal and may change over time.

The ideal profile for high-achieving societies can be described in terms of the cultural dimensions examined in Chapter 4. In particular, two cultural dimensions identified by Hofstede in Chapter 4—uncertainty avoidance and masculinity—best describe high-achieving societies (see Figure 12–7). These societies tend to have weak uncertainty avoidance. People in high-achieving societies are not afraid to take at least moderate risks or to live with ambiguity. These societies also tend to have moderate-to-high masculinity, as measured by the high importance they assign to the acquisition of money and other physical assets and the low value they give to caring for others and for the quality of work life. This combination (see the upper right quadrant of Figure 12–7) is found almost exclusively in Anglo countries or in nations that have been closely associated with them

Figure 12–7

Selected Countries on the Uncertainty-Avoidance and Masculinity Scales

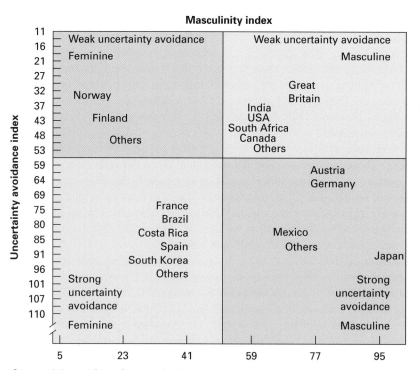

Source: Adapted from Geert Hofstede, "The Cultural Relativity of Organizational Practices and Theories," *Journal of International Business Studies,* Fall 1983, p. 86.

through colonization or treaty, such as India, Singapore, and Hong Kong (countries associated with Great Britain) and the Philippines (associated with the United States).

Countries that fall into one of the other three quadrants of Figure 12–7 will not be very supportive of the high need for achievement. MNCs in these geographic regions, therefore, would be wise to formulate a human resource management strategy for either changing the situation or adjusting to it. If they decide to change the situation, they must design jobs to fit the needs of their people or put people through an achievement motivation training program to create high-achieving managers and entrepreneurs.

A number of years ago, McClelland was able to demonstrate the success of such achievement motivation training programs with underdeveloped countries. For example, in India, he conducted such a program with considerable success. In following up these Indian trainees over the subsequent 6 to 10 months, he found that two-thirds were unusually active in achievement-oriented activities. They had started new businesses, investigated new product lines, increased profits, or expanded their present organizations. For example, the owner of a small radio store opened a paint and varnish factory after completing the program. McClelland concluded that this training appeared to have doubled the natural rate of unusual achievement-oriented activity in the group studied.[34]

If international human resource managers cannot change the situation or train the participants, then they must adjust to the specific conditions of the country and formulate a motivation strategy that is based on those conditions. In many cases, this requires consideration of a need-hierarchy approach blended with an achievement approach. Hofstede offers such advice in dealing with the countries in the various quadrants of Figure 12-7:

> The countries on the feminine side . . . distinguish themselves by focusing on quality of life rather than on performance and on relationships between people rather than on money and things. This means *social motivation:* quality of life plus security and quality of life plus risk.[35]

In the case of countries that are attempting to introduce changes that incorporate values from one of the other quadrants in Figure 12-7, the challenge can be even greater.

In summary, achievement motivation theory provides additional insights into the motivation of personnel around the world. Like the need-hierarchy and two-factor theories, however, achievement motivation theory must be modified to meet the specific needs of the local culture. The culture of many countries does not support high achievement. However, the cultures of Anglo countries and those that reward entrepreneurial effort do support achievement motivation, and their human resources should probably be managed accordingly.

■ Select Process Theories

While content theories are useful in explaining motivation for managing international personnel, process theories can also lead to better understanding. As noted earlier, the process theories explain how employee behavior is initiated, redirected, and halted; and some of these theories have been used to examine motivation in the international arena. Among the most widely recognized are equity theory, goal-setting theory, and expectancy theory. The following briefly examines each of these three and their relevance to international human resource management.

Equity Theory

Equity theory focuses on how motivation is affected by people's perception of how fairly they are being treated. The theory holds that if people perceive that they are being treated equitably, this perception will have a positive effect on their job performance and satisfaction, and there is no need to strive for equity. Conversely, if they believe they are not being treated fairly, especially in relation to relevant others, they will be dissatisfied, and this belief will have a negative effect on their job performance and they will strive to restore equity.

equity theory
A process theory that focuses on how motivation is affected by people's perception of how fairly they are being treated.

There is considerable research to support the fundamental equity principle in Western work groups.[36] However, when the theory is examined on an international basis, the results are mixed. Yuchtman, for example, studied equity perceptions among managers and nonmanagers in an Israeli kibbutz production unit.[37] In this setting everyone was treated the same, but the managers reported lower satisfaction levels than the workers. The managers perceived their contributions to be greater than those of any other group in the kibbutz. As a result of this perception, they felt that they were undercompensated for their value and effort. These findings support the basic concepts of equity theory.

One study, which assumed that Western thought was synonymous with individualism and Eastern thought with collectivism, indicated that there are both similarities and differences between how cultures view the equity model. The model consists of employee inputs, subsequent outcomes, areas employees choose to compare the self to, and the motivation to change any perceived inequity that may exist between the self and the point of comparison (such as co-workers or employees in similar industries and positions).[38] A summary comparison is provided in Table 12–6.

On the other hand, a number of studies cast doubt on the relevance of equity theory in explaining motivation in an international setting. Perhaps the biggest shortcoming is that the theory appears to be culture-bound. For example, equity theory postulates

Table 12–6
Individualistic and Collectivist Approaches to Equity Model

	Western (Individualistic) Cultures	Eastern (Collectivist) Cultures
Inputs	Effort	Loyalty
	Intelligence	Support
	Education	Respect
	Experience	Organizational tenure
	Skill	Organizational status
	Social status	Group member
Outcomes	Pay	Harmony
	Autonomy	Social status
	Seniority status	Acceptance
	Fringe benefits	Solidarity
	Job status	Cohesion
	Status symbol	
Comparisons	*Situation*	*Organizational Group*
	Physical proximity	Similar industry
	Job facet	Similar product/service
	Personal	*In-Group*
	Gender	Status
	Age	Job
	Position	Tenure
	Professionalism	Age
		Position
Motivation to Reduce Inequity	Change personal inputs	*Organizational Group*
	Provoke alternate outcomes	Change points of comparison
	Psychologically distort inputs and outcomes	Psychologically distort inputs and outcomes
	Leave the field	*In-Group*
	Change points of comparison	Alter inputs of self
		Psychologically distort inputs and outcomes

Source: Adapted from Paul A. Fadil et al., "Equity or Equality?..." *Cross-Cultural Management* 12, no. 4 (2005), p. 23.

that when people are not treated fairly, they will take steps to reduce the inequity by, for example, doing less work, filing a grievance, or getting a transfer to another department. In Asia and the Middle East, however, employees often readily accept inequitable treatment in order to preserve group harmony. Additionally, in countries such as Japan and Korea, men and women typically receive different pay for doing the same work, yet because of years of cultural conditioning women may not feel they are being treated inequitably.[39] Some researchers have explained this finding by suggesting that these women compare themselves only to other women and in this comparison feel they are being treated equitably. While this may be true, the results still point to the fact that equity theory is not universally applicable in explaining motivation and job satisfaction. In short, although the theory may help explain why "equal pay for equal work" is a guiding motivation principle in countries such as the United States and Canada, it may have limited value in other areas of the world, including Asia and Latin America, where compensation differences based on gender, at least traditionally, have been culturally acceptable.

Goal-Setting Theory

Goal-setting theory focuses on how individuals go about setting goals and responding to them and the overall impact of this process on motivation. Specific areas that are given attention in goal-setting theory include the level of participation in setting goals, goal difficulty, goal specificity, and the importance of objective, timely feedback to progress toward goals. Unlike many theories of motivation, goal setting has been continually refined and developed.[40] There is considerable research evidence showing that employees perform extremely well when they are assigned specific and challenging goals that they have had a hand in setting.[41] But most of these studies have been conducted in the United States, while few of them have been carried out in other cultures.[42] One study that did examine goal setting in an international setting looked at Norwegian employee participation in goal setting.[43] The researchers found that the Norwegian employees shunned participation and preferred to have their union representatives work with management in determining work goals. This led the researchers to conclude that individual participation in goal setting was seen as inconsistent with the prevailing philosophy of participation through union representatives. Unlike the United States, where employee participation in setting goals is motivational, it had no value for the Norwegian employees in this study.

Similar results to the Norwegian study have been reported by Earley, who found that workers in the U.K. responded more favorably to a goal-setting program sponsored by the union stewards than to one sponsored by management. This led Earley to conclude that the transferability across cultural settings of management concepts such as participation in goal setting may well be affected by the prevailing work norms.[44] In order to further test this proposition, Erez and Earley studied American and Israeli subjects and found that participative strategies led to higher levels of goal acceptance and performance in both cultures than did strategies in which objectives were assigned by higher-level management.[45] In other words, the value of goal-setting theory may well be determined by culture. In the case, for example, of Asian and Latin work groups, where collectivism is very high, the theory may have limited value for MNC managers in selected countries.

Expectancy Theory

Expectancy theory postulates that motivation is largely influenced by a multiplicative combination of a person's belief that (*a*) effort will lead to performance, (*b*) performance will lead to specific outcomes, and (*c*) the outcomes will be of value to the individual.[46] In addition, the theory predicts that high performance followed by high rewards will lead to high satisfaction.[47] Does this theory have universal application? Eden used it in studying workers in an Israeli kibbutz and found some support;[48] and Matsui and colleagues reported that the theory could be applied successfully in Japan.[49] On the other hand, it

goal-setting theory
A process theory that focuses on how individuals go about setting goals and responding to them and the overall impact of this process on motivation.

expectancy theory
A process theory that postulates that motivation is influenced by a person's belief that (*a*) effort will lead to performance, (*b*) performance will lead to specific outcomes, and (*c*) the outcomes will be of value to the individual.

is important to remember that expectancy theory is based on employees having considerable control over their environment, a condition that does not exist in many cultures (e.g., Asia). In particular, in societies where people believe that much of what happens is beyond their control, this theory may have less value. It would seem that expectancy theory is best able to explain worker motivation in cultures where there is a strong internal locus of control (e.g., in the United States). In short, the theory seems culture-bound, and international managers must be aware of this limitation in their efforts to apply this theory to motivate human resources.

■ Motivation Applied: Job Design, Work Centrality, and Rewards

Content and process theories provide important insights into and understanding of ways to motivate human resources in international management. So, too, do applied concepts such as job design, work centrality, and rewards.

Job Design

job design
A job's content, the methods that are used on the job, and the way the job relates to other jobs in the organization.

Job design consists of a job's content, the methods that are used on the job, and the way in which the job relates to other jobs in the organization. Job design typically is a function of the work to be done and the way in which management wants it to be carried out. These factors help explain why the same type of work may have a different impact on the motivation of human resources in various parts of the world and result in differing qualities of work life.

Quality of Work Life: The Impact of Culture Quality of work life (QWL) is not the same throughout the world. For example, assembly-line employees in Japan work at a rapid pace for hours and have very little control over their work activities. In Sweden, assembly-line employees work at a more relaxed pace and have a great deal of control over their work activities. U.S. assembly-line employees are somewhere in between; they typically work at a pace that is less demanding than that in Japan but more structured than that in Sweden.

What accounts for these differences? One answer is found in the culture of the country. QWL is directly related to culture. Table 12–7 compares the United States, Japan, and Sweden along the four cultural dimensions described in Chapter 4. A brief look shows that each country has a different cultural profile, helping explain why similar jobs may be designed quite differently from country to country. Assembly-line work provides a good basis for comparison.

Table 12–7
Cultural Dimensions in Japan, Sweden, and the United States

Cultural Dimension	High/Strong X ←	Moderate — X —	Low/Weak → X
Uncertainty avoidance	J	USA	S
Individualism	USA S		J
Power distance	J USA		S
Masculinity	J	USA	S

Source: From Geert Hofstede, "The Cultural Relativity of the Quality of Life Concept," *Academy of Management Review,* July 1984, pp. 391, 393. Reproduced with permission of Academy of Management via Copyright Clearance Center.

In Japan, there is strong uncertainty avoidance. The Japanese like to structure tasks so there is no doubt regarding what is to be done and how it is to be done. Individualism is low, so there is strong emphasis on security, and individual risk taking is discouraged. The power-distance index is high, so Japanese workers are accustomed to taking orders from those above them. The masculinity index for the Japanese is high, which shows that they put a great deal of importance on money and other material symbols of success. In designing jobs, the Japanese structure tasks so that the work is performed within these cultural constraints. Japanese managers work their employees extremely hard. Although Japanese workers contribute many ideas through the extensive use of quality circles, Japanese managers give them very little say in what actually goes on in the organization (in contrast to the erroneous picture often portrayed by the media, which presents Japanese firms as highly democratic and managed from the bottom up[50]) and depend heavily on monetary rewards, as reflected by the fact that the Japanese rate money as an important motivator more than the workers in any other industrialized country do.

In Sweden, uncertainty avoidance is low, so job descriptions, policy manuals, and similar work-related materials are more open-ended or general in contrast with the detailed procedural materials developed by the Japanese. In addition, Swedish workers are encouraged to make decisions and to take risks. Swedes exhibit a moderate-to-high degree of individualism, which is reflected in their emphasis on individual decision making (in contrast to the collective or group decision making of the Japanese). They have a weak power-distance index, which means that Swedish managers use participative approaches in leading their people. Swedes score low on masculinity, which means that interpersonal relations and the ability to interact with other workers and discuss job-related matters are important. These cultural dimensions result in job designs that are markedly different from those in Japan.

Cultural dimensions in the United States are closer to those of Sweden than to those of Japan. In addition, except for individualism, the U.S. profile is between that of Sweden and Japan (again see Table 12–7). This means that job design in U.S. assembly plants tends to be more flexible or unstructured than that of the Japanese but more rigid than that of the Swedes.

This same pattern holds for many other jobs in these three countries. All job designs tend to reflect the cultural values of the country. The challenge for MNCs is to adjust job design to meet the needs of the host country's culture. For example, when Japanese firms enter the United States, they often are surprised to learn that people resent close control. In fact, there is evidence that the most profitable Japanese-owned companies in the United States are those that delegate a high degree of authority to their U.S. managers.[51] Similarly, Japanese firms operating in Sweden find that quality of work life is a central concern for the personnel and that a less structured, highly participative management style is needed for success. Some of the best examples of efforts to integrate job designs with culture and personality are provided by sociotechnical job designs.

Sociotechnical Job Designs

Sociotechnical designs are job designs that blend personnel and technology. The objective of these designs is to integrate new technology into the workplace so that workers accept and use it to increase overall productivity. Because new technology often requires people to learn new methods and, in some cases, work faster, employee resistance is common. Effective sociotechnical design can overcome these problems. There are a number of good examples, and perhaps the most famous is that of Volvo, the Swedish automaker.

Sociotechnical changes reflective of the cultural values of the workers were introduced at Volvo's Kalmar plant. Autonomous work groups were formed and given the authority to elect their own supervisors as well as to schedule, assign, and inspect their own work. Each group was allowed to work at its own pace, although there was an overall output objective for the week, and each group was expected to attain this goal.[52]

sociotechnical designs
Job designs that blend personnel and technology.

The outcome was very positive and resulted in Volvo building another plant that employed even more sophisticated sociotechnical job-design concepts. Volvo's plant layout, however, did not prevent the firm from having some problems. Both Japanese and North American automakers were able to produce cars in far less time, putting Volvo at a cost disadvantage. As a result, stagnant economies in Asia, coupled with weakening demand for Volvo's product lines in both Europe and the United States, resulted in the firm laying off workers and taking steps to increase its efficiency. More recently, Volvo's performance has rebounded, bolstered in part by its truck sales and reputation for safety in its passenger car division.[53]

Without sacrificing efficiency, other firms have introduced sociotechnical designs for better blending of their personnel and technology. A well-known U.S. example is General Foods, which set up autonomous groups at its Topeka, Kansas, plant to produce Gaines pet food. Patterned after the Volvo example, the General Foods project allowed workers to share responsibility and work in a highly democratic environment. Other U.S. firms also have opted for a self-managed team approach. In fact, research reports that the concept of multifunctional teams with autonomy for generating successful product innovation is more widely used by successful U.S., Japanese, and European firms than any other teamwork concept.[54] Its use must be tempered by the cultural situation, however. And even the widely publicized General Foods project at Topeka had some problems. Some former employees indicate that the approach steadily eroded and that some managers were openly hostile because it undermined their power, authority, and decision-making flexibility. The most effective job design will be a result of both the job to be done and the cultural values that support a particular approach.[55] For MNCs, the challenge will be to make the fit between the design and the culture.

At the same time, it is important to realize that functional job descriptions now are being phased out in many MNCs and replaced by more of a process approach. The result is a more horizontal network that relies on communication and teamwork. This approach also is useful in helping create and sustain partnerships with other firms.

Work Centrality

work centrality
The importance of work in an individual's life relative to other areas of interest.

Work centrality, which can be defined as the importance of work in an individual's life relative to his or her other areas of interest (family, church, leisure), provides important insights into how to motivate human resources in different cultures.[56] After conducting a review of the literature, Bhagat and associates found that Japan has the highest level of work centrality, followed by moderately high levels for Israel, average levels for the United States and Belgium, moderately low levels for the Netherlands and Germany, and low levels for Britain.[57] These findings indicate that successful multinationals in Japan must realize that although work is an integral part of the Japanese lifestyle, work in the United States must be more balanced with a concern for other interests. Unfortunately, this is likely to become increasingly more difficult for Japanese firms in Japan because stagnant population growth is creating a shortage of personnel. As a result, growing numbers of Japanese firms are now trying to push the mandatory retirement age to 65 from 60 and, except for workers in the United States, Japanese workers put in the most hours.[58]

Value of Work   Although work is an important part of the lifestyles of most people, this emphasis can be attributed to a variety of conditions. For example, one reason that Americans and Japanese work such long hours is that the cost of living is high, and hourly employees cannot afford to pass up the opportunity for extra money. Among salaried employees who are not paid extra, most Japanese managers expect their subordinates to stay late at work, and overtime has become a requirement of the job. Moreover, there is recent evidence that Japanese workers may do far less work in a business day than outsiders would suspect.

Many people are unaware of these facts and have misperceptions of why the Japanese and Americans work so hard and the importance of work to them. The same is true of Germans and Americans. In recent years, the number of hours worked annually

Table 12–8		
2007 Annual Salaries: U.S. and Germany		
Grade	**U.S. Salary (Annual, in US$)**	**German Salary (Annual, in US$)**
1	16,630	21,259
2	18,698	23,800
3	20,401	25,532
4	22,902	27,919
5	25,623	30,103
6	28,562	33,625
7	31,740	35,839
8	35,151	38,312
9	38,824	41,248
10	42,755	45,010
11	46,974	50,765
12	56,301	57,213
13	66,951	63,248
14	79,115	70,109
15	93,063	NA

Source: www.opm.gov/oca/07tables/html/gs.asp and calculated from www.per.hqusareur.army.mil/CPD/Pay_Information/LN_Program/Germany/GermanySalary.aspx.

by German workers has been declining, while the number for Americans has been on the rise. What accounts for this trend? Some observers have explained it in cultural terms, noting that Germans place high value on lifestyle and often prefer leisure to work, while their American counterparts are just the opposite. In fact, research reveals that culture may have little to do with it. A study by the National Bureau of Economic Research (NBER) found a far wider range of wages within American companies than in German firms, and this large pay disparity has created incentives for American employees to work harder. For instance, Table 12–8 compares U.S. and German salaries based on a "Step 1" or entry-level pay scale. In particular, many U.S. workers believe that if they work harder, their chances of getting pay hikes and promotions will increase, and there are historical data to support this belief. An analysis of worker histories in the United States and Germany led NBER researchers to estimate that American workers who increase their working time by 10 percent, for example, from 2,000 to 2,200 hours annually, will raise their future earnings by about 1 percent for each year in which they put in extra hours.

Another important area of consideration is the importance of work as a part of overall lifestyle. In the case of Japanese workers, in particular, there has been a growing interest in the impact of overwork on the physical condition of employees. A report by the Japanese government noted that one-third of the working-age population suffers from chronic fatigue, and a recent survey by the Japanese prime minister's office found that a majority of those who were surveyed complained of being chronically tired and feeling emotionally stressed and some complained about abusive conditions in the workplace.[59] Fortunately, as seen in "International Management in Action: Karoshi: Stressed Out in Japan," the effects of overwork or job burnout—**karoshi** in Japanese— are beginning to be recognized as a real social problem. Other Asian countries which are subject to accelerated development are also experiencing job stress. Chinese workers, for example, are exhibiting classic Western signs of stress and overwork. Burnout, substance abuse, eating disorders, and depression abound, not to mention time away from the family. The culture is such that employees will not seek counseling, as it is

karoshi
A Japanese term that means "overwork" or "job burnout."

a sign of weakness and embarrassment. However, like the Japanese, the Chinese are seeing the issue and attempting to approach a solution that will alleviate stress and save face.[60]

Job Satisfaction   In addition to the implications that value of work has for motivating human resources across cultures, another interesting contrast is job satisfaction. For example, one study found that Japanese office workers may be much less satisfied with their jobs than their U.S., Canadian, and EU counterparts are. The Americans, who reported the highest level of satisfaction in this study, were pleased with job challenges, opportunities for teamwork, and ability to make a significant contribution at work. Japanese workers were least pleased with these three factors.[61] Similar findings were uncovered by Luthans and his associates, who reported that U.S. employees had higher organizational commitment than Japanese or Korean workers in their cross-cultural study. What makes these findings particularly interesting is that a large percentage of the Japanese and Korean workers were supervisory employees, who could be expected to be more committed to their organization than nonsupervisory employees, and a significant percentage of these employees also had lifetime guarantees.[62] This study also showed that findings related to job satisfaction in the international arena often are different from expected.[63]

Conventional wisdom not always being substantiated has been reinforced by cross-cultural studies that found Japanese workers who already were highly paid, and then received even higher wages, experienced decreased job satisfaction, morale, commitment, and intention to remain with the firm. This contrasts sharply with U.S. workers, who did not experience these negative feelings.[64] These findings show that the motivation approaches used in one culture may have limited value in another.[65]

Research by Kakabadse and Myers also has brought to light findings that are contradictory to commonly accepted beliefs. These researchers examined job satisfaction among managers from the United Kingdom, France, Belgium, Sweden, and Finland. It has long been assumed that satisfaction is highest at the upper levels of organizations; however, this study found varying degrees of satisfaction among managers, depending on the country. The researchers reported that

> senior managers from France and Finland display greater job dissatisfaction than the managers from the remaining countries. In terms of satisfaction with and commitment to the organization, British, German and Swedish managers display highest levels of commitment. Equally, British and German managers highlight that they feel stretched in their job, but senior managers from French organizations suggest that their jobs lack sufficient challenge and stimulus. In keeping with the job-related views displayed by French managers, they equally indicate their desire to leave their job because of their unsatisfactory work-related circumstances.[66]

On the other hand, research also reveals that some of the conditions that help create organizational commitment among U.S. workers also have value in other cultures. For example, a large study of Korean employees ($n = 1,192$ in 27 companies in 8 major industries) found that consistent with U.S. studies, Korean employees' position in the hierarchy, tenure in their current position, and age all related significantly to organizational commitment. Also, as in previous studies in the United States, as the size of the Korean organizations increased, commitment decreased, and the more positive the climate perceptions, the greater was the commitment.[67] In other words, there is at least beginning evidence that the theoretic constructs predicting organizational commitment may hold across cultures.

Also related to motivation are job attitudes toward quality of work life. Recent research reports that EU workers see a strong relationship between how well they do their jobs and the ability to get what they want out of life. U.S. workers were not as supportive of this relationship, and Japanese workers were least likely to see any connection.

Karoshi: Stressed Out in Japan

Doing business in Japan can be a real killer. Overwork, or *karoshi*, as it is called in Japan, claims 10,000 lives annually in this hard-driving, competitive economic society according to Hiroshi Kawahito, a lawyer who founded the National Defense Council for Victims of Karoshi.

One of the cases is Jun Ishii of Mitsui & Company. Ishii was one of the firm's only speakers of Russian. In the year before his death, Ishii made 10 trips to Russia, totaling 115 days. No sooner would he arrive home from one trip than the company would send him out again. The grueling pace took its toll. While on a trip, Ishii collapsed and died of a heart attack. His widow filed a lawsuit against Mitsui & Company, charging that her husband had been worked to death. Tokyo labor regulators ruled that Ishii had indeed died of karoshi, and the government now is paying annual worker's compensation to the widow. The company also cooperated and agreed to make a one-time payment of $240,000.

The reason that the case received so much publicity is that this is one of the few instances in which the government ruled that a person died from overwork. Now regulators are expanding karoshi compensation to salaried as well as hourly workers. This development is receiving the attention of the top management of many Japanese multinationals, and some Japanese MNCs are beginning to take steps to prevent the likelihood of overwork. For example, Mitsui & Company now assesses its managers based on how well they set overtime hours, keep subordinates healthy, and encourage workers to take vacations. Matsushita Electric has extended vacations from 16 days annually to 23 days and now requires all workers to take this time off. One branch of Nippon Telegraph & Telephone found that stress made some workers irritable and ill, so the company initiated periods of silent meditation. Other companies are following suit, although there still are many Japanese who work well over 2,500 hours a year and feel both frustrated and burned out by job demands.

On the positive side, the Ishii case likely will bring about some improvements in working conditions for many Japanese employees. Experts admit, however, that it is difficult to determine if karoshi is caused by work demands or by private, late-night socializing that may be work-related. Other possible causes include high stress, lack of exercise, and fatty diets, but whatever the cause, one thing is clear: More and more Japanese families no longer are willing to accept the belief that karoshi is a risk that all employees must accept. Work may be a killer, but this outcome can be prevented through more carefully implemented job designs and work processes.

At the same time, recent reports show that there is still a long way to go. In Saku, Japan, for example, the city's main hospital has found that 32 percent of the patients hospitalized in the internal medicine and psychiatric wards are being treated for chronic fatigue syndrome, a diagnosis that is made only after six months of severe, continuous fatigue in the absence of any organic illness. Japanese doctors attribute this explosion of chronic fatigue syndrome to stress. Moreover, during the prolonged economic downturn, a growing number of businesspeople found themselves suffering from these symptoms. And to make matters worse, there is growing concern about alcoholism among workers. Over the past four decades, per capita alcohol consumption in most countries has declined, but in Japan it has risen fourfold. The per capita consumption of alcohol in Japan is equal to that in the United States. Even this comparison is misleading because researchers have found that most Japanese women do not drink at all, but Japanese men in their 50s drink more than twice as much as their American counterparts. Additionally, young Japanese employees find that drinking is considered necessary, and some of them have raised complaints about *alru-hara,* or alcohol harassment (forced/pressured alcohol consumption).

Dealing with overwork will continue to be a challenge both for Japanese firms and for the government. The same is true of the growing problems associated with alcohol that are being brought on by stress and business cultures that have long supported alcohol consumption as a way of doing business and fitting into the social structure.

This finding raises an interesting motivation-related issue regarding how well, for example, American, European, and Japanese employees can work together effectively. Some researchers have recently raised the question of how Japanese firms will be able to have effective strategic alliances with American and European companies if the work values of the partners are so different. Tornvall, after conducting a detailed examination of the work practices of five companies—Fuji-Kiku, a spare-parts firm in Japan; Toyota Motor Ltd. of Japan; Volvo Automobile AB of Sweden; SAAB Automobile AB, Sweden; and the General Motors plant in Saginaw, Michigan—concluded that there were benefits from the approaches used by each. This led him to recommend what he calls a "balance in the synergy" between the partners.[68] Some of his suggestions included the following:

Moving away from	Moving toward
Logical and reason-centered, individualistic thinking	A more holistic, idealistic, and group thinking approach to problem solving
Viewing work as a necessary burden	Viewing work as a challenging and development activity
The avoidance of risk taking and the feeling of distrust of others	An emphasis on cooperation, trust, and personal concern for others
The habit of analyzing things in such great depth that it results in "paralysis through analysis"	Cooperation built on intuition and pragmatism
An emphasis on control	An emphasis on flexibility

In large degree, this balance will require all three groups—Americans, Europeans, and Asians—to make changes in the way they approach work.

In conclusion, it should be remembered that work is important in every society. The extent of importance varies, however, and much of what is "known" about work as a motivator often is culture-specific. The lesson to be learned for international management is that although the process of motivation may be the same, the content may change from one culture to another.

Reward Systems

Besides the content and process theories, another important area of motivation is that of rewards. Managers everywhere use rewards to motivate their personnel. Sometimes these are financial in nature such as salary raises, bonuses, and stock options. At other times they are nonfinancial such as feedback and recognition.[69] The major challenge for international managers is that there are often significant differences between the reward systems that work best in one country and those that are most effective in another. Some of these differences are a result of the competitive environment[70] or of government legislation that dictates such things as minimum wages, pensions, and perquisites.[71] In other cases, the differences are accounted for very heavily by culture.[72] For example, while many American companies like to use merit-based reward systems, firms in Japan, Korea, and Taiwan, where individualism is not very high, often feel that this form of reward system is too disruptive of the corporate culture and traditional values.[73]

Incentives and Culture

Use of financial incentives to motivate employees is very common, especially in countries with high individualism. In the United States, a number of chief executive officers earn over $100 million a year thanks to bonuses, stock options, and long-term incentive payments.[74] These pay systems are common when companies attempt to link compensation to performance. Typically, these systems range from individual incentive-based pay systems in which workers are paid directly for their output to systems in which employees earn individual bonuses based on how well the organization at large achieves certain goals such as sales growth, total revenue, or total profit. These reward systems are designed to stress *equity*. However, they are not universally accepted.

In many cultures compensation is based on group membership or group effort. In these cases the systems are designed to stress *equality*, and employees will oppose the use of individual incentive plans. One example of this is the American multinational corporation that decided to institute an individually based bonus system for the sales representatives in its Danish subsidiary. The sales force rejected the proposal because it favored one group over another and employees felt that everyone should receive the same size bonus.[75] Another example, reported by Vance and associates, was Indonesian oil workers who rejected a pay-for-performance system that would have resulted in some work teams making more money than others.[76]

While financial rewards such as pay, bonuses, and stock options are important motivators, in many countries workers are highly motivated by other things as well. For example, Sirota and Greenwood studied employees of a large multinational electrical equipment manufacturer with operations in 40 countries. They found that in all of these locales the most important rewards involved recognition and achievement. Second in importance were improvements in the work environment and employment conditions including pay and work hours.[77] Beyond this, a number of differences emerged in preferred types of rewards. For example, employees in France and Italy highly valued job security, while for American and British workers it held little importance. Scandinavian workers placed high value on concern for others on the job and for personal freedom and autonomy, but they did not rate "getting ahead" as very important. German workers ranked security, fringe benefits, and "getting ahead" as very important, while Japanese employees put good working conditions and a congenial work environment high on their list but ranked personal advancement quite low.

Very simply, the types of incentives that are deemed important appear to be culturally influenced. Moreover, culture can even affect the overall cost of an incentive system. For example, in Japan, efforts to introduce Western-style merit pay systems typically lead to an increase in the overall labor costs because the companies find that they cannot reduce the pay of less productive workers for fear of causing them to lose face and thus disturb group harmony.[78] As a result, everyone's salary increases. Culture also impacts profit in that people tend to perform better under management systems that are supportive of their own values. Nam, for example, studied two Korean banks that operated under different management systems.[79] One was owned and operated as a joint venture with an American bank, and the other was owned and operated as a joint venture with a Japanese bank. The American bank put into place management practices and personnel policies that were common in its own organization. The Japanese bank put together a blend of Japanese and Korean human resource management policies. Nam found that employees in the joint venture with the Japanese bank were significantly more committed to the organization than were their counterparts in the American joint venture and the Japanese-affiliated bank had significantly higher financial performance.

Sometimes, however, reward systems can be transferred and used successfully. For example, Welsh, Luthans, and Sommer examined the effectiveness of common Western incentive systems in a Russian textile factory.[80] They found that both contingently administered extrinsic rewards and positive recognition and attention from the supervisor led to significantly enhanced job performance, while participative techniques had little impact on job behavior and performance. Similarly, many people believe that large annual financial packages and lucrative golden parachutes are used only in American firms, but this is untrue. Senior-level managers in many MNCs now earn large salaries, and large financial packages for executives who are terminated or whose company is acquired by another firm are gaining in popularity, especially in Europe.[81] In other words, the type of rewards that are used is not culture-bound.

Overall, however, cultures do greatly influence the effectiveness of various rewards. What works in one country may not work in another. For example, research shows that Swedish workers with superior performance often prefer a reward of time off rather than additional money, while high-performing Japanese workers tend to opt for financial incentives—as long as they are group-based and not given on an individual basis.[82] It is also important to realize that the reasons why workers choose one form of motivation over another—for example, days off rather than more money—may not be immediately obvious or intuitively discernible. For example, research has found that Japanese workers tend to take only about half of their annual holiday entitlements, while French and German workers take all of the days to which they are entitled. Many people believe the Japanese want to earn more money, but the primary reason why they do not take all their holiday entitlements is that they believe taking all of those days shows a lack of commitment to their work group. The same is true for overtime: Individuals who refuse to work overtime are viewed as selfish. One of the results of these cultural values is karoshi, discussed earlier in the chapter.

The World of *BusinessWeek*—Revisited

The opening article shows how important it is for MNCs to understand the underlying factors that motivate workers and the sources of employee satisfaction. By ignoring such crucial issues, companies risk losing a vast talent pool and incurring costs through new hires, training, or settling for less experienced personnel. While Indian workers were first lured into lucrative jobs provided by MNCs through salary compensation and the promise of upward mobility, many have become impatient from the lack of institutional follow-through. Companies moving into India may initially save money through introductory wages, but they need to consider the costs involved in retaining the valuable talent. Until recently, this simply consisted of wage incentives, but more and more organizations are realizing that the work environment, intertwined familial relationships, and the opportunity to continue education are of much higher value to the culture. Identifying alternative cultural viewpoints early can help MNCs in any country to grow, and may be the key to continued survival.

The challenge for international managers is to put together a motivational package that addresses the specific needs of the employee or group in each region where an MNC serves. In applying these ideas, answer the following questions: (1) What are some of the things that successful MNCs do to effectively motivate European employees? South Asian (Indian) employees? (2) What kinds of incentives do scientific and technical employees respond to that might not be as meaningful to other categories of employees? (3) What advantages might employees see of working for a truly global company (as opposed to a North American MNC)?

SUMMARY OF KEY POINTS

1. Two basic types of theories explain motivation: content and process. Content theories of motivation have received much more attention in international management research, because they provide the opportunity to create a composite picture of the motivation of human resources in a particular country or region. In addition, content theories more directly provide ways for managers to improve the performance of their human resources.

2. Maslow's hierarchy-of-needs theory has been studied in a number of different countries. Researchers have found that regardless of country, managers have to be concerned with the satisfaction of these needs for their human resources.

3. Some researchers have suggested that satisfaction profiles are not very useful for studying motivation in an international setting, because there are so many different subcultures within any country or even at different levels of a given organization. These researchers have suggested that job categories

are more effective for examining motivation, because job level (managers versus operating employees) and the need hierarchy have an established relationship.

4. Like Maslow's theory, Herzberg's two-factor theory has received considerable attention in the international arena, and Herzberg's original findings from the United States have been replicated in other countries. Cross-cultural studies related to job satisfaction also have been conducted. The data show that job content is more important than job context to job satisfaction.

5. The third content theory of motivation that has received a great amount of attention in the international arena is the need for achievement. Some current findings show that this need is not as widely held across cultures as was previously believed. In some parts of the world, however, such as Anglo countries, cultural values encourage people to be high achievers. In particular, Dutch researcher Geert

Hofstede suggested that an analysis of two cultural dimensions, uncertainty avoidance and masculinity, helps to identify high-achieving societies. Once again, it can be concluded that different cultures will support different motivational needs, and that international managers developing strategies to motivate their human resources for improved performance must recognize cultural differences.

6. Process theories have also contributed to the understanding of motivation in the international arena. Equity theory focuses on how motivation is affected by people's perception of how fairly they are being treated, and there is considerable research to support the fundamental equity principle in Western work groups. However, when the theory is examined on an international basis, the results are mixed. Perhaps the biggest shortcoming of the theory is that it appears to be culture-bound. For example, in Japan and Korea, men and women typically receive different pay for doing precisely the same work, and this is at least traditionally not perceived as inequitable to women.

7. Goal-setting theory focuses on how individuals go about setting goals and responding to them and the overall impact of this process on motivation. There is evidence showing that employees perform extremely well when they are assigned specific and challenging goals that they had a hand in setting. However, most of these goal-setting studies have been conducted in the United States; few of them have been carried out in other cultures. Additionally, research results on the effects of goal setting at the individual level are very limited, and culture may well account for these outcomes.

8. Expectancy theory postulates that motivation is largely influenced by a multiplicative combination of a person's belief that effort will lead to performance, that performance will lead to specific outcomes, and that these outcomes are valued by the individual. There is mixed support for this theory. Many researchers believe that the theory best explains motivation in countries that emphasize an internal locus of control.

9. Although content and process theories provide important insights into the motivation of human resources, three additional areas that have received a great deal of recent attention in the application of motivation are job design, work centrality, and reward systems. Job design is influenced by culture as well as the specific methods that are used to bring together the people and the work. Work centrality helps to explain the importance of work in an individual's life relative to other areas of interest. In recent years work has become a relatively greater part of the average U.S. employee's life and perhaps less a part of the average Japanese worker's life. Research also indicates that Japanese office workers are less satisfied with their jobs than are U.S., Canadian, and EU workers, suggesting that MNCs need to design motivation packages that address the specific needs of different cultures. This idea is also true in the case of rewards. Research shows that the motivational value of monetary and nonmonetary rewards is influenced by culture. Countries with high individualism such as the United States and the U.K. tend to make wide use of individual incentives, while collectivistic countries such as in Asia tend to prefer group-oriented incentives. At the same time, research shows that some motivational approaches in the United States have been successfully used in Russia. So while the importance of focusing on motivation in the international arena is unquestioned, the use of specific applications continues to be challenging for MNC managers.

KEY TERMS

achievement motivation theory, *407*

content theories of motivation, *395*

equity theory, *409*

esteem needs, *396*

expectancy theory, *411*

extrinsic, *394*

goal-setting theory, *411*

hygiene factors, *401*

intrinsic, *394*

job-content factors, *406*

job-context factors, *406*

job design, *412*

karoshi, *415*

motivation, *394*

motivators, *401*

physiological needs, *396*

process theories of motivation, *395*

safety needs, *396*

self-actualization needs, *396*

social needs, *396*

sociotechnical designs, *413*

two-factor theory of motivation, *401*

work centrality, *414*

REVIEW AND DISCUSSION QUESTIONS

1. Do people throughout the world have needs similar to those described in Maslow's need hierarchy? What does your answer reveal about using universal assumptions regarding motivation?

2. Is Herzberg's two-factor theory universally applicable to human resource management, or is its value limited to Anglo countries?

3. What are the dominant characteristics of high achievers? Using Figure 12–7 as your point of reference, determine which countries likely will have the greatest percentage of high achievers. Why is this so? Of what value is your answer to the study of international management?

4. A U.S. manufacturer is planning to open a plant in Sweden. What should this firm know about the quality of work life in Sweden that would have a direct effect on job design in the plant? Give an example.

5. What does a U.S. firm setting up operations in Japan need to know about work centrality in that country? How would this information be of value to the multinational? Conversely, what would a Japanese firm need to know about work centrality in the United States? Explain.

6. In managing operations in Europe, which process theory—equity theory, goal-setting theory, or expectancy theory—would be of most value to an American manager? Why?

7. What do international managers need to know about the use of reward incentives to motivate personnel? What role does culture play in this process?

INTERNET EXERCISE: MOTIVATING POTENTIAL EMPLOYEES

In order for multinationals to continue expanding their operations, they must be able to attract and retain highly qualified personnel in many countries. Much of their success in doing this will be tied to the motivational package that they offer, including financial opportunities, benefits and perquisites, meaningful work, and an environment that promotes productivity and worker creativity. Automotive firms, in particular, are a good example of MNCs that are trying very hard to increase their worldwide market share. So for them, employee motivation is an area that is getting a lot of attention.

Go to the Web, and look at the career opportunities that are currently being offered by Ford Motor (**www.ford.com**), Volvo (**www.volvo.com**), and Volkswagen (**www.vw.com**). All these companies provide information about the career opportunities they offer. Based on this information, answer these three questions: (1) What are some of the things that all three firms offer to motivate new employees? (2) Which of the three has the best motivational package? Why? (3) Are there any major differences between Ford and its European rivals? What conclusion can you draw from this?

Singapore

Singapore is an island city-state that is located at the southern tip of the Malay Peninsula. The small country covers 239 square miles and is connected by train across the Johore Strait to West Malaysia in the north. The Strait of Malacca to the south separates Singapore from the Indonesian island of Sumatra. There are approximately 4.5 million people in Singapore, resulting in a population density per square mile of almost 18,000 people. About three-fourths of Singaporeans are of Chinese descent, 15 percent are Malays, and the remainder are Indian and European. The gross domestic product of this thriving country is over $141 billion, and per capita GDP is around $31,400. One of the so-called newly industrialized countries, Singapore, in recent years has been affected by the economic uncertainty around the world, but the currency and prices have remained relatively stable. The very clean and modern city remains the major commercial and shipping center of Southeast Asia.

An important year for Singapore was 2003. In May 2003, the governments of the United States and Singapore signed the U.S.-Singapore Free Trade Agreement (USS-FTA), the first bilateral free-trade agreement between the United States and an Asian country. However, a SARS breakout in the same year, along with a global recession, reduced tourism and consumer spending in the country. Luckily MNCs were not too fazed by these setbacks, and Singapore continues to be the Southeast Asian financial and high-tech hub, attracting more and more pharmaceutical and medical technology productions from across the globe.

The Madruga Corporation of Cleveland has been producing small electronic toys in Singapore. The small factory has been operated by local managers, but Madruga now wants to expand the Singapore facilities as well as integrate more expatriate managers into the operation. The CEO explained: "We do not want to run this plant as if it were a foreign subsidiary under the direct control of local managers. It is our plant and we want an on-site presence. Over the last year we have been staffing our Canadian and European operations with headquarters personnel, and we are now ready to turn attention to our Singapore operation." Before doing so, the company intends to conduct some on-site research to learn the most effective way of managing the Singapore personnel. In particular, the Madruga management team is concerned with how to motivate the Singaporeans and make them more productive. One survey has already been conducted among the Singapore personnel; this study found a great deal of similarity with the workers at the U.S. facilities. Both the Singapore and the U.S. employees expressed a preference for job-content factors such as the chance for growth, achievement, and increased responsibility, and they listed money and job security toward the bottom of the list of things they looked for in a job.

Madruga management is intrigued by these findings and believes that it might be possible to use some of the same motivation approaches in Singapore as it does in the United States. Moreover, one of the researchers sent the CEO a copy of an article showing that people in Singapore have weak uncertainty avoidance and a general cultural profile that is fairly similar to that of the United States. The CEO is not sure what all this means, but she does know that motivating workers in Singapore apparently is not as "foreign" a process as she thought it would be.
www.sg

Questions

1. What are some current issues facing Singapore? What is the climate for doing business in Singapore today?

2. Based on the information in this case, determine the specific things that seem to motivate human resources in Singapore.

3. Would knowledge of the achievement motive be of any value to the expatriate managers who are assigned to the Singapore operation?

4. If you were using Figure 12–7 to help explain how to motivate Singapore human resources effectively, what conclusions could you draw that would help provide guidelines for the Madruga management team?

Motivation Is the Key

Over the last five years, Corkley & Finn, a regional investment brokerage house, has been extremely profitable. Some of its largest deals have involved cooperation with investment brokers in other countries. Realizing that the world economy is likely to grow vigorously over the next 25 years, the company has decided to expand its operations and open overseas branches. In the beginning, the company intends to work in cooperation with other local brokerages; however, the company believes that within five years, it will have garnered enough business to break away and operate independently. For the time being, the firm intends to set up a small office in London and another in Tokyo.

The firm plans on sending four people to each of these offices and recruiting the remainder of the personnel from the local market. These new branch employees will have to spend time meeting potential clients and building trust. This will be followed by the opportunity to put together small financial deals and, it is hoped, much larger ones over time.

The company is prepared to invest whatever time or money is needed to make these two branches successful. "What we have to do," the president noted, "is establish an international presence and then build from there. We will need to hire people who are intensely loyal to us and use them as a cadre for expanding operations and becoming a major player in the international financial arena. One of our most important challenges will be to hire the right people and motivate them to do the type of job we

want and stay with us. After all, if we bring in people and train them how to do their jobs well and then they don't perform or they leave, all we've done is spend a lot of money for nothing and provide on-the-job training for our competitors. In this business, our people are the most important asset, and clients most often are swayed toward doing business with an investment broker with whom they think they can have a positive working relationship. The reputation of the firm is important, but it is always a function of the people who work there. Effective motivation of our people is the key to our ultimate success in these new branches."

Questions

1. When motivating the personnel in London and Tokyo, is the company likely to find that the basic hierarchical needs of the workers are the same? Why or why not?

2. How could an understanding of the two-factor theory of motivation be of value for motivating the personnel at both locations? Would hygiene factors be more important to one of these groups than to the other? Would there be any difference in the importance of motivators?

3. Using Figure 12–7 as a point of reference, what recommendation would you make regarding how to motivate the personnel in London? In Tokyo? Are there any significant differences between the two? If so, what are they? If not, why not?

Chapter 13

LEADERSHIP ACROSS CULTURES

OBJECTIVES OF THE CHAPTER

Leadership is often credited for the success or failure of international operations. As with other aspects of management, leadership styles and practices that work well in one culture are not necessarily effective in another. For example, the leadership approach used by U.S. managers would not necessarily be the same as that employed in other parts of the world. Even within the same country, effective leadership tends to be very situation-specific; however, also like the other areas studied in international management, certain leadership styles and practices transcend international boundaries. This chapter examines these leadership differences and similarities.

First the basic foundation for the study of leadership is reviewed. Next, leadership in various parts of the world, including Europe, East Asia, the Middle East, and developing countries, is examined. Finally, specific types of leadership are analyzed, drawing from recent research on leadership across cultures. The specific objectives of this chapter are:

1. **DESCRIBE** the basic philosophic foundation and styles of managerial leadership.

2. **EXAMINE** the attitudes of European managers toward leadership practices.

3. **COMPARE** and **CONTRAST** leadership styles in Japan with those in the United States.

4. **REVIEW** leadership approaches in China, the Middle East, and developing countries.

5. **EXAMINE** recent research and findings regarding leadership across cultures.

6. **DISCUSS** the relationship of culture clusters and leader behavior on effective leadership practices, including increasing calls for more responsible global leadership.

The World of *BusinessWeek*

BusinessWeek

China's First Global Capitalist

Lenovo Chairman Yang Yuanqing Is Building a New Breed of Multinational

On a bright September afternoon, a black Mercedes S320 pulls up to a curb in the middle of Beijing's bustling Zhongguancun, the consumer-electronics shopping district. Out steps a man in a conservative gray suit, with ink-black hair, a round face, and wire-rim glasses. He still has the same youthful appearance he had 18 years earlier when, as a shy, bean-thin science student, he first arrived in this neighborhood. Then called Swindler's Alley, the area was a disreputable bazaar for knockoffs and black-market software. Now all that has been replaced by neon, steel, and glass.

Yang Yuanqing, 42, chairman of Lenovo Group Ltd., the leading PC company in China, steps into the Ding Hao Electronics Mall and a dizzying scene. Everywhere there are signs, lights, and swarms of shoppers. Strolling from one shop to another to peruse the displays of his company's devices, Yang, introduced by his handlers, speaks quietly with shopkeepers. But each time he stops, he is immediately surrounded by a scrum of people giddily snapping his picture with tiny digital cameras and camera phones. Yang is a rock-star executive here, a Chinese Bill Gates.

It was in this neighborhood in 1988 that Yang began working for Lenovo—then a tiny company called Legend Group—in a nondescript three-story building. Yang slips back into the Mercedes and is soon gliding past the spot where he once bunked with four roommates in a company dormitory. Looking around, he realizes that the building has been demolished to make way for a parking lot. "Everything has been torn down," marvels Yang. "It's a total changeover."

Yang himself has undergone no less startling a transformation. He grew up poor in Hefei, a backwater city in eastern China, during the Cultural Revolution. Today he leads the world's third-largest PC company, with $13 billion in revenues. He's a rich globe-trotter: His compensation last year topped $2 million. He has a luxury apartment overlooking New York's Central Park and a home in suburban Beijing. In July, Yang moved his family for a few weeks to his apartment in Raleigh, N.C., near Lenovo's headquarters, so his kids could soak up American culture at summer camp. The Forbidden City meets Piggly Wiggly.

Last year, when Lenovo bought IBM PC Co., Yang stepped onto the world stage. He became the first Chinese executive to lead the takeover of an iconic Western business. In one swoop, he took on the world's leading technology companies. Now, as China's first truly global capitalist, he has a chance to help his homeland shed its image as a cheap manufacturing hub.

But Yang Yuanqing may turn out to be much more. From the moment he was tapped at age 29 to shake up the struggling PC unit of Lenovo's predecessor company, Yang has defied the stereotype of a Chinese manager. (That's assuming most American business managers can name even one leader of a Chinese company.) Today he is emerging as the first of a hybrid class of leader, marrying the drive and creativity of Western management with the vast efficiencies of China's manufacturing operations.

If your idea of a Chinese boss is a cautious bureaucrat propped up by the state, Yang is not that guy. He presides over a merit-based culture built on the Silicon Valley blueprint: In an elder-worshipping country, he fearlessly promotes young people and fires employees who aren't up to snuff. He demands that people learn from their mistakes, and he's relentless about self-improvement. When it became clear 18 months ago that he was being hindered by his scant knowledge of English, he hired a tutor, watched CNN obsessively, and went from halting to conversant within a year.

Some of Yang's management techniques would make Jack Welch proud. Shortly after rising to power at Legend, he decided managers needed to reconnect with their staff. Too many had highfalutin titles with the equivalent of "president" in them; Yang wanted everybody addressed by their given name. To make the point, he ordered executives to stand outside the building every morning and greet workers while holding signs with their names written on them. "After two weeks, the change finally stuck," recalls Wang Xiaoyan, who is currently Lenovo's senior vice-president for information services.

The pressure on Yang is intense, and not just from shareholders. In the summer of 2005, a few months after the IBM deal closed, Chinese Premier Wen Jiabao paid a visit to Lenovo's Beijing offices. Yang showed him the latest PCs and cell phones. As the short visit wrapped up, Wen told Yang: "You carry the hopes of China on your shoulders," according to someone who was there.

But Yang is discovering just how hard it will be to translate success in China into success everywhere else. The honeymoon after the IBM PC purchase is long over. This spring, Yang ran into a buzz saw of Beltway politics when congressional concerns about security forced the State Dept. to change the way it used some of the 14,000 PCs it had ordered from Lenovo. Responding to worries that Chinese government snooping technology could be tucked into the machines, the department redirected some of them to less sensitive projects.

There has been plenty of friction inside Lenovo, too. Last December, Yang and the board pushed out his second-in-command, former IBMer Steve Ward, in part because he was too slow to cut costs. Ward's replacement as CEO is the frenetic William J. Amelio, who formerly ran Asian operations for Dell Inc.

It's an oddball management setup. Yang runs the company, and Amelio reports to him. But they share a lot of responsibilities for overseeing this sprawling organization on a near-equal basis. Lenovo sells products in no fewer than 66 countries and develops them at labs in China, the U.S., and Japan. Yang and Amelio also must mix the best people and traits of the old Lenovo with those of IBM. In essence, they're blending two national cultures and, to add to the stress, three corporate ones, since Amelio has been replacing some of the top executives from Lenovo and IBM with his own team, mostly from Dell. Rarely if ever has a corporate leader had to manage such a tangled web of relationships.

Yang answers to an odd mix of shareholders that includes public investors, the Chinese Academy of Sciences, the company's founders, and IBM. Each constituency has its own ax to grind. Private equity investors hold a lot of clout, having sunk $350 million into the company for a 10% stake. Board members William O. Grabe of General Atlantic and James G. Coulter of Texas Pacific Group early on pressed for faster cost-cutting and more decisive decision-making. "This is an unusual melding of what had been a Chinese company, IBM, and some very strong-willed U.S. investors," says Coulter.

Yang's strategy is ambitious. Over the next couple of years, he wants to boost Lenovo's already dominant 35% market share in China while expanding to other emerging markets. In the West, he taps IBM for help in selling to large corporations. But for small and midsize businesses, Lenovo is now mimicking its China strategy and offering a new line of PCs through a host of retailers. Meanwhile, the company is retooling the old IBM PC Co. manufacturing supply chain to make it as efficient as Lenovo's China operations. "We want to extend the business model that was so successful in China out across the world," Yang says.

In the long term, Yang aims to turn Lenovo into a high-profile global brand. He took the first huge step in 2004 when he inked a deal with the International Olympic Committee to be the tech sponsor of the Turin and Beijing Olympic Games. After the merger was completed, he challenged company engineers to come up with a string of hit products for businesses and consumers worldwide in advance of the Beijing event.

At the same time, Lenovo is weaning customers off the IBM brand, which it has the right to use for five years. First, it stopped using IBM in advertising. Now it's gradually shifting the branding on ThinkPad laptop computers to remove IBM and replace it with Lenovo.

Former IBM engineers say things have changed for the better since the merger—and in ways you might not expect. Yang has kept research and development spending constant as a percentage of revenues. But because more of the work is being done in China, where engineers cost one-fifth what they do in the U.S., he gets more bang for the buck. He has also dedicated 20% of his R&D budget for cutting-edge ideas. Under U.S. management, the unit had become focused largely on cost-cutting. "It used to be, 'Can we save a penny?' Now it's, 'What new ideas do you have?'" says David Hill, executive director for corporate identity and design. One novel concept already has come from the Beijing engineers: NovaCenter, a living-room-style combination of PC and TV that's now selling in China. In addition to Microsoft's Windows, it has an entertainment-oriented operating system that was created by Lenovo.

For all its big plans and lofty ambitions, though, Lenovo remains in a precarious position. Sales are still strong in China, which is expected to be one of the fastest-growing markets in coming years. However, Lenovo is up against companies several times its size. Dell alone has sunk $16 billion into Chinese factories and suppliers over the past year—more than Lenovo's worldwide sales. Lenovo's

sales declined by 9% in the U.S. last quarter, signaling that the company is struggling in its efforts to build a global brand. Analysts are troubled by that report, though they expect efficiencies and revenue growth to click in over the long term. The stock (which doesn't trade on U.S. exchanges) is priced around HK$3.30, having zigzagged between $2 and $4 for three years. In September, Lenovo was dropped from the Hong Kong Exchange's Hang Seng Index because of slack trading volumes.

Other Chinese business kingpins are watching closely to see if Yang stumbles. With a domestic economy growing at 10% per year and foreign reserves topping $1 trillion soon, they are hungrily eyeing attractive overseas takeover targets—everything from oil to consumer electronics. But China's early forays into global expansion have been frustrating. Electronics maker TCL Corp.'s 2004 joint venture with France's ThomsonTMS, which owns the famed RCA brand, has bled cash, resulting in shuttered plants and offices. And in 2005 an $18.5 billion bid by CNOOC Ltd. for Unocal never got off the ground; the U.S. Congress put the kibosh on it. Many Chinese executives want to see how Yang does before they, too, plunge into globalization.

Edward Tian, a friend of Yang's and former vice-chairman of telecommunications giant China Netcom Group, explains how others view the Lenovo executive: "In China there's an old saying, 'Don't be the first one to eat the crab.' It's difficult to get the meat out, and you might be poisoned. People see Yuanqing as the guy eating the crab. They're waiting to see if he'll survive."

If Lenovo fizzles, it won't be for lack of intensity. Former IBMers agree that the pace of business and decision-making has picked up since Yang took over. That's visible in the massive third-floor atrium of the Lenovo Building in Beijing's sprawling Shangdi Information Industry Base, where a huge billboard with a map of China is divided into 18 sales regions. Across the bottom are columns showing the sales and ranking of each region. Every day at 7:30 p.m., totals are tallied and messages go out to all of the managers' mobile phones. If a region comes in with less than 100% of its quota, its manager immediately must produce a plan for turning things around.

Sometimes, Yang seems obsessed with details. Before formal dinners, he personally reviews seating arrangements to make sure all protocols are being followed. Last year, during a ceremony launching a summer camp program for kids at Lenovo Beijing, he noticed that the Lenovo flag was attached upside down on a flagpole. To get the attention of the events team, he docked their performance bonuses.

Figuring out exactly what role Yang should play in the company has been tricky. He engineered the IBM acquisition, yet during the transition seemed to fade into the background. Ward became the company's front man with the Western press and analysts. Although Ward and

Yang deny there was ever any tension between them, one industry bigwig recalls that when he had dinner with the two a few months after the deal closed, Ward did nearly all of the talking. "It was really an uncomfortable situation," he says.

Initial encounters between Yang and Amelio were also tense. No wonder: They had been head-to-head competitors in the China market. Amelio recalls their first awkward one-on-one session at a Hong Kong hotel: "Here we were, two guys who have been trying to slit each other's throats talking about doing something together."

At their second meeting, Yang surprised Amelio by pulling out a single sheet of paper listing the roles for Lenovo's chairman and CEO. His job included setting corporate and technology strategy and communicating with investors. Amelio's main task was running the PC business day-to-day. This is not the typical split between chairman and CEO—Yang would be much more hands-on, like a co-CEO. Amelio went along without complaint. "I was surprised that he agreed so quickly," says Yang. "He looked at it for three minutes and said, 'O.K.'"

Now they're a tag team. Yang goes deep on his specialties, which include marketing and distribution. Last July, for instance, he spent two days in Stuttgart, brainstorming with a dozen European salespeople about how to radically make over the way the company plans and prices products in Central Europe. Elements of the new program were launched within two weeks. Longtime IBMer Robert Pasquier, now Lenovo's distribution director for Central Europe, was impressed that Yang was willing to get his hands dirty. He says the company has been transformed culturally since Lenovo took over: "There's more of a sense of urgency with everyone. It used to be we felt pressure only at the end of the year, but now we feel it every month. People want to win."

Amelio, meanwhile, concentrates on fine-tuning the supply chain. "Bill often calls me boss, but I don't want to put myself only in the boss position," says Yang. "I want to contribute more to the company at all levels." Still, Yang's influence has grown over the past year. Shortly after the IBM PC takeover, the board created a powerful strategy committee headed by Yang but packed with other strong voices, including company co-founder Liu Chuanzhi. At first, the committee met monthly; now, it meets just once a quarter. "Today, Yang is the guy who runs the strategy and sets the agenda," says General Atlantic's Grabe.

A confident Yang has emerged as more of a public figure in the West. And he has become more outspoken. Yang was irate during the dustup over the State Dept. computer order. "We are not a government-controlled company," he insisted in a phone call placed to a *BusinessWeek* reporter shortly after the matter came to a head. "The Chinese PC market used to be dominated by state-owned enterprises. We beat them all." Today, the state-run Chinese Academy of Sciences holds 27% of Lenovo's shares, thanks to its early $25,000 investment in Legend. (That compares with 35% for public shareholders, 15% for employees, 13% for IBM, and 10% for private investors.) But the academy has no members on the board, and the company insists it exerts no influence.

Later, Yang made his case directly to Congress on a sweep through Capitol Hill. Last June, at a business conference in San Francisco, he switched name tags at a table so that he could sit next to C. Richard D'Amato, a member of the congressional advisory committee that had raised the security concerns. D'Amato says he was impressed with Yang's earnestness, but "nothing really changed my thinking."

Yang was more successful in brokering a deal to help rein in PC software piracy in China. Microsoft had been struggling for years to get Chinese computer users to pay for software, yet most of them still bought PCs that didn't include Windows and later loaded illegal copies on their machines. In July, 2005, during a meeting at Microsoft headquarters in Redmond, Wash., Gates and Microsoft Chief Executive Steven A. Ballmer asked Yang for help with piracy, and, over the next few months, Yang worked out a deal with Microsoft China executives. They agreed to give him a rebate on Windows and marketing help in exchange for him agreeing to load it on most Lenovo PCs sold in China. Yang gambled that other Chinese makers would follow suit, and, thanks to pressure from the government, they did. Microsoft's sales of Windows shipped on PCs in China have tripled since the deal came together last fall. Says Ballmer: "Yuanqing made a huge difference. He was willing to go out on a limb."

But if Yang is more of a risk taker than one might expect of a person who grew up in a communist state, his style is also highly calculated. Lenovo colleagues who have spent evenings with Yang playing Tuolaji, a Chinese card game, say he studies his cards for a long time before making a move. Even when dealt a bad hand, he tries to figure out a way to win. They see parallels in how Yang runs the company: He's willing to take risks, but only if he has thoroughly studied a situation and figures he has a reasonable chance of prevailing.

It's no mystery where these traits come from. Yang recalls his parents as tough taskmasters who demanded that he study hard and rank at the top of his classes. Both were surgeons, yet in 1960s China they were paid the same as manual laborers and repeatedly sent to the countryside for reeducation and community service.

That forced Yang to grow up fast. Starting at age 8, he cooked meals over a smoky coal fire for himself and two younger siblings on the balcony of the brick housing project where the family lived in a cramped apartment. Yang's only toy was a bag of marbles; if he wanted to play ball, he'd scrunch up a cast-off cigarette package. His mother, Wang Biqin, gave him a tiny allowance each month, but he rarely spent it because he knew that she might have to take it back to buy food. Yang knew nothing of the outside world. "It was a tragedy, but it was also lucky," he says, looking back. "If you don't know what's going on outside, you don't know what you're missing."

Contrast hardscrabble Hefei in the 1960s with Yang's life today. In August he moved his parents, wife, and three children into a Raleigh apartment inside a gated community amid rolling, wooded countryside. On a steamy summer day, the Yangs gather excitedly in the living room around a low glass table spread with fresh fruit and cookies—which the children don't touch. Yang proudly prompts his eldest boy, Yang Yiqi, 11, to list the three goals he had been assigned when he went off to American summer camp. They were: learn English, make new friends, and excel at sports. "And did you reach your target?" Yang asks. The boy's enthusiastic answer: "Yes, I did!"

When asked what Yang was like when he was growing up, his father, Yang Furong, launches into a long tale that makes the whole family chuckle knowingly. Yang studied ferociously for the national university entrance exams. One evening, he accompanied the rest of the family on a rare outing to a movie theater, but when the house lights came up at the end, they discovered that his seat was empty. In mid-movie, he had raced back home to study.

Yang loved reading literature and writing poetry as a teenager, but pursued a computer science degree at university on the advice of a professor friend of his parents. Six years later he was studying in Beijing to finish up his master's degree in computer science and was headed for an academic career when he spotted an ad for a job at Legend in a newspaper. At the time it was a 100-person company that sold Sun Microsystems and Hewlett-Packard computers at retail. Yang signed on as a salesman at one of the few truly market-driven companies in all of China. His pay: $30 a month.

It was a fortuitous choice. Legend's chief executive, Liu, had emerged in the 1980s as one of modern China's first real entrepreneurs. He and 10 other researchers at the science academy formed the company in 1984. Legend had a rocky first few years, but, by the time Yang landed there, it seemed to be on solid footing. He excelled as a salesman, and Liu eventually put him in charge of small businesses and then the company's crucial engineering workstation unit. There, he got to know Americans who worked for Sun and HP, and he scarfed up every bit of knowledge he could about how to run a successful business.

A pivotal moment came in 1994. Liu was laid up in a Beijing hospital suffering from exhaustion and stress. Legend had begun selling its own PCs in 1990, but, when China opened the market to direct imports by foreign PC giants, it was caught in a pincer. As a publicly held company, Legend did not receive government support like state-owned PC outfits. Yet it didn't have the financial strength of foreign PC makers. Flat on his back for weeks, Liu used the time to consult with his underlings. He came away impressed with the youthful Yang's knowledge of the PC business and his Boy Scout–style honesty—not a small consideration at a time when Chinese enterprises were rife with corruption. Upon leaving the hospital, Liu decided to stay in PCs and create a separate division with the 29-year-old Yang in charge.

What Yang accomplished far exceeded Liu's expectations. In just three years he transformed Legend from an also-ran into the leading PC player in China. He switched from using only a direct sales force to also selling through a vast network of retailers. And he focused on innovation. Until then, the technology in PCs sold in China had been a generation behind those sold in the West. Legend shipped PCs based on Intel's new Pentium processor at the same time they were shipped in North America. Yang also opened up the now-vast consumer market with low-cost, super-easy-to-use PCs. One Legend model let PC novices set up an Internet connection with a single push of a button.

Along the way, Yang learned management lessons that would later prove vital. As the new boss of the PC Div., he supervised several of the company's founders. That was hard for them to swallow. To make matters worse, Yang didn't have a diplomatic sinew in his body. He fired half of the staff, forced managers to radically alter the way they did business, bawled out people when they screwed up, and ignored criticism. It was not very Chinese of him. Liu saw that he very nearly had a revolt on his hands, so he called a management meeting to deal with it. "I criticized Yang so severely he almost broke down in tears," recalls Liu. "But this had a good effect. . . . He started to change his work style."

While Yang became more diplomatic, he remained a reformer. When the PC Div. switched buildings in 1997, he used the move to break with the past. He insisted on a more formal dress code and trained all employees in phone etiquette. This is when he made everyone start referring to managers by their given names.

It wasn't until later that Legend employees understood what Yang was up to. He wanted Legend managers and employees to think and act like techies in Silicon Valley, Boston, or Berlin. Yang knew that unless Legend expanded beyond the borders of China, it would not be able to match the clout of the foreign PC giants. So, when Liu handed the CEO job to him in 2001, Yang made globalization one of his long-term goals.

His big opportunity came in 2003, when he learned that IBM was interested in selling off its large but money-losing PC unit as part of its move to services. Yang saw this deal as a way for Legend, which was about to rebrand itself as Lenovo, to leap onto the world stage without having to grind it out country by country. But the entire board of

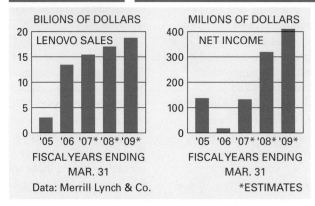

Lenovo: PC Giant Rising

WHAT IT IS: Lenovo Group was created in 1984 as Legend Group, one of China's first capitalist enterprises. It became the world's third-largest PC player when it bought IBM's PC operation in 2005. Today it is run by Chairman Yang and CEO William Amelio, a former Dell executive.

HOW IT'S DOING: Lenovo made only $22 million in 2006, the first year since the IBM acquisition. But analysts expect efficiencies to click in and profits to grow.

WHAT IT SELLS: With a 35% market share, Lenovo sells more PCs than anyone else in China, mostly through stores to consumers and small businesses. Outside China, the company has a 4.7% market share, mostly with large corporations.   Data: IDC, Merrill Lynch & Co.

Source: www.businessweek.com/magazine/content/06_50/b4013064.htm.

directors lined up against Yang. Think about what he was asking the Lenovo elders to do: A $3 billion company based in China would be taking over a $10 billion global behemoth. IBM had practically invented the PC industry; if Big Blue couldn't make money selling these machines worldwide, how could little Lenovo hope to do any better? "We had all built this company, and nobody wanted to take such a big risk," explains Liu.

Yang and his team dug in. They made presentation after presentation to the board until the endless meetings took on the feel of a court trial. Yang was under extreme pressure. One day, when Yang was venting to him in the locker room after a workout, his friend Tian suggested they take a sauna to relax. Yang had something of an epiphany after the two men jumped, naked, into a pool of icy water. "Suddenly Yuanqing was not a serious person anymore. He smiled like a baby," recalls Tian. Eventually, Yang prevailed. He agreed to give up the CEO role to a more worldly Western executive and convinced the board that he could make the former IBM operations more profitable.

Today, Yang's moments of pure bliss are rare. At the end of a long workday in September, he sits at a table in the Bai Family Courtyard Restaurant in Beijing—a setting as far from the smoky balcony in Hefei as you could imagine. The restaurant is decorated in the style of Beijing's Imperial Palace, and the waitresses dress like Qing

Dynasty princesses in elaborate headdresses and lavishly embroidered silk clothing. They bring dish after exquisite dish, an overabundance that seems designed to make up for the privations of China's past.

For a moment, Yang appears relaxed. But that's only temporary. A guest asks what keeps him up at night, and Yang quickly answers: almost everything. "I have a lot of anxiety dreams," he says. "It's the normal emergencies of running a company every day. A customer complains. We're not able to meet demand. There's a shortage of parts. I often wake up, and sometimes I'm up all night."

By Steve Hamm and Dexter Roberts

The opening article provides an excellent example of how effective leadership can transform a company. Yang was born in a time when Chinese businesses were government-owned and -funded, and entrepreneurs were virtually nonexistent. As China moves to a market economy, Yang shows the importance of leadership modernizing a company at all levels. Yang promotes a goal-centric focus as he attempts to employ efficient production methods in overseas operations. Managers are more motivated than ever to succeed, as they are aware of the job losses that may ensue if they do not perform at acceptable levels. Innovation fills the corridors as teams are expected to implement prompt decision-making processes. The hierarchy of the workplace has been broken down, and there exists an atmosphere of camaraderie. Focus has shifted away from simply saving money, and communication among levels is encouraged as ideas flow. The culture of Chinese business has changed within Lenovo's walls, and it can all be attributed to the honest, humble, visionary chairman, Yang Yuanqing. In this chapter we address different leadership styles and address these foundations as a platform for building effective leadership across cultures.

■ Foundation for Leadership

When one realizes that much of history, political science, and the behavioral sciences is either directly or indirectly concerned with leadership, the statement that more research has focused on leadership than nearly any other social science topic becomes believable. Despite all this attention over the years, there still is no generally agreed-on definition, let alone sound answers to the question of which approach is more effective than others in the international arena. For present purposes, **leadership** can be defined as the process of influencing people to direct their efforts toward achievement of some particular goal or goals.[1] Leadership is widely recognized as being very important in the study of international management, which raises the question, What is the difference between being a manager and being a leader? While there is no concise answer, seeing as there is no universally agreed upon definition of "leadership," some interesting perspectives have emerged in this arena.

> **leadership**
> The process of influencing people to direct their efforts toward the achievement of some particular goal or goals.

The Manager-Leader Paradigm

While the terms *manager* and *leader* have often been used interchangeably in the business environment, many believe that there exists distinctions in characteristics and behaviors between the two, adding ambiguity and confusion to an already convoluted situation. Some believe that leaders are born, but managers can be shaped. MNCs that simply sought out employees with appropriate skill sets now face a new challenge: clarifying the unique and integrated components of the seemingly dichotomous roles of managers and leaders to ensure a cohesive vision. The true difficulty is in recognizing how management and leadership are generally distinct from each other and how they overlap.

It has been postulated that managers provide leadership and leaders perform management functions. But managers don't perform the unique functions of leaders.[2] Managerial positions often consist of sheer responsibility. The attributes necessary to make a successful manager can be learned through academic study or observation and training.[3] Behaviors of managers vary greatly, but fundamentally they tend to follow company objectives and rules while attempting to maintain stability as they react to inevitable change. Essentially, management is something that one does, and the journey consists of striving to always do things right. Unfortunately this often results in focusing on failures as a basis for identifying what needs improvement and ignoring success or denying praise.[4]

Leadership is more difficult to summarize as views of what makes a leader are inconsistent across studies. This status is not something that can be learned, but something that must be earned through respect.[5] In other words, people are not hired as leaders, but appointed as such via employee perspective of the individual. Leaders guide and motivate team members and are extremely visible. While managers can be distracted by reaching objectives through financial information, leaders work to get the right people in the right positions; marking money matters as a secondary objective. Proactive behavior is often crucial as these individuals create change and a vision of the future. Overall, leadership is how someone does something and the drive to ultimately do the right thing.[6] Focus tends toward the success and praise of team members, building morale and motivation.

Many firms are beginning to search for an all-encompassing package of skill sets, and while it is imperative for the survival of a business to have both managers and leaders, it is extremely difficult, if not impossible, to find someone who fits the inclusive criteria.[7] Hope exists in the reasonable venture of finding someone who harbors overlapping attributes inherent within the two, and certain training methods can be implemented to magnify the most relevant qualities. Effective communication, planning, organizing, and problem solving are just a few examples of what both leaders and managers should develop in order to live up to their role. The evolution of the manager-leader role will depend on the ability to focus on the future while maintaining current organizational trends along with the support and respect of subordinates, since the leadership role is ultimately determined by team member perspectives.[8]

The concept of whether or not leadership and management are mutually exclusive or if one is a subset of the other is debatable. Table 13–1 provides an outline of perceived differences. The possible implications of continued ambiguity occur when individuals who do not exhibit the capacity of a leader and a manager attempt to fill both shoes. Continuously shifting can lead to inconsistencies and a belief that those in positions of authority may not have the credentials to succeed.[9] However, cultural perspectives are somewhat responsible for how the roles of managers and leaders are seen to overlap, and in some cases, they are synonymous. Furthermore, with the myriad behaviors and styles exhibited by leaders, the two are virtually synonymous. For the purpose of this text, assume a high level of overlap in characteristics, as "supervisor," "leader" and "manager" are used interchangeably. Today, managers that seek to do more than balance the budget can be shaped into the leaders of tomorrow.

Leadership definitions may not be universal, yet relatively little effort has been made to systematically study and compare leadership approaches throughout the world. Most international research efforts on leadership have been directed toward a specific country or geographic area.

Two comparative areas provide a foundation for understanding leadership in the international arena: (1) the philosophical grounding of how leaders view their subordinates and (2) leadership approaches as reflected through use of autocratic-participative characteristics and behaviors of leaders. The philosophies and approaches used in the United States often are quite different from those employed by leaders in overseas organizations, although the differences often are not as pronounced as is commonly believed. First we review historical viewpoints and then move on to exploring new findings.

Table 13–1
Perceived Differences: Managers vs. Leaders

Managers	Leaders
Can learn skills necessary	Harbor innate characteristics
Take care of where you are	Bring you to new horizons
Oversee	Motivate
Point out flaws to improve on	Give recognition for good work
Deal with complexity	Deal with ambiguity
Are fact finders	Are decision makers
Focus on efficiency	Focus on effectiveness
Are given immediate authority	Earn respect through actions
Follow company objectives	Set new standards
Have present vision	Have future vision
Do things right	Do the right things

Philosophical Background: Theories X, Y, and Z

One primary reason that leaders behave as they do is their philosophy or beliefs regarding how to direct their subordinates most effectively. Managers who believe their people are naturally lazy and work only for money will use a leadership style that is different from the style of managers who believe their people are self-starters and enjoy challenge and increased responsibility. Douglas McGregor, the pioneering leadership theorist, labeled these two sets of assumptions "Theory X" and "Theory Y."

A **Theory X manager** believes that people are basically lazy and that coercion and threats of punishment must be used to get them to work. The specific philosophical assumptions of Theory X leaders are:

> **Theory X manager**
> A manager who believes that people are basically lazy and that coercion and threats of punishment often are necessary to get them to work.

1. By their very nature, people do not like to work and will avoid it whenever possible.
2. Workers have little ambition, try to avoid responsibility, and like to be directed.
3. The primary need of employees is job security.
4. To get people to attain organizational objectives, it is necessary to use coercion, control, and threats of punishment.[10]

A **Theory Y manager** believes that under the right conditions people not only will work hard but will seek increased responsibility and challenge. In addition, a great deal of creative potential basically goes untapped, and if these abilities can be tapped, workers will provide much higher quantity and quality of output. The specific philosophical assumptions of Theory Y leaders are:

> **Theory Y manager**
> A manager who believes that under the right conditions people not only will work hard but will seek increased responsibility and challenge.

1. The expenditure of physical and mental effort at work is as natural to people as resting or playing.
2. External control and threats of punishment are not the only ways of getting people to work toward organizational objectives. If people are committed to the goals, they will exercise self-direction and self-control.
3. Commitment to objectives is determined by the rewards that are associated with their achievement.
4. Under proper conditions, the average human being learns not only to accept but to seek responsibility.
5. The capacity to exercise a relatively high degree of imagination, ingenuity, and creativity in the solution of organizational problems is widely distributed throughout the population.
6. Under conditions of modern industrial life, the intellectual potential of the average human being is only partially tapped.[11]

The reasoning behind these beliefs will vary by culture. U.S. managers believe that to motivate workers, it is necessary to satisfy their higher-order needs. This is done best through a Theory Y leadership approach. In China, Theory Y managers act similarly—but for different reasons. After the 1949 revolution, two types of managers emerged in China: Experts and Reds. The Experts focused on technical skills and primarily were Theory X advocates. The Reds, skilled in the management of people and possessing political and ideological expertise, were Theory Y advocates. The Reds also believed that the philosophy of Chairman Mao supported their thinking (i.e., all employees had to rise together both economically and culturally). Both Chinese and U.S. managers support Theory Y, but for very different reasons.[12]

The same is true in the case of Russian managers. In a survey conducted by Puffer, McCarthy, and Naumov, 292 Russian managers were asked about their beliefs regarding work.[13] Table 13–2 shows the six different groupings of the responses. Drawing together the findings of the study, the researchers pointed out the importance of Westerners getting beyond the stereotypes of Russian managers and learning more about the latter's beliefs

Table 13–2
Russian Managerial Beliefs About Work

A. Humanistic Beliefs

Work can be made meaningful.

One's job should give one a chance to try out new ideas.

The workplace can be humanized.

Work can be made satisfying.

Work should allow for the use of human capabilities.

Work can be a means of self-expression.

Work should enable one to learn new things.

Work can be organized to allow for human fulfillment.

Work can be made interesting rather than boring.

The job should be a source of new experiences.

B. Organizational Beliefs

Survival of the group is very important in an organization.

Working with a group is better than working alone.

It is best to have a job as part of an organization where all work together even if you don't get individual credit.

One should take an active part in all group affairs.

The group is the most important entity in any organization.

One's contribution to the group is the most important thing about one's work.

Work is a means to foster group interests.

C. Work Ethic

Only those who depend on themselves get ahead in life.

To be superior a person must stand alone.

A person can learn better on the job by striking out boldly on his own than by following the advice of others.

One must avoid dependence on other persons whenever possible.

One should live one's life independent of others as much as possible.

D. Beliefs About Participation in Managerial Decisions

The working classes should have more say in running society.

Factories would be better run if workers had more of a say in management.

Workers should be more active in making decisions about products, financing, and capital investment.

Workers should be represented on the board of directors of companies.

E. Leisure Ethic

The trend toward more leisure is not a good thing. (R)

More leisure time is good for people.

Increased leisure time is bad for society. (R)

Leisure-time activities are more interesting than work.

The present trend toward a shorter workweek is to be encouraged.

F. Marxist-Related Beliefs

The free-enterprise system mainly benefits the rich and powerful.

The rich do not make much of a contribution to society.

Workers get their fair share of the economic rewards of society. (R)

The work of the laboring classes is exploited by the rich for their own benefit.

Wealthy people carry their fair share of the burdens of life in this country. (R)

The most important work is done by the laboring classes.

Notes: 1. Response scales ranged from 1 (strongly disagree) to 5 (strongly agree).

2. R denotes reverse-scoring items.

3. The 45-individual items contained in the 6 belief clusters were presented to respondents in a mixed fashion, rather than categorized by cluster as shown above.

4. Participation was a subset of Marxist-related values in Buchholz's original study, but was made a separate cluster in his later work.

Source: Adapted from Sheila M. Puffer, Daniel J. McCarthy, and Alexander I. Naumov, "Russian Managers' Beliefs About Work: Beyond the Stereotypes," *Journal of World Business* 32, no. 3 (1997), p. 262.

in order to be more effective in working with them as employees and as joint-venture partners. Obviously, the assumption that Russian managers are strict adherents of Theory X may be common, but it may also be erroneous.[14]

The philosophical assumptions of both the Chinese and the Russian managers help dictate the leadership approach that they use. The assumptions are most easily seen in the managers' behavior, such as giving orders, getting and giving feedback, and creating an overall climate within which the work will be done.

William Ouchi proposed an additional perspective, which he called "Theory Z," that brings together Theory Y and modern Japanese management techniques. A **Theory Z manager** believes that workers seek opportunities to participate in management and are motivated by teamwork and responsibility sharing.[15] The specific philosophical assumptions of a Theory Z leader are:

> **Theory Z manager**
> A manager who believes that workers seek opportunities to participate in management and are motivated by teamwork and responsibility sharing.

1. People are motivated by a strong sense of commitment to be part of a greater whole—the organization in which they work.

2. Employees seek out responsibility and look for opportunities to advance in an organization. Through teamwork and commitment to common goals, employees derive self-satisfaction and contribute to organizational success.

3. Employees who learn different aspects of the business will be in a better position to contribute to the broader goals of the organization.

4. By making commitments to employees' security through lifetime or long-term employment, the organization will engender in employees strong bonds of loyalty, making the organization more productive and successful.

Leadership Behaviors and Styles

Leader behaviors can be translated into three commonly recognized styles: (1) authoritarian, (2) paternalistic, and (3) participative. **Authoritarian leadership** is the use of work-centered behavior that is designed to ensure task accomplishment. As shown in Figure 13–1, this leader behavior typically involves the use of one-way communication from manager to subordinate. The focus of attention usually is on work progress, work procedures, and roadblocks that are preventing goal attainment. There is a managerial tendency toward a lack of involvement with subordinates, where final decisions are in the hands of the higher-level employees. The distance translates into a lack of a relationship where managers focus on assignments over the needs of the employees. At times, the organizational leadership behavior is reflective of the political surroundings, as indicated in one study which focused on Romania.[16] Leaders in this region were slightly more authoritarian (55 percent), which could have been influenced by the Romanian communistic roots that stressed the importance of completing planned productions. Although this leadership style often is effective in handling crises, some leaders employ it as their primary style regardless of the situation. It also is widely used by Theory X managers, who believe that a continued focus on the task is compatible with the kind of people they are dealing with.

> **authoritarian leadership**
> The use of work-centered behavior designed to ensure task accomplishment.

Paternalistic leadership uses work-centered behavior coupled with a protective employee-centered concern. This leadership style can be best summarized by the statement, "Work hard and the company will take care of you." Paternalistic leaders expect everyone to work hard; in return, the employees are guaranteed employment and given security benefits such as medical and retirement programs. Usually, this leadership behavior satisfies some employee needs, and in turn subordinates tend to exhibit loyalty and compliance.[17] Studies have shown that this behavior is seen throughout Latin America, including Argentina, Bolivia, Chile, and Mexico.[18] Paternalistic leaders often are referred to as "soft" Theory X leaders because of their strong emphasis on strictly controlling their employees coupled with concern for their welfare. They often treat employees as strict but caring parents would treat their children. A good example was provided by the chairman of the Daewoo Motor Company of Korea, who laid off thousands of

> **paternalistic leadership**
> The use of work-centered behavior coupled with a protective employee-centered concern.

Figure 13–1

Leader-Subordinate Interactions

One-way downward flow of information and influence from authoritarian leader to subordinates.

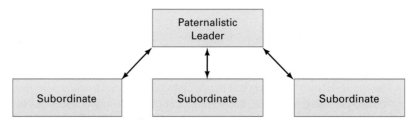

Continual interaction and exchange of information and influence between leader and subordinates.

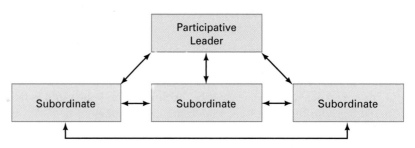

Continual interaction and exchange of information and influence between leader and subordinates and between subordinates.

Source: Adapted from Richard M. Hodgetts, *Modern Human Relations at Work,* 8th ed. (Ft. Worth, TX: Harcourt, 2002), p. 264.

employees in 2002. Having made this decision, the chairman then went throughout the company apologizing for having to take such drastic action and telling each person that he was determined to help him or her find another job. When asked about his approach, he said, "I'm the father of my employees. I need to bring back hope to everyone."[19]

participative leadership

The use of both work- or task-centered and people-centered approaches to leading subordinates.

Participative leadership is the use of both work-centered and people-centered approaches. Participative leaders typically encourage their people to play an active role in assuming control of their work, and authority usually is highly decentralized. The way in which leaders motivate employees could be through consulting with employees, encouraging joint decisions, or delegating responsibilities. Regardless of the method, employees tend to be more creative and innovative when driven by leaders exhibiting this behavior.[20] Participative leadership is very popular in many technologically advanced countries. Such leadership has been widely espoused in the United States, England, and other Anglo countries, and it currently is very popular in Scandinavian countries as well. For example, at General Electric, managers are encouraged to use a participative style that delivers on commitment and shares the values of the firm. This approach is also common in those other nations. One way of characterizing participative leaders is in terms of the managerial grid, which is a traditional, well-known method of identifying leadership styles, as shown in Figure 13–2. Perspectives and preferences of where

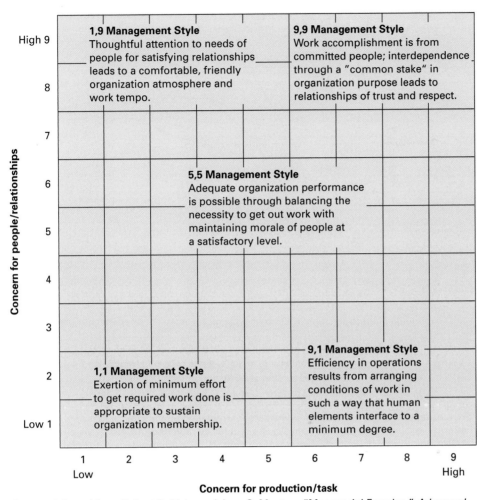

Figure 13–2

The Managerial Grid

Source: Adapted from Robert S. Blake and Jane S. Mouton, "Managerial Facades," *Advanced Management Journal,* July 1966, p. 31.

leaders perform on the grid can be influenced by culture. The next section explores this idea as a way to better illustrate the managerial grid.

The Managerial Grid Performance: A Japanese Perspective

The managerial grid is a useful visual to chart how leadership behaviors compare with one another. Participative leaders are on the 9,9 position of the grid. This is in contrast to paternalistic leaders, who tend to be about 9,5, and autocratic leaders, who are in more of a 9,1 position on the grid. How does this translate into practice, and how effective are these in motivating employees? One early but still relevant study examined the ways in which leadership style could be used to influence the achievement motivation of Japanese subjects.[21] Japanese participants were separated into eight subsets: four groups of high achievers and four groups of low achievers.

Leaders were then assigned to the groups. The first leader focused on performance (called "P supervision" in the study) and mirrored the autocratic style. There was a work-centered focus where subordinates were compared to other groups, and if they were behind, they were pressed to catch up. This correlates to point 9,1 on the grid (high on task, low on people). The second leadership style focused on maintaining and strengthening the group (called "M supervision" in the study). The individual used a 1,9 (low on task, high on people) leadership style on the managerial grid, and created a warm, friendly, sympathetic environment where tensions were reduced, interpersonal relationships strengthened, and suggestions welcomed.

Figure 13–3

Productivity of Japanese Groups with High-Achievement Motivation under Different Leadership Styles

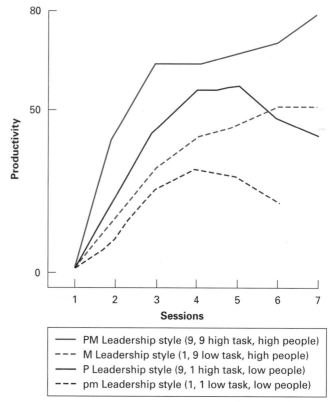

Legend:

——— PM Leadership style (9, 9 high task, high people)
- - - M Leadership style (1, 9 low task, high people)
——— P Leadership style (9, 1 high task, low people)
- - - pm Leadership style (1, 1 low task, low people)

Source: Reprinted from "Effects of Achievement Motivation on the Effectiveness of Leadership Patterns," by Jyuji Misumi and Fumiyasu Seki published in Volume 16, No. 1, March 1971 of *Administrative Science Quarterly*. Copyright © 1971 Johnson Graduate School of Management, Cornell University.

The third leader combined the first two methods into a performance-maintenance style (called "PM supervision" in the study). While pressure to complete tasks was prevalent, supervisors still offered encouragement and support. This style correlates with participative leadership, and is at point 9,9 on the managerial grid. Finally, the fourth leader exhibited more absenteeism, as the focus was neither on performance nor maintenance (called "pm supervision" in the study). This supervisor simply did not get very involved in either the task or the people side of the group being led. In other words, the supervisor used a 1,1 leadership style on the grid.

The results of these four leadership styles among the high-achieving and low-achieving groups are reported in Figures 13–3 and 13–4. In the high-achieving groups, the PM, or participative (9,9) style, was most effective across all phases. The P, or authoritarian (9,1—high on task, low on people), leadership style was second most effective during early and middle phases of the study, but later phases proved M supervision (1,9—low on task, high on people) to be more relevant, possibly suggesting that the more familiar the supervisor and subordinate become with one another, the more significant a personal relationship is over a task-focused objective. Finally, the pm (1,1) leadership style was consistently ineffective.

Among low-achieving groups, the P, or authoritarian (9,1), supervision was most effective. The M (1,9) leadership style was the second most effective during early sessions, but eventually led to negative results. The PM, or participative (9,9), style was moderately ineffective during the first three stages but improved rapidly and was the second most effective by the end of the seventh session. The pm (1,1) leadership style was consistently effective until the fifth session; then productivity began to level off.

So what does this all mean? One can infer from the results that if an individual is high-achieving, then he or she may be driven by intrinsic factors. This translates into being the most motivated when a creative and supportive environment is provided, as

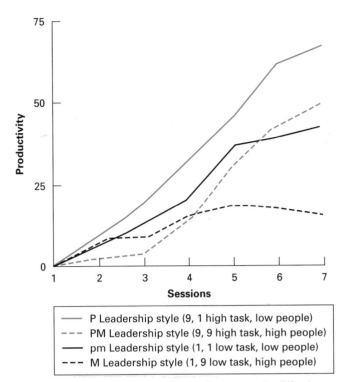

Figure 13–4

Productivity of Japanese Groups with Low-Achievement Motivation under Different Leadership Styles

——— P Leadership style (9, 1 high task, low people)
- - - PM Leadership style (9, 9 high task, high people)
——— pm Leadership style (1, 1 low task, low people)
- - - M Leadership style (1, 9 low task, high people)

Source: Reprinted from "Effects of Achievement Motivation on the Effectiveness of Leadership Patterns," by Jyuji Misumi and Fumiyasu Seki published in Volume 16, No. 1, March 1971 of *Administrative Science Quarterly.* Copyright © 1971 Johnson Graduate School of Management, Cornell University.

indicated by the success of the participative leadership style. This group preferred to be actively challenged, and became unproductive when faced with absentee leadership. On the other hand, low-achieving groups seemed to be driven by extrinsic factors, such as supervisor behavior toward subordinates. The success of the authoritarian style indicates that this group prefers to be told what to do, and a creative environment that encouraged participation was not a successful motivator until after the supervisors and subordinates were familiar with one another. This group tended to be more self-motivated, as absentee leadership initially resulted in satisfactory production, but this did not last throughout the study. This could be an indication that subordinates were active because of the uncertainty involved, but relaxed efforts when it was clear that supervisors would not intervene.

While results of this study were not specific as to what actually occurs in Japan, other studies from high-achieving societies have supported the findings. Korean firms, for example, are relying more heavily on 9,9, or participatory, leadership. Sang Lee and associates have reported that among Korea's largest firms, a series of personality criteria are used in screening employees, and many of these directly relate to 9,9 leadership: harmonious relationships with others, creativeness, motivation to achieve, future orientation, and a sense of duty.[22] These findings have great implication as to what it means to be a leader in different cultures. The next section looks at leadership in the international context in more detail.

■ Leadership in the International Context

How do leaders in other countries attempt to direct or influence their subordinates? Are their approaches similar to those used in the United States? Research shows that there are both similarities and differences. Most international research on leadership has focused on Europe, East Asia, the Middle East, and developing countries such as India, Peru, Chile, and Argentina.

Attitudes of European Managers Toward Leadership Practices

In recent years, much research has been directed at leadership approaches in Europe. Most effort has concentrated on related areas, such as decision making, risk taking, strategic planning, and organization design, that have been covered in previous chapters. Some of this previous discussion is relevant to an understanding of leadership practices in Europe. For example, British managers tend to use a highly participative leadership approach. This is true for two reasons: (1) The political background of the country favors such an approach. (2) Because most top British managers are not highly involved in the day-to-day affairs of the business, they prefer to delegate authority and let much of the decision making be handled by middle- and lower-level managers. This preference contrasts sharply with that of the French and the Germans,[23] who prefer a more work-centered, authoritarian approach. In fact, if labor unions did not have legally mandated seats on the boards of directors, participative management in Germany likely would be even less pervasive than it is, a problem that currently confronts firms like Volkswagen that are trying to reduce sharply their overhead to meet increasing competition in Europe.[24] Scandinavian countries, however, make wide use of participative leadership approaches, with worker representation on the boards of directors and high management-worker interaction regarding workplace design and changes.

As a general statement, most evidence indicates that European managers tend to use a participative approach. They do not entirely subscribe to Theory Y philosophical assumptions, however, because an element of Theory X thinking continues. This was made clear by the Haire, Ghiselli, and Porter study of 3,641 managers from 14 countries.[25] (The motivation-related findings of this study were reported in Chapter 12.) The leadership-related portion of this study sought to determine whether these managers were basically traditional (Theory X, or system 1/2) or democratic-participative (Theory Y, or system 3/4) in their approach. Specifically, the researchers investigated four areas relevant to leadership:

1. *Capacity for leadership and initiative.* Does the leader believe that employees prefer to be directed and have little ambition (Theory X), or does the leader believe that characteristics such as initiative can be acquired by most people regardless of their inborn traits and abilities (Theory Y)?

2. *Sharing information and objectives.* Does the leader believe that detailed, complete instructions should be given to subordinates and that subordinates need only this information to do their jobs, or does the leader believe that general directions are sufficient and that subordinates can use their initiative in working out the details?

3. *Participation.* Does the leader support participative leadership practices?

4. *Internal control.* Does the leader believe that the most effective way to control employees is through rewards and punishment or that employees respond best to internally generated control?

Overall Results of Research on Attitudes of European Managers

Responses by managers to the four areas covered in the Haire, Ghiselli, and Porter study, as noted in Chapter 12, are quite dated but remain the most comprehensive available and are relevant to the current discussion of leadership similarities and differences. The specifics by country may have changed somewhat over the years, but the leadership processes revealed should not be out of date. The clusters of countries studied by these researchers are shown in Table 13–3. Results indicate that none of the leaders from various parts of the world, on average, was very supportive of the belief that individuals have a capacity for leadership and initiative. The researchers put it this way: "In each country, in each group of countries, in all of the countries taken together, there is a relatively low opinion of the capabilities of the average person, coupled with a relatively positive belief in the necessity for democratic-type supervisory practices."[26]

> **Table 13–3**
> **Clusters of Countries in the Haire, Ghiselli, and Porter Study**
>
> NORDIC-EUROPEAN COUNTRIES
> Denmark
> Germany
> Norway
> Sweden
>
> LATIN-EUROPEAN COUNTRIES
> Belgium
> France
> Italy
> Spain
>
> ANGLO-AMERICAN COUNTRIES
> England
> United States
>
> DEVELOPING COUNTRIES
> Argentina
> Chile
> India
>
> JAPAN

An analysis of standard scores compared each cluster of countries against the others, and it revealed that Anglo leaders tend to have more faith in the capacity of their people for leadership and initiative than do the other clusters. They also believe that sharing information and objectives is important; however, when it comes to participation and internal control, the Anglo group tends to give relatively more autocratic responses than all the other clusters except developing countries. Interestingly, Anglo leaders reported a much stronger belief in the value of external rewards (pay, promotion, etc.) than did any of the clusters except that of the developing countries. These findings clearly illustrate that attitudes toward leadership practices tend to be quite different in various parts of the world.

The Role of Level, Size, and Age on European Managers' Attitudes Toward Leadership The research of Haire and associates provided important additional details within each cluster of European countries. These findings indicated that in some countries, higher-level managers tended to express more democratic values than lower-level managers; however, in other countries, the opposite was true. For example, in England, higher-level managers responded with more democratic attitudes on all four leadership dimensions, whereas in the United States, lower-level managers gave more democratically oriented responses on all four. In the Scandinavian countries, higher-level managers tended to respond more democratically; in Germany, lower-level managers tended to have more democratic attitudes.

Company size also tended to influence the degree of participative-autocratic attitudes. There was more support among managers in small firms than in large ones regarding the belief that individuals have a capacity for leadership and initiative; however, respondents from large firms were more supportive of sharing information and objectives, participation, and use of internal control.

There were findings that age also had some influence on participative attitudes. Younger managers were more likely to have democratic values when it came to capacity for leadership and initiative and to sharing information and objectives, although on the other two areas of leadership practices older and younger managers differed little. In specific countries, some important differences were found. For example, younger managers in both the United States and Sweden espoused more democratic values than did their older counterparts; in Belgium, the opposite was true.

Japanese Leadership Approaches

Japan is well known for its paternalistic approach to leadership. As noted in Figure 12–7, Japanese culture promotes a high safety or security need, which is present among home country–based employees as well as MNC expatriates. For example, one study examined the cultural orientations of 522 employees of 28 Japanese-owned firms in the United States and found that the native Japanese employees were more likely than their U.S. counterparts to value paternalistic company behavior.[27] Another study found that Koreans also value such paternalism.[28] However, major differences appear in leadership approaches used by the Japanese and those in other locales.

For example, the comprehensive Haire, Ghiselli, and Porter study found that Japanese managers have much greater belief in the capacity of subordinates for leadership and initiative than do managers in most other countries.[29] In fact, in the study, only managers in Anglo-American countries had stronger feelings in this area. The Japanese also expressed attitudes toward the use of participation to a greater degree than others. In the other two leadership areas, sharing information and objectives and using internal control, the Japanese respondents were above average but not distinctive. Overall, however, this study found that the Japanese respondents scored highest on the four areas of leadership combined. In other words, these findings provide evidence that Japanese leaders have considerable confidence in the overall ability of their subordinates and use a style that allows their people to actively participate in decisions.

In addition, the leadership process used by Japanese managers places a strong emphasis on ambiguous goals. Subordinates are typically unsure of what their manager wants them to do. As a result, they spend a great deal of time overpreparing their assignments. Some observers believe that this leadership approach is time-consuming and wasteful. However, it has a number of important benefits. One is that the leader is able to maintain stronger control of the followers because the latter do not know with certainty what is expected of them. So they prepare themselves for every eventuality. Second, by placing the subordinates in a position where they must examine a great deal of information, the manager ensures that the personnel are well prepared to deal with the situation and all its ramifications. Third, the approach helps the leader maintain order and provide guidance, even when the leader is not as knowledgeable as the followers.

Two experts on the behavior of Japanese management have noted that salarymen (middle managers) survive in the organization by anticipating contingencies and being prepared to deal with them. So when the manager asks a question and the salaryman shows that he has done the research needed to answer the question, the middle manager also shows himself to be a reliable person. The leader does not have to tell the salaryman to be prepared; the individual knows what is expected of him.

> Japanese managers operate this way because they usually have less expertise in a division's day-to-day business than their subordinates do. It is the manager's job to maintain harmony, not to be a technical expert. Consequently, a senior manager doesn't necessarily realize that E, F, G, and H are important to know. He gives ambiguous directions to his subordinates so they can use their superior expertise to go beyond A, B, C, and D. One salaryman explained it this way: "When my boss asks me to write a report, I infer what he wants to know and what he needs to know without being told what he wants." Another interviewee added that subordinates who receive high performance evaluations are those who know what the boss wants without needing to be told. What frustrates Japanese managers about non-Japanese employees is the feeling that, if they tell such a person they want A through D, they will never extract E through H; instead, they'll get exactly what they asked for. Inferring what the boss would have wanted had he only known to ask is a tough game, but it is the one salarymen must play.[30]

Differences Between Japanese and U.S. Leadership Styles

In a number of ways, Japanese leadership styles differ from those in the United States. For example, the Haire and associates study found that except for internal control, large U.S. firms tend to be more democratic than small ones, whereas in Japan, the profile is quite different.[31] A second difference is that younger U.S. managers appear to express more democratic attitudes than their older counterparts on all four leadership dimensions, but younger Japanese fall into this category only for sharing information and objectives

Table 13-4 Japanese vs. U.S. Leadership Styles		
Philosophical Dimension	**Japanese Approach**	**U.S. Approach**
Employment	Often for life; layoffs are rare	Usually short-term; layoffs are common
Evaluation and promotion	Very slow; big promotions may not come for the first 10 years	Very fast; those not quickly promoted often seek employment elsewhere
Career paths	Very general; people rotate from one area to another and become familiar with all areas of operations	Very specialized; people tend to stay in one area (accounting, sales, etc.) for their entire careers
Decision making	Carried out via group decision making	Carried out by the individual manager
Control mechanism	Very implicit and informal; people rely heavily on trust and goodwill	Very explicit; people know exactly what to control and how to do it
Responsibility	Shared collectively	Assigned to individuals
Concern for employees	Management's concern extends to the whole life, business and social, of the worker	Management concerned basically with the individual's work life only

Source: Adapted from William Ouchi, *Theory Z: How American Business Can Meet the Japanese Challenge* (Reading, MA: Addison-Wesley, 1981).

and in the use of internal control.[32] Simply put, evidence points to some similarities between U.S. and Japanese leadership styles, but major differences also exist.

A number of reasons have been cited for these differences. One of the most common is that Japanese and U.S. managers have a basically different philosophy of managing people. Table 13–4 provides a comparison of seven key characteristics that come from Ouchi's *Theory Z,* which combines Japanese and U.S. assumptions and approaches. Note in the table that the Japanese leadership approach is heavily group-oriented, paternalistic, and concerned with the employee's work and personal life. The U.S. leadership approach is almost the opposite.[33]

Another difference between Japanese and U.S. leadership styles is how senior-level managers process information and learn. Japanese executives are taught and tend to use **variety amplification,** which is the creation of uncertainty and the analysis of many alternatives regarding future action. By contrast, U.S. executives are taught and tend to use **variety reduction,** which is the limiting of uncertainty and the focusing of action on a limited number of alternatives.[34] Through acculturation, patterning, and mentoring, as well as formal training, U.S. managers tend to limit the scope of questions and issues before them, emphasize one or two central aspects of that topic, identity specific employees to respond to it, and focus on a goal or objective that is attainable. Japanese managers, in contrast, tend to be inclusive in their consideration of issues or problems, seek a large quantity of information to inform the problem, encourage all employees to engage in solutions, and aim for goals that are distant in the future.

Further, this research found that Japanese focused very heavily on problems, while the U.S. managers focused on opportunities.[35] The Japanese were more willing to allow poor performance to continue for a time so that those who were involved would learn from their mistakes, but the Americans worked to stop poor performance as quickly as possible. Finally, the Japanese sought creative approaches to managing projects and tried to avoid relying on experience, but the Americans sought to build on their experiences.

Still another major reason accounting for differences in leadership styles is that the Japanese tend to be more ethnocentric than their U.S. counterparts. The Japanese think of themselves as Japanese managers who are operating overseas; most do not view themselves as international managers. As a result, even if they do adapt their leadership approach on the surface to that of the country in which they are operating, they still believe in the Japanese way of doing things and are reluctant to abandon it.

variety amplification
The creation of uncertainty and the analysis of many alternatives regarding future action.

variety reduction
The limiting of uncertainty and the focusing of action on a limited number of alternatives.

Despite these differences, managerial practices indicate that there may be more similarities than once believed. For example, in the United States the Saturn has proved to be one of General Motors' most successful new auto offerings. The approach used in managing workers at the Saturn plant was quite different from that employed in other GM plants. Strong attention was given to allowing workers a voice in all management decisions, and pay is linked to quality, productivity, and profitability. Japanese firms such as Sony use a similar approach, encouraging personnel to assume authority, use initiative, and work as a team. Major emphasis also is given to developing communication links between management and the employees and to encouraging people to do their best.

Another common trend is the movement toward team orientation and away from individualism. "International Management in Action: Global Teams" illustrates this point.

Leadership in China

In the past few years a growing amount of attention has been focused on leadership in China. In particular, international researchers are interested in learning if the country's economic progress is creating a new cadre of leaders whose styles are different from the styles of leaders of the past. In one of the most comprehensive studies to date, Ralston and his colleagues found that, indeed, a new generation of Chinese leaders is emerging and they are somewhat different from past leaders in work values.[36]

The researchers gathered data from a large number of managers and professionals ($n = 869$) who were about to take part in management development programs. These individuals were part of what the researchers called the "New Generation" of Chinese organizational leaders. The researchers wanted to determine if this new generation of managers had the same work values as those of the "Current Generation" and "Older Generation" groups. In their investigation, the researchers focused their attention on the importance that the respondents assigned to three areas: individualism, collectivism, and Confucianism. Individualism was measured by the importance assigned to self-sufficiency and personal accomplishments. Collectivism was measured by the person's willingness to subordinate personal goals to those of the work group with an emphasis on sharing and group harmony. Confucianism was measured by the importance the respondent assigned to societal harmony, virtuous interpersonal behavior, and personal and interpersonal harmony.

The researchers found that the new generation group scored significantly higher on individualism than did the current and older generation groups. In addition, the new generation leaders scored significantly lower than the other two groups on collectivism and Confucianism. These values appear to reflect the period of relative openness and freedom, often called the "Social Reform Era," during which these new managers grew up. They have had greater exposure to Western societal influences, and this may well be resulting in leadership styles similar to those of Western managers.

These research findings show that leadership is culturally influenced, but as the economy of China continues to change and the country moves more and more toward capitalism, the work values of managers may also change, as illustrated in the *Business-Week* article that introduced this chapter. As a result, the new generation of leaders may well use leadership styles similar to those in the West, something that has also occurred in Japan as seen by Figures 13–3 and 13–4.

Leadership in the Middle East

Research also has been conducted on Middle East countries to determine the similarities and differences in managerial attitudes toward leadership practices. For example, in a follow-up study to that of Haire and associates, midlevel managers from Arab countries were surveyed and found to have higher attitude scores for capacity for leadership and initiative than those from any of the other countries or clusters reported in Table 13–3.[37]

Global Teams

Institutional productivity used to involve a cavalcade of employees manning factory floors, where meetings with international subsidiaries had to be carefully planned. As technology continues to evolve and the window for decision-making periods quickly closes, the need to instantly connect and coordinate with regional and transnational offices becomes imperative to stay competitive. But how is this implemented? International leaders now put increasing focus on developing global teams that are capable of overcoming cultural barriers and working together in an efficient, harmonious manner. At Dallas-based Maxus Energy (a wholly owned subsidiary of YPF, the largest Argentinean corporation in the world), teams consist of Americans, Dutch, British, and Indonesians who have been brought together to pursue a common goal: maximize oil and gas production. Capitalizing on the technical expertise of the members and their willingness to work together, the team helped the company to achieve its objective and add oil reserves to its stockpiles—an almost unprecedented achievement. This story is only one of many that help illustrate the way in which global teams are being created and used to achieve difficult international objectives.

In developing effective global teams, companies are finding there are four phases in the process. In phase one, the team members come together with their own expectations, culture, and values. In phase two, members go through a self-awareness period, during which they learn to respect the cultures of the other team members. Phase three is characterized by a developing trust among members, and in phase four, team members begin working in a collaborative way.

How are MNCs able to create the environment that is needed for this metamorphosis? Several specific steps are implemented by management, including:

1. The objectives of the group are carefully identified and communicated to the members.

2. Team members are carefully chosen so that the group has the necessary skills and personnel to reinforce and complement each other.

3. Each person learns what he or she is to contribute to the group, thus promoting a feeling of self-importance and interdependency.

4. Cultural differences between the members are discussed so that members can achieve a better understanding of how they may work together effectively.

5. Measurable outcomes are identified so that the team can chart its progress and determine how well it is doing. Management also continually stresses the team's purpose and its measurable outcomes so that the group does not lose sight of its goals.

6. Specially designed training programs are used to help the team members develop interpersonal, intercultural skills.

7. Lines of communication are spelled out so that everyone understands how to communicate with other members of the group.

8. Members are continually praised and rewarded for innovative ideas and actions.

MNCs now find that global teams are critical to their ability to compete successfully in the world market. As a result, leaders who are able to create and lead interdisciplinary, culturally diverse groups are finding themselves in increasing demand by MNCs.

The Arab managers' scores for sharing information and objectives, participation, and internal control, however, all were significantly lower than the scores of managers in the other countries and clusters reported in Table 13–3. The researcher concluded that the results were accounted for by the culture of the Middle East region. Table 13–5 summarizes not only the leadership differences between Middle Eastern and Western managers but also other areas of organization and management.

More recent research provides some evidence that there may be much greater similarity between Middle Eastern leadership styles and those of Western countries.[38] In particular, the observation was made that Western management practices are very evident in the Arabian Gulf region because of the close business ties between the West and this oil-rich area and the increasing educational attainment, often in Western universities, of Middle Eastern managers. A study on decision-making styles in the United Arab Emirates showed that organizational culture, level of technology, level of education, and management responsibility were good predictors of decision-making styles in such an environment.[39] These findings were consistent with similar studies in Western environments. Also,

Table 13–5
Differences in Middle Eastern and Western Management

Management Dimensions	Middle Eastern Management	Western Management
Leadership	Highly authoritarian tone, rigid instructions. Too many management directives.	Less emphasis on leader's personality, considerable weight on leader's style and performance.
Organizational structures	Highly bureaucratic, overcentralized, with power and authority at the top. Vague relationships. Ambiguous and unpredictable organization environments.	Less bureaucratic, more delegation of authority. Relatively decentralized structure.
Decision making	Ad hoc planning, decisions made at the highest level of management. Unwillingness to take high risk inherent in decision making.	Sophisticated planning techniques, modern tools of decision making, elaborate management information systems.
Performance evaluation and control	Informal control mechanisms, routine checks on performance. Lack of vigorous performance evaluation systems.	Fairly advanced control systems focusing on cost reduction and organizational effectiveness.
Personnel policies	Heavy reliance on personal contacts and getting individuals from the "right social origin" to fill major positions.	Sound personnel management policies. Candidates' qualifications are usually the basis for selection decisions.
Communication	The tone depends on the communicants. Social position, power, and family influence are ever-present factors. Chain of command must be followed rigidly. People relate to each other tightly and specifically. Friendships are intense and binding.	Stress usually on equality and a minimization of difference. People relate to each other loosely and generally. Friendships not intense and binding.

Source: From M. K. Badawy, "Styles of Mid-Eastern Managers," *California Management Review*, Spring 1980. Copyright © 1980, by The Regents of the University of California. Reprinted from the California Management review, Vol. 22, No. 3. By permission of The Regents. All rights reserved. This article is for personal viewing by individuals accessing this site. It is not to be copied, reproduced, or otherwise disseminated without written permission from the California Management Review. By viewing this document, you hereby agree to these terms. For permission or reprints, contact: cmr@haas.berkeley.edu.

results indicated a tendency toward participative leadership styles among young Arab middle management, as well as among highly educated managers of all ages.[40]

One study focused on Iran in particular and evaluated not only the preferred leadership style but also the motivating factors that led to worker satisfaction (see Chapter 12) across multiple levels of employment in health care organizations.[41] Results correlated with previous studies in Middle Eastern countries, specifically that the predominant leadership style was participative. Employees reported job satisfaction across a spectrum from "very low" to "high," but the factors which led to these opinions were consistent across the board. That is to say, workers in Iran considered salaries, benefits, working conditions, promotion, and communication as secondary factors leading to satisfaction. Instead, the primary motivators were the nature of the job, co-workers, and supervisory styles. Overall, the study showed that there was a correlation between leadership behaviors and job satisfaction, with higher satisfaction resulting from a participatory environment.

Leadership Approaches in India

India is developing at a rapid rate as MNCs increase investment. India's workforce is quite knowledgeable in the high-tech industry, and society as a whole is moving toward higher education. However, transitions have not allowed sufficient time to pass, and India is still bound by old traditions. This raises the question, What kind of leadership style does India need to satisfy its traditional roots with a high-tech future? One study showed that Indian workers were more productive when managers took a high people and high task approach (participative). Meanwhile, the less productive workers were managed by individuals who showed high people orientation, but low focus on task-related objectives.[42] These findings may indicate that it is important in India to focus on the individual, but in order to be efficient and produce results, managers need to maintain awareness of the tasks that need to be completed.

Because of India's long affiliation with Great Britain, leadership styles in India would seem more likely to be participative than those in the Middle East or in other developing countries. Haire and associates found some degree of similarity between leadership styles in India and Anglo-American countries, but it was not significant. The study found Indians to be similar to the Anglo-Americans in managerial attitudes toward capacity for leadership and initiative, participation, and internal control. The difference is in sharing information and objectives. The Indian managers' responses tended to be quite similar to those of managers in other developing countries.[43]

Other research that focused more on Indian industrial firms indicates that the most effective leadership style used by Indian managers often is a more participative one. One study, for example, found that the job satisfaction of Indian employees increases as leadership style becomes more participative.[44]

These findings from India show that a participative leadership style may be more common and more effective in developing countries than has been reported previously. Over time, developing countries (as also shown in the case of the Persian Gulf nations) may be moving toward a more participative leadership style.

Leadership Approaches in Latin America

Research pertaining to leadership styles in Latin America have indicated that as globalization increases, so does the transitional nature of managers within these regions. One study that compared Latin American leadership styles reviewed past research indicating an initial universality among the countries.[45] In Mexico, leaders tended to have a combination of authoritarian and participative behaviors, while Chile, Argentina, and Bolivia also showed signs of authoritarian behaviors. Typically, Mexican managers who welcomed input from subordinates were viewed as incompetent and weak. This may be the reason that in Mexico, as well as in Chile, managers tend to be socially distant from those working below them. Romero found that Mexican managers who worked close to the U.S. border, however, exhibited even more participative behavior, and that trend enhanced as globalization increased.[46] Overall, the study found that Mexico is moving toward a modern leader style, while other Latin American countries continue to lead based on tradition. However, this is not the only viewpoint.

Haire and associates originally found quite different results for Chile and Argentina, and one can only assume that Peru would be similar to the aforementioned countries due to their geographic and cultural similarities. The results from the Haire and associates study for those two developing countries were similar to those for India.[47] Additional research, however, has found that leadership styles in Peru may be much closer to those in the United States than was previously assumed.

Stephens conducted research among three large textile plants in an urban area in Peru.[48] These three Peruvian plants were matched with three U.S. plants of similar size in urban settings in the southwest United States. Because these Peruvian and U.S. firms all were in the same industry and faced similar competitive pressures, this study was an excellent opportunity to compare intercultural leadership profiles and identify any significant differences. Using the same four dimensions of leadership practice that were used in the Haire and associates study, Stephens found that the leadership profiles of the Peruvian and U.S. managers were similar. Commenting on the results, he noted that:

> There is little reason to conclude that leader styles are much different in Peru than in the U.S. Absolutely, U.S. leaders appear to perceive workers as having more initiative, being more internally motivated, and therefore more capable of meaningful participation. However, the differences for initiative and locus of control were not statistically significant and differences

for sharing of information and objectives showed Peruvians to be statistically more inclined to share than U.S. managers. Taken in total, this does not suggest a more participative, democratic leader style in the U.S. and an authoritarian, external control oriented style in Peru.[49]

As in the case of Middle Eastern managers, these findings in South America indicate there indeed may be more similarities in international leadership styles than previously assumed. As countries become more economically advanced, participative styles may well gain in importance. Of course, this does not mean that MNCs can use the same leadership styles in their various locations around the world. There still must be careful contingency application of leadership styles (different styles for different situations); however, many of the more enlightened participative leadership styles used in the United States and other economically advanced countries, such as Japan, also may have value in managing international operations even in developing countries as well as in the emerging Eastern European countries.

■ Recent Findings and Insights About Leadership

In recent years researchers have begun raising the question of universality of leadership behavior. Do effective leaders, regardless of their country culture or job, act similarly? A second, and somewhat linked, research inquiry has focused on the question, Are there a host of specific behaviors, attitudes, and values that leaders in the 21st century will need in order to be successful? Thus far the findings have been mixed. Some investigators have found that there is a trend toward universalism for leadership; others have concluded that culture continues to be a determining factor and that an effective leader, for example, in Sweden will not be as effective in Italy if he or she employs the same approach, most likely due to motivational factors being different (see Chapter 12). One of the most interesting recent efforts has been conducted by Bass and his associates and has focused on the universality and effectiveness of both transformation and transactional leadership.

Transformational, Transactional, and Charismatic Leadership

transformational leaders
Leaders who are visionary agents with a sense of mission and who are capable of motivating their followers to accept new goals and new ways of doing things.

charismatic leaders
Leaders who inspire and motivate employees through their charismatic traits and abilities.

transactional leaders
Individuals who exchange rewards for effort and performance and work on a "something for something" basis.

Transformational leaders are visionary agents with a sense of mission who are capable of motivating their followers to accept new goals and new ways of doing things. One recent variant on transformational leadership focuses on the individual's charismatic traits and abilities. This research stream, known as the study of **charismatic leaders,** has explored how the individual abilities of an executive work to inspire and motivate her or his subordinates.[50] **Transactional leaders** are individuals who exchange rewards for effort and performance and work on a "something for something" basis.[51] Do these types of leaders exist worldwide, and is their effectiveness consistent in terms of performance? Drawing on an analysis of studies conducted in Canada, India, Italy, Japan, New Zealand, Singapore, and Sweden, as well as in the United States, Bass discovered that very little of the variance in leadership behavior could be attributed to culture. In fact, in many cases he found that national differences accounted for less than 10 percent of the results. This led him to create a model of leadership and conclude that "although this model . . . may require adjustments and fine-tuning as we move across cultures, particularly into non-Western cultures, overall, it holds up as having considerable universal potential."[52]

Simply stated, Bass discovered that there was far more universalism in leadership than had been believed previously. Additionally, after studying thousands of international cases, he found that the most effective managers were transformational leaders and they were characterized by four interrelated factors. For convenience, the factors are referred to as the "4 I's," and they can be described this way:

1. *Idealized influence.* Transformational leaders are a source of charisma and enjoy the admiration of their followers. They enhance pride, loyalty, and

confidence in their people, and they align these followers by providing a common purpose or vision that the latter willingly accept.

2. *Inspirational motivation.* These leaders are extremely effective in articulating their vision, mission, and beliefs in clear-cut ways, thus providing an easy-to-understand sense of purpose regarding what needs to be done.

3. *Intellectual stimulation.* Transformational leaders are able to get their followers to question old paradigms and to accept new views of the world regarding how things now need to be done.

4. *Individualized consideration.* These leaders are able to diagnose and elevate the needs of each of their followers through individualized consideration, thus furthering the development of these people.[53]

Bass also discovered that there were four other types of leaders. All of these are less effective than the transformational leader, although the degree of their effectiveness (or ineffectiveness) will vary. The most effective of the remaining four types was labeled the *contingent reward (CR) leader* by Bass. This leader clarifies what needs to be done and provides both psychic and material rewards to those who comply with his or her directives. The next most effective manager is the *active management-by-exception (MBE-A) leader.* This individual monitors follower performance and takes corrective action when deviations from standards occur. The next manager in terms of effectiveness is the *passive management-by-exception (MBE-P) leader.* This leader takes action or intervenes in situations only when standards are not met. Finally, there is the *laissez-faire (LF) leader.* This person avoids intervening or accepting responsibility for follower actions.

Bass found that through the use of higher-order factor analysis it is possible to develop a leadership model that illustrates the effectiveness of all five types of leaders: I's (transformational), CR, MBE-A, MBE-P, and LF. Figure 13–5 presents this model. The higher the box in the figure and the farther to the right on the shaded base area, the more effective and active is the leader. Notice that the 4 I's box is taller than any of the others in the figure and is located more to the right than any of the others. The CR box

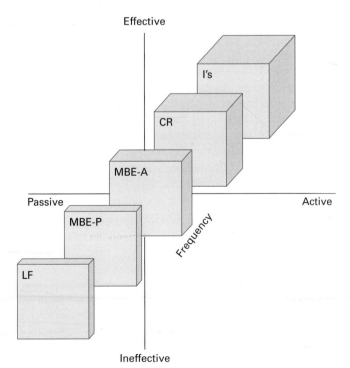

Figure 13–5

An Optimal Profile of Universal Leadership Behaviors

Source: Adapted from Bernard M. Bass, "Is There Universality in the Full Range Model of Leadership?" *International Journal of Public Administration* 16, no. 6 (1996), p. 738.

is second tallest and second closest to the right, on down to the LF box, which is the shortest and farthest from the right margin.

Bass also found that the 4 I's were positively correlated with each other, but less so with contingent reward. Moreover, there was a near zero correlation between the 4 I's and management-by-exception styles, and there was an inverse correlation between these four factors and the laissez-faire leadership style.

Does this mean that effective leader behaviors are the same regardless of country? Bass concluded that this statement is not quite true—but there is far more universalism than people believed previously. In putting his findings in perspective, he concluded that there certainly would be differences in leadership behavior from country to country.[54] For example, he noted that transformational leaders in Honduras would have to be more directive than their counterparts in Norway. Moreover, culture can create some problems in using universal leadership concepts in countries such as Japan, where the use of contingent reward systems is not as widespread as in the West. These reward systems can also become meaningless in Arab and Turkish cultures where there is a strong belief that things will happen "if God wills" and not because a leader has decided to carry them out. Yet even after taking these differences into consideration, Bass contends that universal leadership behavior is far more common than many people realize.[55]

> I cannot and do not want to dismiss the evidence of systematic differences in beliefs, values, implicit theories, traits associated with leadership, decision styles, paternalism, trait and institutional historical and legal differences that shape leader-subordinate relations. Nevertheless, although the model of transformational or transactional leadership may have needs for adjustments and fine-tuning as we move across cultures, particularly into non-Western, overall, it holds up as having a lot of universal potential. Generally speaking, transformation leadership is more effective than managing-by-exception and managing-by-exception is more effective than laissez-faire leadership. Secondly, transformation leadership augments transactional leadership, it does not replace it. Thirdly, the ideals and implicit leadership theories of leadership people carry around in their heads are more transformational than transactional.[56]

Qualities for Successful Leaders

Another recent research approach that has been used to address the issue of international leadership is that of examining the characteristics that companies are looking for in their new executive hires. Are all firms seeking the same types of behaviors or qualities or, for example, are companies in Sweden looking for executives with qualities that are quite different from those being sought by Italian firms? The answer to this type of question can help shed light on international leadership because it helps focus attention on the behaviors that organizations believe are important in their managerial workforce. It also helps examine the impact, if any, of culture on leadership style.

Tollgerdt-Andersson examined thousands of advertisements for executives in the European Union (EU). She began by studying ads in Swedish newspapers and journals, noting the qualities, characteristics, and behaviors that were being sought. She then expanded her focus to publications in other European countries including Denmark, Norway, Germany, Great Britain, France, Italy, and Spain. The results are reported in Table 13–6. Based on this analysis, she concluded:

> Generally, there seem to be great differences between the European countries regarding their leadership requirements. Different characteristics are stressed in the various countries. There are also differences concerning how frequently various characteristics are demanded in each country. Some kind of personal or social quality is mentioned much more often in the Scandinavian countries than in the other European countries. In the Scandinavian advertisements, you often see many qualities mentioned in a single advertisement. This can be seen in other European countries too, but it is much more rare. Generally, the characteristics mentioned in a single advertisement do not exceed three and fairly often, especially in Mediterranean countries (in 46–48% of the advertisements) no personal or social characteristics are mentioned at all.[57]

Table 13–6
Qualities Most Demanded in Advertisements for European Executives

Quality	Sweden (n = 225)	Denmark (n = 175)	Norway (n = 173)	Germany (n = 190)
Ability to cooperate (interpersonal ability)	25	42	32	16
Independence	22	22	25	9
Leadership ability	22		16	17
Ability to take initiatives	22	12	16	
Aim and result orientation	19	10	42	
Ability to motivate and inspire others	16	11		
Business orientation	12			
Age	10	25		13
Extrovert personality/contact ability	10	8	12	11
Creativity	9	10	9	9
Customer ability	9			
Analytic ability		10		
Ability to communicate		12	15	
High level of energy/drive			12	
Enthusiasm and involvement			14	14
Organization skills				7
Team builder				
Self-motivated				
Flexibility				
Precision				
Dynamic personality				
Responsibility				

Quality	Great Britain (n = 163)	France (n = 164)	Italy (n = 132)	Spain (n = 182)
Ability to cooperate (interpersonal ability)	7	9	32	18
Independence			16	4
Leadership ability	10		22	16
Ability to take initiatives			10	8
Aim and result orientation	5			2
Ability to motivate and inspire others		9	26	20
Business orientation				8
Age		12	46	34
Extrovert personality/contact ability				
Creativity	5			4
Customer ability				2
Analytic ability			10	
Ability to communicate	23			8
High level of energy/drive	8			20
Enthusiasm and involvement				
Organization skills		6	12	12
Team builder	10	5		
Self-motivated	10			
Flexibility				2
Precision		7		
Dynamic personality		6		6
Responsibility				10

Note: The qualities most demanded in Swedish, Danish, Norwegian, German, British, French, Italian, and Spanish advertisements for executives are expressed in percentage terms. n = total number of advertisements analyzed in each country. Each entry represents the percentage of the total advertisements requesting each quality.

Source: Adapted from Ingrid Tollgerdt-Andersson, "Attitudes, Values and Demands on Leadership—A Cultural Comparison Among Some European Countries," in *Managing Across Cultures,* ed. Pat Joynt and Malcolm Warner (London: International Thomson Business Press, 1996), p. 173.

At the same time, Tollgerdt-Andersson did find that there were similarities between nations. For example, Italy and Spain had common patterns regarding desirable leadership characteristics. Between 52 and 54 percent of the ads she reviewed in these two countries stated specific personal and social abilities that were needed by the job applicant. The same pattern was true for Germany and Great Britain, where between 64 and 68 percent of the advertisements set forth the personal and social abilities required for the job. In the Scandinavian countries these percentages ranged between 80 and 85.

Admittedly, it may be difficult to determine the degree of similarity between ads in different countries (or cultural clusters) because there may be implied meanings in the messages or it may be the custom in a country not to mention certain abilities but simply to assume that applicants know that these will be assessed in making the final hiring decision. Additionally, Tollgerdt-Andersson did find that all countries expected executive applicants to have good social and personal qualities. So some degree of universalism in leadership behaviors was uncovered. On the other hand, the requirements differed from country to country, showing that effective leaders in northern Europe may not be able to transfer their skills to the southern part of the continent with equal results. This led Tollgerdt-Andersson to conclude that multicultural understanding will continue to be a requirement for effective leadership in the 21st century. She put it this way: "If tomorrow's leaders possess international competence and understanding of other cultures it will, hopefully, result in the increased competitive cooperation which is essential if European commerce and industry is to compete with, for example, the USA and Asia."[58]

Culture Clusters and Leader Effectiveness

Although the foregoing discussion indicates there is research to support universalism in leadership behavior, recent findings also show that effective leader behaviors tend to vary by cultural cluster. Brodbeck and his associates conducted a large survey of middle managers ($n = 6,052$) from 22 European countries.[59] The respondents were given 112 questionnaire items containing descriptions of leadership traits and behaviors. For each attribute the respondents were asked to rate how well it fit their concept of an outstanding business leader. Some of the results, grouped by cluster, are presented in Table 13–7. A close look at the data shows that while there are similarities between some of the cultures, none of the lists of leadership attributes is identical. For example, managers in the Anglo cluster reported that the five most important attributes of an effective manager were a performance orientation, an inspirational style, having a vision, being a team integrator, and being decisive. Managers in the Nordic culture ranked these same five attributes as the most important but not in this order. Moreover, although the rankings of clusters in the North/West European region were fairly similar, they were quite different from those in the South/East European region, which included the Latin cluster, countries from Eastern Europe that were grouped by the researchers into a Central cluster and a Near East cluster, and Russia and Georgia, which were listed separately.

Leader Behavior, Leader Effectiveness, and Leading Teams

Culture is also important in helping explain how leaders ought to act in order to be effective. A good example is provided by the difference in effective behaviors in Trompenaars's categories (covered in Chapter 4) of affective (or emotional) cultures and neutral cultures. In affective cultures, such as the United States, leaders tend to exhibit their emotions. In neutral cultures, such as Japan and China, leaders do not tend to show their emotions. Moreover, in some cultures people are taught to exhibit their emotions but not let emotion affect their making rational decisions, while in other cultures the two are intertwined. Trompenaars explains it this way:

Table 13–7
Rankings of the Most Important Leadership Attributes by Region and Country Cluster

North/West European Region

Anglo Culture (Great Britain, Ireland)	Nordic Culture (Sweden, Netherlands, Finland, Denmark)	Germanic Culture (Switzerland, Germany, Austria)	Czech Republic	France
Performance-oriented	Integrity	Integrity	Integrity	Participative
Inspirational	Inspirational	Inspirational	Performance-oriented	Nonautocratic
Visionary	Visionary	Performance-oriented	Administratively skilled	
Team integrator	Team integrator	Nonautocratic	Inspirational	
Decisive	Performance-oriented	Visionary	Nonautocratic	

South/East European Region

Latin Culture (Italy, Spain, Portugal, Hungary)	Central Culture (Poland, Slovenia)	Near East Culture (Turkey, Greece)	Russia	Georgia
Team integrator	Team integrator	Team integrator	Visionary	Administratively skilled
Performance-oriented	Visionary	Decisive	Administratively skilled	Decisive
Inspirational	Administratively skilled	Visionary	Inspirational	Performance-oriented
Integrity	Diplomatic	Integrity	Decisive	Visionary
Visionary	Decisive	Inspirational	Integrity	Integrity

Source: Adapted from Felix C. Brodbeck et al., "Cultural Variation of Leadership Prototypes Across 22 European Countries," *Journal of Occupational and Organizational Psychology* 73 (2000), p. 15.

Americans tend to exhibit emotion, yet separate it from "objective" and "rational" decisions. Italians and south European nations in general tend to exhibit and not separate. Dutch and Swedes tend not to exhibit and to separate . . . there is nothing "good" or "bad" about these differences. You can argue that emotions held in check will twist your judgments despite all efforts to be "rational." Or you can argue that pouring forth emotions makes it harder for anyone present to think straight. Similarly, you can scoff at the "walls" separating reasons from emotions, or argue that because of the leakage that so often occurs, these should be thicker and stronger.[60]

Researchers have also found that the way in which managers speak to their people can influence the outcome. For example, in Anglo-Saxon cultures it is common for managers to raise their voice in order to emphasize a point. In Asian cultures managers generally speak at the same level throughout their communication, using a form of self-control that shows respect for the other person. Latin managers, meanwhile, vary their tone of voice continually, and this form of exaggeration is viewed by them as showing that they are very interested in what they are saying and committed to their point of view. Knowing how to communicate can greatly influence leadership across cultures. Here is an example:

A British manager posted to Nigeria found that it was very effective to raise his voice for important issues. His Nigerian subordinates viewed that unexpected explosion by a normally self-controlled manager as a sign of extra concern. After success in Nigeria he was posted to Malaysia. Shouting there was a sign of loss of face; his colleagues did not take him seriously and he was transferred.[61]

One of the keys to successful global leadership is knowing what style and behavior works best in a given culture and adapting appropriately. In the case of affective and neutral cultures, for example, Trompenaars and Hampden-Turner have offered the specific tips provided in Table 13–8.

Table 13–8
Leadership Tips for Doing Business in Affective and Neutral Cultures

When Managing or Being Managed in . . .

Affective Cultures	Neutral Cultures
Avoid a detached, ambiguous, and cool demeanor because this will be interpreted as negative behavior.	Avoid warm, excessive, or enthusiastic behaviors because these will be interpreted as a lack of personal control over one's feelings and be viewed as inconsistent with one's high status.
Find out whose work and enthusiasm are being directed into which projects, so you are able to appreciate the vigor and commitment they have for these efforts.	Extensively prepare the things you have to do and then stick tenaciously to the issues.
Let people be emotional without personally becoming intimidated or coerced by their behavior.	Look for cues regarding whether people are pleased or angry and then amplify their importance.

When Doing Business with Individuals in . . .

Affective Cultures (for Those from Neutral Cultures)	Neutral Cultures (for Those from Affective Cultures)
Do not be put off stride when others create scenes and get histrionic; take time-outs for sober reflection and hard assessments.	Ask for time-outs from meetings and negotiations where you can patch each other up and rest between games of poker with the "impassive ones."
When others are expressing goodwill, respond warmly.	Put down as much as you can on paper before beginning the negotiation.
Remember that the other person's enthusiasm and readiness to agree or disagree do not mean that the individual has made up his or her mind.	Remember that the other person's lack of emotional tone does not mean that the individual is uninterested or bored, only that the person does not like to show his or her hand.
Keep in mind that the entire negotiation is typically focused on you as a person and not so much on the object or proposition that is being discussed.	Keep in mind that the entire negotiation is typically focused on the object or proposition that is being discussed and not on you as a person.

Recognize the Way in Which People Behave in . . .

Affective Cultures	Neutral Cultures
They reveal their thoughts and feelings both verbally and nonverbally.	They often do not reveal what they are thinking or feeling.
Emotions flow easily, vehemently, and without inhibition.	Emotions are often dammed up, although they may occasionally explode.
Heated, vital, and animated expressions are admired.	Cool and self-possessed conduct is admired.
Touching, gesturing, and strong facial expressions are common.	Physical contact, gesturing, or strong facial expressions are not used.
Statements are made fluently and dramatically.	Statements are often read out in a monotone voice.

Source: Adapted from Fons Trompenaars and Charles Hampden-Turner, *Riding the Waves of Culture: Understanding Diversity in Global Business,* 2nd ed. (New York: McGraw-Hill, 1998), pp. 80–82.

Cross-Cultural Leadership: Insights from the GLOBE Study

As discussed in Chapter 4, the GLOBE (Global Leadership and Organizational Behavior Effectiveness) research program, a 15-year, multimethod, multiphase research program, is examining the relationships among societal and organizational culture, societal and organizational effectiveness, and leadership. In addition to the identification of nine major dimensions of culture described in Chapter 4, the GLOBE program also includes the classification of six global leadership behaviors. Through a qualitative and quantitative analysis of leadership, GLOBE researchers determined that leadership behaviors can be summarized into six broad categories: Charismatic/Value-Based, Team-Oriented, Participative, Humane-Oriented, Autonomous, and Self-Protective. As is the case in the classification of culture dimensions, these categories build on and extend earlier classifications of leadership styles described earlier in this chapter.

Charismatic/Value-Based leadership captures the ability of leaders to inspire, motivate, and encourage high performance outcomes from others based on a foundation of core values. Team-Oriented leadership places emphasis on effective team building and implementation of a common goal among team members. Participative leadership reflects the extent to which leaders involve others in decisions and their implementation. Humane-Oriented leadership comprises supportive and considerate leadership. Autonomous leadership refers to independent and individualistic leadership behaviors. Self-Protective leadership "focuses on ensuring the safety and security of the individual and group through status-enhancement and face-saving."[62]

The GLOBE study, like earlier research, found that certain attributes of leadership were universally endorsed, while others were viewed as effective only in certain cultures. Among the leadership attributes found to be effective across cultures are being trustworthy, just, and honest (having integrity); having foresight and planning ahead; being positive, dynamic, encouraging, and motivating and building confidence; and being communicative and informed and being a coordinator and a team integrator.[63]

In linking the cultural dimensions of the GLOBE study with the leadership styles described above, the GLOBE researchers investigated the association between cultural values and leadership attributes, and cultural practices and leadership attributes. With regard to the relationship between cultural values and leadership attributes, the GLOBE researchers concluded the following:

- Collectivism I values, as found in Sweden and other Nordic and Scandinavian countries, were likely to view Participative and Self-Protective leadership behaviors favorably while viewing Autonomous leadership behaviors negatively.[64]

- In-Group Collectivism II values, as found in societies such as the Philippines and other East Asian countries, were positively related to Charismatic/Value-Based leadership and Team-Oriented leadership.[65]

- Gender Egalitarian values, as found in countries such as Hungary, Russia, and Poland, were positively associated with Participative and Charismatic/Value-Based leader attributes.[66]

- Performance Orientation values, as found in countries such as Switzerland, Singapore, and Hong Kong, were positively associated with Participative and Charismatic/Value-Based leader attributes.[67]

- Future Orientation values, as found in societies such as Singapore, were positively associated with Self-Protective and Humane-Oriented leader attributes.[68]

- Societal Uncertainty Avoidance values, as found in Germany, Denmark, and China, were positively associated with Team-Oriented, Humane-Oriented, and Self-Protective leader attributes.[69]

- Societal Humane Orientation values, as found in countries such as Zambia, the Philippines, and Ireland, were positively associated with Participative leader attributes.[70]

- Societal Assertiveness values, as found in countries such as the United States, Germany, and Austria, were positively associated with Humane-Oriented leader attributes.[71]

- Societal Power Distance values, as found in countries such as Morocco, Nigeria, and Argentina, were positively correlated with Self-Protective and Humane-Oriented leader attributes.[72]

One of the most influential and possibly universal leadership attributes is future orientation. An extension of the GLOBE project compared the future orientation of select countries, and surprisingly found that "the greater a society's future orientation, the higher its average GDP per capita and its levels of innovativeness, happiness, confidence, and . . . competitiveness."[73] Figure 13–6 illustrates the findings. As shown, Singapore is

Figure 13–6 **Cross-Country Comparison: Future Orientation and Competitiveness**	**Competitive Countries Have an Eye on the Future**

Future Orientation
(cultural support for delayed gratification, planning, and investment)

Source: Reprinted by permission of *Harvard Business Review* from "Forward Thinking Cultures" by Mansour Javidan, July–August 2007, p. 20. Copyright © 2007 by the Harvard Business School Publishing Corporation; all rights reserved.

the most future-oriented country, while Slovenia is the most competitive. Other extremely competitive cultures include Switzerland, the Netherlands, and Malaysia. Conversely, Russia, Argentina, Poland, and Hungary were the least future-oriented, with Germany, Taiwan, Korea, and Ireland posed somewhere in between.

In summarizing the GLOBE findings, researchers suggest that cultural values influence leadership preferences. Specifically, societies that share particular values prefer leadership attributes or styles that are congruent with or supportive of those values, with some exceptions. The studies also resulted in some unexpected findings. For example, societies that valued assertiveness were positively correlated with valuing Humane-Oriented leadership. According to one interpretation, some of these contradictions may reflect desires by societies to make up for or mitigate some aspects of cultural values with seemingly opposing leadership attributes. In the case of societies that value assertiveness, a preference for Humane-Oriented leader attributes may reflect a desire to provide a social support structure in an environment characterized by high competition.[74]

Positive Organizational Scholarship and Leadership

positive organizational scholarship (POS)
A method that focuses on positive outcomes, processes, and attributes of organizations and their members.

Positive organizational scholarship (POS) focuses on positive outcomes, processes, and attributes of organizations and their members.[75] This is a dynamic view that factors in fundamental concerns, but ultimately emphasizes positive human potential, something of obvious relevance as MNCs are increasingly called upon to make contributions to society beyond the bottom line. It consists of three subunits: *enablers, motivations,* and *outcomes or effects.* Enablers could be capabilities, processes or methods, and structure of the environment, which are all external factors. Motivations focus inward, and are categorized as unselfish, altruistic, or as having the ability to contribute without self-regard. Finally, the outcomes or effects in this model accentuate vitality, meaningfulness, exhilaration, and high-quality relationships.[76]

The way POS relates to leadership is encompassed in the name. POS recognizes the *positive* potential that people have within. Constructive behavior will yield desired outcomes, in the sense that those who are able to create meaning in actions and are relatively flexible will be more successful in receiving praise and creating lasting relationships. These are characteristics that could be attributed to leaders, as future vision and relating to employees are positive driving forces that encourage leadership progress. Next, this method outlines positive *organizational* actions. For instance, if a firm is doing financially well due to actions such as downsizing, POS would accentuate the revenue and its potentials, instead of harping on the negative side effects of such a deed. As indicated earlier in the chapter, leaders tend to reward for good things, and deemphasize the general tendency to motivate through pointing out issues. Finally, by accepting a method such as POS, it is implied that there is commitment to every step involved in *scholarship*. In other words, a portion of any whole is not sufficient to reach goals and standards, and devotion or passion to the cause is necessary to form a cohesive vision.

Effective leaders seem to live by the POS model, as they are constantly innovating, creating relationships, striving to bring the organization to new heights, and ultimately working for the greater global good through self-improvement. While positive internal and external factors provide a general framework for what makes a leader, how does one know that the person in power is a true leader?

Authentic Leadership

What makes a leader "authentic"? Researchers have sought to explain what makes a leader authentic and why leaders are important to today's organizations.

As indicated throughout the chapter, leaders tend to be dynamic, forward-thinking, and pioneers on setting new standards. Therefore, individuals who are stagnant or meet the status quo without reaching for higher realms could be considered ineffectual, or inauthentic, leaders. Just as with positive organizational scholarship, authentic leadership accentuates the positive. Authentic leaders are defined by an all-encompassing package which includes elements such as traits, styles, behaviors, and credits.[77] Many interpretations exist as to what makes a leader authentic. For example, authentic leaders could be defined as "those who are deeply aware of how they think and behave and are perceived by others as being aware of their own and others' values/moral perspectives, knowledge, and strengths; aware of the context in which they operate; and who are confident, hopeful, optimistic, resilient, and of high moral character."[78] An interpretation by Shamir and Eilam suggested that authentic leaders have four distinct characteristics: (1) authentic leaders do not fake their actions; they are true to themselves and do not adhere to external expectations; (2) authentic leaders are driven from internal forces, not external rewards; (3) authentic leaders are unique and guide based on personal beliefs, not others' orders; and (4) authentic leaders act based on individual passion and values.[79] However, the authors did not accentuate personal moral drive, which is considered to be of great importance to the authentic leader.

Authentic leaders must possess several interrelated qualities. First, they must have positive psychological aspects, such as confidence and optimism. Next, leaders should have positive morals to guide them through processes. However, these aspects are not effective unless the leader is self-aware, as it is essential for leaders to be cognizant of their duties and be true to themselves. This also means that leaders should periodically check their actions and make sure they are congruous with ultimate goals, and that they do not stray from internal standards or expected outcomes. Authentic leaders are expected to lead by example, and therefore their processes and behaviors should be virtuous and reflect the positive moral values inherent in the leader. However, a leader cannot exist without followers, and if the methods are effective, then the open communication and functionality will motivate followers to exhibit the same characteristics. In other words, followers will become self-aware, and a new clarity will be created in relation to values, morals, and drivers.[80] This could eventually result in followers being indirectly molded into leaders, as inspiration is quite effective. Furthermore, followers will tend toward a sense of trust in their leader, actively engage in processes, and experience a sense of overall workplace well-being.[81]

Environment also plays a role in leadership development, and in order for an authentic leader to succeed, the organization should be evaluated. An optimal situation would be one in which the organization values open communication and sharing, where leaders can both promote the company values and still have room to improve through learning and continued self-development. Finally, an authentic leader consistently performs above expected standards. In other words, in a competitive environment, it is imperative for the leader to sustain innovation, and avoid the tendency to remain stagnant. Future orientation and personal drives will motivate the leader to perform above expectations, as long as he or she remains true to him- or herself and is not simply acting out a part for superiors.[82]

How are authentic leaders different from traditional leaders? We discussed transformational leadership earlier in the chapter. Authentic leadership and transformational leadership are similar with one important difference. Authentic leadership focuses mainly on the internal aspects of the leader, such as morals, values, motivators, and so forth. While transformational leaders may have all the characteristics of an authentic leader, the key to transformational leadership is how the leader motivates others, which is a secondary concern with authentic leadership. In other words, transformational leaders may very well be authentic, but not all authentic leaders are inherently transformational. Charismatic leadership, on the other hand, does not seem to encompass a sense of self-awareness, with either the leader or the follower. Since this is an important component of authentic leadership, it is also a key point of differentiating between the charismatic and authentic leader. Again, charismatic leaders may have similar attributes to the authentic cohorts, but the individual is just not aware of it.[83] Table 13–9 outlines some other areas where these may differ and where they overlap.

Authentic leadership, while similar to traditional leadership, is becoming more important in today's globally marketed world. Through a sense of higher awareness, authentic leadership can create a better understanding within the organization. As cohesive relationships form, understanding is created, and the authentic leaders' drive to reach new standards will motivate everyone to attain their future-oriented goals.

Ethically Responsible Global Leadership

Related to the concept of authentic leadership is ethically responsible leadership. As discussed in Part 1, globalization and MNCs have come under fire from a number of quarters. Criticisms have been especially sharp in relation to the activities of companies—such as Nike, Levi's, and United Fruit—whose sourcing practices in developing countries have been alleged to exploit low-wage workers, take advantage of lax environmental and workplace standards, and otherwise contribute to social and economic degradation. Ethical principles provide the philosophical basis for responsible business practices, and leadership defines the mechanism through which these principles become actionable.

As a result of scandals at Royal Ahold, Andersen, Enron, Tyco, WorldCom, and others, there is decreasing trust of global leaders. A recent public opinion survey conducted for the World Economic Forum by Gallup and Environics found that leaders have suffered declining public trust in recent years and enjoy less trust than the institutions they lead. The survey asked respondents questions about how much they trust various leaders "to manage the challenges of the coming year in the best interests of you and your family." Leaders of nongovernmental organizations (NGOs) were the only ones receiving the trust of a clear majority of citizens across the countries surveyed.[84] Leaders at the United Nations and spiritual and religious leaders were the next-most-trusted leaders; over 4 in 10 citizens said they had a lot or some trust in them. Next most trusted were leaders of Western Europe, "individuals responsible for managing the global economy," those "responsible for managing our national economy," and executives of multinational companies. Those four groups were trusted by only one-third of citizens.[85] Over 4 in 10 citizens reported decreased trust in executives of domestic companies. Figure 3–2 in Chapter 3 summarizes these findings.

The decline in trust in leaders is prompting some companies to go on the offensive and to develop more ethically oriented and responsible leadership practices in their global

Table 13–9
Comparative Leadership Styles

Components of Authentic Leadership Development Theory	TL	CL(B)	CL(SC)
Positive psychological capital	×	×	×
Positive moral perspective	×	×	×
Leader self-awareness			
Values	×	×	×
Congnitions	×	×	×
Emotions	×	×	×
Leader self-regulation			
Intemalized	×		×
Balanced processing	×		
Relational transparency	×		
Authentic behavior	×	×	×
Leadership processes/behaviors			
Positive modeling	×	×	×
Personal and social identification	×	×	×
Emotional contagion			
Supporting self-determination	×	×	×
Positive social exchanges	×	×	×
Follower self-awareness			
Values	×		×
Congnitions	×		×
Emotions	×		×
Follower self-regulation			
Intemalized	×	×	×
Balanced processing	×		
Relational transparency	×		×
Authentic behavior	×		×
Follower development			
Organizational context			
Uncertainty	×	×	×
Inclusion	×		
Ethical	×		
Positive, strengths-based			
Performance			
Veritable			
Sustained	×	×	
Beyond expectations	×	×	

Note: ×—Focal Component.
×—Discussed.
Key: TL—Transformational Leadership Theory.
CL(B)—Behavioral Theory of Charismatic Leadership.
CL(SC)—Self-Concept Based Theory of Charismatic Leadership.
Source: Reprinted from *The Leadership Quarterly,* Vol. 15, Bruce J. Avolio and William L. Gardner, "Authentic Leadership Development: Getting to the Root of Positive Forms of Leadership," p. 323. Copyright © 2005 with permission from Elsevier.

operations. Some researchers link transformational leadership and corporate social responsibility, arguing that transformational leaders exhibit high levels of moral development, including a sense of obligation to the larger community.[86] According to this view, authentic charismatic leadership is rooted in strong ethical values, and effective global leaders are guided by principles of altruism, justice, and humanistic notions of the greater good.

On a more instrumental basis, another research effort linking leadership and corporate responsibility defines "responsible global leadership" as encompassing (1) values-based leadership, (2) ethical decision making, and (3) quality stakeholder relationships.[87] According to this view, global leadership must be based on core values and credos that reflect principled business and leadership practices, high levels of ethical and moral behavior, and a set of shared ideals that advance organizational and societal well-being. The importance of ethical decision making in corporations, governments, not-for-profit organizations, and professional services firms is omnipresent. In addition, the quality of relationships with internal and external stakeholders is increasingly critical to organizational success, especially to governance processes. Relationships involving mutual trust and respect are important within organizations, between organizations and the various constituencies that they affect, and among the extended networks of individuals and their organizational affiliates.

Leaders at many companies have dedicated themselves to responsible global leadership with apparent benefits for their companies' reputations and bottom lines. Even British Petroleum, which has experienced its fair share of disasters over the last few years with factory explosions and pipeline leaks, has attempted to accentuate responsible global leadership. BP will have to work harder now than ever, but keeping a socially responsible and clear objective will certainly aid in its continued global success. Executives at ICI India, a manufacturer and marketer of paints and various specialty chemicals, believe that adhering to global standards, even though doing so increases costs, can boost competitiveness. Aditya Narayan, president of ICI India, explains: "At ICI, standards involving ethics, safety, health, and environment policies are established by headquarters but are adapted to meet national laws. I can benefit by drawing on these corporate policies and in some cases we do far more than required by Indian laws."[88]

Another example of strong global leadership can be found at the Lubrizol Corporation. Lubrizol, a global manufacturer of chemicals, has been praised consistently for its efforts in product stewardship, community relations, and environmental preservation. In 2002 the American Chemistry Council lauded Lubrizol for its successful implementation of Responsible Care, the Council's global and industrywide initiative that sets standards for management of chemicals throughout all aspects of a business.[89] Since its inception in 1988, Lubrizol's Responsible Care programs have resulted in an 85 percent reduction in pollutant emissions per ton of product produced and a 56 percent reduction in safety-related incidents.

Entrepreneurial Leadership and Mindset

As discussed in Chapter 8, an increasing share of international management activities is occurring in entrepreneurial new ventures. Yang Yuanqing's leadership style clearly reflects a strong entrepreneurial bent, and his global vision is a positive illustration of the power of entrepreneurial leadership. But given the high failure rate for international new ventures, what leadership characteristics are important for such ventures to succeed?

Promising start-ups fail for many reasons, including lack of capital, absence of clear goals and objectives, and failure to accurately assess market demand and competition. For international new ventures, these factors are significantly complicated by differences in cultures, national political and economic systems, geographic distance, and shipping, tax, and regulatory costs. A critical factor in the long-term success of a new venture—whether domestic or international—is the personal leadership ability of the entrepreneurial CEO.

Entrepreneurship research has examined some of the key personal characteristics of entrepreneurs, some of which coincide with those of strong leaders. In comparison to nonentrepreneurs, entrepreneurs appear to be more creative and innovative. They tend to break the rules and do not need structure, support, or an organization to guide their thinking. They are able to see things differently and add to a product, system, or idea value that amounts to more than an adaptation or linear change. They are more willing to take personal and business risks and to do so in visible and salient ways. They are opportunity seekers—solving only those problems that limit their success in reaching the vision—and are comfortable with failure, rebounding quickly to pursue another opportunity.[90] Others characterize them as adventurous, ambitious, energetic, domineering, and self-confident.

In addition to these traits, entrepreneurial leaders operating internationally must also possess the cultural sensitivity, international vision, and global mindset to effectively lead their venture as it confronts the challenges of doing business in other countries. Well-known entrepreneurs such as Richard Branson (Virgin Group), Arthur Blank (Home Depot), and Russell Simmons (Def Jam Recordings) have all been successful leading their companies on a global scale while preserving the integrity and values of the host country.[91] As Yang Yuanqing (Lenovo) has shown, this is a trend that is growing, and soon we may see more entrepreneurs emerge from countries where such ventures are not common practice.

VeloCom Inc. is a telecom service company based in Arapahoe County, Colorado, but it has never done any business in Colorado or anywhere else in the United States. In only four years, however, it has become the lead competitor to incumbent telecom giant Telebras in Brazil. David Leonard, VeloCom's chief executive, is a visionary who did not see national borders as an impediment to rapid growth and expansion. Although Leonard says, "We just happened to be in the right place at the right time, and we took advantage of it," entrepreneurial leadership and vision were clearly key to the firm's success.[92] Another start-up, Terracom, has faced numerous setbacks in its effort to provide high-speed Internet service to war-torn Rwanda. Greg Wyler, who made his fortune during the tech boom, has been trying to string fiber-optic cables across Rwanda, connecting schools, government institutions, and homes with low-cost, high-speed Internet service. Wyler had never set foot in Africa, but due to a chance meeting with a Rwandan government official he had met at a wedding, he decided to start a business there. His goal has been to help the war-torn region by turning the small country into a hub of Internet activity. Wyler, and thousands more like him, embody the best of the leadership characteristics described in this chapter.[93]

The World of *BusinessWeek*—Revisited

The opening article outlined just a few challenges that face Yang as he continues to push forward in making Lenovo a globally recognized name. He is a pioneer in China, and while many are cheering for his success, others are awaiting his downfall. Yang's ability to take risks and keep managers on their toes by consistently demanding everyone reach 100 percent of their potential, or immediately find a solution, has certainly helped grow the company. However, his markedly Western-style leadership and management has also brought him Western ailments, such as stress and sleeplessness. Only time will tell if Yang can successfully lead the Lenovo brand across countries and cultures.

In this chapter, it was noted that effective leadership is often heavily influenced by culture. The approach that is effective in Europe is different from approaches used in the United States or Japan. Even so, there are threads of universalism, evident, for example, in the case of Japanese and U.S. leadership styles in managing both high- and low-achieving workers. The research by Bass also lends support to universalism. But can Yang rely on the leadership style that has served him well in China to oversee operations in other countries as he looks to expand? In most cases, leadership styles need to be adjusted to fit the cultural subtleties of disparate markets.

After reviewing the chapter and considering the experience of Yang Yuanqing, respond to the following questions: (1) Does Yang exhibit managerial characteristics, leadership characteristics, or a combination of the two? (2) How do Yang's leadership styles and behaviors compare to other Chinese leaders? (3) Does Yang fit into the expected category postulated by GLOBE for Chinese leaders? What category is the most appropriate? Support your answer with specific examples.

SUMMARY OF KEY POINTS

1. Leadership is a complex and controversial process that can be defined as influencing people to direct their efforts toward the achievement of some particular goal or goals. While some claim that managers and leaders conduct two separate job functions, the lack of a universal definition of leadership allows both to be used interchangeably, especially as the world moves towards a manager-leader model. Two areas warrant attention as a foundation for the study of leadership in an international setting: philosophical assumptions about people in general and leadership styles. The philosophical foundation is heavily grounded in Douglas McGregor's Theories X and Y and William Ouchi's Theory Z. Leadership styles relate to how managers treat their subordinates and incorporate authoritarian, paternalistic, and participative approaches. These styles can be summarized in terms of the managerial grid (1,1 through 9,9).

2. The attitudes of European managers toward dimensions of leadership practice, such as the capacity for leadership and initiative, sharing information and objectives, participation, and internal control, were examined in a classic study by Haire, Ghiselli, and Porter. They found that Europeans, as a composite, had a relatively low opinion of the capabilities of the average person coupled with a relatively positive belief in the necessity for participative leadership styles. The study also found that these European managers' attitudes were affected by hierarchical level, company size, and age. Overall, however, European managers espouse a participative leadership style.

3. The Japanese managers in the Haire and associates study had a much greater belief in the capacity of subordinates for leadership and initiative than managers in most other countries. The Japanese managers also expressed a more favorable attitude toward a participative leadership style. In terms of sharing information and objectives and using internal control, the Japanese responded above average but were not distinctive. In a number of ways, Japanese leadership styles differed from those of U.S. managers. Company size and age of the managers are two factors that seem to affect these differences. Other reasons include the basic philosophy of managing people, how information is processed, and the high degree of ethnocentrism among the Japanese. However, some often overlooked similarities are important, such as how effective Japanese leaders manage high-achieving and low-achieving subordinates.

4. Leadership research in China shows that the new generation of managers tends to have a leadership style that is different from the styles of both the current generation and the older generation. In particular, new generation managers assign greater importance to individualism as measured by such things as self-sufficiency and personal accomplishments. They also assign less importance to collectivism as measured by subordination of personal goals to those of the group and to Confucianism as measured by such things as societal harmony and virtuous interpersonal behavior.

5. Leadership research in the Middle East traditionally has stressed the basic differences between Middle Eastern and Western management styles. Other research, however, shows that many managers in multinational organizations in the Persian Gulf region operate in a Western-oriented participative style. Such findings indicate that there may be more similarities of leadership styles between Western and Middle Eastern parts of the world than has previously been assumed.

6. Leadership research also has been conducted among managers in India and Latin American countries. These studies show that Indian managers have a tendency toward participative leadership styles while Latin America wavers between participative and authoritarian styles. Although there always will be important differences in styles of leadership between various parts of the world, participative leadership styles may become more prevalent as countries develop and become more economically advanced.

7. In recent years, there have been research efforts to explore new areas in international leadership. In particular, Bass has found that there is a great deal of similarity from culture to culture and that transformational leaders, regardless of culture, tend to be the most effective. In addition, the GLOBE study has confirmed earlier research that specific cultural values and practices are associated with particular leadership attributes. Moreover, there is increasing pressure for MNCs to engage in globally responsible leadership that incorporates (*a*) values-based leadership; (*b*) ethical decision making, and (*c*) quality stakeholder relationships. Leaders of international new ventures face particularly challenging obstacles; however, the integration of a global orientation and entrepreneurial flair can contribute to successful "born global" leaders and firms.

KEY TERMS

authoritarian leadership, *435*

charismatic leaders, *448*

leadership, *431*

participative leadership, *436*

paternalistic leadership, *435*

positive organizational scholarship (POS) *456*

Theory X manager, *433*

Theory Y manager, *433*

Theory Z manager, *435*

transactional leaders, *448*

transformational leaders, *448*

variety amplification, *443*

variety reduction, *443*

REVIEW AND DISCUSSION QUESTIONS

1. What cultures would be the most likely to perceive differences between managerial and leadership duties? What cultures would view them as the same? Use evidence to support your answer.

2. Using the results of the classic Haire and associates study as a basis for your answer, compare and contrast managers' attitudes toward leadership practices in Nordic-European and Latin-European countries. (The countries in these clusters are identified in Table 13–3.)

3. Is there any relationship between company size and European managers' attitude toward participative leadership styles?

4. Using the GLOBE study results and other supporting data, determine what Japanese managers believe about their subordinates. How are these beliefs similar to those of U.S. and European managers? How are these beliefs different?

5. A U.S. firm is going to be opening a subsidiary in Japan within the next six months. What type of leadership style does research show to be most effective for leading high-achieving Japanese? Low-achieving Japanese? How are these results likely to affect the way that U.S. expatriates should lead their Japanese employees?

6. What do U.S. managers need to know about leading in the international arena? Identify and describe three important guidelines that can be of practical value.

7. Is effective leadership behavior universal, or does it vary from culture to culture? Explain.

8. What is authentic leadership? What is ethically responsible leadership?

INTERNET EXERCISE: TAKING A CLOSER LOOK

Over the last decade, one of the most successful global firms has been General Electric. Go to the company's Web site at **www.ge.com,** and review its latest annual report. Pay close attention to the MNC's international operations and to its product lines. Also read about the new members on the board of directors, and look through the information on the company's Six Sigma program. Then, aware of what GE is doing worldwide as well as in regard to its quality efforts, answer these questions: On how many continents does the company currently do business? Based on this answer, is there one leadership style that will work best for the company, or is it going to have to choose managers on a country-by-country basis? Additionally, if there is no one universal style that is best, how can current CEO Jeffrey Immelt effectively lead so diverse a group of worldwide managers? In what way would an understanding of the managerial grid be useful in explaining leadership behaviors at GE? Finally, if GE were advertising for new managers in England, Italy, and Japan, what qualities would you expect the firm to be seeking in these managers? Would there be a universal list, or would lists differ on a country-by-country basis?

Germany

The reunification of Germany was a major event of modern times. Despite problems, Germany remains a major economic power. The unified Germany is big, though only about the size of the state of Nevada in the United States. With a population of about 82.5 million, Germany has about three times the population of California. Germany still is far behind the economic size of Japan and 20 percent that of the United States. Because Germany was rebuilt almost from the ground up after World War II, however, many feel that Germany, along with Japan, is an economic miracle of modern times. Unified Germany's GDP of $2.63 trillion is behind that of both the United States and Japan, but Germany exports more than Japan, its gross investment as a percentage of GDP is higher than that of the United States, and its average compensation with benefits to workers is higher than that of the United States or Japan. It is estimated that Germany has direct control of about one-fourth of Western Europe's economy, which gives it considerable power in Europe. The German people are known for being thrifty, hardworking, and obedient to authority. They love music, dancing, good food and beer, and fellowship. The government is a parliamentary democracy headed by a chancellor. Although Germany has experienced a difficult economic environment in recent years, recent governments have pushed through labor reforms designed to improve productivity and stem unemployment.

For the last 13 years, the Wiscomb Company has held a majority interest in a large retail store in Bonn. The store has been very successful and also has proved to be an excellent training ground for managers whom the company wanted to prepare for other overseas assignments. First, the managers would be posted to the Bonn store. Then after three or four months of international seasoning, they would be sent on to other stores in Europe. Wiscomb has holdings in the Netherlands, Luxembourg, and Austria. The Bonn store has been the primary training ground because it was the first store the company had in Europe, and the training program was created with this store in mind.

A few months ago, the Wiscomb management and its German partners decided to try a new approach to selling. The plan called for some young U.S. managers to be posted to the Bonn store for a three-year tour, while some young German managers were sent stateside. Both companies hoped that this program would provide important training and experience for their people; however, things have not worked out as hoped. The U.S. managers have reported great difficulty in supervising their German subordinates. Three of their main concerns are as follows: (1) Their subordinates do not seem to like to participate in decision making, preferring to be told what to do. (2) The German nationals in the store rely much more heavily on a Theory X approach to supervising than the Americans are accustomed to using, and they are encouraging their U.S. counterparts to follow their example. (3) Some of the German managers have suggested to the young Americans that they not share as much information with their own subordinates. Overall, the Americans believe that the German style of management is not as effective as their own, but they feel equally ill at ease raising this issue with their hosts. They have asked if someone from headquarters could come over from the United States and help resolve their problem. A human resources executive is scheduled to arrive next week and meet with the U.S. contingent.

Questions

1. What are some current issues facing Germany? What is the climate for doing business in Germany today?

2. Are the leadership styles used by the German managers really much different from those used by the Americans?

3. Do you think the German managers are really more Theory X–oriented than their U.S. counterparts? Why, or why not?

4. Are the German managers who have come to the United States likely to be having the same types of problems?

5. Using the GLOBE study as a guide, what are some leadership attributes you would expect from the Germans? How does this affect the way German subordinates view U.S. leaders?

An Offer from Down Under

The Gandriff Corporation is a successful retail chain in the U.S. Midwest. The St. Louis–based company has had average annual growth of 17 percent over the last 10 years and would like to expand to other sections of the country. Last month, it received a very interesting offer from a group of investors from Australia. The group is willing to put up $100 million to help Gandriff set up operations Down Under. The Australian investors believe that Gandriff's management and retailing expertise could provide it with a turnkey operation. The stores would be built to Gandriff's specifications, and the entire operation would be run by Gandriff. The investors would receive 75 percent of all profits until they recovered their $100 million plus an annual return of 10 percent. At this point, the division of profits would become 50-50.

Gandriff management likes the idea but feels there is a better chance for higher profit if it were to set up operations in Europe. The growth rate in European countries, it is felt, will be much better than that in Australia. The investors, all of whom are Australian, are sympathetic and have promised Gandriff that they will invest another $100 million in Europe, specifically England, France, and Germany, within three years if Gandriff agrees to first set up and get an Australian operation running. The U.S. firm believes this would be a wise move but is delaying a final decision because it still is concerned about the ease with which it can implement its current approach in foreign markets. In particular, the management is concerned about whether the leadership style used in the United States will be successful in Australia and in European countries. Before making a final decision, management has decided to hire a consultant specializing in leadership to look into the matter.

Questions

1. Will the leadership style used in the United States be successful in Australia, or will the Australians respond better to another?

2. If the retailer goes into Europe, in which country will it have the least problem using its U.S.-based leadership style? Why?

3. If the company goes into Europe, what changes might it have to make in accommodating its leadership approach to the local environment? Use Germany as an example.

Chapter 14

HUMAN RESOURCE SELECTION AND DEVELOPMENT ACROSS CULTURES

The World of *BusinessWeek*

BusinessWeek

Guess Who's Hiring in America

Infosys and Other Indian Companies Are Recruiting More Locals in the U.S.

Bennett Kalcevic's saga offers ample evidence of how the winds of globalization can unexpectedly shift. In the mid-1980s her parents lost their mill jobs when Pittsburgh's steel industry was hit by cheap imports. Now, with a business degree from Michigan State University, Kalcevic has just landed a plum position with Infosys Technologies Ltd., one of the low-cost Indian outfits that many blame for taking jobs from American programmers. After a six-month training stint in India, Kalcevic will return to the U.S. and write software for an Infosys customer. "Outsourcing has angered some people," she says. "It might be easier for clients to deal with Americans locally."

Think of it as offshoring in reverse. In the past, Indian companies almost always transferred Indians to work in the U.S. on temporary visas. But now Infosys and other Indian outfits are hiring aggressively in the U.S.

Wipro Ltd., for instance, is scouting U.S. locations for two big software writing centers that eventually could employ hundreds of programmers each. Cities on its short list include Austin, Tex., and Atlanta, because of their deep tech-talent pools and reasonable salary costs. "The work we're doing requires more and more knowledge of the customers' businesses, and you want local people to do that," says Wipro Chairman Azim H. Premji. Today only 2.5% of Wipro's global workforce is non-Indian, but the company wants to boost that to more than 10% in a few years.

The Indian outsourcers say their U.S. expansion plans predate the latest concerns over immigration and jobs. But they acknowledge the trend might ease tensions as the Senate mulls regulations that would require companies applying for H-1B visas—temporary working papers for foreigners—to try hiring Americans first. "If we can hire close to our clients, we don't have to bring in somebody from India on an H-1B," says S. Padmanabhan, human resources chief for Tata Consultancy Services Ltd. (TCS), India's largest outsourcing firm. About 1,000 of TCS's 10,000 U.S.-based workers are Americans (out of 90,000 total employees worldwide). And it plans to hire an additional 2,000 Americans within three years.

Surprisingly, it often costs more to ship in Indians on a temporary basis than it does to hire Americans. Base salaries are comparable, because Indian companies must by law pay market rates for people they bring in on work visas. But the companies typically have to provide the Indians with housing, and retirement benefits cost more because of India's social security contribution requirements. Also, as the Indian rupee has risen more than 10% against the dollar this year, hiring Americans has gotten cheaper. At the same time, fierce competition for tech talent in India is pushing salaries there up by 12% to 15% per year, although they remain less than a third of those in the U.S.

Allure On Campus

The Indians are recruiting a combination of fresh college grads and experienced vets who have worked at American companies. They're especially active at campus job fairs, and unlike a few years ago students know who these companies are and respect them. In fact, the Indian connection has become an attraction. "I thought this would be a fantastic opportunity, especially because they send you abroad for training," says Brian Oswald, a 23-year-old Rutgers University graduate with a 2006 degree in industrial engineering who joined TCS in February.

The U.S. hiring by the Indians echoes the strategy Japan's auto industry devised after soaring levels of imports sparked political outcry in Washington in December, 2000. "The Indians are doing to the world's IT processes what the Japanese did to manufacturing," says analyst John McCarthy of Forrester Research Inc. And now, like Japan's carmakers before them, the Indians are becoming major employers in the U.S. as well.

By Steve Hamm

The opening news story points out some of the broad impacts of globalization on international human resource selection and development in today's business climate. Originally, MNCs searched overseas for inexpensive labor, but as countries become more developed and citizens in home countries worry about a diminishing labor force, the search has shifted. Once, India was seen as a source of never-ending talent. Today, India is beginning to seek out American workers to take over jobs in the host countries. Companies in India are experiencing the importance of international expansion, and can now appreciate the costly investments of temporarily sending citizens to the United States to work. It is now more efficient to hire U.S. citizens, and many Americans see it as a great opportunity to train in Indian offices. It has been an interesting shift in how offshoring has been created through globalization, and it all has to do with human resources. As more highly skilled workers become available in other countries, MNCs have a growing number of sources for their human resources. In addition, technology now enables work to be conducted at numerous remote locations, making face-to-face contact less essential. In addition to work flowing to other countries, MNCs may also be able to access foreign human resources by hiring them on a temporary or permanent basis in the home country. Often, they will subcontract or outsource work to foreign employees in home and host countries. This complex web of relationships creates significant managerial challenges and opportunities and suggests that there will always be a need for highly skilled, culturally sensitive, and geographically mobile managerial talent.

In this chapter we explore the procedure of international human resource selection and training and examine the difficulties of developing a global human resource management process in the presence of dissimilar cultural norms. At the same time, we survey emerging trends in international human resource management, including the increasing use of temporary and contingent staffing to fill the growing global HR needs of MNCs. We also review training and development programs designed to help employees prepare for and succeed in their foreign assignments and adjust to conditions once they return home.

■ The Importance of International Human Resources

Human resources is an essential part of any organization, since it provides the human capital that keeps operations running. Human resource management is also key to an efficient, productive workplace. We discussed in Chapter 12 how financial compensation can motivate employees, but human resources more broadly plays an important role. By focusing on the employees, or the human resources themselves, organizations have found that the positive organizational structure leads to company success in the market.[1] Sometimes this is recognized through compensation such as competitive salaries, good benefits, promotions, training, education opportunities, and so forth, which has been known to motivate employees and reduce turnover, since there are further incentives to strive for. Other times, companies will provide employees with daily comforts such as meals where an employee's family is welcome to attend, fitness centers, laundry rooms, or even services such as oil changes while at work. Showing the employees that they are not simply cogs in a machine, but their time is valued and they are thanked for it, often builds morale and can increase company sales through a shared drive to succeed. Furthermore, recognizing the potential in employees and encouraging teamwork can lead to greater risk taking and innovations.[2]

Whether managers are trying to increase productivity or decrease turnover rates, it is good to get a sense of how the employees feel they are being treated. Times continue to change, and while employees in the past could be considered one unit, today people are realizing their individual talents and their need to be recognized. For instance, global companies are experiencing a labor shortage as skilled workers are in high demand.[3] In essence, skilled workers can almost walk in and request the kind of compensation they desire, and companies may be willing to accept the terms. Even outside the realm of labor shortages, firms are restructuring how they look at employees. By segmenting the workforce into categories (but avoiding differentiation based on age or gender since that may infer a form of discrimination) and by offering choices, flexibility, and a personal touch to each employee package, employers are able to provide an underlying sense of commitment since the employee is getting what he or she wants. In other words, by focusing on employees and tailoring human resource management to the individual, people stay longer and are more committed to the organization they have joined.[4] However, before a company can keep the employee, it must first hire.

Attracting the most qualified employees and matching them to the jobs for which they are best suited is important for the success of any organization. For international organizations, the selection and development of human resources are especially challenging and vitally important. As prevalent and useful as e-mail and Web- and teleconferencing have become, and despite the increasing incidence of subcontracting and outsourcing, face-to-face human contact will remain an important means of communication and transferring "tacit" knowledge—knowledge that cannot be formalized in manuals or written guidelines. Hence, most companies continue to deploy human resources around the world as they are needed, although the range of options for filling human resources needs is expanding.

One way MNCs are doing this is by sending expatriate managers overseas. There are quite a few costs involved in this, including preassignment training, and potential costs due to failure. According to one estimate, the cost of one assignment failure is between $100,000 and $300,000 per employee.[5] Given these high costs, many MNCs are turning to locally engaged employees or third-country nationals.[6] In addition, the increased education of many populations around the world gives MNCs more options when considering international human resource needs. The emergence of highly trained technical and scientific employees in emerging markets and the increased prevalence of MBA-type training in many developed and developing countries have dramatically expanded the pool of talent from which MNCs can draw. Yet some companies are still having difficulty in winning the "war for talent." A recent report from China noted that despite much greater levels of advanced education, there is still a shortage of skilled management. "We need a lot more people than we have now, and we need a higher caliber of people," said Guo Ming, Coca-Cola's human resource director for Greater China.[7]

Adjustment problems associated with international assignments can be reduced through careful selection and training. Language training and cross-culture training are especially important, but they are often neglected by MNCs in a hurry to deploy resources to meet critical needs.[8] MNCs are also under increasing pressure to keep jobs at home, and their international HR practices have come under close scrutiny. In particular, the "importing" of programmers from India at a fraction of domestic wages, combined with the offshore outsourcing of work to high-tech employees in lower cost countries, has created political and social challenges for MNCs seeking to manage their international human resources efficiently and effectively. Nonetheless, the demand for globally adept managers will likely grow, and MNCs will continue to invest in recruiting and training the best future leaders.

■ Sources of Human Resources

MNCs can tap four basic sources for positions: (1) home-country nationals; (2) host-country nationals; (3) third-country nationals; and (4) inpatriates. In addition, many MNCs are outsourcing aspects of their global operations and in so doing are engaging temporary or contingent employees. The following sections analyze each of these major sources.

Home-Country Nationals

Home-country nationals are managers who are citizens of the country where the MNC is headquartered. In fact, sometimes the term *headquarters nationals* is used. These managers commonly are called **expatriates,** or simply "expats," which refers to those who live and work outside their home country. Historically, MNCs have staffed key positions in their foreign affiliates with home-country nationals or expatriates.[9] Currently, it seems as though in some areas, that trend continues. Major U.S. and European companies such as Cisco Systems have been sending expats to India, and according to a recent estimate, about 1,000 expat senior managers are there now, almost seven times that of two years ago. Furthermore, it has been suggested that by 2009, that will more than double.[10] However, some research has shown that in some instances, host-country nationals may be better suited for the job. Richards, for example, investigated staffing practices for the purpose of determining when companies are more likely to use an expatriate rather than a local manager. She conducted interviews with senior-level headquarters managers at 24 U.S. multinational manufacturing firms and with managers at their U.K. and Thai subsidiaries. This study found that local managers were most effective in subsidiaries located in developing countries or those that relied on a local customer base. In contrast, expatriates were most effective when they were in charge of larger subsidiaries or those with a marketing theme similar to that at headquarters.[11]

home-country nationals
Expatriate managers who are citizens of the country where the multinational corporation is headquartered.

expatriates
Managers who live and work outside their home country. They are citizens of the country where the multinational corporation is headquartered.

There are a variety of reasons for using home-country nationals. One of the most common is to start up operations. Another is to provide technical expertise. A third is to help the MNC maintain financial control over the operation.[12] Other commonly cited reasons include

> the desire to provide the company's more promising managers with international experience to equip them better for more responsible positions; the need to maintain and facilitate organizational coordination and control; the unavailability of managerial talent in the host country; the company's view of the foreign operation as short lived; the host country's multiracial population, which might mean that selecting a manager of either race would result in political or social problems; the company's conviction that it must maintain a foreign image in the host country; and the belief of some companies that a home country manager is the best person for the job.[13]

In the past, expatriates were almost always men, but over the last decade there has been a growing number of female expatriates as companies realize that women want international assignments and are prepared to assume the challenges that accompany these jobs. Stroh, Varma, and Valy-Durbin, for example, recently surveyed 261 female expatriates and 78 of their supervisors and, among other things, found that these women felt that their gender did not stand in the way of their doing their jobs and, in fact, was sometimes an advantage because it gave them greater visibility, enabled them to build stronger interpersonal relationships with clients, and helped them to adapt better to life as an outsider.[14]

In recent years, there has been a trend away from using home-country nationals. This is true even among Japanese firms, which long preferred to employ expats and were reluctant to allow local nationals a significant role in subsidiary management. Beamish and Inkpen conducted an analysis of over 3,200 Japanese subsidiaries and found that the percentage of expats in larger units has been declining steadily over the last four decades.[15] What has caused this? Four reasons for the declining use of Japanese expats have been cited. First, as the number of Japanese subsidiaries worldwide has increased, it has become more difficult to find the requisite number of qualified expats to handle these assignments. Second, the growing number of effective local managers makes it no longer necessary to rely as heavily on expats. Third, the high cost of keeping expats overseas is having a strong negative effect on company profits. Fourth, Japanese human resource management policies are changing, and the old "rice paper ceiling" that prevented non-Japanese from being promoted into the upper management ranks of subsidiaries is now beginning to disappear. This last development, in the United States in particular, is a result of Japanese firms realizing that their American subsidiaries have not been able to compete effectively. Japanese expat managers have been outflanked by their American counterparts. In particular, Japanese managers have not known how to fine-tune products for the U.S. market; did not understand how to tailor market approaches to different customer segments; and were unable to develop the speed, flexibility, and responsiveness needed to compete with the Americans.[16] It is highly likely that MNCs from other countries besides Japan are also following this trend of using local managers in lieu of expats.

Host-Country Nationals

host-country nationals
Local managers who are hired by the MNC.

Host-country nationals are local managers who are hired by the MNC. For a number of reasons, many multinationals use host-country managers at the middle- and lower-level ranks: Many countries expect the MNC to hire local talent, and this is a good way to meet this expectation. Also, even if an MNC wanted to staff all management positions with home-country personnel, it would be unlikely to have this many available managers, and the cost of transferring and maintaining them in the host country would be prohibitive.

Important Tips on Working for Foreigners

As the Japanese, South Koreans, and Europeans continue to expand their economic horizons, increased employment opportunities will be available worldwide. Is it a good idea to work for foreigners? Those who have done so have learned that there are both rewards and penalties associated with this career choice. Here are some useful tips that have been drawn from the experiences of those who have worked for foreign MNCs.

First, most U.S. managers are taught to make fast decisions, but most foreign managers take more time and view rapid decision making as unnecessary and sometimes bad. In the United States, we hear the cliché, "The effective manager is right 51 percent of the time." In Europe, this percentage is perceived as much too low, which helps explain why European managers analyze situations in much more depth than most U.S. managers do. Americans working for foreign-owned firms have to focus on making slower and more accurate decisions.

Second, most Americans are taught to operate without much direction. In Latin countries, managers are accustomed to giving a great deal of direction, and in East Asian firms, there is little structure and direction. Americans have to learn to adjust to the decision-making process of the particular company.

Third, most Americans go home around 5 p.m. If there is more paperwork to do, they take it with them. Japanese managers, in contrast, stay late at the office and often view those who leave early as being lazy. Americans either have to adapt or have to convince the manager that they are working as hard as their peers but in a different physical location.

Fourth, many international firms say that their official language is English. However, important conversations always are carried out in the home-country's language, so it is important to learn that language.

Fifth, many foreign MNCs make use of fear to motivate their people. This is particularly true in manufacturing work, where personnel are under continuous pressure to maintain high output and quality. For instance, those who do not like to work under intense conditions would have a very difficult time succeeding in Japanese auto assembly plants. Americans have to understand that humanistic climates of work may be the exception rather than the rule.

Finally, despite the fact that discrimination in employment is outlawed in the United States, it is practiced by many MNCs, including those operating in the United States. Women seldom are given the same opportunities as men, and top-level jobs almost always are reserved for home-office personnel. In many cases, Americans have accepted this ethnocentric (nationalistic) approach, but as Chapter 3 discussed, ethics and social responsibilities are a major issue in the international arena, and these challenges must be met now and in the future.

This traditional pattern of managerial positions filled by home- and host-country personnel illustrates why it is so difficult to generalize about staffing patterns in an international setting. An exception would be in those cases where government regulations dictate selection practices and mandate at least some degree of "nativization." In Brazil, for example, two-thirds of the employees in any foreign subsidiary traditionally had to be Brazilian nationals. In addition, many countries exert real and subtle pressures to staff the upper-management ranks with nationals. In the past, these pressures by host countries have led companies such as Standard Oil to change their approach to selecting managers.

In European countries, home-country managers who are assigned to a foreign subsidiary or affiliate often stay in this position for the remainder of their career. Europeans are not transferred back to headquarters or to some other subsidiary, as is traditionally done by U.S. firms. Another approach, the least common, is always to use a home-country manager to run the operation.

Sony is trying the host-country approach in the United States. Employees are encouraged to accept or decline styles that emerge from Japanese headquarters, depending on American tastes. Furthermore, innovative creations are birthed at the U.S. site, all with an American flavor. Sony believes that local citizens are the best qualified for the job, as opposed to Japanese managers, because they already have a working knowledge of the language and culture, and it may be difficult for Sony to understand preferred styles otherwise.[17] "International Management in Action: Important Tips on Working for Foreigners" gives examples of how Americans can better adapt to foreign bosses.

Third-Country Nationals

Third-country nationals (TCNs) are managers who are citizens of countries other than the country in which the MNC is headquartered or the one in which they are assigned to work by the MNC. Available data on third-country nationals are not as extensive as those on home- or host-country nationals.

A number of advantages have been cited for using TCNs. One is that the salary and benefit package usually is less than that of a home-country national, although in recent years, the salary gap between the two has begun to diminish. A second reason is that the TCN may have a very good working knowledge of the region or speak the same language as the local people. This helps explain why many U.S. MNCs hire English or Scottish managers for top positions at subsidiaries in former British colonies such as Jamaica, India, the West Indies, and Kenya. It also explains why successful multinationals such as Gillette, Coca-Cola, and IBM recruit local managers and train them to run overseas subsidiaries. Other cited benefits of using TCNs include:

1. TCN managers, particularly those who have had assignments in the headquarters country, can often achieve corporate objectives more effectively than expatriates or local nationals. In particular, they frequently have a deep understanding of the corporation's policies from the perspective of a foreigner and can communicate and implement those policies more effectively to others than can expats.

2. During periods of rapid expansion, TCNs can not only substitute for expatriates in new and growing operations but also offer different perspectives that can complement and expand on the sometimes narrowly focused viewpoints of both local nationals and headquarters personnel.

3. In joint ventures, TCNs can demonstrate a global or transnational image and bring unique cross-cultural skills to the relationship.[18]

Inpatriates

In recent years a new term has emerged in international management—inpatriates. An **inpatriate,** or inpat, is an individual from a host country or a third-country national who is assigned to work in the home country. Even Japanese MNCs are now beginning to rely on inpatriates to help them meet their international challenges. Harvey and Buckley report that:

> The Japanese are reducing their unicultural orientation in their global businesses. Yoichi Morishita, president of Matsushita, has ordered that top management must reflect the cultural diversity of the countries where Matsushita does business. Sony sells 80 percent of its products overseas and recently recognized the need to become multicultural. It has appointed two foreigners to its board of directors and has plans to hire host-country nationals who are to be integrated into the top management of the parent organization. At the same time, the Chairman of Sony has stated that in five years the board-of-directors of Sony will reflect the diversity of countries that are important to the future of the company. Similarly, Toshiba plans to have a more representative top management and board of directors to facilitate long-run global strategies.[19]

This growing use of inpats is helping MNCs better develop their global core competencies. As a result, today a new breed of multilingual, multiexperienced, so-called global managers or transnational managers is truly emerging.[20]

These new managers are part of a growing group of international executives who can manage across borders and do not fit the traditional third-country nationals mold. With a unified Europe and other such developments in North America and Asia, these global managers are in great demand. Additionally, with labor shortages developing in certain regions, there is a wave of migration from regions with an abundance of personnel to those where the demand is strongest.[21]

Subcontracting and Outsourcing

Other potential sources of international management talent are subcontracting and offshore outsourcing (introduced in Chapter 1). Offshore outsourcing is made possible by the increasing organizational and technological capacity of companies to separate, coordinate, and integrate geographically dispersed human resources—whether employed directly by the firm or contracted out—across distant geographic borders. The development of this capacity can be traced to the earlier growth of international subcontracting as well as to the international diffusion of lean production systems (which originated with Japanese auto manufacturers) to other manufacturing and service sectors. In particular, service industries are exploiting inexpensive telecommunications to transmit engineering, medical, legal, and accounting services to be performed in locations previously viewed as remote. Rising levels of educational attainment in developing countries such as China, India, and the Philippines, especially in the scientific and technical fields, make offshoring increasingly attractive for a range of international human resource needs.

On the one hand, offshore outsourcing, as well as the hiring of temporary workers from abroad on special visas, similar to inpatriates, presents significant opportunities for cost savings and lower overhead. On the other hand, the recent wave of media attention has focused on widespread concern that in an age of cheap telecommunications, almost any job—professional or blue collar—can be performed in India for a fraction of U.S. wages. In particular, as discussed in Chapter 1, union groups, politicians, and NGOs have challenged MNCs' right to engage in labor "arbitrage." Offshoring is reaching a new era, and while the top reason that MNCs look to other countries for labor is still to save money, there has been a decline in qualified personnel, which has brought about an emerging focus on other factors, notably access to qualified personnel. Figure 14–1 illustrates this.

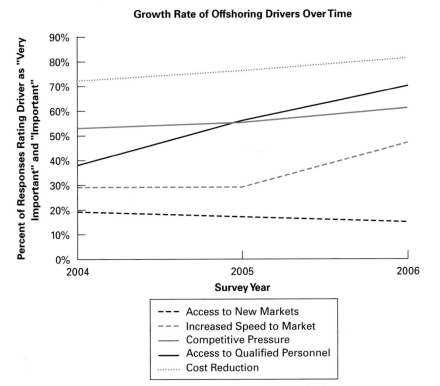

Growth Rate of Offshoring Drivers Over Time

Percent of Responses Rating Driver as "Very Important" and "Important"

Survey Year

- - - Access to New Markets
- - - Increased Speed to Market
—— Competitive Pressure
—— Access to Qualified Personnel
······· Cost Reduction

Figure 14–1

Reasons MNCs Look Abroad for Workforce

Source: Next Generation Offshoring: The Globalization of innovation by Arie Y. Lewin and Vinay Couto, 2006 Survey Report. Booz Allen Hamilton/Duke University Offshoring Research Network 2006 Survey. Reprinted with permission.

Moreover, although the cost for a computer programmer or a middle manager in India remains a small fraction of the cost for a similar employee in the United States (a programmer with three to five years' experience makes about $25,000 in India but about $65,000 in the United States), the wage savings do not necessarily translate directly into overall savings because the typical outsourcing contract between an American company and an Indian vendor saves less than half as much as the wage differences would imply.[22] Microsoft recently revealed that it has been paying two Indian outsourcing companies, Infosys and Satyam, to provide skilled software architects for Microsoft projects. In this case, the work of software architects and developers was being done by employees of the Indian companies working at Microsoft facilities in the United States. Although the actual employees were paid much less than U.S. counterparts ($30,000 to $40,000), Microsoft was billed $90 an hour for software architects, or at a yearly rate of more than $180,000. The on-site work was done by Indian software engineers who came to the United States on H-1B visas, which allow foreign workers to be employed in the United States for up to six years. Microsoft also contracted work in India through the firms, with billing rates of $23 to $36 an hour.[23]

Though politically controversial, outsourcing can save companies significant costs and is very profitable for firms that specialize in providing these services on a contract basis. U.S.-based firms such as EDS, IBM, and Deloitte have developed specific competencies in global production and HR coordination, including managing the HR functions that must support it. These firms combine low labor costs, specialized technical capabilities, and coordination expertise.

Outsourcing can also create quality control problems for some companies, as demonstrated in Dell's decision to repatriate some of its call-center staff from India to Texas because of quality control problems. Because Dell is a company that has little on-site service, the call-center capability is core to Dell's competitive position. "We felt a little noise and angst from our customers, and we decided to make some changes," said Gary Cotshott, vice president of Dell's services division. "Sometimes, we move a little too far, too fast."[24] In addition, as seen in the opening article, Indian companies are beginning to develop their own approaches to outsourcing, including investing in U.S. call centers and business-processing outsourcers. The Indians "are looking to build a global model quickly," said a partner with WestBridge Capital Partners, a Silicon Valley venture-capital firm that invests in outsourcing companies.[25]

Despite these limitations, offshore subcontracting will remain an important tool for managing and deploying international human resources. If anything, the trend is accelerating. Forrester Research recently estimated that U.S. companies would send 3.4 million service jobs offshore by 2015.[26] Although subcontracting provides important flexibility in the human resource practices of MNCs operating globally, it also requires skilled international managers to coordinate and oversee the complex relationships that arise from it.

This is especially true as offshoring begins a new generation. In a survey by Duke University's Offshoring Research Network, significant differences were found in the perspectives of home (source) and host (destination) countries. Specifically, individuals in home countries were often worried about losing jobs to host countries, exacerbated by the fact that higher-end jobs are now being shipped overseas.[27] This is not the case from the organizations' point of view. It is becoming increasingly difficult for managers to find the appropriate talent. More and more, companies are looking overseas in areas such as R&D and procurement to supplement the lack of experts in the home country. This does not take jobs away from home countries; it simply opens jobs globally as managers attempt to fit the skills of the worker to the job itself.[28] Furthermore, companies are very specific about which country they search when looking to fill particular job functions. Figure 14–2 provides a graphical depiction of this reality. Overall, offshoring is a trend that does not appear to be on its way out, but instead is evolving through alternative motivators and continuing to innovatively help the company grow.

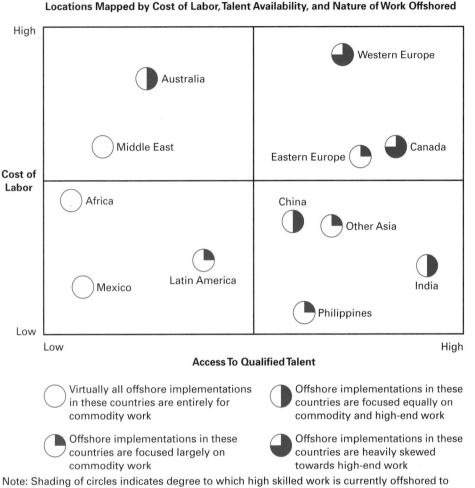

Locations Mapped by Cost of Labor, Talent Availability, and Nature of Work Offshored

Note: Shading of circles indicates degree to which high skilled work is currently offshored to the specific country.

Source: Next Generation Offshoring: The Globalization of Innovation by Arie Y. Lewin and Vinay Couto, 2006 Survey Report. Booz Allen Hamilton/Duke University Offshoring Research Network 2006 Survey. Reprinted with permission.

■ Selection Criteria for International Assignments

Making an effective selection decision for an overseas assignment can prove to be a major problem. Typically, this decision is based on **international selection criteria,** which are factors used to choose international managers. These selections are influenced by the MNC's experience and often are culturally based. Sometimes as many as a dozen criteria are used, although most MNCs give serious consideration to only five or six.[29] Table 14–1 reports the importance of some of these criteria as ranked by Australian, expatriate, and Asian managers from 60 leading Australian, New Zealand, British, and U.S. MNCs with operations in South Asia.[30]

international selection criteria
Factors used to choose personnel for international assignments.

General Criteria

Some selection criteria are given a great deal of weight; others receive, at best, only lip service. A company sending people overseas for the first time often will have a much longer list of criteria than will an experienced MNC that has developed a "short list."

Typically, both technical and human criteria are considered. Firms that fail to consider both often find that their rate of failure is quite high. For example, Peterson, Napier, and Shul-Shim investigated the primary criteria that MNCs use when choosing personnel for overseas assignments and found that the Japanese and American MNCs in their

Table 14–1
Rank of Criteria in Expatriate Selection

	Australian Managers (*n* = 47)	Expatriate Managers* (*n* = 52)	Asian Managers (*n* = 15)
1. Ability to adapt	1	1	2
2. Technical competence	2	3	1
3. Spouse and family adaptability	3	2	4
4. Human relations skill	4	4	3
5. Desire to serve overseas	5	5	5
6. Previous overseas experience	6	7	7
7. Understanding of host-country culture	7	6	6
8. Academic qualifications	8	8	8
9. Knowledge of language of country	9	9	9
10. Understanding of home-country culture	10	10	10

*U.S., British, Canadian, French, New Zealand, or Australian managers working for an MNC outside their home countries.
Source: From Raymond J. Stone, "Expatriate Selection and Failure." Reprinted with permission from *Human Resource Planning,* Vol. 14, Issue 1, 1991, by The Human Resource Planning Society, 317 Madison Avenue, Suite 12509, New York NY 100198.

survey ranked both technical expertise and interpersonal skills as very important.[31] The following sections examine some of the most commonly used selection criteria for overseas assignments in more depth.

Adaptability to Cultural Change

Overseas managers must be able to adapt to change. They also need a degree of cultural toughness. Research shows that many managers are exhilarated at the beginning of their overseas assignment. After a few months, however, a form of culture shock creeps in, and they begin to encounter frustration and feel confused in their new environment. One analysis noted that many of the most effective international managers suffer this cultural shock.[32] This may be a good sign, because it shows that the expatriate manager is becoming involved in the new culture and not just isolating him- or herself from the environment. Here is an example provided by a North American who was assigned to the Middle East:

> My third day in Israel, accompanied by a queasy stomach, I ventured forth into the corner market to buy something light and easy to digest. As yet unable to read Hebrew, I decided to pick up what looked like a small yogurt container that was sitting near the cheese. Not being one hundred percent sure it contained yogurt, I peered inside; to my delight, it held a thick white yogurt-looking substance. I purchased my "yogurt" and went home to eat— soap, liquid soap. How was I to know that soap came in packages resembling yogurt containers, or that market items in Israel were not neatly divided into edible and inedible sections, as I remembered them in the United States. My now "clean" stomach became a bit more fragile and my confidence waned.[33]

As this initial and trying period comes to an end, expatriates tend to identify more with the host-country culture, which only increases as managers become more adept at the position. As seen in Figure 14–3, upon first arrival, the expatriates identify almost wholly with the home country. Over time, they become more familiar with their surroundings and become more of an integral part of the environment. This integration can lead to a higher sense of satisfaction with the job and a lessening of stress and alienation.[34]

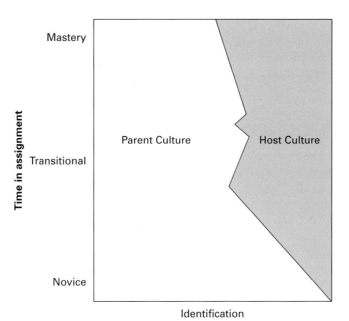

Source: Juan Sanchez, Paul Spector, and Cary Cooper, "Adapting to a Boundaryless World: A Developmental Expatriate Model," *Academy of Management Executive* 14, no. 2 (2000), p. 100.

Organizations examine a number of characteristics to determine whether an individual is sufficiently adaptable. Examples include work experiences with cultures other than one's own, previous overseas travel, knowledge of foreign languages (fluency generally is not necessary), and recent immigration background or heritage. Others include (1) the ability to integrate with different people, cultures, and types of business organizations; (2) the ability to sense developments in the host country and accurately evaluate them; (3) the ability to solve problems within different frameworks and from different perspectives; (4) sensitivity to the fine print of differences of culture, politics, religion, and ethics, in addition to individual differences; and (5) flexibility in managing operations on a continuous basis despite lack of assistance and gaps in information.

In research conducted among expatriates in China, Selmar found that those who were best able to deal with their new situation had developed coping strategies characterized by sociocultural and psychological adjustments including (1) feeling comfortable that their work challenges can be met; (2) being able to adjust to their new living conditions; (3) learning how to interact well with host-country nationals outside of work; and (4) feeling reasonably happy and being able to enjoy day-to-day activities.[35] And Caligiuri, after examining how host nationals help expatriates adjust, reported that certain types of personality characteristics are important in this process. In particular, her findings suggest that greater contact with host nationals helps with cross-cultural adjustment when the person also possesses the personality trait of openness. She also found that sociability was directly related to effective adjustment.[36]

Physical and Emotional Health

Most organizations require that their overseas managers have good physical and emotional health. Some examples are fairly obvious. An employee with a heart condition would be rejected for overseas assignment; likewise, an individual with a nervous disorder would not be considered. The psychological ability of individuals to withstand culture shock also would be considered, as would the current marital status as it affects the individual's ability to cope in a foreign environment. For example, one U.S. oil company operating in the Middle East considers middle-aged men with grown children to be the best able to cope with cultural shock, and for some locations in the desert, people from Texas or southern California make better risks than those from New England.

Age, Experience, and Education

Most MNCs strive for a balance between age and experience. There is evidence that younger managers are more eager for international assignments. These managers tend to be more "worldly" and have a greater appreciation of other cultures than older managers do. By the same token, young people often are the least developed in management experience and technical skills; they lack real-world experience. To gain the desired balance, many firms send both young and seasoned personnel to the same overseas post.

Many companies consider an academic degree, preferably a graduate degree, to be of critical importance to an international executive; however, universal agreement regarding the ideal type of degree is nonexistent. As one expert observed:

> Companies with highly technical products tend to prefer science degrees. Other firms feel that successful management requires depth, drive, imagination, creativity, and character—and that the type of person exemplified by these traits is more likely to be produced by a liberal arts education. But the overall prize-winning combination seems to be an undergraduate degree combined with a graduate business degree from a recognized business school.[37]

MNCs, of course, use formal education only as a point of departure for their own training and development efforts. For example, Siemens of Germany gives members of its international management team specific training designed to help them deal more effectively with the types of problems they will face on the job.

Language Training

One recognized weakness of many MNCs is that they do not give sufficient attention to the importance of language training. English is the primary language of international business, and most expatriates from all countries can converse in English. Those who can speak only English are at a distinct disadvantage when doing business in non-English-speaking countries, however. In other words, language can be a very critical factor, and international experts have referred to it as "a most effective indirect method of learning about a country . . . as well as the value systems and customs of its people."[38]

Traditionally, U.S. managers have done very poorly in the language area. For example, a survey of 1,500 top managers worldwide faulted U.S. expatriates for minimizing the value of learning foreign languages. Executives in Japan, Western Europe, and South America placed a high priority on speaking more than one language. The report concludes that "these results provide a poignant indication of national differences that promise to influence profoundly the success of American corporations."[39]

Motivation for a Foreign Assignment

Although individuals being sent overseas should have a desire to work abroad, this usually is not sufficient motivation. International management experts contend that the candidate also must believe in the importance of the job and even have something of an element of idealism or a sense of mission. Applicants who are unhappy with their current situation at home and are looking to get away seldom make effective overseas managers.

Some experts believe that a desire for adventure or a pioneering spirit is an acceptable reason for wanting to go overseas. Other motivators that often are cited include the desire to increase one's chances for promotion and the opportunity to improve one's economic status. For example, many U.S. MNCs regard international experience as being critical for promotion to the upper ranks. In addition, thanks to the supplemental wage and benefit package, U.S. managers sometimes find that they can make, and especially save, more money than if they remained stateside.

Spouses and Dependents or Work-Family Issues

Spouses and dependents are another important consideration when a person is to be chosen for an overseas assignment. If the family is not happy, the manager often performs poorly and may either be terminated or simply decide to leave the organization. Shaffer and her associates recently collected multisource data from 324 expatriates in 46 countries and found that the amount of organizational support that an expatriate feels he or she is receiving and the interplay between the person's work and family domains have a direct and unique influence on the individual's intentions regarding staying with or leaving the enterprise.[40] For this reason, some firms interview both the spouse and the manager before deciding whether to approve the assignment. This can be a very important decision for the firm because it focuses on the importance of family as an issue. One study found that in Singapore, employees were most heavily influenced by family perspective as to whether or not to accept an expatriate position. The desire to achieve was positively related to the likelihood of accepting the position; however, familial opinions remained the most important.[41] One popular approach in appraising the family's suitability for an overseas assignment is called **adaptability screening.** This process evaluates how well the family is likely to stand up to the rigors and stress of overseas life. The company will look for a number of things in this screening, including how closely knit the family is, how well it can withstand stress, and how well it can adjust to a new culture and climate. The reason this family criterion receives so much attention is that MNCs have learned that an unhappy executive will be unproductive on the job and the individual will want to transfer home long before the tour of duty is complete. These findings were affirmed and extended by Borstorff and her associates, who examined the factors associated with employee willingness to work overseas and concluded that:

> **adaptability screening**
> The process of evaluating how well a family is likely to stand up to the stress of overseas life.

1. Unmarried employees are more willing than any other group to accept expat assignments.
2. Married couples without children at home or those with nonteenage children are probably the most willing to move.
3. Prior international experience appears associated with willingness to work as an expatriate.
4. Individuals most committed to their professional careers and to their employing organizations are prone to be more willing to work as expatriates.
5. Careers and attitudes of spouses will likely have a significant impact on employee willingness to move overseas.
6. Employee and spouse perceptions of organizational support for expatriates are critical to employee willingness to work overseas.[42]

These findings indicate that organizations cannot afford to overlook the role of the spouse in the expat selection decision process. What, in particular, can be done to address their concerns?[43] Table 14–2 provides some insights into this answer. Additionally, the table adds a factor often overlooked in this process—situations in which the wife is being assigned overseas and the husband is the "other" spouse. Although many of the concerns of the male spouse are similar to those of spouses in general, a close look at Table 14–2 shows that some of the concerns of the males are different in their rank ordering.

Table 14–2
Activities That Are Important for Expatriate Spouses
(scale: 1–5, 5 = very important)

Mean Score	Activity
Average	**From All Respondents**
4.33	Company help in obtaining necessary paperwork (permits, etc.) for spouse
4.28	Adequate notice of relocation
4.24	Predeparture training for spouse and children
4.23	Counseling for spouse regarding work/activity opportunities in foreign location
4.05	Employment networks coordinated with other international networks
3.97	Help with spouse's reentry into home country
3.93	Financial support for education
3.76	Compensation for spouse's lost wages and/or benefits
3.71	Creation of a job for spouse
3.58	Development of support groups for spouses
3.24	Administrative support (office space, secretarial services, etc.) for spouse
3.11	Financial support for research
3.01	Financial support for volunteer activities
2.90	Financial support for creative activities
Average	**From Male Spouses**
4.86	Employment networks coordinated with other international organizations
4.71	Help with spouse's reentry into home country
4.71	Administrative support (office space, secretarial services, etc.) for spouse
4.57	Compensation for spouse's lost wages and/or benefits
4.29	Adequate notice of relocation
4.29	Counseling for spouse regarding work/activity opportunities in foreign location
3.86	Predeparture training for spouse and children
3.71	Creation of a job for spouse
3.71	Financial support for volunteer activities
3.43	Financial support for education
3.14	Financial support for research
3.14	Financial support for creative activities
3.00	Development of support groups for spouses

Source: Adapted from Betty Jane Punnett, "Towards Effective Management of Expatriate Spouses," *Journal of World Business* 33, no. 3 (1997), p. 249.

Leadership Ability

The ability to influence people to act in a particular way—leadership—is another important criterion in selecting managers for an international assignment. Determining whether a person who is an effective leader in the home country will be equally effective in an overseas environment can be difficult, however. When determining whether an applicant has the desired leadership ability, many firms look for specific characteristics, such as maturity, emotional stability, the ability to communicate well, independence, initiative, creativity, and good health. If these characteristics are present and the person has been an effective leader in the home country, MNCs assume that the individual also will do well overseas.

Other Considerations

Applicants also can take certain steps to prepare themselves better for international assignments. Tu and Sullivan suggest the applicant can carry out a number of different phases.[44] In phase one, they suggest focusing on self-evaluation and general awareness. This includes answering the question, Is an international assignment really for me? Other questions in the first phase include finding out if one's spouse and family support the decision to go international and collecting general information on the available job opportunities.

Phase two is characterized by a concentration on activities that should be completed before a person is selected. Some of these include (1) conducting a technical skills match to ensure that one's skills are in line with those that are required for the job; (2) starting to learn the language, customs, and etiquette of the region where one will be posted; (3) developing an awareness of the culture and value systems of this geographic area; and (4) making one's superior aware of this interest in an international assignment.

The third phase consists of activities to be completed after being selected for an overseas assignment. Some of these include (1) attending training sessions provided by the company; (2) conferring with colleagues who have had experience in the assigned region; (3) speaking with expatriates and foreign nationals about the assigned country; and (4) if possible, visiting the host country with one's spouse before the formally scheduled departure.

■ International Human Resource Selection Procedures

MNCs use a number of selection procedures. The two most common are tests and interviews. Some international firms use one; a smaller percentage employ both. Theoretical models containing the variables that are important for adjusting to an overseas assignment have been developed. These adjustment models can help contribute to more effective selection of expatriates. The following sections examine traditional testing and interviewing procedures and then present an adjustment model.

Testing and Interviewing Procedures

Some evidence suggests that although some firms use testing, it is not extremely popular. For example, an early study found that almost 80 percent of the 127 foreign operations managers who were surveyed reported that their companies used no tests in the selection process.[45] This contrasts with the more widespread testing that these firms use when selecting domestic managers. Many MNCs report that the costs, questionable accuracy, and poor predictive record make testing of limited value.

Many firms do use interviews to screen people for overseas assignments. One expert notes: "It is generally agreed that extensive interviews of candidates (and their spouses) by senior executives still ultimately provide the best method of selection."[46] Tung's research supports these comments. For example, 52 percent of the U.S. MNCs she surveyed reported that in the case of managerial candidates, MNCs conducted interviews with both the manager and his or her spouse, and 47 percent conducted interviews with the candidate alone. For technically oriented positions, 40 percent of the firms interviewed both the candidate and the spouse, and 59 percent conducted interviews with the candidate alone. German firms also sometimes interview the spouse when hiring into managerial and technical positions, although in a different ratio to U.S. firms. In the case of management positions, 41 percent interviewed both the candidate and the spouse, and 59 percent interviewed the candidate only. For technically oriented positions, these percentages were 62 and 39, respectively. Concerning these findings, Tung concluded:

> These figures suggest that in management-type positions which involve more extensive contact with the local community, as compared to technically oriented positions, the adaptability of the spouse to living in a foreign environment was perceived as important for successful performance abroad. However, even for technically oriented positions, a

sizable proportion of the firms did conduct interviews with both candidate and spouse. This lends support to the contention of other researchers that MNCs are becoming increasingly cognizant of the importance of this factor to effective performance abroad.[47]

The Adjustment Process

In recent years, international human resource management specialists have developed models that help to explain the factors involved in effectively adjusting to overseas assignments.[48] These adjustment models help to identify the underpinnings of the effective selection of expatriates.

There are two major types of adjustments that an expatriate must make when going on an overseas assignment. One is the anticipatory adjustment. This is carried out before the expat leaves for the assignment. The other is the in-country adjustment, which takes place on site.

The anticipatory adjustment is influenced by a number of important factors. One factor is the predeparture training that is provided. This often takes the form of cross-cultural seminars or workshops, and it is designed to acquaint expats with the culture and work life of the country to which they will be posted. Another factor affecting anticipatory adjustment is the previous experience the expat may have had with the assigned country or with countries with similar cultures. These two factors, training and previous experience, help determine the accuracy of the expat's expectations.

The organizational input into anticipatory adjustment is most directly related and concerned with the selection process. Traditionally, MNCs relied on only one important selection criterion for overseas assignments: technical competence. Obviously, technical competence is important, but it is only one of a number of skills that will be needed. If the MNC concentrates only on technical competence as a selection criterion, then it is not properly preparing the expatriate managers for successful adjustment in overseas assignments. Expats are going to go abroad believing that they are prepared to deal with the challenges awaiting them, and they will be wrong.

Once the expatriate is on site, a number of factors will influence his or her ability to adjust effectively. One factor is the expat's ability to maintain a positive outlook in the face of a high-pressure situation, to interact well with host nationals, and to perceive and evaluate the host country's cultural values and norms correctly. A second factor is the job itself, as reflected by the clarity of the role the expat plays in the host management team, the authority the expat has to make decisions, the newness of the work-related challenges, and the amount of role conflict that exists. A third factor is the organizational culture and how easily the expat can adjust to it. A fourth is nonwork matters, such as the toughness with which the expatriate faces a whole new cultural experience and how well his or her family can adjust to the rigors of the new assignment. A fifth and final factor identified in the adjustment model is the expat's ability to develop effective socialization tactics and to understand "what's what" and "who's who" in the host organization.

These anticipatory and in-country factors will influence the expatriate's mode and degree of adjustment to an overseas assignment. They can help to explain why effective selection of expatriates is multifaceted and can be very difficult and challenging. But if all works out well, the individual can become a very important part of the organization's overseas operations. McCormick and Chapman illustrated this by showing the changes that an expat goes through as he or she seeks to adjust to the new assignment.[49] As seen in Figure 14–4, early enthusiasm often gives way to cold reality, and the expat typically ends up in a search to balance personal and work demands with the new environment. In many cases, fortunately, everything works out well. Additionally, one of the ways in which MNCs often try to put potential expats at ease about their new assignment is by presenting an attractive compensation package.

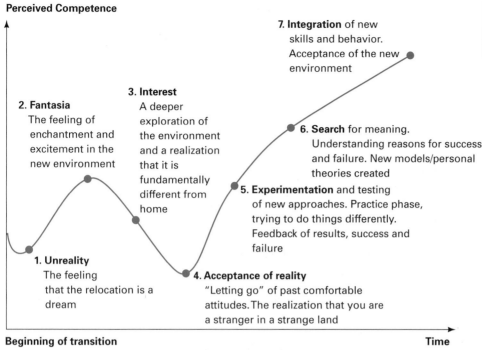

Perceived Competence

7. **Integration** of new skills and behavior. Acceptance of the new environment

3. **Interest**
A deeper exploration of the environment and a realization that it is fundamentally different from home

2. **Fantasia**
The feeling of enchantment and excitement in the new environment

6. **Search** for meaning. Understanding reasons for success and failure. New models/personal theories created

5. **Experimentation** and testing of new approaches. Practice phase, trying to do things differently. Feedback of results, success and failure

1. **Unreality**
The feeling that the relocation is a dream

4. **Acceptance of reality**
"Letting go" of past comfortable attitudes. The realization that you are a stranger in a strange land

Beginning of transition   Time

Figure 14–4

The Relocation Transition Curve

Source: Adapted from Iain McCormick and Tony Chapman, "Executive Relocation: Personal and Organizational Tactics," in *Managing Across Cultures: Issues and Perspectives,* ed. Pat Joynt and Malcolm Warner (London: International Thomson Business Press, 1996), p. 368.

■ Compensation

One of the reasons why there has been a decline in the number of expats in recent years is that MNCs have found that the expense can be prohibitive. Reynolds estimated that, on average, "expats cost employers two to five times as much as home-country counterparts and frequently ten or more times as much as local nationals in the country to which they are assigned."[50] As seen in Figure 14–5, the cost of living in some of the major cities is extremely high, and these expenses must be included somewhere in the compensation package.

Common Elements of Compensation Packages

The overall compensation package often varies from country to country. As Bailey noted:

> Compensation programs implemented in a global organization will not mirror an organization's domestic plan because of differences in legally mandated benefits, tax laws, cultures, and employee expectation based on local practices. The additional challenge in compensation design is the requirement that excessive costs be avoided and at the same time employee morale be maintained at high levels.[51]

There are five common elements in the typical expatriate compensation package: base salary, benefits, allowances, incentives, and taxes.

Base Salary   Base salary is the amount of money that an expatriate normally receives in the home country. In the United States this has been around $175,000 for upper-middle managers in recent years, and this rate is similar to that paid to managers in both Japan and Germany. The exchange rates, of course, also affect the real wages.

Expatriate salaries typically are set according to the base pay of the home countries. Therefore, a German manager working for a U.S. MNC and assigned to Spain would have a base salary that reflects the salary structure in Germany. U.S. expatriates have salaries tied to U.S. levels. The salaries usually are paid in home currency, local currency,

Figure 14–5

Relative Cost of Living in Selected Cities

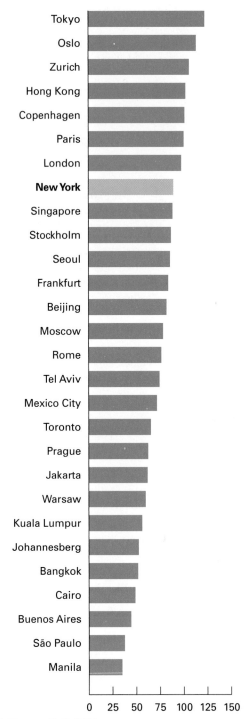

Source: Economist Intelligence Unit, 2000.

or a combination of the two. The base pay also serves as the benchmark against which bonuses and benefits are calculated.

Benefits Approximately one-third of compensation for regular employees is benefits. These benefits compose a similar, or even larger, portion of expat compensation. A number of thorny issues surround compensation for expatriates, however. These include:

1. Whether MNCs should maintain expatriates in home-country benefit programs, particularly if these programs are not tax-deductible.

2. Whether MNCs have the option of enrolling expatriates in host-country benefit programs or making up any difference in coverage.

3. Whether host-country legislation regarding termination of employment affects employee benefits entitlements.

4. Whether the home or host country is responsible for the expatriates' social security benefits.

5. Whether benefits should be subject to the requirements of the home or host country.

6. Which country should pay for the benefits.

7. Whether other benefits should be used to offset any shortfall in coverage.

8. Whether home-country benefits programs should be available to local nationals.

Most U.S.-based MNCs include expatriate managers in their home-office benefits program at no additional cost to the expats. If the host country requires expats to contribute to their social security program, the MNC typically picks up the tab. Fortunately, several international agreements between countries recently have eliminated such dual coverage and expenses.

Additionally, MNCs often provide expatriates with extra vacation and with special leaves. The MNC typically will pay the airfare for expats and their families to make an annual visit home, for emergency leave, and for expenses when a relative in the home country is ill or dies.

Allowances   Allowances are an expensive feature of expatriate compensation packages. One of the most common parts is a cost-of-living allowance—a payment for differences between the home country and the overseas assignment. This allowance is designed to provide the expat with the same standard of living that he or she enjoyed in the home country, and it may cover a variety of expenses, including relocation, housing, education, and hardship.

Relocation expenses typically involve moving, shipping, and storage charges that are associated with personal furniture, clothing, and other items that the expatriate and his or her family are (or are not) taking to the new assignment. Related expenses also may include cars and club memberships in the host country, although these perks commonly are provided only to senior-level expats.

Housing allowances cover a wide range. Some firms provide the expat with a residence during the assignment and pay all associated expenses. Others give a predetermined housing allotment each month and let expats choose their own residence. Additionally, some MNCs help those going on assignment with the sale or lease of the house they are leaving behind; if the house is sold, the company usually pays closing costs and other associated expenses.

Education allowances for the expat's children are another integral part of the compensation package. These expenses cover costs such as tuition, enrollment fees, books, supplies, transportation, room, board, and school uniforms. In some cases, expenses to attend postsecondary schools also are covered.

Hardship allowances are designed to induce expats to work in hazardous areas or in an area with a poor quality of life. Those who are assigned to Eastern Europe, China, and some Middle Eastern countries sometimes are granted a hardship premium. These payments may be in the form of a lump sum ($10,000 to $50,000) or a percentage (15 to 50 percent) of the expat's base compensation.

Incentives   In recent years some MNCs have also been designing special incentive programs for keeping expats motivated. In the process, a growing number of firms have dropped the ongoing premium for overseas assignments and replaced it with a one-time, lump-sum premium. For example, in the early 1990s over 60 percent of MNCs gave ongoing premiums to their expats. Today that percentage is under 50 percent and continuing to

Table 14–3
Employer Incentive Practices Around the World

Percent of MNCs Paying for Moves Within Continents				
Type of Premium	Asia	Europe	North America	Total
Ongoing	62%	46%	29%	42%
Lump sum	21	20	25	23
None	16	27	42	32

Percent of MNCs Paying for Moves Between Continents				
Type of Premium	Asia	Europe	North America	Total
Ongoing	63%	54%	39%	49%
Lump sum	24	18	30	26
None	13	21	27	22

Source: Derived from Geoffrey W. Latta, "Expatriate Incentives: Beyond Tradition," *HR Focus,* March 1998, p. S4.

decline. Peterson and his colleagues, for example, examined the human resource policies of 24 U.S., British, German, and Japanese subsidiaries and found that in only 10 cases did the multinational have a policy of paying expatriates higher compensation than they would have received if they had stayed in their home country.[52]

The lump-sum payment has a number of benefits. One is that expats realize that they will be given this payment just once—when they move to the international locale. So the payment tends to retain its value as an incentive. A second is that the costs to the company are less because there is only one payment and no future financial commitment. A third is that because it is a separate payment, distinguishable from regular pay, it is more readily available for saving or spending.

The specific incentive program that is used will vary, and expats like this. Researchers, for example, have found that some of the factors that influence the type and amount of incentive include whether the person is moving within or between continents and where the person is being stationed. Table 14–3 provides some of the latest survey information related to worldwide employer incentive practices.

Finally, it is important to recognize that growing numbers of MNCs are beginning to phase out incentive premiums. Instead, they are focusing on creating a cadre of expats who are motivated by nonfinancial incentives.

Taxes Another major component of expatriate compensation is tax equalization. For example, an expat may have two tax bills, one from the host country and one from the U.S. Internal Revenue Service, for the same pay. IRS Code Section 911 permits a deduction of up to $80,000 on foreign-earned income. Top-level expats often earn far more than this, however; thus, they may pay two tax bills for the amount by which their pay exceeds $80,000.

Usually, MNCs pay the extra tax burden. The most common way is by determining the base salary and other extras (e.g., bonuses) that the expat would make if based in the home country. Taxes on this income then are computed and compared with the taxes due on the expat's income. Any taxes that exceed what would have been imposed in the home country are paid by the MNC, and any windfall is kept by the expat as a reward for taking the assignment.

Tailoring the Package

Working within the five common elements just described, MNCs will tailor compensation packages to fit the specific situation. For example, senior-level managers in Japan are paid only around four times as much as junior staff members. This is in sharp contrast to the United States, where the multiple is much higher. A similar situation exists in Europe, where many senior-level managers make far less than their U.S. counterparts and stockholders, politicians, and the general public oppose U.S.-style affluence. Can a senior-level U.S. expat be paid a salary that is significantly higher than local senior-level managers in the overseas subsidiary, or would the disparity create morale problems? This is a difficult question to answer and must be given careful consideration. One solution is to link pay and performance to attract and retain outstanding personnel.

In formulating the compensation package, a number of approaches can be used. The most common is the **balance-sheet approach,** which involves ensuring that the expat is "made whole" and does not lose money by taking the assignment. A second and often complementary approach is negotiation, which involves working out a special, ad hoc arrangement that is acceptable to both the company and the expat. A third approach, **localization,** involves paying the expat a salary that is comparable to the salaries of local nationals. This approach most commonly is used with individuals early in their careers who are being given a long-term overseas assignment. A fourth approach is the **lump-sum method,** which involves giving the expat a predetermined amount of money and letting the individual make his or her own decisions regarding how to spend it. A fifth is the **cafeteria approach,** which entails giving expats a series of options and letting them decide how to spend the available funds. For example, expats who have children may opt for private schooling; expats who have no children may choose a chauffeur-driven car or an upscale apartment. A sixth method is the **regional system,** under which the MNC sets a compensation system for all expats who are assigned to a particular region, so that (for example) everyone going to Europe falls under one particular system and everyone being assigned to South America is covered by a different system.[53]

The most important thing to remember about global compensation is that the package must be cost-effective and fair. If it meets these two criteria, it likely will be acceptable to all parties.

■ Individual and Host-Country Viewpoints

Until now, we have examined the selection process mostly from the standpoint of the MNC: What will be best for the company? However, two additional perspectives for selection warrant consideration: (1) that of the individual who is being selected and (2) that of the country to which the candidate will be sent. Research shows that each has specific desires and motivations regarding the expatriate selection process.

Candidate Motivations

Why do individuals accept foreign assignments? One answer is a greater demand for their talents abroad than at home. For example, a growing number of senior U.S. managers have moved to Mexico because of Mexico's growing need for experienced executives. The findings of one early study grouped the participating countries into clusters: Anglo (Australia, Austria, Canada, India, New Zealand, South Africa, Switzerland, United Kingdom, and United States); Northern European (Denmark, Finland, Norway); French (Belgium and France); northern South American (Colombia, Mexico, and Peru); southern South American (Argentina and Chile); and Independent (Brazil, Germany, Israel, Japan, Sweden, and Venezuela).[54] Within these groupings, researchers were able to identify major motivational differences. Some of their findings included:

1. The Anglo cluster was more interested in individual achievement and less interested in the desire for security than any other cluster.

2. The French cluster was similar to the Anglo cluster, except that less importance was given to individual achievement and more to security.

balance-sheet approach
An approach to developing an expatriate compensation package that ensures the expat is "made whole" and does not lose money by taking the assignment.

localization
An approach to developing an expatriate compensation package that involves paying the expat a salary comparable to that of local nationals.

lump-sum method
An approach to developing an expatriate compensation package that involves giving the expat a predetermined amount of money and letting the individual make his or her own decisions regarding how to spend it.

cafeteria approach
An approach to developing an expatriate compensation package that entails giving the individual a series of options and letting the person decide how to spend the available funds.

regional system
An approach to developing an expatriate compensation package that involves setting a compensation system for all expats who are assigned to a particular region and paying everyone in accord with that system.

3. Countries in the Northern European cluster were more oriented to job accomplishment and less to getting ahead; considerable importance was assigned to jobs not interfering with personal lives.

4. In South American clusters, individual achievement goals were less important than in most other clusters. Fringe benefits were particularly important to South American groups.

5. Germans were similar to those in the South American clusters, except that they placed a greater emphasis on advancement and earnings.

6. The Japanese were unique in their mix of desires. They placed high value on earnings opportunities but low value on advancement. They were high on challenge but low on autonomy. At the same time, they placed strong emphasis on working in a friendly, efficient department and having good physical working conditions.

Another interesting focus of attention has been on those countries that expatriates like best. A study conducted by Ingemar Torbiorn found that the 1,100 Swedish expatriates surveyed were at least fairly well satisfied with their host country and in some cases were very satisfied. Five of the countries that they liked very much were Switzerland, Belgium, England, the United States, and Portugal.[55] These countries are still popular today, which makes sense since they are included in the top tier of countries with the highest quality of life. The criteria include such things as family life, economic life, unemployment rates, political stability, and so forth to determine how safe or attractive the country is.

Host-Country Desires

Although many MNCs try to choose people who fit in well, little attention has been paid to the host country's point of view. Whom would it like to see put in managerial positions? One study that compared U.S., Indonesian, and Mexican managers found that behaviors can distinguish them from one another and that host countries would prefer a managerial style similar to that of their country.[56] For example, positive managerial behaviors, such as honesty and follow through with employees, distinguish Indonesian and U.S. managers from Mexican managers. As seen in Chapter 4, this could partially be due to the power distance suggested by Hofstede. Furthermore, negative managerial behaviors, such as public criticism and discipline toward employees, also distinguish Indonesian and U.S. managers from Mexican managers. It has been suggested that the dynamic in the workplace has to do with the familial structure, namely that Mexican workers place a higher value on family over work than the U.S. or Indonesian counterparts. This can be a factor in how the positive and negative behaviors are expressed in each country, as outlined in Table 14–4. Overall, it is important for managers to take the host-country perspectives into consideration, or it could result in an ineffectual endeavor.

■ Repatriation of Expatriates

repatriation
The return to one's home country from an overseas management assignment.

For most overseas managers, **repatriation,** the return to one's home country, occurs within five years of the time they leave. Few expatriates remain overseas for the duration of their stay with the firm.[57] When they return, these expatriates often find themselves facing readjustment problems, and some MNCs are trying to deal with these problems through use of transition strategies.

Reasons for Returning

The most common reason that expatriates return home from overseas assignments is that their formally agreed-on tour of duty is over. Before they left, they were told that they

---

Table 14–4
Comparative Positive and Negative Managerial Behavior by Country

Positive Behaviors	Negative Behaviors
Indonesia	
Is honest with employees	Engages in unfair discrimination
Provides clear work expectations	Disciplines and criticizes in public
Shows confidence in employee	Flaunts power
Provides regular feedback	
Mexico	
Shows respect for employees	Practices favoritism
Shows confidence in employees	Does not understand employee values
Is flexible to individual employee needs	and traditions
Provides clear work expectations	
United States	
Is honest with employees	Disciplines and criticizes in public
Shows loyalty to employees	Flaunts power
Shows respect for employees	
Shows confidence in employees	

Source: From Charles M. Vance and Yongsun Paik, "One Size Fits All in Expatriate Pre-departure Training?" *The Journal of Management Development* 21, No. 7/8, 2002, p. 566. Reprinted with permission of Emerald Insight.

---

would be posted overseas for a predetermined period, often two to three years, and they are returning as planned. A second common reason is that expatriates want their children educated in a home-country school, and the longer they are away, the less likely it is that this will happen.[58]

A third reason why expatriates return is that they are not happy in their overseas assignment. Sometimes unhappiness is a result of poor organizational support by the home office, which leaves the manager feeling that the assignment is not a good one and it would be best to return as soon as possible. Kraimer, Wayne, and Jaworski found that lack of this kind of support has a negative effect on the expat's ability to adjust to the assignment.[59] At other times an expat will want to return home early because the spouse or children do not want to stay. Because the company feels that the loss in managerial productivity is too great to be offset by short-term personal unhappiness, the individual is allowed to come back even though typically the cost is quite high.[60]

A fourth reason that people return is failure to do a good job. Such failure often spells trouble for the manager and may even result in demotion or termination.

Readjustment Problems

Many companies that say that they want their people to have international experience often seem unsure of what to do with these managers when they return. One recent survey of midsize and large firms found that 80 percent of these companies send people abroad and more than half of them intend to increase the number they have on assignment overseas. However, responses from returning expats point to problems. Three-quarters of the respondents said that they felt their permanent position upon returning home was a demotion. Over 60 percent said that they lacked the opportunities to put their foreign experience to work, and 60 percent said that their company had not communicated clearly about what would happen to them when they returned. Perhaps worst of all, within a year of returning, 25 percent of the managers had left the company.[61] These statistics are not surprising to those who have been studying repatriation problems. In fact, one researcher reported the following expatriate comments about their experiences:

> My colleagues react indifferently to my international assignment. . . . They view me as doing a job I did in the past; they don't see me as having gained anything while overseas.
>
> I had no specific reentry job to return to. I wanted to leave international and return to domestic. Working abroad magnifies problems while isolating effects. You deal with more problems, but the home office doesn't know the details of the good or bad effects. Managerially, I'm out of touch.
>
> I'm bored at work. . . . I run upstairs to see what [another returning colleague] is doing. He says, "Nothing." Me, too.[62]

Still another problem is adjusting to the new job back home. It sometimes takes from six months to a year before managers are operating at full effectiveness. Figure 14–6 provides an illustration.

Other readjustment problems are more personal in nature. Many expatriates find that the salary and fringe benefits to which they have become accustomed in the foreign assignment now are lost, and adjusting to this lower standard of living is difficult. In addition, those who sold their houses and now must buy new ones find that the monthly cost often is much higher than when they left. The children often are placed in public schools, where classes are much larger than in the overseas private schools. Many also miss the cultural lifestyles, as in the case of an executive who is transferred from Paris, France, to a medium-sized city in the United States, or from any developed country to an underdeveloped country. Additionally, many returning expatriates have learned that their international experiences are not viewed as important. Many Japanese expatriates, for example, report that when they return, their experiences should be downplayed if they want to "fit in" with the organization. In fact, reports one recent *New York Times* article, a substantial number of Japanese expatriates "are happier overseas than they are back home."[63]

Other research supports the findings noted here and offers operative recommendations for action. Based on questionnaires completed by 174 respondents who had been repatriated from four large U.S. MNCs, Black found the following:

1. With few exceptions, individuals whose expectations were met had the most positive levels of repatriation adjustment and job performance.

2. In the case of high-level managers in particular, expatriates whose job demands were greater, rather than less, than expected reported high levels of repatriation adjustment and job performance. Those having greater job demands may have put in more effort and had better adjustment and performance.

Figure 14–6

Effectiveness of Returning Expatriates

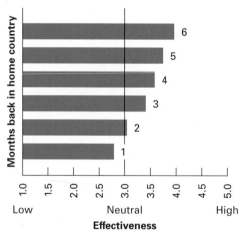

Source: From *International Dimensions of Organizational Behavior,* 2ⁿᵈ Edition by Nancy J. Adler, 1991, pp. 7–8. Reprinted with permission of South-Western, a division of Thomson Learning: www.thomsonrights.com.

3. Job performance and repatriation adjustment were greater for individuals whose job constraint expectations were undermet than for those individuals whose expectations were overmet. In other words, job constraints were viewed as an undesirable aspect of the job, and having them turn out to be less than expected was a pleasant surprise that helped adjustment and performance.

4. When living and housing conditions turned out to be better than expected, general repatriation adjustment and job performance were better.

5. Individuals whose general expectations were met or overmet had job evaluations that placed them 10 percent higher than those whose general expectations were unmet.[64]

Transition Strategies

To help smooth the adjustment from an overseas to a stateside assignment, some MNCs have developed **transition strategies,** which can take a number of different forms. One is the use of **repatriation agreements,** whereby the firm tells an individual how long she or he will be posted overseas and promises to give the individual, on return, a job that is mutually acceptable. This agreement typically does not promise a specific position or salary, but the agreement may state that the person will be given a job that is equal to, if not better than, the one held before leaving.[65]

Some firms also rent or otherwise maintain expatriates' homes until they return. The Aluminum Company of America and Union Carbide both have such plans for managers going overseas. This plan helps reduce the financial shock that often accompanies home shopping by returning expatriates. A third strategy is to use senior executives as sponsors of managers abroad.

Still another approach is to keep expatriate managers apprised of what is going on at corporate headquarters and to plug these managers into projects at the home office whenever they are on leave in the home country. This helps maintain the person's visibility and ensures the individual is looked on as a regular member of the management staff.

One study surveyed 99 employees and managers with international experience in 21 corporations.[66] The findings reveal that cultural reentry, financial implications, and the nature of job assignments are three major areas of expatriate concern. In particular, some of the main problems of repatriation identified in this study include (1) adjusting to life back home; (2) facing a financial package that is not as good as that overseas; (3) having less autonomy in the stateside job than in the overseas position; and (4) not receiving any career counseling from the company. To the extent that the MNC can address these types of problems, the transition will be smooth, and the expatriate's performance effectiveness once home will increase quickly. Some additional steps suggested by experts in this area include:

1. Arrange an event to welcome and recognize the employee and family, either formally or informally.

2. Establish support to facilitate family reintegration.

3. Offer repatriation counseling or workshops to ease the adjustment.

4. Assist the spouse with job counseling, résumé writing, and interviewing techniques.

5. Provide educational counseling for the children.

6. Provide the employee with a thorough debriefing by a facilitator to identify new knowledge, insights, and skills and to provide a forum to showcase new competencies.

7. Offer international outplacement to the employee and reentry counseling to the entire family if no positions are possible.

transition strategies
Strategies used to help smooth the adjustment from an overseas to a stateside assignment.

repatriation agreements
Agreements whereby the firm tells an individual how long she or he will be posted overseas and promises to give the individual, on return, a job that is mutually acceptable.

8. Arrange a postassignment interview with the expatriate and spouse to review their view of the assignment and address any repatriation issues.[67]

Hammer and his associates echo these types of recommendations. Based on research that they conducted in two multinational corporations among expats and their spouses, they concluded that:

> The findings from the present study suggest that one of the key transitional activities for returning expatriates and their spouses from a corporate context should involve targeted communication from the home environment concerning the expectations of the home office toward the return of the repatriate executive and his/her family (role relationships). Further, reentry training should focus primarily on helping the repatriate manager and spouse align their expectations with the actual situation that will be encountered upon arrival in the home culture both within the organizational context as well as more broadly within the social milieu. To the degree that corporate communication and reentry training activities help the returning executive and spouse in expectation alignment, the executive's level of reentry satisfaction should be higher and the degree of reentry difficulties less.[68]

Additionally, in recent years many MNCs have begun using inpatriates to supplement their home-office staff and some of the same issues discussed here with repatriation come into play.

■ Training in International Management

training
The process of altering employee behavior and attitudes in a way that increases the probability of goal attainment.

Training is the process of altering employee behavior and attitudes in a way that increases the probability of goal attainment. Training is particularly important in preparing employees for overseas assignments because it helps ensure that their full potential will be tapped.[69] One of the things that training can do is to help expat managers better understand the customs, cultures, and work habits of the local culture. The simplest training, in terms of preparation time, is to place a cultural integrator in each foreign operation. This individual is responsible for ensuring that the operation's business systems are in accord with those of the local culture. The integrator advises, guides, and recommends actions needed to ensure this synchronization.[70]

Unfortunately, although using an integrator can help, it is seldom sufficient. Recent experience clearly reveals that in creating an effective global team, the MNC must assemble individuals who collectively understand the local language, have grown up in diverse cultures or neighborhoods, have open, flexible minds, and will be able to deal with high degrees of stress.[71] In those cases where potential candidates do not yet possess all these requisite skills or abilities, MNCs need a well-designed training program that is administered before the individuals leave for their overseas assignment (and, in some cases, also on-site) and then evaluated later to determine its overall effectiveness. One review of 228 MNCs found that cross-cultural training, which can take many forms, is becoming increasingly popular. Some of these findings included the following:

1. Of organizations with cultural programs, 58 percent offer training only to some expatriates, and 42 percent offer it to all of them.
2. Ninety-one percent offer cultural orientation programs to spouses, and 75 percent offer them to dependent children.
3. The average duration of the cultural training programs is three days.
4. Cultural training is continued after arrival in the assignment location 32 percent of the time.
5. Thirty percent offer formal cultural training programs.
6. Of those without formal cultural programs, 37 percent plan to add such training.[72]

The most common topics covered in cultural training are social etiquette, customs, economics, history, politics, and business etiquette. However, the MNC's overall philosophy of international management and the demands of the specific cultural situation are the starting point. This is because countries tend to have distinctive human resource management (HRM) practices that differentiate them from other countries. For example, the HRM practices that are prevalent in the United States are quite different from those in France and Argentina. This was clearly illustrated by Sparrow and Budhwar, who compared data from 13 different countries on the basis of HRM factors. Five of these factors were the following:

1. Structural empowerment that is characterized by flat organization designs, wide spans of control, the use of flexible cross-functional teams, and the rewarding of individuals for productivity gains.

2. Accelerated resource development that is characterized by the early identification of high-potential employees, the establishment of both multiple and parallel career paths, the rewarding of personnel for enhancing their skills and knowledge, and the offering of continuous training and development education.

3. Employee welfare emphasis that is characterized by firms offering personal family assistance, encouraging and rewarding external volunteer activities, and promoting organizational cultures that emphasize equality in the workplace.

4. An efficiency emphasis in which employees are encouraged to monitor their own work and to continually improve their performance.

5. Long-termism, which stresses long-term results such as innovation and creativity rather than weekly and monthly short-term productivity.[73]

When Sparrow and Budhwar used these HRM approaches on a comparative country-by-country basis, they found that there were worldwide differences in human resource management practices. Table 14–5 shows the comparative results after each of the 13 countries was categorized as being either high or low on the respective factors. These findings reveal that countries are unique in their approach to human resource management. What

Table 14–5
Human Resource Management Practices in Select Countries

	Structural Empowerment		Accelerated Resource Development		Employee Welfare Emphasis		Efficiency Emphasis		Long-Termism	
	High	Low	High	Low	High	Low	High	Low	High	Low
United States	X		X		X		X			X
Canada	X		X		X			X		X
United Kingdom	X		X			X		X		X
Italy		X	X			X		X		X
Japan		X	X		X		X		X	
India		X	X		X			X	X	
Australia	X			X		X	X		X	
Brazil	X			X	X			X	X	
Mexico	X			X	X			X		X
Argentina		X		X	X			X		X
Germany		X		X		X		X	X	
Korea		X		X		X	X		X	
France		X		X		X	X			X

Source: Adapted from Paul R. Sparrow and Pawan S. Budhwar, "Competition and Change: Mapping the Indian HRM Recipe Against Worldwide Patterns," *Journal of World Business* 32, no. 3 (1997), p. 233.

works well in the United States may have limited value in France. In fact, a close analysis of Table 14–5 shows that none of the 13 countries had the same profile; each was different. This was true even in the case of Anglo nations such as the United States, Canada, Australia, and the United Kingdom, where differences in employee welfare emphasis, accelerated resource development, efficiency emphasis orientation, and long-termism resulted in unique HRM profiles for each. Similarly, Japan and Korea differed on two of the factors, as did Germany and France; and India, which many people might feel would be more similar to an Anglo culture, because of the British influence, than to an Asian one, differed on two factors with Canada, on three factors with both the United States and the United Kingdom, and on four factors with Australia.

These findings point to the fact that MNCs will have to focus increasingly on HRM programs designed to meet the needs of local personnel. A good example is provided in the former communist countries of Europe, where international managers are discovering that in order to effectively recruit college graduates, their firms must provide training programs that give these new employees opportunities to work with a variety of tasks and to help them specialize in their particular fields of interest. At the same time the MNCs are discovering that these recruits are looking for companies that offer a good social working environment. A recent survey of over 1,000 business and engineering students from Poland, the Czech Republic, and Hungary found that almost two-thirds of the respondents said that they wanted their boss to be receptive to their ideas; 37 percent wanted to work for managers who had strong industry experience; and 34 percent wanted a boss who was a good rational decision maker. These findings indicate that multinational human resource management is now becoming much more of a two-way street: Both employees and managers need to continually adjust to emerging demands.[74]

The Impact of Overall Management Philosophy on Training

The type of training that is required of expatriates is influenced by the firm's overall philosophy of international management. For example, some companies prefer to send their own people to staff an overseas operation; others prefer to use locals whenever possible.[75] Briefly, four basic philosophical positions of multinational corporations can influence the training program:

ethnocentric MNC
An MNC that stresses nationalism and often puts home-office people in charge of key international management positions.

polycentric MNC
An MNC that places local nationals in key positions and allows these managers to appoint and develop their own people.

regiocentric MNC
An MNC that relies on local managers from a particular geographic region to handle operations in and around that area.

geocentric MNC
An MNC that seeks to integrate diverse regions of the world through a global approach to decision making.

1. An **ethnocentric MNC** puts home-office people in charge of key international management positions. The MNC headquarters group and the affiliated world company managers all have the same basic experiences, attitudes, and beliefs about how to manage operations. Many Japanese firms follow this practice.

2. A **polycentric MNC** places local nationals in key positions and allows these managers to appoint and develop their own people. MNC headquarters gives the subsidiary managers authority to manage their operations just as long as these operations are sufficiently profitable. Some MNCs use this approach in East Asia, Australia, and other markets that are deemed too expensive to staff with expatriates.

3. A **regiocentric MNC** relies on local managers from a particular geographic region to handle operations in and around that area. For example, production facilities in France would be used to produce goods for all EU countries. Similarly, advertising managers from subsidiaries in Italy, Germany, France, and Spain would come together and formulate a "European" advertising campaign for the company's products. A regiocentric approach often relies on regional group cooperation of local managers. The Gillette MNC uses a regiocentric approach.

4. A **geocentric MNC** seeks to integrate diverse regions of the world through a global approach to decision making. Assignments are based on qualifications, and all subsidiary managers throughout the structure are regarded as

equal to those at headquarters. IBM is an excellent example of an MNC that attempts to use a geocentric approach.

All four of these philosophical positions can be found in the multinational arena, and each puts a different type of training demand on the MNC.[76] For example, ethnocentric MNCs will do all training at headquarters, but polycentric MNCs will rely on local managers to assume responsibility for seeing that the training function is carried out.

The Impact of Different Learning Styles on Training and Development

Another important area of consideration for development is learning styles. **Learning** is the acquisition of skills, knowledge, and abilities that result in a relatively permanent change in behavior.[77] Over the last decade, growing numbers of multinationals have tried to become "learning organizations," continually focused on activities such as training and development. In the new millennium, this learning focus applied to human resource development may go beyond learning organizations to "teaching organizations." For example, Tichy and Cohen, after conducting an analysis of world-class companies such as General Electric, PepsiCo, AlliedSignal, and Coca-Cola, found that teaching organizations are even more relevant than learning organizations because they go beyond the belief that everyone must continually acquire new knowledge and skills and focus on ensuring that everyone in the organization, especially the top management personnel, passes the learning on to others. Here are their conclusions:

> In teaching organizations, leaders see it as their responsibility to teach. They do that because they understand that it's the best, if not only, way to develop throughout a company people who can come up with and carry out smart ideas about the business. Because people in teaching organizations see teaching as critical to the success of their business, they find ways to do it every day. Teaching every day about critical business issues avoids the fuzzy focus that has plagued some learning organization efforts, which have sometimes become a throwback to the 1960s- and 1970s-style self-exportation and human relations training.[78]

Of course, the way in which training takes place can be extremely important. A great deal of research has been conducted on the various types and theories of learning. However, the application of these ideas in an international context often can be quite challenging because cultural differences can affect the learning and teaching. Prud'homme van Reine and Trompenaars, commenting on the development of expats, noted that national cultural differences typically affect the way MNCs train and develop their people. For example, Americans like an experiential learning style, while Germans prefer a theoretical-analytical learning approach.[79] Moreover, there can be sharp learning preferences between groups that are quite similar in terms of culture. Hayes and Allinson, after studying cultural differences in the learning styles of managers, reported, "Two groups can be very similar in ecology and climate and, for example, through a common legacy of colonialism, have a similar language and legal, educational and governmental infrastructure, but may be markedly different in terms of beliefs, attitudes, and values."[80] Moreover, research shows that people with different learning styles prefer different learning environments, and if there is a mismatch between the preferred learning style and the work environment, dissatisfaction and poor performance can result.

In addition to these conclusions, those responsible for training programs must remember that even if learning does occur, the new behaviors will not be used if they are not reinforced. For example, if the head of a foreign subsidiary is highly ethnocentric and believes that things should be done the way they are in the home country, new managers with intercultural training likely will find little reward or reinforcement for using their ideas. This cultural complexity also extends to the way in which the training is conducted.

learning
The acquisition of skills, knowledge, and abilities that result in a relatively permanent change in behavior.

Reasons for Training

Training programs are useful in preparing people for overseas assignments for many reasons. These reasons can be put into two general categories: organizational and personal.

ethnocentrism
The belief that one's own way of doing things is superior to that of others.

Organizational Reasons   Organizational reasons for training relate to the enterprise at large and its efforts to manage overseas operations more effectively.[81] One primary reason is to help overcome **ethnocentrism,** the belief that one's way of doing things is superior to that of others. Ethnocentrism is common in many large MNCs where managers believe that the home office's approach to doing business can be exported intact to all other countries because this approach is superior to anything at the local level. Training can help home-office managers understand the values and customs of other countries so that when they are transferred overseas, they have a better understanding of how to interact with local personnel. This training also can help managers overcome the common belief among many personnel that expatriates are not as effective as host-country managers. This is particularly important given that an increasing number of managerial positions now are held by foreign managers in U.S. MNCs.[82]

Another organizational reason for training is to improve the flow of communication between the home office and the international subsidiaries and branches. Quite often, overseas managers find that they are not adequately informed regarding what is expected of them although the home office places close controls on their operating authority. This is particularly true when the overseas manager is from the host country. Effective communication can help minimize these problems.

Finally, another organizational reason for training is to increase overall efficiency and profitability. Research shows that organizations that closely tie their training and human resource management strategy to their business strategy tend to outperform those that do not.[83] Stroh and Caligiuri conducted research on 60 of the world's major multinationals and found that effective HRM programs pay dividends in the form of higher profits. Additionally, their data showed that the most successful MNCs recognized the importance of having top managers with a global orientation. One of the ways in which almost all these organizations did this was by giving their managers global assignments that not only filled technical and managerial needs but also provided developmental experiences for the personnel—and this assignment strategy included managers from every geographic region where the firms were doing business. Drawing together the lessons to be learned from this approach, Stroh and Caligiuri noted that:

> The development of global leadership skills should not stop with home country nationals. Global HR should also be involved in developing a global orientation among host country nationals as well. This means, for example, sending not only home-country managers on global assignments but host national talent to the corporate office and to other divisions around the world. Many of the managers at the successful MNCs talked about how their companies develop talent in this way. In addition, they described a "desired state" for human resources, including the ability to source talent within the company from around the world. Victor Guerra, an executive at Prudential, commented: *We need to continually recognize that there are bright, articulate people who do not live in the home country. U.S. multinationals are especially guilty of this shortsightedness.* Acknowledging that talent exists and using the talent appropriately are two different issues—one idealist, the other strategic.[84]

Personal Reasons   The primary reason for training overseas managers is to improve their ability to interact effectively with local people in general and with their personnel in particular. Increasing numbers of training programs now address social topics such as how to take a client to dinner, effectively apologize to a customer, appropriately address one's overseas colleagues, communicate formally and politely with others, and learn how to help others "save face."[85] These programs also focus on dispelling myths and stereotypes by replacing them with facts about the culture. For example, in helping expatriates better understand Arab executives, the following guidelines are offered:

1. There is a close relationship between the Arab executive and his environment. The Arab executive is looked on as a community and family leader, and there are numerous social pressures on him because of this role. He is consulted on all types of problems, even those far removed from his position.

2. With regard to decision making, the Arab executive likely will consult with his subordinates, but he will take responsibility for his decision himself rather than arriving at it through consensus.

3. The Arab executive likely will try to avoid conflict. If there is an issue that he favors but that is opposed by his subordinates, he tends to impose his authority. If it is an issue favored by the subordinates but opposed by the executive, he will likely let the matter drop without taking action.

4. The Arab executive's style is very personal. He values loyalty over efficiency. Although some executives find that the open-door tradition consumes a great deal of time, they do not feel that the situation can be changed. Many executives tend to look on their employees as family and will allow them to bypass the hierarchy to meet them.

5. The Arab executive, contrary to popular beliefs, puts considerable value on the use of time. One thing he admires most about Western or expatriate executives is their use of time, and he would like to encourage his own employees to make more productive use of their time.[86]

Another growing problem is the belief that foreign language skills are not really essential to doing business overseas. Effective training programs can help to minimize these personal problems.

A particularly big personal problem that managers have in an overseas assignment is arrogance. This is the so-called Ugly American problem that U.S. expatriates have been known to have. Many expatriate managers find that their power and prestige are much greater than they were in their job in the home country. This often results in improper behavior, especially among managers at the upper and lower positions of overseas subsidiaries. This arrogance takes a number of different forms, including rudeness to personnel and inaccessibility to clients.

Another common problem is expatriate managers' overruling of decisions, often seen at lower levels of the hierarchy. When a decision is made by a superior who is from the host country and the expatriate does not agree with it, the expatriate may appeal to higher authority in the subsidiary. Host-country managers obviously resent this behavior, because it implies that they are incompetent and can be second-guessed by expatriate subordinates.

Still another common problem is the open criticizing by expatriate managers of their own country or the host country. Many expatriates believe that this form of criticism is regarded as constructive and shows them to have an open mind. Experience has found, however, that most host-country personnel view such behavior negatively and feel that the manager should refrain from such unconstructive criticism. It creates bad feelings and lack of loyalty.

In addition to helping deal with these types of personal problems, training can be useful in improving overall management style. Research shows that many host-country nationals would like to see changes in some of the styles of expatriate managers, including their leadership, decision making, communication, and group work. In terms of leadership, the locals would like to see their expatriate managers be more friendly, accessible, receptive to subordinate suggestions, and encouraging to subordinates to make their best efforts. In decision making, they would like to see clearer definition of goals, more involvement in the process by those employees who will be affected by the decision, and greater use of group meetings to help make decisions. In communication, they would like to see more exchange of opinions and ideas between subordinates and managers. In group work, they would like to see more group problem solving and teamwork.

The specific training approach used must reflect both the industrial and the cultural environment. For example, there is some evidence that Japanese students who come to the United States to earn an MBA degree often find this education of no real value back home. One graduate noted that when he tactfully suggested putting to use a skill he had learned during his U.S. MBA program, he got nowhere. An analysis of Japanese getting an outside education concluded:

> Part of the problem is the reason that most Japanese workers are sent to business schools. Whatever ticket the MBA degree promises—or appears to promise—Americans, the diploma has little meaning within most Japanese companies. Rather, companies send students abroad under the life-time employment system to ensure that there will be more English speakers who are familiar with Western business practices. Some managers regard business schools as a kind of high-level English language school, returning students say, or consider the two years as more or less a paid vacation.[87]

However, as the Japanese economy continues to have problems, American-style business education is beginning to receive attention and respect. In the 1980s American managers went to Japan to learn; now Japanese managers are coming to the United States in increasing numbers to see what they can pick up to help them better compete.

■ Types of Training Programs

There are many different types of multinational management training programs. Some last only a few hours; others last for months. Some are fairly superficial; others are extensive in coverage. Organizations can decide what training program works best by determining the effectiveness of the program, and altering it accordingly. Typically, a combination of standardized and tailor-made training and development approaches are used.

Standardized vs. Tailor-Made

Some management training is standard, or generic. For example, participants often are taught how to use specific decision-making tools, such as quantitative analysis, and regardless of where the managers are sent in the world, the application is the same. These tools do not have to be culturally specific. Research shows that small firms usually rely on standard training programs. Larger MNCs, in contrast, tend to design their own. Some of the larger MNCs are increasingly turning to specially designed video and PowerPoint programs for their training and development needs.

Tailor-made training programs are created for the specific needs of the participants. Input for these offerings usually is obtained from managers who currently are working (or have worked) in the country to which the participants will be sent as well as from local managers and personnel who are citizens of that country. These programs often are designed to provide a new set of skills for a new culture. For example, MNCs are now learning that in managing in China, there is a need to provide directive leadership training because many local managers rely heavily on rules, procedures, and orders from their superiors to guide their behaviors.[88] So training programs must explain how to effectively use this approach. Quite often, the offerings are provided before the individuals leave for their overseas assignment; however, there also are postdeparture training programs that are conducted on-site. These often take the form of systematically familiarizing the individual with the country through steps such as meeting with government officials and other key personnel in the community; becoming acquainted with managers and employees in the organization; learning the host-country nationals' work methods, problems, and expectations; and taking on-site language training.

Training approaches that are successful in one geographic region of the world may need to be heavily modified if they are to be as effective elsewhere. Sergeant and Frenkel conducted interviews with expatriate managers with extensive experience in China in order to identify HRM issues and the ways in which they need to be addressed by MNCs going

---

Table 14–6
Human Resources Management Challenges Facing MNCs in China

Human Resource Management Function	Comments/Recommendations
Employee recruitment	The market for skilled manual and white-collar employees is very tight and characterized by rapidly rising wages and high turnover rates. Nepotism and overhiring remain a major problem where Chinese partners strongly influence HR policies; and transferring employees from state enterprises to joint ventures can be difficult because it requires approval from the employee's old work unit.
Reward system	New labor laws allow most companies to set their own wage and salary levels. As a result, there is a wide wage disparity between semiskilled and skilled workers. However, these disparities must be balanced with the negative effect they can have on workers' interpersonal relations.
Employee retention	It can be difficult to retain good employees because of poaching by competitive organizations. In response, many American joint-venture managers are learning to take greater control of compensation programs in order to retain high-performing Chinese managers and skilled workers.
Work performance and employee management	Local managers are not used to taking the initiative and are rarely provided with performance feedback in their Chinese enterprises. As a result, they tend to be risk-averse and are often unwilling to innovate. In turn, the workers are not driven to get things done quickly and they often give little emphasis to the quality of output. At the same time, it is difficult to dismiss people.
Labor relations	Joint-venture regulations give workers the right to establish a trade union to protect employee rights and to organize. These unions are less adversarial than in the West and tend to facilitate operational efficiency. However, there is concern that with the changes taking place in labor laws and the possibility of collective bargaining, unions may become more adversarial in the future.
Expatriate relations	Many firms have provided little cross-training to their people and family, education, and health issues limit the attractiveness of a China assignment. Some of the major repatriation problems include limited continuity in international assignments and difficulties of adjusting to more specialized and less autonomous positions at home, lack of career prospects, and undervaluation of international experience. Management succession and the balancing of local and international staff at Chinese firms are also problematic.

Source: Adapted from Andrew Sergeant and Stephen Frenkel, "Managing People in China: Perceptions of Expatriate Managers," *Journal of World Business* 33, no. 1 (1998), p. 21.

---

into China.[89] As seen in Table 14–6, many of the human resource management approaches that are employed are different from those used in the United States or other developed countries because of the nature of Chinese culture and China's economy.

Some organizations have extended cross-cultural training to include training for family members, especially children who will be accompanying the parents. "International Management in Action: U.S.-Style Training for Expats and Their Teenagers" explains how this approach to cultural assimilation is carried out.

In addition to training expats and their families, effective MNCs also are developing carefully crafted programs for training personnel from other cultures who are coming into their culture. These programs, among other things, have materials that are specially designed for the target audience. Some of the specific steps that well-designed cultural training programs follow include:

1. Local instructors and a translator, typically someone who is bicultural, observe the pilot training program or examine written training materials.

2. The educational designer then debriefs the observation with the translator, curriculum writer, and local instructors.

3. Together, the group examines the structure and sequence, ice breaker, and other materials that will be used in the training.

U.S.-Style Training for Expats and Their Teenagers

One of the major reasons why expatriates have trouble with overseas assignments is that their teenage children are unable to adapt to the new culture, and this has an impact on the expat's performance. To deal with this acculturation problem, many U.S. MNCs now are developing special programs for helping teenagers assimilate into new cultures and adjust to new school environments. A good example is provided by General Electric Medical Systems Group (GEMS), a Milwaukee-based firm that has expatriates in France, Japan, and Singapore. As soon as GEMS designates an individual for an overseas assignment, this expat and his or her family are matched up with those who have recently returned from this country. If the family going overseas has teenage children, the company will team them up with a family that had teenagers during its stay abroad. Both groups then discuss the challenges and problems that must be faced. In the case of teenagers, they are able to talk about their concerns with others who already have encountered these issues, and the latter can provide important information regarding how to make friends, learn the language, get around town, and turn the time abroad into a pleasant experience. Coca-Cola uses a similar approach. As soon as someone is designated for an overseas assignment, the company helps initiate cross-cultural discussions with experienced personnel. Coke also provides formal training through use of external cross-cultural consulting firms that are experienced in working with all family members.

A typical concern of teenagers going abroad is that they will have to go away to boarding school. In Saudi Arabia, for example, national law forbids expatriate children's attending school past the ninth grade, so most expatriate families will look for European institutions for these children. GEMS addresses these types of problems with a specially developed education program. Tutors, schools, curricula, home-country requirements, and host-country requirements are examined, and a plan and specific program of study are developed for each school-age child before he or she leaves.

Before the departure of the family, some MNCs will subscribe to local magazines about teen fashions, music, and other sports or social activities in the host country, so that the children know what to expect when they get there. Before the return of the family to the United States, these MNCs provide similar information about what is going on in the United States, so that when the children return for a visit or come back to stay, they are able to quickly fit into their home-country environment once again.

An increasing number of MNCs now give teenagers much of the same cultural training they give their own managers; however, there is one area in which formal assistance often is not as critical for teens as for adults: language training. While most expatriates find it difficult and spend a good deal of time trying to master the local language, many teens find that they can pick it up quite easily. They speak it at school, in their social groups, and out on the street. As a result, they learn not only the formal language but also clichés and slang that help them communicate more easily. In fact, sometimes their accent is so good that they are mistaken for local kids. Simply put: The facility of teens to learn a language often is greatly underrated. A Coca-Cola manager recently drove home this point when he declared: "One girl we sent insisted that, although she would move, she wasn't going to learn the language. Within two months she was practically fluent."

A major educational benefit of this emphasis on teenagers is that it leads to an experienced, bicultural person. So when the young person completes college and begins looking for work, the parent's MNC often is interested in this young adult as a future manager. The person has a working knowledge of the MNC, speaks a second language, and has had overseas experience in a country where the multinational does business. This type of logic is leading some U.S. MNCs to realize that effective cross-cultural training can be of benefit for their workforces of tomorrow as well as today.

4. The group then collectively identifies stories, metaphors, experiences, and examples in the culture that will fit into the new training program.

5. The educational designer and curriculum writer make the necessary changes in the training materials.

6. The local instructors are trained to use the newly developed materials.

7. After the designer, translator, and native-language trainers are satisfied, the materials are printed.

8. The language and content of the training materials are tested with a pilot group.[90]

In developing the instructional materials, culturally specific guidelines are carefully followed so that the training does not lose any of its effectiveness.[91] For example, inappropriate pictures or scenarios that might prove to be offensive to the audience must be screened out. Handouts and other instructional materials that are designed to enhance the learning process are provided for all participants. If the trainees are learning a second language, generous use of visuals and live demonstrations will be employed. Despite all these efforts, however, errors sometimes occur.

Cultural Assimilators

The cultural assimilator has become one of the most effective approaches to cross-cultural training. A **cultural assimilator** is a programmed learning technique that is designed to expose members of one culture to some of the basic concepts, attitudes, role perceptions, customs, and values of another. These assimilators are developed for each pair of cultures. For example, if an MNC is going to send three U.S. managers from Chicago to Caracas, a cultural assimilator would be developed to familiarize the three Americans with Venezuelan customs and cultures. If three Venezuelan managers from Caracas were to be transferred to Singapore, another assimilator would be developed to familiarize the managers with Singapore customs and cultures.

In most cases, these assimilators require the trainee to read a short episode of a cultural encounter and choose an interpretation of what has happened and why. If the trainee's choice is correct, he or she goes on to the next episode. If the response is incorrect, the trainee is asked to reread the episode and choose another response.

cultural assimilator
A programmed learning technique designed to expose members of one culture to some of the basic concepts, attitudes, role perceptions, customs, and values of another culture.

Choice of Content of the Assimilators   One of the major problems in constructing an effective cultural assimilator is deciding what is important enough to include. Some assimilators use critical incidents that are identified as being important. To be classified as a critical incident, a situation must meet at least one of the following conditions:

1. An expatriate and a host national interact in the situation.
2. The situation is puzzling or likely to be misinterpreted by the expatriate.
3. The situation can be interpreted accurately if sufficient knowledge about the culture is available.
4. The situation is relevant to the expatriate's task or mission requirements.[92]

These incidents typically are obtained by asking expatriates and host nationals with whom they come in contact to describe specific intercultural occurrences or events that made a major difference in their attitudes or behavior toward members of the other culture. These incidents can be pleasant, unpleasant, or simply nonunderstandable occurrences.

Validation of the Assimilator   The term **validity** refers to the quality of being effective, of producing the desired results. It means that an instrument—in this case, the cultural assimilator—measures what it is intended to measure. After the cultural assimilator's critical incidents are constructed and the alternative responses are written, the process is validated. Making sure that the assimilator is valid is the crux of its effectiveness. One way to test an assimilator is to draw a sample from the target culture and ask these people to read the scenarios that have been written and choose the alternative they feel is most appropriate. If a large percentage of the group agrees that one of the alternatives is preferable, this scenario is used in the assimilator. If more than one of the four alternatives receives strong support, however, either the scenario or the alternatives are revised until there is general agreement or the scenario is dropped.

After the final incidents are chosen, they are sequenced in the assimilator booklet and can be put online to be taken electronically. Similar cultural concepts are placed together and presented, beginning with simple situations and progressing to more complex ones. Most cultural assimilator programs start out with 150 to 200 incidents, of which 75 to 100 eventually are included in the final product.

validity
The quality of being effective, of producing the desired results. A valid test or selection technique measures what it is intended to measure.

The Cost-Benefit Analysis of Assimilators   The assimilator approach to training can be quite expensive. A typical 75- to 100-incident program often requires approximately 800 hours to develop. Assuming that a training specialist is costing the company $50 an hour including benefits, the cost is around $40,000 per assimilator. This cost can be spread over many trainees, and the program may not need to be changed every year. An MNC that sends 40 people a year to a foreign country for which an assimilator has been constructed is paying only $200 per person for this programmed training. In the long run, the costs often are more than justified. In addition, the concept can be applied to nearly all cultures. Many different assimilators have been constructed, including Arab, Thai, Honduran, and Greek, to name but four. Most importantly, research shows that these assimilators improve the effectiveness and satisfaction of individuals being trained as compared with other training methods.

Global Leadership Development

Another current trend in human resource development is to focus on leadership, as discussed in Chapter 13. Tichy noted that a number of leadership training approaches can be used.[93] As shown in Figure 14–7, these range from awareness to cognitive and conceptual understanding to the development of skills and then on to new problem-solving approaches and, ultimately, fundamental change. In this process, management development becomes deeper, involves greater risk, incorporates a longer-term time horizon, and focuses on organization (rather than just individual) change.

At the same time, effective MNCs now encourage strong leadership in the areas of both hard and soft organizational issues. Examples of hard issues include the budget, manufacturing, marketing, distribution, and finance; soft issues address values, culture, vision, leadership style, and innovative behavior. In exercising strong leadership on hard organizational issues, attention is focused on becoming a low-cost provider of goods and services. In exercising strong leadership on soft organizational issues, the emphasis is on developing and maintaining innovativeness.

Figure 14–7

The Tichy Development Matrix

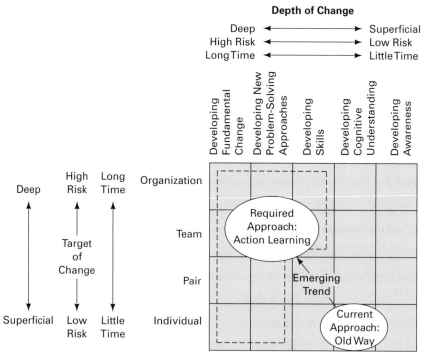

Source: Reported in Noel M. Tichy, "Global Development," in *Globalizing Management,* ed. Vladimir Pucik, Noel M. Tichy, and Carole K. Barnett, John Wiley & Sons, Inc., 1993, pp. 206–224. Reprinted with permission of John Wiley & Sons, Inc.

GLP Program   One of the best examples of the emerging leadership development programs used by MNCs is the Global Leadership Program (GLP), which is a consortium of leading U.S., European, and Japanese firms, global faculty, and participating host countries. Here is how the GLP has been described:

> The companies are part of an ongoing partnership started in 1988 jointly committed to research and development on issues of globalization. The program design, facilities, and support staff are directed by core faculty from universities in the United States, Europe, and Japan. The members of the consortium participate in a research partnership and in an intensive 5-week Global Leadership Program designed for senior executives with CEO potential.[94]

The GLP is designed to provide participants with an intensive international experience to develop a global mindset, instill cross-cultural competency, and provide the opportunity for global networking. The program is five weeks in duration, but before attending, each person is given specially prepared briefing materials about the country that he or she will visit. At the beginning, participants are asked to complete the survey instruments that are designed to assess the individual's perceptions regarding the characteristics of a global organization, dimensions of global leadership, and the way that managers carry out their global responsibilities.

The core of the program is a two-week, on-site, country assessment carried out by cross-cultural teams. Each group of trainees is required to use information from the assessment to produce investment opportunities and entry strategy recommendations as well as video documentaries as part of their country assessment. Among other things, each team of trainees spends two weeks preparing for the country assessment by working on its personal global leadership capabilities and its global mindset and team skills. Preparation also includes a weekend at an Outward Bound school and a two-day assessment in Washington, D.C.

The GLP is designed to blend rigorous intellectual development of global leaders, beginning with each individual's map of his or her own personal global mindset. These are shared with the members of each team, who then are responsible for creating an analytical framework to guide its assessment of a major geopolitical region of the world. By the second week of the program, the teams have started on their country assessment. During the third and fourth weeks, the participants split up and travel to their respective countries. During the fifth and last week of the program, the individuals write their reports and make their video documentaries and presentations. Because of its strong emphasis on involvement and action learning, the GLP has become one of the best-recognized development programs for training global leaders for MNCs.

Positive Organizational Behavior

We discussed in Chapter 13 how leaders can increase motivation and morale if they focus on the positives, or strengths, of individuals. The positive internal traits of the leader, along with the other factors, tended to lead to consistent positive behaviors. Luthans has done extensive research on **positive organizational behavior (POB).** He defines it as:

> The study and application of positively oriented human resource strengths and psychological capacities that can be measured, developed, and effectively managed for performance improvement in today's workplace.[95]

Positivity in the workplace has been connected to employee satisfaction. The positive environment, however, consists of many layers. Luthans and Youssef postulated that in order for an organization to be the most efficient and innovative, it must have positive traits, states, and systems in order to promote in positive behavior. The

positive organizational behavior (POB) The study and application of positively oriented human resource strengths and psychological capacities that can be measured, developed, and effectively managed for performance improvement in today's workplace.

Lessons in Global Leadership Development: The PWC Ulysses Program

PricewaterhouseCoopers (PwC), one of the "Final 4" global accounting firms, has for several years sent top midcareer talent to the developing world for eight-week service projects under its "Ulysses" Program. For a fairly modest investment—$15,000 per person, plus salaries—Ulysses both tests the talent and expands the world view of the accounting firm's future leaders. Since the company started the program in 2000, it has attracted the attention of Johnson & Johnson, Cisco Systems, and other big companies considering their own programs.

In 2003, PwC partner Tahir Ayub was assigned a consulting gig unlike anything he had done before. His job was helping village leaders in the Namibian outback grapple with their community's growing AIDS crisis. Faced with language barriers, cultural differences, and scant access to electricity, Ayub, 39, and two colleagues had to scrap their PowerPoint presentations in favor of a more low-tech approach: face-to-face discussion. The village chiefs learned that they needed to garner community support for programs to combat the disease, and Ayub learned an important lesson as well: Technology isn't always the answer. "You better put your beliefs and biases to one side and figure out new ways to look at things," he said.

Ayub may never encounter as extreme a cultural disconnect at PwC as he did in Namibia. But for the next generation of partners, overcoming barriers and forging a connection with clients the world over will be a crucial part of their jobs. It's those skills that PwC hopes to foster in partners who take part in the program.

While results are hard to quantify, PwC is convinced that the program works. All two dozen of the initial graduates are still working at the company. Half of them have been promoted, and most have new responsibilities. Just as important, all 24 people say they have a stronger commitment to PwC—in part because of the commitment the firm made to them and in part because of their new vision of the firm's values. Says global managing partner Willem Bröcker: "We get better partners from this exercise." The Ulysses Program is PwC's answer to one of the biggest challenges confronting professional services companies: identifying and training up-and-coming leaders who can find unconventional answers to intractable problems. By tradition and necessity, new PwC leaders are nurtured from within. But with 8,000 partners, identifying those with the necessary business savvy and relationship-building skills isn't easy. Just as the program gives partners a new view of PwC, it also gives PwC a new view of them, particularly their ability to hold up under pressure.

For midcareer partners, the rigors of the developing world came as quite a shock. Brian P. McCann, 37, a mergers and acquisitions expert from PwC's Boston office, had never been to a third-world country before his stint in Belize, where he encountered dirt-floored houses, sick children, and grinding poverty.

Ayub, having been born in Africa, considered himself worldly. Even so, long days spent among Africa's exploding HIV-positive population took their psychological toll. With his work confined to daylight hours—there was often no electricity—Dinu Bumbacea, a 37-year-old partner in PwC's Romanian office who spent time in Zambia working with an agricultural center, had plenty of time to dwell on the misery all around him. "Africa is poor, and we all know that," says Bumbacea. "But until you go there, you don't understand how poor it is. We take so much for granted."

For more than 15 years, companies have used social-responsibility initiatives to develop leaders. But PwC takes the concept to a new level. Participants lend their business skills to local aid groups—from an ecotourism collective in Belize to small organic farmers in Zambia to AIDS groups in Namibia. Ulysses also presents participants with the challenge of collaborating across cultures with local clients as well as with PwC colleagues from other global regions. Ayub, for example, was paired with partners from Mexico and the Netherlands.

PwC says the program, now in its third cycle, gives participants a broad, international perspective that's crucial for a company that does business around the world. Traditional executive education programs turn out men and women who have specific job skills but little familiarity with issues outside their narrow specialty, according to Douglas Ready, director of the International Consortium for Executive Development Research. PwC says Ulysses helps prepare participants for challenges that go beyond the strict confines of accounting or consulting and instills values such as community involvement that are fundamental to its corporate culture.

Ulysses is also a chance for partners to learn what they can accomplish without their usual resources to lean on. The program forces them to take on projects well outside their expertise. In the summer 2003, for example, McCann developed a business plan for an ecotourism group in Belize. McCann's most lasting memory is a dinner he shared in the home of a Mayan farmer after they spent a day discussing their plan. "He didn't even have electricity," McCann recalls, "but he made do."

PwC partners say they've already adapted their experiences to the task of managing people and clients. Malaysian partner Jennifer Chang says her team noticed a shift in her managerial style after the Belize trip. She listened more and became more flexible. "Once you see how slowly decisions are made in other places, you gain patience for the people you work with," she says. Ayub, who was promoted in June, now manages 20 partners. He says he favors face-to-face conversations over e-mail because the low-tech approach builds trust. "It made the difference in Namibia," he says. If insights like those ripple out across the firm, Ulysses will be more than a voyage of personal discovery for a handful of partners. It could help build leaders capable of confronting the challenges of an increasingly global business. And that, says PwC, is the whole point.

Source: Reprinted with special permission from Jessi Hempel with Seth Porges, "It Takes a Village—and a Consultant," *BusinessWeek,* September 4, 2005. Copyright © 2005 The McGraw-Hill Companies.

positive traits were covered in Chapter 13 and consist of conscientiousness, emotional stability, extroversion, agreeableness, openness to experience, core self-evaluations, and positive psychological traits. A positive state is domain-specific, and reactions and behaviors may change depending on the environment. Research has shown that other "states" are self-efficacy, hope, optimism, resiliency and psychological capital.[96]

Finally, positive organizations focus on the selection, development, and management of human resources. This positive approach attempts to match employee skills and talents with organizational goals and expectations. When employees are treated well, they will be motivated to give back to the institution. Therefore, when these individual traits, internal and external states, and organizations all focus on the positive, the resulting organizational citizenship behavior (OCB) will also be positive. Furthermore, altruism, conscientiousness, and courtesy will be inadvertently emphasized.[97]

As with most examples, the description above is culturally specific. That is, what seems to be positive internal or external factors in one country may not be the same in another. However, human resources are essential to an organization no matter its location, and MNCs should do all they can to focus on the power of human capital to drive organizational success.

The World of *BusinessWeek*—Revisited

The *BusinessWeek* case that opens this chapter illustrates how the next generation of offshoring is coming of age. In a time of increased globalization, innovation is necessary to remain competitive. As outlined in this chapter, MNCs are realizing the intense challenges associated with the selection, development, and training of international human resources. MNCs have a range of options when selecting employees for overseas assignments, and increasing numbers of tools and resources are available to help develop, train, and deploy those individuals. Human resource selection and development across cultures cannot be taken lightly. Firms that do not invest in their human resource processes will face additional costs related to poor labor relations, quality control, and other issues.

Now that you have read the chapter and reflected on the opening article, answer the following questions: (1) What are the costs and benefits of hiring home-, host-, and third-country nationals for overseas assignments? (2) What skill sets are important for international assignments, and how can employees be prepared for them? (3) What are the implications of offshore outsourcing for the management of human resources globally?

SUMMARY OF KEY POINTS

1. MNCs can use four basic sources for filling overseas positions: home-country nationals (expatriates), host-country nationals, third-country nationals, and inpatriates. The most common reason for using home-country nationals, or expatriates, is to get the overseas operation under way. Once this is done, many MNCs turn the top management job over to a host-country national who is familiar with the culture and language and who often commands a lower salary than the home-country national. The primary reason for using third-country nationals is that these people have the necessary expertise for the job. The use of inpatriates (a host-country or third-country national assigned to the home office) recognizes the need for diversity at the home office. This movement builds a transnational core competency for MNCs. In addition, MNCs can subcontract or outsource to take advantage of lower human resource costs and increase flexibility.

2. Many criteria are used in selecting managers for overseas assignments. Some of these include adaptability, independence, self-reliance, physical and emotional health, age, experience, education, knowledge of the local language, motivation, the support of spouse and children, and leadership.

3. Individuals who meet selection criteria are given some form of screening. Some firms use psychological

testing, but this approach has lost popularity in recent years. More commonly, candidates are given interviews. Theoretical models that identify important anticipatory and in-country dimensions of adjustment offer help in effective selection.

4. Compensating expatriates can be a difficult problem, because there are many variables to consider. However, most compensation packages are designed around four common elements: base salary, benefits, allowances, and taxes. Working within these elements, the MNC will tailor the package to fit the specific situation. In doing so, there are six different approaches that can be used: balance-sheet approach, complementary approach, localization, lump-sum method, cafeteria approach, and regional method. Whichever one (or combination) is used, the package must be both cost-effective and fair.

5. A manager might be willing to take an international assignment for a number of reasons: increased pay, promotion potential, the opportunity for greater responsibility, the chance to travel, and the ability to use his or her talents and skills. Research shows that most home countries prefer that the individual who is selected to head the affiliate or subsidiary be a local manager, even though this often does not occur.

6. At some time, most expatriates return home, usually when their predetermined tour is over. Sometimes, managers return because they want to leave early; at other times, they return because of poor performance on their part. In any event, readjustment problems can arise back home, and the longer a manager has been gone, the bigger the problems usually

are. Some firms are developing transition strategies to help expatriates adjust to their new environments.

7. Training is the process of altering employee behavior and attitudes to increase the probability of goal attainment. Many expatriates need training before (as well as during) their overseas stay. A number of factors will influence a company's approach to training. One is the basic type of MNC: ethnocentric, polycentric, regiocentric, or geocentric. Another factor is the learning style of the trainees.

8. There are two primary reasons for training: organizational and personal. Organizational reasons include overcoming ethnocentrism, improving communication, and validating the effectiveness of training programs. Personal reasons include improving the ability of expatriates to interact locally and increasing the effectiveness of leadership styles. There are two types of training programs: standard and tailor-made. Research shows that small firms usually rely on standard programs and larger MNCs tailor their training. The six major types of training are environmental briefings, cultural orientation, cultural assimilators, language training, sensitivity training, and field experience.

9. A cultural assimilator is a programmed learning approach that is designed to expose members of one culture to some of the basic concepts, attitudes, role perceptions, customs, and values of another. Assimilators have been developed for many different cultures. Their validity has resulted in the improved effectiveness and satisfaction of those being trained as compared with other training methods.

KEY TERMS

adaptability screening, *479*

balance-sheet approach, *487*

cafeteria approach, *487*

cultural assimilator, *501*

ethnocentric MNC, *494*

ethnocentrism, *496*

expatriates, *469*

geocentric MNC, *494*

home-country nationals, *469*

host-country nationals, *470*

inpatriates, *472*

international selection criteria, *475*

learning, *495*

localization, *487*

lump-sum method, *487*

polycentric MNC, *494*

positive organizational behavior (POB), *503*

regiocentric MNC, *494*

regional system, *487*

repatriation, *488*

repatriation agreements, *491*

third-country nationals, *472*

training, *492*

transition strategies, *491*

validity, *501*

REVIEW AND DISCUSSION QUESTIONS

1. A New York–based MNC is in the process of staffing a subsidiary in New Delhi, India. Why would it consider using expatriate managers in the unit? Local managers? Third-country managers?

2. What selection criteria are most important in choosing people for an overseas assignment? Identify and describe the four that you judge to be of most universal importance, and defend your choice.

3. What are the major common elements in an expat's compensation package? Besides base pay, which would be most important to you? Why?

4. Why are individuals motivated to accept international assignments? Which of these motivations would you rank as positive reasons? Which would you regard as negative reasons?

5. Why do expatriates return early? What can MNCs do to prevent this from happening? Identify and discuss three steps they can take.

6. What kinds of problems do expatriates face when returning home? Identify and describe four of the most important. What can MNCs do to deal with these repatriation problems effectively?

7. How do the following types of MNCs differ: ethnocentric, polycentric, regiocentric, and geocentric? Which type is most likely to provide international management training to its people? Which is least likely to provide international management training to its people?

8. IBM is planning on sending three managers to its Zurich office, two to Madrid, and two to Tokyo. None of these individuals has any international experience. Would you expect the company to use a standard training program or a tailor-made program for each group?

9. Zygen Inc., a medium-sized manufacturing firm, is planning to enter into a joint venture in China. Would training be of any value to those managers who will be part of this venture? If so, what types of training would you recommend?

10. Hofstadt & Hoerr, a German-based insurance firm, is planning on expanding out of the EU and opening offices in Chicago and Buenos Aires. How would a cultural assimilator be of value in training the MNC's expatriates? Is the assimilator a valid training tool?

11. Ford is in the process of training managers for overseas assignments. Would a global leadership program be a useful approach? Why or why not?

12. Microsoft is weighing setting up an R&D facility in India to develop new software applications. Should it staff the new facility with Microsoft employees? Indian employees? Or should it subcontract with an Indian firm? Explain your answer and some of the potential challenges in implementing it.

INTERNET EXERCISE: GOING INTERNATIONAL WITH COKE

As seen in this chapter, the recruiting and selecting of managers is critical to effective international management. This is particularly true in the case of firms that are expanding their international operations or currently do business in a large number of countries. These MNCs are continually having to replace managers who are retiring or moving to other companies. Coca-Cola is an excellent example. Go to the company's Web site at **www.coke.com** and look at the career opportunities that it offers overseas. In particular, pay close attention to current opportunities in Europe, Africa, and Asia. Read what the company has to say, and then contact one of the individuals whose e-mail address is provided. Ask this company representative about the opportunities and challenges of working in that country or geographic area. Then using this information, coupled with the chapter material, answer these questions: (1) From what you have learned from the Coca-Cola inquiry, what types of education or experience would you need to be hired by the company? (2) What kinds of international career opportunities does Coke offer? (3) If you were hired by Coke, what type of financial package could you expect? (4) In what areas of the world is Coke focusing more of its attention? (5) What kinds of management and leadership training programs does Coke offer?

Russia

Russia is by far the largest of the former Soviet republics. Russia stretches from Eastern Europe across northern Asia to the Pacific Ocean. The 141 million people consist of 83 percent Russians, 4 percent Tartars, and a scattering of others. The largest city and capital is Moscow, with about 9 million people. At present, there is continuing social and economic turmoil in Russia. Although prices are no longer controlled and privatization is well under way, the value of the ruble continues to deteriorate. At the same time, there are many pockets of prosperity in the country, and under President Vladimir Putin positive efforts are under way to bolster the economy.

By 2006, Russia's GDP had reached $1.75 trillion, and Russia's privatization and liberalization program was attracting substantial foreign investment. One MNC that has been extremely interested in the country is Earth, Inc. (EI), a farm-implement company headquartered in Birmingham, Alabama. EI recently entered into an agreement with the government of Russia to set up operations near Moscow in a factory that was operating at about one-half of capacity. The factory will produce farm implements for the newly emerging Eastern European market. EI will supply the technical know-how and product design as well as assume responsibility for marketing the products. The Russian plant will build the equipment and package it for shipping.

The management of the plant operation will be handled on a joint basis. EI will send a team of five management and technical personnel from the United States to the Russian factory site for a period of 12 to 18 months. After this time, EI hopes to send three of them home, and the two who remain would continue to provide ongoing assistance. At the same time, EI intends to hire four middle-level managers and eight first-level supervisors from Italy and Germany, because the operation will need Europeans who are more familiar with doing manufacturing in this part of the world. Very few locals have inspired EI with confidence that they can get the job done. However, over a two-year period, EI intends to replace the third-country nationals with trained local managers. "We need to staff the management ranks with knowledgeable, experienced people," the CEO explained, "at least until we get the operation up and running successfully with our own people. Then we can turn more and more of the operation over to local management, and run the plant with just a handful of headquarters people on-site."

This arrangement has been agreed to by the Russian government, and EI currently is identifying and recruiting managers both in the United States and in Europe. Initially, the firm thought that this would be a fairly simple process, but screening and selecting are taking much longer than anticipated. Nevertheless, EI hopes to have the plant operating within 12 months.

Questions

1. What are some current issues facing Russia? What is the climate for doing business in Russia today?

2. What are some of the benefits of using home-country nationals in overseas operations? What are some of the benefits of using host-country nationals?

3. Why would a multinational such as EI be interested in bringing in third-country nationals?

4. What criteria should EI use in selecting personnel for the overseas assignment in Russia?

A Selection Decision

The Star Corporation is a California-based manufacturing firm that is going to do business in mainland China. The company's contract with the Chinese government calls for it to supply technical know-how and machinery for producing consumer electronics. These products are not state-of-the-art, but they will be more than adequate for the needs of the Chinese consumers. Star has agreed to sell the Chinese its U.S. plant, which was being closed because it no longer was competitive.

The Chinese will pay to move all the machinery and equipment to the mainland and install it in a factory that currently is being modified for this purpose. The two then will become partners in the venture. Star will provide the management and technical expertise to run the plant, and the Chinese government will provide the workers and be responsible for paying for all output. Star will receive an annual fee of $1 million and 5 percent of all sales.

The Star management is very pleased with the arrangement. Although they are of Chinese descent, they have lived in the United States all their lives and know relatively little about doing business either with or in mainland China. To provide Star with the necessary information and assistance, a native of Beijing, educated there but living in California for the past five years, was brought in. The individual told the company the following facts about mainland China:

- Chinese managers do not plan. They usually are told what to do, and they do it. Planning is handled by others and simply passed on to them.
- Chinese managers are not concerned with profit or loss. They simply do their jobs and let the government worry about whether the operation is making money.
- No rewards are given to workers who perform well; everyone is treated the same. If there is no work, the workers are still paid, although they may not be required to come to the factory.
- There is a basic aversion to individual decision making; most decisions are collective efforts.
- The current government of China would like its managers to learn how to run a profit-oriented operation and eventually eliminate the need for foreign managerial assistance.
- When outsiders tell the Chinese how to do things, they have to be careful not to insult or offend the Chinese, who often are sensitive about the way they are treated.

Questions

1. What selection criteria would you recommend to Star when deciding whom to send to mainland China?
2. What procedures should the company use in making the final selection?
3. What type of repatriation agreement would you recommend the firm use? Be specific regarding some things you would suggest be contained in the agreement.

Brief Integrative Case 1

A Copy Shop Goes Global

After weeks of demonstrations, the Berlin Wall came crashing down on November 9, 1989. The end of Communist rule in Eastern Europe was clearly in sight. At about the same time, Washington, D.C., entrepreneur Paul Panitz was completing his three-year contractual obligation to the purchasers of his typesetting company. After nearly 20 years of running and working in the business he had started, Panitz had no concrete plans for the future.

Paul had two heroes that he looked to for inspiration. One was Duke Snyder of the old Brooklyn Dodgers; the other was Alexander Dubcek, first secretary of the Communist Party of Czechoslovakia from January 5, 1968, until his ouster by Soviet tanks in August of the same year. During his short tenure, known as the "Prague Spring," Dubcek introduced reforms that presaged the "Velvet Revolution," which occurred about 20 years later.

Thinking of his heroes and having both time and money, Panitz wanted to do what he could for the newly freed people of Central and Eastern Europe. He believed in freedom of the press. He also believed that the way to help people was by creating businesses that created jobs. Paul wanted to do something that would advance both beliefs. His first venture was a loan/equity deal to help a Polish daily newspaper modernize its composition department. But this was a passive investment, and he was left with plenty of time to consider his next opportunity.

On a trip to Budapest, Paul visited a government-run copy center, one of the few copy centers available in Hungary. In fact, copiers that members of the public could use were extremely rare—perhaps not surprisingly: In Communist countries the last thing the government had wanted was for ordinary people to have access to a means of sharing information. The opportunity in postcommunist Hungary was obvious to Paul, and on a return visit home, he contacted me [Ken Chaletzky] and Dirck Holscher, college friends of Paul's who operated a successful chain of copy centers in Washington, D.C., called Copy General. Paul asked us if we would like to help him open a copy center in Budapest. We were a little skeptical about the concept, but we signed on.

Copy General in Budapest: The Beginning

It was now early 1990, and the search for a first store location in Budapest was under way. In a major U.S. city, we would have contacted a commercial real estate agent and asked him or her to show us what was available. Not possible in Budapest in 1990. There was no organized real estate market. Nearly all retail space—what there was of it—was owned and controlled by the government. Even if you found vacant space, it was never clear with whom you needed to talk. So we spent most of 1990 and early 1991 being led down one blind alley after another. Every time we thought we had a deal, a new complication would arise. Frequently, potential landlords wanted an equity position in the business. At other times, space we thought would be ours alone was supposed to be shared with the current occupant. On one occasion, we drank a celebratory toast with a government official signifying agreement—only to have that official lose his position the next day. It was very stressful.

In mid-1990, we hired our Hungarian country manager, although at the time we didn't know he was going to be the country manager. Paul and Dirck Holscher were looking at a street map on a Budapest tramcar. They seemed to be in need of assistance, and a young man came over and asked in nearly flawless English if he could help. Erno Duda was barely in his 20s. His parents, both well-traveled physicians, had spent a few years in Canada, where he learned English. Erno spent the afternoon showing Paul and Dirck around and shortly thereafter was hired as translator and aide.

Erno was a natural-born wheeler-dealer. If we needed something, he knew whom to see or where to go. In the early days of 1990s Hungarian capitalism, he was a very useful person to have on our team. As our first country manager, he helped lead us through rapid growth during our first five years. After leaving Copy General, Erno went on to become a successful investment banker and later formed his own biotechnology company. He says he owes much of his success to what he learned working with Paul Panitz and Copy General.

Erno Duda's Recollections

"I met Paul when I was traveling on the subway. I noticed two Americans who were arguing about where to get off. They couldn't figure out from the Hungarian signs which stop was Heroes' Square. I went up to them and helped them out, and we started talking; and when we got off the subway, the guy with the baseball hat asked me if I wanted to have a beer with them. So we drank a few beers and talked about all kinds of things.

He mentioned the idea of starting a copy center in Hungary. I immediately told him that in my opinion it was a lousy idea because they do photocopying on every corner so he should think of something else. Frankly, I thought he didn't have much business sense whatsoever. I changed my mind later. We ended up exchanging phone numbers and had drinks on a few other occasions. He called me up once because his interpreter didn't show up, and he asked me if I was willing to do fill in. Since he was satisfied with me, from then on he used me as his interpreter/translator. He had a market survey done for him by some consulting company. He paid 5,000 bucks for it, and it had maybe five companies listed. I offered to help and got a few friends to go through literally every street in downtown Budapest. We gave him a database of 53 companies (and a lot more detail), and it cost him less than a hundred dollars. I got more and more involved, and after a while it was me who went and figured out things for him and negotiated because every time an American showed up the prices suddenly quadrupled.

"When we were trying to find a bank for Copy General, most banks immediately refused us because they didn't want to deal with companies with only one million forints as base capital, which they thought was not enough. Finally we found a surprisingly flexible bank called Budapest Bank. The shock came when the lady said that she would be really willing to help and the one-million-forint base capital was not a problem, but the bank was full. We just stood there with Paul and stared. Then finally Paul asked me to translate the following sentence: 'If your bank is really full, we've just recently rented a large basement in Lonyai utca, so if you can't store any more money in your bank, we would be willing to help.' It turned out that it was not a matter of where to put the money; the bank had no more space for files (they were installing a computer system and were recording everything twice, on the computer and then on paper). It was interesting to see how the banking system changed in two or three years after this scenario. By the way, in the end we did become a customer of Budapest Bank."

Challenges of Operating in a Postsocialist World

Early in 1991, Paul took charge of the location search and found a small store in the basement of a 19th-century apartment building near the Budapest University of Economic Sciences. Renovations began while we looked for suppliers. We thought that finding them would be easy, but it was not. We contacted Xerox, our main supplier in the United States, to arrange for copiers for our new store. Xerox told us they would be pleased to provide us with equipment as long as we were willing to pay 100 percent cash up front. Of course, the latest models were not available in Budapest, so we would have to accept older models. No new equipment and no equipment leases—not what we were used to.

Then we contacted Kodak, which was then still a major competitor of Xerox in the copier business. At the time it had almost no presence in Hungary and wanted one. Kodak offered to lease equipment to us on very favorable terms. It offered us ramp-up pricing, which meant that the equipment payments would start out very low and then grow as the business grew. Additionally, it asked if it could use our store to showcase its equipment because it didn't have an office in Budapest.

One weakness of the Kodak offer was that it had no service technicians based in Budapest. Service would have to come from Vienna, which meant the next day or so. To compensate, Kodak would provide us with extra equipment at no cost. Another part of our early arrangement with Kodak was that Copy General, which would be open 24 hours a day, would act as backup for machines that Kodak would install at government offices. If a Kodak copier went down at a government office, we would run the copies free for the customer and send the bill to Kodak. This arrangement provided Kodak with a guarantee that its competition couldn't match, and it provided us with extra business and contacts with government agencies. This symbiotic relationship continued for several years.

During all this time in Budapest, Paul and the Copy General people who visited from the United States needed a place to stay. Most Western businesspeople settled in at the Forum, Hyatt, or Gellert hotels, but that was not Paul's style. He said that it would be difficult to expect our local Hungarian staff to help us build a business if we were staying in $200-a-night hotel rooms while they were living off $200-a-month average wages. This attitude was typical of Paul and signaled the type of corporate culture he wanted to create.

Our initial company flat was located in a working-class district of Budapest a few steps from a Metro station. Later, Copy General rented a new apartment around the corner from the first store. Locating near public transportation was important because company policy discouraged the use of taxis and private vehicles. The public transportation system in Budapest goes everywhere, operates frequently, and is cheap. In the early 1990s, a monthly pass cost about $7. With your photo-ID pass in hand, you had unlimited travel rights. You learned a lot about the locals crammed into a tram on a hot summer afternoon.

In June 1991, our first store opened and was an immediate success. We were the first copy shop anyone had seen that offered self-service copiers. It was quite a sight to see people lined up in front of the store and down the sidewalk waiting their turn to use one of our walk-up machines.

Branching Out: Hungary, Czech Republic, and Poland

Shortly after opening in Budapest, we set our sights on Prague. Steven and Teresa Haas partnered with us and moved to the Czech capital. In keeping with company policy, the Haases rented an apartment in the Pancraz district, which was notorious for a prison that had been used by the secret police and the Gestapo. The company flat was in a dull gray Stalinist-era block across the street from a large state-run bakery.

On their first visit to the small retail store that was part of the bakery, the Haases had difficulty choosing. No one at the counter spoke English, and they spoke no Czech. After a few minutes, one of the clerks went to the back of the store and brought out a young bookkeeper who knew a little English. He helped the Haases with their purchases; then they left. The next evening they were back for their daily purchases. One of the counter people handed them a small folded note, which began, "I am the boy from last night . . . ," Roman Petr's way of introducing himself.

Roman became their guide and translator, showing them around Prague. Steve did most of the scouting for new locations. They learned quickly that the best way to find possible retail locations was to knock on the doors of stores in areas in which they were interested. Steve and Roman spent many weeks walking around the center of Prague near Wenceslas Square.

One day they went into an electronics repair shop in Gorky Square. Roman asked a member of the store's staff if he knew of any stores that might be available to rent. He replied, "Yes, this one." Steve and Roman were directed to the government education agency that controlled that building. After much negotiation that store became the first Copy General in Prague. In typical socialist fashion, the store had plywood partitions and two interior levels that disguised the turn-of-the-century architecture. The first step was to gut the store and remove all the "improvements" made by the previous occupants. Uncovered were 15-foot ceilings, curved archways, solid walnut doors and trim, and an intricate tile floor.

Steve and Roman oversaw a major renovation that brought back many long-lost details. The store opened in the late spring of 1992—almost exactly one year after the first Budapest store. It was arguably the most attractive and inviting copy center in Europe, and it was an instant success. Its nonstop hours and friendly, helpful service were a novelty. As you may have guessed, Roman became our country manager, a position he still holds.

With the Czech operation under way successfully, Steve and Roman headed for Warsaw to scout out locations for Copy General in Poland. Again, hard work and shoe leather paid off. A government-run travel agency that needed to downsize offered to share its space in the center of town with us. Our preference was not to share space, but the excellent location made us willing to compromise. Then as time went by and we began our renovations, the travel agency decided it didn't need any of the space, so we had the whole store to ourselves.

For Western businesspeople, the Marriott Hotel was the place to stay. It still is. If a guest at the hotel walks out the front door and continues across the street, he or she will walk right into our front entrance. The airport bus terminal is located in the hotel, which is across the street from the main railway station. At a conference in Washington, [Ken Chaletzky] was talking with the Polish trade minister. He knew Copy General, and he was very curious about how we were able to obtain such an excellent location. It was clear from his tone that he suspected we had bribed someone or had some inside help. Though we had done everything honestly, his comments confirmed what we already knew: There was no better location in Warsaw for our store.

As we opened our first stores in each new country, we continued to expand where we already were. Every bit of profit was reinvested into the business. We kept looking for new opportunities to open Copy General copy centers. By the time we opened our first store in Prague, we had four stores in Budapest. When the Warsaw store opened, there were three stores in the Czech Republic (Slovakia became independent on January 1, 1993).

Russia, China, and Beyond

Copy General now operates eight retail copy centers in Hungary, seven in the Czech Republic, and four in Warsaw, Poland. There are also Copy General locations in Moscow; Riga, Latvia; and Shanghai in the People's Republic of China. In addition to offering in-house facilities management to large corporations, the company has set up on-site facilities for special events. NATO, the World Bank, and the U.S. State Department have all hired Copy General to provide on-site services for their large meetings.

Much of the success of the Copy General in Eastern Europe is due to the vision and persistence of Paul Panitz and the people he chose to join him. Paul seized on an opportunity to "do good" and to make a profit—both among the most noble of American capitalist qualities.

Questions for Review

1. What are some of the general challenges of starting a new business in another country? What specific challenges did Copy General face in Eastern and Central Europe?

2. How important was Paul Panitz's vision to the decision to go into Hungary? How would you characterize his leadership and management style and his commitment to "doing well by doing good"?

3. Compare the recollections of Ken Chaletsky, a U.S. manager with Copy General, and Erno Duda, Copy General's initial country manager in Hungary. How do their perspectives differ, and how do they reflect the cultural values of their respective countries?

4. What lessons (if any) can you derive from Copy General's successful experience in Eastern Europe and beyond?

Source: Reprinted with permission of Kenneth B. Chaletzky, President, Copy General Corporation.

Brief Integrative Case 2

The Road to Hell

John Baker, chief engineer of the Caribbean Bauxite Company of Barracania in the West Indies, was making his final preparations to leave the island. His promotion to production manager of Keso Mining Corporation near Winnipeg—one of Continental Ore's fast-expanding Canadian enterprises—had been announced a month before, and now everything had been tidied up except the last vital interview with his successor, the able young Barracanian, Matthew Rennalls. It was crucial that this interview be successful and that Rennalls leave his office uplifted and encouraged to face the challenge of a new job. A touch on the bell would have brought Rennalls walking into the room, but Baker delayed the moment and gazed thoughtfully through the window, considering just exactly what he was going to say and, more particularly, how he was going to say it.

John Baker, an English expatriate, was 45 years old and had served 23 years with Continental Ore in East Asia, several African countries, Europe, and for the last two years, the West Indies. He hadn't cared much for his previous assignment in Hamburg and was delighted when the West Indian appointment came through. Climate was not the only attraction. Baker had always preferred working overseas (in what were termed "the developing countries"), because he felt he had an innate knack—better than most other expatriates working for Continental Ore—of knowing just how to get along with the regional staff. After 24 hours in Barracania, however, he realized that he would need all this "innate knack" to deal effectively with the problems that awaited him in this field.

At his first interview with Hutchins, the production manager, the problem of Rennalls and his future was discussed. There and then it was made quite clear to Baker that one of his most important tasks would be "grooming" Rennalls as his successor. Hutchins had pointed out that not only was Rennalls one of the brightest Barracanian prospects on the staff of Caribbean Bauxite—at London University he had taken first-class honors in the BSc engineering degree—but being the son of the minister of finance and economic planning, he also had no small political pull.

The company had been particularly pleased when Rennalls decided to work for it rather than the government in which his father had such a prominent post. The company ascribed his action to the effect of its vigorous and liberal regionalization program, which since World War II had produced 18 Barracanians at midmanagement level and given Caribbean Bauxite a good lead in this respect over all other international concerns operating in Barracania. The success of this timely regionalization policy led to excellent relations with the government.

This relationship was given an added importance when Barracania, three years later, became independent—an occasion that encouraged a critical and challenging attitude toward the role that foreign interests would play in the new Barracania. Therefore, Hutchins had little difficulty in convincing Baker that the successful career development of Rennalls was of primary importance.

The interview with Hutchins was now two years old, and Baker, leaning back in his office chair, reviewed his success in grooming Rennalls. What aspects of the latter's character had helped and what had hindered? What about his own personality? How had that helped or hindered? The first item to go on the credit side would, without question, be the ability of Rennalls to master the technical aspects of the job. From the start, he had shown keenness and enthusiasm and often impressed Baker with his ability in tackling new assignments as well as the constructive comments he invariably made in departmental discussions. He was popular with all ranks of Barracanian staff and had an ease of manner that placed him in good stead when dealing with his expatriate seniors. These were all assets, but what about the debit side?

First and foremost, there was his racial consciousness. His four years at London University had accentuated this feeling and made him sensitive to any sign of condescension on the part of expatriates. It may have been to give expression to this sentiment that as soon as he returned from London, he threw himself into politics on behalf of the United Action Party, which later won the preindependence elections and provided the country with its first prime minister.

The ambitions of Rennalls—and he certainly was ambitious—did not lie in politics, because, staunch nationalist that he was, he saw that he could serve himself and his country best—for bauxite was responsible for nearly half the value of Barracania's export trade—by putting his engineering talent to the best use possible. On this account, Hutchins found that he had an unexpectedly easy task in persuading Rennalls to give up his political work before entering the production department as an assistant engineer.

Baker knew that it was Rennalls's well-repressed sense of race consciousness that had prevented their relationship from being as close as it should have been. On the surface, nothing could have seemed more agreeable. Formality between the two men was at a minimum. Baker was delighted to find that his assistant shared his own peculiar "shaggy dog" sense of humor so that jokes were continually being exchanged; they entertained each other at their houses and often played tennis together—and yet the barrier remained invisible, indefinable, but ever present. The existence of this "screen" between them was a constant source of frustration to Baker, because it indicated a weakness that he was loath to accept. If he was successful with all other nationalities, why not with Rennalls?

At least he had managed to "break through" to Rennalls more successfully than any other expatriate. In fact, it was the young Barracanian's attitude—sometimes overbearing, sometimes cynical—toward other company expatriates that had been one of the subjects Baker had raised last year when he discussed Rennalls's staff report with him. He knew, too, that he would have to raise the same subject again in the forthcoming interview, because Jackson, the senior draftsperson, had complained only yesterday about the rudeness of Rennalls. With this thought in mind, Baker leaned forward and spoke into the intercom, "Would you come in, Matt, please? I'd like a word with you." As Rennalls entered the room, Baker said, "Do sit down," and offered a cigarette. He paused while he held out his lighter, then went on.

"As you know, Matt, I'll be off to Canada in a few days' time, and before I go, I thought it would be useful if we could have a final chat together. It is indeed with some deference that I suggest I can be of help. You will shortly be sitting in this chair doing the job I am now doing, but I, on the other hand, am 10 years older, so perhaps you can accept the idea that I may be able to give you the benefit of my longer experience."

Baker saw Rennalls stiffen slightly in his chair as he made this point. Consequently, he added in explanation, "You and I have attended enough company courses to remember those repeated requests by the personnel manager to tell people how they are getting on as often as the convenient moment arises and not just the automatic 'once a year' when, by regulation, staff reports have to be discussed."

Rennalls nodded his agreement, and Baker went on. "I shall always remember the last job performance discussion I had with my previous boss back in Germany. He used what he called the 'plus and minus technique.' His firm belief was that when a senior, by discussion, seeks to improve the work performance of his staff, his prime objective should be to make sure that the latter leaves the interview encouraged and inspired to improve. Any criticism must, therefore, be constructive and helpful. He said that one very good way to encourage a person—and I fully

agree with him—is to tell him about his good points—the plus factors—as well as his weak ones—the minus factors. I thought, Matt, it would be a good idea to run our discussion along these lines."

Rennalls offered no comment, so Baker continued. "Let me say, therefore, right away, that, as far as your own work performance is concerned, the plus far outweighs the minus. I have been most impressed, for instance, with the way you have adapted your considerable theoretic knowledge to master the practical techniques of your job—that ingenious method you used to get air down to the fifth-shaft level is a sufficient case in point—and at departmental meetings I have invariably found your comments well-taken and helpful. In fact, you will be interested to know that only last week I reported to Mr. Hutchins that, from the technical point of view, he could not wish for a more able man to succeed to the position of chief engineer."

"That's very good indeed of you, John," cut in Rennalls with a smile of thanks. "My only worry now is how to live up to such a high recommendation."

"Of that I am quite sure," returned Baker, "especially if you can overcome the minus factor which I would like now to discuss with you. It is one that I have talked about before, so I'll come straight to the point. I have noticed that you are more friendly and get on better with your fellow Barracanians than you do with Europeans. In point of fact, I had a complaint only yesterday from Mr. Jackson, who said you had been rude to him—and not for the first time either.

"There is, Matt, I am sure, no need for me to tell you how necessary it will be for you to get on well with expatriates, because until the company has trained sufficient people of your caliber, Europeans are bound to occupy senior positions here in Barracania. All this is vital to your future interests, so can I help you in any way?"

While Baker was speaking on this theme, Rennalls sat tensed in his chair, and it was some seconds before he replied. "It is quite extraordinary, isn't it, how one can convey an impression to others so at variance with what one intends? I can only assure you once again that my disputes with Jackson—and you may remember also, Godson—have had nothing at all to do with the color of their skins. I promise you that if a Barracanian had behaved in an equally peremptory manner, I would have reacted in precisely the same way. And again, if I may say it within these four walls, I am sure I am not the only one who has found Jackson and Godson difficult. I could mention the names of several expatriates who have felt the same. However, I am really sorry to have created this impression of not being able to get along with Europeans—it is an entirely false one—and I quite realize that I must do all I can to correct it as quickly as possible. On your last point, regarding Europeans holding senior positions in the company for some time to come, I quite accept the situation. I know that Caribbean Bauxite—as it has been doing for many years now—will promote Barracanians as soon as their experience warrants it. And, finally, I would like to assure you, John—and my father thinks the same too—that I am very happy in my work here and hope to stay with the company for many years to come."

Rennalls had spoken earnestly. Although not convinced by what he heard, Baker did not think he could pursue the matter further except to say, "All right, Matt, my impression *may* be wrong, but I would like to remind you about the truth of that old saying, 'What is important is not what is true but what is believed.' Let it rest at that."

But suddenly Baker knew he didn't want to "let it rest at that." He was disappointed once again at not being able to break through to Rennalls and having yet again to listen to his bland denial that there was any racial prejudice in his makeup. Baker, who had intended to end the interview at this point, decided to try another tactic.

"To return for a moment to the 'plus and minus technique' I was telling you about just now, there is another plus factor I forgot to mention. I would like to congratulate you not only on the caliber of your work but also on the ability you have shown in overcoming a challenge which I, as a European, have never had to meet. Continental Ore is, as you know, a typical commercial enterprise—admittedly a big one—which is a product of the economic and social environment of the United States and Western Europe. My ancestors have all been brought up in this environment for the past 200 or 300 years, and I have, therefore, been able to live in a world in which commerce (as we know it today) has been part and parcel of my being. It has not been something revolutionary and new that has suddenly entered my life." Baker went on, "In your case, the situation is different, because you and your forebears have had only some 50 or 60 years in this commercial environment. You have had to face the challenge of bridging the gap between 50 and 200 or 300 years. Again, Matt, let me congratulate you—and people like you—once again on having so successfully overcome this particular hurdle. It is for this very reason that I think the outlook for Barracania—and particularly Caribbean Bauxite—is so bright."

There was a pause, and for a moment, Baker thought hopefully that he was about to achieve his long-awaited breakthrough, but Rennalls merely smiled back. The barrier remained unbreached. There remained some five minutes of cheerful conversation about the contrast between the Caribbean and Canadian climate and whether the West Indies had any hope of beating England in the Fifth Test before Baker drew the interview to a close. Although he was as far as ever from knowing the real Rennalls, he nevertheless was glad that the interview had run along in this friendly manner and, particularly, that it had ended on such a cheerful note.

This feeling, however, lasted only until the following morning. Baker had some farewells to make, so he arrived at the office considerably later than usual. He had no sooner sat down at his desk than his secretary walked into the room with a worried frown on her face. Her words came fast, "When I arrived this morning, I found Mr. Rennalls already waiting at my door. He seemed very angry and told me in quite a peremptory manner that he had a vital letter to dictate that must be sent off without any delay. He was so worked up that he couldn't keep still and kept pacing about the room, which is most unlike him. He wouldn't even wait to read what he had dictated. Just signed the page where he thought the letter would end. It has been distributed, and your copy is in your tray."

Puzzled and feeling vaguely uneasy, Baker opened the confidential envelope and read the following letter:

From: Assistant Engineer

To: Chief Engineer,
Caribbean Bauxite Limited

14 August

*Assessment of Interview Between Baker
and Rennalls*

It has always been my practice to respect the advice given me by seniors, so after our interview, I decided to give careful thought once again to its main points and so make sure that I had understood all that had been said. As I promised you at the time, I had every intention of putting your advice to the best effect.

It was not, therefore, until I had sat down quietly in my home yesterday evening to consider the interview objectively that its main purport became clear. Only then did the full enormity of what you said dawn on me. The more I thought about it, the more convinced I was that I had hit upon the real truth—and the more furious I became. With a facility in the English language which I, a poor Barracanian, cannot hope to match, you had the audacity to insult me (and through me every Barracanian worth his salt) by claiming that our knowledge of modern living is only a paltry 50 years old whereas yours goes back 200 or 300 years. As if your materialistic commercial environment could possibly be compared with the spiritual values of our culture. I'll have you know that if much of what I saw in London is representative of your most boasted culture, I hope fervently that it will never come to Barracania. By what right do you have the effrontery to condescend to us? At heart, all you Europeans think us barbarians; as you say amongst yourselves, we are "just down from the trees."

Far into the night I discussed this matter with my father, and he is as disgusted as I. He agrees with me that any company whose senior staff think as you do is no place for any Barracanian proud of his culture and race—so much for all the company "clap-trap" and specious propaganda about regionalization and Barracania for the Barracanians.

I feel ashamed and betrayed. Please accept this letter as my resignation, which I wish to become effective immediately.

cc: Production Manager
        Managing Director

Questions for Review

1. What mistake did John Baker make? Why did he not realize this mistake when it occurred?

2. What would you recommend that Baker do now? Explain.

3. What does this case illustrate about human resource management in the international environment? Be complete in your answer.

Source: This case was prepared by Gareth Evans and is used with permission.

In-Depth Integrative Case 1

HSBC in China

Introduction

After years of negotiations, China finally acceded to the World Trade Organization (WTO) in December 2001 (see Exhibit 1). This development was a significant milestone in China's integration with the global economy. One of the most important and far-reaching consequences was the transformation of China's financial sector. China's banking, insurance, and securities industries were long due for a major overhaul, and the WTO requirements guaranteed that the liberalization of China's economy would extend to the important financial sector. China's banking sector had become a casualty of the state. Banks and other financial institutions haphazardly extended loans to state-owned enterprises (SOEs) based not on sound credit analysis but favoritism and government-directed policy. As a consequence, crippling debt from bad and underperforming loans mounted, with no effective market disciplines to rein it in.

China recognized that opening up the banking sector could bolster its financial system. Foreign management would help overhaul the banking sector and put the focus on returns, instead of promoting a social agenda. This fiscal agenda would ultimately lead to a stronger and more stable economy. Yet after years of direction from the state, Chinese bank managers did not have the necessary skills to transform the banks on their own. Guo Shuqing, shortly after being promoted to chairman of China Construction Bank, admitted that, "more than 90% of the bank's risk managers are unqualified."[1]

Immediately upon accession to the WTO, China's banking sector began to open to foreign banks. Initially, foreign banks were allowed to conduct foreign currency business without any market access restrictions and conduct local currency business with foreign-invested enterprises and foreign individuals. In addition, the liberalization of foreign investment rules made Chinese banks attractive targets for foreign financial institutions. Sweeping domestic changes have followed. Strong emphasis has been placed on interest rate liberalization, clearer and more consistent regulation, and a frenzy of IPOs of state owned banks has followed. It was in this context that HSBC rapidly expanded its presence in China.

Exhibit 1 China's WTO Commitments

General Cross-Sector Commitments

- ➤ Reforms to lower trade barriers in every sector of the economy, opening its markets to foreign companies and their exports from the first day of accession.
- ➤ Provide national treatment and improved market access to goods and services from other WTO members.
- ➤ Special rules regarding subsidies and the operation of state-owned enterprises, in light of the state's large role in China's economy.
- ➤ Undertake important changes to its legal framework, designed to add transparency and predictability to business dealings and improve the process of foreign market entry.
- ➤ Agreement to assume the obligations of more than 20 *existing* multilateral WTO agreements, covering all areas of trade.
- ➤ Under the acquired rights commitment, agreed that the conditions of ownership, operation, and scope of activities for a foreign company under any existing agreement would not be made more restrictive than they were on the date of China's accession to the WTO.
- ➤ Licensing procedures that were streamlined, transparent, and more predictable.

Commitments Specific to the Financial Services Industry

- ➤ Allow foreign banks to conduct *foreign currency business* without any market access or national treatment limitations.
- ➤ Allow foreign banks to conduct *local currency business* with foreign-invested enterprises and foreign individuals (subject to geographic restrictions).
- ➤ Banking services (with a five-year transitional plan) by foreign banks:
    Within two years after accession, foreign banks would be able to conduct *domestic* currency business with Chinese enterprises (subject to geographic restrictions).
    Within five years after accession, foreign banks would be able to conduct domestic currency business with Chinese individuals, and all geographic restrictions will be lifted.
    Foreign banks also would be permitted to provide financial leasing services at the same time that Chinese banks are permitted to do so.

HSBC, known for its international scope and careful, judicious strategy, made a series of key investments between 2001 and 2005 that arguably gave it the most extensive position in China of any foreign financial group. These investments included two separate transactions that resulted in a 19.9 percent stake in Ping An insurance, and, in June 2004, a $1.8 billion successful tender for a 19.9 percent stake in Bank of Communications, the fifth largest bank in China. HSBC had a long history in Asia, and was uniquely positioned to take advantage of China's vast population and mushrooming middle class, high savings rates (in the range of 40 percent), and huge capital investments (US$50 billion FDI in 2005). HSBC recognized that the current banking system was not capitalizing on this vast opportunity, and sought to get in on the ground floor in this new environment. Perhaps, with further liberalization, however, China would allow future investors to establish even greater claims to Chinese banks. Citigroup's successful effort to gain a controlling stake in Guandgong Development Bank appeared to undermine earlier investors who had been limited by China's rule that allowed foreigners to own no more than 19.9 percent of domestic financial institutions. Did the huge potential rewards of being an early mover in China mitigate the promise of uncertainty and risks of doing business in an emerging market? After being burned in Argentina, could HSBC relax its conservative philosophy in its China strategy? If the economy took a turn for the worse, HSBC could face heavy losses. On the other hand, could HSBC afford not to be an early mover in a region where it had a longstanding presence?

Background on HSBC

History

Thomas Sutherland founded the Hongkong and Shanghai Banking Corporation (Hongkong Bank) in 1865 to finance the growing trade between Europe, India, and China.[2] Sutherland, a Scot, was working for the Peninsular and Oriental Steam Navigation Company when he recognized a considerable demand for local banking facilities in Hong Kong and on the China coast. Hongkong Bank opened in Hong Kong in March 1865 and in Shanghai a month later.

The bank rapidly expanded by opening agencies and branches across the globe, reaching as far as Europe and North America, but maintained a distinct focus on China and the Asia-Pacific region. Hongkong Bank helped pioneer modern banking during this time in a number of countries, such as Japan, where it opened a branch in 1866 and advised the government on banking and currency, and Thailand, where it opened the country's first bank in 1888 and printed the country's first banknotes. By the 1880s, the bank issued banknotes and held government funds in Hong Kong, and also helped manage British government accounts in China, Japan, Penang, and Singapore. In 1876, the bank handled China's first public loan, and thereafter issued most of China's public loans. Hongkong Bank had become the foremost financial institution in Asia by the close of the 19th century.[3]

After the First World War, the Hongkong Bank anticipated an expansion in its Asian markets, and took a leading role in stabilizing the Chinese national currency. The tumultuous Second World War, for its part, saw most of the bank's European staff become prisoners of war to the advancing Japanese.

The Postwar Years

In the postwar years, Hongkong Bank turned to dramatic expansion through acquisitions and alliances in order to diversify. The acquisitions began with the British Bank of the Middle East (Persia and the Gulf states) and the Mercantile Bank (India and Malaya) in 1959, and were followed by acquiring a majority interest in Hong Kong's Hang Seng Bank in 1965. The 51 percent controlling interest in Hang Seng Bank was acquired during a local banking crisis for $12.4 million. As of 2002, HSBC's interest in the bank was 62 percent and was over $13 billion. Hang Seng, which retained its name and management, has been a consistently strong performer. The bank made further acquisitions in the United Kingdom and Europe (from 1973), North America (from 1980), Latin America (from 1997), as well as other Asian markets.

Under Chairman Michael Sandberg, Hongkong Bank entered the North American market with a $314 million, 51 percent acquisition of Marine Midland, a regional bank in upstate New York. In 1987, the bank purchased the remaining 49 percent, doubling Hongkong Bank's investment and providing the bank a significant U.S. presence. As a condition of the acquisition, however, Marine Midland retained its senior management.

Move to London and Acquisitions

In 1991, Hongkong Bank reorganized as HSBC Holdings and moved its headquarters in 1993 to London from Hong Kong. Sandberg's successor, William Purves, led HSBC's purchase of the U.K.'s Midland Bank in 1992. This acquisition fortified HSBC's European presence and doubled its assets. The move also enhanced HSBC's global presence and advanced the bank's reputation as a global financial services company.

Other major acquisitions of the 1990s included Republic Bank and Safra Holdings in the United States, which doubled HSBC's private banking business investments moves in Brazil and Argentina in 1997, and acquisition of Mexico's Bital in 2002. In 2000, HSBC acquired CCF in France. By 2006, HSBC had assets exceeding $1,860 billion, customers numbering close to 100 million, and operations in six continents. In recent years, HSBC has made a major commitment to emerging markets, especially China and Mexico, but also Brazil, India, and smaller developing economies.

Expansion, Acquisition, and Succession

The World's Local Bank

HSBC, holding company set up a group policy in 1991 that established 11 quasi-independent banks, each a separate subsidiary with its own balance sheet.[4] The head office provided essential functions, such as strategic planning, human resource management, and legal, administrative, and financial planning and control. This setup promoted prompter decision making at a local level and greater accountability.[5] HSBC portrays itself as "the world's local bank," recognizing the importance of globalization, flexibility, and local responsiveness.

As of 1998, HSBC established distinct customer groups or lines of business that would overlay existing geographic designations. This encouraged maximizing the benefits of its universal scope, such as sharing best practices of product development, management, and marketing. The geographic perspective was melded closely with a customer group perspective, demanding both global and local thinking.

Traditionally, HSBC's culture has embraced caution, thrift, discipline, and risk avoidance. The bank looked at long-term survival and considered markets in 50-year views. Thrift manifested through the company, and even the chairman flew economy class on flights less than three hours.[6] In 2005, incoming Chairman Stephen Green recognized the company's rule "to follow the letter and spirit of regulations" and signaled his intention to protect the bank's reputation as it extends into consumer finance.[7]

Bond's Rein and Move to "HSBC"

Sir John Bond joined Hongkong Bank in 1961, spent most of his early career in Asia and the United States, and is credited with turning around Marine Midland Bank in the late 1980s. Bond became CEO of HSBC in 1993, and chairman in 1998, bringing with him a hands-on entrepreneurial style and exceptionally ambitious goals.[8] He pursued acquisitions beyond HSBC's traditional core, in pursuit of such attractive financial segments as wealth management, investment banking, online retail financing, and consumer finance. Bond considered shareholder value and economic profit in deciding when acquisition premiums were in order, which was in contrast to his predecessor's "three times book value" rule.[9] By 2001, Bond had authorized investments of over $21 billion on acquisitions and new ventures.[10]

In 1998, Bond adopted the HSBC brand, and preserved "The Hongkong & Shanghai Banking Corp." name only for its bank based in Hong Kong. HSBC branded its subsidiary banks across the world with the parent bank's acronym and greatly expanded marketing efforts in 2000. In March 2002, HSBC's marketing message became "the world's local bank," which would help the brand become one of the world's top 50 most recognizable brands by 2003.[11]

Household Acquisition

In 2003, HSBC's acquisition of Household International became the basis of HSBC's Consumer Finance customer group. Household utilized a unique system to forecast the likelihood that customers would repay debt, which used a 13-year database of consumer behavior. Household was controversial and yet presented great opportunity. HSBC desired to leverage this new skill in developing countries, yet was unable to find all demographic and credit data that Household normally relies on in the United States. HSBC particularly looked to extend the Household model into China and Mexico.

Transitions

In May 2006, Sir John Bond presided over his final board meeting, with CEO Stephen Green poised to replace the retiring chairman. Green had been with HSBC for nearly a quarter century, after also spending several years as a consultant at McKinsey. Green's style is known to be more cerebral and low key than his predecessor.[12] Stephen Green was succeeded as group chief executive by Michael Geoghegan, 52, who joined HSBC in 1973 and was formerly chief executive of HSBC Bank plc, the group's principal subsidiary in the U.K. Geoghegan has a reputation as an aggressive banker who is not afraid to make tough strategic decisions. Shortly after his appointment, Geoghegan traveled around the world visiting more than a dozen countries and meeting with thousands of HSBC employees. Overall, the appointments were met with guarded optimism in the investment community, though not without detractors. One shareholder said: "The question is whether HSBC should have an independent nonexecutive who might make a future chairman and therefore widen the choice in the future."[13]

Managing for Growth

HSBC's strategic plan, "Managing for Growth," was launched in the fall of 2003. This strategy builds on HSBC's global, international scope and seeks to grow by focusing on the key customer groups of personal financial services; consumer finance; commercial banking; corporate, investment banking, and markets; and private banking.[14] "Managing for Growth" is intended to be "evolutionary, not revolutionary," and aims to vault HSBC to the world's leading financial services company. HSBC seeks to grow earnings over the long term, using its peers as a benchmark. It also plans to invest in delivery platforms, technology, its people, and brand name to prop up the future value of HSBC's stock market rating and total shareholder return. HSBC retains its core values of communication, long-term focus, ethical relationships, teamwork, prudence, creativity, high standards, ambition, customer-focused marketing, and corporate social responsibility, all with an international outlook.[15]

Strategic Pillars

As part of the growth strategy, HSBC identified eight strategic pillars:

> *Brand*: continue to establish HSBC and its hexagon symbol as one of the top global brands for customer experience and corporate social responsibility.
> *Personal Financial Services*: drive growth in key markets and through appropriate channels; emerging markets are essential markets with a burgeoning demand.
> *Consumer Finance*: offer both a wider product range and penetrate new markets, such as the emerging country markets.
> *Commercial Banking*: leverage HSBC's international reach through effective relationship management and improved product offerings.
> *Corporate, Investment Banking, and Markets*: accelerate growth by enhancing capital markets and advisory capabilities.
> *Private Banking*: a focus on serving the highest value personal clients.
> *People*: draw in, develop and motivate HSBC's people.
> *TSR*: fulfill HSBC's TSR target by achieving strong competitive performances in earnings per share growth and efficiency.[16]

Challenges in Investment Banking

Within the CIBM group, HSBC had always excelled at the "C" (global corporate banking) and "M" (markets—sales and trading of bonds, foreign exchange, derivatives, and other instruments) but had lagged in its execution of the "IB"(investment banking). Therefore, as part of the managing for growth initiative, HSBC launched an ambitious plan to strengthen IB. Executing the plan proved to be challenging within the HSBC culture. According to a *Wall Street Journal* report, the budget for the first two years—mostly for hiring new talent and improving technology—was around $800 million. The then chairman, Sir John Bond, needed top IB talent to lead the change. He hired John Studzinski, a very experienced banker who had worked for Morgan Stanley. Studzinski was paired with Stuart Gulliver, an experienced veteran of HSBC's international manager program. Because Gulliver had worked for HSBC for 26 years, he was accustomed to HSBC's very strict cost-control policies. Studzinski started building a team from scratch by hiring people from competitor's banks, such as Credit Suisse, Lazard Frères, and Goldman Sachs.[17] According to the *Wall Street Journal* account, spending was drastically increasing and Gulliver was disturbed by this change in HSBC's traditional prudence. For example, although unusual for the banking industry, some bankers were promised fixed bonuses (they are usually paid based on the company's financial performance).[18]

Although expenses were increasing, profits were down. In the first half of 2005, costs for the CIBM unit were up 24 percent to $3.32 billion, whereas pretax profit decreased by 18 percent.[19] HSBC was outranked by other banks in terms of mergers and acquisitions for 2006. The bank ranked number 13 (see Exhibit 2). The IB strategy appeared to stall. In November 2005, Sir John announced his retirement for the next May, and in May 2006, Studzinski announced he would leave in September 2006.

Focus on Emerging Markets

In 2000, HSBC had half of its assets in developing countries.[20] Most earnings, however, stemmed from mature markets, such as Hong Kong and Britain. All but 5 percent of group profits came from five economies, while India and Latin America each only added 1 percent to group profit.[21]

Exhibit 2   HSBC Mergers and Acquisitions Ranking

Adviser	2006 Rank (first nine months)	Value of deals in US$	Number of deals
Goldman Sachs	1	731 b	237
Citigroup	2	659.7	225
J.P. Morgan	3	652.9	313
Morgan Stanley	4	574.2	263
Merrill Lynch	5	543.3	197
Credit Suisse	6	497.1	211
UBS	7	477.0	271
Lehman Brothers	8	430.5	138
Deutsche Bank	9	388.7	161
BNP Paribas	10	292.3	82
HSBC	**13**	**211.2**	**58**

Source: Carrick Mollenkamp, "HSBC Stumbles in Bid to Become Global Deal Maker," *The Wall Street Journal,* October 5, 2006, p. A1.

The Draw of Emerging Markets

Recognition of the impact of emerging markets is an essential thread running throughout the elements of the "Managing for Growth" strategy. Since 2000, many of HSBC's emerging markets' profits have increased dramatically (see Exhibit 3). Across the board, HSBC's pretax profits in emerging markets have increased from $905 million in 2000 to $3,439 million in 2005. China, which lost $26 million in 2000, made $334 million in 2005, an increase of 944 percent from 2004 alone. Mexico has also had great success, increasing from $9 million profit in 2000 to $923 million in 2005. In 2006, this trend continued, as total profit before tax during the first half of 2006 increased by 18 percent over the first half of 2005 (see Exhibit 3). The biggest winners were India (99 percent increase), the Middle East (95 percent increase), and China (74 percent increase), while Indonesia (–51 percent) and Argentina (–50 percent) fell by the greatest percentage.

Incoming Chairman Stephen Green underlined HSBC's focus on the potential of emerging markets: "There is a general rule of thumb that says the emerging markets grow faster than mature markets as economies and the financial services sector grows faster than the real economy in emerging markets because you are starting from very low penetration of financial services in general."[22]

Specifically in consumer finance, Green recognized the importance of importing HSBC's model into markets starved for credit cards and loans, saying, "Any analysis of the demographics of emerging markets tells you that consumer finance is going to be an important part, and a rapidly growing part, of the financial-services spectrum for a long time to come."[23]

Success in Mexico

HSBC has had phenomenal success in Mexico, which led emerging markets with $515 million in pretax profits during the first half of 2006, an increase of 20 percent over the same period in 2005. Indeed, Mexico's market is expanding at a very rapid clip. In 2002, HSBC purchased the undercapitalized Mexican bank Grupo Financiero Bital SA. Four years later, HSBC opened Bital's new headquarters in an impressive tower in Mexico City's Paseo de la Reforma. HSBC's tagline in Mexico City proclaims: "13,500 tons of commitment to Mexico."[24] The slogan works well with the proudly nationalistic Mexican population.

Today, foreign banks control more than 80 percent of Mexico's banking assets. Turning over the assets was the easiest way for policy makers to escape the "Tequila Crisis" of 1994–95, which wiped out half of Mexico's assets. HSBC and other foreign banks that bet on Mexico have won big, as profits in Mexico have skyrocketed. HSBC has taken a long-term view of Mexico, which has a relatively stable economy and a very young population (about 45 percent under age 19), in addition to great opportunities arising from NAFTA. HSBC's plan includes offering credit cards to a customer base that uses primarily debit cards. "That's part of a wide-ranging retail-banking strategy for Mexico, where we are also growing our deposit products [and] remittance products for the very considerable flow of retail remittances," according to Chairman Stephen Green.[25]

Setback in Argentina

Not all emerging markets have been as successful for HSBC as Mexico. A hefty investment in Argentina, for

Exhibit 3   HSBC Emerging Markets

Pretax Profits 2005 vs. 2004, 2002					Pretax Profits 2005 vs. 2006		
Country	2000 (US$ mil)	2004 (US$ mil)	2005 (US$ mil)	% Change 2004–2005	Country	2006 (US$ mil)	% Change (2006 over 2005)
Argentina	112	154	244	58	Argentina	157	−36
Brazil	208	281	406	44	Brazil	526	30
China	−26	32	334	944	China	708	112
India	87	178	212	19	India	393	85
Indonesia	70	76	113	49	Indonesia	71	−37
Malaysia	116	214	236	10	Malaysia	274	16
Mexico	9	774	923	19	Mexico	1009	9
Saudi Arabia	30	122	236	93	Saudi Arabia	181	41
South Korea	65	89	94	6	South Korea	48	−13
Taiwan	45	107	68	−36	Taiwan	(23)	NA
Turkey	59	142	265	87	Turkey	217	−18
UAE	130	192	308	60	Middle East	730	25
Total	**905**	**2,361**	**3,439**	**+46**	Other	166	−15
Total profit before tax (all countries)		18,943	20,966	+10.7	**Total**	**4,533**	**19**
					Total profit before tax (all countries)	22,086	5

example, spiraled out of control. In 1997, HSBC completed its acquisition of Grupo Roberts, becoming one of the major players in the country and expanding its Latin American presence. Four years later, however, Argentina went from seemingly one of Latin America's strongest economies to a stunning failure.

Much of the damage stemmed from a government-mandated conversion of U.S.-dollar-denominated assets into pesos. Argentina removed an 11-year-old mechanism pegging the peso one to one to the dollar, which led to the peso's sharp devaluation, and resulted in massive losses for many banks. In the 2001 meltdown of Argentina's economy, HSBC lost $1.152 billion, with bad debt charges on HSBC's Argentina exposure of $737 million, even though the country only accounted for 0.5 percent of HSBC's assets.[26] Faced with huge losses, HSBC was forced to cut 2001 profit estimates 10 percent and considered exiting the country. Despite its long-term approach, the fluid, unstable economy was daunting, and demonstrates the volatile nature of emerging markets. More recently, HSBC's position in Argentina has recovered somewhat (see Exhibit 3).

Liberalization of China's Banking Sector

China's Banking Sector Pre-WTO

Before the WTO accession negotiations, China's banking industry operated as a cog in China's centrally planned economy. The state commercial banks performed a social function, during China's post-Mao drive to industrialize, instead of operating for economic return. Consequently, the banks adhered to directed lending practices from the government and in turn created some of China's most successful enterprises, but also supported thousands of other, inefficient, and unprofitable state-owned enterprises. This practice left state commercial banks with massive amounts of debt that were largely unrecoverable and hordes of nonperforming loans.

In addition to widespread losses, instability ensued in the banking system overall. To make matters worse, corruption and mismanagement ran rampant throughout the sector, sapping away consumer and investor confidence.

WTO Accession

Following 15 years of negotiation and two decades of economic reform in China, December 11, 2001, marked China's accession to the World Trade Organization. The main objective of the WTO agreement was to open China's market up to foreign competition. The deadline for complete implementation was December 11, 2006.

China made a number of implementations immediately. To begin with, foreign banks were allowed to conduct foreign currency business without any market access restrictions. Also, foreign banks were allowed to conduct local currency business with foreign-invested enterprises and foreign individuals (with geographic restrictions). Within two years of accession, China agreed to allow foreign banks to conduct domestic currency business with Chinese enterprises (geographic restrictions). Within five years, foreign banks could conduct domestic currency business with Chinese individuals (no geographic restrictions); and foreign banks were able to provide financial leasing services at the same time as Chinese banks. Under the WTO investment provisions, China agreed to allow foreign ownership of Chinese banks (up to 25 percent), with no single foreign investor permitted to own more than 20 percent.

"Bank reform has become the most crucial task for the government in pushing forward economic reforms," said Yi Xianrong, an economist at the Chinese Academy of Social Sciences in Beijing.[27] Indeed, bank reform is critical to stabilizing and advancing the Chinese economy.

Domestic Reform

China has undertaken a number of domestic reforms in order to overhaul the banking industry. China has engaged in interest rate liberalization by removing certain interest rate and price controls. Instead of being pegged to the U.S. dollar, as it once was, China's currency exchange rate is now pegged to within 0.3 percent of a basket of currencies, dominated by a group including the U.S. dollar, euro, Japanese yen, South Korean won, British pound, Thai baht, and Russian ruble. The yuan was revalued by 2.1 percent against the dollar in July 2005, but analysts estimate that it remains 10–30 percent undervalued.

Regulation has long been a concern in the Chinese banking industry. China has made major progress by creating regulatory agencies. In 2003, China created a central regulator, the China Banking Regulatory Commission (CBRC), out of the central bank. The regulator's 20,000 staff members endeavor to shift the banks' focus from senseless loans and grow mind-sets to a goal of preserving capital and generating returns. Lenders not meeting a capital ratio of 8 percent of risk-weighted assets (as decreed by Basel I, a global standard) by 2007 may face sanctions, which could include the removal of senior management. Still, the CBRC faces an uphill battle. Han Mingzhi, as head of the CBRC's international department, admitted in 2004 that "we lack people who understand commercial banking and microeconomics. It is a headache for the CBRC."[28]

Concurrently, China is striving to make regulatory and reporting requirements more clear, because they have often proved confusing barriers to foreign investment. Since 1998, China has intensified accounting, prudential, and regulatory standards. Prior to 1998, the banks booked interest income for up to three years even if it was not being paid. Now, the banks can do so for only 90 days, which is the international norm. Still, it has been all too common for Chinese banks to ignore regulations and not monitor loans. As a result of poor accounting, the banks themselves are sometimes unsure of their bad loans. Lai Xiaomin, head of the CBRC's Beijing office, admits that "when our banks disclose information, they don't always do so in a totally honest manner."[29] Indeed, the lack of reliable accounting can hamper investment. As one Hong Kong investor put it, "When you take a state-owned enterprise that has had weak internal controls, it can be enormously labor-intensive to come up with financials we can work with."[30]

In 2006, regulators overhauled the system in which almost one-third of a company's shares were "nontradable." Fixing this problem has helped energize the market and welcome in individual investors.[31]

Recent Regulatory Moves

New regulations also hope to address China's history of dishonesty and embezzlement. With the tight connection of Chinese banks with local governments, corruption has choked the Chinese banking system. Some common practices have historically encouraged corruption, such as allowing the same person to make and approve a loan. Former bank Chairman Zhang Enzhao himself was arrested in June 2005 for allegedly taking bribes. At the China Construction Bank alone, there were more than 100 cases

of theft and embezzlement between 2002 and 2004.[32] These old habits have to be rooted out.

China is working hard to transition its traditional banks into "universal" banks. Most of China's 128 commercial banks have introduced better governance, shareholding, and incentive structures, while also adding independent directors to their boards.[33] Foreign management and knowledge are intended to flush the Chinese banking system with managerial talent. To help encourage foreign banks, China is relaxing some foreign bank restrictions. The Chinese government has also taken steps to eliminate bad loans, by bailing out banks.

IPO Explosion

China has aggressively pursued IPOs of state-owned banks, a policy which has been met with a strong response from investors eager to tap into the populous country and seize first-mover advantages (see Exhibit 4). HSBC's purchase of a 19.9 percent stake in Bank of Communications (BoCOM) in June 2004 was the pioneering, substantial foreign bank investment in China. HSBC previously made large investments in Fujian Asian Bank (50 percent) and Bank of Shanghai (8 percent). In 2005, foreign banks invested $18 billion in several of China's largest banks. The October 2005 listing of China Construction Bank

Exhibit 4 **Foreign Bank Investments in China**

PRC Bank	Foreign Partner	% Stake	Price	Date
Bank of Shanghai	HSBC	8.00	$62.6 m	12/2001
	IFC	7.00	$25.0 m	
	Shanghai Commercial Bank (HK)	3.00	$15.7 m	
Shanghai Pudong Dev Bank	Citigroup	4.62	$72.0 m	12/2003
Fujian Asian Bank	HSBC	50	Less than $20 m[1]	12/2003
Bank of Communications	HSBC	19.90	$1.75 b	6/2004
Xian CCB	Scotia Bank	12.4	$3.2 m	10/2004
Jinan City CCB	Commonwealth Bank of Australia	11.0	$17 m[2]	11/2004
Shenzhen Dev. Bank	Newbridge Capital	17.9	$1.23 b	12/2004
Minsheng Bank	Temasek	4.9		1/2005
Hangzhou CCB	Commonwealth Bank of Australia	19.90	$78.0 m	4/2005
China Construction Bank	Bank of America	9.00	$3.0 b	6/2005
	Temasek	5.1	$1.5 m[3]	
Bank of China	Royal Bank of Scotland	5.00	$3.1 b	8/2005
	UBS	1.6	$500 m[4]	9/2005
	Temasek	10.00	$3.1 b[5]	9/2005
Industrial Commercial BOC	Goldman, Allianz, AmEx			8/2005
Nanjing CCB	BNP Paribas	19.20	$27.0 m	10/2005
Hua Xia Bank	Deutsche Bank	9.9	$329 m[6]	10/2005
	Sal. Oppenheim Jr.	4.1		10/2005
Bank of Beijing	ING	19.90	$214 m	3/2005

[1]HSBC Press Article, accessed October 3, 2006, www.hsbc.com.cn/cn/aboutus/press/content/03dec29a.htm.

[2]Guonan Ma, "Sharing China's Bank Restructuring," *China and World Economy* 14, no. 3 (2006), p. 8.

[3]David Lague and Donald Greenlees, "China's Troubled Banks Lure Investors," *International Herald Tribune*, www.iht.com/articles/2005/09/21/business/bank.php, accessed on October 4, 2006.

[4]"UBS to Invest $500 million in Bank of China," CBS News, www.cbsnews.com/stories/2005/09/27/ap/business/main D8CSHPLO0.shtml, assessed October 4, 2006.

[5]Luo Jun and Xiao Yu, "Temasek to Buy 10% of China Bank," *International Herald Tribune*, www.iht.com/articles/2005/09/01/bloomberg/sxboc.php, accessed on October 4, 2006.

[6]"Deutsche Bank Seals Chinese Deal," BBC News, news.bbc.co.uk/2/hi/business/4348560.stm, accessed October 4, 2006.

(CCB), China largest at the time, raised $8 billion from foreign investors for 12 percent of its shares. CCB further obtained an additional $4 billion ahead of its float by selling stakes of 9 percent to Bank of America and 5.1 percent to Temasek, Singapore's investment agency. In the following months, the Royal Bank of Scotland put $3.1 billion into Bank of China, Temasek another $3.1 billion and Switzerland's UBS $500 million.

In May 2006, Bank of China, the country's second-largest lender, raised $11.2 billion in a Hong Kong stock sale, which was the fifth-largest initial public offering in history. In July 2006, the Chinese government announced approval for an even larger IPO of the country's largest bank, Industrial & Commercial Bank of China, to raise $18 billion or more in one of the largest stock offerings ever.[34] The central bank expects foreigners to bring much needed improvements to the state banks' risk-management and internal control systems, including credit-risk assessment and more transparent reporting. With capital allocated more efficiently, a more stable financial system will follow, and the economy will become more open to foreign competition.

Two Steps Forward

Pulling back from some of its commitments, China indirectly delayed the implementation of its WTO commitments. On February 1, 2002, the People's Bank of China (PBOC) issued regulations and implementation rules governing foreign-funded banks. While these measures met the commitments of the WTO agreement, the PBOC was taking a *very* conservative approach in opening up the banking sector. For example, foreign-funded banks could open only one branch every 12 months.

In the wake of these early obstacles, there have been positive changes. Capital requirements were reduced, additional cities were opened up to foreign banking, and the "one branch every 12 months" restriction was lifted. Central bank officials have indicated willingness to eventually elevate the foreign ownership limit above the current 25 percent, but experts doubt it will ever go beyond 50 percent.[35]

A 2006 study by McKinsey found that underperforming loans with merely negligible returns are also very damaging to the Chinese economy. McKinsey estimates that reforming China's financial system could boost GDP by $321 billion annually.[36]

China's banking sector plays an excessive role in the overall financial system. The share of bank deposits in the financial system ranges from less than 20 percent in developed economies to around half in emerging markets. China, however, has a share of bank deposits at a sky-high 75 percent of the capital in the economy, which practically doubles any other Asian nation (see Exhibit 5).[37]

Capital is still mostly allocated to state-owned enterprises, even though private companies have been China's growth engine. Private companies produce 52 percent of GDP in China, but only account for 27 percent of outstanding loans.[38] By sinking money into state-owned enterprises, China's banks are dragging the economy. China's banks had difficulty lending to private companies in the past, because of challenges related to gathering and processing the necessary information on them. As a response,

Exhibit 5 Financial Depth in Major Market

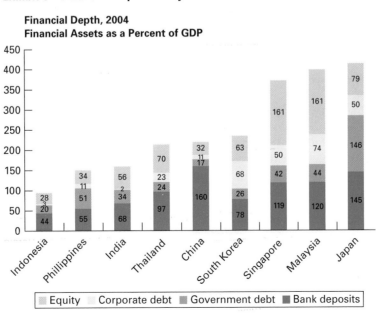

Financial Depth, 2004
Financial Assets as a Percent of GDP

Source: McKinsey.

China launched its first national credit bureau in early 2006. China's banks have been satisfying a social role, but now must allocate capital efficiently in order to generate positive economic return.

Investments in Ping An and BoCOM

With its longstanding presence in China, HSBC was among the most well-positioned financial institutions to take advantage of China's market opening.

Ping An Investments

In October of 2002, HSBC announced that it had taken a 10 percent stake in Ping An Insurance, China's second largest insurer for $600 million. U.S. investment banks Goldman Sachs and Morgan Stanley already had a combined 14 percent stake in Ping An. Chairman Sir John Bond indicated that HSBC was particularly attracted to the long-term prospects in the insurance and asset management sectors.

In May 2005, HSBC indicated it was investing an additional HK$8.1 billion ($1.04 billion) for an additional 9.91 percent stake in Ping An, doubling its holding in the number-two life insurer. HSBC paid HK$13.20 a share for the stakes held by investment banks Goldman Sachs and Morgan Stanley, lifting HSBC's holding to 19.9 percent, the maximum stake allowed by a single foreign investor.

"This is good news for Ping An," said Kenneth Lee, an analyst at Daiwa Institute of Research. "HSBC is buying at a premium and is replacing Goldman Sachs and Morgan Stanley, which are venture capital investors. HSBC is a long-term investor and will help Ping An to develop its insurance platform," he said.

The company's market share of more than 15 percent of the Chinese market puts it behind domestic competitor China Life Insurance Co., which underwrites about half of all Chinese life insurance premiums. In 2005, HSBC Chairman John Bond commented, "We are optimistic about the long-term prospects of the insurance industry in mainland China and believe Ping An is well-positioned to benefit from the sector's development."[39]

In addition to holding a stake in Ping An Insurance, HSBC has applied for its own life insurance license in China. Foreign firms only account for 5 percent of the life insurance market in China, while three domestic firms (China Life Insurance, Ping An Insurance, and China Pacific Insurance) hold 76 percent of the market share. The bank hopes to start operations in 2008, and says it will maintain its relationship with Ping An.[40]

The BoCOM Deal

HSBC invested $1.8 billion for a 19.9 percent stake in BoCOM in June 2004. HSBC's chairman at the time, Sir John Bond, commented on the company's long-term perspective, "[I]t is inevitable that China will become a superpower. And indeed, desirable. And we are positioning our business for the decades ahead accordingly."[41] HSBC wanted a piece of the alluring Chinese market, which Goldman Sachs predicts will overtake the United States as the number-one economy in the world by 2040, and wanted to deepen its international scope in line with the "Managing for Growth" strategy.

Speaking one month after HSBC's big move, then-CEO and future Chairman Stephen Green expounded upon China, "[T]he potential in China's domestic market is the largest in history." China is the "world's manufacturer," and as the population continues to urbanize and industrialize, it increasingly has more disposable income, the workers become greater consumers, and the middle class expands.[42] China has one of the world's highest savings rates, at around 40 percent, and already has around one-third of the $1.2 trillion of central bank foreign exchange reserves sitting in Asia. Further, access to capital is not a problem, as FDI floods the country. The challenge facing China is to recycle and invest its pool of savings efficiently.

HSBC recognized the huge potential in the market for banking services, as well as credit cards. As part of its emerging market strategy, HSBC wanted to feed the demand for credit cards in these markets. Green commented: "[O]ur joint venture with Bank of Communications for credit cards is one which we think has a lot of exciting prospects. Bank of Communications has over 30 million debit cards in issue. Over time, a proportion of those is going to convert to credit cards. And we are issuing co-branded credit cards with the Bank of Communications."[43] HSBC saw an opportunity to shepherd millions of new people into the banking system.

HSBC's Green acquiesced that emerging markets do carry risk. This risk was starkly evident during the HSBC debacle in Argentina during the country's economic crisis. China's epic turnaround could conceivably flop, and heavily invested banks could pay dearly. The banking system in China was and is very fragile. Would China's banks be able to break away from state-directed lending and its lasting effects? The banks further rely on the continued acceleration of the economy, and many rely on volatile real estate loans.[44] HSBC recognized other challenges for China, including the need to strengthen regulations, build social security, stem corruption, and fortify the financial system.[45]

Green contends that "emerging markets growth will continue at quite a rapid clip for the foreseeable future. I think that China will continue on a strong growth path."[46] HSBC, in investing in BoCOM, was wagering beyond continued growth and counting on the financial system finally being fixed. HSBC trusts that the banking cleanup would continue with cleaner, more competent corporate governance, decreased corruption, and more transparent practices.[47]

Margaret Leung, general manager and global co-head commercial banking for the HSBC Group commented,

"[W]e believe we have a unique advantage [in China]. A lot of analysts… have been saying that if any foreign bank is going to succeed in China, that would be HSBC."[48] BoCom's net profit soared from Rmb1.604bn (US$200m) in 2004 to Rmb9.249bn in 2005, and a BoCOM-HSBC credit card has successfully been issued to over 650,000 people.[49] However, with the passing of the WTO deadline, BoCOM now faces greater competition from foreign banks, which are now better able to compete under the new Regulation on Administration of Foreign-Funded Banks (adopted in late 2006). Under these new regulations, foreign banks are allowed to issue local currency loans and are no longer limited in the size and scope of their business.

Recent Developments and Future Competitive Conditions

Current Strategies in China

Foreign banks that operate in China have different strategies. Some of them have purchased smaller stakes of Chinese financial institutions, while some prefer to buy a bigger stake of a small bank. Nevertheless, they all want to be in China. The best strategy, in theory, has turned out to be with a local partner. Bob Edgar, senior managing director at Australia and New Zealand Banking Group Ltd., said that "it would be very difficult to go into a market like that and undertake the cost of establishing a branch network, getting a customer base of hundreds of thousands if not millions of customers. That already exists, so why would we want to set it up again?"[50]

Many foreign banks however experience difficulties when working with a local partner. The credit standards are not as strict as they should be, and there is still high corruption at different levels. In addition, the partners gain influence in the foreign bank. This is the reason why HSBC has decided to invest "outside the Big Four" so it would have bigger control in operations. Peter Wong, executive director of HSBC's Hong Kong and Mainland China operations, has commented: "[T]he state-owned banks would be too big." So only the future will tell what is the best strategy.[51]

Recent Developments

One significant development in the bank sector in China was the IPO of Industrial and Commercial Bank of China IPO. As expected, it was the world's biggest IPO. ICBS raised $19.1 billion, exceeding investors' predictions, valuing the bank at more than $108 billion. The previous IPO record was $18.4 billion and was held by NTT DoCoMo Inc., a Japanese mobile company.[52] The bank has announced that the money will be used to fund its expansion.

The competition in China's banking industry is continuing to grow. Recently, Morgan Stanley announced its expansion into China, given the company's desire to tap into the growing Chinese market and become competitive there. The company chief executive commented, "[T]his platform will allow us to provide a wider array of new product capabilities that are currently offered only by commercial banks with a presence within China."[53]

Another important development was the deal in which a consortium led by Citigroup took control over the Guangdong Development Bank (GDB). The agreement was reached on November 16, 2006, after a year of negotiations. Citigroup and its investors' partners have agreed to pay about $3.1 billon for 85.6 percent of Guangdong Development Bank.[54] The deal is significant since this is the first time that a foreign investor has been able to gain control in a Chinese bank. It is expected that Citigroup alone would purchase only 20 percent of Guangdong Development Bank; however, its partners would split the remaining 65.6 percent. The China Life Insurance Co. and State Grid Corporation each own 20 percent, followed by Citic Trust & Investment Co. with 12.9 percent and Yangpu Puhua Investment and Development Co. with 8 percent. Interestingly, IBM also has a stake at GDB, owning 4.74 percent of Guangdong Development Bank.

Another issue that makes the deal special is the fact that in January 2007, China opened its financial sector to foreign investors, which was one of its last WTO membership commitments. Under the new rules, foreign banks in China finally have the opportunity to offer services in the local currency—yuan—which was previously prohibited.[55] In a statement issued after the deal was announced, William R. Rhodes, the chairman and chief executive of Citibank, said, "The continued emergence of China's economy represents a tremendous opportunity for Citigroup."[56]

Although Citigroup has gained more market opportunities since the deal was approved, analysts say that there are certain risks involved. It is publicly known that the Guangdong Development Bank has been struggling financially, and there is speculation about the amount of bad loans that have not been put on the books. Bad loans have been an issue for the Chinese banks. However, it seems that the experience in banking and asset management that Citigroup possesses, in addition to the IT support offered by IBM, would make this investment beneficial to Guangdong Development Bank and could turn the bank around.[57] In June 2007, the Guangdong Development Bank issued an outline of its five-year plan. The bank aims to reach the average levels of its Chinese bank peers for all major operational indicators in the next two to three years and become a leader among midsized Chinese banks within three to five years.[58]

Other recent developments include the Ping An and China Life Insurance initial public offerings in China. Ping An raised 38.9 billion yuan ($5 billion) with its February 2007 IPO and plans to use those funds to finance operations. In January 2007, its main competitor, China Life Insurance Co., was also listed on the Shanghai Stock Exchange, making an IPO of $3.6 billion.

In July 2006, it was announced that Bank of Communications President Zhang Jianguo had submitted his resignation, and would replace Chang Zhenming as president of the China Construction Bank. It was not clear whether HSBC was consulted in this move.

On September 11, 2006, HSBC opened a new sub-branch in Beijing. With the opening of its fourth branch in Beijing, HSBC became the foreign bank with the most branches in Beijing. Richard Yorke, chief executive officer China at the Hongkong and Shanghai Banking Corporation Limited, commented: "[We] are delighted to be able to further expand our service network in Beijing. It is part of our overall network expansion in China where HSBC has a long-term commitment. Beijing is a key retail market for HSBC in the Mainland and we shall provide diversified products to meet our customers' growing needs for world-class banking services."[59]

Yet another recent development for HSBC was its decision to reduce its exposure to the U.S. subprime lending market in early 2007. HSBC had entered the market when it purchased Household International Inc., a U.S. subprime lender, in 2003. However, since then the subprime lending market has begun to fail as a result of the huge U.S. construction boom and rising interest rates. Delinquencies on subprime mortgages in the United States rose to a four-year high in the fourth quarter of 2006, contributing to a 5.7 percent drop in HSBC's total second-half profits (an 87 percent drop in its North American profits alone).[60] This prompted HSBC's early 2007 announcement that it would stop buying second-charge loans from other lenders. In addition, HSBC has decided to change the management of Household in order to bring the business "under the HSBC model," as Michael Geoghegan, chief executive of the HSBC Group, put it.[61]

In addition to shrinking its U.S. mortage unit, HSBC continues to invest in fast-growing emerging markets, including Asia, Latin America, and the Middle East. Malaysia is one country where HSBC's expansion is quite noticeable. As of March 2007, it operated 40 branches there and was awaiting approval to open eight more. HSBC also has plans to extend its insurance business to other countries.[62]

Future Competitive Conditions

China has the highest foreign direct investment (FDI) in Asia; however, the high growth in FDI is beginning to slow. According to the Ministry of Commerce, for the first eight months of 2006, China drew $37.2 billion in FDI, or 2.1 percent, less than during the same period in 2005. In August 2006, FDI was down 8.5 percent compared to the same month of last year. David Li, an economist from Tsinghua University, argues that "an opposition to FDI is a sign of economic maturity." China's local companies are growing and becoming stronger.[63]

One of the challenges facing foreign firms in China is that foreign mergers and acquisitions are becoming less welcome. The Chinese economy's annual growth is 10 percent, and therefore, the opportunities for local firms are growing. As such, there is a concern with the increasing number of mergers and acquisitions. However, Arthur Kroeber, managing editor of *China Economic Quarterly,* has said that despite this concern, "they are still happy to have you come and build a factory."[64]

HSBC is an institution that actively seeks new opportunities; indeed, HSBC was the first foreign bank to invest in China in 2001. Peter Wong has commented, "[We] are reacting to the evolution of the China market. The government basically opened the door and said, 'Why don't you [foreign banks] start investing and see what happens.' So we invested in the Bank of Shanghai. Then they opened the door in insurance, so we invested in Ping An insurance. Then it was joint-stock banks, and we invested in Bank of Communications."[65] Exhibit 6 summarizes HSBC's strategic stakes in Chinese financial institutions.

Exhibit 6   **HSBC's Stakes in Chinese Financial Institutions**

Date	Target	Amount (millions of US$)	Stake (%)
May 2005	Ping An Insurance Group Co. (second stake)	$1,040	9.9%
August 2004	Bank of Communications	1,750	19.9
December 2003	Industrial Bank Co. Ltd.	205*	16.0
October 2002	Ping An Insurance Group Co. (first stake)	600	10.0
December 2001	Bank of Shanghai	63	8.0

*Investment made by Hang Seng Bank of Hong Kong, which is majority controlled by HSBC.

Source: K. C. Swanson, "Buying into China's Banks," *Corporate Dealmaker,* September–October 2006, p. 18.

HSBC's future development will depend heavily on two things. First, the competition will play a major role in HSBC's strategy. HSBC competitors are aggressively seeking opportunities in China, and HSBC has to constantly work to maintain and expand its market position. Second, HSBC's success will depend on the opportunities that the company sees in the other emerging markets of the world.

Questions for Review

1. How has HSBC adapted its global strategy to operate in China, both before and after China's WTO accession?

2. Discuss HSBC's strategy for entering and operating in other emerging markets. Where has it found success, and where has it faced setbacks? Why?

3. What are the pros and cons of HSBC's "Managing for Growth" strategy?

4. Discuss Stephen Green's leadership style. How does he differ from his predecessor, Sir John Bond? How might Michael Geoghegan lead HSBC going forward?

5. Do you think HSBC should reevaluate its corporate strategy in China, now that the WTO deadline has passed and the new regulations for foreign banks are in place?

Exercise

HSBC is considering asking the government of China (China Banking Regulatory Commission—CBRC) to allow it to increase its state in BoCom above the limit currently in place (25% total foreign ownership; 20% for an individual foreign investor). Break into four groups:

1. HSBC
2. BoCom
3. Citibank
4. CBRC

Groups 1–3 should prepare a 5 minute presentation on whether the government of China should grant the request and, if so, what the ownership limit should be (30%? 50%?) and whether it should be extended to other foreign financial institutions (e.g., Citibank). Then, Group 4 should discuss the question and report its decision.

Source: This case was prepared by Jonathan Doh of Villauora University as the basis for class discussion. Research assistance was provided by Courtney Asher and Elizabeth Stewart. It is not intended to illustrate effective or ineffective managerial capability or administrative responsibility.

In-Depth Integrative Case 2

Chiquita's Global Turnaround

Synopsis

On January 12, 2004, Chiquita named Fernando Aguirre as the company's new president and CEO, replacing Cyrus Freidhem, who had held the position since the company's emergence from bankruptcy in March 2002. In his 23 years with Cincinnati-based Procter & Gamble (P&G), Aguirre served in a variety of positions, including president of P&G Brazil and president of P&G Mexico. In his first remarks to Chiquita employees and investors, Aguirre reiterated the importance of corporate responsibility: "In terms of managing businesses and people, while I am profit-conscious, I make decisions first and foremost based on values and principles. In that respect, I'm proud to be joining a company with Core Values that guide day-to-day operations and one where corporate responsibility is an important part of our company culture."[1]

Over the past several years, social responsibility has become the watchword of this traditional company with midwestern roots but a checkered history. In 2004, Chiquita scarcely resembled the company that once held a reputation as cold, uncaring, and indifferent, frustrated with mediocre returns, a lack of innovation, and a demoralized workforce. Throughout the 20th century, hostile relationships with its labor unions and employees and a reputation for immorality solidified by the actions of its predecessor company, United Fruit, helped to slow Chiquita's growth. In addition, by the late 1990s, consumption of bananas had declined in major markets, and Chiquita's position in Europe had been compromised by the European Union's preferential import relationships with its members' former colonies in the Caribbean, Africa, and the Pacific. These factors helped push Chiquita to seek Chapter 11 bankruptcy protection in November 2001.

Through a serious and dedicated internal analysis, a thorough reevaluation of its core mission and business principles, and a concerted effort to reach out to some of its primary stakeholders—such as employees—who had become disenchanted and alienated, by early 2003, Chiquita had engineered the beginnings of a turnaround. One of the most impressive aspects of this recovery was Chiquita's success in redirecting and redefining its reputation through a more open and transparent approach to its global operations and to the various stakeholder groups with which it interacted. In addition, Chiquita had substantially reformed its labor practices and relations and initiated a set of projects in sustainable development and community action in its various locations around the world.

Both labor unions and nongovernmental organizations (NGOs) lauded these steps.

Yet despite Chiquita's apparent turnaround, lingering problems remained in financial performance, organizational efficiency, and a strategy for the future. How could Chiquita sustain the positive momentum from its turnaround in reputation and employee relations to deliver improved and sustainable business performance in a global industry environment plagued by low margins and intense competition?

Chiquita's Background

Chiquita Brands International Inc. is a multinational producer, distributor, and marketer of bananas and other fresh produce. The company also distributes and markets fresh-cut fruit and other branded, value-added fruit products. Approximately 60 percent of its 2003 revenues of $2.6 billion came from bananas.[2] Since adding new products and acquiring Fresh Express, the U.S. market leader in fresh salads, in 2005, bananas totaled 43 percent of Chiquita's net sales.[3] In 2003, the banana division consisted of 19,000 employees, mainly working on more than 100 banana farms in countries throughout Latin America, including Guatemala, Honduras, Nicaragua, Ecuador, Costa Rica, Panama, and Colombia. Approximately 45 percent of all bananas sold by Chiquita are from Chiquita-owned farms; independent suppliers in Latin America produce the remainder. Chiquita is one of the global market leaders in banana supply and production (see Table 1). Since Chiquita's exports are often a substantial part of the foreign trade of the Latin American countries in which the company operates, relationships with suppliers, workers' unions, and communities are critical elements for success.

Chiquita sources bananas from many developing Latin American countries, countries that historically have struggled with poverty, literacy, access to affordable health care, and limited infrastructure. The image of the banana

Table 1 **Banana World Market Share Leaders, 1999, 2002, and 2005**

	2005	2002	1999
Chiquita	25%	23%	25%
Dole	25	25	25
Del Monte	15	16	15
Fyfess	8	8	8
Noboa	11	11	11

Source: Banana Link.

industry has long been tarnished by its historical support of the failed U.S. invasion of Cuba in 1961, child labor, unsafe working conditions, sexual discrimination, low wages, and accusations of serious brutality against unionizing workers.[4] Chiquita's reputation was damaged by past events, notably those associated with its predecessor company, United Fruit. These included allegations of the company's participation in labor rights suppression in Colombia in the 1920s, the use of company ships in the U.S. government–backed overthrow of the Guatemalan government in 1954, and involvement in a bribery scandal in Honduras in 1975.[5] In the 1980s and 1990s, Chiquita clearly projected a defensive and protective culture, conveying a closed-door impression of its policies and practices.

Because bananas are produced all year long, local communities are closely tied together by the performance of farms. Many employees live in houses owned by the company, most of which are located on the farms themselves. In many areas, Chiquita provides electricity, potable water, medical facilities, and other basic services.[6] However, labor relations remained strained throughout the 1980s and 1990s.

Chiquita's Downward Spiral

Although Chiquita improved its environmental procedures throughout the 1990s, many human rights groups, including Banana Link and US/Labor Education in the Americas, organized an outspoken campaign against all banana companies to improve social conditions on their plantations. One morning in early 1998, executives at Chiquita were devastated to see their company splashed all over the newspapers after an undercover investigation into "dangerous and illegal business practices" throughout Chiquita's Latin American operations. This was a watershed moment for the company.

The *Cincinnati Enquirer,* a paper based in the same town as Chiquita's corporate headquarters, printed an exposé contending that Chiquita was guilty of "labor, human rights, environmental and political violations in Central America."[7] Although the newspaper was later forced to retract the series after it was discovered that a reporter had illegally penetrated Chiquita's voice-mail system, the damage was done. Corporate image was further damaged when the firm emphasized the violation of its privacy instead of addressing the possible validity of the claims made. According to Jeff Zalla, current corporate responsibility officer at Chiquita, the strategy backfired. "It left some people with an unsavory impression of our company," he said.[8]

Damaging media coverage and a renewed desire to evaluate its own ethics performance and gain support for a common set of values and standards for environmental and social performance served as catalysts for the institution of corporate social responsibility policies at Chiquita. After recognizing the need for a complete corporate makeover, Chiquita's then CEO, Steve Warshaw, declared his commitment to leading in the area of corporate responsibility and pledged that the company would do much more than just repair previous damage. Four years later, despite changes in the executive management group, Chiquita's corporate social responsibility programs were a positive example of leading responsibility change in today's multinational business environment.

In January 2001, Chiquita announced that it could no longer pay the interest on its $862 million debt. The fiercely competitive banana industry, downward trends in prices due to excess supply, EU restrictive trade quotas, poor labor-union relations, and the market view of bananas as a low-margin commodity all contributed to Chiquita's bankruptcy filing. Chiquita attributed much of the responsibility to the European Union. In 1993, the EU imposed quotas that gave preferential treatment to banana imports from ACP (Africa, Caribbean, and Pacific) countries that were former European colonies, ostensibly to help these former European colonies boost their international trade and commerce. Before the 1993 act, 70 percent of the bananas sold in Europe came from Latin America, and Chiquita had a 22 percent share of the world's banana market.[9] After the quotas were imposed, Chiquita claimed that its European market share was cut in half, costing $200 million a year in lost earnings.

Although many of its difficulties were intensified by the EU policy, Chiquita's problems had begun to develop before the 1993 decision. Most important, miscalculations of increases in European demand in the 1990s resulted in an oversupply, leading to depressed banana prices worldwide. Although prices recovered somewhat (see Table 2), CEO Keith Linder blamed $284 million in losses in 2001

Table 2 **Banana Prices: Regional Year-over-Year Percentage Change, 2003 vs. 2002**

Region	Q1, 03	Q2, 03	Q3, 03	Q4, 03	Year
North America	3%	−4%	1%	−2%	−1%
European core markets—US$	11	12	5	18	12
European core markets—local currency	−9	−10	−9	0	−7
Central & E. Europe/Mediterranean—US$	4	−3	4	2	−2
Central & E. Europe/Mediterranean—local currency	−15	−22	−10	−14	−19
Asia—US$	−7	0	3	12	0
Asia—local currency	−18	−7	3	6	−5

Source: Company reports.

Table 3   Key Developments in Chiquita's History

1899:	United Fruit Company is created through a merger of fruit companies.
1903:	The company is listed on the New York Stock Exchange; it builds refrigerated ships.
1918:	Thirteen banana ships are lost after being commissioned by Allied forces in World War I.
1941:	Allied forces in World War II commission company ships, and the banana industry nearly shuts down.
1945:	Twenty-seven ships and 275 men on company ships are lost serving Allied forces.
1950:	The company starts massive postwar banana-planting projects.
1961:	Company ships provide support for failed U.S. invasion of Cuba.
1964:	The company begins a large-scale branding program for produce and starts using banana stickers bearing the Chiquita name.
1970:	United Fruit merges with AMK Corp. and becomes United Brands Company.
1975:	United Brands is involved in Honduran bribery scandal, which leads to enactment of U.S. Foreign Corrupt Practices Act. Company stocks plunge, and CEO Eli Black commits suicide.
1990:	United Brands changes name to Chiquita Brands International.
1993:	EU banana regulations cut Chiquita's market share by more than 50 percent. Chiquita begins working with Rainforest Alliance and Better Banana Project.
1994:	Start of the "banana wars" between the EU and WTO. Follows complaints by Chiquita that EU favors Caribbean banana suppliers over Latin American importers.
1998:	Chiquita becomes largest U.S. private-label fruit canner. Becomes first large company to meet with COLSIBA, an affiliation of Latin American banana unions.
1999:	Faces possible auction proposed by large shareholder American Financial Group.
2000:	Adopts expanded code of conduct. All 115 Chiquita-owned farms achieve Better Banana certification.
2001:	Restructures debt after stopping payments on $862 million loan, cites prejudiced trade pacts by EU.
2001:	Files for Chapter 11 bankruptcy protection.
2001:	Issues first (2000) corporate responsibility report.
2002:	Chiquita shareholders and bondholders support reorganization plan.
2002:	Issues 2001 corporate responsibility report.
2003:	Chiquita reports positive net income under reorganized company.
2003:	SustainableBusiness.com names Chiquita one of the top 20 sustainable stock picks for the second year in a row.
2004:	Maintained market leadership in the growing EU.
2005:	Chiquita acquires Fresh Express, U.S. market leader in fresh salads.
2006:	Awarded the Contribution to the Community Award by the American–Costa Rican Chamber of Commerce for its Nature & Community Project in Costa Rica.
2007:	Chiquita faces a $25 million fine from the U.S. Department of Justice for payments made to Colombian paramilitary groups for the protection of its employees.

on a "decline in product quality resulting from an extraordinary outbreak of disease and unusual weather patterns."[10] At the end of 2006, Chiquita still faced financial difficulties as a result of a "perfect storm" of higher tariffs, increased competition in the EU banana market, U.S. consumer concerns about the safety of fresh spinach (another Chiquita product), and higher industry costs overall. While the company expressed dissatisfaction with 2006 results, it also stated that "we firmly believe our 2006 results are not indicative of the underlying strengths of Chiquita's business or our long-term potential."[11] Table 3 provides a comprehensive summary of key developments in Chiquita's history.

Dispute over Access to European Banana Markets

Chiquita has long claimed that its recent struggles are a direct result of the 1993 EU decision to put restrictive quotas on imports from Latin American suppliers. Immediately after the decision by the EU in 1993 to extend preferential quotas to its former Caribbean and African colonies, Chiquita took the issue to the U.S. trade representative, suggesting violations of free trade. In 1994, a

General Agreement on Tariffs and Trade (GATT) panel ruled that the new regime violates GATT obligations, but the EU blocked adoption of the ruling by the full GATT. In 1996, the United States, along with Ecuador, Guatemala, Honduras, and Mexico, challenged the new regime under the new World Trade Organization (WTO) dispute-settlement mechanism, which came into force after the Uruguay Round of GATT negotiations.

In May 1997, a WTO panel ruled that the EU's banana import regime violated WTO obligations under the General Agreement on Trade in Services and the Agreement on Import Licensing Procedures. In September 1997, the WTO Appellate Body upheld the panel ruling, granting the EU 15 months, until January 1, 1999, to comply with the ruling. In January 1999, the deadline for EU compliance expired, and the United States sought WTO authorization to impose retaliatory tariffs. In April 1999, the WTO Dispute Settlement Body authorized U.S. retaliatory tariffs amounting to $191.4 million a year—the level of damage to U.S. companies calculated by arbitrators—and the United States immediately began steps to withhold liquidation of European imports, the first step in the imposition of the tariffs.[12]

In April 2001, the United States and the European Commission announced that they had reached agreement resolving their dispute. The agreement took effect on July 1, 2001, at which time the United States suspended the retaliatory sanctions imposed on EU imports in 1999. Import volumes of bananas were returned to levels comparable to those prior to 1993, and the EU committed to moving to a tariff-only system in 2006 as part of its overall WTO obligations.

The dispute has taken its toll on the banana trade by creating uncertainty for smaller producers reliant on EU markets under the quota system and for large producers such as Chiquita that were forced to expend considerable financial and other resources in the course of the dispute. High tariffs in the EU continue to be a financial burden for Chiquita.

Corporate Responsibility

Chiquita had begun to initiate corporate responsibility projects in 1992 when it adopted Better Banana Project standards designed to improve environmental and worker conditions on its farms. Then after the 1998 exposé in the *Cincinnati Enquirer,* Chiquita management began to conduct a series of broader companywide reviews of its conduct, policies, and internal and external operations and relationships, all designed to integrate corporate responsibility throughout the company's operations.

In 1998, Chiquita initiated several projects aimed at implementing its corporate responsibility efforts worldwide. Two internal groups were formed: the Senior Management Group and the Corporate Responsibility Steering Committee. The former consists of eight top managers of Chiquita's global businesses, including the president/CEO and COO of banana operations. The Senior Management Group is ultimately responsible for providing strategic vision and leadership for corporate responsibility. The Steering Committee, also consisting of eight members, was constructed to help streamline corporate social responsibility policies throughout each operational area of the firm.

In August 1999, Chiquita adopted the four key values that now guide all strategic business decision making worldwide. After a year of discussions, interviews, and debates on the merits of an internal corporate social responsibility policy, Chiquita defined the following four core values:

> *Integrity:* We live by our Core Values. We communicate in an open, honest and straightforward manner. We conduct our business ethically and lawfully.
> *Respect:* We treat people fairly and respectfully. We recognize the importance of family in the lives of our employees. We value and benefit from individual and cultural differences. We foster individual expression, open dialogue and a sense of belonging.
> *Opportunity:* We believe the continuous growth and development of our employees is key to our success. We

> encourage teamwork. We recognize employees for their contributions to the company's success.
> *Responsibility:* We take pride in our work, in our products and in satisfying our customers. We act responsibly in the communities and environments in which we live and work. We are accountable for the careful use of all resources entrusted to us and for providing appropriate returns to our shareholders.[13]

In support of the four core values, Chiquita undertook reforms to link its corporate governance and corporate responsibility policies. These reforms included expanding the role of the board's Audit Committee to oversee the firm's corporate responsibility (CR) mission and to evaluate whether the firm had the right people, policies, and programs in place to properly advance the CR agenda.[14] In addition, in May 2000, Chiquita appointed a full-time vice president and CR officer responsible for all aspects of corporate social responsibility. According to Chiquita, the four core values, supported by the senior management group and CR committee, have helped drive responsibility change throughout the entire organization. Each business decision must be evaluated through the lens of CR policies.

Chiquita also began to realize that a corporate social responsibility platform could mean a competitive advantage in the banana market. Dennis Christou, vice president of marketing–Europe, explained: "Bananas are, by definition, a commodity and U.K. consumers do not generally see fruit as branded. Chiquita is trying to change this. We have a brand because we own certain values and a relationship with consumers. And we communicate with them. They have expectations about Chiquita."[15] In particular, environmental and social performance is of keen interest to some leading European customers. In 2002, 56 percent of Chiquita's sales in northern European markets were to customers who had either inspected farms or formally asked questions about environmental and social performance. This was a 5 percent increase—about 13,000 forty-pound boxes per week—over the prior year.

Chiquita also strengthened its commitment to the Better Bananas Project. Under this program, external auditors audit all Chiquita farms annually. Chiquita has made an important partnership with Rainforest Alliance, which has been integral in assessing Chiquita's environmental practices, especially related to deforestation. The Rainforest Alliance, which claims that the world's rainforests are being deforested at a rate of 1 percent per year (or 2 U.S. football fields every second),[16] has annually accredited every Chiquita farm since 2000. Chiquita also encourages its independent producers, which supply Chiquita with about 50 percent of its bananas, to achieve Rainforest Alliance certification. In 2002, the volume of bananas purchased from certified farms rose from 33 to 46 percent, and farms certified through June 2003 brought the total to 65 percent. In 2006, the percent of Chiquita's independent producers that were Rainforest Alliance–certified

Table 4 **Better Banana Project Principles**

1. **Ecosystem Conservation.** Protect existing ecosystems; recovery of damaged ecosystems in plantation area.

2. **Wildlife Conservation.** Protect biodiversity, especially endangered species.

3. **Fair Treatment and Good Conditions for Workers.** Comply with local and international labor-laws/norms; maintain policy of nondiscrimination; support freedom of association.

4. **Community Relations.** Be a "good neighbor," contributing to the social and economic development of local communities.

5. **Integrated Pest Management.** Reduction in use of pesticides; training for workers in pesticide use/management/risks.

6. **Integrated Waste Management.** Reduction of the production of wastes that contaminate the environment and harm human health; institute recycling.

7. **Conservation of Water Resources.** Reduce and reuse the water used in production; establish buffer zones of vegetation around waterways; protect water from contamination.

8. **Soil Conservation.** Control erosion; promote soil conservation and replenishment.

9. **Planning and Monitoring.** Plan and monitor banana cultivation activities according to environmental, social, and economic measures.

Source: Adapted from Rainforest Alliance, *Normas Generales Para la Certificación del Cultivo de Banano,* May 2002, www.rainforest-alliance.org/programs/cap/socios/banana-s.pdf.

reached 84 percent.[17] Table 4 presents the nine principles of the Better Banana Project. According to insiders, the adoption of third-party standards has helped Chiquita drive a stronger internal commitment to achieving excellence[18]—and to cut costs. In 2003, the Rainforest Alliance estimated that Chiquita reduced production spending by $100 million as a result of a $20 million investment to reduce agrochemical use.[19]

And Chiquita is receiving increasing recognition for its efforts. In 2005, SustainableBusiness.com, publisher of *The Progressive Investor* newsletter, named Chiquita to its list of the world's top 20 sustainable stock picks, known as the SB20, for the fourth year in a row. SustainableBusiness.com identifies its picks by asking leading investment advisers to recommend companies that stand out as world leaders in both sustainability and financial strength. In April 2004, the Trust for the Americas, a division of the Organization of Americas, selected Chiquita Brands as the winner of the 2004 Corporate Citizen of the Americas Award for Chiquita's Nuevo San Juan Home-Ownership Project in Honduras.[20] Also in 2004, Chiquita earned the Ethic Award from the AGEPE Editorial Group and KPMG in Italy for its initiatives in the field of ethics, environmental protection, and workplace improvements.[21]

One recent setback for Chiquita's corporate responsibility profile involved its banana-producing subsidiary in Colombia. After a 2003 probe into the company's finances, Chiquita self-reported to the U.S. Department of Justice (DOJ) that it had made payments to left- and right-wing paramilitary groups in Colombia such as the AUC, ELN, and FARC. These payments, beginning in 1997, were made in order to protect the lives of its employees. Colombia has one of the highest kidnapping rates in the world and a murder rate 11 times that of the United States.[22] "It's certainly a common understanding that in order to do

business in Colombia, payments have to be made for at best security, or at worst extortion," explained Ron Oswald, general secretary of the International Union of Foodworkers, which represents Chiquita workers in Latin America (including many in Colombia).[23]

The U.S. 1996 Anti-Terrorism Act makes it illegal to support any organizations identified as a terrorist threat. As of September 2001, the list of terrorist threats included the Colombian paramilitary groups. In a company press release, Chiquita chairman and CEO, Fernando Aguirre, explained, "The payments . . . were always motivated by our good faith concern for the safety of our employees. Nevertheless, we recognized—and acted upon—our legal obligation to inform the DOJ of this admittedly difficult situation."[24] Officially announced in 2007, Chiquita faced a $25 million fine for the payments it made in Colombia. In anticipation of the decision, the company set aside funds in 2006 to pay the fine. Chiquita does not believe the fines will hurt its operations.[25] Perhaps as a result of the pending DOJ investigation and decision, Chiquita sold its Colombian subsidiary in 2004.

Global Codes of Conduct, Standards, and Labor Practices

In late 2001, Ron Oswald, general secretary of the International Union of Food Workers, was asked if he had seen improvements in Chiquita's internal and external corporate policies. He responded, "Yes. It is a company that is totally unrecognizable from five years ago."[26] Clearly Chiquita had come a long way.

Traditionally, relations between Chiquita and labor unions in Latin America were mired in conflict and mistrust. In 1998, after recognizing the need for change in the way it deals with its line, Chiquita began striving to adhere to SA8000, the widely accepted international labor rights standard. Management struggled with the decision of whether to adopt an outside standard or to develop an internal measurement gauge for corporate responsibility. After much deliberation, management concluded that adopting the SA8000 standard would yield the most credibility with external stakeholders, because SA8000 gives detailed requirements for adequacy of management systems for implementation. Having an external standard forces Chiquita to push CR change down through each organizational level so that the firm is able to meet third-party requirements.

In May 2000 Chiquita expanded its code of conduct to include SA8000. Standards now included areas such as food safety, labor standards, employee health and safety, environmental protection, and legal compliance.[27] Recognizing the importance of labor support and its resounding effect on corporate image, Chiquita began an open dialogue with the International Union of Food Workers and the Coalition of Latin American Banana Workers' Unions (COLSIBA). By June 2001, the firm had reached an agreement with both organizations, pledging to respect worker rights as elaborated in ILO conventions, address longstanding health and safety concerns for workers, and ensure that its independent suppliers do likewise. This made Chiquita the first multinational corporation in the agricultural sector to sign a worker rights agreement.[28] Management credits this agreement as helping to build a positive image, improving relations with both internal and external stakeholders. In mid-2001, Chiquita published its first corporate responsibility report detailing the firm's future CR strategies and goals. Both stakeholders and media outlets have been impressed with the complete turnaround in the transparency of Chiquita's corporate agenda, which has led to a much more favorable impression of the company.

In order to adhere to the organization's own core values and to the SA8000 labor standard, Chiquita routinely performs internal audits in all of its Latin American operations. NGOs also conduct external audits. After the audits are completed, each local management team plans corrective actions using the firm's code of conduct and core values as decision-making guides. At year-end 2003, independent auditors certified Chiquita's operations in Costa Rica, Colombia, and Panama to the SA8000 standard. Chiquita's operations were the first ever to earn SA8000 certification in each of these countries. In its 2006 corporate responsibility report, Chiquita announced that it has maintained 100 percent certification of its banana farms in Latin America in accordance with the Rainforest Alliance, Social Accountability 8000, and EurepGAP standards (environmental, labor, and human rights and food safety standards, respectively).

Marketing the Message

Although it would seem advantageous for Chiquita to communicate and leverage the great strides it has made through its corporate responsibility effort, management seems reluctant to promote its achievements through the typical mass communication vehicles. Indeed, when Chiquita attempted to advertise its certification process with commercials in Denmark that equated its Central American banana farms with a "glorious rainforest," the ads were met with skepticism and thought to be unrealistic.[29]

Instead of mass advertising, the firm has opted for a longer-term marketing strategy based on educating leading opinion makers and critics alike. According to Dennis Christou, vice president of marketing–Europe, there is a natural suspicion among consumers about commercially driven messages. He believes that customers feel more trust in the message if it's delivered by an external body rather than by the company or by a paid advocate of the business.[30] That is a main reason why the firm is relying on viral marketing tactics and third-party testimonials as the means of spreading its message. Retailers are treated differently: They must be exposed to improvements at Chiquita because they determine which exclusive brand to carry on an annual basis. However, Christou believes that creating brand recognition with consumers is possible through nonobtrusive, reputable means.

Defining and conveying a brand's differences in a commodities marketplace is difficult. Nevertheless, Chiquita believes it can carve out its own niche by distinguishing itself as a leader in corporate responsibility. Instead of positioning itself solely on the basis of price, Chiquita is hoping that its distinctive competency in CR will help it stand out from the pack. The company got a boost in this regard in April 2003, when Chiquita, along with Ben and Jerry's, received the first Award for Outstanding Sustainability Reporting presented by the Coalition for Environmentally Responsible Economies (CERES) and the Association of Chartered Certified Accountants.[31] In 2006, Chiquita won Costa Rica's Contribution to the Community Award for its Nature and Community Project, which preserves biodiversity and promotes nature conservation awareness.[32]

Recent Performance and Future Path

Chiquita has drastically shifted its strategic decision-making models and broader corporate operating principles. During its reorganization, debt repayments and other reorganization costs resulted in significant losses. Chiquita made great strides in improving its financial performance by cutting costs and streamlining its local and global operations. In 2003, the year after it filed for bankruptcy, Chiquita's net sales were $2.6 billion, up from $1.6 billion the year before. In 2006, net sales reached a record $4.5 billion (due in part to the acquisition of Fresh Express). Since its emergence from bankruptcy in early 2002, Chiquita has been profitable (see Tables 5 and 6).

Table 5 **Chiquita Brands Balance Sheet as of December 31, 2005, December 31, 2003, December 31, 2002, December 31, 2001, December 31, 2000**

Chiquita Brands International Inc. Balance Sheet as of 12/31/2005 (in thousands)

	2005	2003	2002	2001	2000
Assets					
Cash and equivalents	89,020	—	—	—	26,715
Other current assets	31,388	951	810	732	42,375
Total current assets	900,075	951	810	732	69,090
Investments in and accounts with subsidiaries	—	1,035,915	908,404	1,424,961	1,399,708
Other assets	165,558	5,607	5,429	15,328	29,872
Total assets	2,833,099	1,042,473	914,643	1,441,021	1,498,625
Liabilities and Shareholders' Equity					
Accounts payable and accrued liabilities	569,648	17,182	16,541	10,735	86,930
Total current liabilities	600,857	17,182	16,451	10,735	125,833
Long-term debt	475,000	250,000	250,000	—	772,380
Total liabilities	1,839,598	285,127	285,354	992,427	916,082
Shareholders' equity	993,501	757,346	629,289	448,594	582,543
Total liabilities and shareholders' equity	2,833,099	1,042,473	914,643	1,441,021	1,498,625

Source: Company reports.

Table 6 **Chiquita Income Statement, 2001–2005**

Chiquita Brands International Inc. Income Statement (in thousands)

	Predecessor Company			Reorganized Company	
	Year Ended 12/31/2005	Year Ended 12/31/2003	9 Months Ended 12/31/2002	Three Months Ended 3/31/2002	Year Ended 12/31/2001
Net sales	3,904,361	—	—	—	—
Cost of sales	3,268,128	—	—	—	—
SG&A	(384,184)	(38,500)	(30,443)	(6,545)	(31,188)
Equity in earnings of subsidiaries (loss)		170,398	68,822	(368,899)	32,674
Operating income (loss)	187,633	131,898	38,379	(375,444)	1,486
Interest income	10,255	—	—	—	783
Interest expense	(60,294)	(27,392)	(20,384)	(1,250)	(81,633)
Financial restructuring items	—	—	—	124,394	(33,604)
Income before income taxes and accounting change	134,540	104,506	17,995	(252,300)	(112,968)
Income taxes	(3,100)	(5,300)	(4,800)	(1,000)	(5,800)
Income (loss) before accounting change		99,206	13,195	(253,300)	(118,768)
Cumulative effect of accounting change		—	—	(144,523)	—
Net income (loss)	134,440	99,206	13,195	(397,823)	(118,768)

Source: Company reports.

Chiquita's future financial stability depends, in part, on external market factors such as steady or rising international banana prices and consumer demand. Internally, the company's performance will result from the effectiveness of financial controls on the cost side, and successful marketing, emphasizing differentiation and value-added production, on the revenue side. Although Chiquita has gone to impressive lengths to turn around its reputation and performance, it continues to face a challenging and competitive international business environment and must make continuous progress in its management and operations in order to achieve a healthy and sustainable financial future.

Questions for Review

1. How would you characterize Chiquita's historic approach to global management?

2. Describe Chiquita's approach to human resource management in its global supply chain. What particular human resource challenges does Chiquita face as the purchaser, producer, and supplier of a commodity?

3. Does Chiquita's global corporate responsibility (CR) program create a conflict between shareholders and other stakeholders? Who are Chiquita's main stakeholders in the United States and around the world, and how are they affected by Chiquita's CR program?

4. How would you characterize Chiquita's past and present leadership? How does leadership affect a company's overall reputation?

5. Do you believe Chiquita would have changed its policies without the presence of damaging stories in the media? If not, what does this say about Chiquita's old management style?

6. What challenges does Chiquita's new CEO face in continuing to turn the company around and balance the interests of competing stakeholders?

Exercise

At its annual stakeholder/shareholder meeting, management, represented by Chiquita's CEO, is considering input from various groups about its strategic direction and continued reorganization. Your group represents one of the following interests:

1. Shareholders of the previous company who lost most of the value of the shares after the company declared bankruptcy.

2. Shareholders in the newly reorganized company.

3. Employees and union representatives of North American operations.

4. Employees and union representatives of South American operations.

5. Representatives of the nongovernmental organization Rainforest Action Network.

Spend five minutes preparing two or three requests to the management team about your group's interests and priorities for the company. Then conduct an open forum in which you discuss these requests among the different groups.

Source: © McGraw-Hill Irwin. This case was prepared by Professor Jonathan Doh and Research Associate Erik Holt of Villanova University as the basis for class discussion. Research assistance was provided by Courtney Asher. It is not intended to illustrate either effective or ineffective managerial capability or administrative responsibility. We appreciate assistance from Sherrie Terry and Michael Mitchell of Chiquita International. Any errors remain those of the authors.

SKILL-BUILDING AND EXPERIENTIAL EXERCISES

- Personal Skill-Building Exercises
- In-Class Simulations

1. The Culture Quiz

Objectives

- To stimulate awareness of cultural differences
- To promote consideration of the impact of cultural differences in a global economy
- To stimulate dialogue between domestic and international students
- To explore issues raised by culturally diverse workforces

Background

Few, if any, traditions and values are universally held. Many business dealings have succeeded or failed because of a manager's awareness or lack of understanding of the traditions and values of his/her foreign counterparts. With the world business community so closely intertwined and interdependent, it is critical that managers today become increasingly aware of the differences that exist.

How culturally aware are you? Try the questions below.

Instructions

Working alone or with a small group, answer the questions (without peeking at the answers). When you do look at the answers, be sure to read the explanations. If you are taking the quiz with students from other countries than your own, explore what the answer might be in your country and theirs.

1. In Japan, loudly slurping your soup is considered to be
    - a. rude and obnoxious.
    - b. a sign that you like the soup.
    - c. okay at home but not in public.
    - d. something only foreigners do.

2. In Korea, business leaders tend to
    - a. encourage strong commitment to teamwork and cooperation.
    - b. encourage competition among subordinates.
    - c. discourage subordinates from reporting directly, preferring information to come through well-defined channels.
    - d. encourage close relationships with their subordinates.

3. In Japan, virtually every kind of drink is sold in public vending machines except for
    - a. beer.
    - b. diet drinks with saccharine.
    - c. already sweetened coffee.
    - d. soft drinks from U.S. companies.

4. In Latin America, managers
    - a. are most likely to hire members of their own families.
    - b. consider hiring members of their own families to be inappropriate.
    - c. stress the importance of hiring members of minority groups.
    - d. usually hire more people than are actually needed to do a job.

5. In Ethiopia, when a woman opens the front door of her home, it means
    - a. she is ready to receive guests for a meal.
    - b. only family members may enter.
    - c. religious spirits may move freely in and out of the home.
    - d. she has agreed to have sex with any man who enters.

6. In Latin America, businesspeople
    - a. consider it impolite to make eye contact while talking to one another.
    - b. always wait until the other person is finished speaking before starting to speak.
    - c. touch each other more than North Americans do under similar circumstances.
    - d. avoid touching one another as it is considered an invasion of privacy.

7. The principal religion in Malaysia is
    - a. Buddhism.
    - b. Judaism.
    - c. Christianity.
    - d. Islam.

8. In Thailand
    - a. it is common to see men walking along holding hands.
    - b. it is common to see a man and a woman holding hands in public.
    - c. it is rude for men and women to walk together.
    - d. men and women traditionally kiss each other on meeting in the street.

9. When eating in India, it is appropriate to
    - a. take food with your right hand and eat with your left.
    - b. take food with your left hand and eat with your right.
    - c. take food and eat it with your left hand.
    - d. take food and eat it with your right hand.

10. Pointing your toes at someone in Thailand is
    a. a symbol of respect, much like the Japanese bow.
    b. considered rude even if it is done by accident.
    c. an invitation to dance.
    d. the standard public greeting.

11. American managers tend to base the performance appraisals of their subordinates on performance, while in Iran, managers are more likely to base their performance appraisals on
    a. religion.
    b. seniority.
    c. friendship.
    d. ability.

12. In China, the status of every business negotiation is
    a. reported daily in the press.
    b. private, and details are not discussed publicly.
    c. subjected to scrutiny by a public tribunal on a regular basis.
    d. directed by the elders of every commune.

13. When rewarding a Hispanic worker for a job well done, it is best not to
    a. praise him or her publicly.
    b. say "thank you."
    c. offer a raise.
    d. offer a promotion.

14. In some South American countries, it is considered normal and acceptable to show up for a social appointment
    a. ten to fifteen minutes early.
    b. ten to fifteen minutes late.
    c. fifteen minutes to an hour late.
    d. one to two hours late.

15. In France, when friends talk to one another
    a. they generally stand about three feet apart.
    b. it is typical to shout.
    c. they stand closer to one another than Americans do.
    d. it is always with a third party present.

16. When giving flowers as gifts in Western Europe, be careful not to give
    a. tulips and jonquils.
    b. daisies and lilacs.
    c. chrysanthemums and calla lilies.
    d. lilacs and apple blossoms.

17. The appropriate gift-giving protocol for a male executive doing business in Saudi Arabia is to
    a. give a man a gift from you to his wife.
    b. present gifts to the wife or wives in person.

    c. give gifts only to the eldest wife.
    d. not give a gift to the wife at all.

18. If you want to give a necktie or a scarf to a Latin American, it is best to avoid the color
    a. red.
    b. purple.
    c. green.
    d. black.

19. The doors in German offices and homes are generally kept
    a. wide open to symbolize an acceptance and welcome of friends and strangers.
    b. slightly ajar to suggest that people should knock before entering.
    c. half-opened, suggesting that some people are welcome and others are not.
    d. tightly shut to preserve privacy and personal space.

20. In the area that was formerly West Germany, leaders who display charisma are
    a. not among the most desired.
    b. the ones most respected and sought after.
    c. invited frequently to serve on boards of cultural organizations.
    d. pushed to get involved in political activities.

21. American managers running businesses in Mexico have found that by increasing the salaries of Mexican workers, they
    a. increased the number of hours the workers were willing to work.
    b. enticed more workers to work night shifts.
    c. decreased the number of hours workers would agree to work.
    d. decreased production rates.

22. Chinese culture teaches people
    a. to seek psychiatric help for personal problems.
    b. to avoid conflict and internalize personal problems.
    c. to deal with conflict with immediate confrontation.
    d. to seek help from authorities whenever conflict arises.

23. One wedding gift that should not be given to a Chinese couple would be
    a. a jade bowl.
    b. a clock.
    c. a basket of oranges.
    d. shifts embroidered with dragon patterns.

24. In Venezuela, New Year's Eve is generally spent
    a. in quiet family gatherings.
    b. at wild neighborhood street parties.

c. in restaurants with horns, hats, and live music and dancing.

d. at pig roasts on the beach.

25. If you order "bubble and squeak" in a London pub, you will get

    a. two goldfish fried in olive oil.

    b. a very cold beer in a chilled glass, rather than the usual warm beer.

    c. Alka Seltzer and a glass of water.

    d. chopped cabbage and mashed potatoes fried together.

26. When a stranger in India wants to know what you do for a living and how much you earn, he will

    a. ask your guide.

    b. invite you to his home and, after getting to know you, will ask.

    c. come over and ask you directly, without introduction.

    d. respect your privacy above all.

27. When you feel you are being taken advantage of in a business exchange in Vietnam, it is important to

    a. let the anger show in your face but not in your words.

    b. say that you are angry, but keep your facial expression neutral.

    c. not show any anger in any way.

    d. end the business dealings immediately, and walk away.

28. When a taxi driver in India shakes his head from side to side, it probably means

    a. he thinks your price is too high.

    b. he isn't going in your direction.

    c. he will take you where you want to go.

    d. he doesn't understand what you're asking.

29. In England, holding your index and middle fingers up in a vee with the back of your hand facing another person is seen as

    a. a gesture of peace.

    b. a gesture of victory.

    c. a signal that you want two of something.

    d. a vulgar gesture.

Answers to the Culture Quiz

1. *b.* Slurping your soup or noodles in Japan is good manners in both public and private. It indicates enjoyment and appreciation of the quality. (Source: Eiji Kanno and Constance O'Keefe, *New Japan Solo.* Japan National Tourist Organization: Tokyo, 1990, p. 20.)

2. *b.* Korean managers use a "divide-and-rule" method of leadership that encourages competition among subordinates. They do this to ensure that they can exercise maximum control. In addition, they stay informed by having individuals report directly to them. This way, they can know more than anyone else. (Source: Richard M. Castaldi and Tjipyanto Soerjanto, "Contrasts in East Asian Management Practices." *The Journal of Management in Practice,* 2:1, 1990, pp. 25–27.)

3. *b.* Saccharine-sweetened drinks may not be sold in Japan by law. On the other hand, beer, a wide variety of Japanese and international soft drinks, and so forth, are widely available from vending machines along the streets and in buildings. You're supposed to be at least 18 to buy the alcoholic ones, however. (Source: Eiji Kanno and Constance O'Keefe, *New Japan Solo.* Japan National Tourist Organization: Tokyo, 1990, p. 20.)

4. *a.* Family is considered to be very important in Latin America, so managers are likely to hire their relatives more quickly than hiring strangers. (Source: Nancy J. Adler, *International Dimensions of Organizational Behavior,* 2nd ed., PWS-Kent: Boston, 1991.)

5. *d.* The act, by a woman, of opening the front door, signifies that she has agreed to have sex with any man who enters. (Source: Adam Pertman, "Wandering No More," *Boston Globe Magazine,* June 30, 1991, pp. 10 ff.)

6. *c.* Touching one another during business negotiations is common practice. (Source: Nancy J. Adler, *International Dimensions of Organizational Behavior,* 2nd ed., PWS-Kent: Boston, 1991.)

7. *d.* Approximately 45 percent of the people in Malaysia follow Islam, the country's "official" religion. (Source: Hans Johannes Hoefer, ed., *Malaysia.* Prentice Hall: Englewood Cliffs, NJ, 1984.)

8. *a.* Men holding hands is considered a sign of friendship. Public displays of affection between men and women, however, are unacceptable. (Source: William Warren, Star Black, and M. R. Priya Rangsit, eds., *Thailand.* Prentice Hall: Englewood Cliffs, NJ, 1985.)

9. *d.* In India, as in many Asian countries, toilet paper is not used. Instead, water and the left hand are used, after which the left hand is thoroughly cleaned. Still, the left hand is considered to be polluted and therefore inappropriate for use during eating or touching another person. (Source: Gitanjali Kolanad, *Culture Shock! India.* Graphic Arts Center Publishing Company: Portland, OR, 1996, p. 117.)

10. *b.* This is especially an insult if it is done deliberately, since the feet are the lowest part of the

body. (Source: William Warren, Star Black, and M. R. Priya Rangsit, eds., *Thailand.* Prentice Hall: Englewood Cliffs, NJ, 1985.)

11. *c.* Adler suggests that friendship is valued over task competence in Iran. (Source: Nancy J. Adler, *International Dimensions of Organizational Behavior.* 2nd ed., PWS-Kent: Boston, 1991.)

12. *b.* Public discussion of business dealings is considered inappropriate. Kaplan et al. report that "the Chinese may even have used a premature announcement to extract better terms from executives" who were too embarrassed to admit that there was never really a contract. (Source: Frederic Kaplan, Julian Sobin, Arne de Keijzer, *The China Guidebook.* Houghton Mifflin: Boston, 1987.)

13. *a.* Public praise for Hispanics and Asians is generally embarrassing because modesty is an important cultural value. (Source: Jim Braham, "No, You Don't Manage Everyone the Same," *Industry Week,* February 6, 1989.) In Japan, being singled out for praise is also an embarrassment. A common saying in that country is, "The nail that sticks up gets hammered down."

14. *d.* Though being late is frowned upon in the United States, being late is not only accepted but expected in some South American countries. (Source: Lloyd S. Baird, James E. Post, and John F. Mahon, *Management: Functions and Responsibilities.* Harper & Row: New York, 1990.)

15. *c.* Personal space in most European countries is much smaller than in the United States. Americans generally like at least two feet of space around themselves, while it is not unusual for Europeans to be virtually touching. (Source: Lloyd S. Baird, James E. Post, and John F. Mahon, *Management: Functions and Responsibilities.* Harper & Row: New York, 1990.)

16. *c.* Chrysanthemums and calla lilies are both associated with funerals. (Source: Theodore Fischer, *Pinnacle: International Issue,* March–April 1991, p. 4.)

17. *d.* In Arab cultures, it is considered inappropriate for wives to accept gifts or even attention from other men. (Source: Theodore Fischer, *Pinnacle: International Issue,* March–April 1991, p. 4.)

18. *b.* In Argentina and other Latin American countries, purple is associated with the serious fasting period of Lent. (Source: Theodore Fischer, *Pinnacle: International Issue,* March–April 1991, p. 4.)

19. *d.* Private space is considered so important in Germany that partitions are erected to separate people from one another. Privacy screens and walled gardens are the norm. (Source: Julius Fast, *Subtext: Making Body Language Work.* Viking Penguin Books: New York, 1991, p. 207.)

20. *a.* Though political leaders in the United States are increasingly selected on their ability to inspire, charisma is a suspect trait in what was West Germany, where Hitler's charisma is still associated with evil intent and harmful outcomes. (Source: Nancy J. Adler, *International Dimensions of Organizational Behavior.* 2nd ed., PWS-Kent: Boston, 1991, p. 149.)

21. *c.* Paying Mexican workers more means, in the eyes of the workers, that they can make the same amount of money in fewer hours and thus have more time for enjoying life. (Source: Nancy J. Adler, *International Dimensions of Organizational Behavior.* 2nd ed., PWS-Kent: Boston, 1991, pp. 30 and 159.)

22. *b.* Psychological therapy is not an accepted concept in China. In addition, communism has kept most Chinese from expressing opinions openly. (Source: James McGregor, "Burma Road Heroin Breeds Addicts, AIDS Along China's Border." *Wall Street Journal,* September 29, 1992, p. 1.)

23. *b.* The Chinese regard a clock as a bad omen because the word for clock, pronounced *zhong,* is phonetically similar to another Chinese word that means the end. Jade is highly valued as symbolizing superior virtues, and oranges and dragon patterns are also auspicious symbols. (Source: Dr. Evelyn Lip, "Culture and Customs." *Silver Kris,* February 1994, p. 84.)

24. *a.* Venezuelans do the reverse of what most people in other countries do on Christmas and New Year's. On Christmas, they socialize. While fireworks are shot off on both nights, most restaurants are closed, and the streets are quiet. (Source: Tony Perrottet, ed., *Venezuela.* Houghton Mifflin: Boston, 1994, p. 97.)

25. *d.* Other popular pub food includes Bangers and Mash (sausages and mashed potatoes), Ploughman's lunch (bread, cheese, and pickled onions), and Cottage pie (baked minced meat with onions and topped with mashed potatoes). (Source: Ravi Desai, ed., *Let's Go: The Budget Guide to Britain and Ireland.* Pan Books: London, 1990, p. 83.)

26. *c.* Indians are generally uninhibited about staring at strangers and asking them about personal details in their lives. Social distance and personal privacy are not common social conventions in India. (Source: Frank Kusy, *India.* The Globe Pequo Press: Chester, Conn., 1989, p. 27.)

27. *c.* Vernon Weitzel of the Australian National University advises never to show anger when dealing with Vietnamese officials or businesspeople. Showing anger causes you to lose face and is considered

rude. Weitzel also recommends always smiling, not complaining or criticizing anyone, and not being inquisitive about personal matters. (Source: Daniel Robinson and Joe Cummings, *Vietnam, Laos & Cambodia.* Lonely Planet Publications: Australia, 1991, p. 96.)

28.   *c.* What looks to Westerners like a refusal is really an Indian way of saying "yes." It can also express general agreement with what you're saying or suggest that an individual is interested in what you have to say. (Source: Gitanjali Kolanad, *Culture Shock! India.* Graphic Arts Center Publishing Company: Portland, OR, 1996, p. 114.)

29.   *d.* In England, this simple hand gesture is considered vulgar and obscene. In a report to *The Boston Globe,* an American who had been working in London wrote, "I wish someone had told me before I emphatically explained to one of the draftsmen at work why I needed two complete sets of drawings." (Source: "Finger Gestures Can Spell Trouble," *The Berkshire Eagle:* January 26, 1997, p. E5.)

Source: Copyright © Houghton Mifflin Company. All rights reserved. Exercises 1, 3, 4 and 5 are from Janet W. Wohlberg, Gail E. Gilmore, and Steven B. Wolff, *OB in Action,* 5th ed. (Boston: Houghton Mifflin, 1998). Used with permission.

2. Using Gung Ho *to Understand Cultural Differences*

Background

There is no avoiding the increasing globalization of management. Few, if any, current students of business can expect to pursue a successful career without some encounter of an international nature. Gaining early and realistic exposure to the challenges of cross-cultural dynamics will greatly aid any student of business.

The Pacific Rim will continue to play a dominant role in North American transnational organization and global markets. The opening doors to China offer an unprecedented market opportunity. Korea, Singapore, and Taiwan continue to be unsung partners in mutually beneficial trading relationships. And, of course, Japan will always be a dominant player in the international arena.

An important aspect of cross-cultural awareness is understanding actual differences in interpersonal style and cultural expectations, and separating this from incorrect assumptions. Many embellished stereotypes have flourished as we extend our focus and attention abroad. Unfortunately, many of these myths have become quite pervasive, in spite of their lack of foundation. Thus, North American managers frequently and confidently err in their cross-cultural interactions. This may be particularly common in our interactions with the Japanese. For example, lifetime employment has long been touted as exemplifying the superior practices of Japanese management. In reality, only one-third of Japanese *male* employees enjoy this benefit, and in 1993, many Japanese firms actually laid off workers for the first time. Also, Japan is promoted as a collectivist culture founded on consensus, teamwork, and employee involvement. Yet Japan is at the same time one of the most competitive societies, especially when reviewing how students are selected for educational and occupational placement.

Films can provide an entertaining yet potent medium for studying such complex issues. Such experiential learning is most effective when realistic and identifiable with one's own likely experiences. Case studies can be too sterile. Role plays tend to be contrived and void of depth. Both lack a sense of background to help one "buy into" the situation. Films, on the other hand, can promote a rich and familiar presentation that promotes personal involvement. This exercise seeks to capitalize on this phenomenon to explore cross-cultural demands.

Procedure

Step I (110 minutes) Watch the film *Gung* Ho. (This film can be obtained at any video store.)

Step II (30 minutes) Use one of the following four formats to address the discussion topics.

Option A Address each issue in an open class forum. This option is particularly appropriate for moderate class sizes (40 students) or for sections that do not normally engage in group work.

Option B Divide the class into groups of four to seven to discuss the assigned topics. This is a better approach for larger classes (60 or more students). This approach might also be used to assign the exercise as an extracurricular activity if scheduled class time is too brief.

Option C Assign one group to adopt the American perspective and another group to take the Japanese perspective. Using a confrontation meeting approach, have each side describe its perception and expected difficulties in collaborating with each other. Then, have the two sides break into small mixed groups to discuss methods to bridge the gap (or avoid its extreme escalation as portrayed in the film). Ideas should extend beyond those cited in the movie. Present these separate discussions to the class as a whole.

Option D Assign students to groups of four to seven to watch the film and write a six-page analysis addressing one or more of the discussion topics.

Discussion Topics

1. In the opening scenes, Hunt observes Kaz being berated in a Japanese "management development center." According to at least one expert, this is a close representation of Japanese disciplinary practices. Would such an approach be possible in an American firm? How does this scene illustrate the different perspectives and approaches to motivation? To reinforcement? To feedback?

2. The concepts of multiculturalism and diversity are emerging issues in modern management environments. The importance of recognizing and responding to racial, ethnic, and other demographic factors has been widely debated in the popular press. What does *Gung Ho* offer to the discussion (both within and across the two groups)? How does each culture respond to different races, genders, and cultures?

3. Individualism and collectivism represent two endpoints on a continuum used to analyze different cultural orientations. Individualism refers to a sense of personal focus, autonomy, and compensation. Collectivism describes a group focus, self-subjugation, obligation, and sharing of rewards. How do you see American and Japanese workers

differing on this dimension? You might compare the reactions of the Japanese manager whose wife was about to give birth with those of the American worker who had planned to take his child to a doctor's appointment.

4. How does the softball game illuminate cultural differences (and even similarities)? You might consider this question in reference to topic 3; to approaches to work habits; to having "fun"; to behavioral norms of pride, honor, and sportsmanship.

5. On several occasions we see George Wendt's openly antagonistic responses to the exercise of authority by Japanese managers. Discuss the concept of authority as seen in both cultures. Discuss expectations of compliance. How might George's actions be interpreted differently by each culture? Indeed, would they be seen as different by an American manager as compared with a Japanese manager?

6. Throughout the film, one gains an impression of how Americans and the Japanese might differ in their approach to resolving conflict. Separately describe how each culture tends to approach conflict, and how the cultures might be different from each other.

7. Experienced conflict between work and family demands has also gained attention as an important managerial issue. How do both cultures approach the role of work in one's life? The role of family? How does each approach balance competing demands between the two? Have these expectations changed over time (from twenty years ago, forty years ago, sixty years ago)? How might they change now in the twenty-first century?

8. In reality, Japanese managers would be "shamed" if one of their subordinates was seriously injured on the job (the scene where the American worker's hand is caught in the assembly-line belt). Taking this into account, what other issues in the film might be used to illustrate differences or similarities between American and Japanese management and work practices?

Source: Steven M. Sommer, Pepperdine University. Used with permission.

3. "When in Bogotá ..."

As Jim Reynolds looked out the small window of the Boeing 757, he saw the glimmer of lights in the distance. After a five-hour flight, he arrived in Bogotá, Colombia, at 9:35 P.M. on a clear Friday evening. It had been nearly five years since Jim had seen his best friend, Rodrigo Cardozo. The two had met in college and kept in touch over the years. During their school years, Rodrigo would often accompany Jim when he went home to Chicago for the holidays.

Entering the main terminal, Jim found himself in what looked like a recently bombed building. Piles of debris were everywhere. Lights hung from the ceiling by exposed electrical wires, and the walls and floors were rough, unfinished concrete. "Certainly, aesthetics are not a major concern at the Bogotá International Airport," Jim thought.

As he came to the end of the long, dimly lit corridor, an expressionless customs official reached out his hand and gestured for Jim's travel documents.

"Passaporte, por favor. Bienvenidos a Bogotá, Señor Reynolds. Estás en vacacciones?"

"Sí," Jim replied.

After a few routine questions, Jim was allowed to pass through customs feeling relatively unscathed.

"Loquillo! Loquillo! Estamos aquí! Jim, Jim," a voice shouted.

Trying to find the origin of the voice among the dense crowd, Jim finally spotted Rodrigo. "Hey, man. How've you been? You look great!"

"Jim, it's so good to see you. How've you been? I would like you to meet my wife, Eva. Eva, this is my best friend, Jim. He's the one in all those pictures I've shown you."

Late Night Begins the Day

Close to an hour later, Jim, Rodrigo, and Eva arrived at Rodrigo's parents' house on the other side of Bogotá from the airport. As Jim was aware, it is customary for couples to live with their parents for a number of years after their marriage, and Rodrigo and Eva were part of that custom.

Darío, Rodrigo's father, owned an import/export business in Bogotá. He was a knowledgeable and educated man and, from what Jim knew, a master of business negotiations. Over the years, Darío had conducted business with people in nearly every country in Central and South America, the United States, Europe, Hong Kong, and some parts of Africa. Jim had first met Darío with Rodrigo in Boston in 1989.

"Jim, welcome to my house," Darío boomed effusively as the group walked in. "I am so pleased that you're finally in Bogotá. Would you like something to drink—whiskey, bourbon, Aguardiente?"

"Aguardiente!" Rodrigo urged.

"Yes, Jim would like some Aguardiente. I understand you're going to Bahía tonight," Darío added.

"Where?" Jim asked, looking around. "I didn't know we were going anywhere tonight."

"Don't worry, Jim, todo bien, todo bien," Rodrigo assured him. "We're going dancing, so get dressed. Let's go."

The reality of being in Colombia hit Jim at about 11:15 that night when he and his friends entered Bahía, a Bogotá nightclub. The rhythms of salsa and merengue filled the club. Jim's mind flashed back to the Latin dance parties he and Rodrigo had had in Boston with their friends from Central and South America.

"Jim, this is my cousin, Diana. She'll be your partner tonight," Rodrigo said. "You'll get to practice your Spanish too; she doesn't speak a word of English. Have fun."

For the next six hours, they danced and drank. This is the Colombian way. At 5:30 the next morning, Rodrigo decided it was time to leave to get something to eat. On the drive home, they stopped at an outdoor grill in the mountains where many people had congregated for the same reason. Everyone was eating arepas con queso and mazorca, and drinking Aguardiente.

Next, they continued to an outdoor party just down the street. Here, they danced and drank until the sun crested over the mountains of Bogotá. It was about 7:00 A.M. when they decided to conclude the celebration—for now.

Saturday was spent recovering from the previous evening and also touring some local spots in the country. However, Saturday night was a repeat of Friday. After being in Colombia for three days, Jim had slept a total of about four hours. Fortunately, Monday was a national holiday.

Business Before Pleasure Before Business?

Although Jim was having a great time, he had also scheduled a series of business meetings with directors of business schools at various Bogotá universities for the week to come. Jim worked as an acquisitions editor for Academia Press, a major publisher of college-level business textbooks. The purpose of the meetings was to establish business contacts in the Colombian market. It was hoped that these initial contacts would lead to others in Latin America.

At Academia Press headquarters in New York, Jim and Caroline Evans, his boss, had discussed the opportunities in Latin America. Although Academia Press routinely published international editions of its texts, total international sales never represented more than 15 percent of their gross. Consequently, international markets had never been pursued aggressively. Caroline, however, saw the Latin American markets as having a lot of potential within the next three to five years. She envisioned this market alone, in time, representing 15 to 20 percent of gross sales. Moreover, she felt that within the next ten years, international sales could reach 40 percent if developed properly. With numbers like that, it was evident to Jim that this deal was important, not only to the company but to his career as well. If Jim was able to open these markets, he might receive a promotion and be able to continue to work in Central and South America.

Jim's first meeting was scheduled for 11:00 A.M. on Tuesday, the second on Wednesday at 11:00 A.M., and the third on Friday at 3:00 P.M. At precisely 11:00 A.M. on Tuesday, Jim arrived at Javeriana University, where he was to meet with Professors Emilio Muñoz, Diana Espitia, and Enrique Ronderos. When he arrived, Professor Muñoz was waiting for him in the conference room.

"Señor Reynolds, I am delighted to meet you. How was your flight?"

"Wonderful," Jim replied.

"And how do you like Bogotá so far? Have you been able to sightsee?"

"No, I haven't had the chance to get around the city yet. I hope to see some things later in the week."

"Well, before you leave, you must visit *El Museo de Oro*. It is the finest collection of gold artifacts from the various indigenous Indian tribes in Colombia. Although much of the gold was stolen by the Spanish, many pieces have survived." For the next thirty minutes, Professor Muñoz spoke of everything from the upcoming presidential elections to World Cup soccer.

Jim looked at his watch, concerned about the other professors who had not yet arrived and about the meeting for which he had prepared.

"Is there something wrong, Señor Reynolds?"

"No, no, I was just wondering about the others; it's 11:30."

"Don't worry. They'll be here shortly. Traffic in Bogotá at this hour is terrible. They're probably caught in a traffic jam."

Just then, Professors Espitia and Ronderos walked in. "Muy buenas, Señor Reynolds," Professor Espitia said warmly. "Please forgive us for the delay. Traffic is simply awful at this time of day."

"Oh, that's not necessary. I understand. Traffic in New York can be absolutely horrendous as well," Jim replied. "Sometimes it takes two hours to get from one end of the city to the other."

"Have you had lunch yet, Señor Reynolds?" asked Professor Ronderos.

Jim shook his head.

"Why don't we go to lunch, and we can talk there?" Professor Ronderos suggested.

After discussing the restaurants in the area, the professors decided on El Club Ejecutivo. It was nearly 12:30 P.M. when they arrived.

"It's been an hour and a half, and we haven't discussed anything," Jim thought. He was concerned that the Colombians were not very interested in what he had to offer.

Throughout lunch, Jim grew increasingly concerned that the professors were more interested in his trying typical Colombian dishes and visiting the sights in Bogotá than in Academia's textbooks. They were fascinated that Jim knew how to dance salsa and merengue and impressed that he spoke Spanish with a slight Colombian accent; Señorita Espitia said she found it amusing. That seemed much more important than his knowledge of business textbooks and publishing in general.

By the end of lunch, Jim was nearly beside himself. It was now after 2:30 P.M. and nothing had been accomplished.

"Why don't we all go to Monserate tomorrow? It's absolutely beautiful up there, Señor Reynolds," Professor Ronderos suggested, going on to describe the mountain that overlooks Bogotá and the myths and traditions that surround it.

"That's a wonderful idea," Professor Espitia added.

"Monserate it is then. Jim, it has been a pleasure. I look forward to our meeting tomorrow," Professor Ronderos said with a slight bow.

"Señor Reynolds, would you like a ride home?" Professor Muñoz asked.

"Yes, if it's not too much trouble."

On the way home, Jim was relatively quiet.

"Do you feel okay?"

"It must be jet lag catching up to me. I'm sure it's nothing," Jim responded. Concerned about the way the meeting had gone, Jim realized that he had never even had a chance to mention Academia Press's various titles and how these texts could be used to create a new curriculum or supplement an existing curriculum at the professors' business school.

When in Bogotá

On arriving at the house, Jim went upstairs and sat in the living room glumly sipping a cup of aguapanela. "I just don't get it," he thought. "The Colombians couldn't have been happier with the way the meeting turned out, but we didn't do anything. We didn't even talk about one book. I just don't understand what went wrong."

In a short time, Darío arrived. "Muy buenas, Jim. How did your meetings go today with the directors?" he asked.

"I don't know. I don't know what to think. We didn't do anything. We didn't talk about business at all. We talked more about the sights I should see and the places I should visit before I leave Colombia. I'm supposed to call my boss this afternoon and tell her how the initial meeting went. What am I going to tell her? 'Sorry, we just decided to plan my vacation in Colombia instead of discussing business.' I can't afford to have this deal fall through."

Darío laughed.

"Señor, I'm serious."

"Jim, I understand. Believe me. Tell me about your meeting today."

Jim recounted every detail of the meeting to Darío, who smiled and nodded his head as he listened.

"Jim, you have to understand one thing before you continue negotiating with the directors."

"What's that?"

"You're in Colombia now," Darío said simply.

Jim stared at him with a puzzled look. "And?"

"And what, Jim?"

"Is there something else I should know?"

"That's where you need to start. You let the directors set the tone of the meeting. It's obvious they felt very comfortable with you, or they wouldn't have invited you to Monserate. Here in Colombia, Jim, we do business differently. Right now, you're building friendship. You're building their trust in you. This is very important in doing business in all of Latin America."

"Jim," Darío continued, "would you rather do business with a friend or someone you hardly know?"

As Darío went on to analyze the meeting, Jim realized that his perception of the situation had been formed by his experiences in the United States. "When in Bogotá," he thought, "I guess I had better think like the Colombians."

"Jim, you've gained the respect and the trust of the directors. In my opinion, your first meeting was a complete success."

"What should I expect in the meetings to come?" Jim asked.

"Don't worry," he responded. "Just let the directors worry about that. You'll come to an agreement before the end of the week. I guarantee it."

Questions for Discussion

1. What differences does Jim notice between life in the United States and life in Colombia?

2. What differences does Jim notice between doing business in the United States and doing business in Colombia? How might these same factors differ in other countries?

3. What advice would you give Jim for closing his deals? Why?

Source: Copyright 1994 by Matthew B. Shull. Used with permission.

4. The International Cola Alliances

Objectives

- To introduce some of the complexities involved in doing business across international borders
- To examine what happens when countries seek to do business with one another without the benefit of a common language and customs

Background

Even with a common language, communication can break down, and interpretations of words and actions often can confound understanding and incur negative attributions of purpose. Add to this the differences of personal needs that exist from individual to individual, as well as national and cultural needs that exist from country to country. These limitless variables make cooperation across borders even more complex.

The Story

You are a delegation from a country that would like to enter into a large cooperative effort with a number of other countries for the production and distribution of a popular soft drink produced by the American company International Cola. In the past, countries in your region of the world have been resistant to allowing foreign soft drinks into their markets, despite consumer demands. However, recent thinking is that the advantages of allowing this competition outweigh the disadvantages.

International Cola has expressed an interest in setting up a bottling plant, a regional corporate headquarters, and four distribution depots. Their goal, of course, is to do this in the most economically efficient way possible to maximize profits. However, because the executives at International Cola believe this area to be a rich new market with outstanding potential and are therefore eager to get in, they have ceded to the demands of the various governments in the proposed alliance. These require International Cola to allow for local control of the facilities; to maintain only 49 percent interest in the facilities with local partners holding 51 percent ownership; and to allow the participating governments to work out among themselves the details of where the facilities will be located.

For the countries involved, having one or more of these facilities located within their borders will bring jobs, revenue, and a certain amount of prestige. (It is possible for a single country to have all six of the facilities: regional headquarters, bottling plant, distribution depots.)

Each of the countries involved shares at least two borders with the other countries. This has not always been the most peaceful area. Border skirmishes are frequent, most stemming from minor misunderstandings that became inflated by vast cultural and religious differences.

These distinct cultural differences between your country and your neighbors will likely become even more evident as you pursue the negotiation. It will be up to you to decide how to respond to them. While it is important for you to retain your own cultural integrity—for example, when you first meet a delegate from another country you will likely greet him or her in the cultural style of your country—you understand the importance of being sensitive to one another. If you understand, for example, that the cultural style of another country is to bow on meeting, whereas you shake hands, you may wish to bow instead.

Since you are negotiating the venture across borders, and each country has a different primary language, you have agreed to negotiate in English, but none of you is entirely fluent. Therefore, a few phrases will creep in from your own languages.

Wear your country's flag in a visible place at all times.

Instructions

Step 1 *(30–40 minutes—may be done before class)* Working in small groups (5–7), develop a profile of your country and its people based on profile sheets 1 and 2.

You will also be given a third profile sheet that details cultural norms within your country. Information given will include the ways in which people in your country deal with areas such as time, personal physical space, gender, social mores, and oral communication.

After you have completed profile sheets 1 and 2, briefly discuss them to be sure there is mutual understanding of what the group's behavior and negotiating stance are to be during the negotiation.

Step 2 *(20 minutes—may be done before class)* Based on the profile sheets, decide which International Cola facilities you believe you should have in your country and why you believe they should be in your country rather than one of the others that will be represented. For example, if you have a highly educated population, you may argue that you should be the home of the regional corporate headquarters; be aware, however, that another country might argue that you should not have bottling and distribution facilities because these do not require a highly educated or skilled labor force.

On the negotiation sheet, make a list of the facilities you believe your country should have and some notes as to what your arguments will be for having them. Also, make some notes on what you believe the other countries' counter-arguments will be and how you expect to respond to them.

Step 3 *(30–45 minutes—in class)*   Everyone in your group should pin a copy of your country's flag and motto on himself or herself in a visible place. One to three representatives from your group (delegation) should negotiate the arrangements for International Cola's facilities with the representatives from the other delegations. Be sure to use the cultural norms of your country during the negotiation, but *do not tell* the others what your social norms are.

Representatives should introduce themselves to one another on an individual basis. After personal introductions, representatives should form a circle in the center of the room with their delegations behind them, briefly describe their countries, state their positions, and begin negotiations. During negotiations, representatives should make an effort to use their new language at least three times. They should not use English for any of the six phrases listed.

Delegation representatives and the other members of their groups may communicate with one another at any point during the negotiation, but only in writing. Group members may also communicate among themselves, but only in writing during the negotiation.

Any group or representative may ask for a side meeting with one or more of the other groups during the negotiation. Side meetings may not last more than five minutes.

At any time in the negotiation, the delegation may change its representative. When such a change is made, the new representative and the other delegates must reintroduce themselves and greet one another.

Those members of each delegation who are not directly negotiating should be active observers. Use the observer sheet to record situations in which other groups insulted them, shamed them, or were otherwise offensive.

At the end of 45 minutes, the negotiation should be concluded whether or not an agreement has been reached.

Questions for Discussion

1. What role did cultural differences play in the various phases of the negotiation process? Be careful not to overlook the introductory phase. Was the negotiation frustrating? Satisfying? Other? Why?

2. At any time, did delegations recognize the cultural differences between themselves and the others? If so, was any attempt made to try to adapt to another country's norms? Why? Why not? Would there have been a benefit in doing so? Why?

3. What role did language differences play during the negotiation? What was the effect of lack of understanding or miscommunication on the process?

4. Did the delegations from various countries attempt to find mutual goals and interests despite their differences? In what ways were the best interests of the overall plan subjugated to the individual interests of each country? What rhetoric was used to justify the personal interests?

5. To what degree did groups construct their countries to best justify their position? In situations where this happened, did it work? Why? Why not?

Profile Sheet 1

1. Select a name for your country:

   _____

   Be sure that the name of your country appears on or around the flag (see below).

2. In the space below, design your country's flag or emblem. Make enough copies so that each member of your group has one to wear.

   _____
   _____
   _____
   _____
   _____

3. Write a slogan for your country that best embodies your country's ideals and goals. Include the slogan on or around the flag.

   _____
   _____
   _____

4. Make up a partial language with a vocabulary of up to twenty-five (25) words into which you should translate the following phrases for use during negotiations:

Phrase   *Translation*

I agree. _____

I disagree. _____

This is unacceptable. _____

I don't understand your point. _____

_____

You have insulted me. _____

Please repeat that. _____

5. Briefly describe how people in your country react when they have been insulted.

   _____
   _____
   _____
   _____
   _____

Profile Sheet 2

Describe your country by selecting one element from each of the following lists. After you have made your selections, list the elements that make up your country's description on a separate piece of paper and add any additional elements you wish.

Population Density

_____ high density with overpopulation a problem

_____ moderate density—high end

_____ moderate density—average

_____ moderate density—low end

_____ low density

Average Educational Level

_____ less than 3 years—large percent totally illiterate

_____ 3–6 years—widespread functional illiteracy

_____ 6–9 years—functional illiteracy a problem in scattered areas

_____ 9–12 years—most read and write at functional levels

_____ 12+ years—a highly educated and functioning population

Per Capita Income

_____ under $1,000 per year

_____ $1,000–5,000 per year

_____ $5,000–10,000 per year

_____ $10,000–20,000 per year

_____ $20,000–30,000 per year

_____ $30,000–40,000 per year

_____ $40,000+ per year

Climate

_____ tropical

_____ arctic

_____ mixed in different areas

_____ runs range from season to season

Form of Government

_____ socialist

_____ democratic

_____ communist

_____ monarchy

_____ dictatorship

_____ other (specify)

Dominant Racial-Ethnic Group

_____ Asian

_____ black

_____ white

_____ other (specify)

Dominant Religion

_____ animist

_____ atheist/agnostic

_____ Buddhist

_____ Catholic

_____ Hindu

_____ Jewish

_____ Mormon

_____ Protestant (specify)

_____ other (specify)

Negotiation Sheet

1. What facilities do you believe your country should have?

_____

_____

_____

_____

2. What facilities of those listed above are you willing to relinquish to reach agreement?

_____

_____

_____

3. On what bases will you justify your need or desire for having the facilities you have listed?

_____

_____

_____

_____

_____

_____

_____

_____

Observer Sheet

1. List actions taken by members of other delegations that were insulting, created shame for you and your delegation, or were otherwise offensive based on your country's norms. Include notes on the context in which the actions were taken.

_____

_____

_____

_____

_____

_____

_____

2. Based on the above list, what happened to your interest in forming an alliance and your belief that a mutual agreement could be reached?

_____

_____

_____

_____

_____

_____

_____

_____

_____

_____

_____

5. Who to Hire?

Objectives

- To explore participants' cultural biases and expectations
- To examine cultural differences
- To consider the impact culture has on hiring decisions

Instructions

Step 1 (10–15 minutes) Read the background information and descriptions of each of the applicants. Consider the job and the cultures within which the individual to be hired will be operating. Rank the candidates from 1 to 5, with 1 being your first choice, and enter your rankings on the ranking sheet in the column marked "My Ranking." Briefly, list the reasons for each of your rankings.

Do not discuss your rankings with your classmates until told to do so.

Step 2 (30–40 minutes) Working with three to four of your classmates, discuss the applicants, and rank them in the order of group preference. Do not vote.

Rank the candidates from 1 to 5, with 1 being the group's first choice, and enter your group rankings on the ranking sheet in the column marked "Group Ranking." Briefly list the reasons for each of the group's rankings.

If your group represents more than one culture, explore the ways in which each person's cultural background may have influenced his or her individual decisions.

Step 3 (open-ended) Report your rankings to the class, and discuss the areas of difference that emerged within your group while you were trying to reach consensus.

Questions for Discussion

1. Was your group able to explore openly any culturally based biases that came up—for example, feelings about homosexuality, religion, personality traits, politics?

2. Did you make any comments or observations that you feel would have been fully acceptable in your own culture but were not accepted by the group? Explain.

3. If the answer to number 2 was yes, how did the reaction of the group make you feel about your membership in it? How did you handle the situation?

4. What implications do you believe these cultural differences would have in business dealings?

Background

You are a member of the management committee of a multinational company that does business in 23 countries. While your company's headquarters are in Holland, your offices are scattered fairly evenly throughout the four hemispheres. Primary markets have been in Europe and North America; the strongest emerging market is the Pacific Rim. Company executives would like to develop what they see as a powerful potential market in the Middle East. Sales in all areas except the Pacific Rim have shown slow growth over the past two years.

At present, your company is seeking to restructure and revitalize its worldwide marketing efforts. To accomplish this, you have determined that you need to hire a key marketing person to introduce fresh ideas and a new perspective. There is no one currently in your company who is qualified to do this, and so you have decided to look outside. The job title is "vice-president for international marketing"; it carries with it a salary well into six figures (US$), plus elaborate benefits, an unlimited expense account, a car, and the use of the corporate jet. The person you hire will be based at the company's headquarters and will travel frequently.

A lengthy search has turned up five people with good potential. It is now up to you to decide whom to hire. Although all the applicants have expressed a sincere interest in the position, it is possible that they may change their minds once the job is offered. Therefore, you must rank them in order of preference so that if your first choice declines the position, you can go on to the second, and so on.

Applicants
Park L., age 41, Married with Three Children

Park L. is currently senior vice president for marketing at a major Korean high-technology firm. You have been told by the head of your Seoul office that his reputation as an expert in international marketing is outstanding. The market share of his company's products has consistently increased since he joined the company just over fifteen years ago. His company's market share is now well ahead of that of competing producers in the Pacific Rim.

Park started with his present company immediately after his graduation from the University of Seoul and has worked his way up through the ranks. He does not have a graduate degree. You sense that Park has a keen understanding of organizational politics and knows how to play them. He recognizes that because the company he works for now is family controlled, it is unlikely that he will ever move much higher than his present situation. Park has told you that he is interested in the growth potential offered at your company.

In addition to his native tongue, Park is able to carry on a reasonably fluent conversation in English and has a minimal working knowledge of German and French.

His wife, who appears quiet and quite traditional, and his children speak only Korean.

Kiran K., age 50, Widow with One Adult Child

Kiran K. is a Sikh woman living in Malaysia. She began her teaching career while finishing her DBA (doctorate in business administration) at the Harvard Business School and published her first book on international marketing 10 months after graduation. Her doctoral dissertation was based on the international marketing of pharmaceuticals, but she has also done research and published on other areas of international marketing.

Two months after the publication of her book, Kiran went to work in the international marketing department of a Fortune 500 company, where she stayed for the next 10 years. She returned to teaching when Maura University offered her a full professorship with tenure, and she has been there since that time. Her academic position has allowed her to pursue a number of research interests and to write authoritative books and papers in her field. At present, she is well published and internationally recognized as an expert on international marketing. In addition, she has an active consulting practice throughout Southeast Asia.

You have learned through your office in Kuala Lumpur that Kiran's only child, a 23-year-old son, is severely mentally and physically disabled. You sense that part of her interest in the job with your company is to have the income to guarantee his care should anything happen to her. Her son would go with her to Holland, should she be given the job, where he will need to be enrolled in special support programs.

In addition to fluency in Malay, English, and Hindi, Kiran speaks and writes German and Spanish and is able to converse in Japanese and Mandarin.

Peter V., age 44, Single

Peter is a white South African. He had worked in a key position in the international marketing division of an American Fortune 100 company until the company pulled out of his country eight months ago. While the company wanted to keep him on, offering to move him from Johannesburg to its New York headquarters, Peter decided that it was time to look elsewhere. He had begun to feel somewhat dead-ended in his position and apparently sees the position at your company as an opportunity to try out new territory. Like your other candidates for the position, Peter has a long list of accomplishments and is widely recognized as outstanding in his field. People in your company who have had contacts with him say that Peter is creative, hardworking, and loyal. In addition, you have been told that Peter is a top-flight manager of people who is able to push his employees to the highest levels of performance. And, you are told, he is very organized.

Peter has a PhD in computer science from a leading South African university and an MBA from Purdue's Krannert School of Business.

Peter had been a vehement opponent of apartheid and is still very much a social activist. His high political visibility within South Africa had made his life there difficult, and even now, with the end of apartheid, he would like to get out. His constant male companion, P. K. Kahn, would be coming with him to Holland, and Peter would like your personnel office to help P. K. find an appropriate position.

Peter speaks and reads English, Dutch, Afrikaans, and Swahili and can converse in German.

Tex P., age 36, Divorced with One Child

Tex is currently job hunting. His former job as head of marketing for a single-product high-technology firm—highly specialized workstations for sophisticated artificial intelligence applications—ended when the company was bought out by Texas Instruments. Tex had been with his previous company virtually from the time the company was started six years earlier. Having to leave his job was an irony to Tex as it was largely due to the success of his efforts that the company was bought out. You sense that he is a little bitter, and he tells you that jobs offered to him by TI were beneath him and not worthy of consideration.

Tex has both his undergraduate and MBA degrees from Stanford University. In addition, he was a Rhodes Scholar and won a Fulbright scholarship, which he used to support himself while he undertook a two-year research project on the marketing of high-technology equipment to Third World countries.

You have learned through your New York office that Tex has a reputation for being aggressive and hard driving. Apparently he is a workaholic who has been known to work eighteen to twenty hours a day, seven days a week. He seems to have little time for his personal life.

In addition to his native English, Tex has a minimal command of French—which he admits he hasn't used since his college days.

Zvi C., age 40, Married with Five Children

Zvi began his career after receiving his MBA from the Sloan School of Management at the Massachusetts Institute of Technology (MIT). His first job was as marketing manager for a German company doing business in Israel.

Zvi's phenomenal success with this company led to his being hired away by an international office equipment company in England. Again, he proved to be outstanding, boosting the company's market share beyond all expectations within two years. After five years, Zvi was offered a chance to go back to Israel, this time to oversee and coordinate all the international marketing programs for an industrial park of 14 companies run as an adjunct to Israel's leading scientific research institution. It has been his responsibility to interface the research component with product development and sales as well as to manage the vast marketing department. Again, he has shown himself to be a master.

You have learned through your Haifa office that Zvi is highly respected and has extensive contacts in the scientific and high-tech worlds. He is exception-ally creative in his approach to marketing, often trying bold strategies that most of his peers would dismiss as too risky. Zvi, however, has made them work and work well.

Zvi is a religious man who must leave work by noon on Friday. He will not work Saturdays nor any of his reli-gion's major and minor holidays—about eighteen a year. He will, however, work on Sundays.

In addition to his native language, Dutch (Zvi and his family moved to Israel form Holland when Zvi was six), he speaks and writes fluent Hebrew, English, German, and Arabic.

Ranking Sheet

Rank candidates from one to five with one as your first choice.

Applicant	My Ranking		Group Ranking	
	Rank	Reasons	Rank	Reasons
Park L.				
Kiran K.				
Peter V.				
Tex P.				
Zvi C.				

1. "Frankenfoods" or Rice Bowl for the World: The U.S.–EU Dispute over Trade in Genetically Modified Organisms

This simulation is designed to develop skills at cross-cultural negotiations with an emphasis on multi-stakeholder dialogue and exchange.

Synopsis

On August 18, 2003, members of the World Trade Organization (WTO) met in Geneva to hear a U.S. request for a full-blown dispute-settlement proceeding regarding European Union (EU) restrictions on the import and sale of goods produced with or containing genetically modified organisms (GMOs). In late 1996, Monsanto exported the first genetically modified soybeans to Europe, assuming that consumers would accept them as Americans had. The timing was not good, however, as the GMO issue became linked in the minds of Europeans with "mad cow" disease, an outbreak that was first thought limited to animals but eventually killed several humans. Neither GMO companies nor European authorities were prepared for the reaction, as public sentiment immediately turned against the technology. Britain's *Daily Mirror* ran a front-page headline in 1998 warning against "Frankenfood." In 1998, five European countries said they wouldn't process any more applications for genetically modified crops, and the EU upheld this decision.[1]

In May 2003, the United States filed a complaint with the WTO in hopes of getting the ban lifted. In response, in the summer of 2003, the European Parliament passed groundbreaking legislation that would require detailed labeling of all food products containing as little as 0.9 percent of genetically modified ingredients, and would require origin tracing in order to gain approval. Although these steps were designed to move toward lifting the moratorium, many in the United States charged that these rules would be unworkable, would be discriminatory toward imports, and would violate WTO sanitary and phytosanitary (SPS) agreements.[2]

Paradoxically, both sides claimed to be concerned about public health and environmental safety. The U.S. government and industry argued that the EU was in violation of WTO provisions requiring nondiscriminatory treatment of like or similar goods. The Americans contended that uninformed Europeans were spreading unfounded fears about GMOs.[3] In addition, the U.S. government argued that requiring labels for GMO products would result in segregating GMO foods from non-GMO foods and, in so doing, limit their consumer appeal. Furthermore, the threshold of 0.9 percent was far too restrictive, according to U.S. officials.

Description of Exercise

This exercise provides an interactive case simulation in which you will be assigned to a group that will assume the role of one of several stakeholder groups in the actual dispute between the United States and the EU over trade in GMOs. In this case, the U.S. government, on behalf of U.S. farmers and the biotech industry, argued that the EU is in violation of global trading rules. Europe responded that it has the right to protect the health and safety of its population and domestic crops, given the uncertainties over the effects of GMOs on humans, animals, and plants.

This simulation assumes that the United States and the EU proceed through the WTO dispute-settlement procedures, and it places participants in the roles of the various disputants: the U.S. government, the European Union, a consortium of GMO companies, a group of interested developing countries, a group of NGOs, and a WTO Dispute Settlement Panel.

Genetically Modified Food

According to some estimates, over half the world's soy, a key ingredient in products ranging from candy bars to animal feed, comes from genetically modified strains. In 2005, about 8.5 million farmers in 21 countries were planting genetically altered seeds.[4] The global market value of genetically modified crops in 2006 was $6.15 billion. Yet genetically modified food has quickly become as controversial as cloning. The central feature of a GMO is human alteration of the DNA of an organism through the use of biotechnology. Proponents and opponents in the genetic-modification debate have been eager to weigh in on the benefits and risks associated with using GMOs. Each side has identified a number of key arguments to support its position:

Benefits

- Increased yields.
- Herbicide-tolerant crops encourage less tilling/soil erosion.
- Insecticidal crops encourage less use of harmful pesticides.
- Virus-resistant crops.
- Development of drought-resistant crops.

Risks

- Possible allergic or other health responses in humans/ livestock.
- Creating new or more vigorous pests and pathogens.

- Harm to "nontarget" beneficial species.
- Unwanted gene flow.
- Irreparable changes in species diversity and in genetic diversity within a species.

Genetically engineered products are not new. Insulin used in medicine is an example of genetic engineering. The insulin gene from the intestines of pigs is inserted into bacteria.[5] The bacteria grow and produce insulin, which is then purified and used for medical purposes. Other genetically engineered products include the chemical compound aspartame, used as a sugar substitute, and the hepatitis B vaccine.

A large barrier to the acceptance of GMOs worldwide is the fuzzy international law regulating GMO trade. The Agreement on Sanitary and Phytosanitary Measures (SPS Agreement), part of the 1994 agreement that established the World Trade Organization, requires that food safety regulations be based on scientific risk assessments.[6] Most studies to date seem to point to the conclusion that foods containing GMOs are safe for human consumption. But the fact that a majority of these studies were conducted by or for U.S. biotech firms independent of any third-party overseers suggests to some that the findings are suspect. In 1997, the United States won a complaint with the WTO against the EU concerning an EU ban on hormone-treated beef, but the EU continued to enforce the broader ban on approval of newly introduced GMO products because a large majority of Europeans are steadfastly against the use of GMOs.

The United States, along with Canada and Argentina, filed another complaint with the WTO in 2003, claiming that the EU's ban on genetically modified products violates international trade rules. In 2006 the WTO ruled in favor of the United States, claiming that the EU had indeed violated recognized trade rules. Now the EU is seeking to limit GMO sales through tougher approval processes.

The U.S. Position

In the United States, 86 percent of soy and more than 40 percent of corn are genetically modified. The U.S. government argues that the EU ban on genetically modified food not only is hurting U.S. commerce but also is discouraging developing countries from growing genetically modified crops for export.

The U.S. government believes that genetically modified products could reduce hunger and poverty in the world's poorest nations, and that by restricting the use of GMOs, the EU is aggravating starvation in the developing world.[7] Biotechnology, according to U.S. policy makers and biotech executives, offers the prospect of crops that are more resilient, require less water, and give higher yields. Thus the EU ban on genetically modified foods indirectly contributes to starvation by denying access to more efficient

agricultural techniques.[8] Furthermore, according to Robert B. Zoellick, the U.S. trade representative, uninformed European attitudes continue to spread unfounded fears in developing countries, where the need for the increased yields offered by genetically modified foods is greatest.[9] In addition, according to the U.S. government, GMO technologies would help developing countries dramatically increase export earnings. The U.S. government is not only concerned that Europe will prevent the use of GMOs but also that the EU model could serve as a blueprint for other countries, including those in the developing world, that plan to regulate GMOs.

In its recent WTO dispute with the EU, the United States argued that the EU's ban on GMOs violated international trade rules. In February 2006, the WTO dispute panel ruled in favor of the United States, Canada, and Argentina, deciding that the EU and six member states had broken trade rules by banning the import of genetically modified foods. The ban caused "undue delays" in the approval of GMO products, thereby violating the SPS Agreement.[10]

Along with continued criticism from Europe, the GMO cause has experienced some setbacks in the United States as well. For example, Aventis CropScience, developer of StarLink corn, was forced to pay $10 million to Iowa farmers and grain elevators in premiums and compensation for losses tied to growing and handling genetically modified grain that contaminated the grain supply. Although the government had approved StarLink for use in livestock feed, it was not cleared for human consumption after possibly allergic reactions were reported in people who consumed the protein that StarLink produces. Hundreds of food products were recalled in 2001 after testing showed residues of the StarLink protein in taco shells and other food. Some estimates suggest costs could eventually exceed $200 million.[11] Anti-GMO activists in the United States continue to make progress. In 2007, rice producers in California called for a moratorium on transgenic rice in the state, and a USDA ruling could stop the production of genetically modified alfalfa throughout the United States.[12]

The EU Position

For most Europeans, the debate over genetically modified foods is closely intertwined with cultural, environmental, and health issues. Earlier surveys suggested that nearly 80 percent of Europeans do not want to consume products with GMOs,[13] although European opinion about GMOs seems to be getting more optimistic. A 2006 Eurobarometer survey reported that, of those with a decided opinion on "green" biotechnology, only 58 percent discouraged it. This brings European opinion on GMOs close to that of Canada.[14]

At the heart of the debate over genetically modified products is the growing disagreement between the United

States and Europe over what steps are necessary to protect public health and the environment.[15] A major obstruction to settling this argument is deeply embedded in European culture. Food and culture are closely linked in Europe's historical and contemporary life. Many European regions celebrate their unique food traditions and local produce. Unlike Americans, whose food choices are driven by accessibility and convenience, Europeans try to limit the influence of corporate food companies on their food choices. Respecting their preferences, global food companies such as McDonald's, Burger King, and Coca-Cola have pledged to keep all products for sale in Europe free of GMOs.[16]

Another obstacle to the use of GMOs is the fact that in recent years Europe experienced several health crises—notably the outbreak of bovine spongiform encephalopathy (BSE), commonly known as "mad cow" disease—that alerted people to the possible dangers lurking in the food supply. Experts agreed that beef from cows with the disease was perfectly safe; then dozens of people died. Biotech firms will have difficulty convincing Europeans to consume GMOs in the absence of long-term statistical evidence from third parties supporting their safety claims.

Exacerbating the issue is the persistent view in Europe that the United States continues to engage in a unilateral—some would say imperial—foreign policy. Regardless of the ongoing battle over GMOs, many people in Europe support challenging U.S. positions as a matter of principle—as a demonstration of European strength and cultural unity. These strong views will continue to influence European consumer choices no matter the outcome of the current dispute. Resistance by European customers to all U.S. foods could overshadow any GMO benefits to the U.S. economy if, for example, the labeling provision is not upheld. The EU also argues that U.S. corporations are squeezing farmers around the world through their control of exporting and processing activities with the goal of developing a lower-cost, vertically integrated global supply chain.

European and North American protesters have been seen with banners calling genetically modified products "Frankenfoods," a label that deliberately associates them with frightening and unpredictable risks. Europe formally adopted a "precautionary principle" (described below) that takes a cautious approach to the approval of new bioengineered food, assuming that there may be unforeseen effects unless proven otherwise.

The EU argues the United States is motivated exclusively by economic considerations and that the U.S. government is responding only to the agribusiness and biotech firms that stand to gain financially if current restrictions are lifted. For example, in 2003, ten agricultural conglomerates, many of which are active in GMOs, owned almost 40 percent of the world's seed market.[17]

According to Martin Rocholl, director of Friends of the Earth Europe, "The U.S. Administration, funded by the likes of GMO giant Monsanto, is using the undemocratic and secretive WTO to force-feed the world foods containing GMOs. Decisions about the food we eat should be made in Europe and not in the White House, the WTO or Monsanto's HQ. We welcome the European Commission's commitment to fight this aggressive U.S. policy and ensure that Europe's wildlife and people are protected from the threats of GM crops."[18]

Since the WTO's 2006 decision, which ruled the EU's ban on genetically modified products illegal, the EU has fought to control the presence of GMOs on its own turf. Under the SPS Agreement, the EU originally banned all genetically modified products on the grounds that they could not be proven "safe." However, the WTO decision claimed that enough evidence is now available to perform adequate risk assessments of genetically modified products and, furthermore, that most existing risk assessments do not provide enough of a reason for banning such products.[19] The EU's new authorization process will likely be the stage for new disputes regarding the international sale of genetically modified products.

GMOs are starting to become more prevalent in Europe, with GMO crop area expected to increase over the next decade. "It will be slow but within 10 years GMOs will have reached the point of no return," said Jean-Michel Duhamel, Monsanto's director for southern Europe.[20] But common anti-GMO sentiment is still strong. Some European companies, such as Unilever, produce genetically modified products, but they don't sell those products in Europe because of consumer opposition. Germany's Metro AG chain, like other major European grocery stores, doesn't allow bioengineered ingredients in its store brands.[21] Labeling rules proposed to replace the ban have generated heated responses from European GMO opponents. Greenpeace promised to marshal thousands of volunteers throughout Europe to police grocery stores in the weeks that follow the launch of labeling. "If consumers start buying it and get used to it, we will lose," says Dan Hindsgaul, the head of Greenpeace's effort. In 2006, Greenpeace sent a petition, calling all EU member states to alter their GMO-labeling rules to include products such as meat, eggs, and milk, which come from animals that are fed with genetically modified products. According to Greenpeace, the typical diet of a farm animal in Europe consists of up to 30 percent GMOs.[22]

Substantial Equivalence and the Precautionary Principle

The issue of scientific proof has been a major point of contention. At the heart of the debate are the concepts of substantial equivalence and the precautionary principle. The term *substantial equivalence* was first mentioned in a 1993 Organization for Economic Cooperation and

Development (OECD) report on the safety of biotechnology. Members of the OECD agreed that the most practical approach to determining the safety of foods derived by biotechnology is to consider whether they represent a "substantial equivalent" to analogous traditional products. The term *substantial equivalence* was borrowed from the U.S. Food and Drug Administration's (FDA) definition of a class of new medical devices that do not differ materially from their predecessors and thus do not raise new regulatory concerns. However, after considering the possible unseen effects of foods that contain GMOs, the EU argues that it is difficult to directly apply the FDA definition of *substantial equivalence* in this case. The concept of substantial equivalence was applied for the first time to a GMO in the safety assessment of the Flavr Savr tomato before it went to market in 1994. Data collected revealed that the modified tomato was equivalent to the nonmodified parent plant, and genetically modified tomatoes were accepted under FDA rules.

The EU adopted an approach to health and safety risks known as the "precautionary principle." In common parlance, this approach may be summed up as, "Better safe than sorry." Under this policy, new products are not assumed to be safe unless scientifically shown to be so. According to some in the EU, there is little scientific, third-party evidence that shows foods containing GMOs are safe for consumption. The precautionary principle thus provides justification for restricting GMOs unless they can be shown to be safe in all respects.

Biotech and Agricultural Firms

Because of their international reach, several large U.S. firms, including Monsanto and Du Pont, that support biotech and use biotech crops in their products have pressed the U.S. government to take a strong stand on the issue. The United States is the largest agricultural exporter in the world, and U.S. officials argue that trade restrictions of any kind will only undermine an already sluggish global economy. At stake for large biotech multinationals is a substantial amount of future commerce. These firms have claimed huge losses since the EU ban was put into effect in 1998, projecting that the ban has cost them close to $300 million annually. U.S. government policy has been supportive of biotech firms and a strong advocate of their ability to help alleviate famine in developing countries by producing more abundant yields in areas notorious for infertile soil and a lack of other resources.

The reluctance of key foreign trading partners—the EU, Japan, and other nations—to import genetically modified products has become a significant problem for American farmers as they compete in the international marketplace. (In 2003, Australia joined the United States as a third-party supporter in the WTO dispute against the EU over the ban on GMO products. Australia is a minor producer of GMO crops, including cotton and carnations.[23] Support

for GMOs in Australia primarily comes from the national government, while state governments and public opinion tend to oppose GMOs.) In the United States, genetically modified crops, including corn and soybeans, are now planted on millions of acres of farmland. If current restrictions on genetically modified foods aren't lifted, American farmers will lose millions of dollars from unusable crops. In March 2004, the American Soybean Association (ASA) stepped forward to take a lead role in preparing the WTO challenge of the EU's labeling ban. In addition, the ASA claims the labeling threshold of 0.9 percent is too stringent and lacks statistical backing. Also worsening the farmers' plight is the fact that worldwide commodity prices have dropped over the past decade.[24]

Developing Countries

In developing countries, farmers have been resisting pressure to grow bioengineered crops—even if they could improve their productivity and reduce hunger—for fear of losing their European market.

GMO supporters believe that the modified organisms can resist certain viruses and extreme temperatures, enabling crops to survive with less energy than is normally required with nonmodified seeds. This ability could be very useful in regions that don't have much fertile soil and lack other usable resources. More abundant yields would help feed the large population in most developing countries. For example, yields could be increased by growing insect-resistant crops in regions where bugs have seriously restricted outputs. Proponents believe that foods containing GMOs will be able to alleviate starvation and hunger in needy places. The United States insists that GMOs do not pose a risk to developing nations because the seeds are destined for consumption, not planting.[25] GMO crops are also considered by some to be better for regions such as Africa where lack of education and training in the use of fertilizers and other modern farming techniques hampers agricultural development. Transgenic crops make up for this lack of education because the technology to control insects is already packaged in the seeds and farmers just have to plant them.

Skeptics argue that the skewed food distribution system, not lack of access to GMOs, is responsible for food shortages in developing countries. According to this view, developing countries are underfed because most of the food that they generate is sold in the export market to the wealthy developed nations. Furthermore, they question how poor developing countries will be able to afford the genetically modified seeds. U.S. agricultural firms own the patents, and the suspicion is widespread that U.S. companies will limit the availability of nonmodified seeds in order to support the sale of modified ones. Also, many people in the developing world remain skeptical about the health effects. In late June 2002, Zambia's minister of commerce, trade, and industry, Dipak Patel, proclaimed that African nations would not accept genetically modified food until it has been proved safe for human consumption.[26] South Africa, one of only a few African nations that allow the planting of genetically modified crops, is expected to test a strain of genetically modified maize in late 2007. The prospects for GMOs in Africa, especially maize, could be on the rise since the 2006 maize streak virus, which destroyed anywhere between 5 and 100 percent of African farmers' crops.[27]

In Brazil, controversy surrounded President Lula da Silva's Provisionary Measure 131, which authorized the commercialization of genetically modified soy. Opponents of GMOs in Brazil suggested that the governing administration, notorious for bribery and scandals, was influenced by its relationship with Monsanto, which owns the patent on the most popular genetically modified soy. Brazilian legislators agreed and proposed that genetically modified soy in Brazil be burned and replaced with conventional crops beginning in February 2004. Later, under pressure from some farming interests, the legislators reversed position, and genetically modified crops and seeds are now permitted.

The UN Cartagena Protocol, an agreement intended to educate emerging-market countries about the benefits and risks of genetically modified products, was activated in June 2003 when the Republic of Palau became the 50th country to ratify the bill. The agreement is designed to help educate emerging-market countries about the risks of proliferated GMOs.

Simulation Instructions

You will be assigned to one of six groups:

1. The U.S. government.
2. The European Union.
3. A consortium of companies that manufacture or use GMO products, including Monsanto and Cargill.
4. A group of interested developing countries.
5. A group of nongovernmental organizations (NGOs) opposed to the exchange of GMO products.
6. A WTO Dispute Settlement Panel.

Participants should spend 20 to 30 minutes reviewing the case and formulating arguments that advance the agenda of their group. Refer to the "GATT/WTO Principles" section below and to the background material above for information. After the initial session, groups whose interests may be similar may consult with each other for an additional 10 to 15 minutes to coordinate presentations and minimize duplication. For example, the consortium of GMO companies might consult with the U.S. government. The WTO Dispute Settlement Panel is composed of "judges" and should be treated respectfully. Each group should make an opening presentation of no more than 10 minutes to the WTO panel. The presentation should summarize the main points of the argument and urge a

particular decision by the panel. Panel members may then ask questions of the groups for an additional 15 minutes. After each group presents its argument, the WTO panel will deliberate for 20 minutes and present its findings.

The issue for decision by the WTO Dispute Settlement Panel is whether the EU prohibition on imports of genetically modified products is consistent with WTO principles. Depending on the ruling in this matter, the WTO panel may offer specific remedies for how the ruling should be implemented. Further, the panel may wish to consider whether the proposed labeling and origin requirements (which in theory would allow the resumption of imports of genetically modified products) would or would not resolve the dispute, and whether this ban itself would be consistent with WTO principles.

GATT/WTO Principles: General Obligations

The General Agreement on Tariffs and Trade (now the World Trade Organization) was founded after World War II to establish rules for international trade practices and to resolve disputes among nations. Two fundamental principles govern most GATT/WTO provisions: most-favored-nation treatment and national treatment. *National treatment* refers to the obligations of the contracting parties to treat the nationals of foreign countries no less favorably than they treat the nationals of their own country. A more common term for this obligation is "nondiscrimination." The GATT/WTO also requires that the parties extend *most-favored-nation treatment* to other parties, so that some countries are not treated more favorably than others. Dispute settlement resolution (when one or more countries accuse another contracting party of violating GATT/WTO rules) is carried out by three- to five-member panels that render reports (decisions).

Exceptions

The GATT/WTO provides for limited exceptions to the above-mentioned obligations. For example, preferential trade agreements such as the EU and NAFTA are permitted to extend better than most-favored-nation treatment to their members under certain conditions. There are also "general" exemptions, which excuse otherwise illegal actions if they are designed to protect public morals, preserve national heritage, and limit commerce in goods made with prison labor. Although the word *environment* is never mentioned, the GATT/WTO does offer a basis for deviating from GATT/WTO principles in support of environmental protection. Specifically, Article XX holds that the GATT/WTO does not prevent contracting parties from taking actions (1) necessary to the protection of human, animal, or plant life or health and (2) relating to the conservation of exhaustible natural resources—provided trade measures affecting international commerce are joined by restrictions on domestic production or consumption.

The Uruguay Round agreement established agreements on the application of sanitary and phytosanitary (SPS) measures and technical barriers to trade (TBT). SPS measures are those necessary to safeguard human, animal, and plant health. Typically, when applied by an individual country, they are designed to safeguard its citizens, animal and plant industries, and environment against the risks posed by exotic pests and diseases, and against general threats to health entering from outside, and to control the incidence and spread of pests and diseases already present.

These agreements established the basis for reducing or eliminating nontariff regulatory barriers unless they respect scientifically substantiated and internationally recognized standards and conformance procedures and technical and labeling regulations. As applied to international trade, SPS protocols include a range of control measures—for example, import requirements; methods of treatment, manufacture, handling and packaging, and storage; inspection and certification requirements; and in some cases outright import bans on some products from certain areas. The major areas covered are plant quarantine measures, animal quarantine measures, and food safety standards. Thus governments may restrict imports of products that have been found to pose health or safety risks, based on sound, scientific evidence. Specifically, SPS measures must be designed to accomplish one or more of the following objectives:

1. To protect animal or plant life or health within the territory of the member from risks arising from the entry, establishment, or spread of pests, diseases, disease-carrying organisms, or disease-causing organisms.

2. To protect human or animal life within the territory of the member from risks arising from additives, contaminants, toxins, or disease-carrying organisms in food, beverages, or feedstuffs.

3. To protect human life or health within the territory of the member from risks arising from diseases carried by animals, plants, or products thereof, or from the entry, establishment, or spread of pests.

4. To prevent or limit other damage within the territory of the member from the entry, establishment, or spread of pests.

Questions for Discussion After Conclusion of Simulation

1. How does your solution compare to your expectation of the likely actual outcome? What is different or similar in the two approaches?

2. How would you characterize the cultures of Europe (France and Germany) and the United States in terms of Hofstede's scheme? In what ways are the cultures similar, and in what ways do they differ? How might the differences influence approaches to disputes like this one?

3. Why would an approach emphasizing "substantial equivalence" result in an outcome different from the outcome of a policy driven by the "precautionary principle"?

4. How might the United States and EU resolve differences such as this in the future?

Source: © McGraw-Hill Irwin. This simulation was prepared by Professor Jonathan Doh as the basis for class discussion. It is not intended to illustrate either effective or ineffective managerial capability or administrative responsibility.

■ Notes

1. Scott Miller, "EU's New Rules Will Shake Up Market for Bioengineered Food," *Wall Street Journal,* April 16, 2004, p. A1.

2. Kerry Capell, "The Genetically Modified Food Fight," *BusinessWeek Online,* July 21, 2003, bw.com/news/941856. asp?0dm=C18LB.

3. Elizabeth Becker, "U.S. Contests Europe's Ban on Some Food," *New York Times,* May 13, 2003, p. B4.

4. Nina V. Fedoroff, "Genetically Modified Foods: Making the Earth Say Beans," *Science Journal,* Penn State Eberly College of Science, vol. 26, Spring 2007.

5. *Bacillus thuringiensis,* www.bt.ucsd.edu.

6. John Hulsman, "Cherry-Picking: U.S. and European Relationship," Heritage Foundation, www.heritage.org/research/tradeandforeignaid/tst061103.cfm.

7. Mark Drajem, "EU Pledges to Begin Approving Gene-Modified Crops This Year," *Bloomberg News,* June 17, 2003.

8. Jeremy Rifkin, "The Fight over GMO Crops Exposes the Weaknesses of Globalization," *The Guardian,* June 2, 2003, p. 16.

9. Becker, "U.S. Contests Europe's Ban on Some Food."

10. Regulatory Compliance Systems, LLC, "Precautionary Principle will 'Run in Place' in 2007, Trade Expert Predicts," *Pesticide. net Insider eJournal* 4, no. 2 (January 30, 2007).

11. Jerry Perkins, "Iowa StarLink Costs $9.2 Million—Aventis CropScience Pays Claims to Farmers, Elevators," *Des Moines Register,* September 15, 2001.

12. The Center for Urban Education about Sustainable Agriculture (CUESA), "News about Our Food's Genes," *Weekly Newsletter,* March 3, 2007.

13. Sara Fitzgerald, "Putting the EU in Its Place: Why Filing a GMO Case with the WTO Is Crucial," Heritage Foundation, www.heritage. org/research/Europe/em855.cfm.

14. GMO Compass, "Majority of Europeans Believe Biotech Will Improve Quality of Life," June 20, 2006, www.gmo-compass. org/eng/news/messages/200606.docu.html.

15. John Connor, "GM Corn Variety Classed as Safe," *New Zealand Herald,* July 7, 2002, p. A6.

16. Becker, "U.S. Contests Europe's Ban on Some Food."

17. John Schoen, "Is This Biotech Boom for Real?" www.msnbc.com/news/930313. asp?0dm=L1BmB, June 23, 2003.

18. Press release from Friends of the Earth Europe, www.foeeurope.org/press/2003/AW_18_Aug_ GMO_trade_war.htm, August 18, 2003.

19. Regulatory Compliance Systems, "Precautionary Principle will 'Run in Place' in 2007."

20. Sybille de La Hamaide, "Europe GMO Area to Surge over 10 Years: Monsanto," Reuters, June 25, 2007.

21. Miller, "EU's New Rules."

22. "Better GMO Labelling Backed by a Million Europeans," Euractiv.com, February 5, 2007.

23. "Australia Struggles to Win Support for GMO Crops," Reuters, March 10, 2005.

24. Interview with Keith Dittrich, president of the American Corn Growers Association, June 12, 2003.

25. Arpad Pusztai, "Genetically Modified Foods: Are They a Risk to Human/Animal Health?" http://www.mindfully.org/GE/GE2/Pusztai-Risk-To-Health.htm.

26. Daniel Levine, "Mapping a New Plan for Biotech," *San Francisco Business Times,* March 10, 2003, p. 12.

27. Crystal Davis, "Genetically Modified Crops May Boost African Agriculture," *Earth Trends,* World Resources Institute, January 16, 2007, earthtrends.wri.org/updates/ node/142.

2. Cross-Cultural Conflicts in the Corning–Vitro Joint Venture

This simulation accompanies Brief Integrative Case 1 at the end of Part 2. It is designed to develop skills at international negotiation with an emphasis on cross-cultural communication and negotiation.

Case Summary

During the NAFTA negotiations, many U.S. firms were concerned about the reduction of U.S. tariffs on flat glass, which averaged 20 percent, and the perceived competitive advantages Mexican glass firms would have in the event these tariffs were removed. In the fall of 1991, in the midst of the NAFTA negotiations, Vitro S.A., the $3 billion Mexican glassmaker, signed a tentative $800 million joint venture with Corning Inc. Two mirror companies were established—Corning-Vitro and Vitro-Corning— and each company took an equity stake in each of these joint-venture firms. In addition, the two parent companies agreed to a series of marketing, sales, and distribution relationships to support the activities of each of the new companies.[1] Two years later, the joint venture was in distress, and some of the interested parties were suggesting that it be dissolved. This simulation provides participants with an opportunity to undertake negotiations designed to resolve these differences.

Background

Vitro Sociedad Anonima is a 100-year-old Mexican company with roughly $3.5 billion in sales and 40,000 employees. As Vitro positioned itself to take advantage of the emerging North American market, CEO Ernesto Martens-Rebolledo described the tightrope the company must walk: "We don't want to lose our identity as a Mexican company with a unique culture and relationship with our employees, but we don't want to be battered in the world marketplace either."[2] In 1989 Vitro completed a hostile takeover of Anchor Glass Container Corporation, and in 1992 Vitro laid off some 3,000 workers, an unusual move in Mexico at that time, given traditional notions about labor-management relations and job security.

Corning, an upstate New York maker of glass, traces its roots back to the mid-1800s. In recent years, Corning has diversified into fiber optics and other high-technology applications of glass, ceramics, and composite materials. During the 1980s, Corning's business increasingly relied on sales of fiber optics to telecommunications firms. These firms were beginning construction of the new infrastructure to support high-speed voice and data transmission. At the same time, sales of household, flat glass, and other traditional glass products remained important to the company.

NAFTA and Glass[3]

During the early part of NAFTA negotiations (1989– 1991), U.S. makers of household and flat glass products expressed concern about their ability to compete against cheaper Mexican imports, and some even accused Corning S.A. of unfair trading practices. Guardian Industries Corp., a Michigan-based manufacturer of float glass—the high-quality flat glass used in mirrors, insulated windows, furniture, and automobiles—complained that Vitro, the only Mexican producer of float glass, was engaged in anticompetitive practices by trying to intimidate a Mexican glass distributor that was considering buying a product from Guardian. Vitro exported approximately $120 million in float glass and related products to the United States in 1990. Other glassmakers argued that even with present U.S. duties averaging over 20 percent on household glassware from Mexico, the after-duty prices of the Mexican products were significantly below those of U.S. producers, owing in large part to considerably lower labor and energy costs.

In February 1991, the International Trade Commission (ITC) issued a report on these allegations. Vitro Crisa (an operating subsidiary of Vitro S.A.) allegedly priced its glass beverageware at about 20 to 30 percent below that of U.S. producers in the U.S. market. Vitro Crisa's lower productivity relative to U.S. industry, said the ITC, was offset by considerably lower labor costs (about $1.50 an hour versus $15 an hour in 1987 in the United States), which constituted nearly half of the production costs of the U.S. household glassware industry. The cost of natural gas, another major production input, was about 15 percent lower in Mexico.

Problems Arise[4]

"Vitro and Corning share a customer-oriented philosophy and remarkably similar corporate cultures." This was the characterization of the joint venture offered at the time by Julio Escamez, a Vitro executive. Both companies had long histories of successful joint ventures. Corning Inc. had been an innovative leader in foreign alliances for over 73 years. One of the company's first successes was an alliance with St. Gobain, a French glassmaker, to produce Pyrex cookware in Europe during the 1920s. Corning has formed approximately 50 ventures over the years. Only nine failed (dissolved), an impressive number considering one recent study found that over one-half of foreign and national alliances do not succeed. From 1985 to 1990, Corning's sales from joint ventures were over $3 billion, contributing more than $500 million to its net income. Corning enters into joint ventures primarily to gain access to markets that it cannot penetrate quickly enough to obtain a competitive advantage. In addition, both companies were globally oriented, and both had founding families still at their centers. Yet the joint venture became subject to a series of cultural and other conflicts that began to undermine this vision.

U.S.-Mexico Alliances[5]

"There are many reasons why corporate marriages between Mexican and U.S. companies fail," says Richard Sinkin, managing director of InterAmerican Holdings, a consultancy based in San Diego, California, that advises U.S. companies doing business in Mexico. Sinkin says that U.S. and Mexican companies often get together for the wrong reasons. Unless the two partners contribute essential qualities to the marriage, the alliance soon founders. The second difficulty is corporate control. "Most Mexican firms are still run as family businesses," Sinkin says, "and these firms are often reluctant to share control with an outside investor."

In the case of the Corning/Vitro JV, Corning managers said that they were sometimes left waiting for important decisions about marketing and sales because in the Mexican culture only top managers could make them and at Vitro those people were busy with other matters. Vitro's sales approach was less aggressive than Corning's, the remnant of years in a closed economy, and was sometimes at odds with the pragmatic approach Corning had developed over decades of competition.

NAFTA and Alliances[6]

To varying degrees, such cultural issues have plagued many mergers and alliances with their roots in the North American Free Trade Agreement. "Mexico initially appears to be the United States except that people speak Spanish," said Harley Shaiken, a labor economist who often works in Mexico. "That's just not the case, which everyone finds out in the short term rather than the long term." The trade pact may have created false expectations about how much like the United States Mexico has become. In discussing cultural differences, it's difficult not to slip into stereotypes about "mañana"—Mexicans who move at a slower pace. But what the gap separating the two business cultures really amounts to is a different approach to work, reflected in everything from scheduling to decision making to etiquette.

In the Corning venture, the Mexicans sometimes saw the Americans as too direct, and Vitro managers, in their dogged pursuit of politeness, sometimes seemed to the Americans unwilling to acknowledge problems and faults. The Mexicans sometimes thought Corning moved too fast; the Americans felt Vitro was too slow.

Cultural differences generally, said Richard Sinkin, the corporate consultant, are "the No. 1 problem for doing business in Mexico." That may be an exaggeration, but it underscores the difficulty of transferring a culture across the border. Sinkin's own experience bears that out. He is bilingual and often works in Mexico but finds that it isn't always easy to get paid because the Mexican view of contracts differs markedly from the view commonly held in the United States. In Mexico, the terms of a contract "are kind of ideal things that you strive to achieve," Sinkin said, "while in the U.S. they are law." In general, corporate style is more formal in Mexico than in the United States. Titles are common, and nearly everyone is "licenciado," which loosely refers to having any professional training. Forgetting the honorific can be seen as a serious insult.

In Mexico, executives can expect the unquestioned loyalty of employees, but outsiders are often viewed with mistrust. Horace E. Scherer, director general of Hobart Dayton Mexicana, the Mexican subsidiary of the Hobart Corporation, said his salespeople must often make four trips to complete one transaction because of that lack of trust. To sell the company's scales and other equipment, a salesperson starts with a visit to the client's top official. If a sale is made, a representative of the company itself must deliver the goods because the customer won't accept delivery from DHL or some other service. If all the papers are in order on delivery, the company representative is told to come back on an appointed day to present an invoice, in person; if the invoice is accepted, an appointment is made for the rep to return to receive payment.

Many companies that have formed joint ventures end up creating their own new corporate culture, taking bits and pieces from each side. At Vitro-Whirlpool in Monterrey, assembly-line workers have a long tradition of taking what in Mexico is referred to as "el puente," or the bridge, which commonly extends a formal holiday into a mini-vacation. When, for instance, Mexico's version of Mother's Day fell on Tuesday, May 10, workers did not show up on Monday, bridging the gap to the holiday. (If an American holiday falls on a Tuesday, of course, absenteeism will be high on Monday, but in Mexico the custom is far more entrenched—and can even shut a plant down.) The company now allows workers to take the "puente," but only if they agree to work an extra hour each day for eight days beforehand.

Because their corporate conversations can be filled with so many feints and pleasantries, Mexicans often use memos to convey dissatisfaction. When Labatt's (the Canadian brewer) Mexican manager, Noel Trainor, decided to cut back employees' lunch from two hours to one, he had to do it in a memo that all 30 employees had to sign. Trainor said he abided by a strict holiday policy, priding himself on the degree to which his compatriots had been able to adapt to the expectations of the United States and seemingly only half aware of the degree to which he had compromised. "We only give what we are obligated by law to give," he said, "and of course half a day on Mother's Day."

Financial and Commercial Concerns[7]

Added complications emerged from the relatively strong peso, increased overseas competition, and a reconsideration of marketing strategies by both companies. The joint ventures suffered from the different administrative practices of the two companies. "Managing from two countries was more complicated than we anticipated," said Corning. "There were different (management) structures, styles and accounting systems." Corning said the different needs of customers in the United States and Mexico complicated the integration of sales and distribution. Corning's U.S. customers, especially the large discount stores, expect the timely and regular delivery of products packaged in a certain way; Vitro's Mexican customers are less demanding.

In 1992, Corning-Vitro had sales of approximately $700 million, and Vitro-Corning achieved turnover of about $230 million.

Issues for Decision

As a result of cultural clashes, failure to integrate complementary product lines, and disappointing sales, both Corning and Vitro are contemplating dissolving the joint ventures. Within the two companies, however, there are those who support maintaining the relationship, and others who oppose it. Corning and Vitro must first decide on whether they want to remain in the joint ventures and, if they do, under what conditions. If they decide to dissolve the relationship, they must negotiate the terms of the dissolution. If they decide to remain in the arrangement, some changes must be made to address the growing problems.

Simulation Instructions

You will be assigned to one of four groups.

The groups are ad hoc. Each group represents an ad-hoc committee appointed by the CEO of each company to make recommendations about the future of the alliance. The groups' initial positions can be characterized as follows:

1. Vitro—supports keeping JVs
2. Vitro—against keeping JVs
3. Corning—supports keeping JVs
4. Corning—against keeping JVs

Negotiation 1

The initial negotiation occurs *within* each company. Hence, Vitro Groups (1 and 2) discuss their differing positions, and Corning Groups (3 and 4) exchange their views with each other. Each pair of groups (1/2 + 3/4) should decide whether their company wants to remain within the joint venture or dissolve it. Each pair of groups has 45 minutes to negotiate *within* the respective companies over whether

to stay in or dissolve the JV. Groups 1 and 3 should consider the following:

1. The logic and original rationale for the JV.
2. How that logic may still hold.
3. How the JV could be made to work better.

Groups 2 and 4 should consider the following:

1. What caused the JV relationship to sour.
2. Why the partner has not lived up to expectations.
3. What the terms of dissolution should be.

Each company agrees on a position to bring forward to the partner. This position need not necessarily be a demand to maintain the joint venture or to dissolve it; rather it could be a contingency laying the conditions for maintaining the relationship, or demands for how it should be dissolved. Once each company has decided on its position, representatives from each Corning group (two to four representatives total) will meet with their counterparts from the Vitro groups.

Negotiation 2

Each company must decide, collectively, through negotiation, whether to remain within the joint venture or dissolve it. The representatives from each company have 60 minutes to reach some resolution. *They must consult with the remainder of their company throughout the negotiation to ensure support for the outcome.* The main issues for consideration include:

1. The logic and original rationale for the JV.
2. How that logic may still hold.
3. How the JV could be made to work better.
4. What caused the JV relationship to sour.
5. Why the partner has not lived up to expectations.
6. Whether the JV should be terminated and, if so, what the terms of dissolution should be.

Ultimately, issue 3 or 6 must be resolved. Any solution, whether to maintain the JV, dissolve it, or some hybrid approach, should be comprehensive and address these elements:

- *Financial structure:* Terms for financing existing or new ventures under the arrangement or payments for dissolution of the relationship.
- *Governance:* Board, management, or other top-level changes in ownership and leadership under the present or revised relationship.
- *Marketing:* Agreements about marketing, distribution, and sales relationships either under the current arrangement or in any new structure.
- *Competition/cooperation:* Changes in the way in which each company operates in the other's territories or markets.

Table 1
Hofstede's Cultural Ratings for the United States and Key Latin Countries

	Power Distance	Uncertainty Avoidance	Individualism	Masculinity
United States	40	46	91	62
Mexico	81	82	38	69
Canada	39	48	80	52
Argentina	49	86	46	56
Brazil	69	76	38	49
Colombia	67	80	13	64
Peru	64	87	16	42
Venezuela	81	76	12	73
Spain	57	86	51	42
Portugal	63	104	27	31

Source: Geert Hofstede, *Culture's Consequences: International Differences in Work-Related Values* (Beverly Hills, CA: Sage, 1980).

Questions for Discussion After Conclusion of Simulation

1. Compare your solution to the joint venture's problems with the actual outcome. What is different or similar in the two approaches?

2. How would you characterize the Mexican and U.S. culture in terms of Hofstede's scheme (see Table 1)? In what ways were the cultures similar and in what ways were they different?

3. Compare Corning-Vitro's problems to those of some of the other international joint ventures described in this simulation. How were they similar, different, and more or less challenging?

4. How have other companies in Mexico and Latin America addressed these cultural divisions in the recent past? How should they do so as they go forward with comprehensive regional Latin American strategies?

Source: © McGraw-Hill Irwin. This simulation was prepared by Jonathan Doh of Villanova University as the basis for class discussion. It is not intended to illustrate either effective or ineffective managerial capability or administrative responsibility.

■ Notes

1. "Glassmakers' Complaints Aired in NAFTA Hearings," *LDC Debt Report/Latin American Market,* September 9, 1999, p. 10.

2. Nancy A. Nichols, "From Complacency to Competitiveness: An Interview with Vitro's Ernesto Martens," *Harvard Business Review,* September–October 1993, p. 162.

3. "Glassmakers' Complaints Aired in NAFTA Hearings."

4. Anthony Depalma, "It Takes More than a Visa to Do Business in Mexico," *New York Times,* June 26, 1994, sec. 3, p. 5.

5. Leslie Crawford, "Anheuser's Cross-Border Marriage on the Rocks: Modelo Deal Is the Latest U.S.-Mexican Partnership to Be Soured by Disagreement," *Financial Times,* March 18, 1998, p. 46.

6. Depalma, "It Takes More than a Visa."

7. John Holusha, "Corning to Buy Northern Telecom Assets," *New York Times,* December 16, 1993, sec. D, p. 4.

References

■ Chapter 1

International Management in Action: Tracing the Roots of Modern Globalization Thomas Cahill, *Sailing the Wine Dark Sea: Why Greeks Matter* (New York: Doubleday, 2003), pp. 10, 56–57; Charles W. L. Hill, *International Business,* 4th ed. (New York: McGraw-Hill Irwin, 2003), p. 100; Nefertiti Web site, http://nefertiti.iweland.com/trade/internal_ trade.htm, 2003 (ancient Egypt: domestic trade); Gavin Menzies, *1421: The Year China Discovered America* (New York: William Morrow/HarperCollins, 2003), pp. 26–27; Milton Viorst, *The Great Documents of Western Civilization* (New York: Barnes & Noble Books, 1994), p. 115 (Magna Carta) and p. 168 (Declaration of Independence).

International Management in Action: Telecommunications Privatization in Brazil Simon Romero, "Brazil Still Embraces Globalization," *New York Times,* December 2, 1999, p. C1; "Brazil's Dozen Phone Spinoffs Come to Trade in New York," *New York Times,* November 17, 1998, p. C12; Edward A. Robinson, "Update: Telebras Pieces Fetch High Prices," *Fortune,* September 7, 1998, p. 181; Al Goodman, "Spanish Phone Utility Extends Its Latin American Leadership," *New York Times,* August 4, 1998, p. D7; Jonathan Wheatley, "Brazil: A Hot Incubator For Tech Startups," BusinessWeek online, July 25, 2005, http://www.businessweek.com/magazine/content/05_30/b3944085_mz058.htm?chan=gb.

International Management in Action: Recognizing Cultural Differences Garry Kasparov, "Putin's Gangster State," *Wall Street Journal,* March 30, 2007, p. A15; The Economist Intelligence Unit, *Country Report: Russia* (Kent, UK: EIU, 2007), p. 7; "Trust the Locals," *The Economist* 382, January 25, 2007, pp. 55–56.

In the International Spotlight: India John F. Burns, "India Now Winning U.S. Investment," *New York Times,* February 6, 1995, pp. C1, C5; Rahual Jacob, "India Gets Moving," *Fortune,* September 5, 1994, pp. 101–102; Jon E. Hilsenrath, "Honda Venture Takes the Bumps in India," *Wall Street Journal,* August 2, 2000, p. A18; Manjeet Kripalani and Pete Engardio, "India: A Shocking Election Upset Means India Must Spend Heavily on Social Needs," *BusinessWeek,* May 31, 2004; Steve Hamm, "The Trouble with India,' *BusinessWeek*, March 19, 2007, pp. 48–58.

■ Chapter 2

International Management in Action: The U.S. Goes to the Mat Brian Brenner, "Why Taming the China Dragon Is Tricky," BusinessWeek Online, April 23, 2007; "China Tries to Tap the Brakes on Economic Growth," *Wall Street Journal,* December 26, 2003, p. A9; "US-China Trade Friction Getting Hotter," *China Economic Review,* as appearing in BusinessWeek Online, May 7, 2007; Michael M. Phillips, "Congress Fumes as China Talks Show Few Gains," *Wall Street Journal,* May 24, 2007, p. A1.

In the International Spotlight: Vietnam Frederik Balfour, "Back on the Radar Screen," *BusinessWeek,* November 20, 2000, pp. 56–57; Jon E. Hilsenrath, "U.S. Investors See Hope in Vietnam Trip," *Wall Street Journal,* November 17, 2000, p. A17; Roy Rowan, "25 Years After the Fall," *Fortune,* May 1, 2000, pp. 208–222; Wayne Arnold, "Trade Accord with Vietnam: Exports in Place of Enmity," *New York Times,* July 28, 2000, p. C4; Ha Thank Nguyen and Klaus E. Meyer, "Managing Partnerships with State-Owned Joint Venture Companies: Experiences From Vietnam," *Business Strategy Review* 15 (Spring 2004), p. 39; James Hookway, "WTO Entry No Cure-All for Vietnam," *Wall Street Journal,* November 8, 2006. www.wsj.com.

■ Chapter 3

International Management in Action: Get Tough . . . Or Else Richard Behar, "Beijing's Phony War on Fakes," *Fortune,* October 30, 2000, pp. 189–208; Robin Stanley Snell and Choo-sin Tseng, "Ethical Dilemmas of Relationship Building in China," *Thunderbird International Business Review,* March–April 2001, pp. 171–200; Brian Brenner, "Why Taming the China Dragon Is Tricky," BusinessWeek Online, April 23, 2007; "US-China Trade Friction Getting Hotter," *China Economic Review,* as appearing in BusinessWeek Online, May 7, 2007; Michael M. Phillips, " Congress Fumes as China Talks Show Few Gains," *Wall Street Journal,* May 24, 2007, p. A1; Richard McGregor, "Hu Trip to Seattle Lifts Hopes on Piracy Policy," *Financial Times,* April 19, 2006, p. 4; Bi Mingxin, "Microsoft Unveils Huge China Plans," *Shanghai Daily,* April 23, 2007.

In the International Spotlight: Saudi Arabia Neil Macfarquhar, "After the Saudi Rampage, Questions and Few Answers," *New York Times,* June 1, 2004, p. A6; "Rising Stars," *Airfinance Journal,* September 2002, p. 50.

■ Chapter 4

International Management in Action: Business Customs in South Africa www.kwintessential.co.uk/resources/globaletiquette/south-africa-country-profile.html; Going Global Inc., "Cultural Advice," *South Africa Career Guide, 2006.* Accessed at content.epnet.com.ps2.villanova.edu/pdf18_21/pdf/2006/ONI/01Jan06/22291722.pdf.

International Management in Action: Common Personal Values George W. England, "Managers and Their Value Systems: A Five-Country Comparative Study," *Columbia Journal of World Business,* Summer 1978, pp. 35–44; Geert Hofstede, *Culture's Consequences: International Differences in Work-Related Values* (Beverly Hills, CA: Sage, 1980); Geert Hofstede, *Cultures and Organizations: Software of the Mind* (London: McGraw-Hill U.K., 1991); Martin J. Gannon, *Understanding Global Cultures,* 2nd ed. (Thousand Oaks, CA: Sage, 2001), pp. 35–56.

In the International Spotlight: Taiwan Michael J. Marquardt and Dean W. Engel, *Global Human Resource Development* (Englewood Cliffs, NJ: Prentice-Hall, 1993), pp. 183–186; "China (Taiwan)," *Europa World Year Book 1995,* vol. 1 (London: Europa Publications, 1995), pp. 833–842; Brian Bremmer et al., "Asia: The Big Chill," *BusinessWeek,* April 2, 2001, pp. 48–49; Andy Reinhardt, "A Silicon Chameleon Challenges Intel," *BusinessWeek,* May 29, 2000, pp. 102–106; Raj Aggarwal, "Assessing the Recent Asian Economic Crises: The Role of Virtuous and Vicious Cycles," *Journal of World Business* 34, no. 4 (1999) pp. 392–408; Jason Dean, "Taiwan Economy Is a Winner;

Analysts Are Bullish on Stocks No Matter Election's Outcome," *Wall Street Journal,* March 19, 2004, p. C16; David Lague, "The Result Is Final: A Divided Taiwan," *Far Eastern Economic Review,* April 1, 2004, pp. 14–17.

■ Chapter 5

International Management in Action: Ten Key Factors for MNC Success James F. Bolt, "Global Competitors: Some Criteria for Success," *Business Horizons,* January–February 1988, pp. 34–41; Alan S. Rugman and Richard M. Hodgetts, *International Business,* 2nd ed. (London: Pearson, 2000), chapter 1; and Sheida Hodge, *Global Smarts: The Art of Communicating and Deal Making Anywhere in the World* (New York: Wiley, 2000).

International Management in Action: Managing in Hong Kong J. Stewart Black and Lyman W. Porter, "Managerial Behaviors and Job Performance: A Successful Manager in Los Angeles May Not Succeed in Hong Kong," *Journal of International Business Studies,* 22, no. 1 (First Quarter 1991), pp. 99–112; Geert Hofstede, *Cultures and Organizations: Software of the Mind* (London: McGraw-Hill U.K., 1991), chapters 4–6; Alan S. Rugman and Richard M. Hodgetts, *International Business,* 2nd ed. (London: Pearson, 2000), chapter 20; Benjamin Fulford, "Microwave Missionaries," *Forbes,* November 13, 2000, pp. 136–146.

In the International Spotlight: Mexico David Wessel, Paul B. Carroll, and Thomas T. Vogel Jr., "How Mexico's Crisis Ambushed Top Minds in Officialdom, Finance," *Wall Street Journal,* July 6, 1995, pp. A1, A4; Craig Torres and Paul B. Carroll, "Mexico's Mantra for Salvation: Export, Export, Export," *Wall Street Journal,* March 17, 1995, p. A6; "Mexico," *Europa* (London: Europa Publications, 1995), pp. 429–444; Carlta Vitzthum and Nicole Harris, "Telefonica Makes Its Move into Mexico," *Wall Street Journal,* October 5, 2000, p. A19; Joel Millman, "Mexico Factories See Growth Unchecked," *Wall Street Journal,* November 6, 2000, p. A29; David Luhnow, "Mexico's Economy Hints at Rebound, Aided Once Again by U.S. Ties," *Wall Street Journal,* January 13, 2004, p. A2; Ken Bensinger, "Trade Bandwagon Sweeps Up Mexico, but Critics Say Pacts Create Mixed Results," *Houston Chronicle,* April 2, 2004, p. 1.

■ Chapter 6

International Management in Action: Doing Things the Wal-Mart Way, Germans Say, "Nein vielen Dank" Mark Landler and Michael Barbaro, "Wal-Mart Finds That Its Formula Doesn't Fit Every Culture, " *New York Times,* August 2, 2006, http://www.nytimes.com/2006/08/02/business/worldbusiness/02walmart.html.

International Management in Action: Matsushita Goes Global P. Christopher Earley and Harbir Singh, "International and Intercultural Management Research: What's Next," *Academy of Management Journal,* June 1995, pp. 327–340; Karen Lowry Miller, "Siemens Shapes Up," *BusinessWeek,* May 1, 1995, pp. 52–53; Christine M. Riordan and Robert J. Vandenberg, "A Central Question in Cross-Cultural Research: Do Employees of Different Cultures Interpret Work-Related Measures in an Equivalent Manner?" *Journal of Management* 20, no. 3 (1994), pp. 643–671; Brenton R. Schlender, "Matsushita Shows How to Go Global," *Fortune,* July 11, 1994, pp. 159–166.

In the International Spotlight: Japan Iain McDonald, "Japan's Industrial Production Rises 3.3% Amid Payroll Gains," *Wall Street Journal,* June 1, 2004. p. A14; Ian Rowley, "Japan Isn't Buying the Wal-Mart Idea," *BusinessWeek,* February 28, 2005, www.businessweek.com/magazine/content/05_09/b3922073.htm.

■ Chapter 7

International Management in Action: Doing It Right the First Time www.jetro.gp.ip/JETROINFO/DOING/4.html; Alan Rugman and Richard M. Hodgetts, *International Business,* 2nd ed. (London: Pearson, 2000), chapter 17; Philip R. Harris and Robert T. Moran, *Managing Cultural Differences,* 3rd ed. (Houston: Gulf Publishing, 1991), pp. 393–406; Sheila Hodge, *Global Smarts* (New York: Wiley, 2000), p. 76; Richard D. Lewis, *When Cultures Collide* (London: Nicholas Brealey, 1999), pp. 414–415.

International Management in Action: Communicating in Europe Karen Matthes, "Mind Your Manners When Doing Business in Europe," *Personnel,* January 1992, p. 19; Philip R. Harris and Robert T. Moran, *Managing Cultural Differences: High-Performance Strategies for a New World of Business,* 4th ed. (Houston: Gulf Publishing, 1994), chapter 13; Alan Rugman and Richard M. Hodgetts, *International Business,* 2nd ed. (London: Pearson, 2000), chapter 16; Richard Lewis, *When Cultures Collide* (London: Nicholas Brealey, 1999).

International Management in Action: Negotiating with the Japanese Rosalie J. Tung, "How to Negotiate with the Japanese," *California Management Review,* Summer 1984, pp. 62–77; Carla Rapoport, "You Can Make Money in Japan," *Fortune,* February 12, 1990, pp. 85–92; Margaret A. Neale and Max H. Bazerman, "Negotiating Rationally," *Academy of Management Executive,* August 1992, pp. 42–51; Martin J. Gannon, *Understanding Global Cultures,* 2nd ed. (Thousand Oaks, CA: Sage, 2001), pp. 35–56; Sheila Hodge, *Global Smarts* (New York: Wiley, 2000), chapter 14; and Richard D. Lewis, *When Cultures Collide* (London: Nicholas Brealey, 1999), pp. 400–415.

In the International Spotlight: China Patricia O'Connell, "Huawei vs. Cisco Just Got Nastier," *BusinessWeek,* June 3, 2003; Edward Cody, "China's Government Tries to Calm Economic Boom," *Washington Post,* May 19, 2004, p. E1; Bruce Einhorn and Peter Burrows, "Huawei: Cisco's Rival Hangs Tough," *BusinessWeek,* January 19, 2004, p. 73.

■ Chapter 8

International Management in Action: Point/Counterpoint Wendy Bonds, "Fuji, Accused by Kodak of Hogging Markets, Spits Back: 'You Too,'" *Wall Street Journal,* July 31, 1995, pp. A1, A5; "Photo Wars: Shuttered," *Economist,* August 5, 1995, pp. 59–60; Mark Maremont, "Next a Flap over Film," *BusinessWeek,* July 10, 1995, p. 34; "Japan's Fuji Photo Film's Group Operating Profit Rose in FY 2000," *Asia Pulse,* May 8, 2001; and "Kodak Says Profit Outlook Unchanged," Reuters, May 23, 2001.

International Management in Action: How Telecom Is Revolutionizing Economies at the Base of Pyramid Jack Ewing, "Upwardly Mobile in Africa," *BusinessWeek online,* September 13, 2007.

In the International Spotlight: Poland David Fairlamb and Bogdan Turek, "Poland and the EU: Will the Dynamic Poles Energize Europe or Sink into a Bureaucratic, Slow-Growth Trap?" *BusinessWeek,* May 10, 2004, p. 54; Ben Arisin Prague, "Central European Entrants to EU Have Most to Gain but Are Least Prepared," *Knight Ridder Tribune Business News,* March 14, 2004. p. 1.

You Be the International Management Consultant: Go East, Young People, Go East Amy Borrus et al., "The Asians Are Bracing for a Trade Shoot-Out," *BusinessWeek,* May 1, 1989, pp. 40–41; John W. Verity, "If It Looks Like a Slump and Crawls Like a Slump . . . ," *BusinessWeek,* May 1, 1989, p. 27; Geoff Lewis, "Is the Computer Business Maturing?" *BusinessWeek,* March 6, 1989, pp. 68–78.

■ Chapter 9

International Management in Action: Joint Venturing in Russia
Keith A. Rosten, "Soviet–U.S. Joint Ventures: Pioneers on a New Frontier," *California Management Review,* Winter 1991, pp. 88–108; Steven Greenhouse, "Chevron to Spend $10 Billion to Seek Oil in Kazakhstan," *New York Times,* May 19, 1992, pp. A1, C9; Louis Uchitelle, "Givebacks by Chevron in Oil Deal," *New York Times,* May 23, 1992, pp. 17, 29; Craig Mellow, "Russia: Making Cash from Chaos," *Fortune,* April 17, 1995, pp. 145–151; Daniel J. McCarthy and Sheila M. Puffer, "Strategic Investment Flexibility for MNE Success in Russia," *Journal of World Business* 32, no. 4 (1997), pp. 293–318; R. Bruce Money and Debra Colton, "The Response of the 'New Consumer' to Promotion in the Transition Economies of the Former Soviet Bloc," *Journal of World Business* 35, no. 2 (2000), pp. 189–206.

International Management in Action: Organizing in Germany
Hermann Simon, "Lessons from Germany's Midsize Giants," *Harvard Business Review,* March–April 1992, pp. 115–123; Carla Rapoport, "Europe's Slump Won't End Soon," *Fortune,* May 3, 1993, pp. 82–87; Robert Neff and Douglas Harbrecht, "Germany's Mighty Unions Are Being Forced to Bend," *BusinessWeek,* March 1, 1993, pp. 52–56.

In the International Spotlight: Australia Wayne Arnold, "World Business Briefing: Australia's Jobless Rate Falls," *New York Times,* April 9, 2004, p. W1; "Finance and Economics: A Wonder Down Under—The Australian Economy," *Economist,* March 20, 2004, p. 105.

■ Chapter 10

International Management in Action: Sometimes It's All Politics
John Stackhouse, "India Sours on Foreign Investment," *Globe and Mail,* August 10, 1995, sec. 2, pp. 1–2; Peter Galuszka and Susan Chandler, "A Plague of Disjointed Ventures," *BusinessWeek,* May 1, 1995, p. 55; Marcus W. Brauchli, "Politics Threaten Power Project in India," *Wall Street Journal,* July 3, 1995, p. A14; "Enron, and On and On," *Economist,* April 21, 2001, pp. 56–57; Saritha Rai, "Enron Unit Moves to End India Contract for Power," *New York Times,* May 22, 2001, pp. W1, W7; Enron Properties Outside the U.S. Hit Auction Block, *Wall Street Journal,* January, 22, 2002, p. A6.

In the International Spotlight: Brazil *CIA Factbook* (2001); Jonathan Wheatley, "Is Lula's Honeymoon Winding Down?" *Business-Week,* April 26, 2004, p. 59; "BellSouth's Latin Ambitions," *Business-Week Online,* October 20, 2003; Larry Rohter, "Brrazil's President Re-elected in Landslide," New York Times, October 29, 2006, p. A1.

■ Chapter 11

International Management in Action: Kodak's Corner Wendy Bonds, "Fuji, Accused by Kodak of Hogging Markets, Spits Back: 'You Too,'" *Wall Street Journal,* July 31, 1995, pp. A1, A5; "Kodak Completes Acquisition of Leading Online Photo Service" Kodak Company news release, June 4, 2001.

International Management in Action: How the Japanese Do Things Differently Ford S. Worthy, "Japan's Smart Secret Weapon," *Fortune,* August 12, 1991, pp. 72–75; Brenton R. Schlender, "Hard Times for High Tech," *Fortune,* March 22, 1993, p. 98; Ronald Henkoff, "Companies That Train Best," *Fortune,* March 22, 1993; Jim Carlton, "Sega Leaps Ahead by Shipping New Player Early," *Wall Street Journal,* May 11, 1995, pp. B1, B3; Jeffrey K. Liker and Yen-Chun Wu, "Japanese Automakers, U.S. Suppliers and Supply-Chain Superiority," *Sloan Management Review,* Fall 2000, pp. 81–93.

In the International Spotlight: Spain Angela Sormani, "Hidden Treasure Spain Is Flourishing," *Venture Capital Journal,* October 1, 2003, p. 1.

■ Chapter 12

International Management in Action: McDonald's New Latin Flavor "Putting the Front Line First: McDonald's commitment to employees bolsters the bottom line," *Hewitt,* Vol. 9, Issue 1, http://www.hewittassociates.com/intl/na/en-us/KnowledgeCenter/Magazine/vol9_iss1/departments-upclose.html.

International Management in Action: Karoshi: Stressed Out in Japan Michael Zielenziger, "Alcohol Consumption a Rising Problem in Japan," *Miami Herald,* December 28, 2000, p. 10A; Howard K. French, "A Postmodern Plague Ravages Japan's Workers," *New York Times,* February 21, 2000, p. A4; William S. Brown, Rebecca E. Lubove, and James Kwalwasser, "Karoshi: Alternative Perspectives of Japanese Management Styles," *Business Horizons,* March–April 1994, pp. 58–60; Karen Lowry Miller, "Now, Japan Is Admitting It: Work Kills Executives," *BusinessWeek,* August 3, 1992, p. 35.

In the International Spotlight: Singapore Philip Day, "The Lion Roars," *Far Eastern Economic Review,* June 3, 2004, p. 50; "Business Outlook: Singapore," *Country Monitor,* April 5, 2004, p. 3; "Economic Outlook: Singapore," *Business Asia,* August 11, 2003, p. 7; "Solectron to Open Center in Singapore," *Manufacturing & Technology News,* January 3, 2006.

■ Chapter 13

International Management in Action: Global Teams Jitao Li, Katherine R. Xin, Anne Tsui, and Donald C. Hambrick, "Building Effective International Joint Venture Leadership Teams in China," *Journal of World Business* 34, no. 1 (1999), pp. 52–68; Charlene Marmer Solomon, "Global Teams: The Ultimate Collaboration," *Personnel Journal,* September 1995, pp. 49–58; Andrew Kakabdse and Andrew Myers, "Qualities of Top Management: Comparison of European Manufacturers," *Journal of Management Development* 14, no. 1 (1995), pp. 5–15; Noel M. Tichy, Michael I. Brimm, Ram Chran, and Hiroraka Takeuchi, "Leadership Development as a Lever for Global Transformation," in *Globalizing Management: Creating and Leading the Competitive Organization,* ed. Vladimir Pucik, Noel M. Tichy, and Carole K. Barnett (New York: Wiley, 1993), pp. 47–60; Gloria Barczak and Edward F. McDonough III, "Leading Global Product Development Teams," *Research Technology Management* 46, no. 6 (November/December 2003), pp. 14–18; Michael J. Marquard and Lisa Horvath, *Global Teams* (Palo Alto, CA: Davies-Black, 2001).

In the International Spotlight: Germany "Leaders: Odd European Out; Germany's Economy," *Economist,* February 21, 2004, p. 13; Robert Metz, Rebecca Riley, and Martin Weale, "Economic Performance in France, Germany and the United Kingdom, 1997–2002," *National Institute Economic Review,* April 2004, pp. 83–99.

■ Chapter 14

International Management in Action: Important Tips on Working for Foreigners Martin J. Gannon, *Understanding Global Cultures,* 2nd ed. (Thousand Oaks, CA: Sage, 2001); Richard D. Lewis, *When Cultures Collide* (London: Nicholas Brealey, 1999); Roger E. Axtell, ed., *Do's and Taboos Around the World* (New York: Wiley, 1990); John Holusha, "No Utopia but to Workers It's a Job," *New York*

Times, January 29, 1989, sec. 3, pp. 1, 10; Faye Rice, "Should You Work for a Foreigner?" *Fortune,* August 1, 1988, pp. 123–124; Jeanne Whalen, "American Finds Himself Atop Russian Oil Giant in Turmoil," *Wall Street Journal,* October 30, 2003, p. B1.

International Management in Action: U.S. Style Training for Expats and Their Teenagers   Dawn Anfuso, "HR Unites the World of Coca-Cola," *Personnel Journal,* November 1994, pp. 112–121; Karen Dawn Stuart, "Teens Play a Role in Moves Overseas," *Personnel Journal,* March 1992, pp. 72–78; Richard M. Hodgetts and Fred Luthans, "U.S. Multinationals' Expatriate Compensation Strategies," *Compensation and Benefits Review,* January–February 1993, p. 61; Philip R. Harris and Robert T. Moran, *Managing Cultural Differences: High-Performance Strategies for a New World of Business,* 3rd ed. (Houston: Gulf Publishing, 1991), chapter 9.

International Management in Action: Lessons in Global Leadership Development: The PWC Ulysses Program   Jessi Hempel with Seth Porges, "It Takes a Village—And a Consultant," *BusinessWeek,* September 4, 2004, p. 76, www.businessweek.com.

In the International Spotlight: Russia   "Mixed Signals; Russian Reform," *Economist,* May 29, 2004, p. 39; "Command and Control; Russian Economy," April 10, 2004, p. 70; Jason Bush, "Russia's New Deal," BusinessWeek Online, March 29, 2007, www.businessweek.com/globalbiz/content/mar2007/gb20070329_226664.htm.

You Be the International Consultant: A Selection Decision   William H. Davidson, "Creating and Managing Joint Ventures in China," *California Management Review,* Summer 1987, pp. 77–94; Denis Fred Simon, "After Tiananmen: What Is the Future for Foreign Business in China?" *California Management Review,* Winter 1990, p. 106; S. Gordon Redding, *The Spirit of Chinese Capitalism* (New York: Walter de Gruyter, 1990); James T. Areddy, "Older Workers from U.S. Take Jobs in China," *Wall Street Journal,* June 22, 2004, p. B1.

Endnotes

■ Chapter 1

1. "Ireland's Largest Exporter Dell Is Responsible for 4% of All Expenditure in the Irish Economy," *FinFacts,* June 1, 2006, www.finfacts.com/irelandbusinessnews/publish/article_10006071.shtml.

2. "Solectron to Open Center in Singapore," *Manufacturing & Technology News,* January 3, 2006.

3. Steve Hamm, "IBM Wakes Up to India's Skills," BusinessWeek Online edition, June 5, 2006, www.businessweek.com/magazine/content/06_23/b3987098.htm.

4. "Genpact Is Largest Employer in BPO Sector," *Hindu Business Line,* November 16, 2006, p. 1.

5. Geri Smith, "Wrapping the Globe in Tortillas," *BusinessWeek,* February 26, 2007, p. 54.

6. "India's Fast-Growing Tata Business Empire," *The Economist,* March 31, 2005.

7. Rajesh Mahapatra, "Cisco to Set Up Center in India," Associated Press, December 6, 2006.

8. Joan Lublin, "India Could Provide Unique Opportunities for Expat Managers," *Wall Street Journal,* May 8, 2007, p. B1.

9. Thomas Friedman, *The World Is Flat: A Brief History of the Twenty-first Century* (New York: Farrar, Straus and Giroux, 2005).

10. Thomas Friedman, *The Lexus and the Olive Tree: Understanding Globalization* (New York: Farrar, Straus & Giroux, 1999).

11. Jonathan P. Doh and Hildy Teegen, *Globalization and NGOs: Transforming Business, Government, and Society* (Westport, CT: Praeger, 2003).

12. For discussions of the benefits of globalization, see Jagdish Bhagwati, *In Defense of Globalization* (New York: Oxford University Press, 2004), and Edward Graham, *Fighting the Wrong Enemy: Antiglobal Activists and Multinational Enterprises* (Washington, DC: Institute for International Economics, 2000).

13. For discussion of some of the emerging concerns surrounding globalization, see Peter Singer, *One World: The Ethics of Globalization* (New Haven: Yale University Press, 2002); George Soros, *George Soros on Globalization* (New York: Public Affairs Books, 2002); and Joseph Stiglitz, *Globalization and Its Discontents* (New York: Norton, 2002).

14. Steve Hamm, "The Trouble with India," *BusinessWeek,* March 19, 2007, pp. 48–58.

15. Paul Blustein, "EU Offers to End Farm Subsidies," *Washington Post,* May 11, 2004, p. E1.

16. Jeffrey E. Garten, "Going Up in Flames," *Newsweek* (International Edition), September 29, 2003, p. 38.

17. Christopher Marquis, "Bush Says He'll Press Effort for Hemisphere Trade Pact," *New York Times,* April 18, 2001, p. A4.

18. Office of the United States Trade Representative, "Trade Agreements," www.ustr.gov/Trade_Agreements/Section_Index.html.

19. Ana Campoy, "As EU Expands, It Re-examines Old Ways," *Wall Street Journal,* April 24, 2004, p. A14.

20. Goldman Sachs, "Global Economics Paper No: 134: How Solid Are the BRICs," December 1, 2005.

21. Goldman Sachs, "Global Economics Paper No: 99: Dreaming with the BRICs: The Path to 2050," October 1, 2003.

22. WTO, *International Trade Statistics* (Switzerland, WTO, 2006).

23. David Reilly, "EU's Green-Eyeshade Crusade," *Wall Street Journal,* March 18, 2004, p. A15.

24. "World Watch," *Wall Street Journal,* January 27, 2004, p. A12.

25. Charles W. L. Hill, *International Business* (New York: McGraw-Hill/Irwin, 2007).

26. R. Glenn Hubbard and Anthony Patrick O'Brien, *Essentials of Economics* (Upper Saddle River, NJ: Pearson Prentice Hall, 2007).

27. Ibid.

28. Ibid.

29. Geri Smith, "Bolivia's Risky Game," BusinessWeek Online, May 3, 2006, www.businessweek.com/globalbiz/content/may2006/gb20060503_773605.htm.

30. CIA, *The World Factbook* (2007), www.cia.gov/cia/publications/factbook/geos/mx.html.

31. Simon Romero and Claudia Deutsch, "War and Abuse Do Little to Harm U.S. Brands," *New York Times,* May 9, 2004, p. A1.

32. CIA, *The World Factbook* (2007), www.cia.gov/cia/publications/factbook/geos/ci.html.

33. CIA, *The World Factbook* (2007) www.cia.gov/cia/publications/factbook/geos/ar.html.

34. "The Americas, Still Prickly; Mercosur and the EU," *Economist,* May 1, 2004, p. 54.

35. CIA, *The World Factbook* (2007), www.cia.gov/cia/publications/factbook/geos/ee.html.

36. Brian Brenner, "Why Taming the China Dragon Is Tricky," BusinessWeek Online, April 23, 2007.

37. "China Tries to Tap the Brakes on Economic Growth," *Wall Street Journal,* December 26, 2003, p. A9.

38. "U.S.-China Trade Friction Getting Hotter," *China Economic Review,* as appearing in BusinessWeek Online, May 7, 2007.

39. Economic Commission on Africa, "Economic Report on Africa 2007: Accelerating Africa's Development through Diversification," March 2007.

■ Chapter 2

1. J. Denis and Ian Derbyshire, *Political Systems of the World* (New York: Helicon Publishing, 1996).

2. Charles W. L. Hill, *International Business* (New York: McGraw-Hill/Irwin, 2007).

3. Michael Gundlach, "Understanding the Relationship Between Individualism-Collectivism and Team Performance Through an Integration of Social Identity Theory and the Social Relations Model," *Human Relations* 59, no. 12 (2006), pp. 1603–1632.

4. Donald Ball, Wendell H. McCulloch, et al., *International Business: The Challenge of Global Competition* (New York: McGraw-Hill, 2007).

5. "Survey: The European Union," *The Economist,* March 15, 2007.

6. Henry W. Spiegel and Ann Hubbard, *The Growth of Economic Thought* (Durham, NC: Duke University Press, 1991).

7. Donald Ball, Wendell H. McCulloch, et al., *International Business: The Challenge of Global Competition* (New York: McGraw-Hill, 2007).

8. Daniel J. McCarthy, Sheila M. Puffer, and Alexander I. Naumov, "Russia's Retreat to Statization and the Implications for Business," *Journal of World Business* 35, no. 3 (2000), p. 258.

9. Jason Bush, "Russia's New Deal," BusinessWeek Online, March 29, 2007, www.businessweek.com/globalbiz/content/mar2007/gb20070329_226664.htm.

10. "Russian State Customs Committee Reports Corruption Rate Among Employees," *BBC Monitoring Former Soviet Union,* October 14, 2003, p. 1.

11. "Russian Report Says Corruption Threatens Stability in Country," *Wall Street Journal online,* February 21, 2007, online.wsj.com/article/SB117200984737714064.html; and Garry Kasparov, "Putin's Gangster State," *Wall Street Journal,* March 30, 2007, p. A15.

12. The Economist Intelligence Unit, *Country Report: Russia* (Kent, UK: EIU, 2007), p. 7.

13. "Trust the Locals," *The Economist* 382, January 25, 2007, pp. 55–56.

14. Dean A. Minx and Sandra M. Hawley, *Global Politics* (Belmont, CA: Wadsworth Publishing Company, 1998).

15. J. Denis and Ian Derbyshire, *Political Systems of the World* (New York: Helicon Publishing, 1996).

16. Emad McKay, "U.S. Issues Warning to Partners Who Erect Trade Barriers," *Global Information Network,* April 5, 2004, p. 1.

17. "When Opium Can Be Benign," *The Economist* 382, February 1, 2007, pp. 25–27.

18. John Child and David K. Tse, "China's Transition and Its Implications for International Business," *Journal of International Business Studies,* First Quarter 2001, pp. 5–21.

19. Paul Nadler, "Making a Mystery out of How to Comply with Patriot Act," *American Banker,* May 19, 2004, p. 5.

20. John Graham, "Foreign Corrupt Practices Act: A Manager's Guide," *California Management Review,* Summer 1987, p. 9.

21. For more on this see Tipton F. McCubbins, "Somebody Kicked the Sleeping Dog—New Bite in the Foreign Corrupt Practices Act," *Business Horizons,* January–February 2001, pp. 27–32.

22. Glenn Kessler and Anthony Faiola, "Cheney Lauds Koizumi; Iraq Dominates Talks with Japan," *Washington Post,* April 13, 2004, p. A16.

23. Richard Jerram, "This Time It's Different," *The International Economy* 18, no. 2 (Spring 2004), p. 46.

24. Robert Slate, "Chinese Role Models and Classic Military Philosophy in Dealing with Soldier Corruption and Moral Degeneration," *Journal of Third World Studies* 20, no. 1 (Spring 2003), p. 193.

25. Thomas Friedman, *The World Is Flat: A Brief History of the Twenty-first Century* (New York: Farrar, Straus and Giroux, 2005).

26. Charles W. L. Hill, *International Business* (New York: McGraw-Hill/Irwin, 2007).

27. Carol Sottili, "Have Cell Phone, Will Travel to Europe," *Washington Post,* April 6, 2003, p. E1.

28. Rebecca Buckman, "China Keeps Telecom Firms Waiting on 3G," *Wall Street Journal,* May 13, 2004, p. B4.

29. Nandini Lakshman, "Linux Spreads Its Wings in India," *BusinessWeek,* October 2, 2006, pp. 40–41.

30. Steve Hamm and Spencer E. Ante, "Underwater Peril," *BusinessWeek,* January 15, 2007, pp. 46–47.

31. William M. Bulkeley, "MIT Scientists Pave the Way for Wireless Battery Charging," *The Wall Street Journal,* June 8, 2007, p. B6.

32. Robert A. Guth and Don Clark, "The Shape of Computers to Come?" *The Wall Street Journal,* May 30, 2007, p. B1.

33. "Supercomputers: The Race Is On," *BusinessWeek,* June 7, 2004, p. 76.

34. Bruce Einhorn, "Stem-Cell Refugees," *BusinessWeek,* February 12, 2007, pp. 40–42.

35. Gautam Naik, "Stem-Cell Advance May Skirt Ethical Debate," *The Wall Street Journal,* June 7, 2007, p. B1.

36. Nicholas Zamiska and Eric Bellman, "Ranbaxy Unveils Its Ambition to Be a Generics Powerhouse," *The Wall Street Journal,* January 10, 2007, p. A11.

37. John Carey, Adrienne Carter, and Assif Shameen, "Food vs. Fuel," *BusinessWeek,* February 5, 2007, pp. 80–83.

38. Christopher Leonard, "Monsanto, BASF Join Forces," Business-Week Online, March 21, 2007, www.businessweek.com.

39. Doris De Guzman, "Monsanto Sows More Seeds," *ICIS Chemical Business Americas* 270, no. 2 (2007), p. 26.

40. "World's First BSE-Immune Cow," *Asia Pacific Biotech News* 8, no. 12 (2004), p. 682.

41. www.fda.gov.

42. David Mildenberg, "SDN Sees Growth in High Speed Links," *The Business Journal,* May 14, 2004, p. 1.

43. Jean Halliday, "Car Renters Flock to Internet," *Advertising Age,* October 27, 2003, p. 44.

44. "Deutsche Bank Govvie Honcho: Business as Usual Now," *Bondweek,* June 22, 2003, p. 1.

45. Sebastian Mallaby, "Taming the Wild Web," *Washington Post,* April 2, 2003, p. A19.

46. See "In Peru, a Cellular Revolution," *Miami Herald,* May 22, 1995, p. 6A.

47. Roger Crockett, Andy Reinhardt, and Moon Ihlwan, "Cell Phones: Who's Calling the Shots," *BusinessWeek,* April 26, 2004, p. 48.

48. Matt Richtel, "Wi-Fi Providers Rethink How to Make Money," *New York Times,* June 7, 2004, p. C1.

49. Erika Stuzman, "More Companies Begin to Outsource White-Collar Jobs," *Knight Ridder Tribune Business News,* May 23, 2004, p. 1.

50. Jan Syfert, "Up There with the Best," *Productivity SA,* November–December 1998, p. 49.

51. Ashok Bhattacharjee, "India's Outsourcing Tigers Seek Cover, Markets, in Europe's East," *Wall Street Journal,* December 18, 2003, p. A16.

■ Chapter 3

1. Thomas Donaldson, *The Ethics of International Business* (New York: Oxford University Press, 1989).

2. *Facts on Child Labor—2006* (Geneva: International Labour Organization, 2006).

3. Donald Ball and W. H. McCulloch, *International Business: The Challenge of Global Competition* (New York: McGraw-Hill, 2007).

4. Richard Behar, "Beijing's Phony War on Fakes," *Fortune,* October 30, 2000, p. 193.

5. "Olga Kharif, Microsoft's China Card," *BusinessWeek,* April 26, 2006. Available at http://www.businessweek.com/technology/content/apr2006/tc20060426_405461.htm?campaign_id=bier_tca.

6. Ron Duska and Nicholas M. Rongione, *Ethics and Corporate Responsibility: Theory, Cases and Dilemmas* (New York: Thomas Custom Publishing, 2003).

7. Paul M. Minus, *The Ethics of Business in a Global Economy* (Boston: Kluwer Academic Publishers, 1993).

8. Steve Hamm, "How Accenture One-Upped Bangalore," *Business-Week,* April 23, 2007, pp. 98–99.

9. R. J. Vincent, *Human Rights and International Relations* (New York: Cambridge University Press, 1986).

10. Vladimir Kovalev, "EU Presses Russia on Human Trafficking," *BusinessWeek,* February 23, 2007. Available at http://www.businessweek.com/globalbiz/content/feb2007/gb20070223_311905.htm?chan=globalbiz_europe_more+of+today's+top+stories.

11. Andrew Pollack, "In Japan, It's See No Evil; Have No Harassment," *New York Times,* May 7, 1996, p. C5; and Howard W. French, "Diploma at Hand, Japanese Women Find Glass Ceiling Reinforced with Iron," *New York Times,* January 1, 2001, p. A4.

12. Bob Davis, "The Economy: U.S. Nears Pact on Corruption Treaty," *Wall Street Journal,* August 13, 2003, p. A2. See also Jonathan P. Doh, Peter Rodriguez, Klaus Uhlenbruck, Jamie Collins, and Lorraine Eden, "Coping with Corruption in Foreign Markets," *Academy of Management Executive* 17, no. 3 (2003), pp. 114–127.

13. Tipton F. McCubbins, "Somebody Kicked the Sleeping Dog—New Bite in the Foreign Corrupt Practices Act," *Business Horizons,* January–February 2001, p. 27.

14. Greg Steinmetz, "U.S. Firms Are Among Least Likely to Pay Bribes Abroad, Survey Finds," *Wall Street Journal,* August 25, 1997, p. 5.

15. Edmund L. Andrews, "29 Nations Agree to Outlaw Bribing Foreign Officials," *New York Times,* November 21, 1997, p. C2.

16. "Special Report: The Short Arm of the Law—Bribery and Business," *Economist,* March 2, 2002, p. 85.

17. Abigal McWilliams and Donald Siegel, "Corporate Social Responsibility: A Theory of the Firm Perspective," *Academy of Management Review* 26, no. 1 (2001), pp. 117–127.

18. "Non-governmental Organizations and Business: Living with the Enemy," *Economist,* August 9, 2002, pp. 49–50.

19. Gallup International's 2002 Voice of the People survey, http://www.weforum.org.

20. Pete Engardio, "Beyond the Green Corporation," *BusinessWeek,* January 29, 2007, pp. 50–64.

21. Christopher Power, "A Somber Mood at Warmer Davos," *BusinessWeek,* January 23, 2007.

22. For more information visit www.epa.gov.

23. For more information regarding the role of the UNEP visit www.unep.org.

24. Marc Gunther, "The Green Machine," *Fortune,* August 7, 2006, pp. 42–57.

25. "Environmentalists Get Citigroup Pledge," *New York Times,* January 22, 2004, p. C3.

26. "WTO to Allow Access to Cheap Drug Treatments," *Los Angeles Times,* August 31, 2003, p. A4.

27. Jonathan P. Doh and Terrence R. Guay, "Globalization and Corporate Social Responsibility: How Nongovernmental Organizations Influence Labor and Environmental Codes of Conduct," *Management International Review* 44, no. 3 (2004), pp. 7–30; Petra Christmann and Glen Taylor, "Globalization and the Environment: Strategies for International Voluntary Environmental Initiatives," *Academy of Management Executive* 16, no. 30 (2002), pp. 121–135.

28. Michael Yaziji, "Turning Gadflies into Allies," *Harvard Business Review,* February 2004, pp. 110–115.

29. Debra Dunn and Keith Yamashita, "Microcapitalism and the Megacorporation," *Harvard Business Review,* August 2003, pp. 46–54.

30. Clayton Collins, "Above and Beyond: A Surprising Number of Companies Are Finding It Makes Business Sense to Go Beyond Government Regulations," *Christian Science Monitor,* November 3, 2003, p. 14.

31. Organization for Economic Cooperation and Development, *Corporate Governance: A Survey of OECD Countries* (Paris: OECD), 2003.

32. Stijn Claessens and Joseph P. H. Fan, "Corporate Governance in Asia: A Survey," *International Review of Finance* 3, no. 2 (2002), pp. 71–103.

33. "Putting the World to Rights," *Economist,* June 5, 2004, p. 63.

34. Gustavo Capdevilla, "Development: U.N. Report Calls for Urgent Action on Poverty," *Global Information Network,* July 9, 2003, p. 1.

35. Rachel Zimmerman, "Jack Valenti Will Lobby for AIDS Fight," *Wall Street Journal,* June 3, 2004, p. B1.

■ Part 1 Integrative Cases

Brief Integrative Case 2

1. "Nike CEO Retracts University Donation over Human Rights," SocialFunds.com, May 3, 2000.

2. State of California, San Francisco Superior Court, *Marc Kasky v. Nike Inc.,* 02 C.D.O.S. 3790, www.law.com/regionals/ca/opinions/may/s087859.shtml (accessed May 24, 2007).

3. Linda Greenhouse, "Free Speech for Companies on Justices' Agenda," *New York Times,* April 20, 2003, p. A17.

4. Linda Greenhouse, "Nike Free Speech Case Is Unexpectedly Returned to California," *New York Times,* June 27, 2003, p. A16.

5. "Corporate Social Responsibility—Companies in the News: Nike," www.mallenbaker.net/csr/CSRfiles/nike.html (accessed May 24, 2007).

6. Nike Inc. Press Release, "Nike Foundation Secures Footing in Helping to Reach Millennium Development Goals," www.nikebiz.com (accessed September 15, 2005).

7. Nike Inc. Press Release, "Nike Announces $200,000 Grant to Hillsboro Schools," www.nikebiz.com (accessed March 6, 2007).

In-Depth Integrative Case 1

1. "WTO to Allow Access to Cheap Drug Treatments," *Los Angeles Times,* August 31, 2003, p. A4.

2. Miriam Jordan, "Brazil to Stir Up AIDS-Drug Battle; Nation to Authorize Imports of Generics, Citing the Cost of Big Companies' Products," *Wall Street Journal,* September 5, 2003, p. A3.

3. Sushil Vachani, "South Africa and the AIDS Epidemic," *Vikalpa* 29, no. 1 (January–March 2004), pp. 101–109. *HIV* stands for human immunodeficiency virus; *AIDS* stands for acquired immunodeficiency syndrome.

4. Ibid.

5. UNAIDS, *2002 Report on Global AIDS,* www.unaids.gov.

6. Donald G. McNeil, "Medicine Merchants: A Special Report: Drug Makers and 3rd World: Study in Neglect," *New York Times,* May 21, 2000, p. 1.

7. World Health Organization, *World Health Report, 2003.*

8. Bill Schiller, "Hope," *Toronto Star*, September 18, 1999.

9. Ibid.

10. Vachani, "South Africa and the AIDS Epidemic."

11. Pharmaceutical Research and Manufacturers of America, *Pharmaceutical Industry Profile 2002* (Washington, DC, 2002).

12. McNeil, "Medicine Merchants."

13. Lawrence K. Altman, "In Effort to Save Lives, South Africa Creates an Anti-AIDS Campaign That Minces No Words," *New York Times*, July 9, 2000, p. 8.

14. Ibid.

15. This section draws from Sushil Vachani, "South Africa and the AIDS Epidemic," *Vikalpa*, 29, no. 1 (January–March, 2004), pp. 101–109.

16. www.wto.org/english/tratop_e/trips_e/trips_e.htm (accessed July 26, 2002).

17. Vachani, "South Africa and the AIDS Epidemic."

18. UNAIDS, *2000 Report on the Global AIDS epidemic,* www.unaids.gov.

19. Vachani, "South Africa and the AIDS Epidemic."

20. Pharmaceutical Research and Manufacturers of America, *Pharmaceutical Industry Profile 2002,* p. 36.

21. This section draws from Sushil Vachani, "South Africa and the AIDS Epidemic," *Vikalpa* 29, no. 1 (January–March, 2004), pp. 101–109.

22. Karl Vick, "African AIDS Victims Losers of a Drug War: U.S. Policy Keeps Price Prohibitive," *Washington Post*, December 4, 1999, p. A1.

23. Ibid.

24. Ibid.

25. Sarah Boseley, "Trade Terrorism," *The Guardian*, August 11, 1999.

26. Vick, "African AIDS Victims Losers of a Drug War."

27. Ibid.

28. Victor Mallet, "The Ravaged Continent: AIDS Is Now the Biggest Killer of Young Adults in Africa," *Financial Times*, December 3, 1999, p. 4.

29. Vachani, "South Africa and the AIDS Epidemic."

30. Justin Brown, "Spread of AIDS Raises Moral Issue for U.S.," *Christian Science Monitor*, July 12, 2000.

31. Ibid.

32. Nicol Degli Innocenti, "South Africa Hits Back at EU Criticism of AIDS Policy," *Financial Times*, April 5, 2001, p. 11.

33. Melody Petersen and Larry Rohter, "Maker Agrees to Cut Prices of 2 AIDS Drugs in Brazil," *New York Times*, March 31, 2001, p. 4.

34. Vachani, "South Africa and the AIDS Epidemic."

35. UNAIDS, *2002 Report on the Global AIDS Epidemic,* www.unaids.gov.

36. Vachani, "South Africa and the AIDS Epidemic."

37. Rachel Zimmerman, "Jack Valenti Will Lobby for AIDS Fight," *Wall Street Journal*, June 3, 2004, p. B1.

38. www.wto.org/english/tratop_e/trips_e/pharmpatent_e.htm (accessed July 26, 2002).

39. Julia Flynn and Mark Schoofs, "Glaxo, Boeringer to Let Africa Make More Generics for AIDS," *Wall Street Journal*, December 11, 2003, p. D4.

40. Hollister H. Hovey, "Religious Groups Push Drug Cost to Assess HIV," Dow Jones Newswires, March 24, 2004.

41. World Trade Organization, Press Release, "Members OK Amendment to Make Health Flexibility Permanent," December 6, 2005. www.wto.org/english/news_e/pres05_e/pr426_e.htm.

42. Ibid.

43. Doctors Without Borders, "HIV/AIDS," 2006, www.doctorswithoutborders.org/news/hiv-aids/index.cfm.

44. "Drug Development: Bristol-Myers Squibb Seeks to Expand Access to HIV/AIDS Medicine," *Drug Week,* March 24, 2007, p. 287.

45. Doctors Without Borders, "Access Denied to Crucial New AIDS Medications," March 15, 2006, www.doctorswithoutborders.org/pr/2006/03-15-2006.cfm.

46. Ibid.

47. World Health Organization, "WHO Discussion Paper: The Practice of Charging User Fees at the Point of Service Delivery for HIV/AIDS Treatment and Care," December 2005, www.who.int/hiv/pub/advocacy/promotingfreeaccess.pdf.

48. UNAIDS/WHO Press Release, "HIV Infection Rates Decreasing in Several Countries but Global Number of People Living with HIV Continues to Rise," November 21, 2005, www.who.int/hiv/epiupdate2005/en/index.html.

49. Ibid.

50. James Hookway and Nicholas Zamiska, "Thai Showdown Spotlights Threat to Drug Patents: Abbott Protests Move to Buy Copycat Pills, but It Yields on Price," *Wall Street Journal*, April 24, 2007, p. A1.

51. Ibid.

52. Alastair Stewart, "Brazil Moves to Break Merck AIDS Drug Patent," *Wall Street Journal*, May 5, 2007, p. B6.

53. Ibid.

54. "Clinton, Drug Companies Strike Deal to Lower AIDS Drug Prices," Associated Press, May 8, 2007, lists.essential.org/pipermail/ip-health/2007-May/011142.html.

55. Ibid.

56. Donald G. McNeil, "Plan to Bring Generic AIDS Drugs to Poor Nations," *New York Times,* April 6, 2004, p. F6.

■ Chapter 4

1. Pat Joynt and Malcolm Warner, "Introduction: Cross-Cultural Perspectives," in *Managing Across Cultures: Issues and Perspectives,* ed. Pat Joynt and Malcolm Warner (London: International Thomson Business Press, 1996), p. 3.

2. For additional insights see Gerry Darlington, "Culture—A Theoretical Review," in Pat Joynt and Malcolm Warner, *Managing Across Cutures: Issues and Perspectives* (London: International Thomson Business Press, 1996), pp. 33–55.

3. Fred Luthans, *Organizational Behavior,* 7th ed. (New York: McGraw-Hill, 1995), pp. 534–535.

4. Gary Bonvillian and William A. Nowlin, "Cultural Awareness: An Essential Element of Doing Business Abroad," *Business Horizons,* November–December 1994, pp. 44–54.

5. Roger E. Axtell, ed., *Do's and Taboos Around the World,* 2nd ed. (New York: Wiley, 1990), p. 3.

6. Lillian H. Chaney and Jeanette S. Martin, *Intercultural Business Communication* (Englewood Cliffs, NJ: Prentice-Hall, 1995), p. 115.

7. Fons Trompenaars and Charles Hampden-Turner, *Riding the Waves of Culture: Understanding Diversity in Global Business,* 2nd ed. (New York: McGraw-Hill, 1998), p. 23.

8. Christopher Orpen, "The Work Values of Western and Tribal Black Employees," *Journal of Cross-Cultural Psychology,* March 1978, pp. 99–111.

9. William Whitely and George W. England, "Variability in Common Dimensions of Managerial Values Due to Value Orientation and Country Differences," *Personnel Psychology,* Spring 1980, pp. 77–89.

10. Ibid., p. 87.

11. George W. England and Raymond Lee, "The Relationship Between Managerial Values and Managerial Success in the United States, Japan, India, and Australia," *Journal of Applied Psychology,* August 1974, pp. 418–419.

12. George W. England, "Managers and Their Value Systems: A Five-Country Comparative Study," *Columbia Journal of World Business,* Summer 1978, p. 39.

13. A. Reichel and D. M. Flynn, "Values in Transition: An Empirical Study of Japanese Managers in the U.S.," *Management International Review* 23, no. 4 (1984), pp. 69–70.

14. Yumiko Ono and Bill Spindle, "Japan's Long Decline Makes One Thing Rise: Individualism," *Wall Street Journal,* December 29, 2000, pp. A1, A4.

15. Sang M. Lee and Suzanne J. Peterson, "Culture, Entrepreneurial Orientation, and Global Competitiveness," *Journal of World Business* 35, no. 4 (2000) pp. 411–412.

16. "Confucius makes a comeback," *The Economist,* May 17, 2007. Accessed online at www.economist.com/world/asia/displaystory.cfm?story_id=9202957.

17. Geert Hofstede, *Culture's Consequences: International Differences in Work-Related Values* (Beverly Hills, CA: Sage, 1980).

18. Geert Hofstede, *Cultures and Organizations: Software of the Mind* (London: McGraw-Hill U.K., 1991), pp. 251–252.

19. Ibid.

20. Geert Hofstede and Michael Bond, "The Need for Synergy Among Cross-Cultural Studies," *Journal of Cross-Cultural Psychology,* December 1984, p. 419.

21. A. R. Negandhi and S. B. Prasad, *Comparative Management* (New York: Appleton-Century-Crofts, 1971), p. 128.

22. For additional insights, see Mark F. Peterson et al., "Role Conflict, Ambiguity, and Overload: A 21-Nation Study," *Academy of Management Journal,* June 1995, pp. 429–452.

23. Hofstede, *Culture's Consequences.*

24. Ibid.

25. Ibid.

26. Also see Chao C. Chen, Xiao-Ping Chen, and James R. Meindl, "How Can Cooperation Be Fostered? The Cultural Effects of Individualism-Collectivism," *Academy of Management Review* 23, no. 2 (1998), pp. 285–304.

27. Hofstede, *Culture's Consequences,* pp. 419–420.

28. Ibid., p. 420.

29. Fons Trompenaars, *Riding the Waves of Culture: Understanding Diversity in Global Business* (New York: Irwin, 1994), p. 10.

30. Talcott Parsons, *The Social System* (New York: Free Press, 1951).

31. Also see Lisa Hoecklin, *Managing Cultural Differences* (Workingham, England: Addison-Wesley, 1995).

32. Charles M. Hampden-Turner and Fons Trompenaars, "A World Turned Upside Down: Doing Business in Asia," in *Managing Across Cultures,* ed. Joynt and Warner (London: International Thomson Business Press, 1996), p. 279.

33. Ibid., p. 288.

34. Trompenaars, *Riding the Waves of Culture,* p. 131.

35. Ibid., p. 140.

36. Mansour Javidan and Robert House, "Leadership and Cultures Around the World: Findings from GLOBE: An Introduction to the Special Issue," *Journal of World Business* 37, no. 1 (2002), pp. 1–2.

37. Robert House, Paul J. Hanges, Mansour Javidan, Peter W. Dorfman, and Vipin Gupta, *Culture, Leadership, and Organizations: The GLOBE Study of 62 Societies* (London: Sage, 2004).

38. Kwong Leung, "Editor's Introduction to the Exchange Between Hofstede and GLOBE," *Journal of International Business Studies* 37 (2006), p. 881.

39. Robert House, Paul J. Hanges, Mansour Javidan, Peter W. Dorfman, and Vipin Gupta, *Culture, Leadership, and Organizations: The GLOBE Study of 62 Societies* (London: Sage, 2004).

40. Mansour Javidan and Robert House, "Cultural Acumen for the Global Manager: Lessons from Project GLOBE," *Organizational Dynamics* 29, no. 4 (2001), pp. 289–305.

41. Robert House, Mansour Javidan, Paul Hanges, and Peter Dorfman, "Understanding Cultures and Implicit Leadership Theories Across the Globe: An Introduction to Project GLOBE," *Journal of World Business* 37, no. 1 (2002), pp. 3–10.

42. Ibid.

43. David A. Waldman, Mary Sully de Luque, et al., "Cultural and Leadership Predictors of Corporate Social Responsibility Values of Top Management: A GLOBE Study of 15 Countries," *Journal of International Business Studies* 37 (2006), pp. 823–837.

44. Geert Hofstede, "What Did GLOBE Really Measure? Researchers' Minds versus Respondents' Minds," *Journal of International Business Studies* 37 (2006), pp. 882–896.

45. P. Christopher Earley, "Leading Cultural Research in the Future: A Matter of Paradigms and Taste," *Journal of International Business Studies* 37 (2006), pp. 922–931; Peter B. Smith, "When Elephants Fight, the Grass Gets Trampled: The GLOBE and Hofstede Projects," *Journal of International Business Studies* 37 (2006), pp. 915–921.

46. Mansour Javidan, Peter W. Dorfman, et. al., "In the Eye of the Beholder: Cross Cultural Lessons in Leadership from Project GLOBE," *Academy of Management Perspectives* 20, no. 1 (2006), pp. 67–90.

47. Ibid.

■ Chapter 5

1. Nancy J. Adler, *International Dimensions of Organizational Behavior,* 3rd ed. (Cincinnati, OH: Southwestern, 1997).

2. See Clifford C. Clarke and Douglas Lipp, "Contrasting Cultures," *Training and Development Journal,* February 1998, pp. 21–31.

3. Amy Chozick and John D. Stoll, "U.S. Remains the Bane of Ford and Nissan," *Wall Street Journal,* April 27, 2007, p. A11.

4. "Logan's Run," *Economist,* April 26, 2007. Accessed at www.economist.com/business/displaystory.cfm?story_id=9088309.

5. Owen Brown, "Japan Is Quality Favorite in China," *Wall Street Journal,* June 7, 2004, p. A17.

6. David Gow, "Car Industry at Crossroads in China: Supply Could Outstrip the Huge Demand," *The Guardian,* May 21, 2004, p. 26.

7. David Pearson, "Renault French Car Sales Fall, Hurt by Asian Manufacturers," *Wall Street Journal Online,* April 3, 2007, online.wsj.com/article/SB117554768020257301search.html?KEYWORDS=renault&COLLECTION=wsjie/6month.

8. Jason Bush, "They've Driven a Ford Lately," *BusinessWeek,* February 26, 2007, p. 52.

9. For a more detailed analysis, see Allen J. Morrison, David A. Ricks, and Kendall Roth, "Globalization Versus Regionalization: Which Way for the Multinational?" *Organizational Dynamics,* Winter 1991, pp. 17–28.

10. Lisa Hoecklin, *Managing Cultural Differences: Strategies for Competitive Advantage* (Workingham, England: Addison-Wesley, 1995), pp. 98–99.

11. Linda Leung, "Managing Offshore Outsourcing," *Network World,* December 8, 2003, p. 59.

12. Matt Ackerman, "State St.: New Markets Key to Growth," *American Banker,* May 3, 2004, p. 1.

13. Linda M. Randall and Lori A. Coakley, "Building a Successful Partnership in Russia and Belarus: The Impact of Culture on Strategy," *Business Horizons,* March–April 1998, pp. 15–22.

14. Fons Trompenaars and Charles Hampden-Turner, *Riding the Waves of Culture: Understanding Diversity in Global Business,* 2nd ed. (New York: McGraw-Hill, 1998), p. 202.

15. See, for example, Anisya S. Thomas and Stephen L. Mueller, "A Case for Comparative Entrepreneurship: Assessing the Relevance of Culture," *Journal of International Business Studies,* Second Quarter 2000, pp. 287–301.

16. Adapted from Richard Mead, *International Management* (Cambridge, MA: Blackwell, 1994), pp. 57–59.

17. Derived from www.communicaid.com/Malaysia-business-culture.asp.

18. Fred Luthans, Richard M. Hodgetts, and Stuart A. Rosenkrantz, *Real Managers* (Cambridge, MA: Ballinger, 1988).

19. Fred Luthans, Dianne H. B. Welsh, and Stuart A. Rosenkrantz, "What Do Russian Managers Really Do? An Observational Study with Comparisons to U.S. Managers," *Journal of International Business Studies,* Fourth Quarter 1993, pp. 741–761.

20. Diane H. B. Welsh, Fred Luthans, and Steven M. Sommer, "Organizational Behavior Modification Goes to Russia: Replicating an Experimental Analysis Across Cultures and Tasks," *Journal of Organizational Behavior Management* 13, no. 2 (1993), pp. 15–35; Diane H. B. Welsh, Fred Luthans, and Steven M. Sommer, "Managing Russian Factory Workers: The Impact of U.S.-Based Behavioral and Participative Techniques," *Academy of Management Journal,* February 1993, pp. 58–79.

21. Welsh, Luthans, and Sommer, "Organizational Behavior Modification," p. 31. The summary of positive (17 percent average) performance from O.B.Mod. for U.S. samples can be found in Fred Luthans and Alexander Stajkovic, "Reinforce for Performance," *Academy of Management Executive* 13, no. 2 (1999), pp. 49–57.

22. Steven M. Sommer, Seung-Hyun Bae, and Fred Luthans, "The Structure-Climate Relationship in Korean Organizations," *Asia Pacific Journal of Management* 12, no. 2 (1995), pp. 23–36. Also see Steven Sommer, Seung-Hyun Bae, and Fred Luthans, "Organizational Commitment Across Cultures: The Impact of Antecedents on Korean Employees," *Human Relations* 49, no. 7 (1996), pp. 977–993.

23. Sommer, Bae, and Luthans, "The Structure-Climate Relationship."

24. Trompenaars and Hampden-Turner, *Riding the Waves of Culture,* p. 196.

25. Shari Caudron, "Lessons for HR Overseas," *Personnel Journal,* February 1995, p. 92.

26. Richard M. Hodgetts and Fred Luthans, "U.S. Multinationals' Compensation Strategies for Local Management: Cross-Cultural Implications," *Compensation and Benefits Review,* March–April 1993, pp. 42–48.

27. Rochelle Kopp, "International Human Resource Policies and Practices in Japanese, European, and United States Multinationals," *Human Resource Management,* Winter 1994, p. 590.

28. Philip M. Rosenzweig and Nitin Nohria, "Influences on Human Resource Management Practices in Multinational Corporations," *Journal of International Business Studies,* Second Quarter 1994, pp. 229–251.

29. "Disillusioned Workers Cost Japanese Economy up to $180.18 Billion," *Wall Street Journal,* September 5, 2001, p. B18.

30. Also see Richard W. Wright, "Trends in International Business Research: Twenty-Five Years Later," *Journal of International Business Studies,* Fourth Quarter 1994, pp. 687–701; Schon Beechler and John Zhuang Yang, "The Transfer of Japanese-Style Management to American Subsidiaries: Contingencies, Constraints, and Competencies," *Journal of International Business Studies,* Third Quarter 1994, pp. 467–491.

31. "Books and Arts: The Perils of Pat: Doing Business in China," *Economist,* April 24, 2004, p. 98.

32. Eric W. K. Tsang, "Can Guanxi Be a Source of Sustained Competitive Advantage for Doing Business in China?" *Academy of Management Executive* 12, no. 2 (1998), p. 64.

33. Stephen S. Standifird and R. Scott Marshall, "The Transaction Cost Advantage of Guanxi-Based Business Practices," *Journal of World Business* 35, no. 1 (2000), pp. 21–42.

34. Lee Mei Yi and Paul Ellis, "Insider-Outsider Perspective of Guanxi," *Business Horizons,* January–February 2000, p. 28.

35. Rosalie L. Tung, "Managing in Asia: Cross-Cultural Dimensions," in *Managing Across Cultures: Issues and Perspectives,* ed. Pat Joynt and Malcolm Warner (London: International Thomson Business Press, 1996), p. 239.

36. Richard D. Lewis, *When Cultures Collide* (London: Nicholas Brealey, 1999), p. 390.

37. For more on this topic, see Philip R. Harris and Robert T. Moran, *Managing Cultural Differences,* 3rd ed. (Houston: Gulf Publishing, 1991), pp. 410–411.

38. Ming-Jer Chen, *Inside Chinese Business* (Boston: Harvard Business School Press, 2001), p. 153.

39. Michelle Conlin, "Go-Go-Going to Pieces in China," *Business-Week,* April 23, 2007, p. 88.

40. William B. Snavely, Serguel Miassaoedov, and Kevin McNeilly, "Cross-Cultural Peculiarities of the Russian Entrepreneur: Adapting to the New Russians," *Business Horizons,* March–April 1998, pp. 10–13.

41. Jeanne Whalen and Bhushan Bahree, "How Siberian Oil Field Turned into a Minefield," *Wall Street Journal,* February 9, 2000, p. A21.

42. Snavely, Miassaoedov, and McNeilly, "Cross-Cultural Peculiarities," pp. 10–13.

43. For additional insights into how to interact and negotiate effectively with the Russians, see Lewis, *When Cultures Collide,* pp. 314–318.

44. Snavely, Miassaoedov, and McNeilly, "Cross-Cultural Peculiarities," p. 13.

45. Ashok Bhattacharjee, "India's Outsourcing Tigers Seek Cover, Markets, in Europe's East," *Wall Street Journal,* April 30, 2004, p. A12; Julia Angwin, "AOL's Tech Center in India Is Money Saver," *Wall Street Journal,* August 7, 2003, p. B4.

46. "The Challenges for India," *Chicago Tribune,* May 27, 2004, p. 28; Amy Waldman, "In India, Economic Growth and Democracy Do Mix," *New York Times,* May 26, 2004, p. A13.

47. Adapted from Harris and Moran, *Managing Cultural Differences,* p. 447.

48. Also see Lewis, *When Cultures Collide,* pp. 341–346.

49. Jean-Louis Barsoux and Peter Lawrence, "The Making of a French Manager," *Harvard Business Review,* July–August 1991, pp. 58–67.

50. Adapted from Harris and Moran, *Managing Cultural Differences,* p. 471.

51. Lewis, *When Cultures Collide,* pp. 231–232.

52. T. Lenartowicz and James Patrick Johnson, "A cross-national assessment of values of Latin America managers: Contrasting hues or shades of gray?" *Journal of International Business Studies* 34, no. 3 (May 2003), p. 270.

53. Reed E. Nelson and Suresh Gopalan, "Do Organizational Cultures Replicate National Cultures? Isomorphism, Rejection and Reciprocal Opposition in the Corporate Values of Three Countries," *Organization Studies* 24, no. 7 (September 2003), pp. 1115–1154.

54. Derived from Raul Gouvea, "Brazil: A Strategic Approach," *Thunderbird International Business Review* 46, no. 2 (March–April 2004), pp. 183–184; David Hannon, "Brazil Offers the Best of Both Worlds," *Purchasing,* October 5, 2006, pp. 51–52, www.careerjournaleurope.com/myc/workabroad/countries/brazil.html.

55. Sean Van Zyl, "Global Political Risks: Post 9/11," *Canadian Underwriter* 71, no. 3 (March 2004), p. 16; Marvin Zonis, "Mideast Hopes: Endless Surprises," *Chicago Tribune,* January 18, 2004, p. 1.

56. Changiz Pezeshkpur, "Challenges to Management in the Arab World," *Business Horizons,* August 1978, p. 50.

57. Adapted from Harris and Moran, *Managing Cultural Differences,* p. 503.

■ Chapter 6

1. Lisa Hoecklin, *Managing Cultural Differences: Strategies for Competitive Advantage* (Workingham, England: Addison-Wesley, 1995), p. 146.

2. Edgar H. Schein, *Organizational Culture and Leadership,* 2nd ed. (San Francisco: Jossey-Bass, 1997), p. 12.

3. Fred Luthans, *Organizational Behavior,* 10th ed. (New York: McGraw-Hill/Irwin, 2005), pp. 110–111.

4. In addition see W. Mathew Jeuchter, Caroline Fisher, and Randall J. Alford, "Five Conditions for High-Performance Cultures," *Training and Development Journal,* May 1998, pp. 63–67.

5. Hoecklin, *Managing Cultural Differences,* p. 145.

6. Andre Laurent, "The Cultural Diversity of Western Conceptions of Management," *International Studies of Management and Organization,* Spring–Summer 1983, pp. 75–96.

7. Nancy J. Adler, *International Dimensions of Organizational Behavior,* 2nd ed. (Boston: PWS-Kent Publishing, 1991), pp. 58–59.

8. Robert Frank and Thomas M. Burton, "Cross-Border Merger Results in Headaches for a Drug Company," *Wall Street Journal,* February 4, 1997, p. A1.

9. Brian Bremner and Gail Edmondson, "A Tale of Two Auto Mergers," *BusinessWeek,* May 10, 2004, online edition, www.businessweek.com/magazine/content/04_19/b3882044.htm.

10. Hoecklin, *Managing Cultural Differences,* p. 151.

11. Robert Hughes, "Weekend Journal: Futures and Options: Global Culture," *Wall Street Journal,* October 10, 2003, p. W2.

12. Rita A. Numeroff and Michael N. Abrams, "Integrating Corporate Culture from International M&As," *HR Focus,* June 1998, p. 12.

13. See Maddy Janssens, Jeanne M. Brett, and Frank J. Smith, "Confirmatory Cross-Cultural Research: Testing the Viability of a Corporation-Wide Safety Policy," *Academy of Management Journal,* June 1995, pp. 364–382.

14. Fons Trompenaars, *Riding the Waves of Culture: Understanding Diversity in Global Business* (Burr Ridge, IL: Irwin, 1994), p. 154.

15. Ibid.

16. Ibid., p. 156.

17. Ibid., p. 164.

18. Ibid., p. 167.

19. Ibid., p. 172.

20. For more see Rose Mary Wentling and Nilda Palma-Rivas, "Current Status of Diversity Initiatives in Selected Multinational Corporations," *Human Resource Development Quarterly,* Spring 2000, pp. 35–60.

21. Adler, *International Dimensions of Organizational Behavior,* p. 121.

22. Jean Lee, "Culture and Management: A Study of Small Chinese Family Business in Singapore," *Journal of Small Business Management,* July 1996, p. 65.

23. Noboru Yoshimura and Philip Anderson, *Inside the Kaisha: Demystifying Japanese Business Behavior* (Boston: Harvard Business School Press, 1997).

24. Edmund L. Andrews, "Meet the Maverick of Japan, Inc." *New York Times,* October 12, 1995, pp. C1, C4.

25. Sheryl WuDunn, "Incubators of Creativity," *New York Times,* October 9, 1997, pp. C1, C21.

26. Adler, *International Dimensions of Organizational Behavior,* p. 132.

27. Adele Thomas and Mike Bendixen, "The Management Implications of Ethnicity in South Africa," *Journal of International Business Studies,* Third Quarter 2000, pp. 507–519.

28. John M. Ivencevich and Jacqueline A. Gilbert, "Diversity Management: Time for a New Approach," *Public Personnel Management,* Spring 2000, pp. 75–92.

29. "Over the Rainbow," Economist, November 20, 1997, online edition, www.economist.com/business/displaystory.cfm?story_id=E1_TDGQRP.

30. See, for example, Betty Jane Punnett and Jason Clemens, "Cross-National Diversity: Implications for International Expansion Decisions," *Journal of World Business* 34, no. 2 (1999), pp. 128–138.

31. Adler, *International Dimensions of Organizational Behavior,* p. 137.

32. Wellford W. Wilms, Alan J. Hardcastle, and Deone M. Zell, "Cultural Transformation at NUMMI," *Sloan Management Review,* Fall 1994, p. 103.

33. Ibid., p. 111.

■ Chapter 7

1. E. T. Hall and E. Hall, "How Cultures Collide," in *Culture, Communication, and Conflict: Readings in Intercultural Relations,* ed. G. R. Weaver (Needham Heights, MA: Ginn Press, 1994).

2. Noboru Yoshimura and Philip Anderson, *Inside the Kaisha: Demystifying Japanese Business Behavior* (Boston: Harvard Business School Press, 1997), p. 59.

3. William C. Byham and George Dixon, "Through Japanese Eyes," *Training and Development Journal,* March 1993, pp. 33–36; Linda S. Dillon, "West Meets East," *Training and Development Journal,* March 1993, pp. 39–43.

4. Fons Trompenaars and Charles Hampden-Turner, *Riding the Waves of Culture: Understanding Diversity in Global Business,* 2nd ed. (New York: McGraw-Hill, 1998), p. 204.

5. Nancy J. Adler, *International Dimensions of Organizational Behavior,* 2nd ed. (Boston: PWS-Kent Publishing, 1991), pp. 75–76.

6. Giorgio Inzerilli, "The Legitimacy of Managerial Authority: A Comparative Study," *National Academy of Management Proceedings* (Detroit, 1980), pp. 58–62.

7. Ibid., p. 62.

8. Philip R. Harris and Robert T. Moran, *Managing Cultural Differences,* 3rd ed. (Houston: Gulf Publishing, 1996), pp. 36–37.

9. Richard Tanner Pascale and Anthony G. Athos, *The Art of Japanese Management* (New York: Warner Books, 1981), pp. 82–83.

10. Justin Fox, "The Triumph of English," *Fortune,* September 18, 2000, pp. 209–212.

11. See "Double or Quits," *Economist,* February 25, 1995, pp. 84–85.

12. Brock Stout, "Interviewing in Japan," *HR Magazine,* June 1998, p. 73.

13. Ibid., p. 75.

14. H. W. Hildebrandt, "Communication Barriers Between German Subsidiaries and Parent American Companies," *Michigan Business Review,* July 1973, p. 9.

15. John R. Schermerhorn Jr., "Language Effects in Cross-Cultural Management Research: An Empirical Study and a Word of Caution," *National Academy of Management Proceedings* (New Orleans, 1987), p. 103.

16. Brenda R. Sims and Stephen Guice, "Differences Between Business Letters from Native and Non-Native Speakers of English," *Journal of Business Communication,* Winter 1991, p. 37.

17. James Calvert Scott and Diana J. Green, "British Perspectives on Organizing Bad-News Letters: Organizational Patterns Used by Major U.K. Companies," *The Bulletin,* March 1992, p. 17.

18. Ibid., pp. 18–19.

19. Mi Young Park, W. Tracy Dillon, and Kenneth L. Mitchell, "Korean Business Letters: Strategies for Effective Complaints in Cross-Cultural Communication," *Journal of Business Communication,* July 1998, pp. 328–345.

20. As an example see Jeremiah Sullivan, "What Are the Functions of Corporate Home Pages?" *Journal of World Business* 34, no. 2 (1999), pp. 193–211.

21. Joseph Kahn, "Fraying U.S.-Sino Ties Threaten Business," *Wall Street Journal,* July 7, 1995, p. A6; Nathaniel C. Nash, "China Gives Big Van Deal to Mercedes," *New York Times,* July 13, 1995, pp. C1, C5; and Seth Faison, "China Times a Business Deal to Make a Point to America," *New York Times,* July 16, 1995, pp. 1, 6.

22. David A. Ricks, *Big Business Blunders: Mistakes in Multinational Marketing* (Homewood, IL: Dow Jones/Irwin, 1983), p. 39.

23. Ibid., p. 55.

24. John Kass, "Some Bright Ideas Get Lost in Translation," *Chicago Tribune,* April 20, 2007, online edition, www.chicagotribune.com/news/columnists/chi-0704190692apr20,1,6809930.column.

25. Edwin Miller, Bhal Bhatt, Raymond Hill, and Julian Cattaneo, "Leadership Attitudes of American and German Expatriate Managers in Europe and Latin America," *National Academy of Management Proceedings* (Detroit, 1980), pp. 53–57.

26. Abdul Rahim A. Al-Meer, "Attitudes Towards Women as Managers: A Comparison of Asians, Saudis and Westerners," *Arab Journal of the Social Sciences,* April 1988, pp. 139–149.

27. Sheryl WuDunn, "In Japan, Still Getting Tea and No Sympathy," *New York Times,* August 27, 1995, p. E3.

28. Fathi S. Yousef, "Cross-Cultural Communication: Aspects of the Contrastive Social Values Between North Americans and Middle Easterners," *Human Organization,* Winter 1974, p. 385.

29. Peter McKiernan and Chris Carter, "The Millennium Nexus: Strategic Management at the Crossroads," *European Management Review 1,* no. 1 (Spring 2004), p. 3.

30. R. Bruce Money, "Word-of-Mouth Referral Sources for Buyers of International Corporate Financial Services," *Journal of World Business* 35, no. 3 (2000), pp. 314–329.

31. Yousef, "Cross-Cultural Communication," p. 383.

32. See Roger E. Axtell, ed., *Do's and Taboos Around the World* (New York: Wiley, 1990), chapter 2.

33. Jane Whitney Gibson, Richard M. Hodgetts, and Charles W. Blackwell, "Cultural Variations in Nonverbal Communication," *55th Annual Business Communication Proceedings,* San Antonio, November 8–10, 1990, pp. 211–229.

34. William K. Brandt and James M. Hulbert, "Patterns of Communications in the Multinational Corporation: An Empirical Study," *Journal of International Business Studies,* Spring 1976, pp. 57–64.

35. Hildebrandt, "Communication Barriers," p. 9.

36. See for example George Ming-Hong Lai, "Knowing Who You Are Doing Business with in Japan: A Managerial View of Keiretsu and Keiretsu Business Groups," *Journal of World Business* 34, no. 4 (1999), pp. 423–449.

37. Nicholas Athanassiou and Douglas Nigh, "Internationalization, Tacit Knowledge and the Top Management Teams of MNCs," *Journal of International Business Studies,* Third Quarter 2000, pp. 471–487.

38. Also see Linda Beamer, "Bridging Business Cultures," *China Business Review,* May–June 1998, pp. 54–58.

39. Michael D. Lord and Annette L. Ranft, "Organizational Learning About New International Markets: Exploring the Internal Transfer of Local Market Knowledge," *Journal of International Business Studies,* Fourth Quarter 2000, pp. 573–589.

40. Jennifer W. Spencer, "Knowledge Flows in the Global Innovation System: Do U.S. Firms Share More Scientific Knowledge than Their Japanese Rivals?" *Journal of International Business Studies,* Third Quarter 2000, pp. 521–530.

41. Kenichi Ohmae, "The Global Logic of Strategic Alliances," *Harvard Business Review,* March–April 1989, p. 154.

42. See Hildy Teegen and Jonathan P. Doh, "U.S./Mexican Alliance Negotiations: Cultural Impacts on Trust, Authority and Performance," *Thunderbird International Business Review* 44, no. 6 (2002), pp. 749–775; Elise Campbell and Jeffrey J. Reuer, "International Alliance Negotiations: Legal Issues for General Managers," *Business Horizons,* January–February 2001, pp. 19–26.

43. Nina Reynolds, Antonis Simintiras, and Efi Vlachou, "International Business Negotiations: Present Knowledge and Direction for Future Research," *International Marketing Review* 20, no. 3 (2003), p. 236.

44. *Harvard Business Essentials: Negotiation* (Boston: Harvard Business School Press, 2003), p. 2.

45. Ibid. p. 4.

46. David K. Tse, June Francis, and Ian Walls, "Cultural Differences in Conducting Intra- and Inter-Cultural Negotiations: A Sino-Canadian Comparison," *Journal of International Business Studies,* Third Quarter 1994, pp. 537–555; Teegen and Doh, "U.S./Mexican Alliance Negotiations," pp. 749–775.

47. Adler, *International Dimensions of Organizational Behavior,* p. 197.

48. Daniel Druckman, "Group Attachments in Negotiation and Collective Action," *International Negotiation* 11 (2006), pp. 229–252.

49. Jeanne M. Brett, Debra L. Shapiro, and Anne L. Lytle, "Breaking the Bonds of Reciprocity in Negotiations," *Academy of Management Journal,* August 1998, pp. 410–424.

50. Stephen E. Weiss, "Negotiating with 'Romans'—Part 2," *Sloan Management Review,* Spring 1994, p. 89.

51. Trompenaars and Hampden-Turner, *Riding the Waves of Culture,* p. 112.

52. James K. Sebenius, "The Hidden Challenge of Cross-Border Negotiations," *Harvard Business Review,* March, 2002, pp. 4–12.

53. John L. Graham, "Brazilian, Japanese, and American Business Negotiations," *Journal of International Business Studies,* Spring–Summer 1983, pp. 47–61; John L. Graham, "The Influence of Culture on the Process of Business Negotiations in an Exploratory Study," *Journal of International Business Studies,* Spring 1983, pp. 81–96.

54. William Zartman, "Negotiating Internal, Ethnic and Identity Conflicts in a Globalized World," *International Negotiation* 11 (2006), pp. 253–272.

55. Roger Fisher and William Ury, *Getting to Yes: Negotiating Agreement Without Giving In* (New York: Penguin Books, 1983), p. 11.

56. Ibid., p. 79.

57. Ibid., p. 111.

58. Graham, "Brazilian, Japanese, and American Business Negotiations," pp. 84, 88.

■ Part 2 Integrative Cases

Brief Integrative Case 2

1. Peter Wonacott and Chad Terhune, "Politics & Economics: Path to India's Market Dotted with Potholes; Savvy Cola Giants Stumble over Local Agendas; KFC Climbs Back from Abyss," *Wall Street Journal,* September 12, 2006, p. A6.

2. "CSE Report on Pesticide Residue Inconclusive," *Businessline,* August 27, 2006, p. 1.

3. Rajesh Kumar and Verner Worm, "Institutional Dynamics and the Negotiation Process: Comparing India and China," *International Journal of Conflict Management* 15, no. 3 (2004), p. 304.

4. Wonacott and Terhune, "Politics & Economics."

5. Archna Shukla, "Message Will Always Be More Important than Medium," *Business Today,* August 27, 2006, p. 102.

6. Mark Sappenfield, "India's Cola Revolt Taps into Old Distrust: Behind Contradictory Reports of Pesticides in Coke and Pepsi Is an Underlying Wariness of Foreign Companies," *The Christian Science Monitor,* September 1, 2006, p. 6.

7. Brian Bremner, Nandini Lakshman, and Diane Brady, "India: Behind the Scare over Pesticides in Pepsi and Coke," *BusinessWeek,* September 4, 2006, p. 43.

8. Sappenfield, "India's Cola Revolt Taps into Old Distrust."

9. Bremner, Lakshman, and Brady, "India: Behind the Scare over Pesticides in Pepsi and Coke."

10. Ratna Bhushan, "RC Cola Comes to India," *Businessline,* October 7, 2003, p. 1.

11. "India: Reports of Contaminated Soda Dry up Coke, Pepsi Sales," *Global Information Network,* September 7, 2006, p. 1.

12. Aryn Baker, "India's Storm in a Cola Cup," *Time International,* August 21, 2006, p. 8.

13. Bremner, Lakshman, and Brady, "India: Behind the Scare over Pesticides in Pepsi and Coke."

14. Sappenfield, "India's Cola Revolt Taps into Old Distrust."

15. Wonacott and Terhune. "Politics & Economics."

16. "India: Reports of Contaminated Soda Dry up Coke, Pepsi Sales."

17. Sappenfield, "India's Cola Revolt Taps into Old Distrust."

18. "Coca-Cola Co: India's Kerala State Cancels Ban on Coke, Pepsi Drinks," *Wall Street Journal,* September 25, 2006, p. A11.

19. Ibid.

20. Diane Brady, "Pepsi: Repairing a Poisoned Reputation in India," *BusinessWeek,* June 11, 2007.

21. Ibid.

22. Ibid.

23. Ibid.

24. Amit Srivastava, "Coca-Cola Funded Group Investigates Coca-Cola in India," India Resource Center, April 16, 2007, www.indiaresource.org/campaigns/coke/2007/coketeri.html.

25. Sappenfield, "India's Cola Revolt Taps into Old Distrust."

26. Amelia Gentleman, "For 2 Giants of Soft Drinks, a Crisis in Crucial Market," *New York Times,* August 23, 2006, p. C3.

27. Wonacott and Terhune, "Politics & Economics."

28. "Coca-Cola-India: Key Facts," www.cokefacts.org.

29. Ibid.

30. Ben Blanchard, "Coke Vows to Reduce Water Used in Drink Production," June 5, 2007, www.reuters.com.

31. "The Coca-Cola Company Pledges to Replace the Water It Uses in Its Beverages and Their Production," Press Release, June 5, 2007, www.thecoca-colacompany.com/presscenter/nr_20070605_tccc_and_wwf_partnership.html.

32. "Coca-Cola-India: Key Facts."

33. Gentleman, "For 2 Giants of Soft Drinks, a Crisis in Crucial Market."

34. Kenneth E. Behring, "Water Research; Researchers Are Raising Awareness of the Global Drinking Water Crisis," *Health & Medicine Week,* October 16, 2006, p. 1339.

35. Thalif Deen, "Development: Water, Water Everywhere Is Thing of the Past," *Global Information Network,* August 22, 2006, p. 1.

36. Loretta Chao and Shai Oster, "China Study Says Foreigners Violate Clean-Water Rules," *Wall Street Journal,* October 30, 2006, p. B7.

In-Depth Integrative Cases 1a and 1b

1. Stephen Koepp, "Do You Believe in Magic?" *Time,* April 25, 1988, pp. 66-73.

2. Raymond H. Lopez, "Disney in China Again?" March 2002, appserv.pace.edu/emplibrary/FINAL.Asiacasestudy.doc.

3. Ibid.

4. Ibid.

5. "Disney's Shanghai Park Plan in Doubt: Company Mulls Move to Another Location in China," Msnbc.com, December 11, 2006.

6. Raymond H. Lopez, "Disney in China Again?"

7. Thomas Crampton, "Disney's New Hong Kong Park to be 'Culturally Sensitive': Mickey Mouse Learns Chinese," *International Herald Tribune,* January 13, 2003, www.iht.com/articles/2003/01/13/disney_ed3__0.php.

8. Michael Schuman, "Disney's Hong Kong Headache," *Time Magazine,* May 8, 2006, www.time.com/time/magazine/article/0,9171,501060515-1191881,00.html.

9. Kim Soyoung and George Chen, "Hollywood Chases Asia Theme Park Rainbow," *Turkish Daily News,* May 29, 2007, www.turkishdailynews.com.tr/article.php?enewsid=74352.

10. "Malaysia Discussing Building Disney Park: Would be First Such Attraction in Southeast Asia," *Associated Press,* May 30, 2006, www.msnbc.msn.com/id/13045465/.

11. Soyoung and Chen, "Hollywood Chases Asia Theme Park Rainbow."

12. Ibid.

In-Depth Integrative Case 2

1. "Seiyu Stake Should Pay Off," *MMR,* May 26, 2003, p. 14.

2. "Wal-Mart Bottom Line Hits Mark," *MMR,* June 16, 2003, p. 9.

3. Ann Zimmerman and Martin Fackler, "Wal-Mart's Foray into Japan Spurs a Retail Upheaval," *Wall Street Journal,* September 18, 2003, p. B1.

4. Jennifer McTaggart, "Wal-Mart Versus the World," *Progressive Grocer,* October 15, 2003, p. 20.

5. David Lague, "Unions Triumphant at Wal-Mart in China," *International Herald Tribune,* October 12, 2006, www.iht.com/articles/ 2006/10/12/business/unions.php.

6. Wal-Mart Inc., "China Fact Sheet," www.walmartstores.com.

7. "'Wal-Mart' in Japan Sees Losses," Associated Press, August 23, 2006, www.sptimes.com/2006/08/23/Business/_Wal_Mart__in_Japan_s.shtml.

8. "Wal-Mart to Add 125 Stores in Mexico," *Arkansas Business Staff,* February 14, 2007, www.arkansasbusiness.com/article.aspx?aID=97026.13096.109168.

9. Geri Smith, "In Mexico, Banco Wal-Mart," *BusinessWeek,* November 20, 2006.

10. Clay Chandler, "The Great Wal-Mart of China," *Fortune,* July 25, 2005, money.cnn.com/magazines/fortune/fortune_archive/2005/07/25/8266651/index.htm.

11. Pallavi Gogoi, "Wal-Mart's China Card," *BusinessWeek,* July 26, 2005.

12. "Wal-Mart's Cheap Doubling in China," 24/7 *Wall Street,* February 27, 2007, www.247wallst.com/2007/02/walmarts_cheap_.html.

13. "Wal-Mart Buys China Grocery Chain," *Wire Services,* October 17, 2006, www.sptimes.com/2006/10/17/Business/Wal_Mart_buys_China_g.shtml.

14. Gogoi, "Wal-Mart's China Card."

15. "Wal-Mart Buys China Grocery Chain."

16. Carl Steidtmann, "Wal-Mart Set to Change Retail Face of Japan," *Asia Pulse,* October 27, 2003, p. 12.

17. "Wal-Mart Says Global Going Good," *Home Textiles Today,* September 26, 2003, p. 12.

18. McTaggart, "Wal-Mart Versus the World."

19. Ian Rowley, "Japan Isn't Buying the Wal-Mart Idea," *BusinessWeek,* February 28, 2005, www.businessweek.com/magazine/content/05_09/b3922073.htm.

20. Zimmerman and Fackler, "Wal-Mart's Foray into Japan."

21. Ibid.

22. "Wal-Mart Takes Crack at Japan," *Women's Wear Daily,* July 4, 2003, p. 2.

23. "Wal-Mart Says Global Going Good."

24. "Wal-Mart Takes Crack at Japan."

25. Ibid.

26. "Losses Widen at Wal-Mart in Japan," BBC News Online, February 16, 2007, news.bbc.co.uk/2/hi/business/6367819.stm.

27. "Wal-Mart Japan Reports Fivefold Jump in 1H Losses," *Taipei Times,* August 23, 2006, p. 10.

28. "Wal-Mart Says Global Going Good."

29. Ian Rowley, "Japan Isn't Buying the Wal-Mart Idea."

30. Ibid.

31. Rowley, "Japan Isn't Buying the Wal-Mart Idea."

32. "Wal-Mart Japan?" *Chain Store Age Executive* 78, no. 4 (April 2002), p. 32.

33. Ken Belson, "Wal-Mart Hopes It Won't Be Lost in Translation," *New York Times,* December 14, 2003, sec. 3, p. 1.

34. Tsukasa Furukawa, "Seiyu Eyes Wal-Mart 'Efficiency' Model," *Women's Wear Daily,* April 21, 2003, p. 15.

35. Koji Hirano, "Wal-Mart Might Soon Be Entering Japan," *Women's Wear Daily,* September 24, 2001, p. 10.

36. Mike Troy, "Wal-Mart Invests in Japan, Buys 6 Percent Share of Seiyu," *DSN Retailing Today,* March 25, 2002, p. 2.

37. David Ibison, "Wal-Mart to Expand with Push in Japan," *Financial Times London Edition,* January 2, 2001, p. A10.

38. McTaggart, "Wal-Mart Versus the World."

39. "Aeon to Pay 46 Billion Yen for 15% Daiei Stake," Associated Press, March 10, 2007, search.japantimes.co.jp/cgi-bin/nb20070310a1.html.

40. Wal-Mart Inc., "Global Procurement," www.walmartstores.com.

41. "Japan Food & Drink Report Q4 2006," *Business Monitor International,* February 2007.

42. Gary McWilliams and Ann Zimmerman, "Wal-Mart to Fight Ruling in Suit: Retailing Seeks Rehearing on Class-Action Status: Billions of Dollars in Claims," *Wall Street Journal,* February 7, 2007, p. A3.

43. "Wal-Mart Discrimination Case," June 29, 2007, www.walmart-facts.com.

44. Ibid.

45. Steven Malanga, "The War on Wal-Mart," *Wall Street Journal,* April 7, 2004, p. A18.

46. Patricia O'Connell, "Wal-Mart's Scott: 'We Were Getting Nowhere,'" *BusinessWeek,* September 22, 2005.

47. Marc Gunther, "The Green Machine," *Fortune,* July 31, 2006.

48. Ibid.

49. "Wal-Mart CEO Lee Scott Unveils 'Sustainability 360,'" July 2, 2007, www.walmartstores.com.

■ Chapter 8

1. Charlie Nordblom, "Involving Middle Managers in Strategy at Volvo Group," *Strategic Communication Management* 10, no. 2 (February–March 2006), pp. 26–29.

2. Joel Baglole, "Citibank Takes Risk by Issuing Cards in China," *Wall Street Journal,* March 10, 2004, p. C1.

3. Wang Ming, "Citigroup Sets China Growth," *Wall Street Journal,* March 15, 2007, p. C7.

4. "Foreign Investment Restrictions in OECD Countries" (Paris: Organization for Economic Cooperation and Development, June 2003), p. 167.

5. Matthew Karnitschnig, "Bertelsmann Plans Expansion as All Units Return to the Black," *Wall Street Journal,* March 31, 2004, p. B3.

6. Andrew Collier, "China: Foreign First in China Book Sector," *South China Morning Post,* December 4, 2003, p. A10.

7. Matthew Kamitsching, "Book-of-the-month Club to Turn a New Page," *Wall Street Journal,* April 10, 2007, p. B1.

8. Michael McHugh, "GE Energy Purchase of BHA Fits into Strategy," *Wall Street Journal,* June 1, 2004, p. A4.

9. www.ge.com/en/company/investor.

10. Barry Hopewell, "Strategic Management: A Multi-perspective Approach," *Long Range Planning* 36, no. 4 (July 2003), p. 317.

11. Sharon Watson O'Neil, "Managing Foreign Subsidiaries: Agents of Headquarters, or An Independent Network?" *Strategic Management Journal* 21, no. 5 (May 2000), p. 525.

12. Noel Capon, Chris Christodoulou, John U. Farley, and James Hulbert, "A Comparison of Corporate Planning Practice in American and Australian Manufacturing Companies," *Journal of International Business Studies,* Fall 1984, pp. 41–45.

13. Martin K. Welge, "Planning in German Multinational Corporations," *International Studies of Management and Organization,* Spring 1982, pp. 6–37.

14. Martin K. Welge and Michael E. Kenter, "Impact of Planning on Control Effectiveness and Company Performance," *Management International Review* 20, no. 2 (1988), pp. 4–15.

15. Johanna Mair, "Exploring the Determinants of Unit Performance: The Role of Middle Managers in Stimulating Profit Growth," *Group & Organization Management* 30, no. 3 (June 2005), pp. 263–288.

16. See for example Masaaki Kotabe, "Global Sourcing Strategy in the Pacific: American and Japanese Multinational Companies," in *Trends in International Business: Critical Perspectives,* ed. Michael R. Czinkota and Masaaki Kotabe (Malden, MA: Blackwell, 1998), pp. 237–256.

17. Joan Magretta, "Fast, Global, and Entrepreneurial: Supply Chain Management, Hong Kong Style," *Harvard Business Review,* September–October 1998, p. 108.

18. Nikhil Deogun, "For Coke in India, Thumbs Up Is the Real Thing," *Wall Street Journal,* April 29, 1998, pp. B1, B6.

19. Richard M. Hodgetts, *Measures of Quality and High Performance* (New York: American Management Association, 1998).

20. Sang M. Lee, Fred Luthans, and Richard M. Hodgetts, "Total Quality Management: Implications for Central and Eastern Europe," *Organizational Dynamics,* Spring 1992, pp. 44–45.

21. Yukari Iwatani Kane, "Wii and Nintendo Are Hot Buys, but Can the Good Times Continue?" *Wall Street Journal,* July 4, 2007, p. C5.

22. Lindsay Chappell, "Ford Man Runyon Rewrote the Rules at Nissan," *Automotive News,* May 10, 2004, p. 28.

23. Christine Y. Chen, "How Nortel Stole Optical," *Fortune,* October 2, 2000, p. 144. See also Sam Masud, "Building a Flexible Optical Network," *Telecommunications America* 37, no. 13 (December 2003), p. 18.

24. Leslie Wayne, "Chief Decided to Step Down at Motorola," *New York Times,* September 20, 2003, p. C1.

25. "Hip Cell," *Chicago Tribune,* June 3, 2004, p. 32.

26. Christopher A. Bartlett and Sumantra Ghoshal, *Managing Across Borders: The Transnational Solution,* updated 2nd ed. (Cambridge, MA: Harvard Business School Press, 2002).

27. Ibid.

28. Royal Ford, "Driven by Demand, Vehicle Buyers Want Versatility and Amenities, Too," *Boston Globe,* February 3, 2004, p. G1.

29. Fons Trompenaars and Charles Hampden-Turner, *Riding the Waves of Culture: Understanding Diversity in Global Business,* 2nd ed. (New York: McGraw-Hill, 1998), p. 188.

30. Andrew Pollack, "Japan's Companies Seek a Digital VCR Standard," *The New York Times,* February 16, 1993, online edition, www.nytimes.com; also www.panasonic.com.

31. Kerry Capell, "Thinking Simple at Philips," *BusinessWeek,* December 11, 2006, p. 50.

32. www.monsanto.com.

33. Charles Hill, *Global Business Today,* 3rd ed. (New York: McGraw-Hill, 2004), pp. 376–380.

34. Ibid.

35. See Anne-Wil Harzing, "An Empirical Analysis and Extension of the Bartlett and Ghoshal Typology of Multinational Companies," *Journal of International Business Studies,* First Quarter 2000, pp. 101–120; Julias H. Johnson Jr., "An Empirical Analysis of the Integration–Responsiveness Framework: U.S. Construction Equipment Industry Firms in Global Competition," *Journal of International Business Studies* 26, no. 3 (1995), pp. 621–636.

36. Kendra S. Albright, "Environmental Scanning: Radar for Success," *Information Management Journal* 38, no. 3 (May–June 2004), pp. 38–44.

37. Manuel Yunggar, "Environment Scanning for Strategic Information: Content Analysis from Malaysia," *Journal of American Academy of Business* 6, no. 2 (March 2005), pp. 324–331.

38. Michael Flagg, "U.S. Firm to Pioneer China's Interactive TV," *Wall Street Journal,* May 15, 2001, p. A21.

39. Ben Dolven, "China Grooms Global Players," *Wall Street Journal,* February 25, 2004, p. A12.

40. Gail Edmonson and Kathleen Kerwin, "Can Ford Fix This Flat?" *BusinessWeek,* December 1, 2003, p. 50.

41. David Shephardson, "Ex-Ford Executive Says He Didn't Resign," *Detroit News,* December 19, 2003, p. B1.

42. Gail Edmondson, "For Ford's Mulally, Europe's a Worry, Too," *BusinessWeek,* September 14, 2006, online edition, www.businessweek.com.

43. Sea Jin Chang, "International Expansion Strategy of Japanese Firms: Capacity Building Through Sequential Entry," *Academy of Management Journal,* April 1995, p. 402.

44. www.unctad.org.

45. Jathon Sapsford, "Real-Estate Buyers Circle Japan," *Wall Street Journal,* March 11, 1998, p. B10.

46. Graham Gori, "Investors Are Rushing to Mexico, Despite Slowing Growth," *New York Times,* May 25, 2001, p. W1; Mary Anastasia O'Grady, "Americas: Teamsters Give NAFTA a Flat Tire," *Wall Street Journal,* April 16, 2004, p. A15.

47. Craig Torres, "Foreigners Snap Up Mexican Companies: Impact Is Enormous," *Wall Street Journal,* September 30, 1997, p. A1. See also Joel Millman, "The Economy: Mexican Mergers, Acquisitions Triple from 2001," *Economist,* December 27, 2002, p. A2.

48. John Garland and Richard N. Farmer, *International Dimensions of Business Policy and Strategy* (Boston: Kent Publishing, 1986), pp. 62–63.

49. Harry I. Chernotsky, "Selecting U.S. Sites: A Case Study of German and Japanese Firms," *Management International Review* 23, no. 2 (1983), pp. 45–55.

50. Also see Roland Calori, Leif Melin, Tugrul Atamer, and Peter Gustavsson, "Innovative International Strategies," *Journal of World Business* 35, no. 4 (2000), pp. 333–354.

51. Christos Pantzalis, "Does Location Matter? An Empirical Analysis of Geographic Scope and MNC Market Valuation," *Journal of International Business Studies,* First Quarter 2001, pp. 133–155.

52. Das Narayandas, John Quelch, and Gordon Swartz, "Prepare Your Company for Global Pricing," *Sloan Management Review,* Fall 2000, pp. 61–70.

53. John McCary and Andrew Batson, "Punishing China: Will It Fly?" *Wall Street Journal,* June 23, 2007, p. A4.

54. United Nations Conference on Trade and Development, *World Investment Report 2002* (New York and Geneva: UNCTAD, 2003).

55. United Nations Conference on Trade and Development, *World Investment Report 2006* (New York and Geneva: UNCTAD, 2007).

56. Jeffrey E. Garten, *The Big Ten: The Big Emerging Markets and How They Will Change Our Lives* (New York: Basic Books, 1997).

57. Jonathan P. Doh and Ravi Ramamurti, "Reassessing Risk in Developing Country Infrastructure," *Long Range Planning* 36, no. 4 (2003), pp. 337–353.

58. Jonathan P. Doh, Hildy Teegen, and Ram Mudambi, "Balancing Private and State Ownership in Emerging Markets' Telecommunications Infrastructure: Country, Industry, and Firm Influences," *Journal of International Business Studies* 35, no. 3 (2004), pp. 233–250.

59. See Yudong Luo and Mike W. Peng, "First Mover Advantages in Investing in Transitional Economies," *Thunderbird International Business Review* 40, no. 2 (March–April 1998), pp. 141–163.

60. For a detailed analysis of first-mover effects of this case, see Jonathan P. Doh, "Entrepreneurial Privatization Strategies: Order of Entry and Local Partner Collaboration as Sources of Competitive Advantage," *Academy of Management Review* 25, no. 3 (2000), pp. 551–571.

61. Stuart Hart and Clayton Christensen, "The Great Leap: Driving Innovation from the Base of the Pyramid," *Sloan Management Review* 44, no. 1 (2002), pp. 51–56; C. K. Prahalad and Stuart L. Hart, "The Fortune at the Bottom of the Pyramid," *Strategy + Business* 26 (2002), pp. 54–67.

62. Joan Enric Ricart, Michael J. Enright, Pankaj Ghemawat, Stuart L. Hart, and Tarun Khanna, "New Frontiers in International Strategy," *Journal of International Business Studies* 35, no. 3 (May 2004), pp. 175–200.

63. Ibid., pp. 194–195.

64. Jamie Anderson and Niels Billou, "Serving the World's Poor: Innovation at the Base of the Economic Pyramid," *Journal of Business Strategy* 28, no. 2 (2007), pp. 14–21.

65. Patricia P. McDougall and Benjamin M. Oviatt, "International Entrepreneurship: The Intersection of Two Research Paths," Academy of Management Journal 43 (2000), pp. 902–908.

66. Ibid., p. 902.

67. Erkko Autio, Harry J. Sapienza, and James G. Almeida, "Effects of Age at Entry, Knowledge Intensity, and Irritability on International Growth," *Academy of Management Journal* 43 (2000), pp. 909–924.

68. Shaker A. Zahra, Duane R. Ireland, and Michael A. Hitt, "International Expansion by New Venture Firms: International Diversity, Mode of Market Entry, Technological Learning, and Performance," *Academy of Management Journal* 43 (2000), pp. 925–950.

69. Moen Oystein, "The Born Globals: A New Generation of Small European Exporters," *International Marketing Review* 19, no. 2/3 (2002), pp. 156–175.

70. Gary A. Knight and S. Tamar Cavusgil, "Innovation, Organizational Capabilities, and the Born-Global Firm," *Journal of International Business Studies* 35, no. 2 (2004), pp. 124–141.

71. Ibid.

72. Olli Kuivalainen, Sanna Sundqvist and Per Servais, "Firms' Degree of Born-Globalness, International Entrepreneurial Orientation and Export Performance," *Journal of World Business* 42 (2007), pp. 253–267.

73. Kimberly C. Gleason and Joan Wiggenhorn, "Born Globals: The Choice of Globalization Strategy, and the Market's Perception of Performance," *Journal of World Business* 42 (2007), pp. 322–335.

74. J. de La Torre and R. W. Moxon, "Electronic Commerce and Global Business: Introduction to the Symposium," *Journal of International Business* 32, no. 1 (2001), pp. 617–640.

75. Joseph Weber, "E*Trade Rises from the Ashes," *BusinessWeek,* January 17, 2005, online edition, www.businessweek.com.

■ Chapter 9

1. For more on this see Donald F. Kuratko and Richard M. Hodgetts, *Entrepreneurship: A Contemporary Approach,* 5th ed. (Ft. Worth, TX: Harcourt, 2001), pp. 529-535.

2. J. Contractor, "Contractual and Cooperative Forms of International Business: Towards Unified Theory of Model Choice," *Management International Review* 30, no. 1 (1990), pp. 31–54.

3. Peng S. Chan, "International Joint Ventures vs. Wholly Owned Subsidiaries," *Multinational Business Review* 3, no. 1 (Spring 1995), pp. 37–44.

4. Harrry Barkema and Freek Vermeulen, "International Expansion Through Start-up or Acquisition: A Learning Perspective," *Academy of Management Journal,* February 1998, pp. 7-26.

5. K. Carow, R. Heron, and T. Saxton, "Do Early Birds Get the Returns? An Empirical Investigation of Early-Mover Advantages in Acquisitions," *Strategic Management Journal* 25 (2004), pp. 563–585.

6. "A Post-modern Proctoid," *Economist,* April 12, 2006, online edition, www.economist.com.

7. Youssef M. Ibrahim, "British Petroleum Is Buying Amoco in $48.2 Billion Deal," *New York Times,* August 12, 1998, pp. A1, C5; Charles Goldsmith and Steven Lipin, "BP to Acquire Amoco in a Huge Deal Spurred by Falling Oil Prices," *Wall Street Journal,* August 12, 1998, p. A1.

8. Chip Cumming and Mark Long, "BP Net Rises 14%, Aided by Stock Sales," *Wall Street Journal,* April 28, 2004, p. A2.

9. Jim Carlton, "Claim of Unsafe BP Practices at Prudhoe Bay Probed," *Wall Street Journal,* July 2, 2007, p. A6.

10. Christine T. W. Huang and Brian H. Kleiner, "New Developments Concerning Managing Mergers and Acquisitions," *Management Research News* 27, no. 4–5 (2004), pp. 54–62.

11. Max Colchester, "Alcatel-Lucent Continues to Struggle," *Wall Street Journal,* August 1, 2007, p. B4.

12. For additional insights into alliances and joint ventures, see William Newburry and Yoram Zeira, "General Differences Between Equity International Joint Ventures (EIJVs), International Acquisitions (IAs) and International Greenfield Investments (IGIs): Implications for Parent Companies," *Journal of World Business* 32, no. 2 (1997), pp. 87–102.

13. Also see David Lei, Robert A. Pitts, and John W. Slocum Jr., "Building Cooperative Advantage: Managing Strategic Alliances to Promote Organizational Learning," *Journal of World Business* 32, no. 3 (1997), pp. 203–222.

14. For more on this see Ana Valdes Llaneza and Esteban Garcia-Canal, "Distinctive Features of Domestic and International Joint Ventures," *Management International Review* 38, no. 1 (1998), pp. 49–66.

15. "Singapore Telecommunications: Alcatel, Fujitsu Wins Contract for Undersea Cable Network," *Wall Street Journal,* March 30, 2004, p. 1.

16. John B. Cullen, Jean L. Johnson, and Tomoaki Sakano, "Success Through Commitment and Trust: The Soft Side of Strategic Alliance Management," *Journal of World Business* 35, no. 3 (2000), pp. 223–240.

17. John Markov, "Sony and AOL Join Forces on the Video Game Front," *New York Times,* May 15, 2001, p. C12.

18. For more on this see Hildy J. Teegen and Jonathan P. Doh, "U.S./Mexican Alliance Negotiations: Cultural Impacts on Trust, Authority and Performance," *Thunderbird International Business Review* 44, no. 6 (2002), pp. 749–775; Michael A. Hitt, M. Tina Dacin, Edward Levitas, Jean-Luc Arregle, and Anca Borza, "Partner Selection in Emerging and Developed Market Contexts: Resource-Based and Organizational Learning Perspectives," *Academy of Management Journal* 43, no. 3 (2002), pp. 449–467.

19. Christopher Lawton, "Dell Will Sell PCs in Japan Stores," *Wall Street Journal,* July 27, 2007, p. B4.

20. Jenny Watts, "Is This the End for Coke's 'Think Local' Ad Strategy?" *Campaign,* October 12, 2001, p. 17.

21. Jonathan Wheatley, "Coke Pops the Top off an Emerging Market," *BusinessWeek,* May 2, 2005, online edition, www.businessweek.com.

22. Joan Magretta, "Fast, Global, and Entrepreneurial: Supply Chain Management, Hong Kong Style," *Harvard Business Review,* September-October 1998, p. 106.

23. See George S. Yip, *Total Global Strategy II* (Englewood Cliffs, NJ: Prentice Hall, 2003), chapter 8.

24. A. V. Phatak, *International Dimensions of Management,* 2nd ed. (Boston: PWS-Kent, 1989), pp. 92–93.

25. John Tagliabue, "Renault Agrees to Buy Troubled Samsung Motors of Korea," *New York Times,* April 22, 2000, pp. B1, B3.

26. Stephanie Strom, "DaimlerChrysler Buying a Third of Mitsubishi for $2.1 Billion," *New York Times,* March 28, 2000, p. C4.

27. Also see Andrew C. Inkpen and Adva Dinur, "Knowledge Management Processes and International Joint Ventures," *Organization Science,* July–August 1998, pp. 454–468.

28. See for example John Child, "A Configurational Analysis of International Joint Ventures," *Organization Studies* 23, no. 5 (2002), pp. 781–815.

29. Pien Wang, Chow Hou Wee, and Peck Hiong Koh, "Establishing a Successful Sino-Foreign Equity Joint Venture: The Singapore Experience," *Journal of World Business* 34, no. 3 (1999), pp. 287–306.

30. Gus Gorman and Thurmon Williams, "How Do You Spell Success in Mexico? CALICA," *Business Horizons* 44, no. 1 (January–February 2001), p. 11.

31. For some insights regarding the importance of networking, see "The Battle for Ukraine," *Economist,* February 11, 1995, p. 56.

32. Miki Tanikawa, "Electronics Giants Join Forces in Japan," *New York Times,* May 24, 2001, p. W1.

33. Donald Gerwin, "Coordinating New Product Development in Strategic Alliances," *Academy of Management Review* 29, no. 2 (April 2004), p. 241.

34. Eric Peterson, "New Keiretsu Forum Chapter Links Angels, Entrepreneurs," *Boulder County Business Report* 26, no. 11 (May 11–24, 2007), p. 1A.

35. Craig Zarley, "IBM Outsourcing Rolls On," *CRN,* January 13, 2003, p. 24.

36. Matthew Schifrin, "Partner or Perish," *Forbes,* May 21, 2001, p. 27.

37. Thomas W. Malone and Robert J. Laubacher, "The Dawn of the E-Lance Economy," *Harvard Business Review,* September–October 1998, p. 148.

38. Durward K. Sobek II, Jeffrey K. Liker, and Allen C. Ward, "Another Look at How Toyota Integrates Product Development," *Harvard Business Review,* July–August 1998, p. 49.

39. For more on this see M. Bensaou and Michael Earl, "The Right Mind-Set for Managing Information Technology," *Harvard Business Review,* September–October 1998, pp. 119–128.

40. Anne-Wil Harzing, "An Empirical Analysis and Extension of the Bartlett and Ghoshal Typology of Multinational Companies," *Journal of International Business Studies,* First Quarter 2000, pp. 101–120.

41. Steven M. Sommers, Seung-Hyun Bae, and Fred Luthans, "The Structure-Climate Relationship in Korean Organizations," *Asia Pacific Journal of Management* 12, no. 2 (1995), pp. 23–36.

42. James R. Lincoln, Mitsuyo Hanada, and Kerry McBride, "Organizational Structures in Japanese and U.S. Manufacturing," *Administrative Science Quarterly,* September 1986, p. 356.

43. Rhy-song Yeh and Tagi Sagafi-nejad, "Organizational Characteristics of American and Japanese Firms in Taiwan," *National Academy of Management Proceedings,* 1987, pp. 111–115.

44. Ibid., p. 113.

45. Abbass F. Alkhafaji, *Competitive Global Management: Principles and Strategies* (Delray Beach, FL: St. Lucie Press, 1995), pp. 390–391.

46. Michael Yoshino and N. S. Rangan, *Strategic Alliances* (Boston: Harvard Business School Press, 1995), p. 195.

47. For additional insights, see Anant K. Sundaram and J. Stewart Black, *The International Business Environment: Text and Cases* (Englewood Cliffs, NJ: Prentice-Hall, 1995), pp. 314–315.

48. Lincoln, Hanada, and McBride, "Organizational Structures," p. 349.

49. Vito Racancelli, "Why Hung-Up Nokia Might Still Be Decent Value Play," *Barron's,* May 24, 2004, p. MW6.

50. Mark Lehrer and Kazuhiro Asakawa, "Unbundling European Operations: Regional Management and Corporate Flexibility in American and Japanese MNCs," *Journal of World Business* 34, no. 3 (1999), pp. 267–286.

51. Masumi Tsuda, "The Future of the Organization and the Individual to Japanese Management," *International Studies of Management and Organization,* Fall-Winter 1985, pp. 89–125.

52. Yeh and Sagafi-nejad, "Organizational Characteristics," p. 113.

53. Stephen Christophe and Ray Pfeiffer Jr., "The Valuation of MNC International Operations During the 1990s," *Review of Quantitative Finance and Accounting* 18, no. 2 (March 2002), p. 119.

54. Tsuda, "The Future of the Organization," p. 114.

■ Chapter 10

1. "Finance and Economics: Footloose Firms; Economic Focus," *Economist,* March 27, 2004, p. 99.

2. Seth Faison, "China Applies Brakes on Move Toward Market Economy," *New York Times,* September 30, 1998, p. C3. See also Kathy Chen, "China's Party Line Is Capital," *Wall Street Journal,* February 12, 2004, p. C20.

3. Alfred Hille, "Li Leads Way in China Piracy Battle," *Media,* January 16, 2004, p. 17.

4. Richard Read, "Chinese Knockoffs, Nike Headache," *Knight Ridder Tribune Business News,* July 30, 2006, p. 1.

5. Benjamin Fulford, "Microwave Missionaries," *Forbes,* November 13, 2000, p. 146.

6. Andrew Green, "The Development of Mass Media in Asia-Pacific," *International Journal of Advertising* 22, no. 2 (2002), p. 273.

7. Howard W. French, "Chinese Discuss Plan to Tighten Restrictions on Cyberspace," *The New York Times,* July 4, 2006, p. A3.

8. P. T. Bangsberg, "Hong Kong, China Plant Transport Links," *Journal of Commerce,* June 14, 2004, p. 1.

9. Elisabeth Rosenthal, "U.S. Trade Official Says China Market Is Closed Tighter," *New York Times,* September 23, 1998, p. C2.

10. Andrew Baston and Lauren Etter, "Politics & Economics: Safety Becomes a Hot Trade Issue: As China and U.S. Cite Import Concerns, Fears Grow Rules May Be Abused," *Wall Street Journal,* July 16, 2007, p. A4.

11. Mark Landler, "Back to Vietnam, This Time to Build," *New York Times,* September 13, 1998, sec. 3, pp. 1, 11.

12. "Change Will Come...But Not Yet," *Asia Monitor,* January 2007, online edition, www.asia-monitor.com.

13. Todd Zaun, "The Economy: U.S. Trade Chief Seeks to Reassure a Very Weary Japan on Steel Tariffs," *Wall Street Journal,* April 12, 2002, p. A2.

14. John McKinnon and Neil King, "EU Set to Impose Trade Sanctions If U.S. Fails to Act," *Wall Street Journal,* January 26, 2004, p. A4.

15. "Coca-Cola Co: Settlement of Anti-Trust Case Is Discussed with EU Officials," *Wall Street Journal,* April 19, 2004, p. 1.

16. Edmund L. Andrews, "Why U.S. Giants Are Crying Uncle," *New York Times,* October 11, 2000, p. W1.

17. "EU Blocks Ryanair Bid for Aer Lingus," *USA Today,* June 27, 2007, online edition, www.usatoday.com.

18. Jack N. Kondrasuk, "The Effects of 9/11 and Terrorism on Human Resource Management: Recovery, Reconsideration, and Renewal," *Employee Responsibilities and Rights Journal* 16, no. 1 (May 2004), pp. 25–35.

19. J. Hocking, *Beyond Terrorism: The Development of the Australian Security State* (Sydney: Allen & Unwin Pty Ltd, 1993).

20. Kondrasuk, "The Effects of 9/11."

21. Jack N. Kondrasuk, Daniel Bailey, and Mathew Sheeks, "Leadership in the 21st Century: Understanding Global Terrorism," *Employee Responsibilities and Rights Journal* 17, no. 4 (December 2005), pp. 263–280.

22. Siaw Khiun Then and Martin Loosemore, "Terrorism Prevention, Preparedness, and Response in Built Facilities," *Facilities* 24, no. 5-6 (2006), pp. 157–176.

23. David A. Schmidt, "Analyzing Political Risk," *Business Horizons,* July-August 1986, pp. 43–50.

24. Matthew Brzezinski, "Russia Kills Huge Oil Deal with Exxon," *Wall Street Journal,* August 28, 1997, p. A2.

25. For more, see Thomas A. Pointer, "Political Risk: Managing Government Intervention," in *International Management: Text and Cases,* ed. Paul W. Beamish, J. Peter Killing, Donald J. LeCraw, and Harold Crookell (Homewood, IL: Irwin, 1991), pp. 119–133.

26. See Jonathan P. Doh and Ravi Ramamurti, "Reassessing Risk in Developing Country Infrastructure," *Long Range Planning* 36, no. 4 (2003), pp. 337–353.

27. Ravi Ramamurti and Jonathan Doh, "Rethinking Foreign Infrastructure Investment in Developing Countries," *Journal of World Business* 39, no. 2 (2004), pp. 151–167.

28. Michael M. Schuman, "Indonesia to Pay Reduced Claim to U.S. in Long-Disputed Overseas Insurance Case," *Wall Street Journal,* May 11, 2001, p. A12.

29. Timothy Mapes, "Power Firm's Bid to Collect Funds from Pertamina Raises Hackles," *Wall Street Journal,* April 1, 2002, p. A6.

30. See Jonathan P. Doh and John A. Pearce II, "Corporate Entrepreneurship and Real Options in Transitional Policy Environments: Theory Development," *Journal of Management Studies* 41, no. 4 (2004), pp. 645–664.

31. Doh and Ramamurti, "Reassessing Risk," pp. 344–349.

32. Amy Hillman and Michael A. Hitt, "Corporate Political Strategy Formulation: A Model of Approach, Participation, and Strategy Decisions," *Academy of Management Review* 24, no. 24 (1999), pp. 825–842.

33. Amy Hillman and Gerald Keim, "International Variation in the Business-Government Interface: Institutional and Organizational Considerations," *Academy of Management Review* 20, no. 1 (1995), pp. 193–214.

34. Robert J. Bowman, "Are You Covered?" *World Trade* 8, no. 2 (March 1995), pp. 100–103.

35. Mark A. Hofmann, "Political Risk Market Eases as Supply Outpaces Demand," *Business Insurance* 40, no. 8 (February 20, 2006), pp. 9–10.

36. Jonathan P. Doh and Hildy Teegen, "Nongovernmental Organizations as Institutional Actors in International Business: Theory and Implications," *International Business Review* 11, no. 6 (2002), pp. 665–684.

37. Karl Schoenberge, "Motorola Bets Big on China," *Fortune,* May 27, 1996, pp. 116–121.

38. Matthew Karnitschnig, "Siemens to Expand Business in China and Boost Sales," *Wall Street Journal,* May 18, 2004, p. A6.

39. Peter J. Buckley and Mark Casson, "An Economic Model of International Joint Venture Strategy," *Journal of International Business Studies* 27 (1996), pp. 849–876.

40. Farok J. Contractor and Peter Lorange, eds., *Cooperative Strategies in International Business* (Lexington, MA: Lexington Books, 1998).

41. Andrew C. Inkpen, *The Management of International Joint Ventures: An Organizational Learning Perspective* (London: Routledge, 1995).

42. Shige Makino and Andrew Delios, "Local Knowledge Transfer and Performance: Implications for Alliance Formation in Asia," *Journal of International Business Studies* 27 (1996), pp. 905–927.

43. Hildy Teegen and Jonathan P. Doh, "U.S./Mexican Alliance Negotiations: Cultural Impacts on Trust, Authority and Performance," *Thunderbird International Business Review* 44, no. 6, (2002), pp. 749–775.

44. Harry G. Barkema and Freek Vermeulen, "What Differences in the Cultural Backgrounds of Partners Are Detrimental for International Joint Ventures?" *Journal of International Business Studies* 28, no. 4 (1997), pp. 845–864.

45. Teegen and Doh, "U.S./Mexican Alliance Negotiations," pp. 749–775.

46. Dirk Holtbrugge, "Management of International Strategic Business Cooperation: Situation Conditions, Performance Criteria and Success Factors," *Thunderbird International Business Review* 46, no. 3 (May-June 2004), pp. 255–274.

47. Manuel G. Serapio Jr. and Wayner F. Cascio, "End Games in International Alliances," *Academy of Management Executive* 10, no. 1 (February 1996), pp. 62–73.

48. Julia G. Djarova, "Foreign Investment Strategies and the Attractiveness of Central and Eastern Europe," *International Studies in Management and Organization* 29, no. 1 (Spring 1999), pp. 14–23.

49. Jonathan P. Doh and Hildy Teegen, "Government Mandates and Local Partner Participation in Emerging Markets: Policy and Performance Implications for Government and Business Strategies" (paper presented at the annual meeting of the Academy of International Business, Phoenix, AZ, November 20, 2002).

50. Jonathan P. Doh, Peter Rodriguez, Klaus Uhlenbruck, Jamie Collins, and Lorraine Eden, "Coping with Corruption in Foreign Markets," *Academy of Management Executive* 17, no. 3 (2003), pp. 114–127.

51. Serapio and Cascio, "End Games in International Alliances," pp. 71–72.

52. Edward Norton, "Starbucks in China," *Economist,* October 4, 2001, pp. 80–82.

53. Frederick Balfour, "Back on the Radar Screen," *BusinessWeek,* November 2000, p. 27.

54. Henry Gallagher, "A Private Sector Surfaces in Vietnam," *The World & I* 18, no. 11 (November 2003), p. 56.

55. Trien Nguyen, "From Plan to Market: The Economic Transition in Vietnam," *Journal of Economic Literature* 38, no. 3 (September 2000), p. 683.

56. Klaus E. Meyer, Yen Thi Thu Tran, and Hung Vo Nguyen, "Doing Business in Vietnam," *Thunderbird International Business Review,* March–April 2006, pp. 263–290.

■ Chapter 11

1. Andrew Osborn, "Crash Course in Quality for Chinese Car," *Wall Street Journal,* August 8, 2007, p. B1.

2. Jon E. Hilsenrath, "Ford Designs Ikon to Suit Indian Tastes," *Globe and Mail,* August 8, 2000, p. B10.

3. "Q&A with PetroChina's Huang Yan," *BusinessWeek,* July 2, 2001, online edition, www.businessweek.com.

4. Deborah Ball, "Cadbury Retools to Ward Off a Takeover," *Wall Street Journal,* June 20, 2007, p. A8.

5. Jette Schramm-Nielsen, "Cultural Dimensions of Decision Making: Denmark and France Compared," *Journal of Managerial Psychology* 16, no. 6 (2001), pp. 404–423.

6. Ibid., pp. 410–411.

7. Raghu Nath, *Comparative Management: A Regional View* (Cambridge, MA: Ballinger, 1988), pp. 74–75.

8. Noboru Yoshimura and Philip Anderson, *Inside the Kaisha: Demystifying Japanese Business Behavior* (Boston: Harvard Business School Press, 1997), p. 44.

9. Bill Roberts, "Renesas Merges East and West," *Electronic Business* 30, no. 11 (November 2004), pp. 44–50.

10. Sang M. Lee, Fred Luthans, and Richard M. Hodgetts, "Total Quality Management: Implications for Central and Eastern Europe," *Organizational Dynamics,* Spring 1992, p. 45.

11. Daewoo Park and Herna A. Krishnan, "Understanding Supplier Selection Practices: Differences Between U.S. and Korean Executives," *Thunderbird International Business Review,* March–April 2001, pp. 243–255.

12. Rebecca Blumstein, "Cadillac Has Designs on Europe's Luxury Car Buyers," *Wall Street Journal,* September 9, 1997, p. B1.

13. Christopher Rauwald, "GM to Export Opel Model to North America," *Wall Street Journal,* December 8, 2006, online edition, www.wsj.com.

14. "BMW: Up Close and Personal," *Marketing Week,* July 27, 2002, p. 42.

15. Christopher Gasper, "NEC Seeks Right Fits for Expansion," *Boston Globe,* May 13, 2004, p. C3.

16. Edward Moltzen, "Intel Highlights New Roadmap with Dual-Core Processors," *CRN,* May 31, 2004, p. 35.

17. Jack Ewing, "Siemens' Culture Clash," *BusinessWeek,* January 29, 2007, pp. 42–46.

18. "GM China Has Jump in Car Sales," *Wall Street Journal,* July 3, 2003, p. A1.

19. Bill Spindle, "Cowboys and Samurai: The Japanizing of Universal," *Wall Street Journal,* March 22, 2001, p. B6.

20. Kelly Olsen, "Universal Studios Plans Theme Park in South Korea," *USAToday,* May 23, 2007, online edition, www.usatoday.com.

21. Dana Corporation, *Annual Report* 2003.

22. Dana Corporation, *Annual Report* 2007.

23. Jim Middlemiss, "IT Challenge: Settlement," *Wall Street Week,* April 2004, p. 46.

24. Fons Trompenaars and Charles Hampden-Turner, *Riding the Waves of Culture: Understanding Diversity in Global Business,* 2nd ed. (New York: McGraw-Hill, 1998), pp. 157–159.

25. John D. Daniels and Jeffrey Arpan, "Comparative Home Country Influences on Management Practices Abroad," *Academy of Management Journal,* September 1972, p. 310.

26. Jacques H. Horovitz, "Management Control in France, Great Britain and Germany," *Columbia Journal of World Business,* Summer 1978, pp. 17–18.

27. Ibid., p. 18.

28. William G. Egelhoff, "Patterns of Control in U.S., U.K., and European Multinational Corporations," *Journal of International Business Studies,* Fall 1984, p. 81.

29. Ibid., pp. 81–82.

30. M. Kreder and M. Zeller, "Control in German and U.S. Companies," *Management International Review* 28, no. 3 (1988), pp. 64–65.

31. Lane Daley, James Jiambalvo, Gary L. Sundem, and Yasumasa Kondo, "Attitudes Toward Financial Control Systems in the United States and Japan," *Journal of International Business Studies,* Fall 1985, pp. 91–110.

32. Yoshimura and Anderson, *Inside the Kaisha,* p. 55.

33. A. V. Phatak, *International Dimensions of Management,* 2nd ed. (Boston: PWS-Kent, 1989), p. 154.

34. William Boston and Paul Hofheinz, "Once Again, EU to Take Back Seat to VW," *Wall Street Journal,* February 27, 2002, p. A16.

35. David A. Garvin, "Japanese Quality Management," *Columbia Journal of World Business,* Fall 1984, pp. 3–12.

36. Ibid., p. 6.

37. Jeffrey K. Liker and Yen-Chun Wu, "Japanese Automakers, U.S. Suppliers and Supply-Chain Superiority," *Sloan Management Review,* Fall 2000, pp. 81–93.

38. Cited in John Holusha, "Improving Quality, the Japanese Way," *New York Times,* July 20, 1988, p. 25. See also Richard Dauch, "Recipe for Success," *Manufacturing Engineering* 131, no. 2 (August 2003), p. 69.

39. "Key to Success: People, People, People," *Fortune,* October 27, 1997, p. 232.

40. Golpira Eshgi, "Nationality Bias and Performance Evaluations in Multinational Corporations," *National Academy of Management Proceedings* (San Diego, 1985), p. 95.

41. Jeremiah Sullivan, Terukiho Suzuki, and Yasumasa Kondo, "Managerial Theories and the Performance Control Process in Japanese and American Work Groups," *National Academy of Management Proceedings* (San Diego, 1985), pp. 98–102.

42. Ibid.

■ Part 3 Integrative Cases

Brief Integrative Case 1

1. "Microsoft Restates China Policy," BBC News Online, November 3, 2007, news.bbc.co.uk/go/pr/fr/-/2/hi/technology/6114846.stm.

2. USINFO East Asia, "One-Third of Computer Software Pirated, Industry Says, July 7, 2004," July 9, 2004, italy.usembassy.gov/viewer/article.asp?article=/file2004_07/alia/a4070702.htm; and Tom Braithwaite, "China Defies Trend and Curbs Illicit Software," *Financial Times,* May 23, 2006, p. 7.

3. "China Passes Strategic Plan for Informatization Development," People's Daily Online, November 4, 2006, english.people.com.cn/200511/04/eng20051104_218969.html.

4. "National Economic Security Should Not Be Ignored in the Rush to Open Up," People's Daily Online, August 31, 2006, english.people.com.cn//200608/31/eng20060831_298522.html.

5. Except where noted, this section draws upon Jean-Marc F. Blanchard, "Multinationals versus State Power in an Era of Globalization: The Case of Microsoft in China," *International Financial Review,* Vol. 7, ed. J. Jay Choi and Reid W. Click (Elsevier, 2007), pp. 497–534.

6. "Microsoft's Investment in China Spans the Last Six Years," Microsoft PressPass, November 5, 1998, www.microsoft.com/presspass/features/1998/11-5mschinalab.asp.

7. "Gates Visit to China Highlights Cooperation with Government, Academia, Local Industry Partners," Microsoft PressPass, February 28, 2003, www.microsoft.com/presspass/features/2003/feb03/02-28gates-china.mspx.

8. "Microsoft Eyes China's Government Procurement Deals," People's Daily, June 13, 2002, china.org.cn/english/investment/34523.htm.

9. "Microsoft Prepares to Launch MSN China," Microsoft Press-Pass, May 11, 2005, www.microsoft.com/presspass/press/2005/may05/05-11MSNChinaLaunchPR.mspx.

10. Richard McGregor, "Hu Trip to Seattle Lifts Hopes on Piracy Policy," *Financial Times,* April 19, 2006, p. 4.

11. Bi Mingxin, "Microsoft Unveils Huge China Plans," Shanghai Daily, April 23, 2007, news.xinhuanet.com/english/2007-04/23/content_6014028.htm.

12. Gareth Powell, "Microsoft Unveils Huge China Plans," China IT News, April 24, 2007, www.chinaeconomicreview.com/it/2007/04/24/microsoft-unveils-huge-china-plans.

13. Tom Leander, "Does Microsoft Need China?" CFO.com, August 10, 2004, www.cfo.com/printable/article.cfm/3015475?f=options.

14. "Microsoft in China: Clash of Titans," CNN.com, February 23, 2000, archives.cnn.com/2000/TECH/computing/02/23/microsoft.china.idg.

15. "Reasons for Microsoft's Success in China," NewsGD.com, April 28, 2006, www.newsgd.com/news/china1/200604280042.htm.

In-Depth Integrative Case 1

1. Robyn Weisman, "Problems Mount for Hewlett-Packard," *News-Factor Network,*www.newsfactor.com/perl/story/14668.html, November 8, 2001.

2. Cynthia Webb, "HP's Spin Fails to Appease the Street," www.washingtonpost.com, August 20, 2003.

3. Ibid.

4. Clint Swett, "Hewlett-Packard Seems to Have Digested Compaq," Knight Ridder Tribune Business News, May 13, 2003, p. 1.

5. Keith Reagan, "The HP-Compaq One Year Checkup," *E-Commerce Times,*www.ecommercetimes.com/perl/story/21406.html, May 1, 2003.

6. "About HP," www.hp.com.

7. Ibid.

8. "Assuming HP-Compaq Merger Takes Place . . . ," SV News Services, www.ciol.com/content/news/trends/102032601.asp, March 26, 2002.

9. Shukor Rahman, "Challenges Ahead for the New HP," *Computimes Malaysia,* May 13, 2002, p. 1.

10. Henry Norr, "Cost Cuts Going Fast for New HP," *San Francisco Chronicle,* June 5, 2002, p. B1.

11. "About HP," www.hp.com.

12. Ibid.

13. C. Doyle and S. Lelii, "From Integration to Execution: HP at One," *VAR Business,* May 12, 2003, p. 24.

14. Reagan, "The HP-Compaq One Year Checkup."

15. Swett, "Hewlett-Packard Seems to Have Digested Compaq."

16. Reagan, "The HP-Compaq One Year Checkup."

17. Ibid.

18. www.hp.com.

19. "HP's e-Drive Targets Underprivileged Worldwide," www.computerweekly.com/article123846.htm, July 31, 2003.

20. John Boudreau, "Fiorina Reaffirms HP's Pledge to Philanthropy," www.siliconvalley.com/3205060/asp.?, August 5, 2003.

21. Ibid.

22. Ibid.

23. "HP's e-Drive Targets Underprivileged Worldwide."

24. Melvin Calimag, "HP Philippines Aims to Open Eight HP Stores This Year," *Newsbyte News Network,* February 11, 2003.

25. "HP-Compaq Deal Likely to Clear European Hurdle," www.redding.com/newsarchive/20020131bus013.shtml, January 31, 2002.

26. Paul R. La Monica, "Fiorina Out, HP Stock Soars," CNN/Money, February 10, 2005, money.cnn.com/2005/02/09/technology/hp_fiorina/index.htm, July 1, 2007.

27. Ibid.

28. "The Word from Hurd," *BusinessWeek,* September 1, 2005.

29. Ibid.

30. David A. Kaplan, "Suspicions and Spies in Silicon Valley," *Newsweek,* September 18, 2006.

31. "George Keyworth Resigns as HP Director," HP Press Release, September 12, 2006, www.hp.com.

32. "HP Names Todd Bradley as Executive Vice President of Personal Systems Group," HP Press Release, June 13, 2005, www.hp.com/hpinfo/newsroom/press/2005/050613a.html?jumpid=reg_R1002_USEN.

33. Ibid.

34. Christopher Lawton, "How H-P Reclaimed Its PC Lead Over Dell," *Wall Street Journal*, June 4, 2007.

35. Ibid.

36. Ibid.

37. Ibid.

38. Ibid.

39. Ibid.

In-Depth Integrative Case 2

1. Wayne Arnold, "A Continent Divided by Water, Now United by Air," *New York Times*, January 1, 2004, p. W1.

2. Ibid.

3. Scott Neuman, "Low-Fare Airlines Take Off in Asia," *Wall Street Journal*, February 25, 2004, p. B6G.

4. A. Goldstein and C. Findlay, "Liberalisation and Foreign Direct Investment in Asian Transport Systems: The Case of Aviation," *Asian Development Bank and OECD Development Centre*, no. 26–27 (November 2003), p. 11.

5. Centre for Asia Pacific Aviation, "Outlook 2007: Full Frontal Attack on Flag Carriers Begins," March 6, 2007, www.centreforaviation.com, July 9, 2007.

6. Japan Travel Bureau, "Travel Trends and Prospects for 2003," *JTB Newsletter*, January 5, 2003.

7. Centre for Asia Pacific Aviation, "Low Cost Airlines in the Asia Pacific Region: An Exceptional Intra-regional Traffic Growth Opportunity," September 2002, www.centreforaviation.com.

8. Ibid.

9. Goldman Sachs, "Asia Airlines," *Asia Research*, October 17, 1997, p. 9.

10. Associated Press, "Malaysian Airline Tests Asia's Resistance to No-Frills Flights" (December 2002).

11. Centre for Asia Pacific Aviation, "Low Cost Airlines in the Asia Pacific Region."

12. Associated Press, "Malaysian Airline Tests Asia's Resistance."

13. Interview with Conor McCarthy, April 25, 2003.

14. Comment of William Ng provided on www.airlinequality.com after traveling on AirAsia in March 2003 from Kuala Lumpur to Penang.

15. G. Thomas, "In Tune with Low Fares in Malaysia," *Air Transport World*, May 2003, pp. 45–46.

16. Nicholas Ionides, "Man of the Moment," *Airline Business*, April 2004, p. 29.

17. Arnold, "A Continent Divided by Water."

18. Thomas, "In Tune with Low Fares in Malaysia."

19. Ionides, "Man of the Moment."

20. Interview with Conor McCarthy, May 8, 2003.

21. Ibid.

22. Centre for Asia Pacific Aviation, "Low Cost Airlines in the Asia Pacific Region."

23. www.airasia.com; Centre for Asia Pacific Aviation, "To Malaysia with Love; AirAsia Goes Patriotic," May 31, 2007, www.centreforaviation.com.

24. Centre for Asia Pacific Aviation, "Low Cost Airlines in the Asia Pacific Region."

25. Thomas, "In Tune with Low Fares in Malaysia."

26. Goldman Sachs, "Asia Airlines."

27. Ibid.

28. Centre for Asia Pacific Aviation, "Who's Who in Low Cost Aviation: AirAsia," 2007.

29. Ibid.

30. Nicholas Ionides, "Third Japanese New-Start Fair Inc. Launches Services," *Air Transport Intelligence News* (August 2000).

31. Wayne Arnold. "Qantas Airways Discloses Plan for Low-Cost Singapore Carrier," *New York Times*, April 7, 2004, p. W1.

32. "Having Fun and Flying High," *Economist*, March 11, 2004.

33. Arnold, "A Continent Divided by Water."

34. Centre for Asia Pacific Aviation, "To Malaysia with Love; AirAsia Goes Patriotic," May 31, 2007, www.centreforaviation.com.

35. Centre for Asia Pacific Aviation, "AirAsia & Leisure Cargo Partnership to Generate RM12 million in Revenue per Annum," June 7, 2007, www.centreforaviation.com.

36. "AirAsia IPO Takes Off," *The Standard*, November 23, 2004.

37. AirAsia, "Corporate Profile," www.airaisa.com, July 2, 2007.

38. Centre for Asia Pacific Aviation, "Outlook for 2007: Prepare for Shakeout," November 10, 2006.

39. Centre for Asia Pacific Aviation, "Asian Governments to Open Skies in 2007," March 8, 2007.

40. "Having Fun and Flying High."

41. Neuman, "Low-Fare Airlines Take Off in Asia."

42. Ibid.

43. Centre for Asia Pacific Aviation, "Outlook for 2007: Prepare for Shakeout."

■ Chapter 12

1. David Beswick, "Management Implications of the Interaction Between Intrinsic Motivation and Extrinsic Rewards," Seminar notes, February 16, 2007.

2. Abbass F. Alkhafaji, *Competitive Global Management* (Delray Beach, FL: St. Lucie Press, 1995), p. 118.

3. Nancy L. Adler, *International Dimensions of Organizational Behavior*, 2nd ed. (Boston: PWS-Kent, 1991), p. 160.

4. Dianne H. B. Welsh, Fred Luthans, and Steven Sommer, "Managing Russian Factory Workers: The Impact of U.S.-Based Behavioral and Participative Techniques," *Academy of Management Journal*, February 1993, p. 75.

5. Andrew Sergeant and Stephen Frenkel, "Managing People in China: Perceptions of Expatriate Managers," *Journal of World Business* 33, no. 1 (1998), p. 21.

6. "Economic Tonic: Japan's Economy," *Economist*, May 22, 2004, p. 87.

7. For a more detailed discussion, see Fred Luthans, *Organizational Behavior*, 10th ed. (New York: Irwin/McGraw-Hill, 2004), chapter 8.

8. A. H. Maslow, "A Theory of Human Motivation," *Psychological Review*, July 1943, pp. 390–396.

9. For more information on this topic, see Richard Mead, *International Management: Cross-Cultural Dimensions* (Cambridge, MA: Blackwell, 1994), pp. 209–212.

10. See Richard M. Hodgetts, *Modern Human Relations at Work*, 8th ed. (Hinsdale, IL: Dryden Press, 2002), chapter 2.

11. Mason Haire, Edwin E. Ghiselli, and Lyman W. Porter, *Managerial Thinking: An International Study* (New York: Wiley, 1966).

12. Ibid., p. 75.

13. Edwin C. Nevis, "Cultural Assumption and Productivity: The United States and China," *Sloan Management Review,* Spring 1983, pp. 17–29.

14. Geert H. Hofstede, "The Colors of Collars," *Columbia Journal of World Business,* September 1972, pp. 72–78.

15. Ibid., p. 72.

16. George H. Hines, "Cross-Cultural Differences in Two-Factor Motivation Theory," *Journal of Applied Psychology,* December 1973, p. 376.

17. Donald D. White and Julio Leon, "The Two-Factor Theory: New Questions, New Answers," *National Academy of Management Proceedings,* 1976, p. 358.

18. D. Macarov, "Work Patterns and Satisfactions in an Israeli Kibbutz: A Test of the Herzberg Hypothesis," *Personnel Psychology,* Autumn 1972, p. 492.

19. Peter D. Machungwa and Neal Schmitt, "Work Motivation in a Developing Country," *Journal of Applied Psychology,* February 1983, pp. 31–42.

20. Farhad Analoui, "What Motivates Senior Managers? The Case of Romania," *Journal of Managerial Psychology* 15, no. 4 (2000).

21. G. E. Popp, H. J. Davis, and T. T. Herbert, "An International Study of Intrinsic Motivation Composition," *Management International Review* 26, no. 3 (1986), pp. 28–35.

22. Also see Rabi S. Bhagat et al., "Cross-Cultural Issues in Organizational Psychology: Emergent Trends and Directions for Research in the 1990s," in *International Review of Industrial and Organizational Psychology,* ed. C. L. Cooper and I. Robertson (New York: Wiley, 1990), p. 76.

23. Rabindra N. Kanungo and Richard W. Wright, "A Cross-Cultural Comparative Study of Managerial Job Attitudes," *Journal of International Business Studies,* Fall 1983, pp. 115–129.

24. Ibid., pp. 127–128.

25. Fred Luthans, "A Paradigm Shift in Eastern Europe: Some Helpful Management Development Techniques," *Journal of Management Development* 12, no. 8 (1993), pp. 53–60.

26. For more information on the characteristics of high achievers, see David C. McClelland, "Business Drive and National Achievement," *Harvard Business Review,* July–August 1962, pp. 99–112.

27. For more detail on the achievement motive, see Luthans, *Organizational Behavior,* pp. 253–256.

28. S. Iwawaki and R. Lynn, "Measuring Achievement Motivation in Japan and Great Britain," *Journal of Cross-Cultural Psychology* 3 (1999), pp. 219–220.

29. For more on this, see J. C. Abegglen and G. Stalk, *Kaisha: The Japanese Corporation* (New York: Basic Books, 1985); and R. M. Steers, Y. K. Shin, and G. R. Ungson, *The Chaebol: Korea's New Industrial Might* (New York: McGraw-Hill, 1989).

30. Fred Luthans, Brooke R. Envick, and Mary F. Sully, "Characteristics of Successful Entrepreneurs: Do They Fit the Cultures of Developing Countries?" *Proceedings of the Pan Pacific Conference,* 1995, pp. 25–27.

31. These data were reported in David C. McClelland, *The Achieving Society* (Princeton, NJ: Van Nostrand, 1961), p. 294.

32. E. J. Murray, *Motivation and Emotion* (Englewood Cliffs, NJ: Prentice Hall, 1964), p. 101.

33. David J. Krus and Jane A. Rysberg, "Industrial Managers and nAch: Comparable and Compatible?" *Journal of Cross-Cultural Psychology,* December 1976, pp. 491–496.

34. David C. McClelland, "Achievement Motivation Can Be Developed," *Harvard Business Review,* November–December 1965, p. 20.

35. Geert Hofstede, "Motivation, Leadership, and Organization: Do American Theories Apply Abroad?" *Organizational Dynamics,* Summer 1980, pp. 55–56.

36. For more on this, see Richard M. Steers and Carlos J. Sanchez-Runde, "Culture, Motivation, and Work Behavior" in *Handbook of Cross-Cultural Management,* ed. Martin J. Gannon and Karen L. Newman (London: Basil Blackwell, 2002).

37. E. Yuchtman, "Reward Distribution and Work-Role Attractiveness in the Kibbutz: Reflections on Equity Theory," *American Sociological Review* 37 (1972), pp. 581–595.

38. Paul A. Fadil, Robert J. Williams, Wanthanee Limpaphayom, and Cindi Smatt, "Equity or Equality? A Conceptual Examination of the Influence of Individualism/Collectivism on the Cross-Cultural Application of the Equity Theory," *Cross Cultural Management* 12, no. 4 (2005), pp. 17–35.

39. R. M. Steers, S. J. Bischoff, and L. H. Higgins, "Cross-Cultural Management Research: The Fish and the Fisherman," *Journal of Management Inquiry* 1 (1992), pp. 321–330; and Ken I. Kim, Hun-Joon Park, and Nori Suzuki, "Reward Allocations in the U.S., Japan, and Korea: A Comparison of Individualistic and Collectivistic Cultures," *Academy of Management Journal,* March 1990, pp. 188–198.

40. Luthans, *Organizational Behavior,* p. 520.

41. Edwin A. Locke and Gary P. Latham, *A Theory of Goal-Setting and Task Performance* (Englewood Cliffs, NJ: Prentice Hall, 1990).

42. M. Erez, "The Congruence of Goal-Setting Strategies with Socio-Cultural Values and Its Effect on Performance," *Journal of Management* 12 (1986), pp. 585–592.

43. J. P. French, J. Israel, and D. As, "An Experiment in a Norwegian Factory: Interpersonal Dimension in Decision-Making," *Human Relations* 13 (1960), pp. 3–19.

44. P. C. Earley, "Supervisors and Shop Stewards as Sources of Contextual Information in Goal-Setting," *Journal of Applied Psychology* 71 (1986), pp. 111–118.

45. M. Erez and P. C. Earley, "Comparative Analysis of Goal-Setting Strategies Across Cultures," *Journal of Applied Psychology* 72, no. 4 (1987), pp. 658–665.

46. Victor Vroom, *Work and Motivation* (New York: Wiley, 1964).

47. Lyman W. Porter and Edward E. Lawler III, *Managerial Attitudes and Performance* (Homewood, IL: Irwin, 1968).

48. Dov Eden, "Intrinsic and Extrinsic Rewards and Motives: Replication and Extension with Kibbutz Workers," *Journal of Applied Social Psychology* 5 (1975), pp. 348–361.

49. T. Matsui, T. Kakuyama, and M. L. Onglatco, "Effects of Goals and Feedback on Performance in Groups," *Journal of Applied Psychology* 72 (1987), pp. 407–415.

50. For a systematic analysis of this and other myths of Japanese management, see Richard M. Hodgetts and Fred Luthans, "Japanese HR Management Practices," *Personnel,* April 1989, pp. 42–45.

51. David Nicklaus, "Labor's Pains," *St. Louis Post-Dispatch,* September 2, 2002, p. A1.

52. For more on this topic, see Noel M. Tichy and Thore Sandstrom, "Organizational Innovations in Sweden," *Columbia Journal of World Business,* Summer 1974, pp. 18–28.

53. "Automotive Brief—Volvo AB: Profit Rose 80% in 4th Period, Bolstered by Truck Division," *Wall Street Journal,* February 4, 2004, p. A1; "Cars Brief: Volvo," *Wall Street Journal,* March 16, 2004, p. A1.

54. Edward McDonough, "Market-Oriented Product Innovation," *R&D Management,* June 2004, p. 335.

55. Eric Sundstrom, Kenneth P. DeMeuse, and David Futrell, "Work Teams: Application and Effectiveness," *American Psychologist,* February 1990, pp. 120–133.

56. See Lillian H. Chaney and Jeanette S. Martin, *Intercultural Business Communication* (Englewood Cliffs, NJ: Prentice Hall, 1995), pp. 46–47.

57. Bhagat et al., "Cross-Cultural Issues," p. 72.

58. Jonathan Watts, "Japan's Old Shy Away from Retiring," *The Guardian,* August 5, 2002, p. 12; "U.S. Workers Most Productive; but Study Says Europeans Have More Output per Hour," *Houston Chronicle,* September 1, 2003, p. 27.

59. Howard W. French, "A Postmodern Plague Ravages Japan's Workers," *New York Times,* February 21, 2000, p. A4; "Japanese Workers See Abuses by Bosses," *Los Angeles Times,*" June 30, 2003, p. C5.

60. Michelle Conlin, "Go-Go-Going to Pieces in China," *Business-Week,* April 23, 2007, p. 88.

61. "Satisfaction in the USA, Unhappiness in Japanese Offices," *Personnel,* January 1992, p. 8.

62. Fred Luthans, Harriette S. McCaul, and Nancy G. Dodd, "Organizational Commitment: A Comparison of American, Japanese, and Korean Employees," *Academy of Management Journal,* March 1985, pp. 213–219.

63. For other research on this topic, see Shahid N. Bhuian, Eid S. Al-Shammari, and Omar A. Jefri, "Work-Related Attitudes and Job Characteristics of Expatriates in Saudi Arabia," *Thunderbird International Business Review,* January–February 2001, pp. 21–31.

64. David I. Levine, "What Do Wages Buy?" *Administrative Science Quarterly,* September 1993, pp. 462–483.

65. David Heming, "What Wages Buy in the U.S. and Japan," *Academy of Management Executive,* November 1994, pp. 88–89.

66. Andrew Kakabadse and Andrew Myers, "Qualities of Top Management: Comparisons of European Manufacturers," *Journal of Management Development* 14, no. 1 (1995), p. 6.

67. Steven M. Sommer, Seung-Hyun Bae, and Fred Luthans, "Organizational Commitment Across Cultures: The Impact of Antecedents on Korean Employees," *Human Relations* 49, no. 7 (1996), pp. 977–993.

68. Anders Tornvall, "Work-Values in Japan: Work and Work Motivation in a Comparative Setting," in *Managing Across Cultures: Issues and Perspectives,* ed. Pat Joynt and Malcolm Warner (London: International Thomson Business Press, 1996), p. 256.

69. Stephen Kerr, "Practical, Cost-Neutral Alternatives That You May Know, but Don't Practice," *Organizational Dynamics,* Summer 1999, pp. 61–70.

70. "U.S. Workers Most Productive."

71. Matthew O. Hughes and Andrew Pirnie, "Retirement Reform Worldwide," *LIMRA's MarketFacts Quarterly* 22, no. 2 (Spring 2003), p. 12.

72. In the case of money, for example, see Swee Hoon Ang, "The Power of Money: A Cross-Cultural Analysis of Business-Related Beliefs," *Journal of World Business* 35, no. 1 (2000), pp. 43–60.

73. J. Milliman, S. Nason, M. A. von Glinow, P. Hou, K. B. Lowe, and N. Kim, "In Search of 'Best' Strategies Pay Practices: An Exploratory Study of Japan, Korea, Taiwan, and the United States," in *Advances in International Comparative Management,* ed. S. B. Prasad (Greenwich, CT: JAI Press, 1995), pp. 227–252.

74. Louis Lavelle, "Executive Pay," *BusinessWeek,* April 19, 2004, pp. 106–110.

75. S. C. Schneider, S. A. Wittenberg-Cox, and L. Hansen, *Honeywell Europe* (Insead, 1991).

76. C. M. Vance, S. R. McClaine, D. M. Boje, and H. D. Stage, "An Examination of the Transferability of Traditional Performance Appraisal Principles Across Cultural Boundaries," *Management International Review* 32, no. 4 (1992), pp. 313–326.

77. David Sirota and J. Michael Greenwood, "Understand Your Overseas Workforce," *Harvard Business Review,* January–February 1971, pp. 53–60.

78. D. E. Sanger, "Performance Related Pay in Japan," *International Herald Tribune,* October 5, 1993, p. 20.

79. S. H. Nam, "Culture, Control, and Commitment in International Joint Ventures," *International Journal of Human Resource Management* 6 (1995), pp. 553–567.

80. Dianne H. B. Welsh, Fred Luthans, and Steven Sommer, "Managing Russian Factory Workers: The Impact of U.S.-Based Behavioral and Participative Techniques," *Academy of Management Journal,* February 1993, pp. 58–79.

81. Anita Raghavan and G. Thomas Sims, "'Golden Parachutes' Emerge in European Deals," *Wall Street Journal,* February 14, 2000, pp. A17, A18.

82. Susan C. Schneider and Jean-Louis Barsoux, *Managing Across Cultures,* 2nd ed. (London: Prentice Hall, 2003).

■ Chapter 13

1. Richard M. Hodgetts, *Modern Human Relations at Work,* 8th ed. (Ft. Worth, TX: Harcourt, 2002), p. 255. Also see Daniel Goleman, "What Makes a Leader?" *Harvard Business Review,* November–December 1998, pp. 93–102.

2. Abraham Zaleznik, "Managers & Leaders: Are They Different?" *Harvard Business Review,* March–April 1992, pp. 126–135; and James E. Colvard, "Managers vs. Leaders," *Government Executive* 35, no. 9 (July 2003), p. 82.

3. Caroline Hulme, "The Right Place and the Right Style," *The British Journal of Administrative Management* 55 (October–November 2006), pp. i–iii.

4. Zaleznik, "Managers & Leaders: Are They Different?"

5. Mike Diamond, "Are You a Manager or a Leader?" *Reeves Journal* 87, no. 2 (2007), p. 66.

6. Thomas W. Kent, "Leading and Managing: It Takes Two to Tango," *Management Decision* 43, no. 7–8 (2005), pp. 1010–1017.

7. L. Gary Boomer, "Leadership and Management: Your Firm Needs Both," *Accounting Today* 21, no. 2 (2007), pp. 22–23.

8. Zaleznik, "Managers & Leaders: Are They Different?"

9. Matthew Fairholm, "I Know It When I See It: How Local Government Managers See Leadership Differently," *Public Management* 88, no. 9, pp. 10–14.

10. Douglas McGregor, *The Human Side of Enterprise* (New York: McGraw-Hill, 1960), pp. 33–34.

11. Ibid., pp. 47–48.

12. See Nancy J. Adler, *International Dimensions of Organizational Behavior,* 2nd ed. (Boston: PWS-Kent, 1991), p. 150.

13. Sheila M. Puffer, Daniel J. McCarthy, and Alexander I. Naumov, "Russian Managers' Beliefs About Work: Beyond the Stereotypes," *Journal of World Business* 32, no. 3 (1997), pp. 258–276.

14. For other insights into this area, see Manfred F. R. Kets de Vries, "A Journey into the 'Wild West': Leadership Style and

Organizational Practices in Russia," *Organizational Dynamics,* Spring 2000, pp. 67–80.

15. William Ouchi, *Theory Z: How American Management Can Meet the Japanese Challenge* (New York: Addison-Wesley, 1981).

16. Ingrid Aioanei, "Leadership in Romania," *Journal of Organizational Change Management* 19, no. 6 (2006), pp. 705–712.

17. Jun Yan and James G. Hunt, "A Cross Cultural Perspective on Perceived Leadership Effectiveness," *International Journal of Cross Cultural Management* 5, no. 1 (2005), pp. 49–67.

18. For more, see review in Sergio Matviuk, "A Study of Leadership Prototypes in Columbia," *The Business Review* 7, no. 1 (Summer 2007), pp. 14–19.

19. Yong Suhk Pak, Jiman Lee, and Jung Moo An, "Lessons Learned from Daewoo Motors' Experience in Emerging Markets," *Multinational Business Review* 10, no. 2 (Fall 2002), p. 122.

20. For more, see C. M. Axtell, D. J. Holman, K. L. Unsworth, T. D. Wall, P. E. Waterson and E. Harrington, "Shopfloor Innovation: Facilitating the Suggestion and Implementation of Ideas," *Journal of Occupational and Organizational Psychology* 73 (2000), pp. 265–285; and R. K. Yukl, *Leadership in Organizations* (Englewood Cliffs: Prentice-Hall, 2002).

21. Iyuji Misumi and Fumiyasu Seki, "Effects of Achievement Motivation on the Effectiveness of Leadership Patterns," *Administrative Science Quarterly,* March 1971, pp. 51–59.

22. Sang M. Lee, Sangjin Yoo, and Tosca M. Lee, "Korean Chaebols: Corporate Values and Strategies," *Organizational Dynamics,* Spring 1991, p. 41.

23. Michael Woywode, "Global Management Concepts and Local Adaptations: Working Groups in the French and German Car Manufacturing Industry," *Organization Studies* 23, no. 4 (2002), p. 497.

24. Chris Reiter and Neal Boudette, "VW Delays Launch of Microbus to Reduce Its Production Cost," *Wall Street Journal,* May 20, 2004, p. D3.

25. Mason Haire, Edwin E. Ghiselli, and Lyman W. Porter, *Managerial Thinking: An International Study* (New York: Wiley, 1966).

26. Ibid., p. 21.

27. James R. Lincoln, Mitsuyo Hanada, and Jon Olson, "Cultural Orientation and Individual Reactions to Organizations: A Study of Employees of Japanese-Owned Firms," *Administrative Science Quarterly,* March 1981, pp. 93–115. Also see Karen Lowry Miller, "Land of the Rising Jobless," *BusinessWeek,* January 11, 1993, p. 47.

28. Sangjin Yoo and Sang M. Lee, "Management Style and Practice of Korean Chaebols," *California Management Review,* Summer 1987, pp. 95–110.

29. Haire, Ghiselli, and Porter, *Managerial Thinking,* p. 29.

30. Noboru Yoshimura and Philip Anderson, *Inside the Kaisha: Demystifying Japanese Business Behavior* (Boston: Harvard Business School Press, 1997), p. 167.

31. Haire, Ghiselli, and Porter, *Managerial Thinking,* p. 140.

32. Ibid., p. 157.

33. For more on this topic, see Edgar H. Schein, "SMR Forum: Does Japanese Management Style Have a Message for American Managers?" *Sloan Management Review,* Fall 1981, pp. 55–68.

34. Jeremiah J. Sullivan and Ikujiro Nonaka, "The Application of Organizational Learning Theory to Japanese and American Management," *Journal of International Business Studies,* Fall 1986, pp. 127–147.

35. Ibid., pp. 130–131.

36. David A. Ralston, Carolyn P. Egri, Sally Stewart, Robert H. Terpstra, and Yu Kaicheng, "Doing Business in the 21st Century with the New Generation of Chinese Managers: A Study of Generational Shifts in Work Values in China," *Journal of International Business Studies,* Second Quarter 1999, pp. 415–428.

37. John Politis, "The Role of Various Leadership Styles," *Leadership and Organization Development Journal* 24, no. 4 (2003), pp. 181–195.

38. Darwish A. Yousef, "Predictors of Decision-Making Styles in Non-Western Countries," *Leadership and Organizational Development Journal* 19, no. 7 (1998), pp. 366–373.

39. Ibid.

40. Ibid.

41. Ali Mohammad Mosadegh Rad and Mohammad Hossein Yarmohammadian, "A Study of Relationship Between Managers' Leadership Style and Employees' Job Satisfaction," *Leadership in Health Services* 19, no. 2 (2006), pp. xi–xxviii.

42. James Thomas Kunnanatt, "Leadership Orientation of Service Sector Managers in India: An Empirical Study," *Business and Society Review* 122, no. 1 (2007), pp. 99–119.

43. Haire, Ghiselli, and Porter, *Managerial Thinking,* p. 22.

44. Priyanka Banerji and Venkat Krishnan, "Ethical Preferences of Transformational Leaders: An Empirical Investigation," *Leadership Organization and Development Journal* 21, no. 8 (2000), p. 405.

45. Eric J. Romero, "Latin American Leadership: El Patron & El Lider Moderno," *Cross Cultural Management* 11, no. 3 (2004), pp. 25–37.

46. Ibid.

47. Haire, Ghiselli, and Porter, *Managerial Thinking,* p. 22.

48. D. B. Stephens, "Cultural Variations in Leadership Style: A Methodological Experiment in Comparing Managers in the U.S. and Peruvian Textile Industries," *Management International Review* 21, no. 3 (1981), pp. 47–55.

49. Ibid., p. 54.

50. See Jay A. Conger, *The Charismatic Leader* (San Francisco: Jossey-Bass, 1989).

51. Hodgetts, *Modern Human Relations at Work,* pp. 275–276.

52. Bernard M. Bass, "Is There Universality in the Full Range Model of Leadership?" *International Journal of Public Administration* 16, no. 6 (1996), p. 731.

53. Ibid., pp. 741–742.

54. Ibid., p. 731.

55. For additional insights on recent research by Bass and his associates, see Bruce J. Avolio and Bernard M. Bass, "You Can Drag a Horse to Water but You Can't Make It Drink Unless It Is Thirsty," *Journal of Leadership Studies,* Winter 1998, pp. 4–17.

56. Bass, "Is There Universality?" pp. 754–755.

57. Ingrid Tollgerdt-Andersson, "Attitudes, Values and Demands on Leadership—A Cultural Comparison Among Some European Countries," in *Managing Across Cultures,* ed. Pat Joynt and Malcolm Warner (London: International Thomson Business Press, 1996), p. 172.

58. Ibid., p. 176.

59. Felix C. Brodbeck et al., "Cultural Variation of Leadership Prototypes Across 22 European Countries," *Journal of Occupational and Organizational Psychology* 73 (2000), pp. 1–29.

60. Fons Trompenaars and Charles Hampden-Turner, *Riding the Waves of Culture: Understanding Diversity in Global Business,* 2nd ed. (New York: McGraw-Hill, 1998), p. 74.

61. Ibid., p. 77.

62. Robert J. House and Mansour Javidan, "Overview of GLOBE," in *Culture, Leadership, and Organizations: The GLOBE Study of 62 Societies,* ed. Robert J. House, Paul J. Hanges, Mansour Javidan, et al. (Thousand Oaks, CA: Sage, 2004), p. 14.

63. Peter Dorfman, Paul Hanges, and Felix Brodbeck, "Leadership and Cultural Variation: The Identification of Culturally Endorsed Leadership Profiles," in House et al., *Culture, Leadership, and Organizations,* pp. 669–720.

64. Michele J. Gelfand, D. P. S. Bhawuk, Lisa H. Nishii, and David J. Bechtold, "Individualism and Collectivism," in House et al., *Culture, Leadership, and Organizations,* pp. 437–512.

65. Ibid.

66. Cynthia G. Emrich, Florence L. Denmark, and Deanne Den Hartog, "Cross-Cultural Differences in Gender Egalitarianism," in House et al., *Culture, Leadership, and Organizations,* pp. 343–394.

67. Mansour Javidan, "Performance Orientation," in House et al., *Culture, Leadership, and Organizations,* pp. 239–281.

68. Neal Ashkanasy, Vipin Gupta, Melinda Mayfield, and Edwin Trevor-Roberts, "Future Orientation," in House et al., *Culture, Leadership, and Organizations,* pp. 282–342.

69. Mary Sully De Luque and Mansour Javidan, "Uncertainty Avoidance," in House et al., *Culture, Leadership, and Organizations,* pp. 602–654.

70. Hayat Kabasakal and Muzaffer Bodur, "Humane Orientation in Societies, Organizations, and Leader Attributes," in House et al., *Culture, Leadership, and Organizations,* pp. 564–601.

71. Dean Den Hartog, "Assertiveness," in House et al., *Culture, Leadership, and Organizations,* pp. 395–436.

72. Dale Carl, Vipin Gupta, and Mansour Javidan, "Power Distance," in House et al., *Culture, Leadership, and Organizations,* pp. 513–563.

73. Mansour Javidan, "Forward Thinking Cultures," *Harvard Business Review,* July–August 2007, p. 20.

74. Narda Quigley, Mary Sully De Luque, and Robert J. House, "Responsible Leadership and Governance in a Global Context: Insights from the GLOBE Study," in *Handbook on Responsible Leadership and Governance in Global Business,* ed. Jonathan P. Doh and Stephen A. Stumpf (London: Edward Elgar Publishing, 2005), pp. 352–379.

75. Kim S. Cameron, Jane E. Dutton, and Robert E. Quinn, *Positive Organizational Scholarship* (San Francisco: Berrett-Koehler, 2003), p. 3.

76. Ibid.

77. C. Cooper, T. A. Scandura, and C. A. Schriesheim, "Looking Forward but Learning from Our Past: Potential Challenges to Developing Authentic Leadership Theory and Authentic Leaders," *The Leadership Quarterly* 16, no. 3 (2005), pp. 475–493.

78. B. Avolio, F. Luthans, and F. O. Walumba, *Authentic Leadership: Theory Building for Veritable Sustained Performance* (Gallup Leadership Institute, University of Nebraska–Lincoln, 2004), p. 4.

79. B. Shamir and G. Eilam, "What's Your Story? A Life-Stories Approach to Authentic Leadership Development," *The Leadership Quarterly* 16, no. 3 (2005), pp. 395–417.

80. William L. Gardner, Bruce J. Avolio, Fred Luthans, Douglas R. May, and Fred Walumbwa, "Can You See the Real Me? A Self-Based Model of Authentic Leader and Follower Development," *The Leadership Quarterly* 16 (2005), pp. 343–372.

81. Ibid.

82. Bruce J. Avolio and William L. Gardner, "Authentic Leadership Development: Getting to the Root of Positive Forms of Leadership," *The Leadership Quarterly* 16 (2005), pp. 315–338.

83. Ibid.

84. World Economic Forum, "Declining Public Trust Foremost a Leadership Problem," Press Release, January 14, 2003.

85. Ibid.

86. David Waldman, Donald Siegel, and Mansour Javidan, "Transformational Leadership and Corporate Social Responsibility," in Doh and Stumpf, *Handbook of Responsible Leadership and Governance in Global Business.*

87. Jonathan P. Doh and Stephen A. Stumpf, "Toward a Framework of Responsible Leadership and Governance," in Doh and Stumpf, *Handbook of Responsible Leadership and Governance in Global Business.*

88. Allen Morrison, "Integrity and Global Leadership," *Journal of Business Ethics* 31, no. 1 (May 2001), p. 65.

89. Edward P. Richards, "Developing Socially Responsible Business Leaders: The Lubrizol Experience," *Mid-American Journal of Business* 18, no. 1 (Spring 2003), p. 11.

90. Stephen A. Stumpf, "Career Goal: Entrepreneur?" *International Journal of Career Management* 4, no. 2 (1992), pp. 26–32.

91. T. K. Maloy, "Entrepreneurs Need Moms," United Press International, March 11, 2004.

92. Andrew Backover, "How, Not Where, Is Key Word Now Local Firms Serve Foreign Markets," *Denver Post,* February 27, 2000, p. D14.

93. Ron Nixon, "Africa, Offline: Waiting for the Web," *New York Times,* July 22, 2007, p. A1.

■ Chapter 14

1. "How HR Contributes at Best Small and Midsize Companies to Work For," *Human Resource Department Management Report,* August 2004, p. 2.

2. Ann Pomeroy, "Cooking Up Innovation," *HR Magazine,* November 2004, pp. 46–53.

3. Peter Coy and Jack Ewing, "Where Are All the Workers?" BusinessWeek, April 9, 2007, pp. 28–31.

4. Susan Cantrell, "The Work Force of One," *Wall Street Journal,* June 16, 2007, p. R10.

5. Gary M. Wederspahn, "Costing Failures in Expatriate Human Resources Management," *Human Resource Planning* 15, no. 3 (1992), pp. 27–35.

6. Also see Kenneth Groh and Mark Allen, "Global Staffing: Are Expatriates the Only Answer?" *HR Focus,* March 1998, pp. S1–S2.

7. Leslie Chang, "China's Grads Find Jobs Scarce," *Wall Street Journal,* June 22, 2004, p. A17.

8. Nick Forster, "Expatriates and the Impact of Cross-Cultural Training," *Human Resource Management Journal* 10, no. 3 (2000), pp. 63–78.

9. See, for example, Kenneth Groh and Mark Allen, "Global Staffing: Are Expatriates the Only Answer? *HR Focus,* March 1998, p. 1.

10. Joann Lublin, "India Could Provide Unique Opportunities for Expat Managers," *Wall Street Journal,* May 8, 2007, p. B1.

11. Malika Richards, "U.S. Multinational Staffing Practices and Implications for Subsidiary Performance in the U.K. and Thailand," *Thunderbird International Business Review,* March–April 2001, pp. 225–242.

12. Richard B. Peterson, Nancy K. Napier, and Won Shul-Shim, "Expatriate Management: A Comparison of MNCs Across Four Parent Countries," *Thunderbird International Business Review,* March–April 2000, p. 150.

13. Arvind V. Phatak, *International Dimensions of Management,* 2nd ed. (Boston: PWS-Kent Publishing, 1989), p. 106.

14. Linda K. Stroh, Arup Varma, and Stacey J. Valy-Durbin, "Why Are Women Left at Home: Are They Unwilling to Go on International Assignments?" *Journal of World Business* 35, no. 3 (2000), pp. 241–256.

15. Paul W. Beamish and Andrew C. Inkpen, "Japanese Firms and the Decline of the Japanese Expatriate," *Journal of World Business* 33, no. 1 (1998), pp. 35–50.

16. Ibid., pp. 44–45.

17. Cliff Edwards and Kenji Hall, "Remade in the USA," *Business-Week* May 7, 2007, pp. 44-45.

18. Calvin Reynolds, "Strategic Employment of Third Country Nationals," *HR Planning* 20, no. 1 (1997), p. 38.

19. Michael G. Harvey and M. Ronald Buckley, "Managing Inpatriates: Building a Global Core Competency," *Journal of World Business* 32, no. 1 (1997), p. 36.

20. For some additional insights about inpatriates and worldwide staffing, see Michael Harvey and Milorad M. Novicevic, "Staffing Global Marketing Positions: What We Don't Know Can Make a Difference," *Journal of World Business* 35, no. 1 (2000), pp. 80–94.

21. Jennifer Smith, "Southeast Asia's Search for Managers," *Management Review,* March 1998, p. 9.

22. Noam Scheiber, "As a Center for Outsourcing, India Could Be Losing Its Edge," *New York Times,* May 9, 2004, p. 3.

23. Steve Lohr, "Evidence of High-Skill Work Going Abroad," *New York Times,* June 16, 2004, p. C2.

24. "Dell to Bring Some Jobs Back Home," *Houston Chronicle,* November 23, 2003, p. 2.

25. Manjeet Kripalani, "Now It's Bombay Calling the U.S.," *BusinessWeek,* June 21, 2004, p. 26.

26. Marilyn Geewax, "Outsourcing of Service Jobs Grows Faster than Estimated," *Houston Chronicle,* May 18, 2004, p. 4.

27. Arie Lewin and Vinay Couto, *2006 Survey Report: Next Generation Offshoring, The Globalization of Innovation* (Durham: Booz Allen Hamilton, 2007), pp. 7–10.

28. Ibid.

29. Winfred Arthur Jr. and Winston Bennett Jr., "The International Assignee: The Relative Importance of Factors Perceived to Contribute to Success," *Personnel Psychology,* Spring 1995, pp. 99–114.

30. Also see Michael G. Harvey, Milorad M. Novicevic, and Cheri Speier, "An Innovative Global Management Staffing System: A Competency-Based Perspective," *Human Resource Management,* Winter 2000, pp. 381–394.

31. Peterson, Napier, and Shul-Shim, "Expatriate Management," p. 151.

32. Indrei Ratiu, "Thinking Internationally: A Comparison of How International Executives Learn," *International Studies of Management and Organization,* Spring–Summer 1983, pp. 139–150.

33. Nancy J. Adler, *International Dimensions of Organizational Behavior,* 2nd ed. (Boston: PWS-Kent Publishing, 1991), pp. 228–229.

34. Juan Sanchez, Paul Spector, and Cary Cooper, "Adapting to a Boundaryless World: A Developmental Expatriate Model," *Academy of Management Executive* 14, no. 2 (2000), pp. 96–106.

35. Jan Selmer, "Effects of Coping Strategies on Sociocultural and Psychological Adjustment of Western Expatriate Managers in the PRC," *Journal of World Business* 34, no. 1 (1999), pp. 41–51.

36. Paula M. Caligiuri, "Selecting Expatriates for Personality Characteristics: A Moderating Effect of Personality on the Relationship Between Host National Contact and Cross-Cultural Adjust-

ment," *Management International Review* 40, no. 1 (2000), pp. 61–80.

37. Jean E. Heller, "Criteria for Selecting an International Manager," *Personnel,* May–June 1980, p. 50.

38. Jeffrey L. Blue and Ulric Haynes Jr., "Preparation for the Overseas Assignment," *Business Horizons,* June 1977, p. 64.

39. The survey was conducted by executive recruiters for Korn-Ferry International and the Columbia Business School. Excerpts were reported in "Report: Shortage of Executives Will Hurt U.S.," *Omaha World Herald,* June 25, 1989, p. 1G.

40. Margaret A. Shaffer, David A. Harrison, K. Matthew Gilley, and Dora M. Luk, "Struggling for Balance amid Turbulence on International Assignments: Work-Family Conflict, Support, and Commitment," *Journal of Management* 27 (2001), pp. 99–121.

41. Weichun Zhu, Fred Luthans, Irene K. H. Chew, and Cuifang Li, "Potential Expats in Singaporean Organizations," *Journal of Management Development* 25, no. 8 (2006), pp. 763–776.

42. Patricia C. Borstorff, Stanley G. Harris, Hubert S. Field, and William F. Giles, "Who'll Go? A Review of Factors Associated with Employee Willingness to Work Overseas," *Human Resource Planning* 20, no. 3 (1997), p. 38.

43. See Betty Jane Punnett, "Towards Effective Management of Expatriate Spouses," *Journal of World Business* 33, no. 3 (1997), pp. 243–256.

44. Howard Tu and Sherry E. Sullivan, "Preparing Yourself for an International Assignment," *Business Horizons,* January–February 1994, p. 68.

45. James C. Baker and John M. Ivancevich, "The Assignment of American Executives Abroad: Systematic, Haphazard or Chaotic?" *California Management Review,* Spring 1971, p. 41.

46. Heller, "Criteria for Selecting an International Manager," p. 53.

47. Rosalie L. Tung, "U.S. Multinationals: A Study of Their Selection and Training Procedures for Overseas Assignments," *National Academy of Management Proceedings* (Atlanta, 1979), p. 65.

48. This section is based on J. Stewart Black, Mark Mendenhall, and Gary Oddou, "Toward a Comprehensive Model of International Adjustment: An Integration of Multiple Theoretical Perspectives," *Academy of Management Review,* April 1991, pp. 291–317. For more on this area, see Jaime Bonache, Chris Brewster, and Vesa Suutari, "Expatriation: A Developing Research Agenda," *Thunderbird International Business Review,* January–February 2001, pp. 3–20.

49. Iain McCormick and Tony Chapman, "Executive Relocation: Personal and Organizational Tactics," in *Managing Across Cultures: Issues and Perspectives,* ed. Pat Joynt and Malcolm Warner (London: International Thomson Business Press, 1996), pp. 326–337.

50. Calvin Reynolds, "Expatriate Compensation in Historical Perspective," *Journal of World Business* 32, no. 2 (1997), p. 127.

51. Elaine K. Bailey, "International Compensation," in *Global Perspectives of Human Resource Management,* ed. Oded Shenkar (Englewood Cliffs, NJ: Prentice Hall, 1995), p. 148.

52. Peterson, Napier, and Shul-Shim, "Expatriate Management," p. 155.

53. See Dennis R. Briscoe, *International Human Resource Management* (Englewood Cliffs, NJ: Prentice Hall, 1995), pp. 111–120.

54. David Sirota and J. Michael Greenwood, "Understand Your Overseas Workforce," *Harvard Business Review,* January–February 1971, pp. 53–60.

55. Ingemar Torbiorn, *Living Abroad* (New York: Wiley), p. 127.

56. Charles Vance and Yongsun Paik, "One Size Fits All in Expatriate Pre-departure Training? Comparing the Host Country Voices

of Mexican, Indonesian and U.S. workers," *The Journal of Management Development* 21, no. 7–8 (2002), pp. 557–572.

57. Chi-Sum Wong and Kenneth S. Law, "Managing Localization of Human Resources in the PRC: A Practical Model," *Journal of World Business* 34, no. 1 (1999), pp. 28–29.

58. Torbiorn, *Living Abroad*, p. 41.

59. Maria L. Kraimer, Sandy J. Wayne, and Renata A. Jaworski, "Sources of Support and Expatriate Performance: The Mediating Role of Expatriate Adjustment," *Personnel Psychology* 54 (2001), pp. 71–99.

60. Yoram Zeira and Moshe Banai, "Selection of Expatriate Managers in MNCs: The Host-Environment Point of View," *International Studies of Management & Organization* 15, no. 1 (1985), pp. 33–41.

61. Jobert E. Abueva, "Return of the Native Executive," *New York Times,* May 17, 2000, p. C1.

62. Adler, *International Dimensions of Organizational Behavior,* p. 236.

63. Howard W. French, "Japan Unsettles Returnees, Who Yearn to Leave Again," *New York Times,* May 2, 2000, p. A12.

64. J. Stewart Black, "Coming Home: The Relationship of Expatriate Expectations with Repatriate Adjustment and Job Performance," *Human Relations* 45, no. 2 (1992), p. 188.

65. Wong and Law, "Managing Localization of Human Resources," p. 36.

66. Nancy K. Napier and Richard B. Peterson, "Expatriate Reentry: What Do Expatriates Have to Say?" *Human Resource Planning* 14, no. 1 (1991), pp. 19–28.

67. Charlene Marmer Solomon, "Repatriation: Up, Down or Out?" *Personnel Journal,* January 1995, p. 32.

68. Mitchell R. Hammer, William Hart, and Randall Rogan, "Can You Go Home Again? An Analysis of the Repatriation of Corporate Managers and Spouses," *Management International Review* 38, no. 1 (1998), p. 81.

69. Karen Roberts, Ellen Ernst Kossek, and Cynthia Ozeki, "Managing the Global Workforce: Challenges and Strategies," *Academy of Management Executive,* November 1998, pp. 93–106. See also Mark C. Blino and Daniel C. Feldman, "Increasing the Skill Utilization of Expatriates," *Human Resource Management* 39, no. 4 (Winter 2000), pp. 367–379; Ben L. Kedia and Ananda Mukherji, "Global Managers: Developing a Mindset for Global Competitiveness," *Journal of World Business* 34, no. 3 (1999), pp. 230–251.

70. Robert C. Maddox and Douglas Short, "The Cultural Integrator," *Business Horizons,* November–December 1988, pp. 57–59.

71. Michael Hickins, "Creating a Global Team," *Management Review,* September 1998, p. 6.

72. Charlene Marmer Solomon, "Global Operations Demand That HR Rethink Diversity," *Personnel Journal,* July 1994, p. 50.

73. Paul R. Sparrow and Pawan S. Budhwar, "Competition and Change: Mapping the Indian HRM Recipe Against Worldwide Patterns," *Journal of World Business* 32, no. 3 (1997), p. 231. See also Chi-Sum Wong and Kenneth S. Law, "Managing Localization of Human Resources in the PRC: A Practical Model," *Journal of World Business* 34, no. 1 (1999), pp. 32–33.

74. Bodil Jones, "What Future European Recruits Want," *Management Review,* January 1998, p. 6.

75. Filiz Tabak, Janet Stern Solomon, and Christine Nielsen, "Managerial Success: A Profile of Future Managers in China," *SAM Advanced Management Journal,* Autumn 1998, pp. 18–26.

76. Also see Allan Bird, Sully Taylor, and Schon Beechler, "A Typology of International Human Resource Management in Japanese Multinational Corporations: Organizational Implications," *Human Resource Management,* Summer 1998, pp. 159–176.

77. Fred Luthans, *Organizational Behavior,* 10th ed. (New York: McGraw-Hill/Irwin, 2004), chapter 16.

78. Noel M. Tichy and Eli Cohen, "The Teaching Organization," *Training and Development Journal,* July 1998, p. 27.

79. Peter Prud'homme van Reine and Fons Trompenaars, "Invited Reaction: Developing Expatriates for the Asia-Pacific Region," *Human Resource Development Quarterly* 11, no. 3 (Fall 2000), p. 238.

80. J. Hayes and C. W. Allinson, "Cultural Differences in the Learning Styles of Managers," *Management International Review* 28, no. 3 (1988), p. 76.

81. See for example Jennifer Smith, "Southeast Asia's Search for Managers," *Management Review,* June 1998, p. 9.

82. Also see Schon Beechler and John Zhuang Yang, "The Transfer of Japanese-Style Management to American Subsidiaries: Contingencies, Constraints, and Competencies," *Journal of International Business Studies,* Third Quarter 1994, pp. 467–491.

83. Allan Bird and Schon Beechler, "Links Between Business Strategy and Human Resource Management Strategy in U.S.-Based Japanese Subsidiaries: An Empirical Investigation," *Journal of International Business Studies,* First Quarter 1995, p. 40.

84. Linda K. Stroh and Paula M. Caligiuri, "Increasing Global Competitiveness Through Effective People Management," *Journal of World Business* 33, no. 1 (1998), p. 10.

85. For more on this, see Tomoko Yoshida and Richard W. Breslin, "Intercultural Skills and Recommended Behaviors," in Shenkar, *Global Perspectives of Human Resource Management,* pp. 112–131.

86. Alan M. Barrett, "Training and Development of Expatriates and Home Country Nationals," in Shenkar, *Global Perspectives of Human Resource Management,* p. 135.

87. Yukimo Ono, "Japanese Firms Don't Let Masters Rule," *Wall Street Journal,* May 4, 1992, p. B1.

88. See Chi-Sum Wong and Kenneth S. Law, "Managing Localization of Human Resources in the PRC: A Practical Model," *Journal of World Business* 34, no. 1 (1999), pp. 32–33.

89. See Andrew Sergeant and Stephen Frenkel, "Managing People in China: Perceptions of Expatriate Managers," *Journal of World Business* 33, no. 1 (1998), pp. 17–34.

90. Michael J. Marquardt and Dean W. Engel, *Global Human Resource Management* (Englewood Cliffs, NJ: Prentice Hall, 1995), p. 44.

91. Ingmar Bjorkman and Yuan Lu, "A Corporate Perspective on the Management of Human Resources in China," *Journal of World Business* 34, no. 1 (1999), pp. 20–21.

92. Fred E. Fiedler, Terence Mitchell, and Harry C. Triandis, "The Culture Assimilator: An Approach to Cross-Cultural Training," *Journal of Applied Psychology,* April 1971, p. 97.

93. Noel M. Tichy, "Global Development," in *Globalizing Management,* ed. Vladimir Pucik, Noel M. Tichy, and Carole K. Barnett (New York: Wiley, 1993), pp. 206–224.

94. Ibid., p. 219.

95. Fred Luthans, "Positive Organizational Behavior: Developing and Managing Psychological Strengths," *Academy of Management Executive* 16, no. 1 (2002), p. 59.

96. Fred Luthans and Carolyn M. Youssef, "Emerging Positive Organizational Behavior," *Journal of Management* 33, no. 3 (June 2007), pp. 321–349.

97. Ibid.

■ Part 4 Integrative Cases

In-Depth Integrative Case 1

1. "China's Banking Industry. A Great Big Banking Gamble," *The Economist,* October 25, 2005.

2. "The HSBC Group: A Brief History," Hsbc.com, accessed August 10, 2006.

3. Ibid.

4. Tarun Khanna and David Lane, "HSBC Holdings," *Harvard Business School,* July 18, 2005.

5. Ibid.

6. Kerry Capell and Mark Clifford, "John Bond's HSBC," *Business-Week,* September 20, 1999, www.businessweek.com.

7. Carrick Mollenkamp, "HSBC Plans Push in Emerging Markets," *The Wall Street Journal,* October 24, 2005, B2.

8. Khanna and Lane, "HSBC Holdings."

9. Kevi Hamlin, "The Quiet Revolution at HSBC," *Institutional Investor,* January 2001, p. 54.

10. Ibid.

11. See Interbrand rakings.

12. "The Low-Key Rise of Stephen Green," FT.com, November 28, 2005, p. 1.

13. Katie Burgess and Peter Thal Larsen, "Investor Scrutiny at HSBC" *Financial Times,* February 3, 2006, p. 20.

14. "The HSBC Group: A Brief History."

15. "Strategy," www.hsbc.com/hsbc/investor_centre/strategy, accessed August 11, 2006.

16. Ibid.

17. Carrick Mollenkamp, "HSBC Stumbles in Bid to Become Global Deal Maker," *The Wall Street Journal,* October 5, 2006, p. A1.

18. Ibid.

19. Ibid.

20. John Barha, The Thinking Banker's Thinking Banker," *LatinFinance,* September 2001, p. 10.

21. Karina Robinson, "HSBC's Killer Move," *The Banker,* October 2003, p. 24.

22. Carrick Mollenkamp, "HSBC CEO Discusses the Bank's Expansion Plans," *The Wall Street Journal,* October 23, 2005.

23. Mollenkamp, "HSBC Plans Push in Emerging Markets."

24. John Authers, "Big Betters See Return on Stake Banking," *Financial Times,* June 21, 2006, p. 3.

25. Mollenkamp, "HSBC Plans Push in Emerging Markets."

26. Chris Wright, "What's Argentina Going to Do to HSBC?" *Asiamoney* 13, no. 4 (May 2002), p. 6.

27. Peter S. Goodman, "China Approves Plan for Huge Bank IPO," *The Washington Post,* July 20, 2006, D5.

28. "China's Banking Industry. A Great Big Banking Gamble," *The Economist,* October 25, 2005.

29. Ibid.

30. Barney Jopson, "China Struggles to Overcome Shortage of Good Accountants," *Financial Times,* June 6, 2006, p. 11.

31. Joshua Cooper Ramo, "Chinese Investors Focus on Return, but Not Risk," *Financial Times,* August 11, 2006, p. 13.

32. Brian Bremner, "Betting on China's Banks," *BusinessWeek,* October 20, 2005.

33. "China's Banking Industry. A Great Big Banking Gamble."

34. Peter S. Goodman, "China Approves Plan for Huge Bank IPO," *The Washington Post,* July 20, 2006, p. D5.

35. Abe De Ramos, "View from Asia: Leveling the Chinese Playing Field," *CFO Magazine,* October 15, 2005.

36. "Putting China's Capital to Work: The Value of Financial System Reform," *McKinsey Global Institute,* May 2006.

37. Ibid.

38. Ibid.

39. "HSBC Doubles China Insurer Stake with $1.04b," *China Daily,* May 9, 2005.

40. Amy Or, "HSBC Has Applied for China Life Insurance License," www.marketwatch.com, June 28, 2007.

41. Sir John Bond, "China: The Re-emergence of the Middle Kingdom," Speech, July 19, 2005.

42. Stephen K. Green, "The Financial System and Economic Development: Challenges and Opportunities for China," Speech at China International Financial Services Convention and Expo, Beijing, July 1, 2004.

43. Mollenkamp, "HSBC Plans Push in Emerging Markets."

44. Bremner, "Betting on China's Banks."

45. Stephen K. Green, "Professor Sir Roland Smith Chief Executive Lecture: The Rise and Rise of Asia," Speech, February 14, 2005.

46. Mollenkamp, "HSBC Plans Push in Emerging Markets."

47. Bremner, "Betting on China's Banks."

48. "Managing for Growth in Commercial Banking," *Fair Disclosure Wire,* Conference Call, March 21, 2006.

49. Justine Lau, "Loan Growth Boosts BoCOM," *Financial Times,* March 29, 2006, p. 18.

50. K. C. Swanson, "Buying into China's Banks," *Corporate Dealmaker,* September–October 2006, p. 18.

51. Ibid.

52. Associated Press, "ICBC Raises $19B in World's Biggest IPO," October 20, 2006, www.washingtonpost.com/wp-dyn/content/article/2006/10/20/AR2006102000207.html?nav=hcmodule.

53. Kate Linebaugh, "Morgan Stanley Expands in China with Bank Deal," *The Wall Street Journal,* October 3, 2006, p. C3.

54. David Barboza, "Rare Look at China's Burdened Banks," *The New York Times,* November 15, 2006, www.nytimes.com/2006/11/15/business/worldbusiness/15bank.html?ex=1164344400&en=94836291a17fe947&ei=5070.

55. James Areddy, "Citigroup's Risky Win in China," *The Wall Street Journal,* November 17, 2006, p. C10.

56. David Barboza, "Citigroup Is Part of Deal to Control a Bank in China," *The New York Times,* November 17, 2006, www.nytimes.com/2006/11/17/business/worldbusiness/17bank.html.

57. Barboza, "Rare Look at China's Burdened Banks."

58. Rick Carew, "China's Guangdong Development Bank Sets Five-Year Plan," www.marketwatch.com, June 13, 2007.

59. "HSBC Opens a New Sub-branch in Beijing," Media Release on September 11, 2006, www.hsbc.com.cn/cn/aboutus/press/content/06sep11a.htm, accessed on October 5, 2006.

60. Stephanie Phang and Chia-Peck Wong, "HSBC to Scale Back U.S. Subprime Mortgage Division," *International Herald Tribune,* March 30, 2007.

61. James Moore, "HSBC Fires US Executives as It Works to Get Household in Order," *The Independent,* February 9, 2007.

62. Ibid.

63. Clay Chandler, "China Snubs Foreign Investment," *Fortune Magazine,* October 3, 2006, money.cnn.com/magazines/fortune/fortune_archive/2006/10/16/8388651.

64. Ibid.

65. K. C. Swanson, "Buying into China's Banks," *Corporate Deal-maker,* September–October 2006, p. 16.

In-Depth Integrative Case 2

1. "Chiquita Names New CEO," *Cincinnati Business Courier,* January 12, 2004.

2. Shanon Murray, "Chiquita's Exit Plan Jumps Big Hurdle," *The Daily Deal,* March 5, 2002, p. C3.

3. Chiquita 2006 Annual Report, www.chiquita.com.

4. Marco Were, "Implementing Corporate Responsibility—The Chiquita Case," *Journal of Business Ethics* 44, no. 2–3 (May 2003), p. 247.

5. "Trade Feud on Bananas Not as Clear as It Looks," *New York Times,* February 7, 2001, p. A5.

6. Sonja Sherwood, "Chiquita's Top Executive," *Chief Executive*, June 2002, p. 18.

7. Geert de Lombaerde, "Chiquita Outlook Improves Following EU Deal," *Cincinnati Business Courier,* April 20, 2001.

8. Nicholas Stein, "Yes, We Have No Profits," *Fortune,* November 26, 2001, pp. 182–196.

9. Ruth Mortimer, "A Strategy That's Bearing Fruit: When Is a Banana Not a Banana? When It's a Brand," *Brand Strategy,* May 26, 2003, p. 40.

10. Stein, "Yes, We Have No Profits."

11. Chiquita 2006 Annual Report. www.chiquita.com.

12. Jerome Goldstein, "Greasing the Wheels of Sustainable Business," *In Business Magazine*, March–April 2003, p. 21.

13. "Corporate Social Responsibility," www.chiquita.com.

14. Sherwood, "Chiquita's Top Executive."

15. Were, "Implementing Corporate Responsibility."

16. J. Gary Taylor and Patricia J. Scharlin, *Smart Alliance: How a Global Corporation and Environmental Activists Transformed a Tarnished Brand* (New Haven: Yale University Press, 2004), p. 10.

17. Chiquita Brands International, 2006 Corporate Fact Sheet, www.chiquita.com.

18. "Trade Feud on Bananas Not as Clear as It Looks."

19. Mortimer, "A Strategy That's Bearing Fruit."

20. "Chiquita Earns 2004 Corporate Citizen of the Americas Award," PR Newswire, April 5, 2004.

21. "Chiquita Brands International Corporate Responsibility Awards/ Recognition," News from Chiquita, www.chiquita.com.

22. Cliff Peale, "Protection Payments Ensured Safety: Chiquita Disclosure Revealed a Darker Side of Global Economy," *The Cincinnati Enquirer,* May 12, 2004.

23. Ibid.

24. Michael Mitchell, "Chiquita Statement on Agreement with U.S. Department of Justice," Chiquita Press Release, March 14, 2007, www.chiquita.com.

25. Ibid.

26. Stein, "Yes, We Have No Profits."

27. Were, "Implementing Corporate Responsibility."

28. J. Gary Taylor and Patricia J. Scharlin, *Smart Alliance: How a Global Corporation and Environmental Activists Transformed a Tarnished Brand* (New Haven: Yale University Press, 2004), p. 152.

29. Taylor and Scharlin, *Smart Alliance,* p. 133.

30. Kintto Lucas, "Chiquita Brand Suffers in Banana Wars," Inter-press Service: Global Information Network, November 30, 2001.

31. CERES (Coalition for Environmentally Responsible Economies) Sustainability Awards 2004, www.ceres.org/newsroom/press/rep_award_slist.htm.

32. Chiquita 2006 Annual Report: Corporate Responsibility Section, www.chiquita.com.

Glossary

achievement culture   A culture in which people are accorded status based on how well they perform their functions.

achievement motivation theory   A theory which holds that individuals can have a need to get ahead, to attain success, and to reach objectives.

act of state doctrine   A jurisdictional principle of international law which holds that all acts of other governments are considered to be valid by U.S. courts, even if such acts are illegal or inappropriate under U.S. law.

adaptability screening   The process of evaluating how well a family is likely to stand up to the stress of overseas life.

administrative coordination   Strategic formulation and implementation in which the MNC makes strategic decisions based on the merits of the individual situation rather than using a predetermined economically or politically driven strategy.

alliance   Any type of cooperative relationship among different firms.

ascription culture   A culture in which status is attributed based on who or what a person is.

assessment center   An evaluation tool used to identify individuals with potential to be selected or promoted to higher-level positions.

authoritarian leadership   The use of work-centered behavior designed to ensure task accomplishment.

balance-sheet approach   An approach to developing an expatriate compensation package that ensures the expat is "made whole" and does not lose money by taking the assignment.

base of the pyramid strategy   Strategy targeting low-income customers in developing countries.

bicultural group   A group in which two or more members represent each of two distinct cultures, such as four Mexicans and four Taiwanese who have formed a team to investigate the possibility of investing in a venture.

biotechnology   The integration of science and technology to create agricultural or medical products through industrial use and manipulation of living organisms.

born-global firms   Firms that engage in significant international activities shortly after being established.

cafeteria approach   An approach to developing an expatriate compensation package that entails giving the individual a series of options and letting the person decide how to spend the available funds.

centralization   A management system in which important decisions are made at the top.

chaebols   Very large, family-held Korean conglomerates that have considerable political and economic power.

charismatic leaders   Leaders who inspire and motivate employees through their charismatic traits and abilities.

chromatics   The use of color to communicate messages.

chronemics   The way in which time is used in a culture.

civil or code law   Law that is derived from Roman law and is found in the non-Islamic and nonsocialist countries.

codetermination   A legal system that requires workers and their managers to discuss major decisions.

collectivism   The political philosophy that views the needs or goals of society as a whole as more important than individual desires. (Chapter 2); the tendency of people to belong to groups or collectives and to look after each other in exchange for loyalty (Chapter 4).

common law   Law that derives from English law and is the foundation of legislation in the United States, Canada, and England, among other nations.

communication   The process of transferring meanings from sender to receiver.

communitarianism   Refers to people regarding themselves as part of a group.

conglomerate investment   A type of high-risk investment in which goods or services produced are not similar to those produced at home.

content theories of motivation   Theories that explain work motivation in terms of what arouses, energizes, or initiates employee behavior.

context   Information that surrounds a communication and helps to convey the message.

controlling   The process of evaluating results in relation to plans or objectives and deciding what action, if any, to take.

corporate governance   The system by which business corporations are directed and controlled.

corporate social responsibility (CSR)   The actions of a firm to benefit society beyond the requirements of the law and the direct interests of the firm.

cultural assimilator   A programmed learning technique designed to expose members of one culture to some of the basic concepts, attitudes, role perceptions, customs, and values of another culture.

culture   Acquired knowledge that people use to interpret experience and generate social behavior. This knowledge forms values, creates attitudes, and influences behavior.

decentralization   Pushing decision making down the line and getting the lower-level personnel involved.

decision making   The process of choosing a course of action among alternatives.

democracy   A political system in which the government is controlled by the citizens either directly or through elections.

diffuse culture   A culture in which public space and private space are similar in size and individuals guard their public space carefully, because entry into public space affords entry into private space as well.

direct controls   The use of face-to-face or personal meetings for the purpose of monitoring operations.

distributive negotiations   Bargaining that occurs when two parties with opposing goals compete over a set value.

doctrine of comity   A jurisdictional principle of international law which holds that there must be mutual respect for the laws, institutions, and governments of other countries in the matter of jurisdiction over their own citizens.

downward communication   The transmission of information from superior to subordinate.

economic imperative   A worldwide strategy based on cost leadership, differentiation, and segmentation.

Eiffel Tower culture   A culture that is characterized by strong emphasis on hierarchy and orientation to the task.

emotional culture   A culture in which emotions are expressed openly and naturally.

empowerment   The process of giving individuals and teams the resources, information, and authority they need to develop ideas and effectively implement them.

environmental scanning   The process of providing management with accurate forecasts of trends related to external changes in geographic areas where the firm currently is doing business or is considering setting up operations.

equity theory   A process theory that focuses on how motivation is affected by people's perception of how fairly they are being treated.

esteem needs   Needs for power and status.

ethics   The study of morality and standards of conduct.

ethnocentric MNC   An MNC that stresses nationalism and often puts home-office people in charge of key international management positions.

ethnocentric predisposition   A nationalistic philosophy of management whereby the values and interests of the parent company guide strategic decisions.

ethnocentrism   The belief that one's own way of doing things is superior to that of others.

European Union   A political and economic community consisting of 27 member states.

expatriates   Managers who live and work outside their home country. They are citizens of the country where the multinational corporation is headquartered.

expectancy theory   A process theory that postulates that motivation is influenced by a person's belief that (*a*) effort will lead to performance, (*b*) performance will lead to specific outcomes, and (*c*) the outcomes will be of value to the individual.

expropriation   The seizure of businesses by a host country with little, if any, compensation to the owners.

extrinsic   A determinant of motivation by which the external environment and result of the activity are of greater importance due to competition and compensation or incentive plans.

family culture   A culture that is characterized by a strong emphasis on hierarchy and orientation to the person.

femininity   A cultural characteristic in which the dominant values in society are caring for others and the quality of life.

Foreign Corrupt Practices Act (FCPA)   An act that makes it illegal to influence foreign officials through personal payment or political contributions; made into U.S. law in 1977 because of concerns over bribes in the international business arena.

foreign direct investment (FDI)   Investment in property, plant, or equipment in another country.

formalization   The use of defined structures and systems in decision making, communicating, and controlling.

franchise   A business arrangement under which one party (the franchisor) allows another (the franchisee) to operate an enterprise using its trademark, logo, product line, and methods of operation in return for a fee.

Free Trade Agreement of the Americas (FTAA)   A proposed free-trade agreement among the 34 democratically governed countries of the Western Hemisphere.

geocentric MNC   An MNC that seeks to integrate diverse regions of the world through a global approach to decision making.

geocentric predisposition   A philosophy of management whereby the company tries to integrate a global systems approach to decision making.

global area division   A structure under which global operations are organized on a geographic rather than a product basis.

global functional division   A structure that organizes worldwide operations primarily based on function and secondarily on product.

global integration   The production and distribution of products and services of a homogeneous type and quality on a worldwide basis.

globalization   The process of social, political, economic, cultural, and technological integration among countries around the world.

globalization imperative   A belief that one worldwide approach to doing business is the key to both efficiency and effectiveness.

global product division   A structural arrangement in which domestic divisions are given worldwide responsibility for product groups.

global strategy   Integrated strategy based primarily on price competition.

GLOBE (Global Leadership and Organizational Behavior Effectiveness)   A multicountry study and evaluation of cultural attributes and leadership behaviors among more than 17,000 managers from 951 organizations in 62 countries.

goal-setting theory   A process theory that focuses on how individuals go about setting goals and responding to them and the overall impact of this process on motivation.

groupthink   Social conformity and pressures on individual members of a group to conform and reach consensus.

guanxi   In Chinese, it means "good connections."

guided missile culture A culture that is characterized by strong emphasis on equality in the workplace and orientation to the task.

haptics Communicating through the use of bodily contact.

home-country nationals Expatriate managers who are citizens of the country where the multinational corporation is headquartered.

homogeneous group A group in which members have similar backgrounds and generally perceive, interpret, and evaluate events in similar ways.

honne A Japanese term that means "what one really wants to do."

horizontal investment An MNC investment in foreign operations to produce the same goods or services as those produced at home.

horizontal specialization The assignment of jobs so that individuals are given a particular function to perform and tend to stay within the confines of this area.

host-country nationals Local managers who are hired by the MNC.

hygiene factors In the two-factor motivation theory, job-context variables such as salary, interpersonal relations, technical supervision, working conditions, and company policies and administration.

incubator culture A culture that is characterized by strong emphasis on equality and orientation to the person.

indigenization laws Laws that require nationals to hold a majority interest in an operation.

indirect controls The use of reports and other written forms of communication to control operations.

individualism The political philosophy that people should be free to pursue economic and political endeavors without constraint (Chapter 2); the tendency of people to look after themselves and their immediate family only (Chapter 4).

inpatriates Individuals from a host country or third-country nationals who are assigned to work in the home country.

integrative negotiation Bargaining that involves cooperation between two groups to integrate interests, create value, and invest in the agreement.

integrative techniques Techniques that help the overseas operation become a part of the host country's infrastructure.

international division structure A structural arrangement that handles all international operations out of a division created for this purpose.

international entrepreneurship A combination of innovative, proactive, and risk-seeking behavior that crosses national boundaries and is intended to create value for organizations.

international management Process of applying management concepts and techniques in a multinational environment and adapting management practices to different economic, political, and cultural environments.

international selection criteria Factors used to choose personnel for international assignments.

international strategy Mixed strategy combining low demand for integration and responsiveness.

intimate distance Distance between people that is used for very confidential communications.

intrinsic A determinant of motivation by which an individual experiences fulfillment through carrying out an activity and helping others.

Islamic law Law that is derived from interpretation of the Qur'an and the teachings of the Prophet Muhammad and is found in most Islamic countries.

job-content factors In work motivation, those factors internally controlled, such as responsibility, achievement, and the work itself.

job-context factors In work motivation, those factors controlled by the organization, such as conditions, hours, earnings, security, benefits, and promotions.

job design A job's content, the methods that are used on the job, and the way the job relates to other jobs in the organization.

joint venture (JV) An agreement under which two or more partners own or control a business.

kaizen A Japanese term that means "continuous improvement."

karoshi A Japanese term that means "overwork" or "job burnout."

keiretsu In Japan, an organizational arrangement in which a large, often vertically integrated group of companies cooperate and work closely with each other to provide goods and services to end users; members may be bound together by cross-ownership, long-term business dealings, interlocking directorates, and social ties.

key success factor (KSF) A factor necessary for a firm to effectively compete in a market niche.

kinesics The study of communication through body movement and facial expression.

leadership The process of influencing people to direct their efforts toward the achievement of some particular goal or goals.

learning The acquisition of skills, knowledge, and abilities that result in a relatively permanent change in behavior.

license An agreement that allows one party to use an industrial property right in exchange for payment to the other party.

localization An approach to developing an expatriate compensation package that involves paying the expat a salary comparable to that of local nationals.

lump-sum method An approach to developing an expatriate compensation package that involves giving the expat a predetermined amount of money and letting the individual make his or her own decisions regarding how to spend it.

macro political risk analysis Analysis that reviews major political decisions likely to affect all enterprises in the country.

maquiladora A factory, the majority of which are located in Mexican border towns, that imports materials and equipment on a duty- and tariff-free basis for assembly or manufacturing and re-export.

masculinity A cultural characteristic in which the dominant values in society are success, money, and things.

merger/acquisition The cross-border purchase or exchange of equity involving two or more companies.

micro political risk analysis   Analysis directed toward government policies and actions that influence selected sectors of the economy or specific foreign businesses in the country.

Ministry of International Trade and Industry (MITI)   A Japanese government agency that identifies and ranks national commercial pursuits and guides the distribution of national resources to meet these goals.

mixed organization structure   A structure that is a combination of a global product, area, or functional arrangement.

MNC   A firm having operations in more than one country, international sales, and a nationality mix of managers and owners.

monochronic time schedule   A time schedule in which things are done in a linear fashion.

motivation   A psychological process through which unsatisfied wants or needs lead to drives that are aimed at goals or incentives.

motivators   In the two-factor motivation theory, job-content factors such as achievement, recognition, responsibility, advancement, and the work itself.

multicultural group   A group in which there are individuals from three or more different ethnic backgrounds, such as three U.S., three German, three Uruguayan, and three Chinese managers who are looking into mining operations in South Africa.

multi-domestic strategy   Differentiated strategy emphasizing local adaptation.

national responsiveness   The need to understand the different consumer tastes in segmented regional markets and respond to different national standards and regulations imposed by autonomous governments and agencies.

nationality principle   A jurisdictional principle of international law which holds that every country has jurisdiction over its citizens no matter where they are located.

negotiation   Bargaining with one or more parties for the purpose of arriving at a solution acceptable to all.

neutral culture   A culture in which emotions are held in check.

nongovernmental organizations (NGOs)   Private, not-for-profit organizations that seek to serve society's interests by focusing on social, political, and economic issues such as poverty, social justice, education, health, and the environment.

nonverbal communication   The transfer of meaning through means such as body language and the use of physical space.

North American Free Trade Agreement (NAFTA)   A free-trade agreement between the United States, Canada, and Mexico that has removed most barriers to trade and investment.

oculesics   The area of communication that deals with conveying messages through the use of eye contact and gaze.

offshoring   The process by which companies undertake some activities at offshore locations instead of in their countries of origin.

operational risks   Government policies and procedures that directly constrain management and performance of local operations.

organizational culture   Shared values and beliefs that enable members to understand their roles and the norms of the organization.

outsourcing   The subcontracting or contracting out of activities to endogenous organizations that had previously been performed by the firm.

ownership-control risks   Government policies or actions that inhibit ownership or control of local operations.

parochialism   The tendency to view the world through one's own eyes and perspectives.

participative leadership   The use of both work- or task-centered and people-centered approaches to leading subordinates.

particularism   The belief that circumstances dictate how ideas and practices should be applied and that something cannot be done the same everywhere.

paternalistic leadership   The use of work-centered behavior coupled with a protective employee-centered concern.

perception   A person's view of reality.

personal distance   In communicating, the physical distance used for talking with family and close friends.

physiological needs   Basic physical needs for water, food, clothing, and shelter.

political imperative   Strategic formulation and implementation utilizing strategies that are country-responsive and designed to protect local market niches.

political risk   The unanticipated likelihood that a business's foreign investment will be constrained by a host government's policy.

polycentric MNC   An MNC that places local nationals in key positions and allows these managers to appoint and develop their own people.

polycentric predisposition   A philosophy of management whereby strategic decisions are tailored to suit the cultures of the countries where the MNC operates.

polychronic time schedule   A time schedule in which people tend to do several things at the same time and place higher value on personal involvement than on getting things done on time.

positive organizational behavior (POB)   The study and application of positively oriented human resource strengths and psychological capacities that can be measured, developed, and effectively managed for performance improvement in today's workplace.

positive organizational scholarship (POS)   A method that focuses on positive outcomes, processes, and attributes of organizations and their members.

power distance   The extent to which less powerful members of institutions and organizations accept that power is distributed unequally.

principle of sovereignty   An international principle of law which holds that governments have the right to rule themselves as they see fit.

proactive political strategies   Lobbying, campaign financing, advocacy, and other political interventions designed to shape and influence the political decisions prior to their impact on the firm.

process theories of motivation   Theories that explain work motivation by how employee behavior is initiated, redirected, and halted.

profit   The amount remaining after all expenses are deducted from total revenues.

protective and defensive techniques   Techniques that discourage the host government from interfering in operations.

protective principle   A jurisdictional principle of international law which holds that every country has jurisdiction over behavior that adversely affects its national security, even if the conduct occurred outside that country.

proxemics   The study of the way people use physical space to convey messages.

public distance   In communicating, the distance used when calling across the room or giving a talk to a group.

quality control circle (QCC)   A group of workers who meet on a regular basis to discuss ways of improving the quality of work.

quality imperative   Strategic formulation and implementation utilizing strategies of total quality management to meet or exceed customers' expectations and continuously improve products or services.

regiocentric MNC   An MNC that relies on local managers from a particular geographic region to handle operations in and around that area.

regiocentric predisposition   A philosophy of management whereby the firm tries to blend its own interests with those of its subsidiaries on a regional basis.

regional system   An approach to developing an expatriate compensation package that involves setting a compensation system for all expats who are assigned to a particular region and paying everyone in accord with that system.

repatriation   The return to one's home country from an overseas management assignment.

repatriation agreements   Agreements whereby the firm tells an individual how long she or he will be posted overseas and promises to give the individual, on return, a job that is mutually acceptable.

return on investment (ROI)   Return measured by dividing profit by assets.

ringisei   A Japanese term that means "decision making by consensus."

safety needs   Desires for security, stability, and the absence of pain.

self-actualization needs   Desires to reach one's full potential, to become everything one is capable of becoming as a human being.

simplification   The process of exhibiting the same orientation toward different cultural groups.

social distance   In communicating, the distance used to handle most business transactions.

socialism   A moderate form of collectivism in which there is government ownership of institutions, and profit is not the ultimate goal.

socialist law   Law that comes from the Marxist socialist system and continues to influence regulations in countries formerly associated with the Soviet Union as well as China.

social needs   Desires to interact and affiliate with others and to feel wanted by others.

sociotechnical designs   Job designs that blend personnel and technology.

specialization   An organizational characteristic that assigns individuals to specific, well-defined tasks.

specific culture   A culture in which individuals have a large public space they readily share with others and a small private space they guard closely and share with only close friends and associates.

strategic management   The process of determining an organization's basic mission and long-term objectives, then implementing a plan of action for attaining these goals.

strategy implementation   The process of providing goods and services in accord with a plan of action.

sustainability   Development that meets humanity's needs without harming future generations.

tatemae   A Japanese term that means "doing the right thing" according to the norm.

territoriality principle   A jurisdictional principle of international law which holds that every nation has the right of jurisdiction within its legal territory.

terrorism   The use of force or violence against others to promote political or social views.

Theory X manager   A manager who believes that people are basically lazy and that coercion and threats of punishment often are necessary to get them to work.

Theory Y manager   A manager who believes that under the right conditions people not only will work hard but will seek increased responsibility and challenge.

Theory Z manager   A manager who believes that workers seek opportunities to participate in management and are motivated by teamwork and responsibility sharing.

third-country nationals (TCNs)   Managers who are citizens of countries other than the country in which the MNC is headquartered or the one in which the managers are assigned to work by the MNC.

token group   A group in which all members but one have the same background, such as a group of Japanese retailers and a British attorney.

totalitarianism   A political system in which there is only one representative party which exhibits control over every facet of political and human life.

total quality management (TQM)   An organizational strategy and the accompanying techniques that result in the delivery of high-quality products or services to customers.

training   The process of altering employee behavior and attitudes in a way that increases the probability of goal attainment.

transactional leaders   Individuals who exchange rewards for effort and performance and work on a "something for something" basis.

transfer risks   Government policies that limit the transfer of capital, payments, production, people, and technology in and out of the country.

transformational leaders   Leaders who are visionary agents with a sense of mission and who are capable of motivating their followers to accept new goals and new ways of doing things.

transition strategies   Strategies used to help smooth the adjustment from an overseas to a stateside assignment.

transnational network structure   A multinational structural arrangement that combines elements of function, product, and geographic designs, while relying on a network arrangement to link worldwide subsidiaries.

transnational strategy   Integrated strategy emphasizing both global integration and local responsiveness.

two-factor theory of motivation   A theory that identifies two sets of factors that influence job satisfaction: hygiene factors and motivators.

uncertainty avoidance   The extent to which people feel threatened by ambiguous situations and have created beliefs and institutions that try to avoid these.

universalism   The belief that ideas and practices can be applied everywhere in the world without modification.

upward communication   The transfer of meaning from subordinate to superior.

validity   The quality of being effective, of producing the desired results. A valid test or selection technique measures what it is intended to measure.

values   Basic convictions that people have regarding what is right and wrong, good and bad, important and unimportant.

variety amplification   The creation of uncertainty and the analysis of many alternatives regarding future action.

variety reduction   The limiting of uncertainty and the focusing of action on a limited number of alternatives.

vertical investment   The production of raw materials or intermediate goods that are to be processed into final products.

vertical specialization   The assignment of work to groups or departments where individuals are collectively responsible for performance.

wholly owned subsidiary   An overseas operation that is totally owned and controlled by an MNC.

work centrality   The importance of work in an individual's life relative to other areas of interest.

World Trade Organization (WTO)   The global organization of countries that oversees rules and regulations for international trade and investment.

Name Index

Note: Page numbers followed by "n" indicate material in source notes and footnotes.

Subject Index

Note: Page numbers followed by "n" indicate material in source notes and footnotes.

611

ACRONYM	PROPER NAME
ADB	Asian Development Bank
AfDB	African Development Bank
AFIC	Asian Finance and Investment Corporation
AFTA	Asian Free Trade Agreement
ASEAN	Association of Southeast Asian Nations
ATPA	Andean Trade Preference Act
BIS	Bank for International Settlements
BOP	Balance of Payments
CIM	Computer-Integrated Manufacturing
CIS	Commonwealth of Independent States
CISG	UN Convention on Contracts for the International Sale of Goods
CEMA	Council for Mutual Economic Assistance
CRA	Country Risk Assessment
DB	Development Bank
DC	Developed Country
DFIs	Development Finance Institutions
DISC	Domestic International Sales Corporation
EBRD	European Bank for Reconstruction and Development
ECOWAS	Economic Community of West African States
EMU	Economic and Monetary Union
EEA	European Economic Area
EFTA	European Free Trade Association
EMCs	Export Management Companies
EMCF	European Monetary Cooperation Fund
EMS	European Monetary System
EPO	European Patent Organization
ETC	Export Trading Company
ETUC	European Trade Union Confederation
EU	European Union
FCPA	Foreign Corrupt Practices Act
FDI	Foreign Direct Investment
FSC	Foreign Sales Corporation
FTAA	Free Trade Agreement of the Americas
FTZ	Foreign Trade Zone
Fx	Foreign Exchange
G7	Group of Seven
GATT	General Agreement on Tariffs and Trade
GC	Global Company
GDP	Gross Domestic Product
GNP	Gross National Product
GSP	Generalized System of Preferences
IAC	International Anti-counterfeiting Coalition
IC	International Company
IDA	International Development Association
IDB	Inter-American Development Bank
IEC	International Electrotechnical Commission
IFC	International Finance Corporation
IMF	International Monetary Fund
IPLC	International Product Life Cycle
IRC	International Revenue Code
ISA	International Seabed Authority
ISO	International Organization for Standardization
ITA	International Trade Administration
JIT	Just-in-Time
JV	Joint Venture
LAIA	Latin American Integration Association (formerly LAFTA)
LDC	Less Developed Country
LIBOR	London Interbank Offer Rate
LOST	Law of the Sea Treaty
MERCOSUR	Free Trade Agreement between Argentina, Brazil, Paraguay, and Uruguay
MNC	Multinational Company
MNE	Multinational Enterprise
NAFTA	North American Free Trade Agreement
NATO	North Atlantic Treaty Organization
NIC	Newly Industrializing Country
NTBs	Nontariff Barriers
OECD	Organization for Economic Cooperation and Development
OPEC	Organization of Petroleum Exporting Countries
PPP	Purchasing Power Parity
PRC	People's Republic of China
PTA	Preferential Trade Area for Eastern and Southern Africa
SACC	Southern African Development Coordination Conference
SBA	Small Business Administration
SBC	Strategic Business Center
SBU	Small Business Unit
SDR	Special Drawing Rights
SEZ	Special Economic Zone
TQM	Total Quality Management
UN	United Nations
UNCTAD	UN Conference on Trade and Development
VAT	Value Added Tax
VER	Voluntary Export Restraint
VRAs	Voluntary Restraints Agreements
WEC	World Energy Council
WIPO	World Intellectual Property Organization
WTO	World Trade Organization